Lecture Notes in Computer Science 3842

Commenced Publication in 1973
Founding and Former Series Editors:
Gerhard Goos, Juris Hartmanis, and Jan van Leeuwen

Heng Tao Shen Jinbao Li Minglu Li
Jun Ni Wei Wang (Eds.)

Advanced Web and Network Technologies, and Applications

APWeb 2006 International Workshops:
XRA, IWSN, MEGA, and ICSE
Harbin, China, January 16-18, 2006
Proceedings

Springer

Heng Tao Shen
University of Queensland
School of Information Technology and Electrical Engineering
Brisbane QLD 4072, Australia
E-mail: shenht@itee.uq.edu.au

Jinbao Li
Heilongjiang University
Department of Computer Science and Technology
74 Xue Fu Road, Harbin 150080, China
E-mail: jbli@hlju.edu.cn

Minglu Li
Shanghai Jiao Tong University
Department of Computer Science and Engineering
1954 Hua Shan Road, Shanghai 200030, China
E-mail: li-ml@cs.sjtu.edu.cn

Jun Ni
University of Iowa
Department of Computer Science, College of Liberal Arts and Science
Iowa City, IA 52242, USA
E-mail: jun-ni@uiowa.edu

Wei Wang
University of New South Wales
School of Computer Science and Engineering
NSW 2052 , Australia
E-mail: weiw@cse.unsw.edu.au

Library of Congress Control Number: Applied for

CR Subject Classification (1998): H.3, H.4, H.5, C.2, K.4

ISSN 0302-9743
ISBN-10 3-540-31158-0 Springer Berlin Heidelberg New York
ISBN-13 978-3-540-31158-4 Springer Berlin Heidelberg New York

Springer is a part of Springer Science+Business Media

springer.com

Printed in Germany

Typesetting: Camera-ready by author, data conversion by Scientific Publishing Services, Chennai, India
Printed on acid-free paper SPIN: 11610496 06/3142 5 4 3 2 1 0

APWeb 2006 Workshop Chair's Message

APWeb conferences are premier international conferences on theoretical and practical aspects of Web engineering with a focus on the Asia Pacific region. Previous APWeb conferences were held in Beijing (1998), Hong Kong (1999), Xi'an (2000), Changsha (2001), Xi'an (2003), Hangzhou (2004) and Shanghai (2005). From this year, under the leadership of APWeb 2006 General Chair Masaru Kitsuregawa, APWeb will have co-located workshops on specialized and emerging topics. It is my pleasure to serve as the Workshop Chair for APWeb 2006.

This volume comprises papers from four APWeb 2006 workshops:

1. Workshop on Metropolis/Enterprise Grid and Applications (MEGA)
2. Workshop on Sensor Network (IWSN)
3. Workshop on Web-Based Internet Computing for Science and Engineering (ICSE)
4. Workshop on XML Research and Applications (XRA)

These four workshops were selected from a public call-for-proposals process. The workshop organizers put a tremendous amount of effort into soliciting and selecting research papers with a balance of high quality and new ideas and new applications. We have asked all workshops to follow a rigid paper selection process, including the procedure to ensure that any Program Committee members (including workshop Program Committee Chairs) are excluded from the paper review process of any papers they are involved in. A requirement about the overall paper acceptance ratio was also imposed on all workshops. This is the first year that APWeb experimented with a workshop program. I hope you will enjoy this program.

I am very grateful to Heng Tao Shen, Hong Gao, Winnie Cheng, Miranda Lee, Xin Zhan, Wenjie Zhang, Yanchun Zhang, Qing Li, Rikun Wang and many other people for their great effort in supporting the conference organization. I would like to take this opportunity to thank all workshop organizers and Program Committee members for their great effort in putting together the workshop program of APWeb 2006, and in particular Minglu Li, Jinbao Li, Jun Ni and Wei Wang.

January 2006

Jeffrey X. Yu
APWeb 2006 Workshop Chair

International Workshop on XML Research and Applications (XRA 2006) Program Chairs' Message

The First International Workshop on XML Research and Applications (XRA 2006) was held in Harbin, China, on January 15, 2006, in conjunction with the 8th Asia Pacific Web Conference (APWEB 2006). XRA 2006 provided a forum for international researchers and practitioners interested in XML to meet and exchange research ideas and results. It also provided an opportunity for participants to present their research papers and to take part in open discussions. The workshop received 45 submissions from 10 countries and regions. All submissions were peer reviewed by at least two Program Committee members. The Program Committee selected 12 full papers and 8 short papers for inclusion in the proceedings. The accepted papers covered a wide range of research topics and novel applications related to XML. Among them, the paper "Early Evaluating XML Trees in Object Repositories" by Sangwon Park was chosen for the best paper award.

We are grateful to National ICT Australia (NICTA) for sponsoring the workshop and donating the prize for the best paper award. We would also like to thank all authors who submitted papers and all the participants in the workshop program. We are grateful to members of the Program Committee who contributed their expertise and ensured the high quality of the reviewing process. We are thankful to the APWEB organizers for their support and local arrangement.

January 2006

Wei Wang
Raymond Wong

International Workshop on Sensor Networks (IWSN 2006) Program Chairs' Message

Recent advancements in digital electronics, microprocessors and wireless technologies enable the creation of small and cheap sensors which have processor, memory and wireless communication ability. This accelerates the development of large-scale sensor networks and brings new challenges in ways we do computing and service. The First International Workshop on Sensor Networks (IWSN 2006) provided a forum for researchers to exchange information regarding advancements in the state of the art and practice of sensor networks, as well as to identify the emerging research topics and directions for future research and development work.

IWSN 2006 received 126 submissions from the USA, Korea, Australia, China among other countries, and selected 24 regular papers and 14 short papers for publication after a rigorous and careful review process. The papers accepted cover a wide range of exciting topics, including protocol, data management, security, and applications.

The excellent program of IWSN 2006 comes from the hard work and collective effort of many PC members and organizers. We would like to express our special thanks to Heilongjiang University, China, and Harbin Institute of Technology, China. We would also like to thank all the authors, many of whom traveled a great distance to participate in this workshop and make their valuable contributions. We hope that all participants enjoyed the technical program and the culture of Harbin. We warmly welcome your comments and suggestions.

January 2006

Jinbao Li
Yingshu Li
Xiaohua Jia

International Workshop on Metropolis/Enterprise Grid and Applications (MEGA 2006) General Chairs' Message

In the last few years, the field of metropolis/enterprise grid and applications has been developing very rapidly. This goes along with the growing popularity of the Internet, the availability of powerful computers and high-speed networks, and is changing the way we do computing and service. The First International Workshop on Metropolis/Enterprise Grid and Applications (MEGA 2006) was held in Harbin, in cooperation with the 8th Asia Pacific Web Conference (APWEB 2006), during January 16-18, 2006.

MEGA 2006 provided a forum to present current and future work as well as to exchange research ideas by researchers, developers, practitioners, and users in metropolis/enterprise grid and applications. It was created with the firm objective of becoming a major international forum of discussion of the theory and applications of the above-mentioned fields. MEGA 2006 received 63 papers from the USA, Korea and China, and selected 12 regular papers and 18 short papers from these three countries after a strict and careful review process. The papers accepted covered a wide range of exciting topics, including architecture, software, networking, and applications.

The excellent program was the result of the hard work and collective effort of many people and organizations. We would like to express our special thanks to the Science and Technology Commission of Shanghai Municipality, Shanghai Jiao Tong University, China, and the Technical Committee on Services Computing of IEEE Computer Society. We would also like to thank all the authors, many of whom traveled a great distance to participate in this workshop and make their valuable contributions. We hope that all participants enjoyed the program and found it worthwhile. We warmly welcome any comments and suggestions to improve our work.

January 2006

Minglu Li
Xian-He Sun
Junwei Wu
Liang-Jie Zhang

International Workshop on Web-Based Internet Computing for Science and Engineering (ICSE 2006) Organizers' Message

Computational science is an important field with multidisciplinary research. It focuses on algorithm development and implementations of computing for scientists and engineers. Its impact is already being felt in many science and engineering disciplines. Current research in computational science requires multidisciplinary knowledge, not only in sciences and engineering but also in cutting-edge computing technologies. Many science and engineering explorations rely on mature, efficient computational algorithms and implementations, practical and reliable numerical methods, and large-scale computation systems.

With the above paradigm and goal of promoting Web-Based scientific and engineering computing, we organized the International Workshop on Web-Based Internet Computing for Science and Engineering (ICSE 2006), held on January 15, 2006, Harbin, China, in conjunction with The 8th Asia Pacific Web Conference (APWEB 2006).

The workshop focuses on scientific computations and applications on the Web-Based Internet, enhancing cyberinfrastructure-based scientific and engineering collaborations. It offered academic researchers, developers, and practitioners an opportunity to discuss various aspects of computational science and engineering-related computational methods and problem-solving techniques for science and engineering research.

We selected about 40 regular and 18 short papers contributed from 8 countries or regions, representing 66 universities or institutions. The selected papers in these proceedings cover a broad range of research topics presented in four presentation sessions and two poster sessions.

We would like to thank the members of the Program Committee and the additional reviewers. We are grateful to the following APWEB 2006 organizers, Masaru Kitsuregawa, Jianzhong Li, Xiaofang Zhou, Heng Tao Shen, Chengfei Liu, and Ge Yu. A special thanks to APWeb 2006 workshop organizer Jeffrey X. Yu, who provided valuable support and help in promoting this workshop.

The workshop organizers deeply appreciate President Zhigang Liu and Vice-President Wei Lin of Harbin Engineering University for their support and sponsorship of this workshop.

Thanks go to all who contributed their papers and provided unforgettable cooperation.

January 2006

General Co-chairs: Jack Dongarra and Yao Zhen
Program Co-chairs: Jun Ni and Shaobin Huang

Organization

International Workshop on XML Research and Applications (XRA 2006)

Program Co-chairs
Wei Wang, University of New South Wales, Australia
Raymond Wong, National ICT Australia, Australia

Program Committee
James Bailey, University of Melbourne, Australia
Sourav S. Bhowmick, Nanyang Technological University, Singapore
Shuyao Chien, Yahoo! Inc., USA
Gillian Dobbie, University of Auckland, New Zealand
Patrick Hung, University of Ontario IT, Canada
Haifeng Jiang, IBM Almaden Research Lab, USA
Hasan Jamil, Wayne State University, USA
Franky Lam, National ICT Australia, Australia
Xiaofeng Meng, Renmin University of China, China
Mukesh Mohania, IBM India Research Lab, India
Mehmet Orgun, Macquarie University, Australia
Keun Ho Ryu, Chungbuk National University, South Korea
Vlad Tosic, Lakehead University, Canada
Guoren Wang, Northeastern University, China

International Workshop on Sensor Networks (IWSN 2006)

Program Committee Co-chairs
Jinbao Li, Heilongjiang University, China
Yingshu Li, Georgia State University, USA
Xiaohua Jia, City University of Hong Kong, Hong Kong

Program Committee
S. Makki, University of Toledo, USA
Weifa Liang, Australian National University, Australia
Xuemin Lin, University of New South Wales, Australia
Ophir Frieder, Illinois Institute of Technology, USA
Yongbing Zhang, University of Tsukuba, Japan
Weijia Jia, City University of Hong Kong, Hong Kong
Chuanhe Huang, Wuhan University, China
Limin Sun, Chinese Academy of Sciences, China

Li Cui, Chinese Academy of Sciences, China
Bin Zhang, Northeastern University, China
Jinli Cao, La Trobe University, Australia
Xiao Bin, Hong Kong Polytechnic University, Hong Kong
Hong Gao, Harbin Institute of Technology, China
Weili Wu, University of Texas at Dallas, USA
Longjiang Guo, Heilongjiang University, China
Hua Wang, University of Southern Queensland, Australia
Qing Zhang, e-Health Center/CSIRO, Australia

International Workshop on Metropolis/Enterprise Grid and Applications (MEGA 2006)

General Co-chairs
Minglu Li, Shanghai Jiao Tong University, China
Xian-He Sun, Illinois Institute of Technology, USA
Junwei Wu, Science and Technology Commission of Shanghai Municipality, China
Liang-Jie Zhang, IBM T.J. Watson Research Center, USA

Program Committee
Wentong Cai, Nanyang Technological University, Singapore
Jiannong Cao, The Hong Kong Polytechnic University, Hong Kong
Xiaowu Chen, Beihang University, China
Qianni Deng, Shanghai Jiao Tong University, China
Guangrong Gao, University of Delaware Newark, USA
Yadong Gui, Shanghai Supercomputer Center, China
Minyi Guo, The University of Aizu, Japan
Weijia Jia, City University of Hong Kong, Hong Kong
Changjun Jiang, Tongji University, China
Hai Jin, Huazhong University of Science and Technology, China
Chung-Ta King, National Tsing Hua University, Taiwan
Francis C. M. Lau, The University of Hong Kong, Hong Kong
Jysoo Lee, KISTI, Korea
Jianzhong Li, Harbin Institute of Technology, China
Xinda Lu, Shanghai Jiao Tong University, China
Junzhou Luo, Southeast University, China
Xiangxu Meng, Shandong University, China
Lionel M. Ni, The Hong Kong University of Science and Technology, Hong Kong
Yi Pan, Georgia State University, USA
Hong Shen, Japan Advanced Institute of Science and Technology, Japan
Weiqin Tong, Shanghai University, China
Cho-Li Wang, The University of Hong Kong, Hong Kong
Xingwei Wang, Northeastern University, China
Jie Wu, Florida Atlantic University, USA

Xinhong Wu, Shanghai Urban Transportation Information Center, China
Zhaohui Wu, ZheJiang University, China
Nong Xiao, National University of Defense Technology, China
Chengzhong Xu, Wayne State University, USA
Laurence Tianruo Yang, St. Francis Xavier University, Canada
Ling Zhang, South China University of Technology, China
Xiaodong Zhang, Ohio State University, USA
Yanchun Zhang, Victoria University, Australia
Aoying Zhou, Fudan University, China
Xiaofang Zhou, University of Queensland, Australia
Hai Zhuge, Institute of Computing Technology, CAS, China

International Workshop on Web-Based Internet Computing for Science and Engineering (ICSE 2006)

General Co-chairs
Jack Dongarra, University of Tennessee, USA
Yao Zhen, Zhejiang University, China

Program Co-chairs
Jun Ni, University of Iowa, USA
Shaobin Huang, Harbin Engineering University, China

Program Committee
Akiyo Nadamoto, NICT, Japan
Alex Vazhenin, University of Aizu, Japan
Beniamino Di Martino, Second University of Naples, Italy
Changsong Sun, Harbin Eng. University, China
Choi-Hong Lai, University of Greenwich, UK
Daxin Liu, Harbin Eng. University, China
Deepak Srivastava, NASA Ames Research Center USA
Enrique Quintana-Orti, University of Jaime I, Spain
George A. Gravvanis, Democritus University of Thrace, Greece
Gudula Rnger, Chemnitz University of Technology, Germany
Guochang Gu, Harbin Eng. University, China
Anand Padmanabhan, University of Iowa, USA
Hamid R. Arabnia, University of Georgia, USA
Jack Dongarra, University of Tennessee, USA
Joan Lu, The University of Huddersfield, UK
Joe Zhang, University of Southern Mississippi, Hattiesburg, USA
Jerry Jenkin, CFD Research Corporation, USA
Julien Langou, University of Tennessee, USA
Laurence T. Yang, St. Francis Xavier University, Canada

Luciano Tarricone, University of Lecce, Italy
M. P. Anantram, NASA Ames Research Center USA
Michael Ng, University of Hong Kong, China
Nadamoto Akiyo, NICT, Japan
Rodrigo de Mello, University of Sao Paulo, Brazil
Sabin Tabirca, University College Cork, Ireland
Shaowen Wang, University of Iowa
Thomas Rauber, University of Bayreuth, Germany
Layne Watson, Virginia Tech. USA
Xing Cai, University of Oslo, Norway
Yi Pan, George State University, USA
Jin Li, Harbin Engineering University, China
Junwei Cao, MIT, USA
Wenyang Duan, Harbin Engineering University, China
Xing Cai, Harbin Engineering University, China

Table of Contents

International Workshop on Sensor Networks (IWSN 2006)

International Workshop on Metropolis/Enterprise Grid and Applications (MEGA 2006)

International Workshop on Web-Based Internet Computing for Science and Engineering (ICSE 2006)

Clustered Absolute Path Index for XML Document: On Efficient Processing of Twig Queries

Hongqiang Wang, Jianzhong Li, and Hongzhi Wang

School of Computer Science and Technology,
Harbin Institute of Technology, Harbin 150001
whqwzy@yahoo.com.cn, Lijz@mail.banner.com.cn,
wangzh@hit.edu.cn

Abstract. Finding all the occurrences of a twig pattern in an XML document is a core operation for efficient evaluation of XML queries. A number of algorithms have been proposed to process twig queries based on region encoding. While each element in source document is given two or more numbers in region-encoding-form index, the size of index grows linearly to the source document. The algorithms based on region encoding perform worse when the source document grows large. In this paper, we address the problem by putting forward a novel index structure, called Clustered Absolute Path Index (CAPI for brief). This index can extremely reduce the size of index and grows slowly as the source document grows large. Based on CAPI, we design novel join algorithms, called Path-Match to process queries without branches, Branch-Filter and RelatedPath-Join to process queries with branches. Experimental results show that the proposed algorithms based on CAPI outperform twig join significantly and have good scalability.

1 Introduction

XML is widely used a standard of information exchange and representation in web. All standard XML query languages, e.g., XPath and XQuery, can retrieve a subset of the XML data nodes satisfying certain path constraints. For example, XPath query "//book[author]/title" will retrieve all "title" nodes appeared under "book" that have a child "author". In the past few years, many algorithms have been proposed to address the problem. One of important methods is to use labeling scheme to accelerate path query processing. Such method has two steps: (i) first develop a labeling scheme to capture the structural information of XML documents, and then (ii) perform pattern matching based on labels alone without traversing the original XML documents.

In order to solve the first sub-problem of designing a proper labeling scheme, existing region encoding[3, 4, 5, 6] encode every XML node by a pair of numbers such that the ancestor-descendant relationship between two nodes can be determined simply by comparing intervals. The level of the node is also used to distinguish the parent-child relationship from the ancestor-descendant relationship. However, region encoding represents each node in source document as a tuple in index, the total number of tuples in index grows linearly to the number of elements in source document. Performance of processing of queries against large document brings challenges.

H.T. Shen et al. (Eds.): ADWeb 2006, LNCS 3842, pp. 1 – 10, 2006.

```
<bib>
  <book>
    <title>TCP/IP
Illustrated</title>
    <author><last>Stevens<
/last>
      <first>W.</first></a
uthor>
  </book>
  <book>
    <title>Data on the
Web</title>
    <author><last>Abitebou
l</last>
      <first>Serge</first>
</author>
    <author>
      <last>Buneman</last>
      <first>Peter</first>
</author>
  </book>
</bib>
```

(a) book.xml

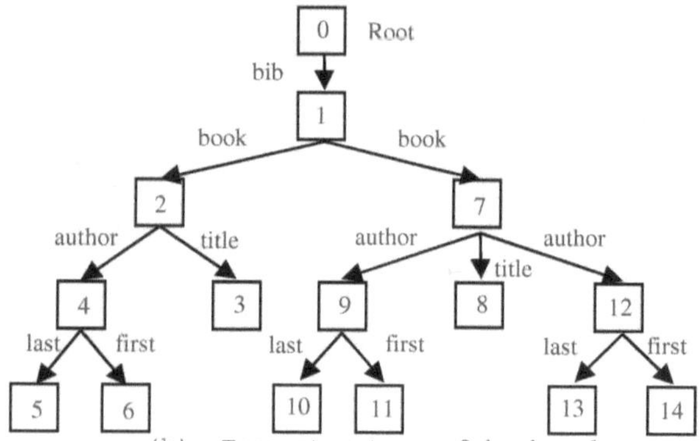

(b) Tree structure of book.xml

Fig. 1. Book.xml and it's tree structure

In this paper, we propose a powerful index, Clustered Absolute Path Index (CAPI for brief). We label each node in source document with an absolute path expression, which is composed of tags and its relative positions of nodes on the path from Root to the given node. For example, we mark node &2 with absolute path "/bib[1]/book[1]" (Figure 1). Further, we use the clustered absolute path (CAP for brief) "/bib[1]/book[1, 2]" to mark nodes &2 and &7 in the document, While the CAP "/bib[1]/book[1, 2]" is a combination of absolute path "/bib[1]/book[1]" and "/bib[1]/book[2]". An immediate benefit of this feature is that, we can use a single CAP in index to mark lots of nodes in the document. As a result, an index with fewer objects against a document with millions of nodes is built. Experimental results show that the number of CAPs in CAPI is less than 1% of the number of nodes in the document. Compared with region encoding when processing a query, there are fewer disk accesses. Algorithms based on CAPI perform better. Besides, the number of CAPs in CAPI grows slowly as the document grows large, algorithms based on CAPI have good scalability.

In this paper, we make the following contributions:

- We propose a novel index structure: CAPI, which contains a few objects even though XML document contains a large number of elements. A CAPI index can be efficiently organized and accessed in external memory.
- We develop novel algorithms, Path-Match, Branch-Filter and RelatedPath-Join, based on CAPI to process XPath expressions with or without twig queries.
- Our experimental results demonstrate that our proposed CAPI index can scale up to large data size with excellent query performance. Algorithms Path-Match, Branch-Filter and RelatedPath-Join based on CAPI outperform other join-based query processing systems.

Organization. The rest of the paper proceeds as follows. We first discuss preliminaries in Section 2. The CAPI index structure is presented in Section 3. We present query processing algorithms in Section 4. Section 5 is dedicated to our experimental results and we close this paper by the related works and a conclusion.

2 Preliminaries

2.1 Data Model

XML data are usually modeled as labeled trees: elements and attributes are mapped to nodes in the trees and direct nesting relationships are mapped to edges in the trees. In this paper, we only focus on the element nodes since it is easy to generalize our methods to the other types of nodes.

All structural indexes for XML data take a path query as input and report exactly all those matching nodes as output, via searching within the indexes.

2.2 Absolute Path Labeling Scheme

We propose absolute path labeling scheme to mark nodes in an XML document. In absolute path labeling scheme, each element is presented by a string: (i) the root is labeled by a empty string, (ii) for a non-root element u, label(u)=label(s)/tag(u)[p], where u is the p-th child with tag(u) of node s. Absolute path supports efficient evaluation of structural relationships between elements. That is, element u is an ancestor of element s if and only if label(u) is a prefix of label(s).

We can prove that a CAPI induces a straightforward one-to-one correspondence between nodes in XML document and CAPs in CAPI. This property is useful for query processing.

3 CAPI Data Structure

In an XML document, there are lots of nodes with similar absolute path labeling, such as &2 (/bib[1]/book[1]) and &7 (/bib[1]/book[2]) in book.xml, we can use a single path (/bib[1]/book[1, 2]) to represent both nodes. The composed path is not an absolute path any more, we call it Clustered Absolute Path (CAP for brief) and the nodes whose labeling can be composed are called Bi-Structured Nodes.

Definition 1. (Bi-Structured Nodes) A node v_1 with absolute path $/e_1[p_1]/e_2[p_2]\ldots/e_k[p_k]$ and another node v_2 with absolute path $/f_1[q_1]/f_2[q_2]\ldots/f_h[q_h]$ are Bi-Structured Nodes if k=h and $e_i=f_i$ and $p_i \neq q_i$ stands for at most once.

Definition 2. (Clustered Absolute Path) A CAP $(/e_1[P_1]/e_2[P_2]\ldots/e_k[P_k])$ is a set of absolute paths $(/e_1[p_1]/e_2[p_2]\ldots/e_k[p_k]$, where P_i are sets of natural numbers, $p_i \in P_i$, $1 \leq i \leq k)$.

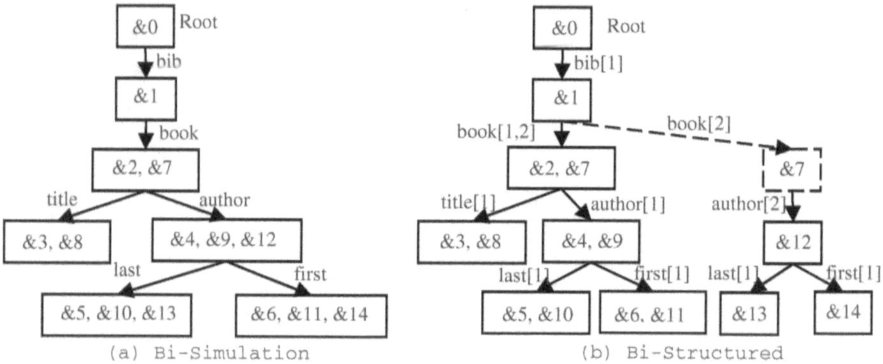

Fig. 2. 1-index and CAPI against book.xml

Bi-Structured nodes are different from Bi-Simulation in 1-index [7]. Bi-Simulation classifies nodes only by their labeled path, while Bi-Structured nodes classify nodes by their absolute paths, which contains positional information of nodes.

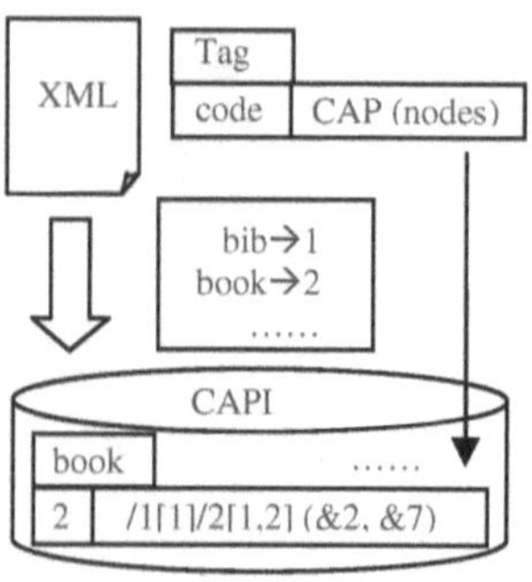

Fig. 3. CAPI data structure

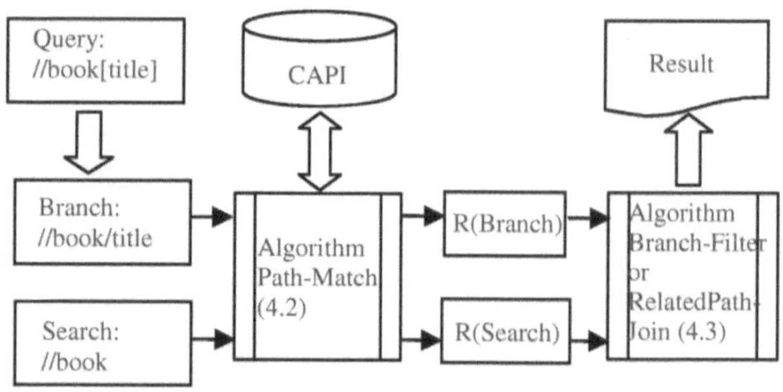

Fig. 4. Query processing based on CAPI

4 Query Processing Based on CAPI

4.1 Introduction of Query Processing Based on CAPI

We illustrated the steps of query processing with an example.

Example 1. We consider an XPath expression "//book[title]", which means we need to find all the "book" element with child "title". Now we need to access both "book" and "title" CAPs in CAPI. We access CAPI and fetch CAPs set with tag "title", which contains all absolute paths contained in "//title", we call it A(Branch). We match "//book/title" with each CAP in A(Branch). We call the set of matched CAPs in A(Branch) as R(Branch). The detail of matching is presented in 4.2. Similarly, we get

R(Search) for evaluating "//book". Next, we need to filter R(Search) with R(Branch) and obtain the query results, we will introduce how to join R(Search) and R(Branch) to get our final result in 4.3. □

4.2 Path-Match Algorithm Based on CAPI

It's a co-NP problem to judge the containment of two XPath expressions [8]. But the problem in our paper is to judge the containment relationship between a general XPath expression and an absolute path or CAP. Based on this feature, we propose Path-Match algorithm based on CAPI.

To make the problem simple, we introduce the concept of broken XPath expression.

Definition 3. (Broken XPath Expression) An XPath expression is decomposed into a equence of sub expressions by "//".

Example 2. As an example, consider a query "//book/title", we get all CAPs matching "//title" with CAPI, which is "/bib[1]/book[1, 2]/title[1]". To perform path matching, we first break the query expression into a sequence of simple XPath (Root, book/title), second, we add "Root" into the CAP and match the CAP with the first simple path, in the example, we use CAP P="Root/bib[1]/book[1, 2]/title[1]" to match P_1="Root", the first tag of P matches P_2 (Figure5 (a)). Then we remove the matched part from P and continue matching next simple XPath P_2="book/title" with P="bib[1]/book[1, 2]/title[1]". This time, the first tag in P is "bib", which can't match the first tag "book" in P_2. We remove the first tag in P and continue matching P="book[1, 2]/title[1]" and P_2="book/title" (Figure5 (b)). Since the first tag in P matches the first tag in P_2, we keep matching the left parts in P and P_2. When the second tag in P matches the second tag in P_2, P matches P_2 (Figure5 (c)). □

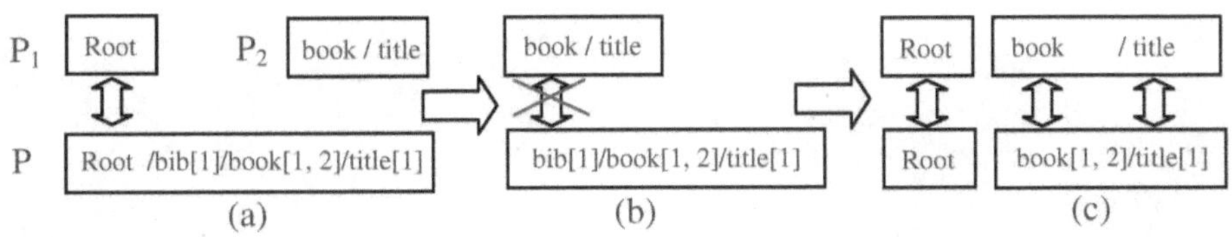

Fig. 5. Example of algorithm Path-Match

We omit the detail of algorithm Path-Match here for the sake of the space of the paper. The time complexity of algorithm Path-Match is O(length(P)×length(QP)) where length(P) is the number of elements in CAP and length(QP) is the number of elements in query XPath.

4.3 Processing Twig Queries

Twig query like P="//a[//b]/c" can be decomposed into two parts which are P_1="//a/c" and P_2="//a//b". In our algorithm, we evaluate P_1 and P_2 separately and join the results to get the result of P.

We use an example to illustrate the procedure of processing of twig queries in example 3.

Example 3. We consider query expression "//book[//last]/title". The query retrieves all "title" elements with a parent "book" which has a descendant "last". First, we retrieve query expression "//book/title" and branch expression "//book//last", they are related with path "//book". We retrieve branch expression "//book//last" first. With CAPI and Path-Match algorithm, we get R(Branch)={ /bib[1]/book[1, 2]/author[1]/last[1], /bib[1]/book[2]/author[2]/last[1]}. Next, we retrieve query expression "//book/title", similarly we get R(Search)={ /bib[1]/book[1, 2]/title[1] }. Second, we filter R(Search) with R(Branch), we analyze it in detail:

(1) We pick out a CAP "/bib[1]/book[1, 2]/title[1]" from R(Search), we call it candidate.
(2) We build a temporal target: "/bib[ ]/book[ ]/title[1]", which delete the positions in related path segment in candidate.
(3) We pick out a CAP "/bib[1]/book[1, 2]/author[1]/last[1]" from R(Branch), we call it filter. We check each element in related path segment in candidate and filter from beginning of the CAPs. The related path is "//book". If the corresponding element matches each other, we put the intersection of their position sets into corresponding position set of the temporal target. The target in this case will be "/bib[1]/book[1, 2]/title[1]". If every element in related path segment in temporal target has non-null position set, the temporal target is a target and will be put into result set. If there is one filter that turns the temporal target into a target, we say that filter satisfies the candidate.
(4) Continue to do (3) until there is no filter in R(Branch). □

The detail of the algorithm is omitted for the sake of the space of the paper. Note that in algorithm Branch-Filter, only the related path segment in temporal target is used. Usually, the related path segment in candidates in R(Search) may have similar structure, so does the related path segment in filters in R(Branch). That means we have done many repetitive operations if the related path segment are same with different candidates and filters. We can avoid these repetitive operations by taking out the related path segment in R(Search) and R(Branch) before join operation. We will analyze this point in detail in example 4.

Example 4. We consider the query expression "//book[//last]//first". This query retrieves all "first" elements with a parent "book" which has a descendent "last". First, we retrieve "//book//last" and we get R(Branch) = {/bib[1]/book[1, 2]/author[1]/last[1], /bib[1]/book[2]/author[2]/last[1]}, then we retrieve "//book//first" and we get R(Search)={/bib[1]/book[1, 2]/author[1]/first[1], /bib[1]/book[2]/author[2]/first[1] }, the related path is "//book". We put all the related path segments of CAPs in R(Search) into a set which we called RP(Search). A related path segment of a CAP is still a CAP, when it's putted into RP(Search), it can combine with some CAP in RP(Search) if they are the same one or they are Bi-Structured nodes. In this case, RP(Search)={ /bib[1]/book[1, 2]}. Similarly, we get related path segment set of R(Branch) which we called RP(Branch)={ /bib[1]/book[1, 2]}. Now we only use RP(Branch) to filter RP(Search) instead of using R(Branch) to filter R(Search). After filtering, we get filtered related path RP(Filtered) ={ /bib[1]/book[1, 2]}, we have to join R(Search) and RP(Filtered) to get our targets. □

We call the algorithm shown in example 4 RelatedPath-Join. We omit the detail of algorithm RelatedPath-Join here for the sake of the space of the paper.

Comparison of These two Algorithms. We compare these two algorithms by their time complexity analysis. Suppose there is only one branch in the query expression, for Branch-Filter, the number of candidates in R(Search) is S and after join with related path is s in RP(Search), the number of filters in R(Branch) is B and after join with related path is b in RP(Branch), the length of related path is RPL, the number of positions is AP. The complexity of Branch-Filter is O(B×S×RPL×AP). For Related-Path-Join, the complexity is O((B+S)+b×s+S) ×RPL×AP), So we can figure out that when B and S are much bigger than b and s, the algorithm RelatedPath-Join performs better than algorithm Branch-Filter.

5 Experiments and Conclusion

All of our experiments are performed on a PC with AMD64 2800+, 512M DDR400 memory and 120G SATA hard disk. The OS is WindowsXP Professional sp2. We implemented our system using JDK1.5. We implemented our Path-Match, Branch-Filter and RelatedPath-Join algorithms. We obtained the source code of TwigStack [3] from the original authors. The dataset we tested is the standard XMark benchmark dataset [16]. It has a fairly complicated schema, with several deeply recursive tags.

Table 1. Dataset of experiments

Dataset	Elements	File Size	CAPs	CAPs/Elements	CAPI File Size
XMark10.xml	167865	11.6M	3976	2.4%	0.8M
XMark20.xml	336244	23.4M	5414	1.6%	1.59M
XMark30.xml	501498	34.9M	6248	1.2%	2.37M
XMark40.xml	667243	46.4M	7034	1.1%	3.13M
XMark50.xml	832911	57.6M	7451	0.9%	3.93M
XMark60.xml	1003441	69.9M	8404	0.8%	4.77M
XMark70.xml	1172640	81.6M	8698	0.7%	5.56M
XMark80.xml	1337383	93.0M	9341	0.7%	6.36M
XMark90.xml	1504685	104.6M	9701	0.6%	7.18M
XMark100.xml	1666315	115.8M	9776	0.6%	8.01M

We can find out that CAPI index grows very slow when XMark file grows to large scale with table 1. This slowness is not only in relative amount but in absolute amount, the number of elements in dataset is 1666315 when the file size grows to 115M, the CAPs in the index is only 9776, 0.6% of the elements in the dataset. The number of elements increases 161630 when the size of document grows from 104M to 115M, while the number of CAPs grows only 75.

Table 2. Query expressions

Query	Query expression
Q1	//listitem
Q2	/site/regions/asia/item/mailbox/mail
Q3	/site/regions/asia/item/description/parlist/listitem/parlist/listitem/text/bold
Q4	//asia/item[//mail]//bold
Q5	//asia/item[//mail]/description/parlist[//bold]//keyword
Q6	//asia/item[mailbox/mail]/description/parlist[listitem]//parlist[//text/bold]//keyword

We choose 6 query expressions as the input of the experiment, within them Q1, Q2, Q3 with no branch query expressions but with different expression length, Q4, Q5, Q6 are query expressions with 1, 2, 3 branch query expressions. We run the experiments separately from XMark10.xml to XMark100.xml the experimental result is showed in Figure 6.

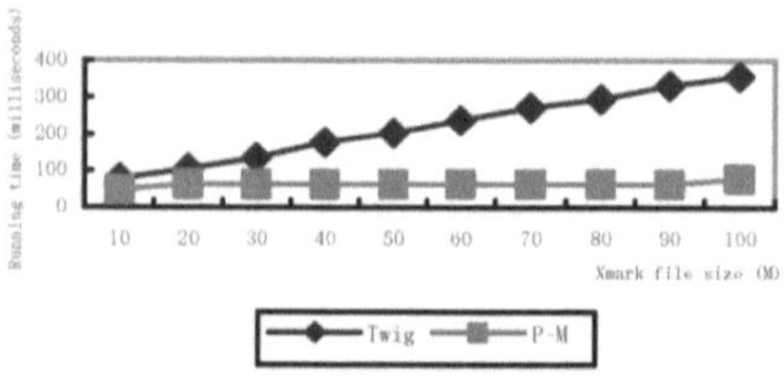

Running time of Q1

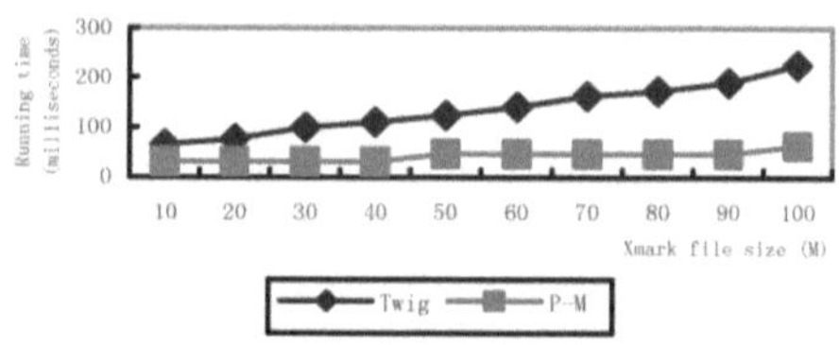

Running time of Q2

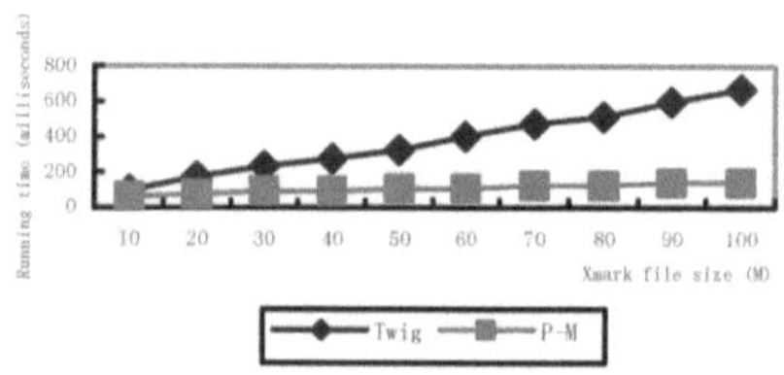

Running time of Q3

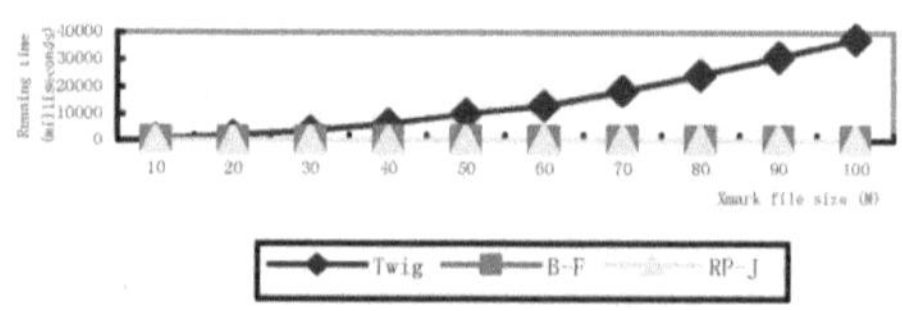

Running time of Q4

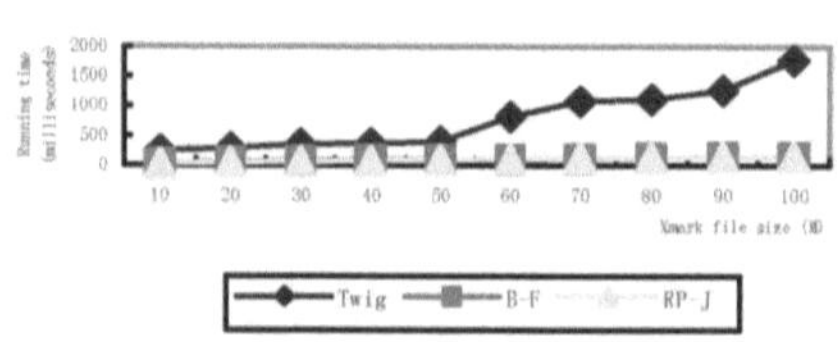

Running time of Q5

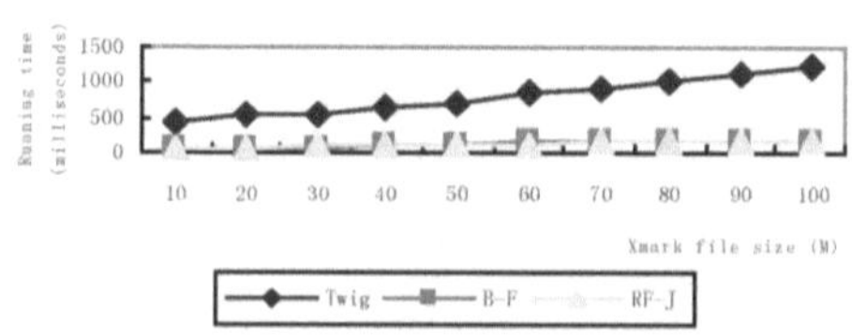

Running time of Q6

Fig. 6. Experimental results,Twig is TwigStack, P-M is Path-Match, B-F is Branch-Filter, RP-J is RelatedPath-Join

From the experimental results of Q1, Q2 and Q3, we conclude that the algorithms based on CAPI perform better than Twig join, especially when the XML document is large. The reason why algorithms based on CAPI is better is that most of the costs of each algorithm is used on disk access, Since CAPI index fewer objects compared with twig join encoding every elements, and algorithms based on CAPI have less disk access than twig join. Besides, in spit of high efficiency of ancestor-descendant relationship judgment from region encoding, twig join need to retrieve every element in the query expression and do join operation one by one, this leads to lots of disk access and mediate results, while algorithm Path-Match processes query by only searching the leaf element in the query expression without any mediate results. Although the matching procedure is not as efficient as region encoding, it need less disk access and performs well.

From the experimental results of Q4, Q5 and Q6, we conclude that both algorithm Branch-Filter and RelatedPath-Join performs better than twig join. Like the analysis before, the advantage comes from less disk access and less mediate results. The reason why algorithm RelatedPath-Join does not perform better than Branch-Filter is the high clustering of CAPI, the number of CAPs in R(Search) and R(Branch) is not much bigger than that in RP(Search) and RP(Branch).

We conclude that the algorithms based on CAPI perform better than twig join on queries with or without branch. The advantage comes from (1)labeling scheme, which combines large amount of elements into few objects; (2)slow growth of the size of index when the document grows large, which guarantees the algorithms efficient even though the document grows large.

6 Related Work

O'Neil et al.[14] introduced a hierarchical labeling scheme called ORDPATH that is implemented in RDBMS. ORD-PATH is also a variation of prefix labeling scheme. But unlike our CAPI, the main goal of ORDPATH is to gracefully handle insertion of XML nodes in the database. They did not show any new algorithm for XML twig pattern matching.

N.Bruno et al. [3] proposed a holistic twig join algorithm based on region encoding. The performance of twig join has been showed in our experiments.

BLAS by Chen et al. [5] proposed a bi-labelling scheme: D-Label and P-Label for accelerating parent-child relationship processing. Their method decomposes a twig pattern into several parent-child path queries and then merges the results. Note that BLAS may have the problem of the large useless intermediate results. Further, it is also difficult for BLAS to handle branching wildcard queries.

1-index [19] is based on the backward bi-simularity relationship. It can answer all simple path queries. F&B Index [12] uses both backward and forward bisimulation and has been proved as the minimum index that supports all branching queries (i.e., twig queries). A(k)-index [15] is an approximation of 1-index by using only k-bisimularity instead of bisimularity. D(k)-index [20] generalizes A(k)-index by using different k according to the workload. M(k)-index further optimize the D(k)-index by taking care not to over-refining index nodes under the given workload. These indexes can't process twig queries except F&B index. While F&B index model nodes in the document as nodes in a tree and algorithms based on F&B index are tree-travel algorithms. CAPI model nodes in the document as CAPs and algorithms based on CAPI are string-match algorithms.

7 Conclusion and Future Work

In this paper, we have proposed a novel index structure, called CAPI. It can extremely reduce the size of index and grows slowly as the source document grows large. Based on CAPI, we design novel join algorithms, called Path-Match to process queries without branches, Branch-Filter and RelatedPath-Join to process queries with branches. We implement the algorithms and compare the performance with twig join. From the experimental results, we conclude that the algorithms based on CAPI perform better than twig join on queries with or without branch. The advantage comes from less disk access due to high clustering of CAPI.

We try to find integer labeling scheme based on CAPI to improve the performance of algorithm Path-Match.

References

[1] J. Clark and S. DeRose, eds. XML Path Language (XPath) Version 2.0 – W3C Working Draft, 2003.

[2] S. Boag, D. Chamberlin, M. F. Fernandez, D. Florescu, J. Robie, and J. Simeon. XQuery 1.0: An XML query language. Technical report, W3C, 2002.

[3] N. Bruno, D. Srivastava, and N. Koudas. Holistic twig joins: optimal XML pattern matching. In SIGMOD Conference, pages 310-321, 2002.

[4] H. Jiang et al. Holistic twig joins on indexed XML documents. In Proc. of VLDB, pages 273-284, 2003.

[5] H. Jiang, H. Lu, and W. Wang. Efficient processing of XML twig queries with OR-predicates. In Proc. of SIGMOD Conference, pages 274-285, 2004.

[6] Q. Li and B. Moon. Indexing and querying XML data for regular path expressions. In Proc. of VLDB, pages 361-370, 2001.

[7] T. Milo and D. Dan Suciu. Index structures for path expressions. In ICDT, pages 277-295, Jerusalem, Israel, 1999

[8] G. Miklau and D. Suciu. Containment and equivalence for an XPath fragment. In PODS, pp. 65–76, 2002.

[9] P. O'Neil et al. ORDPATHs: Insert-friendly XML node labels. In SIGMOD, pages 903-908, 2004.

[10] Y. Chen, S. B. Davidson, and Y. Zheng. BLAS: An efficient XPath processing system. In Proc. of SIGMOD, pages 47-58, 2004.

[11] Extensible Markup Language (XML) 1.0 http://www.w3.org/TR/2004/REC-xml-20040204/

[12] R. Kaushik, P. Shenoy, P. Bohannon, and E. Gudes. Exploiting local similarity for efficient indexing of paths in graph structured data. In ICDE 2002.

[13] C. Qun, A. Lim, and K. W. Ong. D(k)-index:An adaptive structural summary for graph-structureddata. In ACM SIGMOD, pages 134-144, San Diego,California, USA, 2003.

[14] H. He and J. Yang. Multiresolution indexing of XML for frequent queries. In ICDE 2004.

[15] R. Kaushik, P. Bohannon, J. F. Naughton, and H. F. Korth. Covering indexes for branching path queries. In SIGMOD 2002.

[16] XMark: The XML-benchmark project.http://monetdb.cwi.nl/ xml, 2002.

Positioning-Based Query Translation Between SQL and XQL with Location Counter

Joseph Fong[1], Wilfred Ng[2], San Kuen Cheung[1], and Ivan Au[1]

[1] Computer Science Department, City University of Hong Kong, Hong Kong
csjfong@cityu.edu.hk
[2] Computer Science Department, Hong Kong University of Science and Technology
Wilfred@cs.ust.hk

Abstract. The need for interoperation and data exchange through the Internet has made Extensible Markup Language (XML) a dominant standard language. Much work has already been done on translating relational data into XML documents and vice versa. However, there is not an integrated method to combine them together as a unifying technology for database interoperability on the Internet. Users may not be familiar with various query language syntax. We propose database gateways built on the top of a Relational Database (RDB) and an XML Database (XMLDB). Users can access both databases at the same time through the query language SQL or XQL (an XML query language) to access data stored in either RDB or XMLDB. The translation process adopts query graph translation between a RDB and an XMLDB. Thus, a stepwise procedure of query translation is devised and amenable to implementation. The procedure also provides an XML interface to a RDB as well as a relational interface to XMLDB. A location counter sequence number is used to position tuples in a RDB for subsequent transforming the tuples into the corresponding positioning element instances in the XML documents. As a result, both XMLDB and RDB can co-exist, and be accessible by the users.

1 Introduction

This paper proposes a stepwise approach to query translation that constructs a gateway between relational and XML database systems. One of the keys to success in migration strategy is the ability that copes with the changes imposed by business requirements. We address the issue of such changes by partitioning the process of database migration and query translation into three phases as shown in Figure 1. Phase I is the translation of the source relational schema into a target XML schema. Phase II is an inverse mapping that is represented as augmented views. These augmented views are similar to relational views but it is more flexible for users to select their root-based XML documents. Phase III transforms a query from relational SQL into an equivalent XQL query over the target XML database. The rationale for defining phases I and II is that a relational schema is not wholly compatible with an XML schema. As a result, we need to partition a relational schema into an augmented view of XML tree structure in order to make them compatible. A methodology is developed to allow users to interoperate RDB and XMLDB through query translation.

H.T. Shen et al. (Eds.): ADWeb 2006, LNCS 3842, pp. 11 – 18, 2006.

The database gateways receive the input queries before they are sent to the underlying databases. Query translation will be done through the gateways. The translated query will be sent to the appropriate database. Users can rely on one data model and his or her familiar query language to access data in both the RDB and the XMLDB.

The query translation process consists of two main steps of schema translation and query translation. The system allows users to input SQL query which is translated into XPath for selecting the data on XMLDB. The architecture composes of two gateways, the XML Gateway and the Relational Gateway, as shown in Figure 2. There is a common interface between these gateways, which connect to a XMLDB server and a RDB server.

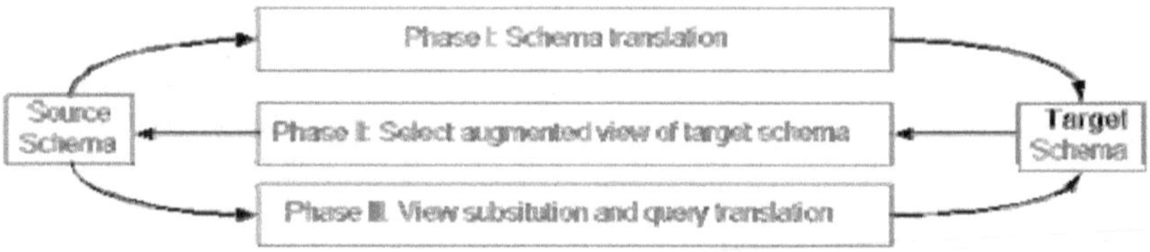

Fig. 1. The three steps for database reengineering query translation

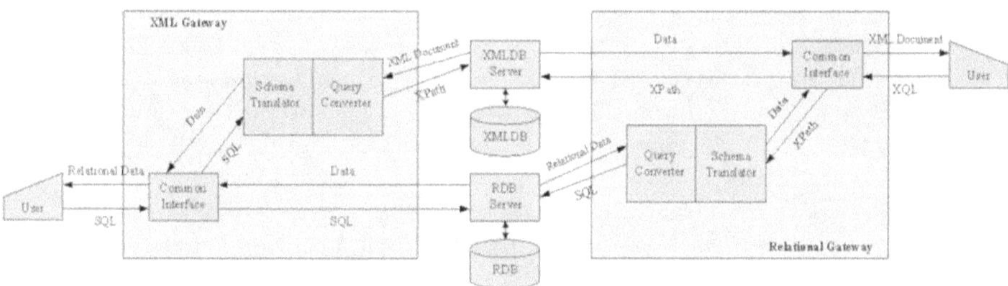

Fig. 2. XML and Relational Gateways

1.1 Related Work

Shanmugasundaram [2] presents three inlining algorithms that focus on the table level of the schema while Florescu and Kossmann [3] investigate various performance issues among five algorithms that focus on the attribute and value level of the schema. They all transform the given XML DTD to a relational schema. Collins [4] describes two algorithms for mapping relational and network models schemas into XML schema using the relational mapping algorithm. Such an approach allows the data in the relational and network database system. Tatarinov [5] studies how XML's ordered data model can be supported using an unordered RDB system. They propose three order encoding methods (Global Order, Local Order and Dewey Order) for representing XML in the relational model. Tseng and Hwung [6] developed a system called XML meta-generator (XMG) that is an extraction scheme to store and retrieve XML documents through object-relational databases. WebReader [7] is a middleware for automating the search and collecting information and manipulation in XSL, WebReader also provides the users with a centralized, structured, and categorized means to specify for querying web information.

2 Methodology of Query Translation Between SQL and XQL

As shown in Figure 1, we need to abstract an augmented view of the target XML tree structure into a relational schema in phases I and II. We have a compatible tree structure in a partitioned relational schema and a mapped target XML schema. Then in phase III, we translate an SQL to XQL according to the mapped XML schema. Similarly, we can translate an XQL to SQL according to the partitioned relational schema. These three phases are further detailed in the subsequent subsections.

2.1 Phase I: Schema Translation Between Relational and XML Data

We add a sequence number into a relational table for data position in XML document. For any table that is used for query translation, an extra column - *seqno* is required. This column is used by the XML gateway described as follows:

For each table, the last column is *seqno*. This *seqno* column is used to ensure that the records returned from database are in the right order. The column is also used for translation of XQL location index functions (e.g. *position()*). The *seqno* column is incremented by one for each new record of the same key value and maintained by using the insert trigger. The records in the repository table *node_table-column_mapping* is used for mapping the column of the table that is used for maintaining the *seqno* value.

node_tablecolumn_mapping Table

Table name	Node key column
CLIENT	ClientID
CLIENTACCOUNTEXECUTIVE	ClientID
ACCOUNTEXECUTIVE	AEID
BALANCE	ClientID

CLIENTACCOUNTEXECUTIVE Table

ClientID	AEID	*Seqno*
600001	AE0001	1
600001	AE0002	2
600002	AE0001	1
600003	AE0003	1

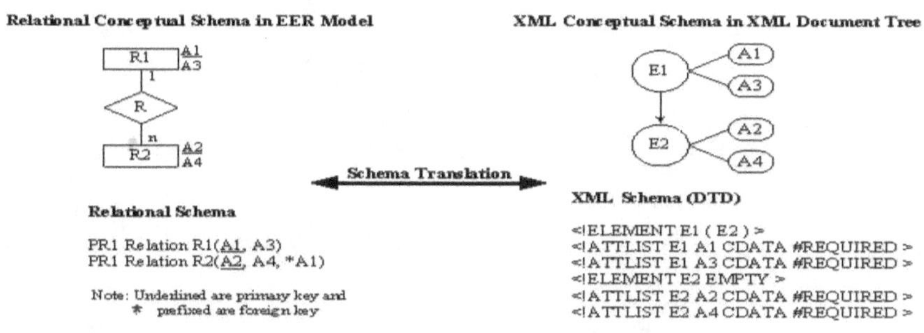

Fig. 3. Translation of Functional Dependency between Relational and XML Schemas

On inserting a new record into a table, the insert trigger first locates that the column is used for counting *seqno* from the *node_tablecolumn_mapping* table. Then, the trigger selects the maximum *seqno* value for the new record. The maximum *seqno* value plus one is assigned as the *seqno* value of the new record. There is no need to update the *seqno* value in case the record is deleted. In XQL, the location index function (e.g. *position()*) counts the order of the record relative to the parent node. Given receiver's relations R1(A1, A3) and R2(A2, A4, *A1) with an FD (functional dependency): R2.A1 → R1.A1. R1 and R2 are classified and joined into a relation R(A1, A2, A3, A4), which is then translated into a single sub-element topological XML document by mapping parent relation R1 into element E1, and child relation R2 into sub-element E2 as shown in Figure 3.

2.2 Phase II: Select Augmented View of Target XML Schema in Mapping RDB to XML Schema

To convert a relational database into an XML document tree, we integrate the translated XML document trees into an XML document tree, select an element as root and put its relevant information into a document. We load the relational database into the object instances of the XML documents. Each XML document focuses on a root class upon user requirements. The selection is driven by some business requirements. Relevance concerns elements that are related to a root selected by the users among the integrated XML document tree (DOM tree). Figure 4(a) shows an integrated XML document tree. The user can select root A1 with its relevant classes to form a partitioned XML document tree.

Select augmented view of target RDB schema in mapping XML to RDB schema. Similar to convert an XML schema to RDB schema, we allow user select an augmented view of the EER model of target RDB schema as shown in Figure 4(b).

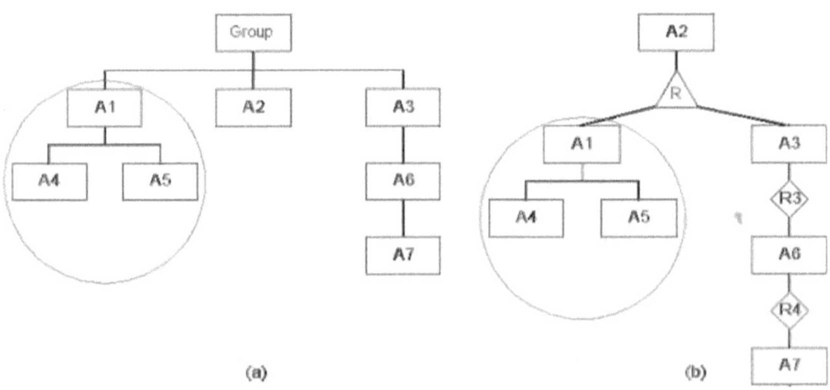

Fig. 4. Select augment view of target (a) XML schema and (b) relational schema in cycle

2.3 Phase III: Query Translation Between XQL and SQL

2.3.1 Query Translation from SQL to XQL

In query transformation, a syntax-directed parser converts the SQL into multi-way trees. The transformation process is performed, based on the subtree matching and replacement technique. The process of SQL query transformation is given in Figure 5.

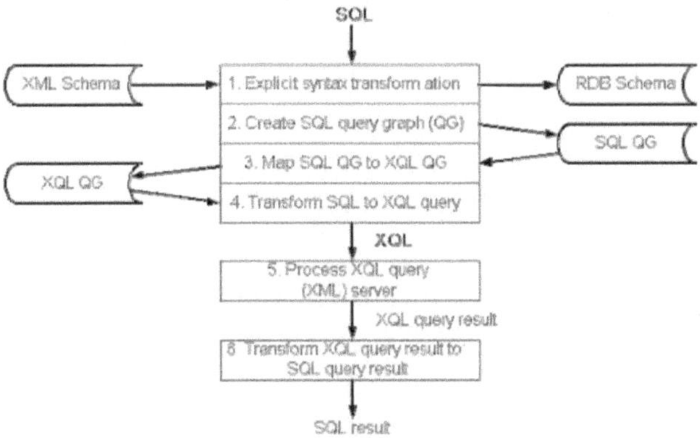

Fig. 5. Process for SQL to XQL Transformation

Translation of SQL Query to XPath Query

After the schema is done, SQL query can be translated to XPath query by the following steps:

Step 1 Decompose SQL Query Transaction: The basic syntax SQL SELECT statement is given as follows:

SELECT {attribute-list-1} FROM {relation-list}
WHERE {join-condition} AND / OR {search-condition-1}
ORDER BY {attribute-list-2} GROUP BY {attribute-list-3}
HAVING {search-condition-2}

Step 2 Create the SQL Query Graph: Based on the relation-list and the join-condition in the SQL query transaction, the SQL query graph is created. The join condition is based on the natural join or based on the search condition specified in the SQL query [1].

Step 3 Map the SQL Query Graph to XPath Query Graph: The SQL query graph is mapped to the XPath query graph. The table joins from the SQL query graph forms the XPath location path, which are the steps for navigating down the document tree from root node.

Step 4 Transform SQL to XPath Query: In this step, the SQL query is transformed into XPath syntax as follows:

/root/node1[@attribute1=condition]/…/node2[@attribute2=condition]/@attribute3

The attribute-list in the SQL query is mapped to the leaf attribute node at the bottom of the document tree. If all the attributes of the element node are selected, "@*" is mapped to select all the attributes from the leaf element node. If more than one attributes are selected, the union operator is used to get the result. For example:
/root/node1/@attribute1 | /root/node1/@attribute2

Step 5 Transform XPath Query Data into SQL Query Data: The XML document returned from XMLDB is formatted into tables before the document returning to user. The format of the result is based on the data stored in the table *table_column_seq* (prepared in pre-processed schema translation).

2.3.2 Query Translation from XQL to SQL

To translate query from XQL to SQL, document tree nodes in XQL query are replaced by the relational JOIN in SQL. The XQL allows data retrieval using path expressions, and data manipulation using methods. A syntax-directed parser converts the XQL into multi-way trees. The transformation process is performed, based on the subtree matching and replacement technique. The process of XQL query transformation is given in Figure 6.

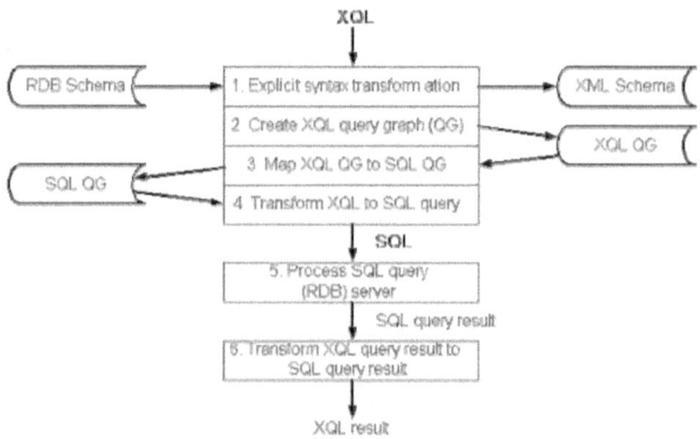

Fig. 6. Process for XQL to SQL Transformation

2.3.3 Query Translation from XPath to SQL

XPath views a document as a tree of nodes consisting of elements and attributes. Based on the generated XML schema, the XPath query graph of node navigation is converted to SQL query graph of table joins. Below is a stepwise procedure of how XPath query is translated to SQL query:

Step 1 Decompose the XPath Transaction: Each slash-separated (/) path component of XPath query is a step. The following nodes and predicates are identified from the descendent axis:

1. * - selects all element children of the context node
2. @name – selects the name attribute of the context node
3. @* - selects all the attributes of the context node

Orderid	Exe_sequence	Quantity	Price	Time	*Seqno*
300001	1	10000	21.6	200204031001	1
300002	1	2000	10.85	200204031002	1

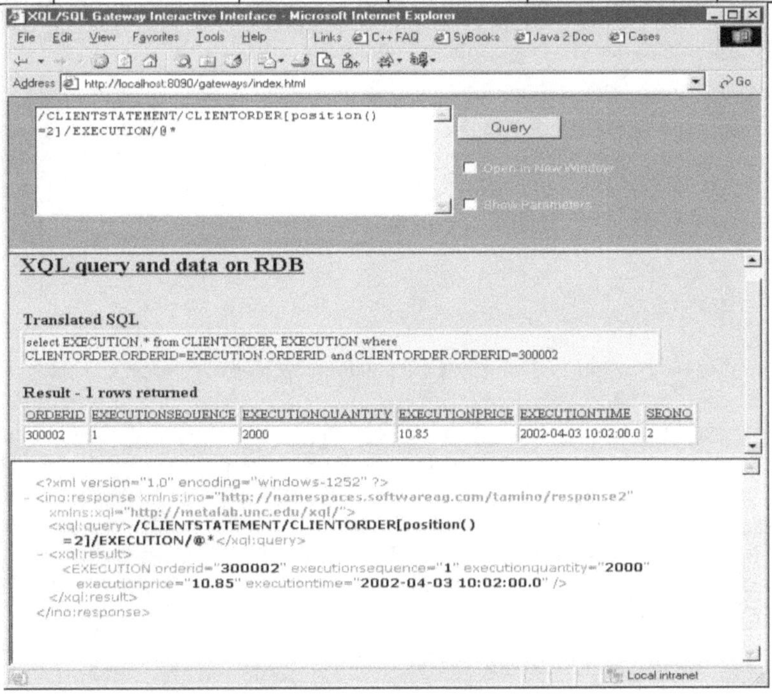

Fig. 7. XQL Query with Position Value Translated into SQL

4. [method] – built-in functions to create more expressive queries. They are text(), *position()*=n, or last() where n is index of the location of element instance starting from 0.
5. [@name="attributeValue"] – the value of the name attribute is equal to "attributeValue"

Step 2 Create XPath Query Graph: The query graph of the XPath expression or query is created in this step. Based on the translated XML schema, a navigation path is created to indicate the relationship between nodes by stepping down the XML document tree hierarchy. From the node_sequence table, all the nodes down from the root element are identified.

Step 3 Map the XPath Query Graph to SQL Query Graph: From the XPath query graph, the root node and its descendant child node are located. For each node, the elements are mapped to their corresponding relation in the RDB.

Step 4 Translate XPath Query to SQL Queries: From the mapped XML schema, each XML document has a key for retrieving the data for each element node. A key cursor is created for first retrieving the keys for the XML documents. This key is stored in the table xml_document_key and each value fetched from this cursor is used subsequently for each translated SQL query. It is constructed by the following replacements:

- Replacing XML document tree node navigation path by SQL join relations path.
- Replacing the XML tree elements by their corresponding SQL relations.
- Replacing XML document tree node filtering by SQL WHERE clause.
- Replacing the XML document instance location index function by embedded SQL query cursor. By counting the number of time result set is fetched from cursor, the location index of XML document is emulated.

Step 5 Map the Retrieved Relation Data into XML Document Format: The result set returned from SQL query is mapped into the translated XML schema. The tags for the data returned from SQL query are identified from the table xml_document_node. The result is formatted into XML document returned to user[1],

3 Conclusions

This paper describes a methodology that translates XQL query to SQL query and vice versa. Sequence numbers are applied to indicate the position of the relational tuples that are involved in the schema translation. The approach provides flexibility for users to query on a selected (focused on root based) XML view of a relational database when translating SQL to XQL, or to query a set of selected relational tables in translating XQL to SQL. The benefit of our approach is that the sequential processing of both the relational database and the XML database are compatible due to the added positioning *SEQNO* in the relational side. Our approach has a distinct feature that XDB and RDB are able to co-exist, and XQL and SQL can be employed to access both systems. As shown in Figure 7, a prototype of the database gateways is developed. It shows that query translation between SQL and XQL with the proposed methodology is feasible. For example, we want to fetch its second tuple of the following Execution table.

References

[1] Ivan Au, Feasibility Study of Query Translation between SQL and XQL, M.Sc. dissertation of C.S. Department at City University of Hong Kong, 2002

[2] Jayavel Shanmugasundaram et al, RDBs for Querying XML Documents: Limitations and Opportunities, 25th VLDB Conference, 1999, Page(s): 302-314.

[3] D. Florescu, and D. Kossman, Storing and Querying XML Data Using an RDBMS, IEEE Data Engineering Bulletin, 22(3), 1999, Page(s): 27-34

[4] Samuel Robert Collins et al, XML Schema Mappings for Heterogeneous Database Access, Information and Software Technology, Volume 44, Issue 4, March 2002, Page(s): 251-257

[5] Igor Tatarinov et al, Storing and Querying Ordered XML Using a RDB System, 2002 ACM SIGMOD int'l conference on Management of data, June 2002

[6] Frank S. C. Tseng and Wen-Jong Hwung, An Automatic Load/Extract Scheme for XML Documents through Object-Relational Repositories, Journal of Systems and Software, Volume 64, Issue 3, December 2002, Page(s): 207-218

[7] J. Chan and Q. Li, WebReader: A Mechanism for Automating the Search and Collecting Information from the World Wide Web, 1st International Conference on Web Information Systems Engineering, Volume 2, 2000, Page(s): 47-56

Integrating XML Schema Language with Databases for B2B Collaborations

Taesoo Lim and Wookey Lee*

Dept. of Computer, Sungkyul University,
Anyang-8 Dong, Manan-Gu, Anyang-city, Kyunggi-Do, South Korea
{tshou, wook}@sungkyul.edu

Abstract. In this paper, we propose a series of rules for transforming XML Schema language into standard database schema, specifically based on ODMG 3.0 specifications. Our rules have the following characteristics: First, the rules use XML Schema as a document structure description language because the XML Schema has much stronger capabilities in exchanging data than the DTD has. Second, the rules support both structured and unstructured requests for XML documents, since the types of XML documents can be varied according to the level of integration among enterprises. We expect the rules will be an enabler technology for integrating distributed applications, in which the storage and retrieval of transmitted XML documents are mission-critical.

1 Introduction

Distributed organizations can collaborate with each other by exchanging data related to product, planning, control, and so forth. However, organizations may often have different data formats and communication methods with one another. This diversity has been an obstacle to effective collaboration among trading partners [9]. An information integration technology between heterogeneous information sources would substantially assist collaborative interactions between distributed organizations. The advent of both the World Wide Web (WWW) and XML removed to some extent the barriers of communication between heterogeneous applications. The WWW provides easy access channels between distributed organizations, and XML plays an important role as a standard B2B communication format. However, often enterprises have created their own databases with underlying organizational models, including relational, object-oriented, network, and hierarchical models. Furthermore, these databases use their own data formats, which are not defined in the form of XML. Consequently, to support its wide use, XML needs to be integrated effectively with legacy databases.

This paper proposes a schema transformation method of integrating XML documents with legacy databases. This method may act as a base technology to support collaborative work processes. Specifically, in this paper, we propose a generic model that complies with various requests that occur in B2B transactions. Previous integration methods have been focused on the relational transformation for structured

* Corresponding author.

H.T. Shen et al. (Eds.): ADWeb 2006, LNCS 3842, pp. 19–28, 2006.

documents declared by DTD language. However, the types of XML documents can be varied according to the level of integration among enterprises, and structured documents require XML Schema language more than DTD. Therefore, to effectively support B2B transactions, it is needed to comply with both structured and unstructured requests for XML documents represented by XML Schema language.

This paper is organized as follows: Section 2 describes the characteristics of XML documents in the B2B collaborations. In section 3, we compared our model with previous transformation models for XML documents. Section 4 proposes in detail the transformation rules with illustrative examples. Finally, Section 5 presents conclusions.

2 XML Documents in Collaborative B2B Environments

B2B transactions are usually binary collaborations performed by sellers and buyers. A buyer purchases products through a series of operations: requisitions, Request For Quotation (RFQ), Purchasing Order (PO), and product arrival. A seller performs corresponding actions: proposal, quotation, order receipt, shipping, and invoicing. Although buying and selling activities are done at the front end, information flow is connected with the internal production process. For example, material specification information from the manufacturing process flows into the purchasing process, and the information on material arrival is transferred into the manufacturing process. Order information from the sales process is integrated into production planning in the manufacturing process, and product delivery information is sent to the shipping department in the sales division. Therefore, to carry out an effective B2B collaboration, front-end applications need to be properly implemented, which means seamless integration with the back-end information systems

There are numerous research papers on the patterns of B2B collaboration. The special issue of Production Planning and Control (2001, v.12, no. 5) on enterprise collaboration in extended manufacturing is especially helpful. Jagdev and Thoben [6] classified three main types of B2B collaborations according to the level of applied IT and CT: supply chain, extended enterprise, and virtual enterprise. In a supply chain type of collaboration, material and information flows are streamlined by means of data sharing through an entire supply chain. An extended enterprise type of collaboration is a higher level of cooperation between organizations and requires process integration on top of existing long-term partnerships. A virtual enterprise type of collaboration is temporarily constructed in response to the customer needs. The supply chain type can be defined as a loosely coupled collaboration, whereas the extended enterprise can be defined as a tightly coupled collaboration. From the viewpoint of partnership, the virtual enterprise is different from the first two types. The format of XML document generated in B2B transactions can be varied according the integration level of the collaborations. The more tightly integrated the trading partners are, the more they prefer structured documents.

Bertino and Catania [1] had two views on the types of XML documents: one type was seen as a document and the other as a data envelope. As a document type, an XML document needs to be processed as a whole rather than in parts. Its representation is more critical than its structure, and it is characterized by irregular and roughly structured content and importance in the sequence of elements. As a data envelope type, the XML instance acts as neutral information interchange format with the shape of a document. Therefore, it is important also to have structural information, such as well-ordered, standardized, and more finely structured content. In addition, the data envelope type features strict type definition, and the sequence of elements is unimportant. Fig. 1 shows the positioning of XML documents according to the requirements of the document and data envelope types.

An unstructured XML document has been used to generate Standard Generalized Markup Language (SGML), which preceded XML. It is critical to fulfill the requirements as a document and is rarely used as a data envelope. On the other hand, a structured XML document is required as a data exchange format. The XML document is used as the standard and neutral envelope format only to carry the data inside, not as a whole document. Because a semi-structured XML document is structured as well as unstructured, both the value and the order of the elements are equally important. The format of the XML document generated in B2B transactions can be either structured or semi-structured. The more tightly integrated the trading partners are, the more they prefer structured documents. Therefore, it is necessary to support both document-centric and data-centric characteristics of XML documents.

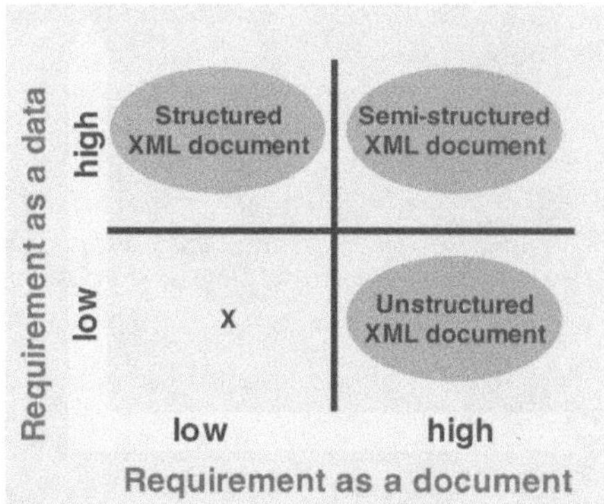

Fig 1. Types of XML documents

3 Previous Transformation Models for XML Documents

Since XML was highlighted as an information interchange format, many requirements have emerged for the tightly coupled integration of XML and traditional databases. Primary requirements are how data transferred by XML documents can be read, stored, and queried [1] [12]. To support those requirements, most of the conventional approaches have been applied to relational databases (RDB) or object-relational databases [3] [7] [13] [15] [14]. However, some limitations were found in combining tree-structured XML with RDB, and the object-oriented model was found to be more appropriate for processing the complex data structure of XML. Especially, relational models can represent document-centric characteristics of XML documents such as implicit order, nesting, and hyperlinks but only with costly time and space transformations [10].

Previous researches using an object-oriented model have concentrated on DTD (see table 1) except Varlamis and Vazirgiannis [14]'s X-Database system. However, our model focused on XML Schema, which was developed as an alternative and to complement the drawbacks of DTD [11]. Its latest version has been approved as a W3C Recommendation in October, 2004.

Table 1. Object-oriented models for XML documents

Models	Input type	Features	Remarks
OEM model[4]	instance	Adopting OEM (Object Exchange Model) data model with Dataguide	More spaces may be needed to store Dataguides than actual XML data.
ORM model[5]	DTD and instance	Adopting ORM (Object Representation Model) data model with super classes and class methods	Modeling attributes as classes will increase space complexity.
CDM model[8]	DTD and instance	Adopting mediator-wrapper approach with CDM (Common Data Model)	Confusions between terminal element and attributes.
Chung Model[2]	DTD	Composing a class hierarchy using inheritance	No support for attribute and sequence information.
Our model	XML Schema	Support for essential characteristics of XML Schema	Limited to structure-mapping approach.

As shown in table 1, previous work has concentrated on DTD. Our model differs from previous research on object-oriented models for XML because it supports, in addition to the essential components of DTD, other resources of XML Schema that are not included in DTD. Our model provides a generic data model to manage both document-centric and data-centric XML documents generated from B2B transactions. The model is designed on the basis of the ODMG 3.0 object-oriented model independent of specific DBMSs. Furthermore, the proposed model supports bi-directional transformation between XML documents and legacy DBMSs and attempts to reduce the generated number of classes and instances, which are advantages over previous models.

4 XML Schema Transformation Methods

This paper proposes type conversion and constraint preservation transformation rules for XML Schema. The type conversion rules handle transformation of types and elements described by XML Schema into an object-oriented model. The constraint preservation rules deal with preservation of the constraints restricting the types or elements in the object-oriented model. We describe type conversion rules in sec. 4.1 and constraint preservation rules in sec. 4.2.

4.1 Type Conversion Rules

This section discusses the rules that convert various types specified by an XML Schema into types and classes in an object-oriented model. These XML Schema-based types are divided into pre-defined built-in types and user-defined types and are also classified into simple types and complex types according to their content. A complex type defines sub-elements or attributes, whereas a simple type does not. Built-in data types are simple types, and user-defined types can be either simple or complex types depending on their content model. We explain the conversion rules of built-in data types, user-defined simple types, and user-defined complex types, successively.

4.1.1 Built-In Types

Built-in data types are derived from anySimpleType that is a restricted type of anyType, a super type. Built-in data types are classified into primitive data types derived directly from anySimpleType and data types derived from those primitive types. Refer to http://www.w3.org/TR/xmlschema-2/#typesystem for the details of each type.

Because the XML Schema was developed in different domains from the ODMG 3.0 standard, it provides data types different from the standard types. The XML Schema supplies many data types to express both document and data. On the other hand, the ODMG standard provides more generic types than the XML Schema does. The ODMG standard represents pre-defined built-in types as literals. Atomic literals are the primary built-in types that bind to the implementation programming language. Collection literals are the types that gather homogeneous types, and structured literals include a user-defined structure collecting heterogeneous types. Comparing XML Schema with ODMG type system, we can see that the XML Schema provides richer pre-defined types than the ODMG 3.0 standard.

We divided the built-in data types into four categories as follows.

Common data type: There are two kinds of methods to handle the common data type. A float type can be directly mapped into a float literal. On the other hand, both decimal and integer types are mapped into long long literal, the longest integer type of ODMG 3.0. Most primitive types like long, int, float, double, etc. belong to the common data type.

Constrained data type: The constrained data type needs a checking method for its constraint. For instance, the nonPositiveInteger type requires that its value be less than or equal to zero. The checking methods can be defined by the stored procedure of a DBMS, and the detail implementation codes for the methods depend on the selected DBMS. Detail types are omitted.

Decomposed data type: This type is mapped into an ODMG 3.0 literal by combining several built-in data types of the XML Schema. The XML Schema decomposes a date type into several types, such as gYearMonth, gYear, gMonthDay, gDay and gMonth. But, ODMG 3.0 only provides a date literal. Therefore, the functions to combine these types need to be provided.

Combined data type: QName, NOTATION, NMTOKENS, IDREFS, and ENTITIES are converted by using other types. They are defined by using struct, set, and list according to the combination type.

4.1.2 Simple Types

Simple types are classified into three types: an atomic type specified by a built-in data type, a list type of an atomic type, and a union type of atomic types or list types. A simple type can be either an anonymous simple type that is only applicable to a specific element or a global simple type that is reusable. A global simple type must be recorded, but an anonymous simple type does not have to be.

A class does not need to be created for a type because the type does not have its instance. On the contrary, it is natural to transform an element into a class because the element has its instance. However, the element specified by the simple type is a terminal element, and therefore, is modeled as an attribute of its parent element or type to reduce the number of classes.

An element can be either a simple type element or a complex type element according to its type. Because the category of the element depends on the chosen type, rules for combining a type and an element are given. Rule 1 explains how to convert a simple type into an ODMG model.

Rule 1. Simple type and simple type element
The simple type element specified by a simple type is not converted into a class. Its parent element or complex type has the element as an attribute, and the simple type as the type of the attribute. When the simple type is a global type, a typedef declarer defines it.

Fig. 2 shows that the Product element of RFQ.xsd reuses the list type defined in Product.xsd. It also represents the result modeled by Rule l.

```
<element name='RFQ' type='RFQType'/>
<complexType name=RFQType>
<element name=Product type=PRODUCT:listOfProductID/>
```

(a) RFQ.xsd

```
<simpleType name="listOfProductID">
    <list itemType="ProductID"/>
</simpleType>
<simpleType name='ProductID' base='string'>
    <pattern value='[A-Z]{1}d{6}'/>
</simpleType>
```

(b) Product.xsd

```
typedef string ProductID;
typedef        list<ProductID>
listOfProductID;
class RFQ{
        Attribute  listOfProductID
Product;
};
```

(c) ODMG expression

Fig. 2. Simple type description and its modeling

4.1.3 Complex Types

A complex type element needs to instantiate its object. It is a non-terminal element so that it is modeled as a class. Because a complex type has embedded elements or attributes, we cannot use a typedef declarer that has defined a simple type. Instead, the complex type is converted into an abstract class that does not have its instance and makes the complex type element inherit the class. Rule 2 represents the conversion rule for the complex type.

Rule 2. Complex type and complex type element
The attribute of a complex type is represented as an attribute with prefix 'private_'. The sub-element of the type is modeled as a relationship. If the type has a value, it is represented as an attribute with prefix 'terminal_'.

The complex type element specified by the complex type is converted into a class. When the complex type is a global type, the type is modeled as an abstract class and the element class extends it.

We already have made a terminal element an attribute of its parent element (Refer to sec. 4.1.2). Because a complex type can have its own attributes, the attributes need to be distinguished from the terminal element attributes. The attributes enclosed by a tag in XML documents are not visible information to users, but rather are invisible components used for processing the document. The model uses a private keyword to represent these components. A private keyword is used by most object-oriented languages to encapsulate attributes in a class. . Because there is no clear private declaration in the ODMG 3.0 standard, the prefix could be used for indication in the implementation phase. For a complex type that has its own value, it is also natural to represent it as an attribute. This attribution causes the same problem; therefore, a terminal prefix is used to prevent misunderstandings. It looks slightly unnatural, however, when a complex type element has a value; it is generally the lowest level element possessing an attribute. Fig. 3 shows an example applying Rule 2.

```
<element name='RFQ' type='RFQType'/>
<complexType name=RFQType> ...
   <element name=Payement type=Payment_info/>..
   <attribute name=Quotation_req_num
    type=Doc_num/>
   <attribute name=Quotation_req_date
         type=Standard_date/>
</complexType>
<simpleType name=Doc_num base=string>
   <pattern value=[A-Z]{1}d{6}/>
</simpleType>
<simpleType name=Standard_date base=date>
   <pattern value=d{2}-d{3}-d{4}/>
</simpleType>
<complexType name=Payment_info>
   <element name=Payment_terms_code
         type=Standard_terms_code/>
   <element name=Payement_due
   type=Standard_date/>
</complexType>
<simpleType name=Standard_terms_code
base=decimal>
   <totalDigits value=6/>
</simpleType>
```

```
typedef string Doc_num;
typedef date Standard_date;
typedef decimal Standard_terms_code;
class abstract_RFQ{
   ....
   attribute Doc_num
   private_Quotation_req_num;
   attribute Standard_date
            private_Quotation_req_date;
   relationship Payment super
            inverse shipTo::sub;
};
class RFQ extends abstract_RFQ{
};
class Payment extends
     abstract_Payment_info{
   relationship RFQ sub
            inverse Payment::super;
};
class abstract_Payment_info{
  attribute Standard_terms_code
              Payment_terms_code;
  attribute Standard_date Payment_due;
};
```

Fig. 3. Complex type description and its modeling

4.2 Constraint Preservation Rules

The XML Schema provides various and plentiful constraints, which can be used to design an elaborate data interchange format. Among these constraints, those restricting the most essential constructs, types and elements, can be classified into two categories. The first category includes the constraints indicating the sequence or occurrence of sub-elements originating from DTD. The second category includes constraints defining new types by restriction or extension for the reusability of the existing types.

4.2.1 Sequence and Occurrence

Sequence constraint is needed to keep document characteristics, and the occurrence indictor was devised to avoid a redundant description of the same element. The XML Schema obviously specifies the order through the sequence element and provides more precise occurrence specification than that of DTD.

Sequence constraint requests that sub-elements are ordered sequentially within a parent element. The parent element is a complex type element and sub-elements are either a complex type or a simple type element. Because a single element can be used as sub-elements for several parent elements, the parent elements keep the sequence structure of their sub-elements. For the same reason, occurrence constraints of sub-elements are preserved in their parent elements. Rule 3 defines the modeling method for these sequence and occurrence constraints.

Rule 3. Sequence and occurrence constraints
The parent element indicates the sequence and occurrence constraints of sub-elements by adding attributes. The occurrence constraint of each sub-element is represented as an ODMG struct named 'occurrence_constraint'. To indicate whether the sequential flow of the sub-elements is required or not, we define two collection literal types: list and set. The list type represents an ordered collection of the occurrence_constraint struct, and the set type represents an unordered collection of the occurrence_constraint struct. When the complex type is a global type, its corresponding abstract class has the attribute, and the element class extends it.

4.2.2 Restriction and Extension

Both restriction and extension resources are newly introduced in XML Schema. We derive a new type from a base type by restriction. For example, to restrain the occurrence of an embedded element, assign '2' to minOccurrs. Derived types by restriction have a limited domain value, which is a subset of the base type domain. However, extension adds new elements or attributes to the base type definition. For instance, adding attributes to a decimal built-in type can derive a new complex type.

Base type can be simple type or complex type as well as derived type. Additionally, both derivations of extension and restriction are also possible, and all the feasible combinations are as shown in table 2.

Table 2. Derivation patterns

Derived type \ Base type		Simple type	Complex type
Restriction	Simple type	Constraining facets	N/A[a]
	Complex type	N/A[b]	extends + constraints
Extension	Simple type	N/A[c]	N/A[a]
	Complex type	Complex + attributes	extends + attributes

Regardless of methods of restriction and extension, a complex type cannot be a simple type because it has sub-elements and attributes ([a]). The complex type cannot be generated from a simple type by restriction because restriction limits the domain ([b]). Furthermore, because extension adds new elements or attributes, a derived type cannot become a simple type ([c]). Consequently, there are four types, and the processing rules for each type are as shown in Rule 4.

Rule 4. Restriction and extension
The constraint preservation rules involved with restriction and extension are as follows:

Case1. Derive a simple type from the simple type by restriction. Use constraint struct.
Case2. Derive a complex type from the simple type by extension. Refer to Rule 2.
Case3. Derive a complex type from the complex type by restriction. Make a new abstract class that extends the class corresponding to the base type, and redefine the changed elements and attributes using Rules 1, 2, and 3.
Case4. Derive a complex type from the complex type by extension. Make a new abstract class that extends the class corresponding to the base type, and add new attributes according to Rule 2.

5 Conclusions

This paper proposes an object-oriented document model that can integrate XML documents with legacy databases without losing any characteristics of the documents. The model has the following characteristics: First, it conforms to the ODMG 3.0 specifications that are the international standard for an object-oriented data model. With that standard, a tree-structured XML document can be modeled more naturally rather than using a relational model. Second, it uses the XML Schema as a document structure description language. The XML Schema has much stronger capabilities in exchanging data than has DTD. Third, the meta-model can store XML documents into databases maintaining both characteristics of the documents: document-centric and data-centric; consequently, it can serve as a medium to exchange data and to keep documents.

We expect that the model can be used to integrate distributed applications, in which the storage and retrieval of transmitted XML documents are critical. The model is focused on business documents generated from trading activities, which are front-end transactions between collaborating enterprises. Messages or documents generated from back-end applications might have different aspects from the business documents. Therefore, it is necessary to analyze specific messaging structures required in manufacturing applications, and to expand the model to support the structure.

Acknowledgement

This work was supported by the Ministry of Science and Technology (MOST)/ Korea Science and Engineering Foundation (KOSEF) through the Advanced Information Technology Research Center (AITrc).

References

1. Bertino, E., Catania, B.: Integrating XML and databases, IEEE Internet Computing, 5 (4), (2001) 84-88
2. Chung, T.-S., Park, S., Han, S.-Y., Kim, H.-J.: Extracting Object-Oriented Schemas from XML DTDs Using Inheritance, LNCS (Springer-Verlag), (2001) 49-59
3. Florescu, D., and Kossmann, D.: Storing and querying XML data using an RDBMS. IEEE Data Engineering Bulletin, 22 (3), (1999) 27-34
4. Goldman, R., Mchugh, J., Widom, J.: From semistructured data to XML: migrating the Lore data model and query language, In: Proc. International Workshop on the Web and Databases, (1999) 25-30
5. Hou, J., Zhang, Y., Kambayashi, Y.: Object-oriented representation for XML data, In: Proc. Cooperative Database Systems and Applications, (2001) 43-52
6. Jagdev, H. S., Thoben, K.-D.: Anatomy of enterprise collaborations, Production Planning and Control, 12 (5), (2001) 437-451
7. Lee, D., Mani, M., Chu, W.: Schema Conversion Methods between XML and Relational Models, Knowledge Transformation for the Semantic Web, (2003) 1-17
8. Lin, H., Risch, T., and Katchaounov, T.: Object-oriented mediator queries to XML data, In: Proc. Web Information Systems Engineering, (2000) 38-45
9. Mcivor, R., Humphreys, P., Mccurry, L.: Electronic commerce: supporting collaboration in the supply chain?, Journal of Materials Processing Technology, 6736, (2003) 1-6
10. Nambiar, U., Lacroix, Z., Bressan, S., Lee, M. L., Li, Y.: Current approaches to XML management, IEEE Internet Computing, 6(4), (2002) 43-51
11. Roy, J., Ramanujan, A.: XML Schema language: taking XML to the next level. IEEE IT Professional, March-April, (2001) 37-40
12. Seligman, L., Roenthal, A.: XML's impact on databases and data sharing, IEEE Computer, 34 (6), (2001) 59-67
13. Sha, F., Gardarin, G.., Nemirovski, L.: Managing semi-structured data in object-relational DBMS, Networking and Information Systems Journal, 1 (1), (2000) 7-25
14. Varliamis, I., Vazirgiannis, M.: Bridging XML-Schema and relational databases. A system for generating and manipulating relational databases using valid XML documents. In: Proc. DocEng'01, (2001) 9-10
15. Yoshikawa, M., Amagasa, T., Shimura, T., and Uemura, S., XRel: A path-based approach to storage and retrieval of XML documents using relational databases. ACM Transactions on Internet Technology, 1, (2001) 110-141

Functional Dependencies in XML Documents

Ping Yan[1] and Teng Lv[1,2]

[1] College of Mathematics and System Science,
Xinjiang University, Urumqi 830046, China
[2] Teaching and Research Section of Computer,
Artillery Academy, Hefei 230031, China
lt0410@163.com

Abstract. This paper analyzes and points out the differences of functional dependencies when they are applied in XML documents and relational databases. A concept of functional dependency in XML documents based on path expressions is proposed. The advantage of this definition is that it can represent the functional dependencies not only between the values of attributes and elements, but also between the nodes of elements in an XML documents. Some inference rules of XML functional dependencies also given as a start point and foundation for further research.

1 Introduction

XML (eXtensible Markup Language)[1] has become one of the primary standards of data exchange on the World Wide Web and is widely used in many fields. Although XML is flexible, extensible, self-explanatory, etc, which are its advantages, it is hard for XML to express semantic information as little mechanism is provided for XML. So it is necessary to study such problem in XML research field. One of topics of XML semantic is functional dependency, which is fundamental to other related XML research fields, such as normalizing XML documents [2, 3], Querying XML documents, mapping between XML documents and other data forms [15-17], etc. There are some schemas for XML documents are proposed, such as XML-Data [4], XML Schema [5], DTD (Document Type Definition)[6], etc. In recent years, XML Schema has become one of the primary schemas for XML documents and is widely supported by many applications and product providers. Although the theory of functional dependencies in relational database world has matured, there is no such mature and systematic theory for XML world because XML is new comparing to relational databases, and there are so many differences between relational schemas and XML schemas in structure.

Related work. The theory of functional dependencies [7] for relational databases can not be directly applied in XML documents as there are significant differences in their structures: relational model are flat while XML schemas are nested. Refs. [3,13] propose a definition of XML functional dependencies. Unfortunately, it does not differentiate between global functional dependencies and local functional dependencies for XML, which is a major characteristic of functional dependencies in XML documents considering their nested structure. Ref. [8] also gives a definition of XML functional

H.T. Shen et al. (Eds.): APWeb Workshops 2006, LNCS 3842, pp. 29 – 37, 2006.

dependencies which only considers the string values of attributes and elements of XML documents, but XML documents have elements as well. The definition of XML functional dependencies proposed in our paper overcomes the shortcomings of the above definitions in the following aspects: (1) it captures the characteristics of XML structure and differentiates between global functional dependencies and local functional dependencies for XML. (2) it considers not only the string values of attributes and elements but also the elements themselves of XML documents. Ref.[14] proposes a definition of XML functional dependencies based on sub-graph which are orthogonal to our definition of XML functional dependencies which are based on path expressions. Refs. [9-11] propose the concept of XML keys, but XML functional dependencies is more complicated and has more applications than XML keys.

This paper studies the problem of functional dependencies in XML documents with XML Schema as their schemas. First, we give an example to demonstrate the difference of functional dependencies when they are applied in relational databases and XML documents and points out the main characteristics of functional dependencies in XML documents. Then we give the formal definition of XML functional dependencies which are defined on path expressions of XML documents. The functional dependencies in XML documents proposed in our paper differentiate between global XML functional dependencies and local XML functional dependencies. Moreover, The XML functional dependencies in our paper can express the functional dependencies not only on string values of elements and attributes but also on elements themselves, which have more applicability than those only considering string values of elements and attributes. We also give some inference rules of XML functional dependencies as a start point for further research.

Organization. The rest of the paper is organized as follows. One motivating example is given in section 2 to demonstrate the difference of functional dependencies when they are applied in relational databases and XML documents. The definition of XML functional dependencies and their inference rules are given in Section 3. Section 4 concludes the paper and points out the directions of future work.

2 An Example

Example 1. Consider the following XML Schema $\$_1$, which describes the information of course, student, and teacher:

```
<xs:schema xmlns:xs='http://www.w3.org/2001/XMLSchema'>
<xs:element name='course'>
  <xs:complexType>
   <xs:sequence>
     <xs:element ref='title'/>
     <xs:element ref='takenby'/>
   </xs:sequence>
  <xs:attribute name='cno' use='required'/>
  </xs:complexType>
 </xs:element>
 <xs:element name='courses'>
  <xs:complexType>
```

```
    <xs:sequence>
      <xs:element ref='course' minOccurs='0' maxOc-
curs='unbounded'/>
    </xs:sequence>
   </xs:complexType>
  </xs:element>
  <xs:element name='sname'>
   <xs:complexType mixed='true'>
   </xs:complexType>
  </xs:element>
  <xs:element name='student'>
   <xs:complexType>
    <xs:sequence>
      <xs:element ref='sname'/>
      <xs:element ref='teacher'/>
    </xs:sequence>
   <xs:attribute name='sno' use='required'/>
   </xs:complexType>
  </xs:element>
  <xs:element name='takenby'>
   <xs:complexType>
    <xs:sequence>
      <xs:element ref='student' minOccurs='0' maxOc-
curs='unbounded'/>
    </xs:sequence>
   </xs:complexType>
  </xs:element>
  <xs:element name='teacher'>
   <xs:complexType>
    <xs:sequence>
      <xs:element ref='tname'/>
    </xs:sequence>
   <xs:attribute name='tno' use='required'/>
   </xs:complexType>
  </xs:element>
  <xs:element name='title'>
   <xs:complexType mixed='true'>
   </xs:complexType>
  </xs:element>
  <xs:element name='tname'>
   <xs:complexType mixed='true'>
   </xs:complexType>
  </xs:element>
</xs:schema>
```

For clarity, we use two elements "sname" and "tname" to represent a student's name and a teacher's name, respectively. In fact, we can just use one element "name" to represent a student's name or a teacher's name here as elements "sname" and "tname" have the same definition, which does not cause name clash.

Figure 1 is an XML document conforming to XML Schema $\$_1$. Suppose we want to express functional dependencies such that a student's number (@sno) can uniquely determines a student node within the sub-tree rooted on a course node, which can be expressed by a functional dependency as the following form:

(courses.course,[courses.course.takenby.student.@sno]→
[courses.course.takenby.student]).

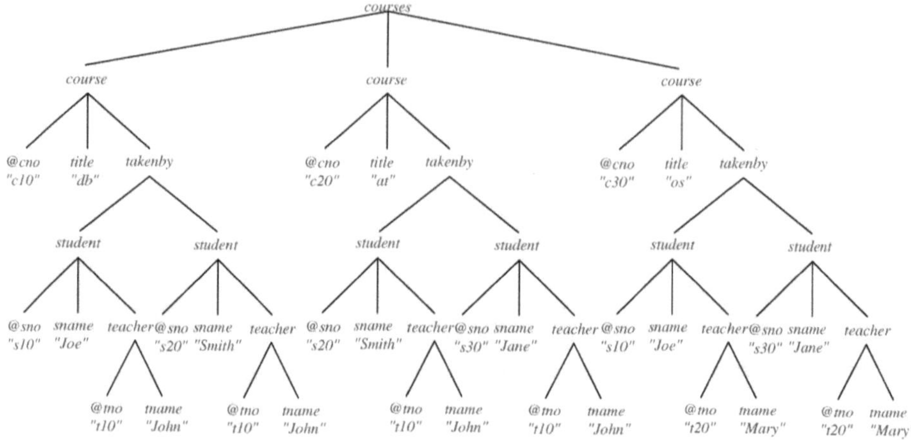

Fig. 1. An XML tree T_1 conforming to $\$_1$

The above functional dependency has its scope (a specific course here). Moreover, it is involved in nodes comparisons (comparing student nodes here). We can see from the above observation that functional dependency in XML documents has two major characteristics when comparing with that in relational databases: (1) functional dependencies have no scope in relational databases as relation schemas are flat, while they often have scopes in XML documents as XML Schemas are nested and tree-structured; (2) functional dependencies only consider string values in relational databases as relation attributes are simple data types, while they consider not only string values of elements and attributes but also nodes themselves in XML documents as XML Schemas not only have simple data types but also nodes.

3 Functional Dependencies in XML Documents

3.1 Notations

As an XML Schema can be always simplified as a set of elements, attributes, and string values, we give the definition of XML Schema, path, XML tree similar to the counterpart definitions proposed in Ref. [12].

Definition 1. An XML Schema is defined as $\$=(E, A, P, R, r)$, where (1) E is a finite set of element types; (2) A is a finite set of attributes; (3) P is a mapping from E to element type definitions. For each $\tau \in E$, $P(\tau)$ is a regular expression α defined as $\alpha ::= S \mid \varepsilon \mid \tau^1 \mid \alpha|\alpha \mid \alpha,\alpha \mid \alpha^*$, where S denotes string types , ε is the empty sequence ,

$\tau^1 \in E$, "|", "," and "*" denote union (or choice), concatenation and Kleene closure, respectively; (4) R is a mapping from E to the power set P(A); (5) $r \in E$ is called the element type of the root.

Example 2. According to Definition 1, XML Schema $\$_1$ in Example 1 is defined as $\$_1 = (E_1, A_1, P_1, R_1, r_1)$, where

E_1= {*courses, course, title, takenby, student, sname, teacher, tname*}
A_1= {*cno, sno, tno*}
$P_1(courses)=course^*$
$P_1(course)=title, takenby$
$P_1(title)= P_1(sname)= P_1(tname)=S$
$P_1(takenby)=student^*$
$P_1(student)=sname, teacher$
$P_1(teacher)=tname$
$R_1(course)=\{@cno\}$
$R_1(student)=\{@sno\}$
$R_1(teacher)=\{@tno\}$
$R_1(courses)= R_1(title)= R_1(takenby)= R_1(sname)= R_1(tname)=\Phi$
$r_1=courses$.

A path in XML Schema is defined as:

Definition 2. A path p in XML Schema $\$=(E, A, P, R, r)$ is defined to be $p=\omega_1.\cdots.\omega_n$, where (1) $\omega_1=r$; (2) $\omega_i \in P(\omega_{i-1})$, $i \in [2,n-1]$; (3) $\omega_n \in P(\omega_{n-1})$ if $\omega_n \in E$ and $P(\omega_n) \neq \Phi$, or $\omega_n=S$ if $\omega_n \in E$ and $P(\omega_n)=\Phi$, or $\omega_n \in R(\omega_{n-1})$ if $\omega_n \in A$.

For a path p, *last*(p) denotes the last symbol of p. For two paths p and q, $p \supseteq_{Path} q$ denotes q is a prefix of p, but not necessarily a proper prefix. Let $paths(\$)=\{p \mid p$ is a path in $\$ \}$.

Example 3. Paths *courses, courses.course, courses.course.@cno, courses.course.title, courses.course.title.S*, and *courses.course.takenby* are some paths in $paths(\$_1)$, and *courses.course.title* $\supseteq_{Path}$ *courses.course*.

An XML tree conforming to an XML Schema is defined as:

Definition 3. Let $\$=(E, A, P, R, r)$. An XML tree T conforming to $\$$ (denoted by $T \models \$$) is defined to be $T=(V, lab, ele, att, val, root)$, where (1) V is a finite set of vertexes; (2) *lab* is a mapping from V to $E \cup A$; (3) *ele* is a partial function from V to V^* such that for any $v \in V$, $ele(v)=[v_1,\ldots,v_n]$ if $lab(v_1),\ldots, lab(v_n)$ is defined in $P(lab(v))$; (4) *att* is a partial function from V to A such that for any $v \in V$, $att(v)=R(lab(v))$ if $lab(v) \in E$ and $R(lab(v))$ is defined in $\$$; (5) *val* is a partial function from V to S such that for any $v \in V$, $val(v)$ is defined if $P(lab(v))=S$ or $lab(v) \in A$; (6) $lab(root)=r$ is called the root of T.

Example 4. Figure 1 is an XML tree T_1 conforming to $\$_1$ in Example 1 (Note: Each node is marked by its *lab* mapping value for clarity here). According to Definition 3, T_1 is defined as $T_1=(V_1, lab_1, ele_1, att_1, val_1, root_1)$, where V_1 is the finite set of nodes of Figure 1, $lab_1(root)=r=courses$, for the leftmost *course* node in Figure 1,

$ele_1(course)$=*title,takenby*,
$att_1(course)$=*@cno*,

and for the leftmost *title* node, $val_1(title)$=*db*.

Definition 4. Given an XML Schema $ and an XML tree T|=$, a path p in T is defined to be $p= v_1.\cdots.v_n$, where (1) $v_1=root$; (2) $v_i \in ele(v_{i-1})$, $i\in[2, n-1]$; (3) $v_n\in ele(v_{n-1})$ if $lab(v_n)\in E$, or $v_n\in att(v_{n-1})$ if $lab(v_n)\in A$, or $v_n=S$ if $P(lab(v_{n-1}))=S$. Let $paths(T)=\{p \mid p$ is a path in $T\}$.

If n is a node in an XML tree T|=$ and p is a path in $, then the last node set of path p passing node n is $n[[p]]$. Specifically, $root[[p]]$ is just simplified as $[[p]]$. A path p is denoted as $p(n)$ if its last node is node n. For paths $p_1, p_2,\ldots,$ and p_n in an XML tree T, the maximal common prefix is denoted as $p_1\cap p_2\cap\ldots\cap p_n$, which is also a path in T.

Example 5. *courses*, *courses.course*, *course.course.@cno*, *courses.course.title*, and *courses.course.title.S* are some paths in T_1 (Figure 1), and *courses*∩*courses.course*∩ *course.course.@cno*∩*courses.course.title*∩*courses.course.title.S*= *courses*. [[*course.course*]] is the three *course* nodes in Figure 1. For the first *course* node, *p*(*course*)=*courses.course*, which is the leftmost path in T_1.

We give the definition of value equality of two nodes. Intuitively, two nodes are value equal iff the two sub-trees rooted on the two nodes are identical.

Definition 5. Two nodes x and y are value equal denoted as $x=_v y$ iff (1) $lab(x)=lab(y)$; (2) $val(x)=val(y)$ if $x, y\in A$ or $x=y=$S; (3) if $x, y\in E$, then (a) for any attribute $a\in att(x)$, there exists $b\in att(y)$ and satisfies $a=_v b$, and vice versa; (b) If $ele(x)=v_1,\ldots,v_k$, then $ele(y)=w_1,\ldots,w_k$, and for any $i\in[1, k]$, there exists $v_i=_v w_i$, and vice versa.

Example 6. In Figure 1, the leftmost two *teacher* nodes are value equal as the two sub-trees rooted on the two nodes *teacher* are identical.

3.2 The Definition of XML Functional Dependencies

Definition 6. Given an XML Schema $, a functional dependency (FD) f over $ has the form $(S_h,[S_{x1},\ldots,S_{xn}]\rightarrow[S_{y1},\ldots,S_{ym}])$, where

(1) $S_h\in paths(\$)$ is called header path of f, which defines the scope of f over $. $last(S_h)\in E$. If $S_h\neq\Phi$ and $S_h\neq r$, then f is called a local FD which means that the scope of f is the sub-tree rooted on $last(S_h)$; otherwise, f is called a global FD which means the scope of f is the overall $.
(2) $[S_{x1},\ldots,S_{xn}]$ is called left paths of f. For $i=1,\ldots,n$, it is the case that $S_{xi}\in paths(\$)$, $S_{xi} \supseteq_{Path} S_h$, $S_{xi}\neq\Phi$, and $last(S_{xi})\in E\cup A\cup S$.
(3) $[S_{y1},\ldots,S_{ym}]$ is called right paths of f. For $j=1,\ldots,m$, it is the case that $S_{yj}\in paths(\$)$, $S_{yj} \supseteq_{Path} S_h$, $S_{yj}\neq\Phi$, and $last(S_{yj}) \in E\cup A\cup S$.

For an XML tree T |=$, we call T satisfies FD f (denoted as T |= f) iff for any nodes $H\in[[S_h]]$(let $H=root$ if $S_h=\Phi$) and $X_1, X_2\in H[[S_{x1}\cap\ldots\cap S_{xn}]]$ in T, if there exist nodes $X_1[[S_{x1}]]=_v X_2[[S_{x1}]]$, …, $X_1[[S_{xn}]]=_v X_2[[S_{xn}]]$, and it is the case that for any nodes Y_1, $Y_2\in H[[S_{y1}\cap\ldots\cap S_{ym}]]$ and $H(p(X_1)\cap p(Y_1))$, $H(p(X_2)\cap p(Y_2))\in H[[S_{x1}\cap\ldots\cap S_{xn}\cap S_{y1}\cap\ldots\cap S_{ym}]]$ such that $Y_1[[S_{y1}]]=_v Y_2[[S_{y1}]]$, …, $Y_1[[S_{ym}]]=_v Y_2[[S_{ym}]]$.

Example 7. In Figure 1, we have the following FDs:

F_1: [*courses.course.@cno*] →[*courses.course*],
F_2: (*courses.course*, [*courses.course.takenby.student.@sno*]→ [*courses.course.takenby.student*]),
F_3: [*courses.course.@cno*] →[*courses.course.takenby.student.teacher.@tno*],
F_4: (*courses.course.takenby.student*, [*courses.course.takenby.student.@sno*]→ [*courses.course.takenby.student.teacher*]),
and
F_5: [*courses.course.takenby.student.teacher.@tno*]→ [*courses.course.takenby.student.teacher.tname.*S],

where F_1 is a global FD, which implies that a course number (@cno) can uniquely determines a course node within the whole XML document; F_2 is a local FD, which implies that a student number (@sno) can uniquely determines a student node within the sub-tree rooted on a course node; F_3 is a global FD, which implies that a course number (@cno) can uniquely determines a teacher number within the whole XML document; F_4 is a local FD, which implies that a student number (@sno) can uniquely determines a teacher node within the sub-tree rooted on a student node; and F_5 is a global FD, which implies that a teacher number (@tno) can uniquely determines a teacher's name within the whole XML document.

3.3 Inference Rules of XML Functional Dependencies

From the definition of XML functional dependencies, it is easy to get the following theorems:

Theorem 1. Given an XML Schema $ and a FD $f\,(S_h,[S_{x1},\ldots,S_{xn}] \rightarrow [S_y])$ over $, we have the following inference rules:

(1) FD $[S_h, S_{x1}, \cdots, S_{xn}] \rightarrow [S_y]$.

(2) FD $(S_h,[S_{x1},\ldots,S_{xn}] \rightarrow [S_y.e])$ if $e \in P(last(S_y)) \in E$ and $e^* \notin P(last(S_y))$.

(3) FD $(S_h,[S_{x1},\ldots,S_{xn}] \rightarrow [S_y.@a])$ if $R(last(S_y)) = a \in A$.

(4) FD $(S_h,[S_{x1},\ldots,S_{xn}] \rightarrow [S_y.S])$ if $last(S_y) \in E$ and $P(last(S_y)) = S$.

(5) FD $(S_h,[S_{x1},\ldots,S_{xn}] \rightarrow [S_y/last(S_y)])$ if $last(S_y) \in E$, $last(S_y) \neq r$ and $S_y/last(S_y) \supseteq_{path} S_h$.

(6) FD $(S'_h,[S_{x1}, \cdots, S_{xn}] \rightarrow [S_y])$ if $S'_h \supseteq_{Path} S_h$, $\forall S_{xi} \supseteq_{Path} S'_h$ ($i \in [1,n]$), and $S_y \supseteq_{Path} S'_h$.

(7) FD $(S_h,[S_{x1}, \cdots, S_{xn}, S] \rightarrow [S_y, S])$ if $S_h \subseteq_{Path} S \in paths(\$)$.

(8) FD $(S_h,[S_{x1}, \cdots, S_{xn}] \rightarrow [S'_y])$ if $(S'_h,[S_y] \rightarrow [S'_y])$, $S'_h \subseteq_{Path} S_h$, and $S_h \subseteq_{Path} S'_y$.

Theorem 2. It is trivial that

(1) FD [p]→[r]if $p \in paths(\$)$.

(2) FD $[S_{x1},\cdots,S_{xn}] \rightarrow [S_y]$ if $S_y \in \{S_{x1},\cdots,S_{xn}\} \subseteq paths(\$)$.

4 Conclusions and Future Work

Functional dependencies are very important semantic information in XML documents, which are fundamental to other related XML research topics such as normalizing XML documents and query optimization. This paper extended the theory of functional dependencies in relational database world to the XML world and proposes the formal definition of functional dependencies in XML documents which are based on path expressions. The XML functional dependencies in our work deal with not only string values but also elements themselves in XML documents and differentiate between global functional dependencies and local functional dependencies in XML documents.

The future work should be done on the issues of relationship between functional dependencies and keys in XML documents and the complete inference rules for XML functional dependencies.

Acknowledgements

This work is supported by National Natural Science Foundation of China (No.60563001) and Science Research Foundation for Young Teachers of Xinjiang University (No. QN040101).

References

1. Extensible Markup Language (XML) 1.0.2nd Edition. http://www.w3.org/TR/REC-xml. Oct. 2000.
2. Teng Lv, Ning Gu, and Ping Yan. Normal forms for XML documents. Information and Software Technology, 2004(46), 12: 839~846.
3. Marcelo Arenas and Leonid Libkin. A Normal Form for XML Documents. Symposium on Principles of Database Systems (PODS'02), Madison, Wisconsin, U.S.A. ACM press, 2002, 85~96.
4. Teng Lv and Ping Yan. Mapping DTDs to relational schemas with semantic constraints. Information and Software Technology (In press and to be appear).
5. D. Lee, M. Mani, and W. W. Chu. Schema conversion methods between XML and relational models. Knowledge Transformation for the Semantic Web, Frontiers in Artificial Intelligence and Applications, Vol. 95, IOS Press, 2003, pp.1-17.
6. S. Lu, Y. Sun, M. Atay, and F. Fotouhi. A new inlining algorithm for mapping XML DTDs to relational schemas. ER workshops 2003, Spinger, Lecture Notes in Computer Science, Vol. 2814, 2003, pp366-377.
7. W3C XML-Data. http://www.w3.org/TR/1998/NOTE-XML-data-0105/, Jan. 1998.
8. XML Schema Part 0: Primer Second Edition. W3C Recommendation, http://www.w3.org/TR/2004/REC-xmlschema-0-20041028/.

9. W3C XML Specification DTD. http://www.w3.org/XML/1998/06/xmlspec-report-19980910.htm, Jun, 1998.
10. Serge Abiteboul, Richard Hull, and Victor Vianu. Foundations of Databases. Addison-Wesley, Reading, Massachusetts 1995.
11. M. Vincent, J. Liu, and C. Liu. Strong functional dependencies and their application to normal forms in XML. ACM Transactions on Database Systems, 2004, 29(3): 445-462.
12. Mong Li Lee, Tok Wang Ling, Wai Lup Low. Designing Functional Dependencies for XML, in VIII Conference on Extending Database Technology (EDBT'02), Springer, 2002, pp124~141.
13. Sven Hartmann and Sebastian Link. More functional dependencies for XML. In: Proc. of ADBIS 2003, LNCS 2798. Germany: Springer, 2003, 355~369.
14. Peter Buneman, Susan Davidson, Wenfei Fan, Carmem Hara, and Wang-chiew Tan. Keys for XML. Computer Networks, 2002, Volume 39, Issue 5: 473~487.
15. Peter Buneman, Wenfei Fan, J. Simeon, and S. Weistein. Constraints for semistructured data and XML. ACM SIGMOD Record, 2001, Volume 30, Issue 1: 47~54.
16. Peter Buneman, Susan Davidson, Wenfei Fan, Carmem Hara, and Wang-chiew Tan. Reasoning about keys for XML. Lecture Notes in Computer Science (LNCS), 2001, Volume 2397 : 133~148.
17. Wanfei Fan and Leonid Libkin. On XML Integrity Constraints in the Presence of DTDs, Journal of the ACM (JACM), 2002, Volume 49, Issue 3: 368~ 406.

Querying Composite Events for Reactivity on the Web

François Bry, Michael Eckert, and Paula-Lavinia Pătrânjan

University of Munich, Institute for Informatics,
Oettingenstr. 67, D-80538 München
{bry, eckert, patranjan}@pms.ifi.lmu.de
http://www.pms.ifi.lmu.de

Abstract. Reactivity, the ability to detect events and respond to them automatically through reactive programs, is a key requirement in many present-day information systems. Work on Web Services reflects the need for support of reactivity on a higher abstraction level than just message exchange by HTTP. This article presents the composite event query facilities of the reactive rule-based programming language XChange. Composite events are important in the dynamic world of the Web where applications, or Web Services, that have not been engineered together are composed and have to cooperate by exchanging event messages.

1 Introduction

Reactivity, the ability to detect events or situations of interest and respond to them automatically through reactive programs, is a key requirement in many present-day information systems. The World Wide Web, undoubtedly by far the largest information system, has become a basis for many applications requiring reactivity, e.g., in commerce, business-to-business, logistics, e-Learning, and information systems for biological data.

It is natural to represent events that are exchanged between Web sites as XML messages. The Web's communication protocol, HTTP, provides an infrastructure for exchanging events or messages. Still, until recently the Web has been commonly perceived as a passive collection of HTML and XML documents; reactivity had to be implemented largely "by hand" (e.g., CGI scripts) and was limited to single Web sites (e.g., filling out forms on a shopping Web site). There is little support for reactivity on a higher abstraction level, e.g., in the form of reactive programming languages. Research and standardization in the Web Services area reflect the need to overcome what one might call the Web's passiveness.

XChange [1, 2, 3] is a rule-based reactive language for programming reactive behavior and distributed applications on the Web. Amongst other reactive behavior it aims at easing implementation and composition of Web Services. XChange is based on *Event-Condition-Action* rules (ECA rules). These specify that some *action* should be performed in response to some (class of) *events* (or situations of interest), provided that the *condition* holds.

H.T. Shen et al. (Eds.): ADWeb 2006, LNCS 3842, pp. 38–47, 2006.

To specify situations that require a reaction, XChange provides *event queries*, which describe classes of events. But event queries do more: they also extract and make available data from the events' XML representation that is relevant for the particular reaction. Considering a tourism application, it is not only important to detect when a flight has been canceled, but also to know its flight number and similar information in the reaction to the event.

Often, the situations are not given by a single atomic event, but a temporal combination of events, leading to the notion of *composite events* and *composite event queries*. Support for composite events is very important for the Web: In a carefully developed application, designers have the freedom to choose events according to their goal. They can thus often do with only atomic events by representing events which might by conceptually composite with a single atomic event. In the Web's open world however many different applications which have not been engineered together are integrated and have to cooperate. Situations that require a reaction might not have been considered in the original design of the applications and thus have to be inferred from many atomic events.

Consider again a tourism scenario: an application might want to detect situations where a traveler has already checked out of his hotel (first atomic event) but his flight has been canceled (second atomic event). On the Web the constituent events are emitted from independent Web sites (the airline and the hotel), which have not designed together. Hence an application has to infer the composite event from the given atomic events.

Similar motivating scenarios for composite events are filtering of stock trade reports, e.g., "recognize situations where the NASDAQ rises 10 points and the Dow Jones falls 5 points", or work-flow-management, e.g., "a student has fulfilled her degree-requirements if she has handed in her thesis and taken the final exams (which in turn can be a composite event)."

The remainder of this paper is structured as follows. We first give a short overview of XChange (Sect. 2), and then explain the event query language in detail. We introduce the syntax and intuitive meaning of its language constructs (Sect. 3), before turning to the formal semantics (Sect. 4) and the event query evaluation (Sect. 5). Conclusions (Sect. 6) complete this article.

2 XChange: ECA Rule-Based Reactivity

XChange programs consist of ECA rules running locally at some Web site. In reaction to events, they can query and modify local and remote XML data and raise new events, which are sent as XML messages to other remote Web sites (in a push-manner).

XChange ECA rules have the general form *Action – Event Query – Web Query*. They specify to automatically execute the action (an update to a Web resource or rasing of a new event) as response to a situation specified by the event query (a query over the stream of incoming event messages), provided the Web query (a query to persistent Web data) evaluates successfully.

```
<flight-cancellation>
   <number> UA917 </number>
   <date> 2005-02-20 </date>
</flight-cancellation>
```

```
flight-cancellation [
   number [ "UA917" ]
   date [ "2005-02-20" ]
]
```

```
flight-cancellation {{
   number [ var N ]
}}
```

Fig. 1. An event message in XML and term representation, and an atomic event query

Atomic event queries (queries to a single incoming event message) and Web queries rely on the query language *Xcerpt* [4]. Also, update specifications are an extension to Xcerpt. Xcerpt queries describe *patterns* of the queried XML data and are represented in a term-like syntax. Fig. 1 depicts a small XML document, its term representation, and a query term against this data. In the term syntax, square brackets indicate that the order of child elements is significant, while curly braces indicate it isn't. Double braces or brackets indicate a partial match, i.e., other children may exists, while single braces or brackets indicate a total match, i.e., no other children may exist. Queries can contain free variables (indicated by the keyword `var`) which are bound during the evaluation, which is based on a novel method called *Simulation Unification* [5].

XChange can provide the following benefits over the conventional approach of using imperative programming languages to implement Web Services:

- ECA rules have a highly declarative nature, allow programming on a high level of abstraction, and are easy to analyze for both humans and machines (see [6], for example).
- Event queries, Web queries, and updates follow the same paradigm of specifying patterns for XML data, thus making XChange an elegant, easy to learn language.
- Both atomic and composite events can be detected, the latter being an important requirement in composing an application from different Web Services (cf. Sect. 1) and relevant data extracted.
- Having an XML query language embedded in the condition part allows to access Web resources in a natural way. Also Xcerpt's *deductive rules* allowing to reason with data and to query not only pure XML but also RDF [7].
- A typical reaction to some event is to update some Web resource; XChange provides an integrated XML update language for doing this.
- ECA rules of XChange enforce a clear separation of persistent data (Web resources with URIs) and volatile data (event messages, no URIs). The distinction is important for a programmer: the former relates to *state*, while the latter reflects *changes in state*.

3 Event Queries and Composite Events

Event queries detect atomic events (receptions of single event messages) and composite events (temporal patterns in the reception of event messages) in the stream of incoming events and extract data in the form of variables bindings from them.

3.1 Atomic Events and Atomic Event Queries

Atomic events are received by XChange-aware Web sites as XML messages. Typically these messages will follow some standardized envelope format (e.g., SOAP format) providing information like the sender or the reception time of the message; in this paper we skip such details for the sake of brevity.

Atomic event queries are query terms (as introduced in the previous section). On reception of an incoming event message, XChange tries to simulation unify the query term and the message. If successful, this results in a set of substitutions for the free variables in the query.

3.2 Composite Event Queries

Composite event queries are built from atomic (and smaller composite) event queries (`EQ`) by means of composition operators and temporal restrictions. They describe a pattern of events that have to happen in a some time frame. Composite events are sequences of atomic events that answer a given composite event query; they happen over a period of time and thus have a starting and ending time.

Temporal Restrictions limit the time frame in which events are considered relevant. XChange supports absolute and relative temporal restrictions. Absolute restrictions are introduced by the keyword `in` and a time interval specification, e.g., `[1978-02-20 .. 2005-02-20]` following an (atomic or composite) event query. Answers to the event query are only considered if they happen in the specified time interval. Relative restrictions are introduced by the keyword `within` and a specification of a duration, e.g., `365 days`. They limit the duration (difference between starting and ending time) of answers to the event query.

XChange requires every (legal) composite event query to be accompanied by a temporal restriction specification. This makes it possible to release each (atomic or semi-composed composite) event at each Web site after a finite time. Thus, language design enforces the requirement of a bounded event lifespan and the clear distinction persistent vs. volatile data.

Composition Operators express a temporal pattern of atomic event occurrences. XChange provides a rich set of such composition operators, a selection of which is presented here.

Conjunctions of event queries detect instances for each specified event query regardless of their order. They have the form: `and` { $\mathtt{EQ}_1$, ..., $\mathtt{EQ}_n$ }.

Inclusive Disjunctions of event queries detect instances of any of the specified event queries. They have the form: `or` { $\mathtt{EQ}_1$, ..., $\mathtt{EQ}_n$ }.

Temporally Ordered Conjunctions of event queries detect successive instances of events: `andthen [` $\mathtt{EQ}_1$, ... , $\mathtt{EQ}_n$ `]` and `andthen [[` $\mathtt{EQ}_1$, ... , $\mathtt{EQ}_n$ `]]`.

A total specification (using `[ ]`) expresses that only instances of the $\mathtt{EQ}_i$ ($i = 1, \ldots, n$) are of interest and are included in the answer. Instances of other events that possibly have occurred between the instances of the $\mathtt{EQ}_i$ are not of interest and thus are not contained in the answer. In contrast, a partial specification (using `[[ ]]`) expresses interest in all incoming events that have been received between the instances of the $\texttt{EQ}_i$. Thus, all these instances are contained in the event query's answer.

Example. The composite event query on the right side detects notifications of flight cancellations that are followed, within two hours of reception, by notifications that the airline is not granting accommodation. Note the use of the variable `P` to make sure that the notifications apply to the *same* passenger.

```
andthen [
     flight-cancellation {{
          number { var N },
          passenger { var P }
     }},
     no-accommodation {{
          passenger { var P },
     }}
] within 2 hours
```

Event Exclusions enable the monitoring of the *non-occurrence* of (atomic or composite) event query instances during an absolute time interval or the answer to another composite event query: `without EQ during CompositeEQ` or `without EQ during [`s `..` t`]`.

Other operators include n `times EQ` to detect n occurrences of the same event, and m `of {EQ1, ... EQn}` to detect occurrences of m instances in a given set of event queries.

4 Semantics of Event Queries

Comparisons of (composite) event query languages such as [8] show that interpretation of similar language constructs can vary considerably. To avoid misinterpretations, clear semantics are indispensable.

The notion of answers to event queries is twofold. An answer to some query consists of (1) a sequence s of atomic events that allowed a successful evaluation of the query on the one hand, and (2) a set of variable substitutions Σ on the other hand. Variable substitutions can influence the reaction to some event specified in the remaining part of an XChange ECA rule. The sequence of events allows for events not being specified in the query to become a part of the answer (e.g., a partial `andthen[[`EQ_1`, `EQ_2`]]` returns not only answers to EQ_1 and EQ_2 but also any atomic events in-between) and gives answer closedness, i.e., the result of a query can be in turn queried by further queries.

We define a declarative semantics for XChange's event query language similar to a model-theoretic entailment relation. Unlike the traditional binary entailment relation $\models$, which relates models to queries (under some environment giving bindings for the free variables), however, our answering relation has to be ternary: it relates the stream of incoming event messages (which corresponds to a model), queries, *and answers* (as discussed above these include the "environment" Σ). The reason for the need of answers is that in our event query language answers cannot be simply obtained from queries by applying the variables substitutions to them, since they may contain events not having a corresponding constituent query. The answering relation is defined by induction on the structure of a query.

This allows easy recursive evaluation of composite (event) queries, where each constituent query can be evaluated independently of the others.

We now give a formal account of the declarative semantics.

Answers. An answer to an event query q is a tuple (s, Σ). It consists of a (finite) sequence s of atomic events happening in a time interval $[b..e]$ that allowed a successful evaluation of q and a corresponding set of substitutions Σ for the free variables of q. We write $s = \langle a_1, \ldots a_n \rangle_b^e$ to indicate that s begins at time point $begin(s) := b$, ends at $end(s) := e$, and contains the atomic events $a_i = d_i^{r_i}$, which are data terms d_i received at time point r_i. We have $b \leq r_1 < \ldots < r_n \leq e$; note that $b < r_1$ and $r_n < e$ are possible.

Observe that the answer is an event sequence, and it is possible for instances of events not specified in the query to be returned. For example, a partial match `andthen[[a,b]]` returns not only event instances of `a` and `b`, but also all atomic events happening between them. This cannot be captured with substitutions alone.

Substitution Sets. The substitution set Σ contains substitutions σ (partial functions) assigning variables to data terms. Assuming a standardisation of variable names, let V be the set of all free variables in a query having at least one defining occurrence. A variable's occurrence is *defining*, if it is part of a non-negated sub-query, i.e. does not occur inside a `without`-construct, and thus can be assigned a value in the query evaluation. Let $\Sigma |_V$ denote the restriction of all substitutions σ in Σ to V. For triggering rules in XChange, we are interested only in the maximal substitution sets.

Event Stream. For a given event query q, all atomic events received after its registration form a *stream of incoming events* (or, *event stream*) $\mathcal{E}$. Events prior to a query's registration are not considered, as this might require an unbounded event life-span. Thus, since it fits better with the incremental event query evaluation (described in the next section), we prefer the term "stream" to the term "history" sometimes used in related work. Formally, $\mathcal{E}$ is an event sequence (as s above) beginning at the query's registration time.

Answering-Relation. Semantics of event queries are defined as a ternary relation between event queries q, answers (s, Σ), and event stream $\mathcal{E}$. We write $q \lhd_{\mathcal{E}} (s, \Sigma)$ to indicate that q is answered by (s, Σ) under the event stream $\mathcal{E}$. Definition of $\lhd_{\mathcal{E}}$ is by induction on q, and we give only a few exemplary cases here.

<u>q is an atomic event query:</u> $q \lhd_{\mathcal{E}} (s, \Sigma)$ if and only if (1) $s = \langle d^r \rangle_r^r$, (2) d^r is an atomic event in the stream $\mathcal{E}$, (3) the data term d simulation unifies ("matches") with the query q under all substitutions in Σ. For a formal account of (3) see work on Xcerpt [9].

<u>$q =$ **and**$[q_1, \ldots, q_n]$:</u> $q \lhd_{\mathcal{E}} (s, \Sigma)$ iff there exist event sequences $s_1, \ldots s_n$ such that (1) $q_i \lhd_{\mathcal{E}} (s_i, \Sigma)$ for all $1 \leq i \leq n$, (2) s comprises all event sequences $s_1, \ldots s_n$ (denoted $s = \bigcup_{1 \leq i \leq n} s_i$).

<u>$q =$ **andthen**$[[q_1, q_2]]$:</u> $q \lhd_{\mathcal{E}} (s, \Sigma)$ iff there exist event sequences s_1, s', and s_2 such that (1) $q_i \lhd_{\mathcal{E}} (s_i, \Sigma)$ for $i = 1, 2$, (2) $s = s_1 \cup s' \cup s_2$, (3) $end(s_1) \leq begin(s_2)$, and (4) s' is a continuous extract of $\mathcal{E}$ (denoted $s' \sqsubset \mathcal{E}$) with (5) $begin(s') =$

$end(s_1)$ and $end(s') = begin(s_2)$. The event sequence s' serves to collect all atomic events happening "between" the answers to q_1 and q_2 as required by the partial matching `[[ ]]`. The n-ary variant of this binary **andthen** is defined by rewriting the n-ary case associatively to nested binary operators.

$q =$ `without` $\{q_1\}$ `during` $\{q_2\}$: $q \triangleleft_{\mathcal{E}} (s, \Sigma)$ iff (1) $q_2 \triangleleft_{\mathcal{E}} (s, \Sigma)$, (2) there is no answer (s_1, Σ_1) to q_1 ($q_1 \triangleleft_{\mathcal{E}} (s_1, \Sigma_1)$) such that Σ contains substitutions for the variables V with defining occurrences that are also in Σ_1 ($\Sigma\, |_V \subseteq \Sigma_1\, |_V$).

$q = q'$ `within` w: $q \triangleleft_{\mathcal{E}} (s, \Sigma)$ iff (1) $q' \triangleleft_{\mathcal{E}} (s, \Sigma)$ and (2) $end(s) - begin(s) \leq w$.

Discussion. Our answering relation approach to semantics allows the use of advanced features in XChange's event query language, such as free variables in queries, event negation, and partial matches. Note that due to the latter two, approaches where answers are generated by a simple application of substitutions to the query would be difficult, if not impossible to define.

The declarative semantics provide a sound basis for formal proofs about language properties. In particular, we have used it for proving the *bounded event lifespan* property for all legal event queries. Legal event queries are atomic event queries and composite event queries that are accompanied by temporal restrictions, such as q `within` d, q `in` $[t_1..t_2]$, q `before` t_2, or `without` q `during` $[t_1..t_2]$. All legal event queries are such that no data on any event has to be kept forever in memory, i.e., the lifespan of every event is bounded.

More exactly, to evaluate any legal event query q at some time t correctly, only events of bounded life-span are necessary; that is, it suffices to consider the restriction $\mathcal{E}\, |_{t-\beta}^{t}$ of the event stream $\mathcal{E}$ to a time interval $[(t - \beta) .. t]$. The time bound β (a length of time) is only determined from q and does not depend on the incoming events $\mathcal{E}$. A more formal account of this and detailed proofs can be found in [10].

5 Evaluation of Composite Event Queries

Evaluation of composite event queries against the stream of incoming event messages should be performed in an incremental manner: work done in one evaluation step of an event query on some incoming atomic event should not be redone in future evaluation steps on further incoming events. Following the ideas of the rete algorithm [11] and previous work on composite event detection like [12], we evaluate a composite event query incrementally by storing all partial evaluations in the query's operator tree. Leaf nodes in the operator tree implement atomic event queries, inner nodes implement composition operators and time restrictions. When an event message is received, it is injected at the leaf nodes; data in the form of event query answers (s, Σ) (cf. Sect. 4) then flows bottom-up in the operator tree during this evaluation step. Inner nodes can store intermediate results to avoid recomputation when the next evaluation step is initiated by the next incoming event message.

Leaf nodes process an injected event message by trying to match it with their atomic event query (using Simulation Unification). If successful, this results in a substitution set $\Sigma \neq \emptyset$, and the answer (s, Σ), where s is an event sequence

```
SetOfCompositeEvents evaluate( AndNode n, AtomicEvent a ) {
    // receive events from child nodes
    SetOfCompositeEvents newL := evaluate( n.leftChild, a );
    SetOfCompositeEvents newR := evaluate( n.rightChild, a );

    // compose composite events
    SetOfCompositeEvents answers := ∅;
    foreach ((s_L, Σ_L), (s_R, Σ_R)) ∈(newL × n.storageR) ∪
                                      (n.storageL × newR) ∪
                                      (newL × newR) {
            SubstitutionSet Σ := Σ_L ⋈ Σ_R;
            if (Σ ≠ ∅) answers := answers ∪ new CompositeEvent( s_L ∪ s_R, Σ );
    }

    // update event storage
    n.storageL := n.storageL ∪ newL;
    n.storageR := n.storageR ∪ newR;

    // forward composed events to parent node
    return answers;
}
```

Fig. 2. Implementation of a (binary) and inner node in pseudo-code

containing only the one event message, is forwarded to the parent node. Inner nodes process events they receive from their children following the basic pattern:

1. attempt to compose composite events (s, Σ) (according to the operator the inner node implements) from the stored and the newly received events,
2. update the event storage by adding newly received events that might be needed in later evaluations,
3. forward the events composed in (1) to the parent node.

Fig. 2 sketches an implementation for the evaluation of a (binary) and inner node in java-like pseudo-code. Consider it in an example of evaluating the event query q =`and{ a{{var X}}, b{{var X}} } within 2h` in Fig. 3. (Keep in mind, Fig. 2 covers only the and-node; `within` is a separate node with a separate implementation)

In Fig. 3, we now let event messages arrive at time points $t = 1, 2, 3$. For simplicity, these are each one hour apart; this is of course not the normal case in practice and not an assumption made by the algorithm.

Fig. ?? depicts receiving `a{1,2}` at time $t = 1$. It does not match with the atomic event query `b{{var X}}` (right leaf in the tree). But it does match with the atomic event query `a{{var X}}` (left leaf) with substitution set Σ_1 and is propagated upwards in the tree as answer (s_1, Σ_1) to the parent node and (Fig. ?? defines s_i and Σ_i). The and-node cannot form a composite event from its input, yet, but it stores (s_1, Σ_1) for future evaluation steps.

At $t = 2$ we receive `b{2,3}` (Fig. ??); it matches the right leaf node and (s_2, Σ_2) is propagated upwards. The and-node stores (s_2, Σ_2) and tries to form a composite event (s_3, Σ_3) from (s_1, Σ_1) and (s_2, Σ_2). To be able to compose the events they have to agree on the variables substitutions with a common Σ_3. This can be computed as a (variant of a) natural join ($\perp$ denotes undefined): $\Sigma_3 = \Sigma_1 \bowtie \Sigma_2 = \{\sigma_1 \cup \sigma_2 \mid \sigma_1 \in \Sigma_1, \sigma_2 \in \Sigma_2, \forall X.\ \sigma_1(X) = \sigma_2(X) \vee \sigma_1(X) = \perp \vee \sigma_2(X) = \perp\}$. Σ_3 now contains all substitutions that can be used simultaneously

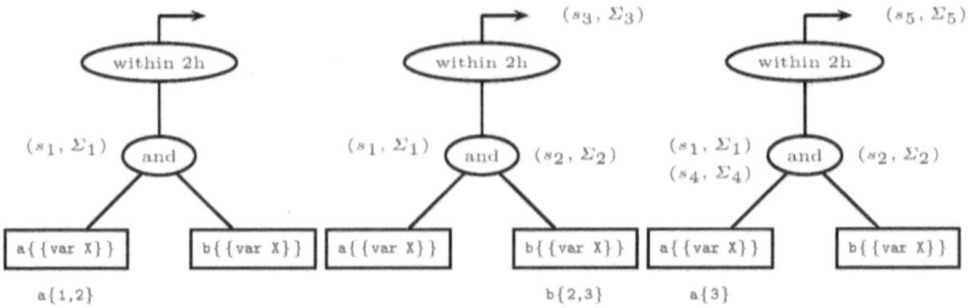

(a) t=1 (b) t=2 (c) t=3

$s_1 = \langle$a{1,2}$\rangle$, $\Sigma_1 = \{\{X \mapsto 1\}, \{X \mapsto 2\}\}$; $s_2 = \langle$b{2,3}$\rangle$, $\Sigma_2 = \{\{X \mapsto 2\}, \{X \mapsto 3\}\}$;
$s_3 = \langle$a{1,2}, b{2,3}$\rangle$, $\Sigma_3 = \{\{X \mapsto 2\}\}$; $s_4 = \langle$a{3}$\rangle$, $\Sigma_4 = \{\{X \mapsto 3\}\}$; $s_5 = \langle$b{2,3}a{4}$\rangle$, $\Sigma_5 = \{\{X \mapsto 3\}\}$.

Fig. 3. Incremental evaluation of an event query using bottom-up data flow in a storage-augmented operator tree

in all atomic event queries in and's subtree. $\Sigma = \emptyset$ would signify that no such substitution exists and thus no composite event can be formed. In our case however there is exactly one substitution $\{X \mapsto 2\}$ and we propagate (s_3, Σ_3) to the `within 2h`-node. This node checks that $end(s_3) - begin(s_3) = 1 \leq 2$ and pushes (s_3, Σ_3) up (there is no need to store it). With this (s_3, Σ_3) reaches the top and we have our first answer to the event query q.

Fig. ?? shows reception of another event message a{3} at $t = 3$, which results in another answer (s_5, Σ_5) to q. After the query evaluation at $t = 3$, we can release (delete) the stored answer (s_1, Σ_1) from the operator tree: any composite event formed with use of (s_1, Σ_1) will not pass the `within 2h`-node. Event deletion is performed by top-down traversal of the operator tree. Temporal restriction operator nodes put restrictions on $begin(s)$ and $end(s)$ for all answers (s, Σ) stored in their subtrees. In our example, all events (s, Σ) in the subtree of `within 2h` must satisfy $t - 2 \leq begin(s)$, where t is the current time.

6 Conclusions

This article has presented the event query facilities of the reactive rule-based language XChange. Event queries detect (composite) events in the stream of incoming event messages and extract data from them for use in the subsequent reaction. The event query language is tailored for the Web: Events are represented as XML messages, so it is necessary to extract data from them with an XML query language. When composing Web Services or other reactive applications in an ad-hoc manner, situations that require a reaction oftentimes are not given through a single atomic event, requiring support for composite events.

While composite event detection has been explored in the active database community, this work doesn't consider or extract data contained in events. An important novelty in the XChange event query language are the free variables, which allow to "correlate" data from different events during the composite event detection and to extract data in the form of variable bindings for use in the rest of a reactive rule. This work has defined declarative semantics for composite event queries in the presence of free variables. Existing approaches to composite event detection have been extended to incrementally evaluate such queries.

Acknowledgments

This research has been funded by the European Commission and by the Swiss Federal Office for Education and Science within the 6th Framework Programme project REWERSE number 506779 (`http://rewerse.net`).

References

1. Bry, F., Pătrânjan, P.L.: Reactivity on the Web: Paradigms and applications of the language XChange. In: Proc. 20th ACM Symp. on Applied Computing. (2005)
2. Bailey, J., Bry, F., Eckert, M., Pătrânjan, P.L.: Flavours of XChange, a rule-based reactive language for the (Semantic) Web. In: Proc. Intl. Conf. on Rules and Rule Markup Languages for the Semantic Web. (2005)
3. Pătrânjan, P.L.: The Language XChange: A Declarative Approach to Reactivity on the Web. PhD thesis, Institute for Informatics, University of Munich (2005)
4. Schaffert, S., Bry, F.: Querying the Web reconsidered: A practical introduction to Xcerpt. In: Proc. Extreme Markup Languages. (2004)
5. Bry, F., Schaffert, S.: Towards a declarative query and transformation language for XML and semistructured data: Simulation Unification. In: Proc. Int. Conf. on Logic Programming. (2002)
6. Bailey, J., Poulovassilis, A., Wood, P.T.: Analysis and optimisation of event-condition-action rules on XML. Computer Networks **39** (2002)
7. Berger, S., Bry, F., Bolzer, O., Furche, T., Schaffert, S., Wieser, C.: Querying the standard and Semantic Web using Xcerpt and visXcerpt. In: Proc. European Semantic Web Conf. (2005)
8. Zimmer, D., Unland, R.: On the semantics of complex events in active database management systems. In: Proc. 15th Int. Conf. on Data Engineering. (1999)
9. Schaffert, S.: Xcerpt: A Rule-Based Query and Transformation Language for the Web. PhD thesis, Institute for Informatics, University of Munich (2004)
10. Eckert, M.: Reactivity on the Web: Event queries and composite event detection in XChange. Master's thesis, Institute for Informatics, University of Munich (2005)
11. Forgy, C.L.: A fast algorithm for the many pattern/many object pattern match problem. Artificial Intelligence **19** (1982)
12. Chakravarthy, S., Krishnaprasad, V., Anwar, E., Kim, S.K.: Composite events for active databases: Semantics, contexts and detection. In: Proc. 20th Int. Conf. on Very Large Data Bases. (1994)

Efficient Evaluation of XML Twig Queries

Ya-Hui Chang*, Cheng-Ta Lee, and Chieh-Chang Luo

Department of Computer Science, National Taiwan Ocean University
yahui@ntou.edu.tw

Abstract. With rapid acceptance of XML technologies, efficient query processing is a critical issue for XML repositories. In this paper, we consider the XML query which can be represented as a query tree with twig patterns. The proposed approach will first quickly retrieve data satisfying fragment paths which consist of only the parent-child relationship, and deal with the ancestor-descendent constraint in the later gluing stage. This approach focuses on where the data need to be "glued" and thus is very efficient. We conduct several experiments to evaluate the performance of the proposed approach. The results show that our system is more efficient than the holistic approach.

1 Introduction

As XML (eXtensible Markup Language) technology emerged as the de facto standard for information sharing on the World-Wide-Web (WWW) and for data exchange in e-business, XML data management and query processing have attracted a lot of attention from the academic and business communities.

In XML, *elements* are the basic constructs of data, which form a nested hierarchy and can be captured by the tree model. Queries are typically specified in the form of *path expressions* to retrieve data from the XML tree. Consider the XQuery statement: "*for $a in input()//article where $a/title = "XML" return $a/author, $a/year*". The path expression *//article/title="XML"* restricts element contents under the path *//article/title* to be "XML" and *//article/author* and *//article/year* project the authors and the year of publication for the selected articles. We can observe that XML queries do not only specify *value constraints* on data contents as in the relational databases, but also implicitly specify a *structural constraint* on data elements involved in the query. In general, all the path expressions in a query constitute a twig pattern.

An intuitive approach to process queries with structural constraints is *pointer-chasing* [7], where the elements are represented as nodes and edges and the tree-traversal functionality is supported. To expedite the decision of the structural relationship between elements, the numbering schemes are proposed to encode each node based on the *preorder* and *postorder* traversal sequences [1, 4, 6], and partial results are joined together to satisfy the structural constraints. These numbering schemes mainly alleviate the cost of pointer-chasing on simple path queries but do not perform well enough on the more general twig queries. To resolve this problem, the holistic approach [2] proposes a chain

* This work was partially supported by the National Science Council under Contract No. NSC 94-2422-H-019-001.

H.T. Shen et al. (Eds.): ADWeb 2006, LNCS 3842, pp. 48–57, 2006.

of linked stacks that compactly represent the final results, and achieves the optimal performance when elements only present the ancestor-descendent structural relationship (or called AD in short). However, the holistic approach does not always guarantee a good performance when elements present more local relationship, particularly the parent-child relationship (or called PC in short), which is actually the most common structural relationship specified in XML queries [9].

In this paper, we will discuss how to efficiently process XML twig queries, with either the PC or AD structural relationships between elements. The main idea of our approach is to decompose the query into *pieces*. We first identify those paths consisting of only PC structural relationships, which are called *fragment paths*. These paths could efficiently obtain the satisfied elements via our specially designed path-based indexes, as will be explained later. We then *glue* these paths up to the *branching points* to form the *glued paths*, and combine these glued paths to construct the complete twig patterns. In contrast to the holistic approach, which first glue elements into *root-to-leaf* paths before combining them, our approach requires less element accesses and thus achieves better performance. The experimental study shows that the proposed technique not only outperforms the holistic approach in the PC cases to a large extent, but is also more efficient in the AD cases.

The remaining of this paper is organized as follows. The index structures used in our system are discussed in Section 2. The decomposing and combining algorithms are presented in Section 3 and 4. The performance evaluation is described in Section 5. Finally, a brief summary is given in Section 6.

2 Representations of XML Data

In this section, we discuss how data and the associated indexes are represented in our system. The XML document is modeled as a rooted labeled tree, where each node corresponds to an element and the edge represents the nesting relationship between elements. To quickly determine the structural relationship between two elements, each of which is encoded as *(Start, End, Level)*, where the first component represents its preorder se-

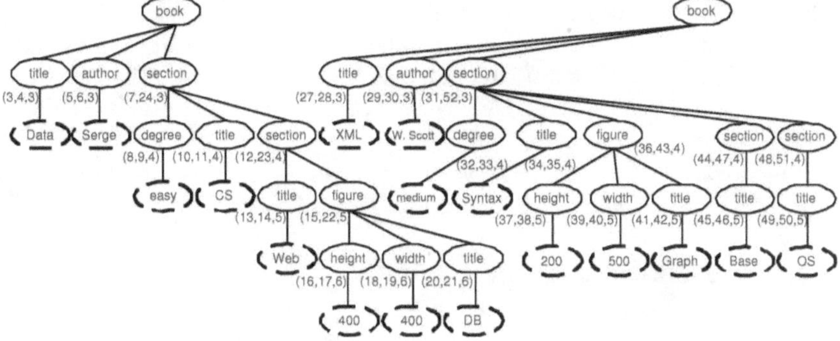

Fig. 1. The sample XML tree

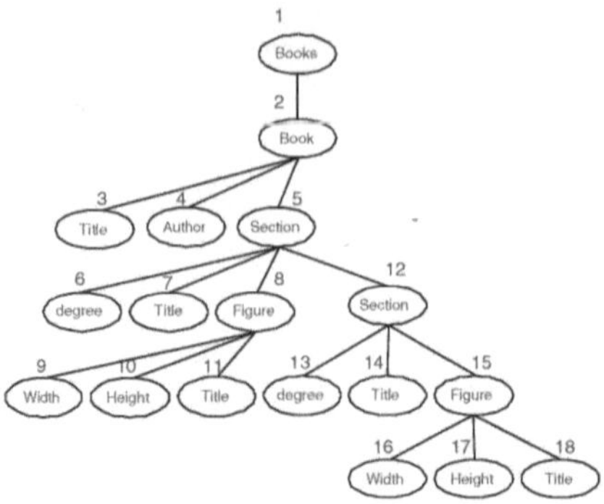

(a) The EP-tree

Tag	Path Encoding
books	1
book	2
title	3, 7, 11, 14, 18
author	4
section	5, 12
degree	6, 13
figure	8, 15
width	9, 16
height	10, 17

(b) The Tag-table

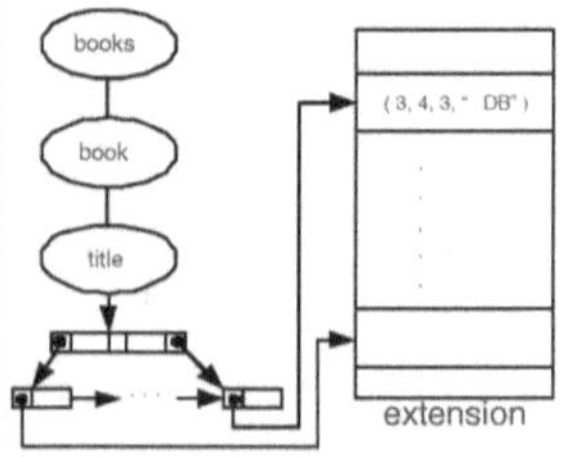

(c) The Value Index

Fig. 2. The index structures

quence in the XML tree, the second component represents its postorder sequence, and the third component is its level. For example, the leftmost *title* element in Figure 1 is encoded as (3, 4, 3).

Although XML data are self-explanatory, many efforts are on defining the standard format, such as in DTD description, to make the data interchange more easily. In this research, we express the DTD also as a tree. The one corresponding to the XML tree in Figure 1 is depicted in Figure 2(a). To represent the element which is recursively defined, *e.g.*, *section*, we expand the cycle into a longer path. We also encode each node of the tree based on the *preorder traversing sequence*, and call the tree an *EP-tree*. The EP-encoding is used to succinctly represent a path from the root to a particular node. For example, the EP-encoding 7 represents the path */Books/Book/Section/Title*.

The EP-tree is designed for top-down processing. To facilitate the bottom-up usage, we construct another structure, called the *Tag-table* (Figure 2(b)). It records the correspondence of an element tag and the paths (in EP-encoding) ended at the element. For the paths which do not start from the root, *e.g.*, *//figure/title*, we will first identify the EP-encodings for the last tag *title*, which are $\{3, 7, 11, 14, 18\}$. We then check if these nodes have the parent with the tag *figure*. The final results are $\{11, 18\}$.

The EP-tree summarizes and encodes all the possible paths in the XML repository. For each path in the EP-tree, we collect and index (using B^+-tree) all the values corresponding to the end-point of the path in order to efficiently locate those elements storing those values, as illustrated in Figure 2(c). The collection of B^+-trees is named the Value index. During query processing, we will traverse the EP-tree based on the given path, and reach the associated B^+-tree. The value constraint associated with the given path will guide the traversal of the B^+-tree to get the corresponding elements.

3 The Query Tree and Fragment Paths

The input XML query will be transformed into a *query tree*, where all the path expressions specified in the query are represented as paths in the tree. Particularly, the AD structural relationship "//" will be represented as a "| |" edge, and the PC structural

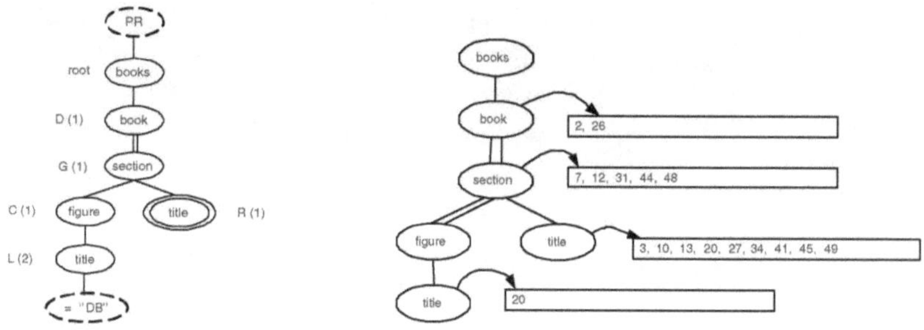

(a) with nodetypes (b) with streams

Fig. 3. The query tree

relationship "/" will be represented as a "|" edge. The query tree in Figure 3(a) is transformed from the following XML query (in Xpath): */books/book//section[//figure/title = "DB"]/title*, which retrieves the title of a section presenting a figure with the title *"DB"*.

Among the nodes in the query tree, the *root* refers to the top element in the query tree, *i.e.*, *books*. We attach a *pseudo root (PR)* on top of the root and connect it with the root by the PC edge. We will see its usage later. The other node depicted by dashed lines represents the value constraint, *e.g.*, = *"DB"*. It is represented as a child node of the path's end-point. The value constraint associated with each path will be resolved by the Value index, as shown in Figure 2(c).

All nodes of the query tree will be given a specific type. First, the type RN refers to a node to return, which is denoted by double circles, *e.g.*, the *title* on the right. The leaf node (LN) is self-explanatory, *e.g.*, the *title* on the left. The type GN is associated with the branching node (or called the gluing node), *e.g.*, *section*. For an internal node, if its following step is an AD relationship, it will be called an descendent node (DN). Otherwise, the following step will be a PC relationship, and the type is CN.

The type of each node is denoted in Figure 3(a). The number following the type is its *distance*, which is defined as the distance to the nearest GRLD ancestor. (A GRLD node means that it can be either GN, RN, LN, or DN.) For example, the node *figure* is right below the gluing node *section*. Therefore, its distance is 1. We will also explain its usage later.

After the query tree is constructed, it will be decomposed as a set of *Fragment paths*, which are defined as follows:

Definition 1. *Given a path $N_0E_0N_1 \cdots N_nE_nN_{n+1}$ in the query tree, where N_k is the parent node of N_{k+1}, $0 \leq k \leq n$, we will define the path $E_0N_1 \cdots N_nE_nN_{n+1}$ as a Fragment Path, or called FP in short, if the following conditions hold: (1) N_0 is a GRLD node or the pseudo root; (2) N_{n+1} is a GRLD node; (3) if $n \geq 1$, N_k is not a GRLD node, where $1 \leq k \leq n$; .*

Based on the third condition and the definition of node types, the structural relationship between elements in a fragment path will be all PC. For example, the query tree in Figure 3(a) will be decomposed into the following four FPs: "/books/book", "//section", "//figure/title", and "/title".

After identifying all the FPs, we will retrieve those elements which correspond to each FP, called *streams*, based on the index strucutre described in Section 2. The query tree along with the streams for the running example is depicted in Figure 3(b), where elements are represented and sorted by their *start* encoding. Note that all the GRLD nodes are associated with streams.

4 Building and Combining Glued Paths

We will discuss how to construct the final data based on the streams associated with each fragment path in this section. The notations *Glued Paths (GP)* and the *Glued Node Paths (GNP)* are first introduced as follows:

Definition 2. *Given a query tree and a sequence of FP: $FP_1, \cdots, FP_n$, $n \geq 1$, where the first node and the last node of each FP_k are represented as SN_k and EN_k, respectively. We will call the sequence of the FPs a Glued Path, and the sequence of their last nodes $< FN_1, \cdots, FN_n >$ a Glued Node Path, if the following conditions hold: (1) $SN_{k+1} = FN_k$, where $1 \leq k \leq n-1$, if $n \geq 2$; (2) FN_k is not GL, where $2 \leq k \leq n-1$, if $n \geq 3$; (3) FN_n is a GRL node; (4) FN_1 is a GN, or SN_1 is the root.*

The first condition requires that the input sequence of FPs forms a continuous path in the query tree. Other conditions basically make the GNP expand from a GN node to a GRL node, such as < section, title >. Note that each FN_K is a GRLD node (Definition 1), and the intermediate FN_k is not GL (condition 2). Therefore, we can conclude that the intermediate FN_k is a RD node.

Based on this definition, we identify each GP from the query tree, and store the corresponding GNP in the *list* structure in the *reverse* order. That is, for the GNP < section, title >, the operation *first*, which returns the first node in the list, will identify *title*, and the operation *last* will return *section*, as seen in Figure 4(a). Other operations defined for the node in the list include the following: (1) next: the next node; (2) pre: the previous node; (3) distance: the distance to its nearest GRLD ancestor, as explained in Section 2.

Each node n in the list is also associated with a stream and a stack, identified as $n.Stream$ and $n.Stack$, respectively. Recall that the streams associated with a GRLD node consist of those elements satisfying the corresponding FP, as shown in Figure 3(b).

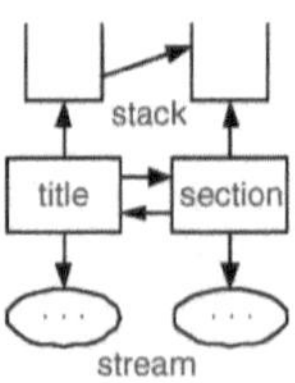

(a) The List

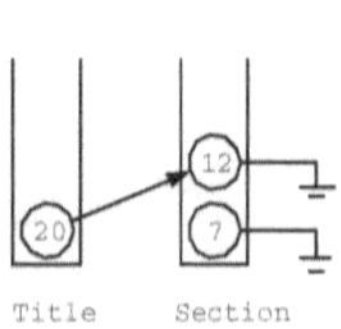

(b) The Stack

/books/book	//section
2	7, 12
*26	31, 44, 48

//section	//figure/title
7	20
12	20

//section	/title
7	10
12	13
*31	34
*44	45
*48	49

(c) The GP-Table

Fig. 4. The intermediate data structures

```
Algorithm getPGP
 1: while !end(List.first) do
 2:    Nmin=getMin(List); //in preorder sequence
 3:    for N = Nmin to List.last do
 4:       CleanStack(N.Next.Stack, Nmin.Stream.cur); //only ancestors are kept in stacks
 5:    end for
 6:    if ((Nmin = List.last or !(Nmin.Next.stack.isEmpty())) and (Nmin.stream.cur.level-
       Nmin.Next.stack.bottom.level >=Nmin.distance)) then
 7:       Nmin.stack.Push(Nmin.Stream.cur, getPLink(Nmin.Next.stack, Nmin.Stream.cur,
          Nmin.Distance));
 8:       Nmin.Stream.advance();
 9:       if Nmin=List.first then
10:          result = NULL; OutputPGP(Nmin, Nmin.Stack.Top, result);
11:          Nmin.Stack.Pop();
12:       end if
13:    else
14:       Nmin.Stream.advance();
15:    end if
16: end while
17: mark the delete flag for those unmatched elements;
```

```
Algorithm end: return List.first.stream.eof;
Algorithm getMin: return N in List node
  where N.stream.cur is minimal;
Algorithm CleanStack: while (!Stack.isEmpty)
  and (Stack.Top.End < E.Start) do Stack.Pop();
Algorithm getPLink:
  for M=Stack.top to Stack.bottom do
    if E.Level-M.Level>=D then return M;
```

```
Algorithm OutputPGP:
for M=N.Stack.bottom to SN do
  if N.pre=NULL then result=M endif;
  if N.next = NULL then GP-Table.insert(M, result);
  else if ((N.next.next = Null) and (N.PEdge=/ and
    M.Level-M.PLink.Level=N.distance)) then
    GP-Table.insert(M.PLink,result);
  else OutputPGP(N.Next, M.Plink, result);
```

Fig. 5. Algorithms for building Physical GNPs

We define several operations for each stream as follows: (1) cur: the element currently under processing; (2) advance: the next element; (3) reset: the first element. Each element in the stream is associated with one more flag *delete*. If an element does not find any other elements to match, its flag will be set to *false*. During the next matching process, the procedure will skip it to avoid unnecessary matching.

All the stacks associated with the node in the list are linked to compactly represent the physical GNP, *e.g.*, $< 20, 12 >$, as seen in Figure 4(b). In addition to the common operations *push* and *pop* defined for each stack, we also define the *top (bottom)* operation which reads the top (bottom) element without removing it. For an element n in the stack, $n.Plink$ will point to an element m in the next stack, where the pair (n, m) is part of a physical GNP, and m is the element with the largest $start$ encoding among all the qualified elements.

The list structure will be passed to Algorithm getPGP (Figure 5) to formulate physical GNPs. The statement in line 1 shows that we will continue processing as long as there are elements associated with the first stream. In line 2, we identify the query node which has the smallest start-encoding element. This causes the elements to be processed in the preorder sequence. The identified query node is called Nmin, and the current element is Nmin.stream.cur. In the FOR loop in line 3, we make sure only the ancestors of the current element are kept in the stacks to the end of the list.

We then determine if the current element is part of a physical GNP. The conditions specified in line 6 require that in the following stack, there exists an ancestor which is *old* enough, *i.e.*, the level difference above the current element exceeds the *distance* associated with the query node. If there exists such ancestor, we will move the current element to the stack and set its PlinK, as discussed before.

If we reach the last query node of the GNP, we will call algorithm OutputPGP to produce the physical GNPs and represent them in the structure GP-table. Each GP-table consists of two columns, where the first column corresponds to the first node of the GNP, and the second column represents the last node of the GNP. All the GP-tables for our running example are shown in Figure 4(c). Note that each tuple in the GP-table corresponds to a physical GNP, with the elements represented and sorted by their *start* encoding.

Based on the elements represented in the GP-Table, we will combine them and represent them based on the preorder sequence, *e.g.*, (2, 7, 10, 20). The detailed algorithms are omitted due to space limitation.

5 Experimental Results

We have implemented the algorithms in Borland C++. We will perform several experiments to evaluate the efficiency of our system (denoted as *Glued*) and compare it with the holistic approach (denoted as *Holistic*) [2]. All experiments are performed on a Pentium Cerelon 2.8GHz computer, with 512 MB of RAM and the Linux Red Hat 8 operating system.

The first experiment is based on an artificial DTD (Figure 6(a)). We vary the length of the projection path of the query, and fix all the structural relationships to be PC, to study how the performance of both approaches is affected. Take the query */E1/E2[E3 = 'Answer']/E4/E5/E6* as an example. Its path length will be regarded as 5. In this experiment, the stream sizes of Glued remain the same, but Holistic needs to process more elements when the path is longer (Figure 6(b)). This is the main reason that Holistic performs more element access than Glued does (Figure 6(c)). The execution time is measured for the building stage and the combining stage respectively, which are compared in Figure 6(d). We can see that Glued outperforms Holistic in both stages.

Based on the same data set, we modify the query to examine how the structural relationship AD affects the performance. The first change is to let the structural relationship between elements be all AD. The other change is to make the two structural relationships, AD and PC, occur alternatively. In Figure 6(e), we compare the combining time for all cases. We can see that the combining time of Glued is not affected by the structural relationship, but Holistic presents some differences. The reason is that Holistic examines the PC relationship in the combining stage, and will need to spend more time in the pure PC case. The total execution time is compared in Figure 6(f). We can see that Glued performs best in the pure PC case, but still outperforms Holistic in the respective case no matter what the structural relationship is.

Note that the major execution time for both systems are on building physical GNPs. In the second experiment, we will mainly discuss the building stage. We adopt the XBench schema about catalog information [8], and use the IBM XML generator [5] to

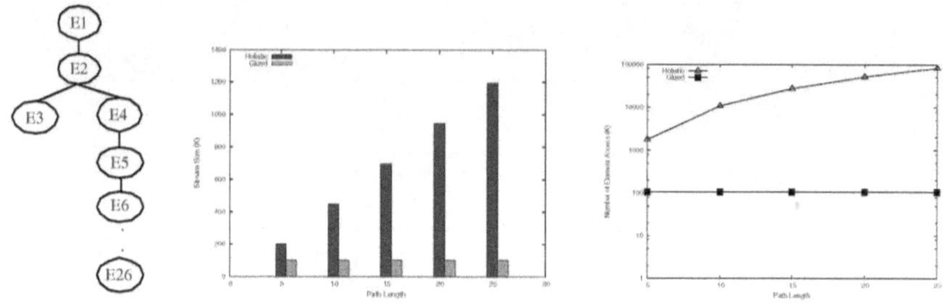

(a) DTD (b) Stream sizes (c) Element access in Build

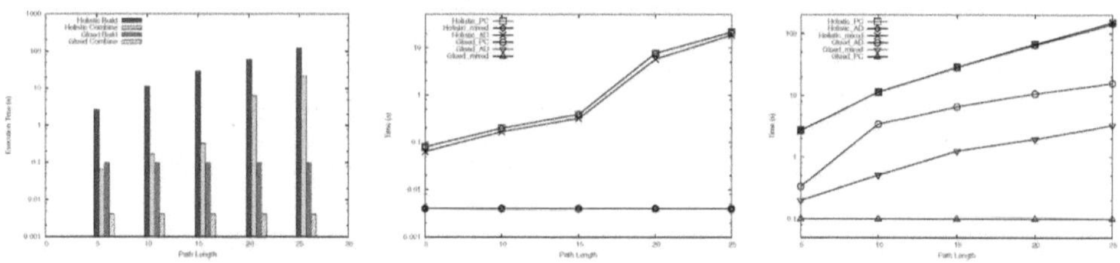

(d) Execution time (e) Comparison of combining time (f) Comparison of total time

Fig. 6. Analysis of path lengths

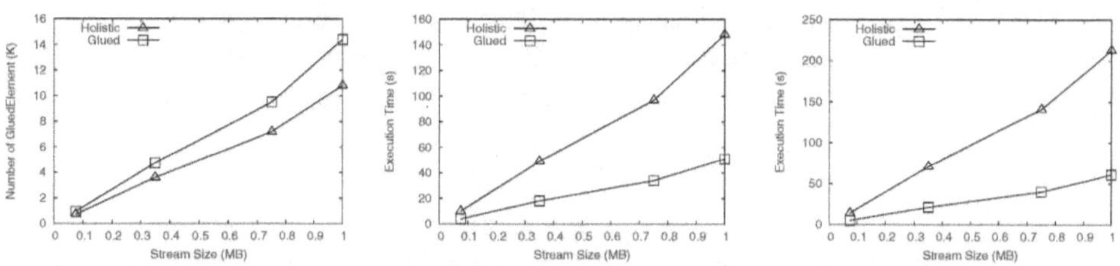

(a) # of elements to glue (b) Building time (c) Total time

Fig. 7. Analysis of stream sizes

produce five data sets, with the sizes 1M, 5M, 10M, and 15M, respectively. The same query */catalog//item[//title = "Book1"]//data_of_release* is run against each data set, and the stream sizes are 75K, 350K, 750K and 1MB, respectively. We fix the structural relationship between elements in the query to be AD in this case, so the stream sizes for both approaches are the same.

Although the input sizes of the building stage are the same for both approaches, we can see that the output size of Glued is actually larger (Figure 7(a)). This is because some elements in the GP-Table do not contribute to the final answers. However, this only presents a linear effect and the building time is still less (Figure 7(b)), and so is the total execution time (Figure 7(c)).

		Stream Size (K)	Retrieval Time (s)	Element Access (k)	Building Time (s)	Result	Combining Time (s)	Total Time (s)
Q1	Holistic	250.3	0.807	925.1	1.733	5	0	2.54
	Glued	250.3	0.807	1275.6	1.967	5	0.015	2.789
	Glued New	50	0.159	74.9	0.231	5	0.015	0.404
Q2	Holistic	288.63	1.013	365.71	0.937	659	0.5	2.45
	Glued	288.63	1.013	1778.5	2.346	659	0.025	4.397
	Glued New	25.6	0.174	76.1	0.106	659	0.025	0.305
Q3	Holistic	250.3	0.851	2457.7	3.92	2	0	3.92
	Glued	250.3	0.851	640.2	0.693	2	0.014	1.558
	Glued New	125	0.385	374.6	0.468	2	0.014	0.867
Q4	Holistic	75	0.257	100	0.498	1	0	0.755
	Glued	75	0.257	50	0.044	1	0	0.301
	Glued New	50	0.158	50	0.044	1	0	0.202

Fig. 8. Analysis of real data

In the last experiment, we use the tool provided by XBench [8] to produce the data set which simulates real XML data. The size is 100mb. We also design several queries with different twig patterns and structural relationship to run the experiments. In general, the amount of returned elements is quite small, so the combining time is sometimes negligible. The performance of different systems on these queries is summarized in Figure 8. Note that the system "Glued_New" is an improved version of Glued, which expands all the regular expressions in the EP-tree first so that the load of retrieval time and building time could be reduced. Although there are cases where Holistic beats Glued due to particular data distribution, Glued_New always has the best performance.

6 Conclusion

Efficient query processing of XML data is a very important research issue. In this paper, we consider the most common XML query which presents a twig pattern with PC or AD structural relationships. We propose to decompose the query into fragment paths to get the partial data, and then combine them back based on the gluing nodes. Such approach is more efficient than the state-of-the-art holistic approach since the elements to process are less. In the future, we plan to modify the algorithm to allow different combining sequences. We will also investigate how to extend the current system to support more complicated queries.

References

1. S. Al-Khalifa, H. V. Jagadish, N. Koudas, J. M. Patel, D. Srivastava, and Y. Wu. Structural joins: A primitive for efiicient xml query pattern matching. In *Proceedings of the ICDE Conference*, 2002.
2. Nicolas Bruno, Nick Koudas, and Divesh Srivastava. Holistic twig joins: Optimal xml pattern matching. In *Proceedings of the ACM SIGMOD conference*, 2002.

3. Zhimin Chen, H. V. Jagadish, Laks V. S. Lakshmanan, and Stelios Paparizos. From tree patterns to generalized tree patterns: On efficient evaluation of xquery. In *Proceedings of the 29th VLDB conference*, 2003.
4. Shu-Yao Chien, Zografoula Vagena, Donghui Zhang, Vassilis J. Tsotras, and Carlo Zaniolo. Efficient structural joins on indexed xml documents. In *Proceedings of the VLDB*, 2002.
5. Angel Luis Diaz and Douglas Lovell. Xml generator. http://www.alphaworks.ibm.com/tech/xmlgenerator, 1999.
6. Q. Li and B. Moon. Indexing and querying xml data for regular path expressions. In *Proceedings of the 27th VLDB Conference*, 2001.
7. J. McHugh and J. Widom. Query optimization for xml. In *Proceedings of the 25th VLDB Conference*, 1999.
8. B. B. Yao, M. T. Ozsu, and J. Keenleyside. Xbench – a family of benchmarks for xml dbmss. In *Proceedings of EEXTT 2002 and DiWeb 2002*, 2002.
9. Ning Zhang, Varun Kacholia, and M. Tamer Ozsu. A succinct physical storage scheme for efficient evaluation of path queries in xml. In *Proceedings of the IEEE ICDE conference*, 2004.

Early Evaluating XML Trees in Object Repositories *

Sangwon Park

Hankuk University of Foreign Studies, Youngin, Korea
swpark@hufs.ac.kr

Abstract. Data on the Internet are usually represented and transfered as XML. The XML data is represented as a tree and therefore, object repositories are well-suited to store and query them due to their modeling power. XML queries are represented as regular path expressions and evaluated by traversing each object of the tree in object repositories. Several indexes are proposed to fast evaluate regular path expressions. However, in some cases they may not cover all possible paths because they require a great amount of disk space. In order to efficiently evaluate the queries in such cases, we propose an signature based block traversing which combines the signature method and block traversing. The signature approach shrink the search space by using the signature information attached to each object, which hints the existence of a certain label in the sub-tree. The block traversing reduces disk I/O by early evaluating the reachable objects in a page. We conducted diverse experiments to show that the hybrid approach achieves a better performance than the other naive ones.

1 Introduction

XML is an emerging standard for data representation and exchange on the Internet. A database system is required for efficient manipulation of XML data, as large quantities of information are represented and processed as XML. The XML data is similar to semistructured data[2, 4] which is intensively studied in recent years by the database research community. The XML data model is a tree, so object-oriented data model is suitable for its data model because of excessive modeling power compared to a relational data model. For example, object repositories such as Lore[12], eXcelon[7] and PDOM[8] use object-oriented data model to store XML data.

The XML queries contain regular path expressions and are evaluated by traversing the trees, where each node is stored as an object in the object repositories. For efficient evaluation of the XML query, shrinking the search space of the tree and reducing page I/O are highly important.

```
SELECT x.(telephone|company.*.tel)
FROM person x;
```

* This work is supported by Hankuk University of Foreign Studies research fund of 2005.

H.T. Shen et al. (Eds.): ADWeb 2006, LNCS 3842, pp. 58–67, 2006.

The above is an example of an XML query, which is similar to XQuery[3]. This query retrieves person's telephone numbers. It contains regular path expressions [1, 5, 6], which are supported by general XML query languages. Some syntaxes, such as star(*) in XML queries, enlarge the search space because almost all nodes under `company` must be visited by `company.*`. Therefore, regular path indexes have been studied to solve this problem.

We developed the signature technique[13] to shrink the search space when we could not use indexes. But even the search space is reduced, lots of page I/O are occurred when the objects are un-clustered in repository. For reducing the page I/O, we evaluate the objects stored in same page ahead of others, which is called *block traversing*. The former shrink the search space, the latter reduce disk I/O by changing navigation order. We combine two techniques called signature based block traversing technique to reduce a great number of page I/O regardless of the object distribution in the object repository. This technique could be adopted to semistructured indexes to reduce the number of traversing index nodes.

2 Preliminaries

2.1 Data Model and Query Language

The XML data model is represented as a tree of which sibling objects are an ordered list. DOM is a standard interface of XML data, which has interfaces to traverse the tree. DOM is the data model used in this paper.

Figure 1 is an example of a DOM tree which can be traversed from a certain node to its parent, child or sibling nodes. Each node is an object and stored in object repositories. Each object has an OID that is represented by '&' as depicted in Figure 1. There are element nodes, attribute nodes and text nodes in DOM, in which each node has a name or a value and is stored in disk pages. For example, &1, &2 and &6 are stored in the page A. Simple definitions useful for describing the mechanism described in this paper are:

Definition 1 (label path). *A label path of a DOM object o is a sequence of one or more dot-separated labels, $l_1.l_2...l_n$, such that we can traverse a path of n nodes ($n_1...n_n$) from o, where node n_i has a label l_i, and the type of node is element or attribute.*

Definition 2 (regular path expression). *A regular path expression is a path expression that has regular expressions in the label path.*

2.2 Evaluating Regular Path Expressions Using NFA

In this paper, we evaluate the regular path expression by translating it to an NFA(non-deterministic automata). A regular expression can be represented by an NFA[11]. A regular path expression is a regular expression as well, and can be translated to an NFA. Any complex NFA can be constructed by composition of $L(r_1)L(r_2)$, $L(r_1+r_2)$ and $L(r*)$ as depicted in Figure 3[11]. $L(r?)$ and $L(r+)$

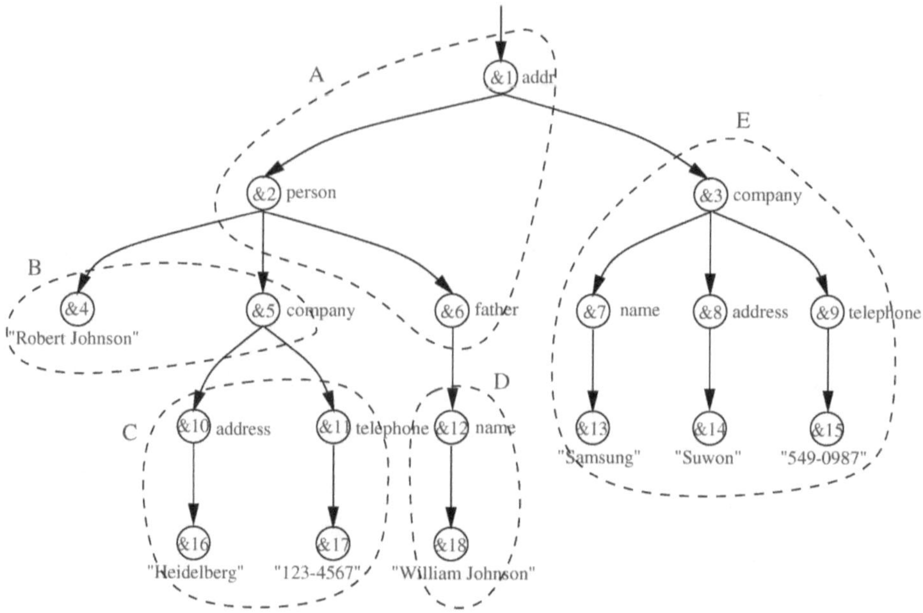

Fig. 1. DOM graph

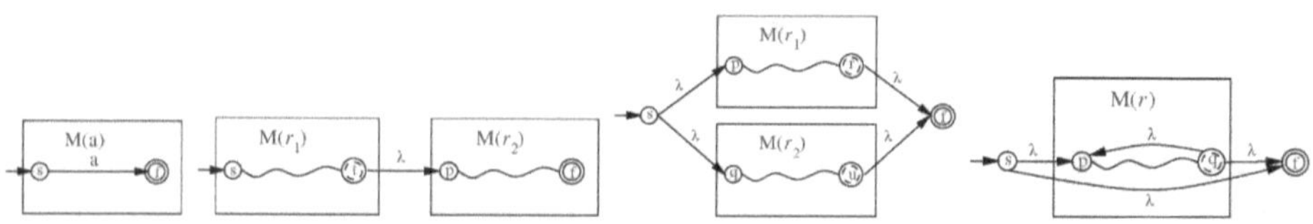

(a) L(a) (b) $L(r_1)L(r_2)$ (c) $L(r_1 + r_2)$ (d) $L(r^*)$

Fig. 2. NFA

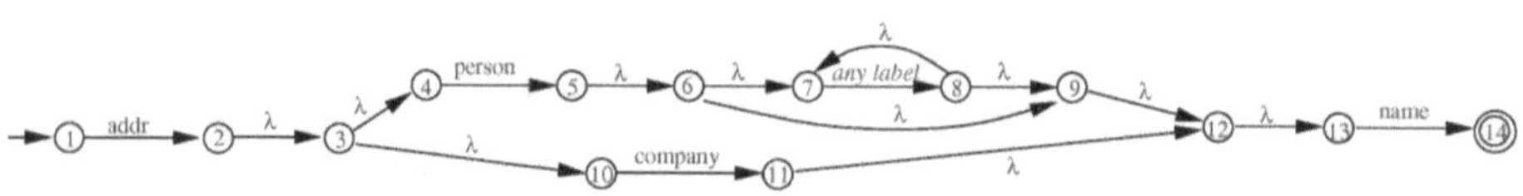

Fig. 3. The NFA of `addr.(person.*|company).name`

are the variations of $L(r^*)$. $L(r?)$ can be derived by removing an edge λ from a state q to a state p in Figure 2(d). $L(r+)$ is an $L(r^*)$ where an edge λ is removed from a state s to a state f in Figure 2(d). A regular path expression used in this paper is `addr.(person.*|company).name` and the NFA of this query is depicted in Figure 3.

Definition 3 (state set). *The state set is a set of state nodes of NFA, elements of which are the results of transition in NFA by a certain label path.*

2.3 The OID Table of Object Repositories

Each object in the object repository has an OID which is the information of its physical location. There are two types of OID, one is a logical OID(LOID) and the other is a physical OID(POID)[10]. The logical OID is a pseudo number created by the system. In this case, there is an OID table which maps LOID to physical location of the object. In this paper, it is assumed that an object has an LOID and there is an OID table. POID means physical location of an object, and the OID table is not needed. We propose two techniques in this paper. One is block traversing, the other is the signature based traversing. LOID or POID can be used for the block traversing.

We additionally add a signature to each object in the OID table, which is the hint of what labels are existed in the sub-tree[14]. If we use the POID approach, then the OID table is unnecessary and the signature has to be stored in each object[13]. Let the hash value of the name of an object n be H_n, and the signature of the object be S_n. $S_n = \bigvee_{child\ i\ of\ n} H_i$, which is the ORing of all the hash values of child objects of the object n. The existence of a certain label l in the sub-tree of the object i can be estimated by comparison of $H_l \wedge S_i$. If $H_l \wedge S_i \equiv H_l$ then there may be an object whose name is l in the sub-tree. Otherwise, if $H_l \wedge S_i \neq S_i$, then it assures that the objects with the name l does not exist in the sub-tree.

3 New Object Navigating Techniques

In this section, we present the signature based traversing and the block traversing. In addition, the signature based block traversing is proposed, which combines the above two techniques.

3.1 Block Traversing

Each node in the DOM tree is stored as an object in the object repository. All objects can be clustered when they are stored for the first time. However, after lots of update operations, the objects are scattered over pages. As a result, when adjacent objects may be stored in different pages. Fetching these objects makes page faults. For example, the objects &2, &4, &5 and &6 in Figure 1 are visited in order. The object &2 and &6 are stored in the page A, and the objects &4 and &5 are stored in the page B. The object &6 have to be visited after processing the objects in the page B and their child objects by depth-first search. Then the page A could be replaced by the buffer manager after traversing the child objects of &2, resulting in causing a page fault. This is because we ignore the locality information between objects.

It is the best if we can process all objects in a fetched page at a time like the block nested loop join[9] in relational database. However, for evaluating a regular path expression, the state set of an object has to be made from its parent object, which means that an object can not be processed before processing its

Algorithm 1. block::next()

```
/* SS is the state set of NFA */
node ← Queue.remove()
while node is not NULL do
   SS ← traverse NFA by the label of node
   /* if SS is empty then the sub-tree of node can not be query result */
   if SS is not empty then
      Queue.addChildren(node, SS)
      if a final state node exists ∈ SS then
         return node
      end if
   end if
   node ← Queue.remove()
end while
return NULL
```

all parent objects. An object in the object repository has an OID which is the information of physical location in disk. We can determine whether two objects are existed in a same page by their OIDs or not. An object in the DOM tree has OIDs of its child objects. This means that we can find which child objects exist in the same page with their parent object. Therefore, we can early evaluate such objects, reducing lots of page faults.

Definition 4 (next-door object). *If the two objects o_i and o_j are stored in a same page, then o_i is a next-door object of o_j, vice versa.*

Algorithm 1 is a scan operator that returns a node accepted by the regular path expression. Before calling this function, a pair of (the OID of root object, { }) has to be inserted to the queue which stores the pair of (OID, the state set of its parent). The hash table is implemented to retrieve an object to find a next-door object rapidly. A path stack manages the path from the root to the current processing object. The top object o_t of the path stack is the one processed just before. The function `remove` returns one of next-door objects of the object o_t. If there is no next-door object of o_t in the queue, then it returns an arbitrary object which is an element of the largest group. We can group the objects in the queue by the page number. Let a state set of the object &i be SS_i and one of child nodes of &i be c_i. The function `addChildren` stores pairs of (the OID of c_i, SS_i) in the queue to retrieve the next-door objects.

Example 1 *Let OID of an object* `&i` *be OID_i and the state set of* `&i` *be SS_i. When the root object in Figure 1 is fetched and traverse the NFA depicted in Figure 3, the state set SS_1 is $\{4, 10\}$. The pairs of its child nodes and this state set, (OID_2, SS_1) and (OID_3, SS_1) are inserted to the queue. The function* `remove` *returns* `&2` *because a next-door object of* `&1` *is* `&2`*. After processing* `&2`*,*

SS_2 is obtained as {7, 13}. Then (OID_4, SS_2), (OID_5, SS_2) and (OID_6, SS_2) are inserted to the queue. The `remove` *function returns* `&6` *and it is processed before* `&4` *even if* `&4` *is the first child of the* `&2` *because the next-door object of* `&2` *is* `&6`*. The pair of (OID_{12}, SS_6) is inserted after processing the object* `&6`*. Then there is no next-door objects of the object* `&6`*. We use a heuristic to select an object in the queue by the number of the objects stored in each page. By this heuristic, the function* `remove` *returns the object* `&2`.

3.2 Signature Based Traversing

We have developed the signature based traversing called s-NFA[13] for XML query processing. The signature based traversing shrinks the search space and reduce the page I/O during query processing. We modify this technique in order to apply it to the object repository by adding a signature column in the OID table.

The regular path expressions allows wild card operators such as *, + and ?. The scan operator is provided for searching the objects matching with the given regular path expression when processing the query. For the query like `person.*.name`, all child objects of `person` have to be visited because of star(*). If we know what labels exist in the sub-tree below an object in advance, we can prune the graph and shrink the search space of the tree.

Definition 5 (NFA path). *The NFA path P_n is a path from a state node n to the final state node in an NFA.*

Definition 6 (path signature). *The path signature PS_n of a state node n in the NFA is defined as $PS_n = \{ x \mid x$ is a signature which is ORing the hash values of all the labels along an NFA path P_n in the NFA$\}$*

Let the path signature of the state node n be PS_n and the signature of the object &i be S_i. Let one signature of PS_n be S_j. If $S_j \wedge S_i \equiv S_j$, then we may guess that we can arrive the final state node when traversing the sub-tree of object &i. If not, the final state node can not be arrived when traversing all objects in the sub-tree of object &i. Therefore, we can prune the tree by checking the signature while evaluating the queries.

Figure 2 describes how to build the various types of NFA. Therefore, if path signatures of that NFA in Figure 2 can be made, then path signatures of any complicated NFA can be built. The rules for making path signatures are described below[13].

Rule 1 (L(a)) $PS_s = \{ H_a \}$, $PS_f = \{ 0 \}$

Rule 2 (L($r_1 + r_2$)) $PS_s = PS_p \cup PS_q$, $PS_f = \{ 0 \}$

Rule 3 (L(r*)) $PS_s = \{ 0 \}$, $PS_f = \{ 0 \}$ *The path signature of L(r?) is same as the Rule 3.*

Rule 4 (L(r+)) $PS_s = PS_p$, $PS_f = \{ 0 \}$.

Algorithm 2. signature-block::next()

```
/* SS is the state set of NFA */
node ← Queue.remove()
while node is not NULL do
    SS ← forward(node, node.SS) /* using Signature */
    /* if SS is empty then the sub-tree of node can not be query result */
    if SS is not empty then
        Queue.addChildren(node, SS)
        if a final state node exists ∈ SS then
            return node
        end if
    end if
    node ← Queue.remove()
end while
return NULL
```

Rule 5 (L(r_1)L(r_2)) *$L(r_1)L(r_2)$ is the concatenation of two NFAs. While traversing from the start state node to the final state node, the state node p in $M(r_2)$ should be visited. So a path signature PS_i of a state node i in $M(r_1)$ has to be changed by ORing PS_p; that is, $PS_i = PS_i \times_{\vee} PS_p$. It is the Cartesian product ORing with the path signature of each state node in $M(r_1)$ and PS_p. It is called as signature propagation. The path signatures of $M(r_2)$ are not changed. Therefore, the path signature PS_i of each state node i in $M(r_1)$ is $PS_i = \{ (x \vee y) \mid PS_i^{'}$ is the path signature of a state node in $M(r_1)$, x is a signature of $PS_i^{'}$, y is a signature of PS_p $\}$.*

3.3 The Signature Based Block Traversing

The signature based traversing shrinks the search space by pruning the subtree using the signature information. The block traversing reduces page I/O

Algorithm 3. forward(*node*, *SS*)

```
SS ← forward by label
for each state node n which can go forward by λ in SS do
    for each signature S_i of PS_n do
        if S_i ∧ node.signature ≡ S_i then
            m ← the state node moved from n by λ
            add m to SS
            break
        end if
    end for
    remove n from SS
end for
```

by changing the traversing order of objects. Both of them reduce page I/O but are based on different mechanism. We combine these techniques which are complementary to each other. We call it the *signature based block traversing*.

Algorithm 2 is a scan operator that returns an object which is accepted by the regular path expression by the signature based block traversing. This scan operator calls `forward` described in Algorithm 3. This algorithm is the same as Algorithm 1 except the function `forward` to prune the sub-tree by the signature information.

4 Experimental Results

The simulation program in this paper is implemented in Java and evaluates the queries in the main memory. We store nodes of DOM as objects and fetch them by scan operator, of which input is a regular path expression. The scan operator requests objects from the object cache, which is built on the buffer manager. We only count the number of page I/O in the buffer manager as a performance metric. The processing time for managing siganture or block traversing can be ignored because they are processed in the main memory. The page size is 4K bytes and the buffer size is 20 pages.

The objects may be clustered when they are stored for the first time in the object repository. However, as times go by, they will be scattered over the repository after many update operations. At first we store the objects as depth-first, which are fully clustered. The performance is differenct when objects are fully clustered in depth-first and breadth-first[13]. This performance gap get smaller as the un-clustered ratio becomes larger. Considering the implementation, depth-first is more applicable to store large XML files. The data used in this paper are Shakespeare, The Book of Mormon, and part of Michael Ley's bibliography, which are all translated into XML. The numbers of nodes of XML data are 737,621, 19,854 and 142,751, respectively. The sizes of each data are 7.5 Mbytes, 247 Kbytes and 6.7 Mbytes.

Six queries are used in the experiments and described in Table 1. In these queries, '*[2]' means that two arbitary label strings exist between PLAY and PERSONA. The Q1, Q2 and Q5 retrieve the data that are located in a specific string. The rest queries retrieves the data located at any depth of the tree.

There are four scan operators for naive, signature based, block or signature based block traversing(optimal), respectively. The naive operator fetches objects by depth first search The signature based traversing predicts the existence of a

Table 1. Queries used in simulation

Q1	Shakespeare	PLAY.*[2].PERSONA	Q4	Bibliography	*.author
Q2	Shakespeare	*.TITLE	Q5	Mormon	tstmt.*[1].(title|ptitle)
Q3	Bibliography	bibliography.paper.*[1].pages	Q6	Mormon	*.chapter

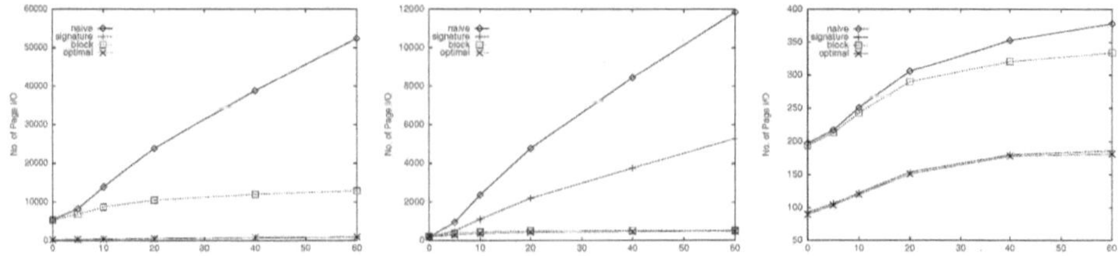

(a) Q1 (b) Q3 (c) Q5

Fig. 4. Performance results (queue size : 4,000)

certain label in regular path expressions. The block scan operator fetches next-door objects early while navigating the tree. It reduces disk I/O by changing the navigating sequence. The signature based block scan operator combines the last two techniques.

Figure 4 shows the results of the performance test. There are only three results for Q1, Q3 and Q5 because Q2, Q4 and Q6 are very similar to Q3. The objects are clustered by depth first when the un-clustered ratio is zero and scattered by the ratio depicted as x-axis in Figure 4. The queue size and the signature size are fixed as 4,000 and 4 bytes, respectively. The page I/O is counted at each un-clustered ratio.

Figure 4 shows that the block traversing reduces page I/O with the growth of the un-clustered ratio. However, the sub figures (a) and (c) show that the signature based traversing highly shrinks the search space, that is, its performance is much better than the block traversing. The reason is that with the signature based traversing, the objects are pruned at the shallow depth of the tree and leading to cause shrink search space a lot. In Figure 4(a), the signature based traversing is better than the block traversing, while in Figure 4(b), the latter outperforms the former. However in the figures, the signature based block traversing always a winner among the four techniques. By this fact, the signature based block traversing is favorable to evaluating the XML queries.

The block traversing uses a queue to manage next-door objects and memorizes their state sets. If the queue size is huge, the number of page I/O will be the fewest.

5 Conclusion

Each node of the DOM tree is stored as an object in object repositories. The page I/O can be reduced when these objects are clustered in the repositories. However, after lots of update operations, objects in a same page may be scattered over several pages. When the objects are un-clustered, a page fault per object fetching may happen in worst case. The characteristic of the XML query is the regular path expressoins. Three different scan operators are made to efficiently evaluate the regular path expressions. We introduce the block traversing to reduce page I/O by early evaluation of next-door objects which are located in the same page.

The location of objects are determined by the OID table of the object repository. By using this, the block traversing reduces lots of page I/O even when the objects are un-clustered. We deverloped the signature based traversing which shrink the search space. The signature based block traversing which combines the above two techniques is superior to any other methods. We significantly reduce the number of page I/O by this signature based block traversing, which is very useful in evaluating the XML queries.

References

1. S. Abiteboul, D. Quass, J. McHugh, J. Widom, and J. Wiener. The Lorel Query Language for Semistructured Data. *International Journal on Digital Library*, 1(1), 4 1997.
2. Serge Abiteboul. Querying Semistructured Data. *International Conference on Database Theory*, January 1997.
3. Scott Boag and et al. XQuery 1.0: An XML Query Language. *W3C*, 2005.
4. P. Buneman. Semistructured Data. *ACM SIGACT-SIGMOD-SIGART Symposium on Principles of Database Systems*, May 1997.
5. Peter Buneman, Susan Davidson, Gerd Hillebrand, and Dan Suciu. A Query Language and Optimization Techniques for Unstructured Data. *SIGMOD*, 1996.
6. V. Christophides, S. Abiteboul, S. Cluet, and M. Scholl. From Structured Documents to Novel Query Facilities. *SIGMOD*, 1994.
7. eXcelon. An XML Data Server For Building Enterprise Web Applications. *http://www.odi.com/products/white_papers.html*, 1999.
8. GMD-IPSI. GMD-ISPI XQL Engine. *http://xml.darmstadt.gmd.de/xql*, 2000.
9. Won Kim. A New Way to Compute the Product and Join of Relations. *SIGMOD*, 1980.
10. Won Kim. *Introduction to Object-Oriented Databases.* The MIT Press, 1990.
11. Peter Linz. *An Introduction to Formal Languages and Automata.* Houghton Mifflin Company, 1990.
12. Jason McHugh, Serge Abiteboul, Roy Goldman, Dallan Quass, and Jennifer Widom. Lore: A Database Management System for Semistructured Data. *SIGMOD Record*, 26(3), 9 1997.
13. Sangwon Park and Hyoung-Joo Kim. A New Query Processing Technique for XML Based on Signature. *DASFAA*, 2001.
14. Hwan-Seung Yong, Sukho Lee, and Hyoung-Joo Kim. Applying Signatures for Forward Traversal Query Processing in Object-Oriented Databases. *ICDE*, 1994.

Caching Frequent XML Query Patterns

Xin Zhan, Jianzhong Li, Hongzhi Wang, and Zhenying He

Department of Computer Science and Engineering, Harbin Institute of Technology, China
zhanxin2003@hotmail.com, {lijzh, Wangzh, hzy}@hit.edu.cn

Abstract. As XML becomes prevailing on the Internet, efficient management of XML queries becomes more important. Caching frequent queries can expedite XML query processing. In this paper, we propose a framework to address an NP-hard optimization problem, caching frequent query patterns. We develop several algorithms to respectively generate query subpatterns, check query containment, and choose query subpatterns for caching. Experimental results show that our algorithms are efficient and scalable.

1 Introduction

With rapid growth of XML management systems on the Internet, XML is increasing used as model of data representation and data exchange. Due to growing demand for retrieving data from multiple remote XML sources, caching techniques [2,3] are employed. Consider that when frequent queries and their answers are reserved in local cache, new queries can be answered locally by reasoning query containment, instead of accessing remote sources. In this way, response latency caused by data transmission over the Internet can be reduced.

XQuery [1] is a XML query language proposed by W3C. It contains special characters wildcard (*) and descendant path (//). Each instance of XQuery can be transformed to a *query pattern tree*. For example, Figure 1 shows an instance of XQuery and an equivalent query pattern tree, which defines the following navigation: starting from root node **bib**, we pass its child node **book** from which we can reach a node **author** by means of any path, and return **price** of these books.

In this paper, we address an NP-hard optimization problem, *caching frequent XML query patterns*, that is by mining previous user query pattern trees stored in database, a set of frequent XML *query subpatterns* is discovered for caching, which satisfies two conditions: these subpatterns are most frequent, and total result size of corresponding queries are smaller than cache capacity. This problem is at least as complicated as *Knapsack* problem.

We propose a framework for caching frequent XML query patterns. First, we develop an algorithm to generate all the query subpatterns. Next we use a *position histogram* scheme [7] to estimate sizes of query answers. We also present a *query containment* algorithm [8,9] based on *homomorphism* to compute *frequencies* of query subpatterns. At last, a *fully polynomial approximation scheme* (FPTAS) [22] is developed to choose query subpatterns for caching. Experimental results show that our algorithms are computationally efficient and scalable.

H.T. Shen et al. (Eds.): ADWeb 2006, LNCS 3842, pp. 68 – 75, 2006.

```
for $b in doc("bib.xml")/bib/book,
    $a in $b/author,
    $p in $b/price
return
    <result>
        {$t}
    </result>
```

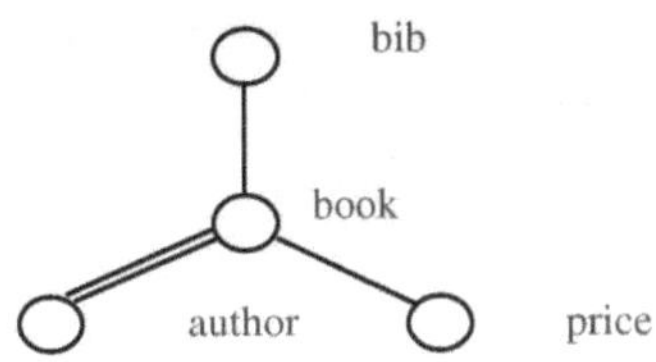

Fig. 1. An example of XQuery and its pattern tree

The rest of this paper is organized as follows. In Section 2, we provide formal problem definition. In Section 3, we present a framework for our problem and develop several algorithms. We introduce cache replacement strategy and an optimization heuristic in Section 4. In Section 5, we experimentally evaluate our algorithms. Finally, we discuss related works in Section 6 and conclude in Section 7.

2 Problem Definition

In this section, we present several important definitions. We model XML documents as ordered node-labeled trees over an infinite alphabet Σ in this paper.

Query Pattern Trees. A *query pattern tree* is a rooted tree *QPT* = <*N*, *E*> where:

1. *N* is the node set. Each node in it has a label string over alphabet $\Sigma \cup \{*\}$.
2. *E* is the edge set, which can be partitioned into two disjoint subsets, the child edge set and the descendant edge set.

Query Subpattern Trees. Given a query pattern tree *QPT*, a *query subpattern tree* *SPT* = <*N'*, *E'*> is a subtree of *QPT*, where:

1. *Root*(*SPT*) = *Root*(*QPT*), that is *SPT* and *QPT* share the same root node.
2. $N' \subseteq N$ and $E' \subseteq E$.

A query subpattern tree is called a query subpattern in short. Its answer refers to result of the XML query equivalent to this subpattern tree.

Caching Frequent Query Patterns. Given a set of user query pattern trees $Q = \{QPT_1, QPT_2, \ldots, QPT_m\}$, and a cache capacity *C*, our goal is to discover frequent query subpattern trees, cache such query subpatterns and their answers under restriction that total size must not exceed cache capacity.

We obtain *frequency* of a query subpattern SPT, denoted as *freq*(*SPT*), by checking query containment between *SPT* and each query pattern tree in *Q*. If *k* query pattern trees are contained by *SPT*, then *freq*(*SPT*) is *k*. For a set of query subpatterns *SQ*, we obtain frequency of *SQ*, *freq*(*SQ*), by summing up frequencies of its elements. When *freq*(*SQ*) is maximized, we say *SQ* is a set of *frequent query subpatterns*.

To be precise, our problem is as follows: we first generate a set of query subpatterns $SQ=\{SPT_1, SPT_2, \ldots, SPT_n\}$ from *Q*. For each SPT_i, we denote its frequency as $freq(SPT_i)$ and result size as $size(SPT_i)$. With specified frequency and result size, our problem is to find a subset of *SQ*, *SQ'*, whose frequency is maximized, and total result size of query patterns in *SQ'* is bounded by the cache capacity. That is,

$$\sum_{SPT_i \in SQ} size(SPT_i) < C \text{ and maximize}\{ \sum_{SPT_i \in SQ} freq(SPT_i) \} \quad (1)$$

3 A Framework for Caching Frequent XML Query Patterns

In this section, we propose a framework for the caching frequent query patterns, which basically contains several problems: how to generate all query subpatterns, how to compute frequency, how to estimate answer size and select what query patterns for caching. A sequence of solutions is provided below to address each problem respectively.

3.1 Query Subpattern Generation

Here we introduce the solution to generate all the query subpatterns. First, merge user query pattern trees into a global pattern tree *G-QPT* with a dummy node as the root and each query pattern tree as a subtree. Next, generate query subpatterns of *G-QPT*. We propose an effective algorithm shown in Figure 2. It takes the root node of *G-QPT* as input, visits each node of *G-QPT*, set it true and then set it false. Whenever a node is assigned with a boolean value, output current *G-QPT* made up of true-value nodes. Note that *right sibling*(*r*) refers to the right sibling node of node *r*, *first child*(*r*) refers to the first child node of node *r*.

This algorithm systematically generates all the query subpatterns of *G-QPT* with no redundancy. When workload grows, the number of query subpatterns expands rapidly. So we propose a pruning heuristic, as is discussed in Section 4.

Rooted-Subtree-Generation (node *r*)
Input: node *r*, the root of global pattern tree *G-QPT*
Output: *SQ*, the set of query subpatterns of *G-QPT*
let *r* is false;
if *r* has right siblings
then Rooted-Subtree-Generation(*right sibling*(*r*));
else output current *G-QPT* made up of true nodes;
let *r* is true;
if *r* has children
then Rooted-Subtree-Generation(*first child*(*r*));
if r has right siblings
then Rooted-Subtree-Generation(*right sibling*(*r*));
if *r* has neither siblings nor children
then output current *G-QPT* made up of true nodes;

Fig. 2. Algorithm Rooted-Subtree-Generation

3.2 Frequency Computation

Now we introduce the solution to compute frequency. When generating each query subpattern, we need to compute its frequency by checking query containment. The containment problem for query patterns are equivalent to the containment problem for a fragment of *XPath* [10], which consists of node tests, the child axis (/), the descendant axis (//) and wildcards (*). Previous research [8,9] showed that such problem has PTIME algorithms. Here we use *homomorphism* between patterns to reason about containment. A homomorphism is a mapping which is root-preserving, respects node labels, and obeys edge constraints. The existence of a homomorphism is always a sufficient condition for containment.

Compute-Frequency ()
Input: a query subpattern *SPT*
Output: the frequency of *SPT*, *freq*(*SPT*)

```
for each QPT_i in Q
   check homomorphism from SPT to QPT_i ;
   if there exist a homomorphism
   then freq(SPT)+1;
return freq(SPT);
```

Fig. 3. Algorithm Compute-Frequency

In Figure 3, we present an algorithm for computing frequency based on homomorphism. This algorithm takes a query subpattern *SPT* as input, counts its frequency by checking homomorphism from it to each user query pattern tree. Its running time is polynomial in the number of nodes of *SPT*.

3.3 Selection of Frequent Query Subpatterns for Caching

So far, we have introduced how to generate query subpatterns and compute their frequencies. In terms of result size estimation, we make use of an estimation algorithm based on *position histogram* [7]. Given query subpatterns with their specified frequencies and answer sizes, we need to decide which subpatterns are selected for caching. This selection problem is a NP-hard optimization problem, for which a fully polynomial approximation scheme is the best solution.

As shown in Figure 4, we develop a FPTAS algorithm for selection. It modifies the frequency of each query subpattern in *SQ*, then use *Knapsack* style dynamic programming approach [22] to find the most frequent subset *SQ'*, whose total result size is bounded by cache capacity *C*. Running time of this algorithm is polynomial in n and 1/ε, where ε is a error parameter.

$$O(n^2 \left\lfloor \frac{F}{K} \right\rfloor) = O(n^2 \left\lfloor \frac{n}{\varepsilon} \right\rfloor) \tag{2}$$

Frequency of the outputted subset *SQ'*, *freq*(*SQ'*), is at least (1-ε)•OPT. [22]

```
Choose_Patterns ()
Input: the set of query subpattern SQ, each query subpattern in SQ has
       specified frequency and result size, cache capacity C, error
       parameter ε>0.
Output: subset SQ'
  F = max {freq(SPT_i)}, for SPT_i ∈ SQ ;
  K = εF/n ;
  for each SPT_i in SQ
    freq'(SPT_i) = freq(SPT_i)/K ;
  Use dynamic programming to find the most frequent subset SQ' ;
  Output SQ' ;
```

Fig. 4. Algorithm Choose_Patterns

Caching_Frequent_Query_Patterns( )
Input: a set user query patterns Q, cache capacity C, error parameter ε
Output: the most frequent subset SQ', whose result size bounded by C

1 Generate the set of query subpatterns SQ and compute frequency of each query subpattern in SQ.
2 Estimate answer size of each query subpattern in SQ.
3 Find the most frequent subset of SQ, SQ', and total answer size of SQ' is smaller than C.
4 Output SQ'.

Fig. 5. Algorithm Caching_Frequent_Query_Patterns

So far, we have introduced how to address the problems within our framework. By combining the solutions presented above, we propose an algorithm for caching frequent XML query patterns in Figure 5.

4 Caching Frequent Query Patterns

In this section, we present cache replacement strategy and a heuristic for subpattern generation. After frequent query subpatterns are found by Caching Frequent Query Patterns algorithm, we load cache with these query subpatterns and their answers. When a new user query *QPT* arrives, it is compared with cached query patterns. If *QPT* is contained by a cached query pattern *QPT'*, we rewrite *QPT* and use result of *QPT'* to answer *QPT*.

Replacement Strategy. When cache replacement is needed, we first replace result of the most infrequent query subpattern. If space for admitting the result of new query is still not enough, result of the second most infrequent pattern is replaced. We repeatedly replace infrequent patterns until new query result can be cached. Such replacement strategy is called *leastFreq*.

Cache must be periodically updated to keep the cached data fresh. Thus periodically we rerun our algorithms upon recent user query patterns and reload the cache. However, as workload increases, the number of generated query subpatterns becomes very large. To improve the efficiency of our algorithms, we propose the following heuristic.

Heuristic for subpattern generating. While generating query subpatterns, we compute the frequency of each newly generated subpattern. If its frequency is lower than a predefined threshold λ, then this subpattern is discarded. We define λ according to the least frequency of cached query subpatterns in last period. That is, let *SQ'* be the set of frequent query subpatterns discovered for caching in last period.

$$\lambda = \min\{freq(SPT_i)\}, \text{ for each } SPT_i \in SQ' \tag{3}$$

5 Experimental Evaluations

In this section, we experimentally demonstrate that our framework is effective, and evaluate performances of our algorithms. We implemented our algorithms and simulated a cache system in C++. All the experiments were carried out on Pentium IV 2.4 GHz with 256MB RAM under Windows XP. We use public standard dataset DBLP [23], convert its DTD file into a global pattern tree by importing some wildcards and descendant edges. Characteristics of this global pattern tree are shown in Table 1. We generate all the query subpatterns of global pattern tree, and use them to produce the set of user query pattern trees which follow a Zipfian distribution.

Table 1. Characteristics of Dataset

Num of nodes	Max depth	Num. of *	Num. Of //	Max fanout
185	4	12	15	22

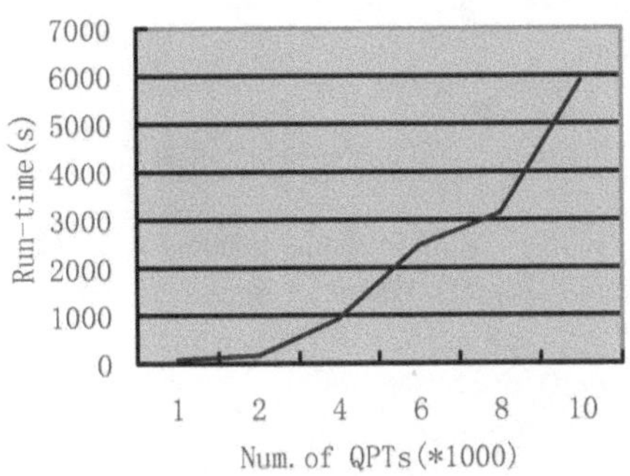

Fig. 6. Impact of the number of QPTs on the running time of algorithm

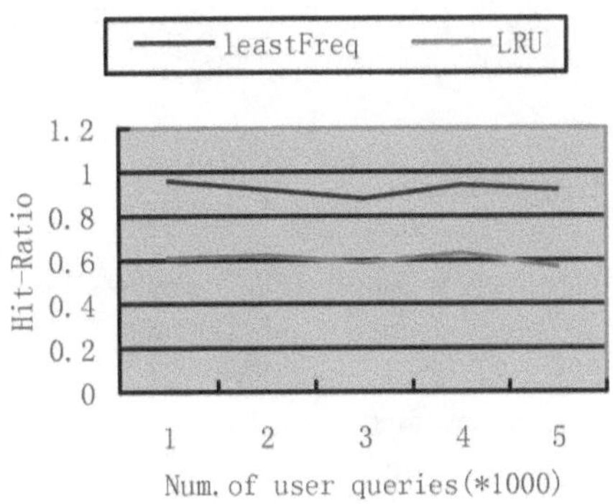

Fig. 7. Impact of caching frequent query patterns on Hit-Ratio

First, we investigate scalability of our algorithms. We set ε 0.5. In Figure 6, horizontal coordinate represents the number of user query pattern trees (QPTs), vertical coordinate represents running time of Caching_Frequent_Query_Patterns algorithm. As the number of QPTs varies from 1000 to 10000, the running time of our algorithm increases less than eight times. Therefore, our algorithm has good scalability.

Next, we investigate how caching frequent query patterns would impact the hit ratio of cache system. In Figure 7, horizontal coordinate represents the number of user queries, and vertical coordinate represents value of hit ratio. We compare two cases. In the first case, cache is loaded with frequent query patterns and their answers, and *leastFreq* strategy is employed when processing new user queries. In the second case, cache is not loaded in advance, and LRU is employed as replacement strategy. As the number of new user query increases, the hit ratio of *leastFreq* is nearly twice higher than that of LRU. Therefore, caching frequent query patterns discovered by our algorithms can greatly improve caching system performance.

6 Related Works

Semantic/query cache [2,3,4,5,6] is different from traditional tuple or page-based caching systems, because data cached at the client side of the former is logically organized by queries, instead of physical tuple identification or page number. Work on semantic/query caching examines how user queries, together with the corresponding answers can be cached for future reuse.

Mining frequent substructure of graphs and trees [11,12,13,14] has also drawn a great deal of attention from the research community. Paper [15] presents an efficient algorithm *FastXMiner*, to discover frequent XML query patterns. But issue of cache capacity is not considered in it. In the field of selectivity estimation and estimating answer sizes for XML queries, various techniques have been used including pruned suffix trees[16], set hashing [17,18], and histogram [7]. In paper [7], a histogram is introduced to catch the position information native to XML data. In terms of pattern containment, prior results [19,20,21] show that for any combination of two of the constructs '*', '//' and '[...]', containment problem is in PTIME, while the containment problem for XP{*, // and [...]} is *co-NP complete* [8,9].

7 Conclusions

In this paper, we propose a framework for an NP-hard optimization problem, *caching frequent query patterns*. Within the framework, we first develop an algorithm to generate all the query subpatterns. Next we use a *position histogram* scheme to estimate sizes of query answers. We also present a *query containment* algorithm based on *homomorphism* to compute frequency of query subpatterns. A *fully polynomial approximation scheme* is developed to choose query subpatterns for caching. Experimental results show that our algorithms are computationally scalable and our framework is effective to improve performances of cache system. In future, we will study how to process XML queries using materialized XPath views.

References

1. W3C. XQuery 1.0: An XML Query Language. April, 2005.
2. L.Chen, E.A.Rundensteiner. A Fine-Grained Replacement Strategy for XML Query Cache. In WIDW, MeLean, Virginia, 2002
3. L.Chen, E.A.Rundensteiner. ACE-XQ: A CachE-aware XQuery Answering System. In Proc.of WebDB, Madison, WI, pages 31-36, 2002.
4. S.Dar, M.J.Franklin, and B.Jonsson. Semantic Data Caching and Replacement. In VLDB, Bombay, India, pages 330-341, 1996.
5. L.M.Haas and D. Kossmann and I. Ursu. Loading a Cache with Query Results. In Proceedings of the 25th VLDB Conference, Edinburgh, Scotland, 1999.
6. B.Chidlovskii, U.M.Broghoff. Semantic Caching of Web Queries, VLDB Journal 9(1): 2-12, 2000.
7. Y. Wu, J. M. Patel, H. V. Jagadish. Estimating Answer Sizes for XML Queries. EDBT 2002.
8. G.Miklau, D.Suciu, Containment and Equivalence for an XPath Fragment, Proc. of the 21st ACM SIGACT-SIGMOD-SIGART Symp. on Principles of Database Systems(PODS), Madison, Wisconsin, USA, June 3-5, 2002.
9. S. Flesca, F. Furfaro, E. Masciari. On the minimization of XPath queries. VLDB, Berlin, Germany, 2003.
10. W3C. XPath 1.0: XML Path Language. http://www.w3.org/TR/xpath, November 1999.
11. L. Dehaspe, H. Toivonen, R. D. King. Finding Frequent Substructures in Chemical Compounds. Proc. of ACM SIGKDD, pages 30-36, 1998.
12. M. Kuramochi and G. Karypis. Frequent Subgrapf Discovery. IEEE Int. Conference on Data Mining, pages 313-320, 2001.
13. R. Agrawal and R. Srikant. Fast algorithms for mining association rules. VLDB, September 1994.
14. M. Zaki. Efficiently Mining Frequent Trees in a Forest. ACM SIGMOD, 2002.
15. L. N. Yang, M. L. Lee, Wynne Hsu. Efficient Mining of XML Query Patterns for Caching. VLDB, Berlin, Germany, 2003.
16. H.V.Jagadish, L.V.S.Lakshmanan, T.Milo, D.Srivastava, and D.Vista. Querying network directories. In Proceedings of the ACM SIGMOD Conference on Management of Data, Philadelphia, PA, June 1999.
17. A.Beoder. On the Resemblance and Containment of Documents. IEEE SEQUENCES '97, pages 21-29, 1998.
18. Z.Chen, F.Korn, N.Koudas, and S.Muthukrishnan, R.T.Ng, D.Srivastava. Counting Twig Matches in a Tree, ICDE, 2001.
19. M.Yannakakis. Algorithm for acyclic database scheme, VLDB, Morgan Kaufman pubs.(Los Altos CA), Zaniolo and Delovel(eds), 1981.
20. S.Amer-Yahia, S.choo, L. V. S. Lakshmanan, and D.Srivastava. Minimization of tree pattern queries. SIGMOD, 2001.
21. T. Milo and D. Suciu. Index structures for path expressions. In ICDT, pages 277-295, 1999.
22. Appromixation Algorithms. Springer-Verlag Berlin Heidelberg 2001.
23. DBLP data set. Available at http://www.informatik.uni-trier.de/ley/db/index.html

Efficient Evaluation of Distance Predicates in XPath Full-Text Query

Hong Chen, Xiaoling Wang, and Aoying Zhou

Department of Computer Science and Engineering,
Fudan University, Shanghai 200433, China
{davidchen, wxling, ayzhou}@fudan.edu.cn

Abstract. In recent years, more and more XML repositories are emerging, e.g., XML digital library, SIGMOD and DBLP document collections. Since XML is good at representing both structured and unstructured data, to facilitate the usage of this kind of information, it is necessary to support structure-based and content-based (full-text) queries/retrievals over XML repositories. With existing XPath/XQuery Full-Text, user could do search based on cardinality, proximity or distance predicates. In this paper, we propose an efficient approach for the Information Retrieval (IR) style search, especially distance predicates search, on XML documents. Numbering technique is employed to encode XML documents, and then three algorithms are designed to evaluate queries with distance predicates. To improve the performance, some optimization techniques are introduced. Extensive experiments show the effectiveness and efficiency of the proposed approach.

1 Introduction

XML query languages has been studied in previous reasearch, such as Lorel, XML-QL [12], XPath [5] and XQuery [6]. Though most of these query languages can express some powerful structured queries, they don't support full text retrieval tasks very well. For example, there is no way to express distance predicates in XPath. On the other hand, in order to describe an XML query, users must have a profound knowledge about the schema of the underlying XML data and claim the query path exactly, which is somehow burdensome and unpractical for novice and ordinary users.

Unified structured data query and text retrieval is a promising field in XML. Recently, Information Retrieval (IR) style query languages over XML documents have been studied by TeXQuery[13] and XKSearch[14]. XPath/XQuery Full-Text [7, 8, 9] is a well-known language designed to support integration of structure query and text retrieval over XML documents. In XQuery Full-Text Use Cases, it is very important to support IR-like search based on distance predicates, stemming and scoring. Consider the following example in the W3C XPath/XQuery Full-Text Use Cases Document.

"Find all books whose content contains the phrases 'users', 'feeling' and 'well-served' within an ordered window of up to 15 words." This query can be

H.T. Shen et al. (Eds.): ADWeb 2006, LNCS 3842, pp. 76–85, 2006.

expressed by XPath Full-Text syntax: "doc("http://bstore1.example.com/full-text.xml")/books/book[count(.//content ftcontains "users" && "feeling" && "well-served") with window at most 15 words ordered>0]."

Distance operation is an important and frequently required condition in full-text query. How to evaluate IR style query with distance limitations in large XML collections is a key factor in XQuery Full-Text search. Former work mostly focuses on query language syntax and semantic definition; nonetheless, there are a lot of challenging research topics left about implementation.

In this paper, we devise some techniques for processing the combination of the traditional structured query and Full-Text query. The distance is more significant than matching the keywords or phrase. This paper studies this problem in detail and presents some algorithms to evaluate efficiently the distance predicates in XPath Full-Text.

The main contributions of this paper can be summarized as follows:

1. The Numbering encode approach explores both structure and content information for IR style query over a large collection of XML documents. Based on this approach, we present algorithms to process distance predicates in XPath Full-Text.
2. A Window-based approach is proposed to improve the performance. Some optimization techniques are employed to reduce the search space.
3. Experimental results show window-based approach and optimization techniques are effective and efficient.

The rest of the paper is organized as follows. Related work is introduced in Sect. 2. Sect. 3 is for the problem statement and some preliminaries. The encoding approach is introduced in Sect. 4, and the definition about distance is also given as well. In Sect. 5, the proposed approach and associated optimization techniques on handling distance predicates in XPath Full-Text queries are presented. Sect. 6 is for the description of the experimental results and related analysis. Finally, Sect. 7 concludes the whole paper.

2 Related Work

There are a few of previous research works on IR style query over XML documents. XRank[10] uses the inverted list as index to support keyword search over XML documents. XXL[3] and XIRQL[4] are examples of systems that focus on using approximation techniques in combining IR search with XML structure information. XQuery-IR[15] is an extension of XQuery that supports restriction of phrase matching on document fragments. Phrase Matching[2] uses the labelling method and ignores some useless elements to support efficient phrase query. W3C proposes XPath/XQuery with Full-Text requirements, language syntax and use cases[7, 8, 9] for full-text query in XPath/XQuery, such as boolean conjunctions, distance predicates, stemming and scoring.

The XPath/XQuery Full-Text queries could be divided into two parts: the first one is structured path query, and the second part is IR style keyword search. For the first part, there is a lot of previous research works in the field to accelerate the evaluation of path expressions over XML data, such as structural indexing. For the second part, although IR style query has been well studied in text/hypertext retrieval field, traditional IR approaches can't be adopted for XML XPath Full-Text directly, for in this scenario, structure information also plays an important role in evaluation and ranking. So, an efficient approach should unify structure information and content information. Based on this consideration, in this paper, we propose some approaches to handle queries with distance predicates efficiently.

3 Problem Statement and Preliminaries

After modelling XML documents as ordered labelled trees in which each node corresponds to an element or the content value of an element. XML repositories containing a large number of XML documents are actually huge forests. Intuitively, the goal of XML document retrieval is in fact to get some XML elements/nodes that meet the structure and content requirement.

For structured XPath query, we adopt path expression evaluation techniques. A label-path is a sequence of labels $l_1 \cdots l_p (p \geq 1)$, separated by separators (/). It is known from previous work that path expression can be evaluated efficiently based on XML structure index. Here, for space limitation, we will not discuss path expression evaluation in detail.

For the IR style requirement, keywords search has been proven to be the user-friendly and helpful way. IR style XML query requires that the content of elements satisfy both the keywords, and distance or other Full-Text constraints. The query results are a set of smallest XML segments or XML elements containing all keywords within the distance limitation.

Here, we give the description of distance predicates in XPath Full-Text. Distance matching on the content require not only containing all query keywords, but also satisfying the distance limitation, where distance predicates mean the number of intervening words between the query keywords. Take an XML fragment from XPath Full-Text Use Cases as an example, the query is asking for all the contents that contain the keywords "web" and "usability" under the $< book >$ element and the distance among three keywords are less than 3. Fig.1 illustrates all the matching results on the content in bold.

4 Numbering XML Documents

In this section, XML encoding approach is introduced, which lays a foundation of our distance predicates evaluation algorithms.

It is natural way to encode each word in XML content by numbering approach, Fig.1 is a numbering example. When parsing all the content of the XML, we label the words in the content in sequence, then an inverted keyword list for all the words is built up. The result is presented in Table 1, where the first column represents the word, and the second keeps its appearance locations. The positions for each word are stored in an ascending order.

```
<book number="1">
 1      2    3
  <title> Improving the usability of a Web Site Through Expert Reviews and Usability
     4        5          6       7      8 9  10  11     12          13        14        15    16
 Testing
   17
  </title>
  <author>Millicent Marigold: </author>
  ......
  <content>
        <p>The usability of a Web ......well-served: </p>
        <p> Expert reviewers ...
           <footnote>...
              <citation>Research-Based Web Design and Usability Guidelines:
                                      116         117   118   119     120          121
              </citation> ...
</book>
```

Fig. 1. XML fragement

Table 1. Keywords Invert List

Keyword	Positions
best	88
...	...
web	6 24 39 103 117
while	51

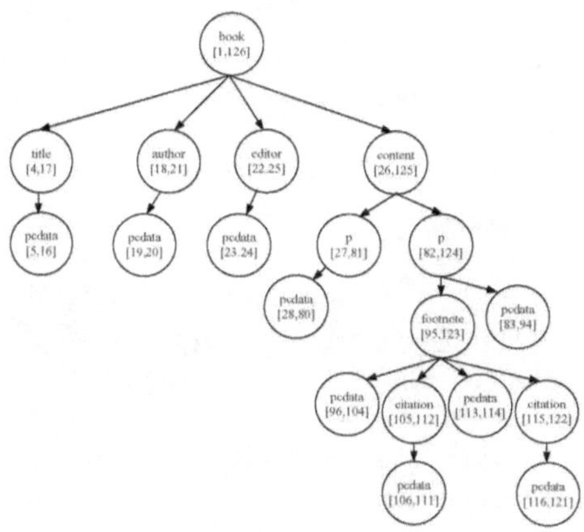

Fig. 2. XML Labeling Tree

Now we are at the point to describe how to make use of encoding approach to index XML data. With this numbering approach, each element n is labelled by a pair of integers (n_{start}, n_{end}), which stands for the range of all the words this element contains, n_{start} is the start word position of element's content, and n_{end} is the end word position. If node y is the ancestor of node x, $y_{start} < x_{start} < x_{end} < y_{end}$. Under this consideration, given the labels of two nodes x and y, x is the descendent of y if $x_{start} \in (y_{start}, y_{end})$. For example, the encoding example in Fig.1 can be labelled as the tree shown in Fig.2. The procedure of executing path expression is in fact traversing XML label tree.

Then, after numbering the content and labelling the tree, we can unify content and structure queries. XML structure queries are handled by the XML label tree, and inverted list can be used for evaluation IR style query. Next section will present algorithms to take advantage of this encoding approach for distance predicates in XPath Full-Text.

5 Distance Predicates Evaluation

Take query "doc('http://example.com/full-text.xml')//book[count(.//content ftcontains "users" && "feeling" && "well-served") with window at most 15 words ordered] > 0) " as an example, the evaluation process for distance predicates is illustrated in this section.

As discussed above, this query can be divided into structure query part and IR style keywords part. For the structure part in the query, traditional structure index can be used to evaluate the path expression, and consequently the target elements and the global range from the elements' range labels could be obtained. For IR style keywords, one naïve approach is to get the word positions from the inverted list for each keyword in query, such as keyword 1: pos_{11}, $\text{pos}_{12...}$, pos_{1L_1},keyword 2: pos_{21}, $\text{pos}_{22...}$, pos_{2L2}, and keyword m: pos_{m1}, $\text{pos}_{m2...}$, pos_{mL_m}, where L_i is the position numbers of i-th keyword, then the distance among these keyword position lists could be computed. In this section, three different approaches will be presented to address this problem.

5.1 Naïve Approach - DBP

Intuitively, this problem can be transformed to compute distance based on several position lists, that is, computing the distance for each composition [pos_{11}, pos_{21},..., pos_{m1}],..., [pos_{1L1}, ..., pos_{mL_m}] where pos_{ij} is got from k_i's position list; therefore, the time complexity is $O(L_1 * L_2 * \ldots * L_m)$. This approach is called Distance Based Processing, abbreviated as DBP, which is to find regions satisfying the distance requirement. DBP algorithm is depicted in Algorithm 1.

However this algorithm is time-consuming, some optimizations approaches will be considered in the next sections.

5.2 Window-Based Approach

First of all, some definitions associated with window-based (WB) approach is given before discussion.

Definition 1. *Position Pointer (PP): Each position list for a keyword have a pointer to indicate the current position. Initially, all position pointers point to the first position of each list.*

Algorithm 1. `findAllComposition(partPos,allPos,depth)`

Input:
allPos /*all position lists for all keywords, $[k_1 : pos_{11}, pos_{12...,}, pos_{1L1}] \ldots [k_m : pos_{m1}, pos_{m2...,} pos_{mLm}]$, all positions are sorted in ascending order*/
Output: *allComps* /*keep all results*/

```
get the position list from keyword k_depth;
for all each position pos_cur ∈ k_depth's position list as current position do
   if distance between pos_cur and partial keywords composition partPos <= N then
      add pos_cur into partial keywords composition partPos;
      if depth < all keyword numbers then
         depth = depth + 1;
         findAllComposition(partPos, allPos, depth);
         remove the pos_cur from partial keywords composition partPos;
         depth = depth − 1;
      else
         add the result into allComps;
         remove the pos_cur from partial keywords composition partPos;
      end if
   else
      break;
   end if
end for
return allComps;
```

Notes:
partPos: partial of keywords composition satisfing the distance, initially is null
depth: current keyword to be composited is k_{depth}, initially is 1 for k_1

Definition 2. *Current Smallest Position(CSP): The smallest position in all PPs is called Current Smallest Position and represented as* pos_{start}.

Definition 3. *Distance Window(DW): If the number of the distance predicates is N, the distance window is defined as a window with width N and position rang* $[pos_{start}, pos_{start} + N - 1]$.

If positions in a keyword's position list do not fall in the range $[pos_{start}, pos_{start} + N - 1]$, the corresponding composition result is empty. We call this kind of DW *Empty Window (EW)*.

Initially, PP for each position list points to the first position. When the current position has been processed, PP moves forward to next position.

The procedure of WB approach can be described as follows. We find the CSP pos_{start} and get a DW from pos_{start} $[pos_{start}, pos_{start} + N - 1]$, if the DW is an empty window EW, the PP which points pos_{start} moves forward to next position, until getting a new CSP pos_{start} and the DW is not a EW, then we get the composition results from this DW, and move the PP pointing to pos_{start} forward to next position, this process repeats. If any PP arrives at the last position of its corresponding list, the program halts.

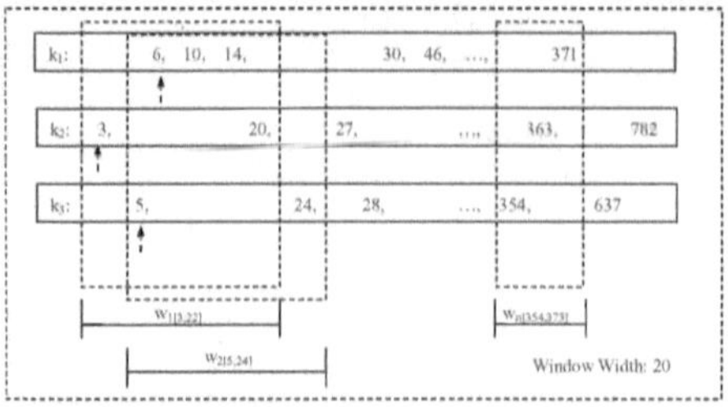

Fig. 3. WB processing

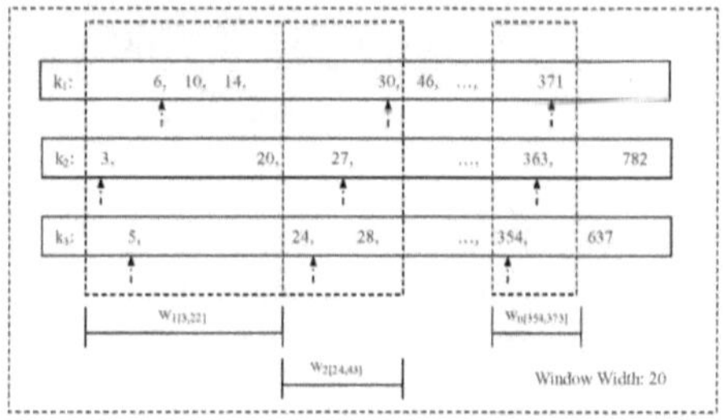

Fig. 4. EWB processing

Algorithm 2. `getAllWindowResult`

Input: *allPos* /*position lists for all keywords, $[k_1 : pos_{11}, pos_{12...}, pos_{1L1}] \ldots [k_m : pos_{m1}, pos_{m2...}, pos_{mLm}]$, all positions are sorted in ascending order*/
Output: *allComps* /*keep all results*/

```
while CSP pointer not points the last position of one keyword's position list do
    obtain a DW from CSP;
    if DW is EW then
        move CSP pointer to point next position;
    else
        find all results in DW and add them into allComps;
        /*it may appear redundant result, simply discard it*/
        move CSP pointer to point next position;
    end if
end while
return allComps;
```

Figure 3 is an example, where the query distance is 20. Initially, the CSP is 3 in k_2's position list, we find DW w_1 $[3, 22]$(list k_1 includes 6,10 and 14, list k_2 includes 3 and 20, list k_3 includes 5 in this window), it's not an EW. After finding all results for w_1, we move the CSP's PP forward to next position 20. We find the new CSP is 5 in k_3's position list and get a new DW w_2 $[5, 24]$. If the current window is EW, move the CSP's PP forward and find next DW provided that this DW is a non-empty window, then process it as described above. Algorithm 2 describes the WB algorithm.

Compared with DBP which scans all the keywords position lists many times, WB move the windows forward and only scan all position once; therefore, this can reduce the redundant composition number greatly.

5.3 Enhanced Window Based Approach

To improve the performance, an enhanced window based (EWB) approach, which is an extension of WB, is proposed here. The goal of EWB algorithm is to reduce the redundant generation of compositions. When we move to a no-empty window w_1 (as shown in Fig.4) and find all compositions in this window, we move all PPs out of w_1(in Fig.4, PP for k_1 points 30, PP for k_2 points 27, PP for k_3 points 24) and find the CSP, which is 24. Then use this CSP to get the next DW w_2, we compute the composition using the positions in w_2 with former window w_1, at least one new position must appear in the composition, so the new composition won't be overlapped with the existing composition. We can find all the compositions in w_2 by repeating the above processing. EWB approach reduce the redundant compositions greatly than WB.

In next section, some extensive experiments are conducted to show the efficiency of the proposed approaches.

6 Experiments

We implement these three algorithms in Java and conduct the experiments on a DELL PC with 2GHz CPU, 1532M memory, 50G drive and run window2000. Our data sets are obtained from TREC[16], which contains a large number of XML documents excepted from Compute Magazine and PC weeks.

For the first experiment, we test the performance of DBP and WB. Given a query "doc(http://trec.nist.gov/ziff.xml)/docs [count(.// ftcontains "compute" && "service" distance at most 100 words)>0].", we vary the XML documents whose size range from 10-50M. The execution time for the query is shown in the Fig.5, and the result shows the WB algorithm is obviously outperform DBP algorithm. Fig.5 shows the results in logarithmic time.

In the second experiment, we fix the collection size 50MB and vary the distance predicates for given queries. The window distance N ranges from 10-500, the experiment result is shown in Fig.6, which betrays that WB is also far faster than DBP and WB approach is robust for any distance range.

The third experiment is to test the algorithms for different keyword numbers in query. For a fixed XML document whose size is 50M and a fixed distance predicates 100, the result is shown in Fig.7, and the WB algorithm is more efficient, even for many keywords.

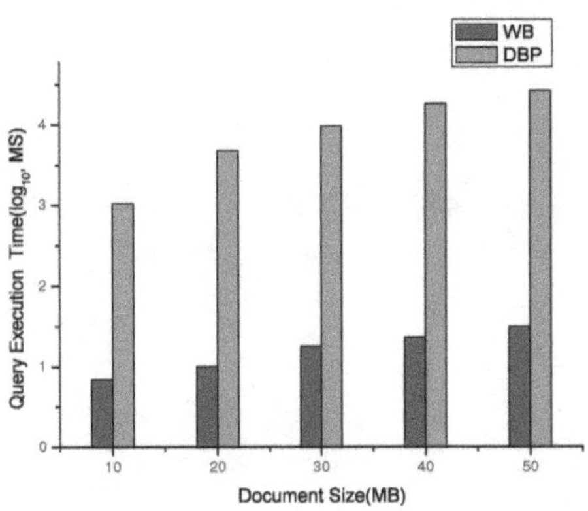

Fig. 5. Execution time over various document sizes

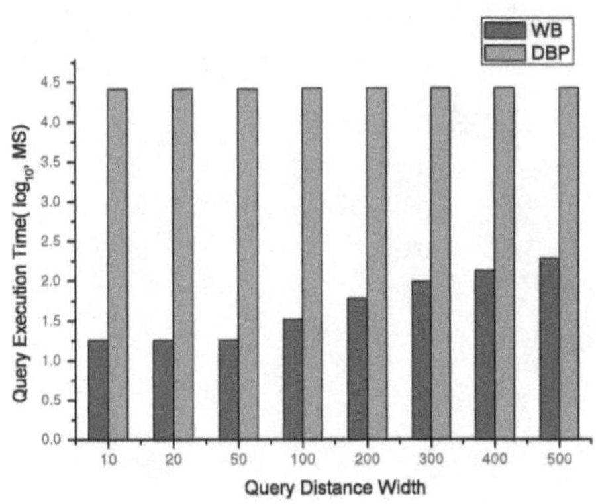

Fig. 6. Execution time for different distances

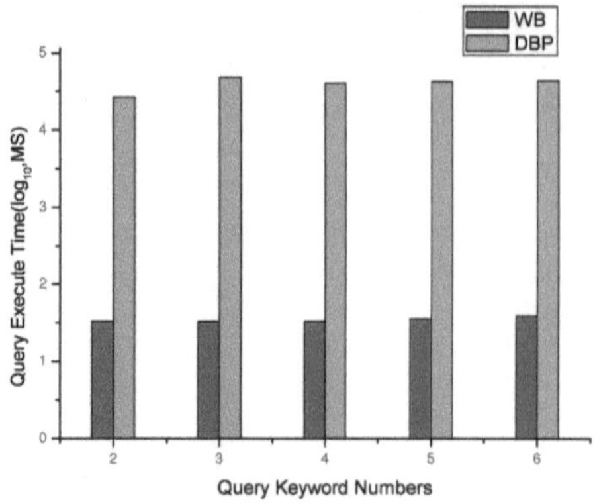

Fig. 7. Execution time for various keyword numbers

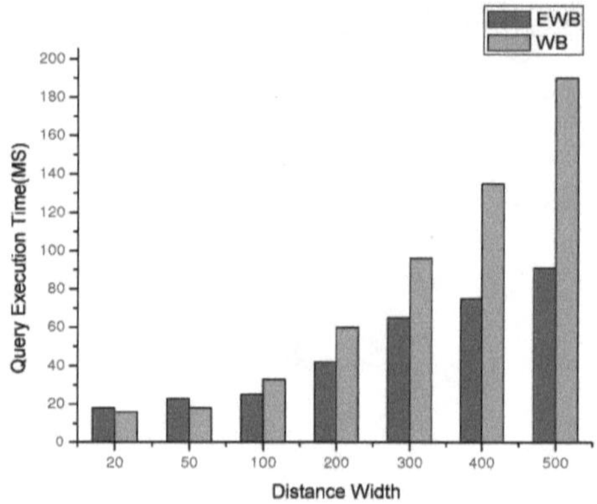

Fig. 8. Execution time for WB and EWB algorithm

Fourthly, we conduct some experiments to compare WB and EWB over the same query. By changing the distance width over a fix XML with size of 50M, we compare the execution time shown in Fig.8. When the distance width is large, the EWB outperforms WB.

7 Conclusions and Future Work

This paper presents efficient approaches for XPath query with distance predicates. XPath/XQuery Full-text has been proposed by W3C and distance predicates are very most important in XPath Full-Text. This paper presents window-based approach to support distance predicates very well after modelling XML documents with numbering schema. We also conduct a series of experiments and verify that our proposed approach is efficient and practical for distance predicates evaluation in XML IR style search. In the future work, based on numbering schema, we will extend our approach to exploit ranking metric and more XML IR style query in XPath/XQuery Full-Text.

Acknowledgement

This work is partially supported by NSFC under grant No. 60228006 and 60496325, and the Foundation of Lab. of Computer Science, ISCAS under grant No. SYSKF0408.

References

1. Amer-Yahia, S., Lakshmanan, L.V. S., Pandit, S., FleXPath : Flexible Structure and Full-Text Querying for XML. SIGMOD 2004, 83–94
2. Amer-Yahia, S., Fernndez, M.F., Srivastava, D., Xu, Y., PIX : Exact and Approximate Phrase Matching in XML. SIGMOD 2003, 664–664

3. Theobald, A., Weikum, G., The XXL Search Engine : Ranked Retrieval of XML Data Using Indexes and Ontologies. SIGMOD 2002, 615–615
4. Fuhr, N., Grojohann, K., XIRQL : An XML Query Language Based on Information Retrieval Concepts. TOIS 2004, 313–356
5. Clark, J., DeRose, S., XML Path Language (XPath) Version 1.0, 1999, http://www.w3.org/TR/xpath
6. Chamberlin, D., Berglund, A., Boag, S., XQuery 1.0: An XML Query Language, 2005, http://www.w3.org/TR/xquery/
7. Case, Pat., Amer-Yahia, S., Botev, C., XQuery 1.0 and XPath 2.0 Full-Text, 2005, http://www.w3.org/TR/xquery-Full-Text/
8. Buxton, S., Rys, M., uery and XPath Full-Text Requirements, 2003, http://www.w3.org/TR/xquery-Full-Text-requirements/
9. Amer-Yahia, S., Case, P., XQuery 1.0 and XPath 2.0 Full-Text Use Cases, 2005, http://www.w3.org/TR/xmlquery-Full-Text-use-cases/
10. Guo, L., Shao, F., Botev, C., Shanmugasundaram, J., XRANK : Ranked Keyword Search over XML Documents. SIGMOD 2003, 16–27
11. Hristidis, V., Papakonstantinou, Y., Balmin, A., Keyword Proximity Search on XML Graphs. ICDE 2003, 367-378
12. Deutsch, A., Fernandez, M., Florescu, D., Levy, A., Suciu, D., XML-QL: A Query Language for XML, 1998, http://www.w3.org/TR/NOTE-xml-ql/.
13. Amer-Yahia, S., Botev, C., Shanmugasundaram, J., Texquery : A Full-Text Search Extension to XQuery . WWW 2004, 583–594
14. XKSearch. http://www.db.ucsd.edu/projects/xksearch.
15. Bremer, J. M., Gert, M., XQuery/IR: Integrating XML Document and Data Retrieval. WebDB 2002, 1-6
16. TREC. http://trec.nist.gov

A Web Classification Framework Based on XSLT

Atakan Kurt and Engin Tozal

Fatih University, Computer Eng. Dept.,
Istanbul, Turkey
{akurt, engintozal}@fatih.edu.tr

Abstract. Data on the web is gradually changing format from HTML to XML/XSLT driven by various software and hardware requirements such as interoperability and data-sharing problems between different applications/platforms, devices with vairous capabilities like cell phones, PDAs. This gradual change introduces new challenges in web page and web site classification. HTML is used for presentation of content. XML represents content in a hierarchical manner. XSLT is used to transform XML documents into different formats such as HTML, WML. There are certain drawbacks in HTML and XML classifications for classifying a web page. In this paper we propose a new classification method based on XSLT which is able to combine the advantages of HTML and XML classifications. We also introduce a web classification framework utilizing XSLT classification. Finally we show that using Naïve Bayes classifier XSLT classification outperfoms both HTML and XML classifications.

1 Introduction

Web mining is an active and challenging branch of *data mining* that deals with analyzing, classifying, clustering and extracting useful information from web pages based on their content, structure and usage.

Web pages consist of text content and tags for presentation of content. A number of methods based on text classification, HTML (Hyper Text Markup Language) classification, XML (eXtensible Markup Language) classification have been proposed to classify web pages [8, 9].

The simplest web page classification method is *text-only* classification. All markup are removed from the HTML document and the classification is based on the remaining textual content. [6] proposes a method where a document is represented as a feature vector. The documents are analyzed and all stop words are removed, and the features are generated. At the end, all low frequency (*frequency* < *4*) features are deleted and Naïve Bayes algorithm is used to classify those documents.

Hypertext approach analyzes presentation information as well as text information. HTML tags are features considered in classification [7]. For example, information between *<b></b>* tags or the text has greater font size can be more important than theothers. [8] shows that the title and the anchor words in an HTML document are important. They use *support vector machines* to classify web pages.

H.T. Shen et al. (Eds.): ADWeb 2006, LNCS 3842, pp. 86–96, 2006.

Link analysis classifies pages according to the text on the link and the documents referred by links [10, 11]. A web page has *in-neighbors* pages referring to it and *out-neighbors* pages that it refers to. In-neighbors and out-neighbors may contain valuable information in classification.

XML or semi-structured document classification deals with the problem of classifying documents in XML format. A simple XML document is given in Figure 1. The element/attribute names and the structure of document i.e. the nesting of elements play an important role in addition to the text content of the document. Methods bassed on component tagging and component splitting are proposed in classfying XML documents [4, 5].

As the web exploits XML and XSL technologies, it becomes important to incorporate those technologies into web mining. A great number of studies have been published for classification of XML documents and HTML pages; however a classification based on XSLT stylesheet have not been considered yet. This paper discusses a framework which exploits the information embedded into XSLT stylesheets to classify web pages, instead of text only, HTML-only, or XML-only classification approaches.

```
<?xml version="1.0" encoding="UTF-8"?>
<!DOCTYPE resume SYSTEM "sample.dtd">
<!-- Sample Resume for illustration purpose -->
<resume id="10050808" language="EN" category="Software Architect">
   <type>Functional</type>
   <create-date>March,13,2005</create-date>
   <modification-date>July,9,2005</modification-date>
   <copyright>All content contained within this document is protected
      by copyright laws &#x00A9; Acme Resume Corp. 2005</copyright>
   <personal name="Engin" last-name="Tozal">
      <objective>To hold a Ph.D. in Distributed Systems area and become
      an expert in Distributed Systems issues as a researcher</objective>
      <education start="1997" end="1999">
         <collage>Fatih University</collage>
         <department>Mathematics</department>
      </education>
      <education start="1999" end="2003">
         <collage>Fatih University</collage>
         <department>Computer Engineering</department>
      </education>
      <language>Turkish</language>
      <language>English</language>
   </personal>
   <experience>
      <project>
         <name>High-Level Data Link Control Simulation</name>
         <technology>Berkeley  Sockets, C</technology>
      </project>
      <project>
         <name>Visual XPath</name>
         <technology>Java, XML, XPath, DOM, SAX,
         Xerces, Xalan, XSLT</technology>
      </project>
   </experience>
</resume>
```

Fig. 1. Simple XML Document

The paper is organized as follows: We discuss how web mining can benefit from XSLT as more and more applications are using XML/XSLT in Section 2. Section 3 present the new framework based XSLT web classification. Section 4 discusses experiments designed to compare HTML, XML and XSLT classification approaches. Section 5 is reserved for conclusion and the future work.

2 Web Mining and XSLT

Web applications are getting more complex due to interoperability problems among different platforms, languges, browsers, diverse client devices such as mobile phones, PDAs, TV sets. and vairous GUI requirements. Most of these problems can be solved by separating content data from presentation markup which can be achieved with XSLT.

XSLT[1] (eXtensible Stylesheet Language Transformation) is part of XSL (Extensible Stylesheet Language) technology that defines a set of rules used to transform XML documents into different formats as shown in Figure 2. XML captures only the content and the structure, not the presentation which is defined using HTML.

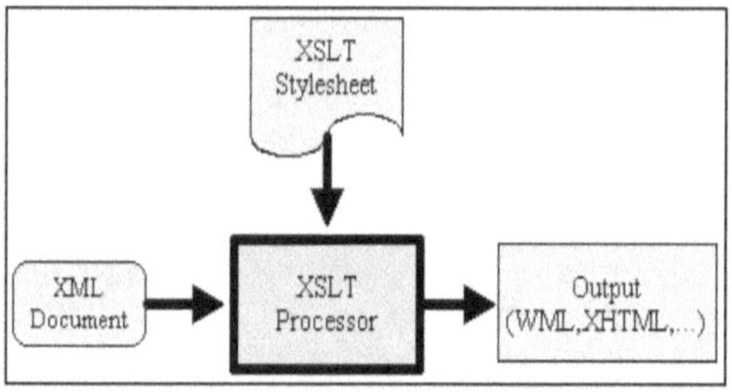

Fig. 2. XSL Transformation

When the information is kept in XML format, a different stylesheet can be used to transform the same information into different presentation formats according to client application's capabilities or requirements. The other clear advantage is; the people developing business logic can work independently from those who are developing user interface.

Web application addresses some important problems faced by todays requirements using XSLT in the following manner: Data is produced in XML format by the serving web application and fed into an XSLT processor which applies an XSLT stylesheet to it and produces an output appropriate for the client application. This computational model allows three web page classification options*; HTML Classification, Semi-Structured Document (XML) Classification and XSLT classification* –a classification scheme where XSLT related data is utilized-. There are many studies on the first two options, however the last is not considered yet to the best of our knowledge, and it is the starting point of our novel proposition.

XSLT classification; is a hybrid classification technique that exploits both structure of XML document and markup features embedded in result XHTML document.

[1] http://www.w3.org/TR/xslt

We believe that XSLT classification can produce better results than HTML classification because (1) the XML document itself contains valuable structural information about content, (2) tag and attribute names in XML are important for text classification and can not be ignored in the process

We believe that XSLT classification is more promising than XML classification because; (1) An XML document usually contains meta-data that are not related to actual content but used internally for different purposes by the generators of document, usually those data are not presented to end-user, and should be omitted in classification process. Elements; *type, id, create-date, modification-date and copyright* are examples of meta-data in sample XML document given in Figure 1, (2) some of the information presented to end-user does not come from any XML document but are string literals embedded directly into the HTML tags used in XSLT stylesheets. That information can be useful in classification process; (3) sometimes an XML document is a large document with lots of information, but different parts are presented to different users while the rest is suppressed, so each transformed version should be considered and classified as a different document, rather than classifying the complete document as a whole, (4) sometimes the information generated to end-user is merged from different XML documents, so considering and classifying the transformed document as a single page can be more appropriate than classifying each document separately.

3 A Web Classification Framework Based on XSLT

A web classification framework based on XSLT is implemented (Figure 3). The framework consists of three modules; *Preprocessor, Semi-Structured Document Modeler, and Classifier*. The system accepts blocks of, one or more source XML documents and an XSLT stylesheet which transforms these documents into XHTML to be viewed by end-user.

Firstly, the original XSLT document is passed to the Preprocessor which produces a new XSLT document named *formatted XSLT stylesheet*. Formatted XSLT is a version of original XSLT stylesheet which has xsl templates to produce ancestor-or-self hierarchies of referenced XML fragments. This information will be used to prefix content with its ancestors while generating term frequency vectors for documents. Secondly, an XSLT processor applies the formatted XSLT stylesheet to the original XML documents to generate *formatted XML documents*. Formatted XML documents consist of all string literals embedded into the original XSLT stylesheet, content of HTML *meta, title, anchor* tags and source XML fragments that are referenced only in original XSLT stylesheet. The textual content of each source XML fragment is surrounded with its ancestor-or-self-hierarchies separated by "-_-" character sequence (See Figure 4). Thirdly, formatted XML documents are given to Semi-Structured Document Modeler which generates term frequency vectors for each document. Lastly, term frequency vectors are given to the classifier for building classification model.

3.1 Preprocessor

In the preprocessing step an XSLT-to-XSLT stylesheet is applied to the original XSLT stylesheet to generate another XSLT stylesheet called *formatted stylesheet*. Because an XSLT document is an XML document, XSLT-to-XSLT stylesheet simply traverses each element of the original XSLT document and does the following;

- If the current node is an *xsl:element* node, it is used to print out an HTML tag or a tagged text so if it is an HTML element remove it otherwise insert it into result tree and process its child-nodes.
- If the current node is an *xsl:vlaue-of* element than the *select* attribute of the *xsl:vlaue-of* can refer to an element or attribute node in the source XML document, so normalize space and remove all punctuation characters of the content and insert it into the result tree with all its *ancestor-or-self* hierarchy. If the current node is an attribute, then the name of the attribute is considered to be part of *ancestor* hierarchy.

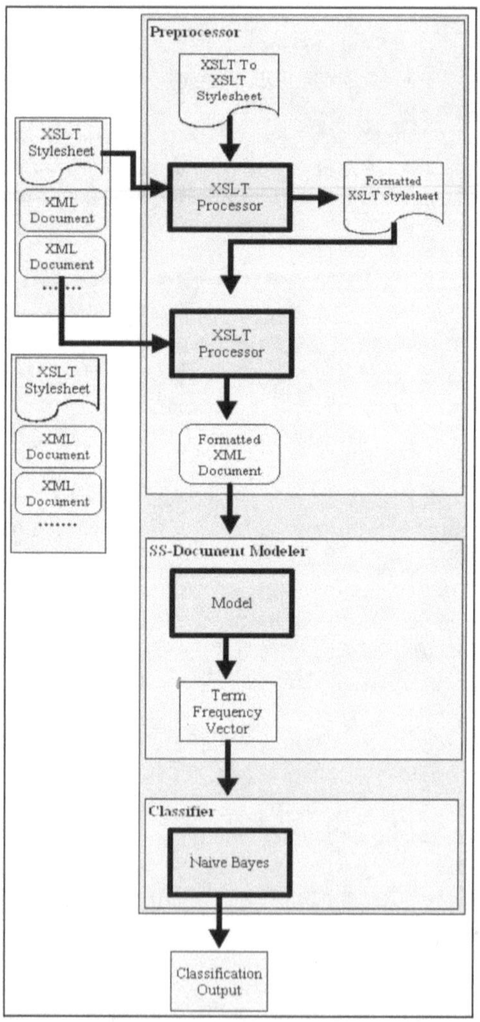

Fig. 3. XSLT Framework Architecture

```xml
<?xml version="1.0" encoding="UTF-8"?>
<document-root>
resume career experience cv education jobAcme resume and
career services Acme Resume Corp ACME Resume Corp Logo Acme Resume Corp
provides fully customized resume services based on peoples background
education work experience and career goals presenting peoples details in the
most effective way possible Resume Templates Multiple Resume Versions Write
a Resume Draft Sections of a Resume Data Mining  Name
 <resume-_-personal-_-name>Engin</resume-_-personal-_-name> Last Name
 <resume-_-personal-_-last-name>Tozal</resume-_-personal-_-last-name>
 Objective
 <resume-_-personal-_-objective>To hold a Ph D in Distributed Systems area
 and become an expert in Distributed Systems issues as a researcher
 </resume-_-personal-_-objective> Education
 <resume-_-personal-_-education-_-department>Mathematics
 </resume-_-personal-_-education-_-department>
 <resume-_-personal-_-education-_-collage>Fatih University
 </resume-_-personal-_-education-_-collage>
 <resume-_-personal-_-education-_-start>1997
 </resume-_-personal-_-education-_-start>
 <resume-_-personal-_-education-_-end>1999
 </resume-_-personal-_-education-_-end>
 <resume-_-personal-_-education-_-department>Computer Engineering
 </resume-_-personal-_-education-_-department>
 <resume-_-personal-_-education-_-collage>Fatih University
 </resume-_-personal-_-education-_-collage>
 <resume-_-personal-_-education-_-start>1999
 </resume-_-personal-_-education-_-start>
 <resume-_-personal-_-education-_-end>2003
 </resume-_-personal-_-education-_-end> Experience  Project Technology
 <resume-_-experience-_-project-_-name>
 High Level Data Link Control Simulation
 </resume-_-experience-_-project-_-name>
 <resume-_-experience-_-project-_-technology>Berkeley Sockets C
 </resume-_-experience-_-project-_-technology>
 <resume-_-experience-_-project-_-name>Visual XPath
 </resume-_-experience-_-project-_-name>
 <resume-_-experience-_-project-_-technology>Java XML XPath DOM SAX Xerces
  Xalan XSLT</resume-_-experience-_-project-_-technology> Spoken Languages
  <resume-_-personal-_-language>Turkish</resume-_-personal-_-language>
 <resume-_-personal-_-language>English</resume-_-personal-_-language>
</document-root>
```

Fig. 4. Formatted XML Document

- If the current node is an *xsl:text* element normalize space and remove all punctuation characters of the content and insert it into the result tree with all its *ancestor-or-self* hierarchy. If the identified node is an attribute, then the name of the attribute is considered to be part of *ancestor* hierarchy.
- If the current node is any other XSLT element *-xsl:variable, xsl:param, xsl:with-param, xsl:if, xsl:when, xsl:choose, xsl:otherwise, xsl:copy, xsl:copy-of, xsl:sort, xsl:for-each-* put it directly into the result tree and process its children.
- If the current node is an HTML *meta* tag whose name attribute is *keyword* or *description* insert its content into the result tree.
- If the current node is an HTML *img* tag insert its *alt* attribute value into the result tree.
- If any other string literals exist in the XSLT document, simply normalize space and remove all punctuation characters of the string and insert it into the result tree.

The result of XSLT-to-XSLT transformation is a formatted XSLT stylesheet which is used to transform source XML documents into formatted XML documents, instead of HTML. Figure 4 shows the formatted XML document generated by applying an

XSL stylesheet to the XML document given in Figure 1. The ancestor hierarcy of XML fragments referenced all string literals, and the content of *meta, title,* and *img* tags from the XSLT stylesheet are captured.

3.2 Semi-structured Document Modeler

Semi-Structured Document Modeler generates term frequency vectors from formatted XML documents using the word prefixing model explained below.

When a document doesn't any tags. Only the frequency of the words is important. When we try to classify XML/HTML documents the structural elements or tags/attributes become important. The names of element/attributes and nesting of elements in an XML document play crutial roles in classification.

There are a number of alternatives to incorporating structural information into document classification such as prefixing the word with the innermost enclosing tag or all inclosing tags etc. The strength of each alternative model is affected both by how the structure is represented in the word frequency vectors and by the variations of element or attribute names, removal, insertion of inter elements, or the swap of elements in the document. We skip these models here, because of space limitations and show how a document is represented in word frequency vectors in our framework. The example below is based on XML document given in Figure 1. `resume`, `personal`, `language` are tags, `english` is a text content.

```
resume
personal
resume.personal
personal.resume
language
personal.language
language.personal
resume.language
language.resume
english
language.english
personal.english
resume.english
```

We prefix each word, element, and attribute with each of its ancestor in addition to the word, element, and attribute names. Elements in ancestor hierarchy are prefixed with each of its ancestor. Also descendants of elements in ancestor hierarchy are used to prefix the element. Although the structure is captured in a loose manner (i.e. we do not capture ancestor hierarchy in a strict manner), complete document hierarchy is captured. Inter-element structure is captured in two ways (i.e. from ancestor to descendant and from descendant to ancestor) as well. This is resistant to structural alterations to some degree. Moreover, this model is resistant to inter element swaps.

3.3 Classifier

The Classifier accepts term frequency vectors produced by Semi-Structured Document Modeler and builds a classification model before classifying documents. We used Naïve Bayes Classifier, since it is a widely used classification technique in IR community due to both its simplicity and accuracy. However any other classifier can be plugged into the framework instead of Naïve Bayes.

A document classifier simply maps a document to a predefined category (class) or estimates the probability that a given document belonging to one of those categories.

Given a document database $D=\{d_1,d_2,...,d_n\}$ and a set of categories $C=\{c1,c2,...,cm\}$ the classification problem is to define a mapping $f: D \rightarrow C$ where each d_i is assigned to one category. A category contains those documents mapped to it; that is $c_j = \{d_i \mid f(d_i) = c_j,\ 1 \leq i \leq n$ and $d_i \in D,\ cj \in C\}$.

In Naïve Bayes IR text classification technique [1, 2]; given the set of categories $c=\{c_1,c_2,...,c_m\}$, and a set of documents $d=\{d_1,d_2,...,d_k\}$ a document d is represented as an n dimensional feature vector $d=\{w_1,w_2,....w_n\}$ where the occurrence frequency of ith word is kept as value of a feature w_i, $1 \leq i \leq n$. An estimation of conditional class probability of document d_j belongs to category c_i is obtained by formula

$$P(c_i \mid d_j) = \frac{P(c_i) * P(d_j \mid c_i)}{P(d_j)},\quad 1 \leq i \leq m, \text{ and } 1 \leq j \leq k$$

$P(d_j)$ which is prior document probability is same for each class i so there is no need to calculate. Prior class probabilities $P(c_i)$ for each class i can be estimated from the frequencies of documents belonging to class c_i in the training data. Estimating the probability of the feature vector document d_j given the class c_i, $P(d_j|c_i)$ is expensive to compute, due to the fact that; a feature w_r can take a big number of values. In order to make the calculation simple each feature is assumed to be independent, this is the core of Naïve Bayes Classifier model. So $P(d_j|c_i)$ is calculated under Naïve Bayes multinomial model [3] by formula;

$$P(d_j \mid c_i) = \prod_{w \in d_j} P(w \mid c_i)^{f(w,d_j)}$$

$f(w,d_j)$ is the number of occurrences of word w in document d_j.

4 Experimental Results and Evaluation

Experiments are conducted for comparing HTML XML and XSLT classification approaches to web page classification. using the framework which is implemented in this study is based on Weka 3.4[2] and Saxon-B 8.4[3]. We used 2/3 of documents for training and 1/3 for testing the classification model. We used 10-fold cross validation to further improve the classification. The element and attribute names and the text content are stemmed (taking the root of a word) in all experiments, as it is a common practice in text mining.

4.1 Dataset

Current dataset repositories on the web do not provide a proper dataset for our experiment. We generated XML/XSLT version of web pages from 20 different sites

[2] http://www.cs.waikato.ac.nz/~ml/weka/
[3] http://www.saxonica.com

belonging to 4 different categories; *Automotive, Movie, Software, News & Reference*. The sites belonging to *News & Reference* contains news and articles about movies, automobiles and software health and literature to make the classification more difficult. The list of sites and all dataset can be viewed and downloaded[4] from the web site. 100 XML documents that hold the information published on web sites are generated. These documents are evenly distributed among categories. Headers in HTML page are used to surround the content as attributes or elements in XML documents. XML documents have variant structures, element and attribute names, and nesting to mimic that, they are generated by different people. For each site an XSLT stylesheet producing exactly the same presentation with all links, images, embedded objects, literal strings and non-printable data like meta, style, script tags and their contents of actual HTML page is generated. When the XSLT is applied to the XML document it produces all static content in each page of a site and brings the dynamic content from XML documents to produce a valid XHTML document.

4.2 Evaluation

The experimental results are shown in Figure 5. XSLT classification yields considerably higher accuracy rate than both HTML and XML classification, while XML classification produced slightly better accuracy rate than HTML classification for the reasons explanied below.

Instead of any advanced HTML classification technique mentioned at Section 1, a simple hypertext approach that uses text content and the values of *title*, *anchor*, *meta* and *img* tags in HTML is applied in this experiment.

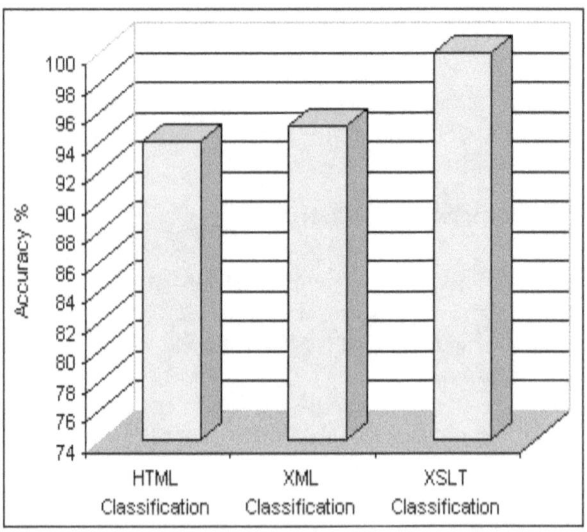

Fig. 5. The HTML, XML, and XSLT Classifications

[4] http://www.fatih.edu.tr/~engin

XML classification uses the structural tagging explained in Section 3.2 to represent an XML document as a feature vector. It does not include any string literals in the presentation markup (the HTML content defined in the XSLT stylesheet). It adds all meta data (e.g. copyright notice, author, creation and last modification date, type, and category in Figure 1) and irrelevant data from the source XML documents into term frequency vector.

XSLT classification uses *formatted XML* documents generated by applying *formatted XSL* stylesheets to the original XML documents at the preprocessing step. All string literals in presentation markup (HTML tags) in XSLT stylesheet are included in this classification. In addition, only the referenced XML fragments in XSLT stylesheet are inserted into term frequency vectors. All meta and irrelevant data fragments in source XML documents are suppressed. XSLT classification uses the same structural tagging method used in XML classification. By exploiting these options, XSLT classification prodeces the highest accuracy rate of 99.6%.

5 Conclusion

Web applications producing output using XML/XSLT technology allows three types of classification options; classification at the source (XML classification), classification at the destination (HTML classification), or a new alternative, that is, classification at the point of XSLT transformation. We have explored the third option for classifying web pages and showed that it is not only viable but a preferable approach to the others as it takes advantages of both approaches because this thechnique is able use both the source and the destination document for better classification. More spefically, it is able utilize both structural data in XML and relevant data in HTML using the transformation rules in XSLT stylesheets. As a result a technique with a considerably higher classification rate is obtained.

We implemented a framework that incorporates the XSLT classification in a practical manner to classify web pages. The framework uses an XSLT stylesheet to tweak the original XSLT stylesheet around so that a structural tagging of content is produced which is basically a feature vector of stemmed words in the document. Finally feature vector can be classified any appropriate classification technique, in our case Naïve Bayes.

As future work we need to work with bigger and various other data sets. Alternatives to Naïve Bayes classifier can be plugged to the system for further experimentaiton. Various structural tagging techniques need to be explored further to produce feature vectors. The clustering of web pages using XSLT is one of the many open research problems.

References

[1] David D. Lewis, *"Naive (Bayes) at Forty: The Independence Assumption in Information Retrieval"* Lecture Notes in Computer Science; Vol. 1398, 1998.

[2] Irina Rish, *"An empirical study of the naive Bayes classifier"*, IJCAI 2001 Workshop on Empirical Methods in Artificial Intelligence, 2001.

[3] Andrew McCallum and K. Nigam, *"A comparision of event models for naive bayes text classification"*, AAAI-*98 Workshop on Learning for Text Categorization, 1998.*

[4] Jeonghee Yi and Neel Sundaresan, *"A classifier for semi-structured documents"*, Proceedings of the sixth ACM SIGKDD international conference on Knowledge discovery and data mining, 2000.

[5] Ludovic Denoyer and Patrick Gallinari, *"Bayesian network model for semi-structured document classification"*, Information Processing and Management, Volume 40, Issue 5, 2004.

[6] Dunja Mladenic, *"Turning Yahoo to Automatic Web-Page Classifier"*, European Conference on Artificial Intelligence, 1998

[7] F. Esposto, D. Malerba, L. D. Pace, and P. Leo. *"A machine learning apporach to web mining"*, In Proc. Of the 6th Congress of the Italian Association for Artificial Intelligence, 1999

[8] A. Sun and E. Lim and W. Ng, *"Web classification using support vector machine"*, Proceedings of the fourth international workshop on Web information and data management. ACM Press, 2002

[9] Arul Prakash Asirvatham, Kranthi Kumar Ravi, *"Web Page Classification based on Document Structure"*, 2001

[10] H.-J. Oh, S. H. Myaeng, and M.-H. Lee, *"A practical hypertext categorization method using links and incrementally available class information"*, Proceedings of the 23rd ACM International Conference on Research and Development in Information Retrieval, 2000

[11] Soumen Chakrabarti and Byron E. Dom and Piotr Indyk, *"Enhanced hypertext categorization using hyperlinks"*, Proceedings of {SIGMOD}-98, {ACM} International Conference on Management of Data, 1998

Logic-Based Association Rule Mining in XML Documents

Hong-Cheu Liu[1], John Zeleznikow[2], and Hasan M. Jamil[3]

[1] School of Economics and Information Systems, University of Wollongong, Wollongong, NSW 2522, Australia
hongcheu@uow.edu.au
[2] School of Information Systems, Victoria University, Melbourne, Vic. 8001 Australia
John.Zeleznikow@vu.edu.au
[3] Department of Computer Science, Wayne State University, Detroit, MI 48202, USA
jamil@cs.wayne.edu

Abstract. In this paper, we propose a new framework, called XLogic-Miner, to mine association rules from XML data. We consider the generate-and-test and the frequent-pattern growth approaches. In XLogic-Miner, we propose an novel method to represent a frequent-pattern tree in an object-relational table and exploit a new join operator developed in the paper. The principal focus of this research is to demonstrate that association rule mining can be expressed in an extended datalog program and be able to mine XML data in a declarative way. We also consider some optimization and performance issues.

1 Introduction

The integration of data mining with Web database systems is an emerging trend in database research and development area. The eXtensible Markup Language (XML) has been a popular way for representing semi-structured data and emerged as a standard for data exchange over the Web. The fast-growing amount of available XML data raises a pressing need for languages and tools to manage collections of XML documents, as well as mine interesting information.

Knowledge discovery from large databases has gained popularity and its importance is well recognized. Most efforts have focused on developing novel algorithms and data structures to aid efficient computation of mining tasks. While research into such procedural computation of mining rules has been extensive, object-relational machinery has yet been significantly exploited in mining XML data even though XML data is often stored in (object)-relational databases. It was pointed out in the literature that current SQL systems are unable to compete with ad-hoc file processing algorithms in general purpose data mining systems such as the well known Apriori algorithm and its variants [1, 2]. However, database management systems already provide powerful techniques

H.T. Shen et al. (Eds.): ADWeb 2006, LNCS 3842, pp. 97–106, 2006.

to deal with huge datasets and database-coupled mining systems provide query processing capabilities for nontrivial mining queries. Therefore database system vendors try to integrate data analysis functionalities to some extent into their query engines in order to exploit object-relational technologies and narrow the gap between raw data and analysis processing.

Several encouraging attempts at developing methods for mining XML data have been proposed [3, 4, 5, 6]. In principle, we can express and implement association rule mining in conventional SQL language (XML data has been transformed into a relational database) or XQuery (native XML documents). These approaches were examined by [7, 4], for instance. However, the resulting SQL (or XQuery) codes are less than intuitive, unnecessarily long and complicated. An XML-enabled association rule mining framework is presented in [5]. The authors of [6] propose a framework for mining association rules from XML documents. However, there is no relational optimization exploited in the above proposals. The major problems with the state-of-the-art methods are: (1) some approaches select data from native XML documents, thus the efficient performance is difficult to gain as a huge volume of XML data needs to be scanned in the mining process, (2) the SQL or XQuery implementation of association rule mining is very intricate and may affect the efficiency of the rule mining as no detailed optimization have been supported in these approaches. To address the above problems, we propose a new framework, called XLogic-Miner, to effectively mine association rules from XML documents. In XLogic-Miner, XML data are extracted and stored in organized tables that are suitable for association rule mining.

The main idea of our framework is to combine relational query languages with data mining primitives in an overall framework capable of specifying data mining tasks as object-relational queries. Logic-based database languages provide a flexible model of representing, maintaining and utilizing high-level knowledge. This motivates us to study a logic-based framework for data mining tasks.

Frequent itemset mining is a core problem in many data mining tasks, and a huge number of algorithms have been developed. In this paper, we investigate DBMS-based mining process and focus on frequent itemset mining by using the logic programming paradigm. The main contributions of our work are: (1) We propose a framework to mine association rules from XML data by exploiting object-relational technologies. (2) We develop new join operators for frequent itemsets mining in object-relational tables, (3) We consider optimization and performance issues and propose a heuristic strategy to prune a large candidate frequent itemsets. The principal focus of this work is to demonstrate that association rule mining can be expressed in an extended datalog program.

The presentation of the paper is organized as follows. We briefly review the basic concepts in Section 2. We then present datalog implementation for frequent itemset mining in Section 3. A brief discussion on performance and optimization issues is presented in Section 4 before we conclude in Section 5.

2 Problem Revisit

In this section, we first briefly review the frequent itemset mining problem and the widely established terminology for association rule mining, then focus on the candidate generate-and-test and the frequent-pattern growth approaches.

2.1 Association Rules

While many forms of rule inductions are interesting, association rules were found to be appealing because of their simplicity and intuitiveness. In this paradigm, the rule mining process is divided into two distinct steps - discovering *large item sets* and generating rules.

The first work on mining association rules from large databases is the support-confidence framework established by Agrawal et al. [8]. Let $I = \{i_1, ...i_n\}$ be a set of item identifiers. An association rule is an implication of the form

$$X \Rightarrow Y, \text{ where } X, Y \subseteq I, \text{ and } X \cap Y = \emptyset$$

Association rules are characterized by two measures. The rule $A \Rightarrow B$ holds in the transaction set D with support s, where s is the percentage of transactions in D that contain $A \cup B$. This is taken to be the probability, $P(A \cup B)$. The rule $A \Rightarrow B$ has confidence c in the transaction set D if c is the percentage of transactions in D containing A that also contain B. This is taken to be the conditional probability, $P(B \mid A)$. That is,

$$support(A \Rightarrow B) = P(A \cup B)$$
$$confidence(A \Rightarrow B) = P(B \mid A)$$

The task of mining association rules is to generate all association rules that satisfy two user-defined threshold values: a minimum support and a minimum confidence.

We summarize the basic concepts of association rule in the context of XML data. We introduce an XML document described in Figure 1.

We consider the problem of mining frequent associations among parts which have the same company source. Let $\mathcal{X}$ be the set of XML fragments in an XML document which are mapped to an object-relational database. For example, Figure 1 is mapped to three nested relational tables as shown in the Figure 2.

2.2 The Candidate Generate-and-Test-Approach

The candidate generate-and-test approach essentially consists of a sequence of steps that proceed in an iterative manner. In each iteration, the output of the previous step is used as seeds to generate the candidate set of the following step. For example, in the k-th pass of the Apriori algorithm a set of potential frequent k-itemsets is computed from the output of the k-*1*-th pass. Then the transaction database and the candidate k-itemsets C_k are joined to generate frequent k-itemsets L_k.

```
<Corporation>
  <Products>
    <Product id = "prod-A">
      <prod-name> LCD monitor ( </prod-name>
      <Warranty>
        <premium> $ 120 </premium>
        <country> Taiwan </country>
        <w-period> 3 years </w-period>
      </Warranty>
      <Composition id = "c-1">
        <c-name> comp-1 </c-name>
        <Component>
          <part idref = "p-1" />
          <quantity > 2 </quantity>
          <part idref = "p-2" />
          <quantity > 3 </quantity>
        </Component>
      </Composition>
      <Distributor>
        <company> DHS </company>
        <fee> $1,000 </fee>
      </Distributor>
    </Product >
          .
          .
          .
  </Products>
  <Parts>
    <part id = "p-1", >
      <part-name> screen </part-name>
      <weight> 1 kg </weight>
      <Warranty>
        <country> Japan </country>
        <w-period> 1 years </w-period>
      < /Warranty>
      <Source>
        <company> TNT </company>
        <cost> $500 </cost>
      < /Source>
    < /part >
          .
          .
          .
  </Parts>
</Corporation>
```

Fig. 1. An example of XML document

```
TABLE Corporation = (Doc-id, Sub-doc)
TABLE Products = (Product-id, prod-name, Warranty,
                  Composition, Distributor)
        Warranty = (premium, country, w-period)
        Composition = (Composition-id, c-name,
                       Component)
        Component = (part, quantity)
        Distributor = (company, fee)
TABLE Parts = (Part-id, part-name, weight, Warranty,
               Source)
        Warranty = (country, w-period)
        Source = (company, cost)
```

Fig. 2. Three mapped nested relational schemes

One of the most well known algorithms is the *Apriori* algorithm which uses an anti-monotone property to reduce the computational cost of candidate frequent itemset generation. In many cases, the Apriori candidate generate-and-test method reduces the size of candidate sets significantly and leads to good performance. However, it may suffer the following drawbacks: (1) huge computation involved during the candidate itemset generation, (2) massive I/O disk scans, and (3) high memory dependency. The basic operations in the candidate generate-and-test approach are join and subset checking. Both are expensive operations especially when itemsets are very long. Some Apriori-like algorithms make improvements.

2.3 The Frequent-Pattern Growth Approach

The frequent-pattern growth (FP-growth) approach adopts a divide-and-conquer strategy to compress the database representing frequent items into a frequent-pattern tree and then divides such a compressed database into a set of conditional databases. Each conditional database associates with one frequent item (suffix pattern). Then it mines each such conditional database separately. The FP-growth method transforms the problem of finding long frequent patterns to looking for shorter ones recursively and then concatenating the suffix. The frequent-pattern growth approach avoids generating and testing a large number of candidate itemsets. The basic operations in the frequent-pattern growth approach are counting frequent items and new conditional database construction. The performance of a frequent-pattern growth algorithm depends on the number of conditional databases constructed and the mining cost of each individual conditional database.

2.4 Datalog$^{cv,\neg}$

In this paper, we consider the logic programming paradigm and use Datalog^{cv} with negation as a representative. The complex value model has been proposed as a significant extension of the relational one and forms a core structure of object-relational databases. Complex values allow the application of the tuple and set constructor recursively. We consider an extension of datalog to incorporate complex values. The Datalog for complex values is denoted Datalog^{cv}. The formal syntax and semantics of Datalog^{cv} are straightforward extensions of those for Datalog. Datalog^{cv} with negation is denoted Datalog$^{cv,\neg}$. A Datalog $^{cv,\neg}$ rule is an expression of the form $A \leftarrow L_1, ..., L_n$, where A is an atom and each L_i is either a positive atom B_i or a negated atom $\neg B_i$. A Datalog$^{cv,\neg}$ program is a nonempty finite set of Datalog$^{cv,\neg}$ rules. The detailed theoretical foundation can be found in [9].

3 Datalog$^{cv,\neg}$ Implementation for Frequent Itemset Mining

In this section, we present an operational semantics for association rule mining queries expressed in Datalog$^{cv,\neg}$ programs using the candidate generate-and-test and the FP-growth approaches. The challenge is to develop declarative means of computing association rules so that we can mine interesting information from XML documents which are stored in object-relational databases.

3.1 The Candidate Generate-and-Test Approach

We expect to have a function **sub** available in the next generation database systems that takes three arguments, two sets of values (Items) V_1 and V_2, and a natural number k such that $|V_2| \leq k \leq |V_1|$, and returns the degree-k subsets of the set V_1 that include V_2. For any two sets S and s, s is said to be a degree-k subset of S if $s \in \mathcal{P}(S)$ and $|s| = k$. $\mathcal{P}(S)$ denotes the powerset of S.

We define a new join operator called *sub-join*.

Definition 1. *Let us consider two relations with the same schemes* $\{Items, Support\}$.

$$r \bowtie^{sub,k} s = \{t \mid \exists u \in r, v \in s \text{ such that } u[Items] \subseteq v[Items] \\ \wedge \exists t' \in unnest(sub(v, u, k)),\ t = < t', v[Support] > \}$$

Here, we treat the result of $r \bowtie^{sub,k} s$ as *multiset* meaning, as it may produce two tuples of t' with the same support value. In the mining process we need to add all support values for each item.

r

Items	*Support*
$\{a\}$	0
$\{b, f\}$	0
$\{d, f\}$	0

s

Items	*Support*
$\{a, b, c\}$	3
$\{b, c, f\}$	4
$\{d, e\}$	2

$r \ltimes^{sub,2} s$

Items	*Support*
$\{a, b\}$	3
$\{a, c\}$	3
$\{b, f\}$	4

Fig. 3. An example of sub-join

Example 1. *Given two relations* r *and* s*, the result of* $r \ltimes^{sub,2} s$ *is shown as in figure 3.*

We present a Datalog program, as shown below, which can compute the frequent itemsets.

1. $cand(J, C) \leftarrow freq(I, C),\ J \subset I,\ |J| = 1$
2. $large(J, C) \leftarrow cand(J, C),\ C > \delta$
3. $T(genid(), x, C_2) \leftarrow large(J, C_1),\ freq(I, C_2),$
   $k = max(|J|) + 1,\ sub\_join(J, I, k, x)$
4. $cand(x, sum < C >) \leftarrow T(id, x, C)$
5. $large(x, y) \leftarrow cand(x, y), y > \delta$

The rule 1 generates the set of *1-itemset* from the input frequency table. The rule 2 selects the frequent *1-itemset* whose support is greater than the threshold. Let us assume that we have a *sub-join* relation, where $sub\_join(J, I, k, x)$ is interpreted as 'x is obtained by applying **sub** function to two operands J and I, i.e., $x = J \ltimes^{sub,k} I$. The rule 3 performs the *sub-join* operation on the table *large* generated in the rule 2 and the input frequency table.

Datalog system is of set semantics. In the above program, we treat T facts as multisets, i.e., bag semantics, by using system generated *id* to simulate multiset operation. The rule 4 counts the total of all supports corresponding to each candidate itemset generated in table T so far. Finally, rule 5 computes the large item sets by selecting them in the candidate set whose support is greater than the threshold. Suppose that n is the maximum cardinality of the item sets in the frequency table. The above program is bounded by n.

We now show the program that defines *sub-join*:

$$to\_join(J, I) \leftarrow A(J),\ B(I),\ J \subset I$$
$$sub\_join(J, I, k, x) \leftarrow to\_join(J, I),\ J \subset I,\ x \subset I,\ |x| = k$$

Once the large itemset table has been generated, we can easily apply the following rule, which was proposed in [10], to produce all association rules.

$$rules(I, J - I, support, conf) \leftarrow large(I, C_I), large(J, C_J),$$
$$support = C_J, conf = C_J/C_I, conf > \delta$$

In the final step, the above generated rules will be represented in the XML format.

(a) D

company	*parts*
c1	p_1, p_2, p_5
c2	p_2, p_4
c3	p_2, p_3
c4	p_1, p_2, p_4
c5	p_1, p_3
c6	p_2, p_3
c7	p_1, p_3
c8	p_1, p_2, p_3, p_5
c9	p_1, p_2, p_3

(b) L_1

part	*count*
p_2	7
p_1	6
p_3	6
p_4	2
p_5	2

(c) FP

part	*count*	pattern-base	
		pattern	count
p_5	2	$< p_2, p_1 >$	1
		$< p_2, p_1, p_3 >$	1
p_4	2	$< p_2, p_1 >$	1
		$< p_2 >$	1
p_3	6	...	...
p_1	6	...	...
p_2	7	...	...

Fig. 4. An object-relational table representing FP-tree

3.2 The FP-Growth Approach

The FP-growth mining process consists of two steps [11]:

- Construct a compact frequent-pattern tree which retains the itemsets about association information in less space.
- Mine the FP-tree to find all frequent patterns recursively.

When the database is large, it is unrealistic to construct a main memory-based FP-tree. An interesting alternative is to store a FP-tree in an object-relational table.

Example 2. *We reexamine the task of mining frequent associations among parts which have the same company source, which was stated in Section 2. The first scan of the relevant database (i.e., the Parts table in Figure 1) is the same as Apriori, which creates a task-relevant table, D, and derives the set of frequent 1-itemsets and their support counts as shown in Figure 4(a) and (b). A FP-tree table is then constructed as follows. We scan the relevant table D a second time. The parts supplied by each company are processed in L_1 order (i.e., sorted according to descending support count) and a tuple is created for each 1-itemset (i.e., part). We represent an FP-tree in an object-relational table with three attributes: item identifier (part), the number of companies that contain this part (count), and conditional pattern bases (i.e., prefix).*

For example, during the scan process, we get two patterns "p_1, p_2, p_5" and "p_1, p_2, p_3, p_5, which contains two conditional pattern bases (i.e., prefix): "p_2, p_1" and p_2, p_1, p_3" in L_1 order, leads to the construction of the first tuple with three attribute values: $< p_5, 2, \{<< p_2, p_1 >, 1 >, << p_2, p_1, p_3 >, 1 >\} >$ as shown in Figure 4. The mining of the FP-tree proceeds as follows. Start from each frequent 1-itemset (as an initial suffix pattern), perform mining by applying a special kind of join, called fp-join which is defined below, on the pattern base attribute in the FP-tree table.

Definition 2. *Given two arrays $a =< a_1, ..., a_m >$ and $b =< b_1, ..., b_n >$, where $m \leq n$, the join of two arrays is defined as $a \bowtie b =$*

- $< a_1, ..., a_j >$, *if* $(a_1 = b_1,...,a_j = b_j)$ *and* $a_{j+1} \neq b_{j+1}$ *where* $j < m$; *or*
- $< a_1, ..., a_m >$, *if* $a_1 = b_1,...,a_m = b_m$

For example, given two arrays $< i_2, i_1, i_5 >$ and $< i_2, i_1 >$, then $< i_2, i_1, i_5 > \bowtie < i_2, i_1 > = < i_2, i_1 >$. Then we define fp-join for the conditional pattern base attribute in the FP-tree table.

Definition 3. *Given two relations* u_1 *and* u_2 *with schemas* $\{< pattern : array, count : integer >\}$, *the fp-join of two relations is defined as follows:*

$$\begin{aligned} u_1 \bowtie^{fp} u_2 = \{t \mid\ & \exists t_1 \in u_1 \text{ and } t_2 \in u_2 \text{ such that} \\ & (t[pattern] = t_1[pattern] \bowtie t_2[pattern] \\ & \wedge t[count] = t_1[count] + t_2[count]) \\ & \vee (t \in u_1 \wedge (\forall t' \in u_2, t[pattern] \bowtie t'[pattern] = \emptyset) \\ & \vee (t \in u_2 \wedge (\forall t' \in u_1, t[pattern] \bowtie t'[pattern] = \emptyset)\} \end{aligned}$$

Example 3. *Suppose there is a relation* $R = \{<< i_2, i_1 >, 2 >, << i_2 >, 2 >, << i_1 >, 2 >\}$. $R \bowtie^{fp} R = \{<< i_2, i_1 >, 2 >, << i_2 >, 4 >, << i_1 >, 2 >\}$

We present a Datalog program as shown in the figure 5 which can compute the frequent itemsets by using the FP-growth approach.

Similar to the candidate generate-and-test approach, the rules 1 and 2 produce the frequent 1-itemset L_1. The rule 3 produces the prefix patterns for each item (i.e., part). The rule 4 counts the number of patterns for each prefix. The nest operator is applied to create nested schema *FP-base*$(J, C, pattern\text{-}base < K, PC >)$ in rule 5. The rule 6 applies the fp-join operator defined before to create the conditional pattern base, called $CondFP$. Finally, rules 7 and 8 form the frequent patterns by concatenating with the suffix pattern. In the program we use *Powerset* function which can be implemented in a sub-program and an aggregate function *min* to select the minimum support of the prefix patterns.

Similarly, we can pre-process the input XML tree and convert it into an object-relational database. Then we can mine frequent pattern subtrees by using the above deductive paradigm.

1.	$freq(parts, count < company >)$	$\leftarrow D(company, parts)$
2.	$L_1(J, C)$	$\leftarrow freq(I, C),\ J \subset I,\ \lvert J\rvert = 1,\ C > \delta$
3.	$FP\text{-}pattern(J, C, T, K)$	$\leftarrow L_1(J, C),\ D(T, I),\ J \subset I,\ K = I - J$
4.	$FP\text{-}tree(J, C, K, count < T >)$	$\leftarrow FP\text{-}pattern(J, C, T, K)$
5.	$FP\text{-}base(J, C, pattern\text{-}base < K, PC >$	$\leftarrow FP\text{-}tree(J, C, K, PC)$
6.	$Cand\text{-}FP(J, C, CondFP < base, count >)$	$\leftarrow FP\text{-}base(J, C, B),\ B \bowtie^{fp} B = CondFP$
7.	$FP(I, PC)$	$\leftarrow Cand\text{-}FP(J, C, CondFP < K, C >),$ $Powerset(CondFP.K) \cup J = I,\ PC = C,$ $C > \delta$
8.	$FP(I, min(PC))$	$\leftarrow FP(I, PC)$

Fig. 5. The FP-growth approach to frequent pattern mining

4 Optimization and Performance Issues

The main disadvantage of the deductive approach to data mining query languages is the concern of its performance. However, optimization techniques from deductive databases can be utilized and the most computationally intensive operations can be modularized. We have presented our preliminary ideas first and comprehensive query optimization and experimental work will be carried out at a later stage.

There exist some opportunities for optimization in the expressions and algorithms expressed in the deductive paradigm. Like in the algebraic paradigm, we may improve performance by exploiting algebraic optimization techniques, for example, optimizing subset queries [12], algebraic equivalences for nested relational operators [13]. In the deductive paradigm, we may also apply pruning techniques by using the 'anti-monotonicity'. However, it is not easy to achieve in a declarative way as pruning of any itemset depends on its support value which may not be finalized until at a later stage.

In the datalog program expressed in the preceding section, we used an explicit generation of the powerset of each item to be able to compute the large item set. This is a huge space overhead. Therefore, we require optimization techniques that exploit 'anti-monotonicity' or other heuristic rules to prune a large set of items. We propose the following rules to optimize the program using the candidate generate-and-test approach.

$$last\_step\_large(I, C) \leftarrow large(J, C),\ I \subseteq J,\ |I| = max(|J|)$$

We add the above rule to between rule 2 and rule 3 in the program using the candidate generate-and-test approach and modify rule 3 as follows.

$$3'\ \ T(genid(), x, C_2) \leftarrow last\_step\_large(J, C_1),\ freq(I, C_2),\ k = max(|J|) + 1,\ sub\_join(J, I, k, x)$$

Then, during the step k, we use only frequent itemset inserted in the large table during the previous iteration $k-1$ to perform sub-join operation with the input frequent table. This can avoid unnecessary computing.

We can also consider the following heuristic rules to prune the useless candidate itemsets.

$$\begin{aligned} not\_large(id, x, C) &\leftarrow T(id, x, C), y \subset x, |y| = |x| - 1, \\ &\quad\ \neg large(y, C) \\ cand(x, sum < C >) &\leftarrow T(id, x, C), \neg not\_large(id, x, C) \end{aligned}$$

In order to perform the fp-join efficiently, we need to devise indexing scheme and exploit optimization techniques developed in nested relational databases.

5 Conclusion

We have proposed a framework, called XLogic-Miner, to mine association rules from XML documents by using the logic programming paradigm. Two approaches, the generate-and-test and the frequent-pattern growth, have been utilized in our work. In this paper, we have also demonstrated that XML data can be mined in a declarative way. The results of our research provide an alternative method for the data mining process in DBMS-based mining systems. It could be helpful for the next generation of Web-based database systems with data mining functionality.

References

1. Tsur, D., Ullman, J.D., Abiteboul, S., Clifton, C., Motwani, R., Nestorov, S., Rosenthal, A.: Query flocks: A generalization of association-rule mining. In: Proceedings of ACM SIGMOD. (1998) 1–12
2. Rantzau, R.: Processing frequent itemset discovery queries by division and set containment join qperators. In: Proceedings of the 2003 ACM DMKD. (2003) 20–27
3. Braga, D., Campi, A., Ceri, S.: Discovering interesting information in xml data with association rules. In: Proceedings of ACM symposium on applied computing. (2003)
4. W.W.Wan, J., Dobbie, G.: Mining association rule from xml data using xquery. In: Proceedings of the Fifth International Workshop on Web Information and Data Management. (2003)
5. Feng, L., Dillon, T., Weigand, H., Chang, E.: An xml-enabled association rule framwork. In: Proceedings of DEXA'03. (2003) 88–97
6. Zhang, S., Zhang, J., Liu, H., Wang, W.: Xar-miner: efficient association rules mining for xml data. In: Proceedings of ACM WWW2005. (2005) 894–895
7. Jamil, H.M.: Ad hoc association rule mining as sql3 queries. In: Proceedings of IEEE international conference on data mining. (2001) 609–612
8. Agrawal, R., Imielinski, T., Swami, A.: Mining association rules between sets of items in large databases. In: Proceedings of ACM SIGMOD conference on management of data. (1993) 207–216
9. Abiteboul, S., Hull, R., Vianu, V.: Foundations of databases. Addison Wesley (1995)
10. Jamil, H.M.: Mining first-order knowledge bases for association rules. In: Proceedings of 13th IEEE International conference on tools with Artificial intelligence. (2001)
11. Han, J., Pei, J., Yin, Y.: Mining frequent patterns without candidate generation. In: Proceedings of ACM SIGMOD Conference on Management of Data. (2000) 1–12
12. Masson, C., Robardet, C., Boulicaut, J.F.: Optimizing subset queries: a step towards sql-based inductive databases for itemsets. In: Proceedings of the 2004 ACM symposium on applied computing. (2004) 535–539
13. Liu, H.C., Yu, J.: Algebraic equivalences of nested relational operators. Information Systems **30** (2005) 167–204

XML Document Retrieval System Based on Document Structure and Image Content for Digital Museum*

Jae-Woo Chang and Yeon-Jung Kim

Dept. of Computer Engineering, Research Center for Advanced LBS Technology,
Chonbuk National University, Chonju, Chonbuk 561-756, South Korea
jwchang@chonbuk.ac.kr, yjkim@dblab.chonbuk.ac.kr

Abstract. In this paper, we design an XML document retrieval system for a digital museum. It can support unified retrieval on XML documents based on both document structure and image content. To achieve it, we perform the indexing of XML documents describing Korean porcelains used for a digital museum, based on not only their basic unit of element but also their image color and shape features. In addition, we provide index structures for the unified retrieval based on both document structure and image content. Finally, we implement our XML document retrieval system designed for a digital museum and analyze its performance in terms of insert time and retrieval time for simple queries and composite queries.

1 Introduction

Because the XML (eXtensible Markup Language) has become a standard markup language to represent Web documents [1], it is necessary to develop a digital information retrieval system which provides services in the Web. An XML document not only has a logical and hierarchical structure, but also contains its multimedia data, such as image and video. In this paper, we design an XML document retrieval system used for a digital museum. It can support unified retrieval on XML documents based on both document structure and image content. In order to support retrieval based on document structure, we perform the indexing of XML documents describing Korean porcelains for a digital museum, based on their basic unit of elements. For supporting retrieval based on image content, we also do the indexing of the documents describing Korean porcelains, based on color and shape features of their images. Finally, we provide index structures for the unified retrieval based on both document structure and image content. This paper is organized as follows. In Section 2, we introduce related work. In Section 3 and 4, we design and implement an XML document retrieval system for a digital museum, respectively. In Section 5, we draw conclusions and provide future work.

* This work is financially supported by the Ministry of Education and Human Resources Development(MOE), the Ministry of Commerce, Industry and Energy(MOCIE) and the Ministry of Labor(MOLAB) though the fostering project of the Lab of Excellency.

H.T. Shen et al. (Eds.): ADWeb 2006, LNCS 3842, pp. 107 – 111, 2006.

2 Related Work

Because an element is a basic unit that constitutes an XML document, it is essential to support not only retrieval based on element units but also retrieval based on logical inclusion relationships among elements. First, Univ. of Wisconsin in Madison proposed a new technique to use the position and depth of a tree node for indexing each occurrence of XML elements [2]. Secondly, IBM T.J. Watson research center in Hawthorne proposed ViST, a novel index structure for searching XML documents [3]. Finally, Univ. of Singapore proposed D(k)-Index, a structural summary for general graph structured documents [4]. There have been a lot of studies on content-based retrieval techniques for multimedia or XML documents. First, the *QBIC(Query By Image Content) project* of IBM Almaden research center studied content-based image retrieval on a large on-line multimedia database [5]. Secondly, the Pennsylvania State Univ. presented a comprehensive survey on the use of pattern recognition methods for content-based retrieval on image and video information [6]. Finally, the Chinese Univ. of Hong Kong presented a multi-lingual digital video content management system, called iVIEW, for intelligent searching and access of English and Chinese video contents [7].

3 Design of XML Document Retrieval System

We design an XML document retrieval system for a digital museum, which is mainly consists of three parts, such as an indexing part, a storage manager part, and a retrieval part. When an XML document is given, we parse it and perform image segmentation from it through the indexing part, in order that we can index its document structure consisting of element units and can obtain the index information of color and shape features of its image. The index information for document structure and that for image content are separately stored into its structure-based and content-based index structures, respectively. Using the index information extracted from a set of XML documents, some documents are retrieved by the retrieval part in order to obtain a unified result to answer user queries.

3.1 Indexing

To support a query based on a logical inclusion between elements and based on the characteristic value of elements, we construct a document structure tree for XML documents describing Korean porcelains used for a digital museum, after analyzing XML documents based on DTD. To build a document structure tree for XML documents describing Korean porcelains, we parse the XML documents by using sp-1.3 parser [8]. For content-based indexing of images contained in XML documents, we extract images from XML documents and analyze them for obtaining image feature vectors. To achieve it, we first separate a salient object, i.e., a Korean porcelain, from the background of an image by using the fuzzy c-mean (FCM) algorithm [9]. The FCM algorithm has an advantage that the separation of a salient object of an image from its background can be performed well. In order to obtain an image feature vector for shape, we obtain a salient object from an image and generate a 24-dimensional feature vector from it.

3.2 Index Structure

For answering structured- and content-based queries, it is required to design index structures for structure-based retrieval as well as those for content-based retrieval. The index structures for structure-based retrieval consist of keyword, structure, element, and attribute index structures. The keyword index structure is composed of keyword index file containing keywords extracted from data token element (e.g., PCDATA, CDATA) of XML documents, posting file including the IDs of element where keywords appear, and location file containing the location of keyword in elements. The structure index structure is used for searching an inclusion relationship among elements. We propose an element unit parse tree structure representing the hierarchical structure of a document. In this structure, we easily find an inclusion relationship among elements because an element contains the location of its parent, its left sibling, its right sibling, and its first left child. The element index is used for locating a start element and plays an important role in mapping the element IDs obtained from the attribute index structure into an actual element name. The attribute index structure is used for retrieval based on an attribute name and an attribute value assigned to an element. Meanwhile, the index structure for content-based retrieval is a high-dimensional index structure based on the CBF method so as to store and retrieve both color and shape feature vectors efficiently. The CBF method [10] was proposed as an efficient high-dimensional index structure to achieve good retrieval performance even though the dimension of feature vectors is high.

3.3 Retrieval

There is little research on retrieval models for integrating structure- and content-based information retrieval. To answer a query for retrieval based on document structure, a similarity measure (S_w) between two elements, say q and t, is computed as the similarity between the term vector of node q and that of node t by using a cosine measure [11]. Supposed that a document can be represented as $D = \{ E_0, E_1, \ldots, E_{n-1} \}$ where E_i is an element i in a document D. Thus, a similarity measure (D_w) between an element q and a document D is computed as follows.

$$D_w = \text{MAX} \ \{ \ COSINE \ (NODE_q, NODE_{E_i}), 0 \le i \le n-1\}$$

To answer a query for retrieval based on image content, we first extract color or shape feature vectors from a given query image. Next, we compute Euclidean distances between a query color (or shape) feature vector and the stored image color (or shape) vectors. A similarity measure, $C_W(q, t)$, between a query image q and a target image t in the database is calculated as (1- Distc(q, t))/ Nc in case of color feature where Distc(q, t) is a color vectors distance and Nc is the maximum color distances for normalization. Finally, when α is the relative weight of retrieval based on document structure over that based on image content, a similarity measure (T_w) for a composite query is calculated as follows.

$$T_w = \begin{cases} C_w \times \alpha + D_w \times (1-\alpha), & \text{if results are document for user query} \\ C_w \times \alpha + S_w \times (1-\alpha), & \text{if results are element for user query} \end{cases}$$

4 Implementation and Performance Analysis

We implement our XML document retrieval system for a digital museum, under SUN SPARCstation 20 with GNU CCv2.7 compiler. For this, we make use of O_2-Store v4.6 [12] as a storage system and Sp-1.3 as an XML parser. For constructing a prototype digital museum, we make use of 630 XML documents describing Korean porcelains with an XML DTD for a museum. They are extracted from several Korean porcelain books published by Korean National Central Museum. To evaluate the efficiency of our XML document retrieval system for a digital museum, we measure insertion time and retrieval time. Our system requires about 6 seconds on the average to insert an XML document into keyword, attribute, structure, and element indexes. It also requires less than 1 second on the average to insert one image content into color and shape index. The retrieval time for the structure-based query is 6.5 seconds. But the retrieval times for the keyword-based, attribute-based, image content-based queries are less than 2 seconds. We also measure retrieval times for composite queries, such as query containing keywords in hierarchical tree structure (structure + key), query containing attribute values in hierarchical tree structure (structure + attr), query containing both keywords and color features (keyword + color), and query containing shape features in hierarchical tree structure (structure + shape). Figure 1 shows retrieval times for composite queries.

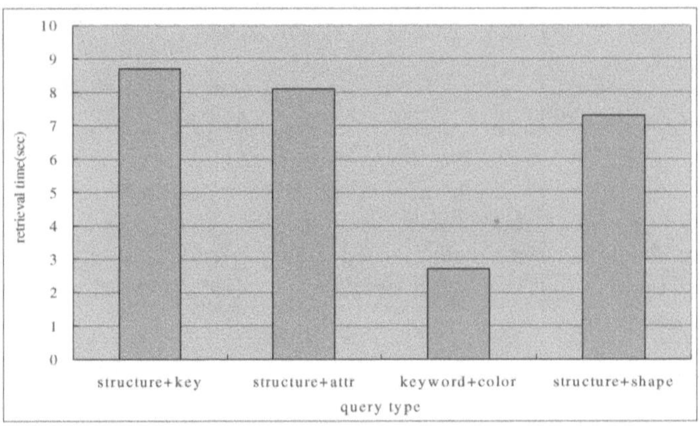

Fig. 1. Retrieval time for complex queries

The retrieval time for a keyword + color query is less than 3 seconds. However, the retrieval times for the other composite queries are about 8 seconds. It is shown that a composite query containing structure-based retrieval requires large amounts of time to answer it.

5 Conclusions and Future Work

In this paper, we designed and implemented an XML document retrieval system for a digital museum. It can support efficient retrieval on XML documents for both structure- and content-based queries. In order to support structure-based queries, we performed the indexing of XML documents describing Korean porcelains for a digital museum, based on their basic unit of element. In order to support content-based queries, we also performed the indexing of XML documents based on both color and shape features of their images. We also provided index structures for good retrieval to a composite query, based on both document structure and image content. Our system for a digital museum requires about up to 8 seconds for answering a composite query. Future work can be studied on new information retrieval models for integrating preliminary results acquired from both structure- and content-based queries, which can be achieved by dealing with MPEG-7 compliant XML documents [13].

References

[1] eXtensible Markup Language(XML), http :// www.w3.org/TR/PR-xml-971208.
[2] C. Zhang, J. Naughton, D. DeWitt, Q. Luo, and G. Lohman, "On Supporting Containment Queries in Relational Database Management Systems," In Proc. ACM Int'l Conf. on Management of Data. pp 425-436, 2001.
[3] H. Wang, S. Park, W. Fan, and P.S. Yu, "ViST: A Dynamic Index Method for Querying XML Data by Tree Structures," In Proc. ACM Int'l Conf. on Management of Data. pp 110-121, 2003.
[4] Q. Chen, A. Lim, and K.W. Ong, "D(k)-Index: An Adaptive Structural Summary for Graph-structured Data," In Proc. ACM Int'l Conf. on Management of Data. pp 134-144, 2003.
[5] M. Flickner, et. al., "Query by Image and Video Content: The QBIC System," IEEE Computer, Vol. 28, No.9, pp. 23-32, 1995.
[6] S. Antani, R. Kasturi, and R. Jain, "A Survey on the Use of Pattern Recognition Methods for Abstraction, Indexing and Retrieval of Images and Video," Pattern Recognition. Vol. 35, No. 4, pp 945-965. (2002).
[7] M.R. Lyu, E. Yau, and S. Sze, "A Multilingual, Multimodal Digital Video Library System," In Proc. ACM/IEEE-CS Joint Conf. on Digital Libraries, pp 145-153, 2002.
[8] http://www.jclark.com/sp.
[9] J.C. Bezdek and M.M. Triedi, "Low Level Segmentation of Aerial Image with Fuzzy Clustering," IEEE Trans. on SMC, Vol. 16, pp 589-598, 1986.
[10] S.G. Han and J.W. Chang, "A New High-Dimensional Index Structure using a Cell-based Filtering Technique," In LNCS 1884 (ADBIS-DASFAA 2000), pp 79-92, 2000.
[11] G. Salton and M. McGill, "An Introduction to Modern Information Retrieval," McGraw-Hill, 1983.
[12] O. Deux et al. "The O_2 System," Communication of the ACM, Vol. 34, No. 10, pp 34-48, 1991.
[13] U. Westermann and W. Klas, "An Analysis of XML Database Solutions for the Management of MPEG-7 Media Descriptions," ACM Computing Surveys. Vol. 35, No. 4, pp 331-373, 2003.

Meta Modeling Approach for XML Based Data Integration

Ouyang Song and Huang Yi

Department of Computer Science, Central South University,
Changsha, Hunan, P.R. China 410083
Tel. +86 731 8876887
ouyangsong@yahoo.com

Abstract. Meta modeling is in nature more suitable for enterprises' large applications and has many advantages over the traditional OO modeling. Up to now how to provide meta modeling support in an XML based data integration has not yet been addressed systematically This paper describes the most distinguished features of meta modeling from the traditional OO modeling and the key issues in the meta modeling enabled XML based data integration applications. Two algorithms: a semantic constraint parsing algorithm and an XML Schema mapping algorithm are discussed in detail.

1 Introduction

The rapid development of enterprise infrastructure has led to an ever-growing data being processed in various enterprises' applications. To use the data more efficiently, lot of effort has been paid in enterprise data integration [1][2]. As XML provides a natural way of structuring data, based on hierarchical representations, and has the ability to represent structured, unstructured, and semi-structured data, it has been adopted as a common model in many data integration applications.

Although XML can greatly help the task of data integration, before using XML based data, two issues must be solved first. One is how to represent the object using XML. In existing XML based data integration applications, various representations of XML for object have been used. This can result in more confusion. To solve this problem, XML Metadata Interchange (XMI) [3] has been proposed by OMG. XMI defines a consistent way to create XML schemas from models and XML document instances from objects that are instances of those models. The other one, as the XML data abstract model, which is a tree model, replaces the flat relational object model, how to deal with the problem of semantic integrity becomes much more complicated. Many research works have dealt with this issue [4][5].

In most of existing data integration applications, the basic modeling approach is traditional OO modeling. A new trend in software engineering is meta modeling. The fundamental difference between traditional OO modeling and the meta modeling is that the primary artifacts of meta modeling are meta-model and models, while in traditional OO modeling the primary artifacts are models. Meta modeling is in nature more suitable for enterprises' large applications and has many advantages over the traditional OO modeling. Up to now how to support meta modeling in an XML based

H.T. Shen et al. (Eds.): ADWeb 2006, LNCS 3842, pp. 112 – 116, 2006.

data integration has not yet been addressed systematically This paper analyses the main features of meta modeling; works out the key issues for an XML based data integration to be able to use meta modeling; and develops a semantic constraint parsing algorithm and an XML Schema mapping algorithm to support meta modeling in XML based data integration.

2 Basic Concepts of Meta Modeling Approach

The framework for meta modeling is based on a four layers architecture specified in OMG's MOF specification [6]. These layers are: M_0 layer (object layer), M_1 layer (model layer), M_2 layer (meta model layer), M_3 layer (meta-meta-model layer).

Two features of meta modeling have closer relations with data integration:

- A meta-model defines not only the meta-objects for models, but also the containment and the inherent relationships among meta-objects in M_2 layer. When developers design the models in M_1 layer, the relationships may conflict with those defined in M_2 layer. So the system should guarantee that the containment and the inherent relationships defined in M_1 layer are not violated those defined in M_2 layer.
- With meta-modeling the only operation between two adjacent layers of MOF architecture is "instance-of". In strict meta-modeling [7] every element of an M_n layer model is an "instance-of" exactly one element of the M_{n+1} layer model. The system based on meta modeling approach should support this restriction.

The data integration application based on meta modeling should has at least two abilities: (i) to guarantee that the containment and the inherent relationships designed in M_1 layer are not conflict with that defined in M_2 layer; (ii) to fulfill the strict meta-modeling. More discussions about meta modeling can be found in [7].

3 Mappings Between MOF Model and XML Schema

The prerequisite work for XML based data integration is the mappings between the data of various formats and the data of XML format. The most important one is the mapping between MOF model and XML Schema. The current version of XMI standard is only for traditional OO modeling. In the following subsections, a mapping method supporting the meta modeling is developed. The technique used in this paper is to add a semantic constraint parsing process before mapping, and to make an extension to the normal XML Schema mapping process. The component to fulfill theses functionalities is called XML Adaptor in our system.

3.1 Relation Simplifying

One of the purposes of semantic constraint parsing process is to enable the system to insert a check point to check the containment and the inherent integrity that are expressed ether explicitly or implicitly between adjacent meta layer's meta objects in meta modeling before XML Schema mapping. To make passing more efficient, some simplifications are made in the AML Adaptor.

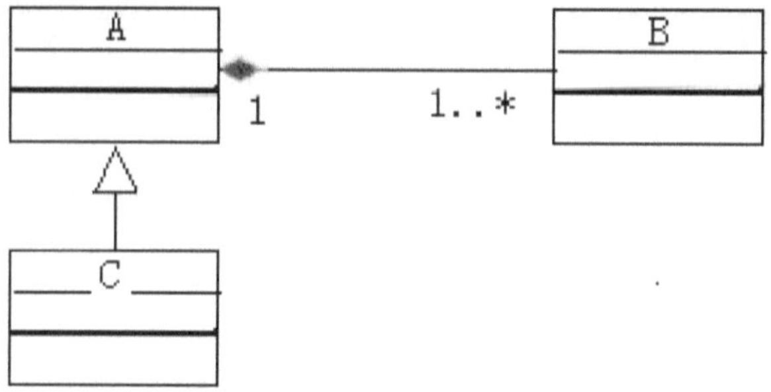

Fig. 1. A fragment of model with simple semantics

In Fig.1 C includes a reference to B. This is because that C is an instance of A and B is a part of A. This information may be lost in the XML Schema mapping if C does not know the relation between A and B as the inheritance information is kept in B.

If all relations (containment or inherent) between current processed element and other elements are analyzed at the time of being processed, then it is obvious that the efficiency is very poor since other elements may have relations remained to be analyzed. It is necessary to simplify the relations between model elements before parsing.

Four rules defined to simplify the four basic relations defined in MOF:

- Composite: An element that is part of a model element (composite association) will be treated as a component of that element.
- Reference: It is an identity that allows objects to be referenced from other objects. A link to the other object will be used.
- Aggregation: It is treated in the same way as reference.
- Generalization: If element B is generalized from element A, then B will contain all of the components that A possesses.

Then the parsing process can analyze model elements and simplify the analysis of linkages among model elements. The next step is to choose a start point for parsing. To explain the start point, two propositions are presented below:

Proposition 3-1. Parsing a model element at random sequence when the full relationship analysis has not completed can result in semantic conflicts.

Proposition 3-2. A set of digraphs can be built from elements of a model, with generalization relations as its edges and the elements as the vertexes. This set can be sorted with a classical topology-sorting algorithm.

3.2 Semantic Constraint Parsing Algorithm

The main purpose of the algorithm is to get the normalized semantic constraints of the model, and the information can then be used in the checking process to guarantee the semantic consistency between adjacent meta layers.

Algorithm GSCP (Generic Semantic Constraint Parsing):
Input: Model elements with simplified semantic constraints information.
Output: Model elements with normalized complete semantic information.

1. Build the vertexes (nodes) for every element in the model, and build a set of edges for generalization between elements. Then build a digraph.
2. Divide the digraph into one or more connected graphs G_0, G_1... G_N, then parse the relations of sub graphs with only one vertex, produce a sequence for the vertex.
3. Use topology algorithm on other sub graphs and get the sequences of them named S_0, S_1... S_N.
4. If all the sequences are handled, the algorithm finishes successfully and exits. If there are sequences that are not handled, then choose a sequence S_x $(0<x<N)$; parse the vertex V_0 whose out edges is zero. Add all the components of the vertex to a temp node N_t.
5. If all the vertexes in current sequence are handled then turn to step 4, otherwise get the next vertex N_m of the sequence and add all components of N_t into N_m.

This algorithm can guarantee that XML Adaptor gets complete semantic constraints in arbitrary MOF layer before the XML Schema mapping.

3.3 XML Schema Mapping Algorithm

The algorithm XMLSchemaProcess is used to map parsed model data to XML data.

In MOF model, packages are the main containment elements of model; they are used to organize classes and relationships information. An XML Adaptor should follow the correct package containment orders to convert the classes into XML data. Two concepts about mapping start points are defined below:

Definition 3-1. Outer Most Package (OMP): An OMP is the package that is not contained in any other packages via nesting or clustering relations [6].

Definition 3-2. Outer Most Class (OMC): An OMC is the class not contained by either classes via composite associations or an attribute type of any other classes.

The OMP and the OMC concepts are used in the XML Schema mapping process. The algorithm to produce XML Schema is described below:

Algorithm XMLSchemaProcess:

The main purpose of this algorithm is to convert the model elements into XML Schema. It can be considered as an extension to the normal XML Schema mapping.

Input: OMP and OMC information, the normalized semantic constraint information.

Output: XML Schema for the source model.

The XMLSchemaProcess algorithm is described as following steps:

1. Generate root element declaration for XML schema.
2. Read parsed information of model elements and the collection of the OMP.
3. Do the follow steps for each package in the collection:
4. Generate element declarations for the package, add the declaration to its parent node as a sub node. The declaration will be added to the root node if it is an OMP.

5. Generate containment declarations for all of the classes and the sub packages included in the package; then add them to the package declaration node as sub nodes. The OMC should be processed first.
6. Generate reference declarations for all of the package-class relations within the package and add the declarations to the package declaration node as its sub nodes.
7. Do step 4 to 6 to every sub packages of this package.
8. Call the checker to check the semantic constraint specified for source model. If the checking passed, do following steps for every sequence.
9. Generate XML element declarations for all the model classes in the sequence then add these declarations into root element node.
10. Generate XML element and/or attribute declarations for model class components and attributes, add declarations to the element node of the classes possess them.
11. Generate XML reference declarations for the relations within the classes and add them to class element nodes.
12. If all of the packages and classes are processed, return successfully.

4 Conclusion

From above discussion the main conclusion is that adding a semantic constraint parsing process before mapping and making an extension to the normal XML Schema mapping process are the basic means for the data integration application to use the meta modeling approach.

References

1. Grahne, G.: Information Integration and Incomplete Information. Survey in IEEE Computer Society Bulletin on Data Engineering, (September 2002), pp. 46-52.
2. Lenzerini, M.:Data Integration: A Theoretical Perspective. Survey in Proc. ACM Symposium on Principles of Database Systems (PODS), (2002), pp. 233-246.
3. OMG: XML Metadata Interchange (XMI) Specification Version 2.0, (May 2003), http://www.omg.org/docs/ formal/03-05-02.pdf
4. W. Fan, L. Libkin: On XML Integrity Constraints in the Presence of DTDs. In 20th ACM Symp. On Principles of Database Systems, 114"C125, ACM, (2001).
5. M. Arenas, W. Fan, L. Libkin: On Verifying Consistency of XML Specifications. In 20th ACM Symposium on Principles of Database Systems, ACM Press, (2002).
6. OMG: Meta Object Facility (MOF) Specification Version 1.4, (April 2002), http://www.omg.org/docs/formal/02-04-03.pdf
7. Colin Atkinson and Thomas Kühne: The Essence of Multilevel Meta-modeling, Proceedings of the 4th International Conference on the Unified Modeling Lan-guage, Toronto, Canada, (October 2001).

XML and Knowledge Based Process Model Reuse and Management in Business Intelligence System

Luan Ou and Hong Peng

School of Computer Science and Engineering,
South China University of Technology, 510641, Guangzhou, China
hrddn2005@126.com

Abstract. As a kind of data-driven decision support systems, business intelligence tools focus too much on data. In order to provide the business intelligence system with the ability of process-driven decision making, we introduce the concept of business process management to the current business intelligence system. With the implementation of case-base reasoning and rule-base reasoning technology, the process models can be built and managed efficiently. In this paper we also provide a strategy for data mining experience reuse. Process models in our system are all defined based on XML.

1 Introduction

As a kind of data-driven decision support systems [1], business intelligence tools focus too much on the data layer. However, today's companies are more process-oriented than in the past [3]. In order to provide business intelligence system with the ability of process-driven decision making, we add process models in our business intelligence system. Our business process models are defined based on ontology. With the implementation of case-base reasoning and rule-base reasoning technology, the process models can be built and managed efficiently. We also store data mining process models in the model base, which can be reused. XML technology is used as the foundational representation method in our system.

The remainder of this paper is organized as follows. In section 2, framework of XML and knowledge based process model management system and related approaches are provided. In section 3, we will draw a conclusion.

2 XML and Knowledge Based Process Model Management

Reuse of existing business process model has attracted researchers' interest [2]. However the recent management and reuse of business process are limited to the level of workflow and lack of formal guidance.

For the above reasons, we define extensible process models based on ontology [7] and XML at the business process level. In our knowledge based process model management system (KBPMS), we use hybrid technology of case-based reasoning (CBR) and rule-based reasoning (RBR) to facilitate reuse and management of process models.

H.T. Shen et al. (Eds.): ADWeb 2006, LNCS 3842, pp. 117 – 121, 2006.

2.1 Overview of Approach and System Framework

Case-based reasoning (CBR) is a method that reuses similar past experiences and adapts them to suit the current problems [4] [5]. According to the characteristics of process model management and limitations of CBR and RBR, we combine these two reasoning methods to obtain more satisfactory results.

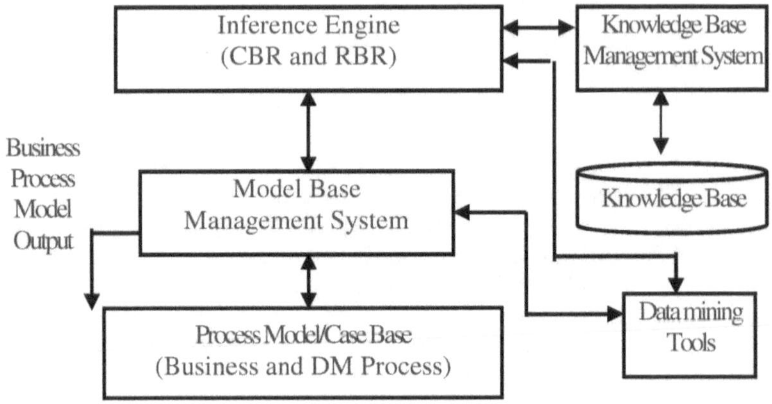

Fig. 1. Frame of KBPMS

The framework of our XML and knowledge based process model management system KBPMS is shown in Fig.1. We combine the process model base and case base for CBR as one system. Each process model in the process model base is a case for case-base reasoning.

2.2 Business Process Model Representation

Our business process model includes a combination of four main ontologies: domain ontology, task ontology, activity ontology and event ontology.

The Domain ontology defines a set of concept and relationships describing the application domain. It has a hierarchy structure composed of domain terms.

The task ontology defines the goal of the process.

The activity ontology describes operations taken for specified kind of tasks. It also has a hierarchy structure.

The event ontology includes all kinds of input and output events of business process.

We use RDF [8] to define these ontologies. RDF Schema vocabulary consists of classes, subclasses and properties, which can be used to define complicated term hierarchies.

For example, we can use RDF schema to define an activity class: <rdfs:class rdf:ID="Activity" /> and define a property of this class:

```
<rdf:Property ID="proprety1">
<rdfs:range rdf:resource="......"/>
<rdfs:domain rdf:resource="#Activity"/>
</rdf:Property>
```

We can define an instance of the above class: <Activity rdf:ID="Activity1" >. Then, Activity1owns all properties of the Activity class.

We use XML (Extensible Markup Language) to describe the process model because XML can easily shape hierarchy structure and can be conveniently exchanged between different systems. Since most current workflow definition languages are based on XML, our process model can be transformed into standard workflows easily. A simplified process model template is shown below:

```
<Process>
  <Domain>...</Domain>
  <Task>...</Task>
  <Activity>...</Activity>
  <Inputevent>...</Inputevent>
  <Dataobject>...</Dataobject>
  <Constrains>...</Constrains>
  <Outputevent>...</Outputevent>
</Process>
```

This process model template can be reused and specialized to make more sophisticated models. As an ontology-based model, our process model can be inherited. Inheritance behaviors of process model mainly include process component specializing, component deletion and component removing.

2.3 Business Process Model Retrieval and Generation

According to different input of users, there are two kinds of methods for case retrieval: goal-driven case retrieval and attribute-driven case retrieval. If the user only provides the aim of the process he wanted, goal-driven case retrieval will be used and related cases will be selected based on the combination of domain and task. If the user knows part of the structure of the target process, attribute-driven case retrieval can be used. Attribute-driven case retrieval is based on similarity matching. The similarity evaluation method employed in our system is based on the nearest-neighbor idea [5].

If no satisfactory process model is obtained, the user can develop his process from the beginning. Domain terms and task items from domain ontology and task ontology are provided to the user and related process models are shown. In every step, relevant candidate process models are given based on task attribute. After the user has finished process model composition, domain knowledge and business rules are used to verify whether a new process model is reasonable. Measures for feasibility judgment include activity sequence reasonability; constrain satisfaction and other domain dependent requirements. If the process model can fulfill the requirements of evaluation and is confirmed by the user, it is then stored in the process model base.

2.4 Knowledge Based Data Mining Process Model Reuse and Management

Data mining technology plays a very important role in business intelligence systems. In most current data mining tools, mining models to be used are always determined by data mining experts. At the same time, few researchers pay enough attention on the experience gained in data mining process. In fact, the experiential knowledge obtained during the data mining procedure is very helpful for solving new problems.

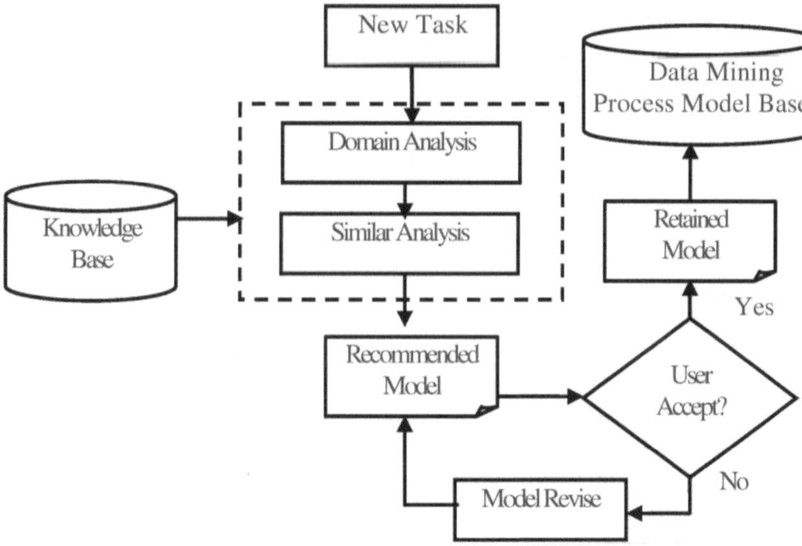

Fig. 2. Schematic Diagram of Knowledge Based Data Mining Process Management System

We store data mining process models in the model base. We extend the PMML [6] standard to describe our data mining process model by adding domain attribute. PMML is a XML based application and system independent interchange format for statistical and data mining models and it is the most widely deployed data mining standard.

For a new data mining task, the most similar model will be retrieved based on predefined measures. The whole procedure is shown in Fig. 2. The first step is domain analysis. In this step, the new task is identified based on domain attribute. After domain analysis, only the models of relevant domain are selected for similarity evaluation. Similarity evaluation is based on the nearest-neighbor algorithm [5]. Weights and measures are defined based on domain knowledge. Retrieved data mining process model can be revised to meet the requirement of the user. After the confirmation of the user, the revised model can be stored in the model base.

3 Conclusion

We have described the KBPMS system, a framework for facilitating model-driven process design implementing hybrid of RBR and CBR techniques. The innovative features proposed are: ontology based business process models representation that is flexible and can be easily extended and inherited; combination of rule-based reasoning and case-base reasoning that can overcome the limitations of these two methods and get more satisfactory results; strategy for data mining experience reuse that makes data mining process more efficient. Currently, we are implementing the KBPMS on a prototype of CRM (Customer Relationship Management).

Acknowledgments

This paper is supported by the Provincial High-tech Program of Guangdong, China under Grant No. A10202001 and the High-tech Program of Guangzhou, China under Grant No. 2004Z2-D0091.

References

1. Power, D.J. A Brief History of Decision Support Systems. DSSResources.COM, World Wide Web, http://DSSResources.COM/history/dsshistory.html, version 2.8, May 31, 2003.
2. G. Joeris and O. Herzog. Managing evolving workflow specifications. In Proceed-ings.3rd IFCIS International Conference on Cooperative Information Systems, pages 310 –319, 1998. 1998.
3. Baina, K., Tata, S., and Benali, K. A Model for Process Service Interaction. In Proceedings 1st Conference on Business Process Management (EindHoven, The Netherlands, 2003).
4. Aamodt, A., Plaza, E., 1994. Case-based reasoning: foundational issues, methodological variations and system approaches. AI Communications 7 (l), 39-59.
5. Kolodner, J.L., 1993. Case-Based Reasoning. Morgan Raufmann Publishers, San Mateo, CA.
6. http://www.dmg.org, August 2005
7. http://www-ksl.stanford.edu/kst/what-is-an-ontology.html, August 2005
8. http://www.w3.org/RDF/, August 2005

Labeling XML Nodes in RDBMS

Moad Maghaydah and Mehmet A. Orgun

Department of Computing,
Macquarie University, Sydney,
NSW 2109, Australia
{moad, mehmet}@comp.mq.edu.au

Abstract. Relational Database storage for XML data is the most affordable and available solution. Meanwhile supporting document order and structure for dynamic XML data in RDBMS still needs more work. We present a new labeling approach for nodes in XML documents, which we call XMask, where each element is identified by two values (1) node Id (2) and node Mask. XMask can efficiently maintain the document structure and order with a short-length label that can fit in a 32-bit integer. We performed experimental evaluation between our approach and an interval approach model using XML data (XRel). Our approach outperformed the interval approach for complex queries.

1 Introduction

As the number and size of XML documents grow, it is critical to have efficient mechanisms for storing, querying and updating XML documents. However, Enabled XML Management Systems, RDBMS based systems, are still the most available and affordable solutions.

XML document order is an important feature in XML data model which is not supported in the relational data model. To maintain the document order, the nodes and the attributes of XML documents have to be identified and numbered.

We can classify the numbering methods into two main categories; the intervals approach and the Dewey based approach. In the intervals approach [2, 3, 6], each node is identified by a pair (S, E) of numerical start and end values. The S value represents the order when the node is visited for the first time and E represents the order when the node is visited for the second time; that means after visiting all of its children and sub children. A node X is descended from node Y iff:

$$(S_Y < S_X) \; AND \; (E_Y > E_X)$$

The intervals approach provides better representation for static XML documents.

The Dewey coding concept for XML trees, which was introduced in [5], provides a semantic labeling scheme with paths like (1.4.9.1) and it can reduce the cost of relabeling in case of dynamic XML data. The authors encoded the order information in UTF-8 strings and they used the prefix match functions, as in [4], to evaluate ancestor-descendent relationship between any two nodes. The major drawback of UTF-8 is its inflexibility since its compression is poor for small ordinals, e.g. the label

H.T. Shen et al. (Eds.): APWeb Workshops 2006, LNCS 3842, pp. 122 – 126, 2006.

(1.1.1.1) uses four one-byte components. Another issue is the complexity of translated queries especially for queries that involve local order.

In this paper we introduce a new fixed-schema approach, which we call XMask, using RDBMS at the backend. XMask adapts the idea of the IP network addressing technique where each computer can be uniquely identified by two values: an IP address and a network Mask. For our system the analogous values will be (Node ID, Node Mask). We use the Dewey labeling scheme for the node ID, but we handle the resulting label as an integer value instead of a binary string. XMask can efficiently maintain the document structure and order with a short-length label that can fit in a 32bit integer. Even if we use fixed width integer values, XMask has the ability of numbering large and deeply nested documents effectively. XMask also simplifies the procedure for translating XML queries into SQL queries by reducing the number of joins required for complex queries.

The rest of the paper is organized as follows. Section 2 describes the outline of our XML management system and discusses the proposed XMask approach. In section 3 we compare the performance of XMask against an intervals approach. Section 4 concludes this paper.

2 XMask: An Enabled XML Management System

The structure of a complete Enabled XML management system is shown figure 1. An RDBMS sits at the heart of this system. The other major components of the system would be XML document's Parsing Manager which parses an XML document and shreds it down based on certain mapping rules and stores it into the RDBMS. The Data Guide is a structure descriptor outside the RDBMS, which provides useful information during translation of XML queries into SQL queries. And finally the XML formatter processes the query result to produce the required format, tags, and/or order.

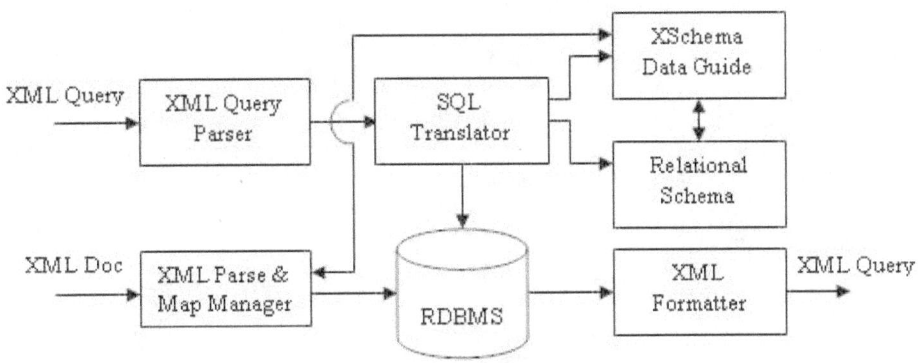

Fig. 1. Structure of an enabled XML management system

2.1 Node ID and Node Mask Approach

The hierarchical structure of an XML document resembles the structure of the World Wide Web, where every computer has a unique identifier (IP address) and a subnet mask, represented using 32-bits. Any two computers are considered to be on the same network (siblings) if and only if they have the same network mask and the same network identifier.

A similar idea can be adapted and modified to identify the nodes of an XML document. Each node in the document will be given an Id and an associated Mask. Since an XML document has some other features that must be preserved (i.e. ancestor-descendent relationship) beside parent-child relationship, the node's identifier and node's mask would be calculated in a different manner using arithmetic and bitwise operations.

Proposal 1: A node N within an XML document can be uniquely identified using two values:

1- Node ID: gives information about the node's local order and the ids of ancestor nodes. In other words, the node ID is the mathematical concatenation of the local sequence for each node on the path from the Root to node N.
2- Node MASK: gives information about how to interpret the Node ID. And it is the mathematical concatenation of the local mask for each node on the path from the Root to node N. The mask is a sequence of zeros and ones with the set bits referring to the positions of new node ids that are concatenated.

For path p1 with sequence (N_0, N_1, N_2...N_k) with local numbering sequence (i_0, i_1, i_2... i_k) and masks (m_0, m_1, m_2...m_k) then the node id for node N_k is $i_0i_1i_2...i_k$ with node mask: $m_0m_1m_2...m_k$.

As example the node id (1.3.7.2) in Dewey representation would be (1.01.001.00), using compressed binary, and the node mask would become (1.10.100.10). The resulting values that would be stored in the database are:

Node id: 10100100
Node Mask: 11010010

Proposal 2: Assuming a node *N* with node ID *I* and node Mask *M* as in proposal 1, the pair *(I, M)* is unique regardless of the starting point of the sequences *I* and *M*. In other words, if the length of *I* is *L* and that implies the length of *M*, and if *I* and *M* are shifted to left by number *K* of units (or right padded by a special number; i.e. 0s or 1s) then the new pair (I_1, M_1) with length $L+K$ is still unique and that will have no impact on the total number of nodes that can be labelled, because only one pair but not both of them can happen in the same document.

2.2 Database Schema

In our solution a fixed database schema is used to store the XML document structure. A basic database schema of three tables is proposed as follows: a table for all possible path combinations in an XML document associated with unique path ids. The Second table contains identification information about all nodes in the document (no attribute nodes). And the third table contains the values for text nodes and attributes; parent nodes will not show up in this table.

***Path** (Path id, PathExp);*
***All nodes** (Node ID, Node Mask, Path id, Forward index);*
***Value** (Node ID, Node Mask, Path id, Value);*

The Forward index in All_nodes table holds the local order for the nodes of the same type (i.e. the same tag value). That might be useful in queries similar to query Q5 in table 1.

2.3 Data Processing and Query Translation

Due to the mismatch between the relational model and XML data model, we use some User Defined Functions to process the data that is stored in the relational database.

XML queries need to be translated into SQL queries. With our model, the translated queries would contain join operations on functions. We can have as many functions as we like, but what we recommend is to carefully determine what to be done by functions (to be more specific when to join on functions) and what to be done by the normal select and join operations. The XMask approach can reduce the number of joins. Due to space limitations, query translation algorithms are not presented in this paper.

3 Performance Evaluation

In order to assess the effectiveness of the node ID and Mask approach, experimental studies have been carried out. The tests were conducted using MYSQL database on 2.7MHz Pentium 4 machine with 256MB RAM. For performance comparison we also implemented XRel the same way it was implemented in [3]. The Bosak's collection for Shakespeare plays [7], 37 documents with 8MB approximate size, was used as the experimental data.

We conducted an experimental study using the same queries that were used in XRel and shown in table 4. We ran every query 10 times. We excluded the first run; then we calculated the average run time for each query.

Table 1. The queries that were used in the test and query performance (seconds)

Query	Query Expression	XRel	XMask
Q1	/PLAY/ACT	0.0012	0.00112
Q2	/PLAY/ACT/SCENE/SPEECH/LINE/STAGEDIR	0.0029	0.00285
Q3	//SCENE/TITLE	0.00355	0.00296
Q4	//ACT//TITLE	0.00379	0.00305
Q5	/PLAY/ACT[2]	0.00185	0.00129
Q6	(/PLAY/ACT)[2]/TITLE	1.06315	0.10787
Q7	/PLAY/ACT/SCENE/SPEECH[SPEEKER='CURIO']	0.0789	0.0008
Q8	/PLAY/ACT/SCENE[//SPEAKER='Steward']/TITLE	0.43588	0.00562

We found that our approach outperformed XRel approach for all complex queries. For simple path queries either for short or long paths as in Q1 and Q2 or for queries with double path notation (//) as in Q3 and Q4, the two systems performed at the same level because they both benefit from the path table.

Q6 is a more complicated order query where the potential tuples are selected based on the document order and not based on the order within the same parent node. XRel did worse than our system due to the number of θ joins. In Q7 and Q8, our system ran faster than XRel because the translated SQL queries for our system contained joins on functions so the query optimizer started with matching tuples from Path table and joined back on All_nodes and Value tables. We also needed fewer numbers of joins.

4 Concluding Remarks

We have described the components of our proposed XML management system. We also proposed a new model-mapping approach called XMask, which is able to maintain the document structure and document order using only two encoded integer values (the node ID and node Mask). As we used the Dewey concept for the node ID we have introduced the Mask concept which makes it possible to label large XML documents using binary sequences and keep these sequences as numeric values rather than strings.

The performance evaluation test showed that our solution outperformed an intervals approach (XRel). Our solution has several advantages: the translation of queries is simpler and the resulting SQL queries contain a fewer number of joins. Second our solution has the ability to identify very large deeply nested documents with a friendly update labeling scheme. Future work will involve extensive performance evaluation against other approaches using established benchmarks.

References

1. Florescu, D. and D. Kossmann, *Storing and Querying XML data using an RDBMS.* IEEE Data Engineering Bulletin, 1999. **22**(3).
2. Li, Q. and B. Moon. *Indexing and Querying XML Data for Regular Path Expressions.* in *The 27th VLDB Conference.* 2001. Roma, Italy.
3. YoshiKawa, A., *XRel: A path-based approach to Storage and Retrieval of XML Documents using Relational Database.* ACM Transactions on Internet Technology, 2001. **1**(1).
4. Cohen, E., H. Kaplan, and T. Milo. *Labeling Dynamic XML Trees.* in *Twenty-first ACM SIGACT-SIGMOD-SIGART Symposium on Principles of Database Systems.* 2002. Madison, Wisconsin, USA.
5. Shanmugasundaram, J., et al., *Storing and Querying Ordered XML Using a Relational Database System*, in *ACM SIGMOD.* 2002. p. 204-215.
6. Zhang, C., et al. *On Supporting Queries in Relational Database Management Systems.* in *SIGMOD.* 2001. Santa Barbara, California USA.
7. Bosak, J., *Shakespeare 2.00.* 1999, http://www.cs.wisc.edu/niagara/data/shakes/shaksper.htm.

Feature Extraction and XML Representation of Plant Leaf for Image Retrieval

Qingfeng Wu, Changle Zhou, and Chaonan Wang

Institute of Artificial Intelligence, Computer Science Department,
Xiamen University, 361005, Fujian, P.R. China
qfwu@xmu.edu.cn

Abstract. Leaf recognition and retrieval plays an important role in plant recognition and retrieval and its key issue lies in whether selected features are stable and have good ability to discriminate different kinds of leaves. From the view of plant leaf morphology, domain-related visual features and semantic features of plant leaf are analyzed and extracted first. Then these features are translated into a hierarchy that is easily represented by XML. On such a basis, the leaf image retrieval system proposed in this paper provides two types of retrieval methods, which could give better precision and flexibility. Experiment results prove the effectiveness of selected features and performance superiority of the leaf image retrieval system.

1 Introduction

The recognition of plant has great significance to explore genetic relationship of plant. However it is a very time consuming task People expect to fulfill the recognition of plant automatically or semi-automatically by computers [1].

As an important organ of plants, recognition of leaves is an important step for plant recognition and most of related work focuses on it [2, 3, 4, 5]. The problem of the above methods lies in the simplicity of the description of leaf feature and the lack of representation of domain-related features of leaves.

The key issue of leaf image retrieval, same as that of plant recognition, is whether extracted features are stable and can distinguish individual leaves. Following this idea, visual features and semantic features are extracted first in this paper to represent leaves. And the visual features include features of shape, margin, and vein of leaf image; Then these features are translated into a hierarchy that is easily and naturally represented by XML; The proposed system in this paper provides two types of image retrieval methods. The prototype of retrieval system has been implemented and the architecture of leaf image retrieval system is described as Fig. 1.

The rest part of the paper is organized as follows. Leaf image features, including domain-related visual features and semantic features, are analyzed and extracted in Section 2. In Section 3 leaf image features are presented by XML and two types of retrieval method in leaf image retrieval system are described. In Section 4, experimental results and discussions are presented. In Section 5, conclusions and further work are given.

H.T. Shen et al. (Eds.): ADWeb 2006, LNCS 3842, pp. 127–131, 2006.

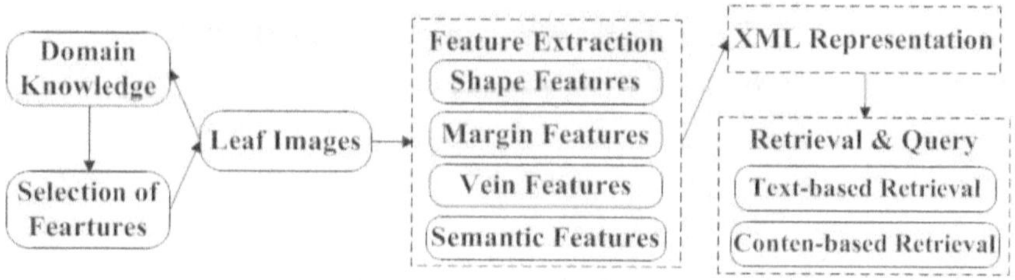

Fig. 1. Architecture of Leaf Image Retrieval System

2 Extraction of Leaf Image Features

Combined with the morphology characteristic of leaves, several domain-related visual features and semantic features are analyzed and extracted in the following.

2.1 Domain-Related Visual Features

Solidity: Solidity expresses the degree of splitting depth in a leaf.

$$Shape\_solidity = \frac{S_1}{S_2}, \tag{1}$$

where, S_1 is the internal area connecting the valley points of leaf dents; S_2 is the external area connecting the top points.

Moment invariants: Classical shape representation uses a set of moments which are invariant to translation, rotation, and scale. This paper adopts moment invariants as shape describer. Please refer to ref. [6] for the detailed formula.

Coarseness: This feature expresses the coarseness of the leaf margin.

$$Margin\_coarseness = \frac{P}{P'}, \tag{2}$$

where, P is the perimeter of leaf contour, and P' is the length of internal border.

In reference [4], modality of leaf venation can be extracted accurately by trained neural network. Based on this work, further features are extracted to present the leaf vein.

Ramification: The number of ramification of the main vein can be used to measure the complexity of venation [7,8]. It is defined as the following Formula 3.

$$Vein\_ramification = \frac{fc_i}{l_i}, \tag{3}$$

where, l_i is the length of main vein, and fc_i is the number of ramification.

Camber: Camber expresses the degree of crook of main vein. $T = \{t_0, t_1, ..., t_n\}$ represents a main vein, and t_{i-1}, t_i, t_{i+1} are the three continuing points. Supposing the positions of t_{i-1} and t_i are determined, t_{i+1} may have seven directions If t_{i-1}, t_i and t_{i+1} are located in a line, the main vein has no turning at the point of t_{i+1}. Otherwise, vein has turning at the point of t_{i+1} [7,8].

Camber is defined as:

$$Vein\_camber = \frac{rn_T}{n+1}, \quad (4)$$

where rn_T is the number of turning of main vein.

2.2 Leaf Semantics

To describe the information of leaf image more accurately, text is also adopted to describe such information as plant name, specie, the collection time, region and so on. Through text descriptions, users can query images based on standard Boolean queries.

3 XML Hierarchical Representation and Leaf Image Retrieval

XML and its associated technologies open new avenues of electronic communications between people and machines. One of the main advantages of XML is that XML format is hierarchical rather than relational which is used in traditional relational database. After the features have been extracted for leaf images, XML files will be generated to represent the leaf hierarchy.

The representation of plant leaf features with a standardized XML format can be parsed and searched by any of the standard XML tools. The searching and comparing of XML files is far superior to HTML in that more context information can be used thus providing far more focused search results.

There are two main image retrieval methods: text-based image retrieval and content-based image retrieval. To meet the different needs of users, the proposed system provides these two retrieval methods.

Text-based Image Retrieval: The XML files can be easily loaded into database by utilizing the XML tools for large-scale leaf retrieval, thus applying the flexibility and power provided by SQL and PL/SQL. Text-based image retrieval allows users to post their queries either simply using keywords or using a form of natural languages [9]. Queries are analyzed and executed automatically. When queries match results, the system will return and automatically transform the retrieval results into the form suitable for the various user environments, such as web browser or mobile browser, using XSLT. In an advanced search, the query is expected to take longer to execute due to the number of extra conditions included in the query, but on the other hand it allows a better accuracy of the search.

Content-based Image Retrieval: Users gather leaf images of unknown plant by digital camera, and input them into the leaf image retrieval system with portable devices such as PDA and notebook PC. Visual features of the query image are extracted and represented by XML. And the visual features are compared with those of all leaf images in the XML file by computing the similarity with Euclidean distance between the features. The existing leaf images are ranked and chosen by the values of the distance. The system automatically transforms the retrieval results into the form suitable for the various user environments.

4 Experiments and Results

4.1 Validity Evaluation of Visual Features

To examine the validity of leaf visual features, neural network is adopted to conduct the task of leaf recognition. The selected neural network has 3 layers, input layer with 11 nodes, hidden layer with 25 nodes and output layer with 6 nodes. Back propagation algorithm is used to train the neural network [10,11]. And minimize the error between real output and expect output by adjusting the weight of connections.

We collected six kinds of plant leaf images, and there are thirty images in each category. These images are separated into the training set and the test set respectively with the ratio of 6:4. The experiment results in Table 1 demonstrate the recognition performance is improved after trained with different size of training set and validate the high ability of extracted visual features to distinguish different kinds of leaves.

Table 1. Recognition Performance of Visual Features with Different Size of Training Set

Plant Species	Recognition Accuracy Rate (%)	
	54 (50%)	108 (100%)
P1	89.6%	92.4%
P2	92.6%	93.8%
P3	88.1%	89.7%
P4	90.3%	94.5%
P5	93.2%	96.6%
P6	94.5%	95.7%

4.2 Experiment of Leaf Image Retrieval

The prototype system has been implemented based on Web with JAVA. The image database contains 4500 leaf images. Experiment results demonstrate that the retrieval methods presented in this paper can achieve retrieval results that are similar to the results from human visual perception.

5 Conclusions

In this paper, from the view of plant morphology, domain-related visual features and semantic features of plant leaf are analyzed and extracted. Features are conveniently and naturally organized by the XML hierarchy. The leaf image retrieval system proposed in this paper provides two types of retrieval methods, which could give better precision and flexibility. From the experimental results, it is shown that the performance of our methods is advantageous.

Our future work will focus on: 1) the extraction of plant leaf from the images with complex background consisting of various objects; 2) the study on XML representation of leaf images for visual data miming.

References

1. Hengnian Qi, Tao Sh., Shuihu Jin: Leaf Characteristics-based Computer-aided Plant Identification Model. Journal of Zhejiang Forestry College. 20(3), (2003) 281-284
2. Im. C., Nishida, H., Kunii T.L.: Recognizing Plant Species by Leaf Shapes- A Case Study of the Acer Family. In Proceedings of IEEE International Con. On Pattern Recognition (1998) 1171-1173
3. Wang Z, Chi Z, Feng D, Wang Q: Leaf Image Retrieval with Shape Features. In: Laurini R. (ed.): Advances in Visual Information Systems. Lecture Notes in Computer Science, vol. 1929. Springer-Verlag, Berlin Heidelberg (2000) 477-487
4. Fu H, Chi Z, Chang J, Fu X: Extraction of Leaf Vein Features Based on Artificial Neural Network-Studies on the Living Plant Identification I. Chinese Bulletin of Botany. 21(4), (2004) 429-436
5. Zhang B., Zhang H.: Content Based Image Retrieval of Standard Tobacco Leaf Database. Computer Engineering and Application.38 (7), (2002) 203-205
6. Ming-Kei Hu: Visual Pattern Recognition by Moment Invariants. IEEE Trans. on Information Theory. 8(2), (1962) 179-187
7. X.S. Zhou, T.S. Huang: Edge-based Structural Features for Content-based Image Retrieval. Pattern Recognition Letters. 22(5), (2001) 457-468
8. J.W Han, L. Guo: A Shape-based Image Retrieval Method Using Salient Edges, Signal Processing: Image Communication. 18(2), (2003) 141-156
9. A. Tam, C.H.C. Lcung: Structured Natural Language Content Retrieval of Visual Materials. Journal of American Society for Information Science and Technology (2001) 930-997
10. B.D.Ripley: Pattern Recognition and Neural Networks. Cambridge University Press (1996)
11. K. Mehrotra, C. K. Mohan, S. Ranka: Elements of Artificial Neural Networks. A Bradford Book, The MIT Press, Cambridge, Massachusetts, London, England (1997)

A XML-Based Workflow Event Logging Mechanism for Workflow Mining

Kwanghoon Kim

Collaboration Technology Research Lab.,
Department of Computer Science,
Kyonggi University
kwang@kyonggi.ac.kr

Abstract. In this paper[1], we propose a XML-based workflow event logging mechanism, and describe the implementation details of the mechanism so as to be embedded into the e-Chautauqua system that has been recently developed by the CTRL research group as a very large scale workflow management system. Finally, we explain how the XML-based workflow event logs will be applied and used to the workflow mining and rediscovery framework.

Keywords: Workflow Event Log Information, XML-based Log Schema, workflow Mining and Rediscovery, Quality of Workflow, EJB-based Very Large-Scale Workflow Management Systems.

1 Introduction

In fact, workflow design and automation technologies are becoming one of the hottest technologies in the enterprize information technology arena, which means that workflow systems have been widely adopted by many organizations with the belief that they enable large organizations to improve dramatically the way they operate, and the evidence that their effectiveness has also come under our observation in numerous deployments. Consequently, according for those workflow design and automation technologies to swiftly grow and be increasingly used by both traditional and newly-formed web-based enterprizes, we need to deal with and attempt to analyze a new and advanced type of requirements and demands concerning workflow intelligence and quality in terms of not only the design-time workflow verification and validation issues but also the runtime workflow execution issues. That is, the newly emerging requirement in recent has been set-up as a new toughest challenge - Quality of Workflow (QOW)[5].

Particularly, many successful large scale workflow customers found out that as they tried to scale up from pilot test mode to enterprize-wide mode, there were severe symptoms of inflexibility, non-recoverability, and non-verifiability.[3][4] That is, it is necessary for the systems to be equipped with advanced features

[1] This work was supported by Grant No. C1-2003-03-URP-0005 from the University Fundamental Research Program of MIC in the Republic of Korea.

H.T. Shen et al. (Eds.): ADWeb 2006, LNCS 3842, pp. 132–136, 2006.

to effectively trace and observe the runtime behaviors of workflow procedures. The event logging mechanism ought to be the right solution for the advanced features like the workflows' runtime behaviors trace and observation, and the workflow quality improvement [5]. Based upon these practical backgrounds and motivations, this paper conceives a workflow execution event logging mechanism and implants it into the e-Chautauqua workflow management system [3] that has recently developed by the author's research group. Especially, in the mechanism, the workflow execution events log information [2][4] being stored by the system's engine components is formatted in XML. That is, we identified all types of events possibly happened in the system, classified them based upon the statuses of workflow instances running on and being managed by the system, and defined their XML schema to represent the log information.

2 The XML-Based Workflow Event Logging Mechanism

As a functional part of the e-Chautauqua workflow management system [3], we have developed a XML-based event logging mechanism. In this section, we describe the functional structure of log agents, and explain about how the engine components take events, generate the events' log message formats, and finally store them on log database. Finally, we also introduce the asynchronous logging message queue mechanism that is used for the engine components to store their event log information formatted in XML.

2.1 Structure of the Mechanism

The functional structure of the workflow event logging mechanism is depicted in Fig. 1. It consists of the following three types of components:

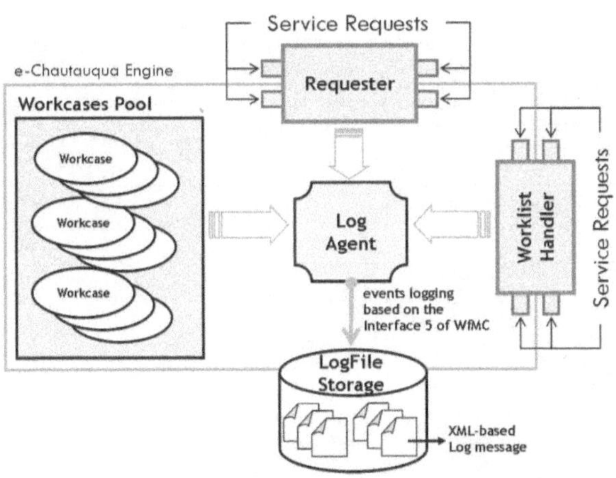

Fig. 1. e-Chautauqua's Events Logging Mechanism

- *Event triggering components* — Requester and Worklist Handler
- *Event formatting components* — Workcase Pool
- *Event logging components* — Log Agent and Log File Storage

The *event triggering components* handle the workflow enactment services requested from workflow clients, and, these services are able to be categorized into three levels of classification — Workcase level class, Running activity level class, and Workitem level class. The *event formatting components* try to compose event log messages according to the service classes after performing the requested services. Finally, the *event logging components*, especially the log agents, take in charge of the responsibility of the event logging mechanism. Once, a log agent receives event logs and then transforms them into XML-based log messages, and store the transformed messages onto the Log File Storage.

2.2 Workflow Events Classification and XML Representation

As shortly explained in the previous section, the workcase components, which are taking a role of the event formatting component, compose event log messages after executing the requested services from the event triggering components —

Table 1. Workcase Level Class's Events Log Message and Its XML Representation

Log Element	XML Tag	Description
WorkcaseLog	<WorkcaseLog> ... </WorkcaseLog>	Event Log on Workcase
WorkcaseID	<WorkcaseID> `workcaseID` </WorkcaseID>	Unique ID of current workcase
ParentWorkcaseID	<ParentWorkcaseID> `ParentWorkcaseID` </ParentWorkcaseID>	Unique ID of initial(parent) workcase
WorkcaseName	<WorkcaseName> `WorkcaseName` </WorkcaseName>	Name of current workcase
State	<State> `State = { INACTIVE | ACTIVE | SUSPENDED | COMPLETED | TERMINATED | ABORTED }` </State>	Current state of workcase
PackageID	<PackageID> `PackageID` </PackageID>	Package ID identifying the definition used for creating this workcase
WorkflowID	<WorkflowID> `WorkflowID` </WorkflowID>	Process Definition ID identifying the definition used for creating this workcase
EventCode	<EventCode> `EventCode = { WMCreatedWorkcase | WMStartedWorkcase | WMChangedWorkcaseState | WMCompletedWorkcase | WMTerminatedWorkcase | WMAbortedWorkcase }` </EventCode>	This message code is associated with event of workcase
EventTimestamp	<EventTimestamp> `EventTimestamp` </EventTimestamp>	Timestamp at the time when the event was recorded
CreatedTimestamp	<CreatedTimestamp> `CreatedTimestamp` </CreatedTimestamp>	Timestamp at the time when the workcase was created
StartTimestamp	<StartTimestamp> `StartTimestamp` </StartTimestamp>	Timestamp at the time when the workcase was started

the requester and the worklist handler. After doing the formatting job, they transmit the formatted event log messages to the event logging components — the log agents. Based on the formatted messages, the log agents form the XML-based event log information. In order to efficiently perform these logging-related jobs, we classify the events into three levels of classes — workcase level event class, running activity level event class, and workitem level event class. Due to the page limitation, only the workcase level event class's message formats and their XML representations are precisely described in Table 1. The detailed names of the events that are captured and logged by the mechanism are summarized as the following:

- *Workcase Level Events* : WMCreatedWorkcase, WMStartedWorkcase, WMChangedWorkcaseState, WMCompletedWorkcase, WMTerminatedWorkcase, WMAbortedWorkcase
- *Running Activity Level Events*: WMChangedActivityInstanceState, WMCompletedActivityInstance, WMTerminatedActivityInstance, WMAbortedActivityInstance
- *Workitem Level Events*: WMAssignedWorkitem, WMGetWorkitem, WMChangedWorkitemState, WMCompletedWorkitem

2.3 XML Schema of the Mechanism

Based upon the workflow event classes and their XML-based message formats, we are able to design a XML schema of the event log information to be used by the log agents. Fig. 2 is to represent the structure, XML schema and samples of the workflow event log information. Especially, because of that we implemented the mechanism as embedded components of e-Chautauqua workflow management system, it was possible to be able to show you the samples in the right-hand side of the figure.

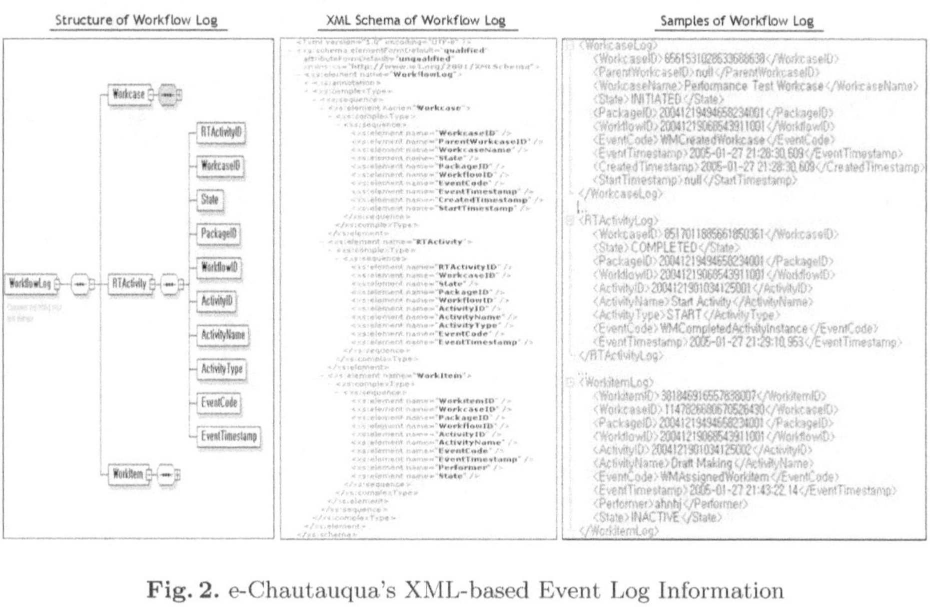

Fig. 2. e-Chautauqua's XML-based Event Log Information

3 Conclusions

In this paper, we have newly proposed the XML-based workflow logging mechanism. And, in order to show that the mechanism properly works in the real computing environment, we have implemented and implanted in the e-Chautauqua workflow management system that has recently implemented by the author's research group. Especially, the event level classes and their XML representations suggested in this paper should have to be a guideline for the XML-based workflow log message formats that are possibly referred by other workflow research groups who have plans to develop such a workflow logging mechanism. In recent, the literature needs various, advanced, and specialized workflow mining techniques and rediscovery algorithms that are used for finally providing feedbacks of their analysis results in order to the redesign and reengineering phase of the existing workflow and business process models. we strongly believe that this work might be one of those impeccable attempts and pioneering contributions for those efforts.

Notes and Comments. This work was supported by Grant No. C1-2003-03-URP-0005 from the University Fundamental Research Program of the Ministry of Information & Communication in the Republic of Korea.

References

1. Workflow Management Coalition Specification Document, "The Workflow Reference Model," Version 1.1, (1994)
2. Workflow Management Coalition Specification Document, "Workflow Management Coalition Audit Data Specification," Version 1.1, Document Number: WFMC-TC-1015, (1998)
3. K. Kim and H. Ahn, "An EJB-based Very Large Scale Workflow System and Its Performance Measurement", The Proceedings of the 6th International Confernece on Web-Age Information Management (LNCS Springer-Verlag), Hangzhou China, (2005, To be Published)
4. W.M.P. van der Aslst, et al, "Workflow Mining: Which processes can be rediscovered?", Technical Report, Department of Technology Management, Eindhoven University of Technology, (2002)
5. K. Kim and C. A. Ellis, "Workflow Reduction for Reachable-path Rediscovery in Workflow Mining", The Foundations and Novel Approaches in Data Mining, Series of Studies in Computational Intelligence, Vol.9, Springer-Verlag (2005)

XML Clustering Based on Common Neighbor

Tian-yang Lv[1,2], Xi-zhe Zhang[1], Wan-li Zuo[1], and Zheng-xuan Wang[1]

[1] College of Computer Science and Technology,
Jilin University, Changchun, China
[2] College of Computer Science and Technology,
Harbin Engineering University, Harbin, China
raynor1979@163.com, zxzok@163.com

Abstract. Clustering on XML documents is an important task. However, it is difficult to select the appropriate parameters' value for the clustering algorithms. By integrating outlier detection with clustering, the paper takes a new approach for analyzing the XML documents by structure distance. After stating the XML tree distance, the paper proposes a new clustering algorithm, which stops clustering automatically by utilizing the outlier information and needs only one parameter, whose appropriate value range can be decided in the outlier mining process. The paper adopts the XML dataset with different structure and other real-life datasets to compare it with other clustering algorithms.

Keywords: XML Structure; Clustering; Common Neighbor.

1 Introduction

It becomes an interesting topic to retrieval information from the semi-structured data. And clustering XML documents according to their structural homogeneity can help in devising indexing techniques for such documents and improving the query plans.

Several works applied clustering algorithms in analyzing XML documents by structure [1, 2]. However, they encounter the following difficulties. First, it is difficult to select appropriate parameter's value for clustering algorithm, because of lacking the valuable prior knowledge of the collected XML documents. Second, current clustering algorithms are short at detecting outliers. Some have no such ability, while others prune the small clusters. This is treating outlier-detection as the byproduct of clustering and cannot mine outliers effectively.

Thus, the paper addresses the problem of clustering structurally similar XML documents and proposes a new strategy that stops clustering automatically according to the dissimilarity degree implied by the detected outliers. It is based on the following observation: with the progressing of clustering, the dissimilarity $D(\boldsymbol{C}_{NN\text{-}A}, \boldsymbol{C}_{NN\text{-}B})$ between the two most similar clusters $\boldsymbol{C}_{NN\text{-}A}$ and $\boldsymbol{C}_{NN\text{-}B}$ is increasing. And the clustering should stop at the moment when $\boldsymbol{C}_{NN\text{-}A}$ and $\boldsymbol{C}_{NN\text{-}B}$ are so diverse from each other. The outlier-mining process can provide that suitable "diverse degree", since outliers are detected according to the great difference from the others.

The rest of paper is organized as follows: after introducing the weighted tree distance in section 2, the paper develops the concept of *common-neighbor* based

H.T. Shen et al. (Eds.): ADWeb 2006, LNCS 3842, pp. 137 – 141, 2006.

outlier and proposes a clustering algorithm As-ROCK. Section 4 applies As-ROCK in analyzing the XML documents and states the comparison experimental results; section 5 summarizes the paper.

2 Weighted Tree Distance of XML

Some researches discuss the topic of computing the distance between XML documents. [1] proposes a method for clustering the DTDs of XML data source based on the similarity of structures and semantics of DTDs. But, it can't be directly applied to XML documents. [2] proposes a clustering technique for schemaless XML documents. Some researches try to extract common structures from XML documents.

This paper modifies the algorithm of [3] to reduce the complexity for computing the distance and exploits the weight label ordered tree in the distance metric. First, nesting reduce: if a node is the same to its ancestor, delete this node and remove its sub-tree to the ancestor, while add one weight to this ancestor; second, repetition reduce: suppose there are *n* repetition nodes at the one level, only the first node remains and set its weight *n*. Thus, we got a weight label ordered tree T_i' which can be considered as a representative of the original XML document. Fig. 1 is an example.

In clustering XML, the paper adopts the following equation to compute the distance, which satisfies the requirement that the similarity is less if data are similar:

$$Sim(T_1,T_2)=1-\frac{S(T_1,T_2)}{Max[S(T_i,T_j)]},\quad S(T_1,T_2)=\frac{D(T_1,T_2)}{D_{\max}(T_1,T_2)} \tag{1}$$

Where $Max[S(T_i,T_j)]$ equals to maximum distance among all XML data. And $D(T_1, T_2)$ is the tree edit distance and $D_{max}(T_1; T_2)$ be the maximum cost between the costs of all possible sequences of tree edit operations that transform T_1 to T_2.

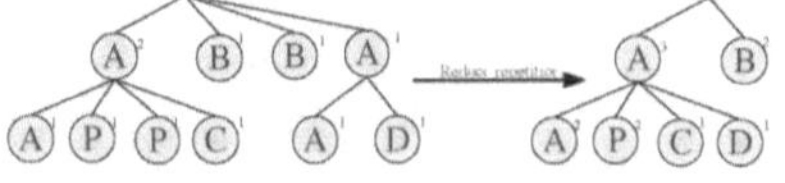

Fig. 1. Construction weight label ordered tree

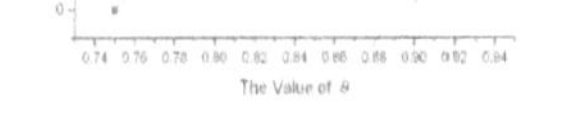

Fig. 2. The vary of n_{out} under different θ

3 The Auto-stopped Algorithm Based on Common Neighbor

This section proposes the new concept of *common-neighbor* based outlier and makes several improvements on ROCK algorithm. Then, the clustering algorithm As-ROCK (Auto-Stopped ROCK) is constructed.

3.1 ROCK Algorithm

The clustering algorithm ROCK is proposed [5] to deal with categorical attribute by adopting the novel concepts of *common neighbor*. Its main idea is as follows: $sim[a_1, a_2] = |a_1 \cap a_2| / |a_1 \cup a_2|$ for data a_1 and a_2; a_1 and a_2 are *neighbor* if $sim(a_1, a_2) \geq \theta$; a_3 is a *common neighbor* of a_1 and a_2, if a_3 is the neighbor of both a_1 and a_2; $link(a_1, a_2)$ is defined as the number of the *common neighbors* of a_1 and a_2. ROCK will first merge the clusters with the largest number of *common neighbors*. Let $link[\boldsymbol{C_i}, \boldsymbol{C_j}]$ be the sum of the number of *common neighbors* of data in C_i and C_j; then

$$D(C_i, C_j) = \frac{link[C_i, C_j]}{(n_i + n_j)^{1+2f(\theta)} - n_i^{1+2f(\theta)} - n_j^{1+2f(\theta)}}, \quad f(\theta) = \frac{1-\theta}{1+\theta} \tag{2}$$

And the way to compute the *common neighbors* of C_{new} and a cluster C_p is:

$$link[C_{new}, C_p] = link[C_i, C_p] + link[C_j, C_p] \tag{3}$$

Although ROCK is good at clustering categorical data, it has several shortcomings: needing the user-specified k; interfered by the outliers before they are pruned.

3.2 Outlier Mining Based on Common Neighbor

In the clustering mechanism based on *common neighbor*, the parameter θ can be used to detect outliers. But this is not fully explored in [5]. Suppose each data corresponds to a node; the weight of the edge linking a_i and a_j equals to $sim(a_i, a_j)$; since all edges with weight less than θ are removed, an appropriate θ will make some data/node isolated from the others. Obviously, these data should be recognized as outliers. Thus, the *common-neighbor based* outlier is defined as follows:

Data a is a *common-neighbor based* outlier, if $\forall\, b$, $link(a, b) = 0$.

For any data a with an edge connected with a *common-neighbor based* outlier o_i, $link(a, b)=0$ for any b except o_i. Thus, an extended definition of outliers is as follows:

Data a is an outlier, if $sim(a, o_i) \geq \theta$ and o_i is a *common-neighbor based* outlier.

3.3 Similarity Between Clusters

In the clustering process, ROCK approximately calculates the *common neighbors* between $\boldsymbol{C}_{new}$ and a cluster $\boldsymbol{C_i}$ according to equation 3. However, in some cases, the sum of $link[\boldsymbol{C}_{NN\text{-}A}, \boldsymbol{C_i}]$ and $link[\boldsymbol{C}_{NN\text{-}B}, \boldsymbol{C_i}]$ is larger than the number n of all data. That is unreasonable in real-life dataset.

Therefore, As-ROCK approximate $link[\boldsymbol{C}_{new}, \boldsymbol{C_i}]$ by evaluating its value range: its lower limit *minLink* equals the smaller one of $link[\boldsymbol{C}_{NN\text{-}A}, \boldsymbol{C_i}]$ and $link[\boldsymbol{C}_{NN\text{-}B}, \boldsymbol{C_i}]$, while its upper limit *maxLink* equals the smaller of $(link[\boldsymbol{C}_{NN\text{-}A}, \boldsymbol{C_i}]+link[\boldsymbol{C}_{NN\text{-}B}, \boldsymbol{C_i}])$ and n. Thus, $link[\boldsymbol{C}_{new},\boldsymbol{C_i}]=(minLink+maxLink)/2$ and $D(\boldsymbol{C}_{new}, \boldsymbol{C_i})$ is computed according to equation 2.

3.4 Automatically Decide θ

The only parameter θ of As-ROCK influences the outlier mining process and the clustering procedure. A method is proposed to determine the appropriate value range of θ: outliers are extremely dissimilar from the others.

In mining the *common-neighbor based* outliers, it means that outliers have much smaller *link* with others, while *link* of normal data are much bigger. Therefore, after outliers are detected, the detected outlier number n_{out} will increases much faster with further increasing of θ. And the appropriate value range of θ should be the stable period of n_{out} before the greatly increase. Fig. 2 is the change of n_{out} under different value of θ for the dataset zoo [8]. The big-jump can be clearly observed at 0.88 and the appropriate value range is [0.82, 0.87].

4 Experiment and Analysis

The XML documents with 8 different kinds of DTDs [6] and 2 real-life datasets Zoo and Vote from [8] are adopted to perform the experimental comparison with ROCK and the algorithm of [7], which is nicknamed as Frozen algorithm.

To measure the clustering results' quality, two criterions of [4] are adopted:

$$Entropy=\sum_{i=1}^{k}\frac{n_i}{N}\left(-\frac{1}{\log q}\sum_{j=1}^{q}\frac{n_i^j}{n_i}\log\frac{n_i^j}{n_i}\right),\quad Purity=\sum_{i=1}^{k}\frac{1}{N}\max_j(n_i^j) \tag{4}$$

n_i^j is the number of data of j th original class assigned to the i th cluster. The better the clustering result, the smaller is the *Entropy* and the bigger is the *Purity*.

The clustering performance of As-Rock, plus the best clustering results of other algorithms under all possible parameters' value, is listed in Table 1 with the appropriate value range of θ and the detected number of outlier etc.. To be more persuasive, let the parameter k of K-Means equal to the number of final clusters of As-Rock. It can be seen that As-Rock is the best for almost each dataset. And the final clusters it obtained is also acceptable comparing to the original class number.

Table 1. The clustering results overview

	Dataset	**Parameter(s)**	***k***	**Entropy**	**Purity**	**Range of θ**
As-ROCK	Zoo	θ=0.86	7	0.0717	0.9394	[0.82,0.86]
	Vote	θ=0.67	8	0.3679	0.9052	[0.57,0.68]
	XML	θ=0.10	11	0.1186	0.8843	[0.10,0.19]
ROCK	Zoo	θ=0.82, k=7	--	0.1046	0.8812	--
	Vote	θ=0.73, k=8	--	0.3988	0.8598	--
	XML	θ=0.70, k=14	--	0.2014	0.8023	--
Frozen	Zoo	α=0.7	10	0.2945	0.7822	--
	Vote	α=0.7	21	0.5220	0.8230	--
	XML	α=1.5	16	0.3041	0.7024	--
K-Means with Random Initial Points	Zoo	k=7	--	0.2816	0.7822	--
	Vote	k=8	--	0.1677	0.8988	--
	XML	k=14	--	0.1453	0.8433	--

5 Conclusion

To overcome the shortcomings of traditional approaches in clustering XML documents, the paper proposes a new auto-stopped clustering algorithm As-Rock, which integrates outlier detection with clustering and needs only one parameter, whose value range can be automatically decided during outlier mining. Experimental results show its good performance for both XML dataset and other datasets.

Acknowledgements

This work is sponsored by the Natural Science Foundation of China under grant number 60373099 and the Natural Science Research Foundation of Harbin Engineering University under the grant number HEUFT05007.

References

1. Lee, M. L., Yang, L. H., Hsu, W., Yang, X.: XClust: Clustering XML Schemas for Effective Integration. Proc. 11th ACM Int. Conf. on Information and Knowledge Management (2002) 292-299
2. Shen, Y., Wang, B.: Clustering Schemaless XML Document. Proc. of the 11th Int. Conf. on Cooperative Information System (2003) 767-784
3. Dalamagas, T., et al., Clustering XML documents by structure, in Methods and Applications of Artificial Intelligence, Proceedings. 2004. p. 112-121.
4. Ying Zhao, George Karypis. Criterion Functions for Document Clustering: Experiment and Analysis. Technical Report #01-40, 2001, University of Minnesota.
5. S. Guha, R. Rastogi, K. Shim. ROCK: a robust clustering algorithm for categorical attributes. In Proc. of the 15th Int'l Conf. on Data Eng., 1999.
6. http://www.cs.wisc.edu/niagara/data.html
7. Ana L.N. Fred, José M.N. Leitão. A new Cluster Isolation criterion Based on Dissimilarity Increments. IEEE Transactions on Pattern Analysis and Machine Intelligence, VOL. 25, No. 8, August 2003: pp944-958.
8. http://www.ics.uci.edu/~mlearn/MLRepository.html

Modeling Dynamic Properties in the Layered View Model for XML Using XSemantic Nets

R. Rajugan[1], Elizabeth Chang[2], Ling Feng[3], and Tharam S. Dillon[1]

[1] eXel Lab, Faculty of IT, University of Technology, Sydney, Australia
{rajugan, tharam}@it.uts.edu.au
[2] School of Information Systems, Curtin University of Technology, Australia
Elizabeth.Chang@cbs.cutin.edu.au
[3] Faculty of Computer Science, University of Twente, The Netherlands
ling@ewi.utwente.nl

Abstract. Due to the increasing dependence on semi-structured data, there exists a requirement to model, design, and manipulate self-describing, schema-based, semi-structured data models (e.g. XML) and the associated semantics at a higher level of abstraction than at the instance level. In this paper, we propose to model dynamic properties of a layered XML view model, at the conceptual level, using eXtensible Semantic (XSemantic) nets.

1 Introduction

Object-Oriented (OO) conceptual modeling offers the power in describing and modeling real-world data semantics and their inter-relationships in a form that is precise and comprehensible to users [1]. Conversely, XML [2] is becoming the dominant standard for storing, describing and interchanging data among various Enterprises Information Systems and databases. With the increased reliance on such self-describing, schema-based, semi-structured data language/(s), there exists a requirement to model, design, and manipulate XML data and the associated semantics at a higher level of abstraction than at the instance level.

However, existing Object-Oriented conceptual modeling languages provide insufficient modeling constructs for utilizing XML schema like data descriptions and constraints, while most semi-structured schema languages lack the ability to provide higher levels of abstraction (such as conceptual models) that are easily understood by humans. To this end, it is interesting to investigate conceptual and schema formalisms as a means of providing higher level semantics in the context of XML-related data engineering. In this paper, we use XML view as a case in point and propose to model dynamic properties of a layered XML view model [3] using eXtensible Semantic (XSemantic) nets.

In data molding, we can group the existing view models into four categories, namely [3]; (a) classical (or relational) views, (b) Object-Oriented (OO) views, (c) semi-structured (namely XML) view models [4-6, 3] and (d) view models for Semantic Web. A comprehensive discussion on existing view models can be found in our work [3]. Here, we focus only on view models for XML.

H.T. Shen et al. (Eds.): ADWeb 2006, LNCS 3842, pp. 142–147, 2006.

Many researchers have attempted to solve semi-structured view models by using graph based [7] and/or semi-structured data models [8, 9]. But, as in the case of relational and OO, the actual view definitions are only available at the lower levels of the implementation and not at the conceptual and/or logical level. Also, it is interesting to note that, of all the XML view models such as in [4, 5, 10, 11, 6], all provide discussion on static properties of views and only one (Active XML views [11]) provides some discussion on capturing, specifying and/or modeling dynamic nature of view properties, that have potential real-world applications in XML data engineering. In the Active XML view system, views are based on simple active rules (using non-standard, declarative ActiveView language) rather than native (XML) data or document centric view definitions. Thus, it is interesting to investigate modeling and specifying dynamic properties for XML views in a systematic manner, similar to that of describing/specifying real-world data objects in OO conceptual models.

The rest of this paper is organized as follows. In section 2 we describes our view model, followed by section 3, where we present the view modeling notation; *XSemantic nets*, with emphasis on modeling dynamic properties. Section 4 concludes the paper with some discussion on our future research directions.

2 Our Work

Our view model for XML comprised of three levels of abstraction, namely [3], *conceptual level, logical or schema level*, and *document or instance level.*

The top conceptual level describes the structure and semantics of views in a way that is more comprehensible to human users. It hides the details of view implementation and concentrates on describing objects, relationships among the objects, as well as the associated constraints upon the objects and relationships. This level can be modelled using some well-established modelling languages such as UML/OCL [12], or our own XML-specific XSemantic nets [13, 14]. The output of this level is a well-defined *valid* conceptual model in UML or XSemantic nets which can be either visual or textual (in the case of XMI models). The middle level of the view model is the schema (or logical) level describes the schema of views for the view implementation, using the XML Schema (XSD) [15] definition language. Views at the conceptual level are mapped into the view schemas at the schema level via the schemata transformation mechanism developed in previous works such as [13, 16]. The output of this level will be in either textual (XSD) or some visual (graph) notations that comply from the schema language. In our previous works such as [3, 17], we have shown how conceptual views are mapped to XSD. This includes mapping UML (view specific) stereotypes, constraints (both UML and XSemantic nets) and constructional constructs (such as bag, set, list etc.) to XSD. The third level is the document or instance level, implies a fragment of instantiated XML data, which conforms to the corresponding view schema defined at the upper level. Here, the *conceptual operators* [18] (and other view dynamic properties) are mapped to language specific query expressions (e.g. XQuery [19]), which are syntax specific.

There are two types of dynamic properties we address in our layered view model, namely; (a) view constructs: These are the sequence of one ore more conceptual operators that constructs the views and (b) internal class methods such as generic and user defined method. In this paper we address only the view constructs and the generic methods and their declarative transformation to query expression.

To illustrate our concepts in this paper, we use the description of a simple Conference Publishing System (CPS) for managing, distributing and archiving conference proceedings such as ACM, LNCS, IEEE etc. The system is similar to that of existing systems such as SpringerLink [20] or IEEE Xplore® [21].

3 Modeling Views with XSemantic Nets

The eXtensible Semantic (XSemantic) net based view design methodology comprised of three design levels: (1) semantic level, (2) schema level and (3) instance level. The aim is to enforce conceptual modeling power of semi-structured data (and views) in order to narrow the gap between real-world objects and XML document structures. The XSemantic net notation used in this paper is shown in Fig. 1.

The first level corresponds to the OO conceptual level and composes of two models, namely, the XML domain model and the XML view model. This level is based on modified semantic network [13] that provides semantic modeling of XML domains. The second level of the proposed methodology is concerned with detailed XML schema design for both domain and view objects defined at the semantic level, including *element/attribute declarations* and *simple/complex type definitions*. The mapping between these two design levels are extension of the schemata transformation proposal stated in [13] and proposed to transform the semantic models into the XML Schema, based on which XML documents can be systematically created, managed, and validated. The third level of the design methodology is concern with detailed query design for the views defined at the semantic level, including query language specific expressions and syntax declarations. The *declarative transformation* between the semantic level and the instance level are proposed to transform valid conceptual operators (and other dynamic properties) into native XML query lanague expressions, such as XQuery FLOWR expressions, Java or SQL 2003/SQLX statements. The resulting query expressions/statements are able to construct imaginary XML documents that can be validated against the XML (view) schemas, developed at the schema level of the design methodology.

The original "modified" semantic network based design methodology for XML was proposed in [13],to enforce conceptual modeling power in XML domains. It was a modified semantic net notation, to model XML domains using Object-Oriented conceptual modeling principles. The modification includes; (i) the removals of cycles in the original semantic network concept and (ii) the addition of clusters [13] (connection, connection cluster and connection cluster set) to realistically capture real-world objects and their properties or descriptions (i.e. attributes constraints etc.). By doing so, the designers can differentiate the different levels of complex and simple nodes that are used to represent real-world *objects* (e.g. PAPER) and their *properties* (e.g. PaperID, Title etc.). Later, in order to model views for XML, the "modified" semantic network was extended (called XML Semantic (XSemantic) net [14]) to include a set of conceptual operators [18] to systemically construct conceptual views from a given collection set of nodes and edges. The conceptual operators include; (i) a set of binary conceptual operators, namely union, intersection, difference Cartesian product and join and (ii) a set of unary conceptual operators, namely projection, selection, rename and restructure.

Since OO models describe both structure and behavior of an object, in order to capture dynamic properties of the views, we further extended XML Semantics nets with a new node type called ***event node***. An example of an *event node* is shown in Fig. 1-3. An *event node* is a node that describes a dynamic property (i.e. methods, messages, or triggers) associated with a complex node, using one more conceptual operators, user defined and/or generic methods (i.e. get, set, update or delete). An event node may be described as; (i) an event node $en \in N_{ode}$, is a 4-tuple, $en = (n_{id}, n_{name}, n_{category}, n_{content})$, (ii) $n_{category}$ indicating if the node is an "*event*" (this is in comparison to "*basic*" or "*complex*" categories), (iii) $n_{content}$ is a textual description of the methods. For example, the select conceptual operator node may be stated as, $n_{content} = \sigma_{paper\text{-}type=\text{"}journal\text{"}}$ and (iv) the parent of the event node is always of type complex. A complex node may have one or more simple nodes that may contain data values. Conversely, each simple node is connected to a complex node (or the root node). Thus, the event nodes associated with a complex node may be able to provide weak encapsulation for accessing and the simple nodes that are connect to the complex node in question. An XML Semantic net model with event nodes is called ***eXtensible Semantic*** (XSemantic) ***net***. A detail discussion on modeling static properties, constraints and relationships of the conceptual views can be found in [13, 17]. Here, we only discuss modeling dynamic properties using XSemantic nets.

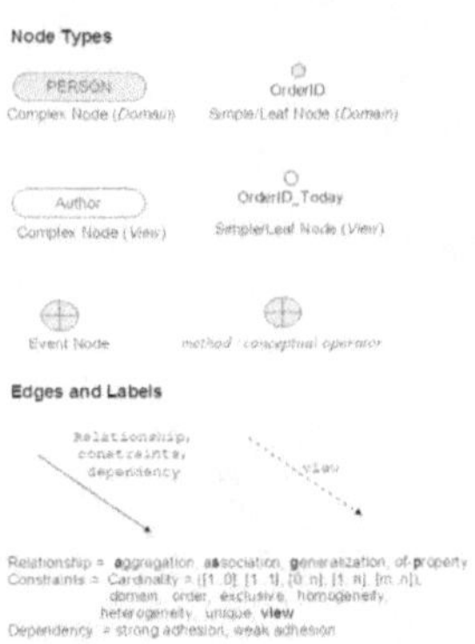

Fig. 1. XSemantic net notation

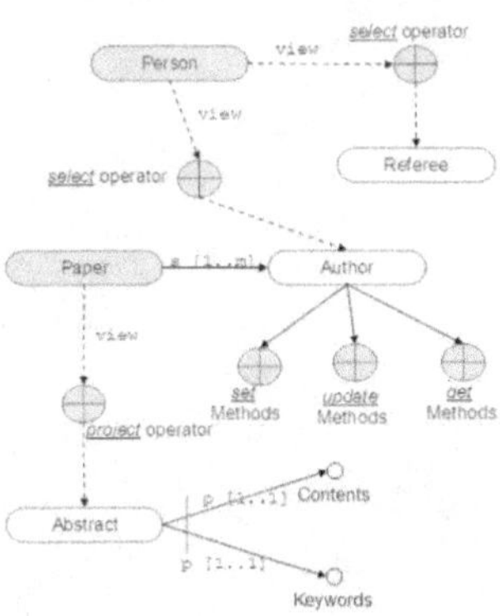

Fig. 2. Generic method examples

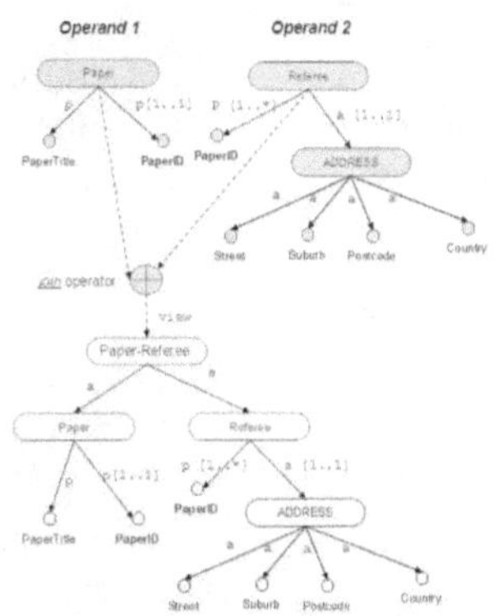

Fig. 3. JOIN operator example

Example 1: In Fig. 2, "`Referee`" is a valid XML conceptual view, named in the context of "`Person`". It is constructed using the conceptual SELECT operator, which can be shown as; $\sigma_{type=\text{"}referee\text{"}}$.

Example 2: In the case of conceptual JOIN operator with join conditions (Fig. 3), where x = `Paper` and y = `Referee/*`; $x \rightarrow_{x.PaperId\,=\,y.paperID}\, y$.

In this paper, we use XQuery as the document view construction language and for generic methods (namely the *get* or *retrieve* methods). However, unlike SQL in relational data model, XQuery standard do not fully support XML data manipulation (for *set* and *update* operations). But, we choose XQuery as it is gaining momentum as the language of choice for XML databases and repositories, and in the future it will support many of the data manipulation features. The following examples demonstrate some of these declarative transformations.

Example 3: To transform the *get* method in the person node (Fig. 2), the following code return a person's first name; `doc ("person.xml")//firstName`.

Example 4: As shown in Fig. 2, the conceptual view operators of the view "`Referee`" can be mapped to the document view construct (XQuery expression) as shown below in the code segment.

```
for     $type in document ("person.xml")//type
where   $type = "referee"
return  <referee> {$role} </referee>
```

Example 5: As shown in example 2 (Fig. 3), we can show the conditional join conceptual operator can be mapped to the following XQuery expression, at the document level as;

```
for     $paper in document ("paper.xml"),
        $ref in document ("referee.xml")
where   $paper//papered = $ref//paperID
return  <join-example> {$paper} <referee> {$ref} </referee> </join-example>
```

4 Conclusion and Future Work

In this paper, we presented a modeling notation to capture dynamic properties in the layered view model using XSemantic nets. We also have shown a declarative transformation of such dynamic properties into document view (query) expressions.

For future work, some issues deserve investigation. First, the investigation of a formal mapping approach to conceptual view (dynamic) properties to query expressions and the automation (including efficient query constructs) of such transformation. Second, is the investigation into dynamic perspectives of the conceptual view formalism that can be applied to traditional data, Semantic Web and web services.

References

1. T. S. Dillon and P. L. Tan, *Object-Oriented Conceptual Modeling*: Prentice Hall, Australia, 1993.
2. W3C-XML, "XML 1.0, (http://www.w3.org/XML/)," 3 ed: The W3C Consortium, 2004.
3. R.Rajugan, E. Chang, T. S. Dillon, and L. Feng, "A Three-Layered XML View Model: A Practical Approach," 24th Int. Conf. on Conceptual Modeling (ER '05), Klagenfurt, Austria, 2005.
4. S. Abiteboul, "On Views and XML," Proc. of the eighteenth ACM PODS '99, USA, 1999.
5. S. Abiteboul, et al., "Active Views for Electronic Commerce," Proc. of Int. Conf. on VLDB, Scotland, 1999.
6. Y. B. Chen, et al., "Designing Valid XML Views," Proc. of the 21st Int. Conf. on ER '02, Tampere, Finland, 2002.

7. Y. Zhuge and H. Garcia-Molina, "Graph structured Views and Incremental Maintenance," Proc. of the 14th IEEE Conf. on Data Engineering (ICDE '98), USA, 1998.
8. S. Abiteboul, et al., "Views for Semistructured Data," Wrk.. on Management of Semistructured Data, USA, 1997.
9. H. Liefke and S. Davidson, "View Maintenance for Hierarchical Semistructured," Proc. of DaWak '00, UK, 2000.
10. S. Cluet, et al., "Views in a Large Scale XML Repository," Proc. of the 27th VLDB Conf. (VLDB '01), Italy, 2001.
11. S. Abiteboul, et al., "Active XML: A Data-Centric Perspective on Web Services," BDA, 2002.
12. OMG-UML™, "UML 2.0 Final Adopted Specification (http://www.uml.org/#UML2.0)," 2003.
13. L. Feng, E. Chang, and T. S. Dillon, "A Semantic Network-based Design Methodology for XML Documents," *ACM Transactions on Information Systems (TOIS)*, vol. 20, No 4, pp. 390 - 421, 2002.
14. R.Rajugan, et al., "Semantic Modelling of e-Solutions Using a View Formalism with Conceptual & Logical Extensions," 3rd Int. IEEE Conf. on INDIN '05, Perth, Australia, 2005.
15. W3C-XSD, "XML Schema (http://www.w3.org/XML/Schema)," vol. 2004, 2 ed: W3C, 2001.
16. L. Feng, E. Chang, and T. S. Dillon, "Schemata Transformation of Object-Oriented Conceptual Models to XML," *Int. Journal of Computer Systems Science & Engineering*, vol. 18, No. 1, pp. 45-60, 2003.
17. R.Rajugan, et al., "Alternate Representations for Visual Constraint Specification in the Layered View Model," The Int. Conf. on Information Integration and Web Based Applications & Services (iiWAS '05), Malaysia, 2005.
18. R.Rajugan, E. Chang, T. S. Dillon, and L. Feng, "A Layered View Model for XML Repositories & XML Data Warehouses," The 5th Int. Conf. on Computer and Information Technology (CIT '05), Shanghai, China, 2005.
19. W3C-XQuery, "XQuery 1.0 (http://www.w3.org/XML/Query): The World Wide Web Consortium (W3C), 2004.
20. Springer, "SpringerLink: http://www.springerlink.com," Springer, 2005.
21. IEEE, "IEEE Xplore®: http://ieeexplore.ieee.org," Rel 1.8 ed: IEEE, 2004.

VeriFLog: A Constraint Logic Programming Approach to Verification of Website Content

Jorge Coelho[1] and Mário Florido[2]

[1] Instituto Superior de Engenharia do Porto & LIACC
[2] University of Porto, DCC-FC & LIACC,
Rua do Campo Alegre, 823, 4150-180 Porto, Portugal
Tel. +351 2260778830, Fax. +351 226003654
{jcoelho, amf}@ncc.up.pt

Abstract. Web site semantic content verification can be a tedious and error prone task. In this paper we propose a framework for syntactic validation and semantic verification based on the logic programming language XCentric. The high declarative model of this language based on a new unification algorithm along with an interface to semistructured data provides an elegant framework for semantic error detection. The result is an easy to follow model to improve website quality and management.

1 Introduction

Managing the semantic content of a website is not easy and it is even harder when it is built by many different persons. Consider for example a website of a university. There, different persons such as, teachers and administrative staff have access to some part of the website, for example their homepage. The website manager or the university administration may impose some constraints in the website construction, for example, every person must have his/her curriculum in his/her homepage or every teacher must have information about his/her teaching activities. Verifying these constraints may be a difficult task when we have a high number of pages to look up. Another question arises from usefulness of the information available in the website: can it be used to infer more information? For example, in our research laboratory, technical reports and other publications are added to a central web page. It is desirable to infer some statistical data about scientific production activities. Both of these tasks can be accomplished by a logic-based language with an interface to semistructured data and an inference engine to impose semantic constraints and infer new data.

In this work we propose a framework for web site verification based on a constraint-logic programming language named XCentric [3]. This language achieves a high level of expressivity through a new unification model based on flexible arity function symbols and sequence variables. It provides a very pleasant way to query data in html/xml documents and to write verification rules. The framework works by translating documents to terms (an internal representation for documents), and then optionally applying syntactic validation, verifying semantics and inferring new data. All the different modules are implemented in

H.T. Shen et al. (Eds.): ADWeb 2006, LNCS 3842, pp. 148–156, 2006.

XCentric which is built on top of SWI-Prolog [11], thus the programmer can use all the potential of SWI-Prolog in addition to XCentric.

As motivation, consider the following simple example: suppose we want to verify if the teachers of our university have in their XML-based home pages a correct email address. We have an XML file generated from our database with their data and can use the following code:

```
check(N,URL):-
    http2pro(URL,T),
    T =*= hpage(_,email(E),_),
    xml2pro('dbase.xml',DB),
    DB =*= db(_,record(name(N),_,email(E),_),_).
```

This program, starts by using *http2pro* to retrieve from the web address in *URL* the XML code, translating it to an internal notation and storing it in variable *T*. Then the non-standard unification operator =*= is used to find the teacher's email and store it in variable *E*. Note that the anonymous variable '_' allows the programmer to ignore parts of the document (this is not possible with standard unification). Using *xml2pro* the database file is translated to the internal representation and stored in variable *DB*. Then the record of the teacher named *N* is searched and the program succeeds only if both the email found in the web page and the one found in the database are the same. We can easily generalize the program to accept a list of teachers, verify the entire website and output error messages.

In the rest of the paper we assume that the reader is familiar with logic programming ([10]) and XML ([13]).

We start in section 2 by presenting terms with flexible arity symbols and sequence variables. Then, in section 3 we present our framework along with some examples. In section 4 we propose XCentric as the intermediate language for another language based in XML itself. Then, in section 5 we present related work and in section 6 we conclude.

2 Terms with Flexible Arity Symbols and Sequence Variables

Here we present briefly the concept behind XCentric along the lines presented in [4].

2.1 Constraint Logic Programming

Constraint Logic Programming (CLP) [7] is the programming paradigm used in a class of languages based on rule-based constraint programming. Each different language is obtained by specifying the domain of discourse and the functions and relations on the particular domain. This framework extends the logic programming framework because it extends the Herbrand universe, the notion of *unification* and the notion of equation, accordingly to the new computational domains. A complete description of the major trends of the fundamental concepts about CLP can be found in [7].

2.2 XCentric

XCentric extends Prolog with terms with flexible arity symbols and sequence variables. We now describe the syntax of XCentric programs and their intuitive semantics.

In XCentric we extend the domain of discourse of Prolog (trees over uninterpreted functors) with finite sequences of trees.

Definition 21. *A* sequence $\tilde{t}$, *is defined as follows:*

- ε *is the empty sequence.*
- $t_1, \tilde{t}$ *is a sequence if* t_1 *is a term and* $\tilde{t}$ *is a sequence*

Example 21. *Given the terms* $f(a)$, b *and* X, *then* $\tilde{t} = f(a), b, X$ *is a sequence.*

Equality is the only relation between trees. Equality between trees is defined in the standard way: two trees are equal if and only if their root functor are the same and their corresponding subtrees, if any, are equal.

We now proceed with the syntactic formalization of XCentric, by extending the standard notion of Prolog term with flexible arity function symbols and sequence variables.

We consider an alphabet consisting of the following sets: the set of standard variables, the set of sequence variables (variables are denoted by upper case letters), the set of constants (denoted by lower case letters), the set of fixed arity function symbols and the set of flexible arity function symbols.

Definition 22. *The set of terms over the previous alphabet is the smallest set that satisfies the following conditions:*

1. *Constants, standard variables and sequence variables are terms.*
2. *If* f *is a flexible arity function symbol and* $t_1, \ldots, t_n$ $(n \geq 0)$ *are terms, then* $f(t_1, \ldots, t_n)$ *is a term.*
3. *If* f *is a fixed arity function symbol with arity* n, $n \geq 0$ *and* $t_1, \ldots, t_n$ *are terms such that for all* $1 \leq i \leq n$, t_i *does not contain sequence variables as subterms, then* $f(t_1, \ldots, t_n)$ *is a term.*

Terms of the form $f(t_1, \ldots, t_n)$ where f is a function symbol and $t_1, \ldots, t_n$ are terms are called *compound terms.*

Definition 23. *If* t_1 *and* t_2 *are terms then* $t_1 = t_2$ *(standard Prolog unification) and* $t_1 = * = t_2$ *(unification of terms with flexible arity symbols) are constraints.*

A constraint $t_1 = * = t_2$ or $t_1 = t_2$ is solvable if and only if there is an assignment of sequences or ground terms, respectively, to variables therein such that the constraint evaluates to *true*, i.e. such that after that assignment the terms become equal.

Remark 21. *In what follows, to avoid further formality, we shall assume that the domain of interpretation of variables is predetermined by the context where they occur. Variables occurring in a constraint of the form* $t_1 = * = t_2$ *are interpreted in the domain of sequences of trees, otherwise they are standard Prolog variables. In XCentric programs, therefore, each predicate symbol, functor and variable is used in a consistent way with respect to its domain of interpretation.*

XCentric programs have a syntax similar to Prolog extended with the new constraint $=*=$. The operational model of XCentric is the same of Prolog.

2.3 Constraint Solving

Constraints of the form $t_1 = * = t_2$ are solved by a non-standard unification that calculates the corresponding minimal complete set of unifiers. Details about the implementation of this non-standard unification can be found in [3]. As motivation we present some examples of unification:

Example 22. *Given the terms $f(X, b, Y)$ and $f(a, b, b, b)$ where X and Y are sequence variables, $f(X, b, Y) = * = f(a, b, b, b)$ gives three results:*

1. $X = a$ *and* $Y = b, b$
2. $X = a, b$ *and* $Y = b$
3. $X = a, b, b$ *and* $Y = \varepsilon$

Example 23. *Given the terms $f(b, X)$ and $f(Y, d)$ where X and Y are sequence variables, $f(b, X) = * = f(Y, d)$ gives two possible solutions:*

1. $X = d$ *and* $Y = b$
2. $X = N, d$ *and* $Y = b, N$ *where N is a new sequence variable.*

Note that this non-standard unification is conservative with respect to standard unification: in the last example the first solution corresponds to the use of standard unification. Soundness and completeness of this non-standard unification were proved in [8] and [4].

2.4 XML Processing

In XCentric an XML document is translated to a term with flexible arity function symbol. This term has a main functor (the root tag) and zero or more arguments. Although our actual implementation translates attributes to a list of pairs, since attributes do not play a relevant role in this work we will omit them in the examples, for the sake of simplicity. Consider the simple XML file presented bellow:

```
<addressbook>
        <record>
                <name>John</name>
                <address>New York</address>
                <email>john.ny@mailserver.com</email>
        </record>
    ...
</addressbook>
```

The equivalent term is:

```
addressbook(record(name('John'),address('New York'),
                   email('john.ny@mailserver.com')),...)
```

Example 24. *Suppose that the term Doc is the XCentric representation of the document "addressbook.xml". If we want to gather the names of the people living in New York we can simply solve the following constraint:*

$$Doc = * = addressbook(\_, record(name(N), address('New\ York'), \_), \_).$$

All the solutions can then be found by backtracking.

Note that '_' is an unnamed sequence variable which unifies with any sequence. Further details and examples can be found in [3, 4].

3 Website Verification Framework

The main idea of this work is to provide an interface to semistructured data, syntactic validation and use XCentric as the rule language for semantic verification. By semantic verification we mean verifying if the content of a website is correct with relation to a given criteria. For example, we have a web page with all the staff of the department grouped by category (Senior researcher, Phd researcher, Researcher and Assistant researcher), one verification we can do, is searching for people catalogued as one of the above mentioned categories but that doesn't belong to that category.

With our framework the programmer can also use the high declarative model of XCentric to infer new knowledge from web pages. For example, if every researcher of our department has its own publications in his/her homepage we can easily retrieve this data and get new statistical data from it, for example, how many publications in journals and international conferences by year.

3.1 Examples

Due to space limitations, we only present some simple examples of how this framework can be used. We encourage the reader to test the full versions of these examples and many others available at:

`http://www.ncc.up.pt/~jcoelho/veriflog/examples.html`.

There are four ways to retrieve HTML/XML data: directly from the web using *http2pro(URL, Term)*; directly from the web with validation using *http2pro(URL, DTDFile, Term)*, where the file in *URL* is validated against the DTD given in *DTDFile*; from an xml file using *xml2pro(XMLFile, Term)* and from an xml file with validation using *xml2pro(XMLFile, DTDFile, Term)*.

Example 31. *In our department website we have an HTML page with a list of technical reports indexed by year. A similar page can be found in* `http://www.ncc.up.pt/~jcoelho/veriflog/examples/techreports.html`. *Suppose that we want to know if some publications are out of place with respect to the year of publication. We can simply do:*

```
verify(URL):-
     http2pro(URL,TR),
     TR =*= html(_,body(_,h4(Y1),Seq,h4(Y2),_),_),
     atom_number(Y1,N1),atom_number(Y2,N2),
     N2 is N1 - 1,write('Year: '),write(Y1),nl,
     process(Seq,Y1).

process(Seq,Y):-
      Seq =*= ul(_,li(C),_),
      not(substring(Y,C)),write(C).
```

We start by using http2pro/2 to translate the web page given in variable URL into its internal representation, then we get the sequences of elements (variable Seq), between two adjacent years (variables Y1 and Y2). Note that the way we use variables (unifying with zero or more elements) is not the standard way in Prolog but very useful for XML queries:

```
TR =*= html(_,body(_,h4(Y1),Seq,h4(Y2),_),_),
```

We then check if some string (variable C) describing a technical report does not include the year that indexes that report (variables '_' are used to ignore sequences of elements):

```
Seq =*= ul(_,li(C),_),
not(substring(Y,C)),
```

Running this program over the previously mentioned web page will present the following output:

```
Year: 2005
Year: 2004
Sandra Alves and Mario Florido. Type Inference for Programming
Languages: A Constraint Logic Programming Approach, Technical
Report DCC -  FC & LIACC, Universidade do Porto
```

Meaning that for the year 2004 it was found one publication that doesn't have a reference to the year it was published or the year is different from 2004.

Example 32. *Given a teacher homepage, for example this one:*

```
<teacher>
   <name>Mario</name>
   <phone>+351 123456789</phone>
   <email>amf@ncc.up.pt</email>
   <courses>
     <name>Compilers</name>
   </courses>
</teacher>
```

We want to know if it includes information about the classes he teaches. We get that information from our database (in an XML file) and compare both:

```
DBase =*= staff(_,teacher(_,name(N),_,courses(_,class(C),_),_),_),
write('Database: '),write(C),
XML =*= teacher(_,name(N),_,courses(_,name(C),_),_),
write('>Found in XML<'),nl.
```

Here we query the database file stored in variable DBase *and for each teacher we store his name in variable* N *and the classes he teaches one by one in variable* C. *Then, we query the teacher homepage, stored in variable* XML *trying to find the same classes which were found in the database. The output follows:*

```
Database: Compilers >Found in XML<
Database: Logic
Database: Programming Languages
```

Meaning that, from the three courses found in the database only Compilers *was found in the teacher homepage. This can be easily generalized to a set of teachers (using http2pro/2 to retrieve each ones data).*

4 XCentric as an Intermediate Language

Although a lot of the framework power is inherited from XCentric itself, a user less experienced with logic programming but used to XML can have some trouble figuring out how to do verification. However, note that our framework can be used as an intermediate language for another language based in XML itself. We can build an XML-like syntax for a new language and then translate it to our framework. For example, given the following query in a language similar to the one presented in [5]:

```
<pubs>
  _
  <pub>
       _
       <publisher> X </publisher>
       _
  </pub>
  _
</pubs>
=> X
```

This can be translated to our framework as (note that '_' ignores sequences of elements):

```
XML =*= pubs(_,pub(_,publisher(X),_),_).
```

Due to the power of constraint solving for terms with arbitrary arity, XCentric revealed to be a better language than Prolog as the target of a pre-processing step for XML based verification language such as [5].

5 Related Work

Imposing criteria in website creation using logic programming approach was addressed in several previous works. In [5] the author proposed the use of a simple pattern-matching-based language and its translation to Prolog as a framework for website verification. Our work also uses Prolog but our syntax smoothly integrates with it, thus our framework inherits all the power of Prolog. We also provide a richer interface to semistructured data. In [12] logic was proposed as the rule language for semantic verification, there the authors provide a mean for introducing rules in a graphical format. In contrast, our work provides a powerful programming language and thus a richer and more flexible way to write rules. In [1] it was presented a rewriting-based framework that uses simulation [6] in order to query terms, this was a new rewriting-based language quite different from ours. In [9] the author proposed an algorithm for website verification similar to [2] in expressiveness but based in a different theoretical approach. The idea was to extend sequence and non-sequence variable pattern matching with context variables, allowing a more flexible way to process semistructured data but the author doesn't provide an implementation.

6 Conclusion

Our main contribution is a framework for website verification applying concepts from a language that revealed to be quite appropriate for this task (this is shown by the quite simple code presented in this paper to perform some standard verification tasks). We presented examples of application and proposed the use of this framework as an intermediate language where a more "XML-programmer friendly" language is used on top of the framework. As far as we know this is the most complete approach to website verification based in logic programming in the sense that it integrates an interface to semi structured data, syntactic validation and semantic verification. We are now working to improve our work namely by building an automatic website crawler and a graphical interface in order to increase the ease of use of this tool. Another novelty of this approach is that it smoothly integrates with Prolog and thus it inherits all the power of the language. Moreover we are convinced that XML-based websites will increase in number in the next years increasing the utility of verification tools such as VeriFLog.

References

1. M. Alpuente, D. Ballis, and M. Falaschi. A Rewriting-based Framework for Web Sites Verification. In *Electronic Notes in Theoretical Computer Science*, pages 41–61. Elsevier Science, 2005.
2. F. Bry and S. Schaffert. Towards a Declarative Query and Transformation Language for XML and Semistructured Data: Simulation Unification. In *International Conference on Logic Programming (ICLP)*, volume 2401 of *LNCS*, 2002.
3. Jorge Coelho and Mário Florido. CLP(Flex): Constraint Logic Programming Applied to XML Processing. In *Ontologies, Databases and Applications of SEmantics (ODBASE)*, volume 3291 of *LNCS*. Springer Verlag, 2004.
4. Jorge Coelho and Mário Florido. CLP(Flex): Constraint logic programming applied to XML processing. Technical Report 06, DCC-FC, LIACC. University of Porto, (available from www.ncc.up.pt/~jcoelho/clpflex.pdf), July 2004.

5. Thierry Despeyroux. Practical semantic analysis of web sites and documents. In Stuart I. Feldman, Mike Uretsky, Marc Najork, and Craig E. Wills, editors, *WWW*, pages 685–693. ACM, 2004.
6. Monika Rauch Henzinger, Thomas A. Henzinger, and Peter W. Kopke. Computing simulations on finite and infinite graphs. In *FOCS*, pages 453–462, 1995.
7. Joxan Jaffar and Michael J. Maher. Constraint logic programming: A survey. *Journal of Logic Programming*, 19/20:503–581, 1994.
8. T. Kutsia. Unification with sequence variables and flexible arity symbols and its extension with pattern-terms. In *Joint AICS'2002 - Calculemus'2002 conference*, LNAI, 2002.
9. Temur Kutsia. Context sequence matching for xml. In *Proceedings of the 1th International Workshop on Automated Specification and Verification of Web Sites*, pages 103–119, Valencia, Spain, 14–15 March 2005.
10. J. W. Lloyd. *Foundations of Logic Programming*. Springer-Verlag, second edition, 1987.
11. SWI Prolog. http://www.swi-prolog.org/.
12. Frank van Harmelen and Jos van der Meer. Webmaster: Knowledge-based verification of web-pages. In Ibrahim F. Imam, Yves Kodratoff, Ayman El-Dessouki, and Moonis Ali, editors, *IEA/AIE*, volume 1611 of *Lecture Notes in Computer Science*, pages 256–265. Springer, 1999.
13. Extensible Markup Language (XML). http://www.w3.org/XML/, 2003.

Bandwidth Guaranteed Multi-tree Multicast Routing in Wireless Ad Hoc Networks

Huayi Wu[1], Xiaohua Jia[1,2], Yanxiang He[1] and Chuanhe Huang[1]

[1] Computer School of Wuhan University
whylei429@hotmail.com
[2] Dept of Computer Science, City University of Hong Kong
jia@cs.cityu.edu.hk

Abstract. This paper investigates the issues of QoS multicast routing in wireless ad hoc networks. Due to limited bandwidth of wireless nodes, a QoS multicast call will be blocked if there does not exist a single multicast tree that has the requested bandwidth, even though there is enough bandwidth in the system to support the call. We propose a new QoS multicast routing scheme that uses multiple trees. The aggregate bandwidth of multiple trees can meet the bandwidth requirement and the delay from the source to the farthest destination node shall not exceed a pre-specified bound. Two strategies for constructing multiple trees are studied. The simulation results show that the new scheme significantly improves the request success rate and makes a better use of network resources.

1 Introduction

Mobile Ad hoc Networks (MANETs) are collections of wireless mobile nodes constructed dynamically without the use of any existing network infrastructure or centralized administration [1]. QoS multicast routing is to find a multicast tree rooted from the source and spanning to all destinations and every internal path satisfies the QoS requirements. Many advanced MANET applications require QoS multicast such as multimedia meeting or real-time data dissemination.

Many multicast protocols have been proposed for MANETs. 1) Proactive methods, such as the AMRoute [2], the FGMP [3] and the MCEDAR [4]; 2) Reactive methods, such as the ODMRP [5, 6] and the MAODV [7]; 3) Hybrid methods, such as the ZRP [8]. Some multi-path protocols for MANETs have been proposed in [9-13]. Some other multicast protocols like [14-16] use multi-tree methods. The RoMR protocol in [14] builds multiple reliable multicast trees that adapt to dynamic topology changes. Studies in [15, 16] use multiple subtrees in WDM networks.

In a MANET, there may not exist a single multicast tree that meets the QoS requirements due to the limited bandwidth and a call could be blocked. In [17], a multi-path multicast routing scheme was proposed to improve the success rate of calls. In this paper, we propose a new multicast routing scheme that directly utilizes multiple trees to meet the bandwidth requirement of a single QoS call.

The rest of the paper is organized as follows. In Section 2, we present the formulation of the problem. Section 3 describes the new multi-tree multicast routing protocol

H.T. Shen et al. (Eds.): ADWeb 2006, LNCS 3842 , pp. 157 – 166, 2006.

and different routing strategies are presented in Section 4. Simulation results and analysis are discussed in the Section 5. Finally, Section 6 concludes the paper.

2 Problem Formulation

In this paper, we assume the MAC sub-layer adopts the CDMA-over-TDMA channel model [18]. In CDMA, each node uses a pre-assigned code for communication with neighbours in a conflict free fashion [19]. The transmission and reception between two neighbours are governed by the TDMA model, where a time frame is divided into fix-sized timeslots. Fig. 1. (b) shows a good case of slot assignment. The timeslot assignment algorithm on a path follows the method proposed in [18].

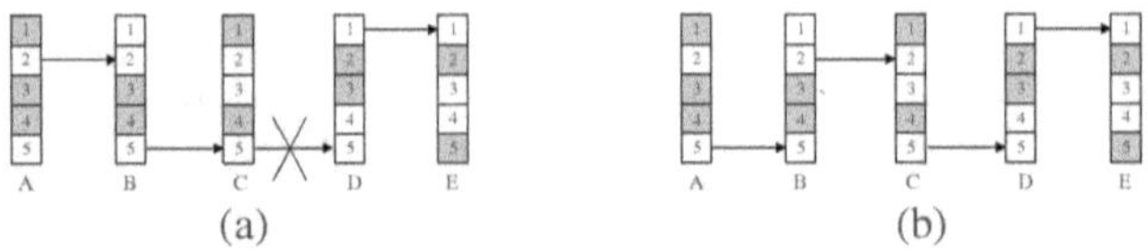

Fig. 1. Two examples of timeslot assignment (timeslots in grey are occupied)

The topology of the network is modeled as a directed graph $G = (V, E)$ with positive edge costs (the available bandwidths of the links).

Definition 1. The available bandwidth of a link $b(l)$ is the number of free timeslots over the link.

Definition 2. The available bandwidth of a path, called the bandwidth of the path, is the minimum bandwidth of the links in the path.

Definition 3. The available bandwidth of a tree, called the bandwidth of the tree, is the minimum bandwidth of the links in the tree.

Definition 4. The network cost of a path P is defined as the value of the bandwidth times the number of hops of P:

$$c(P) = B(P) \times H(P), \tag{1}$$

where $B(P)$ and $H(P)$ are the bandwidth and the number of hops of P, respectively.

Definition 5. The network cost of a multicast tree T is defined as the value of its bandwidth times the total number of hops (i.e., links) in T:

$$c(T) = B(T) \times H(T)\ , \tag{2}$$

where $B(T)$ and $H(T)$ are the bandwidth and the number of hops of T, respectively.

Notice that the actual *bandwidth consumed* over a tree is the bandwidth reserved for the tree, which is less than or equal to the *available bandwidth*.

Definition 6. The delay of a tree, denoted by $d(T)$, is the number of hops from the root to the farthest leaf node in T.

In our multi-tree routing scheme, multiple trees are used in parallel to transmit data for one multicast communication.

Our problem is: given a QoS multicast request from source s to a set of destinations $D=\{ d_j | 1\leq j\leq m \}$ with bandwidth requirement B and delay bound Δ, to find a set of subtrees $T=\{ T_i | 1\leq i\leq k \}$, where each T_i is a tree rooted from s and spanning to all nodes in D, such that the following objective is achieved:

$$Min\sum_{i=1}^{k} c(T_i)\,, \tag{3}$$

subject to:

$$\sum_{i=1}^{k} B(T_i) = B \tag{4}$$

$$\sum_{i=1}^{k} \delta_l B(T_i) \leq b(l),\ \text{where } \delta_l = \begin{cases} 1, \text{if } l\in T_i, \\ 0, \text{otherwise.} \end{cases} \quad (l\in E) \tag{5}$$

$$\forall T_i \in T\ ,\ d(T_i)\leq \Delta \tag{6}$$

3 Multi-tree Multicast Routing Protocol

At first, when a source node receives a request from the application layer to set up a QoS multicast connection to a group of destination nodes with bandwidth requirement B and maximal delay bound Δ, it prepares a RR (route-request) packet by setting the *TTL* (time to live) value in the packet to Δ and floods the RR packet to its neighbors. When a node receives a RR packet, it checks if there is any common free timeslot between the last hop-sender and this node. If not, the RR packet is dropped. Otherwise, if the RR packet is received by the first time, this node appends its own address to the RR packet, decreases *TTL* by one and refloods this RR packet out. This operation is repeated node by node until *TTL* is reduced to zero. If the RR packet was received before, this node will record the information about this path, but will not reflood the packet. It will wait either for a pre-specified timeout or the reception of a certain number of RR packets, and send back a RP (route-reply) packet including all the information about multiple paths going through it.

When a destination node receives the first RR packet, it will wait either for a pre-specified timeout or the reception of a certain number of RR packets, and then sends back a RP packet to the source via the shortest path. If the source cannot receive any more RP packets, the route reply phase completes. The source has the picture of a *partial network topology* to all destinations. There is no need for the source to maintain the information about the global network topology. Fig. 2 is an example of such a partial network graph, where S is the source and C, E, J and N are destination nodes. The integer number represents the bandwidth of the link. Our routing algorithms are based on this partial topology G.

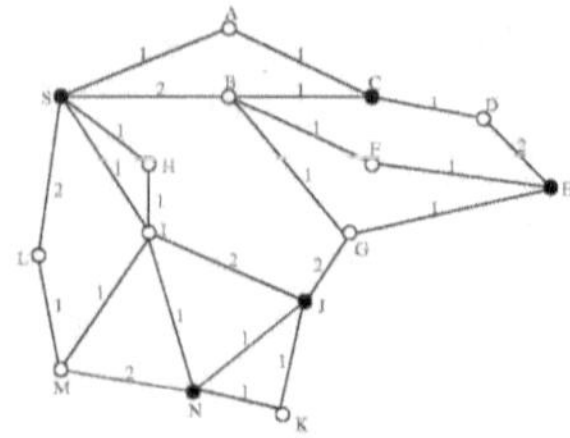

Fig. 2. A partial network graph discovered in route discovery and reply phases

4 Multi-tree Multicast Routing Algorithms

When the source node learned the partial network topology towards all destinations, it computes multiple suitable trees for the multicast communication. We propose two strategies for constructing multiple trees, namely MSPT and MMST.

If a multicast tree meeting the QoS requirements does not exist, a call will be blocked in a single tree scheme. The MSPT heuristic will continue to search for SPTs until the aggregate bandwidth of all the SPTs can satisfy B.

We assume that the bandwidth requirement is 2 and the delay bound is 5. The source first finds a SPT of G as shown in Fig. 3. (a). The bandwidth of the SPT is 1 that is less than the requirement. The source continues to find a second SPT as shown in Fig. 3. (b). The aggregate bandwidth of the two SPTs meets the requirement.

MSPT Algorithm

Input: partial topology $G = (V, E)$ and a multicast request $(s, D, B, \bullet)$.

Output: A set of shortest path trees $T=\{T_i \mid 1 \le i \le k\}$.

While $(\sum_{i=1}^{k} B(T_i) < B)$ && (G is connected) **do**

Find a shortest path tree T_{k+1} of G rooted from s and spanning to D;

Reserve $B(T_{k+1})$;

Deduct the reserved bandwidth from the available bandwidth of all links in T_{k+1};

Remove from G the links that has no more bandwidth;

$k=k+1$;

End-while

The MMST heuristic is based on the minimum spanning tree heuristic. The basic idea of the MMST heuristic is to keep on computing an MST of G' and to reserve the bandwidth of the MST until all destinations have enough bandwidth to flow data in.

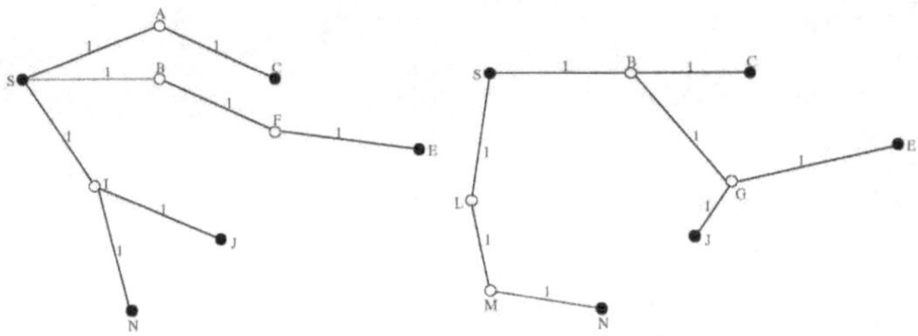

(a) (b)

Fig. 3. Multiple shortest path trees

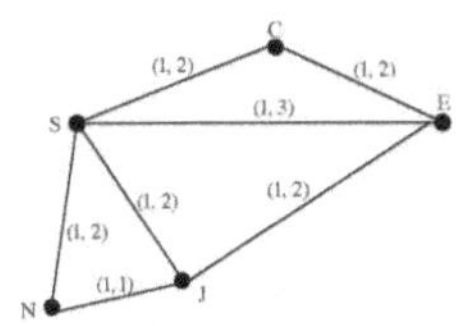

Fig. 4. Induced graph G' derived from G

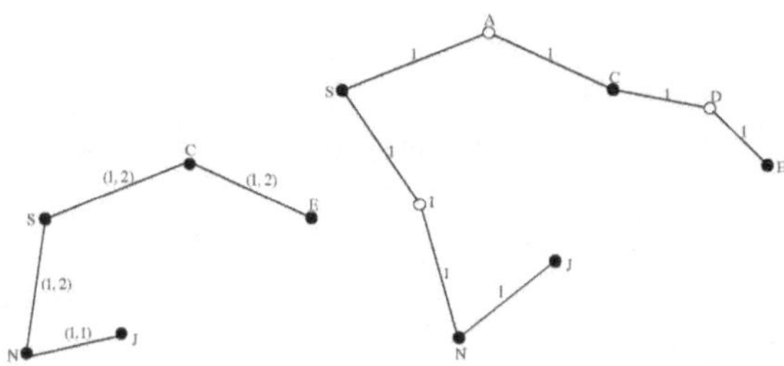

(a) (b)

Fig. 5. An MST of G' and its original tree in G

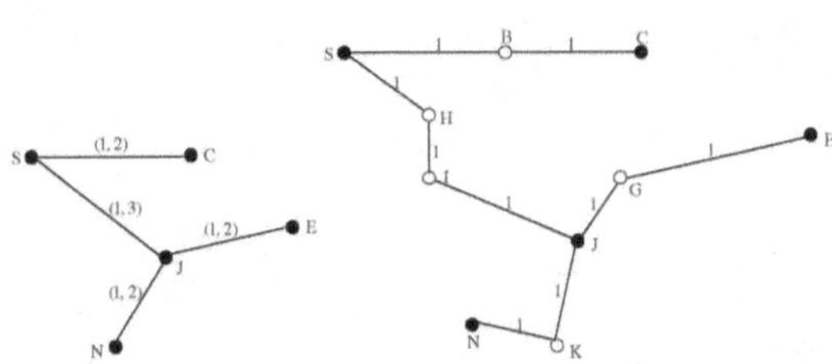

(a) (b)

Fig. 6. Another MST and its original tree in *G*

Fig. 4 is the induced graph *G'* derived from *G*. Fig. 5. (a) is an MST of Fig. 4 and (b) is the original tree in *G* by replacing each edge of the MST in Fig. 5. (a). Since the MST in Fig. 5. (a) does not have enough bandwidth, another MST is found in Fig. 6.

MMST Algorithm

Input: partial topology $G = (V, E)$ and a multicast request $(s, D, B, \bullet)$.

Output: A set of subtrees $T=\{T_i \mid 1 \le i \le k\}$, $T_i \subseteq G$.

While $(\sum_{i=1}^{k} B(T_i) < B)$ && (G is connected) **do**

Transform $G(V, E)$ to $G'(V', E')$;

Compute an MST T_{k+1}' on G';

Map T_{k+1}' to T_{k+1} in G by replacing each edge in T_{k+1}' by the corresponding path in G;

Reserve $B(T_{k+1})$;

Deduct the reserved bandwidth from the available bandwidth of all links in T_{k+1};

Remove from G the links that has no more bandwidth;

$k=k+1$;

End-while

After all the above steps, the reservation of timeslots along the routes can be done and the data can begin to be transmitted.

5 Simulations

We introduce a single tree (SGT) routing protocol as a performance benchmark. SGT adopts a least-cost-tree heuristic. The performance is evaluated in two aspects: a) success ratio of the call; b) average cost of network resources. The call success ratio is the value of the number of successful QoS multicast requests divided by the total number of requests. Network cost is defined in (2).

5.1 Simulation Setup

The simulation is conducted in a 100×100 2-D free-space by randomly allocating N nodes (N = 100). The radius of the transmission range of all nodes is set to 30 throughout the simulation process. Once the nodes are placed and their transmission ranges are decided, a network graph is formed where two nodes within each other's transmission range will have a link. Any graph that is not connected will be discarded. The number of timeslots at each node is set to be 16. The network load used in the simulation is defined as the average percentage of occupied timeslots in all nodes in the system that varies between 0 and 1. During the simulations, we randomly generate traffics and inject them into the network. As the period of a route setup phase is very short, mobility of nodes has little effect on the success ratio.

Throughout the simulations, a QoS multicast call setup request is generated as follows. A source and a group of destination nodes are randomly picked up from the network graph. The multicast group size is represented as the number of destination nodes. We simulate three types of requests, namely low, medium and high bandwidth requests, whose bandwidth requirements are set to 2, 4, and 6 timeslots, respectively. The values in the following figures are the average values of 100 runs. Each time, a request is generated as above and all the multicast routing algorithms are executed.

5.2 Simulation Results and Analysis

In the first experiment, the multicast group size is simulated against two parameters: network cost and success ratio. When the multicast group size is one, unicast is requested in fact. We assume that the network load and QoS requirements are unchanged throughout the experiment. In the initiation phase, the network load is set to 0.4, bandwidth requirement set to 4 (timeslots) and delay bound set to 3 (hops).

The simulation results are shown in Fig. 7. From the figures, the following observations can be made:

1) The MMST method performs better than the other two methods in network cost. This matches the original goal of the MMST method. The SGT method also aims at minimizing the network cost. As some links with smaller costs are not selected because of their lower bandwidth, the SGT method may result in higher network cost than the MMST method in the same condition.
2) The SGT method requires every link in the tree to meet the bandwidth requirement. So it is more difficult for SGT to find proper paths successfully and the success ratio by using the SGT method is also much lower than by using the MSPT or MMST method. This proves that our multi-tree routing scheme greatly increases the success ratio of the QoS requests.

In the second experiment, we study the changes of the success ratio in different network environment. We assume the multicast group size is 10. The delay bound is set to 4 and the low, medium and high bandwidth requirements are all considered.

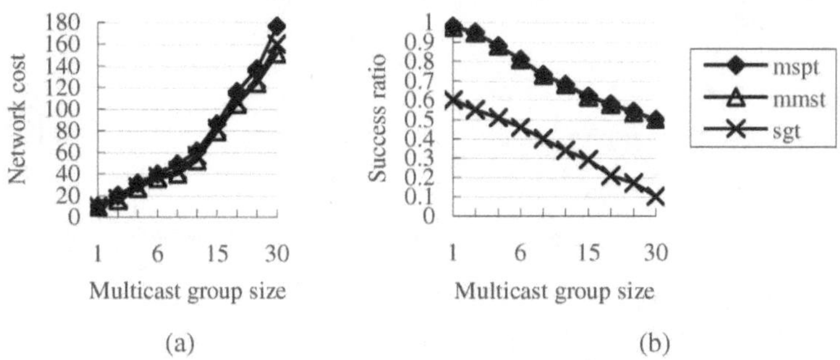

Fig. 7. Network cost and success ratio versus multicast group size

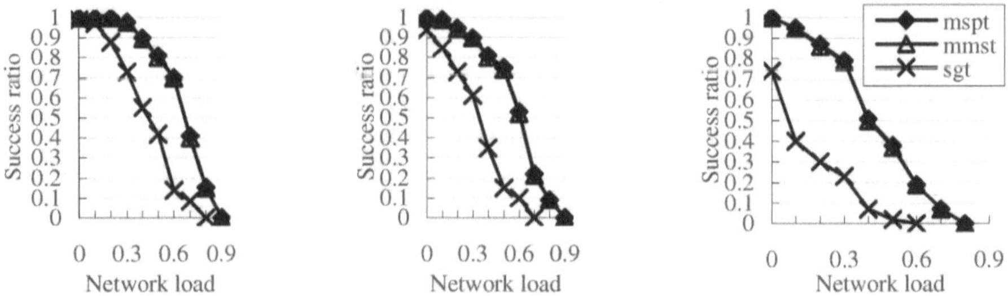

(a) Low-bandwidth requests (b) Medium-bandwidth requests (c) High-bandwidth requests

Fig. 8. Success ratio versus network load

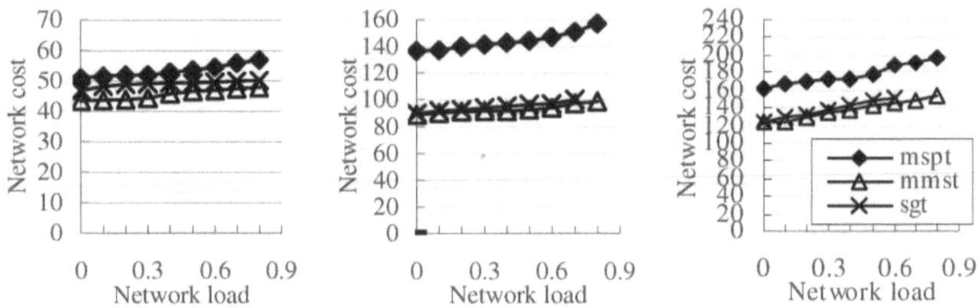

(a) Low-bandwidth requests (b) Medium-bandwidth requests (c) High-bandwidth requests

Fig. 9. Network cost versus network load

The simulation results are shown in the above figures (Fig. 8). From the figures, the following observations can be made:

1) The multi-tree routing scheme greatly reduces blockings of the requests in different network load environment. This reduction becomes even more significant when the network load is heavy or when the bandwidth requirements of requests are high.
2) By using the SGT method, the success ratio reaches to the zero more quickly with the increase of network load. This is because when using the MSPT or MMST method, those links with lower bandwidths have chances to be selected and thus the free network resources are more efficiently utilized. In a long run, the system will have more resources for later requests.
3) The success ratio is pretty high initially as the network load is light. It decreases sharply when the network load reaches a certain level. Beyond this level, the network is saturated and most of the new requests will be blocked. This threshold is much higher for the MSPT or MMST method than for the SGT method.

In the third experiment, we study the changes of the network cost in different network environment. We still assume the multicast group size is 10. The delay bound is set to 4 and the low, medium and high bandwidth requirements are all considered.

From simulation results shown in Fig. 9, we can make the following observations:

1) At the same level of network load, the cost of network resources is less by using the MMST and SGT methods than by using the MSPT method, because the goals of MMST and SGT are to make the network cost minimum while the purpose of MSPT is to make the delay from the source to each destination shortest.
2) The MMST method performs better than the other two methods in network cost of a call. This matches the original goal of MMST, which minimizes the cost of network resources for each request. As multiple trees are used in the MMST method, there are more choices to select links with lower cost than in the SGT method. This also shows that the network resources are better utilized in the multi-tree scheme.

6 Conclusions and Discussions

In this paper, we have discussed the QoS multicast routing in wireless ad hoc networks. A new scheme that uses multiple trees to meet the QoS requirements of a call has been proposed. It has three major advantages: 1) It greatly reduces the system blockings and system resources can be better utilized; 2) Multicast routing is in a distributed fashion. Even though the computation of routing trees is done at the source node, the source collects the network information in a distributed and on-demand fashion. There is no need for the source to maintain the information about the global network topology. 3) The proposed routing protocol follows the similar method as the traditional on-demand multicast routing protocols for ad hoc networks, which makes it easy to be incorporated into them. We also proposed two strategies for constructing multiple trees as the route of a call, namely, MSPT and MMST. Each of the two strategies has a different objective, such as minimizing the delay of a call or minimizing the overall network cost. The two strategies can be used in different network environment and for meeting different application needs. Extensive simulations have been conducted to evaluate the performance of the proposed scheme. Simulation results have demonstrated the effectiveness of our method in reducing the network blockings.

References

1. P. Pham and S. Perreau, "Performance Analysis of Reactive Shortest Single-path and Multi-path Routing Mechanism with Load Balance", *Proceedings of IEEE INFOCOM,* Sun Francisco, 2003.
2. J. Xie, R. R. Talpade, A. Mccauley, and M. Liu, "AMRoute: Ad Hoc Multicast Routing protocol," *ACM Mobile Networks and Applications*, Vol. 7, Issue 6, Dec. 2002.
3. C.-C. Chiang, M. Gerla and L. Zhang, "Forwarding Group Multicast Protocol (FGMP) for Multihop, Mobile Wireless Networks", *Cluster Computing* 1(2), 1998, pp. 187–196.
4. Sinha, P. Sivakumar, R. Bharghavan, "MCEDAR: Multicast Core-Extraction Distributed Ad hoc Routing", *IEEE Wireless Communications and Networking Conference*, September 1999.
5. S.-J. Lee, M. Gerla and C.-C. Chiang, "On-Demand Multicast Routing Protocol", *Proceedings of IEEE WCNC'99,* New Orleans, LA, September 1999, pp. 1298–1302.

6. S. Lee, W. Su, and M. Gerla, "On-Demand Multicast Routing Protocol in Multihop Wireless Mobile Networks", *Internet Draft draft-ietf-manet-admrp-02.txt,* work in progress, June 1999.
7. E. Royer and C. Perkins, "Multicast Operation of the Ad-hoc On-Demand Distance Vector Routing Protocol", *Proceedings of ACM/IEEE MOBICOM'99,* Aug. 1999, pp. 207–18.
8. ZJ Haas and MR Pearlman, "The Zone Routing Protocol (ZRP) for Ad Hoc Networks", work in progress, *internet draft,* draft-ietf-manet-zone-zrp-02.txt, *IETF*, June 1999.
9. Yuh-Shyan Chen, Yun-Wen Ko, and Ting-Lung Lin, "A Lantern-Tree-Based QoS Multicast Protocol with Reliable Mechanism for Wireless Ad-Hoc Networks", *Proceedings of IEEE ICCCN'02*, Miami, Florida, U. S. A., Oct. 14–16, 2002.
10. S. J. Lee and M. Gerla, "Aodv-br: Backup Routing in Ad Hoc Network", *IEEE WCNC'00*, Chicago, USA, September 2000; 1311–1316.
11. S. J. Lee and M. Gerla, "Split Multi-path Routing with Maximally Disjoint Paths in Ad Hoc Networks", in *ICC'01*, 2001.
12. W. Lou, W. Liu and Y. Fang, "SPREAD: Enhancing Data Confidentiality in Mobile Ad Hoc Networks", *Proceedings of IEEE INFOCOM,* Hong Kong, March 2004.
13. Y. Ganjali, A. Keshavarzian, "Load Balancing in Ad Hoc Networks: Single-path Routing vs. Multi-path Routing", *Proceedings of IEEE INFOCOM,* Hong Kong, March 2004.
14. Gretchen H. Lynn and Taieb F. Znati, "RoMR: A Robust Multicast Routing Protocol for Ad-Hoc Networks", *26th Annual IEEE Conference on Local Computer Networks (LCN'01),* November 14–16, 2001 Tampa, Florida, pp. 260.
15. G. Xue and R. Banka, "Bottom-up Construction of Dynamic Multicast Trees in WDM Networks", Performance, Computing, and Communications Conference 2003, Conference Proceedings of the 2003 IEEE International, pp. 49–56.
16. X. D. Hu, X. Jia, TP. Shuai and MH Zhang, "Multicast Routing and Wavelength Assignment in WDM Networks with Limited Drop-offs", *Proceedings of IEEE INFOCOM,* Hong Kong, March 2004.
17. H. Wu, X. Jia, Y. He and C. Huang, "Multi-tree QoS Multicast Routing in Ad Hoc Wireless Networks", *Proceedings of First ACM SIGCOMM ASIA WORKSHOP 2005*, Beijing, China, April 2005; 132-140.
18. C. R. Lin, "Admission Control in Time-slotted Multihop Mobile Networks", *IEEE Journal on Selected Areas in Communications*, Vol. 19, Issue. 10, Oct. 2001, pp. 1974 –1983.
19. Limin Hu, "Distributed Code Assignment for CDMA Packet Radio Networks", *IEEE/ACM Transactions on Networking*, Vol. 1, No. 6, pp. 668–677, Dec. 1993.

Finding Event Occurrence Regions in Wireless Sensor Networks*

Longjiang Guo[1], Jianzhong Li[1,2], and Jinbao Li[1,2]

[1] Harbin Institute of Technology 150001, Harbin, China
[2] Heilongjiang University 150080, Harbin, China
guolongjiang@mail.banner.com.cn, lijzh@hit.edu.cn

Abstract. Wireless sensor networks have emerged as a promising solution for a large number of monitoring applications. Sensor nodes are capable of measuring real world phenomena, storing, processing and transferring these measurements. However, users are interested in event monitored by sensors, but not the sensor itself or the massive irrelevant readings from sensors. Users often issue event queries such as "Where did happen hailstone in sensor network from 3:00 to 5:00?" Since battery supply of sensors is limited, energy-efficient query processing in sensor networks has become an important research problem. This paper presents an improved data-centric storage strategy, called CM-DCS, and also proposes two event query processing algorithms based on CM-DCS and local storage. The energy consumption of sensors for three storage strategies namely external storage, local storage and data-centric storage are analyzed and compared. The paper also studies the influence of the number of sensor nodes and node density on energy consumption. Analytical and experimental results show that in most cases the event query processing algorithm based on CM-DCS can save more energy than those algorithms based on external storage and local storage strategies.

1 Introduction

Sensor networks are an important and emerging area of research. The purpose of sensor networks is monitoring, collecting and processing the sensing data in the covered area coordinately and sending data to users [1]. In sensor networks, users are interested in event monitored by sensors, but not the sensor itself or the massive irrelevant readings from sensors. An example of an interesting event is "Fire at 10:00 am in area R". Users normally do not issue queries like "What is the temperature of sensor whose ID is 70?", but only event queries such as "Where did frost occur from 2:00 to 8:00 o'clock in the covered area?" The computing ability, storage capacity and power of sensors are limited. Communication bandwidth of sensor networks is limited too. Under the constraints of limited resources, how to store and manage events and answer event queries efficiently becomes an urgent challenge.

---

* Supported by Key Program of the National Natural Science Foundation of China, Grant No.60533110; the National Natural Science Foundation of China under Grant No.60473075; the key project of the Natural Science Foundation of Heilongjiang province under Grant No.ZJG03-05; the research project of Heilongjiang educational office under Grant No.10551246.

H.T. Shen et al. (Eds.): ADWeb 2006, LNCS 3842, pp. 167 – 175, 2006.

[2, 3] introduced spatio-temporal queries such as "Which events did happen in region R from 10:00 to 12:00? " and proposed the local storage based spatio-temporal query processing algorithm and the corresponding energy consumption model. Three different algorithms, WinFlood, WinDepth, and FullFlood, are proposed. The experimental results showed that WinFlood is more energy efficient in most situations than simple FullFlood and WinDepth.

Event information should be stored in advance and extracted from the sensor networks when query comes. We highlight the recent research work on storage in sensor networks. [4] introduced DCS (Data Centric Storage) that maps an event to a physical location (x, y) in sensor networks through HASH function. All the events with the same type are saved in the node nearest to (x, y). (x, y) is called Home Node. When query is sent out from Sink, the same HASH function is used to calculate the location where events with the same type are stored. Then the modified GPSR routing algorithm is used to get the corresponding event information from certain nodes. In this storage strategy, queries are not sent in a Flood manner to save energy. One disadvantage of DCS is that all the events and the queries with the same type are sent to the Home Node resulting in consumption of energy by the Home Node and its surrounding nodes. [5] proposed a Ring-based index to solve this problem. Another disadvantage in DCS is that it didn't consider where to map event type to save more energy. Section 2.1 of this paper gives a mapping method, called CM-DCS, for energy saving. [6] proposed an improved DCS storage strategy called resilient data-centric storage strategy, which reduced the average storage capacity of nodes and average communication cost to receive data. [7] and [8] proposed the hierarchical storage strategy named dimensions. Wavelets-based compression is adopted in each leaf node to compress the data based on temporal similarity. Each middle node accepts data from multiple leaf nodes and compresses them based on temporal similarity using wavelets. In this way, a hierarchy is constructed from lower level to a higher level, which is a hierarchical structure from low-resolution to high-resolution. This structure is suitable for drill down operation. Users send query on the highest level firstly. If an interesting event is found, a detailed query can be made through drill down operation. [9] proposed a distributed index for features in sensor networks, named DIFS. It is very efficient for range queries. [10] proposed a spatial index structure named DIM, which supports range query on multi-dimensional data. Most of the research works focus on how to save energy when storing sensing data. All works on storage in wireless sensor networks didn't consider how to support event queries. An improved data-centric storage, CM-DCS (Center Mapping Data-Centric Storage), is proposed in this paper, and two new event query processing algorithms based on CM-DCS and local storage are presented in this paper. To the best of our knowledge, there are no other research works on event query in sensor networks environment.

2 Event Storage Strategy

In sensor networks, if monitoring data satisfies the event occurrence condition, the events will be stored in the sensor networks. The nodes collecting measurements and checking event occurrence condition are called **event fusion nodes**. The nodes storing events are called **event storage nodes**.Event fusion node needs to route an event to the event storage node.

In this paper we propose a data-centric storage strategy, called center mapping data-centric storage (CM-DCS), and an energy efficient hash strategy: logically, the area of sensor networks can be divided into $m \times n$ grids where each grid is called an **observation zone**. All the observation zones are coded, and the events belonging to the same type are hashed to an observation zone lying in the center of the sensor network. The observation zone node nearest to the center of the sensor networks will be used as the event storage node of an event type. The following theorem proves that this kind of event storage strategy can minimize the energy consumption.

Lemma 1: *In wireless sensor networks, the total energy consumption for events routed from the event fusion node to the event storage node is proportional to the distance between the event fusion node and the event storage node.*

Proof: The distance D between the event fusion node and the event storage node can be represented by $D = n * d$, where n is the number of hops from the event fusion node to the event storage node; d is the average per hop distance. If the energy consumption for the sensor to receive and transmit an event is v, the events will be transmitted from the event fusion node to the event storage node approximately n times, hence the energy consumption is $V = n * v = (D/d) * v$. From this formula we can see the energy consumption is proportional to the distance D between the event fusion node and the event storage node.

Lemma 2: *If observation nodes are distributed uniformly in the observation zone, the position of the event fusion node can be considered to be located in the center of observation zone.*

Proof: Because the nodes are distributed uniformly in the observation zone, the position of observation nodes (X,Y) can be considered as a two dimensional random variable from the two dimensional uniform distribution $U(a,c,b,d)$, where (a,b) is the left down corner of observation zone and (c,d) is the right up corner of observation zone. In order to distribute the energy consumption evenly among the observation nodes, every observation node acts as the event fusion node one by one. The event fusion node's position (CX,CY) can be considered as a two dimensional random variable following the two dimensional uniform distribution $U(a,c,b,d)$.The expectation of CX and CY are $E(CX) = 0.5*(a+c)$, $E(CY) = 0.5*(b+d)$. $(E(CX), E(CY))$ can be considered as the center of observation zone.

Theorem 1: *If the observation nodes are distributed uniformly in the observation zone, the event storage nodes should be located near the center of the sensor networks so that the event transmission energy consumption can be minimized.*

Proof: From lemma 2 we know that every center of observation zone can be seen as the position of event fusion nodes. The centers of each observation zone are (X_1,Y_1), (X_2,Y_2), ..., $(X_{m\times n},Y_{m\times n})$, let (X,Y) is the position of the event storage node for event type ET_i. The events of ET_i detected in each observation zone are fused by event fusion nodes and routed to the event storage node at (X,Y). From lemma 1 we know that the energy consumption of each event transmission is proportional to the distance between the event fusion node and event storage node. So the problem is to choose a coordinate (X,Y) which satisfy the formula: $\min\sum_{i=1}^{m\times n}(X_i - X)^2 + (Y_i - Y)^2$. We derivate the formula and get: $X = \frac{1}{m\times n}\sum_{i=1}^{m\times n} X_i$ $Y = \frac{1}{m\times n}\sum_{i=1}^{m\times n} Y_i$. From these results we find that (X,Y) is the center of the sensor networks. So if we use the nodes located near the center of the sensor networks as the event storage nodes, these nodes can minimize the energy consumption.

Fig. 1 illustrates that the sensor network observes 4 event types: ET_1, ET_2, ET_3, ET_4, the zone covered by sensor network is divided into 4×4 observation zones which are coded as { Z_1, Z_2, ..., Z_{16} }. Constructing a mapping { $ET_1 \to Z_6$; $ET_2 \to Z_{10}$; $ET_3 \to Z_{11}$; $ET_4 \to Z_7$ } where Z_6, Z_{10}, Z_{11}, Z_7 lie in the center of the sensor network and are shaded in Fig. 1. The nodes with dark color in Fig. 1 whose positions are nearest to the center of the sensor network are appointed as the event storage nodes for each event type. If events of the same type occur frequently, the nodes lying around the event storage nodes will consume more energy. After a period of time, it is necessary to adjust the mapping for balanced energy consumption. For example, as illustrated in Fig. 1, if events belonging to event type ET_1 frequently happen then energy consumption of the event storage node of ET_1 will be faster. After a period of time, sensor network will construct a new mapping { $ET_1 \to Z_2$; $ET_2 \to Z_{10}$; $ET_3 \to Z_{11}$; $ET_4 \to Z_7$ }. As shown in Fig. 2, Z_2 is the neighbor of Z_6 and it is appointed as the new mapping zone of event type ET_1. The node lying nearest to the center of sensor network in zone Z_2 will be the new event storage node for event type ET_1

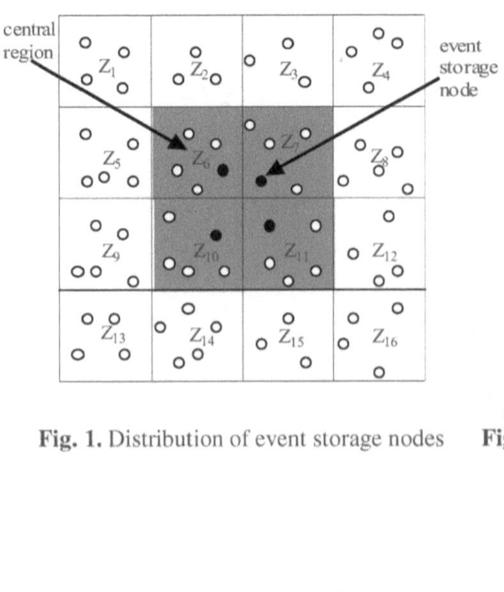

Fig. 1. Distribution of event storage nodes

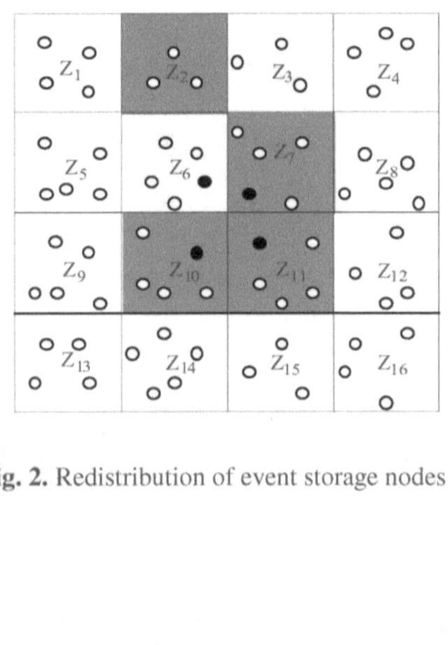

Fig. 2. Redistribution of event storage nodes

3 Event Query Processing

In this section we propose two event query processing algorithms describing how to extract information from the sensor networks for query $Q\{[t_1,t_2],ET_i\}$, which means find all observation zones where the events, whose event type is ET_i, occurred from round t_1 to round t_2.

3.1 Event Query Processing Based on CM-DCS

The algorithm for the event query $Q\{[t_1,t_2],ET_i\}$ based on CM-DCS is composed of four phases.

Phase 1: Calculating the routing destination. According to mapping $ET_i \to Z_j$, compute the position of the corner (x_i, y_i) of Z_j, it meets that the distance between (x_i, y_i) and the center of the sensor network are nearest.

Phase 2: Routing event query $Q\{[t_1,t_2],ET_i\}$ from the sink to the event storage node p whose position is nearest to (x_i, y_i).

Phase 3: Answer event query $Q\{[t_1,t_2],ET_i\}$. If the event storage node p receives the event query, p will choose those vectors $A=\{(I,t)\mid t\in[t_1,t_2]\}$ from $B(ET_i)$, where $B(ET_i)=\{(I,t)\mid$ I is a vector containing $m\times n$ bits, t is the round of sensor networks, $t\geq 0\}$. If the bits $j_1, j_2,..., j_k$ of vector I are 1 and the other bits are 0 which means observation zones $Z_{j_1}, Z_{j_2},..., Z_{j_k}$ has detected the event of type ET_i. So (I,t) means the observation zones detect the event belonging to event type during round t, then $I_p = \underset{(I,t),t\in[t_1,t_2]}{\oplus I}$ will be computed. Here $\oplus$ denotes the bitwise OR operator and I_p denotes result vector. If the bits $j_1, j_2,..., j_k$ of vector I_p are 1 and the remaining bits are 0 then it means nodes in $Z_{j_1}, Z_{j_2},..., Z_{j_k}$ has detected the event of event type ET_i.

Phase 4: Node p routes I_p to the sink.

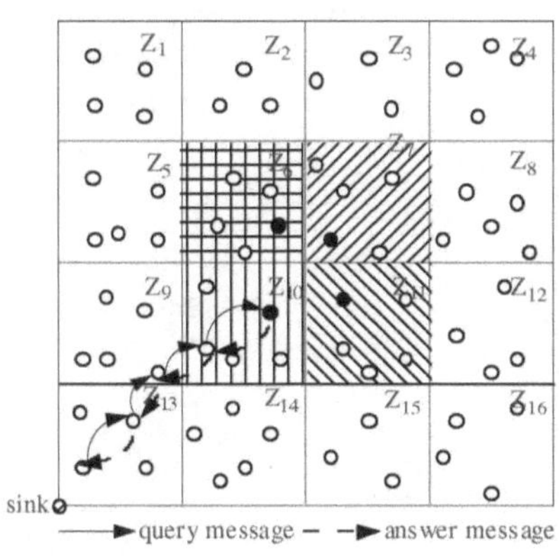

Fig. 3. Routing query based on CM-DCS

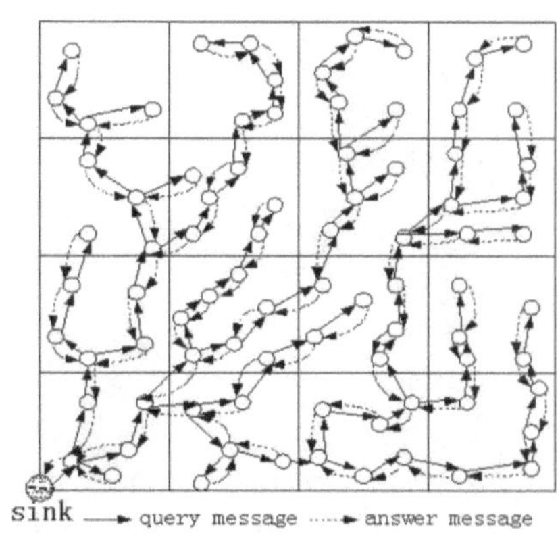

Fig. 4. Routing query based on local storage

Fig.3 illustrates the procedure of routing event query based on CM-DCS. Suppose event query is $Q\{[t_1,t_2],ET_2\}$, since $ET_2 \rightarrow Z_{10}$, the event query packet is routed in the event storage nodes lying in Z_{10}, and the result will be returned to the sink.

3.2 Event Query Processing Based on Local Storage

The algorithm for the event query $Q\{[t_1,t_2],ET_i\}$ based on local storage is explained below in four phases.

Phase 1: Event query dissemination. Query $Q\{[t_1,t_2],ET_i\}$ is issued from the sink to the sensor network. A routing tree rooted at the sink is constructed. Initially, the sink broadcasts query packet to its neighbors. The sink adds its ID in query packet. When a node p receives a query packet from a node q, p regards q as its father, and p replaces ID in the query packet with its ID, then p broadcasts the query packet to its neighbors. p will drop the query packet, if p receives same query packet.

Phase 2: Getting children's ID. Node p broadcasts information $<p, fp>$ to its neighbors, where fp is p 's father's ID. We assume that p 's neighbors are $\{q_1,q_2,\ldots,q_m\}$, and p receives $\{<q_1,fq_1>,<q_2,fq_2>,\ldots,<q_m,fq_m>\}$, then p 's children set is $Children(p)=\{q_i \mid <q_i,fq_i>, it\ meets\ fq_i = p\}$.

Phase 3: Combination of query result. If the event storage node p receives the event query, p will choose those vectors $A=\{(I,t) \mid t\in[t_1,t_2]\}$ from $B(ET_i)$, then p computes $I_p = \bigcup_{(I,t),t\in[t_1,t_2]} I$. If $Children(p)$ is null, p will send I_p to his father, otherwise p will wait for its children's query results. When p receives all its children's answers, p will combine I_p with its children's answers using bitwise OR operator. Finally, p will send combined query result to its father.

Phase 4: The sink receives final answers from its children.

Fig.4 illustrates the procedure of routing event query packet based on local storage. A routing tree rooted at the sink is built when the event query $Q\{[t_1,t_2],ET_i\}$ is disseminated in the sensor network, and the query result is returned from leaves to the sink, the root of routing tree.

4 Experiments

In this section, we present the implementation of event query processing algorithms based on CM-DCS and local storage as in ns-2. The simulated experiments were done using a Pentium-4 PC with 512MB RAM, running WindowsXP and having cygwin1.59 installed. We have used 802.15.4 as MAC protocol, rather than traditional 802.11 and SMAC. Table 1 lists the simulation parameters used in ns-2.

(1) Effect of node density ρ on node energy consumption. In the experiment, network topology area is set to $X = Y$, and the node density is varied. Five different random network topologies are given, with node density ρ increasing, the number of

nodes N and boundary length of sensor network topology X and Y also increases. Table 2 shows the corresponding relationship among network topology areas, the number of nodes and node density of five network topologies in detail. Note that sensor nodes are deployed uniformly at random to the $X \times X$ square area. We use CMU's version of setdest in *ns*-2 to generate randomly five wireless scenarios shown in table 2 and define sink to be the node closest to (0,0). Fig. 5 shows the effect of node density on energy consumption in each node as network node density increases. Fig. 5 also indicates that the CM-DCS proposed in this paper for answering event queries can save more energy as compared to other storage strategies.

Table 1. Simulation parameters used in ns-2

Parameters	Values
Radio range	10m
Sleeping power in watts	0.035W
Transmitting power in watts	0.66W
Initial energy per node in joules	10000J
Receiving power in watts	0.4W
Number of bit vector saved by node	50

Table 2. Sensor network field size and the number of nodes when node density varies

Sensor network field size	Number of nodes (N)	Node density (ρ)
64×64	100	$8 nodes / 314m^2$
90×90	250	$10 nodes / 314m^2$
110×110	460	$12 nodes / 314m^2$
127×127	720	$14 nodes / 314m^2$
142×142	1020	$16 nodes / 314m^2$

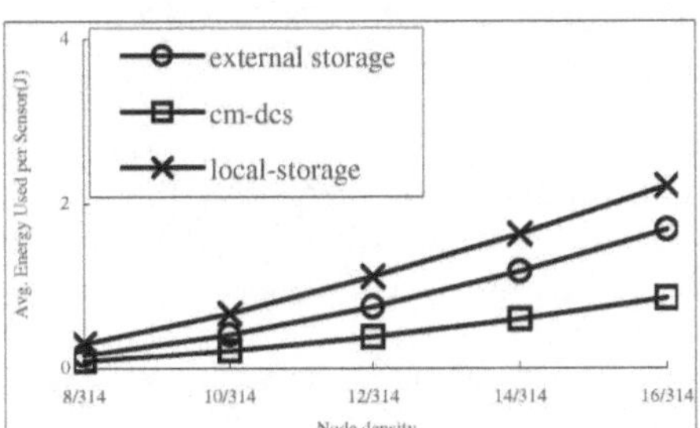

Fig. 5. Energy varies with node density

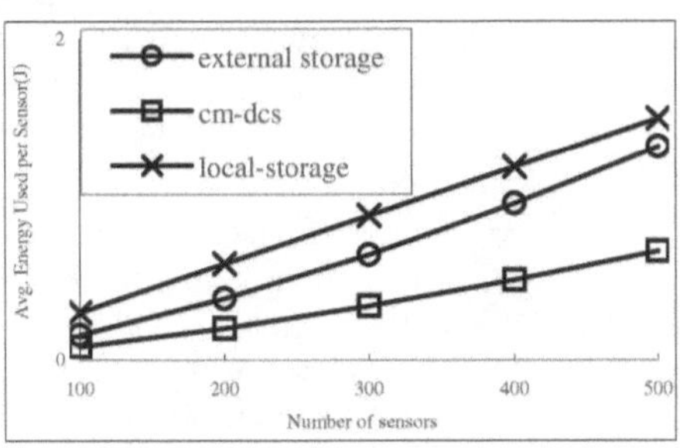

Fig. 6. Energy varies with number of nodes

Table 3. Sensor network field size and the number of nodes when $\rho = 8nodes/314m^2$

Sensor network field size	Number of nodes (N)
64×64	100
90×90	200
110×110	300
127×127	400
142×142	500

(2) Effect of number of sensors on node energy consumption. In this experiment, network topology area is set to be a square (i.e. $X = Y$). Five different random network topologies are shown in Table 3. Note that N increases in proportion to an increase of boundary length of sensor network topology. For all these network topologies, we hold node density ρ fixed ($\rho = 8nodes/314m^2$). Table 3 shows a corresponding relationship between sensor network topology area and the number of nodes when $\rho = 8nodes/314m^2$. Fig.6 shows that during each round, how average energy consumption of each node change when $\rho = 8nodes/314m^2$ and increase the number of nodes. We can see that CM-DCS proposed in this paper for answering event queries is the most energy-economizing as the number of nodes increases.

5 Conclusion

This paper presents an CM-DCS strategy and also proposes two event query processing algorithms based on CM-DCS and local storage. Analytical and experimental results show that in most cases the event query processing algorithm based on CM-DCS can save more energy than those algorithms based on other storage.

References

1. Li JZ, Li JB, Shi SF. Concepts, issues and advance of sensor networks and data management of sensor networks. Journal of software, 2003, 14(10):1717-172.
2. Alexandru C, Mario AN, Jörg S. A framework for spatio-temporal query processing over wireless sensor networks. In: Alexandros L, Samuel M, ed. Proceedings of the 1st international workshop on data management for sensor networks in conjunction with VLDB 2004. New York: ACM Press, 2004. 104-110.
3. Alexandru C, Jörg S, Mario AN. An analysis of spatio-temporal query processing in sensor networks. In: Ramesh G, Cyrus S, ed. 1st IEEE International Workshop on Networking Meets Databases in cooperation with 21st IEEE Conference on Data Engineering (ICDE 2005). Washington: IEEE Computer Society, 2005. 120-125.
4. Scott S, Sylvia R, Brad K, Ramesh G, Deborah E. Data-Centric Storage in Sensornets. ACM SIGCOMM Computer Communication Review, 2003,33(1): 137-142.
5. Wensheng Z, Guohong C, Tom LP, Data Dissemination with Ring-Based Index for Wireless Sensor Networks, In: Kevin A, Ken C, ed. IEEE International Conference on Network Protocols (ICNP 2003). Washington: IEEE Computer Society,2003. 305-314.

6. Abhishek G, Jens G, John C. Resilient Data-Centric Storage in Wireless Ad-Hoc Sensor Networks. In: Arkady Z, ed. Proceedings of the 4th International Conference on Mobile Data Management (MDM2003). London: Springer-Verlag, 2003.45-62.
7. Deepak G, Deborah E, John H. Dimensions: why do we need a new data handling architecture for sensor networks. ACM SIGCOMM Computer Communication Review, 2003,33(1): 143-148.
8. Deepak G, Ben G, Denis P, Deborah E, John H. An Evaluation of Multi-resolution Storage for Sensor Networks. In: Ian A, Deborah E,ed. The 1st international conference on Embedded networked sensor systems. New York: ACM Press, 2003. 89-102.
9. Benjamin G, Deborah E, Ramesh G, Sylvia R, Scott S. DIFS: A Distributed Index for Features in Sensor Networks. In: Erdal C, Taieb Z, Eylem E, ed. Proceedings of the first IEEE International Workshop on Sensor Network Protocols and Applications Anchorage. Washington: IEEE Computer Society, 2003. 163-173.
10. Xin L, Young JK, Ramesh G, Wei H. Multi-dimensional Range Queries in Sensor Networks. In: Ian A, Deborah E, ed. Proceedings of the 1st international conference on Embedded networked sensor systems. New York: ACM Press, 2003. 509-517.

Energy Efficient Protocols for Information Dissemination in Wireless Sensor Networks*

Dandan Liu[1], Xiaodong Hu[2], and Xiaohua Jia[1,3]

[1] Computer School, Wuhan University, Wuhan 430072, China
liudd2004@hotmail.com
[2] Academy of Math and System Science, CAS, Beijing 100080, China
xdhu@amss.ac.cn
[3] Dept of Computer Science, City Univ of Hong Kong, Hong Kong, China
jia@cs.cityu.edu.hk

Abstract. In this paper we consider a distributed and efficient information dissemination and retrieval system for wireless sensor networks. In such a system each sensor node operates autonomously with no central node of control in the network, and it can be a data source as well as a data sink. We aim at developing energy efficient protocols that disseminate information to any nodes that are interested in. Two protocols are proposed, one is based on the quorum scheme and the other is based on the home-agent scheme. The proposed protocols have two advantages: 1) High success rate for data retrieval; 2) Fully distributed. The theoretical analysis and simulation results show their significant improvements on energy efficiency over the previous protocols.

1 Introduction

A Wireless Sensor Network (WSN) [1] consists of hundreds or thousands of sensor nodes deployed across a physical space, providing functions of data sensing, information processing and communication. There are many applications of WSN [2], such as environment monitoring, target surveillance and object tracking.

A WSN works as a distributed database system. Each sensor node senses data, processes the data and advertises the data to others that are interested in. When a user needs to access the data, it makes a query to the network, and whoever holding the data will pass the data to it. In this paper, we discuss a distributed processing system of WSNs that provides distributed information services on sensed data efficiently. In such a system each sensor node operates autonomously with no central control in the network. Each node can be a data source (producing data) as well as a data sink (consuming data). In such an environment, the system is robust and fault tolerant. It can continue to function properly in the presence of failures of individual sensor nodes.

* Supported in part by Research Grants Council of Hong Kong Project No. CityU 114505 and the NNSF of China under Grant No. 70221001 and 60373012.

H.T. Shen et al. (Eds.): ADWeb 2006, LNCS 3842, pp. 176–185, 2006.

There are several challenges in the design and implementation of such a distributed information system for resource constrained WSNs. The energy capacity of WSNs and bandwidth capacity of sensor nodes are limited, and nodes don't have global topology information.

In this paper, we aim at developing energy efficient protocols that disseminate sensed information from a source node to any other nodes that are interested in such information. We propose two distributed protocols, one is based on the quorum scheme and the other is based on the home-agent scheme. None of them use the flooding (or zone flooding) method, which makes them different from the previous ones.

The rest of paper is organized as follows. Section 2 summarizes the related works and our contributions. Section 3 specifies the network model. Section 4 introduces the quorum based and home-agent based protocols, respectively. Sections 5 and 6 study the performances of the proposed protocols through theoretical analysis and simulations, respectively. Section 7 concludes the paper.

2 Related Works and Contributions

The simplest method for disseminating information in WSNs is by flooding. However, it incurs heavy cost and message implosion problem. Gossiping [3] is an alternative that achieves energy efficiency through randomization [4-5]. However, it disseminates information slow and cannot guarantee the eventual delivery of data to destinations.

To overcome those deficiencies, Heinzelman et al [6] proposed a family of adaptive protocols, called *Sensor Protocols for Information via Negotiation* (SPIN). Meta-data that describes the observed data or queries are exchanged among sensors through advertisement (ADV) and request (REQ) message. These negotiation helps ensure that only useful information will be transmitted. It is an event-driven method. Another important data-centric routing, called *directed diffusion* [7], was proposed to diffuse data queries in an on-demand fashion. An interest message is broadcasted by a sink node to its neighbors when it needs to access data. Data then starts to report back after receiving such interest message. The ADV messages in SPIN and the initial interest in directed diffusion are broadcasted or flooded throughout the network. They will cause severe performance penalties in wireless networks.

Although quorum scheme [8, 9] and home-agent scheme [10, 11] have previously been used for location management in wireless ad hoc networks, they can be quite complicated to be applied to WSNs due to those challenges. Recently, some pseudo-quorum methods are used to find matched data in sensor networks [12, 13], but with poor success rate.

The main contributions of this paper include: 1) Applying the general quorum and home-agent scheme to information dissemination protocols for WSNs, which achieves high energy efficiency; 2) Employing recovery scheme in geometric routing, which helps achieve high querying success rate with low message cost; 3) Fully distributed design of the protocols with no need of any sensor node to keep the global information of the network.

3 Network Model And Preliminaries

We consider a sensor network, where sensor nodes are stationary and have a fixed transmission radius R. The network is modelled by Unit Disk Graph, denoted by $G = (V, E)$. V represents the set of sensor nodes in the network and there is an edge $e = (u, v) \in E$ between nodes u and v if and only if the Euclidean distance between them $||uv|| \leq R$. Each node obtains its neighbors' locations by sending out probing messages (or hello messages).

There are two models of information dissemination in WSNs: event-driven (proactive) and query-driven (on-demand). Our method is a combination of these two models. Three types of messages for data query or data transmission are used, which are very similar to those introduced in [3, 7]:

1. ADV - advertisement of data, which is event-driven. It contains its location and the description of the data.
2. REQ - request for data, which is query-driven. It contains its location and the description of its interest.
3. DATA - data message. Data messages contain the actual data.

The ADV and REQ messages also include information about the data rate, the duration and expiration time of data, and some other necessary information for routing.

Our protocols use a geometric routing to recover from the failure of Greedy forwarding (discussed in section 4). Since the geometric routing always requires the network topology to be a planar graph, we construct the Gabriel Graph [14] when the recovery scheme is executed.

4 Energy Efficient Protocols

In the following, we will present our quorum based and home-agent based protocols, respectively. The basic idea of them is that the negotiation messages, ADV and REQ, are sent to potentially different groups of nodes in the network. Note that there is no need of ordering ADV and REQ for the matched data. Arrived message will be stored for future matching until expiration time is reached. The key challenge is how to ensure that any two matching groups will meet at some rendezvous by using less cost.

4.1 Quorum Based Protocol

Given a set S of n servers, a quorum system is a partition of S consisting of a set of mutually disjoint subsets of S whose union is S. When one of servers requires information from the other, it suffices to query one server from each quorum. Some variations of this method have been proposed. Aydin and Shen [12] proposed a match-making method for ad hoc networks and WSNs. In this method, the threshold angle is a key parameter that limit the probability of the intersection between

ADV and SUB quorums. In a more recent work, Liu et al [13] proposed a comb-needle query support model. However, in an irregular network, the REQ messages can hardly follow a comb shape, and the comb may miss the needle. This problem will be more severe in the presence of 'voids' in the network.

Through a simpler mechanism than the match-making and comb-needle methods, we proposed a novel quorum based protocol that achieves much higher success rate. A quorum system is used to advertise data and find the location of the data without any sort of flooding or broadcasting. By this quorum system, the message cost for new data dissemination can be greatly reduced. To save energy, when a node selects its neighbors to forward an ADV/REQ, it will not consider those neighbors that have already been requested to forward the same message before. It is called *non-duplicate forwarding policy*. Under this policy, any message will be forwarded at most $|V| - 1$ times.

Transmission of ADV message. When a node s has sensed new data, it broadcasts an ADV to its neighbors in northward and southward directions. All its neighbors, upon receiving the message, will record the message together with the location of s. As for the northward direction, the neighbor with the largest y-coordinate will broadcast the message further to its neighbors. This operation is carried on by the neighbors in northward direction and the ADV is propagated northward hop by hop until it reaches the node at the north boundary of the network. At the same time with the message going northward, the same operation is taken to propagate the ADV in southward direction until reaching the south boundary of the network.

Transmission of REQ message. When a node intends to acquire the data that it is interested in, it broadcasts a REQ to its neighbors. Similarly to ADV propagation, the REQ is propagated in both eastward and westward directions until it reaches the west and east boundaries. When the message propagation terminates, all nodes have received the REQ, they form an east-west row dividing the network. The most important fact is that when the row and column intersect, some nodes (as rendezvous nodes) must have received both ADV and REQ.

Transmission of DATA message. When a node receives a new REQ (or ADV), it always first checks whether this message matches an ADV (or REQ) it has received before. When such a matching is found, the node will send the REQ to the source node along the route where the matched ADV was transmitted. Upon receiving the REQ, the source node transmits the DATA to the querying node along the route that the REQ was transmitted. By using the same route for data transmission as the REQ, it avoids extra routing for the DATA, which could save significant routing overhead in sensor networks. An alternative method used after ADV and REQ are matched is geometric routing, such as Greedy Perimeter Stateless Routing (GPSR) [15], Geometric Adaptive Face Routing (GOAFR) [16], or Greedy-Face-Greedy (GFG) [17].

To implement the quorum based protocol, we must solve a couple of technical problems that we have not addressed in the description above. We will consider only the ADV propagation; the case of REQ can be implemented in the same way.

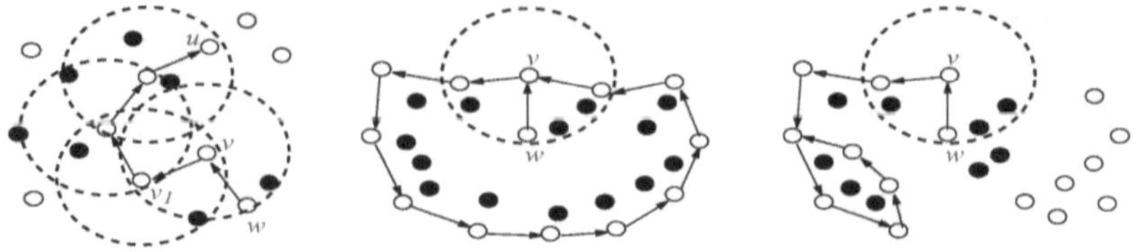

Fig. 1. Implementation of quorum based protocol

Suppose that a node v (Fig.1(a)) receives an ADV from node w that should be forwarded northward, but none of node v's direct neighbors is located further north than v itself. In this case, the ADV cannot be propagated any further towards north, even though there exists a node u at its further north direction in the column. The ADV reaches a local maximum with respect to the direction to the north. This situation will occur when the deployment of sensor nodes has some "void areas". In order to direct the message to leave out of the local maximum v, the protocol executes a recovery scheme on the Gabriel graph. It applies the right-hand rule of face routing [15], but with the non-duplicate forwarding policy. Specifically, when node v finds that no neighbor is further north than itself, it forwards the message to its neighbor v_1 that has the largest angle a formed from wv to vv_1 in clockwise direction. After v_1 receives the message, it will perform the same operation as node v. Eventually, u will receive the message (Fig.1(a)).

Notice that this is different from the traditional face routing in [15-17], the aim of which is to make sure that messages will reach the destination. But in our protocol, it is only required to deliver the ADV or REQ message to enough nodes such that at least one rendezvous exists.

The handling of "void areas" in sensor network would introduce extra overhead to the quorum system. Now suppose that node v is truly located at the north boundary of the network. Consider the case when it receives an ADV and tries to propagate it to further north. Since node v does not have the global topology of the entire network, it is unable to tell whether it is in the case of local maximum or it actually reaches the north boundary. As the result, node v still follows the right-hand rule to propagate the message hop by hop along the boundary of the network until the message traverses back to either node v (Fig.1(b)), or meets some node at its traversed route (Fig.1(c)). In either case, the message travels a lot of unnecessary distance. However, this overhead is inevitable if our protocol has to handle the case of "void areas".

From the above discussion, we find that in the quorum system, the ADV does not actually travel in the ideal fashion following the north-south directions. But what makes the protocol working is that when a source node has the data that another node is interested, there always exists a rendezvous node for the data. Notice that in the real scenario, only the ADV needs to traverse along the perimeter of the network. The REQ will stop being forwarded when meet the rendezvous inside the network (or immediately at a boundary node), except the REQ is sent out before its matched ADV is advertised. This makes the cost for propagating the ADV asymmetric from the REQ.

Unfortunately, the quorum-based protocol with our non-duplicate forwarding policy doesn't guarantee successful information dissemination in some pathological cases. Alternatively, we can introduce some routing techniques (similar to face routing in [15-17]) to ensure information delivery. However, this will incur high message cost (e.g., face routing requires $4|E|$ steps to reach the destination node in the worst case). Moreover, our simulation study shows that the proposed protocols can create at least one rendezvous in most cases. It is thus unnecessary to introduce the over conservative and high cost message forwarding policy.

4.2 Home-Agent Based Protocol

The home-agent scheme was introduced to ad hoc networks for maintaining location information of mobile nodes in [10]. However, since each node should have the initial global location information of other nodes in the network, the protocol has extra requirements on node storage and energy consumption.

We now propose another protocol, called *home-agent based protocol.* When a node needs to advertise new data, it sends an ADV to the home agent; and any node that wishes to access the data sends a REQ to the same agent. The home agent serves as the rendezvous. Our home-agent based protocol is different from the one used in [10]. The system has only one home agent shared by all sensor nodes in the network, and it can be easily extended to a distributed version of home-agent method by using a hash table [18].

The home agent will consist of all nodes that reside within the circle of the radius (a network parameter). There are two possible ways to choose the center of the circle: 1) A real node - such that the maximal distance from any node to it is minimal; 2) A virtual home - the geometric center of the network whose maximal Euclidean distance to the location of any node is minimal, or the geometric center of the geographical field where the sensors are deployed.

When a virtual home agent is used, it is possible that there is no sensor node at the selected center. Two cases may occur: 1) ADV/REQ is propagated to some nodes within the circle of radius 1/2. In this case, any node located inside the circle can be a rendezvous after the message is broadcasted within the circle; 2) ADV/REQ cannot be propagated to any node inside the circle. In this case, the non-duplicated face routing will propagate the message along a closed route encompassing the circle. Some of the nodes on the route can be rendezvous.

Like the quorum-based protocol, the home-agent based protocol cannot guarantee the successful information dissemination in all cases either. But instead of traversing the perimeter of the network, it only produces rendezvous within a much smaller home region. This incurs fewer transmissions. Although, the home-agent based protocol imposes heavy communication load on nodes around the home agent, its performance is almost independent of the nodes number and transmission radius of node and its implementation complexity is low.

5 Theoretical Analysis

In this section, we will study the performances of the two proposed protocols in $(n \times n)$-grid and $(n \times n)$-hexagonal grid, respectively. Both topologies are very popular in wireless communications, where many ad hoc networks or randomly deployed sensor networks can be approximated by them. We evaluate two performance metrics associated with energy efficiency: 1) The number of nodes that are required to forward an ADV/REQ, denoted by f_Q and f_H, respectively; 2) The hop counts of the route between the source node and querying node, denoted by h_Q and h_H, respectively. The hop counts indicate the distance that data would travel. Each node in the network is supposed to have the same independent possibility to disseminate and inquire the information, and the expected values of f_Q, f_H, h_Q and h_H are denoted by $E[f_Q]$, $E[f_H]$, $E[h_Q]$ and $E[h_H]$. The following theorems are given without proofs due to page limit.

Theorem 1. *For $(n \times n)$-grids of any $n \geq 2$, $E[f_Q] < 5n$, $E[f_H] < n/2$, $E[h_Q] < 4n/3$ and $E[h_H] < n$.*

Theorem 2. *For $(n \times n)$-hexagonal grids of any $n \geq 2$, $E[f_Q] < 68n/9$, $E[f_H] < 2n/3$, $E[h_Q] < 41n/45$ and $E[h_H] < 4n/3$.*

From above theorems, we can see that the quorum-based protocol needs only $O(\sqrt{|V|})$ nodes to forward the messages in grids. The home-agent based protocol requires even fewer forwarding nodes. They achieve significant energy savings when compared with the classic flooding-based methods, which requires $O(|V|)$ nodes. However, since under the home-agent based protocol, data must be transmitted from the source to querying node via the agent, it probably produces a longer path for final data transmission.

6 Simulation Study

In Section 6 we have analyzed the performances of the proposed protocols in some special cases where the success of information dissemination is guaranteed. In this section we will study their performances in general case where the success of information dissemination is not guaranteed. We also compare their performances with the match-making method [12], a method based on the quorum system concept. The comb-needle method [13] has the similar problems as that in [12] in randomly deployed sensor networks, such as poor success rate due to the irregularity of the network and the presence of "void areas". Moreover, it incurs higher message cost than that in [12], because it has to form many teeth of the "comb". Therefore, we did not simulate the comb-needle method.

The performances of all protocols are measured by success rate and energy efficiency. Success rate shows the probability of the existence of at least one rendezvous node, or equivalently the probability of successful delivery of data packets to the interested nodes. Energy efficiency is evaluated respectively by forwarding nodes and hop counts, which are defined as that in section 6. The data are obtained when success rate is 1.

6.1 Description of Simulation Method

We use the simulation programs written in C++ program language to evaluate the performance of proposed protocols, considering an idealized network environment. Three methods are simulated and compared, our proposed quorum-based and home-agent based methods, and the match-making method [12].

Two network parameters are varied over a wide range: the number of nodes in the network (N) and the transmission radius of nodes (R). For the home-agent based protocol, we use the geometric center as the virtual home agent. For the match-making protocol, the threshold angle is set to degree 15.

The simulation is conducted in an 100×100 2-D free-space by randomly placing N nodes, which are assumed to have idealized energy consumption. Transmission radius R starts from 13, since it is difficult to generate a connected graph when R is smaller than 13. In each run of the simulations, for given N and R, we randomly place N nodes in the square, and randomly pick two nodes (one sending ADV and the other REQ). All unconnected topologies are discarded. The following analysis is based on the averages of 200 separate runs.

6.2 Analysis of Simulation Results

The success rates of both quorum-based and home-agent based protocols keep at a high level, and rise up to 100% quickly as R or N increases (Fig2). Because when more nodes can get messages from their neighbors in one transmission, more nodes can be added into the quorum. Moreover, the recovery scheme in our protocols is able to extend each quorum to pass the 'void area' and reach the extreme point of networks, which increases the probability of intersection between two quorums. However, the match-making protocol has much lower success rate, since the threshold angle limits the extension of each directions and no recovery scheme is used when further forwarding fails.

The number of forwarding nodes required in home-agent based protocol decreases as R increases (Fig3(a)) by the method of greedy (it requires about 5% forwarding nodes). But the number of forwarding nodes in quorum-based protocol increases as R increases. This seems to be contrary to our expectation, but

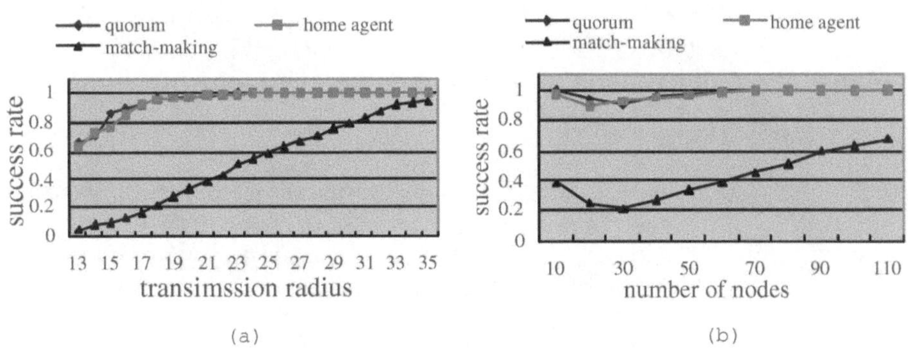

Fig. 2. Success rate of protocols

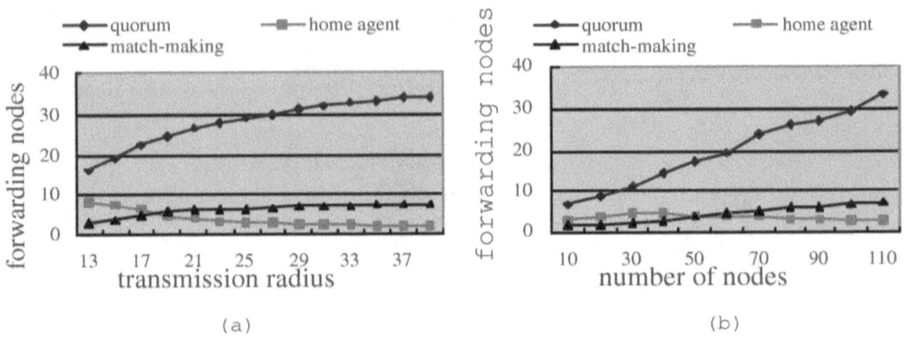

Fig. 3. Energy efficiency of protocols

it is right. First, increasing R yields a denser network. A node has more neighbors and more choices to select one of them to be the next forwarding node. Thus each direction can be extended much further. Second, as R increases, face routing is more likely to be triggered on the outer boundary, on which more and more nodes will be added to the quorum as well. Finally, after R increases enough so that face routing will be executed by all nodes along the perimeter of the network, the number tends to steady eventually (it requires about 30% forwarding nodes). Although the match-making protocol requires fewer nodes to forward packets, it is at the sacrifice of much lower success rate, since fewer nodes can be selected as rendezvous.

When N increases, the number of forwarding nodes involved increases almost proportionally to the number of nodes in the network under the quorum based protocol, but it is not fluctuated much under the home agent based protocol (Fig3(b)). Because home-agent method only requires messages to be transmitted to the home, the hop distance between a source node and the home agent node is not significantly affected by the nodes number.

Since the route considered for hop counts between a source node and the querying node is a part of the route composed by forwarding nodes, the figures for hop counts have similar tendency as Fig3 (the results could not be included due to the limited space). The difference is that the hop counts in quorum-based protocol decreases as R increases. Because it is more influenced by the part of quorum system which is constructed by the greedy method.

7 Conclusions

In this paper, we proposed two information dissemination protocols by negotiation in WSNs. Negotiations ensure that nodes only disseminate information when necessary so that lots of energy could be saved. The proposed protocols are based on the quorum and home-agent schemes, respectively. A novel recovery scheme, known as non-duplicated face routing, is also presented to handle 'voids' in the networks. It reduces large amount of control overhead encountered in traditional face routing. We have studied and compared their performances through both mathematical analysis in some special cases and simulation in general case. As demonstrated, both proposed protocols achieve very high success rate and energy efficiency, and at the same time they can overcome the implosion problem occurring in the classic flooding.

References

1. D. Culler, D. Estrin, and M. Srivastava, Overview of sensor networks, *Computer*, **37** (8) (2004), 41-49.
2. K. Martinez, J. K. Hart, and R. Ong, Sensor network applications, *Computer*, **37** (8) 2004, 50-56.
3. S. M. Hedetniemi, S. T. Hedetniemi, and A. L. Liestman, A survey of gossiping and broadcasting in communication networks, *Networks*, **18** (4) (1988), 319-349.
4. B. S. Chlebus, Randomized communication in radio networks, *Handbook of Randomized Computing*, **1-2** (2001), 401-456, Kluwer Academic Publishers, Dordrecht.
5. L. Orecchia, A. Panconesi, C. Petrioli, and A. Vitaletti, Localized techniques for broadcasting in wireless sensor networks, *MOBICOM*, Philadelphia, PA, 2004.
6. W. R. Heinzelman, J. Kulit, and H. Balakrishnan, Adaptive protocols for information dissemination in wireless sensor networks, *MOBICOM*, Seattle, WA, 1999.
7. C. Intanagonwiwat, R. Govindan, and D. Estrin, Directed diffusion: a scalable and robust communication paradigm for sensor networks, *MOBICOM*, Boston, MA, 2000.
8. G. Krishnamurthy, A. Azizoglu, and A. K. Somani, Optimal location management algorithms for mobile networks, *MOBICOM*, Dallas, Texas, 1998.
9. I. Stojmenovic, A scalable quorum based location update scheme for routing in ad hoc wireless networks, *Technical Report* 99-09, SITE, University of Ottawa, Ontario, Canada, 1999.
10. I. Stojmenovic, Home agent based location update and destination search schemes in ad hoc wireless networks, *Technical Report* 99-10, SITE, University of Ottawa, Ontario, Canada, 1999.
11. G. Pei and M. Gerlan, Mobility management for hierarchical wireless networks, *Mobile Networks and Applications*, **6** (4) (2001), 331-337.
12. I. Aydin and C. C. Shen, Facilitating Match-Making Service in Ad hoc and Sensor Networks Using Pseudo Quorum, *ICCCN*, Miami, FL, 2002.
13. X. Liu, Q. Huang, and Y Zhang, Combs, needles, haystacks: balancing push and pull for discovery in large-scale sensor networks, *SenSys*, Baltimore, MD, 2004.
14. K. Gabriel and R. Sokal, A new statistical approach to geographic variation analysis, *Systematic Zoology*, **18** (1969), 259-278.
15. B. Karp and H. T. Hung, GPSR: Greedy perimeter stateless routing for wireless networks, *MOBICOM*, Boston, MA, 2000.
16. E. Kranakis, H. Singh, and J. Urrutia, Compass routing on geometric networks, *CCCG*, Vancouver, Canada, 1999.
17. P. Bose, P. Morin, I. Stojmenovic, and J. Urrutia, Routing with guaranteed delivery in ad hoc wireless networks, *Wireless Networks*, **7** (2001), 609-616.
18. S. Ratnasamy, B. Karp, S. Shenker, D. Estrin, R. Govindan, L. Yin and F. Yu, Data-centric storage in sensornets with GHT, a geographic hash table, *Mobile Networks and Applications*, **8** (2003), 427-442.

Hierarchical Hypercube-Based Pairwise Key Establishment Schemes for Sensor Networks

Wang Lei[1], Junyi Li[1,2], J.M. Yang[1], Yaping Lin[1], and Jiaguang Sun[2]

[1] College of Software, Hunan University 410082, Chang sha, Hunan, P.R. China
wanglei_hn@hn165.com
http://www.hnu.cn
[2] Department of Computer Science & Technology, Tsinghua University 100084, Beijing, P.R. China

Abstract. Security schemes of pairwise key establishment, which enable sensors to communicate with each other securely, play a fundamental role in research on security issue in wireless sensor networks. A general framework for key predistribution is presented, based on the idea of Key Distribution Center and polynomial pool schemes. By utilizing nice properties of Hierarchical Hypercube model, a new security mechanism for key predistribution based on such model is also proposed. Theoretic analysis and experimental figures show that the new algorithm has better performance and provides higher possibilities for sensors to establish pairwise key, compared with previous related works.

1 Introduction

The security issue in wireless sensor networks has become research focus because of their tremendous application available in military as well as civilian areas. However, constrained conditions existent in such networks, such as hardware resources and energy consumption, have made security research more challenging compared with that in traditional networks.

Current research focus on such security schemes as authentication and key management issues, which are essential to provide basic secure service on sensor communications. Pairwise key establishment enables any two sensors to communicate secretly with each other. However, due to the characteristics of sensor nodes, it is not feasible to utilize traditional pairwise key establishment schemes.

Eeschnaure et al [9] presented a probabilistic key predistribution scheme for pairwise key establishment. This scheme picks a random pool (set) of keys S out of the total possible key space. For each node, m keys are randomly selected from the key pool S and stored into the node's memory so that any two sensors have a certain probability of sharing at least one common key. Chan [10] presented two key predistribution techniques: *q-composite* key predistribution and random pairwise keys scheme. The *q-composite* scheme extended the performance provided by [9], which requires at least q predistributed keys any two sensor should share. The random scheme randomly pickes pair of sensors and assigns each pair a unique random keys. Liu et al [11] developed the idea addressed in previous works and proposed a general framework of

H.T. Shen et al. (Eds.): ADWeb Workshops 2006, LNCS 3842, pp. 186–195, 2006.

polynomial pool-based key predistribution. Based on such a framework, they presented random subset assignment and hypercube-based assignment for key predistribution.

However, it still requires further research on key predistribution because of deficiencies existent in those previous works. Since sensor networks may have dramatic varieties of network scale, the *q-composite* scheme would fail to secure communications as a small number of nodes are compromised. The random scheme may requires each sensor to store a large number of keys, which would be contradicted with hardware constraints of sensor nodes. The random subset assignment would not ensure any two nodes to establish a key path if they do not share a common key. Though the hypercube-based assignment can make sure that there actually exist a key path, however, the possibilities of direct pairwise key establishment are not perfect, leading to large communication overhead.

In order to improve possibilities of direct pairwise key establishment, and depress communication overhead on indirect key establishment, we propose a *H*2 (Hierarchical Hypercube) framework, combined with a new key predistribution scheme, which is proved to be of better working performance on probabilities of pairwise key establishment between any two sensors.

2 Preliminaries

Definition 1 (key predistribution). Cryptographic algorithms are pre-loaded in sensors before node deployment phase.

Definition 2 (pairwise key). When any two nods share a common key denoted as *E*, we call that the two nodes share a pairwise key *E*.

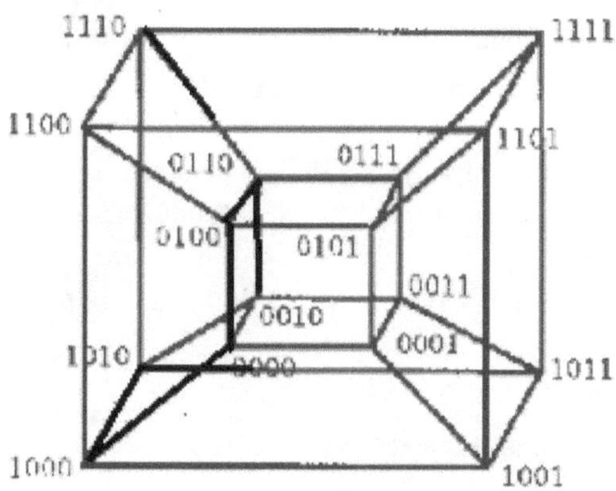

Fig. 1. A 4-dimensional hypercube interconnection network

Definition 3 (key path). Given two nodes A_0 and A_k, which do not share a pairwise key, if there exists a path in sequence described as A_0, A_1, A_2,……,A_{k-1}, A_k and any two nodes A_i, A_j ($0 \leq I \leq k$-1, $1 \leq j \leq k$) share at least one pairwise key, we call that path as a key path.

Definition 4 (*n*-dimensional hypercube interconnection network). *n*-dimensional hypercube interconnection network H_n(abbreviation as *n–cube*) is a kind of network topology that has the following characteristics: (1) It is consisted with 2^n nodes and $n{\cdot}2^{n-1}$ links; (2) Each node can be coded with a different binary string with n bits such as $b_1b_2\ldots b_n$; (3) For any pair of nodes, there is a link between them iif there is just one bit different between their corresponding binary strings.

Fig.1 illustrates the topology of a 4-dimensional hypercube interconnection network, which is consisted with 2^4=16 nodes and $4{\cdot}2^{4-1}$=32 links. And the nodes are coded from 0000 to 1111.

3 Hierarchical Hypercube Model

Definition 5 (*H*2 (Hierarchical Hypercube) Model). Assume that there exist 2^n nodes, the construction algorithm of *n*-dimension *H*2 (*n*) is illustrated as follows:

1) Each $2^{\lceil n/2\rceil}$ nodes are connected as a $\lceil n/2\rceil$ dimensional hypercube, in which nodes are coded from $\underbrace{00...0}_{\lceil n/2\rceil}$ ~ $\underbrace{11...1}_{\lceil n/2\rceil}$, and such kind of node code is called Inner-Hypercube-Node-Code. As a result, $2^{\lfloor n/2\rfloor}$ different such kind of $\lceil n/2\rceil$ dimensional hypercubes can be formed, where $\lceil\ \rceil$ represents the upper integer operation, and $\lfloor\ \rfloor$ means the lower integer operation.

2) The obtained $2^{\lfloor n/2\rfloor}$ different such kind of $\lceil n/2\rceil$ dimensional hypercubes are codes from $\underbrace{00...0}_{\lfloor n/2\rfloor}$ ~ $\underbrace{11...1}_{\lfloor n/2\rfloor}$, and such kind of node code is called Outer-Hypercube-Node-Code. And then, the nodes in the $2^{\lfloor n/2\rfloor}$ different such kind of $\lceil n/2\rceil$ dimensional hypercubes with the same Inner-Hypercube-Node-Code are connected as a $\lfloor n/2\rfloor$ dimensional hypercube, so we can obtain $2^{\lceil n/2\rceil}$ different such kind of $\lfloor n/2\rfloor$ dimensional hypercubes.

3) The graph constructed through the above two steps is called a *H*2 graph. And it is obvious that each node in the *H*2 graph is coded as (*r*, *h*), where *r* ($\underbrace{00...0}_{\lfloor n/2\rfloor} \le r \le \underbrace{11...1}_{\lfloor n/2\rfloor}$) is the node's Inner-Hypercube-Node-Code, and *h* ($\underbrace{00...0}_{\lceil n/2\rceil} \le h \le \underbrace{11...1}_{\lceil n/2\rceil}$) is the node's Outer-Hypercube-Node-Code.

Theroem 1. There exist 2^n nodes in *H*2 (*n*) diagram.

Proof. The conclusion is naturally held as $2^n = 2^{\lfloor n/2\rfloor} * 2^{\lceil n/2\rceil}$.

Theorem 2. The diameter of *H*2 (*n*) is *n*.

Proof. As the diameter of $\lceil n/2\rceil$ dimension hypercube is $\lceil n/2\rceil$, and it is naturally held for the case of $\lfloor n/2\rfloor$ dimension hypercube. Thus the diameter of *H*2(*n*) is $\lceil n/2\rceil+\lfloor n/2\rfloor=n$ according to definition 5.

Theorem 3. The distance of any two nodes $A(r_1, h_1)$ and $B(r_2, h_2)$ in $H2(n)$ is expressed as $d(A,B)= d_h(r_1, r_2)+d_h(h_1, h_2)+1$ where d_h is *Hamming* distance.

Proof. Since the distance of any two nodes is the *Hamming* distance of their corresponding codes, it is held according to definition5.

4 Pairwise Key Establishment Scheme Based on *H*2 Model

As addressed above, polynomial-based and polynomial pool-based schemes have some limitations. In this section we propose a new pairwise key establishment and predistribution scheme based on *H*2 model. The new algorithm is composed of three phases: polynomial pool generation and key predistribution, direct key establishment, and path key establishment.

4.1 Polynomial Pool Generation and Key Predistribution

Assume that there are N nodes in a wireless sensor network, where $2^{n-1} < N \le 2^n$. A n-dimension $H2$ (n) is then generated and we construct a polynomial pool with the following method:

1. The key setup server randomly generates $n*2^n$ bivariate t-degree polynomial pool over a finite fields F_q, denoted as $F= \{ f^i_{<i_1,i_2,\ldots,i_{\lfloor n/2 \rfloor -1}>}(x,y)$, $f^j_{<j_1,j_2,\ldots,j_{\lceil n/2 \rceil -1}>}(x,y) \mid 0 \le i_1 \le i_2 \le \ldots \le i_{\lfloor n/2 \rfloor -1} \le 1,\ 1 \le i \le \lfloor n/2 \rfloor$, $0 \le j_1 \le j_2 \le \ldots \le j_{\lceil n/2 \rceil -1} \le 1, 1 \le j \le \lceil n/2 \rceil \}$.
2. The $2^{\lceil n/2 \rceil -1}$ bivariate polynomials, denoted as $\{ f^j_{<j_1,j_2,\ldots,j_{\lceil n/2 \rceil -1}>}(x,y) \mid 0 \le j_1 \le j_2 \le \ldots \le j_{\lceil n/2 \rceil} \le 1\}$, where $1 \le j \le \lceil n/2 \rceil$, are assigned to the *jth* dimension of the $(i_1, i_2, \ldots, i_{\lfloor n/2 \rfloor})$ th hypercube in *H*2 (*n*).
3. The $2^{\lfloor n/2 \rfloor -1}$ bivariate polynomials, denoted as $\{ f^i_{<i_1,i_2,\ldots,i_{\lfloor n/2 \rfloor -1}>}(x,y) \mid 0 \le i_1 \le i_2 \le \ldots \le i_{\lfloor n/2 \rfloor -1} \le 1\}$ where $1 \le i \le \lfloor n/2 \rfloor$, are assigned to the *ith* dimension of the $(j_1, j_2, \ldots, j_{\lceil n/2 \rceil})$ th hypercube in *H*2(*n*).
4. For any nodes $((i_1, i_2, \ldots, i_{\lfloor n/2 \rfloor}), (j_1, j_2, \ldots, j_{\lceil n/2 \rceil}))$ in *H*2 (*n*), the polynomial shares, denoted as $\{ f^1_{<j_2,\ldots,j_{\lceil n/2 \rceil}>}(x,y)$, $f^2_{<j_1,j_3,\ldots,j_{\lceil n/2 \rceil}>}(x,y)$,…, $f^{\lceil n/2 \rceil}_{<j_1,j_2,\ldots,j_{\lceil n/2 \rceil -1}>}(x,y) \} \cup \{ f^1_{<i_2,i_3,\ldots,i_{\lfloor n/2 \rfloor}>}(x,y)$, $f^2_{<i_1,i_3,\ldots,i_{\lfloor n/2 \rfloor}>}(x,y)$,…, $f^{\lfloor n/2 \rfloor}_{<i_1,i_2,\ldots,i_{\lfloor n/2 \rfloor -1}>}(x,y) \}$, are assigned and pre-loaded before deployment phase.
5. The server assigns a unique ID, denoted as $((i_1, i_2, \ldots, i_{\lfloor n/2 \rfloor}), (j_1, j_2, \ldots, j_{\lceil n/2 \rceil}))$, to every node in sequence, where $0 \le i_1 \le i_2 \le \ldots \le i_{\lfloor n/2 \rfloor} \le 1$, $0 \le j_1 \le j_2 \le \ldots \le j_{\lceil n/2 \rceil} \le 1$.

4.2 Direct Key Establishment

If any two nodes $A\ ((i_1,i_2,\ldots,i_{\lfloor n/2\rfloor}),(j_1,j_2,\ldots,j_{\lceil n/2\rceil}))$ and $B((i'_1,i'_2,\ldots,i'_{\lfloor n/2\rfloor}),(j'_1,j'_2,\ldots,j'_{\lceil n/2\rceil}))$ want to establish pairwise key, the node A can achieve the pairwise key with B by processing the following procedures:

Node A first computes the *Hamming* distance between B and itself, as $d_1=d_h((i_1,i_2,\ldots,i_{\lfloor n/2\rfloor}),(i'_1,i'_2,\ldots,i'_{\lfloor n/2\rfloor}))$,$d_2=d_h((j_1,j_2,\ldots,j_{\lceil n/2\rceil}),(j'_1,j'_2,\ldots,j'_{\lceil n/2\rceil}))$. If d_1=1 or d_2=1, the node can establish the pairwise with the peer according to the conclusion of the theorem4.

Theorem 4. For any two nodes $A((i_1,i_2,\ldots,i_{\lfloor n/2\rfloor}),(j_1,j_2,\ldots,j_{\lceil n/2\rceil}))$ and $B((i'_1,i'_2,\ldots,i'_{\lfloor n/2\rfloor}),(j'_1,j'_2,\ldots,j'_{\lceil n/2\rceil}))$, If the *Hamming* distance $d_h((i_1,i_2,\ldots,i_{\lfloor n/2\rfloor}),(i'_1,i'_2,\ldots,i'_{\lfloor n/2\rfloor}))=1$, or $d_h((j_1,j_2,\ldots,j_{\lceil n/2\rceil}),(j'_1,j'_2,\ldots,j'_{\lceil n/2\rceil}))=1$, then there exists certainly pairwise key between A and B.

Proof

1) $dh\ ((i_1,i_2,\ldots,i_{\lfloor n/2\rfloor}),(i'_1,i'_2,\ldots,i'_{\lfloor n/2\rfloor}))=1$: Assume that $i_t= i'_t$, where $1\le t\le \lfloor n/2\rfloor$-1. Since $i_{\lfloor n/2\rfloor}\neq i'_{\lfloor n/2\rfloor}\Rightarrow f^{\lfloor n/2\rfloor}_{<i_1,i_2,\ldots,i_{\lfloor n/2\rfloor-1}>}(i_{\lfloor n/2\rfloor},i'_{\lfloor n/2\rfloor})=f^{\lfloor n/2\rfloor}_{<i'_1,i'_2,\ldots,i'_{\lfloor n/2\rfloor-1}>}(i'_{\lfloor n/2\rfloor},i_{\lfloor n/2\rfloor})$. So, There exists a pairwise key $f^{\lfloor n/2\rfloor}_{<i_1,i_2,\ldots,i_{\lfloor n/2\rfloor-1}>}(i_{\lfloor n/2\rfloor},i'_{\lfloor n/2\rfloor})$ between A and B.

2) $d_h((j_1,j_2,\ldots,j_{\lceil n/2\rceil}),(j'_1,j'_2,\ldots,j'_{\lceil n/2\rceil}))=1$: Imitating the step 1), it is easy to prove that there exists a pairwise key between A and B.

4.3 Indirect Key Establishment

If $d_h\ ((i_1,i_2,\ldots,i_{\lfloor n/2\rfloor}),(i'_1,i'_2,\ldots,i'_{\lfloor n/2\rfloor}))>1$ and $d_h\ ((j_1,j_2,\ldots,j_{\lceil n/2\rceil}),(j'_1,j'_2,\ldots,j'_{\lceil n/2\rceil}))>1$ then node A can establish indirect pairwise key with B according to Theorem5. In order to make it clear, we will provide a lemma before the illustration of Theorem5.

Lemma 1. For any two nodes $A((i_1,i_2,\ldots,i_{\lfloor n/2\rfloor}),(j_1,j_2,\ldots,j_{\lceil n/2\rceil}))$ and $B((i'_1,i'_2,\ldots,i'_{\lfloor n/2\rfloor}),(j'_1,j'_2,\ldots,j'_{\lceil n/2\rceil}))$, assume that d_h=k, then there exists a k-distance path denoted as $I_0(=A)$, $I_1,\ldots,I_{k-1}$, $I_k(=B)$, where $d_h\ (I_i, I_j)$=1.

Proof. According to Theorem3, d_h can be expressed as $d_h((i_1,i_2,\ldots,i_{\lfloor n/2\rfloor}),(i'_1,i'_2,\ldots,i'_{\lfloor n/2\rfloor}))+d_h((j_1,j_2,\ldots,j_{\lceil n/2\rceil}),(j'_1,j'_2,\ldots,j'_{\lceil n/2\rceil}))=k$. Assume that $d_h((i_1,i_2,\ldots,i_{\lfloor n/2\rfloor}),(i'_1,i'_2,\ldots,i'_{\lfloor n/2\rfloor}))=h$, then $d_h((j_1,j_2,\ldots,j_{\lceil n/2\rceil}),$

$(j'_1, j'_2, ..., j'_{\lceil n/2 \rceil})$)=*k-h*. According to definition5, node $C((i_1, i_2, ..., i_{\lfloor n/2 \rfloor})$, $(j'_1, j'_2, ..., j'_{\lceil n/2 \rceil}))$ and *A* are located in a $\lfloor n/2 \rfloor$-dimensional hypercube *H*, and node *C* and B are located in a $\lceil n/2 \rceil$-dimensional hypercube H'. According to the properties of hypercube[13,14], there exist a path described as $I_0(=A)$, $I_1, \ldots, I_{h-1}$, $I_h(=C)$ in *H*, where $d_h(I_i, I_j)=1$. Similarly, another path with the same property is existed in H', denoted as $I_h(=A)$, $I_{h+1}, \ldots, I_{k-1}$, $I_k(=B)$, where $d_h(I_i, I_j)=1$.

Thus there exist a integrated path in *H2* diagram from node *A* to *B*, described as $I_0(=A)$, $I_1, \ldots, I_{k-1}$, $I_k(=B)$ where $d_h(I_i, I_j)=1$.

Theorem 5. Assume that any two nodes can communicate directly in a wireless sensor networks, and there is no compromised node in the networks, then there exist a key path for any node $A((i_1, i_2, ..., i_{\lfloor n/2 \rfloor}), (j_1, j_2, ..., j_{\lceil n/2 \rceil}))$ and node $B((i'_1, i'_2, ..., i'_{\lfloor n/2 \rfloor}), (j'_1, j'_2, ..., j'_{\lceil n/2 \rceil}))$.

Proof. According to Lemma1, there exist a path for any two nodes where $d_h=k$ in *H2* diagram. Thus the conclusion is held.

We propose the algorithm for indirect key establishment as follows. Assume the two nodes $A((i_1, i_2, ..., i_{\lfloor n/2 \rfloor}), (j_1, j_2, ..., j_{\lceil n/2 \rceil}))$ and node $B((i'_1, i'_2, ..., i'_{\lfloor n/2 \rfloor}), (j'_1, j'_2, ..., j'_{\lceil n/2 \rceil}))$ want to establish indirect pairwise key in the network, we propose the algorithm for indirect key establishment illustrated as follows.

Indirect_Key_Establishing_Algorithm(){

1) Node A computes a set *L* which records the dimensions in which node A and B have different sub-indexes. The set can be expressed as $L=\{(d_1, d_2, \ldots, d_k), (g_1, g_2, \ldots, g_w)\}$ where $d_1 < d_2 < \ldots < d_k$, $g_1 < g_2 < \ldots < g_w$.
2) Node A maintains a path set *P* with initial vale of $P=\{A\}$.
3) Assume that $U((u_1, u_2, ..., u_{\lfloor n/2 \rfloor}), (u'_1, u'_2, ..., u'_{\lceil n/2 \rceil}))=A$; $s=1$.
4) Node *A* computes intermediate nodes expressed as $V=((u_1, u_2, \ldots u_{d_s-1}, i'_{d_s}, u_{d_s+1}, ..., u_{\lfloor n/2 \rfloor}), (u'_1, u'_2, ..., u'_{\lceil n/2 \rceil}))$. And $P=P \cup \{V\}$.
5) Assume that $U=V$.
6) If $s<k$, then $s=s+1$, and repeats the step 4, otherwise turns to step7).
7) Node *A* computes intermediate nodes $V=((u_1, u_2, ..., u_{\lfloor n/2 \rfloor}), (u'_1, u'_2, \ldots u'_{g_s-1}, j'_{g_s}, u'_{g_s+1}, ..., u'_{\lceil n/2 \rceil}))$, and let $P=P \cup \{V\}$.
8) Let $U=V$.
9) If $s<w$, then $s=s+1$, and repeats step7); otherwise go on step10).
10) Let $P=P \cup \{B\}$.

}

According to Theorem5, any node can compute a key path to it destination when there is no compromised node in the network. Once the path *P* is achieved, the two nodes can exchange secret information to generate pairwise key between them.

For example, the node $A((001),(0101))$ and the node $B((100),(1100))$ can establish pairwise key along the following key path: $A((001),(0101)) \rightarrow ((101),(0101)) \rightarrow ((100),(0101)) \rightarrow ((100),(1101)) \rightarrow B((100),(1100))$.

According to the algorithm described above, the following conclusion is naturally held.

Theorem6: Assume that any two nodes can communicate with each other directly, and there is no compromised node in a network. If the distance between the two nodes is k, then there exists a key path with distance of k. That is, the two nodes can establish pairwise key through k-1 intermediate nodes.

5 Analysis

5.1 Feasibilities of the Algorithm

Theorem 7. In our algorithm, the possibility of direct key establishment for any two nodes can be expressed as $P_{H2} \approx (2^{\lfloor n/2 \rfloor} + 2^{\lceil n/2 \rceil}) / (N\text{-}1)$.

Proof. As the algorithm has assigned any node, denoted as $((i_1, i_2, \ldots, i_{\lfloor n/2 \rfloor}), (j_1, j_2, \ldots, j_{\lceil n/2 \rceil}))$, shares of polynomials expressed as $F_A =$ $\{ f^1_{<j_2,\ldots,j_{\lceil n/2 \rceil}>}(j_1, y),\ f^2_{<j_1,j_3,\ldots,j_{\lceil n/2 \rceil}>}(j_2, y), \ldots,\ f^{\lceil n/2 \rceil}_{<j_1,j_2,\ldots,j_{\lceil n/2 \rceil - 1}>}(j_{\lceil n/2 \rceil}, y)\} \cup$ $\{ f^1_{<i_2,\ldots,i_{\lfloor n/2 \rfloor}>}(i_1, y),\ f^2_{<i_1,i_3,\ldots,i_{\lfloor n/2 \rfloor}>}(i_2, y), \ldots,\ f^{\lfloor n/2 \rfloor}_{<i_1,i_2,\ldots,i_{\lfloor n/2 \rfloor - 1}>}(i_{\lfloor n/2 \rfloor}, y)\}$. It's clear that there are $2^{\lfloor n/2 \rfloor} + 2^{\lceil n/2 \rceil}$ nodes which can establish direct pairwise key with the node A. Thus $P_{H2} \approx (2^{\lfloor n/2 \rfloor} + 2^{\lceil n/2 \rceil})/(N\text{-}1)$ as the network scale is within the area $2^{n-1} < N \le 2^n$.

Suppose that a sensor network has N=10000 sensor nodes, then n=14. The possibility of direct key establish is about $P_{H2} \approx 2.56\%$ according to the conclusion drawn by Theorem6. However, the possibility decreases to $P_H \approx 0.14\%$ if the algorithm addressed in [11] is used.

Theroem 8. Assume that the possibility of direct key establishment in $H2$-based scheme is defined as P_{H2}, while the possibility in hypercube is denoted as P_H, then $P_{H2} >> P_H$.

Proof. Suppose the number of a network is within the area of $2^{n-1} < N \le 2^n$, and $P_H \approx \frac{n}{N-1}$ as addressed in [11]. Thus $\lim_{n\to\infty} \frac{P_H}{P_{H2}} = \lim_{n\to\infty} \frac{n}{2^{\lfloor n/2 \rfloor} + 2^{\lceil n/2 \rceil}} = 0$.

5.2 Overhead Analysis

1. Node's storage overhead

1) Any node is required to store t-degree bivariate polynomials whose number is n over the finite fields q, which occupies $n(t+1)\log q$ bits.

2) In order to keep the security of the Keys, for any bivariate polynomial $f(x,y)$, node A is required to store the ID information of the compromised nodes that can

establish direct key with A by using $f(x,y)$. Since the degree of $f(x,y)$ is t, then $f(x,y)$ will be divulged when there are more than t nodes are compromised. So, for any bivariate polynomial $f(x,y)$, node A needs only to store the ID information of n compromised nodes that can establish direct key with A by using $f(x,y)$. In addition, since the node's ID is a vector of n bits, and from theorem 4, we can know that node A needs only to store one bit for each compromised node to determine the whole ID information of the compromised node. So, the total storage cost is *nt bits*.

3) Also the node's own ID information occupies about *n bits* storage space, as it is expressed as $((i_1,i_2,...,i_{\lfloor n/2 \rfloor}),(j_1,j_2,...,j_{\lceil n/2 \rceil}))$.

All of the storage overhead address above sum up to $n(t+1)\log q+nt+n= n(t+1)\log 2q$ *bits*.

Theorem 9. The $H2$-based and the hypercube-based schemes have the same storage overhead.

Proof. According to the analysis on storage overhead addressed in Section5.4 in [11], the result is certainly held.

2. Communication Overhead

In a sensor network, sending a unicast message between two arbitrary nodes may involve the overhead of establishing a route. In case of no compromised node existent in the network, any one node can communicate with the others directly. Assume that the overhead for a hop is defined as 1, then for two arbitrary nodes whose Hamming distance is L, the minimum communication overhead is L. We further inspect average communication overhead on $H2$-based path key establishment.

Suppose there are two nodes A $((i_1,i_2,...,i_{\lfloor n/2 \rfloor}),(j_1,j_2,...,j_{\lceil n/2 \rceil}))$ and $B((i'_1,i'_2,...,i'_{\lfloor n/2 \rfloor}),(j'_1,j'_2,...,j'_{\lceil n/2 \rceil}))$ In the formal part of node's code, the probability of $i_e = i'_e$, $e \in \{1,...,\lfloor n/2 \rfloor\}$ is 1/2; Similarly, the probability of $j_e = j'_e$, $e \in \{1,...,\lceil n/2 \rceil\}$ is also 1/2 in the latter code part. Thus the probability for the two nodes to have i different sub-index in the formal part is expressed as P [*i different sub-indexes in former part*] $= \frac{1}{2^{\lfloor n/2 \rfloor}} \frac{(\lfloor n/2 \rfloor)!}{i!(\lfloor n/2 \rfloor - i)!}$. In the latter part, we also have:

$$P\,[j \textit{ different sub-indexes in later part}] = \frac{1}{2^{\lceil n/2 \rceil}} \frac{(\lceil n/2 \rceil)!}{j!(\lceil n/2 \rceil - j)!}.$$

Thus the average communication overhead can be summarized as:

$$L= \sum_{i=1}^{\lfloor n/2 \rfloor} (i-1)\times P[i \text{ different sub-indexs in former part}] +$$
$$\sum_{j=1}^{\lceil n/2 \rceil} (j-1)\times P[j \text{ different sub-indexs in former part}].$$

Theroem 10. The average communication overhead in the $H2$-based scheme is less than that in the hypercube-based scheme.

Proof. According to the analysis on communication overhead addressed in Section5.4 in [11], the result is certainly held.

Fig.2 shows that the comparison on communication overhead between the $H2$-based scheme and the hypercube-based scheme.

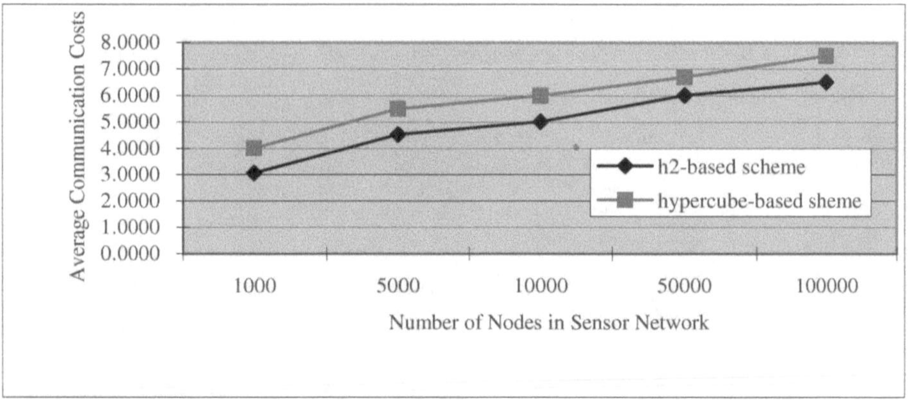

Fig. 2. The comparison on average communication overhead between the $H2$-based and the Hypercube-based schemes

6 Conclusions

Security schemes of pairwise key establishment, which enable sensors to communicate with each other securely, play a fundamental role in research on security issue in wireless sensor networks.A $H2$ –based key predistribution scheme is proposed, and based on which some useful path key establishing algorithms are designed at the same time. Compared with polynomial and polynomial pool-based schemes, the new algorithm can improve the working performances on probability of direct key establishment without additional storage requirement. Moreover, experimental results show that our new algorithms have lower communication costs than previous related works simultaneously.

References

1. G. Pottie and W. Kaiser. Wireless Sensor Networks. Communications of the ACM. Vol.43,(2000)51–58.
2. Estrin,D., Govindan,R., Heideman,J., Kumar,S. Next century challenges: Scalable Coordination in Sensor Networks. Proceedings of the 5th annual ACM/IEEE international conference on Mobile computing and networking. (1999)263-270.
3. LIN Yaping, WANG Lei, A Distributed Data-Centric Hierarchical Routing Algorithm based on Location Information for Sensor Networks, Acta Electronica Sinica, Vol.32, (2004)1801-1805.

4. Liu,D., Ning,P., Efficient Distribution of Key Chain Commitments for Broadcast Authentication in Distributed Sensor Networks, In Proceedings of the 10th Annual Network and Distributed System Security Symposium.(2003)263-276.
5. Perrig,A., Szewczyk,R., et.al. SPINS: Security Protocols for Sensor Networks. In Proceedings of the 7th Annual International Conference on Mobile Computing and Networks. (2001).
6. Karlof,C., Wangner,D., Secure Routing in Wireless Sensor Networks: Attacks and Countermeasures. In Proceedings of 1st IEEE International Workshop on Sensor Networks Protocols and Application. (2003).
7. Pietro,R.D., Mancini,L.V., Mei,A. Random Key Assignment for Secure Wireless Sensor Networks. In 2003 ACM Workshop on Security in Ad Hoc and Sensor Networks. (2003).
8. Du,W., Deng,J., Han,Y.S. et.al. A Pairwise Key Predistribution Scheme for Wireless Sensor Networks, In Proceedings of 10th ACM Conference on Computer and Communication Security. (2003)42-51.
9. Eeschnaure,L., Gligor,V.D. A Key-management Scheme for Distributed Sensor Networks, In proceedings of the 9th ACM Coference on Computer and Communication Security. (2002)41-47.
10. Chan,H., Oerrig,A., Song,D. Random Key Predistribution Schemes for Sensor Networks, In IEEE Syposium on Research in Security and Privacy. (2003)197-213.
11. Donggang Liu, Peng Ning, Rongfang Li, Establishing Pairwise Keys in Distributed Sensor Networks, ACM Journal Name. Vol.20, (2004)1-35.
12. Blundo,C.., Desantis,A., Kutten,S., et.al. Perfectly Secure Key Distribution for Dynamic Conferences. Lecture Notes in Computer Science.Vol.740, (1992) 471-486.
13. WANG Lei, LIN Yaping, Maximum Safety-Path Matrices based Fault-Tolerant Routing for Hypercube Multi-Computers, Journal of Software. Vol.15, (2004)994-1004.
14. WANG Lei, LIN Yaping, A Fault-Tolerant Routing Strategy Based on Maximum Safety-Path Vectors for Hypercube Multi-Computers, Journal of China Institute of Communications. Vol.16, (2004)130-137.

Key Establishment Between Heterogenous Nodes in Wireless Sensor and Actor Networks

Bo Yu[1], Jianqing Ma[2], Zhi Wang[1], Dilin Mao[1], and Chuanshan Gao[1]

[1] Department of Computer Science and Engineering,
Fudan University 200433, China
{boyu, 031021071, dlmao, cgao}@fudan.edu.cn
[2] Department of Computer Information Technology,
Fudan University 200433, China
jqma@guanghua.sh.cn

Abstract. WSAN (Wireless Sensor and Actor Network) has become a promising direction in research. However, up to now, little work has been done in WSAN, especially in security issues. In this paper, we first discuss several challenges in security of WSAN. Aiming at these challenges, we propose our key establishment scheme for heterogeneous nodes in WSAN. In our scheme, authentication and key establishment can be finished with just one round-trip communication. Further more, our scheme is especially designed for heterogeneous architectures. Capability of resource-rich actors are fully used. Finally, our scheme and existing schemes for Ad Hoc Networks and WSN (Wireless Sensor Network) are compared and analyzed.

1 Introduction

A promising research direction called WSAN (Wireless Sensor and Actor Network) is first proposed by Akyildiz [1]. WSAN consists of a group of sensors and actors linked by wireless medium to perform distributed sensing and acting tasks. In such a network, sensors gather information about the physical world, while actors take decisions and then perform appropriate actions upon the environment, which allows a user to effectively sense and act at a distance. A civilian application example is the wild fire handling: sensors relay the information about the exact origin and fire intensity to water sprinkler actors so that the fire can be extinguished before spreading uncontrollably [2].

WSAN has its unique characteristics compared to traditional Ad Hoc Networks and WSN (Wireless Sensor Network), such as heterogeneity, real-time, mobility, and cooperation, etc. However, to our knowledge, little work has been done for WSAN, especially in security issue. Traditional security schemes for Ad Hoc Networks usually are based on decentralized CA (Certificate Authority) or self-organization [12,13,14], which is too complicated to implement in resource-constrained sensor nodes. In the other side, most of existing key management schemes for WSN are based on probabilistic approaches [8,9,11]. Security performance degrades dramatically, when a certain probabilistic threshold is exceeded.

H.T. Shen et al. (Eds.): ADWeb 2006, LNCS 3842, pp. 196–205, 2006.

Further more, the nature attributes of WSAN such as heterogeneity, real-time, also require that new security schemes must be proposed to secure this heterogeneous system.

In this paper, we propose a key establishment scheme for heterogeneous nodes in WSAN. Our scheme is based on PKC (Public Key Cryptography) and Merkle-tree authentication. Our scheme is simple and efficient. Both authentication and session key establishment is finished through just one round-trip communication. We also provide analysis and comparison for our scheme and existing schemes for Ad Hoc Networks and WSN. To the best our knowledge, our approach might be the first attempt to design a heterogeneous key establishment scheme for WSAN.

The main contributions of this paper are:

- Discussing the challenges in security issues in WSAN.
- Designing the key establishment scheme for heterogeneous nodes in WSAN, which provides both identity authentication and key establishment.
- Analyzing and comparing our schemes with the existing schemes for traditional Ad Hoc Networks and WSN.

The rest of this paper is organized as follows. Section 2 provides a simple overview of WSAN, and then proposes several research challenges in security issues for WSAN. We present our key establishment scheme in section 3. Section 4 presents analysis and comparison for our schemes. Related work is briefly introduced in section 5. Finally we draw the conclusion and lay out our future work in section 6.

2 Challenges in Security

Existing security schemes in WSN or Ad Hoc Networks [8,9,11,12,13,14] are not well-suited for WSAN. Due to resource constrains, most of the existing key management schemes in WSN are probabilistic approaches based on pair-wise keys [8,9,10,11], which means sensor nodes might be compromised at a certain probability. This security level is far from enough for nodes, especially actors, in WSAN. Compromised actor would cause more loss than compromised sensor nodes, because of their capability of reacting to the environment. Security schemes in Ad Hoc Networks are also not suitable for WSAN. Most of them are based on asymmetric cryptography and decentralized Certification Authority (CA) [12], which are too complicated and inefficient for heterogeneous nodes in WSAN.

To secure WSAN, we should consider the following attributes:

- Heterogeneous. More work which need complicated computation and large memory space could be transferred from resource-constrained sensor nodes to resource-rich actors.
- Efficient and simple. Security schemes should be efficient and simple enough to meet the realtime and mobile requirement of WSAN.

- Resilient. Strengthened resilience against attacks should be guaranteed to actors, for actors are capable of reacting to the environment, and compromised actors would be much more harmful than compromised sensor nodes.

Although there are many security issues in WSAN, e.g. key management, secure routing, and intrusion detection, in this paper we mainly focus on key establishment for heterogeneous WSAN.

3 Key Establishment

3.1 Assumptions

Before we provide our key establishment approach, we describe several basic assumptions. First, sensor nodes are assumed to be static after deployment, while actors are assumed to be able to move around in a wide area. Sensors are resource-constrained nodes such as MICA2 motes, which have quite limited computation, storage, and wireless communication capabilities. Actors are resource-rich mobile nodes such as unmanned vehicles and robots, which are equipped with powerful CPUs and abundant power supply as well as long-distance wireless communication modules. Actors can communicate with each other within just one hop, while a sensor nodes need to reach a remote node through multi-hops. Finally, we assume that sensor nodes are divided into groups, and they are deployed group by group. Each sensor group will be allocated with one actor. The actor can move around in its home group and the neighboring groups. Deployment information such as the width and length of the target area, can be acquired before deployment.

3.2 Background: Merkle-Tree Based Authentication

Our key establishment scheme is based on a Merkle-Tree algorithm proposed by Du in [7]. We briefly describe how Du's public key authentication scheme works. The Merkle tree is a complete binary tree equipped with a function *hash* and an assignment Φ, which maps a set of nodes to a set of fixed-size strings. Fig. 1 depicts an example of the Merkle tree. The leaves, $L_1, ..., L_N$, represent N sensor nodes. Each leaf contains the bindings between the identity of its corresponding node and the public key of the node. The Φ value of each node is defined as follows:

$$\Phi(L_i) = hash(id_i, pk_i),\ \ for\ i = 1, ..., N$$

$$\Phi(V) = hash(\Phi(V_{left})||\Phi(V_{right}))$$

Let pk be Alice's public key, and L be Alice's corresponding leaf node in the tree. Let λ denote the path from L to the root, and let H represent the length of the path. For each tree node $v \in \lambda$, Alice sends $\Phi(v's\ sibling)$ to Bob, along with the public key pk. We use $\lambda_1, ..., \lambda_H$ to represent these Φ values, and we call these Φ values the proofs. In Fig. 1, the solid dots represent the proofs for Alice. To verify the authenticity of Alice's public key pk(assume Alice's identity

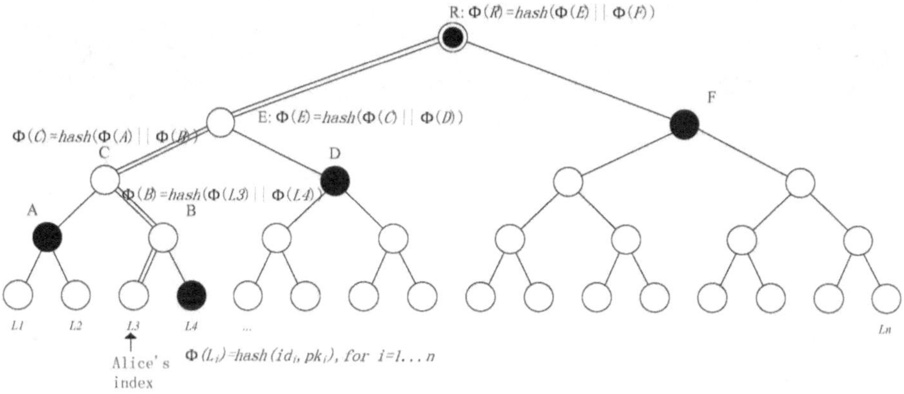

Fig. 1. Merkle-Tree based Authentication

is id), Bob computes $hash(id, pk)$; he then uses the results and $\lambda_1, ..., \lambda_H$ to reconstruct the root of the Merkle tree R' with $\Phi(R')$. Bob will trust that the binding between id and pk is authentic only if $\Phi(R') = \Phi(R)$.

Du proposes an efficient authentication scheme. However, his scheme is designed for homogeneous WSN and not suitable for heterogeneous WSAN. In the next subsection, we introduce our authentication and key establishment scheme for WSAN.

3.3 Our Approach

Key establishment for WSAN can be classified into three categories: actor-actor, sensor-sensor, and sensor-actor key establishments. Due to page limits, in the following we mainly focus on the sensor-actor key establishment which is the most challenging issue.

Key Pre-distribution
We propose a Merkle forest for our key establishment scheme. We suppose that all actor and sensor nodes are divided into N groups, and each group consists of M sensor nodes and one actor. As shown in Fig. 2, our Merkle forest consists of one actor tree and a number of sensor trees. N leaves of the actor tree, $L_1, ..., L_N$, represent N actor nodes, while each leaf contains the bindings between the identity of the corresponding actor and the public key of the actor.

In practice, it is quite common that nodes are deployed in groups. In our work, we divide the target field into grids, and each grid will be deployed with one group of sensor nodes and one actor. We assume that deployment knowledge can be acquired before deployment. Location information has been discussed and proved to be a good technique to strengthen security schemes [10,11]. We propose our key pre-distribution rules based on our Merkle forest and location-aware deployment model as follows:

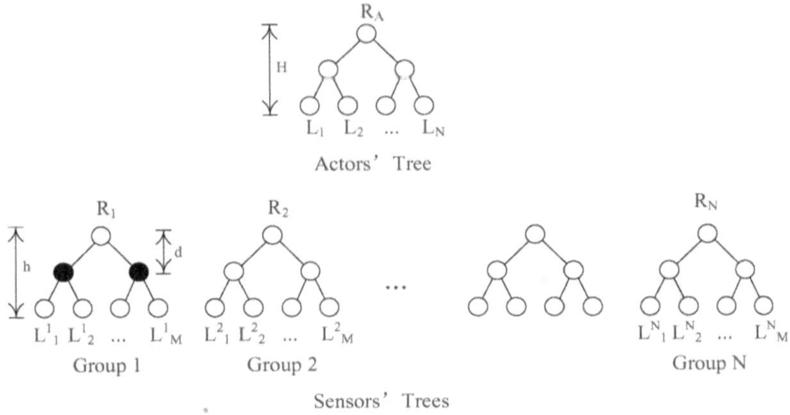

Fig. 2. Merkle Forest for our Key Establishment Scheme

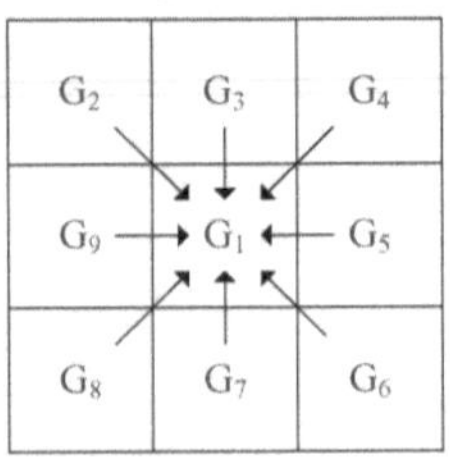

Fig. 3. Group-based Deployment

1. **For sensor nodes.** Suppose that sensor s_i^1, $1 \leq i \leq M$, belongs to group G_1 in Fig. 3. We load $\Phi(R_2), \Phi(R_3), ..., \Phi(R_9)$, $\Phi(L_1)$and $\Phi(R_A)$ into s_i^1's memory. These values are used to help s_i^1 to authenticate identities of other sensor nodes or actors. The proofs for s_i^1, $\lambda_1, ..., \lambda_h$, are also loaded into s_i^1's memory, which can help s_i^1 authenticate itself to other nodes. h refers to the height of sensors' tree, which are decided by the number of sensors in one group. In this way, there are $(10 + h)$ values in total pre-distributed into the memory of each sensor node.
2. **For actor nodes.** Suppose that actor a_1 is deployed together with group G_1 in Fig. 3. We call G_1 a_1's home group. First, the Φ values of the black dots in Fig. 3. are loaded into a_1's memory. There are 2^d Φ values. These values helps a_1 authenticate identities of sensors in its home group. Then, $\Phi(R_2), \Phi(R_3), ..., \Phi(R_9)$ are loaded into s_i^1's memory, which help authenticate identities of sensors in a_1's neighboring groups. Finally, the proofs from actors' tree, $\lambda_1, ..., \lambda_H$, are loaded into a_1's memory, where H refers to the height of the actors' tree. In this way, there are $(2^d + 8 + H)$ values pre-distributed into the memory of each actor.

Because only $\Phi(R)$ values of neighboring groups are loaded for each sensor or actor, less memory will be required, while resilience in security is also strengthened. We will give more analysis in Section 4.

Authentication and Key Establishment
Authentication and key establishment in our scheme is quite simple and efficient. When an actor move into a new area, it tries to set up a secure communication link with sensor nodes in the area. The actor sends its proofs $(\lambda_1, ..., \lambda_H)$, its public key and ID to the target sensor node in plain text. In case of replay attack, a nonce is also generated and sent.

$$\{\lambda_1, ..., \lambda_H, ActPubKey, ActID\} \longrightarrow Plaintext1$$

$$\{nonce, checksum\, of\, Plaintext1\}_{ActPvtKey} \longrightarrow Cyphertext1$$

$$\{Plaintext1, Cyphertext1\} \stackrel{send}{\Longrightarrow} SensorNode$$

After the sensor node receives the message, it use $\lambda_1, ..., \lambda_H$ to authenticate the identity of the actor and use the nonce and checksum to insure the message integrity. If the actor's identity is proved, the sensor node generates a random number as the session key, and encrypts the random number, the nonce, sensor id and its proofs with the actor public key. Some public key operations such as RSA, are proved to be fast enough for sensor nodes, while the private key operations take a quite long time [5,6]. We are in favor of RSA as the public key algorithm in our scheme.

$$\{\lambda_1, ..., \lambda_{h-d}, SenID, random, nonce\}_{ActPubKey} \stackrel{send}{\Longrightarrow} Actor$$

The actor can decrypt the message with its private key. The sensor's identity can be authenticated by its proofs, and the random number is saved in the actor's memory as the future session key.

The process of our key establishment is only one round-trip. It's quite simple and efficient.

4 Analysis

4.1 Security

Compared with existing key management schemes for WSN (Wireless Sensor Network), our scheme is based on PKC (Public Key Cryptography), which is hard in computability for the adversary to break down. Most of the existing key management schemes are based on a probabilistic approach such as random key pre-distribution. Security resilience will be degraded dramatically, when the number of compromised nodes is great than a certain security threshold. What's more, existing key management schemes for WSN is lack of effective authentication, which inevitably lead to its vulnerability to selective node attacks and node replication attacks [9,10]. Although challenge-response techniques are used in existing schemes to implement authentication, they also incur much more communication overhead. On the contrary, both authentication and key establishment is based one round-trip in our scheme.

Compared with existing key management schemes for Ad Hoc Networks, our scheme is simple and efficient. Most of the existing key management schemes [12,13,14] for Ad Hoc Networks don't take heterogeneity into account, and suppose that nodes move together with their users. Zhou [12] proposea an approach based on decentralized CA, which is too complicated for heterogeneous WSAN. Capkun's scheme [13] requires side channels and users' operations to issue certificates. On the contrary, WSAN are widely-deployed and unattended autonomous system. It's impossible to let users to config certificates for thousands of sensors and actors respectively in WSAN.

4.2 Communication vs. Memory

We should make full use of the heterogeneous attributes of WSAN to enhance the performance of the WSAN systems. Actors are resource-rich nodes, while sensors are resource-constrained nodes. So we can move more complicated calculation and mass storage to actors to reduce the communication and memory overhead in sensor nodes.

From section 3.3, we know that each sensor node loads $(10 + h)$ Φ values and each actor loads $(2^d + 8 + H)$ Φ values. We depict several example memory usages of Φ values in Table 1. We suppose that $H = 4$, which means that there are 16 actors in total. From Table 1, We can find that in the case when network size scales up, memory usage in each sensor node increase just a little. We suppose that each Φ value occupies 16 bytes (MD5 length), RSA keys occupy 64 bytes, and there are 1024 sensor nodes in each group and 16 groups (actors) in total. Then memory usage is about $20 \times 16 + 64 = 384$ bytes for each sensor node and $1036 \times 16 + 64 = 16408$ bytes for each actor. Actors store much more Φ values than sensor nodes. Abundant memory resource of actors is fully used. Memory usage of 384 bytes is equal or less than most of the existing probabilistic approaches for WSN [8,9,10,11]. We can tune up d $(0 \leq d \leq h)$ to decide how many memory will be used for Φ values in actors. A great d will help sensor nodes reduce communication overhead, while a small d will help memory-constrained actors free their memory.

In Figure 4, we explore the relationship between communication overhead and d. The overhead refers to the messages for authentication and key establishment introduced in Section 3.3. Communication overhead between a sensor and an

Table 1. The number of Φ values loaded in each node, when network size scales up

# of sensors in each group	Sensor	Actor($d \leq 5$)	Actor($d \leq 10$)
$2^3 = 8$	13	20(d=3)	20(d=3)
$2^7 = 128$	17	44(d=5)	140(d=7)
$2^{10} = 1024$	20	44(d=5)	1036(d=10)

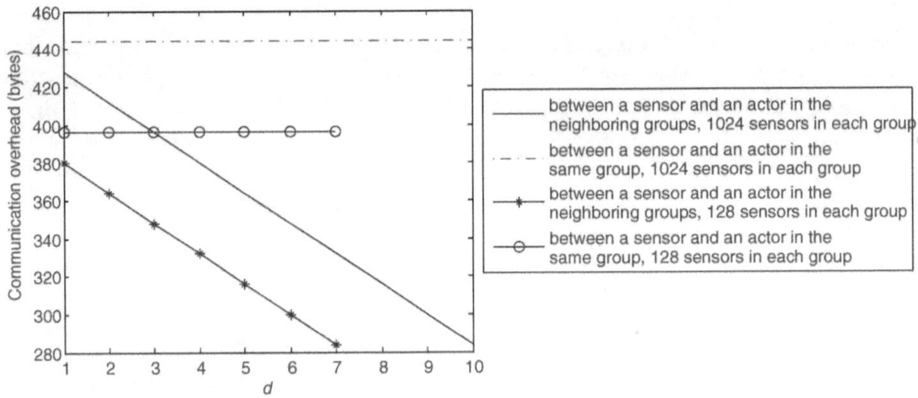

Fig. 4. Communication overhead vs. d. we fix lengthofΦ=16, lengthofPK=64, ActorID(SensorID)=64, nonce=4, checksum=16 (bytes).

actor belonging to the neighboring group is usually a constant (about 400 or 440 bytes in Figure 4), because the sensor and the actor need to send all its proofs (λ values). However, communication overhead can be effectively reduced, if the sensor and the actor belongs to the same group and a greater d is chose. We can have a tradeoff point between actors' memory usage and sensors' communication overhead. Almost 40% overhead can be saved at most if a proper d is chose.

4.3 Analysis Conclusion

Compared with existing key management schemes for Ad Hoc Networks or WSN, our key establishment scheme has following characteristics:

- **Heterogeneous design.** Resource-rich actors is fully used, while communication and computation overhead in sensor nodes are reduced.
- **PKC based.** Our scheme has better security performance in resilience against attacks, compared with existing probabilistic approaches.
- **Simple and efficient.** Both authentication and session key establishment is implemented through just one round-trip communication.

5 Related Work

We first review work in security in Ad Hoc Networks, then review work in key management in WSN.

Zhou and Hass [12] present a distributed public-key management scheme for Ad hoc Networks, which is based on decentralized CA(Certificate Authority). Capkun [13] proposes a self-organized public-key management scheme for mobile Ad Hoc Networks. His scheme has an important precondition that certificates are issued by users and transferred through side channels. Bechler [14] provides a cluster-based security scheme for Ad Hoc Networks, which is based on clustering algorithm.

Eschenauer and Gligor [8] present a key management scheme for sensor networks based on probabilistic key pre-deployment. Chan et al [9] extend this scheme and present three new mechanisms for key establishment based on the framework of probabilistic key pre-deployment. Du [7] and Huang [10] propose location-aware key management schemes, which strengthen the resilience against node selective attacks and node replication attacks. In [5,6], how to apply PKC (Public Key Cryptography) to resource-constrained sensor nodes is studied.

6 Conclusion

In this paper, several challenging issues in WSAN(Wireless Sensor and Actor Network) are proposed first. Security schemes for WSAN are required to be simple, efficient and suitable for heterogeneous architectures. Aiming at these goals, we present our key establishment schemes between heterogeneous nodes for WSAN. Authentication and session key establishment in our scheme can be finished through just one round-trip communication. We also provide analysis and comparison for our scheme and existing schemes. Our scheme is proved to be simple and efficient. To our knowledge, little work, especially in security issues, has been done in WSAN. Our approach may be the first attempt to design a heterogeneous key management scheme for WSAN.

References

1. I. F. Akyildiz and I. H. Kasimoglu, Wireless sensor and actor networks: research challenges, Ad hoc networks 2 (2004), 2004.
2. Fei Hu, Xiaojun Cao, Security in Wireless Actor & Sensor Networks (WASN): Towards A Hierarchical Re-Keying Design. ITCC (2), 2005.
3. I. F. Akyildiz, D. Pompili, T. Melodia, Underwater Acoustic Sensor Networks: Research Challenges, Elsevier's Journal of Ad Hoc Networks, Vol. 3, Issue 3, pp. 257-279. 2005.
4. A. Durresi, M. Durresi, L. Barolli, Sensor Inter-vehicle Communication for Safer Highways. In Proc. of the First International Workshop on Ubiquitous Smart Worlds USW 2005, 2005.
5. N. Gura, A. Patel, A. Wander, H. Eberle, and S. C. Shantz, Comparing Elliptic Curve Cryptography and RSA on 8-bit CPUs. In Proc. of CHES'04, 2004.
6. R.Watro, D. Kong, S. fen Cuti, C. Gardiner, C. Lynn, and P. Kruus, TinyPK: Securing Sensor Networks with Public Key Technology. In Proc. of ACM SASN, 2004.
7. Wenliang Du, Ronghua Wang, and Peng Ning, An Efficient Scheme for Authenticating Public Keys in Sensor Networks. In Proc. of The 6th ACM International Symposium on Mobile Ad Hoc Networking and Computing (MobiHoc), 2005.
8. L. Eschenauer and V. Gligor, A Key-Management Scheme for Distributed Sensor Networks. In Proc. Of ACM CCS, 2002.
9. Haowen Chan, Perrig A., Song D., Random key predistribution schemes for sensor net-works. In Proc. of Symposium on Security and Privacy, 2003.

10. D. Huang, M. Mehta, D. Medhi, L. Harn, Location-aware Key Management Scheme for Wireless Sensor Networks. In Proc. of ACM Workshop on Security of Ad Hoc and Sensor Networks (SASN'04), 2004.
11. Wenliang Du, Jing Deng, Yunghsiang S. Han, Shigang Chen and Pramod Varshney, A Key Management Scheme for Wireless Sensor Networks Using Deployment Knowledge. In Proc. of IEEE Infocom'04, 2004.
12. Lidong Zhou and Zygmunt J. Haas. Securing Adhoc Networks. IEEE Network Magazine, 13(6):24-30, November/December 1999.
13. S. Capkun, L. Buttyan, and J. P. Hubaux, Self-Organized PublicKey Management for Mobile Ad Hoc Networks. IEEE Trans. Mobile Computing, vol. 2, no. 1, pp. 52-64, Jan-Mar. 2003.
14. Marc Bechler, Hans-Joachim Hof, Daniel Kraft, Frank Pahlke, Lars Wolf, A Cluster-Based Security Architecture for Ad Hoc Networks. In Proc. of IEEE Infocom'04, 2004.

A Self-management Framework for Wireless Sensor Networks*

Si-Ho Cha[1], Jongoh Choi[2], and JooSeok Song[2]

[1] Department of Computer Engineering, Sejong University, Korea
sihoc@sejong.ac.kr
[2] Department of Computer Science, Yonsei University, Korea
{jochoi, jssong}@emerald.yonsei.ac.kr

Abstract. In wireless sensor networks (WSNs), a large number of sensor nodes are deployed over a large area and long distances and multi-hop communication is required between nodes. So managing numerous wireless sensor nodes directly is very complex, and is not efficient. The management of WSNs must be autonomic self-managed with a minimum of human interference, and robust to changes in network states. To do this, we propose a scalable self-management framework for WSNs called SNOWMAN (SeNsOr netWork MANagement) framework. Our SNOWMAN framework is based on hierarchical management architecture and on the policy-based network management (PBNM) paradigm. SNOWMAN can reduce the costs of managing sensor nodes and of the communication among them using hierarchical clustering architecture. SNOWMAN can also provide administrators with a solution to simplify and automate the management of WSNs using PBNM paradigm.

1 Introduction

Wireless sensor networks (WSNs) form a new kind of ad hoc network with a new set of characteristics and challenges. Unlike conventional wireless ad hoc network, a WSN potentially comprises hundreds to thousands of nodes. Different from nodes of a traditional ad hoc network, sensor nodes are less mobile after deployment, and are required higher density. During periods of low activity, the network may enter a dormant state in which many nodes go to sleep to conserve energy. Also, nodes go out of service when the energy of the battery runs out or when a destructive event takes place [1].

A WSN consist of a large number of sensor nodes, which are tiny, low-cost, low-power radio devices dedicated to performing certain functions such as collecting various environmental data and sending them to sink nodes, gateway nodes, or base stations.

In this WSN, radio bandwidth is scarce, computational power is limited, and energy efficient is paramount. Such limitations are challenges to overcome. In

* This research was supported by the MIC (Ministry of Information and Communication), Korea, under the ITRC (Information Technology Research Center) support program supervised by the IITA (Institute of Information Technology Assessment).

H.T. Shen et al. (Eds.): ADWeb 2006, LNCS 3842, pp. 206–213, 2006.

particular, one of the essential needs is for a system that autonomously manages the limited energy and bandwidth of WSNs. One of the major goals of network management is to promote productivity of network resources and maintain the quality of service [2]. In WSNs, a large number of sensor nodes are deployed over a large area and long distances and multi-hop communication is required between nodes and sensor nodes have the physical restrictions in particular energy and bandwidth restrictions. So managing numerous wireless sensor nodes directly is very complex and is not efficient. To intelligent self-management, sensor nodes should be organized and managed automatically and dynamic adjustments need to be done to handle changes in the environment. The self-management of WSNs must be able to know the changes in networks and to deal with the changes in a minimum of human interference.

From these backgrounds, we propose a self-management framework for WSNs called SNOWMAN (SeNsOr netWork MANagement), which is based on policy-based network management (PBNM) paradigm and hierarchical clustering architecture. PBNM paradigm of SNOWMAN can provide administrators with a solution to simplify and automate the management of WSNs. However, the cost of PBNM paradigm can be expensive to some WSN architecture. SNOWMAN employs therefore hierarchical clustering management architecture, which can reduce the costs of managing sensor nodes and of the communication among them, using clustering mechanisms.

This paper is structured as follows. Section 2 discusses the management requirements of WSNs and the architecture and components of the proposed SNOWMAN. Section 3 presents the implementation of the SNOWMAN and the testbed of a WSN. Finally in section 4 we conclude the paper.

2 Design

2.1 Management Requirements

The management of WSNs introduces various requirements due to scare network resources, dynamic topology, traffic randomness, energy restriction, and a large amount of network elements. These requirements are follows [3].

- Minimal control overhead. Any network management system involves a certain amount of additional control traffic to regulate the various operational characteristics of the network. In WSNs, it is extremely important to minimize this signaling overhead, ensuring that the links are not congested and the energy consumption is not increase with management traffic.
- Lightweight. Sensor nodes have limited battery life, limited storage and/or processing capabilities. Hence, a lightweight computation is required in order to alleviate the demand on the battery power.
- Automated, Intelligent and Self-organizing. Given the dynamic nature of most WSNs, an adaptive management framework that automatically reacts to changes in network conditions is required.

– Robustness. The divers and hostile environments of WSNs require a network management system that is able to react to them in order to provide fault-tolerance.

2.2 SNOWMAN: SeNsOr netWork MANagement

To facilitate scalable and localizable management of sensor networks, SNOWMAN constructs 3 tier regional hierarchical cluster-based senor networks: regions, clusters, and sensor nodes as shown in Fig. 1.

In the architecture, a WSN is comprised of a few regions and a region covers many clusters has several cluster head nodes. Sensor nodes should be aggregated to form clusters based on their power levels and proximity. That is, a subset of sensor nodes are elected as cluster heads. In 3 tier regional hierarchical architecture of SNOWMAN, cluster heads constitute the routing infrastructure, and

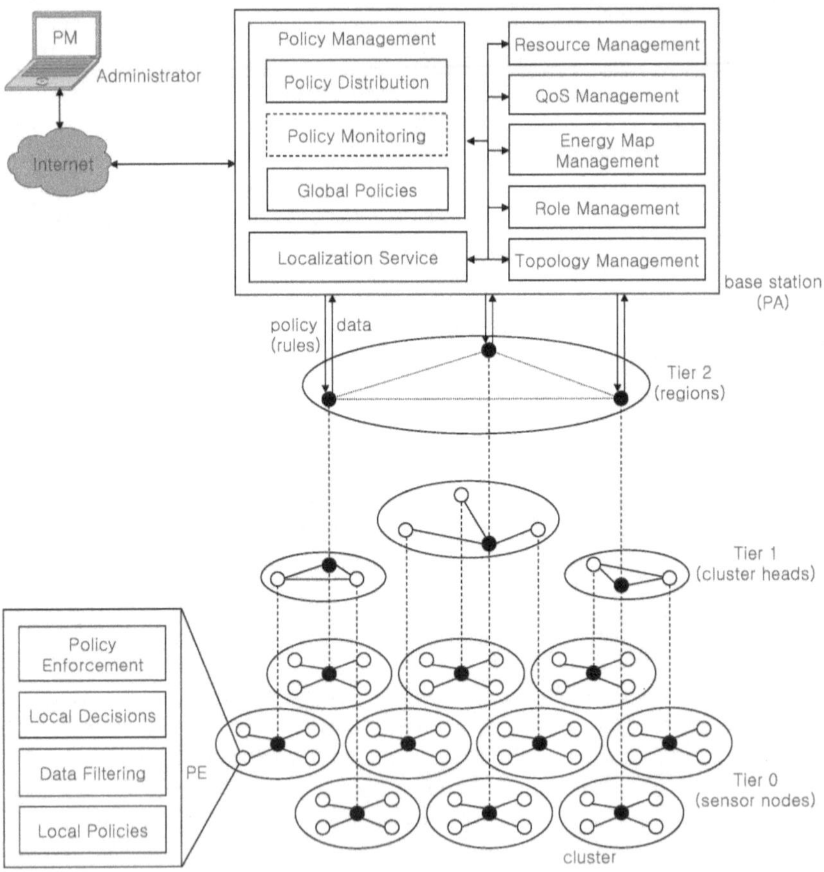

Fig. 1. SNOWMAN Architecture for Self-Management

aggregate, fuse, and filter data from their neighboring common sensor nodes. The PA can deploy specific policies into particular areas (or clusters) to manage just singular regions or phenomena by more scalable manner. So, SNOWMAN framework is very useful to regionally manage the sensor networks.

Our SNOWMAN framework includes a policy manager (PM), one or more policy agent (PA) and a large number of policy enforcers (PEs) as shown in Fig. 1. The PM is used by an administrator to input different policies, and is located in a manager node. A policy in this context is a set of rules that assigns management actions to sensor node states. The PA and the PE reside in the base station and in the sensor node, respectively. The PA is responsible for interpreting the policies and sending them to the PE. The enforcement of rules on sensor nodes is handled by the PE. In a WSN, individual nodes will not be able to maintain a global view of the network. Such a task is well suited for a machine not constrained by battery or memory. This is the reason for having the PA on the base station.

It is the job of the PA to maintain this global view, allowing it to react to larger scale changes in the network and install new policies to reallocate policies (rules). If node states are changed or the current state matches any rule, the PE performs the corresponding local decisions based on local rules rather than sends information to base station repeatedly. Such policy execution can be done efficiently with limited computing resources of the sensor node. It is well known that communicating 1 bit over the wireless medium at short ranges consumes far more energy than processing that bit.

2.3 Hierarchical Clustering: SNOWCLUSTER

The idea of clustering in WSNs is not new. We propose a clustering scheme solely from a management viewpoint. Each sensor node autonomously elects cluster heads based on a probability that depends on its residual energy level. The role of a cluster head is rotated among nodes to achieve load balancing and prolong the lifetime of every individual sensor node. To do this, SNOWMAN re-clusters periodically to re-elect cluster heads that are richer in residual energy level, compared to the other nodes. We assume all sensor nodes are stationary, and have knowledge of their locations.

SNOWMAN constructs hierarchical cluster-based senor network using SNOW CLUSTER clustering algorithm as seen in Table 1. SNOWCLUSTER takes a couple of steps to accomplish the hierarchical clustering: 1) cluster head selection and 2) region node selection. In order to elect cluster heads, each node periodically broadcasts a discovery message that contains its node ID, its cluster ID, and its remaining energy level.

A node declares itself as a cluster head if it has the biggest residual energy level of all its neighbor nodes, breaking ties by node ID. Each node can independently make this decision based on exchanged discovery messages. Each node sets its cluster ID (*c_id*) to be the node ID (*n_id*) of its cluster head (*c_head*). If a node i hears from a node j with a bigger residual energy level (*e_level*) than itself, node i sends a message to node j requesting to join the cluster of node j. If node j already has resigned as a cluster bead itself, node j returns a rejection, otherwise node j returns a confirmation. When node i receives the confirmation, node i resigns as a cluster head and sets its cluster ID to node j's node ID. After forming clusters, region nodes are elected from the cluster heads.

Table 1. SNOWCLUSTER Algorithm

```
// CLUSTER HEAD SELECTION
∀x[node(x).role ← c_head]
∀x[node(x).c_id ← node(x).n_id]
∀x[node(x).bcast(dis_msg)]
 if node_i.hears_from(node_j)
     if node_i.e_level < node_j.e_level
         node_i.req_join(node_j)
 if node_j.role ≠ c_head
     node_j.rej_join(node_j)
 else
     node_j.conf_join(node_j)
 if node_i.rec_conf(node_j)
     node_i.role ← c_member, node_i.c_id ← node_j.n_id

// REGION NODE SELECTION
∀x[ if node(x).role = c_head]
     ∃x[node(x).bcast(c_info_msg)]
 if PA.rec(c_info_msg)
     PA.assign(r_node), PA.bcast(r_dec_msg)
 if node_k.rec(r_dec_msg)
     if node_k.role = c_head
         if node_k.n_id = r_dec_msg.r_id
             node_k.role ← r_node, node_k.r_id ← node_k.n_id
         else if node_k.n_id ∈ r_dec_msg.r_list
             node_k.r_id ← r_dec_msg.r_id
         node_k.bcast(r_conf_msg)
```

When the cluster head selection is completed, the entire network is divided into a number of clusters. A cluster is defined as a subset of nodes that are mutually reachable in at most 2 hops. A cluster can be viewed as a circle around the cluster head with the radius equal to the radio transmission range of the cluster head. Each cluster is identified by one cluster head, a node that can reach all nodes in the cluster in 1 hop.

After the cluster heads are selected, The PA should select the region nodes in the cluster heads. The PA receives cluster information messages (c_info_msgs) that contain cluster ID, the list of nodes in the cluster, residual energy level, and location data from all cluster heads. The PA suitably selects region nodes according to residual energy level and location data of cluster heads. If a cluster head k receives region decision messages (r_dec_msgs) from the PA, the node

k compares its node ID with region ID (r_id) from the messages. If the previous comparison is true, node k declares itself as a region node (r_node) and sets its region ID to its node ID. Otherwise, if node k's node ID is included in a special region list (r_list) from the message, node k sets its region ID to a corresponding region ID of the message. The region node selection is completed with region confirmation messages (r_conf_msgs) broadcasted from all of cluster heads.

2.4 Functional Components of SNOWMAN

The PA consists of several functional components: policy distribution, policy monitoring, resource management, energy map management, QoS management, topology management, role management, and localization service. Localization service in the context implies the scalability of management to regionally manage the sensor networks. It is achieved via role management and topology management. Global policies are specified by a network administrator in a logically centralized fashion, and are expected to be static.

Policy distribution is the first essential task in ensuring that nodes are managed consistently with the defined policies. We design and implement a TinyCOPS-PR protocol that is similar to COPS-PR [7] protocol to deploy policies into sensor nodes. COPS-PR protocol is an extension for the COPS protocol to provide an efficient and reliable means of provisioning policies. The PA communicates with the PE using the TinyCOPS-PR protocol to policy distribution. TinyCOPS-PR allows asynchronous communication between the PA and the PEs, with notifications (reports, changes in policies, etc.) conveyed only when required. However, to provide robust management of the network, it is desirable to have an independent policy monitoring process to ensure that the deployed policies behave well as defined in them. Though the policy monitoring is desirable, it is achieved via passive methods because of the resources of WSNs are scarce. Energy map management continuously updates the residual energy levels of sensor nodes, especially of cluster heads and region nodes. This energy map management is also achieved via topology management process. Topology management consists of a topology discovery, resource discovery, and role discovery. Resource management and role management manage the detected resources and roles, respectively. QoS management is a part of policy management using QoS policies like bandwidth allocation for emergency. Energy map management and/or QoS management go through an aggregation and fusion phase when energy and/or QoS information collected are merged and fused into energy and/or QoS contours by means of cluster heads.

The PE enforces local policies assigned by the PM to make local decisions and filter off unessential redundant sensed data. To do this, the PE consists of policy enforcement function, local decision function, data filtering function, and local policies. The PE communicates with the PA via TinyCOPS-PR protocol to be assigned local policies.

3 Implementation

3.1 Testbed Network

Our current work has focused on validating some of our basic ideas by implementing components of our architecture on Nano-24 [8] platform using the TinyOS programming suite. The Nano-24 uses Chipcon CC4220 RF for transmission and support 2.4 Ghz, Zigbee. The sensor node uses atmega 128L CPU with 32KBytes main memory and 512 Kbytes flash memory. The Nano-24 also supports Qplus-N sensor network development environment support that ETRI (Electronics and Telecommunications Research Institute) developed. We organized a testbed network was composed 12 Nano-24 nodes. Each node contains SNOWMAN's PE to support policy-based management. All sensor nodes are configure the hierarchical clustering architecture according to the SNOWCLUSTER clustering mechanism.

3.2 SNOWMAN

The PM and PA of SNOWMAN architecture are implemented on Windows XP systems using pure JAVA. The PE is implemented on TinyOS in the Nano-24 nodes using gcc.

Fig. 2 shows the input forms for policy information on the PM. We use the XML technologies to define and handle global policies. There are several advantages of using XML in representing global policies. Because XML offers many

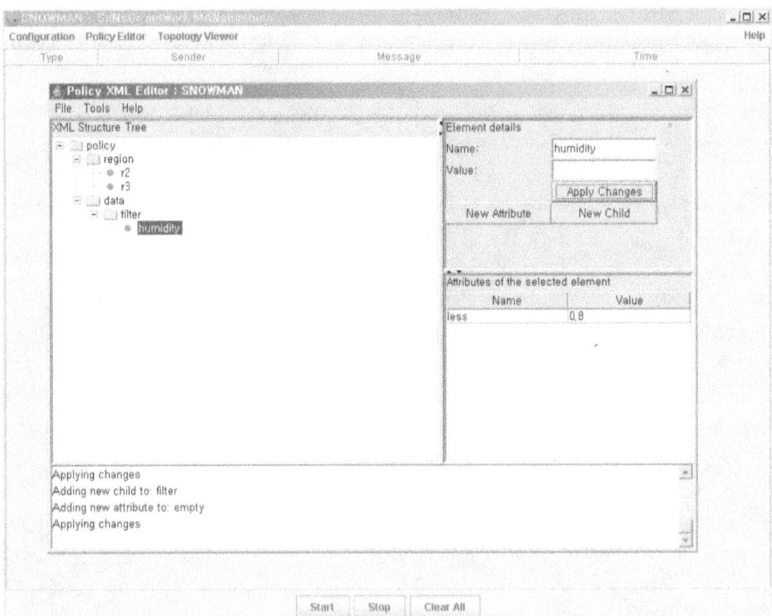

Fig. 2. Snapshot of SNOWMAN Policy Manager (PM)

useful parsers and validators, the efforts needed for developing a policy-based management system can be reduced. To define XML policies, we customized and used the Scott's XML Editor [9]. The defined policies are stored locally in the policy storage of the PM and are stored remotely in the policy storage of the PA. PM communicates with PA via simple ftp for policy transmissions. To policy distribution to sensor nodes, we also design and implement TinyCOPS-PR that is simplified suitably for wireless sensor networks.

4 Conclusion

In this paper, we presented a scalable self-management framework for wireless sensor networks called SNOWMAN. The SNOWMAN framework integrated the policy-based management paradigm and hierarchical cluster-based management architecture to simplify and automate scalable management of WSNs. In SNOWMAN framework, the policies are distributed form PA to PE using TinyCOPS-PR to facilitate intelligent management of sensor networks.

We are currently at the stage of implementation of the business logic of SNOWMAN. We plan to experiment with and demonstrate the system on laboratory testbeds using Nano-24 sensor nodes. This project is still in its early stages. Much work remains to be done on all components of our framework. The eventual goal is to deploy this system in its entirety and to perform a detailed analysis of the results.

References

1. Raquel A. F. Mini, Antonio A. F. Loureiro, Badri Nath, The distinctive design characteristic of a wireless sensor network: the energy map, Elsevier Computer Communications, Faburary 2004.
2. Linnyer B. Ruiz, José M. Nogueira, Antonio A. F. Loureiro, MANNA: A Management Architecture for Wireless Sensor Networks, IEEE Communications Magazine, Volume 41, Issue 2, February 2003.
3. Kaustubh S. Phanse, Luiz A. DaSilva, Extending Policy-Based Management to Wireless Ad Hoc Networks, 2003 IREAN Research Workshop, April 2003.
4. R. Yavatkar, D. Pendarakis, R. Guerin, A Framework for Policy-based Admission COntrol, IETF RFC 2753, January 2000.
5. Linnyer B. Ruiz, Fabircio A. Silva, Thais R. M. Braga, José M. Nogueira, Antonio A. F. Loureiro, On Impact of Management in Wireless Sensors Networks, IEEE/IFIP NOMS 2004, Volume 1, 19-23 April 2004.
6. D. Durham et al., The COPS (Common Open Policy Service) Protocol, IETF 2748, January 2000.
7. K. Chen et al., COPS usage for Policy Provisioning (COPS-PR), IETF RFC 3084, March 2001.
8. Nano-24: Sensor Network, Octacomm, Inc., http://www.octacomm.net
9. Scott Hurring, XML Editor, http://hurring.com/code/java/xmleditor/.

Behavior-Based Trust in Wireless Sensor Network

Lei Huang[1], Lei Li[1], and Qiang Tan[2]

[1] Institute of Software, Chinese Academy of Sciences
{huanglei04, lilei}@ios.cn
[2] Chinese Academy of Space Technology
tqhlff@public3.bta.net.cn

Abstract. The resource constraints of wireless sensor network make it easy to attack and hard to protect. Although carefully designed cryptography and authentication help to make WSN securer, they are not good at dealing with compromised node and ageing node, whose misbehavior may impair the function of WSN. Behavior-based trust mechanism, which is a variant of reputation-based trust in eCommerce, can be used to address this problem. The framework and related techniques of behavior-based trust are discussed in this paper.

1 Introduction

Wireless sensor network is made up of a lot of tiny resources-limited sensors. The shortage of energy, storage and computing capability make strong security mechanism infeasible in WSN. Sensor node is susceptible to be compromised by adversaries, especially in unattended deployments. But node compromise is hard to detect even cryptography mechanism is applied, because most low-cost tiny nodes are not tamper-resistant and the legitimate keys are easy to be cracked by the adversary. Although the cracking may need some time, it is hard to discover because others may think the node is dozing. So the only way to detect a compromised node is by observing its behavior.

Besides compromised nodes, there is another kind of nodes that behave differently from normal ones - the ageing node. With ageing components or decreasing energy, the node cannot work normally during the last period of its lifetime. Both kinds of nodes will not do as expected, and we refer to them as misbehaving nodes.

The existence of misbehaving nodes is harmful to WSN. They may drop packets, provide false reports, and even make part of WSN unworkable. They should be excluded from task allocation whenever there are alternatives. So some kind of mechanism should be applied to predict the future behavior of a sensor node.

Reputation-based trust model[1][2], which measures trustworthiness based on reputation, is used in eCommerce to reduce the risk of dishonest customer or vendor. The concept can also be applied in WSN. But there are some differences. First of all, it's very simple to evaluate single transaction in eCommerce, but that is very difficult in WSN. Secondly, it needs large amount of communication to exchange opinions to achieve a common reputation, which is too expensive to implement in WSN. Third,

H.T. Shen et al. (Eds.): APWeb Workshops 2006, LNCS 3842, pp. 214–223, 2006.

the accuracy of evaluation in eCommerce is much higher than that in WSN. To differentiate the concept from that in eCommerce, we refer to it as behavior-based trust in WSN.

The behavior-based trust is basically a close control loop embedded in WSN. The history of node's past behavior is recorded in term of trust degree, which determine the role of this node in future task allocation. Due to the resource constraints, trust comes mainly from direct interactions. But indirect information is also included in this model, which make the combination more complex.

The paper is organized as follows: The behavior-based trust framework is discussed in section 2. Section 3,4,5 will focus on the related technique: authentication, behavior evaluation, evaluation combination. Conclusion and open issues are addressed in section 6.

2 Behavior-Based Trust Framework

Trust degree is the core of behavior-base trust framework. It represents the accumulative performance of the node in past tasks and decides the role of the node in future tasks. The term "task" here means transaction and interaction between two or more nodes. Various tasks are carried out in WSN, such as communicating, routing, data processing, locating, etc. A node may be involved in one or more tasks. A reasonable assumption is that nodes behave consistently in different tasks, i.e., if a node functions poorly in one kind, it is very likely to misbehave in others. So evaluations of different tasks can be combined together to predict its future behavior.

2.1 Process

The process of the behavior-based trust is depicted in figure 1.After every task, the behavior of the node is evaluated. The evaluation result is combined with old trust degree to form a new one. The new degree is considered in the next task allocation in term of weight. For example, the data from node with high degree should play a more important role in data fusion, and the trustworthy nodes should be chosen to transmit data with higher probabilities than untrustworthy ones.

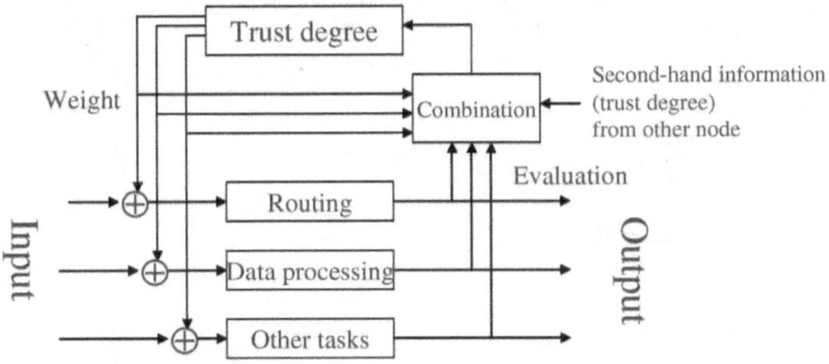

Fig. 1. The process of behavior-based trust management

Second-hand information is also included in this framework to accelerate the convergence of trust degree, assuming that evaluations of a specific behavior conducted by different nodes are fairly consistent. When combining second-hand evaluations, the node must take the trust degree of its source into consideration in case of fraud.

So the trust degree is a function of old trust degree, current evaluation, second-hand information.

$$T^t_{i,j} = F(T^{t-1}_{i,j}, e^t_{i,j}, \alpha \sum_{k \neq i} T^{t-1}_{i,k} T^{t-1}_{k,j}) \tag{1}$$

$T^t_{i,j}$ is the trust degree of node *j* hold by node *i* at time *t*. Note $T^t_{i,j}$ is not necessary to equal $T^t_{k,j}$. $e^t_{i,j}$ is node *i*'s evaluation of node *j* after an interaction. α is a constant representing the weight of second-hand information in the calculation of trust degree.

2.2 Components

A behavior-based trust model is made up of two major parts: evaluation of single task and the evaluation combination. But to make the model work, an effective authentication mechanism must exist to ensure all the identities are trustworthy. Figure 2 depicts the components of the model.

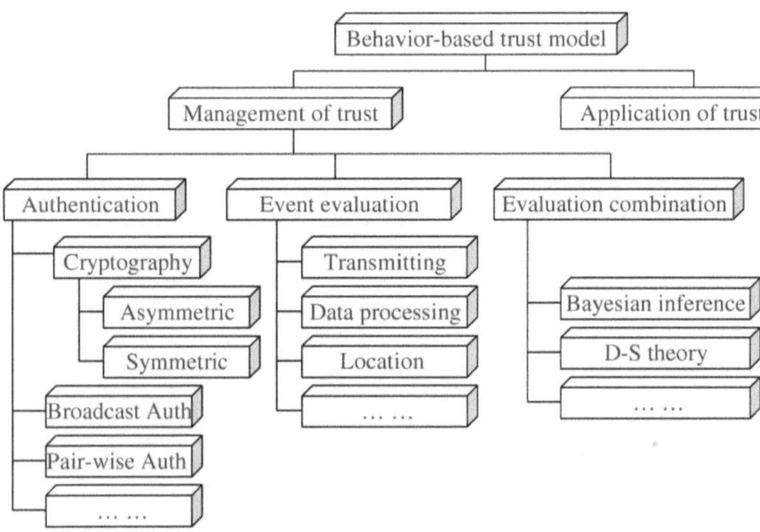

Fig. 2. The components of behavior-based trust

The management of trust and the application of trust are top-level components. While the former is related to the creation, update and deletion of trust degree, the latter cares about how to use it. This paper will focus on the former.

The management of trust can be divided into three components:

- Authentication component assures that the identity of the subject is unique and trustworthy , on the base of cryptographic primitives.
- Task evaluation component evaluates the performance of the node after a task. The tasks here include but not confine to transmitting, data processing, locating and others. Different task needs different evaluation method.
- Evaluation combination component combines the evaluation result with old trust degree and second information from neighbors to form the new trust degree which is used in future task allocation and evaluation.

2.3 Deployment Issues

In essence, trust is a relationship between two peers. Collaboration is not necessary to get common awareness about whether a node is trustworthy or not. Although collaboration helps to accelerate the trust decision process and make the trust more accurate to ground truth, it is achieved by mutual communications which needs high energy cost. So the architecture of trust management in WSN must balance between trust convergence and energy cost.

Trust management can be distributed or central. In totally distributed mode, every node maintains its trust table of other nodes. Evidence of trust comes from direct observations of those nodes. In the central mode, every node reports its observations to a central node which acts as a trust authority in the WSN. While the former needs a long time to get the real estimation of a node's trustworthiness, the latter invokes a quantity of communication and subsequent high energy cost.

Hybrid architecture may be much preferable than the former two. Because most interaction in WSN happens within neighborhood, a reasonable mode is that every node maintain itself 's trust of neighbors while exchanging opinions with each other intermittently within the neighborhood.

3 Authentication

Authentication is closely connected to cryptography. Asymmetric cryptography is widely used in identification and authentication. Although it is regarded as unsuitable for WSN due to the resource constraints, the effort to make it work in WSN has never stopped. [3] argues that asymmetric cryptography works well in WSN with suitable algorithm, parameter, hardware and careful optimization. On the other hand, symmetric cryptography, which demands secure key exchange, must be carefully designed too, to avoid the risks brought by wireless channel of WSN. There are currently three kinds of solutions: key pre-distribution before deployment[4] [5] [6], key creation and distribution during the initial phase after deployment[7], server-based key management[8][9].

Based on cryptography, many authentication mechanisms have been developed. [10] proposed an authentication framework μTESLA for broadcasting, which used a delayed disclosure of symmetric keys to achieved an asymmetry needed by valid authentication. [11] made all the nodes that were involved in relaying sensor report to the base station to authenticate the report in an interleaved, hop-by-hop fashion in order to detect data injection or modification. [12] used one-way hash key chain for one hop broadcast and probabilistic challenge scheme to authenticate received packet. A lot of literature [13][14][15] proposed various authentication scheme used in different scenario and for different purpose. Comparatively, authentication technique is more mature than the other two components of WSN.

4 Behavior Evaluation

A general behavior evaluation process is composed of four steps: expectation definition, actual output observation, difference calculation, and normalization of various task-specific evaluations. Although behavior evaluation is task-specific, energy-efficiency and fault-tolerance are basic requirements.

4.1 Behavior Evaluation in Routing

Node's behavior in routing can be simply expressed by two discrete values: good or bad. The former means forwarded packet reaches the destination successfully, and the later means the packet is dropped somewhere along the path. Behavior in routing is evaluated either by adding active feedback mechanism to protocol or by observing node's behavior pattern passively.

[16] assumed that misbehaving node would consistently drop queries and data packets. With this misbehavior model, if the sink found replies from a certain location were consistently dropped, the sink would initiate en-route probing. Every node received the probing packet should send acknowledge to the sink. The one who didn't answer was regarded as malfunction or compromised, and should be excluded from the routing table consequently. Although the algorithm is proposed for location-based routing mechanism, it can be easily extended to other types. But its misbehavior model is very simple, and the algorithm cannot deal effectively with other undesirable behavior, such as partial or selective dropping, which may be caused by malicious attack or component aging.

[17] used acknowledgments (ACKs) of the data packets to detect fault link. If a valid ACK was not received within a defined period, it was assumed that the packet had been lost. If packet loss rate exceeded a certain threshold, it was assumed that there was a fault node and the protocol probed along the faulty path to locate the misbehaving node. This algorithm is under the same assumption as the one in [16] that the adversary node will always drop packet and will not ACK to the probing packet.

[18] assumed that node worked with promiscuous mode and could hear its neighbor's total communication whether it was destined to it or not. When a node sent a packet to its neighbor, it also cached one locally. Then the node listened to its neighbor's communication. If the neighbor didn't forward the same packet to another node within a period, it was misbehaving. This algorithm judges a node's behavior by passive listening and receiving. Although no additional communication is need, this algorithm is not so energy efficient as it seems to be, because listening and receiving incur relatively high energy costs. And it doesn't work when the neighbor performs some in-network processing or when the communication is encrypted.

[19] combined collision ratio, probability of data packet successful transmission, data packet's waiting-time, RTS packets arrival ratio into a integrated metric to detect whether there were DOS attack. Although this paper doesn't care about the source of attack, some measurement here can be used to locate the malicious node. For example, the node that retransmits RTS packet to exhaust the receiver's resource is malicious. So is the node that occupies the channel for abnormally long time.

4.2 Behavior Evaluation in Data Processing

The quality of the data reported by a node can be used to represent the node's behavior in data processing task. Opposite to the discrete measurement of node's behavior in routing, this metric is continuous. The provider of high quality data is given a value close to good, while provider of outlier data is given a value close to bad. If we can detect that the data reported from a node is false, the node's behavior is evaluated to be bad.

Outlier detection is an integrated part of data processing or data fusion. [20] proposed to predict a node's reading on the base of its own past readings and the readings from its neighbors. It detected possible outliers by comparing the prediction and real report. It is similar to the trust management component in this paper. Although the method proposed in [20] is within the data processing scope, it can be easily extended to other cases.

Some researches on security data processing or data fusion focus mainly on using cryptographic primitives to filter out false report or intermediate result [21][22][23]. They don't care about which node makes the false modification or injection. But the information created in the filtering process can be used to locate the misbehaving node. For example, [24] proposed that a couple of nodes did the same fusing as the witness of each other. The base station decided whether a fusing result was legitimate by an m out of n scheme. Cryptography was used to prevent intermediate modification and assure the node's identification. Although the malfunction node could be detected by this way, no further punishment would be carried out to the wrongdoer. The way to deal with false data or injected data was simply discarding. In the behavior-based trust model, the trust degree of the wrongdoer will be degraded, and its following report is less believable.

5 Combination Framework

The behavior evaluation methods are task-specific, and differ from each other. To a given task, the evaluation result may be accurate or inaccurate. And sometimes there is no accessible evaluation at all. So it's very difficult to combine these measurements into an integrated trust degree that reflects the essential trustworthiness of the node.

A naïve combination method is to record the result of recent tasks, i.e., the number of good and bad behavior, the number of total tasks. If the ratio of good behavior to total numbers surpasses a certain threshold, the node is thought to be trustworthy and is qualified for future assignment. Otherwise, the node will be excluded from future tasks as long as there are alternatives. This simple method has several drawbacks: 1) It treats all the measurement as a two-value function, which is not sufficient under some situation; 2) All evaluation types are treated equally, while in practice some are more important than others; 3) This method can't deal effectively with the second-hand information such as the trust degree given by other node.

Combination algorithms from "Mathematic Theory of Evidence [25]" can serve the purpose better, and actually they have been used in some researches.

5.1 Bayesian Inference

Bayesian inference is used in [26] to combine the observations. The behavior was described by a binary variable *{cooperative, uncooperative}*. The reputation, $R_{ij}=P(node\ j\ is\ trustworthy\ at\ node\ j)$,was calculated from past observations. It assumed that R_{ij} obeyed the beta distribution, $R_{ij}=Beta(\alpha_i,\beta_i)$, and initial $\alpha_0=\beta_0=1$. After α_i cooperative and β_i uncooperative behaviors had been observed, the reputation was refreshed to be $R_{ij}=Beta(\alpha_i+1,\beta_i+1)$. The impact of second-hand information was also expressed by a new α and β which took the trust value of the source into consideration. The trust value of a node was $T=E[R_{ij}]$.

5.2 Dempster-Shafer Theory of Evidence

The DS theory of evidence was first introduced by Dempster and formalized by Shafer. Suppose there is a focal set of mutually exclusive and exhaustive propositions, which is also called frame of discernment F. The inference space Θ is a power set of F. For $F=\{a,b,c\},\Theta=\{a.b.c,\{a,b\},\{a,c\},\{b,c\},\{a,b,c\},\emptyset\}$. Mass function $m(A)$ is the degree of confidence to each element A in Θ, and

$$\sum_{A\subset\Theta} m(A)=1 \tag{2}$$

The belief of A is

$$Bel(A)=\sum_{\forall B:A\subseteq B} m(A) \tag{3}$$

For different observers, mass function may be different. The combination rule is as follows:

$$m(A)=m_1(A)\oplus m_2(A)=\frac{\sum_{B_1\cap B_2=A} m_1(B_1)m_2(B_2)}{1-\sum_{B_1\cap B_2=\phi} m_1(B_1)m_2(B_2)} \tag{4}$$

[27] was an example of the above theory to combine evidences from different source to detect flood attack. The focal set was *F={NORMAL, SYN-flood, UDP-flood, ICMP-flood}*. UDP-flood detection node defined different *m1({UDP}*, *m1({F})* according to the ratio between incoming and outgoing UDP packet. Active flow monitor node assigned *m2({UDP,SYN, ICMP})=1* when there were excessive flood and the type of flood is unknown. Final decision was deduced from the combined mass function from two observation sources.

Although several combination methods have been proposed, they are neither general nor mature. For example, the assumption in [26] that reputation obeyed the beta distribution may not hold for all scenarios. So the method of [26] can only be used in special cases. [27] just outlined the combination rules, and some details are not specified in the paper such as the definition of mass function and its relationship with probability. Further studies should be carried out on the existing and novel methods.

6 Conclusion and Future Work

Node compromise and node ageing is hard to detect in WSN because authentication and cryptography cannot differentiate them from legitimate operation. Behavior-based trust is an effective solution. This paper outlines the behavior-based trust model from the view of process, component and deployment. Current techniques of authentication, evaluation of behavior, evaluation combination are also discussed in this paper.

The study of behavior-based trust in WSN has just begun. There are still many open issues left for future research.

- Behavior evaluation: it is very difficult to evaluate a node's behavior without feedback. But feedback always incurs undesirable additional traffic. How much feedback is the optimum? What kind of feedback is more suitable? To develop evaluation methods with high accuracy and low overhead, WSN protocol must be studied to include optimal feedback.
- Evaluation combination: behavior evaluation is task-specific in essence. How to normalize different types of evaluations and combine them into an integrate trust degree is a topic of future research. The weight of second information in combination should also be studied, and so does the information exchange frequency, which further decides the deployment architecture.

References

[1] Tyrone Grandison , Morris Sloman, Imperial Colege, A Survey of Trust in INTERNET Applications, IEEE Communications Surveys, http://www.comsoc.org/pubs/surveys , Fourth Quarter 2000

[2] Li Xiong, Ling Liu, A Reputation-Based Trust Model for Peer-to-Peer eCommerce Communities, Proceedings of the ACM Conference on Electronic Commerce, 2003, pp228-229

[3] G. Gaubatz, J.-P. Kaps, and B. Sunar, Public key cryptography in sensor networks-revisited.1st European Workshop on Security in Ad-Hoc and Sensor Networks (ESAS 2004), LNCS 3313, 2004.

[4] Laurent Eschenauer, Virgil D. Gligor. A key-management scheme for distributed sensor networks. Proceedings of the 9th ACM conference on Computer and communications security, 2002.

[5] Wenliang Du, Jing Deng, Yunghsiang S. Han, Pramod Varshney, Jonathan Katz, and Aram Khalili, A Pairwise Key Pre-distribution Scheme for Wireless Sensor Networks. The ACM Transactions on Information and System Security (TISSEC), 2005.

[6] Kalidindi R, Paruchuri V., Sub-grid based key vector assignment: A key pre-distribution scheme for distributed sensor networks, Proceedings of the International Conference on Wireless networks(ICWN'04), 2004, p 440-446
[7] Ross Anderson, Haowen Chan, Adrian Perrig. Key Infection: Smart Trust for Smart Dust. IEEE International Conference on Network Protocols ,ICNP 2004
[8] Bhuse Vijay, Gupta Ajay, Pidva, Rishi, A distributed approach to security in sensornets, 2003 IEEE 58th Vehicular Technology Conference, p 3010-3014
[9] M. Eltoweissy, M. Younis, and , K. Ghumman, Lightweight Key Management for Secure Wireless Sensor Networks, IEEE Workshop on Multi-hop Wireless Networks, 2004.
[10] A. Perrig, R. Szewczyk, D. Tygar, V. Wen, D. Culler, SPINS: security protocols for sensor networks, Wireless Networks, vol. 8, no. 5, pp.521–534, 2002.
[11] Sencun Zhu, Sanjeev Setia, Sushil Jajodia, and Peng Ning, An Interleaved Hop-by-Hop Authentication Scheme for Filtering of Injected False Data in Sensor Networks. Proceedings of. IEEE Symposium on Security and Privacy, 2004.
[12] S. Zhu, S. Setia and S. Jajodia. LEAP: Efficient Security Mechanisms for Large-Scale Distributed Sensor Networks. 10th ACM Conference on Computer and Communications Security (CCS'03), 2003.
[13] Mathias Bohge and Wade Trappe. An Authentication Framework for Hierarchical Ad Hoc Sensor Networks. International Conferecnce on Web Information System Engineering(WiSe03),2003
[14] Qian Huang, Johnas Cukier, Hisashi Kobayashi, Bede Liu, Jinyun Zhang, Fast Authenticated Key Establishment Protocols for Self-Organizing Sensor Networks. Proceedings of the 2nd ACM international conference on Wireless sensor networks and applications(WSNA'03), 2003, pp.141-150
[15] Jing Deng, Richard Han, and Shivakant Mishra, Security Support for In-Network Processing in Wireless Sensor Networks. 2003 ACM Workshop on Security of Ad Hoc and Sensor Networks (SASN '03) ,2003
[16] S. Tanachaiwiwat, P.Dave, R. Bhindwale, Location-centric Isolation of Misbehavior and Trust Routing in Energy-constrained sensor networks. IEEE Workshop on Energy-Efficient Wireless Communications and Networks (EWCN04), 2004.
[17] Baruch Awerbuch, David Holmer, Cristina Nita-Rotaru and Herbert Rubens. An on-demand secure routing protocol resilient to byzantine failures. Proceedings of the ACM workshop on Wireless security, 2002, pp 21-30
[18] Marti, Sergio, iuli, T.J., Lai, Kevin, Baker, Mary, Mitigating routing misbehavior in mobile ad hoc networks, Proceedings of the Annual International Conference on Mobile Computing and Networking, MOBICOM, 2000, pp 255-265
[19] Ren, Qingchun,Liang, Qilian, Secure media access control (MAC) in Wireless Sensor Networks: Intrusion detections and countermeasures, IEEE International Symposium on Personal, Indoor and Mobile Radio Communications, PIMRC, 2004,pp 3025-3029
[20] Eiman Elnahrawy, Badi Nath, Context_Aware Sensors, Proceeding of First European Workshop, EWSN2004, pp77-93
[21] Baruch Awerbuch, David Holmer, Cristina Nita-Rotaru and Herbert Rubens. An on-demand secure routing protocol resilient to byzantine failures. In Proceedings of the ACM workshop on Wireless security, 2002, pages 21-30.
[22] F. Ye, H. Luo, S. Lu, L. Zhang, Statistical En-route Detection and Filtering of Injected False Data in Sensor Networks. Proc. of IEEE INFOCOM 2004.
[23] Przydatek Bartosz, Song Dawn, Perrig Adrian, SIA: Secure information aggregation in sensor networks, Proceedings of the First International Conference on Embedded Networked Sensor Systems, 2003, pp 255-265

[24] Wenliang Du, Jing Deng, Yunghsiang S. Han, and Pramod Varshney. A Witness-Based approach For Data Fusion Assurance In Wireless Sensor Networks. Global Communications Conference (GLOBECOM), 2003.
[25] G. Shafer. A mathematical theory of evidence. Princeton University, 1976.
[26] Saurabh Ganeriwal and Mani B. Srivastava, Reputation-based Framework for High Integrity Sensor Networks, 2004 ACM Workshop on Security of Ad Hoc and Sensor Networks (SASN'04), 2004
[27] Christos Siaterlis,Basil Maglaris, Towards Multisensor Data Fusion for DoS detection, International Workshop on Selected Areas in Cryptography(SAC '04),2004

Compromised Nodes in Wireless Sensor Network*

Zhi-Ting Lin **, Yu-Gui Qu, Li Jing, and Bao-Hua Zhao

University of Science and Technology of China,
MOE-Microsoft Key Laboratory of Multimedia Computing and Communication,
Department of Electronic Engineering and Information Science, Hefei, Anhui 230027, China
Ph. 86-0551-3607462, Fax 86-0551-3607462
duanmanni@ustc.edu

Abstract. Sensor webs consisting of nodes with limited battery power and wireless communication are deployed to collect useful information from a variety of environments. A new challenge in the wireless sensor networks (WSN) is the compromised nodes problem. Compromised nodes may exhibit arbitrary behavior and may collude with other compromised nodes. In this paper, we propose a novel security strategy with assistant cluster heads, SSACH, which focuses on limiting the attack from compromised nodes. It adds the Assistant Cluster Heads (ACH) so as to monitor Cluster Head (CH) and take precautions against the inside attack.

1 Introduction

Sensor networks offer economically practicable solutions for many applications. For instance, current implementations include monitoring factory instrumentation, pollution levels, freeway traffic, and the structural integrity of buildings [1].The privacy and security issues posed by sensor networks represent a rich field of research problems [2].

Sensor nodes are susceptible to physical capture [3]. And as a consequence of their targeted low cost, tamper-resistant hardware is unlikely to prevail. So, when designing a secure sensor network we should assume that the nodes within it may be compromised by an attacker. If a node is compromised, all the information it holds will also be leaked out. With nodes compromised, an adversary can carry out an inside attack. In contrast to disabled nodes, compromised nodes actively seek to paralyze the network [4].

Furthermore, wireless sensor network often utilizes message aggregation to reduce communication overhead. But message aggregation makes security more difficult. Each intermediate node can modify, forge or discard messages, or simply transmit false aggregation values, so one compromised node is able to significantly alter the final aggregation value [5][6].

---

* This paper is supported by the National Natural Science Foundation of China under Grant No. 60241004 ,the National Grand Fundamental Research 973 Program of China under Grant No. 2003CB314801, and the State Key Laboratory of Networking and Switching Technology.

** Corresponding author.

H.T. Shen et al. (Eds.): ADWeb 2006, LNCS 3842, pp. 224 – 230, 2006.

In this paper, we propose a novel framework for secure information aggregation in large sensor networks. Security Strategy with Assistant Cluster Head focuses on limiting the attack from compromised node. SSACH adds the Assistant Cluster Heads so as to monitor Cluster Head and take precautions against the inside attack. ACH utilizes the proportionate sampling to testify that the answer given by the CH is a good approximation of the true value. SSACH will be shown to exhibit excellent performance via simulations.

The remainder of this paper is organized as follows. Section 2 presents our strategy in detail. In Section 3, we examine the performance of our scheme, and finally draw a conclusion from our work in Section 4.

2 SSACH Description

2.1 Key Distribute Mechanism of SSACH

Pre-distribution of secret keys are adopted in SSACH. Table 1 displays the notation used in the scheme descriptions.

Table 1. Notation used in SSACH

Notation	Description
S_i	Sensor node i
$F_m(i,j)$	Key generating function shared between sensor nodes i and j
ω	The number of the symmetric matrices
nonce	Random nonce value
E(K,…	Symmetric encryption function using key K
α	The challenge code
Id_i	Identifier for node i
||	Concatenation operator

There are M key generating functions in the entire network. Each node stores a key, K_i, shared with the base station, and a subset of the key generating functions $F_m(i,x)$ [7] [8], $m \in M$. Nodes S_i and S_j sharing the same key generating function F_m, can calculate the shared key $F_m(i,j)=F_m(j,i)$ [9][10]. The other nodes S_p, $p \neq i, j$, are unable to calculate $F_m(i,j)$. For example, we could construct a $(\lambda + 1) * N$ matrix G over a finite field GF(q) and ω symmetric matrices $D_1, D_2, ..., D_\omega$ of size $(\lambda+1)*(\lambda+1)$. Because D_n ($1 \leq n \leq \omega$), is symmetric, it is easy to see:

$$A_n * G = (D_n * G)^T * G = G^T * D_n^T * G = G^T * D_n * G = (A_n * G)^T \quad (1)$$

Let $A_n(j)$ represent the *j*th row of A_n. Then the base station could randomly select t distinct key spaces from the key spaces (A(j)) for each node. Up to now, $F_m(i,j)$ can be calculate in the following manner:

$$F_m(i,j) = A_n(i) * G(j) = A_n(j) * G(i) = F_m(j,i) \quad (2)$$

Despite the fact that some nodes may compromise, they have limited effects on the security of the network. SSACH uses the challenge-response technique to evade the smart attack [11]. Smart attack means the attacker attempts to compromises the sensor that stores the largest number of keys which are not known.

$$\{\alpha, E_{F_m(i,j)}(\alpha), m \in M\} \tag{3}$$

The decryption with the proper key by sensor s_b would reveal the challenge α and the information that s_b shares that particular key with sensor s_a. So far, the nodes succeed in obtaining the following keys:

Key shared with the base station: K_i
Key shared with the Cluster Head: $K_{i,CH}=F_m(i,CH)$
Key shared with the Assistant Cluster Head: $K_{i,ACH}=F_m(i,ACH)$
Key shared with the neighbors nodes: $K_{i,\ neighbour}=F_m(i,\ neighbour)$

2.2 Data Transmission and Compression Based on SSACH

As Fig. 1 shows, the wireless sensor network employs the hierarchical clustering model. Cluster Head and Assistant Cluster Head are selected in turn from nodes within cluster. Gathered data are encrypted and transmitted to the CH and ACHs separately.

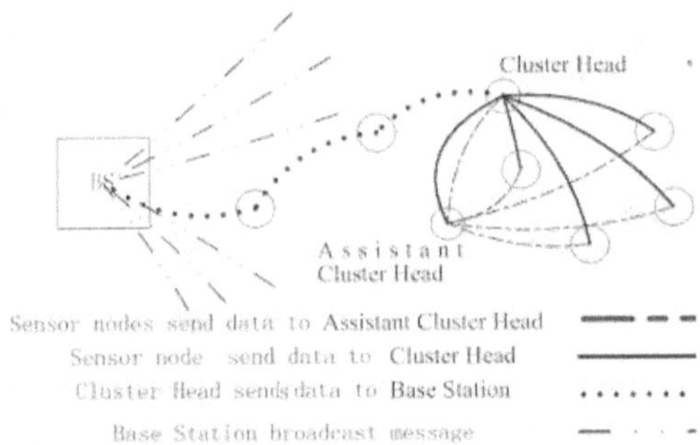

Fig. 1. Structure of wireless sensor network

After collecting results from a group of sensors, the CH calculates a smaller message, $id_{CH}||E(K_{CH,ACH},nounce'||id_{CH}||Aggregation\_message)$, which summarizes the important information and transmits the result to ACHs. Then ACHs validate the compressive message making use of the data collected from certain sensor nodes. If accurate, the ACHs construct an agreement encrypted with the key K_{ACH}, and pass $id_{ACH}||MAC(K_{ACH},nounce''||id_{ACH}||Aggregation\_message)$ on to CH. On the contrary, an alarm would be sent out. The cluster head wouldn't convey the aggregation data to the base station in a relay way, until it has collected adequate agreements. The aggregation datum is denoted as:

$Report: id_{CH} || E(K_{CH}, nounce'' || id_{CH} || Aggregation\_message || XMAC || ACH\_list)$
where,

$$XMAX = MAC(K_{ACH1}, nounce'' || id_{ACH1} || Aggregation\_message) \oplus \\ MAC(K_{ACH2}, nounce'' || id_{ACH2} || Aggregation\_message) \oplus \\ \ldots \\ MAC(K_{ACHk}, nounc'' || id_{ACHk} || Aggregation\_message) \quad (4)$$

If the CH is compromised, and it simply ignores the advice of the ACHs and sends compromised data without enough agreements. The base station would also send out an alarm unhesitatingly. At the same time, the relaying nodes between CH and BS should calculate and store data summary. If a certain relaying node compromises, it may inject wrong message into the sensor network or discard message on purpose. As a result, follow-up nodes must turn into different summaries or have no summary. If the base station receives incorrect information, it can broadcast alarm and collect the summaries in order to isolate the suspicious nodes.

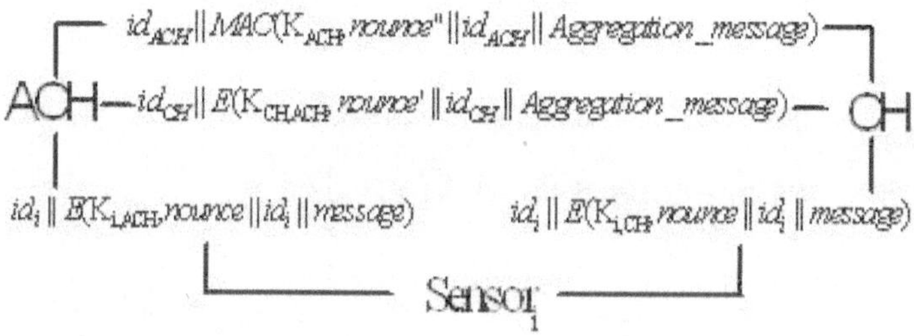

Fig. 2. Message Aggregation

The process of data transmission and compression based on SSACH is shown in Fig.2. Obviously, a distinguishing feature of SSACH is that ACHs and data summaries are added to supervise the behavior of CH and the relaying nodes. SSACH can take precautions against CH launching the inside attack, and provide an effective method of confining the compromised relaying node. The algorithm is rendered useless if the CH and all ACH nodes are compromised. It is stated that the election algorithm must be designed very carefully. The same set of sensor node should not always act as the CH or the ACHs. For instance, sensor nodes can queue up to be header according to their IDs.

Here, it is supposed that there are n nodes compromised in certain cluster which is made up of m sensor nodes. So the probability that the compromised node becomes the cluster head is: P=n/m, which means that n/m of the data may be invalid. SSACH adds k associate cluster head. So the probability of compromised node occupying the CH and all the ACHs turns into:

$$P = \frac{C_n^{k+1}}{C_m^{k+1}} = \frac{n!(m-k-1)!}{m!(n-k-1)!} \quad (5)$$

It points out the amount of invalid data would be much less, whereas such technique will cause the increasing of communication quantity. Keeping in mind that communication between nodes consumes a significant amount of the energy resources, applications and system software are expected to achieve a required level of performance while minimizing the amount of traffic in the network [12]. Therefore, SSACH utilizes the proportionate sampling to reduce energy consumption. The wireless sensor network is divided into k groups. An ACH selects one group of the sensor nodes at random, and the nodes being selected are required to send data of low precision to the ACH. For instance raw data (10bit) are collected by CH, and low precision data (4bit) are gathered by ACH. Subsequently, it will reduce the total of communication. However, error must be brought into while making use of sampling. If the high precision samples are used, mean error of the average of the samples is as follows, where the σ is the total standard deviation.

$$\mu_x = \sqrt{\frac{\sigma^2}{m/k}\left(\frac{m-m/k}{m-1}\right)} = \sqrt{\frac{\sigma^2(k-1)}{m-1}} \tag{6}$$

And in the case that low precision samples are adopted, the formula shows the lower bound of the mean error.

3 Simulation Experiments and Analysis

In this section, we simulated the SSACH described in Section 2. First, we considered a sensor cluster made up of 100 nodes has 1~3 ACHs and 5~30 compromised nodes. The probability of the valid transmission is as follows Fig.3.

It exemplifies that SSACH is able to restrict attack from inside effectively. When the quantity of ACHs is large enough, the data can almost convey correctly. Data transitions are nearly free of the impact of the compromised node.

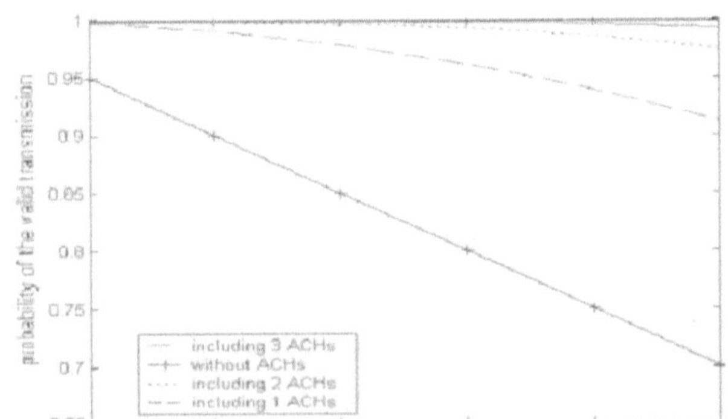

Fig. 3. Performance of resisting compromised node

In order to test the performance of SSACH from different points of view, the error caused by sampling was taken into account. We consider a sensor cluster made up of 200 nodes contains 1~5 ACHs. And the raw data range between [0.0, 100.0]. The results plotted in Figure 4 show that if the data bit is reduced properly, the mean error of the average of the sample can be acceptable.

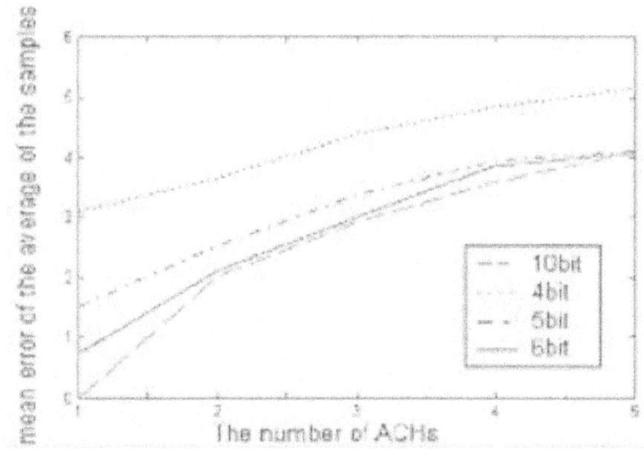

Fig. 4. Mean error of the average of the sample

Simulations above illustrate that SSACH is efficient with respect to the security it provides and allows a tradeoff between security and performance.

4 Conclusions

Wireless sensor networks are often deployed in unattended environments. Node compromise is the central problem that uniquely characterizes the sensor network's threat model. So, in this paper a straightforward but effective scheme, SSACH, is presented. SSACH focuses on secure information aggregation in sensor networks that can handle a malicious CH and malevolent sensor nodes. SSACH has been demonstrated to exhibit excellent performance.

References

1. Haowen Chan, Perrig, A.: Security and Privacy in Sensor Networks. Computer Vol.36, Issue 10. (2003) 103 – 105.
2. Sencun Zhu, Setia, S, Jajodia, S, Peng Ning: An interleaved hop-by-hop authentication scheme for filtering of injected false data in sensor networks. Security and Privacy 2004, Proceedings, 2004 IEEE Symposium. (2004) 59 - 271
3. Shi, E.; Perrig, A.: Designing secure sensor networks. Wireless Communications, IEEE. Vol.11, Issue 6, (2004) 38 – 43.
4. Qingchun Ren, Qilian Liang: Secure media access control (MAC) in wireless sensor networks: intrusion detections and countermeasures. Personal, Indoor and Mobile Radio Communications, 2004. PIMRC 2004. 15th IEEE International Symposium, Vol.4 (2004) 3025 – 3029.

5. Slijepcevic, S., Potkonjak, M., Tsiatsis, V., Zimbeck, S., Srivastava, M.B.: Secure Aggregation for Wireless Networks. Enabling Technologies. Infrastructure for Collaborative Enterprises, 2002. WET ICE 2002. Proceedings. Eleventh IEEE International Workshops. (2002) 139 – 144.
6. B. Przydatek, D. Song, and A. Perrig,: SIA: Secure Information Aggregation in Sensor Networks. Proc. of Embedded Networked Sensor Sys (2003) 255-265.
7. R. Blom.: An Optimal Class of Symmetric Key Generation Systems. Advances in Cryptology, EUROCRYPT'84, LNCS 209. (1984) 335-338.
8. C. Blundo, A. Santis, A. Herzberg, S. Kutten, U. Vaccaro, and M. Yung.: Perfectly-secure key distribution for dynamic conferences. In Advances in Cryptology CRYPTO 92, LNCS 740 (1993) 471-486.
9. D. Liu and P. Ning.: Establishing Pairwise Keys in Distributed Sensor Networks. In Proc. of the 10th ACM Conference on Computer and Communications Security (CCS '03) (2003).
10. Wenliang Du, Jing Deng, Yunghsiang S. Han, Pramod K. Varshney.: A Pairwise Key Pre-distribution Scheme for Wireless Sensor Networks. Proceedings of the 10th ACM conference on Computer and communications security (2003) 42 – 51
11. Di Pietro, R., Mancini, L.V., Mei, A.:Efficient and resilient key discovery based on pseudo-random key pre-deployment. Parallel and Distributed Processing Symposium 2004 Proceedings (2004) 217
12. Slijepcevic S., Potkonjak M., Tsiatsis V., Zimbeck S., Srivastava M.B.: On communication security in wireless ad-hoc sensor networks. Enabling Technologies: Infrastructure for Collaborative Enterprises, 2002. WET ICE 2002. Proceedings. Eleventh IEEE International Workshops (2002) 139 - 144

Reservation CSMA/CA for QoS Support in Mobile Ad-Hoc Networks*

Inwhee Joe

College of Information and Communications,
Hanyang University
iwjoe@hanyang.ac.kr

Abstract. This paper presents the design and performance of a novel medium access control (MAC) protocol, called Reservation CSMA/CA for QoS (Quality of Service) support in mobile ad-hoc networks. The reservation CSMA/CA protocol is based on a hierarchical approach consisting of two sublayers. The lower sublayer of the protocol is designed to support asynchronous data traffic using CSMA/CA, while the upper sublayer is designed for QoS support by making a slot reservation via the three-way handshake. The bandwidth efficiency can be maximized with the slot reuse as much as possible. The proposed protocol has been validated using the ns network simulator with wireless and mobility extensions. The simulation results show that the reservation CSMA/CA offers the higher throughput with the higher load for real-time periodic traffic compared to the IEEE 802.11 standard, while providing deterministic delay performance.

1 MAC Protocol for QoS Support

The reservation CSMA/CA protocol is designed for QoS support in mobile ad-hoc networks, based on a hierarchical approach consisting of two sublayers as shown in Fig. 1. Like the IEEE 802.11 standard, the lower sublayer of the MAC protocol is the DCF to support asynchronous data traffic using a random access method CSMA/CA. The upper sublayer RCF is implemented on top of the DCF to support real-time traffic with QoS requirements by making a slot reservation prior to actual data transmission. It replaces the original PCF of the IEEE 802.11 standard, because the PCF will not work for mobile ad-hoc networks with no centralized coordinator.

The objective of RCF is to make a slot reservation for real-time periodic traffic over mobile ad-hoc networks. The channel bandwidth is time-slotted and time slots are grouped into frame cycles with duration matched to the basic rate of periodic voice packets. Each slot is recognized as reserved or available in the slot table maintained on each mobile node. For real-time periodic traffic, the node attempts to make a slot reservation dynamically by using a three-way handshake.

* This work was supported by grant No. D00174 from the Basic Research Program of the Korea Science & Engineering Foundation.

H.T. Shen et al. (Eds.): ADWeb 2006, LNCS 3842, pp. 231–235, 2006.

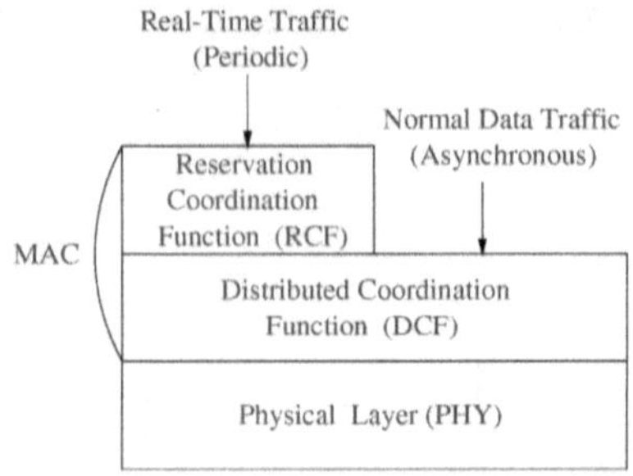

Fig. 1. Reservation CSMA/CA Architecture

If the reservation is done successfully, it continues to reserve the same slots in future frame cycles without any contentions, until the transmission of this traffic is completed. The reserved slot is released automatically when it is left empty. Under limiting cases such that most nodes are transmitting real-time periodic traffic, the reservation CSMA/CA closely resembles TDMA. For asynchronous traffic, on the contrary, its behavior is similar to that of pure CSMA/CA.

Over the last decade, many algorithms have been proposed to solve the problem with slot reservation for wireless networks [2, 4]. Some are identified as a centralized algorithm relying on the existence of a centralized coordinator that maintains a global clock and assigns time slots, which is not appropriate for mobile ad-hoc networks with no centralized concept. Because of the hidden terminal problem with mobile ad-hoc networks, existing schemes will suffer from significant performance degradation. Therefore, our reservation scheme is a distributed algorithm and it is based on the three-way handshake in making a slot reservation for mobile ad-hoc networks. In the handshake procedure, the hidden terminal problem can be fixed by announcing the reserved slot to all the neighbor nodes in the transmission regions of the sender and the receiver, when control frames are exchanged between them.

In addition to the existing three control frames (i.e., RTS, CTS and ACK frames) in the DCF of IEEE 802.11, the RCF introduces three more control frames to make a slot reservation by the three-way handshake: RFS (Request for Slot Reservation) frame, RAC (Reservation Acknowledgment) frame, and RAN (Reservation Announcement) frame. When a mobile node wants to transmit real-time periodic traffic (e.g., voice or video), it initiates the handshake procedure by first sending an RFS frame to the receiver in order to request a reservation for an available slot. The RFS frame contains a bitmap indicating whether each slot is reserved or not from the sender's standpoint. If the RFS frame is received correctly, the receiver searches for an available slot in the slot table. If there is any available slot found in the slot table and at the same time it is not reserved yet from the bitmap of the RFS frame, the receiver grants the reservation by marking it as "reserved" in the slot table and by responding with an RAC frame. Otherwise, the receiver remains silent as if nothing happened, thereby causing the sender to time out and then to retry a slot reservation with retransmission of the RFS frame.

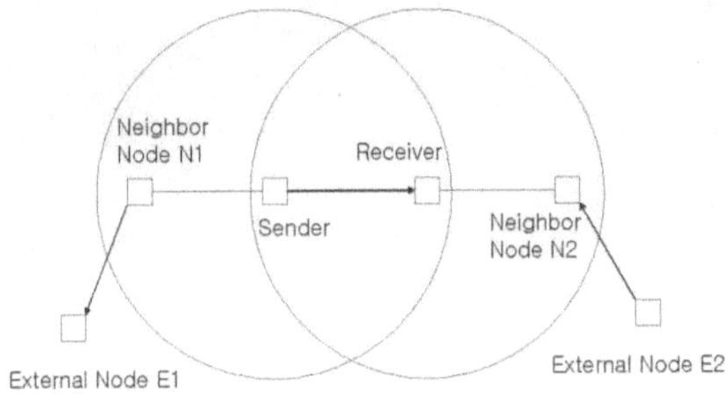

Fig. 2. Slot Reuse Model

Under certain circumstances, the same slots can be reused even for the neighbor nodes located in the transmission range of the sender and the receiver, although they are already reserved for real-time traffic. As shown in Fig. 2, if the neighbor nodes want to communicate with the nodes outside the range, the reserved slots for the transmission from the sender to the receiver can be reused, especially for the neighbor nodes $N1$ and $N2$ because they do not interfere each other. In particular, the neighbor node $N1$ can transmit data to the external node $E1$, while the external node $E2$ can transmit data to the neighbor node $N2$ using the same slots reserved for the transmission from the sender to the receiver without causing any interference. This way the bandwidth efficiency can be maximized, which is very important in that the bandwidth is a scarce resource in the wireless environment.

To carry out the feature of the slot reuse above, the region field of each slot is used from the slot table, indicating in which region the node of this slot table is located, sender, receiver, or both. For example, as shown in Fig. 2, if the neighbor node $N1$ wants to transmit real-time traffic to the external node $E1$, first it needs to make a slot reservation via the three-way handshake procedure. Since this node knows that it belongs to the sender's region in terms of the reserved slots for transmission from the sender to the receiver, these same slots can be reused here by making them available in the bitmap field of the RFS frame. Likewise, if the external node $E2$ wants to transmit real-time traffic to the neighbor node $N2$, the same reserved slots can be reused in this situation, as long as they are available on the external node $E2$. Since the neighbor node $N2$ knows that it is located in the receiver's region, it can allow the slots to be reused by allocating them in the slot number field of the RAC frame. For the neighbor nodes in the common region, the reserved slots cannot be reused due to the interference with the original transmission.

2 Performance Evaluation

The objective of our simulation is to evaluate the performance of the reservation CSMA/CA protocol (R-CSMA/CA in short form) in terms of QoS support. In

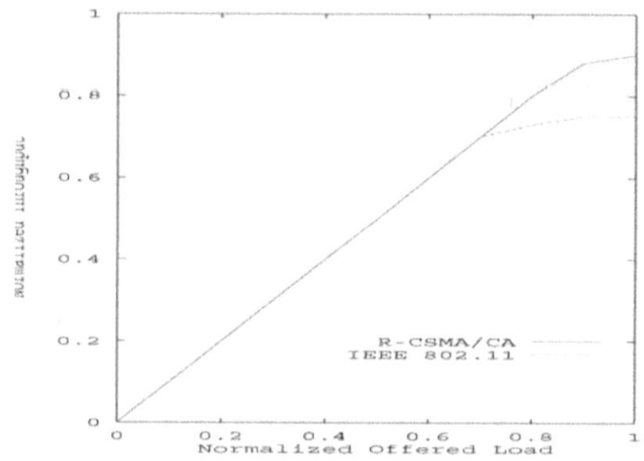

Fig. 3. Normalized Throughput as a function of Offered Load

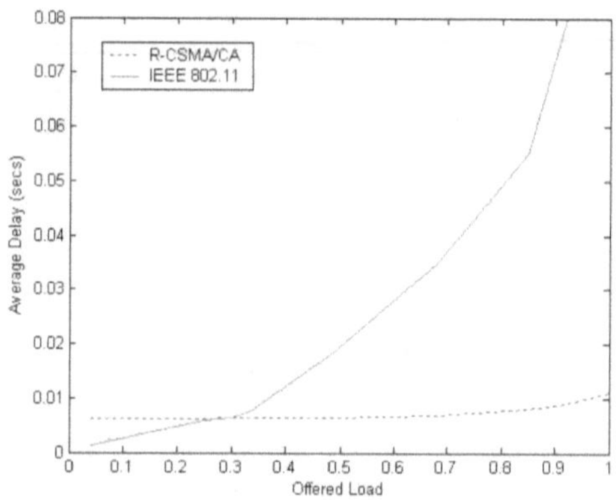

Fig. 4. Average Delay as a function of Offered Load

literature, the DCF performance has been studied extensively for asynchronous data traffic over wireless local area networks and mobile ad-hoc networks [1]. Here, we focus on the real-time periodic traffic over mobile ad-hoc networks, as a preliminary work especially for real-time voice traffic over wireless ad-hoc networks without any mobility. Furthermore, we compare the performance of the proposed protocol with that of the DCF alone as in the IEEE 802.11 standard for ad-hoc networks, as far as real-time traffic is concerned.

The voice stream is modeled as CBR (Constant-Bit-Rate) traffic with the coding rate of 25.6 Kbps. After obtaining a slot reservation, a mobile node is expected to carry a voice stream by transmitting one voice packet per frame cycle. Since the frame cycle is 20 ms and the payload of a voice packet is 512 bits, it can provide the speech coding rate of 25.6 Kbps. For each voice packet, 88 bits are added to the payload as the physical layer overhead including preamble bits. The proposed protocol was validated using the ns network simulator with wireless and mobile extensions.

Fig. 3 presents the normalized throughput as a function of the normalized offered load at the MAC layer for R-CSMA/CA versus IEEE 802.11 over wireless ad-hoc networks. The normalized throughput is defined as the ratio of the throughput to the channel bit rate of 2 Mbps and so is the normalized offered load. As shown in Fig. 3, the proposed protocol gives a higher throughput, especially as the offered load becomes higher. In particular, the throughput of R-CSMA/CA is as high as 0.9 for an offered load of 1.0 in comparison with 0.75 of IEEE 802.11. Since there is no waste of bandwidth due to the contention once the slot reservation is made, it can make a higher throughput possible with the R-CSMA/CA scheme. On the other hand, Fig. 4 shows that R-CSMA/CA provides deterministic delay performance regardless of the offered load to the network, while IEEE 802.11 diverges with the increasing load. However, R-CSMA/CA causes a little longer delay than IEEE 802.11 at the lower load, because each node should wait for its reserved slot to come.

3 Conclusions

In this paper, we have discussed the design and performance of a novel MAC protocol (called Reservation CSMA/CA) for QoS support in mobile ad-hoc networks. The key idea in the proposed protocol is to implement a reservation scheme on top of the fundamental access method CSMA/CA by using the three-way handshake. We have also presented simulation results with the ns network simulator. The simulation results have shown that the reservation CSMA/CA offers the higher throughput with the higher load for real-time periodic traffic compared to the IEEE 802.11 standard, while providing deterministic delay performance.

References

1. B.P. Crow *et al.*: IEEE 802.11 Wireless Local Area Networks, *IEEE Communications Magazine*, pp. 116-126, September (1997)
2. D.J. Goodman *et al.*: Packet Reservation Multiple Access for Local Wireless Communications, *IEEE Transactions on Communications*, Vol. 37, No. 8, pp. 885-890, August (1989)
3. IEEE 802.11: Wireless LAN Medium Access Control and Physical Layer Specifications, *Standard 802.11*, November (1997)
4. S. Ramanathan and E.L. Lloyd: Scheduling Algorithms for Multihop Radio Networks, *IEEE/ACM Transactions on Networking*, Vol. 1, No. 2, pp. 166-177, April (1993)

On Studying Partial Coverage and Spatial Clustering Based on Jensen-Shannon Divergence in Sensor Networks

Yufeng Wang[1] and Wendong Wang[2]

[1] College of Telecommunications and Information Engineering, Nanjing University of Posts and Telecommunications (NUPT), Nanjing 210003, China

[2] State Key Laboratory of Networking & Switching Technology, Beijing University of Posts and Telecommunications (BUPT), Beijing 100876, China

Abstract. The idea of partial coverage is provided in this paper, which means that the distance among data trends gathered by neighbor sensors is so small that, in some period, we can cluster those sensors, and replace the cluster with certain sensor in this cluster to form the virtual sensor network topology. But adopting this approach, we need to solve two problems: 1) how to characterize the distance among data trends (rather than raw data) of different sensors; 2) based on the distance, how to form the cluster and use the virtual network to represent the whole sensor network within certain error range. For the first problem, the Jensen-Shannon Divergence (JSD) is used to characterize the distance among different distributions which represent the data trend of sensors. Then, based on JSD, a hierarchical clustering algorithm is provided to form the virtual sensor network topology. Finally, the performance of our approach is evaluated through simulation.

1 Introduction

Sensor networks of the future are fundamental tools to aware various several physical phenomena over large geographic regions. However, the energy constrained of the sensor nodes presents major challenges in gathering and routing data. So a great deal of studies has been made on aggregating data in wireless sensor network [1][2]. Ref. [3] offers a new aggregation method named Statistical Aggregation Method (SAM) from another perspective, in which sensor nodes transmit to sink only when the difference between previous and current data exceeds threshold. A main drawback in this work is that it only deals with the raw data, but didn't consider the data trends gathered by sensors. There are several applications that apply clustering to sensor networks [4][5]. Spatial clustering algorithms are extensively investigated in [6][7], which is extremely

* Research supported by the NSFC Grants 60472067 and 2003CB314806, and State Key Laboratory of Networking and Switching Technology, Beijing University of Posts and Telecommunications (BUPT).

H.T. Shen et al. (Eds.): ADWeb 2006, LNCS 3842, pp. 236 – 240, 2006.

useful for monitoring physical phenomena in large geographical area. Our work partially adopts the idea of spatial clustering, but in this paper, the spatial clustering is applied to our proposal of partial coverage, furthermore, JSD is used to characterize the distance among data trends of sensors. From information theory filed, JSD is found to be useful to measure distance between distributions [8].

This paper is organized as follows: In section 2, we introduce the definition of JSD, which lay foundation for measuring the distance between two data trends. The hierarchical clustering algorithm based on JSD is provided in section 3. In section 4, from the metrics of average energy consumption and clustering fidelity, the performance of our partial coverage approach is evaluated through simulation, and then compared with Statistical Aggregation Method (SAM). Finally, we briefly conclude the paper in section 5.

2 Basic Concept About JSD

A good partial coverage algorithm should group nodes in the sensor network based on data semantics. In order to cluster based on data trend rather than on raw data, we regress data to build data models, which is expressed as certain probability distribution. We use the following measures of distance between distributions:

Definition 1. The Kullback-Leibler Divergence (KL) and the Jensen-Shannon Divergence (JSD) between two probability distributions $P(x)$ and $Q(x)$ on certain data set X are defined as:

$$D_{KL}(P \| Q) \stackrel{def}{=} \sum_{x \in X} P(x) \log \frac{P(x)}{Q(x)} \tag{1}$$

$$JSD(P,Q) = \frac{1}{2}\left(D_{KL}\left(P \| (\frac{P+Q}{2}) \right) + D_{KL}\left(Q \| (\frac{P+Q}{2}) \right) \right) \tag{2}$$

The function D_{KL} is the KL divergence, which measures the average inefficiency in using one distribution to code for another (This measure produces a scalar value between zero and infinity, with a lower value signifying higher similarity). However, KL divergence, used in its traditional form, requires a workaround to prevent a division by zero. So we use JSD (Equation 2) to characterize the distance between two data trends inferred from data collected by different sensors.

That is: $d(i,j)=JSD(P_i,P_j)= JSD(i,j)$, where i,j denote different sensors, P_i, P_j the corresponding probability distribution inferred from sensor i, j. Without confusion, denote $JSD(P_i,P_j)$ as $JSD(i,j)$.

3 Hierarchical Clustering Algorithm Based on JSD

The idea in our partial coverage approach is to classify the whole sensor network into several clusters. In each cluster, the distance between two geographical neighbor sensors is less than α, and the distance between any pair of sensors is less than β ($\beta \geq \alpha$), when β is small enough, then we can use one sensor with more residual energy to replace the whole cluster to monitor spatial area, and transmit data to sink. Such cluster is called α~β cluster.

Definition 2. (α~β cluster) Cluster containing several sensors with geographical proximity is called α~β cluster if the following two conditions hold.

1. For neighbor pair of nodes i and j, the distance d(i,j) $<\alpha$;
2. For every pair of nodes i and j, d(i,j)$<\beta$.

We adopt hierarchical clustering algorithm to form the virtual sensor network topology. In this clustering, we merge the most similar pair of clusters in a hierarchical manner. For a cluster, every neighboring cluster is a candidate for merger if the resulted cluster doesn't violate the definition of α~β cluster. A *ranking* value is defined for all the candidates. The candidate with the minimum *ranking* is called the best candidate. A pair of clusters merges if they are best candidates with respect to each other. In a round of clustering, all such pairs of clusters merge. This continues recursively until there is either a single cluster of the whole network or no two neighboring clusters can merge.

We explain the details of the algorithm. Assume r rounds of clustering have been completed and there are k clusters (trees). We now explain how two neighboring trees C_i and C_j merge in the (r +1)st round. We assume the following notations:
edge e_{xy} connects C_i and C_j with length less then α, and at their leaf nodes x (of cluster C_i) and y (of cluster C_j); r_i (r_j) is the root of corresponding cluster; m_i(m_j) denotes the maximum distance of the root to any node in the cluster. All nodes in cluster C_i maintain r_i and m_i. Leaves x and y exchange both their root information and the maximum distance. Then x and y locally verify the following condition:

$$(m_i + JSD(r_i,r_j) + m_j) < \beta \tag{3}$$

If they do not satisfy the condition (3), then C_i and C_j rule out each as candidates for merger, else they evaluate the ranking of the possible merger. The ranking of the merger is determined by m_{ij}, the maximum distance of the (new) root to any node in the merged cluster, which is given as equation (4):

$$m_{ij} = \begin{cases} \max\left(m_i, m_j + JSD(r_i, r_j)\right) \text{ if } m_i \geq m_j \\ \max\left(m_j, m_i + JSD(r_i, r_j)\right) \text{ if } m_i \leq m_j \end{cases} \tag{4}$$

Leaf x sends m_{ij} to its root r_i. Root r_i receives m_{ij} (from several leaves) from all candidate clusters Cj . It chooses the optimal candidate $best\_candidate_i$, such that

$$best\_candidate_i = C_j \text{ if } \min_{C_k \in Candidates(C_i)} m_{ik} = m_{ij} \tag{5}$$

Two such clusters C_i and C_j merge if $best\_candidate_i = C_j$ and $best\_candidate_j = C_i$ in the (r+1)st round; Else this merger is stalled in this round. The root of the merged cluster r_{ij}, is the root of the old cluster which has the maximum of m_i and m_j.(If m_i=m_j, we select node with greater degree to act as root of the merged clusters) The new root r_{ij} sends a message (m_{ij}; r_{ij}) to all the nodes of old clusters C_i and C_j to update their attributes.

4 Performance Metrics and Simulations

In this section, we evaluate our algorithms from two measurements: energy consumption and relative clustering error (clustering fidelity).

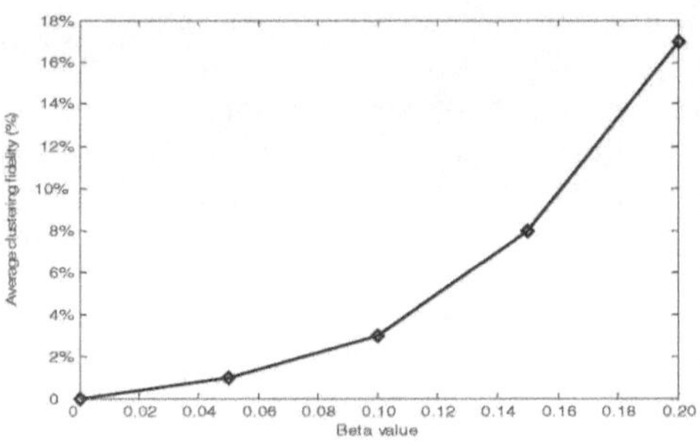

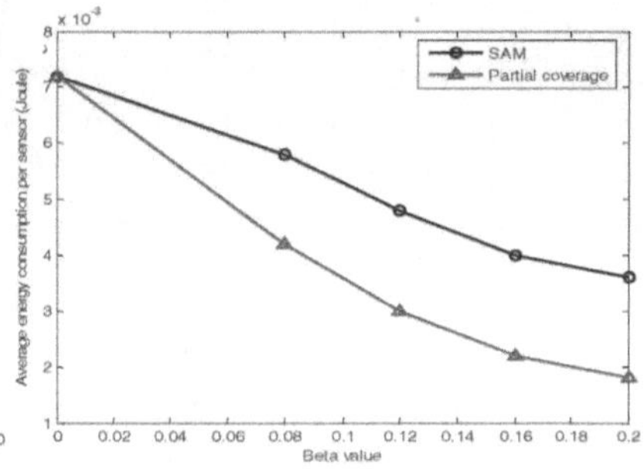

Fig. 1. β value vs. Average energy consumption **Fig. 2.** β value vs. Average clustering fidelity

Energy: Energy is consumed in four main activities in sensor networks: transmitting, listening, processing, and sampling. We focused on transmission and listening power.

Relative clustering error (Clustering fidelity): The clustering fidelity is a measure of how close the exact answer and the approximate answer are. The clustering fidelity is measured in the following way: Assume after k rounds clustering, a cluster C is formed. Denote $JSD(r, r+1)$ (r=1...k-1) the maximal distance between partial cluster formed in the rth round and the partial cluster formed in the (r+1)th round, so the clustering fidelity can be characterized as equation (6):

$$RCM = 1 - \prod_{r=1}^{k-1} \left(1 - JSD(r, r+1)\right) \tag{6}$$

The performance of our partial coverage algorithms is evaluated through simulation on synthetic data set. The simulated network was configured as a grid of sensors (15*15 grids). Each node could transmit data to sensors that were at most one hop away from it. In a grid this means it could only transmit to at most 8 other nodes. We generate data at every node i according to two kinds of distribution: uniform distribution $U(40,50)$, and normal distribution $N(a, \delta^2)$. The mean in normal distribution follows uniform distribution with range between 25 and 30, and variance constantly equals 2. In our simulation, we assumed that each sensor will start listening at the beginning of each round (each round has 30ms), when a node is covered by other sensors from interest sense, it sleeps to save energy. In each simulation, let $\alpha=\beta/3$.

From the viewpoint of average energy consumption, we compare our algorithms with Statistical Aggregation Method (SAM), which is partially similar with our ideas. In Fig.1, we can see that our algorithm save more than 50% energy than SAM, which is wasted in SAM or other similar data aggregation schemes for listening to the almost same spatial data. Fig.2 shows that, with β value increase, the average clustering fidelity increase greatly. It is obvious that this is tradeoff between data precision and energy saving in partial coverage scheme, but, for large spatial area with almost same phenomenon, our approach is significantly useful.

5 Conclusion

In this paper, the idea of partial coverage is provided to save energy in sensor network that monitors the physical phenomena in large geographical area which can be partitioned into a set of spatial regions with similar observations. By partial coverage it means, from viewpoint of data semantics, the divergence between two data trends gathered by pair of geographical neighbor sensors is so small that one sensor is completely covered by another sensor. Based on the idea, within certain error range, we can cluster the neighbor sensors that observe similar data trends, and replace the whole cluster with one representative sensor in this cluster to listening to and transmitting data (depending on the transmission range of sensor and cluster diameter, more sensor may participate in routing data).

In this paper, we use to Jensen Shannon Divergence (JSD) to characterize the similarity between two data trends (rather than raw data). It has been proven in information theory that JSD is appropriate to measure the similarity among probability distributions. Based on the JSD obtained, Hierarchical clustering algorithm is offered to form the cluster. From simulation, we obtain that our partial coverage approach gains more than 50% energy saving than Statistical Aggregation Method (SAM).

References

[1] Antonios Deligiannakis, Yannis Kotidis and Nick Roussopoulos, Hierarchical in-Network Data Aggregation with Quality Guarantees, In Proc. of the 9th Conference on Extending Database Technology (EDBT), Heraklion, Greece, March 2004

[2] Tri Pham, Eun Jik Kim and Melody Moh, On Data Aggregation Quality and Energy Efficiency of Wireless Sensor Network Protocols-Extended Summary, First International Conference on Broadband Networks, 2004.

[3] SangHak Lee and TaeChoong Chung, Energy Efficient Data Aggregation in Wireless Sensor Networks, First International Workshop on Networked Sensing Systems (INSS), 2004, Japan.

[4] W. R. Heinzelman, A. Chandrakasan, and H. Balakrisnan, Energy-efficient Communication Protocol for Wireless Microsensor Networks, In Proc. of the 33rd International Conference on System Sciences, 2000.

[5] Jamil Ibriq and Imad Mahgoub, Cluster-Based Routing in Wireless Sensor Networks: Issues and challenges, In Proc. of the 2004 Symposium on Performance Evaluation of Computer Telecommunication Systems. 2004.

[6] Meka and A. K. Singh, Distributed Spatial Clustering in Sensor Networks, Technical Report of University of California Santa Barbara (UCSB), 2005.

[7] Wokoma, L. Shum, L. Sacks, and I. W. Marshall, A Biologically-Inspired Clustering Algorithm Dependent on Spatial Data on Sensor Networks. In European Workshop on Wireless Sensor Networks (EWSN), 2005.

[8] P. Majtey, P. W. Lamberti, D. P. Prato, Jensen-Shannon divergence as a measure of distinguishability between mixed quantum states, arXiv:quant-ph/0508138 vol. 2, Aug 2005.

Quasi-bottleneck Nodes: A Potential Threat to the Lifetime of Wireless Sensor Networks*

Le Tian, Dongliang Xie, Lei Zhang, and Shiduan Cheng

State Key Lab of Networking and Switching, P.O. Box 79,
Beijing University of Posts & Communications, Beijing 100876, China
tlwhx@126.com,
{xiedl, zhangl, chsd}@bupt.edu.cn

Abstract. Enlightened by the congestion linkage in the traditional Internet, the novel concept of bottleneck node is proposed in this paper, which is crucial to the lifetime of the wireless sensor network deployed randomly. Due to the computation complexity and the operational deployment, the quasi-bottleneck node is presented to replace the theoretical bottleneck node in the practical scenario. Theoretical analysis shows the probability of the presence of quasi-bottleneck nodes stands at high level and an algorithm to find out this kind of nodes is presented. Simulation proves the correctness of the algorithm and shows the effect of these nodes on the network behavior, such as energy consumption and packet lost rate. At last, two effective solutions to decrease the energy consumption of the quasi-bottleneck nodes are presented.

1 Introduction

The fast growth of wireless communications and electronics has fueled up the extensive research and system development on wireless sensor networks. In most applications of wireless sensor networks, sensor nodes are powered by irrechargeable batteries and deployed randomly and unattended[1][2]. So the key concern of such wireless sensor network is its lifetime, which is determined by the energy supply level and the speed of energy consumption.

Because of randomness of deployment, there always have some nodes connecting two or more partitions without any other nodes as backup. When these nodes die, the whole network will be partitioned, and the application will fail. We call these nodes *bottleneck nodes*. It's difficult to find all bottleneck nodes without global topology information. In this paper a distributed, scalable algorithm to find these nodes is proposed. The algorithm can be executed correctly using only local information of

* The work is supported partly by Nokia (China) Research Center, the Collaborative Construction Program of Beijing Municipal Commission of Education (XK100130438), Natural Science Foundation of China under Grant No. 90204003 and No.60402012, the Postdoctoral Science Foundation of China under Grant No.2003034111.

H.T. Shen et al. (Eds.): APWeb Workshops 2006, LNCS 3842, pp. 241 – 248, 2006.

connectivity, and requires no extra information such as node's physical location. The nodes found using this algorithm are called *quasi-bottleneck nodes*, which have similar effect on the network as bottleneck nodes do. To our best knowledge, there have no other work concerning this problem.

The rest of this paper is organized as follows. In section 2 we discuss the related works having been done by other people. In section 3 the definition of the quasi-bottleneck node and its probability of presence are given. Section 4 proposes an algorithm to find out all quasi-bottleneck nodes. Section 5 shows our simulation about the correctness of our algorithm and the effect of those nodes on the network performance. In section 6 two feasible methods are presented to prolong the lifetime of quasi-bottleneck nodes. Section 7 is our conclusion.

2 Related Work

Bottleneck nodes problem has been studied extensively in Internet area[4-6]. However, in Internet, the emphasis of these studies is how to avoid congestion and how to improve the capacity of data flow, while in wireless sensor network, the emphasis is how to decrease energy consumption and how to prolong the network's lifetime.

Konstantinos Kalpakis et al. presented an algorithm to maximize the lifetime of wireless sensor networks for gathering data from every node in the network[7]. Given a base station, n sensor nodes deployed randomly, Kalpakis defined the lifetime of a wireless sensor network as that during which the base station could gather data from every node. However, in most applications, most nodes are working as forwarding nodes. The dead of one or more such nodes does not affect the network's behavior, unless the sink could not gather any data from the source nodes any more.

Jae-Joon Lee et al. studied the impact of the non-uniform individual energy depletion on the connectivity of a wireless sensor network in [8]. They found that various levels of data gathering tree with the sink as the root had various levels of energy consumption rate. More closer to the sink, the nodes consumed energy more quickly. However, in our simulation, we show that this is not always true. Those nodes (we call quasi-bottleneck nodes) which have to forward lots of packets and have no time to rest are more dangerous than the sink's neighbors.

3 Definition and Theoretical Analysis

Bottleneck nodes are defined as the nodes which lie on the critical path of transmission and act as the determinative role on the energy consumption of the whole network. Naturally, these nodes are cut set in graph theory, which can be gotten using MINCUT algorithm proposed by Karger[3]. The prerequisite of the algorithm is that any of nodes knows the information of the whole topology, which is difficult, even impossible in a practical situation.

However, the bottleneck nodes have a common feature, which is their neighbors can be divided into disjoined nonempty sets. So naturally, a node having this feature will be thought to be a candidate bottleneck node, which is defined as the *quasi-bottleneck node* in this paper. Compared with the bottleneck node, the quasi-bottleneck node can be found using distributed algorithm easily.

Definition 1: Assuming the transmission radius of node O is R, the neighbors of O are those nodes whose Euclidean distance with O is less than R, i.e.:

$$Nr(O) = \{u \mid distance(u,O) < R\}$$

Definition 2: A quasi-bottleneck node is such a node that all its neighbors can be divided into disjointed nonempty sets, and none of neighbors belonging to one set is a neighbor of other nodes belonging to other sets.

Now we deduce the probability of a node to be a quasi-bottleneck node. We assume the nodes are deployed randomly, uniformly and independently, they have the same transmission radius *R*, and two nodes can communicate with each other when their Euclidean distance is less than *R*., we can get the following lemma.

Lemma 1: Assume a node O has N neighbors, then this node has the probability p^{qBN} to be a quasi-bottleneck node, which p^{qBN} can be described as:

$$p^{qBN} = \sum_{n=1}^{N-1}\left\{\binom{N}{n}\left(1-\frac{\bigcup_{i=1}^{n} A_i}{A}\right)^{N-n}\left(\frac{\bigcup_{i=1}^{n} A_i}{A}\right)^{n}\right\} \tag{1}$$

Where A denotes the region covered by the node O, A_i denotes the intersection region covered by node O and its ith neighbor.

Lemma 2: In the rectangular coordinates shown in Fig.1(a), the center of the circle is node O, R is node O's coverage radius, N_i is its ith neighbor and its coordinates is (x, y). For a given r, the probability of x<r is (As Fig.1(b) shows):

$$p_r = p\{x < r\} = 1 - \frac{1}{\pi}\arccos\frac{r}{R} + \frac{r\sqrt{R^2 - r^2}}{\pi R^2} \quad (-R < r < R) \tag{2}$$

Definition 3: In a selected rectangular coordinates randomly, P1 is used to denote the set of points mapped on X axis by neighbors in set S1, P2 is used to denote the set of points mapped on X axis by neighbors in set S2, then the distance of P1 and P2 on X axis is $|x_{p1}-x_{p2}|$, where x_{p1} and x_{p2} denote the nearest points of set P1 and set P2 to node O on X axis respectively.

Lemma 3: For a given r ranging from –R to R, the probability of the distance of set P1 and P2 is greater than R is (As Fig.1(c) shows):

$$p_b = (p_1 + p_2)^N - p_1^{\,N} - p_2^{\,N} \tag{3}$$

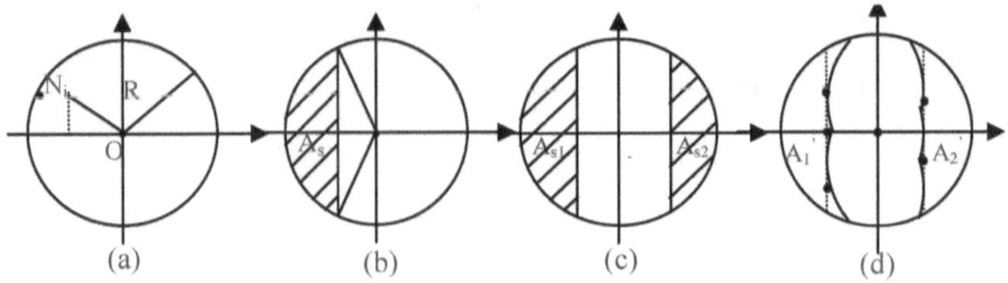

Fig. 1. The distribution of nodes in a rectangular coordinates

Where:

$$\begin{cases} p_1 = \dfrac{1}{\pi}\arccos\dfrac{r}{R} - \dfrac{r}{\pi R^2}\sqrt{R^2 - r^2} \\ p_2 = \dfrac{1}{\pi}\arccos\dfrac{R-r}{R} - \dfrac{R-r}{\pi R^2}\sqrt{2Rr - r^2} \end{cases} \quad 0 \le r < R$$

$$\begin{cases} p_1 = \dfrac{1}{\pi}\arccos\dfrac{-r}{R} + \dfrac{r}{\pi R^2}\sqrt{R^2 - r^2} \\ p_2 = \dfrac{1}{\pi}\arccos\dfrac{R+r}{R} - \dfrac{R+r}{\pi R^2}\sqrt{-2Rr - r^2} \end{cases} \quad -R < r < 0$$

Theorem: While $N \to \infty$, then:

$$\lim_{N\to\infty} E(p^{qPN}) = 2\pi \int_{-R}^{R} p_b dp_r \tag{4}$$

Proof: As shown in Fig.1(d), the direction of x axis is chosen randomly. The direction of x axis distributes uniformly and the value ranges from 0 to 2π, so in planar region, the probability of the distance of two sets is greater than R.is $2\pi p_b$.

For a given r, while $N \to \infty$, number of nodes located on two dashed line is infinity also, so the region $A_1' \to A_{s1}$, and the region $A_2' \to A_{s2}$.

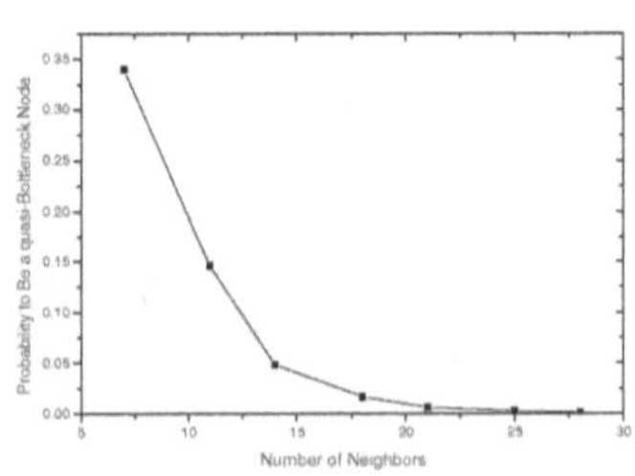

Fig. 2. The probability of a certain node to be a quasi-bottleneck node

While r is a variable ranging from -R to R, and its distribution function is p_r, so we get the result. □

Fig.2 shows the result of the probability of a certain node with N neighbors to be a quasi-bottleneck node. From Fig.2 can we see that even a node has up to 7 neighbors, it still risks high probability to be a quasi-bottleneck node.

4 Algorithm Proposed

This section a distributed, simple and scalable algorithm to find all quasi-bottleneck nodes is proposed. The algorithm includes three phases: neighborhood discovery phase, linkage information exchange phase and self-decision phase. The whole algorithm is described as follows:

1. Neighborhood discovery phase: Based on sending probe packet, every node could know how many neighbors it has and caches them into a neighborhood table.
2. Linkage information exchange phase: After neighborhood discovery phase, every node has known its neighborhood information. Then it can exchange its neighborhood table with its neighbors to get the local topology information in 2 hops.
3. Self-decision phase: After two phases above, every node could decide if it is a quasi-bottleneck node by the following self-decision algorithm:

```
Initialize two sets S1, S2;
Put all neighbors into set S2;
Removing a neighbor from S2 into S1 randomly;
For neighbor i in S2
  For neighbor j in S1
    If i is j's neighbor, then remove i from s2 into s1;
  End
End
If ( set S2 is empty) then
  I am not a quasi-bottleneck node;
Else
  I am a quasi-bottleneck node;
```

5 Simulation Result

This section we compare quasi-bottleneck nodes(qBNs) with ordinary forwarding nodes (OFNs) and one hop away nodes from the sink (OANs) about their energy consumption using simulator NS-2[9]. We show that our algorithm to find qBNs is correct and these nodes do have more significant impact on the performance of the network.

We consider the following scenario: 150 nodes which transmission radius is 30m are deployed in a 200x200m^2 region uniformly, assuming the sink is located at the top right corner of the region, and the source nodes are located in the middle of the region. Fig.3 shows one of the topologies. Adopting energy model from [7], a sensor consumes 400μJ to receive a byte and 720μJ to send a byte. The initial energy of every node is 5.4J. Finally, we assume the load of network is light weight.

In our simulation, a simplified Directed Diffusion[10] protocol is used as routing protocol. The gradient is hops from the sink, and the upstream node is selected randomly to balance energy consumption. When the sink has not received any packets from source nodes for a duration which is 10s in our simulation, it would rebroadcast the interest to rebuild the forwarding tree. If the sink can't receive any packets even it has rebroadcasted the interest for several times, we think the network is dead.

Fig.4 tells us that qBNs consume energy 2 times rapidly compared with OANs, and 3 times rapidly compared with OFNs. And Fig.5 shows the residual energy on average when the sink can not receive any packets from the source nodes, where 1 2 3 stand for qBNs OANs OFNs respectively, we can see that eventually all qBNs in paths died, while other nodes still had many residual energy. So, in contrast to early conclusions[11], it is qBNs that have potential threat to the life of the network.

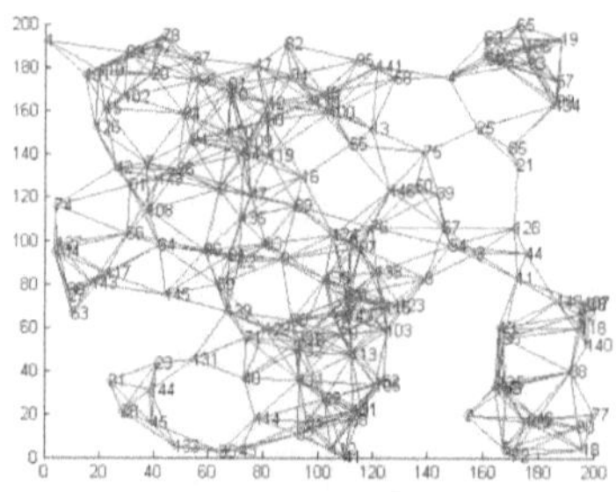

Fig. 3. One of topologies we simulated

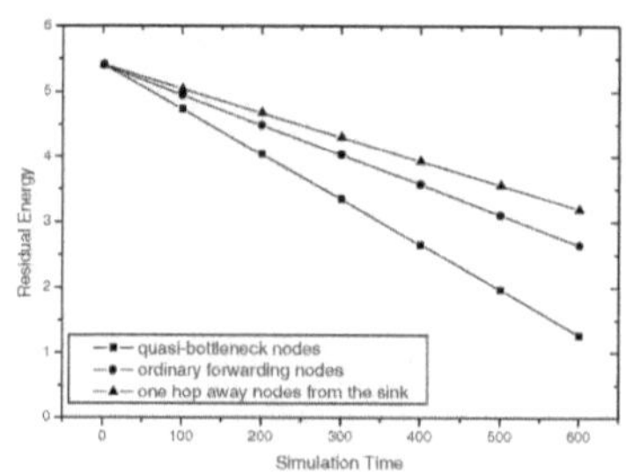

Fig. 4. Energy consumption

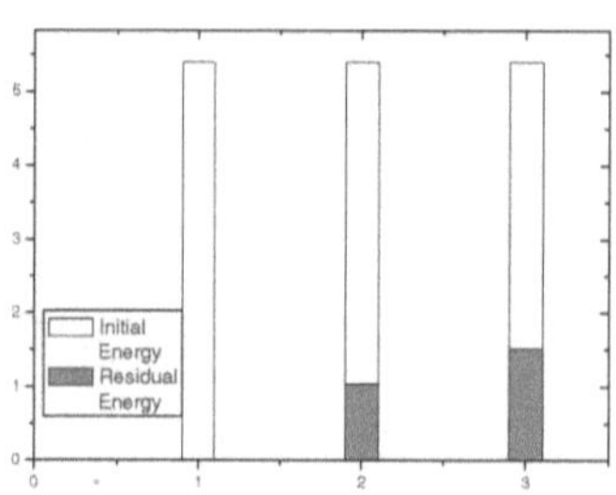

Fig. 5. Final residual energy

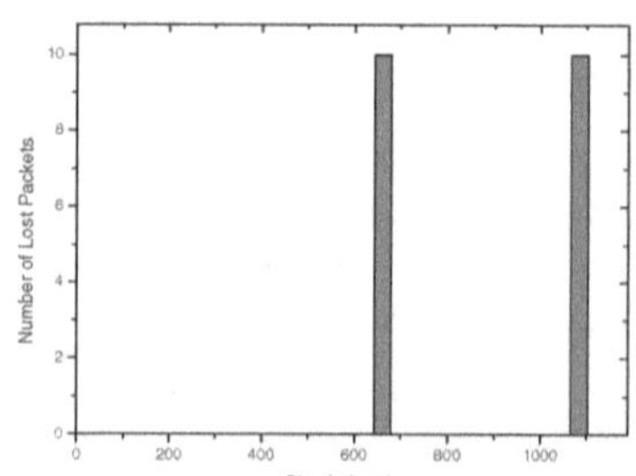

Fig. 6. Number of packets lost

Fig.6 shows when the first qBN in routing path died at 661st second, ten packets were lost, and when another qBN died at 1085th second, ten packets were lost again. The reason is that when a qBN dies, the path through it is broken up, the packets sent to it will be lost until the children nodes finally find out the problem and get rid of this node from its gradient table.

It should be pointed out that not all quasi-bottleneck nodes have so crucial impact on the network performance, only those nodes lying on the forwarding path will affect the behavior of the network.

6 Feasible Methods

The quasi-bottleneck nodes having more important effect on the network's behavior has been proven through simulation. Then how can we eliminate the effect of those nodes on the network while finding out all of them? Here, two feasible methods are presented to tackle this problem.

6.1 Data Aggregation Before Quasi-Bottleneck Nodes

One of the methods is to use data aggregation studied extensively in [7][8][11]. When a node on the forwarding path realizes that it is a quasi-bottleneck node, it can send a notifying packet to its children nodes to pronounce its status. Once a child node knows that its upstream node is a quasi-bottleneck node, it will aggregate packets periodically and send aggregated data to its parent node. By doing so, the quasi-bottleneck nodes will transmit less packets than non-aggregation.

Various aggregation ratios will bring various energy consumption rates. Fig.7 is our simulation result using various aggregation ratios, while 1 stands for without data aggregation. We can see that energy consumption is deeply decreased using data aggregation, while it will bring longer time delay. In our simulation, the delay is increased by 1.5s on average.

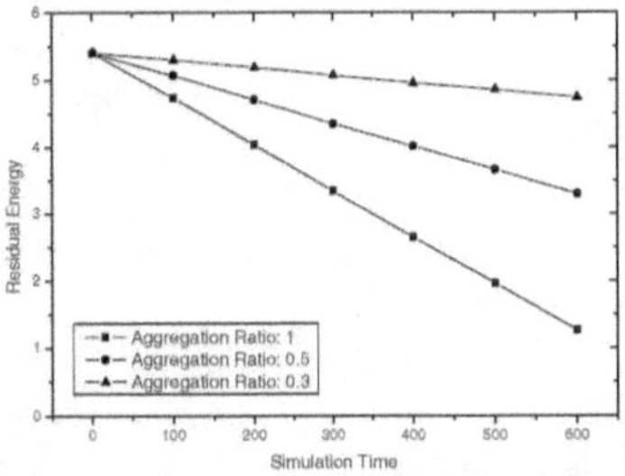

Fig. 7. Energy consumption with data aggregation

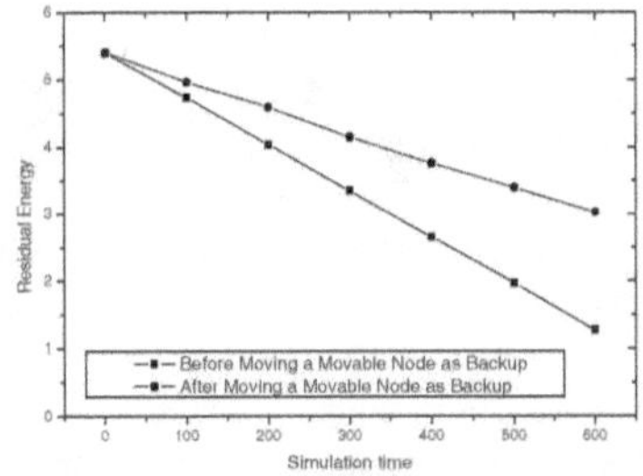

Fig. 8. Energy consumption with backup

6.2 Moving a Movable Node to the Neighboring Region as a Backup

The other method is to move a movable node to the adjacent area of the quasi-bottleneck node. This movable node acts as a backup or fireman. Robomote[12] which is compatible with mote[1] is an example. Readers can refer to [13] to learn how to move nodes efficiently in a wireless sensor network.

Fig.8 shows the simulation result when we use a movable node as a backup of the quasi-bottleneck node. This bottleneck node consumes only half of energy compared with without backup. Thus this method is a feasible choice to prolong the lifetime of the network too.

7 Conclusion

In this paper, we consider the effect of bottleneck nodes. Because bottleneck Nodes are difficult to find, quasi-bottleneck nodes are presented and a simple and scalable algorithm is proposed to find them out. Simulation shows that the correctness of our algorithm and quasi-bottleneck nodes do have crucial effect on the lifetime of a wireless sensor network. Then two feasible methods are presented to decrease the energy consumption of quasi-bottleneck nodes to prolong the lifetime of the network.

References

1. Hill J., Szewczyk R., et al., "System architecture directions for networked sensors", in Proceedings of Architectural Support for Programming Languages and Operating Systems-IX. ACM, 2000.
2. E. Shih, S. Cho, et al., "Physical layer driven protocol and algorithm design for energy-efficient wireless sensor networks", in Proceedings of ACM MobiCom'01, 2001.
3. Lizhi Xu et al., "Computer Mathematics of Modern Mathematics Handbook", Huazhong University of Science and Technology Press, P539.
4. S. Floyd and V. Jacobson, "Random early detection gateways for congestion avoidance". IEEE/ACM Transactions on Networking, 1(4):397--413, August 1993.
5. Laurent Massoulie and James Roberts, "Bandwidth sharing: Objectives and algorithms", In Proceedings of IEEE Infocom1999, 1999.
6. Ningning Hu, Li (Erran) Li, Zhuoqing Morley Mao, Peter Steenkiste and Jia Wang, " A Measurement Study of Internet Bottlenecks", in Proceeding of IEEE Infocom2005, 2005.
7. Konstantinos Kalpakis, Koustuv Dasgupta, and Parag Namjoshi, "Efficient Algorithms for Maximum Lifetime Data Gathering and Aggregation in Wireless Sensor Networks", Computer Networks, vol. 42, no. 6, pp. 697--716, 2003.
8. Bhaskar Krishnamachari, Deborah Estrin and Stephen Wicker, "The Impact of Data Aggregation inWireless Sensor Networks", International Workshop on Distributed Event-Based Systems, (DEBS '02), Vienna, Austria, July 2002.
9. NS-2 simulator, http://www.isi.edu/nsnam.
10. Chalermek Intanagonwiwat, et al., "Directed Diffusion for Wireless Sensor Networking", IEEE/ACM Transactions on Networking, WOL. 11, No. 1, February 2003.
11. Jae-Joon Lee, et al., "Impact of Energy Depletion and Reliability on Wireless Sensor Network Connectivity", SPIE Defense & Security Symposium April 2004
12. Gabe T. Sibley, Mohammed H. Rahimi, and Gaurav S. Sukhatme. "Robomote: A tiny mobile robot platform for large-scale ad-hoc sensor networks. " In Proceedings of the IEEE International Conference on Robotics 158 and Automation (ICRA-2002), 2002..
13. Guiling Wang, Guohong Cao, Tom La Porta, and Wensheng Zhang, "Sensor Relocation in Mobile Sensor Networks", in Proceeding of IEEE Infocom2005, 2005

Adaptive Data Transmission Algorithm for Event-Based Ad Hoc Query*

Guilin Li[1], Jianzhong Li[1,2], and Jinbao Li[1,2]

[1] School of Computer Science and Technology, Harbin Institute of Technology, China
[2] School of Computer Science and Technology, Heilongjiang University, China
{liguilin, lijzh}@hit.edu.cn

Abstract. Event-based ad hoc query processing is one of the most important functions of wireless sensor networks. Data centric storage algorithm is carried out to solve the problem but the traditional algorithm neglects that events will last for a time. During this time, the relationship between the query frequency and the data production frequency will change, which is an important feature to affect the energy consumption of the event-based ad hoc query processing in sensor networks. In this paper, we propose an adaptive data transmission algorithm, which takes the relationship into account. Experiments shows that our adaptive algorithm can save more energy than the traditional data centric storage algorithm.

1 Introduction

Recently wireless sensor networks have been widely used in various applications. Many researchers considered the sensor networks as a new kind of database [1,2] and developed a lot of query processing algorithms. As the energy of each sensor is very limited, energy consumption is the most important factor to think about when designing query processing algorithms.

Event-based ad hoc query is one of the most important applications of sensor networks. An event is a group of predefined conditions that the observed object must satisfy. If the data sampled by the sensor satisfy these predefined conditions, an event occurs and the event-based ad hoc query refers to the query about the event's data proposed by user at anytime.

[3,4] presented the data centric storage to solve the event-based ad hoc query processing. Data centric storage is a distributed algorithm and is composed of three parts, which execute on sink, home node and source node respectively. When source nodes detect events, they use a predefined system hash function to hash the event name detected to a location in the sensor network. The node nearest to the hash location, called home node, will receive the data about an event sent by source nodes. When sink receives users' queries about an event, sink uses the same hash function to find the home node to the same event and sends query to the home node. Finally the home

* Supported by the National Natural Science Foundation of China under Grant No.60273082; the National Natural Science Foundation of China under Grant No.60473075; the Natural Science Foundation of Heilongjiang Province of China under Grant No.ZJG03-05.

H.T. Shen et al. (Eds.): ADWeb 2006, LNCS 3842, pp. 249 – 256, 2006.

node returns the answer to the sink. [5] presented an algorithm called ring-based index, which expands the home node to a circle of nodes surrounding the home node. As the algorithm stores the events' data in different nodes, queries can be answered in different nodes, which solves the hop spot problem of traditional data centric storage. [6] gave an distributed index called DIFS (Distributed Index for Features in Sensor Networks), which is used to answer range queries about events with a single attribute. The index can uniformly distribute the uses' queries to different entries in the distributed index. [7] described another distributed index called DIM (Distributed Index for Multi-dimensional Data) which is used to answer range queries about events with multiple attributes. [8] introduced a concept called "Dimensions" based on which it built a hierarchical storage structure. This structure is suitable for queries such as "Drill Down" operation.

But all the algorithms proposed did not consider that events always last for some time, which is an important feature to affect the energy consumption of event-based ad hoc query processing. For example, the sensor network is used to observe the rainfall of some area. When it rains, the user will submit queries such as "tell me the rainfall of some place now". The rain can last for a long time and the rainfall may change from time to time. If the rain is heavy, the user may send more queries, otherwise the user may send fewer queries, which means during the raining time the user's query rate about the event may change from time to time. At the same time, source nodes sample data during this time at a predefined frequency. It is unreasonable for the source nodes to send event data to the home node no matter the user asks for the data or not.

In this paper, we propose an adaptive data transmission algorithm. By considering the relationship between queries sent by users and the data sampled by source nodes during the event time, our algorithm can adaptively change the data transmission mode of the source node. The experimental results shows that such kind of change can save a lot of energy.

The paper is organized as follows. In Section 2, we analyze the relationship between the data sampled by source nodes and queries sent by users. In Section 3 we develop a distributed adaptive algorithm to answer the event-based ad hoc query. Experimental results to measure the algorithm's performance are given in Section 4. Finally we conclude the paper in Section 5.

2 Relationship Between the Sampled Data and the Query

As the traditional data centric storage does not consider that event will last for some time, it neglects to consider the relationship between the data sampled by sensors and queries sent by users during this time. By analyzing the relationship, we find that the traditional data centric storage will waste energy when it is directly used in the conditions that events last for some time.

2.1 Two Types of Data Transmission Modes

There are two kinds of data transmission mode: active and inactive data transmission mode. They are suitable to different conditions according to the relationship with the query sent by the home node and data sampled by the source node. In traditional data centric storage, when source node finds some event, it will actively send the data about the event to the home node of the event. We call such kind of data transmission "active data transmission mode". On the contrary, another kind of data transmission is "inactive data transmission mode", which means the data about an event is sent to the home node only when the home node sends a query to the source node.

2.2 Energy Consumption Analysis of the Two Data Transmission Modes

As energy is the most important factor to measure the performance of any algorithm for sensor networks, we analyze the energy consumption of these two data transmission mode. The number of hops a packet being transmitted is used as the metric to measure the energy consumption and we assume the number of hops between the source node and home node is h.

For active data transmission mode, data about an event is directly sent by source node, so when doing query processing the home node does not need to send any query to the source node. During this procedure, only source node sends a packet from source to home node, so for the active data transmission mode the energy consumption to do the query processing one time is h.

For inactive data transmission mode, data about an event is sent by source node only when it receives the query from the home node. During this procedure, both of the source node and the home node send a packet and the two packets travel for h hops respectively, so the energy consumption for inactive data transmission mode to do the query processing one time is $2h$.

2.3 Relationship Between Data and Queries

In order to do the query processing for event-based ad hoc query efficiently, we analyze the relationship between the data sampled by the source node and the queries sent by the home node and give the suitable conditions to use different kind of data transmission modes. The following theorem gives the proper conditions for the two kinds of data transmission modes, using the relationship between the users' query frequency and the source's data sample frequency.

Theorem 1: When the ratio between the query frequency and the data sample frequency is beyond 1:2, source nodes should use the active data transmission mode which can save more energy than inactive mode; on the contrary, when the ratio is less than 1:2, source nodes should use inactive data transmission mode; and when the ratio is equal to 1:2, the two modes consume the same energy.

Proof: Assume that the query frequency is f_q, the data sample frequency is f_d and the event being queried lasts for time t.

When a source node uses the inactive data transmission mode, the source node sends out data only if it receives queries from the home node, so the energy consumption of the query processing is controlled by the query frequency. In section 2.2, we analyzed that the energy consumption to do the query processing using the inactive data transmission one time is $2h$, so during the time t, the total energy consumed by the sensor network is $2hf_qt$. In the same way, when source node uses the active data transmission mode, the source node directly sends data to the home node, so the energy consumption is determined by the data sample frequency. As the energy consumption for the active data transmission mode is h for a time, during the time t, the total energy consumed by the sensor network is hf_dt.

If $f_q:f_d > 1:2$, we get the result $2hf_qt > hf_dt$, which means the inactive data transmission mode consumes more energy than the active mode and the source node should use active data transmission mode. Otherwise, if $f_q:f_d <1:2$ the source node should use the inactive data transmission mode. If $f_q:f_d=1:2$ two types of data transmission modes consume the same energy.

3 Adaptive Data Transmission Protocol

In this section we give an adaptive data transmission algorithm, which can make the source node adaptively change its data transmission mode according to the ratio between the data sample frequency and the query frequency to save energy.

Step 1. Register: when a source node detects the occurrence of some event, it will use a system hash function to hash the event name and gets the event's home node's position. Then the source node sends a registration packet, which contains the position of the source node and the data about the detected event, to the home node. When the home node receives the packet, it stores the position of the source node in its local cache. The source node will adopt the inactive data transmission mode as the default data transmission mode after its registration.

Step 2. Query Processing: After the registration, when sink receives queries about some event from the users, it will use the same hash function to hash the queried event and get the home node's position. Sink sends queries to the home node. When home node receives the query, it will check the source node's data transmission mode. If the mode is the inactive one, the home node will send queries to the source nodes according to the source nodes' position registered in step 1. After source nodes receive the queries, they return the results to the home node and the home node return the result to sink. Otherwise, source nodes actively send data to the home node when they detect the event. When the home node receives the query, it directly returns the data to sink. Next, we present the condition of the source node to change its data transmission mode.

In the beginning the source node uses the inactive data transmission mode. During this time, the source nodes answer queries presented by home node, source nodes observe the ratio between the query frequency and the data sample frequency. When the ratio is beyond 1:2, the source node will change the data transmission mode from inactive to active according to theorem 1.

After the source nodes change their data transmission mode from inactive to active, the home node can directly answer the users' queries using its local cache and it has the function to change the source nodes' data transmission mode. During the time the home node directly answers the users' queries, the home node observes the ratio between the query frequency and the data sample frequency. When the ratio is less than 1:2, the home node will send a "mode change" packet to all registered source nodes to change their data transmission mode from active to inactive.

Step 3. Unregister: when the source node detects that an event is over, it will transmit a packet to remove its position in the home node's local cache. After that time, the home node will not send queries to such nodes and energy can be saved.

Another problem is how to detect the ratio between the query frequency and the data sample frequency. The source node or the home node can calculate the query number it received in the most recent t' periods, and the ratio can be estimated by n/t'. But if the value of t' is not set proporly, the adaptive protocol may consume more energy than traditional protocol. How to set proper value for t' is our future work.

4 Experiment and Results Analysis

4.1 Experimental Setup

In the experiments we use energy consumption as the metric to compare our adaptive data transmission algorithm with the traditional data centric storage algorithm. The energy consumption metric is measured by the hop number a message transmitted. We use ns2 [9] as the simulation platform and implement our adaptive data transmission algorithm. The topology of our experiments is that the distance between the source node and the home node is 3 hops and the distance between the sink and the home node is 1 hop. We do two groups of experiments to show the effectiveness of our algorithm. The first experiment is to prove different data transmission modes are suitable to different conditions; the second experiment is to show our adaptive algorithm is more energy efficient than the traditional data centric storage algorithm.

4.2 Experiment I

We set the ratio between the query frequency and the data sample frequency to 1:1 and 1:10 respectively. When the frequency ratio is set to 1:1, the experimental result is shown in Fig.1 (a). It showed that the IADTM (InActive Data Transmission Mode) consumes much more energy than the ADTM (Active Data Transmission Mode). On the contrary, when the ratio is 1:10, the IADTM consumes only about one fourth of the energy consumed by ADTM as shown in Fig.1 (b). This experiment also proves the correctness of theorem 1 in practice.

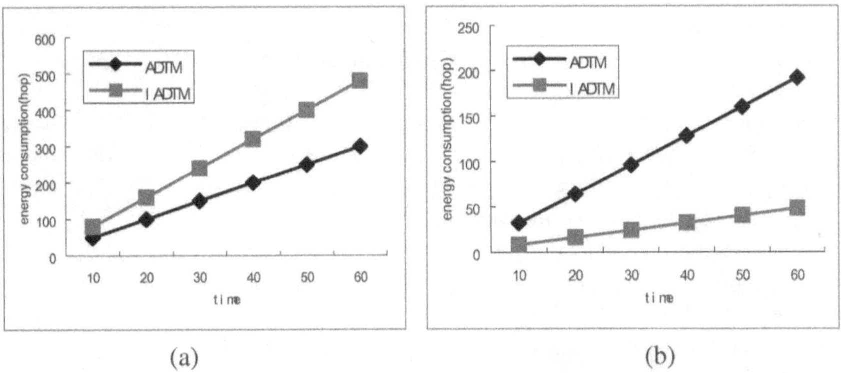

Fig. 1. Energy consumption comparison between different kinds of data transmission modes

4.3 Experiment II

In this experiment we change the query's frequency and show the energy saving of our adaptive data transmission algorithm.

The frequency ratio between the query and data changes between 1:1 and 1:10. Assume that the time duration each frequency ratio lasts for a time is *t''*. The time *t'* to detect the change of frequency ratio is set to be 2 and 4 periods respectively. The experimental results are shown in Fig.2 (a) and (b). The difference between them is the time duration of each frequency ratio (1:1&1:10) *t''* is set to 10 and 20 respectively. In Fig.2 (a), the frequency ratio between the query and data is 1:1 during the 0-10, 20-30, 40-50 periods and is 1:10 during the 10-20, 30-40, 50-60 periods. In Fig.2 (b), the frequency ratio between the query and data is 1:1 during the 0-20, 40-60 periods and is 1:10 during the 20-40, 40-80 periods.

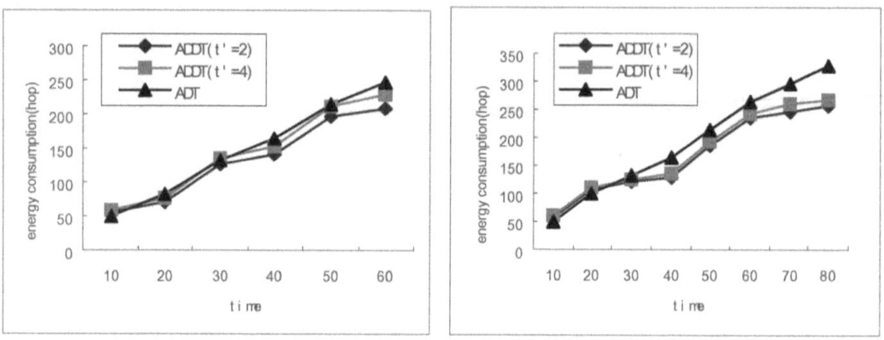

(a) (b)

Fig. 2. Energy consumption comparison between different adaptive data transmission algorithm and traditional data centric storage algorithm

The experimental results showed that when the frequency ratio is 1:1, the ADDT (ADaptive Data Transmission algorithm) consumes more energy than or the same as the ADT (pure Active Data Transmission algorithm) because the ratio detection procedure may consume more energy. When the frequency ratio is 1:10, the ADDT algorithm saves more energy than the ADT algorithm. But overall the ADDT saves more energy than ADT. The results also showed that when *t'* is small (*t'*=2), as the adaptive algorithm can detect the change of frequency ratio quickly at this time, it saves more energy than the adaptive algorithm when *t'* is large (*t'*=4).

In this experiment, we set the time duration of each frequency ratio (1:1&1:10) *t''* to 10, 20, 30 and set *t'* to 2 periods. The adaptive algorithm is simulated for 120 periods. We also simulate the ADT for the same time and compare the total energy consumption of the two algorithms in Fig.3. From the experimental results we can see that our adaptive algorithm can save more energy than ADT algorithm and the longer the time duration of each frequency ratio *t''* lasts, the more energy our adaptive algorithm can save.

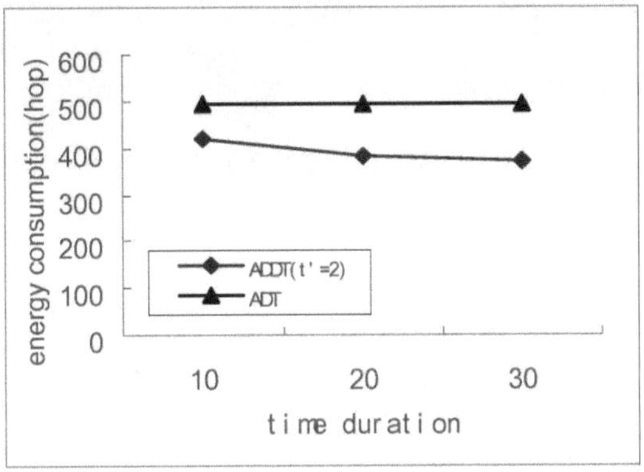

Fig. 3. Energy consumption comparison between adaptive data transmission algorithm and traditional data centric storage algorithm

5 Conclusion

In this paper we propose an adaptive data transmission algorithm. This algorithm can solve the problem of the event-based ad hoc query when the event lasts for some time by using adaptive data transmission mode selection. We analyze the frequency ratio between the query sent by the user and data sampled by the sensor and the ratio's affection to the energy consumption then we give an adaptive data transmission protocol. The experimental results showed the proposed algorithm can save more energy than the traditional data centric storage algorithm.

References

1. S. Madden and H. Kung. The design of an acquisitional query processor for sensor networks. In Proc. of ACM SIGMOD, pages 491-502, 2003.
2. R. Govindan, J. Hellerstein, W. Hong, S. Madden, M. Franklin, and S. Shenker. The Sensor Network as a Database. Technical Report 02-771, Computer Science Department, University of Southern California, September 2002.
3. S. Shenker, S. Ratnasamy, B. Karp, R. Govindan and D. Estrin. Data-Centric Storage in Sensornets. ACM SIGCOMM, Computer Communications Review, Vol. 33, Num. 1, 2003.
4. S. Ratnasamy, B. Karp, Y. Li, F. Yu, R. Govindan, S. Shenker and D. Estrin. GHT: A Geographic Hash Table for Data-Centric Storage. In Proceedings of the First ACM International Workshop on Wireless Sensor Networks and Applications (WSNA 2002), Oct. 2002.
5. W.S. Zhang, G.h. Cao, and T.L. Porta, Data Dissemination with Ring-Based Index for Wireless Sensor Networks, IEEE International Conference on Network Protocols (ICNP), November 2003.
6. B. Greenstein and D. Estrin and R.Govindan and S. Ratnasamy and S. Shenker. DIFS: A Distributed Index for Features in Sensor Networks. In the Proceedings of First IEEE International Workshop on Sensor Network Protocols and Applications Anchorage, AK. May 2003.

7. X.L. Young, J. Kim, R. Govindan, W. Hong, Multi-dimensional Range Queries in Sensor Networks, In Proceedings of the ACM SenSys Conference, pp. 63-75. Los Angeles, California, USA, ACM. November, 2003.
8. D. Ganesan, D. Estrin, J. Heidemann, Dimensions: why do we need a new data handling architecture for sensor networks, ACM SIGCOMM Computer Communication Review, Volume 33 Issue 1, January 2003.
9. UCB/LBNL/VINT Network Simulator – ns (Version 2). http://www-mash.cs.berkeley.edu/ns/, 1998.

Determination of Aggregation Point Using Fermat's Point in Wireless Sensor Networks

Jeongho Son, Jinsuk Pak, and Kijun Han*

Department of Computer Engineering,
Kyungpook National University, Korea
{jhson, jspak}@netopia.knu.ac.kr,
kjhan@knu.ac.kr

Abstract. We propose a method for determining where to aggregate data from sensor nodes using Fermat's point to save energy in wireless sensor networks. Unlike most aggregation schemes, our method does not need to construct any tree for aggregation of data. Simulation results show that Fermat's point can be the most effective aggregation point in terms of energy efficiency and thus the network lifetime.

1 Introduction

A wireless sensor network consists of many sensor nodes with sensing, processing, and communication capabilities, which communicates in ad-hoc mode and can be used in a variety of applications from defense systems to environmental monitoring [1]. Wireless sensor networks must minimize the energy consumption since sensor node has limited battery power.

To extend network lifetime in wireless sensor networks, energy inefficiency must be confronted and eliminated. We need the ways to prolong network lifetime by saving within the node and collaborative processing among nodes to reduce the overall energy dissipated in the network. The most dominant factor concerned with energy consumption in wireless sensor networks is transmission of data or flooding an interest message [2].

There are many dissemination protocols proposed to overcome the energy constraint for wireless sensor networks [3]. Data aggregation is one of methods used to save energy in wireless sensor networks by eliminating redundant transmissions from sources to a sink. *Data aggregation is defined as the task of merging messages while they are traveling through the sensor network.* Reducing the number of messages transmitted by data aggregation in a network can greatly save the amount of energy consumed [4].

Our method is described in section 2. Section 3 contains simulation results, and we make some conclusions in Section 4.

---

* Correspondent author.

H.T. Shen et al. (Eds.): ADWeb 2006, LNCS 3842, pp. 257 – 261, 2006.

2 Aggregation Point Determination Using Fermat's Point

Considering that we have two sources and sink, then we have to decide where to aggregate data to minimize the sum of hops from each source node to the sink. Determining an aggregation point to minimize the sum of hops boils down to find a point which would minimize the sum of the distances to the vertices P_1, P_2, and P_3 in a triangle ($\Delta P_1 P_2 P_3$). Fermat's point gives a solution for this.

The Fermat point is defined as an interior point X from which each side subtends an angle of 120 degrees [5][6], i.e.,

$$\angle P_1 X P_3 = \angle P_1 X P_2 = \angle P_2 X P_3 = 120^\circ$$

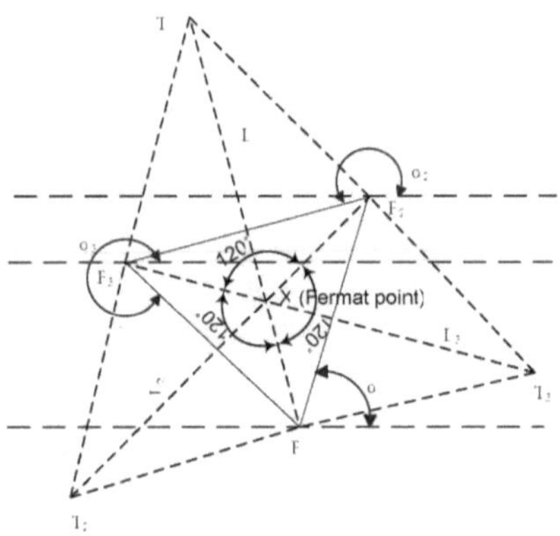

Fig. 1. The Fermat's point

To solve Fermat's point, we should first construct three equilateral triangles $\Delta T_1 P_2 P_3$, $\Delta P_1 T_2 P_3$, $\Delta P_1 P_2 T_3$ on each side of the given triangle $\Delta P_1 P_2 P_3$ (actually only two are needed).

We can find coordinates of $T_1(x_1', y_1')$, $T_2(x_2', y_2')$, and $T_3(x_3', y_3')$ by

$$\begin{aligned} x_1' &= d_{23}\cos(\alpha_2 - \frac{\pi}{3}) + x_2, & y_1' &= d_{23}\sin(\alpha_2 - \frac{\pi}{3}) + y_2 \\ x_2' &= d_{31}\cos(\alpha_3 - \frac{\pi}{3}) + x_3, & y_2' &= d_{31}\sin(\alpha_3 - \frac{\pi}{3}) + y_3 \\ x_3' &= d_{12}\cos(\alpha_1 - \frac{\pi}{3}) + x_1, & y_3' &= d_{12}\sin(\alpha_1 - \frac{\pi}{3}) + y_1 \end{aligned} \tag{1}$$

where d_{12}, d_{23}, and d_{31} mean the distances between each vertex P_1, P_2, and P_3, and α_1, α_2 *and* α_3 mean the slope of each side P_{12}, P_{23}, P_{31}, respectively.

And we draw three segments connecting P_1-T_1, P_2-T_2, and P_3-T_3. Now, we get the Fermat point at the intersection of three segments. The Fermat's point $F(x, y)$ is

$$
\begin{aligned}
x &= \frac{y'_2 - y'_1 + \dfrac{y'_1 - y_1}{x'_1 - x_1}x'_1 - \dfrac{y'_2 - y_2}{x'_2 - x_2}x'_2}{\dfrac{y'_1 - y_1}{x'_1 - x_1} - \dfrac{y'_2 - y_2}{x'_2 - x_2}} \\
y &= \frac{y'_1 - y_1}{x'_1 - x_1}\left(\frac{y'_2 - y'_1 + \dfrac{y'_1 - y_1}{x'_1 - x_1}x'_1 - \dfrac{y'_2 - y_2}{x'_2 - x_2}x'_2}{\dfrac{y'_1 - y_1}{x'_1 - x_1} - \dfrac{y'_2 - y_2}{x'_2 - x_2}} - x'_1 \right) + y'_1
\end{aligned}
\tag{2}
$$

If the largest angle of the triangle $\Delta P_1 P_2 P_3$ reaches 120 degree or more, then the vertex with the largest angle becomes the Fermat's point.

3 Simulation

In this section, we evaluate the performance of our scheme by comparing with GIT. Each node is assumed to have a transmission range of 17*m* and battery power of 10,000*mW*. And, it spends 400*mW* of battery power to transmit data. Each source sends its data every 1 minute for 10 minutes. Two sources whose data are to be aggregated are randomly selected for test.

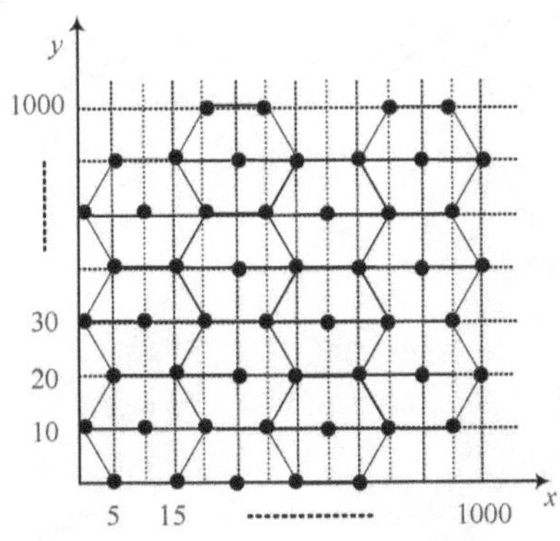

Fig. 2. Network topology for simulation

Fig. 3 illustrates how much the energy consumption to transmit depends on the location of aggregation point. For simulation, a network topology is constructed with 10,000 nodes on 1000×1000*m* field in shape as shown in Fig. 2. All nodes except nodes on the border have 6 neighbors connected in a hexagonal shape.

When we place two sources at (20,980) and (980,980) as shown in Fig. 3(a), the Fermat's point will be (215, 781). So, the node located at (220, 780) closest the Fermat's point is selected as the aggregation point. However, when we place two sources at (650,550) and (980,980) as depicted in Fig. 3(b), then the aggregation node will be at (655, 550) since the node at (655,550) has an angle exceeding 120 degrees. Fig. 3 shows that the Fermat's point can be the best choice of aggregation point in terms of transmission power to delivery data from sources to the sink.

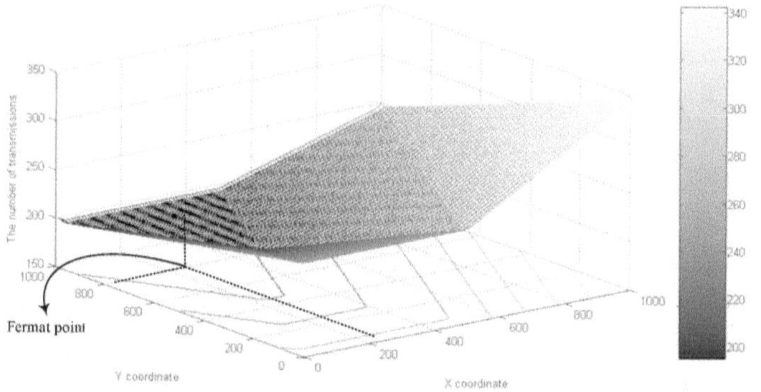

(a) When all angles < 120 degree

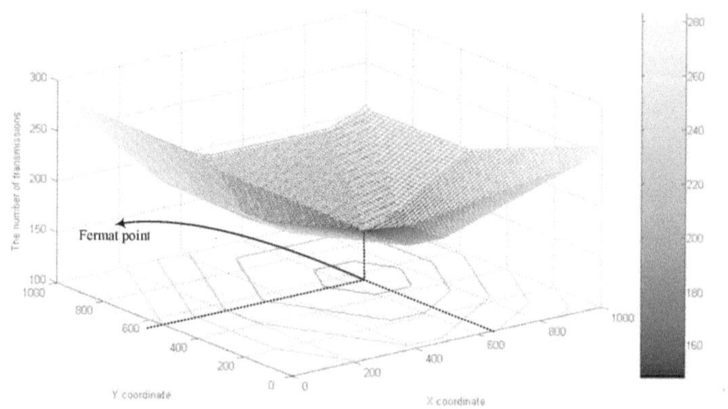

(b) When any angle > 120 degree

Fig. 3. The mount of energy consumption as a function of location of aggregation point

Fig. 4 (a) and (b) show the network lifetime as the number of nodes in the network is varied. The network lifetime is defined as the number of rounds until all sources complete the transmissions to the sink. The network size is $100 \times 100\ m$. In this simulation, the location of the sink is located at (0, 0) or (50, 50). We can observe a more significant aggregation effect to extending the network lifetime when nodes are densely deployed in the network since we can more likely aggregate data near the Fermat's point. We can also see that our scheme can prolong the network lifetime than the GIT scheme. In addition, we show that our scheme is more effective when the sink is located at the center of network than when it is located at (0, 0). This is because there will be more available paths when the sink is located (50, 50).

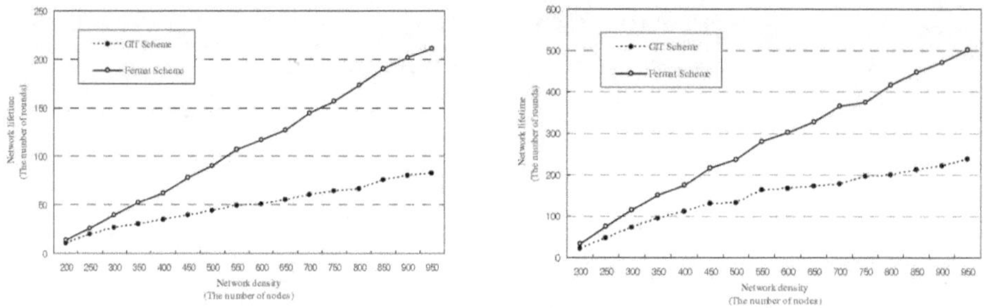

(a) When the sink is located at (0,0) (b) When the sink is located at (50,50)

Fig. 4. Network lifetime

4 Conclusions

In this paper, we have proposed an aggregation scheme which uses the Fermat's point to minimize the number of transmissions. Simulation results assure that Fermat's point can be the best choice of aggregation point in terms of transmission power to delivery data from sources to the sink. We can see that our scheme can prolong the network lifetime than the GIT scheme.

We will study a more delicate method for aggregating data from many sources in the real situation.

Acknowledgement. This research is supported by Program for the Training of Graduate Students for Regional Innovation.

References

[1] Tatiana Bokareva, Nirupama Bulusu, Sanjay Jha, "A Performance Comparison of Data Dissemination Protocols for Wireless Sensor Networks," *Global Telecommunications Conference Workshops, 2004. GlobeCom Workshops 2004. IEEE 29*, Dec 2004, pp. 85 - 89.
[2] R. Min, M. Bhardwaj, S.-H. Choi, N. Ickes, E. Shih, A. Shinha, A. Wang and A. Chandrakasan, "Energy-centric enabling technologies for wireless sensor networks," *IEEE Wireless Communications*, Aug 2002, pp. 28 - 39.
[3] Chalermek Intanagonwiwat, Ramesh Govindan, Deborah Estrin, John Heidemann, "Directed Diffusion for Wireless Sensor Networking," *Networking, IEEE/ACM Transactions on Volume 11*, Feb 2003 pp. 2 - 16.
[4] Min Ding, Xiuzhen Cheng, Guoliang Xue,"Aggregation Tree Construction in Sensor Networks," *Vehicular Technology Conference, VTC 2003-Fall. 2003 IEEE 58th Volume 4*, Oct 2003, pp. 2168 - 2172.
[5] http://mathsforeurope.digibel.be/fermat.htm, Oct 2005.
[6] http://mathworld.wolfram.com/FermatPoints.html, Oct 2005.

Inductive Charging with Multiple Charger Nodes in Wireless Sensor Networks

Wen Yao, Minglu Li, and Min-You Wu

Dept. of Computer Science and Engineering
Shanghai Jiao Tong University, Shanghai 200030, P.R. China
yaowen@sjtu.edu.cn, li-ml@cs.sjtu.edu.cn, wu-my@cs.sjtu.edu.cn

Abstract. Energy consumption in Wireless Sensor Network (WSN) remains a challenging problem. Better Solutions of this problem not only can prolong the lifetime of WSNs, but also can support more complex protocols to improve the network performance. We propose an approach of inductive charging, by using mobile nodes to deliver power to deployed active sensors. Infrequently visited by mobile nodes, the sensors can perpetually work without any human intervention. In order to power a WSN of a large number of sensor nodes in wide geographical range effectively, we propose three schemes for inductive charging. Simulation results demonstrate the effectiveness of these algorithms.

1 Introduction

Lack of continuous energy supply is an obvious limitation of wireless sensor networks. Now, there are many approaches to deal with the power efficiency problems. Normally, sensors are deployed with batteries that will not be recharged or replaced. In this scenario, the network is considered disposable and power conservation is paramount. Energy efficient design techniques have been studied for sensor networks at all levels from hardware design to protocols for medium access control [1], routing [2], data gathering [3], topology control [4], etc.

However, in some applications, the sensor network is not treated as disposable. It is possible to sustain the sensors by recharging or replacing batteries when needed. For example, Schwiebert et al. are considering biomedical monitoring via wireless sensors implanted in the body. Because sensors are intended for long-term use, they use radio frequencies (RF) or infrared (IR) signals to inductively charge the implanted sensors from an external power source [5].

Some have taken a further step to extract energy directly from the deployment environment. These "scavenging" techniques power sensors via solar power [6], kinetic energy [7], floor vibration [8], acoustic noise etc. However, scavenging techniques are only becoming capable of generating the level of power required to sustain some of current wireless sensor applications. Usually it simply cannot generate sufficient energy for sustained operation. The application situation of scavenging techniques is limited by environments. Not all deployment environments are conducive to such techniques.

Actually most of WSNs should run unassisted for long periods of time. They can neither be treated as disposable nor depend on an administrator who can perform

H.T. Shen et al. (Eds.): ADWeb 2006, LNCS 3842, pp. 262 – 270, 2006.

recharging or battery replacement. Due to the deficiency of the approach listed above, we need a more effective approach to deal with the power problems. We propose using mobile nodes to deliver power to deployed active sensors in WSNs when it is needed. The approach is to outfit mobile nodes with charging equipment to inductively recharge sensors. Infrequently visited by the mobile nodes, the wireless sensor nodes can work perpetually.

We propose the system model and three schemes to solve this inductive charging problem in WSNs. The rest of this paper is organized as follows. Related works are discussed in section 2. In section 3, we describe the system model. Three schemes RPC, RIC and DEC for inductively charging are proposed in section 4. In section 5, the schemes are validated by simulations. We finally conclude the paper in section 6.

2 Related Works

The inductive electrical energy transmission has been used in mining and underwater environments, electric vehicle battery-recharging application, some medical applications [9], cordless electric toothbrushes, portable telephone, PDA [10] and the RFID tags.

Inductance technique has also been used to power sensors to increase the longevity of the WSN as a whole. Chevalerias et al. have proposed an approach using one charger to provide power and fast data communication to off-the-shelf sensors, which is based on the well-established inductive coupling principle. In the approach, inductive coupling provides both a power and a communication solution, so the module being powered has no need for an on-board energy source. Chevalerias et al. have demonstrated the hardware feasibility of the approach using inductance to deliver power to sensors [11].

There are also many applications using inductance technique to deliver power to the sensors in WSNs. LaMarca et al. use robot to inductively charge sensors in a WSN for the plant care application. In this application, a mobile service robot, which is used to water plants, is equipped to inductively charge the deployed sensor nodes [12]. The measured efficiency of inductively charging the sensors is around 70% of the baseline efficiency achieved with a shielded cable. The WSNs in this application is in small geographical range and has a small number of sensor nodes. So the inductive charging for sensors in these applications can be simply implemented with a single power source. But many WSNs are deployed in a wide geographical range and have a large number of sensor nodes. Then, in order to inductively charge sensors in time and to minimize the energy consumption and to maintain the WSNs running effectively, a well-designed scheme for inductive charging is needed.

3 System Model

We consider the sensor network consisting of two kinds of nodes, sensor nodes and charger nodes. We assume that the sensor nodes are stationary and have been added inductive coil to support power reception. Charger nodes are mobile nodes which have been equipped to inductively charge the sensor nodes. Because inductive field strength falls off at a rate proportional to the square of the distance, close alignment of the inductive coils is required for achieving more efficient power transfer. So when a sensor node needs charging, the charger node moves to the sensor node, inductively charges the sensor node nearby.

Problems:

1. When a sensor node needs charging, how to choose a unique charger node to charge this sensor node?
2. When a charger node has more than one sensor node to charge at a certain time period, how to figure out a charging sequence for the charger node?

We try to minimize two performance parameters:

1. The moving distance of charger nodes.
2. The charge latency (the time interval from the instant when the sensor node asks for being charged until the time when one charger node starts to charge it).

We assume that during the bootstrapping process, all the sensor nodes and charger nodes are assigned unique IDs. All nodes are location-aware using some localization algorithm or equipped with GPS-capable parts. There is an energy threshold to identify the energy state of sensor nodes. The sensor nodes are able to aware of their low-power states when the remaining energy of a sensor node is under the energy threshold. We assume the network region is a rectangular area. Sensor nodes are randomly dispersed in the region. The number of sensor nodes in the system is M. The number of charger nodes is N and $N << M$.

4 Charging Schemes

4.1 Region Patrol Charge Scheme (RPC)

We divided the network region into N rectangular areas. Put the N charger nodes into each rectangular area respectively. Every charger node only charges the sensor nodes in its rectangular charge area. During the bootstrapping process, sensor nodes in the rectangular charge area inform the charger node about their location. With the location information of sensor nodes, each charger node calculates a shortest round path which links all the sensor nodes in its charge area. Then charger nodes patrol along these paths and check if there are any sensor nodes in the state of low power. When a charger node detects the sensor node nearby is in low power status, it will inductively charge the sensor node immediately.

When a charger node patrols along its path, it uses the information of present energy and energy consumption rate of the nearby normal sensor to predict when the remaining energy of the sensor will be under the energy threshold. The charger node records the minimal low power time. After a circuit of patrolling along the path, the charger node rests for a while, and starts the new circuit at the minimal low power time it recorded. By this way, the charger node moves less and energy is saved.

PRC is a simple scheme. It needs little data communication between nodes. But sensor nodes often can not be charged in time. In fact, some sensor nodes are energy exhausted before being charged. Charger nodes unnecessarily waste energy when moving a long distance for patrolling.

4.2 Region Inquire Charge Scheme (RIC)

This scheme is an improvement of the region patrol charge scheme. The difference between RIC and RPC is that during the patrolling process, a charger node sends packet to inquire the next sensor node in its round path about whether the sensor node is low power before any movement. The sensor node sends a packet to inform the charger node of its energy state. If the sensor node is in the state of low power, the charger node moves towards it; otherwise the charger node inquires of the next sensor node in the path.

We describe RIC in Fig.1. In the description, *Path* denotes the charger node's shortest round path, which links all the sensor nodes in its charge area. The number of sensor nodes in *Path* is *m*. Node i denotes the sensor node i in *Path*. $Low\_Power\_Time_i$ denotes the time when the energy of Node i is under the energy threshold. *Min_Time* denotes the minimal $Low\_Power\_Time_i$ of sensor nodes in *Path*. *T* denotes the present time.

```
1. Initialization
  Receive the location packet of sensor nodes in its area;
  Compute Path;
2. Charge patrolling
While (true)
  Min_Time=infinite;
  For (i=1; i<=m; i++)
   Inquire about energy state of Node i;
   If (Node i is in the state of low power) Move to and charge Node i;
   Predict the Low_Power_Time_i;
   If (Low_Power_Time_i<Min_Time) Min_Time= Low_Power_Time_i;
  EndFor
  If (T< Min_Time) Wait until T=Min_Time;
EndWhile
```

Fig. 1. The RIC algorithm

Compared with RPC, RIC has an obvious improvement in charger nodes moving distance and charge latency. But it increases communication amount.

4.3 Distance and Energy Aware Charge Scheme (DEC)

In this scheme, we do not divide the network region. The N charger nodes manage all the M sensor nodes together. The scheme includes two parts. Part one is to choose a unique charger node to charge the sensor node that is short of energy. Part two is to figure out a charging sequence for the charger node that has more than one sensor node to charge at a certain period.

Part 1. Choose a unique charger node

When sensor node S detects that its energy is less than the energy threshold, it broadcasts a *Request packet* to inform all the charger nodes that it needs to be charged. The charger node which receives the *Request packet* will set up a back-off timer *T*.

$$T=kd,$$

Where *d* is the distance between the sensor node S and the charger node; k is a constant. When the timer expires, the charger node informs the sensor node S that it will charge S. Once the sensor node S receives reply from a charger node, it broadcasts a *Repeal packet* with ID of the charger node, to tell all the charger nodes that this charger node will charge it. After receipt of a *Repeal packet* from sensor node S, a charger node compares the charger node ID in the packet with its own ID. If it is matched, the charger node then puts the sensor node information into its task list. Or the charger node cancels the back-off timers set up for the sensor node S and do not respond to the sensor node S's *Request packet*. Then the unique charger node C to charge sensor node S is elected.

Every charger node maintains a task list. The task list includes the information of sensor nodes that the charger node should charge. The items in the list contain sensor node ID, sensor node location, the time sensor node sends the *Request packet*, sensor node energy when requesting and sensor node energy consumption rate as shown in Table 1.

Table 1. An entry in task list

Sensor node ID	Location	Request time	Energy when requesting	Energy consumption rate

Every sensor node has three states: *Normal* indicates sufficient energy store of the sensor node; *Low_power* indicates energy level of the sensor node is lower than the energy threshold, and the node needs charging; *Waiting_for_charge* indicates the senor node has found a charger node to charge it, and is waiting for being charged.

There are three kinds of packets used in this scheme. *Request packet* is sent from a sensor node to inform all charger nodes that it needs charging. It includes sensor node ID and sensor node location. *Reply packet* is sent from a charger node to inform a sensor node that the charger node will charge it. The package includes charger node ID. *Repeal packet* is sent from a sensor node to inform all charger nodes which charger node will take the charge task. The packet includes sensor node ID, sensor node location, the time sensor node sends the *Request packet*, sensor node energy when requesting, sensor node energy consumption rate and charger node ID.

We describe the algorithm in Fig.2. Sensor node part describes how a sensor node works in DEC. Charger node part describes how a charger node works.

Part 2. Figure out a charging sequence

When a charger node C has more than one sensor node to charge at a certain time period, it has to decide which sensor node should be charged first and which should be charged later. The charging sequence is decided by a function *f*. Every sensor node in the charger node C's task list has a value of function *f* calculated by the charger node C. The charger node C will choose the sensor node with the smallest *f* to be the next charge target.

$$f= [e- v(t_n -t)]\log(d) ,$$

Where e denotes sensor node energy when the sensor node requests for charging; t_n denotes the present time; t denotes the time when sensor node sends the Request packet; v denotes the sensor node energy consumption rate; d denotes the distance between the sensor node and the charger node C. All the parameters used to calculate the value of function f can be found in the task list.

```
Sensor node part
If (Detected energy< energy threshold and state is Normal)
  Update state to Low_power
  Broadcast Request packet
If(receive Reply packet from charger node C)
   Update its state to Waiting_for_charge
   Record charger node C's ID
   Broadcast Repeal package
```

Fig. 2(a). Sensor node part of DEC

```
Charger node part
If(receive Request packet from sensor node S)
  Set back-off timer T
  If (T expires)
   Send Reply packet to S
If(receive Repeal packet from sensor node S)
  If(its ID= the charger node ID in the Repeal packet)
    Add information of S in the Repeal packet to the task list
```

Fig. 2(b). Charger node part of DEC

When a charger node finishes charging a sensor node, it deletes information of this sensor node from its task list, and then calculates the values of function *f* of all the sensor nodes in its task list. It chooses the sensor node S with the smallest function value to be the next charge target. Then it moves to the sensor node S and charges it.

The function *f* is decided by two factors: present energy of the sensor node and distance between the sensor node and the charger node. Energy plays a more important role in deciding the value of the function. It means that the charger node would charge the sensor node with the lowest energy first instead of the sensor node that is the nearest to the charger node. Therefore with this function the charger node works more efficiently.

5 Simulations

In this section, we study the performance of the three proposed charging schemes. The surveillance region is 1000×1000 m². Five hundred sensor nodes are deployed in the region randomly. The energy consuming rate is different in each sensor node. It is randomly generated between 0.1~0.2(J/min). Our simulation starts from the time network starts to work and ends at the time all the sensor nodes in the network are charged at least once. The parameters in the simulation are list in Table 2:

Table 2. The parameters in the simulation

Parameter	Value
Region(m²)	1000*1000
Number of sensor nodes	500
Full energy of sensor node(J)	15000
Energy threshold(J)	5000
Energy consumption rate(J/min)	0.2~1.0
Charger node moving speed(m/min)	4
Inductively charging rate(J/min)	80

The performance metrics of interest are:

1. Average Moving Distance: average moving distance of charger nodes throughout the simulation.
2. Charge Latency: the time interval from the instant when a sensor node asks for charge until the time when a charger node starts to charge it.
3. Total Number of Messages: The total number of charge control messages sent throughout the simulation.

Fig.3 shows that the Average Moving Distance of RPC is much longer than that of RIC and DEC. It is because that in RPC a charger node moves to every sensor node in its path no matter it is low power or not during the patrolling process, while in RIC and DEC the charger node only moves to the low power sensor nodes. Charger nodes in DEC move less than that in RIC especially when there are more charger nodes.

In Fig.4 we can see that the gaps between the average charge latency of RPC and that of RIC and DEC are big. When the number of charger nodes is less than 8, average Charge Latency of DEC is larger than that of RIC. When there are more charger nodes, the performance of DEC is better than that of RIC.

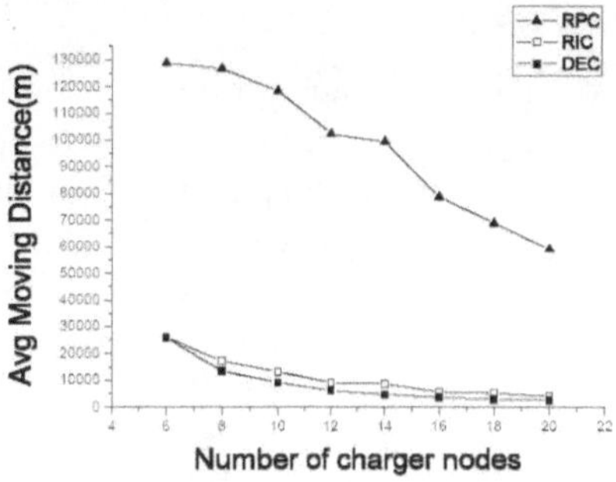

Fig. 3. Average Moving Distance of RPC, RIC and DEC under different numbers of charger nodes

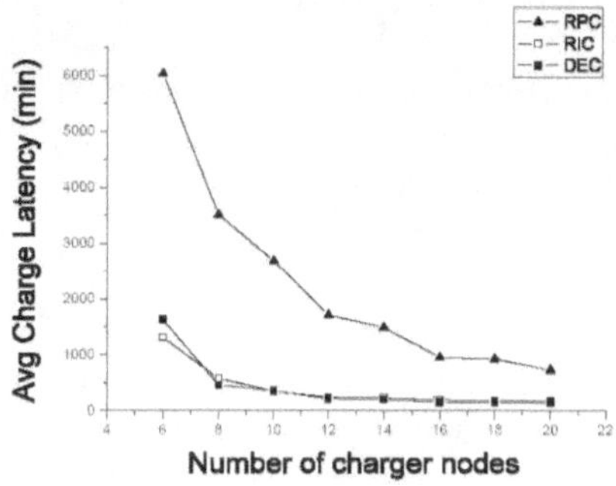

Fig. 4. Average Charge Latency of sensor nodes of RPC, RIC and DEC under different numbers of charger nodes

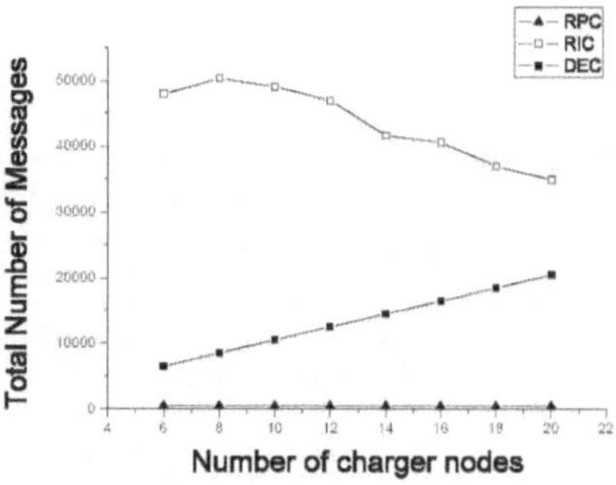

Fig. 5. Total Number of Messages of RPC, RIC and DEC under different numbers of charger nodes

Whatever the number of the change node is, total message sent in RPC is always 500. These messages are the packets sent during the bootstrapping process for charger nodes to compute the shortest round paths. In Fig.5 we can see that the total of message sent in RIC is much larger than that in DEC. This is because that in RIC, every time a charger node moves to the next position, two messages need to be sent to inquire a sensor node in its path.

Though RPC needs the least messages exchange, the performance of RPC on charger nodes moving distance and charge latency is worse than that of RIC and DEC. The performance of DEC on every aspect is better than RIC, especially on total number of messages sent. As a conclusion, RPC is a simple scheme, however the Average Moving Distance and the Average Charge Latency are big. RIC and DEC both can solve the inductively charging problem effectively. DEC has the best performance and better inflexibility.

6 Conclusions and Future Work

In this paper, we reviewed current approaches to dealing with the power problem in WSNs. As inductance technique is well-established and widely used in power delivery system, we propose an approach using multiple mobile nodes to inductively charge the deployed active sensors. We propose three schemes, RPC, RIC and DEC, for inductive charging, which can effectively solve the power problem with low cost. We demonstrate the performance of the schemes by simulation. The result shows RPC is the simplest scheme with lowest cost but relatively poor performance. RIC and DEC both can inductively charge sensor nodes in time and minimize the energy consumption. DEC has better performance than RPC especially in data communication amount. In the near future, we will focus on how many charger nodes are needed at least for inductive charging in WSNs. Then, we will consider the load balance between charger nodes of DEC and improving the performance of PRC especially on moving distance of charger nodes.

References

[1] J. Polastre, J. Hill, D. Culler, "Versatile low power media access for wireless sensor networks", Proc. ACM International Conference on Embedded Networked Sensor Systems. (2004) 95–107.

[2] R. C. Shah ,J. M. Rabaey, "Energy aware routing for low energy ad hoc sensor networks", Proc. IEEE Wireless Comm. and Networking Conference (2002) 350–355.

[3] K. Kalpakis, K. Dasgupta, P. Namjoshi, "Maximum lifetime data gathering and aggregation in wireless sensor networks", Proc. IEEE International Conference on Networking (2002) 685–696.

[4] C. Schurgers, V. Tsiatsis, S. Ganeriwal, M. Srivastava, "Optimizing sensor networks in the energy-density-latency design space", IEEE Transactions on Mobile Computing (2002) 70–80.

[5] L. Schwiebert, S. K. Gupta, J. Weinmann,,"Research Challenges in wireless networks of biomedical sensors", Proc. ACM MOBICOM (2001) 151–165.

[6] J. M. Kahn, R. H. Katz, K. S. J. Pister. "Next Century Challenges: Mobile Networking for "Smart Dust"", Proc. MobiCom (1999) 271-278.

[7] J. Paradiso, M. Feldmeier, "A Compact, Wireless, Self-Powered Pushbutton Controller", Proc. International Conference on Ubiquitous Computing (2001) 299-304.

[8] Meninger, S., Mur-Mirands, J.O., Amirtharajah, R., Chandrakasan, A.P., Lang, J.H. "Vibration-to-electric energy conversion", Proc. ACM/IEEE International Symposium on Low Power Electronics and Design (1999) 48–53.

[9] A. Ghahary, B.H. Cho, "Design of Transcutaneous Energy Transmission System Using a Series Resonant Converter", Proc. IEEE Power Electronics Specialist's Conf. (1990) 1 – 8.

[10] Splashpower, Ltd. (http://www.splashpower.com/solution/overview.html)

[11] Chevalerias, O. Oapos Donnell, T. Power, D. Oapos Donovan, N. Duffy, G. Grant, G. Oapos Mathuna, "Inductive telemetry of multiple sensor modules", Proc. Pervasive Computing,(2005) Vol. 4, 46- 52.

[12] A. LaMarca, D. Koizumi, M. Lease, S. Sigurdsson, G. Borriello, W. Brunette, K. Sikorski, D. Fox, "Making Sensor Networks Practical with Robots," LNCS 2414 (2002) 152-166.

SIR: A New Wireless Sensor Network Routing Protocol Based on Artificial Intelligence

Julio Barbancho, Carlos León, Javier Molina, and Antonio Barbancho

Department of Electronic Technology, University of Seville,
C/ Virgen de Africa, 7. Seville 41011, Spain
Tel: (+034) 954 55 71 92, Fax: (+034) 954 55 28 33
{jbarbancho, cleon, fjmolina, ayboc}@us.es

Abstract. Currently, Wireless Sensor Networks (WSNs) are formed by hundreds of low energy and low cost micro-electro-mechanical systems. Routing and low power consumption have become important research issues to interconnect this kind of networks. However, conventional Quality of Service routing models, are not suitable for ad hoc sensor networks, due to the dynamic nature of such systems. This paper introduces a new QoS-driven routing algorithm, named **SIR**: **S**ensor **I**ntelligence **R**outing. We have designed an artificial neural network based on Kohonen self organizing features map. Every node implements this artificial neural network forming a distributed intelligence and ubiquitous computing system.

Keywords: Wireless sensor networks (WSN); Ad hoc networks, Quality of service (QoS); Routing; Artificial neural networks (ANN); Self-Organizing Map (SOM).

1 Introduction

Due to the sensor features (low-power consumption, low radio range, low memory, low processing capacity, and low cost), self-organizing network is the best suitable network architecture to support applications in such a scenario. Goals like efficient energy management, high reliability and availability, communication security, and robustness have become very important issues to be considered.

Many research centers in the whole world have focused their investigations in this kind of networks [1]. We present in this paper a new routing algorithm which introduces artificial intelligence (AI) techniques to measure the QoS supported by the network.

The wireless sensor networks (WSN) architecture as a whole has to take into account different aspects, such as the protocol architecture; Quality-of-Service, dependability, redundancy and imprecision in sensor readings; addressing structures, scalability and energy requirements; geographic and data-centric addressing structures; aggregating data techniques; integration of WSNs into larger networks, bridging different communication protocols; etc. [2].

H.T. Shen et al. (Eds.): ADWeb 2006, LNCS 3842, pp. 271–275, 2006.

2 SIR: Sensor Intelligence Routing

The necessity of connectivity among nodes introduces the routing problem. In a WSN we need a multi-hop scheme to travel from a source to a destiny. The problem is solved by a technique called *network backbone formation.*

We propose a modification on Dijkstra's algorithm to form the network backbone, with the minimum cost paths from the base station or *root*, r, to every node in the network. We have named this algorithm Sensor Intelligence Routing, **SIR**, which is described as follows in table 1.

Table 1. SIR algorithm

#1: Set up phase: $d(r) = 0$ $d(v_i) = \begin{cases} w_{ri} & if \quad v_i \in \Gamma(r) \\ \infty & if \quad v_i \notin \Gamma(r) \end{cases}$ $\Gamma_p(v_i) = \begin{cases} r & if \quad v_i \in \Gamma(r) \\ 0 & if \quad v_i \notin \Gamma(r) \end{cases}$ **#2:** Find a $v_j \in T$ such as $d(v_j) = \min\{d(v_i) \mid v_i \in T\}$ Do $T = T - \{v_j\}$	**#3:** $\forall \quad v_i \in T \cap \Gamma(v_j)$ calculate $t_i := d(v_j) + w_{ji}$ If $t_i < d(v_i)$ do $d(v_i) = t_i$ **#4:** If $\|T\| > 0$ go to #2 If $\|T\| = 0$ stop

Once it is designed the backbone formation algorithm, we have to define the way of measuring the edge weight parameter, w_{ij}.

We use a QoS definition based on three types of QoS parameters: timeliness, precision and accuracy. Due to the distributed feature of sensor networks, our approach measures the QoS level in a spread way, instead of an end-to-end paradigm. Each node tests every neighbor link quality with the transmissions of a specific packet named *ping*. With these transmissions every node obtains mean values of latency, error rate, duty cycle and throughput. These are the four metrics we have define to measure the related QoS parameters.

Once a node has tested a neighbor link QoS, it calculates the distance to root using the obtained QoS value. The expression 1 represents the way a node v_i calculates the distance to root through node v_j, where qos is a variable which value is obtained as an output of a neural network. This tool is described in section 2.1.

$$d(v_i) = d(v_j) \cdot qos \tag{1}$$

2.1 SOM: Self Organizing Map

One of the most powerful mechanism developed in AI is the Self-Organizing Map (SOM) model [3], created by Teuvo Kohonen in 1982, at the University of Helsinky, Finland.

In SOM we can distinguish two phases: *learning phase*, and *execution phase.*

SOM gives an output denoted by qos. This value is returned by a function Θ defined by the SOM user, according to his aims. Θ depends on the winning neuron: $qos = \Theta\ (\boldsymbol{g})$. In section 3 we define this function.

3 Performance Evaluation by Simulation

Due to the desire to evaluate the SIR performance, we have created two simulation experiments running on our wireless sensor network simulator OLIMPO. Every node in OLIMPO implements a neural network (online processing).

We have focused our simulation on a wireless sensor network composed by 4000 nodes covering an area of 87 Km^2. This is the typical area of a european medium size city like Seville (Spain) or Zurich (Switzerland). The density of nodes which are within the transmission radius of a node es 7.

Noise influence over a node has been modelled as an Additive Gaussian White Noise, (AWGN). Noise power has been modelled as a stochastic variable with a mean value expressed as a percentage of the antenna sensibility; and a standard deviation expressed as a percentage of its mean value.

Our SOM has a first layer formed by four input neurons, corresponding with every metric (latency, throughput, error rate and duty cycle); and a second layer formed by twelve output neurons forming a 3x4 matrix.

Next, we detail our SOM implementation process.

Learning Phase. In order to organize the neurons in a two dimensional map, we need a set of input samples $\boldsymbol{x}(t)$=[latency(t),throughput(t),error-rate(t),duty-cycle(t)]. This samples should consider all the QoS environments in which a link communication between a pair of sensor nodes can work. For that reason we have to create the special environments. These scenarios are implemented by different noise simulations. In our research we created a WSN over OLIMPO composed by 4000 sensor nodes. In this network, we chose a pair of nodes (let us denote them as v_{800} and v_{1250}) and introduced a low power noise into one of them (e.g. v_{1250}). According to the input requirements, we had to measure the QoS metrics. In that sense, we ran a ping application 50 times at node v_{800}. This application pings are sent from node v_{800} to node v_{1250}. Ping requires acknowledgment (ACK). The way node v_{800} receives ACKs will determine a specific QoS environment, expressed on the four elected metrics: latency (seconds), throughput (bits/sec), error rate (%) and duty cycle(%) [4]. This process was repeated 100 times while increasing the noise power.

With the set of 100 input samples we trained our neural network. This process was implemented on a personal computer using the MATLAB® neural toolbox (offline processing).

Once we had ordered the neurons on the Kohonen layer, we identified each one of the set of 100 input samples with an output layer neuron. According to this procedure the set of 100 input samples were distributed over the SOM. We realized that input samples obtained from a similar noisy environment and with similar QoS features were allocated in a specific region of the SOM. Consequently we obtained a map formed by clusters, where every cluster corresponded with a noise level introduced at the environment and consequently a specific QoS. Furthermore, a synaptic-weight matrix is formed, where every synapsis identifies a connection between input and output layer.

In order to quantify the QoS level we studied every cluster features and assigned a value between 0.2 and 10, according to the level of noise introduced. This assignment was based on our experience as experts in networks. In that way we defined the output function $\Theta(i,j), i \in [1,3], j \in [1,4]$ with twelve values corresponding with every neuron $(i,j), i \in [1,3], j \in [1,4]$.

Execution Phase. Every sensor node measures the QoS of its links collecting input samples and running the wining neuron election algorithm. For example, if a specific input sample is quite similar than the synaptic-weight-vector of neuron (2,2), this neuron will be activated. After the winning neuron is elected, the node uses the output function Θ to assign a QoS estimation, qos. Finally this value is employed to modified the distance to root (eq. 1).

Our SIR algorithm has been evaluated by the realization of two experiments detailed as follows.

Experiment #1. First, a wireless sensor network with 4000 nodes is created. The network backbone is formed using SIR algorithm, as detailed in table 2. However, no SOM is applied, so, the distance from a node v_i to root $d(v_i)$ is not modified by the neighbor link quality, qos (eq.1). We have called this algorithm as *No AI* algorithm.

Next, a high level of noise is introduced at nodes v_{100} and v_{200}, figure 1.c.

Finally, a specific node (e.g. node number v_{300}) runs the 'Transmit clock to base station' application. Node v_{300} sends 10 packets to root to measure the latency. Every packet contains 'clock' information.

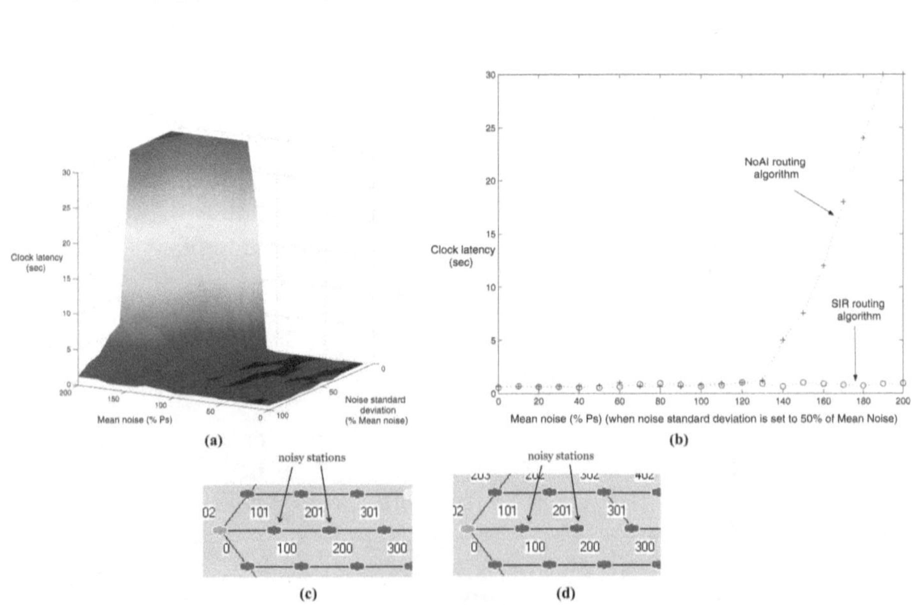

Fig. 1. (a) Clock latency measurement: No AI performance (b) Clock latency measurement: SIR versus No AI (c) Network backbone formation based on No AI algorithm (d) Network backbone formation based on SIR algorithm.

Figure 1.a represents clock latency depending on the level of the noise power introduced at nodes v_{100} and v_{200}.

Experiment #2. This experiment is similar than experiment #1, but in this case, the distance $d(v_i)$ is modified by the neighbor link quality, using equation 1. The network backbone is formed in such a way that the path created from the node v_{300} to root does not contain the noisy nodes, figure 1.d.

Figure 1.b shows SIR algorithm performance compared with No AI algorithm performance. As depicted in this figure, if the mean noise is low, both algorithm performances are excellent. In this case, the path from the node v_{300} to root contains nodes v_{100} and v_{200}. However, when the mean noise grows up above the antenna sensibility SIR algorithm performance improves No AI algorithm performance, maintaining the QoS. In this case, the path from the node v_{300} to root does not contain the noisy nodes.

4 Conclusion and Future Works

SIR has been presented in this paper as an innovative QoS-driven routing algorithm based on artificial intelligence. This routing protocol can be used over wireless sensor networks standard protocols, such as IEEE 802.15.4 and Bluetooth®, and over other well known protocols such as *Arachne*, SMACS, EAR, LEACH, etc.

The inclusion of AI techniques (e.g. neural networks) in wireless sensor networks has been proved to be an useful tool to improve network performances. An additional advantage is the low cost the AI implementation represents.

The great effort made to implement a SOM algorithm inside a sensor node means that the use of artificial intelligence techniques can improve the WSN performance. According to this idea, we are working on the design of new protocols using this kind of tools.

References

1. I.F. Akyildiz, Y. Su, W. Sankarasubramaniam, and E. Çayirci. Wireless sensor networks: A survey. *Computer Networks, Elsevier*, 38:393–422, December 2002.
2. F.J. Molina, J. Barbancho, and J. Luque. Automated meter reading and SCADA application. *Lecture Notes in Computer Science, Springer Verlag*, 2865:223–234, October 2003.
3. T. Kohonen. The self-organizing map. In *Proccedings of the IEEE*, volume 78, pages 1464–1480, 1990.
4. R. Iyer and L. Kleinrock. QoS control for sensor networks. In *IEEE International Conference on Communications, ICC'03*, volume 1, pages 517–521. IEEE Press, May 2003.

A Limited Flooding Scheme for Query Delivery in Wireless Sensor Networks

Jaemin Son, Namkoo Ha, Kyungjun Kim, Jeoungpil Ryu, Jeongho Son, and Kijun Han*

Department of Computer Engineering, Kyungpook National University Daegu, Korea
{jmson, adama2, kjkim, goldmunt, jhson}@netopia.knu.ac.kr, kjhan@knu.ac.kr

Abstract. In query-driven sensor networks, query is generally disseminated to the whole sensor. When the query needs information on a specific area, it is unnecessary for the query to be flooded over the entire network. In this paper, we propose a query delivery scheme which does not flood the query over the entire area but only to a restricted area. Also, our scheme also offers fault tolerance capability in order to prolong the network lifetime and to provide reliability for query transmissions. A performance evaluation shows that the total energy consumption can be significantly reduced and the sensor network lifetime can be prolonged by our scheme.

1 Introduction

A wireless sensor network (WSN) is a collection of hundreds or thousands of sensor nodes that communicate together to achieve and assign tasks. Since the amount of energy available to the sensor nodes is limited, the sensor routing protocols for these networks have to be energy efficient [1-3].

Recently, some data report methods have been proposed for a WSN, i.e. time-driven, event-driven, query-driven, or a hybrid of these methods. Query-driven method responds to a query that is generated by the sink or another node in the network [3]. Most of the existing routing protocols that are categorized in this method only focus on energy-efficient data delivery, such as data aggregation. Energy-efficient query delivery to sensor nodes that have observed a particular event, however, is also important in a query-driven method.

In a query-driven method, the query is generally disseminated to the whole sensor network. When the query, however, needs information on a specific area, it is unnecessary for them to be flooded over the entire sensor network (e.g. "What is the humidity in the lobby?"). If these kinds of queries are flooded in the whole network, the energy of the sensor nodes is rapidly drained because of unnecessary packet relaying. In this paper, we propose a query delivery scheme, which does not flood the query in the entire area but only in the restricted area in order to increase the lifetime of the network. Also, our scheme offers fault tolerance to cope with broken-link during query delivery.

---

* Correspondent author.

H.T. Shen et al. (Eds.): ADWeb 2006, LNCS 3842, pp. 276 – 280, 2006.

The organization of this paper is as follows: Section 2 presents the limited flooding scheme. Computer simulations that can validate our scheme are explained in Section 3. Finally, the conclusion is presented in Section 4.

2 Limited Flooding Scheme for Query Delivery

In this section, we propose a limited flooding scheme for query delivery in order to increase the lifetime of the network. We assume that all nodes know their own location through the GPS and GPS-free positioning, and that the sink is located at the center of the sensor network.

For our scheme, the sensor network is first divided into equi-angular(60 degree) sectors when it is initialized. The sink floods Sector Setup Packet (SSP) contains its own location information and its angular size. Each sensor node that receives a SSP from the sink or other intermediate nodes, decides its own sector (*S*) and track (*T*) by using this information. If we denote coordinates of the sink and sensor nodes by $\{S_x, S_y\}$, $\{N_x, N_y\}$, respectively, the distance between the sensor node and the sink is denoted by

$$d = \sqrt{d_x^{\,2} + d_y^{\,2}} \tag{1}$$

$$\theta_{node} = \cos^{-1}\frac{d^2 + d_x^{\,2} - d_y^{\,2}}{2d \cdot d_x} = \cos^{-1}\frac{d_x}{\sqrt{d_x^{\,2} + d_y^{\,2}}} \tag{2}$$

where $d_x = N_x - S_x$, $d_y = N_y - S_y$. From Fig. 1, the angle of direction, θ_{node}, which indicates where the sensor node is located from the sink, can be calculated by

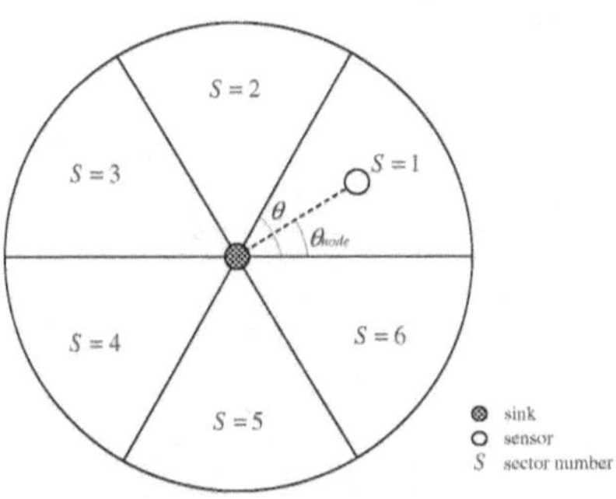

Fig. 1. Direction angle (θ_{node}) and sector number

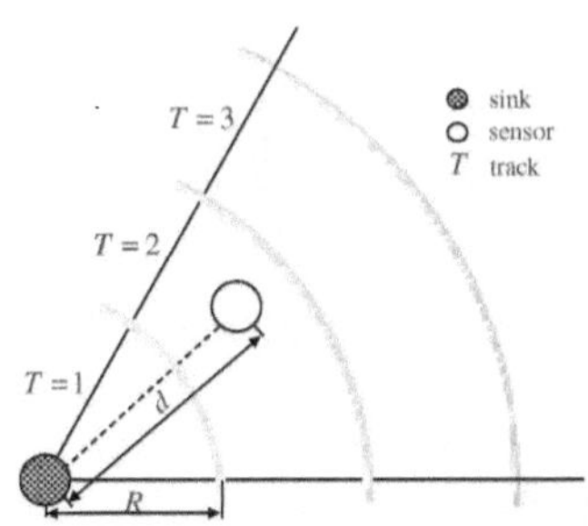

Fig. 2. Track number

Assuming that there is a sector boundary every degree, as depicted in Fig. 1 then, we can acquire sector number, *S*, by solving the following inequality:

$$(S-1)\theta < \theta_{node} \le S\theta \tag{3}$$

Also, we can get track number by $T = \lceil d / R \rceil$ where R is the transmission range, as shown in Fig. 2. In this way, each sensor node memorizes its own sector and track numbers unless until its energy is drained.

The sink forms an OHN (One Hop Node) list which consists of an ID, a sector number, and the amount of remaining energy, as shown in Table 1. The OHN list is updated every time an implicit ACK is received. The sink locates a broken-link by checking an implicit ACK which is received during the RTT.

Table 1. The list of one-hop nodes (OHN list)

Node ID	Sector number	Remaining energy
DEV_001	1	10 mJ
DEV_004	2	13 mJ
:	:	:

When the sink needs information on a specific area, it disseminates a query including a sector number and track number as illustrated in Fig. 3. Each sensor node that receives a query from the sink or another node decides whether it has to relay to its neighbor or discard the query. If the sector number included in the query is equal to that of the sensor node and if the track number contained in the query is higher than that of the sensor node, the sensor node forwards the received query to its neighbors. Otherwise, it discards the query. In other words, the query is restricted to a specific sector and track.

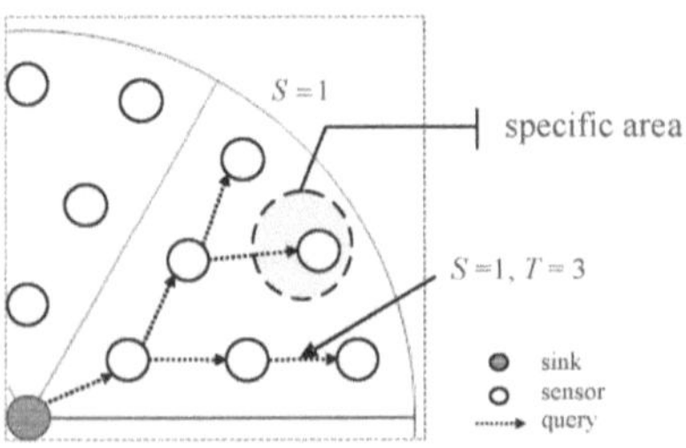

Fig. 3. Dissemination of query to a specific area

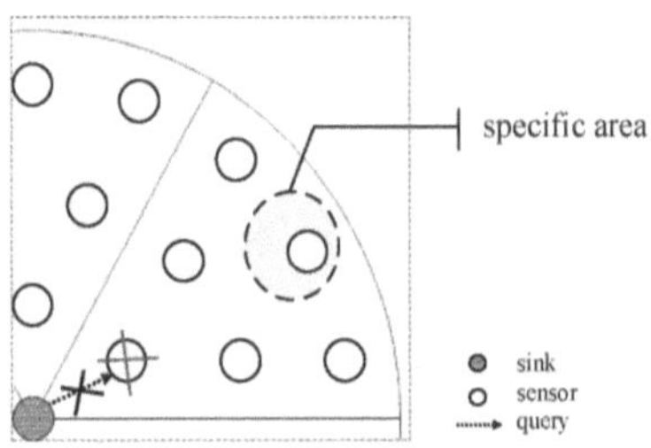

Fig. 4. Node breakdown in a sector

However, if the connection from the sink to the OHNs in the sector is broken and the OHNs in the sector die, as shown in Fig. 4, all of the nodes in the sector cannot receive the query. To cope with this situation, the sink selects one node with the largest energy by looking up its OHN list. The sink selectively sends the query to the node with the largest amount of energy in the OHN list. We call this node the "RELAY" node. The RELAY node floods the query received from the sink. The other OHNs in the sector can increase the lifetime by reducing the number of transmissions. Fig. 5 depicts an example where the sink selects Node-2 as the RELAY node in its OHN list. If there is no OHN in the sector, the sink detours the query via an alternative path. The sink can find the alternative path by extending the sector using the OHN list, and then, the sink sends the query to one node in the extended sector with T=2 as shown in Fig. 6. Therefore, this method can guarantee reliability of transmission.

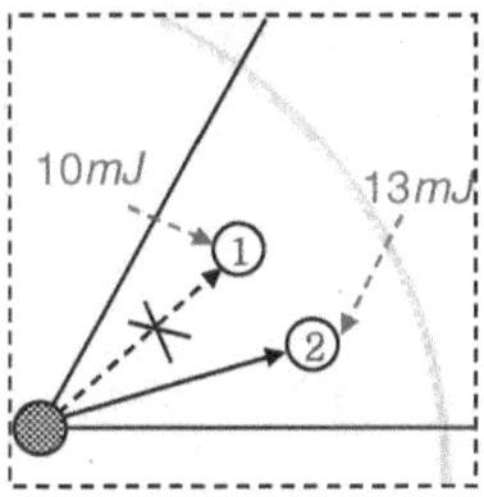

Fig. 5. Selection of the RELAY node

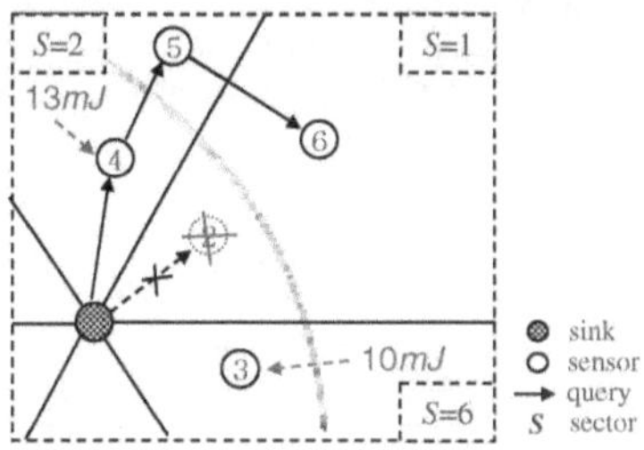

Fig. 6. The extension of the sector

3 Simulations

In this section, we evaluate the performance of our scheme by computer simulations. Our simulation is run on a circlet-topology network, in size of 30 × 30m^2. We randomly deployed 240 nodes with a 5m transmission range to evaluate. We assume that the sink generates the query at a fixed rate. The queries uniformly request the sensing data from the whole network. In general, each query requests to particular area in order to achieve sensing data. We assume that the sizes of the *SSP*, query and data packets are 11, 36 and 64 *bytes*, respectively [5]. In our simulation, we used the first-order radio model presented in LEACH [4].

First, we evaluate the network lifetime by examining the number of rounds until all nodes die. Here, we define one round as the duration from the time the sink sends a query to nodes to the time when it receives sensing data from all of the nodes. Fig. 7 shows that our scheme offers a much longer lifetime than the conventional flooding query method. From Fig. 8, we can see that the conventional flooding method consumes energy faster than the limited flooding scheme by 4~5 times.

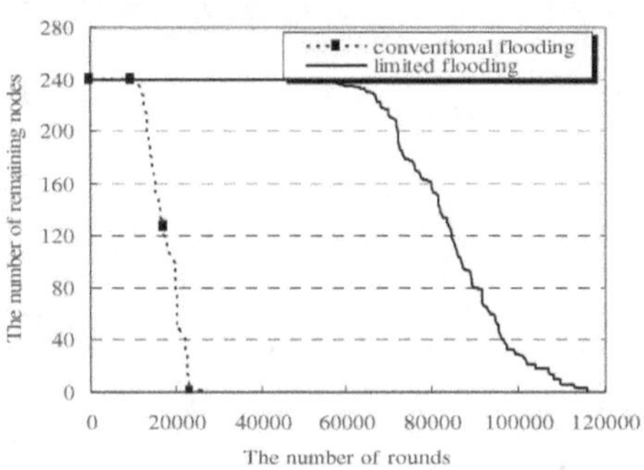

Fig. 7. The number of alive nodes

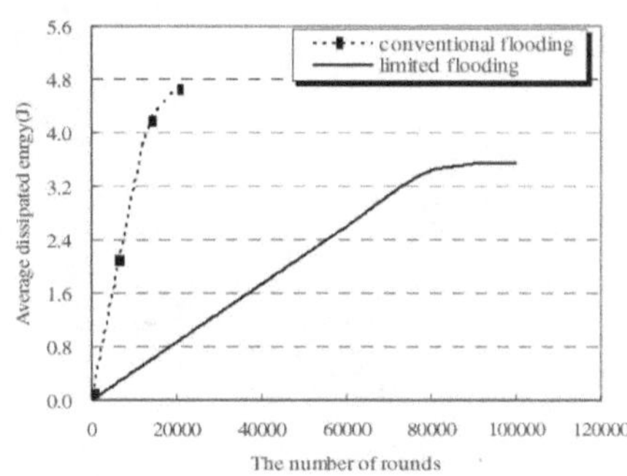

Fig. 8. Average dissipated energy

In most practical surveillance or monitoring applications, we do not want coverage gaps to sense. We therefore measured the First Node Dies (FND) of our schemes when the degrees vary $\theta = 90$, 60, 45 and 30. Fig. 9 shows that the smaller the degree is, the longer the lifetime of the sensor nodes becomes. If the degree is too small (specifically $\theta < 30$ degrees), however, extending the sector is not a sufficient solution to successfully send the query to all nodes.

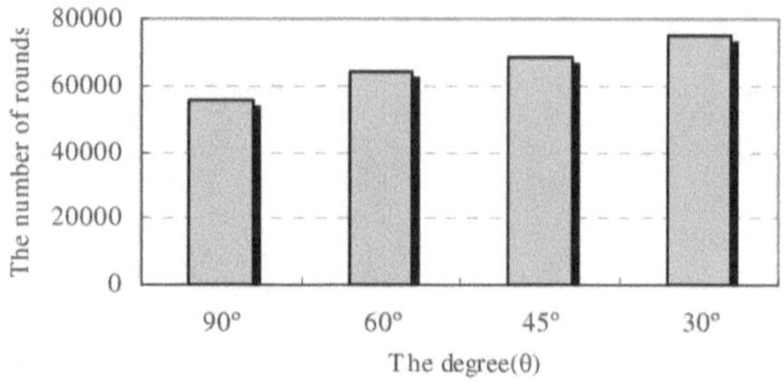

Fig. 9. The FND of each sector

4 Conclusions

We propose a query delivery scheme restricting query transmission to a specific sector. If there is no OHN in the sector where the query is transmitted, however, the query cannot be sent to any nodes. To solve this problem, we propose that the sink selects an alternative path in the neighbor sector, if the sink cannot send the query to the sector.

Our results show that limited flooding can provide lower energy consumption and a longer network. We will further investigate the impact of the parameters on system performance and efficient data reporting methods for our scheme.

Acknowledgement

The authors would like to thank Ministry of Commerce, Industry and Energy and Ulsan Metropolitan City which partly supported this research through the Network-based Automation Research Center (NARC) at University of Ulsan.

References

1. Akyildiz I.F., Weilian Su, Sankarasubramaniam Y. and Cayirci E., "A survey on sensor networks," Communications Magazine, IEEE, Aug. 2002, pp.102-114.
2. J.M. Kahn, R.H. Katz and K.S.J. Pister, "Mobile Networking for Smart Dust," Proc. ACM/IEEE Intl. Conf. Mobile Computing and Networking (MOBICOM), Aug. 1999.
3. l-Karaki J.N., Kamal A.E., "Routing techniques in wireless sensor networks: a survey," Wireless Communications, IEEE, Dec. 2004, pp.6-28.
4. W. H., A. C. and H. B., "Energy-Efficient Communication Protocol for Wireless Microsensor Networks," Proc. 33rd Hawaii Int'l. Conf. Sys. Sci., Jan. 2000.
5. C. I., R. G. and D. E., "Directed Diffusion: A Scalable and Robust Communication Paradigm for Sensor Networks," Proc. 6th Ann. ACM/IEEE. MOBICOM, Aug. 2000, pp.56-67.

Sampling Frequency Optimization in Wireless Sensor Network-Based Control System

Jianlin Mao[1], Zhiming Wu[1], Xing Wu[2], and Siping Wang[1]

[1] Department of Automation, Shanghai Jiao Tong University,
Shanghai, China 200030
{jlmao, ziminwu, wangsiping}@sjtu.edu.cn
[2] School of Mechanical and Electrical Engineering,
Kunming University of Science and Technology,
Kunming, Yunnan Province, China 650093
km_wx@yahoo.com

Abstract. The application of wireless sensor network in control systems can bring some advantages, such as the flexibility and the feasibility of network deployment at low costs. While it also raises some new challenges. First, the limited communication resources are shared by several control loops. Second, the wireless and multi-hop character of sensor network makes the resources scheduling more difficult. Thus, how to allocate the limited communication and computing resources effectively is an important problem. In this paper, this problem is formulated as an optimal sampling frequency assignment problem, where the objective function is to maximize the effectiveness of control systems, subject to channel capacity constraints. Then an iterative distributed algorithm based on local buffer information is proposed, which has features of low computational complexity and well scalability. Finally, the simulation results show that the proposed solution can achieve the optimal quality of the control system in a distributed way. Meanwhile, it is capable of seeking the optimal point automatically when the network load changes.

1 Introduction

With the rapid development of wireless communication technology, the combination of wireless communication and control systems becomes a new trend of networked control systems. Among these kinds of wireless technology, wireless sensor network(WSN) has attracted a lot of interest and visibility due to its huge application space. Wireless sensor network is a kind of wireless ad-hoc network which connect embedded sensors, actuators, processors and in which each node consists of a wireless communication device[1][2]. It allows rapid deployment, flexible installation, fully mobile operation and prevent the cable wear and tear problem. WSN will play an increasingly important role in constructing complex industry control systems.

While introducing WSN into control systems (see Fig.1) will raise some new challenges. First, the limited communication resources of WSN are shared by

H.T. Shen et al. (Eds.): ADWeb 2006, LNCS 3842, pp. 281–290, 2006.

all the control tasks. Second, this kind of network is generally a wireless and multi-hop network, which means that the wireless communication resources are distributed but strongly coupled. Third, the sensor node has limited computation capability. These challenges make it harder to efficiently allocate communication resources to those control loops.

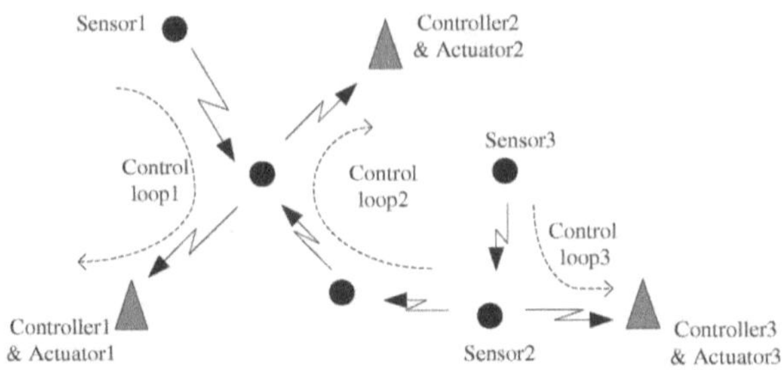

Fig. 1. WSN-based Control System model

To this resource allocation problem, we use nonlinear optimization theory to solve. The idea of using optimization in the context of network system has been explored in wired networks[3][4], ad hoc networks[5][6][7] and sensor networks [8][9] etc. Kelly et al. [3] presented overall optimization framework to realize a proportionally-fair rate control for wireline network. To the same problem, Low et al. [4] proposed a distributed approach. In wireless area, based on [3]or [4], references [5][6][7][9][8] set up several different utility-based models to address the rate control problem. Qiu et al. [5] investigated a simplified ad hoc network model, where the total communication tasks of one node can not exceed its given capacity. In comparison, Xue et al. [6] thought that the resource constraints is topology-dependent, and presented a constraint that the total communication tasks within a clique should not excess the capacity of this space. Yi et al. [7] formulated the wireless link as a wire-line link with a given and unchanged capacity, then presented a multi hop-by-hop algorithm. For sensor networks, chen et al. [9] presented a model with an energy constraint and the node communication capacity constraints, where those nodes' communication capacities are derived from the given network topology. In [8], liu et al. presented an optimization framework for a cellular real-time sensor network, where the constraints comes from the schedulability of period tasks. Compared with them, our optimization model and solving method are different with them.

The rest of paper is organized as follows. Section 2 formulates the problem and presents an optimization model. Section 3 proposes an iterative distributed algorithm based on local buffer information and its realization. The simulation results are given in section 4. Finally, some conclusions are presented.

2 Problem Formulation

To present clearly, the following notations are firstly defined:

s : a session. Each session means a periodic sampling task for a control system.
f_s : the sampling frequency of a session.
x_s : the flow rate of the data of session s in the network.
$C_n^{channel}$: the channel capacity of node. It should be addressed that the channel capacity $C_n^{channel}$ is topology-dependant.

Consider a WSN-based control system, shown in Fig.1, where the controllers are set on the actuator nodes. Based on a CSMA/CA channel access scheme, there is a tradeoff with the sensors' sampling frequencies. Worst case frequencies will lead to a low QoC of the control system, while too high frequencies will result to a congestion in network, which is company with large delay and high drop ratio. This also degrade the QoC of the control system.

Therefore, a proper sensor frequencies and data transmission rates should be set. This problem is then formulated as a constrained nonlinear optimization problem P, where the objective is to maximize the performance of control systems, subject to the node channel capacity.

$$P: \quad \min \quad \sum_{s=1}^{N} \omega_s U_s(f_s) = \sum_{s=1}^{N} \omega_s \alpha_s e^{-\beta_s f_s} \tag{1}$$

$$s.t. \qquad \mathbf{f}_s \leq \mathbf{x}_s \tag{2}$$

$$\mathbf{A} * \mathbf{x}_s \leq \mathbf{C}_n^{channel} \tag{3}$$

$$over \qquad \mathbf{f}_s^{min} \leq \mathbf{f}_s \leq \mathbf{f}_s^{max} \tag{4}$$

where in the objective function (1), ω_s is the weight of the control loop, $U_s(f_s) = \alpha_s e^{-\beta_s f_s}$ is a control performance index[10], which is derived by Seto[11]. Parameter α_s is the magnitude coefficient, β_s is the decay rate. To the most control systems, this control performance index can describe the relationship between the QoC and the sampling frequency in a discrete digital control system . The less the index is, the better the QoC is. This objective function is strictly decreasing differential convex function with regard to frequency f_s.

In formula (2)-(4), the symbols in bold font represent the vector of the corresponding variables. The constraint in formula(2) means each session flow should be transmitted with a rate which is larger than or equal to the sensor's sampling frequency, or the sensor data would jam at some nodes.

In formula(3), A is a node burden matrix. $A_{ij} = 2$, if node i is a router of session j, node i need to use the wireless channel twice to receive and transmit a packet. $A_{ij} = 1$, if node i is the source/destination of session j, node i only need to use the channel once to transmit/receive a packet. Otherwise, $A_{ij} = 0$.

Formula(3) means the total communication tasks of a sensor node should not exceed its communication capability $C_n^{channel}$, which is a topology-dependant parameter.

The formula(4) defines the feasible set scope, i.e., each sensor node has a maximum and a minimum sampling frequency.

3 Iterative Distributed Algorithm Based on Local Buffer Information (IDALBI)

3.1 Transform of the Constrained Optimization Problem

Firstly, some notations are listed as follows:

$R(s)$: the route of session s, i.e. the set of those nodes by which the session s passes.
r_n : the utilization ratio of the node n's buffer.
$D^n(x_s)$: means how many packets of the session s are deposited in the buffer of node n.
C_n^b : the total buffer capacity of node n.

To solve the constrained nonlinear programming problem P, we use barrier function methods[13]. Barrier function is defined that if the constraint is broken, this function will go to the infinite, else, it will be a very small number.

In a wireless network, it is noticed that if the aggregate communication task at any node n exceeds its capacity, then the buffer of its preceding nodes will overflow. Based on this observation and the definition of the barrier function, we construct a barrier function B_s:

$$B_s = \sum_{n\in R(s)} \left(\frac{1}{1-r_n}\right)^w \tag{5}$$

$$= \sum_{n\in R(s)} \left(\frac{1}{1-(\sum\limits_s D^n(x_s))/C_n^b}\right)^w \tag{6}$$

such that it will limit to the infinite if the constraint in (3) is not satisfied at any node on the route of session s, where w is a constant larger than 1. $\sum\limits_s D^n(x_s)$ is the sum of the $D^n(x_s)$ value of all the sessions passing by node n. If any node's buffer overflows, i.e., $r_n = 1$, then directly let the corresponding B_s be a very large value.

According to the barrier function methods and the barrier functions derived above, the constrained nonlinear optimization problem P can be transformed into an unconstrained problem Q:

$$Q: \quad \min \; Q(f) = \sum_{s=1}^{N} \omega_s U_s(f_s) + \sum_{s=1}^{N} \xi_s B_s, \quad \xi_s > 0$$

$$over \qquad \mathbf{f}_s^{min} \le \mathbf{f}_s \le \mathbf{f}_s^{max}$$

3.2 Iterative Solution of the Optimization Problem

According to the gradient projection method, the iterative solution of problem Q is derived as follow:

$$f_s(t+1) = \underset{f_s^{min} \le f_s \le f_s^{max}}{argmin} \{f_s(t) - k_s \frac{\partial Q(f)}{\partial f_s}\}, \forall f_s \forall f_s \tag{7}$$

where $k_s > 0$, $\frac{\partial Q(f)}{\partial f_s} = \frac{\partial \sum_{s=1}^{N} \omega_s U_s(f_s)}{\partial f_s} + \frac{\partial \sum_{s=1}^{N} \xi_s B_s}{\partial f_s}$.

Take f_s as its upper bound in constraint(2), i.e., $f_s = x_s$.

Let:

$$h_s = -\frac{\partial \sum_{s=1}^{N} \omega_s U_s(f_s)}{\partial f_s} = \omega_s \alpha_s \beta_s e^{-\beta_s f_s} \tag{8}$$

$$g_s = \frac{\partial \sum_{s=1}^{N} \xi_s B_s}{\partial f_s} = \xi_s \cdot \frac{\partial B_s}{\partial f_s}$$

$$= \xi_s \cdot \sum_{n \in R(s)} \frac{w}{C_n^b} \cdot (\frac{1}{1-r_n})^{w+1} \cdot \frac{\partial \sum_s D^n(x_s)}{\partial x_s}$$

$$= \xi_s \cdot \sum_{n \in R(s)} \frac{w}{C_n^b} \cdot (\frac{1}{1-r_n})^{w+1} \cdot \frac{dD^n(x_s)}{dx_s}$$

$$= \xi_s \cdot \sum_{n \in R(s)} \frac{w}{C_n^b} \cdot (\frac{1}{1-r_n})^{w+1} \cdot \frac{D^n[x_s(t)] - D^n[x_s(t-1)]}{x_s(t) - x_s(t-1)}$$

$$= \xi_s \cdot \sum_{n \in R(s)} \frac{w}{C_n^b} \cdot (\frac{1}{1-r_n})^{w+1} \cdot \frac{D^n[x_s(t)] - D^n[x_s(t-1)]}{I_s^n(t) - I_s^n(t-1)} \cdot t \tag{9}$$

Where I_s^n is the packet amount of session s flowing into node n during the iteration interval t, thus the flow rate x_s is substituted by I_s^n/t. Here, g_s can be interpreted as the price that the source node s should charge for the change of the sampling frequency to its route.

Let

$$g_n^s = \frac{w}{C_n^b} \cdot (\frac{1}{1-r_n})^{w+1} \cdot \frac{D^n[x_s(t)] - D^n[x_s(t-1)]}{I_s^n(t) - I_s^n(t-1)} \cdot t \tag{10}$$

then,

$$g_s = \xi_s \cdot \sum_{n \in R(s)} g_n^s \tag{11}$$

Substitute (8)(11) to (7), the final iterative solution is as follow:

$$f_s(t+1) = \underset{f_s^{min} \le f_s \le f_s^{max}}{argmin} \{f_s(t) + k_s(h_s - \xi_s \cdot \sum_{n \in R(s)} g_n^s)\}, \forall f_s \tag{12}$$

To the above iteration algorithm, a termination criterion is adopted: if $\|f_s(k)-f_s(k-1)\|_n \leq \varepsilon$ is satisfied, then the iteration procedure stops, where ε is a sufficiently small real number. $\|v\|_n$ is the nth-norm of vector $v = [v_1, v_2, ..., v_k]$.

In addition, to the variables in (12), some comments should be pointed out:

1. g_n^s defined in (10) is only concerned with the local information of node n, like C_n, r_n, $D^n(x_s)$, I_s^n etc. Thus, g_n^s can be computed by node n locally.
2. In (12), all the variables are only concerning with the source sensor node except the $\sum_{n \in R(s)} g_n^s$. Therefore, if the source node could get this value, the iterative computation process can be accomplished at each source node in a distributed way.

3.3 Distributed Realization of IDALBI

The main idea of the distributed realization is firstly to design a price accumulating packet (PAP), which can collect and accumulate the individual prices g_s^n at the router nodes, and send $\sum_{n \in R(s)} g_n^s$ to the source node of session s. Thus each source node can adjust its sampling frequency by an iterative and distributed way according to the formula (12).

The structure of PAP is shown in table 1. It includes four parts: the common header of packet, the PAP flag, the session ID and the price data, where the common header of packet includes basic information of a packet, like the source node ID, the destination node ID and packet ID etc, the price data field ships the accumulated value of g_s^n.

Table 1. PAP packet structure

Common header	PAP flag	Session ID	Price data

Based on the idea of PAP packet, the IDALBI algorithm can be realized by a distributed way. The realization has three local parts:

Destination Node Procedure:

- At each iteration time, the destination puts zero into the price field of PAP, then sends it with the highest priority to the source nodes along the route of the session.

Router Node Procedure:

- Upon the reception of the PAP, the node need to: (a)count its buffer to get r_n, $D^n(x_s)$ and I_s^n, which should be saved for the next iteration; (b)compute its g_n^s value according to formula(10); (c)add the result into the price data in PAP; (d)pass forward this PAP.

Source Node Procedure:

- At the reception of a PAP, the source node gets the price data g_s. Then it updates its sampling frequency according to the iteration formula (12) and the termination criterion.

4 Performance Evaluation

4.1 System Settings

In this section, we evaluate the performance of the IDALBI algorithm using the ns-2 [14]. In order to avoid the effectiveness of routing, the network structure used in simulation is depicted in Fig.2, where each sensor need to send its data to the corresponding controller. The MAC layer adopts CSMA/CA channel access scheme. The other network settings are as follows: a packet length is set as 120B, the data transmission rate of wireless channel is assumed to be 1000Kbps. The buffer capacity of a node is set as 100 packets.

In these control loops, the parameters in the performance index are: $\omega = [1, 2, 3, 4, 5]$, $\alpha = [0.98, 0.98, 0.98, 0.98, 0.98]$, $\beta = [1, 0.71, 0.58, 0.5, 0.45]$. The frequency scopes of these sensors are all in 2Hz$\sim$40Hz.

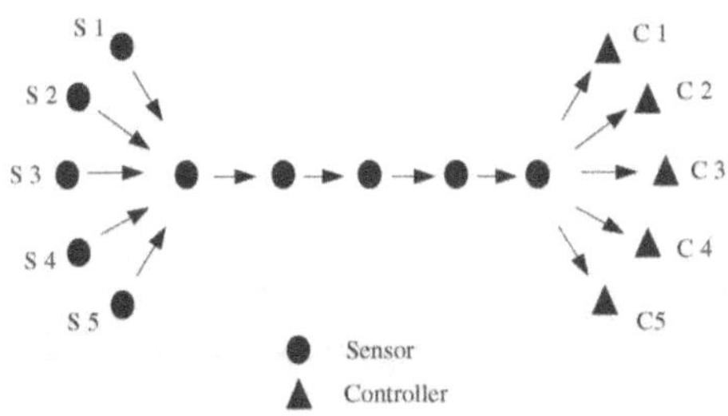

Fig. 2. System structure for simulation

4.2 Validation of Convergency and Uniqueness of IDALBI

Two experiments are run to validate the convergency and uniqueness of the IDALBI algorithm, the results are shown in Fig.3 and Fig.4. In the first situation, the network runs from an initial frequencies 10hz. The result (see Fig.3) shows that these five curves can gradually converge to a stable state [7.30 11.10 13.43 15.44 17.10]. During this procedure, the value of $Q(f)$ decreases from 0.486 (at 44s) to 0.020 (at 332s), and finally reaches a minimum value 0.018(at 580s), i.e., those control systems can get optimal QoCs.

In addition, to compare with the results of IDALBI, we adopt the method in reference[7] to set up a centralize model. The channel utility is set to 30%. Solving by the optimal toolbox in MATLAB, the optimal resolutions are [7.62 11.22 14.01 15.69 17.57], which are close with the results of IDALBI.

In Fig.4, only two nodes' results are given in order to make the figure clear. The first group of curves with the dot line are the results with an initial frequencies of 40Hz, the other group with the real line are the results from the randomly selected frequencies. The results depict: (1)the result of IDALBI from different initial values can converge to a unique value; (2)IDALBI can quickly eliminate the network congestion which is caused by those high sampling frequencies.

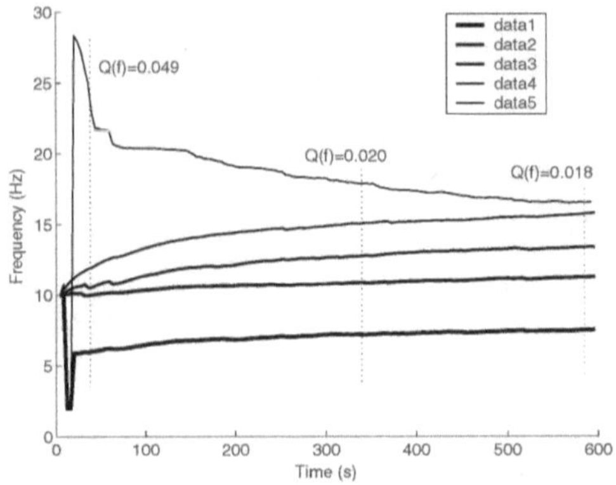

Fig. 3. Sampling frequency ($k_s = 25$, $\xi_s = 0.08$)

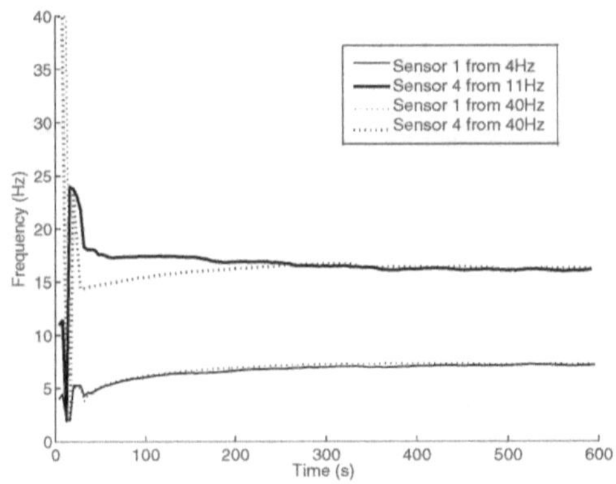

Fig. 4. Sampling frequency ($k_s = 25$, $\xi_s = 0.08$)

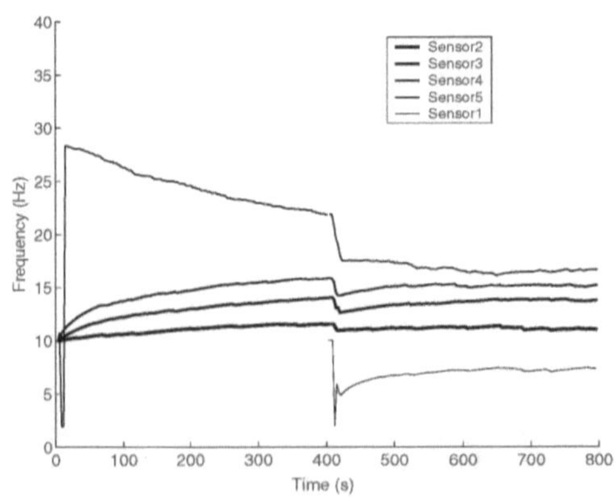

Fig. 5. Adaptive to the change of the traffic($k_s = 30, \xi_s = 0.5$)

4.3 Adaptability Evaluation

In WSN, network load would change because the node may be mobile or new-coming or energy-exhausted. Hence, whether a algorithm can adapt to such changes is important in WSN-based control systems.

In this experiment, we change the network load by adding a new session into the running network at 400s. As Fig.5 shown, the four curves are gradually converging before 400s, while new-coming session breaks the coming balance, these five sessions begin to allocate the resources, and reach a new balance state soon. It is showed that the IDALBI algorithm can adapt to the change of network load.

5 Conclusion

This paper presents a system model of WSN-based control system, upon which an optimization problem is proposed. To maximize the QoC of the control systems under the network limitation, we formulate this problem as a constrained nonlinear programming problem, and solve it by a barrier function method. Then we propose a buffer-based iterative distributed algorithm IDALBI. The simulation results show that this algorithm can automatically seek the optimal point of the system, and it can adapt to the change of network load. Moreover, to each sensor node, only the local buffer information is needed and the computation is simple. Accordingly this algorithm is practical in WSN.

In future we will consider more constraints, like the energy consuming problem and some new MAC constraints including the sleep status, to improve the performance of such networked control system.

References

1. John A. Stankovic. Real-time communication and coordination in embedded sensor networks. PROCEEDINGS OF THE IEEE, 2003, vol. 91, pp. 1002-1022.
2. Ian F.Akyildiz, Ismail H. Kasimoglu, Wireless sensor and actor networks: research chanllenges. Ad Hoc Networks (Elsevier), vol. 2, no. 4, pp. 351–367, October 2004.
3. F.P. Kelly, A.Maulloo, and D. Tan, *Rate control in communication networks: shadow prices, proportional fairness and stability*, Journal of the Operational Research Society, vol.49,pp.238-252,1998
4. S.H.Low and D.E.Lapsley,*Optimization Flow Control,i:Basic Algorithm and Convergence*,IEEE/ACM Tran.on Networking,vol.7,no.6,pp.861-875,Dec,1999.
5. Ying Qiu, Peter Marbach. *Bandwidth Allocation in Ad Hoc Networks: A Price-Based Approach.* IEEE INFOCOM 2003, San Francisco, April 2003.
6. Yuan Xue, Baochun Li, Klara Nahrstedt. *Price-based Resource Allocation in Wireless Ad Hoc Networks*, Proceedings of the Eleventh International Workshop on Quaulity of Service (IWQos03).
7. Yung Yi and Sanjay Shakkottai, *Hop-by-hop congestion control over a wireless multi-hop network*,INFOCOM 2004
8. Xue Liu,Qixin Wang,Liu Sha et al,*Optimal QoS Sampling Frequency Assignment for Real-time Wireless Sensor Networks*,Proceedings of the 24th IEEE International Real-Time Systems Symposium,2003.

9. Weipeng Chen and Lui Sha,*An Energy-Aware Data-Centric Generic Utility Based Approach in Wireless Sensor Networks*,IPSN 04,April 26-27,2004,Berkeley,California,USA
10. Sanfridson M., Timing problems in distributed control, Licentiate Thesis, TRITA-MMK 2000:14, Mechatronics Lab, KTH, May 2000.
11. D.Seto et al, *On Task Schedulability in Real-Time Control Systems*,Proceeding of IEEE Real-Time System Symposium,1996.
12. D. Bersekas, Nonlinear Programming, Belmont, MA. Athena Scientific, 1995.
13. M.S. Bazaraa, C.M. Shetty, *Nonlinear Programming: Theory and Algorithm*, John Wiley & Sons, 1979.
14. Network Simulator - ns (version 2). Available at: http://www.isi.edu/nsnam/ns

MIMO Techniques in Cluster-Based Wireless Sensor Networks

Jing Li[1], Yu Gu[1], Wei Zhang[1], and Baohua Zhao[1,2]

[1] Department of Computer Science, University of Science &Technology of China, Hefei, Anhui, 230027 China
[2] Laboratory of Computer Science Institute of Software Chinese Academy of Sciences
{ajing, guyu, bho}@mail.ustc.edu.cn, bhzhao@ustc.edu.cn

Abstract. Advances in microsensor and radio technology will enable small but smart sensors to be deployed for a wide range of environment monitoring applications. Most architectures of wireless sensor networks (WSN) are built as homogeneous networks, where all sensor nodes have the same structure. But it is not suitable for cluster-based WSN. By using multi-antenna sensor node (MASN) as the cluster head (CH), we import multi-input-multi-output (MIMO) and single-input-multi-output (SIMO) communication modes into WSN. In this network scenario, tremendous energy saving is possible when transmission range is larger than a given threshold. This paper motivates and describes the realization of the inhomogeneous network, special communication scheme and simulation of energy consumption and delay model of it.

1 Introduction

Wireless sensor networks (WSN) has been considered as a hot topic in the research of wireless networks. In recent years, most investigations are focused on homogeneous WSN, where all sensor nodes have the same architecture, thus in cluster-based networks cluster head (CH) is the common sensor node with constrained energy, processing ability and transmission range. Since CHs take more responsibilities than sensor nodes (SNs) such as collecting cluster state information and forwarding inner-cluster messages to base station (BS), they are more appropriate to be special nodes for the sake of better reliability and longer transmission range, which is called inhomogeneous network [1]. To achieve a scalable and long-lived network, this paper presents a new solution to inhomogeneous WSN.

On the other hand, multi-antenna systems have been studied intensively in recent years due to their potential to dramatically increase the channel capacity in fading channels. Alamouti diversity codes in [2] provide a good performance on interference reduction, which is the basis of our paper. Compared to single-input-single-output (SISO) mode, multi-input-multi-output (MIMO) has better SNR and higher data rate. Shuguang Cui analyzes the total energy consumption per bit of multi-antenna nodes transmitting messages under the same bit-error-rate performance requirement and represents that SISO systems use more energy than MIMO as the communication

H.T. Shen et al. (Eds.): ADWeb 2006, LNCS 3842, pp. 291 – 296, 2006.

distance increases [3]. Based on these researches, we apply multi-antenna nodes as CH to WSN by virtue of its adaptation to long-range transmission and energy savings. The primary contributions of our design are:

- A novel architecture of inhomogeneous WSN with multi-antenna CHs is provided, especially to react to large-scale applications;
- The use of MIMO and single-input-multi-output (SIMO) communication techniques in sensor networks enhances the transmission performance, energy efficiency and other capabilities of the network.

2 Inhomogeneous WSN Model and Realization

We consider a cluster-based WSN shown in Fig.1, which consists of BS, CHs and SNs. In inner-cluster layer, SNs are responsible for detecting and transmitting information gathered around them to CH; in inter-cluster layer, CHs forward the composite data toward BS.

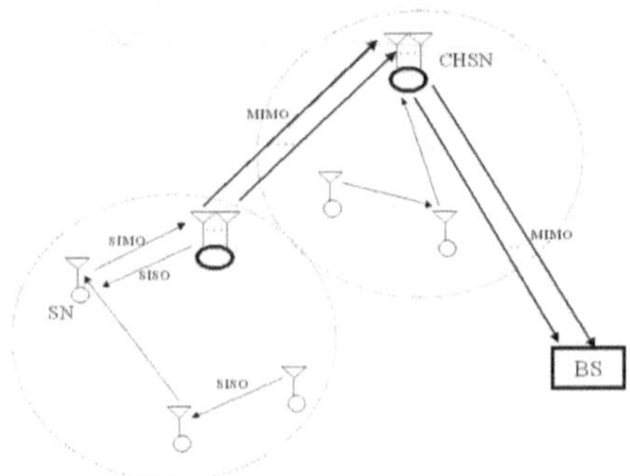

Fig. 1. Communication model of inhomogeneous WSN

As described in Fig.1, SNs transmit messages to each other in a cluster by SISO communication mechanism while they communicate with CH by SIMO scheme. CHs are multi-antenna sensor nodes (MASNs). They communicate each other by MIMO and send messages to SN by SISO scheme. Both nodes contain sense, transmitter and receiver modules.

SN is a single antenna sensor node with SISO encoding and decoding circuit blocks, while MASN makes use of space-time encoding and decoding modules, signal synthesizer (that is also the SIMO decoding circuit block), and determining circuit block. Before transmission, MASN should decide by determining circuit which kind of nodes it will transmit to: MASN or SN. If it is MASN, it encodes messages by space-time coding mode and sends data simultaneously through several antennas; if it is SN, it should transmit directly, i.e., the SISO mode. In the receiver process of MASN, signals received by antennas and demodulated into multi-path sub streams should be judged whether they are from SN or MASN, which can be realized by judging the identification added and encoded into signals when transmitting messages. If they are from SN, it can obtain original signals by signal synthesizer; otherwise, using space-time decoder we can combine multi-path sub streams into original stream.

After the deployment of network, MASNs compete to be CH, whose duty is to wake SNs nearby, divide clusters and calculate routings. At first, MASNs initiate to gather sensing information from surroundings. If messages they collect do not reach the threshold and they have not received the startup message from BS, they go into sleep after T_i. When T_i expires, they move into idle state again [4]. When the quantity or intensity of data collected reach the threshold, indicating that some incidents are taking place nearby, the MASN sends *head announcement message* including intensity of messages to compete for the CH. If it receives head announcement messages from other MASNs that are within the cluster radius $R_{mm}/2$ (R_{mm} is the transmission range of MIMO) before t_1 expires, node with higher intensity of messages or the same intensity but larger ID remains in competitive state; otherwise, it recedes from this round of competition. When t_1 expires, competitive MASNs become to be CHs and broadcast *establishing cluster message*.

SN may receive several establishing cluster messages from CHs in the period of t_2. It should choose the nearest to be its cluster head judged by the intensity of signals. As soon as a node decides to transit to the state of active [4], it sends *join message* and state information to cluster head; otherwise, it will save cluster head ID and remain idle. Since the distance between SN and the CH may be farther than its transmission radius, the course makes use of direct transmission protocol, i.e., SN broadcasts join message to CH and waits for the *relay message*. Its neighbors who receive the message and are in contact with the CH (including CH) will send back relay message to it. It considers the node that first responds to it as its relay. Having acquired inner-cluster topology, CH figures out routing table for cluster members according to minimal link cost algorithm in [5] and sends it to every SN. Routing between clusters is similar to inner-cluster means.

Dynamic cluster sleep mechanism is adaptive to special applications like target tracking, which is triggered by BS sending *sleep message* to CH or CH transiting states automatically according to information gathered from the cluster. In the latter case, CH bases on the quantity of messages Q transmitted by SNs in a period of time (control and state messages are omitted) and message priority P (related to message type and intensity) to decide whether the cluster will go to sleep for energy saving. When Q and P are both under the threshold, CH broadcasts *cluster sleep message* to sleep the cluster.

When a CH's residuary energy falls bellow the threshold, it sends *head change message* to other MASNs. If several MASNs simultaneously compete for it, node in the cluster with the least link cost will win. After task delivered to new cluster head, new CH will re-divide the cluster.

3 Network Energy Consumption and Delay Model

We should make following assumptions and constraints before constructing the energy consumption and delay model of the inhomogeneous WSN:

- Only consider the energy consumption and delay of nodes in active state in time T, thus the energy consumption of idle or sleep nodes is omitted [4].
- Assume we have known interior and inner cluster routing, link cost and quantity of messages transmitted by nodes.
- Make use of the node energy consumption and delay model provided in [3].

Assume that there is a constant set of active nodes, $U = M \cup S$, where M and S represent the set of MASNs and SNs, respectively. r_{ij} corresponds to directional path from node i to node j, and R_t is the set of paths in routing table. The distance between nodes is $d\left(r_{ij}\right): R_t \rightarrow R^+$, and message quantity on the link from i to j is $Q\left(r_{ij}\right): R_t \rightarrow N$. $q(i): U \rightarrow N$ denotes the number of messages produced at node i. Thus the total energy consumption per bit can be obtained as $E_{bt} = f(d(r_{si}), M_t, M_r)$ [3]. $b(r_{ij}): R_t \rightarrow N$ is the optimal value obtained by calculating the minimal value of E_{bt} based on the quantity of messages and deadline T between link i to j [3].

Thus, the total energy consumption of node i in T time is

$$E_i = Q_i E_{bt} = \left[q(i) + \sum_{r_{si} \in R_t} Q\left(r_{si}\right) \right] f(d(r_{ij}), M_t, M_r) \tag{1}$$

The delay formula of node i can be obtained as

$$D_i = T_s \frac{Q_i}{b\left(r_{ij}\right)} \approx \frac{1}{B} \sum_{r_{ij} \in R_t} \frac{Q\left(r_{ij}\right)}{b\left(r_{ij}\right)} \tag{2}$$

As we discussed in Section 2, in tracking applications some clusters may find that the target has already past them, thus they can turn into the state of sleep for the sake of energy saving. Assume that every node can and only can join one cluster and in the period of T the set of active clusters is U_A. Then we obtain that $|U_A| = \gamma |M + N|$, where the average percent of active clusters in network is $\gamma \in (0,1]$ (when in full-scale monitoring application γ equals 1). Thus, the total energy consumption of network in T is given by

$$E_T = \sum_{i \in U_A} E_i = \sum_{i \in U_A} Q_i E_{bt} = \sum_{i \in U_A} \left\{ \left[q(i) + \sum_{r_{si} \in R_t} Q\left(r_{si}\right) \right] f(d(r_{ij}), M_t, M_r) \right\} \tag{3}$$

Since the delay of SN is the same as homogeneous network, we do not discuss it here. The delay of cluster heads in period of T is given as

$$D_{CH} = \sum_{i \in (U_A \cap M)} D_i \approx \frac{1}{B} \sum_{i \in (U_A \cap M)} \sum_{r_{ij} \in R_i} \frac{Q(r_{ij})}{b(r_{ij})} \quad (4)$$

4 Analysis and Simulation

Deriving from formula in [3], we can compare transmit radius of SISO, SIMO and MIMO at a fixed rate. The exact transmit distances are calculated by setting P_{out} as the rated power. Mica2 node with single antenna has a transmit radius of about 15m. From computing, we know that the transmit radiuses of SIMO and MIMO are approximately 2 and 4 times the distance of SISO, respectively. So, the MASN-based WSN might have the maximal radius 4 times the range of homogeneous one.

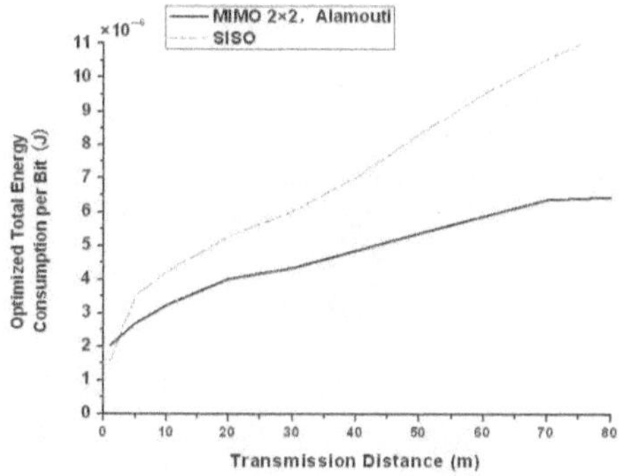

Fig. 2. Transmission energy per bit over d

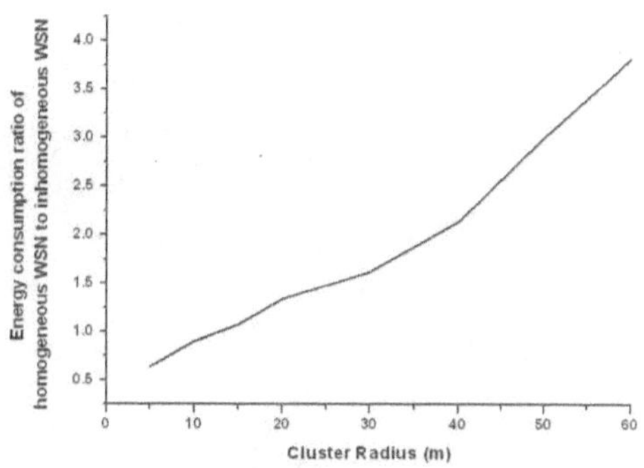

Fig. 3. Energy consumption ratio

Energy consumption per bit of MIMO and SISO can be obtained by the optimized value of b. From Fig.2, we find that the multi-antenna node is adaptive to far-range transmission. When the transmission distance is farther than 5m, the energy consumption per bit of multi-antenna node is obviously smaller than the node with single antenna.

In order to demonstrate the energy efficiency of inhomogeneous WSN, we randomly generate 500 sensor nodes in a surveillance area of $50 \times 50m^2$ for simulation, where the total number of CHs is changing according to different cluster radiuses under the same dynamic cluster division algorithm (SN parameters are according to Mica2 node made by Berkeley University [6] and other parameters can be referred to [3]). Routing mechanism is the direct transmission protocol.

Fig.3 gives us the energy consumption ratio of homogeneous WSN to inhomogeneous WSN under the same cluster division and routing strategies. We can derive from it that as the divided cluster radius increases, MASN-based WSN becomes more adaptive to far-range communications, i.e., when the cluster radius is larger than approximately 15m, the energy consumption of inhomogeneous network is lower than the common cluster-based network. In addition, when BS is deployed farther from surveillance area, the inhomogeneous WSN are also superior to homogeneous one.

5 Conclusion and Future Work

In this paper, we introduce MASN to be the cluster head, import MIMO and SIMO communication modes into WSN, and discuss corresponding mechanisms. We establish system model, simulate and conclude that this network design is superior to homogeneous one in energy efficiency. However, there are still some challenges demanding deep investigations: special communication protocols, efficient routing algorithms and further evaluation between it and other topologies, such as non-clustered WSN.

Acknowledgement

This paper is supported by the National Natural Science Foundation of China under Grant No. 60241004, the National Grand Fundamental Research 973 Program of China under Grant No. 2003CB314801, and the State Key Laboratory of Networking and Switching Technology.

References

[1] Wei-Peng Chen; Hou, J.C.; Lui Sha; Dynamic Clustering for Acoustic Target Tracking in Wireless Sensor Networks[J].Mobile Computing[J].IEEE Transactions on, Volume: 03 , Issue: 3, July 2004, 258 – 271.

[2] Alamouti, S.M.;A simple transmit diversity technique for wireless communications[J].Selected Areas in Communications, IEEE Journal on , Volume 16 , Issue: 8 , Oct. 1998,1451 – 1458.

[3] Shuguang Cui; Goldsmith, A.J.; Bahai, A.;Energy-efficiency of MIMO and cooperative MIMO techniques in sensor networks[J].Selected Areas in Communications, IEEE Journal on , Volume 22 , Issue 6 , Aug. 2004 ,1089 – 1098.

[4] Alberto Cerpa; Deborah Estrin; ASCENT: Adaptive Self-Configuring sEnsor Networks Topologies[J]. mobile computing, IEEE transactions on, vol. 3, no. 3, july-september 2004.

[5] Jae-Hwan Chang; Tassiulas, L. maximum lifetime routing in wireless sensor networks[J]. Networking, IEEE/ACM Transactions on , Volume: 12 , Issue: 4 , Aug. 2004 , 609 – 619.

[6] Thomas Kriz, Oliver Gabel.kluedo.ub.uni-kl.de/volltexte/2004/1687/pdf/MICA2.pdf

An Energy Efficient Network Topology Configuration Scheme for Sensor Networks

Eunhwa Kim, Jeoungpil Ryu and Kijun Han*

Department of Computer Engineering,
Kyungpook National University, Daegu, Korea
Tel: 82-53-950-5557,
Fax: 82-53-957-4846
{ehkim, goldmunt}@netopia.knu.ac.kr,
kjhan@knu.ac.kr

Abstract. Since sensor nodes have limited battery power, it is desirable to select a minimum set of working sensor nodes which should be involved in sensing and forwarding data to the sink. In this paper, we propose a topology scheme which selects a minimum set of working nodes in the sensor network field to avoid wasting excessive energy by turning off too many redundant nodes. Our scheme offers a solution for configuring network topology with a minimal number of working nodes. Simulations show that our scheme extends the lifetime of the dense sensor networks, and achieves the desired robust coverage as well as satisfactory connectivity to the sink in an energy efficient fashion.

1 Introduction

Recent advancements in sensor technologies and wireless communications have enabled the development of wireless sensor networks which can be used for various applications such as the battlefield, health, and the home [1-2]. In sensor networks, many topics have been studied in several fields such as MAC, network configuration, query disseminating, data routing and aggregation, topology, and QoS [3-7]. Most work seriously investigated the efficient use of energy in the sensor network to prolong the network lifetime. In this paper, we focus on the efficient use of energy in the aspect of the network topology configuration. Some emerging sensor network application scenarios including battlefield surveillance and monitoring in agriculture involve a large sensor population to monitor a vast, sometimes hostile environment [10].

In a large-scale sensor network, we need to deploy numerous sensor nodes densely in the sensing field and maintain them in proper way. One of the most important issues in such high-density sensor networks is *density control* [11]. Density control means the function that controls the distribution density of the working sensors at certain level [12]. Density control selects working nodes to enable satisfactory coverage as well as full communication. It can save energy by turning off redundant nodes and it can prolong the system lifetime by replacing the failed nodes with some sleeping nodes.

* Correspondent author.

H.T. Shen et al. (Eds.): ADWeb 2006, LNCS 3842, pp. 297–305, 2006.

Several algorithms have been proposed for sensing coverage in sensor networks [9-12]. In ASCENT, active nodes stay awake all the time and perform multi-hop packet routing, while the rest of the nodes stay "passive" and periodically check if they should become active [9]. However it does not consider the issue of complete coverage of the monitored region [12].

PEAS[10,11] is based on a probing mechanism to control working node density. This algorithm guarantees that the distance between any pair of working nodes is at least the probing range [11]. But, it does not ensure that the coverage area of a sleeping node is completely covered by working nodes [12].

OGDC algorithm is fully localized and can maintain coverage as well as connectivity, and it transforms the problem of minimizing the number of working nodes into one of minimizing overlap, and then derives the optimal conditions for minimizing overlap [12]. But it assumes that transmission range is greater than twice the sensing range for complete coverage to imply connectivity in an arbitrary network.

This paper proposes an algorithm which selects a minimum set of working nodes to configure the network topology in an energy efficient way while guaranteeing full coverage and providing satisfactory connectivity to the sink. In this way, we can prolong the network lifetime and achieve full coverage and good connectivity to the network.

The rest of this paper is organized as follows. In Section 2, we propose our topology control scheme and present the algorithm in details. In Section 3, we evaluate the proposed algorithm through simulation and finally conclude the paper in Section 4.

2 Our Topology Control Scheme

Regarding coverage problem, our goal is to achieve a full coverage with a minimum number of working nodes. Working nodes are here defined as those nodes which are involved in sensing and transmitting sensory data. Given a set of sensors and a target area, no coverage hole exists in the target area, if every point in that target area is covered by at least one sensor. A sensor network should be connected at all times so that the nodes are able to communicate with each other [13] (Fig. 1).

Now, we explain our topology control scheme which tries to distribute working nodes in a hexagonal shape to obtain a full coverage and a satisfactory connectivity with a minimum set of working nodes. For this, we first assume a sensor network where

- the sensor nodes are all homogeneous and energy constrained and stationary.
- the sensing range and the radio transmission range of sensor node are equal.
- the sensor nodes are located arbitrarily in the dense network.
- each sensor nodes knows its position information, and knows its one-hop neighbor's position information using hello messages.

With a selected set of working nodes, there should be no sensing hole in the network to guarantee full coverage. In addition, all working nodes must be connected

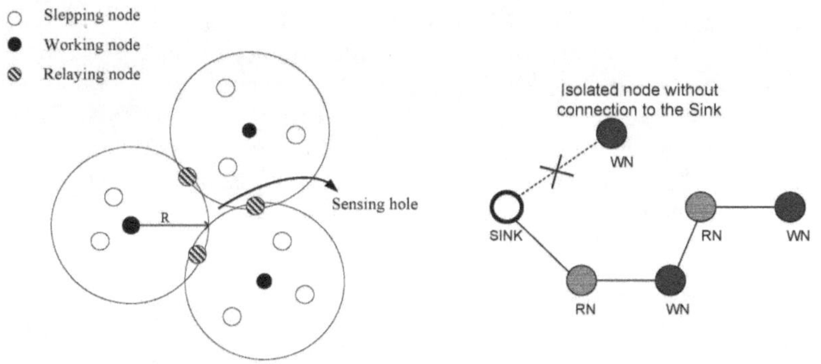

(a) Sensing hole (b) Communication hole

Fig. 1. Scenarios where a sensing hole or a communication hole is generated

to the sink to forward the sensing data. For this, we introduce the concept of relay node which is defined as a node that provides interconnection between two working nodes. We consider two extreme scenarios for selecting working nodes in the sensor network.

(i) If we select working nodes in such a way that their transmission ranges (ideally given by a circle) border on each other as seen in Fig. 2(a), we need to place a relay node at the point of tangency of two ranges to provide connectivity among working nodes. In this way, we can minimize the number of working nodes in the network. However, we will have a sensing hole (marked as shaded area) as shown in the figure.

(ii) If we select working nodes in such a way that they are very closely located as illustrated in Fig. 2(b), we do not need to worry about coverage problems. However, we have to pay the cost for the redundancy of sensory data since the range of each working node is overlapped.

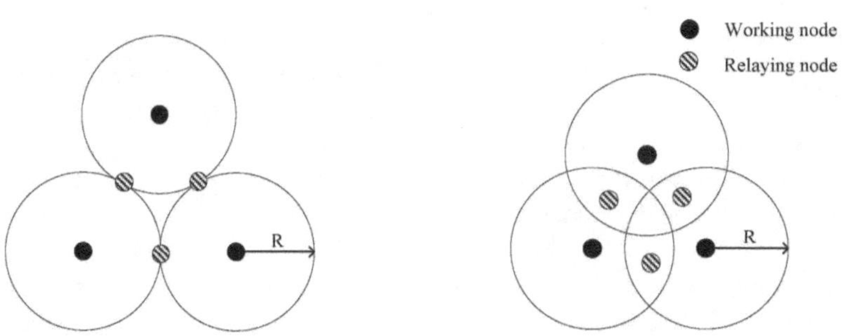

(a) When transmission ranges of nodes border on each other (b) When transmission ranges of nodes are too much overlapped

Fig. 2. Two extreme scenarios in selecting working nodes

Therefore, to configure a network topology with no sensing holes or redundant coverage problems, the working nodes must be distributed in such a way that their ranges intersect at two points making 60 degrees through the working node, as illustrated in Fig. 3. At the same time, we have to position a relay node in each intersected area to obtain connectivity. In other words, the working nodes must be distributed so that their transmission ranges intersect in a hexagonal shape, as shown in Fig. 3.

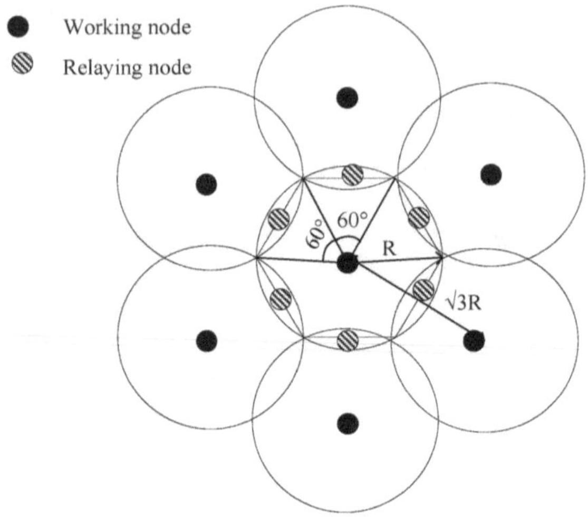

Fig. 3. Distribution of working nodes in a hexagonal shape

To implement the basic idea of our scheme, the sink is automatically selected as the first member of the working node set. Then, 2-hop neighbors located within $\sqrt{3}R$ of the sink are considered as candidates of the next working node where R means the sensing range. At this time, to maximize the sensing coverage while avoiding the sensing hole problem, the node that is farthest from the sink is selected from those 2-hop neighbors as the next working node. Following this, a relay node is chosen from the nodes in the intersected area of two working nodes to guarantee connectivity between these two working nodes, as illustrated in Fig. 3.

Once the first two working nodes are selected in this way, the next working node is chosen from each working node(marked as shaded area) in the intersection of two circular bands between R and $\sqrt{3}R$, as shown in Fig. 4. This is intended to make the duplicated coverage as small as possible while preventing the sensing hole problem. If there are two or more nodes in the shaded intersection area, the node whose transmission range is the least overlapped with those of other working nodes is selected as the next working node, as shown in Fig. 4.

Similarly, another working node is newly selected from any two working nodes in the intersection of two circular bands between R and $\sqrt{3}R$. This process is repeated until there are no working nodes to be selected any more.

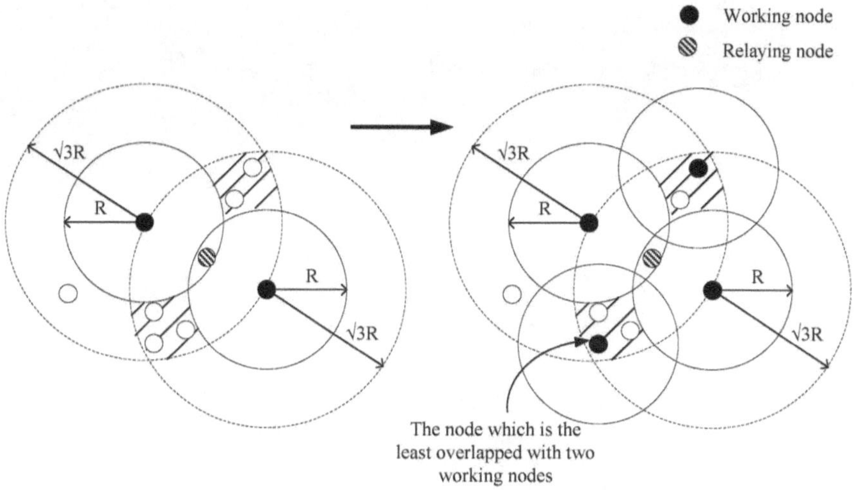

Fig. 4. Selection of working nodes

Our scheme provides fault tolerance capability to cope with a situation in which some working node is dead. If a working node consumes its energy completely or fails in a sudden environment, any other node must replace it. In our algorithm, the substitution is determined in the same way as used for selection of working nodes, as explained above. The substitution is chosen in the intersection of two circular bands between R and $\sqrt{3}R$ from working nodes neighboring to the dead node. If there are several nodes in the intersection area, the node whose transmission range is the least overlapped with those of other working nodes is selected as the substitution node.

For this, when a node does not hear a one-hop message from any working nodes within some time specified by threshold T_w, it assumes that there is no working node within its one-hop range. It can join in the competition to become a working node only if it receives two-hop messages from two or more working nodes which are less than $\sqrt{3}R$ away. Among such candidate nodes, the one whose transmission range is the least overlapped with those of other working nodes is selected (substitution of the dead working node).

Our scheme can be formally described using the following notations.

$N(x)$: one-hop neighbor set of node x,
$N^2(x)$: two-hop neighbor set of node x
S_W : set of working nodes ,
S_R : set of relay nodes
$| x - y |$: distance between two nodes x and y
$overlap(x, y, z)$: intersected transmission area of three nodes x, y, z

Step 1 : Start with Sw having the sink node as its first member (Fig. 5).
$$S_W \leftarrow Sink$$

Step 2 : Select a two-hop neighbor node which is the farthest but within √3R of the sink.

$$\textit{Select } x \textit{ and } S_W \leftarrow x \textit{ such that maximizes} \left| Sink - x \right|, x \in N^2(Sink)$$
$$\textit{while satisfying the condition } R < \left| Sink - x \right| \le \sqrt{3}R$$

Select a relaying node which is the closest to the two working nodes.

$$\textit{Select } r \textit{ and } S_R \leftarrow r \textit{ such that minimizes } (\left| r - Sink \right| + \left| r - x \right|), r \in N(Sink) \cap N(x)$$

Step 3 : For any two members of a working node set, that is, $\forall (y_i, y_j) \subset S_w$, select the one whose transmission range is the least overlapped with those of other working nodes in the intersection of two circular bands between R and √3R of any two working nodes.

$$\textit{Select } x \textit{ and } S_W \leftarrow x \textit{ such that minimize } overlap(x, y_i, y_j), x \in N^2(y_i) \cap N^2(y_j)$$
$$\textit{while satisfying the condition } R < \left| x - y_i \right| \le \sqrt{3}R \textit{ and } R < \left| x - y_j \right| \le \sqrt{3}R$$

Select relaying nodes which connect a new working node to other working nodes.

$$\textit{Select } r \textit{ and } S_R \leftarrow r \textit{ such that minimize}(\left| r - x \right| + \left| r - y \right|), r \in N(x) \cap N(y)$$

Step 4 : Repeat step 3 until a new working node is not generated anymore.

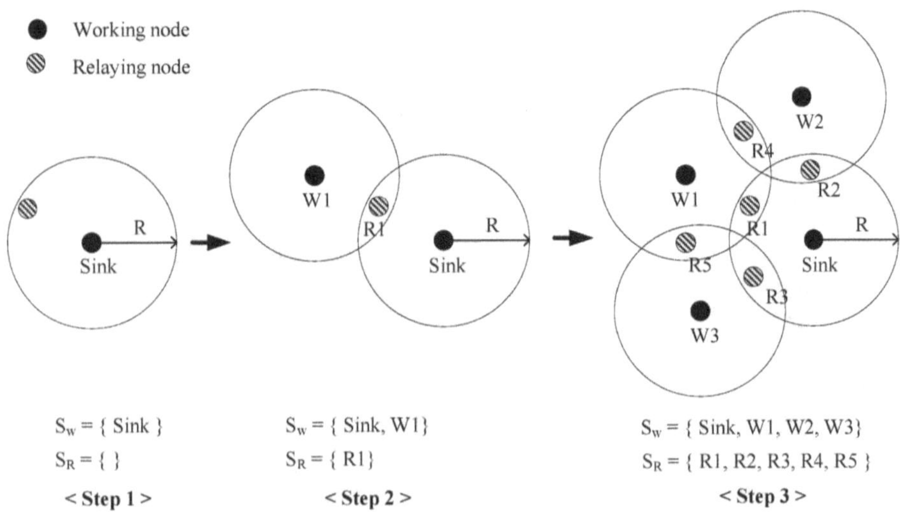

Fig. 5. An example of working node selection

After setup of the network topology each node is in one of four modes: working, relaying, sleeping, and listening, as shown in Fig. 6. Working nodes periodically transmit hello message to all two-hop neighbors. Other nodes except working nodes and relaying nodes will switch between sleeping and listening modes to prepare for replacing a working node that has died due to energy depletion or other hard failures [10]. A sleeping node wakes up after sleeping for a time specified by threshold T_s and hears the one-hop hello messages sent from working nodes. If the listening node hears one-hop hello message from working nodes, it will go back to sleeping mode. The threshold T_s is recalculated based on the remaining energy of the working node.

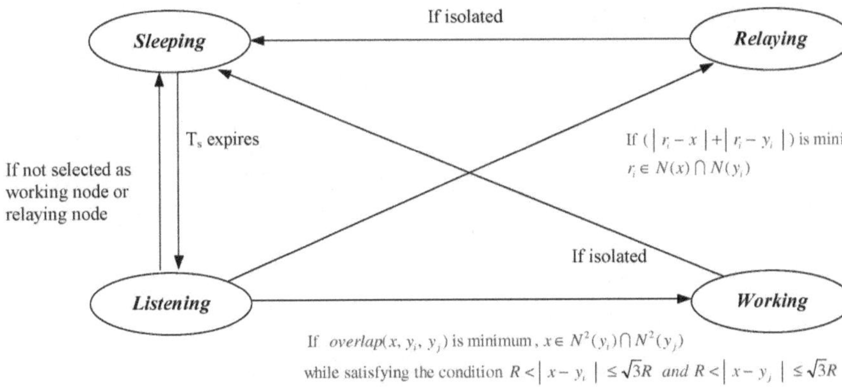

Fig. 6. State transition diagram of node

3 Simulation

To evaluate our topology control algorithm, we carried out experiments to measure coverage and connectivity of the network. We used a network that had n nodes arbitrarily deployed in an area of 500 by 500, where n is in the range of [100, 1000]. The sensing range and transmission radio range are 50.

Fig. 7 shows the number of working nodes as we varied the number of deployed nodes in the network. As we count the number of working nodes which are connected to the sink in the sparse network with less than 500 deployed nodes, we can see that the number of working nodes is small. From Fig. 7, we can see that the random selection scheme generates too many working nodes. On the other hand, the network can be successfully configured with a smaller number of working nodes even in the dense network in our scheme. This can be more clearly seen in the sparse network by comparing it with the number of working nodes (N_{hexa}) needed when the network topology is configured in such a way that all working nodes are connected in the hexagonal shape. The value of N_{hexa} is given by

$$N_{hexa} = \frac{Network\ Size}{3\sqrt{3}R^2/2} \quad (1)$$

In our scheme the network lifetime can be extended by turning off too many redundant nodes. In this test, we do not consider the number of relaying nodes since it is dependent on how many working nodes are selected.

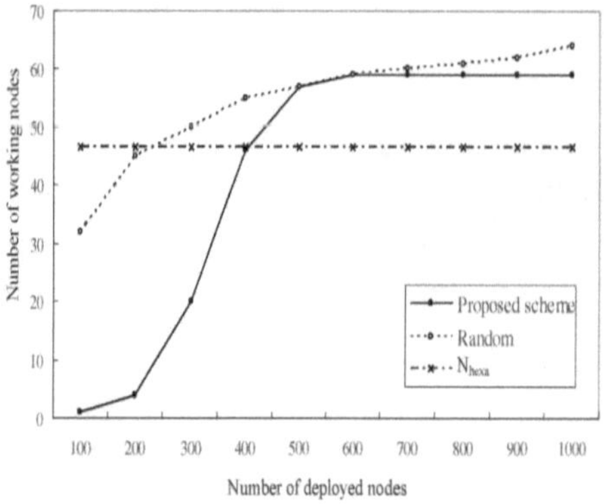

Fig. 7. Number of working nodes

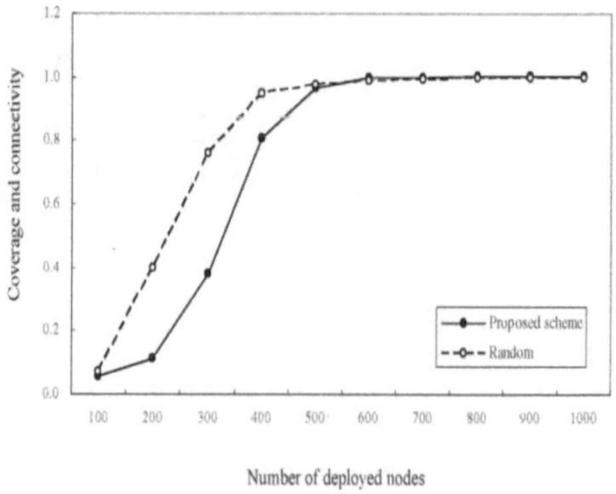

Fig. 8. Coverage and connectivity ratio

To measure coverage, we count the number of points which are included in the range of any working node which is connected to the sink node. In order to measure connectivity, we check if each sensor node is connected to the sink directly or through some working nodes or relaying nodes. Fig. 8 shows the coverage as expressed by the proportion of the number of covered nodes relative to the number of sensor nodes deployed in the network. The connectivity ratio is expressed in a similar way. As shown in Fig. 8, our schem achieves full coverage and good connectivity to the network with a small set of working nodes. Even a dense network with more than 600 deployed nodes can be fully covered with the working nodes selected by our scheme.

In Fig. 9, we examine the number of working nodes in the network as the network size grows. As expected, the number of working nodes increases in accordance with the network size. We can see that the proposed algorithm generates a smaller number of working nodes compared with the random selection scheme regardless of the network size.

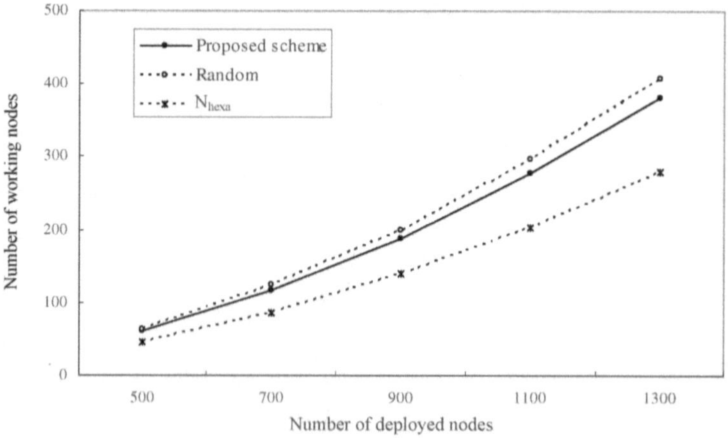

Fig. 9. Number of working nodes versus network size

4 Conclusion

In this paper, we propose a topology scheme which selects a minimum set of working nodes in the sensor network field to avoid wasting excessive energy by turning off too many redundant nodes. Our scheme does not generate communication holes or sensing holes. Simulations showed that our scheme achieves the desired robust coverage as well as satisfactory connectivity to the sink with a small number of working nodes in an energy efficient fashion.

Acknowledgement. University Fundamental Research Program supported by Ministry of Information and Communication in Republic of Korea.

References

1. Ian F. Akyildiz, W. Su, Y. Sankarasubramaniam, E. Cayirci, A survey on sensor networks, *IEEE Communications Magazine,* pp. 102–114, 2002.
2. Chee-Yee Chong, Srikanta P. Kumar, Sensor networks: Evolution, opportunities, and challenges, *Proceedings of the IEEE,* vol 91, pp 1247–1256, August 2003.
3. W. Ye, J. Heidemann, and D. Estrin, An energy-efficient MAC protocol for wireless sensor networks, *INFOCOM 2002,* Vol.3, pp. 1567-1576, New York, NY, USA, June, 2002
4. K. Akkaya and M. Younis, A survey on routing protocols for wireless sensor networks, *Elsevier Ad Hoc Network Journal, 2004.*
5. A. Qayyum, L. Viennot, and A. Laouiti, Multipoint relaying: An efficient technique for flooding in mobile wireless networks. *Technical Report 3898, INRIA - Rapport de recherche*, 2000.
6. TJ Kwon and M. Gerla, Efficient flooding with passive clustering-An Overhead-Free Selective Forward Mechanism for Ad Hoc/Sensor Network, *Proceedings of the IEEE*, vol. 91, no. 8, 2003
7. X. Li, P.Wan, O. Frieder, Coverage in Wireless Ad Hoc Sensor Networks, *IEEE Trans. Computers,* vol. 52, no.6, 2003
8. F. Xue and P. R. Kumar, The number of neighbors needed for connectivity of wireless networks, *ACM Journal of Wireless Networks, vol.* 10, pp. 169-181, 2004
9. A. Cerpa and D. Estrin, Ascent: Adaptive self-configuring sensor networks topologies, *Proc. of Infocom,* 2002.
10. F. Ye, G. Zhong, S. Lu, and L. Zhang, Energy Efficient Robust Sensing Coverage in Large Sensor Networks, *Technical Report UCLA* , 2002.
11. F. Ye, G. Zhong, S. Lu, and L. Zhang. Peas: A robust energy conserving protocol for long-lived sensor networks, *ICDCS,* 2003.
12. H. Zhang and J. C. Hou, Maintaining Sensing Coverage and Connectivity in Large Sensor Networks, *Technical Report UIUC, UIUCDCS-R-2003-2351*, 2003.
13. N. Ahmed, S. S. Kanhere, S. Jha, The Holes Problem in Wireless Sensor Networks: A Survey, *ACM SIGMOBILE Mobile Computing and Communications Review,* vol. 9, no 2, 2005

Robust Multipath Routing to Exploit Maximally Disjoint Paths for Wireless Ad Hoc Networks

Jungtae Kim[1], Sangman Moh[2,*], Ilyong Chung[1], and Chansu Yu[3]

[1] Dept. of Computer Sci., Chosun University,
375 Seoseok-dong, Dong-gu, Gwangju 501-759 Korea
[2] Dept. of Internet Eng., Chosun University,
375 Seoseok-dong, Dong-gu, Gwangju 501-759 Korea
[3] Dept. of Electrical and Computer Eng., Cleveland State U., OH 44115
smmoh@chosun.ac.kr

Abstract. This paper proposes a new multipath routing protocol called *maximally disjoint multipath AODV (MDAODV)*, which exploits maximally node- and link-disjoint paths. The key idea is to extend the route request (RREQ) message by adding source routing information and to make the destination node select two paths from multiple RREQs received. Our simulation study shows that MDAODV outperforms the conventional multipath routing protocol based on AODV as well as the basic AODV protocol in terms of packet delivery ratio, and results in about 15 ~ 50 % less routing overhead.

1 Introduction

A *mobile ad hoc network (MANET)* [1, 2, 3] is a collection of mobile nodes without any fixed infrastructure or any form of centralized administration. MANETs can be effectively applied to ad hoc sensor networks, military battlefields, emergency disaster relief, and commercial applications.

The ad hoc on-demand distance vector routing (AODV) protocol [4, 5], which is one of the most popular routing protocols for MANETs [3], is an on-demand protocol. Like other routing protocols, AODV also has inherently unstable routing paths which are dynamically changed and frequently broken. To resolve this problem by providing *multiple paths* for backup routing, the ad hoc on-demand multipath distance vector routing (AOMDV) protocol [6, 7] was proposed, where multiple paths are guaranteed to be loop-free and link-disjoint. In the AOMDV protocol, however, node-disjointness is not fully exploited and intermediate nodes actively participate in the process of multipath establishment, increasing the overhead incurred at intermediate nodes.

This paper proposes a new multipath routing protocol which exploits maximally node- and link-disjoint paths and outperforms AOMDV as well AODV. In this paper, we call it *maximally disjoint multipath AODV (MDAODV)* protocol. Compared to conventional approaches, the proposed MDAODV provides *reliable*

* Corresponding author.

H.T. Shen et al. (Eds.): APWeb 2006, LNCS 3842, pp. 306–309, 2006.

and *robust routing paths* and *higher performance* because both the alternative path may be used if the current path is broken and it is maximally node- and link-disjoint from the main path. Moreover, MDAODV makes the destination node determine the main and alternative paths, reducing the overhead incurred at intermediate nodes.

2 Maximally Disjoint Multipath Routing

In this paper, the key idea to provide maximally node- and link-disjoint paths is to extend RREQ by adding source routing information and to make the destination node select two paths from multiple RREQs received for a predetermined time period. After receiving the first RREQ, the destination node receives and collects subsequent RREQ copies for the predetermined time period. It forms reverse paths in the same way as at intermediate nodes. Then, it determines two paths. For cost-efficient implementation, the *path selection algorithm* selects the first-received path (also regarded as the shortest path) as the main path and then finds an alternative path that is maximally node- and link-disjoint from the main path. Algorithm 1 describes the path selection algorithm run in the destination node.

Algorithm 1. Select_Path(R, m_s, m_d, n)

1. Let $R = \{r_1, r_2, \ldots, r_n\}$ be the set of the RREQs received by m_d for a predetermined time period, m_s be the source node, m_d be the destination node, and n be the number of RREQs, where the i-th-received RREQ r_i contains a path composed of an ordered list of mobile nodes (m_s, $m_{i,1}$, $m_{i,2}$, $\ldots$, $m_{i,k(i)-1}$, m_d) with the path length of $k(i)$.
2. For the n paths, define the node set Q_i and the link set L_i of the i-th path; *i.e.*, let $Q_i = \{q_{i,1}, q_{i,2}, \ldots, q_{i,k(i)+1}\}$ be the set of an ordered list of $k(i) + 1$ nodes (m_s, $m_{i,1}$, $m_{i,2}$, $\ldots$, $m_{i,k(i)-1}$, m_d) contained in r_i and $L_i = \{l_{i,1}, l_{i,2}, \ldots, l_{i,k(i)}\}$ be the set of $k(i)$ links $((q_{i,1}, q_{i,2}), (q_{i,2}, q_{i,3}), \ldots, (q_{i,k}, q_{i,k(i)+1}))$, where $i = 1, 2, \ldots, n$ and $k(i)$ is the number of links in the i-th path (*i.e.*, $k(i) = |L_i|$).
3. Select the first path $P_1 = (m_s, m_{1,1}, m_{1,2}, \ldots, m_{1,k(1)-1}, m_d)$ as the main path.
4. For the j-th path $P_j = (m_s, m_{j,1}, m_{j,2}, \ldots, m_{j,k(j)-1}, m_d)$, calculate the number of the joint nodes of Q_1 and Q_j, $v_j = |Q_1 \bigcap Q_j|$, and the number of the joint links of L_1 and L_j, $e_j = |L_1 \bigcap L_j|$, where $j = 2, 3, \ldots, n$.
5. Determine the minimum value of v_j, v_{min}, such that $v_{min} \leq v_j$ for all j, where $j = 2, 3, \ldots, n$. Then, from the $n - 1$ paths from P_2 through P_n, select the path with v_{min}. If $v_{min} \neq 0$ and there are two or more paths with v_{min}, select the path with the minimum number of joint links from them.
6. In case of tie, select the path corresponding to the earliest-received RREQ.

---

3 Performance Evaluation

The *network simulator* 2 (*ns*-2) [8] has been used in our simulation study. Our simulation is based on the simulation of mobile nodes moving over a square area of 1,000 meter × 1,000 meter. The radio transmission range is assumed to be 250 meters and a free space propagation channel is assumed. With a data transmission rate 2 Mbps, each run has been executed for 1000 seconds of simulation time. The CBR source sends 1 packet per second and the data payload of the packets is 512 bytes long. Mobile nodes are assumed to move randomly according to the random *waypoint model* [9]. Note that a 95 % confidence level is used for the probabilistic processing of our simulation results.

Fig. 1 shows the packet delivery ratio of AODV, AOMDV and MDAODV. MDAODV has slightly higher packet delivery ratio than AOMDV. The difference is larger and larger as the number of nodes increases. This is mainly due to the fact that higher node density allows more node- and link-disjoint paths between the source and destination nodes. As one of the four simulation factors increases, the packet delivery ratio decreases for all the three protocols. Higher node mobility induces more frequent link breakage resulting in more packets dropped. In addition, the larger number of connections, the heavier offered load and the larger number of nodes increase the probability of link breakage causing more traffic and interference.

Fig. 1. Packet delivery ratio

In this paper, the routing overhead is defined as the total number of routing packets transmitted per second. Each hop-wise transmission of a routing packet is counted as one transmission. According to the simulation results, MDAODV causes less routing overhead than AOMDV and AODV by up to 14 and 50 %, respectively. Furthermore, MDAODV has less routing overhead than AOMDV for the four factors and the difference becomes slightly larger as one of the four simulation factors increases. That is, it is easily inferred that MDAODV has less overhead than AOMDV in worse operational environments. As one of the four simulation factors increases, the routing overhead increases for all the three protocols. Notice that higher node mobility induces more frequent link breakage resulting in more control packets for routing. Note that the routing overhead of AODV is larger than that of MDAODV for all cases because the former to discover a new routing path is larger than the latter to establish an alternative path.

4 Conclusion

A new multipath routing protocol called *maximally disjoint multipath AODV (MDAODV)* has been proposed, which exploits maximally node- and link-disjoint. Compared to AOMDV, the proposed MDAODV provides more *reliable* and *robust routing paths* and higher performance because both the alternative path may be used if the current path is broken and it is maximally node- and link-disjoint from the main path. Our extensive simulation study shows that MDAODV outperforms the conventional AOMDV protocol in terms of packet delivery ratio, and results in about 15 $\sim$ 50 % less routing overhead.

References

1. Perkins, C.E.: Ad Hoc Networking. Addison Wesley (2000)
2. Toh, C.-K.: Ad Hoc Mobile Wireless Networks: Protocols and Systems. Prentice Hall (2002)
3. IETF Mobile Ad Hoc Networks (MANET) Working Group Charter. http://www.ietf.org/html.charters/manet-charter.html (2005)
4. Perkins, C.E., Royer, E.M., Das, S.R.: Ad Hoc On-Demand Distance Vector (AODV) Routing. Internet-Draft, draft-ietf-manet-aodv-13.txt (2003)
5. Belding-Royer, E.M., Perkins, C.E.: Evolution and Future Directions of the Ad Hoc on-Demand Distance-Vector Routing Protocol. Ad Hoc Networks. **1** (2003) 125–150
6. Marina, M.K., Das, S.R.: On-Demand Multipath Distance Vector Routing for Ad Hoc Networks. Proc. of the Int. Conf. on Network Protocols (2001) 14–23
7. Ad hoc On-demand Multipath Distance Vector (AOMDV) Routing. http://www.cs.sunysb.edu/ mahesh/aomdv/ (2004)
8. The Network Simulator ns-2. http://www.isi.edu/nsnam/ns/ (2005)
9. Broch, J., Maltz, D., Johnson, D., Hu, Y.-C., Jetcheva, J.: A Performance Comparison of Multi-Hop Wireless Ad Hoc Network Routing Protocols. Proc. of the 4th Annual Int. Conf. on Mobile Computing and Networking (1998) 56–67

Energy Efficient Design for Window Query Processing in Sensor Networks*

Sang Hun Eo[1], Suraj Pandey[1], Soon-Young Park[1], and Hae-Young Bae[2]

[1,2] Department of Computer Science and Information Engineering, Inha University, Yonghyun-dong, Nam-gu, Incheon, 402-751, Korea
{eosanghun, suraj, sunny}@dblab.inha.ac.kr, hybae@inha.ac.kr

Abstract. In this paper, we propose an energy efficient design for window query processing in sensor networks. A new design is structured to process the window queries. The use of distributed form of spatial indexing introduces greater flexibility and robustness as compared to the previous centralized approach, which lacked proper semantics and evaluation of window queries, in sensor networks. A distributed spatial routing tree efficiently distributes the structure to each node in the sensor network. The MBR of the region where its children and the node itself are located is stored by each parent. The measure of the extent of overlapping determines the inclusion/exclusion of sensor nodes to evaluate the query. Reduction in the number of nodes participating in the query reduces the communication power seeked, thus elongating the life of the embedded sensor system.

1 Introduction

Wireless sensor networks are finding substratial uses in large ares of research and monitoring applications. Sensor nodes, such as the Berkeley MICA Mote [1] which already support many functionalities, are getting smaller, cheaper, and able to perform more complex operations, including having mini embedded operating systems. Taking advantage of these emerging technologies we can readily see much work to be done in the field. New algorithms and designs are thus foreseeable. In this context, the theme tradionally followed by the database community [7, 10] placed a centralized control over the system's operation. But due to limited storage, limited network bandwidth, poor inter-node communication, limited computational ability, and limited power of sensor networks, it is infeasible to use the centralized architecture. We transform them into distributed design with careful consideration of performance and power gauge.

The Cougar project at Cornell [2] discusses queries over sensor networks, which has a central administration that is aware of the location of all the sensors. Madden et.al., in [13] introduced Fjord architecture for management of multiple queries processing, information stored in a catalog. TAG [5] was proposed for an aggregation

* This research was supported by the MIC (Ministry of Information and Communication), Korea, under the ITRC (Information Technology Research Center) support program supervised by the IITA (Institute of Information Technology Assessment).

H.T. Shen et al. (Eds.): APWeb 2006, LNCS 3842, pp. 310–314, 2006.

service as a part of TinyDB [1], which is a query processing system for a network of Berkeley motes. Adaptive querying using Semantic Routing Trees (SRT) was described. Directed diffusion [4], a data centric framework, uses flooding to find paths from the query originator node to the data source nodes. Interestingly, [8] has an R-tree based scheme, but no verification or evaluation is presented. Our work is most closely related to geographic hash-tables (GHTs) [16], DIFS [14] and DIMENSIONS [12]. DIMENSIONS and DIFS can be thought of as using the same set of primitives as GHT (storage using consistent hashing). Tributaries and delta approach [3] is more efficient for routing. For sensor networks, we emphasize that a centralized index for window queries is not feasible for energy-efficiency. So we use distributed index. The algorithm for traversal of nodes resembles that of the tradional R-tree[7].

The remainder of this paper is structured as follows. In section 2, we propose the structure and query processing under the DSR-tree. Section 3 discusses the performance evaluation. Finally, we conclude in Section 4.

2 Energy Efficient Design for Window Queries

In this section, we propose the Distributed Spatial Routing tree (DSR-tree) used for querying with spatial attributes. Considering a static sensor network distributed over a large area, all sensors are aware of their geographical position. Each sensor could be equipped with GPS device or use location estimation techniques. The network structure, as in Cougar and TinyDB, consists of nodes connected as a tree. Also, nodes within the same level do not communicate with each other. This communication relationship is viable to changes due to moving nodes, the power shortage of the nodes, or when new nodes appear. TinyDB has a list of parent candidates. The parent changes if link quality degrades sufficiently. Also in Cougar, a parent sensor node will keep a list of all its children, as a *waiting list,* and will not report its reading until it hears from all the sensor nodes on its waiting list. We follow Cougar's approach.

A DSR-tree is an index designed to allow each node to efficiently determine if any of the nodes below it will need to participate in a given query over some queried window. The routing protocol used, e.g. the tributary-delta approach, determines the parent-child relationship. However, for spatial querying we need additional parameters to be stored by individual nodes. Each node must store the calculated[1] MBR of its children along with the aggregate values as have already been existing in each node under the in-network query processing paradigm and noted by several literatures,[9,15] in particular. Each parent node has a structure in the form *<child-pointers, child-MBRs, overall-MBR, location-info>*. The *child-pointers* helps traverse the node structure just as the *waiting-list* in Cougar. In addition, we have added the MBR in each node which confines the children into a bounded box. The confinement algorithm distributes the sensor nodes into the appropriate MBR taking proximity to their respective parent and dead space of the resulting MBR into account.

[1] Each MBR is updated during the ascending of the tree so that the modified MBR is stored in each node.

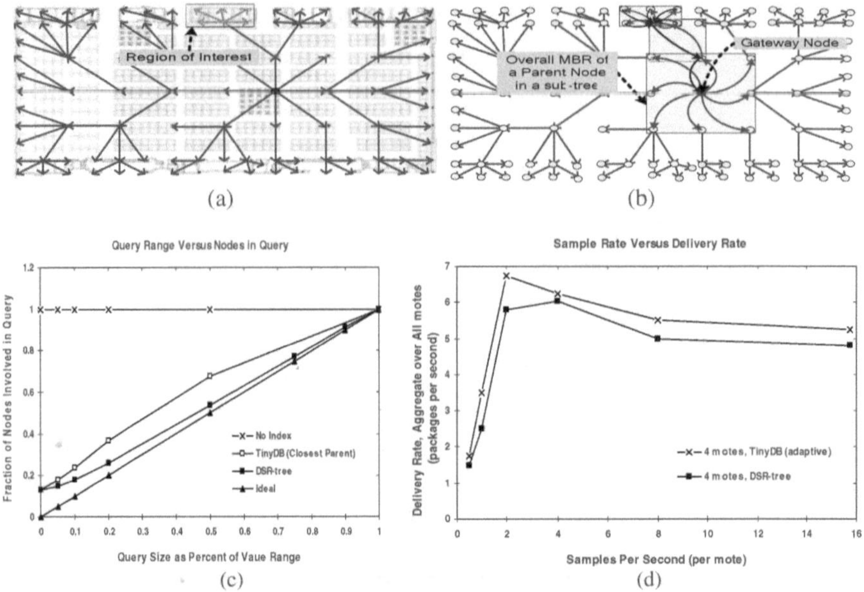

Fig. 1. (a) Simulated Physical Environment showing sensor nodes in our test bed. (b) The MBR under each parent node of a sub tree. (c) Number of nodes participating in window queries of different sizes (20 × 20 grid, 400 nodes). (d) Aggregate delivery rate.

Figure 1 shows our emulated environment design. In the descending stage of construction, a MBR which overlaps the children and the parent is stored by each parent in that region. Each descent correspondingly stores the MBR of the region until the leaf node is reached. When all the nodes have been traversed, the parent node of each region is notified about their child nodes' MBR. Hence, in the ascending stage the parent of each region gets updated the new MBR of their children which now should include the sub-tree under that node, and a distributed R-tree like structure is formed among the sensor nodes. One critical operation of DSR-tree, called *energy efficient forwarding*, is to isolate the regions containing the sensor nodes for window querying. Our prime objective is to maintain the minimum count of nodes taking part in the query which is large dependent upon the construction of the DSR-tree. Using GPRS [16] algorithm the packets are delivered to a node at a specified location.

A window query returns all the relevant data collected/relayed that is associated with regions within a given window W. To process it with the DSR-tree, initially the root node receives the query; originating at any node. The child nodes that receive the request are those whose *overall-MBR* overlaps W. Each parent under that overlapping region floods the sub-tree. The *child-MBR* is used to decide the particular regions which need precise selection for limiting unnecessary node traversal. The optional parameter *location-info* should help to pin-point exact node positions. Its inclusion is based on the type of sensor network and its scalability factor. Additional parameters e.g., time *t*, location attributes etc., can act as a filter. Figure 1 also shows the path for node selection. The code isn't included so as to leverage the robustness in choosing efficient algorithm for independent implementations of our design.

3 Performance Evaluation

To study the performance of the proposed scheme in sensor networks, we created an emulation environment using AVRORA [6]. Following typical sensor network simulation practices, the emulated network of sensors was chosen to be consisting of regular tessellation, as like grid squares. Each node could transmit data to sensors that were at most one hop away from it. Our calculations are based on sensor nodes distributed over a large area where scability factor determines the cost, efficiency and quality of data thus obtained. The query delivery cost directly depends upon the size of the window query. As we base our experiments upon the TinyDB, mote characteristics are identical for our test bed. Light and humidity values are sensed and transmitted.

In the emulation we evaluated the performance of our proposed scheme, DSR-tree, against the *best-case* approach and *closest parent* as used by TinyDB. We used the random distribution to select the query range. As due to the lack of any benchmarks for evaluating query performance in sensor networks, we selected the queries that would be regarded as suitable for window queries, resembling to Sequoia 2000. Figure 1 shows the number of nodes that participate in queries over variably sized window query. It is drawn over the average values obtained after the emulation. TinyDB concludes that only 1% of the 81% energy spent is on processing, 41% of which just spent in communication. Our design reduces 20% of that cost. But, the processing time is increased due to the addition of extra message bits, approximately 17 bits, and the related algorithms. Nevertheless, this slight increase over shadows the significant decrease in communication. So, the number of nodes that are involved in the query is significantly reduced in comparison to the closest parent approach of TinyDB in its SRT. For the partially aggregated value for in-network aggregation and power reduction, we also simulated the performance following the TiNA [15] scheme which improved the delivery rate in resemblance to that of TinyDB shown in fig 2. We can readily conclude that our approach is up to 20% more energy efficient than the centralized version as evident from the graph.

4 Conclusion and Future Work

In this paper, we contribute a new technique to group the sensors in a region for spatial window queries. We proposed an energy efficient design for window query processing using the DSR-tree in sensor networks. DSR-tree reduces the number of nodes that participate in communication over queried window by nearly an order of magnitude by isolating the overlapping regions of sensor nodes covered by the window query. Only the sensor nodes leading to the path of the requested region are communicated, and hence substantial reduction in power is achieved due to reduced number of sub-trees involved. In addition, the aggregate values for the region of interest are collected. Since data transmission is the biggest energy-consuming activity in sensor nodes, using DSR-tree results in significant energy savings. Adoption of distributed redundant architecture for efficient processing of parallel queries and for supporting join operations, are challenges which are under scrutiny as the capabilities of sensor nodes reaches higher levels.

References

1. S.R.Madden, M.J.Franklin and J.M.Hellerstein, TinyDB: An Acquisitional Query Processing System for Sensor Networks. ACM Transasctions on Database Systems, Vol. 30, No. 1, March 2005, Pages 122-173.
2. Y.Yao and J.Gehrke, The Cougar Approach to In-Network Query Processing in Sensor Networks, SIGMOD'02.
3. A.Manjhi, S.Nath, P.B.Gibbons, Tributaries and Deltas: Efficient and Robust Aggregation in Sensor Network Streams. In SIGMOD 2005, USA.
4. C. Intanagonwiwat, R. Govindan and D. Estrin, Directed Diffusion: A Scalable and Robust Communication Paradigm for Sensor Networks, ACM MobiCom'00.
5. S.R.Madden, M.J.Franklin, J.M. Hellerstein, and W.Hong, TAG: a Tiny AGgregation Service for Ad-Hoc Sensor Networks, OSDI, 2002.
6. B.L.Titzer, D.K.Lee, and J.Palsberg, Avrora: Scalable Sensor Network Simulation with Precise Timing. In Proc. of IPSN, April 2005.
7. A. Guttman, R-Trees: A Dynamic Index Struc-ture for Spatial Searching. In Proc. ACMSIGMOD 1984, Annual Meeting, USA, pages 47–57. ACM Press, 1984.
8. A. Coman et al. A framework for spatio-temporal query pro-cessing over wireless sensor networks. In Proc. DMSN Workshop (with VLDB), pages 104–110, 2004.
9. J.Beaver,M.A.Sharaf,A.Labrinidis and P.K.Chrysanthis, Power-Aware In-Network Query Processing for Sensor Data, Proc. 3rd ACM MobiDE Workshop, 2003.
10. D.Comer, The Ubiquitous B-tree. ACM Computing Surveys, 11(2):121-137, 1979.
11. S.Nath, P.Gibbons, S.Seshan, Synopsis Diffusion for Robust Aggregation in Sensor Networks. In Proc. ACM Symposium on Networked Embedded Systems, 2004.
12. D.Ganesan, D.Estrin, and J.Heidemann, DIMENSIONS: Why do we need a new Data Handling architecture for Sensor Networks? In Proc. First Workshop on Hot Topics In Networks (HotNes-I), Princeton, NJ, October 2002.
13. S.Madden and M.J.Franklin, Fjording the Stream: An Architecture for Queries over Streaming Sensor Data. In Proc.18th International Conference on Data Engineering, pp.555-566, 2002.
14. B.Greenstein, D.Estrin, R.Govindan, S.Ratnasamy, and S.Shenker, DIFS: A Distributed Index for Features in Sensor Networks. In Proc.1st IEEE International Workshop on Sensor Network Protocols and Applications, Anchorage, AK, 2003.
15. M. A. Sharaf, J. Beaver, A. Labrinidis, P.Chrysanthis, TiNA: A Scheme for Temporal Coherency-Aware in-Network Aggregation. In Proc. of 2003 International Workshop in Mobile Data Engineering.
16. B.Karp and H.T.Kung, GPRS: Greedy Perimeter Stateless Routing for Wireless Networks. In Proc. Sixth Annual ACM/IEEE International Conference on Mobile Computing and Networking (Mobicom 2000), Boston, MA, August 2000.
17. S.Singh and C.Raghavendra, PAMAS: Power aware multi-access protocol with signaling for ad hoc networks. ACM Computer Comm. Review, 28(3).

A Novel Localization Scheme Based on RSS Data for Wireless Sensor Networks*

Hongyang Chen[1,2], Deng Ping [2], Yongjun Xu[1], and Xiaowei Li[1]

[1] Advanced Test Technology Lab, Institute of Computing Technology, Chinese Academy of Sciences, Beijing 100080
[2] Institute of Mobile Communications, Southwest Jiaotong University, Chengdu 610031
freedove2001@163.com, pdeng115@vip.sina.com, {xyj, lxw}@ict.ac.cn

Abstract. Sensor localization has become an essential requirement for realistic applications over Wireless Sensor Networks (WSN).In this paper, we propose a novel location algorithm based on mean received signal strength (RSS) measurements. It incorporates Chan's hyperbolic position location algorithm and the extended Kalman filtering to achieve an accurate estimation. We have verified the scheme mentioned in the paper performed better than conventional received signal strength indicator (RSSI) location algorithm for the static location estimator in indoor sensor networks.

1 Introduction

Location information plays a crucial role in understanding the application context in Wireless Sensor Networks (WSN), and many localization algorithms for WSN have been proposed to provide per-node location information [1]. With regard to the mechanisms used for estimating location, we divide these localization protocols into two categories: range-based and range-free. Ranging is the process of estimating the distance between two nodes. RSS-based ranging is attractive as a means of distance estimation because it is essentially free, wireless sensor nodes already have radios, and signal strength is often being measured for each radio packet anyway. In contrast, other ranging and localization technologies such as acoustic, AOA, TDOA [2], GPS, and laser require specialized hardware and sometimes sophisticated processing.

As can be seen, each of the localization schemes on its own has their set of weaknesses. Based on the above notes and results it is our opinion that radio localization can play an active role in several indoor applications provided that the accuracy requirement in terms of spatial resolution is not too strict. As such, we will discuss RSSI location algorithm and the performance of the algorithm applied in indoor sensor networks. In the paper we propose a new methodology which using mean value of RSS data to estimate the position of target node with only 3 anchor nodes. This paper makes the following three main contributions. First, we present a practical, fast and easy-to-use localization scheme with relatively high accuracy and

* This paper was supported in part by National Basic Research Program of China under Grant No.2005CB321604, and in part by National Natural Science Foundation of China under Grant No.90207002.

H.T. Shen et al. (Eds.): APWeb 2006, LNCS 3842, pp. 315 – 320, 2006.

low cost for indoor wireless sensor networks. Second, we develop a novel Extended Kalman Filter (EKF), based state estimation algorithm for node localization in our indoor WSN. Third, we implement and validate our scheme on the GAINS sensor node platform, which achieves errors of about 1.16 meter as shown in our experiments. (GAINS sensor nodes are all independently developed by our WSN group of Institute of Computing Technology, Chinese Academy of Sciences.)

2 Localization System Model and Parameters Obtain

In the section, we assume an indoor sensor network model as depicted in Fig. 5. The network proposed in the paper consists of sensor nodes (SN), which are located in random, and three anchor nodes, which have a priori knowledge of their own position with respect to some global coordinate system.

One of the most common radio propagation is the log-normal shadowing path loss model which also will be adopted in our system [3]. The model is given by:

$$PL(d) = PL(d_0) - 10n\log_{10}(d / d_0) - X_\sigma \tag{1}$$

Where d is the transmitter-receiver separation distance, d_0 a reference distance, n the path loss exponent, and $X_б$ a zero-mean Gaussian RV (in dB) with standard deviation б (multi-path effects). $PL(d_0)$ is the signal power at reference distance d_0 and PL(d) is the signal power at distance d. The value of $PL(d_0)$ can either be derived empirically or obtained from the WSN hardware specifications.

A theoretically accurate model would model RSSI as having logarithmic attenuation over distance. The specifications from our radio indicate that the output voltage V_{RSSI} on the RSSI pin is proportional to the received power as

$$RSSI = -51.3V_{RSSI} - 49.2 \text{ [dBm]} \tag{2}$$

The procedure for our scheme to obtain RSSI measurements will be introduced as follows: Anchor node periodically transmits radio frequency (RF) beacon signal to sensor node, which will be located. During this period, sensor node will constantly sample received signal strength from each anchor nodes orderly and store it for later use. After obtains enough information, we can calculate the target sensor node through our localization scheme by the Pentium-based PC rather than sensor node itself. Then we can employ more sophisticated algorithms to improve location performance.

3 Localization Algorithm

In our localization system, we will not adopt traditional RSSI algorithm but present signal strength difference of arrival (SSDOA) algorithm. When RSSI parameters have been obtained, they are converted into range difference measurements and these measurements can be converted into nonlinear hyperbolic equations. Superficially, there doesn't seem to be any advantage in converting RSS measurements into SSDOA measurements, as we can triangulate the position of the target node using the RSS measurements, directly. However, this may give us some increased accuracy when errors due to multiple signal reflections in pairs of RSS measurements are positively correlated because of having a common signal reflector. The more similar the errors in pairs of RSSs are, the more we can gain by changing them into SSDOAs. After compared the location performance of Fang's algorithm with Chan's algorithm, we will calculate the target sensor node using Chan's algorithm based on mean received signal strength (RSS) measurement to improve the location accuracy [4]. In the paper, we named above means improved-Chan algorithm. The mathematical model of traditional RSSI algorithm will not be introduced in detail here. After briefly introduce mathematical model for SSDOA location algorithms, we will focus on our simulation results.

3.1 Mathematical Model for Hyperbolic SSDOA Equations

A general model for two dimensional (2-D) position location estimation of a source using M anchor nodes is developed. Let (x, y) be the source node location and (X_i, Y_i) be the known location of the i'th anchor node receiver. The range difference between anchor nodes with respect to the anchor node where the signal arrives first, is

$$d_{i,1} = d_i - d_1 = \sqrt{(X_i - x)^2 + (Y_i - y)^2} - \sqrt{(X_1 - x)^2 + (Y_1 - y)^2} \tag{3}$$

Where $d_{i,1}$ is the range difference between the first anchor node and the i'th anchor node, d_1 is the distance between the first anchor node and the source node. This defines the set of nonlinear hyperbolic equations whose solution gives the 2-D coordinates of the target source node.

3.2 Extended Kalman-Filter (EKF) Algorithm

In order to utilize the KF equations in the non-linear case, the non-linear equation has to be linearized. A KF that linearizes about the current state and covariance is referred to as an extended Kalman filter or EKF. So the paper deals with target sensor node location tracking using the Extended Kalman filtering based on RSS measurements. EKF tends to increase the robustness of the state estimation process and reduce the chance that a small deviation from the Gaussian process in the system noise causes a significant negative impact on the solution. However, we lose optimality and our solution will be just sub-optimal. The detailed mathematical procedure for EKF algorithm is presented in [5] [6].

4 Simulation Results and Performance Analysis

As described in Fig.5, assume the three anchor nodes are located at (0, 0), (200, 0), and (100,173), so the distance between arbitrary two anchors R is 200 meter. The parameters of propagation model adopted for our simulation scenario are n=2.3, $PL(d_0)$=-56.6519dB, б=2.3875[7]. We average the sensor location results computed from our scheme over 1000 trials, so we will obtain 1000 RSS measurements. We use a sliding window of 10 samples to compute the mean signal strength on a continuous basis which will be adopted in our improved-Chan algorithm. We study the performance of our algorithm based on Gaussian noise environment. Suppose the speed of target sensor node is very low and can be considered as no relative movement, RSS error caused by target node and all network devices is assumed to be Gaussian distributed with mean 0 and variance 1*i dB (where i=1,2,…5).

As can be seen from the simulation results of Fig.1, the Chan's algorithm achieves better performance than RSSI and Fang algorithms based on indoors LOS environment. The root mean square error increases as variance of the RSS measuring errors increase. From Fig.2, we will sure the location accuracy improved when using improved- Chan algorithm compared with using Chan's algorithm. Furthermore, it can be stated that important improvements in the positioning accuracy are obtained using EKF instead of static estimator. The performance of our scheme exceed traditional RSSI location algorithm from our simulation results.

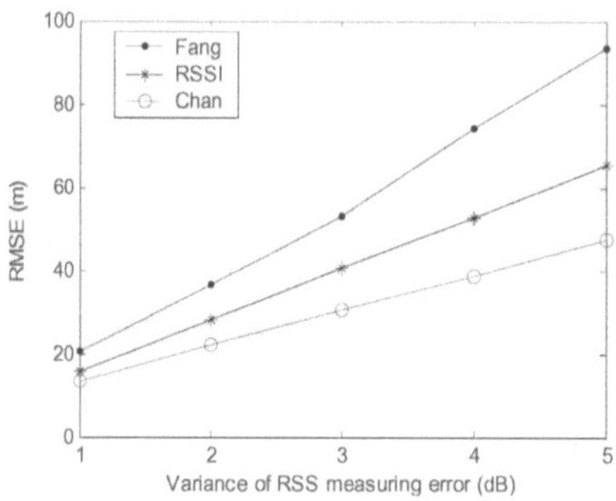

Fig. 1. Position errors of algorithm in LOS environment

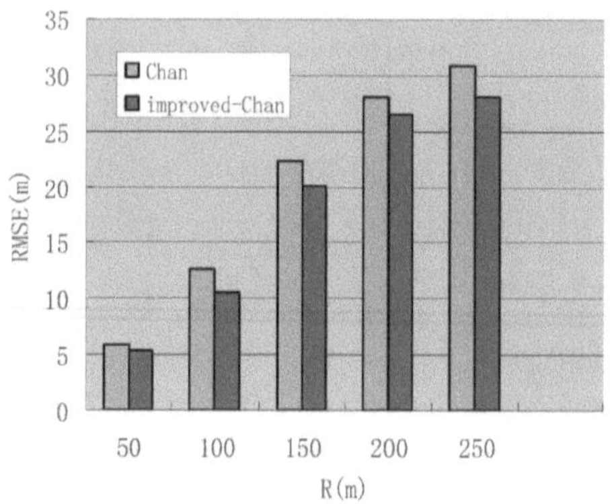

Fig. 2. Analysis localization errors

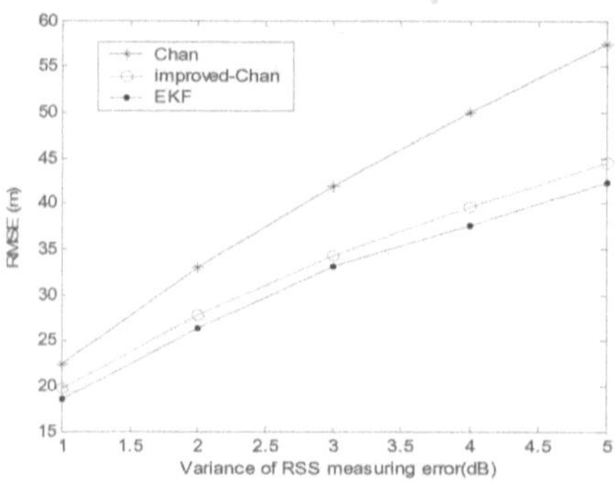

Fig. 3. Comparison of location performance based on different algorithms

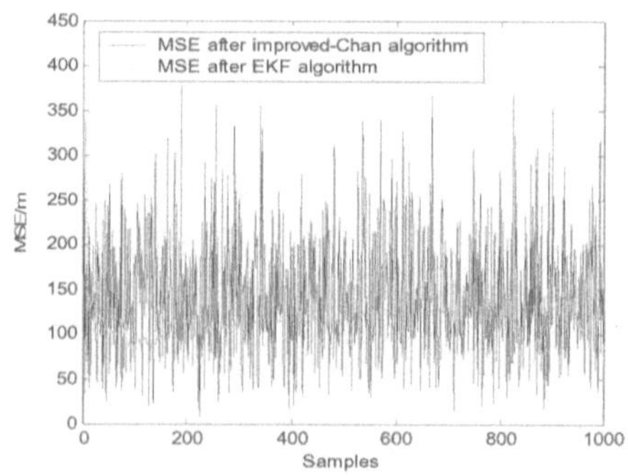

Fig. 4. Comparison of location performance

Absolute Estimation Accuracy: To evaluate estimation accuracy, we report on an experiment with three anchor nodes and one target sensor node, since the visualization of estimation convergence is clearer with a smaller number of sensors.

The three anchor nodes are positioned at (0, *0*) *m*, (10, 0) *m*, (5, 8.6603) *m* in our large boardroom. Fig.6 shows the localization accuracy of our EKF based scheme with approximate 1.16 m. From the observation of our experimental results, we will find when target sensor node close to the center of the triangle which formed by three anchor nodes, the localization accuracy is high. But at some area, the network failed to localize at all.

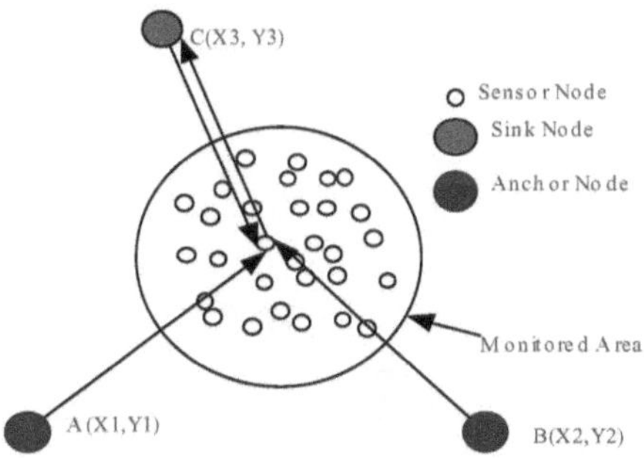

Fig. 5. An example of an indoor sensor networks

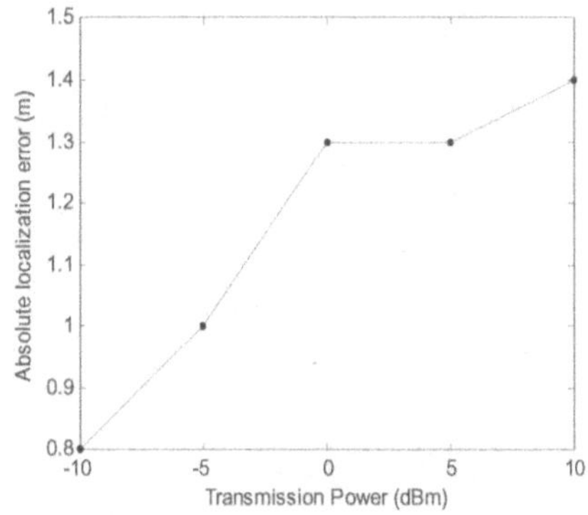

Fig. 6. Localization error for real system

5 Conclusions

In the paper, we presented a novel EKF-based positioning scheme using mean RSS for indoor sensor networks. Our positioning scheme doesn't need sensor node make radio transmission constantly but listen to three beacon signals passively. This efficiently reduces sensor energy cost and also improves using ratio of RF channels. Real experiments in a large indoor boardroom area show that the location accuracy is approximately 1.16m. Now that we have validated our ideas through simulation, implementation and experiment, it can be stated that the approach is effective and obviously has good application foreground in some special indoor sensor networks area.

References

[1] C.Liu and K. Wu.: Sensor Localization with Ring Overlapping Based on Comparison of Received Signal Strength Indicator, Proceedings of The 1st IEEE International Conference on Mobile Ad-hoc and Sensor Systems (MASS04), Fort Lauderdale, Florida, October, 2004

[2] Chen Hongyang, Deng Ping, Xu Yongjun, Li Xiaowei.: A Robust Location Algorithm with Biased Extended Kalman Filtering of TDOA Data for Wireless Sensor Networks, IEEE International Conference on Wireless Communications, Networking and Mobile Computing (WCNM 2005), Wuhan China, September 23-26, 2005.

[3] Thedore S. Rappapport. : Wireless Communications: Principles and Practice, Prentice Hall.
[4] P. Z. Fan, P. Deng and L. Liu.: Radio Location for Cellular Mobile Communications Networks (in Chinese), Publishing House of Electronics Industry, 2002, pp. 52-79.
[5] E. Brookner.: Tracking and Kalman Filtering Made Easy, Ch.2, Wiley, 1998.
[6] Torrieri. D. J.: Statistical theory of passive location systems, IEEE Trans. on AES. Vol. AES-20. No.2. pp. 183-198. Mar.1984.
[7] K. Sohrabi, B. Manriquez, and G. Pottie. : Near ground wideband channel measurement in 800-1000 mhz, IEEE 49th Vehicular Technology Conference, 1:571–574, March 1999.

Threshold Authenticated Key Configuration Scheme Based on Multi-layer Clustering in Mobile Ad Hoc*

Keun-Ho Lee[1], Sang-Bum Han[1], Heyi-Sook Suh[2], Chong-Sun Hwang[1], and SangKeun Lee[1]

[1] Department of Computer Science and Engineering, Korea University,
5-ga, Anam-dong, Sungbuk-gu, Seoul 136-701, Korea
{root1004, topflite, hwang, yalphy}@korea.ac.kr,
[2] Ministry of Education & Human Resources Development, Information Technology,
77-6, Sejong-ro, Jongro-gu, Seoul 110-760, Korea
suh@moe.go.kr

Abstract. In this paper, we describe a secure cluster-routing protocol based on clustering scheme in ad hoc networks. This work provides scalable, threshold authentication scheme in ad hoc networks. We present detailed security threats against ad hoc multi-layer routing protocols. Our proposed protocol designs an end-to-end authentication protocol that relies on mutual trust between nodes in other clusters. The scheme strategy takes advantage of threshold authenticated key configuration in large ad hoc networks. We propose an authentication scheme that uses certificates containing an asymmetric key using the threshold cryptography scheme, thereby reducing the computational overhead and successfully defeating all identified attacks.

1 Introduction

Securing an ad hoc routing protocol presents challenges because each user brings its own mobile unit to the network, without the centralized policy or control of a traditional network. Mobile ad hoc networks security issues have became a central concern and are increasingly important. Ad hoc networks cannot be used in practice if they are not secure, because ad hoc networks are subject to various attacks. Wireless communication links can be intercepted without noticeable effort, and communication protocols in all layers are vulnerable to specific attacks [4]. Studies of secure cluster routing based on multiple layers in ad hoc networks have been carried out using [4-6].

In this paper, we demonstrate possible ways to exploit ad hoc routing protocols, define various security environments, and offer a secure solution with *'Threshold Authenticated Key Configuration Scheme'* (TAKCS). We detail the ways to exploit protocols that are under consideration by [1-6].

Our proposed scheme detects and protects against malicious actions by multi-layer parties in one particular ad hoc environment. We propose an authentication protocol

* This work was done as a part of Information & Communication Fundamental Technology Research Program, supported by Ministry of Information & Communication of Korea.

H.T. Shen et al. (Eds.): APWeb 2006, LNCS 3842, pp. 321 – 329, 2006.

that uses certificates containing a Diffie-Hellman key agreement and a multi-layer architecture so that CCH(Control Cluster Head) is achieved using the threshold scheme, so that the number of essential encryptions reduces the computational overhead and successfully defeats all identified attacks.

Our performance analysis show that TAKCS has minimal performance costs in terms of processing and networking overhead for the increased security that it offers. While this basic idea has been proposed before [2,4,5], we are the first to apply it to a clustered network. Our scheme addresses issues of authentication and multi-layer security architecture and helps to adapt the complexity to the scalability of mobile end systems. Moreover, an extensive evaluation involves the reduction of CH traffic using for threshold authenticated key configuration scheme of the CCH.

We first overview cluster routing protocols in ad hoc networks, and threshold cryptosystems, as well as related work for securing ad hoc networks. We describes our security concept in detail as a CCH construction algorithm

In this paper, we show how our proposed TAKCS reduces the computational overhead and successfully defeats all identified attacks in a large networks area.

2 CH and CCH Selection Algorithm

2.1 CH Selection Algorithm

The selection of the CH and CCH uses the modification of the DMAC algorithm in [3]. The DMAC in our clustering algorithm includes only two conditions to change the CH.

Here, we use the same two types of message used in the DCA(namely, Ch(v) and Join(v, u))[3]. In the following we use Cluster(v) and Clusterhead to indicated the set of nodes in the cluster whose clusterhead is v and the clusterhead of a node's cluster, respectively. v's Boolean variable Ch(v) is set to true if v has sent a Ch message. Its variables Clusterhead, Ch(-), and Cluster(-) are initialized to nil, false and Ø, respectively. The following is the description of the two M-procedures as executed at each node v. On receiving a Ch message from a neighbor u, node v checks if it has received from all its neighbors z such that $w_z > w_u$, a Join(z,x) message. In this case, v will not receive a Ch message from these z, and u is the node with the biggest weight in v's neighborhood that has sent a Ch message.

At the clustering set up, or when a node *v* is added to the network, it executes the procedure CH selection in order to determine its own role. If its neighbors include at least one CH with a greater weight, then *v* will join it. Otherwise it will be a CH[3].

At the clustering set up, or when a node v is added to the network, it executes the procedure Initialize in order to determine its own role. If among its neighbors there is at least a clusterhead with bigger weight, then v will join it. Otherwise it will be a clusterhead. Notice that a neighbor with a bigger weight that has not decided its role yet, will eventually send a message. If this message is a Ch message, then v will affiliate with the new clusterhead. When a neighbor u becomes a clusterhead, on receiving the corresponding Ch message, node v checks if it has to affiliate with u, it checks whether w_n is bigger than the weight of v's clusterhead or not. In this case, independently of its current role, v joins u's cluster[3].

PROCEDURE CH selection;	PROCEDURE CCH selection;

Initialize
begin
if $\{z \in, (v) : w_z \rangle w_v \wedge Ch(z)\} \neq \phi$
then begin
$x := \max_{w_z > w_v} \{z : Ch(z)\}$;
send Join (*v, x*);
$ClusterHead := x$
end
else begin
send *Ch(v)*
$Ch(v) :=$ true;
$ClusterHead := v$;
$Cluster(v) := \{v\}$
end
end;
Repeat – *On receiving ClusterHead(u)*
begin
if $(w_u > w_{ClusterHead})$ then begin
send Join(*v, u*));
$ClusterHead := u$;
if *Ch(v)* then *Ch(v)* := false
end
end;
	begin
	if Ch(v)
	then if $z = v$
	then $Cluster(v) := Cluster(v) \cup \{u\}$
	else if $u \in Cluster(v)$
	then
	$Cluster(v) := Cluster(v) \setminus \{u\}$
	else if $ControlClusterHead = u$
	then
	if
	$\{z \in, (v) : w_z \rangle w_v \wedge Ch(z)\} \neq \phi$
	then begin
	$x := \max_{w_z > w_v} \{z : Ch(z)\}$;
	send Join (v, x);
	$ControlClusterHead := x$
	end
	else begin
	send $CH(v)$
	$Ch(v) :=$ true;
	$ContronlClusterHead := v$;
	$Cluster(v) := \{v\}$
	end
	end

2.2 CCH Selection Algorithm

On receiving the message Join(u,z), the behavior of node v depends on whether it is a clusterhead or not. In the affirmative, v has to check if either u is joining its cluster(z=v : in this case, u is added to Cluster(v)) or if u belonged to its cluster and is now joining another cluster(z≠v: in this case, u is removed from Cluster(v)). If v is not a clusterhead, it has to check if u was its clusterhead. Only if this is the case, v has to decide its role: It will join the biggest clusterhead x in its neighborhood such that $w_x > w_v$ if such a node exists. Otherwise, it will be a CCH(Control ClusterHead). The CCH is v. The CCH roles need slowly mobility, lowest of ID and enough of Energy in CHs. u parameter contents included mobility, ID and energy.

3 End-to-End Threshold Authenticated Key Configuration

We use the notation listed to describe the proposed scheme this paper as the following:

Table 1. Variables and notation used in TAKCS

- CH_A : Cluster Head in cluster A
- ID_X : Identity of X
- $K_{S,CH}$: Secret key shared with S and CH
- $Time_1$: Current time
- S : Member node in CH_A
- X : Member node in CH_B
- K_{A+} : Public-key of node A
- $cert_A$: Certificate belonging to node A
- e : Certificate expiration time
- N_A : Nonce issued by node A

In our case, the n CHs of the key management service share the ability to sign certificates. For the service to tolerate t compromised CHs, we use an $(n, t+1)$ threshold cryptography scheme and divide the private key, k, of the service into n shares (CH_A, CH_B, CH_C), assigning one share to each CH. We call (CH_A, CH_B, CH_C) sharing of K. Figure 1 illustrates how the service is configured.

Given a service consisting of three *CHs*, let K/k be the public/private key pair of the service. Using a (3,2) threshold cryptography scheme, each CH_i gets a share s_i of the private key k.

For a message m, CH_i can generate partial signatures $PS(m, s_i)$ using its share s_i. The correct CH_A and CH_C both generate partial signatures and forward the signatures to a combiner, c. Although CH_B fails to submit a partial signature, c can generate the signature $(m)_k$ of m signed by CH using the private k.

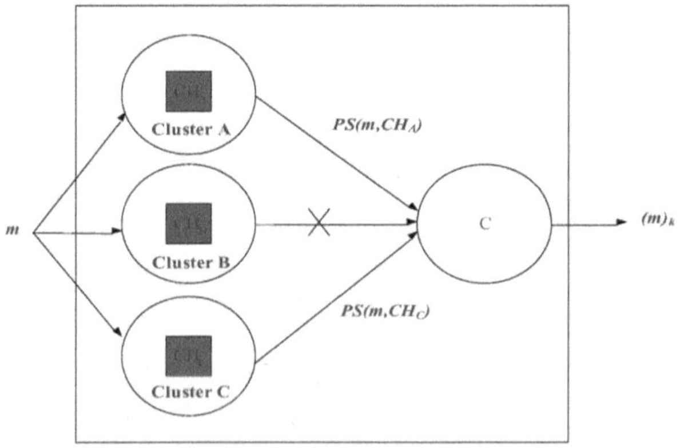

Fig. 1. Threshold authenticated key configuration signature

TAKCS consists of a preliminary certification processes, a mandatory end-to-end authentication step, and an optional second step that provides threshold cryptosystem. The optional step is considerably more reduce overhead than providing end-to-end authentication of other clustering routing protocol.

CCH requires the use of a trusted certificate server *T*[5]. All CHs receive a certificate from *CCH*. A *CH* certificate has the following form:

$$CCH \rightarrow CH_A : cert_{CHA} = [ID_{CHA} \,||\, K_{CCH+} \,||\, e \,||\, Time_1]$$

The certificate contains the ID address of the CH, the public key of the *CCH*, timestamp $Time_1$ for when the certificate was created, and time e at which the certificate expires. These variables are concatenated and signed by the *CCH*. Every *CH* must maintain fresh certificates with the trusted server and must know the *CCH* public key. CH_A sends a request message with a timestamp to *CCH* for a public key request to communicate with CH_B. If sending an encrypted message *CCH* uses a private key that CH_A decrypts using the *CCH* public key.

So far, we have considered security services for communication from one cluster member to a cluster head. In an ad hoc network environment, securing the end-to-end path from one mobile user to another is the primary concern. The end-to-end security service minimizes the interference from intermediate nodes, especially malicious nodes. In this section, we present secure end-to-end authentication using threshold authenticated key configuration. The end-to-end key exchange progress is described in Figure 2. The end-to-end key exchange uses the Diffie-Hellman key as the public key.

Figure 2 shows the authentication process for multiple layers in large ad hoc networks. The CCH authenticates CHs. There are 7 steps required to implement TAKCS. Figure 2 shows the end-to-end authentication between CHs communicating after authentication using the CCH.

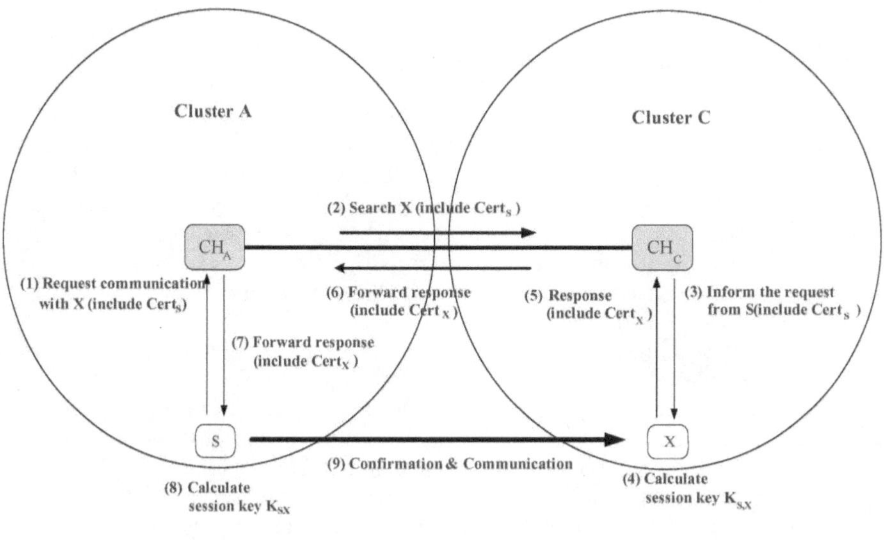

Fig. 2. End-to-end authentication between clusters after the CHs are authenticated from the CCH

First, using a previously shared secret key K_{S,CH_A}, *S* sends a message to CH_A requesting communication with *X*. Since ID_s is encrypted using K_{S,CH_A}, other nodes except S and CH_A do not know the node with which S wishes to communicate. As $Cert_S$ and N_S are also encrypted, they can be transferred securely.

Upon receiving the request, CH_A checks that S is a member. If so, this equals the progress leaving out steps 2 and 6 (*i.e.*, $CH_A = CH_C$). Otherwise, CH_A asks the other cluster heads where X is using the CH_C public key, which was previously established in step 3 between cluster heads. Let X be a member of CH_B.

In step 3, X is informed of the request from S to communicate with him. CH_C sends S's certificate along with N_{CH_C}. Upon deriving the public key for S from the certificate, X calculates the session key $K_{X,S} = (PK_S)^{k_X} \bmod p$, which will be shared between S and X. X uses $K_{S,X}$ in step 4 to let CH_C know that it accepts S's request for communication. CH_C and CH_A pass to S the part of the message in step 4 that contains X's confirmation using $K_{S,X}$. CH_C and CH_A also forward X's certificate to S. Upon receiving a message including X's certificate, S can calculate the session key $K_{S,X} = (PK_X)^{k_S} \bmod p$ using PK_X derived from $Cert_X$.

Finally, S and X share the same secret key, and S communicates with X by sending back X's nonce encrypted using the shared key $K_{S,X}$. We propose a reliable algorithm that runs strong authentication for each packet. This time, *CCH* performs authentication for all *CH*s, and *CH* authenticates the certification authority (CA) for all nodes in a cluster. The *CH* key is used to exchange the session key secretly. Therefore, all the messages described above can be forwarded for reference by appending them to routing packets when a route is discovered.

4 Simulation and Performance Analysis

4.1 Experiment of Energy and Mobility Becoming a CCH

We used tools within MATLAB to simulate the algorithm described in Section 3 for networks with varying node density (λ) and different values of the parameters p and k. Each node in the network chooses to become a CH with probability p and advertises itself as a CH to the nodes within its radio range. This advertisement is forwarded to al the nodes that are no more than k hops away from the CH. Any node that receives such advertisements and is not itself a CH joins the cluster of the closest CH. Any node that is neither a CH nor has joined any cluster itself becomes a CH. Because we have limited the advertisement forwarding to k hops, if a node does not receive a CH advertisement within time duration t (where t units is the time required for data from the CH to reach any node k hops away) it can infer that it is not within k hops of any volunteer CH and hence become a forced CH. Moreover, this limit on the number of hops allows the CH to schedule periodic transmissions to the processing center. To generate the network for each simulation experiment, the location of each node is found by generation two random numbers uniformly distributed in [0, 2a], where 2a is the length of a side of the square area in which the nodes are distributed. In all of these experiments, the communication range of each node was assumed to be 1 unit. To verify that the optimal values of the parameters p and k of our algorithm computed according to [1] formula (11) and (13) do minimized the energy spent in the system, we simulated our clustering algorithm on node networks with 50, 100 and 200 nodes distributed uniformly in a square area of 10 square units.

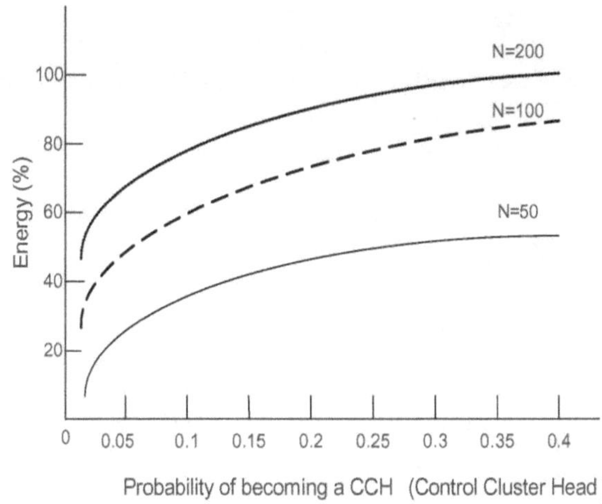

Fig. 3. Total energy in a network of n nodes distributed in an area of 10 square units for different values of probability of become a CCH in algorithm in Section 2

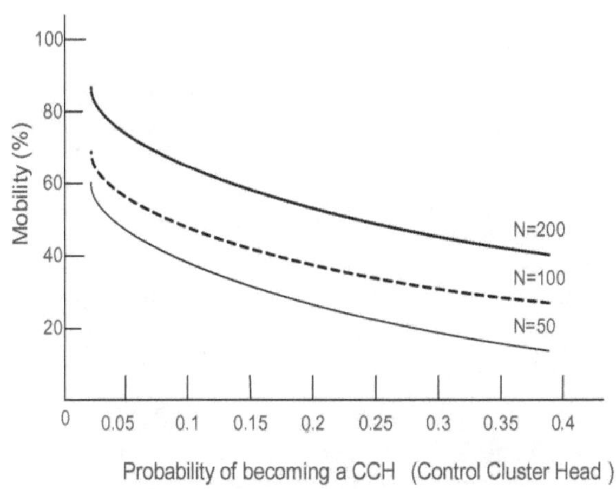

Fig. 4. Mobility in a network of n nodes distributed in an area of 10 square units for different values of probability of become a CCH in algorithm in Section 2

We have, without loss of generality, assumed that the cost of transmitting 1 unit of data is 1 unit of energy. The processing center is assumed to be located at the center of the square area. For the first set of simulation experiments, we considered a range of values for the probability p of becoming a CH in the algorithm proposed in Section 2. For each of these probability values, we computed the maximum number of hops k allowed in a cluster using (13) and used these values for the maximum number of hops allowed in a cluster in the simulations. We simulated in a cluster in the simulations. We simulated the clustering algorithm 100 times for each density and each of the probability values and used the average energy consumption over the 100 experiments to plot the graph in Figure 3, 4.

4.2 Security Analysis of the TAKCS

In this section, we compare the efficiency properties of the existing CCH key establishment protocol and our proposed scheme. We also compare end-to-end security and move distance within a cluster. The efficiency numbers for existing solutions are given in tables for each protocol. None of the existing solutions achieve end-to-end security. In TAKCS, variable *c* is the number of CHs. As TAKCS also establishes authentication based on a trust layer, it also achieves end-to-end security.

We evaluated the performance of our protocol and identified the advantages and limitations of the proposed approach. The CH establishes a member node that is worthy of trust by the members of a CH. Falsehood certification in the certification process can be achieved. TAKCS is a little more stable for certification of CH using CCH and has fewer processing operations. TAKCS is superior for large networks as it was designed for use in such networks. The TAKCS protocol has strong security as it uses the CCH to obtain a higher level of security than other clustering routing protocol.

An analysis of its stability verified its authentication, efficiency, safety and scalability. Authentication and non-repudiation use a cryptographic certificate. Each node receives a certificate from the CH.

We evaluated three performance metrics:

- Unauthorized participation: TAKCS participation accepts only packets that have been signed with a certified key issued by a trusted authority. There are many mechanisms for authenticating users to a trusted certificate authority. The trusted authority is also a single point of failure attack.
- Spoofed Route Signaling: Since only the source node can sign using its own private key, nodes cannot spoof other nodes in route instantiation. Similarly, reply packets include the destination node's certificate and signature, ensuring that only the destination can respond to route discovery.
- Reply Attacks: Reply attacks are prevented by including a nonce and a timestamp with the routing message.

TAKCS minimizes changes in the certificate process of cluster networks. The analysis of scalability verified the authentication, efficiency, safety, and scalability of the method.

Protocol Analysis

We need to show that the above protocol is an TAKCS.

Lemma 1: the protocol described in Section 3 is designed for TAKCS.

Proof: the protocol can be performed as follows: Receiver CH_C authenticates $ID_S \| ID_{CH_A} \| Cert_S \| N_S$ for inter-cluster. Sender CH_A sends *CCH* including $ID_{CH_A} \| ID_{CH_C} \| time_1 \| N_{CH_A}$. TAKCS further improves the stability by the use of a nonce. TAKCS can reduce system energy use by dividing the parts to be handled in each *CH*. The *CCH* offers safe authentication of each node through management of the *CH*s.

Computation costs : The computation costs are calculated as $K_{S,X} = (PK_X)^{k_s} \bmod p$, and our protocol uses an encryption/decryption protocol that requires a total of 1 operation of $K_{S,X} = (PK_X)^{k_s} \bmod p$, which can be computed efficiently using the standard TAKCS. The CCH is achieved using the threshold scheme, thereby reducing the computation overhead because the ARAN protocol step has 12 step but the AMCAN protocol step has 7 step.

5 Conclusion

We showed ways to exploit two protocols that are under consideration for clustering-based routing protocols. Clustering-based protocols are efficient in terms of network performance. Our proposed protocol, called TAKCS, detects and protects against malicious actions across multiple layers and by peers in one particular ad hoc environment. In this paper, we examined the certification process for clustering routing protocols in ad hoc networks, and designed a certification protocol for TAKCS. The basic idea of TAKCS is to propose a CCH that has top-layer authority. We propose an authentication protocol that uses certificates containing an asymmetric key and a multi-layer architecture so that the CCH is achieved using the threshold scheme, thereby reducing the computational overhead and successfully defeating all identified attacks. We also use a more extensive area, such as a CCH, using an identification protocol to build a highly secure, highly available authentication service.

References

1. Seema Bandyopadhyay, Edward J. Coyle, "Minimizing communication costs in hierarchically-clustered networks of wireless sensors", *Elsevier, Computer Networks* 44, 2004
2. E. M. Belding-Royer, "Multi-level hierarchies for scalable ad hoc routing," *Wireless Networks,* Vol.9, no. 5, pp. 461-478, September 2003
3. S. Basagni, "Distributed clustering for ad hoc networks," in *Proc of the 1999 International Symposium on Parallel Architectures, Algorithms, and Networks(ISPAN '99)*,pp. 310-315, Fremantle, Australia, June. 1999.
4. M. Bechler, H.-J. Hof, D. Kraft, F. Rahlke, L. Wolf, "A Cluster-Based security architecture for Ad Hoc networks," in *Proc. 23rd Annual Joint Conference of IEEE Computer and Communications Societies (INFOCOM'04)*, vol. 4, pp.2393-2403, Hong Kong, March. 2004.
5. K. Sanzgiri, B. Dahill, B.N. Levine, C. Shields, E.M. Belding-Royer, "A secure routing protocol for ad hoc networks," in *Proc 10th IEEE International Conference on Network Protocols (ICNP '02)*, pp. 78-87, Paris, France, November 2002.
6. A.C.-F. Chan, "Distributed symmetric key management for mobile ad hoc networks," in *Proc. 23rd Annual Joint Conference of IEEE Computer and Communications Societies (INFOCOM'04)*, vol. 4, pp. 2414-2424, Hong Kong, March 2004
7. L. Zhou and Z. J. Hass, "Securing ad hoc network," *IEEE Network*, vol. 13, no. 6, pp. 24-30, 1999

Connecting Sensor Networks with TCP/IP Network

Shu Lei, Wang Jin, Xu Hui, Jinsung Cho*, and Sungyoung Lee

Department of Computer Engineering,
Kyung Hee University, Korea
{sl8132, wangjin, xuhui, sylee}@oslab.khu.ac.kr,
chojs@khu.ac.kr

Abstract. Wireless sensor networks cannot have meaningful work without connecting with TCP/IP based network. In this paper, we analyze and compare all the existing solutions for connecting sensor networks with TCP/IP network, then based on the analysis result we present the basic design principle and key idea for connecting sensor networks with TCP/IP network. After comparing with related researches we claim that our solution can cover most of the benefits of related researches.

1 Introduction

In the desired 4G paradigm, all kinds of heterogeneous wireless networks and current existing IP based Internet should be integrated into one pervasive network to provide transparent accessibility for users. Sensor networks as a family member of wireless networks should also be integrated. In the new appeared pervasive computing paradigm, by using ubiquitous sensor networks as the underlying infrastructure, middleware which is considered as the key solution to realize the ubiquitous computing paradigm has been invested in many famous research projects, such as Gaia, Context Toolkit, Aura, TOTA, etc. Ubiquitous sensor networks play an important role in our daily life to provide the seamless pervasive accessibility to users. Therefore, in this paper we propose a novel gateway based approach to connect sensor networks with TCP/IP network. In next section, we present related researches. In section 3, presents the key idea and detailed description of our *Virtual – IP Gateway*. In section 4, we present the comparison with related researches, and conclude this paper in section 5.

2 Related Work

***Gateway-based approach*:** This is the common solution to integrate sensor networks with an external network by using *Application-level Gateways* [1] as the inter face. Different protocols in both networks are translated in the application layer as the Figure 1 shows. The advantage is: the communication protocol used in the sensor

* Corresponding author.

H.T. Shen et al. (Eds.): APWeb 2006, LNCS 3842, pp. 330 – 334, 2006.

networks may be chosen freely. However, the drawback is: Internet users cannot directly access any special sensor node. Another research work, Delay Tolerant Network [2], also follows this *Gateway-based approach*. The key different point from [1] is that a *Bundle Layer* is deployed in both TCP/IP network and non-TCP/IP network protocol stacks to store and forward packets, as Figure 2 shows. It is very easy to integrate with different heterogeneous wireless networks by deploying this *Bundler Layer* into their protocol stacks. But the drawback also comes from the deployment of *Bundle Layer* into existing protocols, which is a costly job.

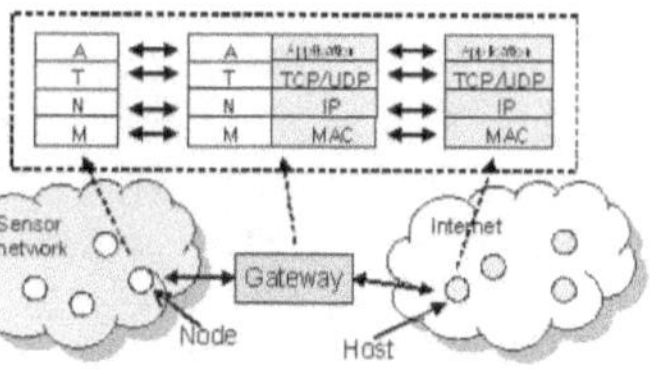

Fig. 1. Application-level Gateway

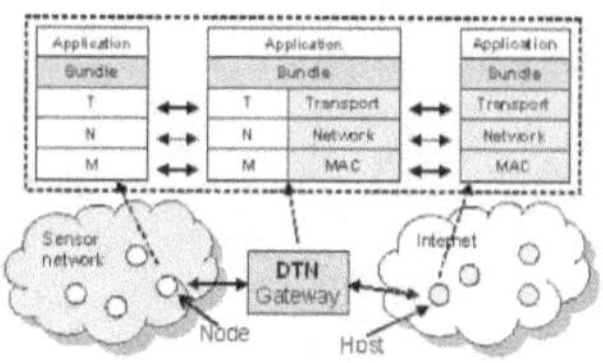

Fig. 2. Delay Tolerant Network

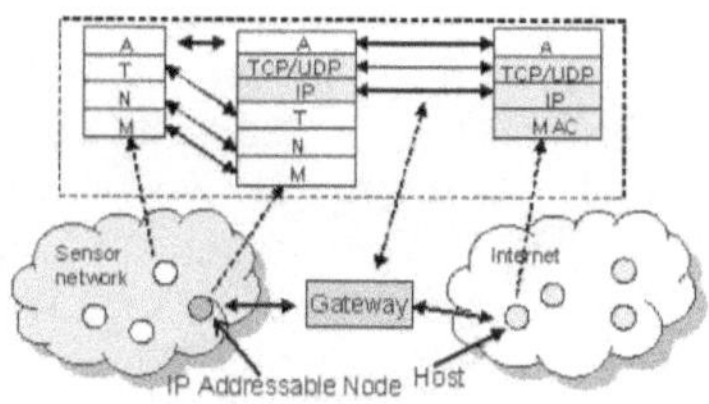

Fig. 3. TCP/IP overlay sensor networks

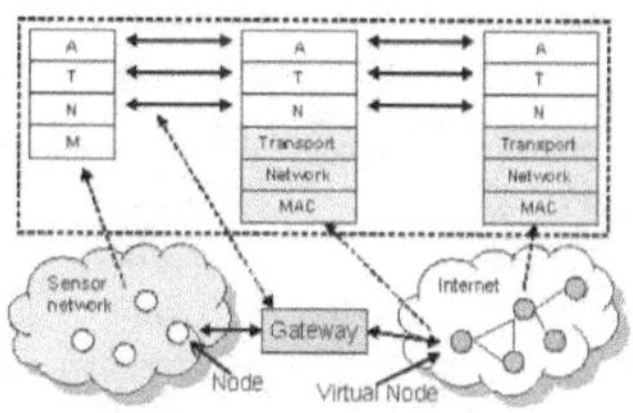

Fig. 4. Sensor networks overlay TCP/IP

***Overlay-based approach*:** There are two kinds of overlay-based approaches for connecting sensor networks with TCP/IP network: 1) *TCP/IP overlay sensor networks*; 2) *sensor networks overlay TCP/IP*. Research work in [3] provides a solution to implement IP protocol stack on sensor nodes which is named as **u-IP**. The key advantage is: Internet host can directly send commands to some particular nodes in sensor networks via IP address. However, this **u-IP** can only be deployed on some sensor nodes which have enough processing capabilities. We show **u-IP** approach in Figure 3. The *sensor networks overlay TCP/IP* is proposed in [4]. As Figure 4 shows, sensor networks protocol stack is deployed over the TCP/IP and each Internet host is considered as a virtual sensor node. By doing so, Internet host can directly communicate with sensor node and Internet host will process packets exactly as sensor nodes do. The problem of [4] is: it has to deploy an additional protocol stack into the Internet host, which brings more protocol header overhead to TCP/IP network.

3 Virtual – IP Gateway

After having these aforementioned analyses, we create our key idea Virtual – IP Gateway: Basing on Node-Centric or Location-Centric communication paradigm, mapping the node label (ID) or location address with IP address in gateway. The IP address will not be physically deployed on sensor node, but just store in gateway as a virtual IP address for Internet users. In this *Virtual – IP Gateway*, there are two major components to translate packets for both sides, as Figure 5 shows: *1) TCP/IP Network -> Sensor Networks (T->S) Packet Translation,* translating packets from TCP/IP network into the packet format of sensor networks; *2) Sensor Networks -> TCP/IP Network (S->T) Packet Translation*, translating packets from sensor networks into the packet format of TCP/IP network. The packet format of original *T->S Packet* has four major fields: 1) *User IP*, used to represent the IP address of user's who sends this packet; 2) *Sensor IP/Gateway IP*, used to represent the destination of this packet, which can be the gateway IP address or some special sensor node's IP address; 3) *Q/O*, used to represent packet type: *Query Command* or *Operation Command*; 4) *Complicated/Simple Data Request / Operation Command*, used to represent the real content that is carried by this packet. The packet format of created *T->S Packet* has the following four major fields: 1) *Gateway ID/Location*, used to represent the ID or location address of Gateway, which sends the packet to sensor networks; 2) *Sensor ID/Location*, used to represent the ID or location of data source; 3) *Q/O*, used to represent packet type: *Query Command* or *Operation Command*; 4) *Complicated/Simple Data Request / Operation Command*, used to represent the real content that is carried by this packet. The *Query Command* is used to request data from sensor networks, it can be as simple as query data just from one special sensor node, or it can be as complicated as query data from many sensor nodes at the same time. *Operation Command* is used to remote control one special sensor node's working status. Similarly, the packet format of *S->T Packet* also has four major fields: 1) *Sensor ID/Location*, used to represent the ID or location of data source; 2) *Gateway ID/Location*, used to represent the ID or location address of Gateway, which is the destination of this packet; 3) *D/A*, used to represent packet type: *Data Packet* or *Acknowledgement Packet*; 4) *Data/Acknowledgement*, used to represent real content carried by this packet. The packet format of created *S->T Packet* has the following four major fields: 1) *Gateway IP*, used to represent the IP address of Gateway, which sends the packet to TCP/IP network; 2) *User IP*, used to represent the IP address of receiver's; 3) *D/A*, used to represent packet type: *Data Packet* or *Acknowledgement Packet*; 4) *Data/Acknowledgement*, used to represent real content carried by this packet. A *Node ID/Location Address* is the node ID or location address of a sensor node. A *Data Information* is a description about what kind of data can be provide by this sensor node. An *IPv6 Address* is the assigned IP address for this special sensor node. *Virtual – IP Gateway* will actively collect *Node ID/Location Address*, *Data Information* for all sensor nodes, and also actively assign *IPv6 Address* for these sensor nodes. All these information are stored in a database which physically locating in the *Virtual – IP Gateway* and mapped with each other.

TCP/IP Network -> Sensor Networks Packet Translation: After receiving packets from TCP/IP network, there are two ways to translate them into the packet format that used by sensor networks: 1) *Data Information Based Discovery*; 2) *IPv6 Address Based Discovery*. Gateway will analyze these received packets based on the field "*Q/O*" to categorize them into *Query Command* and *Operation Command*. If a packet is an *Operation Command*, then gateway can base on the *Sensor IP* to search the database to find out the corresponding *Node ID/Location Address* of this sensor node through the mapping between *IPv6 Address* and *Node ID/Location Address*. If a packet is a *Query Command*, then gateway can base on *Complicated/Simple Data Request* to search the database to find out the corresponding *Node ID/Location Address* of this sensor node through the mapping between *Data Information* and *Node ID/Location Address*. After knowing *Node ID/Location Address* of this sensor node, we can easily create the new packet for sensor networks. Before sending created packet to sensor networks, we backup this new *T->S packet*, and map it with the original *T->S packet* in gateway. These saved packets will be used when we translate packets that come from sensor networks into the packet format of TCP/IP network.

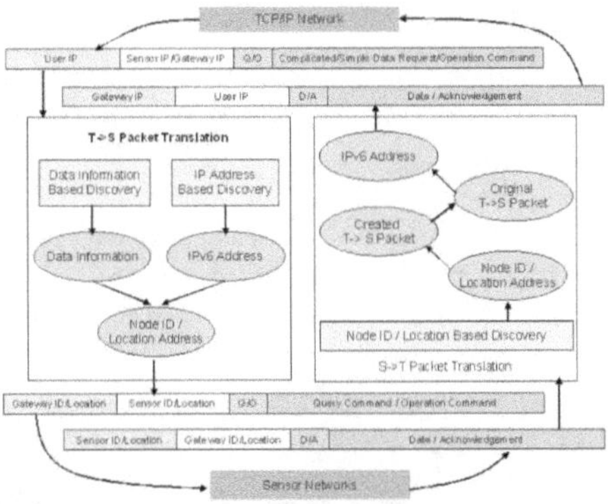

Fig. 5. Architecture of virtual – IP gateway

Sensor Networks -> TCP/IP Network Packet Translation: After receiving the *S->T Packet* from sensor networks, gateway first bases on packet's *Sensor ID/Location* to find out the created *T->S Packet*, then through the mapping between the created *T->S Packet* and the original *T->S Packet*, gateway can easily find out the original *T->S Packet*. By analyzing the original *T->S Packet*, gateway can get the *User IP*, and then create the new *S->T Packet*. Before sending this new *S->T Packet*, gateway will delete the corresponding original and created *T->S Packets* to save the storage space of the database.

4 Comparison with Related Researches

A table based comparison with related researches is essentially necessary to prove that our solution can cover most of the benefit of related researches, as Figure 6 shows. After the integration of sensor networks and TCP/IP network, we can still keep the consistency with the IP based working model by hiding the sensor ID. Because in the view of Internet users, the sensor networks is IP based, they don't need to know which kind of routing protocol is used in sensor networks. Since we only deploy virtual IP addresses in gateway, rather than bring any modification to sensor networks protocols, sensor networks can still freely choose the optimized routing protocol which is *Node-Centric* or *Location-Centric* based. Furthermore, Internet users can easily and directly access some special sensor nodes via *virtual IP ad*

	Application level gateways	Delay Tolerant Network	TCP/IP overlay sensor networks	Sensor networks overlay TCP/IP	Virtual IP
Consistent with Internet working model	No	No	Yes	No	Yes
Transparent for Internet users	Yes	Yes	Yes	No	Yes
Freely choose routing protocol in sensor networks	Yes	Yes	No	Yes	Yes
Directly accessibility some special sensor node	No	No	Yes	Yes	Yes
Easy to integrate different sensor networks	No	Yes	No	Yes	Yes

Fig. 6. Comparison with related researches

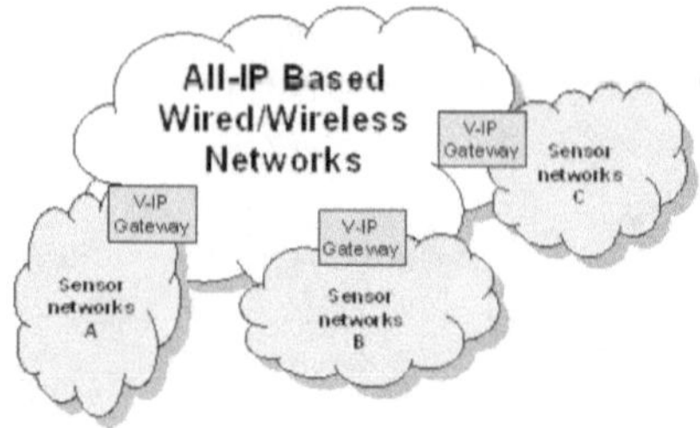

Fig. 7. Integration of Several sensor networks

dresses. Sensor networks which are physically located in different locations may use totally different routing protocols for their specific applications, as Figure 7 shows. If these sensor networks have gateways which have *virtual IP addresses*, then it is very easy to integrate them into one virtual network without modification on existing protocols.

5 Conclusion

Sensor networks as a family member of wireless networks should be integrated with TCP/IP network to provide meaningful services. In this paper we present a new solution to connecting ubiquitous sensor networks with TCP/IP network. By comparison with related researches we claim that our new solution can cover most of the benefits of related researches.

Acknowledgement

This work was supported by the Korea Research Foundation Grant funded by the Korean Government (MOEHRD)"(KRF-2005-003-D00205)

References

1. Z. Z. Marco, K. Bhaskar, "Integrating Future Large-scale Wireless Sensor Networks with the Internet", *USC Computer Science Technical Report CS 03-792*, 2003.
2. K. Fall, "A Delay-Tolerant Network Architecture for Challenged Internets". *In Proceedings of the SIGCOMM 2003 Conference*, 2003
3. 6. A. Dunkels, J. Alonso, T. Voigt, H. Ritter, J. Schiller, "Connecting Wireless Sensornets with TCP/IP Networks", In *Proceedings of WWIC2004*, Germany, February 2004.
4. H. Dai, R. Han, "Unifying Micro Sensor Networks with the Internet via Overlay Networking", in *Proc. IEEE Emnets-I*, Nov. 2004.

Key Establishment and Authentication Mechanism for Secure Sensor Networks*

Inshil Doh and Kijoon Chae

Dept. of Computer Science and Engineering, Ewha Womans University
isdoh@ewhain.net, kjchae@ewha.ac.kr

Abstract. For secure sensor network communication, we propose a key establishment mechanism applying polynomial-based key predistribution scheme under the clustered sensor network architecture, and propose authentication mechanism. Every pair of neighboring nodes can calculate its own pairwise key using polynomial shares predistributed. Gateway nodes interconnecting the clusters play the role of stepping stones. For hop-by-hop authentication, every node adds MAC computed using pairwise key between its upstream node and itself. Broadcast authentication can be achieved using one-time digital signature.

1 Introduction

Distributed sensor networks are expected to be the core technology for ubiquitous computing, and have received a lot of attention recently. Sensor networks usually consist of a large number of ultra-small wireless devices called sensor nodes. A sensor node is battery powered and equipped with integrated sensors, data processing capabilities, small storages, and short-range radio communications. They can be used to gather a lot of information in various environments after being distributed in great scale. However, because of their constraints, they are very vulnerable to various attacks especially when they are deployed in hostile area[1]. Sensor networks have a lot of applications, most of which are dependent on the secure operation of sensor networks. Security services such as authentication and key management are critical to secure the communications between sensor nodes especially in hostile environments. In this paper, we propose a pairwise key establishment and an authentication mechanism based on sensor network architecture exploiting clustering technology for secure sensor communication.

The rest of this paper is organized as follows. Section 2 gives an overview of key predistribution schemes and authentication techniques related to our research. Assumptions and hierarchical architecture for our mechanism are given

* This research was supported by the MIC(Ministry of Information and Communication), Korea, under the ITRC(Information Technology Research Center) support program supervised by the IITA(Institute of Information Technology Assessment).

H.T. Shen et al. (Eds.): APWeb 2006, LNCS 3842, pp. 335–344, 2006.

in section 3. Section 4 describes our proposal for key predistribution and establishment. Authentication mechanism is presented in section 5. Security and overhead analyses are described in section 6. In section 7, we conclude the paper and present some future research directions.

2 Related Work

In the basic random key predistribution scheme by L. Eschenauer and V. Gligor[2], each sensor node receives a random subset of keys from the key pool before deployment. Every pair of nodes is able to establish pairwise key through direct key setup using common key and through path keys with nodes in their vicinity whom they did not happen to share keys with in their key rings. By doing this, two sensors can have a certain probability to share at least one key. These approach has some limitations which a small number of compromised sensors may reveal a large fraction of pairwise keys shared between non-compromised sensors, and the maximum supported network size is strictly limited by the storage capacity for pairwise keys and the desired probability to share a key between two sensors[2].

D. Liu, P. Ning developed a framework to predistribute pairwise keys using bivariate polynomials and proposed two efficient schemes, a random subset assignment scheme and a grid-based key predistribution scheme, to establish pairwise keys in sensor networks[3]. A random subset assignment scheme randomly chooses polynomials from a polynomial pool and assigns polynomial shares to sensors. In this scheme, there is a unique key between each pair of sensors. If no more than t shares on the same polynomial are disclosed, no pairwise key constructed using this polynomial between any two non-compromised sensor nodes will be disclosed. Grid-based key predistribution scheme generates and distributes polynomials from which keys can be derived[3]. If two sensor nodes share a same t-degree polynomial, they can derive common key value from the polynomial. Sensor nodes on the same row or a column can perform share discovery and path discovery based on this information.

Another polynomial based key predistribution scheme by D. Liu and P. Ning partitions the target field into small areas called cells, each of which is associated with a unique random bivariate polynomial[4]. The setup server distributes to each sensor a set of polynomial shares belonging to the cells closest to the one in which the sensor is expected to locate. After deployment, if two sensors can find at least one such a polynomial, a common pairwise key can be established directly using the basic polynomial-based scheme. By using polynomial-based key predistribution scheme, instead of distributing pairwise keys themselves, polynomial shares are assigned and security levels can be enhanced. However, even if we choose polynomials from a polynomial pool, the probability that common polynomial does not exist is high and the pool size affects the key establishment probabilities[2][3]. In addition, in grid-based key predistribution scheme, when several polynomials are disclosed, all sensor nodes on the same row or column using the disclosed polynomials can be under attacks[2]. Location-based key predistribution scheme also has limitations that sensors located in five neighbor cells share the same polynomials and disclosure of a polynomial could lead to large fraction of sensor nodes are disclosed to attacks[4].

For sensor network authentication, a protocol named μTESLA has been proposed for broadcast authentication. It has been adapted from a stream authentication protocol called TESLA[5]. μTESLA employs a chain of authentication keys linked to each other by a pseudo random function, which is by definition a one way function. Each key in the key chain is the image of the next key under the pseudo random function. μTESLA achieves broadcast authentication through delayed disclosure of authentication keys in the key chain. The efficiency of μTESLA is based on the fact that only pseudo random function and secret key based cryptographic operations are needed to authenticate a broadcast message. However, it still has the basic shortcomings of the need for time synchronization and authentication delay.

3 Assumptions and Hierarchical Architecture of Sensor Network

3.1 Assumptions

- All nodes are static and located at the predefined positions.
- All nodes are clustered and the clusters are interconnected by gateway nodes which are included in more than two clusters.
- Clusterheads have more powerful computation ability and have larger storage capacity than normal sensor nodes.
- Routing protocol is not considered in the research. After routing paths are set up, every node becomes aware of its upstream and downstream nodes on the route to the base station.
- Only base station or clusterhead can generate broadcast messages.

3.2 Hierarchical Architecture of Sensor Network

All nodes except the base station are included in more than one cluster and every clusterhead at the center of each cluster gathers data from its member nodes and delivers the data along a routing path to the base station. Gateway nodes are the ones which are located between two clusters and belonging to both clusters. Every routing path from a cluster to another one has to include the gateway between the two clusters. Because normal sensor node cannot establish pairwise key with another node in different cluster, gateway node needs to relay the packets using pairwise keys with each of sensor nodes belonging to different clusters. This will be explained in section 4 in more detail. Fig. 1 shows the sensor network structure.

4 Key Establishment

We combine polynomial-based key predistribution and clustering scheme.

Fig. 1. Hierarchical architecture of sensor network

4.1 Key Material Predistribution

In our mechanism, we cluster our network field and each of the cluster is associated with a unique random polynomial. Key setup server generates bivariate t-degree polynomials $f(x,\ y)$ over a finite field Fq, where q is a prime number that is large enough to accommodate a cryptographic key, such that it has the property of $f(x,\ y) = f(y,\ x)$, assigns a unique polynomial to every cluster and predistributes related polynomial shares to each sensor node in the cluster. Every pair of nodes including clusterhead in a same cluster can compute its own pairwise key using the assigned polynomial share and each other's id when two sensor nodes want to communicate with each other. Key setup server also chooses a polynomial only for clusterheads including the base station and predistributes the shares to each clusterhead. Gateway nodes are predistributed more than two polynomial shares derived from different polynomials because they belong to multiple clusters and connect the clusters as in fig. 1. They need to compute and store more than two pairwise keys derived from different shares from different polynomials with each cluster respectively. After the routing paths are set up, every node computes pairwise keys with its upstream node and downstream node on the paths. Pairwise keys used in our mechanisms are in Table 1.

Steps for network pairwise key setup are as follows.

1. key material predistribution
   a. Normal sensor nodes are predistributed polynomial shares according to their predefined position.
   b. Clusterheads are assigned two different shares, one for communication between clusterheads, another for communication with its member sensor nodes.
   c. Gateway nodes are predistributed more than two different polynomial shares from different polynomials associated with different clusters.

Table 1. Pairwise Keys used in our mechanism

$KEYS$	Concerned Nodes
$K_{CH-CH}(or K_{CH-BS})$	key between two clusterheads or between a clusterhead and the base station
$K_{CH-SN}(or K_{CH-GW})$	key between a clusterhead and its member sensor node or a Gateway node
$K_{SN-SN}(or K_{SN-GW})$	key between two sensor nodes in a cluster or between a sensor node and a Gateway node

2. Nodes deployment and Key establishment
   a. After deployment, routing paths are setup after each node finds its neighbor nodes through Hello messages.
   b. Pairwise keys for communication are computed using assigned polynomial shares ($K_{CH-CH}, K_{CH-SN}, K_{SN-SN}$).

5 Authentication Mechanism

5.1 Unicast Authentication

Sensor nodes to Clusterhead. When each sensor node senses an event, it computes and adds a MAC using a pairwise key between the sensor node and its clusterhead. In raw data delivery phase, hop-by-hop authentication is not used to decrease transmission overhead and delay. Intermediate nodes just relay the data to their clusterhead, and the clusterhead verifies the MACs of the data packets from each sensor node, aggregates the data when the MAC value is verified.

$$SN \longrightarrow CH : (message \| MAC(K_{SN-CH}, message))$$

Clusterhead to Base Station. The clusterhead computes a new MAC using a pairwise key between itself and the base station, and it computes and adds another MAC using the key with its upstream node. Aggregated information is transmitted along the routing path through hop-by-hop authentication. Intermediate node verifies the MAC and adds a new MAC. This message is transmitted up to the base station and verified by the it.

$CH \longrightarrow upstreamSN : (message \| MAC(K_{CH-BS}, message) \| MAC(K_{CH-SN}, message))$

$SN \longrightarrow SN : (message \| MAC(K_{CH-BS}, message) \| MAC(K_{SN-SN}, message))$

$SN \longrightarrow BS : (message \| MAC(K_{CH-BS}, message) \| MAC(K_{SN-BS}, message))$

5.2 Broadcast Authentication

Broadcast authentication is an essential service in distributed sensor networks. It is usually desirable for the base station or clusterheads to broadcast commands and data to the sensor nodes because of the large number of sensor nodes and the broadcast nature of wireless communication. The authenticity of such commands and data is critical for the normal operation of sensor networks. And authenticating broadcast messages is very important because forged broadcast messages can cause DoS and energy exhaustion attacks. Public key based digital signatures (e.g.,RSA), which are typically used for broadcast authentication in traditional networks, are too expensive to be used in sensor networks due to the intensive computation involved in key generation and signature verification. For sensor network broadcast authentication, μTESLA has been proposed[5]. However, in μTESLA protocol, all receiving nodes must synchronize their clocks with the sender. This could cause additional strain on a nodes energy supply, resulting in decreased sensor network lifetime. In addition, because of its characteristics of delayed disclosure of authentication keys, μTESLA causes time delay in message authentication. To overcome these disadvantages, we propose a different broadcast authentication mechanism applying one-time digital signature.

One-time digital signature. One-time signature schemes are based on a public function f that is easy to compute but computationally infeasible to invert. The scheme was first introduced by Lamport[6]. Merkle[7][10] proposed an improvement which reduces the number of public key components in the Lamport method. In Merkle's method, the signer can generate only one x and one y for each bit of the message to be signed, and when one of the bits in the message to be signed is a '1', the signer releases the corresponding value of x; but when the bit to be signed is a '0', the signer releases nothing. To prevent repudiation attack, the signer must also sign count of the '0' bits in the message. Because the count field has only $\log_2 n$ bits in it, the signature size is $n + \lfloor \log_2 n \rfloor + 1$ when the message length is n. K. Zhang, applied one-time digital signature mechanism for signing routing messages in wired networks[8].

Broadcast authentication mechanism. During the communication process, all the broadcast messages are signed by one-time digital signature. When nodes get the messages, they verify the messages by repeated hashing of the key elements delivered.

Signing and verification process runs as follows. Let Mi be the broadcast message to be sent and two hash functions f and h are known to all nodes. we applied MD5[9] for getting hashed information. Hash function f is applied to the message Mi to obtain its hash *f(Mi)*. This hash value *f(Mi)* is to be signed to provide authenticity and integrity of message Mi. Suppose the output of hash function f is l-bit long. Using Merkle's scheme, we need $n(= n + \lfloor \log_2 n \rfloor + 1)$ one-time public key components to sign *f(Mi)*. In order to sign more than one message, we need multiple sets of these one-time public key components. We derive multiple sets of public key components from hash chains by repeated hashing of the public key components in the first set to decrease the storage overhead. Fig. 2 shows signing and verifying process using one-time digital signature.

Signing the broadcast messages

1. *f(Mi)* is concatenated with a count field of 0's using Merkle's method.
2. One-time digital signature is attached to *f(Mi)*. One-time digital signature is the hash values in the $(k\text{-}i)$th row of the hash table where bit-value is 1.

Fig. 2. Signing and verification of message applying one-time digital signature

Verifying the broadcast message

1. When a node receives signed broadcast message, it first obtains the bit string g by concatenating *f(Mi)* with counter field, using Merkle's method.
2. For all j such that g_j=1, check if one-time digital signature is correct by repeated hashing of received signature values.

For one-time digital signature, base station and clusterheads generate hash tables. After the hash tables are generated, public key elements of the base station or clusterheads can be delivered to every other clusterheads encrypted by pairwise keys with each other clusterheads and again delivered to every sensor node encrypted by pairwise keys between clusterhead and its member sensor nodes. After all key elements in the hash table are used up, new hash table is generated by each clusterhead or base station and new public key element is delivered to every sensor node. The hash table format is showed in Fig. 3.

Fig. 3. Hash table generated by each Clusterheads and Base Station

Hash table creation process is as follows.

1. Each node randomly chooses private key components x_j when $j = 1, , n$.

$$n = [l + \log_2 l] + 1,\ l : \text{length of } f(Mi)$$

2. Each node creates a table of n hash chains of length k as in Fig. 3. k is hash table length.
3. Each node broadcasts k'th row as public key elements encrypted using pairwise keys.
4. When receiving messages, every node decrypts the messages and stores them as v_j, $j = 1...n$. These v_j's are the one-time public key components of the corresponding node.

6 Evaluation

6.1 Security Analysis

In our mechanism, sensor nodes sharing the same polynomial are limited in one cluster, and even if some nodes are captured, the effect could be confined in one cluster. In the basic polynomial-based key predistribution scheme, when more than t nodes are captured, the polynomial can be disclosed. However, by limiting the number of sensor nodes located in a cluster less than t, our proposal provides perfect resistance against node capture. And any pair of sensor nodes in the same cluster can setup pairwise key even if the polynomial pool size is small. This is superior to polynomial pool-based mechanism in which pairwise key setup probability can be affected by the polynomial pool size.

For authentication mechanism, if aggregated data is verified just by the base station, attacks such as DoS or energy exhaustion can be possible. In our proposal, through unicast authentication, modified data can be filtered on route from the clusterhead to the base station. By broadcast authentication using one-time digital signature, modified or forged commands can be detected effectively without time synchronization or delay which are major drawbacks of μTESLA.

6.2 Overhead Analysis

Key establishment overhead. For pairwise key establishment, polynomial shares are predistributed before sensor node deployment. Time and computation overhead can be ignored because substituting the other node's id for the variable of the polynomial share causes little overhead. The computation overhead is not that heavy even for clusterheads which need more computations than normal nodes because the computation is very simple. For storage, clusterheads need to store as many keys as the number of its member sensor nodes and other clusterheads. This can be a burden on clusterheads compared to normal sensor nodes which need to store only as many keys as their neighbor nodes. However, on the assumption that clusterheads have superior ability than normal nodes, this can be tolerable.

Authentication overhead. For unicast authentication, hop-by-hop MAC computations are needed. The performance depends on the specification of sensor nodes and the number of hop count from the clusterhead to the base station. This can consume some energy of sensor nodes, but is also worth applying considering damage caused by malicious attacks. Broadcast authentication requires additional hash tables for base station and clusterheads. Usually when MD5 is applied, the time for signing and verification of one-time digital signature is less than one-tenth of the simplest PKI-based digital signature generation and verification. We need encryption and decryption of one-time public key components only when new hash table is generated by base station or clusterhead. This decreases the time overhead considerably. Additional time and computation overhead needed is for generation of new hash table when all the key components are used up. The computation overhead for new table generation depends on the length of the table and the specification of the base station and clusterheads. If broadcast messages are not generated very often, new hash table generation is not requested frequently and can be further decreased if the length is properly adjusted considering tradeoff between the storage and computation overhead. In addition, using the characteristics of hash function, receiver node can further decrease hashing by keeping recently delivered signature values. The storage overhead for one-time public key components is $(l + [\log_2 l] + 1)$ x m bits for each clusterheads and base station, where l and m are the output length of hash function f and h, respectively. When we apply MD5, it requires 2KB and each clusterhead needs $2k$KB storage where k is the length of hash table. The length of the hash table can be properly determined considering the number of broadcast messages. For normal nodes, only the final public key components need to be kept, and this space can be neglected.

7 Conclusion and Future Work

For security of sensor network, we propose pairwise key establishment and authentication mechanism. In our mechanism, we apply polynomial pool-based key predistribution and increase security level by clustering and limiting the area for which a polynomial is used. Unicast authentication can be achieved by adding MAC value using pairwise keys established, and for efficient broadcast authentication, we propose new approach of applying one-time digital signature. By applying one-time digital signature, we can overcome the disadvantages of time synchronization and verification delay caused by μTESLA.

For future research, we would like to simulate our mechanisms and analyze the results in detail. And we will consider mobile situation under various attack scenarios, and also research on secure data aggregation and delivery.

References

1. I. F. Akyildiz, W. Su, Y. Sankarasubramaniam and E. Cayirci : A Survey on Sensor Networks, IEEE Communications Magazine (2002).
2. L. Eschenauer, V. D. Gligor : A Key-Management Scheme for Distributed Sensor Networks, Proc. of the 9th ACM Conference on Computer and Communications Security, 41-47 (2002).
3. D. Liu and P. Ning : Establishing Pairwise Keys in Distributed Sensor Networks, Proc. of the 10th ACM Conference on Computer and Communications Security (CCS), 52-61 (2003).

4. D. Liu, P. Ning : Location-Based Pairwise Key Establishments for Static Sensor Networks, SASN'03 First ACM Workshop on the Security of Ad Hoc and Sensor Networks (2003).
5. A. Perrig, R. Szewczyk, V. Wen, D. Culler, and J. Tygar : SPINS: Security Protocols for Sensor Networks, Proc. of 7th ACM International Conference on Mobile Computing and Networks(Mobicom) (2001).
6. L. Lamport : Construction digital signatures from one-way function, Technical Report SRI-CSL-98, SRI International, October (1979).
7. R. C. Merkle : A Digital Signature Based on a Conventional Encryption Function, Proc. of CRYPTO'87, LNCS 293, pp. 369-378, (1987).
8. K. Zhang : Efficient protocols for signing routing messages, Proc. of the 1998 Internet Society (ISOC) Symposium on Network and Distributed System Security, San Diego, California, March (1998).
9. Ronald Rivest: The MD5 Message Digest Algorithm, RFC1321, April (1992), ftp://ftp.rfc-editor.org/in-notes/rfc1321.txt.
10. R. C. Merkle : A Certified Digital Signature, Proc. of CRYPTO'89, LNCS 435, Springer Verlag, pp. 218-238, (1990).

Energy-Aware Routing Analysis in Wireless Sensors Network

Chow Kin Wah, Qing Li, and Weijia Jia

Department of Computer Science,
City University of Hong Kong,
Kowloon, Hong Kong
50309865@student.cityu.edu.hk,
{itqli, itjia}@cityu.edu.hk

Abstract. Applications of sensor networks have become an emerging technology which can monitor a specific area and collect environmental data around the district. The energy of sensor nodes is tightly constrained so that there is a need to control the power consumption in node operations such as transmission and routing. In this paper, we carry out analysis on energy-aware routing in order to minimize the path loss. Our goal is to prolong the network lifetime and ease the management of sensor networks.

1 Introduction

Sensor networks are highly energy constrained. The sensor nodes are expected to work for a year or more using the power supplied from the on-board batteries. Since it is impractical to replace the batteries on thousands of sensor nodes, we need an appropriate solution to manage the energy consumed by sensor nodes so that the lifetime of the network can be extended.

All the operations in a sensor node consume certain amount of energy. But the most amount of energy is dissipated in the radio circuit, especially during transmission. Therefore, when determining the next hop during routing, the sensor nodes should use as much local information as possible and make less data exchange with neighbours in order to conserve energy.

In this paper, we carry out analysis on energy-aware routing in order to minimize the path loss. Our goal is to prolong the network lifetime [5] and ease the management of sensor networks. The rest of our paper is organized as follows. In section 2, we classify the basic terminologies to be used in the subsequent sections. In section 3, analysis on energy-aware routing for minimizing the path loss is conducted in depth, including such issues as zone-based management, layer-based management, and path loss with the free space model. Finally, we conclude this paper and suggest some further research issues in the last section.

H.T. Shen et al. (Eds.): APWeb 2006, LNCS 3842, pp. 345 – 349, 2006.

2 Energy-Aware Routing

2.1 Zone-Based Management

In a sensors network, we want to monitor a specific area and collect the required environmental data. To achieve this goal efficiently, the target environment is often divided into *zones* and only one sensor node is deployed in each zone. In R-DCS [2][6], there are three types of sensor mode: monitor, replica and normal. Each zone has one monitor node for each event-type and at most one replica node for each event-type. Zones are divided into Z squares with equal size and identified with $z_j : j = 1, \ldots, Z$.

When we define zones in this way, we assign the zone ID arbitrarily or in ascending order. The zone ID cannot provide any geographical meaning and there is no relationship between adjacent zones. Nodes cannot make use of zone information to aid energy-aware routing. A rule is needed to classify the zones so that any zone can tell its physical location and energy-related information through its ID.

2.2 Layer-Based Management

Based on the requirements, we change the zones into layers in which the power required for the sensor nodes to transmit data directly to the access point is within the same range. Nodes should route data towards the layer which is closer to the access point (AP). Each node should maintain: (1) its direct P_{Tx} to AP, or if direct link is not possible, the direct P_{Tx} to its upper layer; (2) its upper layer's direct P_{Tx} to AP. As shown in Fig.2, we use circular lines to denote the boundary of layers and there are three layers. In the center there is the access point. The distance between the boundary of layer 1 and the access point is r_1. Now we have layer number $L = 3$ and layers l_j: $j = 1, \ldots, L$ and radius r_j: $j = 1, \ldots, L$. A node m_{ij} belongs to layer j if

$$d(m_{ij}, AP) \le r_k, \qquad \forall k \ge j \tag{1}$$

and

$$d(m_{ij}, AP) > r_h, \qquad \forall h < j \tag{2}$$

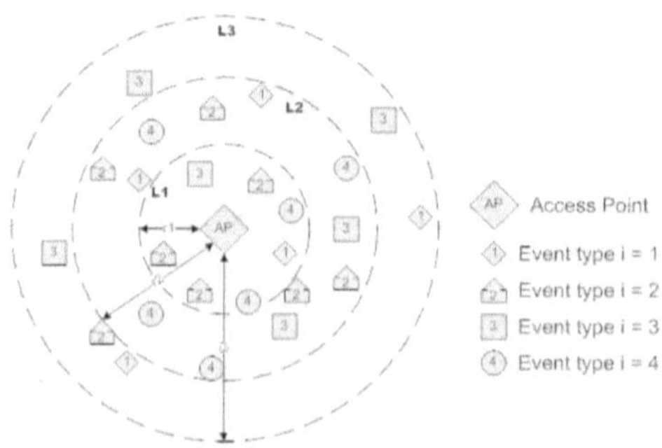

Fig. 1. Use layers instead of zones to divide the areas

where m_{ij} is the monitor node of event type *i* at layer *j*. In Fig.2, we have 4 event types and each node is responsible for sensing a particular event type.

2.3 Path Loss with Free Space Model

We use the free space model [3][4] to analyze the differences between layers through the following equation:

$$P_r = P_t G_t G_r \left(\frac{\lambda}{4\pi d}\right)^2 \tag{3}$$

or equivalently:

$$P_r(dBW) = P_t(dBW) + G_t(dBW) + G_r(dBW) + 20\log_{10}\left(\frac{\lambda}{4\pi}\right) - 20\log_{10}(d) \tag{4}$$

The last two terms are the path loss between the transmitter and receiver. Assume sensor nodes are uniformly distributed around AP and r_1=10, r_2=20 and r_3=30, the distribution of nodes and path loss in each layer are shown in Table 1.

Table 1. Path loss of routing data via upper layer and transmitting directly to the AP

Layer	Radius	Probability	Directly to AP		Route via upper layer	
			$20\log_{10} d(dBW)$	$1/d^2$	$20\log_{10} d(dBW)$	$1/d^2$
1	10	0.11	20	0.01	20	0.01
2	20	0.33	26.02	0.0025	20	0.01
3	30	0.56	29.54	0.0011	20	0.01

Over 50% of nodes are located in the outer-most layers. If they need to transmit data directly to AP, the path loss is 29.54dBW which means 10 times of loss in absolute power when compared with layer 1. Three times of distance can introduce 10 times of path loss in this small area. The greater the path loss, the larger amount of energy we need to supply to achieve the same SINR (Signal-to-Interference- and-Noise-Radio). This addresses the importance of multi-hop routing in a wireless sensors network.

When we move to routing indirectly through upper layer nodes, we find that path loss can be fixed in a small value if nodes in the lower layer can reach the nodes in upper layer within a constant distance. According to [1], the overall rate of energy dissipation is minimized when all the hop distances are equal to *D/K* where *D* is the total distance traveled, and *K* is the number of relays plus one.

In Fig.3, the direct receiving area of the AP is depicted in the dashed circle. Nodes outside this circle have to relay their data through the other nodes. The numbers on the arrows indicate the path loss between two nodes. We define the average path loss from node *i* to AP through node *j* as follows:

$$\overline{E}_{ij}^{n} = \begin{cases} \overline{E}_{ii}^{0} & \text{if \#relay n = 0} \\ \dfrac{1}{n+1}\left[E_{ij} + \overline{E}_{j}^{n-1}(n-1)\right] & \text{if \#relay n > 0} \end{cases} \quad (5)$$

We calculate the average path loss of two paths <C, D, E> and <C, J, E>, and find that <C, J, E> has always a smaller value. But if we look at the average path loss of <C, J, I> and <C, K, I>, the values are the same when it is calculated upon node I. When this happens we need to check the variances along both paths, and the path with smaller variance should be chosen. This is because the path loss along this path is more similar to the *D/K* and less energy will be consumed.

Fig. 2. Path loss between different nodes

Table 2. Average path loss along <C, D, E> and <C, J, E>

Path	Average path loss		
<C, D, E>	$\overline{E}_{CC}^{0}=8$	$\overline{E}_{CD}^{1}=7$	$\overline{E}_{DE}^{2}=8$
<C, J, E>	$\overline{E}_{CC}^{0}=8$	$\overline{E}_{CJ}^{1}=6.5$	$\overline{E}_{JE}^{2}=7.67$

Table 3. Average path loss along <C, J, I> and <C, K, I>

Path	Average path loss		
<C, J, I>	$\overline{E}_{CC}^{0}=8$	$\overline{E}_{CJ}^{1}=6.5$	$\overline{E}_{JI}^{2}=7.67$
<C, K, I>	$\overline{E}_{CC}^{0}=8$	$\overline{E}_{CK}^{1}=10$	$\overline{E}_{KI}^{2}=7.67$

3 Conclusion

In this paper, we have discussed the layer-based approach to manage the sensors network and the path loss in routing through nodes of different layers. Based on our study, it is advantageous by using the average path energy with the aid of variance of path loss to determine the path in energy-aware routing. In the future, we will not only consider energy consumption but also plan to investigate routing based on the data attributes and event types.

Acknowledgement

This work is supported by CityU SRG grant no. 7001709.

References

1. M. Bhardwaj, T. Garnett, and A. P. Chandrakasan, "Upper Bounds on the Lifetime of Sensor Networks", in Proc. of the International Conference on Communications(ICC'01), 2001.
2. A. Ghose, J. Grossklags, and J. Chuang, "Resilient Data-Centric Storage in Wireless Ad-Hoc Sensor Networks", in Proc. of the International Conference on Mobile Data Management(MDM'03), 2003.
3. K. Lassonen, "Radio Propagation Modelling", 2003.
4. T. Rappaport, "Wireless Communications: Principles & Practice", Prentice-Hall, 1996.
5. S. Singh, M. Woo and C. Raghavendra, "Power-Aware Routing in Mobile Ad Hoc Networks", MOBICOM '98, 1998.
6. A. Hac, "Wireless Sensor Network Designs", Wiley, 2003.

A Density-Based Self-configuration Scheme in Wireless Sensor Networks

Hoseung Lee[1], Jeoungpil Ryu[1], Kyungjun Kim[2], and Kijun Han[1,*]

[1] Department of Computer Engineering, Kyungpook National University, Korea
{leeho678, goldmunt}@netopia.knu.ac.kr, kjhan@bh.knu.ac.kr
[2] School of Information & Communication, Daegu University, Korea
kjkim@daegu.ac.kr

Abstract. A sensor network application that should be deployed densely selects particular nodes and configures network topology with them to construct a long-lived network. Only the active nodes participate in message transmission through a routing path and the other nodes turn off their radios to save energy. Previous approaches have been tried to reduce the number of active nodes to construct an energy efficient network topology. However, they preclude the existence multiple active nodes within a small area. The crowded active nodes can reduce network efficiency since they make frequent collisions of messages. In this paper, we propose a self-configuring sensor network topology scheme, that can achieve scalable, robust and energy efficient sensor network based on distance between active nodes. Our scheme may uniformly distribute active nodes in a sensor field and get good energy utilization.

1 Introduction

The advances in micro-sensors and low-power wireless communication technology will enable the deployment of densely distributed sensor networks for a wide area monitoring applications. The sensor nodes gather various sensor data and process them, forward the processed information to a user or, in general a data sink. This forwarding is typically carried out via other nodes using multi-hop path. The node density issues interesting challenges for sensor network research. One of the challenges arises from the energy efficiency to achieve scalable, robust and long-lived networks. As the sensor nodes operate on a small battery with limited capacity, they will do some processing to save power consumption.

Topology management is an important issue because the best way to save power consumption in the wireless network is to completely turn off the node's radio, as the idle mode is almost as power hungry as the transmit mode [1].

S-MAC [2] is an approach that all of the nodes periodically repeat listen and sleep, turning radio on and off, respectively. STEM [3] and PTW [7] improve S-MAC by using a second radio as paging channel. When a node has some message to be transmitted, it waits the destination node radio turning on, and then sends message. So, there is a trade off between energy saving and transmission delay. STEM and

[*] Correspondent author.

H.T. Shen et al. (Eds.): APWeb 2006, LNCS 3842, pp. 350 – 359, 2006.

PTW are designed for sparsely distributed network but can be combined with a topology scheme that exploits the node density.

For a densely distributed sensor network, ASCENT, GAF and Span were suggested [4, 5, 6]. They select some specific node and turn on their radios during some duration. These nodes, called active nodes, join routing infrastructure. The other nodes periodically repeat listen and sleep. And, they decide whether or not to become active by using only local information in a distributed manner for scalable networks. These schemes may produce crowded active nodes within a small area, which increases energy consumption. Furthermore, they cannot detect a network connectivity partition and repair neither, which results in low network utilization [6].

Clustering techniques such as LEACH [8] and HEED [9] can also reduce energy consumption. These techniques suggested algorithms to select a best set of clustering heads to save energy for constructing routing topology.

In this paper, we suggest a self-configuring sensor network topology scheme that can uniformly distribute active nodes over the whole network. Our scheme adaptively selects active nodes in a distributed manner and prevents too many active nodes from being crowded within a small area by keeping the distance between active neighbor nodes above some minimum requirement. In our scheme, we assume each sensor node has two different frequency radio channels similar to STEM frequency setup [4] to exchange the distance information between active nodes.

The rest of this paper is organized as follows. Section 2 summarizes the related works. The details of the proposed scheme are presented in Section 3. In Section 4, we validate our scheme through computer simulations. Section 5 concludes the paper.

2 Related Works

There have been many approaches to managing sensor network topology. STEM (Sparse Topology and Energy Management) [3] is an event/traffic driven wakeup scheme. This mechanism is suited for the applications where events occur rather infrequently. It uses two radios, one is functioned as a wakeup radio and the other is used for data transmission. Each node periodically turns on their wakeup radio. When a node needs data transmission, it sends a beacon on the wakeup radio to explicitly wake up the target node. This gives some delays in path-setup time in exchange for energy saving. PTW (Pipelined Tone Wakeup Scheme) [7] is an advanced wakeup scheme of STEM to save the packet delay. PTW wakes up the next hop node during data transmission plane, and this can reduce the end-to-end packet delay. The STEM and PTW are applicable to sparse networks but can be combined with the schemes which exploit the node density [6].

There have been other approaches to managing sensor network topology to exploit node density. With Span [5], a limited set of nodes forms a multi-hop forwarding backbone that tries to preserve the original capacity of the underlying ad-hoc network. Other nodes transition to sleep states more frequently, as they no longer carry the burden of forwarding data of other nodes. To balance out energy consumption, the backbone functionality is rotated between nodes, and as such, there is a strong interaction with the routing layer.

In ASCENT (Adaptive Self-Configuring sEnsor Networks Topologies) [4], particular nodes are selected by some mechanism and they keep radio on active state for some duration and perform multi-hop packet routing, while the rest remain passive or sleep state and they periodically check if they can become active. In this approach, the sensor network consumes more energy as the numbers of active nodes are increased. Furthermore, it can produce a serious packet loss, called communication hole, when there are too fewer active nodes. To solve this problem, the sink sends a help message when it finds out a communication hole. However, the ASCENT mechanism does not detect, nor repair network partitions. Furthermore, it precludes network dynamics such as node movement. So, there may be multiple active nodes within a small area. This can reduce network efficiency since this makes frequent collisions of messages and loss.

GAF (Geographic Adaptive Fidelity) [6] exploits the fact that nearby nodes can perfectly and transparently replace each other in the routing topology. The sensor network is subdivided into small grids, such that nodes in the same grid are equivalent from a routing perspective. At each point in time, only one node in each grid is active, while the others are in the energy-saving sleep mode. The GAF depends on location information and uniform radio propagation. In many settings, however, location information is not available such as indoors or under trees and a planet such as Mars. In addition, geographic proximity does not always lead to network connectivity.

3 Density-Based Topology Scheme

In this section, we propose a network topology scheme for a wireless sensor network where there are lots of sensor nodes deployed to connect the entire region. Our scheme selects active sensors in such a way that they will be uniformly distributed over the wireless sensor network for robust performance and long network lifetime. In our scheme, only the active nodes join the packet routing.

3.1 Basic Concept

We use two separate radio frequency bands, f_1 and f_2 that have different propagation ranges, R_1 and R_2, respectively. These setups are similar to STEM [4] which use two different radios but an identical propagation range. The short propagation range radio frequency band (f_1) is used for active advertisement and the other radio (f_2) is for data transmission.

If a node becomes activated, for example N_1 in Figure 1, it broadcasts an advertisement message using f_1. The propagation range of the active node is called restricted area. In the restricted area, any other nodes are not allowed to become active. So, more than two active nodes can not be selected simultaneously within a restricted area. For example, node N_3 located inside the restricted area cannot become active, while node N_2 located outside the restricted area can be active. Sometimes, however, there may be more than two active nodes within a restricted area when more than two nodes located outside the restricted area wake up each other at the same time. At this time, they become active and send advertisements simultaneously. In this case, only one of them can remain active state and the other should sleep immediately.

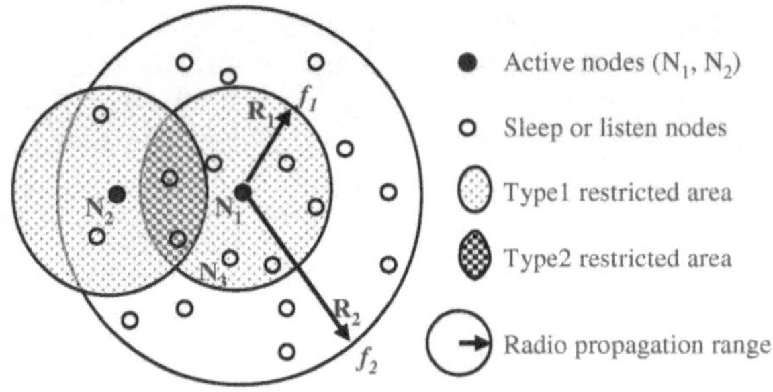

Fig. 1. Restricted area

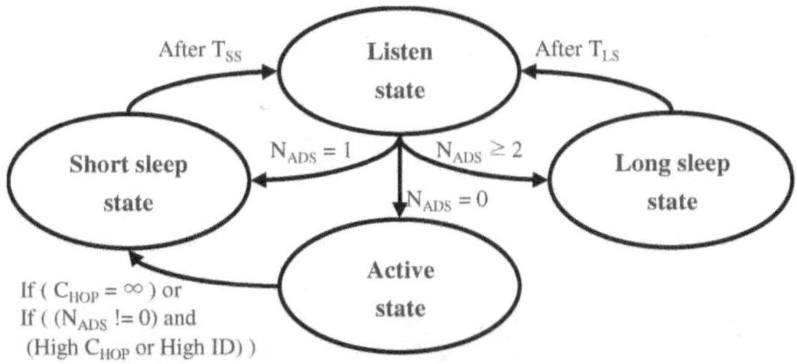

N_{ADS}: the number of advertisement messages received from adjacent active nodes
C_{HOP}: the hop count to the data sink
T_{SS}: the duration time of short sleep state
T_{LS}: the duration time of long sleep state

Fig. 2. State transition diagram

The restricted area is further classified into two types: Type 1 and 2. Type 1 restricted area is where a single advertisement message from only one active node is heard. In this area, nodes sleep for a respectively short time since they should become active after an active node nearby it dies. On the other hand, type 2 is a restricted area where more than two advertisement messages from different active nodes are heard. The nodes within the type 2 restricted area could sleep for a long time.

3.2 State Transition of Node

In our scheme, a node can be in one of four states as illustrated in Figure 2; listening, active, short sleep, and long sleep states. Initially, node starts from the listening state. In this state, it first turns on f_1 radio and off f_2 radio and then sets up a listening status timer (T_L). While the timer T_L goes on, the node counts the number of advertisement messages (denoted by N_{ADS}) that it receives from adjacent active nodes. After the timer is expired, the next state is determined based on the value of N_{ADS} as shown in Figure 2. If $N_{ADS} \geq 2$, the node goes the long sleep status since the node is currently located at type 1 restricted area. When $N_{ADS} = 1$, it goes to the short sleep status because the node is located within type 2 restricted area. If a node does not receive any advertisement messages (that is, $N_{ADS} = 0$), then it transits to the active state.

In the active status, the node turns on f_1 and f_2 radios and periodically sends an advertisement message through f_1 radio to announce that a restricted area has been established. In this state, it can forward data and routing packets until it runs out of energy. The advertisement message contains node ID, active duration time, and the hop count (C_{HOP}) to the data sink. The active duration time is estimated by the amount of residual power. The hop count, which means the number of hops to the sink, is used to avoid collision of advertisement messages from multiple active nodes.

In the sleep status, the node turns off f_1 and f_2 radios and sets up a sleep timer (T_{LS} or T_{SS}). After the timer expires, it goes to the listening status. The long sleep timer (T_{LS}) is set with a larger timer value than the short sleep timer (T_{SS}). T_{LS} can be set with the time during which the active nodes are expected to be active simultaneously. There can be a node in the long sleep on the overlapped area as shown in Figure 1.

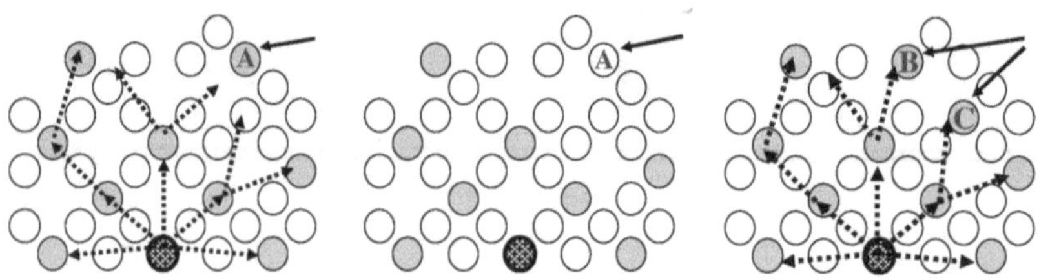

(left) The sink broadcasts a sink message and node A detects a communication hole since it does not receive it. (middle) Node A exits from active state and goes to sleep state. (right) Node B and C newly become active and consequentially reconfigure network.

Sink node Active node Passive node Sink message

Fig. 3. Detection and repair process of network partition

3.3 Topology Connectivity Adjustment

The sink node periodically broadcasts a sink message to examine network connectivity. If an active node has not received a sink message before a timer T_A is expired, it goes to the sleep status since this means that the node is no more reachable to the sink node. A network partition (communication hole) problem is the situation where some data cannot be forwarded to the sink because of the absence of active node in that area. The ASCENT precludes network partition detection, but it tries to solve this problem only the area within one hop distance from the sink node. Our mechanism can detect network partition in the whole network and tries to repair it as shown in Figure 3. In our scheme, if there is a communication partition, some active node cannot receive a sink message during some period. In this case, it regards this situation as a network connectivity failure and changes its state to sleep and gives a chance to any other node to become active. This process will be continued until the network partition is eliminated.

Sometimes, an active node may hear advertisement messages from other active nodes nearby it. This situation can happen when there are more than two active nodes within a restricted area. In this case, it examines the hop count contained in the received advertisement message to determine which one is closer to the sink. If its own hop count is higher than the nearby active node's hop count, it goes to sleep status. If their hop counts are the same, then they compare their node ID's. The node with a lower ID will remain active and the other will go to sleep status. In this way, there is no probability that there are multiple active nodes within a small area.

3.4 Analysis for Energy Consumption

We analyze performance of our scheme via mathematical analysis. Here, we will investigate the effects of some parameters on the power consumption in the wireless sensor network. For analysis in the actual situation, we use some representative values of these parameters as shown in Figure 4 [1].

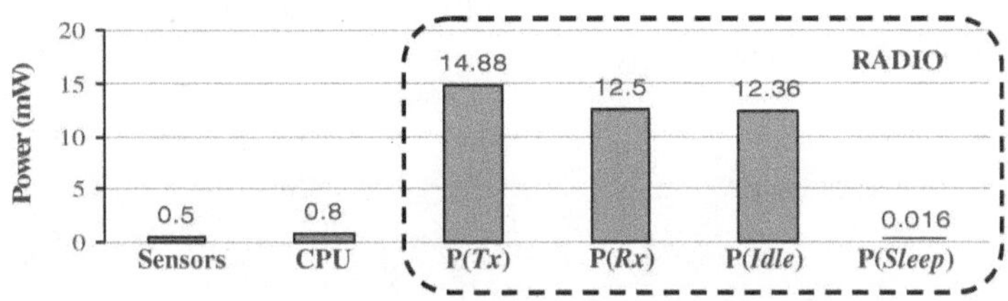

P(*Tx*): Transmission power consumption
P(*Rx*): Receiving power consumption
P(*Idle*): Idle listening power consumption,
P(*Sleep*): Sleep power consumption

Fig. 4. Power consumption at sensor node

Let $P_{f1}(\delta)$, $P_{f2}(\delta)$ mean the power consumed on the f_1 and f_2 radios, respectively, at each node for a short time δ. Also, we define $P_A(\delta)$, $P_L(\delta)$, and $P_S(\delta)$ as the power consumptions in the active, listen and sleep states, respectively, at each node for a short time δ. From Figure 4, we can see that P(*Tx*) $\approx$ P(*Rx*) $\approx$ P(*Idle*) $\gg$ P(*Sleep*) ≈ 0. So, we define the energy consumption at each state as

$$P_A(\delta) = P_{f1}(\delta) + P_{f2}(\delta) \tag{1a}$$

$$P_L(\delta) = P_{f1}(\delta) \tag{1b}$$

$$P_S(\delta) = 0 \tag{1c}$$

Let N_A, N_L, N_{SS} and N_{LS} denote the number of nodes in active state, listen, short sleep and long sleep state, respectively. Then, the power consumption and the power saving in the entire sensor network for a short time δ can be obtained by

$$P_{Consume}(\delta) = \left(P_{f1}(\delta) + P_{f2}(\delta)\right) \cdot N_A + P_{f1}(\delta) \cdot N_L \tag{2}$$

$$P_{Save}(\delta) = \left(P_{f1}(\delta) + P_{f2}(\delta)\right) \cdot (N_{LS} + N_{SS}) + P_{f2}(\delta) \cdot N_L \tag{3}$$

The Eq (2) implies that the power consumption is dependent on the number of active nodes and the number of the listening nodes. The Eq (3) indicates that the power saving of the entire sensor network mainly relies on the number of sleeping nodes.

4 Simulations

To validate our scheme, we perform simulation study. We distribute N nodes over a field of size 50 x 50m in a uniformly random fashion. The data sink node is located in the middle of bottom corner and sends a sink message every 2 seconds. Our setup uses a CSMA MAC protocol for data transmission. And we assume that an advertisement message is always followed by a sink message. In addition, it is assumed that an event arises at the middle of the top corner and the node closest to the event detects it and sends data to the sink per second.

Each node has two radios which have transmission range R_2 and R_1 for the data transmission radio (f_2) and active advertisement radio (f_1), respectively. We define α to be the ratio of the radio propagation range R_2 to R_1 as follows;

$$\alpha = \frac{R_2}{R_1}, (\alpha > 1.0) \tag{4}$$

We simulate with R_2 = 30m and give variance α = 1.5 ~ 3.0 to see the effect of restricted area which is controlled by range R_1.

Let T_L, T_{SS}, T_{LS} denote the duration times of listen, short sleep and long sleep states, respectively. Then, two types of duty ratios, λ_{SS} and λ_{LS} , are defined by

$$\lambda_{SS} = T_L / (T_{SS} + T_L) \tag{5a}$$

$$\lambda_{LS} = T_L / (T_{LS} + T_L) \tag{5b}$$

These equations can be rearranged by

$$T_L = \frac{\lambda_{SS}}{1 - \lambda_{SS}} \cdot T_{SS} = \frac{\lambda_{LS}}{1 - \lambda_{LS}} \cdot T_{LS} \tag{6}$$

We simulate with T_{SS} = 50 seconds and T_L = 5 seconds. In addition, the long sleep timer (T_{LS}) is set with the estimated time during which multiple nodes are in active state simultaneously.

Figure 5 shows the probabilities of active and sleep state in our scheme. From this figure, we can see that the probability of active state increases with α but decreases with the node density. But, the probability of sleep state shows an exactly opposite pattern of the active state, which produces an interesting shape with a symmetric axis. From p(Active)+p(Listen)+p(Sleep) = 1, we can guess the probability of listen state will not vary with α and the node density.

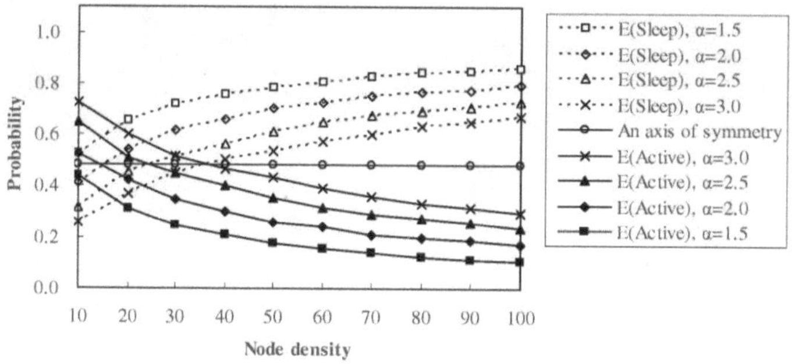

Fig. 5. The state probabilities of active and sleep

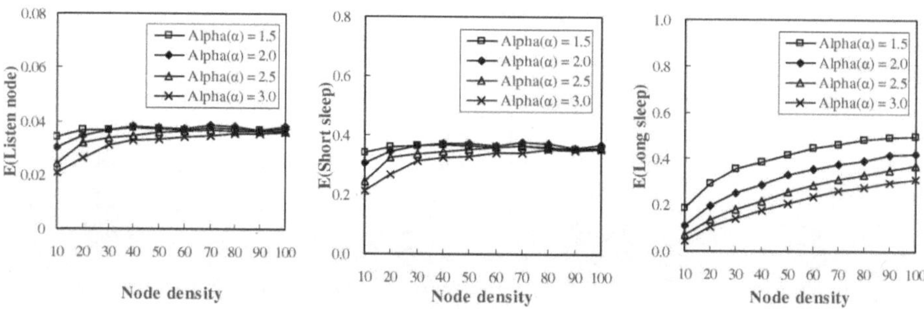

(a) Listen state probability (b) Short sleep probability (c) Long sleep probability

Fig. 6. The state probabilities of listen, short sleep and long sleep states

The probabilities of listen state and short sleep state are shown in Figure 6 (a) and (b). At low densities, the four different values of α yield a somewhat different probabilities. But, as the node density becomes higher, we cannot observe any significant difference in the state probabilities. Figure 6 (c) shows the probabilities of long sleep state and we can see that the probability increases with the node density but decreases with α .

If we denote the numbers of nodes staying in the short and the long sleep states by N_{SS} and N_{LS}, respectively, then we can find the number of nodes in listen states (N_L) from Eq (6). If the duration of the long sleep state is much longer than the duration time of the listen state, then λ_{LS} becomes almost zero. So, we have

$$N_L = \frac{\lambda_{SS}}{1-\lambda_{SS}} \cdot N_{SS} + \frac{\lambda_{LS}}{1-\lambda_{LS}} \cdot N_{LS} \approx \frac{\lambda_{SS}}{1-\lambda_{SS}} \cdot N_{SS} \quad (7)$$

Since T_{SS} = 50s and T_L = 5s, the duty ratio λ_{SS} is given by 0.0909. So, $N_L = 0.1 \times N_{SS}$ from Eq (7). Figure 6 (a) and (b) confirm the fact that the probability of listen status is dependent on only the number of nodes in the short sleep state.

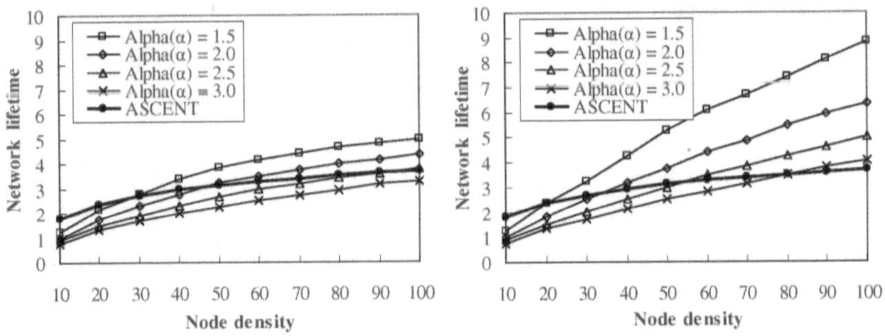

(a) when $T_{SS} = T_{LS}$ (b) when $T_{SS} << T_{LS}$

T_{SS}: the duration time of short sleep state
T_{LS}: the duration time of long sleep state

Fig. 7. The network life time

The life time of sensor network when $T_{SS} = T_{LS}$ is shown in Figure 7 (a), where we cannot tell that the network lifetime with this setting is not bad compared with ASCENT [4].

However, when $T_{SS} << T_{LS}$, we get a different result as shown in Figure 7 (b). When the node density goes high, the network lifetime is much longer than ASCENT. We can also see that α is inversely proportional to the network life. When the state probabilities of active and (or) listen state become higher, the network lifetime becomes shorter. On the contrary, as the state probability of sleep goes higher, the network works for a longer time. From these results, we can say that our scheme offers a long network life time by using short and long sleep states separately.

5 Conclusion

In this paper, we have proposed a self-configuring sensor network topology scheme which uniformly distributes active nodes over the sensor network. In our scheme, an active node announces a restricted area by an advertisement message to prevent other nodes from becoming active. Non-active nodes adaptively select their duration times to stay in the sleep state depending on the number of adjacent active nodes around them.

Simulation and analytical results showed that our scheme could offer very high energy efficiency in highly dense networks. The simulation also showed very sensitive results with the difference between the data frequency propagation range and advertisement frequency propagation range. So, the application using our scheme should adapt the number of deployed sensor nodes and radio propagation range difference according to the application needs.

We are currently carrying out a further study to improve our scheme by considering different power consumption depending on the propagation range and sensor node mobility.

Acknowledgement

This work was supported by grant No. (R01-2005-000-10722-0) from the Basic Research Program of the Korea Science & Engineering Foundation.

References

1. A. Savvides, C.-C. Han, M. Srivastava, "Dynamic fine-grained localization in ad-hoc networks of sensors," *MobiCom 2001*, Rome, Italy, pp. 166 -179, July 2001.
2. Wei Ye, John Heidemann, and Deborah Estrin. "An energy-efficient MAC protocol for wireless sensor networks." In *Proceedings of the Twenty First Annual Joint Conference of the IEEE Computer and Communications Societies (INFOCOM)*, pp. 1567-1576, New York, NY, USA, June 2002.
3. C Schurgers, V Tsiatsis, and M Srivastava. "Stem: Topology management for energy efficient sensor networks." In *IEEE Aerospace Conference*, pp. 78-89, March 2002.
4. A. Cerpa and D. Estrin, "ASCENT: Adaptive self-configuring sensor network topologies." *IEEE Transactions on Mobile Computing*, Vol. 03 , No. 3 , pp. 272-285, July 2004.
5. B. Chen, K. Jamieson, H. Balakrishnan, R. Morris, "Span: an energy-efficient coordination algorithm for topology maintenance in ad hoc wireless networks," *MobiCom 2001*, Rome, Italy, pp. 70-84, July 2001.
6. Y. Xu, J. Heidemann, D. Estrin, "Geography-informed energy conservation for ad hoc routing," *MobiCom 2001*, Rome, Italy, pp. 70-84, July 2001.
7. Xue Yang; Vaidya, N.H.; "A Wakeup Scheme for Sensor Networks: Achieving Balance between Energy Saving and End-to-end Delay," *RTAS 2004. 10th IEEE*, pp.19-26, May 2004.
8. W. Heinzelman, A. Chandrakasan, and H. Balakrishnan, "An Application-Specific Protocol Architecture for Wireless Microsensor Networks," *IEEE Trans. Wireless Comm.*, vol. 1, no. 4, pp. 660-670, Oct. 2002.
9. O. Younis, S. Fahmy, "HEED: A Hybird, Energy-Efficient, Distributed Clustering Approach for Ad Hoc Sensor Networks," *IEEE Transactions on Mobile Computing*, Vol. 03 , No. 4 , pp. 366-378, Oct 2004.

IPv6 Stateless Address Auto-configuration in Mobile Ad Hoc Network*

Dongkeun Lee[1], Jaepil Yoo[1], Keecheon Kim[1,**], and Kyunglim Kang[2]

[1] Dept. of Computer Science & Engineering, Konkuk University,
Gwang-Jin Gu, Seoul, Korea
{dklee, willow, kckim}@konkuk.ac.kr
[2] Communication & Network Lab, Samsung Advanced Institute of Technology
klkang@samsung.com

Abstract. This paper describes global IPv6 address auto-configuration mechanism for MANET(Mobile Ad-hoc Network) nodes connected to the Internet via one or more gateways. IPv6 Duplicate Address Detection(DAD) process cannot be applicable for MANET without modification either because of the multi-hop problem or DAD time bound. In this paper, we propose a stateless auto-configuration that overcomes multi-hop problem. We solve the multi-hop problem by having some ad-hoc routable nodes doing DAD for the new node that is willing to accept DAD. These auto-configuration steps specifically include generation of link-local address and verification of its uniqueness. It further defines the processes of creating globally routable address and a new duplicate address detection mechanism. Once a host configures its interfaces, it becomes possible to communicate in multi-hop environment. We call this new scheme as Tunneled DAD (T-DAD).

1 Introduction

Mobile ad-hoc networks(MANET) are envisioned to have dynamic, sometimes rapidly changing, random, multi-hop topologies which are likely composed of relatively bandwidth-constrained wireless links[1]. Significant research in this area has been focused on the design of efficient routing protocols such as DSDV [2], DSR [3], AODV [4], etc. The majority of routing protocols assume that mobile nodes in ad hoc networks are configured a priori with IP addresses before they begin communications in the network. Thus, address auto-configuration is a desirable goal in implementing MANET[5].

Typically, dynamic configuration in a wired network is accomplished by using the Dynamic Host Configuration Protocols such as DHCP[6] and DHCPv6[7]. These require the existence of a centralized server to provide dynamic address assignment and maintenance for the network.

* This research was supported by the Samsung Advanced Institute of Technology and was partially supported by the MIC(Ministry of Information and Communication), Korea, under the ITRC(Information Technology Research Center) support program supervised by the IITA(Institute of Information Technology Assessment).

** Corresponding Author.

H.T. Shen et al. (Eds.): APWeb Workshops 2006, LNCS 3842, pp. 360–367, 2006.

Because of the mobility of nodes in an ad hoc network, however, nodes in these networks do not have access to a centralized server to acquire IP addresses. Furthermore, nodes may join or leave the network at any time, and network partitions and merges may occur frequently.

In IPv6, stateless address auto-configuration[8] can be used in MANET. This mechanism allows a node to pick a tentative address randomly and then use a Duplicate Address Detection(DAD) procedure to detect duplicate addresses. In a wired single network, DAD is suitable because all the nodes are directly linked and the round-trip bound for DAD message exists. However, in mobile ad-hoc network, we cannot guarantee link state between two nodes and we do not know the round trip bound time between two nodes. These characteristics prevent MANET from address auto-configuration.

Stateless auto-configuration cannot resolve the multi-hop routing problem as well. Multi-hop routing in wireless ad-hoc network can be accomplished by using ad-hoc routing protocol such as AODV. Needless to say, ad-hoc routing protocols operate on routable IP addresses. Therefore, a node that has not received IP address yet cannot send to nor receive DAD messages from indirectly linked node.

Another challenging issue in MANET is connecting to the Internet through the nodes of an ad-hoc network [9]. This MANET topology could be an ordinary situation if we think of our real life depending on the Internet.

In this paper, we investigate a MANET topology that all the nodes in MANET want to connect to the Internet through a special node called the Internet Gateway and we propose a new IPv6 address auto-configuration mechanism in MANET similar to stateless auto-configuration that overcomes multi-hop problem. We solved the multi-hop routing problem by some ad-hoc routable nodes doing the DAD process for the new node that is willing to accept the DAD process. We call this DAD process as Tunneled DAD(T-DAD) from now on. This T-DAD process is lighter than DHCPv6 process and has DAD bound time. So, T-DAD can be a good alternative stateless auto-configuration scheme in MANET that is connected with the Internet through Internet Gateways.

The paper is organized as follows. In section 2, related works are presented. In section 3, the T-DAD for link-local address is described. We describe T-DAD for global address in detail in section 4. Finally, conclusions with future research work are presented in section 5.

2 Related Work

The IETF Zeroconf working group already standardized a stateless auto-configuration mechanism for IPv6 [8]. However, this protocol was not designed for mobile ad hoc networks. In the wireless ad-hoc network, we cannot determine how many nodes will exist, and how long will it take for DAD messages to be returned to the originate node. Hence, DAD waiting time is a big problem of this standard.

DAD based on the stateless auto-configuration in MANET is presented in [5], in which addresses are randomly selected. Duplicate Address Detection(DAD) is performed by each node to guarantee the uniqueness of the selected address. However, this approach uses timeouts, so it has DAD timeout bound problem. The scheme in [5] supports both IPv4 and IPv6.

There is another DAD process to compensate the DAD time. Weak Duplicate Address Detection[10] aims at lowering the overhead needed for the DAD by integrating it with the routing protocol. Weak DAD is an approach to prevent a packet from being routed to a wrong destination, even if duplicate addresses exist. In weak DAD, the nodes do the DAD process with direct linkable nodes first. After that, with the aids of routing protocol, node can detect duplicate address with itself from others. This system is based on the use of a single key that is assigned to each node. Nodes in the network are identified not only by the IP address, but also additionally by a key. If two nodes with the same address choose the same key, a conflict is not detectable because the key is only generated once by each node.

The MANETconf[11] presents an address assignment scheme for ad hoc networks based on a distributed mutual exclusion algorithm that treats IP addresses as a shared resource. In this work, each node maintains a list of all IP addresses in use in the network. A new node obtains an IP address through an existing node in the network. Assignment of a new address requires an approval from all other known nodes in the network. When the network partition is detected, every node in each partition cleans up the addresses in other partitions, and then the nodes agree on a unique identifier for the network. When partitions merge, nodes are required to exchange the set of allocated addresses in each partition. MANETconf produces complex and bandwidth-consuming process by maintaining common address pool information depending on the mobility parameters and also requires the use of timeouts for several operations.

Two agent-based IPv6 auto-configuration mechanisms in mobile ad hoc networks are presented in [12] and [13]. In these approaches, each node acquires a subnet ID from the agent, and generates a link-local address based on its MAC address.

3 Duplicate Address Detection (DAD) for Link-Local Addresses

The DAD for link-local address is done by the same mechanism as described in [8]. That is, a node sends a Neighbor Solicitation to one-hop neighbors with a tentative address. After sending Neighbor Solicitation, it sets a timer for DAD_TIME. During that time, it waits to receive a Neighbor Advertisement. If no Neighbor advertisement is returned for the tentative address within a timeout period, the node retries sending the Neighbor Solicitation up to SEDING_RETRIES times. If, after all retries, no Neighbor Advertisement is still received, the node assumes that the address is not in use, and that the address is taken for its own.

Fig.1 illustrates an example that two or more nodes choose the same link-local address. In fig.1, node B has chosen a link-local address *a*, and node D has chosen a link-local address *a* as well. Now there are two nodes that have the address *a* in one-hop area of node C, thus node C cannot discriminate between node B and node D with link-local address.

So in our solution, after neighbors receive Neighbor Solicitation from a node, they compare the address in Target Address field with its own link-local address and addresses in their neighbor table formed by receiving Ad-hoc Node Advertisements that neighbors broadcast periodically. If there is a same address in their list, receivers send

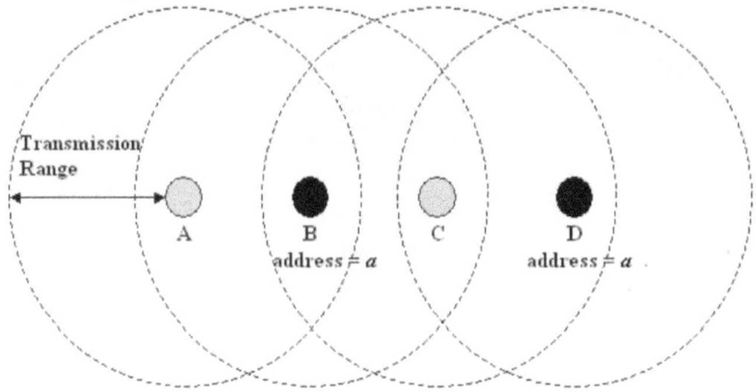

Fig. 1. An example: *node B* and *node D* choose the same IPv6 link-local address *a*

a Neighbor Advertisement to the source. Thus a node in MANET can be convinced that all nodes in its one-hop area have different link-local address each other.Let's look at the fig.1 once again. If node D tries the ad-hoc DAD procedure with a tentative address *a*, node C will send a Neighbor Advertisement to D as node B's proxy. And then node D will randomly choose another address and retry the ad-hoc DAD procedure for link-local addresses.

Link-Local addresses are designed to use for a single link, thus link-local addresses cannot be used for multi-hop routing in MANET. In our solution, link local addresses are used only for communicating with other nodes in one-hop link.

4 Tunneled Duplicate Address Detection (T-DAD) for Global Addresses

After assigning a link-local address, the node makes a tentative global address by appending its interface identifier to the 64 bits-long global prefix[14]. The global prefix is obtained by periodic Ad-hoc Node Advertisements from neighbors.

The basic idea of T-DAD is as follows. The Internet Gateway of ad-hoc network has a table that includes address information of all nodes in a MANET. We call this table as MANET DAD Table. The MANET DAD Table includes global addresses of all nodes in a MANET. The Internet Gateway collects this table information during T-DAD procedures. Thus, if an ad-hoc node wants to verify the uniqueness of its global address, it just asks the Internet Gateway to do that.

An ad-hoc node without a global address, however, cannot send a packet through multi-hop, so it selects a neighboring node that has a global address and sends a Neighbor Solicitation to the selected node. And then the selected neighbor node establishes a tunnel between itself and the Internet Gateway in order to perform T-DAD on behalf of the previous node.

When the Internet Gateway receives a tunneled Neighbor Solicitation from an ad-hoc node, it checks whether the target address in the Neighbor Solicitation is unique or not by scanning its MANET DAD table. Since this looks similar to normal IPv6 DAD, the process of T-DAD looks transparent to the new node seeking a global address.

4.1 Ad-Hoc Node Advertisement

In order to obtain a global prefix of Internet Gateway, nodes in ad-hoc network use Ad-hoc Node Advertisement messages. Internet Gateway's Router Advertisement messages cannot be transmitted over multi-hop link. For that reason, the Internet Gateway's neighbors include the received Router Advertisements in its Ad-hoc Node Advertisement message and periodically broadcast it to its neighbors. If a node receives an Ad-hoc Node Advertisements from its neighbors, it extracts the Router Advertisement message from the received message and then broadcasts the Router Advertisement to its neighbors using Ad-hoc Node Advertisements.

Ad-hoc Node Advertisement message contains its lifetime, preference, and Internet Gateway's advertisement of the ad-hoc network. Link-local address is used for source address of Ad-hoc Node Advertisement. Neighbor nodes cache this source address into their neighbor table. Preference is a value of hop counts from Internet Gateway.

All nodes in ad-hoc network broadcast Ad-hoc Node Advertisement messages periodically or non-periodically. When a node receives a Router Solicitation message form its neighbor nodes, it sends its Ad-hoc Node Advertisement immediately in order to inform Internet Gateway's information to neighbor nodes.

After a node assigns a link-local address to its interface, it starts to broadcast Ad-hoc Node Advertisement to its neighbor nodes using all nodes multicast address at ADVERTISE_INTERVAL millisecond intervals. If the node doesn't configure a global address yet, it sets *preference* field in its Ad-hoc Node Advertisements to maximum value in order to inform its neighbor nodes that it cannot perform T-DAD procedure yet.

4.2 Sending a Global Neighbor Solicitation

After assigning a link-local address, a node makes a tentative global address by appending its interface identifier to the 64 bit-long global prefix. The global prefix is obtained by a periodic or non- periodic Ad-hoc Node Advertisements message from neighbors as defined before in 4.1.

When a node checks for the uniqueness of the address, it selects a neighboring node that has a global address and then it unicasts a Neighbor Solicitation to the selected node. The neighbor selection method is as follows. The node that needs address auto-configuration selects a neighbor that has the smallest value in the *preference* field of Ad-hoc Node Advertisement message.

And the node sets the timer for DAD_TIME. During that time, it waits to receive a Neighbor Advertisement. If no Neighbor advertisement is responded for the selected address within a timeout period, the node retries to send the neighbor solicitation up to SEDING_RETRIES times. If, after all the retries, no Neighbor Advertisement is still received, the node assumes that the address is not in use, and that the address can be taken for its own use.

If the node can receive Internet Gateway's advertisement directly, it can send Neighbor Solicitation to the gateway directly.

In order to distinguish T-DAD messages from normal IPv6 DAD messages, we add *T* flag in reserved field of Neighbor Discovery[15] messages. So, if a node receives Neighbor Discovery messages with the value of 1 in *T* flag, it treats these messages as T-DAD messages.

4.3 Receiving a Global Neighbor Solicitation

On receiving a Neighbor Solicitation with the value of 1 in *T* flag, the selected neighbor node encapsulates received message in *Address Request* message and sends this request message to the Internet Gateway.

When the Internet Gateway receives an Address Request message, it decapsulates the message and extracts encapsulated Neighbor Solicitation. And then the Internet Gateway checks whether the target address in the Neighbor Solicitation is identical with any IP address in its MANET DAD table. If there is no same address in MANET DAD table, Internet Gateway adds an entry with the requested address information in MANET DAD table and does not send Neighbor Advertisement.

If there is a same address with the target address in MANET DAD table, the Internet Gateway sends encapsulated Neighbor Advertisement using *Address Reply* message. After that, the Internet Gateway checks whether the corresponding target address is currently used by another node or not. *Refresh Request* and *Address Refresh* message is used to confirm whether other nodes own that address or not. If the Internet Gateway finds out that any other nodes do not use the corresponding target address, it deletes the corresponding entry in MANET DAD table.

Address Request, *Address Reply*, *Refresh Request* and *Address Refresh* messages are new messages used in this paper.

4.4 Receiving a Global Neighbor Advertisement

When the previously selected neighbor node receives an Address Reply message from the Internet Gateway, it decapsulates the message and then forwards the decapsulated Neighbor Advertisement message to the original source node.

If the original source node receives the Neighbor Advertisement from the selected neighbor node, the node randomly chooses another address and retries T-DAD procedure for the global address.

Although Internet Gateway sends Neighbor Advertisement, the source node may not receive the message if the selected node moved to other link during T-DAD procedure. Even in this case, the source node may set its tentative address as a global address. In order to prevent this, the connection between the source node and the selected node should be checked by periodic Ad-hoc Node Advertisement messages as below. Once the selected node receives a global Neighbor Solicitation Message from the new node, it sends its Ad-hoc Node Advertisement Messages just before DAD_TIME expiration and just after DAD_TIME expiration. In this case, the selected node may set the destination address of the Ad-hoc Node Advertisement Message as a link-local address of the new node, if it doesn't want to send the message to others. In case of not receiving any Ad-hoc Node Advertisement Messages during DAD_TIME, the new node assumes that it does not have connection with the selected node. Therefore it selects new neighbor node and tries T-DAD process again with a randomly generated tentative address.

5 Conclusion and Future Works

In this paper, we have presented the method for the stateless auto-configuration of IPv6 global address for the scenario where Internet Gateway is available in the mobile ad-hoc network.

Because we use stateless approach, the address allocation delays of all nodes in MANET are identical with DAD_TIME x SEDING_RETRIES. However, in our solution, every node in MANET knows hop counts between itself and the Internet Gateway, and uses unicasting when performing T-DAD, thus every node can estimate the DAD time bound according to the hop counts. So, T-DAD is more useful than other solutions using broadcasting.

T-DAD does not change the existing ad-hoc routing protocols and does not use the specific functions of ad-hoc routing protocols, thus T-DAD is flexible enough to be integrated with many different routing protocols.

T-DAD may need some more processing time. The overhead and memory usage of Internet Gateway increases as the network size increases as well, however, this is a case for all kind of network.

T-DAD requires the existence of a centralized server and the new nodes need selected neighbors for auto-configuration. In this situation, some security problems may occur. Hence, we need to specify the possible security issues that may be related to the proposed protocol. Finding a solution to these security issues will be the focus of our future research.

References

1. S. Corson, J. Macker : Mobile Ad hoc Networking (MANET): Routing Protocol Performance Issues and Evaluation Considerations. Request for Comments 2501, Internet Engineering Task Force (1999)
2. C. Perkins, P. Bhagwat : Highly Dynamic Destination-Sequenced Distance-Vector Routing (DSDV) for Mobile Computers. In Proceedings of the ACM SIGCOMM'94 Conference on Communications Architectures, Protocols and Applications (1994)
3. D. B. Johnson, D. A. Maltz : Dynamic Source Routing in Ad Hoc Wireless Networks. In: T. Imielinski, H. Korth(eds.): Mobile Computing, Kluwer Academic Publishers (1996) 153–181.
4. C. Perkins, E. Royer : Ad Hoc On-Demand Distance Vector Routing. In Proceedings of the 2nd IEEEWorkshop on Selected Areas in Communication (1999) 90–100
5. C.E. Perkins, J.T. Malinen, R. Wakikawa, E.M. Belding-Royer, Y. Sun : IP Address Autoconfiguration for Ad Hoc Networks. Internet Draft, Internet Engineering Task Force (2001) Work in Progress
6. R. Droms : Dynamic Host Configuration Protocol. Request for Comments 2131, Internet Engineering Task Force (1997)
7. R. Droms, J. Bound, B. Volz, T. Lemon, C. Perkins, M. Carney : Dynamic Host Configuration Protocol for IPv6 (DHCPv6). Request for Comments 3315, Internet Engineering Task Force (2003)
8. S. Thomson, T. Narten : IPv6 Stateless Address Autoconfiguration. Request for Comments 2462, Internet Engineering Task Force (1998)
9. Y.Sun, E. M. Belding-Royer, C. Perkins : Internet Connectivity for Ad hoc Mobile Networks. Intenational Joulnal of Wireless Information Networks special issue on Mobile Ad hoc Networks (2002)
10. N. H. Vaidya : Weak Duplicate Address Detection in Mobile Ad Hoc Networks. In Proceedings of the 3rd ACM International Symposium on Mobile Ad Hoc Networking and Computing (MobiHoc'02) (2002) 206–216

11. S. Mesargi, R. Prakash : MANETconf: Configuration of Hosts in a Mobile Ad Hoc Network. In Proceedings of the IEEE Conference on Computer Communications (INFOCOM) (2002)
12. M. Gunes, J. Reibel : An IP Address Configuration Algorithm for Zeroconf. Mobile Multi-hop Ad-Hoc Networks. In Proceedings of the International Workshop on Broadband Wireless Ad-Hoc Networks and Services (2002)
13. K. Weniger, M. Zitterbart : IPv6 Autoconfiguration in Large Scale Mobile Ad-Hoc Networks. In Proceedings of European Wireless 2002 (2002)
14. R. Hinden, S. Deering : IP Version 6 Addressing Architecture. Request for Comments 2373, Internet Engineering Task Force (1998)
15. T. Narten, E. Nordmark, W. Simpson : Neighbor Discovery for IP Version 6 (IPv6). Request for Comments 2461, Internet Engineering Task Force (1998)

Fast Collision Resolution MAC with Coordinated Sleeping for WSNs

Younggoo Kwon

Sejong University, 98 Gunja-Dong, Gwangjin-Gu, Seoul 143-747, Korea
ygkwon@sejong.ac.kr

Abstract. Development of energy efficient MAC algorithms that provide both high reliability and easy implementation property is the current major focus in wireless sensor network research. In this paper, the general coordinated sleeping algorithm is combined with fast collision resolution MAC algorithm to achieve high energy efficiency and high performance at the same time. By observing that the sporadic traffic characteristic of WSNs and the operational characteristic of the station in packet transmission in perfectly scheduled algorithm, we propose the fast collision resolution MAC with coordinated sleeping algorithm. Through the various simulation studies, the proposed algorithm shows significant performance improvements in wireless sensor networks.

1 Introduction

Wireless Sensor Networks (WSNs) have recently drawn significant research attention. These sensors are operated on battery power, and energy is not always renewable due to cost, environmental and form-size concerns. The traffic inherent to WSNs is highly sporadic and does not necessarily follow any specific traffic pattern [7]-[9]. To design a good MAC protocol for WSNs, we focus on two main attributes. At first, we use the general coordinated sleeping algorithm to achieve the energy efficiency. By considering the sporadic traffic pattern of WSNs, the actual duty cycle of each node is pretty small, which needs energy for operations. Therefore, by using a simple coordinated sleeping algorithm, we can improve the energy efficiency significantly in WSNs. Secondly, we use an efficient collision resolution algorithm which achieves highly efficient transmission procedure. We will use the operational characteristic of the perfect scheduling algorithm, and induce the fast collision resolution CSMA algorithm. Based on these two design attributes, we present an energy efficient MAC algorithm that provides significantly high energy efficiency for WSNs.

In the next section, we explain related research works. Then, we present the newly proposed algorithm in Section 3. The performance evaluations is given in Section 4. In the final section, we present the conclusions.

2 Related Works

Many MAC protocols to save power consumption in WSNs have been proposed [7]-[9]. The PAMAS [8] protocol was one of the first attempts to reduce

H.T. Shen et al. (Eds.): APWeb 2006, LNCS 3842, pp. 368–372, 2006.

unnecessary power consumption by turning overhearing nodes to sleep. Ye et. al [7] proposed the S-MAC protocol that combines scheduling and contention with the aim of improving collision avoidance and scalability. The power saving is based on scheduling sleep/listen cycles between the neighbor nodes. After the initial scheduling, synchronization packets are used to maintain the inter-node synchronization. The S-MAC operation and frame is divided into two periods; the active period and the sleep period. During the sleep period all nodes that share the same schedule sleep and save energy. The sleep period is usually several times longer than the active period. Nodes listen for a SYNC packet in every frame and the SYNC packet is transmitted by a device infrequently to achieve and maintain virtual clustering.

Cali et. al [3] and Bianchi [2] present the performance analysis of DCF, and derive the optimal value of the contention window that maximizes the aggregate throughput, under the assumption that all stations have the same average contention window size of transmitting a packet in steady state. They derive the following formula for the aggregate network throughput:

$$\rho = \frac{\bar{m}}{\frac{(1-p)}{Mp}t_s + \frac{1-(1-p)^M - Mp(1-p)^{M-1}}{Mp(1-p)^{M-1}}[E[coll] + \tau + DIFS] + E[S]} \quad (1)$$

where $\bar{m}$ is the average packet length, M is the number of active stations, τ is the maximum propagation time, q is the parameter for the geometric distribution of packet length, t_s is the length of a slot (i.e., aSlotTime), $E[coll]$ is the average collision length, and $E[S](= \bar{m} + 2\tau + SIFS + ACK + DIFS)$ is the average time to complete a successful packet transmission without any collisions.

Now, the aggregate network throughput ρ is derived as a function of the probability of a packet transmission p and the number of active stations M from (1), because all other parameters (τ, t_s, $\bar{m}$, q) are determined by the simulation configuration. This means that if the number of active stations M is fixed and given, then we can obtain the optimal p value, which maximizes the network throughput[3].

3 Fast Collision Resolution MAC with Coordinated Sleeping

3.1 Coordinated Sleeping

Periodic sleeping effectively reduces energy waste on idle listening in WSNs. We use the general coordinated sleeping algorithm to combine with fast collision resolution MAC algorithm [7]-[9]. Before each node starts its periodic listen and sleep, it needs to choose a schedule and exchange it with its neighbors. Each node maintains a schedule table that stores the schedules of all its known neighbors. A node first listens for a fixed amount of time, which is at least the synchronization period. If it does not hear a schedule from another node, it immediately chooses its own schedule and starts to follow it. Meanwhile, the node tries to announce the schedule by broadcasting a SYNC packet. Broadcasting a

SYNC packet follows the normal contention procedure. The randomized carrier sense time reduces the chance of collisions on SYNC packets. If the node receives a schedule from a neighbor before choosing or announcing its own schedule, it follows that schedule by setting its schedule to be the same. Then the node will try to announce its schedule at its next scheduled listen time. There are two cases if a node receives a different schedule after it chooses and announces its own schedule. If the node has no other neighbors, it will discard its current schedule and follow the new one. If the node already follows a schedule with one or more neighbors, it adopts both schedules by waking up at the listen intervals of the two schedules. The node who starts first will pick up a schedule first, and its broadcast will synchronize all its peers on its schedule. If two or more nodes start first at the same time, they will finish initial listening at the same time, and will choose the same schedule independently. No matter which node sends out its SYNC packet first, it will synchronize the rest of the nodes.

3.2 Fast Collision Resolution

To reduce the idle slots for the transmitting station and to reduce the collision probability when the number of stations increase, we manipulate the existing access algorithm as follows.

- *Small random backoff timer for the station which has successfully transmitted a packet at current contention cycle*
- *Large random backoff timer for stations that are deferring their packet transmissions at current contention period*: The contention window size of a station will increase not only when it experiences a collision but also when it is in the deferring mode and senses the start of a new busy period. Therefore, all stations which have packets to transmit (including those which are deferred) will increase quickly their contention window sizes at each contention period.
- *Fast change of random backoff timer according to its current state: transmitting or deferring*: When a station transmits a packet successfully, its random backoff timer should be set small. When the station transmission is deferred, its random backoff timer should be set large to avoid the future collisions.

After the random backoff timer is chosen from the large contention window range, it will be realigned to reduce the unnecessary wasted idle backoff time. If a station, which has just performed a successful packet transmission, runs out of packets for transmission or reaches its maximum successive packet transmission limit, then, all stations may have very large contention window ranges (large backoff timers). However, the wasted idle time is limited to a certain predetermined value because all backoff timers are realigned.

4 Performance Evaluations

In this section, we present the simulation studies for the proposed algorithm and IEEE 802.11 by using ns2. The simulation duration is 1000 seconds, and the

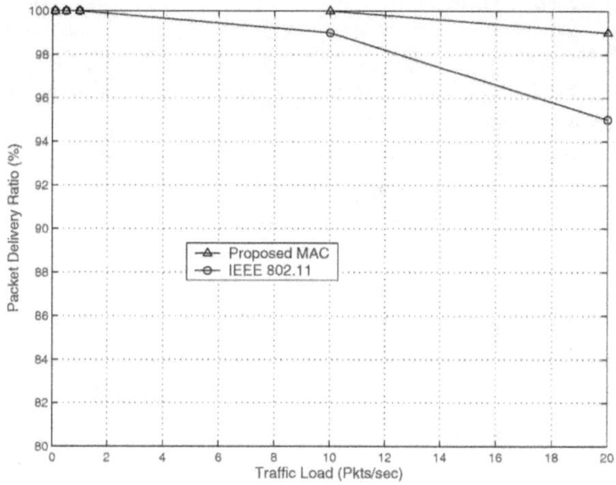

Fig. 1. Packet Delivery Ratio

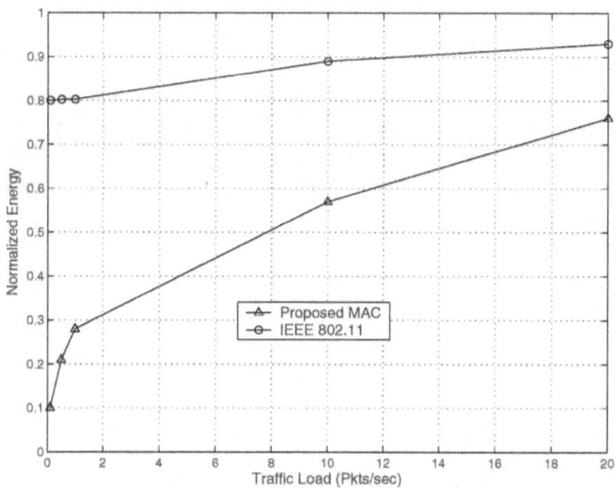

Fig. 2. Normalized Energy vs. Traffic

application traffic runs from 100 to 900 second. 100 nodes evenly distributed with fixed position. Randomly chosen 10 Poisson traffic flows are used and the packet size is 90 bytes. The transmission range only covers the neighbors along diagonal direction. Figure 1 and 2 show that the packet delivery ratio and normalized energy vs. traffic load for the proposed MAC and the IEEE 802.11 respectively.

In Figure 1, the packet delivery ratio of the IEEE 802.11 is decreased as the traffic load increases. The packet delivery ratio of the proposed algorithm is not decrease much by resolving contention efficiently as traffic load increases. In Figure 2, the normalized energy vs. traffic load is shown. We can see that the proposed MAC improves the energy efficiency significantly in low duty cycle areas compared with the IEEE 802.11.

5 Conclusions

By considering sporadic traffic patterns in WSNs, the coordinated sleeping algorithm provides significantly high energy efficiency. The general assumption that all stations have the same contention window range in steady state results in sub-optimal solutions for performance analysis of distributed contention-based MAC algorithms because of its inherent limitations. We combined two important attributes in WSNs and present the fast collision resolution MAC with coordinated sleeping algorithm. The proposed MAC algorithm significantly improves the energy efficiency and still provides easy implementation property in WSNs. Extensive performance analysis and simulation studies for various performance factors have demonstrated that the proposed algorithm reduces the energy consumptions and the wasting overheads come from each contention procedure.

References

1. Bharghavan, V.: MACAW: A Media Access Protocol for Wireless LAN's. SIGCOMM'94, London, England, Aug. (1994) 212-225
2. Bianchi, G.: Performance Analysis of the IEEE802.11 Distributed Coordination Function. IEEE Journal on Selected Areas in Commun. **18** (2000) 535-547
3. Cali, F., Conti, M., Gregori, E.: Dynamin Tuning of the IEEE 802.11 Protocol to Achieve a Theoretical Throughput Limit. IEEE/ACM Trans. on Networking **8** (2000) 785-799
4. Chandra, A., Gummalla, V., Limb, J.: Wireless Medium Access Control Protocols. IEEE Communi. Sur. (2000)
5. Crow, B., Widjaja, I., Kim, J., Sakai, P.: IEEE 802.11 Wireless Local Area Networks. IEEE Commun. Mag. **35** (1997) 116-126
6. Dam, T., Langendoen, K.: An adaptive energy efficient MAC protocol for wireless sensor networks. Proc. 1st international conf. an embedded networked sensor systems (2003) 171-180
7. Ye, W., Heidemann, J., Estrin, D.: Medium access control with coordinated adaptive sleeping for Wireless Sensor Networks. IEEE/ACM Trans. Networking **vol.12** (2004) 493-506
8. Singh, S., Raghavendra, C.: Pamas: Power avare multi access protocol with signalling for ad hoc network (1998) 5-26
9. Fullmer, C., Garcia-Luna-Aceves, J.: Floor acquition multiple access (FAMA) for packet-ratio networks. Proc. SIGCOMM, Cambridge, MA. (1995) 262-273
10. Goodman, D., Valenzuela, R., Gayliard, K., Ramamurthi, B.: Packet Reservation Multiple Access for Local Wireless Communications. IEEE Trans. Commun. **37** (1989) 885-890

Energy-Efficient Deployment of Mobile Sensor Networks by PSO

Xiaoling Wu, Shu Lei, Wang Jin, Jinsung Cho*, and Sungyoung Lee

Department of Computer Engineering, Kyung Hee University, Korea
{xiaoling, sl8132, wangjin, sylee}@oslab.khu.ac.kr,
chojs@khu.ac.kr

Abstract. Sensor deployment is an important issue in designing sensor networks. In this paper, particle swarm optimization (PSO) approach is applied to maximize the coverage based on a probabilistic sensor model in mobile sensor networks and to reduce cost by finding the optimal positions for the cluster-head nodes based on a well-known energy model. During the coverage optimization process, sensors move to form a uniformly distributed topology according to the execution of algorithm at base station. The simulation results show that PSO algorithm has faster convergence rate than genetic algorithm based method while achieving the goal of energy efficient sensor deployment.

1 Introduction

Mobile sensor networks consist of sensor nodes that are deployed in a large area, collecting important information from the sensor field. Communication between the nodes is wireless. Since the nodes have very limited energy resources, the energy consuming operations such as data collection, transmission and reception must be kept at a minimum.

In most cases, a large number of wireless sensor devices can be deployed in hostile areas without human involved, e.g. by air-dropping from an aircraft for remote monitoring and surveillance purposes. Once the sensors are deployed on the ground, their data are transmitted back to the base station to provide the necessary situational information.

The deployment of mobile sensor nodes in the region of interest (ROI) where interesting events might happen and the corresponding detection mechanism is required is one of the key issues in this area. Before a sensor can provide useful data to the system, it must be deployed in a location that is contextually appropriate. Optimum placement of sensors results in the maximum possible utilization of the available sensors. The proper choice for sensor locations based on application requirements is difficult. The deployment of a static network is often either human monitored or random. Though many scenarios adopt random deployment for practical reasons such as deployment cost and time, random deployment may not provide a uniform sensor distribution over the ROI, which is considered to be a desirable distribution in mobile sensor networks. Uneven node topology may lead to a short system lifetime.

* Corresponding author.

H.T. Shen et al. (Eds.): APWeb 2006, LNCS 3842, pp. 373–382, 2006.

The limited energy storage and memory of the deployed sensors prevent them from relaying data directly to the base station. It is therefore necessary to form a cluster based topology, and the cluster heads (CHs) provide the transmission relay to base station such as a satellite. And the aircraft carrying the sensors has a limited payload, so it is impossible to randomly drop thousands of sensors over the ROI, hoping the communication connectivity would arise by chance; thus, the mission must be performed with a fixed maximum number of sensors. In addition, the airdrop deployment may introduce uncertainty in the final sensor positions. These limitations motivate the establishment of a planning system that optimizes the sensor reorganization process after initial random airdrop deployment, which results in the maximum possible utilization of the available sensors.

There are lots of research work [1], [2], [3], [4], [12] related to the sensor nodes placement in network topology design. Most of them focused on optimizing the location of the sensors in order to maximize their collective coverage. However only a single objective was considered in most of the research papers, other considerations such as energy consumption minimization are also of vital practical importance in the choice of the network deployment. Self-deployment methods using mobile nodes [4], [9] have been proposed to enhance network coverage and to extend the system lifetime via configuration of uniformly distributed node topologies from random node distributions. In [4], the authors present the virtual force algorithm (VFA) as a new approach for sensor deployment to improve the sensor field coverage after an initial random placement of sensor nodes. The cluster head executes the VFA algorithm to find new locations for sensors to enhance the overall coverage. They also considered unavoidable uncertainty existing in the precomputed sensor node locations. This uncertainty-aware deployment algorithm provides high coverage with a minimum number of sensor nodes. However they assumed that global information regarding other nodes is available. In [1], the authors examined the optimization of wireless sensor network layouts using a multi-objective genetic algorithm (GA) in which two competing objectives are considered, total sensor coverage and the lifetime of the network. However the computation of this method is not inexpensive.

In this paper, we attempt to solve the coverage problem while considering energy efficiency using particle swarm optimization (PSO) algorithm, which can lead to computational faster convergence than genetic algorithm used to solve the deployment optimization problem in [1]. During the coverage optimization process, sensor nodes move to form a uniformly distributed topology according to the execution of algorithm at the base station. To the best of our knowledge, this is the first paper to solve deployment optimization problem by PSO algorithm.

In the next section, the PSO algorithm is introduced and compared with GA. Modeling of sensor network and the deployment algorithm is presented in section 3, followed by simulation results in section 4. Some concluding remarks and future work are provided in section 5.

2 Particle Swarm Optimization

PSO, originally proposed by Eberhart and Kennedy [5] in 1995, and inspired by social behavior of bird flocking, has come to be widely used as a problem solving method in engineering and computer science.

The individuals, called, particles, are flown through the multidimensional search space with each particle representing a possible solution to the multidimensional problem. All of particles have fitness values, which are evaluated by the fitness function to be optimized, and have velocities, which direct the flying of the particles. PSO is initialized with a group of random solutions and then searches for optima by updating generations. In every iteration, each particle is updated by following two "best" factors. The first one, called *pbest*, is the best fitness it has achieved so far and it is also stored in memory. Another "best" value obtained so far by any particle in the population, is a global best and called *gbest*. When a particle takes part of the population as its topological neighbors, the best value is a local best and is called *lbest*. After each iteration, the *pbest* and *gbest* (or *lbest*) are updated if a more dominating solution is found by the particle and population, respectively.

The PSO formulae define each particle in the D-dimensional space as $X_i = (x_{i1}, x_{i2}, x_{i3}, \ldots\ldots, x_{iD})$ where *i* represents the particle number, and *d* is the dimension. The memory of the previous best position is represented as $P_i = (p_{i1}, p_{i2}, p_{i3} \ldots\ldots p_{iD})$, and a velocity along each dimension as $V_i = (v_{i1}, v_{i2}, v_{i3} \ldots\ldots v_{iD})$. The updating equation [6] is as follows,

$$v_{id} = \varpi \times v_{id} + c_1 \times rand() \times (p_{id} - x_{id}) + c_2 \times rand() \times (p_{gd} - x_{id}) \qquad (1)$$

$$x_{id} = x_{id} + v_{id} \qquad (2)$$

where ϖ is the inertia weight, and c_1 and c_2 are acceleration coefficients.

The role of the inertia weight ϖ is considered to be crucial for the PSO' s convergence. The inertia weight is employed to control the impact of the previous history of velocities on the current velocity of each particle. Thus, the parameter ϖ regulates the trade-off between global and local exploration ability of the swarm. A large inertia weight facilitates global exploration, while a small one tends to facilitate local exploration, i.e. fine-tuning the current search area. A suitable value for the inertia weight ϖ balances the global and local exploration ability and, consequently, reduces the number of iterations required to locate the optimum solution. Generally, it is better to initially set the inertia to a large value, in order to make better global exploration of the search space, and gradually decrease it to get more refined solutions. Thus, a time-decreasing inertia weight value is used [7].

PSO shares many similarities with GA. Both algorithms start with a group of a randomly generated population, have fitness values to evaluate the population, update the population and search for the optimum with random techniques. However, PSO does not have genetic operators like crossover and mutation. Particles update themselves with the internal velocity. They also have memory, which is important to the algorithm [8].

Compared with GA, PSO is easy to implement, has few parameters to adjust, and requires only primitive mathematical operators, computationally inexpensive in terms of both memory requirements and speed while comprehensible. It usually results in faster convergence rates than GA. This feature suggests that PSO is a potential algorithm to optimize deployment in a sensor network.

3 The Proposed Algorithm

First of all, we present the model of mobile sensor network. We assume that each node knows its position in the problem space, all sensor members in a cluster are homogeneous and cluster heads are more powerful than sensor members. Communication coverage of each node is assumed to have a circular shape without any irregularity. The design variables are 2D coordinates of the sensor nodes, $\{(x_1, y_1), (x_2, y_2), \ldots\ldots\}$. Sensor nodes are assumed to have certain mobility. Many research efforts into the sensor deployment problem in mobile sensor networks [4, 9] make this sensor mobility assumption reasonable.

3.1 Optimization of Coverage

We consider coverage as the first optimization objective. It is one of the measurement criteria of QOS of a sensor network.

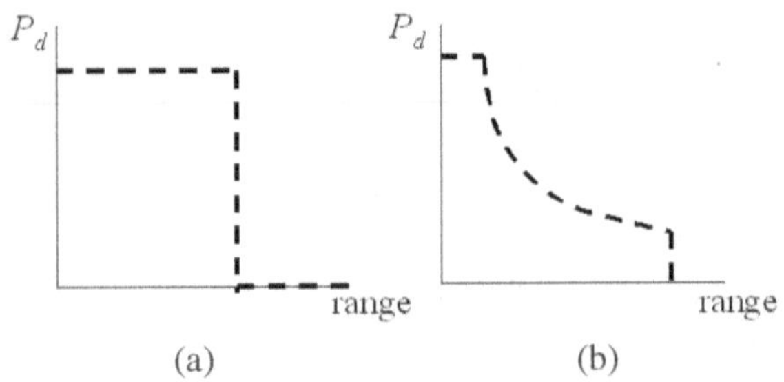

Fig. 1. Sensor coverage models (a) Binary sensor and (b) probabilistic sensor models

The coverage of each sensor can be defined either by a binary sensor model or a probabilistic sensor model as shown in Fig. 1. In the binary sensor model, the detection probability of the event of interest is 1 within the sensing range, otherwise, the probability is 0. Although the binary sensor model is simpler, it is not realistic as it assumes that sensor readings have no associated uncertainty. In reality, sensor detections are imprecise, hence the coverage needs to be expressed in probabilistic terms. In many cases, cheap sensors such as omnidirectional acoustic sensors or ultrasonic sensor are used. Some practical examples [4] include AWAIRS at UCLA/RSC Smart Dust at UC Berkeley, the USC-ISI network, the DARPA SensIT systems/networks, the ARL Advanced Sensor Program systems/networks, and the DARPA Emergent Surveillance Plexus (ESP). For omnidirectional acoustic sensors or ultrasonic sensors, a longer distance between the sensor and the target generally implies a greater loss in the signal strength or a lower signal-to-noise ratio. This suggests that we can build an abstract sensor model to express the uncertainty in sensor responses. In other words, a sensor node that is closer to a target is expected to have a higher detection probability about the target existence than the sensor node that is further away from the target.

In this paper, the probabilistic sensor model given in Eq (3) is used, which is motivated in part by [11].

$$c_{ij}(x, y) = \begin{cases} 0, & if \quad r + r_e \le d_{ij}(x, y); \\ e^{-\lambda a^{\beta}}, & if \quad r - r_e < d_{ij}(x, y) < r + r_e; \\ 1, & if \quad r + r_e \ge d_{ij}(x, y). \end{cases} \tag{3}$$

The sensor field is represented by an $m \times n$ grid. An individual sensor node s on the sensor field is located at grid point (x, y). Each sensor node has a detection range of r. For any grid point P at (i, j), we denote the Euclidean distance between s at (x, y) and P at (i, j) as $d_{ij}(x, y)$, i.e., $d_{ij}(x, y)=\sqrt{(x-i)^2+(y-j)^2}$. Eq (3) expresses the coverage $c_{ij}(x, y)$ of a grid point at (i, j) by sensor s at (x, y), in which $r_e(r_e<r)$ is a measure of the uncertainty in sensor detection, $a = d_{ij}(x, y)-(r-r_e)$, and λ and β are parameters that measure detection probability when a target is at distance greater than r_e but within a distance from the sensor. This model reflects the behavior of range sensing devices such as infrared and ultrasound sensors. The probabilistic sensor detection model is shown in Figure 1(b). The distances are measured in units of grid points. Figure 1(b) also illustrates the translation of a distance response from a sensor to the confidence level as a probability value about this sensor response. The coverage for the entire grid sensor field is calculated as the fraction of grid points that exceeds the threshold c_{th}.

3.2 Optimization of Energy Consumption

After optimization of coverage, all the deployed sensor nodes move to their own positions. Now our goal is to minimize energy usage in a cluster based sensor network topology by finding the optimal cluster head positions. For this purpose, we assume a power consumption model [10] for the radio hardware energy dissipation where the transmitter dissipates energy to run the radio electronics and the power amplifier, and the receiver dissipates energy to run the radio electronics. This is one of the most widely used models in sensor network simulation analysis. For our approach, both the free space (*distance*^{2} power loss) and the multi-path fading (*distance*^{4} power loss) channel models were used. Assume that the sensor nodes inside a cluster have short distance *dis* to cluster head but each cluster head has long distance *Dis* to the base station. Thus for each sensor node inside a cluster, to transmit an l-bit message a distance *dis* to cluster head, the radio expends

$$E_{TS}(l, dis) = lE_{elec} + l\varepsilon_{fs} dis^2 \tag{4}$$

For cluster head, however, to transmit an l-bit message a distance *Dis* to base station, the radio expends

$$E_{TH}(l, Dis) = lE_{elec} + l\varepsilon_{mp} Dis^4 \tag{5}$$

In both cases, to receive the message, the radio expends:

$$E_R(l) = lE_{elec} \tag{6}$$

The electronics energy, E_{elec}, depends on factors such as the digital coding, modulation, filtering, and spreading of the signal, here we set as E_{elec}=50*nJ/bit*, whereas the amplifier constant, is taken as $\varepsilon_{fs}=10pJ/bit/m^2$, $\varepsilon_{mp}=0.0013pJ/bit/m^2$.

So the energy loss of a sensor member in a cluster is

$$E_s(l,dis)=l(100+0.01dis^2) \tag{7}$$

The energy loss of a CH is

$$E_{CH}(l,Dis)=l(100+1.3\times10^{-6}\times Dis^4) \tag{8}$$

Since the energy consumption for computation is much less than that for communication, we neglect computation energy consumption here.

Assume m clusters with n_j sensor members in the jth cluster C_j. The total energy loss E_{total} is the summation of the energy used by all sensor members and all the m cluster heads:

$$E_{total}=l\sum_{j=1}^{m}\sum_{i=1}^{n_j}(100+0.01dis_{ij}^2+\frac{100}{n_j}+\frac{1.3\times10^{-6}Dis_j^4}{n_j}) \tag{9}$$

Because only 2 terms are related to distance, we can just set the fitness function as:

$$f=\sum_{j=1}^{m}\sum_{i=1}^{n_j}(0.01dis_{ij}^2+\frac{1.3\times10^{-6}Dis_j^4}{n_j}) \tag{10}$$

4 Performance Evaluation

The PSO starts with a "swarm" of sensors randomly generated. As shown in Fig. 3 is a randomly deployed sensor network with coverage value 0.31 calculated using approximate method mentioned in section 3.1. A linear decreasing inertia weight value from 0.95 to 0.4 is used, decided according to [6]. Acceleration coefficients c_1 and c_2 both are set to 2 as proposed in [6]. For optimizing coverage, we have used 20 particles, which are denoted by all sensor nodes coordinates, for our experiment in a 50×50 square sensor network, and the maximum number of generations we are running is 500. The maximum velocity of the particle is set to be 50. The other parameters of sensor models are set to be r=5, r_e=3, λ=0.5, β=0.5, c_{th}=0.7. The coverage is calculated as a fitness value in each generation.

After optimizing the coverage, all sensors move to their final locations in setup phase. Now the coordinates of potential cluster heads are set as particles in the sensor network. The communication range of each sensor node is 15 units with a fixed remote base station at (25, 80). We start with a minimum number of clusters acceptable in the problem space to be 4. The node, which will become a cluster head, will not have any restriction on the transmission range. The nodes are organized into clusters by the base station. Each particle will have a fitness value, which will be evaluated by the fitness function (10) in each generation. Our purpose is to find the optimal location of cluster heads. Once the position of the cluster head is identified, if there is no node in that position then a potential cluster head nearest to the cluster head location will become a cluster head.

We also optimized the placement of cluster head in the 2-D space using GA. We used a simple GA algorithm with single-point crossover and selection based on a roulette-wheel process. The coordinates of the cluster head are the chromosomes in the population. For our experiment we are using 10 chromosomes in the population. The maximum number of generations allowed is 500. In each evolution we update the number of nodes included in the clusters. The criterion to find the best solution is that the total fitness value should be minimal.

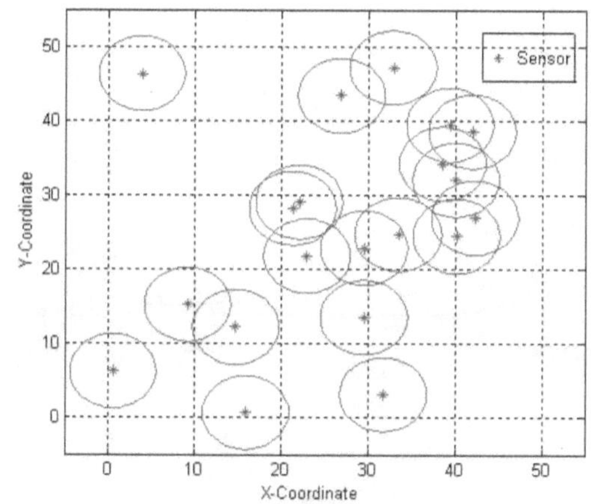

Fig. 3. Randomly deployed sensor network with r=5 (Coverage value=0.31)

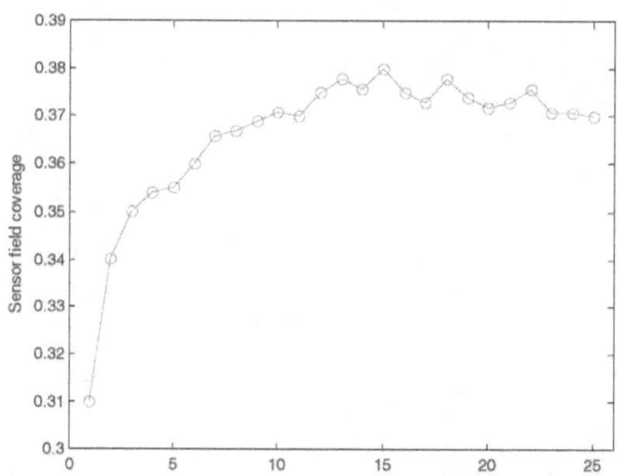

Fig. 4. Optimal coverage achieved using PSO algorithm (probabilistic sensor detection model)

Fig. 4 shows the improvement of coverage during the execution of the PSO algorithm. Note that the upper bound for the coverage for the probabilistic sensor detection model (roughly 0.38) is lower than the upper bound for the case of binary sensor detection model (roughly 0.628). This due to the fact that the coverage for the binary sensor detection model is the fraction of the sensor field covered by the circles. For the probabilistic sensor detection model, even though there are a large number of grid points that are covered, the overall number of grid points with coverage probability greater than the required level is fewer.

Fig. 5 shows the convergence rate of PSO and GA. We ran the algorithm for both approaches several times and in every run PSO converges faster than GA, which was used in [1] for coverage and lifetime optimization. The main reason for the fast convergence of PSO is due to the velocity factor of the particle.

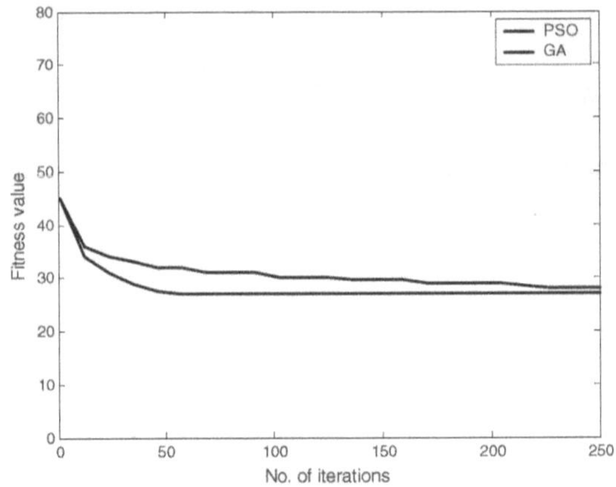

Fig. 5. Comparison of convergence rate between PSO and GA based on Eq. (10)

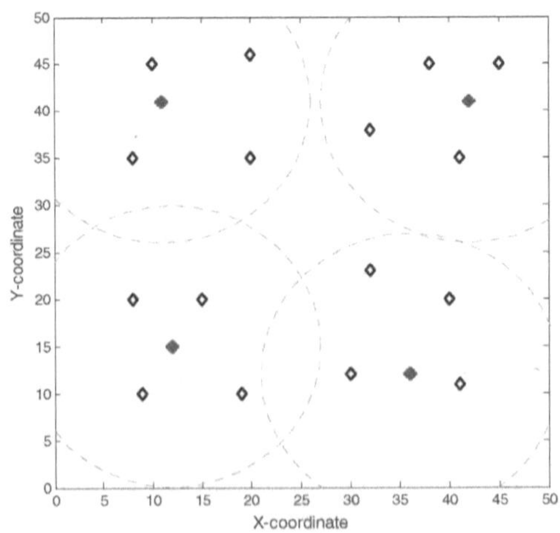

Fig. 6. Energy efficient cluster formation using PSO

Fig. 6 shows the final cluster topology in the sensor network space after coverage and energy consumption optimization when the number of clusters in the sensor space is 4. We can see from the figure that nodes are uniformly distributed among the clusters compared with the random deployment as shown in Fig 3. The four red stars denote cluster heads, the blue diamonds are sensor members, and the dashed circles are communication range of sensor nodes. The energy saved is the difference between the initial fitness value and the final minimized fitness value. In this experiment, it is approximately 16.

5 Conclusions and Future Work

The application of PSO algorithm to optimize the coverage in mobile sensor network deployment and energy consumption in cluster-based topology is discussed. We have used coverage as the first optimization objective to place the sensors uniformly based on a realistic probabilistic sensor model, and energy consumption as the second objective to find the optimal cluster head positions. The simulation results show that PSO algorithm has faster convergence rate than GA based layout optimization method while demonstrating good performance.

In the future work, we will take sensor movement energy consumption into account. Moreover, other objectives, such as time and distance for sensor moving will be further studied.

Acknowledgement

This research was supported by the Kyung Hee University Research Fund in 2005 (KHU-20050370).

References

1. Damien B. Jourdan, Olivier L. de Weck: Layout optimization for a wireless sensor network using a multi-objective genetic algorithm. IEEE 59th Vehicular Technology Conference (VTC 2004-Spring), Vol.5 (2004) 2466-2470
2. K. Chakrabarty, S. S. Iyengar, H. Qi and E. Cho: Grid coverage for surveillance and target location in distributed sensor networks. IEEE transactions on computers, Vol.51 (2002) 1448-1453
3. A. Howard, M.J. Mataric and G. S. Sukhatme: Mobile sensor network deployment using potential fields: a distributed, scalable solution to the area coverage problem. Proc. Int. Conf. on distributed Autonomous Robotic Systems (2002) 299-308
4. Y. Zou and K. Chakrabarty: Sensor deployment and target localization based on virtual forces. Proc. IEEE Infocom Conference, Vol. 2 (2003) 1293-1303
5. Kennedy and R. C. Eberhart: Particle Swarm Optimization. Proceedings of IEEE International Conference on Neural Networks, Perth, Australia (1995) 1942-1948
6. Yuhui Shi, Russell C. Eberhart: Empirical study of Particle Swarm Optimization. Proceedings of the 1999 Congress on Evolutionary Computation, Vol. 3 (1999) 1948-1950
7. K.E. Parsopoulos, M.N. Vrahatis: Particle Swarm Optimization Method in Multiobjective Problems. Proceedings of the 2002 ACM symposium on applied computing, Madrid, Spain (2002) 603- 607

8. http://www.swarmintelligence.org/tutorials.php
9. Nojeong Heo and Pramod K. Varshney: Energy-Efficient Deployment of Intelligent Mobile Sensor Networks. IEEE Transactions on Systems, Man, and Cybernetics—Part A: Systems And Humans, Vol. 35, No. 1 (2005) 78 - 92
10. Wendi B. Heinzelman, Anantha P. Chandrakasan, and Hari Balakrishnan: An Application-Specific Protocol Architecture for Wireless Microsensor Networks. IEEE Transactions on Wireless Communications, Vol. 1, No. 4 (2002) 660 - 670
11. A. Elfes: Sonar-based real-world mapping and navigation. IEEE Journal of Robotics and Automation, Vol. RA-3, No. 3 (1987) 249–265
12. Archana Sekhar, B. S. Manoj and C. Siva Ram Murthy: Dynamic Coverage Maintenance Algorithms for Sensor Networks with Limited Mobility. Proc. PerCom (2005) 51-60

Object Finding System Based on RFID Technology

Lun-Chi Chen[1], Ruey-Kai Sheu[2], Hui-Chieh Lu[3], Win-Tsung Lo[1], and Yen-Ping Chu[3]

[1] Department of Computer Science and Information Engineering, Tunghai University, Taichung, Taiwan, China
[2] Department of Computer Science, National Chiao-Tung University, Hsin-chu, Taiwan, China
[3] Insititute of Computer Science, National Chung Hsing University, Taichung, Taiwan, China
g922823@thu.edu.tw, rksheu@cis.nctu.edu.tw, phd9111@cs.nchu.edu.tw

Abstract. Locations of moving or missing objects are getting important information for context-aware applications which try to get the locality of an object, and then provide services pertaining to the object. To position an object, most systems use a predefined coordinate to compute object location while sensing the appearance of the target object. Usually, it is troublesome and costs much to define the base coordinate in advance for most object positioning systems, especially when the target object is locating in an unknown environment. To reduce the cost and complexity of object locating system and improve the accuracy of location, this paper proposed an Object Finding System based on RFID technology to identify the localities of target objects in buildings. In this paper, we introduce the design concepts of the proposed system as well as the algorithms used to calculate the object locations. In addition, the experimental results show that it is a feasibility study.

Keywords: RFID, wireless networks, user location and tracking, location estimation, indoor localization.

1 Introduction

With Locations of moving or missing objects, we obtain important information for context-aware applications which can get the locality of an object, and then provide services pertaining to the object. A well-known sample of object locating application is the positioning system for locating patients of severe acute respiratory syndrome (SARS) [1][2]. To prevent from the proliferation of SARS, doctors suggest restricting the motions of SARS patients. To make sure that no SARS patients violate the rule, they are forced to wear a sensible tag, which will be detected once they go across restriction area.

Currently, object locating solutions can be classified into two dimensions, which are positioning techniques and sensing systems [3][4]. From the viewpoint of positioning techniques, there are at least three methods can be used, alone or combined, such as:

Triangulation: Based on time of flight or angle of arrival of a signal against some baseline, the difference in distance from each receiver and transmitter can be measured using time difference of arrival or signal strength. ***Scene analysis***: This method

H.T. Shen et al. (Eds.): APWeb 2006, LNCS 3842, pp. 383 – 396, 2005.

measure the location by a particular vantage point of a viewed scene. ***Proximity***: The object can be measured by a set of points which is near known locations. Our approach is similar to proximity and introduces the geometry to locate the object.

As for the dimension of sensing system, most positioning systems use off-the-shelf solutions such as IEEE 802.11 series, Wireless Ethernet, Ultrasound, and Infrared technologies. For example, R. Want designed an infrared sensor which can detect objects carried with active infrared badges [5]. It is an early idea using active signal to locate objects. But, the infrared device is limited to sunlight and fluorescent light. The RADAR system measures the radio signal as a function of the user's position at the base stations and then triangulates the object's coordinate within a building [6]. Users do not need to build many base stations while locating objects. It must be in wireless LAN while tracking objects. Therefore there are drawbacks of the solution which are the power consumption and the size of carried adapter embedded in the target object. Besides, the tracked object needs to wear a sensible device but the cost would increase much. A.M. Ladd et al used wireless Ethernet adapters to locate the position of mobile devices, such as laptops, PDA and the likes [7][8].

In general, users should deploy many sensors to be the pre-defined coordinates before running the object positioning system. The target object will be found using positioning technologies and the object location will be reported in absolute or relative coordinate location value [3]. It is expensive to build the sensor infrastructure of these kinds of systems, and the detected object location is lack of accuracy due to abated signals which is affected by moisture or in-door obstacles [9]. To reduce the cost and deployment complexity of object positioning systems, and improve the accuracy of the returned object location, we try to use radio frequency identification (RFID) tags and readers to build the infrastructure of the proposed Object Finding System (OFS). The proposed OFS can find out target objects using only one moving reader using proximity algorithm.

In section2, this paper will introduce related object location systems. Section3 describes our design concepts and algorithms. Section4 describes the architecture of positioning system. Finally, our designed OFS and experimental results are introduced.

2 Related Work

Highly cost-efficiency rate and accuracy are the main reasons why we choose RFID as the infrastructure. There are also several features which are suitable to implement an object finding system using RFID. These features include the RFID tags are affordable, small size and light-weight, the RFID reader's signal strength is altered which can decide the distance between tag and reader.

The LANDMARC (LocAction iDentification based on dynamic Active Rfid Calibration) mainly raises the accuracy of locating without placing lots of RFID readers [9]. It is the first and most famous locating system based on RFID technology which mainly contains deployment of reference tags and reader. Afterward it can be used to calculate the position of tags with Euclidian distance. Fig.1 shows the object positioning method used by LANDMARC. Users need to install many readers and reference tags in advance and then readers can detect the locations of target objects by scaling up the strength of signals. At least three readers are needed to calculate the location of a target object and it is best to have the target object location if four readers are used to calculate the responded signal information.

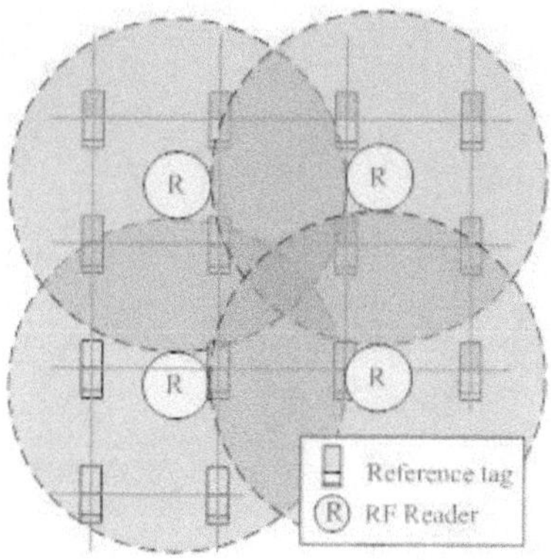

Fig. 1. The deployment of LANDMARC RFID tags and readers

The advantage of this approach is improving the accurate locating with cheaper reference tags instead of the expensive RFID readers. However, the system needs to be deployed RFID tags for each position of the pre-defined coordinate. And, it is sometimes unacceptable to set up several RFID readers inside buildings in the real world. Especially, it is not suitable for existent factories with unknown obstacles which will affect the accuracy of RFID signals. The objective of this paper is to propose an RFID based object finding system to be feasibility of LANDMARC-like systems and reduce both the cost and deployment complexity of object positioning systems.

3 The Proposed OFS Method

We try to use RFID tags and readers to build the infrastructure of the proposed Object Finding System (OFS). The proposed OFS can find out target objects using only one movable reader using proximity algorithm. This paper attempt to classify the indoor positioning system into two dimensions which are positioning the reader is like RADAR system through wireless network and positioning the object through RFID. That's will decrease the cost which consists of detected objects and the deployment of readers. The following will present the method of positioning the object. Beside this paper also consider the path of the reader moving to achieve optimum.

3.1 Method of Locating Tag

Suppose the reader emits at a rate of one time per second and the radius of the read range is $\boldsymbol{r}$. The system would record reader's location on the go. In Fig. 2.1, the coordinate P_{t+1} is the reader's position at time $t+1$ when the reader is detecting the tag first. The reader in the P_t doesn't detect the tag at time t. The average coordinate $P_{avg1}(x_1,y_1)$ is calculated between P_{t+1} and P_t as shown in Fig. 2.2. In Similar, we can also get the average coordinate $P_{avg2}(x_2,y_2)$ between $P_{t'}$ and $P_{t'+1}$. It can get a linear distance d between P_{avg1} and P_{avg2}. By using these two coordinates the position of tag is estimated via coordinate geometry (1). In fact, the system will obtain two coordinates t_1, t_2 via above-mentioned step.

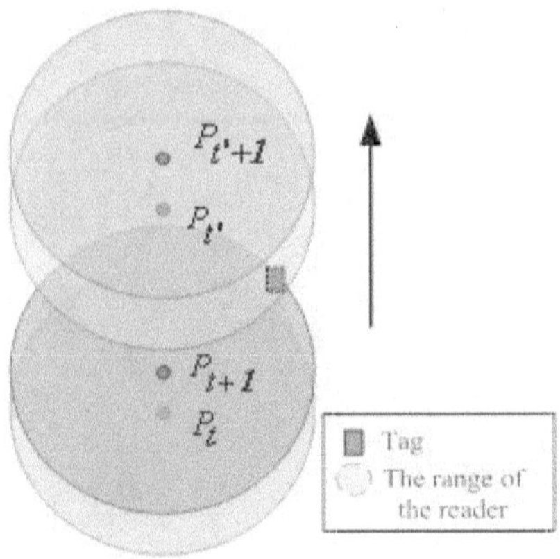

Fig. 2.1. The case of the reader detecting a tag

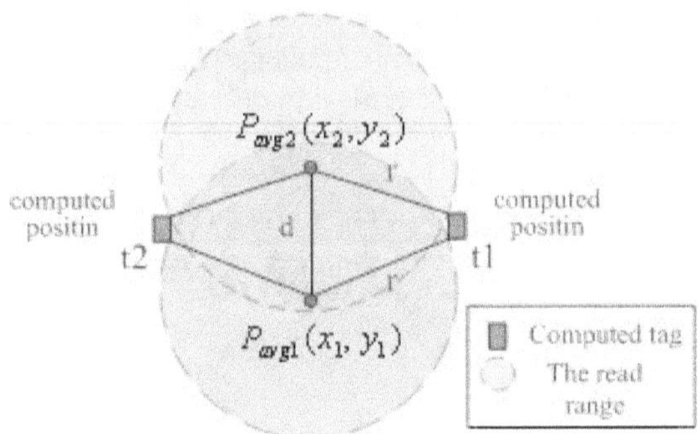

Fig. 2.2. Using coordinate geometry to compute the tag's position

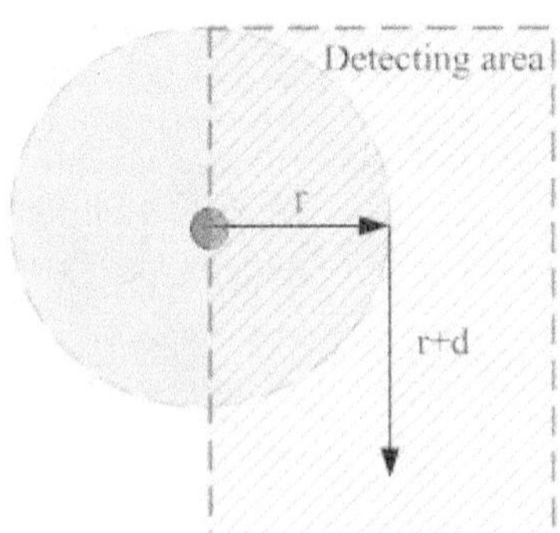

Fig. 3.1. Using shifting to detect the tag

Two of the unknown tag's coordinates (x,y) are obtained by:

$$(x, y) = \begin{cases} (x - x_1)^2 + (y - y_1)^2 = r^2 \\ (x - x_2)^2 + (y - y_2)^2 = r^2 \end{cases} \quad (1)$$

Therefore the reader is commanded to turn right a distance of r to decide one coordinate of both. The tag is placed at right side of the reader if the reader turns right and detects the tag. Otherwise, the tag is placed in left as shown in Fig. 3.1. However, if the P_{avg1} is more than $2r$ apart from P_{avg2}, tag's position maybe close to the beeline between both P_{avg1} and P_{avg2}. At this time the reader doesn't need to turn right. Coordinate of the tag is calculated directly and its coordinate is $(x,y)=(x_2+x_1/2, y_2+y_1/2)$.

When the reader has decided the reader's position, the reader will move back the position where it just turned. And then move to detect next object. This method could also use the other way is similar to Pioneer 2 robot [13] as shown in Fig. 3.2. The two readers equipped with mobile robot can not only detect the object but know which side of the mobile robot the object is placed.

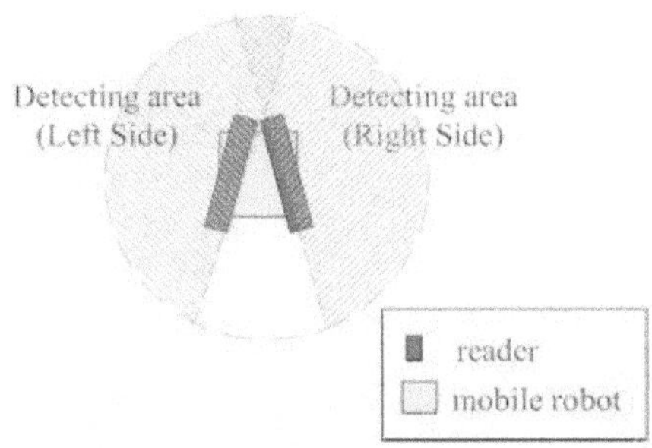

Fig. 3.2. Attaching two readers to robot

3.2 Path of the Reader Moving

A path of the reader affects the computed position of the object and the cost of the reader's path. Therefore the system has to find the optimal path of the reader. First

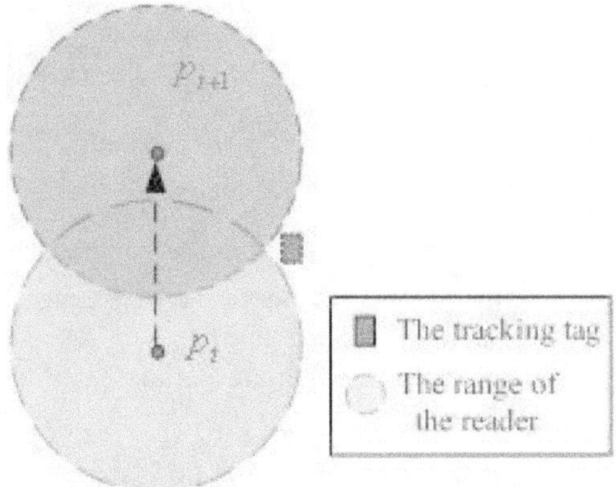

Fig. 4.1. The case of no detecting the tag

this paper presents the situation that the reader doesn't trigger the tag. If the tracking tag appears in the read range within the reader non-triggered time, the reader doesn't detect the tracking tag as shown in Fig. 4.1. This figure shows that the reader triggers to detect the tag in the coordinate P_t at time *t*, and then it triggers again in P_{t+1} at time $t+1$. But the tracking tag will not be detected. The reader would lose the tracking tag.

Therefore this paper proposes a method in order to solve above question. In this method, read range of the reader is overlapped when the reader travels the building as shown in Fig. 4.2. Our approach can find the optimum distance between $P_t^{'}$ and $P_{t'}^{'}$. The distance is $2\left(r^2-(d'/2)^2\right)^{1/2}$. The *d'* is a constant movement distance of the reader once. In this case, the $P_{t'}^{'}$ will detect it if the $P_t^{'}$ doesn't detect the tracking tag with a distance *d'* per second.

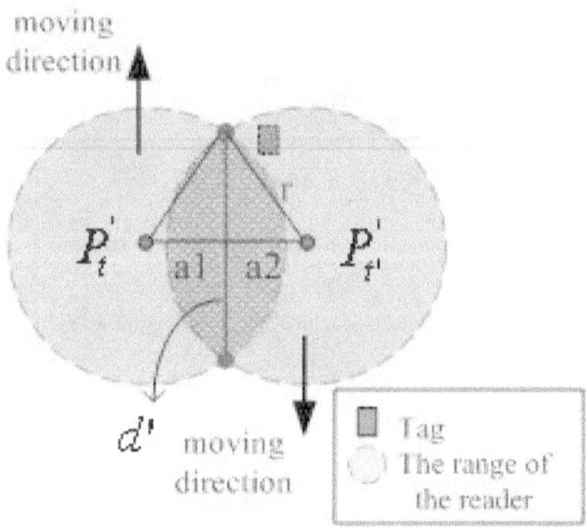

Fig. 4.2. The case of two read ranges overlapping

We then discuss the reader's path in two general areas as follows. In a square area the reader moves parallel with the left wall with a distance $\left(r^2-(d'/2)^2\right)^{1/2}$. When the reader moves to the front of wall, it moves according to the vector of $\vec{g}$ with a distance $2\left(r^2-(d'/2)^2\right)^{1/2}$. The reader then moves the whole square area according to this method as shown in Fig. 5. If the system sets up in the triangular area, the path will be similar to that in the square area as shown in Figure 6.

Let $\vec{f}$, $\vec{g}$, and $\vec{h}$ denote the vectors which are parallel with the wall according to Fig. 6. We define the vector as $\vec{f}=a\vec{x}+b\vec{y}$ and get the vector $\vec{u}=b\vec{x}-a\vec{y}$ which is perpendicular to $\vec{f}$. This paper proposes the travelling path algorithm is shown in table1.

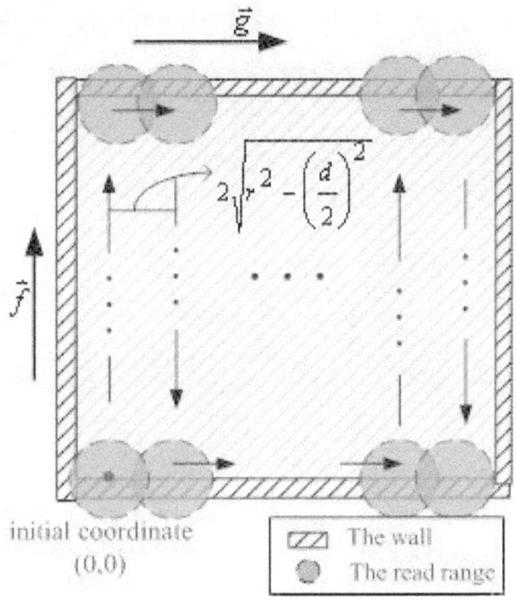

Fig. 5. The path of the reader travelling in the square area

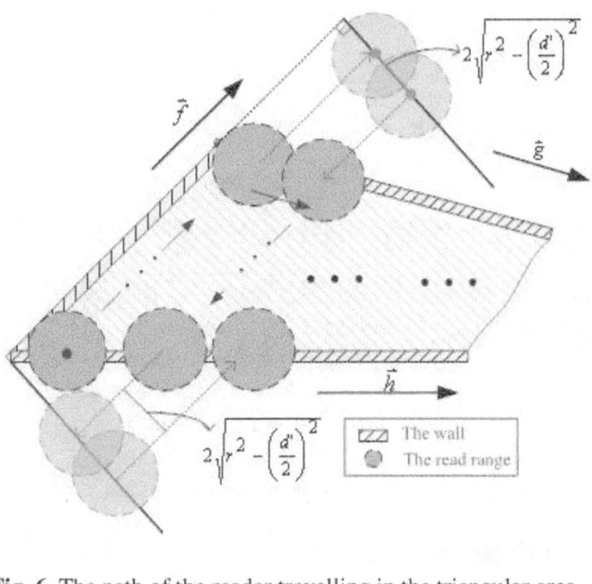

Fig. 6. The path of the reader travelling in the triangular area

Table 1. Travelling Path Algorithm

```
Set Coordinate of the reader (0,0)
  goVector = f̄ // a vector the reader moves
  move with goVector until reach the wall
  do
 if goVecotr = f̄ then
 turn right with ḡ and distance 2(r^2 - (d'/2)^2)^{1/2} / (ḡ·ū/|ḡ|·|ū|)
  goVecotr = -f̄
  move with goVector until reach the wall
else if goVector = -f̄ then
  turn left with h̄ and distance 2(r^2 - (d'/2)^2)^{1/2} / (h̄·ū/|h̄|·|ū|)
  goVecotr = f̄
  move with goVector until reach the wall
  end if
Until travelling all area
```

4 The OFS Architecture

The implement of our approach has to have some equipments which are consists of RFID devices, the mobile robot (machine or people), Position System, and wireless network.

Radio Frequency Identification (RFID) is a system that assists in transmitting the identity of the object, through a three-part of components consisting of a reader, a tag and software application [10]. The reader is a bridge between the application and the antenna. RFID reader emits a radio signal towards the tags, and then would read data emitted from tags. The reader reads all the incoming tag data then sends this information in real-time to a computer to inventory tracking object via wireless network. RFID tags are classified into active and passive. RFID tags may be active or passive depending on whether they have a battery or not. Read ranges of passive tags are shorter than active tags because they don't contain the battery [11]. Active tags possess a battery and they can transmit data to far range. The useful life of a battery can last generally from two to seven years [12]. Since active tags are very suitable for regarding as the identification of objects in RFID positioning system. We attach the active tag written usable information to the object to communicate with positioning system.

The mobile robot which our approach needs is similar to Pioneer 2 robot [13] in order to let the reader move around in the building. But our mobile robot just needs simple equipments are consist of a reader, the mobile device to connect wireless network. The function of the mobile robot is equipping reader to move. The reader would transmit the information which includes detected tag to positioning system. In addition the main subject of Position System is to determine the object's position through that information gathered from the reader.

Beside, we have to construct the environment with wireless network. It can communicate between the reader and Position System.

Object Finding System Framework. To position the object's location, the information received from the reader has to be transferred into positioning data. When the Position System collects suitable data, it will estimate the probable object's position thorough a serious of model from Position System. All process is as shown in Fig. 7. The reader equipped the mobile robot moves and detects the tracking object which wears a sensible tag. When the reader is detecting the tag, it will transmit the information to Position System through wireless network.

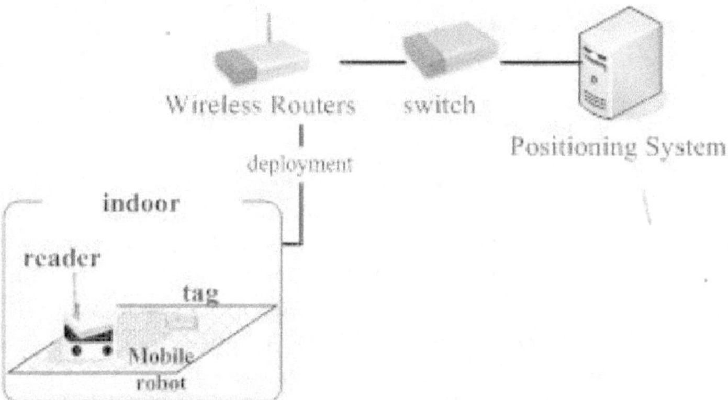

Fig. 7. OFS Framework

Position System uses a serious of model to transfer signal information into object's position. The main subjects of Position System is gathering the transmitted data, providing the travelling path to the mobile robot, and positioning the tracking tag. The Event Module is an event manager in the Position System to operate all processes as shown in Fig. 8.

There are four major modules designed in the Position System to complete above-mentioned subjects as below:

- *Event Module:* This module will analyses all the incoming data from the reader and then communicates the other modules to operate.

- *Map Module:* This module contains the coordinating system. It can display the position of the object in the e-map through the object's coordinate obtained from Position Module.
- *Position Module:* This module is implemented with our positioning method to position the object. It would use the useful information gathered from the reader to assist in positioning.
- *Path Module:* The path of the reader is decided according to this module. This module is designed to divide the e-map into several blocks and decide the path through our path algorithm. Its major function can provide the path information to reader.

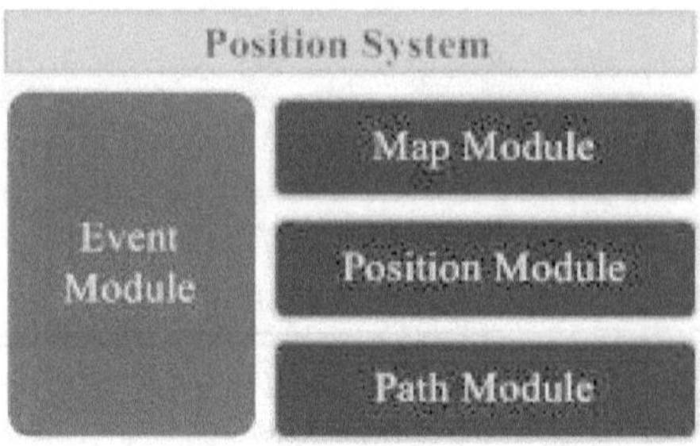

Fig. 8. Modules for object finding system.

5 Experiment

We have presented my positioning method before, but there are more factors to affect the accuracy of the positioning of the system. This paper will discuss these factors are relative to the performance of the positioning are as follows. Afterward we will design a virtual environment programmed by Java to simulate our positioning method just focus on positioning the object. Moreover, the clocks on the reader and the Position System are synchronized and the reader emits the information of the positioning at a rate of one time per second.

In the experiment, we analyze the performance of the positioning using the *error distance*, which is the linear distance between the physical location of the object and the estimated location from the Position System. We suppose the physical coordinate of the object (x,y) and the estimated coordinate (x',y'), and so the function of the error distance is

$$e = \sqrt{(x - x')^2 + (y - y')^2} \tag{2}$$

We set one hundred coordinates as experimental samples, and group them into ten types. They are P1, P2, …, P10.

5.1 Effect of the Movement Distance of the Reader

The movement distance of the reader has a greater effect. Therefore we want to find a suited movement distance once. This movement distance can make both the error distance and the time which the robot spends to move around the building are short. The system defines the radius of the read range is 2 meter and the size of virtual environment is 20m by 20m. We use this environment to complete our experiments. We choose four movement distance as 50cm, 70cm, 90cm, and 110cm. Table 2 shows that the reader spends approximately using the four kinds of different movement distances.

Table 2. The mobile robot spends time with individual movement distance

Distance(cm)	50	70	90	110
Time(minute)	≅ 8	≅ 6	≅ 5	≅ 4

Fig. 9 shows the results of using different movement distance. Obviously, the error distances are lower as the movement distances are 50cm and 70cm. Among of two values the error distance of 70cm is more stable than other. Besides, in Table1 the mobile robot only spends approximately six minutes with the movement distance of 70cm. In fact, the movement distance of the reader is according with the acceptable error distance.

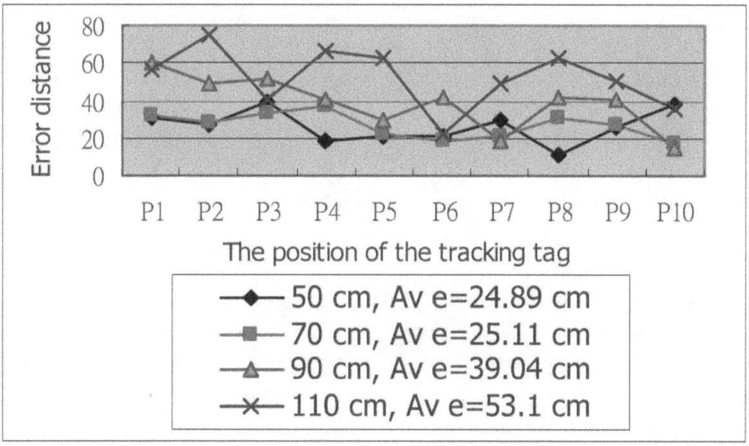

Fig. 9. Error distance with four movement distances

5.2 Effect of the Read Range of the Reader

This experiment is order to know whether or not the range of the reader influences the performance of locating system. First the movement distance of the reader moves is assigned 70cm. We choose four read ranges of the reader such as r = 1m, 2m, 3m, and 4m.

The results show that there is no significant difference from these choices except the radius 1m. The result of this experiment is shown as fig. 10. The radius 1m is so short

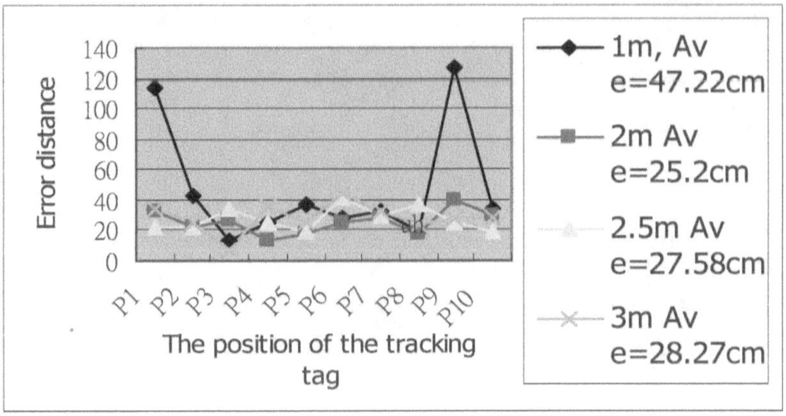

Fig. 10. Error distance with four read range

that the estimated coordinate is wrong direction. Among ten error distances the error distance of P1 and P9 are longer because two groups are marked in the corner of the room.

5.3 Comparison of Current Location Sensing Technologies

Many researches are deployment of static sensor in the room. Therefore, the cost would increase much. They can position all objects which are both dynamic and static. The accuracy of position depends on the deployment of sensors and the factors of environment.

Active Badges [5] designs an infrared sensor which can detect objects carried with active infrared badges. But, the infrared device is limited to sunlight and fluorescent light.

RADAR [6], based on the IEEE 802.11 requires only a few sensors and just uses the infrastructure of Wireless LAN [4]. But, the tag attached the tracking object must be small or power-constrained device. Besides, it necessary for predefined signal-strength database as operating in different environment. The median error distance is 2 to 3 meters and it needs to set up 3 bases per floor.

LANDMARC [9], similar to our methodology uses RFID technology. It mainly contains deployment of reference tags and reader. At least three readers are needed to calculate the location of a target object. The advantage of this approach is improving the accurate locating with cheaper reference tags instead of the expensive RFID readers. However, the system needs to be deployed RFID tags for each position of the pre-defined coordinate.

Our methodology OFS is to propose an RFID based object finding system. We use the RFID tag to be attached the object to reduce the cost and use mobile reader to reduce deployment of readers. At most two readers are needed to operate this system and the median error distance is shorter according to section 5.1 and 5.2.

6 Conclusions and Future Work

We presented an Object Finding System based on RFID technology to identify the localities of target objects in buildings and the concept of dividing indoor positioning into two dimensions. The one is positioning the reader through wireless network and the other is positioning the object through RFID. Our aim focuses on dimension of positioning the object. Also, at most two movable readers are used to position the object to reduce the system cost and improve the accuracy of position. The cost of positioning object with RFID is greatly reduced since the tag attached to the object is cheaper than other sensor devices. Although this system needs to be deployed with base sensors to position reader, its cost is still cheaper than the positioning method of reader deployment. Deploying the reference tag is more difficult in the building since the more factors of the environment will be involved. These factors consist of the deployment place and obstacles. Therefore we use the movable reader to position the object without deploying with reference tag and readers.

In our experiment the system finds the suited movement distance of the reader and reader range. In addition, the system also discovers the error distance will be unstable when a read range is near or smaller than the movement distance. The experiment data is according with the size of detected area, nevertheless, the difference of the size of detected indoor areas in building is not big. In the future we will analyze dissimilar the size of detected area and generalize from them.

Although our methodology is difficult in the dynamic environment, it provides another way in the static environment for positioning system.

Presently, our approach use RADAR to position reader. In the future we will propose a more suitable algorithm is similar to RADAR.

References

1. C. J. Li et al.: Mobile Healthcare Service System Using RFID. Proceedings of the 2004 IEEE Intl. Conference on Networking, Sensing & Control, March 21-23, 2004.
2. M. D. Rodriguez et al.: Location-Aware Access to Hospital Information and Services. IEEE Transactions on Information Technology in Biomedicine, VOL. 8, NO 4, December 2004.
3. K. Kolodziej, J. Danado: In-Building Positioning: Modeling Location for Indoor World. Proceedings of the 15th International Workshop on Database and Expert Systems Applications (DEXA'04), pp. 830 – 834 Sept. 2004
4. J. Hightower, G. Borriello: Location systems for ubiquitous computing. Computer, Volume: 34 , Issue: 8, pp. 57 – 66 Aug. 2001
5. R. Want:The Active Badge Location System. ACM Transactions on Information Systems, pp.91-102 January 1992
6. P. Bahl and V. N. Padmanabhan: RADAR: An In-building RF-based User Location and Tracking System. IEEE INFOCOM 2000, VOL. 2, pp. 775-784 March 2000
7. A. M. Ladd et al.: Using Wireless Ethernet for Localization. The 2002 IEEE/RSJ Intl Conference in Intelligent Robots and Systems,
8. S. S. Manapure et al.: A Comparative Study of Radio Frequency-Based Indoor Location Sensing Systems. International Conference on Networking, Sensing & Control, March 21-23, 2004.

9. L. M. Ni et al.: LANDMARC: Indoor Location Sensing Using Active RFID. Proceedings of the First IEEE Intl. Conference on Pervasive Computing and Communications, pp.407~415 March 2003.
10. Radio Frequency Identification (RFID) home page. http://www.aimglobal.org/technologies/ rfid/
11. Accenture: Radio Frequency Identification (RFID) White Paper, 2001, http://www.accenture.com/xdoc/en/services/technology/vision/rfidwhitepapernov01.pdf
12. RFID Journal, http://www.rfidjournal.com/article/findvendor?region=Canada&function=Other&p=6
13. D. Hahnel et al.: Mapping and Localization with RFID Technology. Robotics and Automation, 2004. Proceedings. ICRA '04. 2004 IEEE International Conference on , Volume: 1 , pp.1015 – 1020, April 26-May 1, 2004

Low Energy Consumption Security Method for Protecting Information of Wireless Sensor Network*

Jaemyung Hyun and Sungsoo Kim

Graduate School of Information and Communication, Ajou University,
Suwon, Gyeonggi-do 443-749, Korea
{jmhyun78, sskim}@ajou.ac.kr

Abstract. Location information is very important in the sensor network. Therefore, cryptography methods are being used to protect the information in wireless sensor network even though cryptography methods consume the large amount of additional energy. One of the final goals in the wireless sensor network is to maximize the life time of sensor node because sensor nodes have very limited power. Therefore, this paper proposes the energy efficient security method which uses relative coordinate instead of physical coordinate to reduce the energy consumption. Location information description with relative coordinate makes the caught data meaningless and can protect the data without using cryptography methods.

1 Introduction

As the wireless sensor network becomes popular recently, it is expected to be widely used in many fields. Main purpose of the wireless sensor network is to collect data from the environment where the sensor node is placed. If the collected data are exposed to attacker, it causes the invasion of personal privacy [1][2][3]. Therefore, cryptography methods are being used to protect data of sensor node in most wireless sensor networks. According to P. Ganeasn [4], most of the cryptography methods consume large amount of energy in wireless sensor network with the limited resource. In this situation, if one sensor node loses the capacity due to the additional energy consumption, the other nodes must work more to send data to sink-node in wireless sensor network. Because it affects the whole wireless sensor network, finally sensor network would lose its ability. To solve both energy problem and security of wireless sensor network, some energy efficiency security methods have been proposed : Energy Efficient Security Protocol [5] and Energy-Efficient Secure Pattern Based Data Aggregation [6]. Both methods can reduce amount of energy consumption, but, energy consumption is still large because they still use cryptography methods. Thus, this paper presents energy efficient security method to solve the problems without any cryptography method.

Our method uses relative coordinate, because relative can hide the location information. For the determination of relative coordinate, GPS-free algorithm [7] and

* This research is supported by the Ubiquitous Autonomic Computing and Network Project, the Ministry of Information and Communication (MIC) 21st Century Frontier R&D Program in Korea.

H.T. Shen et al. (Eds.): APWeb 2006, LNCS 3842, pp. 397–404, 2005.

Relative Location estimation in Wireless Networks [7] are proposed. GPS-free algorithm can estimate relative coordinate without GPS, but it doesn't have any reference physical coordinate. Therefore GPS-free algorithm needs amount of calculation to estimate relative coordinate, and it is larger than Time of Arrival (TOA) algorithm [9] or 3/2 Neighbor Algorithm (3/2NA) [9] does. The Relative Location Estimation in Wireless Networks shown in previous research can also estimate relative coordinate and has reference coordinate from which GPS. However many GPS are used in this system, the cost to build sensor network is expensive. Thus, we developed EESMRC (Energy Efficient Security Method using Relative Coordinate) for energy efficient and inexpensive security in sensor network. In EESMRC, each node maintains relative coordinate table which is estimated by TOA and 3/2NA instead of GPS free algorithm, and it can reduced amount of calculation. Also just 3 GPS are used to get reference coordinated which can change relative coordinate to physical coordinate, therefore the cost to build sensor network with EESMRC is lower than Relative Location Estimation in Wireless Networks [8].

The remainder of the paper is organized as follows : In Section 2, we describe the determination of relative location and physical location and section 3 describes network generation for our security method (EESMRC). In section 4, we present the point of security view and section 5 presents a result of simulation. Finally, section 6 summarizes with concluding remarks and possible extensions to our study.

2 Relative Location and Physical Location

Location information is very important in the wireless sensor network, so our method describes location information as relative coordinate instead of using physical coordinate. If the collected data by sensor nodes are serviced without location information, user wouldn't know where the data are from. Therefore the data without information is useless [10]. We use this point for our energy efficient security method. Location information description with relative coordinate makes the caught data meaningless even though the attacker catches the data. This is example. In the location tracking system, the main data of this system are Object ID and location information. The detail information of object can be supported by Sink-Node and only object ID and location information will be used during the tracking. The Object ID can not have any meaning without location information, so cryptography methods are not needed to protect the data and hiding location information can protect the data of the system.

This section shows how each node can get its relative distance from relative coordinates and how Sink-Node estimates physical coordinate from relative coordinate.

2.1 Relative Distance and Relative Coordinate Determination

Determination of relative coordinate is started from knowing reference coordinate and then relative coordinate can be estimated from reference coordinates. These reference coordinates are from specially equipped nodes which consist of one Sink-Node and two GPS-Equipped nodes. Fig. 1 shows the procedure of determination of node's relative coordinate. The Sink-Node(PS), GPS-Node1($P1$) and GPS-Node2($P2$) have to be grouped and should be able to communicate each other directly (in one hop). We separate procedure into two parts. One part is procedure of Sink-Node group and the other is procedure of every node.

At first, GPS-Nodes use its GPS to gain its own physical coordinate and then send its physical coordinates to Sink-Node. After sending the information, the nodes turn off its GPS to save power, but the nodes are still alive and can communicate with other nodes. As a result, Sink-Node has three physical coordinates of nodes and it will never send to other nodes. To estimate relative coordinate, setting of basis position is mandatory. Therefore, we set Sink-Node as a center of network (0,0) and set relative coordinate of GPS-Node1 to lie on the positive x axis of the Sink-Node. As the Sink-Node already knows the physical coordinate of GPS-Node2, so GPS-Node2's relative coordinate can be estimated easily. The relative coordinates of the Sink-Node group which consists of Sink-Node, GPS-Node1, and GPS-Node2 are:

Sink-Node = (0, 0), GPS-Node1 = ($D_{ps\sim p1}$, 0), GPS-node2 = (R_x , R_y)

We describe the algorithm to estimate GPS-node2 coordinate in 3.2, because it is the same way to determine physical coordinate from relative coordinate.

It is second step. If node i and j can communicate directly (in one hop), node j is called a one-hop neighbor of node i. We define $\forall i \in N$, a set of nodes K_i such that $\forall j \in K_i$, $j \neq i, j$ is a one-hop neighbor of i , whereas N is a set of all the nodes in the network. We call K_i the set of one-hop neighbors of node i . We define $\forall i \in N$ the set D_i as a set of distances measured from the node i to the node $j \in K_i$. The distances between the nodes are measured by TOA.

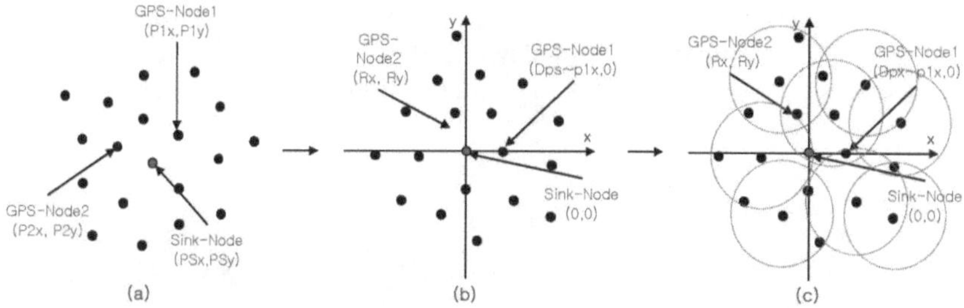

Fig. 1. (a) Using GPS, gain the physical coordinate of GPS nodes (b) Mapping to relative coordinate (c) Using reference nodes calculate other nodes' relative coordinate

Table 1. Relative distance table of NodeA

NodeA(x,y)	
ID	Relative Distance
NodeE-1	NodeA(x,y) − NodeB-1(x,y)
NodeE-2	NodeA(x,y) − NodeB-2(x,y)
NodeE-3	NodeA(x,y) − NodeB-3(x,y)

We assume that nodes already know own relative coordinate by two step of relative coordinate estimation. Node makes a relative information table. This table has relative distance of other nodes which can communicate and it is used during communication. Only relative distance is used during communication and relative coordinate is stored in node. Table 1 shows estimation of relative distance.

2.2 Physical Coordinate Determination

In EESMRC, only relative distance is used and relative coordinate is stored in the node to hide physical coordinate during communication with other nodes. Sink-Node estimates physical coordinate when Sink-Node receives relative coordinate of node. Sink-Node has to know at least 2 relative coordinates and 2 physical coordinates can be matched each other. From these coordinates, Sink-Node can get angle between relative coordinate and physical coordinate and can estimate physical coordinate from relative coordinate. Now we show how to estimate physical coordinate of NodeA. At first, Sink-Node needs coordinate of Sink-Node, GPS-Node1 and NodeA.

Relative coordinate		**Physical coordinate**
Sink-Node $(0,0)$	→	(PS_x, PS_y)
GPS-Node1 $(R1_x, R1_y)$	→	$(P1_x, P1_y)$
NodeA (RA_x, RA_y)	→	(PA_x, PA_y)

α is angle between relative coordinate and physical coordinate of GPS-Node1. β is angle between NodeA and x axis. If NodeA is rotated by angle α, NodeA can be placed at new coordinate. The angle between new position of NodeA and x axis is $\alpha+\beta$. However, still this new coordinate is not a real physical coordinate and we call this coordinate as $RAN(x,y)$. It is the same as coordinate ($PA_x - PS_x, PA_y - PS_y$). $RAN(x,y)$ can be calculated by

$$RAN_x = \cos(\alpha+\beta)\cdot\sqrt{RA_x^2 + RA_y^2} = (\cos(\alpha)\cos(\beta) - \sin(\alpha)\sin(\beta))\cdot\sqrt{RA_x^2 + RA_y^2}$$

$$RAN_y = \sin(\alpha+\beta)\cdot\sqrt{RA_x^2 + RA_y^2} = (\sin(\alpha)\cos(\beta) + \cos(\alpha)\sin(\beta))\cdot\sqrt{RA_x^2 + RA_y^2}$$

As we already know PS, $R1$, $P1$, and RA, so we can estimate values of $\cos\alpha, \cos\beta, \sin\alpha$, and $\sin\beta$. Finally we get the physical coordinate of NodeA by adding physical coordinate of Sink-node to $RAN(x,y)$.

$$PA(x,y) = RAN(x,y) + PS(x,y)$$

3 Network Generation and Communication Method

EESMRC aims at an external environment and a centralized Sensor Network. Most nodes just collect information, and most computation is processed by Sink-Node. Every node has an ID. We assume that the network consists of N sensor nodes in unknown location and sensors are assumed to be equipped with omni-directional antennas which have a sensor-to-sensor communication range r. Sink-Node and two nodes which have GPS are one group, and this group is placed at center of network. In this security method, we use TOA and 3/2NA algorithms to determine relative coordinate. TOA and 3/2NA use three nodes to determine location of node, so the whole number of nodes are set to satisfy that one node can have at least 3 neighbor nodes [11].

Each node has relative information table. Relative coordinate, relative distance and node ID (relative distance and ID of nodes which can communicate) are stored in this table. When node sends data to Sink-Node, the data is passing through several nodes to arrive at Sink-Node, unless node can communicate directly with Sink-Node. Fig. 2 shows this method.

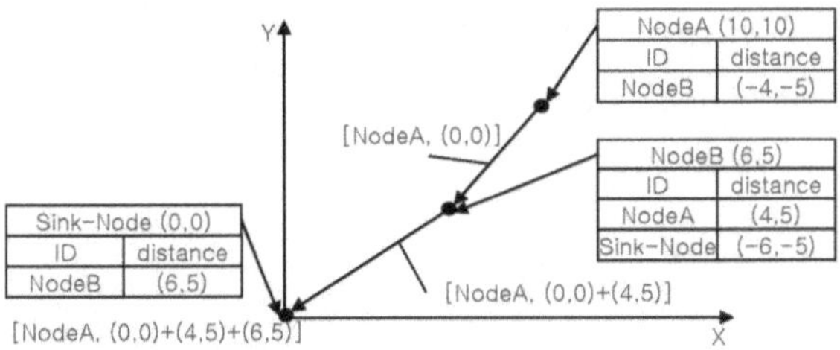

Fig. 2. Additional Method of Communication

4 Security View

When relative coordinate of Sink-Node is estimated, we can make Sink-Node as a center of EESMRC without any physical coordinate. Therefore relative coordinate of Sink-Node can be at any position of geographic position. Even though attacker can get the relative coordinate of whole nodes, they can only know the shape of whole node unless attacker has two physical and relative coordinates which can match each other. These methods which determine relative coordinate of Sink-Node group can make many possibility of getting relative coordinate of nodes and guarantee security of information of location. Also we use relative distance during communication, because the most important node is Sink-Node. Every node sends data to Sink-Node and Sink-Node manages these data. Therefore, protection of Sink-Node is one of the most important job in sensor network. If relative coordinate is used during communication between nodes, attacker can easily estimate distance of Sink-Node when attacker gets relative coordinate. If attacker gets relative distance, it would be the distance between receiving node and sending node when relative distance is used during communication.

5 Simulation and Performance Evaluation

This section shows the Simulation and the performance of using EESMRC. To evaluate performance of our method, we compare our method with the established results [3]. Hardware platform, Sparc 440 node is used to simulate. The amount of computational energy consumed by a security function on a given microprocessor is primarily determined by the number of clocks consumed by the processor to compute the security function. To calculate performance, we use the next formula [2][12].

Table 2. Parameter of performance evaluation

a	Overhead of initialization
b	Time spent in operations
Text_length	Size of the plaintext in bytes
Blocksize	Size of cryptographic data
Processor_freq	Processor clock
Bus_width	processor bus width

Table 3. Parameter of other cryptography

Algorithm	Value A (instruction)	Value B (instruction)	Blocksize (bit)
MD5	203656	86298	512
SHA1	77337	233082	512
RC4	69240	13743	8
EESMRC	11204	597	512

$$amount\ of\ enery\ consumption \approx execution\ time \approx \frac{A + B \cdot \lceil Text\_length / Blocksize \rceil}{Processor\_freq \cdot Bus\_width} \quad (1)$$

Table 2 presents the parameters used in formula (2). The value A, B and Blocksize affect the execution time. Parameter A includes all the initialization overheads while B captures the time spent in operations repeated for each block. Hence, as the value A is bigger, the execution time is increased.

Table 3 presents the overhead of cryptography algorithms compared with others. The value A is the biggest in the MD5 cryptography algorithms and the value B is the biggest in the SHA1 cryptography algorithms. EESMRC's value A and B are small compared with others. Blocksize of RC4 is very small compared with others in the table 3. RC4 cryptography algorithms need a large amount of computation.

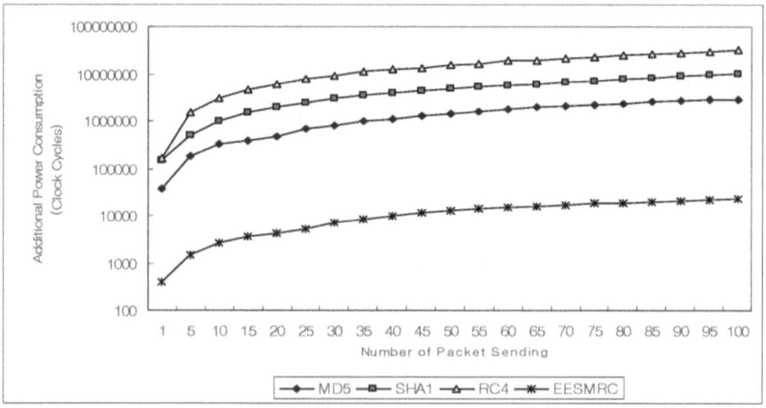

Fig. 3. Power Consumption Comparing with Other Cryptography

Fig. 3 shows additional power consumption with packet sending. EESMRC doesn't need high additional power during communication, while RC4, SHA1 and MD5 spend a large amount of additional power compared with EESMRC. RC4 uses the biggest additional energy consumption because the block size of RC4 is only 8, so

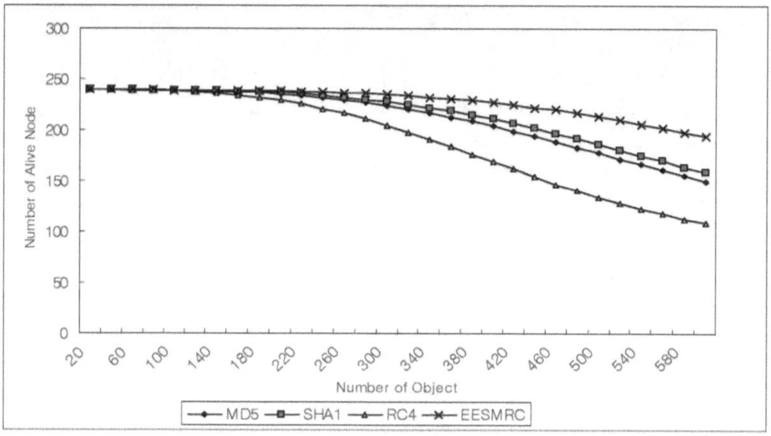

Fig. 4. Alive node per object

every 8 bits in plain text, the parameter B (time spending in operation) in the formula (2) must be repeated. However EESMRC only adds relative distance to received data from their neighbor instead of using cryptography method.

We simulate wireless sensor network with cryptography to analyze the lifetime of sensor node in wireless network. In the simulation, node placement is constant node placement and 240 sensor nodes are placed in the wireless sensor network uniformly. 600 objects appear and when sensor node detects the object, sensor node sends this information. Each cryptography algorithm is used for comparing with EESMRS. We count every 20 objects as the number of alive sensor node. Fig 4 presents the result of simulation. After appearing of 600 objects, the biggest number of sensor node is alive in the simulation using EESMRC while only 100 sensor nodes are alive in the simulation using RC4 cryptography algorithm.

With EESMRC method, sensor node uses a little amount of additional energy, so most of sensor nodes are alive after finishing simulation but with RC4 cryptography algorithm, sensor node uses large amount of additional energy and the sensor node loses the capacity. Other nodes must do the computation instead of the sensor node which loses the capacity. As a result the number of alive sensor node in wireless sensor network declines dramatically. It means the lifetime of wireless sensor network also decreases.

EESMRC is applied with application layer, so it can be used with other cryptography methods, if EESMRC can be used with other cryptography methods, the graph of EESMRC will be same as other graph of cryptography methods. However the wireless sensor network can have more security because the location information is hidden one more by cryptography method. Therefore, if adversary can crack the cryptography methods, adversary can not know the real meaning of the data.

6 Conclusion

In this paper, we present energy efficient security method to take advantage of low power consumption for security by hiding location information using relative coordinate in sensor network. Due to the limited resources in wireless sensor network, cryptography algorithms make large amount of additional power consumption, and it causes short life time of sensor network node. As a result the life time of sensor network is declined. In order to overcome these shortcomings, hiding location information by using relative coordinate technique is introduced. Using relative coordinate for security in sensor network provides better spectral efficiency to the system. And it can take advantage of saving of power in sensor node accordingly. We expect our method will be useful in wireless sensor network with limitation of resource.

We only simulate the energy consumption about using EESMRC in wireless sensor network. But only using hiding information of location for having a security will make problem in dangerous environment. We must study the case of attacking in wireless sensor network and then, study the influence of attacking wireless sensor network with using EESMRC.

References

1. Akyildiz, L., et al.,: A Survey on Sensor Networks. IEEE Communications Magazine (2002) 102-114
2. Perring, A., et al.,: SPINS:Security Protocols for Sensor Networks. Proceedings of Seventh Annual International Conference on Mobile Computing and Networks (2001) 189-199
3. Yin, C., et al., : Secure Routing for Large-scale Wireless Sensor Networks. Proceedings of the International Conference on Communication Technology (2003)
4. Ganeasn, P., et al.,: Analyzing and Modeling Encryption Overhead for Sensor Network Nodes. Proceedings of ACM Workshop on Wireless Sensor Networks and Applications (2003) 151-159
5. Cam, H.,et al,. : Energy-Efficient Security protocol for Wireless Sensor Networks. Proceedings of IEEE VTC Fall 2003 Conference (2003)
6. Cam, H., et al.,: Energy-Efficient Secure Pattern Based Data Aggregation for Wireless Sensor Networks. Proceeding of IEEE International Performance Computing and Communications Conference (2005)
7. Capkun, S., et al.,: GPS-free Positioning in Mobile Ad-Hoc Networks. Proceedings of the 34th Annual Hawaii International Conference on System Sciences (2001) 1-10
8. Patwari, N., et al.,: Relative Location Estimation in Wireless Sensor Networks. IEEE Transactions on Signal Processing, Special Issue on Signal Processing in Networks (2003) 2137-2148
9. Barbeau, M., et al., : Improving Distance Based Geographic Location Techniques in Sensor Networks. International Conference on Ad Hoc Networks and Wireless (2004) 197-210
10. Beutel, J.: Location Management in Wireless Sensor Networks. Chapter in Handbook of Sensor Networks: Compact Wireless and Wired Sensing Systems, CRC Press (2004)
11. Slijepcevic, S et al., : On Communication Security in Wireless Ad-Hoc Sensor Networks. 11th IEEE International Workshop on Enabling Technologies: Infrastructure for Collaborative Enterprises (2002) 139-144.
12. Park, S., and Kim, S.: Self-Protection Scheme in Sensor Network with Autonomic Computing. Technical Report, Ajou University (2004)

Process Scheduling Policy Based on Rechargeable Power Resource in Wireless Sensor Networks*

Young-Mi Song, Kyung-chul Ko, Byoung-Hoon Lee, and Jai-Hoon Kim

Graduate School of Information and Communication,
Ajou University, Suwon, Republic of Korea
{ymsong, amazing, componer, jaikim}@ajou.ac.kr

Abstract. Many multi-process scheduling schemes have been developed to utilize system resources efficiently. In the previous researches, most of the scheduling schemes were focused on how to allocate computing resources efficiently. However, in the environment of wireless sensor networks, scheduling policy for power resources of mobile device is also essential as high power drain of mobile sensor device will lead to immediate non-functioning of device due to limited capacity of its battery. Sensor nodes can also be powered by rechargeable power resources such as solar cell or gravitation. In these cases, residual energy of rechargeable power resource is dynamic over time. This motivated us to design a scheduling policy based on rechargeable power resource for increasing the network life time and reducing the response time of service. In this paper, we present and evaluate six process scheduling schemes based on execution time and energy consumption of process.

1 Introduction

In the area of sensor networks, the power resource management is important factor that determines the longevity of the network life time because sensor nodes are battery-driven [1], [2]. However, sensor nodes can also be powered by rechargeable power resources. For an example, smart dust motes can have a solar cells or gravitation as power resource [3], [4]. These rechargeable power resources have the potential of increasing operational life time of sensor devices.

Rechargeable power resource has special features unlike other resources such as CPU, memory and communication bandwidth, etc. These non-rechargeable resources have fixed amount of available resource per time unit. Besides, if the resource is not used, it becomes wasted. For an example, if the CPU is sleep for a while even though some processes want to use the CPU, it is clearly the waste of CPU. On the other hand, rechargeable power resource is preserved even if it is not used, so it can be used later. Also available amount of rechargeable power resource per time unit is variable. These features motivated us to design a scheduling policy for the power resource management. Most of the process scheduling scheme have been focused on how to

* This work was supported by grant no. R01-2003-000-10794-0 from the Basic Research Program of the Korea Science & Engineering Foundation, by IITA Professorship for Visiting Faculty Positions in Korea (International Joint Research Project), and by the Ubiquitous Computing and Network Project (part of the MIC 21st Century Frontier R&D Program).

H.T. Shen et al. (Eds.): APWeb 2006, LNCS 3842, pp. 405 – 409, 2006.

allocate CPU resources to increase the computing performance (e.g., throughput and response time). For an example, First-Come-First-Served (FCFS), Round Robin, etc [5]. However, in this paper, we focus on how to assign the rechargeable power resource to processes based on its unique features.

This paper proposes six process scheduling schemes that are categorized by execution time and the amount of energy consumption of each process as follows.

1. A scheduler selects a process first that has the largest energy consumption (LEC).
2. A scheduler selects a process first that has the smallest energy consumption (SEC).
3. A scheduler selects a process first that has the longest execution time (LET).
4. A scheduler selects a process first that has the shortest execution time (SET).
5. A scheduler selects a process first that has the largest energy consumption per time unit (LECPT).
6. A scheduler selecting a process first that has the smallest energy consumption per time unit (SECPT).

Through evaluation and simulation of these schemes, we find that the most efficient scheme is the SECPT. Our simulation results can be used to select proper scheduling schemes for rechargeable power resource in wireless sensor networks.

Most of previous schemes for power management focused on minimizing power consumption [6], [7]. These approaches exclude the methods which use rechargeable power resource. Reference [3] suggests the routing protocol for supporting the environment in which several sensor nodes can recharge their power resource by solar cells. This protocol selects the routing path which includes nodes that can recharge its energy in order to increase the network life time. The scheme in [3] is related to ours from the aspect of rechargeable energy. However, we are focused on process scheduling scheme based on rechargeable power resource. We also improve the response time by reducing the waiting time caused insufficient power to complete its tasks on the rechargeable nodes.

2 Proposed Scheduling Scheme

Our scheme has assumptions as follows:

- The amount of energy recharge per time unit is the same for simplification.
- The scheduler must have an estimation of both execution time and energy consumption of processes in the node. Since sensor node's processes perform predefined functions such as sensing or networking, this assumption is practical.
- Process can be executed after checking whether the amount of *residual energy* is enough to finish its tasks. The *residual energy* means the energy that sensor node currently holds. In the environment using solar panels, the weather or other obstacles have influence on the amount of recharged energy. It means that the amount of energy which will be recharged varies. So, if the process is executed without sufficient energy to finish its tasks, it can be stopped during execution of the process causing significant performance degradation. Therefore, if the amount of residual energy is not enough to finish its tasks, the node

has to wait until the required energy is recharged. We define this waiting time as *pause time* in this paper. Pause time also means the 'sleep time' of the sensor node. This is very important factor for improving performance in addition to the network operational life time. We use this pause time as performance evaluation parameter.

The amount of residual energy can be changed dynamically according to process scheduling schemes as unused power resource is preserved. Longer execution time of a process (the amount of recharged energy is grown over time) and the less energy a process consumes, more energy will remain. As large energy is remained, the sensor node can reduce the pause time.

Fig. 1 shows the amount of residual energy and pause time when the scheduler selects a process based on its consumed energy. Table 1 shows the execution time and consumed energy of each process. To analyze how the consumed energy of process affects the pause time, we assumed that all processes have the same execution time. The initial energy of sensor node is 100 J and the recharged energy per time unit is 15 J. In LEC (Fig. 1(a)), process A spends 80 J, but 15 J is recharged while execution time of process A passed. So, residual energy is 35 J (100 - 80 + 15). Next, process B checks residual energy but it is not enough. So, sensor node has to wait 3 time units for recharging the energy by more than 35 J (70 - 35). Rest part of process execution is performed similarly. SEC (Fig. 1(b)) can reduce 2 time units of pause time against LEC. Since the processes required smaller energy are executed ahead in SEC, SEC can preserve more energy than LEC.

Table 1. Execution time and consumed energy

Process ID	A	B	C	D
Consumed energy	80	70	5	5
Execution time	1	1	1	1

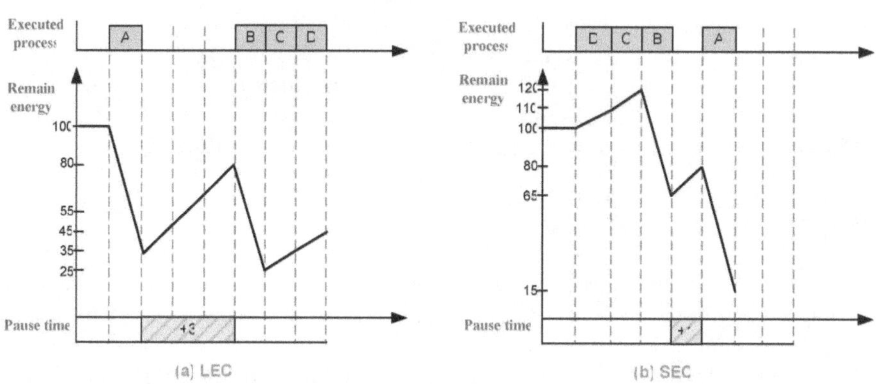

Fig. 1. Comparing two scheduling schemes based on consumed energy

Table 2. Execution time and consumed energy

Process ID	A	B	C	D
Consumed energy	100	100	100	100
Execution time	1	3	5	7

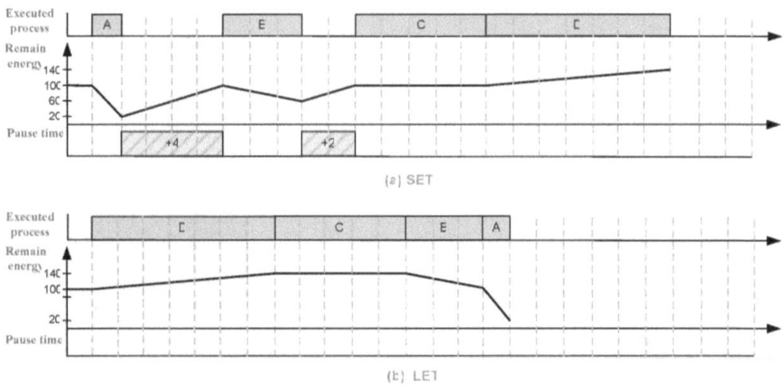

Fig. 2. Comparing two scheduling schemes based on execution time

Another example is represented by Fig. 2 and Table 2. In this case, it presents how process execution time affects the pause time. There are also two process scheduling policies, SET (Fig. 2(a)) and LET (Fig. 2(b)). In this case, we assume that every process consumes the same energy and the recharged energy per time unit is 20 J. As shown Fig. 2(b), LET can reduce 6 time units of pause time against SET. Since the processes executed ahead in LET have longer execution time than SET, LET can reduce pause time by preserving more energy than SET.

In conclusion, we observe that when the scheduler selects a process by order of smallest consumed energy or longest execution time, we can reduce pause time. The process with the smallest consumed energy and the largest execution time means preserving the largest energy per time unit. The 'consumed energy per time unit' is calculated by dividing the total consumed energy by the total execution time of process. LECPT and SECPT are based on this consumed energy per time unit.

3 Performance Evaluation

In this section, we simulate six proposed process scheduling schemes for comparing the performance of these policies in terms of pause time. In Fig. 3, we show the change in pause time by increasing the number of processes. We choose randomly the execution time of processes in the range of [1, 10] time unit and energy consumption in the range of [10, 100] J. The amount of energy recharge per time unit is 10 J. In Fig. 3, the performance gap between those schemes increases as the number of process increases. SECPT achieves the best performance among schemes. It can reduce pause time up to 96% in compare to the worst case, LECPT and up to 33% in compare to LET.

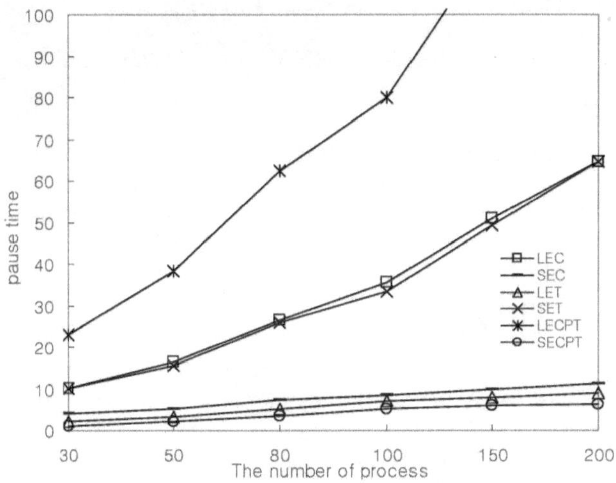

Fig. 3. Performance comparison among scheduling schemes as increasing the number of processes

4 Conclusion

In this paper, we present six different scheduling schemes on the aspect of execution time and energy consumption of processes in the environment of rechargeable power resource. We prove that scheduling scheme choosing a process with the smallest energy consumption per time unit performs the best. Reduction pause time increases throughput and network operational life time by decreasing the sleep time of sensor node in the wireless sensor networks. Future work would include researches about the new recharge aware routing scheme and process scheduling scheme using the various system parameters to improve performance.

References

1. I. F. Akyildiz, W. Su, Y. Sankarasubramaniam and E. Cayirci, "Wireless Sensor Networks : A Survey", *Computer Networks*, vol.38, 2002, pp.392-422.
2. Y. Zhao, R. Govidan and D. Estrin, "Residual Energy Scan for Monitoring Sensor Networks", *IEEE WCNC,* vol.1, 2002, pp.356-362.
3. T. Voigt, H. Ritter and J. Schiller, "Solar-aware Routing in Wireless Sensor Networks", *Personal Wireless Communication,* 2003.
4. J. M. Rabaey, M. J. Ammer, J. L. Da, S. Jr, D. Patel, and S. Roundy, "Picoradio Supports Ad Hoc Ultra-Low Power Wireless Networking", *IEEE Computer Magazine,*vol.33, 2000, pp.42-48.
5. W. Stallings, "Operating Systems, Internals and Design Principles", Prentice Hall, 2001.
6. W. Ye, J. Heidemann, and D. Estrin. "An Energy-Efficient MAC Protocol for Wireless Sensor Networks", *INFOCOM,* vol.3, 2002, pp.1567-1576.
7. R. C. Shah and J. Rabaey, "Energy Aware Routing for Low Energy Ad Hoc Sensor Networks", *IEEE WCNC,* vol.1, 2002, pp. 350-355.

An Energy Efficient Cross-Layer MAC Protocol for Wireless Sensor Networks*

Changsu Suh, Young-Bae Ko, and Dong-Min Son

Graduate School of Information and Communication,
Ajou University, Republic of Korea
{scs, youngko, haeroo83}@ajou.ac.kr

Abstract. In the area of wireless sensor networks, achieving minimum energy consumption is a very important research issue. A number of energy efficient protocols have been proposed, mostly based on a layered design approach, which means that they are focused on designing optimal strategies for "single" layer only. In this paper, we take an alternative approach i.e., a cross-layer design, and present a new MAC protocol named MAC-CROSS. In this new approach, the interactions between MAC and Routing layers are fully exploited to achieve energy efficiency for wireless sensor networks. More precisely, in the proposed MAC-CROSS algorithm, routing information at the network layer is utilized for the MAC layer such that it can maximize a sleep duration of each node. Through implementation on a Mica Mote platform and simulation study using the NS-2, we evaluate a performance of the presented MAC-CROSS and prove its substantial performance gains.

1 Introduction

A wireless sensor network consists of a number of smart sensors equipped with limited battery power and inexpensive short-range radio communication. Due to their energy critical characteristics and high probability of failures, wireless sensor networks require a design of the efficient MAC protocol. Especially, it is a primary goal for any proposed sensor MAC protocol to minimize energy consumption because a power drain of each sensor node may cease all the necessary functions of the sensor network.

There has been recent attention on developing energy efficient MAC protocols in wireless sensor networks [1]. They are generally based on a mechanism of turning off their radio transceivers whenever they are not involved in communication. Also, they are mainly focused on how to optimize the MAC layer's energy efficiency without fully exploiting the potential synergies of the interaction among different layers. In this paper, we instead follow a cross-layer design approach and propose a new MAC protocol that utilizes a routing policy information from the network layer - hence, we call the proposed MAC protocol as

* This research was supported by the MIC (Ministry of Information and Communication), Korea, under the ITRC (Information Technology Research Center) support program supervised by the IITA (Institute of Information Technology Assessment).

H.T. Shen et al. (Eds.): APWeb 2006, LNCS 3842, pp. 410–419, 2006.

"MAC-CROSS". By doing so, we believe that the overall performance gain in terms of energy efficiency can be maximized.

The basic idea of the proposed MAC-CROSS is to minimize the number of nodes that are supposed to wake up when their NAV (Network Allocation Vector) value expires. Remind that, by using NAV information of RTS/CTS packets sent by a data source and a destination, a shared wireless medium can be reserved during the time for exchanging their data packets. Other nodes except for these two communicating nodes are supposed to enter a sleep mode, which is good for saving their energy sources. Now, the problem comes from the fact that all these sleeping nodes must be awake when their NAV timers expire, regardless of whether they are willing to participate in the next packet transmission or not. Such a mandatory and compulsory wake-up strategy may cause some negative effect on the energy perspective, especially for those nodes which are not supposed to be involved in the upcoming transmission phase and therefore will come back to their sleep mode again. In order to solve this problem, our scheme makes only a subset of nodes perform such a mandatory wake-up. The subset of nodes here are the ones, not only whose NAV value becomes expired but also whose current location is along a routing path from a source to a final destination. All other nodes which do not belong to the routing path can stay in their sleep mode until the beginning of the next duty cycle. To decide which node is on the routing path, the proposed scheme utilizes the routing information through a cross-layer design approach. For evaluating analyze the performance, we have implemented the MAC-CROSS over the Mica Mote [15] platform and also the well-known network simulator NS-2 [13]. The results of both tests demonstrate that our scheme is consistently superior more than the adaptive S-MAC protocol [3] in terms of energy efficiency.

2 Related Works

One of the famous energy efficient protocols for wireless sensor network is S-MAC [2, 3]. It is a contention-based random access protocol with a fixed listen/sleep cycle and uses a coordinated sleeping mechanism. A time frame in S-MAC is divided into two parts: one for a listen period and the other for a sleep period. During the listen period, SYNC and RTS/CTS control packets are transmitted based on the CSMA/CA mechanism for the purpose of a synchronization and an announcement for the following data packet transmission. Any two nodes exchanging RTS/CTS packets in the listen period need to keep in an active state and start an actual data transmission without entering a sleep mode. Otherwise, all other nodes can enter the sleep mode in order to avoid any wasteful idle listening and overhearing problems. [1] The basic operation of S-MAC protocol is illustrated in Fig. 1-(a), where the two nodes A and B are keeping awake to

[1] There are four main cases of energy waste: Collision, Control packet overhead, Idle listening and Overhearing. Idle listening is defined as continuously staying in the receive mode even if there is no data traffic, whereas overhearing is defined as receiving a packet that are not destined for the node. For further details, refer to [2].

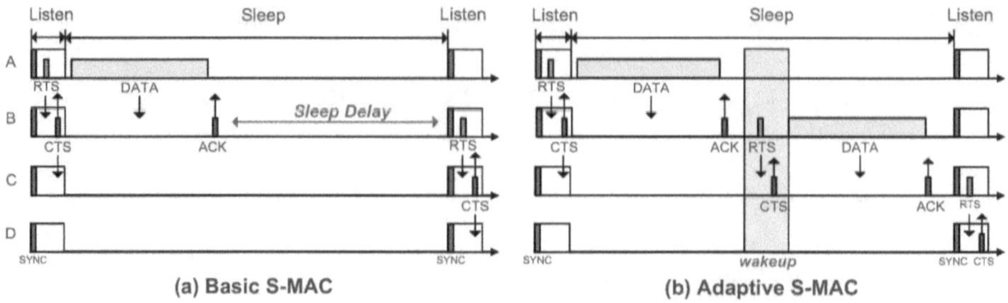

Fig. 1. Operation of basic and adaptive S-MAC [2,3]

exchange their DATA and ACK packets. Note that in S-MAC, the duration of a listen period is always fixed and therefore causes unnecessary energy waste. For solving this problem, another protocol named T-MAC has been proposed [4]. It can be thought as a variation of S-MAC in that it is yet based on a periodic active/inactive mechanism, but with an adaptive length of active state by fine time out, called TA.

In general, periodic listen/sleep-based schemes have some trade-offs between the energy saving and the latency. To reduce a long end-to-end delay, [3] suggests the adaptive listening scheme in which a node receiving NAV information of RTS or CTS packets will wake up when its NAV timer expires and then try to communicate with its neighbors without waiting for the next listen/sleep cycle. Fig. 1-(b) shows the operation of the adaptive S-MAC [3]. It also has the timeout policy like T-MAC, therefore adaptive S-MAC can be said to have both properties of basic S-MAC [2] and T-MAC [4]. The adaptive S-MAC can provide a solution for the latency problem but produce some disadvantage in the energy saving perspective a unnecessary energy consumption because even nodes that do not participate in communication should wake up when their NAV timers expire. We call this problem as "compulsory wake-up problem."

A number of papers have discussed about a cross layer design among different layers to improve the performance of wireless ad hoc networks [5]. It is an active research field wireless sensor networks as well. For instance, [6] suggests the two routing algorithms based on the success/failure of CTS or ACK packet. [7] proposes a variable length TDMA scheme where the slot length is assigned according to traffic information and distance between each node pair. [8] suggests a clustered network architecture where the nodes that have the same hop count to the sink is grouped. [9] proposes a new scheduling algorithm that is fully distributed and works through the cooperation with routing and MAC protocols. Overall, these previous works have focused on searching for the new routing metric or establishing more efficient sleep schedules. However, our proposed scheme focuses more on the cross layer solution of compulsory wake-up problem.

For example, in Fig. 2, we assume that a routing path (A, B and C) is already established, and nodes (D-K) that do not participate in communication are outside of the routing path. First, A sends data to B by four handshake communication, and then other nodes enter to sleep during NAV time. After NAV timer expires, B tries to transmit data to C along the routing path. However, other nodes (D-K) also wake up and causes compulsory wake-up problem. If MAC protocol knows the routing path information from its routing agent, only node C which is the next hop for data delivery can be woken up. To support that, our proposed scheme is designed with cross layer concept for getting routing information. Our scheme can cooperate with any routing protocols such as Diffusion [10] or GPSR [11].

3 The Proposed Scheme: MAC-CROSS

A design goal of MAC-CROSS is to minimize energy consumption by continuously turning off the radio interface of unnecessary nodes that are not included in the routing path. In this paper, we categorize nodes into three types depending upon the state defined by data transmission: Communicating Parties, Upcoming communicating Parties and Third Parties. A state may dynamically change whenever data traffic is transmitted.

- **Communicating Parties (CP):** Any node currently participating in the actual data transmission. (like nodes A and B in Fig. 2).
- **Upcoming communicating Parties (UP):** Any node to be involved in the actual data transmission. (like node C in Fig. 2).
- **Third Parties (TP):** Any nodes that are not included on a routing path and hence not involved in the actual data transmission at all. (like nodes D-K in Fig. 2).

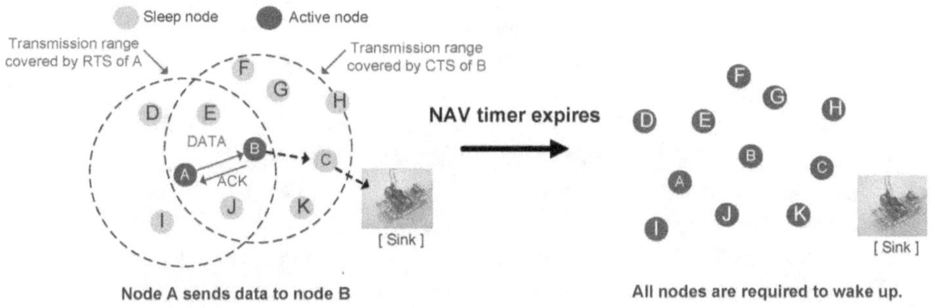

Fig. 2. A drawback of the adaptive S-MAC (in terms of energy efficient)

3.1 The Basic Operation of MAC-CROSS

Now, we explain the proposed MAC-CROSS scheme with the help of the following example. Remind that, in Fig 2 illustrating the main drawback of the adaptive S-MAC, all nodes are being awake when their NAV timer expire and consume unnecessary energy. The proposed MAC-CROSS can overcome this problem, as represented in Fig. 3 with the same scenario to Fig. 2. Thus, with

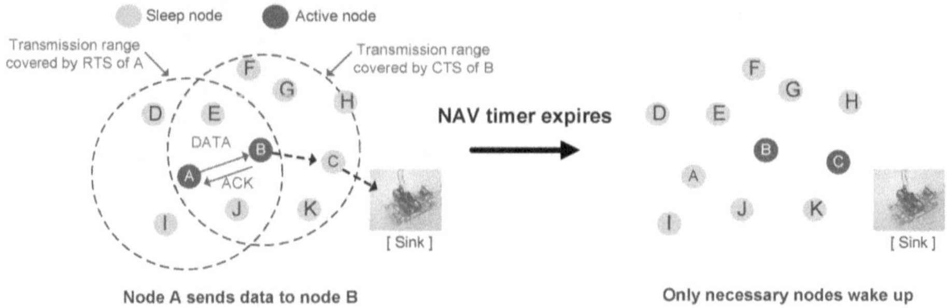

Fig. 3. The main advantage of the proposed MAC-CROSS

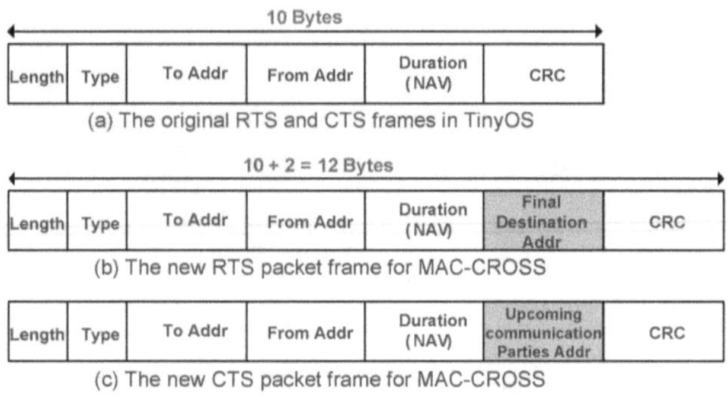

Fig. 4. RTS and CTS frames modification in MAC-CROSS

the MAC-CROSS, only a few nodes concerned of the actual data transmission (i.e., the necessary UP nodes like nodes B and C in Fig 3) are asked to wake up, while other TP nodes can continuously remain in their sleep modes.

Before describing further details about the MAC-CROSS operation, it should be aware that a format of RTS/CTS control frames needs to be slightly modified from their originals in S-MAC protocol family. This modification is for informing a node the fact that its state is changed to UP or TP in the corresponding listen/sleep period. Fig 4-(a) shows the original RTS and CTS control packet formats for adaptive S-MAC in TinyOS [14] as operation of Mica Mote. Fig 4-(b) and (c) show the new RTS and CTS control packet formats for MAC-CROSS. The new RTS and CTS packet add only one field to the original packets. The newly added field in RTS is Final_Destination_Addr, by which the receiver's routing agent can search for the next hop address. The new field of CTS is UP_Addr and it informs which node is UP to its neighbors.

Referring back to Fig 3, when node B receives A's RTS packet including the final destination address of sink, its routing agent refers to the rouging table for getting the UP (node C) and informs back to its own MAC. The MAC agent of node B then transmits CTS packet including the UP information. After receiving the CTS packet from the B, node C changes its state to UP and other neighbor nodes become aware of the fact that they are TP nodes. UP node has to wake up when NAV timer expires for receiving data, but other nodes continuously sleep even if NAV timer expires for saving energy. Otherwise, if no such information about UP is available in node B's routing agent, it means the routing path is broken or has not yet been established. In this case, MAC-CROSS is performed just like S-MAC without cross layer concept.

3.2 Some Optional Features of the MAC-CROSS

If different addressing mechanisms are assumed on MAC and routing layers separately, our MAC-CROSS needs some address conversion schemes like ARP protocol [12] between the two layers (See Fig. 5). For example, any WLAN-based IPv4 devices have 4-bytes IP address as their network addressing mechanism and 6-bytes NIC address as their MAC addressing mechanism. In this case, MAC-CROSS refers to the address conversion scheme for describing the Final_Destination_Addr of RTS packet. However, in wireless sensor networks, most of paper [2, 3, 4, 8, 9] generally assume the node ID as the address of network as well as MAC. In this case, there is no extra overhead.

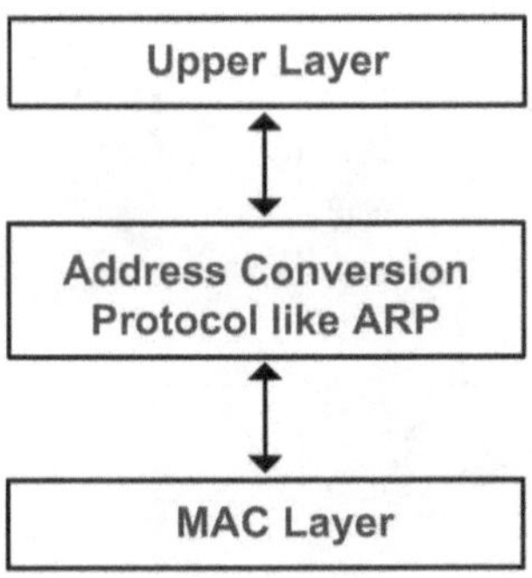

Fig. 5. Address conversion scheme in difference of address mechanisms

In our scheme, if a node obtains the medium access right by contention, the next hop node including the routing path monopolizes the medium access right for reducing compulsory wake-up problem. This solution may cause the unfairness problem. However, most of wireless sensor networks assume that data traffic is very low [10]. So, fairness issue is less important than energy efficiency. If some sensor application requires the fairness, our scheme needs to be modified accordingly. For example, if a node obtains the medium access rights, that node tries to decrease its medium access possibility by increasing its contention window size in the next cycle.

4 Performance Evaluation

4.1 Protocol Implementation on Mica Mote

Mica Mote sensor node has been developed at U.C. Berkeley and is now commercially available from Crossbow Inc [15]. It is equipped with a low-power microprocessor, 128K of program memory, 4 K of SRAM, and low power transceiver for wireless communication. For the purpose of performance comparison with the adaptive S-MAC, we implemented MAC-CROSS modules on Mica Motes. We set a duty cycle of both MAC protocols to be 10% as in [3]. We set the energy model based on S-MAC, which consumes 13.5mW, 24.75mW and 15uW, per receiving, transmitting and sleeping modes, respectively.

The test was performed on a static topology with seven sensor nodes, as illustrated in Fig. 6. Data is transmitted from 1 to 7, and source node 1 generates a packet in every 5 seconds. We measure the total energy consumption of sensor nodes when a data packet arrives at the sink node. Fig. 7 shows the energy consumption results. From the figure, we can observe that: when a number of arrived messages increase, MAC-CROSS consumes less energy than adaptive S-MAC. The reason is that our scheme dose not waste energy by compulsory wake-up, but adaptive S-MAC consumes unnecessary energy when NAC timer

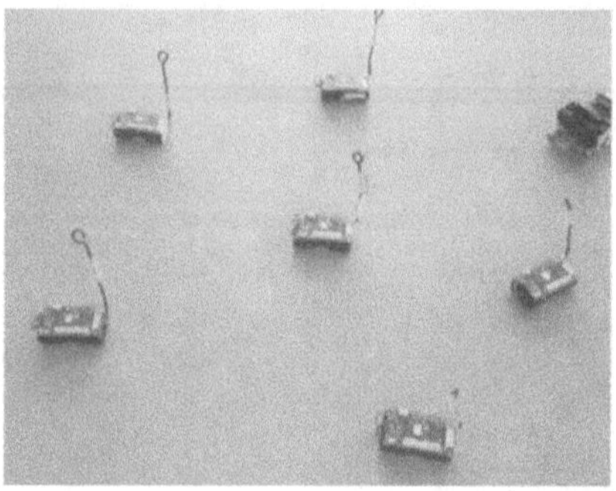
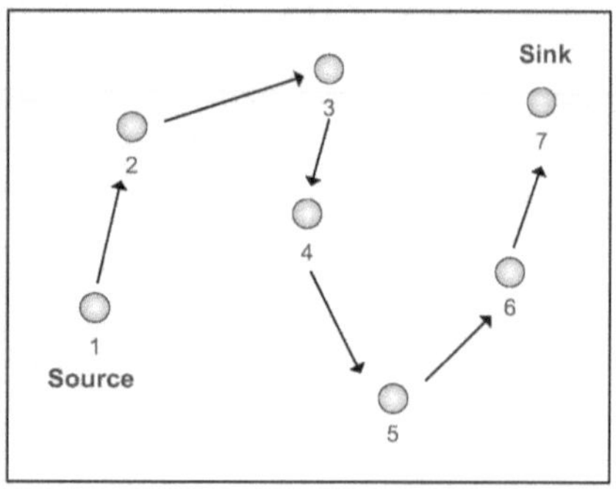

Fig. 6. Mica Mote Test-bed

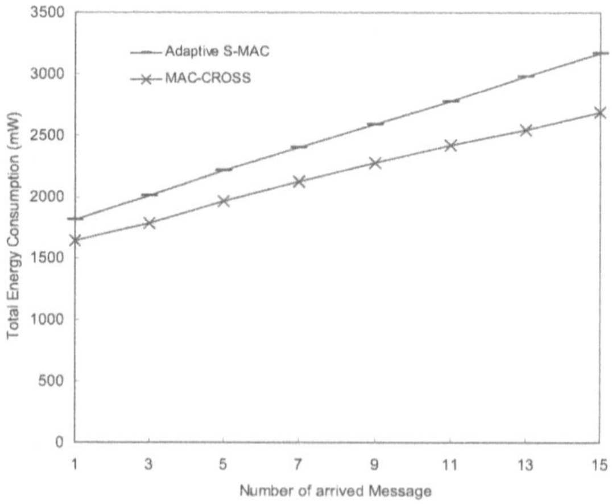

Fig. 7. Total energy consumption according to number of arrived message

expires. Therefore, our proposed scheme is more efficient than adaptive S-MAC as the number of arrived data packets increase.

4.2 Simulation Study

The simulations are done in random topologies with different sets of 30 to 100 nodes. A node transmission range is defined as 40m and its energy model and duty cycle are defined as the same as in implementation test. The routing protocol is based on the greedy approach. Therefore, a next hop node is the nearest neighbor node to the final destination. The size of data packet is fixed at 100 bytes. A sink node is located in the middle of the network and 4 source nodes are

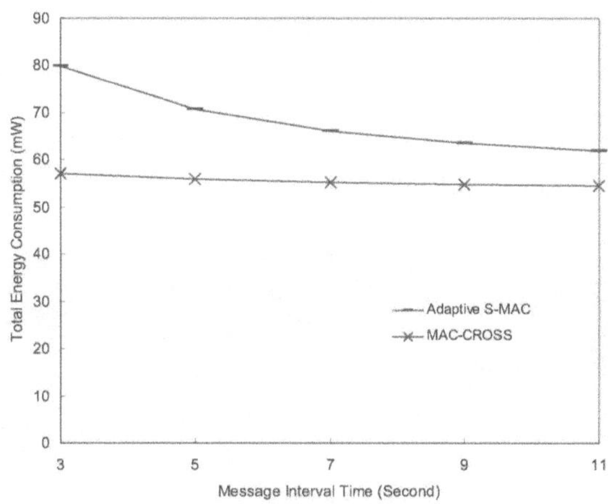

Fig. 8. Energy vs. Message Interval

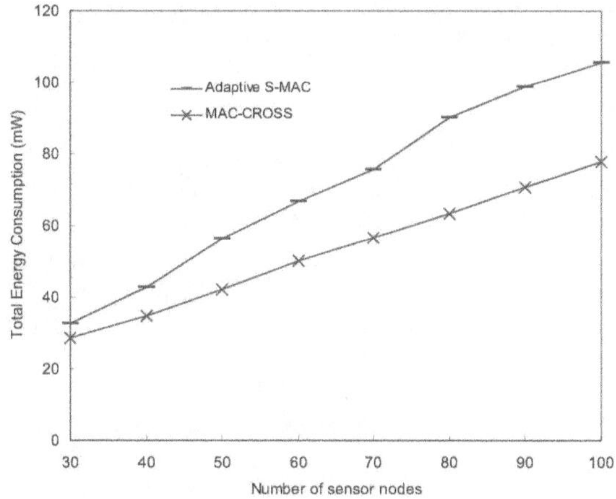

Fig. 9. Energy vs. Number of nodes

deployed in each edge of network. The message interval also varied to analyze the performance of both MAC protocols. The simulation runs for 400 seconds.

In Fig. 8, we show a total energy consumption as the message interval time is increased. When the message interval is 3 seconds, each source generates its data packet in every 3 second during the total simulation time. According to the figure, the performance of our scheme is better than adaptive S-MAC in the environment of high traffic. Since adaptive S-MAC consumes energy by compulsory wake-up whenever data packet is transmitted, our proposed scheme is more efficient as data traffic is increased. In Fig. 9, we change the number of nodes for analyzing the energy consumption of two MAC protocols according to the node density. In the high node density, the number of nodes that receive RTS/CTS control packets increase, meaning that the number of TP nodes also increase when NAV timer expires. In this case, adaptive S-MAC may consume more energy by compulsory wake-up. Therefore, MAC-CROSS results in less energy consumption than the adaptive S-MAC as the number of nodes increase.

5 Conclusion

In this paper, we propose a new MAC protocol for wireless sensor networks, named MAC-CROSS. Our proposed scheme does not have compulsory wake-up problem and maximize sleep duration of sensor nodes by cross-layer design approach. We have implemented the MAC-CROSS on the Mica Mote hardware and NS-2 simulator. Our experimental results demonstrate that our scheme works well and saves significant amount of the energy compared to adaptive S-MAC.

References

1. I. Demirkol, C. Ersoy, and F. Alagoz, "MAC Protocols for Wireless Sensor Networks: a Survey," *in IEEE Communications Magazine*, 2005.
2. W. Ye, J. Heidemann, and D. Estrin, "An energy-efficient MAC protocol for wireless sensor networks," *in IEEE INFOCOM'02*, June 2002.
3. W. Ye, J. Heidemann, and D. Estrin, "Medium Access Control With Coordinated Adaptive Sleeping for Wireless Sensor Networks," *in IEEE/ACM Transactions on Networking*, June 2004.
4. T. V. Dam and K. Langendoen, "An adaptive energy-efficient MAC protocol for wireless sensor networks," *in ACM SenSys'03*, Nov. 2003.
5. L. Qin and T. Kunz, "Survey on Mobile Ad Hoc Network Routing Protocols and Cross-Layer Design, " *in Technical Report of Carleton University*, Aug. 2004.
6. A. Safwat, H. Hassanein, H. Mouftah, "ECPS and E2LA: new paradigms for energy efficiency in wireless ad hoc and sensor networks," *in IEEE GLOBECOM'03*, Dec. 2003.
7. S. Cui, R. Madan, A. J. Goldsmith and S. Lall, "Joint Routing, MAC, and Link Layer Optimization in Sensor Networks with Energy Constraints," *in IEEE ICC'05*, May. 2005.
8. J. Ding, K. Sivalingam, R. Kashyapa and L. J. Chuan, "A multi-layered architecture and protocols for large-scale wireless sensor networks," *in IEEE VTC'03-Fall*, Oct. 2003.

9. M. L. Sichitiu, "Cross-Layer Scheduling for Power Efficiency in Wireless Sensor Networks," *in IEEE INFOCOM'04*, Mar. 2004.
10. C. Intanagonwiwat, R. Govindan, and D. Estrin, "Directed Diffusion: a Scalable and Robust Communication Paradigm for Sensor Networks," *in ACM MOBICOM'00*, Aug. 2000.
11. B. Karp and H. T. Kung, "GPSR: Greedy Perimeter Stateless Routing for Wireless Sensor Networks," *in ACM MOBICOM'00*, Aug. 2000.
12. D.C. Plummer, "Ethernet Address Resolution Protocol: Or converting network protocol addresses to 48.bit Ethernet address for transmission on Ethernet hardware," *in RFC826*.
13. The CMU Monarch Project, "The CMU Monarch Project's Wireless and Mobility Extensions to NS."
14. TinyOS, http://webs.cs.berkeley.edu/tos/.
15. Mica Mote, http://www.xbow.com/

Power-Efficient Node Localization Algorithm in Wireless Sensor Networks*

Jinbao Li[1,2], Jianzhong Li[1,2], Longjiang Guo[1,2], and Peng Wang[1]

[1] Harbin Institute of Technology, 150001, Harbin, China
[2] Heilongjiang University, 150080, Harbin, China
jbli@hlju.edu.cn, lijzh@hit.edu.cn

Abstract. Sensor networks is an Ad-Hoc network consist of large amount of sensors. These sensors are distributed in a huge area. Each of the small, cheap, intelligent sensors has processor, memory and wireless transmission ability. These sensors collect or monitor the surroundings in real-time and process these data to obtain the detailed and accurate information from their covered area. Information from sensors must be combined with its location to make sense, so the location of sensors is very important in sensor network applications. Localization of sensors becomes one of the key techniques in sensor networks. A power-efficient localization algorithm is proposed in this paper. It uses few anchors(the sensors whose location is known) to implement the localization of other nodes without special devices such as GPS. This algorithm not only has the lower time cost and communication cost, but also needs only a few anchor nodes whose distribution is independent. Experimental results and analysis show that the localization algorithm proposed in this paper has higher accuracy, lower power cost and better expansibility. It is very suitable for large scale sensor networks.

1 Introduction

Recent advancement in digital-electronics, micro-processors and wireless technologies enable the creation of small and cheap sensors which has processor, memory and wireless communication ability. This accelerates the development of large scale sensor networks. Sensor networks integrate sensor technique, computer technique, distributed information processing technique and communication technique. It is an Ad-Hoc network composed of large amount of sensors[1]. These sensors are distributed in a huge area and obtain the detailed and accurate information of their surroundings. Various sensors which have different functions are distributed to some given area to collect, monitor and process information. For example, by obtaining the geographical features such as hardness and humidity of the jungle of enemies in battlefield, the blue print of battle can be made. There are a lot of attractive features of sensors such as small, cheap, flexible, movable and wireless communication ability, so the sensor

* Supported by the key project of the National Natural Science Foundation of China, Grant No.60533110; the National Natural Science Foundation of China under Grant No.60473075 and No.60273082; the key project Natural Science Foundation of Heilongjiang Province of China under Grant No.ZJG03-05 and No.QC04C40.

H.T. Shen et al. (Eds.): APWeb 2006, LNCS 3842, pp. 420 – 430, 2006.

network can be used to obtain detailed and reliable information in any time, location, hypsography or environment. In military affairs, sensor networks can be used to monitor the action of enemies and the existence of dangerous features such as poison gas, radiation, exploder, etc. In environment monitoring, sensors can be set at plain, desert, mountain region or seas to monitor and control changes in the environment. In traffic applications, sensors can be used to monitor and control the traffic in freeway or crowed area in cities. Sensors can also be used in security supervising of large shopping center, carport and other devices and in supervising the occupying of parking spaces in parks.

Sensors generally have limited processing, storing and communication ability. They connected with each other by wireless network. Sensors in the network can move, which makes the topology structure of the network change. The nodes communicate with each other by Ad-Hoc manner. Each node can act as a router and has the ability of search, localization and reconnection dynamically. Sensor networks is a special kind of wireless Ad-Hoc network, which has the features such as frequent moving, connection and disconnection, limitation of power, large distributed area, large amount of nodes, limitation of own resources.

Area covered by sensors is often not suitable for human being, such as swampland, or the enemy area in a battle. Sensors have to be thrown to the given places by planes, so the position is randomized. Bulusun pointed out that data from sensors must be combined with the location of them. The data without location information is almost useless[2]. Moreover, in sensor network applications, queries are often related with the location or area of sensors, such as "Where the thickness of the poison gas is beyond the limit?" and "How about the distribution of pine tree in virgin forest?" It can be concluded that power efficient node localization algorithm is very crucial in sensor network applications.

Power saving is an important optimizing target in sensor networks. Each sensor is power by battery. Battery cannot be replaced when it is exhausted because of the deserted or dangerous environment it lies. So the limited power of sensors should be efficiently used to prolong the lifetime of the sensor networks. This paper researches on node localization technique in sensor networks and proposes a node localization algorithm for large scale sensor networks. This algorithm is independent for special localization devices and only few anchor nodes are used to determine the locations of other nodes in the network.

The main contribution of the paper is as follows. (1) It proposes a power efficient localization algorithm. Compared with other algorithms, it has lower time cost and communication cost and has higher localization accuracy. (2) It can determine the positions of other nodes in the network using only few anchor nodes. The number of anchor nodes is almost independent with the number of nodes in the whole network. (3) It is independent with the distribution of anchor nodes or all the other nodes in the network. In general, only three nodes are needed to determine the positions of other nodes. The algorithm proposed in this paper is extendable and suitable for localization in large scale sensor networks.

The paper is organized as follows. Section 1 introduces sensor networks and the localization problem. Section 2 is the related work. Section 3 proposes the node localization algorithm. Then the experiments and analysis is given in section 4. The last section is the conclusion.

2 Related Works

Global Positioning System(GPS) is often used to determine the location of nodes. For the price and the size of sensors and its limited power, it is difficult to integrate GPS with sensors[3]. Most current localization methods use anchor nodes(the location of the anchor nodes are known) to determine the locations of other nodes. These methods are divided into two types. One is based on the connectivity among sensor nodes. It estimates the location of sensors by the connectivity. The other is based on measurement. A sensor sends out messages to measure the distance between other anchor node and itself, then geometry localization methods are used to determine its location. In following parts, the sensor whose location is about to be determined are named as unknown node.

Bulusu in South California University proposed a connectivity-based localization algorithm, called GPS-less LCO[4]. In this method, the connectivity between unknown node and the anchors near it are detected. *k* anchors with the best connectivity are found, which are denoted by $R_1(x_1,y_1)$, $R_2(x_2,y_2)$,…,$R_k(x_k,y_k)$. The unknown node thought of lying in the overlapping region of anchors $R_1,R_2,\ldots,R_k$. The estimated location of the unknown node is calculated by $(x,y)=(\frac{x_1+x_2+\ldots+x_k}{k},\frac{y_1+y_2+\ldots+y_k}{k})$. This algorithm must ensure that there are enough anchors around the unknown node and the anchors must be sorted by grid. Otherwise, the accuracy cannot be ensured. This algorithm need a lot of anchors and has large communication cost. It is not suitable for randomly distributed sensor networks.

C.Savarese proposed a directed triangulation localization algorithm[5,6]. In this algorithm, if the distance between unknown node and anchors can be detected, triangulation can be used to determine the location of the unknown node. If the distances from more than three anchors to the unknown node are known, the coordinates of the unknown node can be determined. Suppose the coordinates of the unknown node is (X_u,Y_u), the coordinates of its three anchors are (X_1,Y_1),(X_2,Y_2) and (X_3,Y_3). The unknown node has got the distance to three anchors by some manner. Suppose the three distances are D_1,D_2 and D_3, we have the following equation:

$$\begin{cases} D_1 = \sqrt{(X_1 - X_u)^2 + (Y_1 - Y_u)^2} \\ D_2 = \sqrt{(X_2 - X_u)^2 + (Y_2 - Y_u)^2} \\ D_3 = \sqrt{(X_3 - X_u)^2 + (Y_3 - Y_u)^2} \end{cases}$$

The coordinates of the unknown node can be obtained by solving the equations.

If the distances between nodes can be detected accurately, directed triangulation localization algorithm determines the location of nodes accurately. This method has the shortcomings described below. (1) It needs the distances between the unknown node and at least three anchors, which requires the number of anchors beyond a threshold. (2) It solves quadratic equations, which makes it more time consuming and not suitable for sensors that have limited power.

Aim at the shortcoming of directed triangulation localization algorithm, D.Niculescu proposed a node localization algorithm, named DV-Hop[7,8,11]. It obtains the distance between unknown node and an anchor node by multiplying the hop count with an average hop distance between them. Then geometry is used to get the location of each node. Based on Euclid distance, the following equations are derived.

$$\begin{cases} hop-distance*H_1=\sqrt{(X_1-X_u)^2+(Y_1-Y_u)^2} \\ hop-distance*H_2=\sqrt{(X_2-X_u)^2+(Y_2-Y_u)^2} \\ \vdots \\ \vdots \\ hop-distance*H_n=\sqrt{(X_3-X_u)^2+(Y_3-Y_u)^2} \end{cases}$$

The coordinates of the unknown node is (X_u,Y_u). The coordinates of the anchors are $(X_1,Y_1),(X_2,Y_2),\ldots,(X_n,Y_n)$. n is the number of anchors. H_i is the number of hops between the unknown node and the i_{th} anchor node. The unknown variables in the above equation are coordinates of unknown node. When $n>3$, the least square method is used to get the approximation of (X_u,Y_u). This algorithm needs not to detect the accurate distance between unknown node and anchors. The number of anchors needed by it is less than that of directed triangulation localization algorithm. The algorithm will get accurate result when the sensors distributed uniformly. But when sensors are distributed asymmetrically or the cover rate of anchors is low, the localization error will be very big.

Lateration is quite expensive in the number of floating point operations that is required. Min-Max method is presented by Savvides et al.[9]. The main idea is to construct a bounding box for each anchor, say $a_i(x_i,y_i)$, $1<=i<=n$, where n is the number of anchors. So n bounding boxes are constructed. The left-top corner of rectangle i is (x_i-d_i,y_i-d_i) and the right-bottom corner is (x_i+d_i,y_i+d_i), where di is the distance between anchor node and unknown node. Then the intersection of these boxes is determined, the left-top corner of which is $(\max(x_i-d_i), \max(y_i-d_i))$, the right-bottom corner of which is $(\min(x_i+d_i),\min(y_i+d_i))$. The location of the unknown node is set to the center of the intersection box. Min-Max is accurate for nodes among the area bounded by the anchor nodes. But when the nodes lie in the outside, the error is bigger.

3 Power Efficient Adaptive Extendable Localization Algorithm

3.1 Distance Measure Algorithm

Distances between nodes are needed in node localization algorithm. We first introduce some general distance measure algorithms.

Sum-dist algorithm[9,10] is the most simple solution for determining the distance to anchors. It simply adds the distances between any two neighbors in the shortest path from unknown node to an anchor, which is used as the final measure distance. There are two factors affects the accuracy of the algorithm. (1) There are almost multiple tops between unknown node and anchor, which makes the nodes in the path are not in line. So the measured distance is always a bit longer than the actual distance. (2) Range errors accumulate when distance information is propagated over multiple hops. This cumulative error becomes significant for large networks with few anchors. To minimize the error, the distance between unknown node and the anchor should be minimized also. This algorithm is adopted in Min-Max.

DV-hop[7] is a algorithm without accumulating error when measure distance. It calculates the average distance of one hop by calculating the distance between two anchors. Because the location of each anchor is known, the distance D between any two anchors and the number of nodes n in the shortest path between them can be calculated. The average distance between any two nodes in the network is D/n. So, from the hop count m between unknown node and an anchor, the distance between them can be determined by $m*D/n$. IF the nodes in the network distributed uniformly, the measured distance is accurate. Otherwise it has big error.

We do not concern the distribution when determining the locations of nodes including anchors, so DV-hop like algorithms are discarded. Even though Sum-dist cares about the distribution of nodes, it cannot control the propagation of error when calculating distance between multi-hop nodes, which results in the big cumulative error. The decreasing of the hop count between unknown node and anchor causes the reducing of errors.

3.2 AELA : Anchor Extending Based Localization Algorithm

The main idea of AELA is to implement node localization in power efficient large scale sensor networks by extending the existing anchors. Suppose u_i is an unknown node whose 3 (or more than 3) neighbors are anchors. AELA firstly determine the location of node u_i. Based on the directed triangulation localization algorithm, the location of u_i can be determined almost accurately. If the error is less than a threshold, we say that the location of node u_i is accurately determined. Node u_i can be extended as an anchor. That is to say, other nodes can regard u_i as a anchor when determining their locations. The set of anchor nodes are extended recursively based on the above idea. So locations of lot of nodes in the network can be determined by directed triangulation localization algorithm and few nodes need to determine their location by multi-hop distance measure algorithm.

The advantage of AELA is that it does not concern the distribution of nodes in the network and almost dose not concern the number of anchors when the network is enlarged. AELA pulls other nodes around anchors into the anchor set. This process continues and the cover rate and the covered area of anchors are enlarged. As a result, most nodes in the network determined their location by anchors 1 hop from them. This avoids the cumulated error and saves the communication cost efficiently. The power is saved and the lifetime of the network is prolonged.

AELA extends anchor set from nodes that the localization error is within a given threshold. We give the error estimation method below.

For any function $Y=f(x_1, x_2, \dots, x_n)$, if the error of independent variables $x_1,x_2, \dots ,x_n$ is $\Delta x_1, \Delta x_2, \dots , \Delta x_n$, the error of Y caused by $x_1,x_2, \dots ,x_n$, denoted by ΔY, is calculated as follows: $Y+\Delta Y = f(x_1+\Delta x_1, x_2+\Delta x_2, \dots , x_n+\Delta x_n)$. Based on Taylor Formula,

$$Y+\Delta Y = f(x_1+\Delta x_1, x_2+\Delta x_2,\cdots,x_n+\Delta x_n) = f(x_1,x_2,\cdots,x_n)+$$
$$\Delta x_1\frac{\partial f}{\partial x_1}+\Delta x_2\frac{\partial f}{\partial x_2}+\cdots+\Delta x_n\frac{\partial f}{\partial x_n}+\frac{1}{2}[(\Delta x_1)^2\frac{\partial^2 f}{\partial x_1^2}+(\Delta x_2)^2\frac{\partial^2 f}{\partial x_2^2}+\cdots+(\Delta x_n)^2\frac{\partial^2 f}{\partial x_n^2}+2\Delta x_1\Delta x_2\frac{\partial^2 f}{\partial x_1 \partial x_2}+\cdots]+\cdots$$

The items that has higher power is omitted, we get

$$Y+\Delta Y = f(x_1+\Delta x_1, x_2+\Delta x_2,\cdots,x_n+\Delta x_n) = f(x_1,x_2,\cdots,x_n)+\Delta x_1\frac{\partial f}{\partial x_1}+\Delta x_2\frac{\partial f}{\partial x_2}+\cdots+\Delta x_n\frac{\partial f}{\partial x_n}$$
$$\Delta Y = \Delta x_1\frac{\partial f}{\partial x_1}+\Delta x_2\frac{\partial f}{\partial x_2}+\cdots+\Delta x_n\frac{\partial f}{\partial x_n} \quad (1)$$

Equation (1) gives the estimated error.

Suppose $u\ (x, y)$ is the unknown node. $a_1(x_1, y_1)$,$a_2(x_2, y_2)$,$a_3(x_3, y_3)$ are three anchors which are all neighbors of u. d_1, d_2 *and* d_3 are the distances from u to a_1,a_2 *and* a_3 separately. Then we get the following equation.

$$\begin{cases} d_1 = \sqrt{(x_1 - x)^2 + (y_1 - y)^2} \\ d_2 = \sqrt{(x_2 - x)^2 + (y_2 - y)^2} \\ d_3 = \sqrt{(x_3 - x)^2 + (y_3 - y)^2} \end{cases}$$

By solving the equation we get the coordinates of the unknown node $u(x,y)$, where $x=\theta(d_1,d_2,d_3)$, $y=\varphi(d_1,d_2,d_3)$.

Suppose $(x+\Delta x, y+\Delta y)$ is the measured coordinates of node u, Δx and Δy are the measure errors. d_{1m}, d_{2m} and d_{3m} are the measured values of d_1, d_2 and d_3, Δd_1, Δd_2 and Δd_3 are the distance measure error. From the above supposition, we get $d_1=d_{1m}+\Delta d_1$, $d_2=d_{2m}+\Delta d_{2m}$, $d_3=d_{3m}+\Delta d_3$. From equation (1), we get

$$\Delta x = \Delta d_1 \frac{\partial\theta}{\partial d_1} + \Delta d_2 \frac{\partial\theta}{\partial d_2} + \Delta d_3 \frac{\partial\theta}{\partial d_3},\ \Delta y = \Delta d_1 \frac{\partial\phi}{\partial d_1} + \Delta d_2 \frac{\partial\phi}{\partial d_2} + \Delta d_3 \frac{\partial\phi}{\partial d_3} \quad (2)$$

d_{1m}, d_{2m}, d_{3m} are got through measurement. Δd_1, Δd_2, Δd_3 are the given distance measure error. So Δx and Δy can be derived from equation (2).

The proposed anchor extension based power efficient node localization algorithm AELA is described below. In this algorithm, equation (2) is used to evaluate the error when extend a node to anchor.

Algorithm AELA

Input: $a_1(x_1, y_1)$, $a_2(x_2,y_2)$, $a_3(x_3,y_3)$,..., u, // a_i is the anchor node or extended anchor node, u is the unknown node

Output: $u(x,y)$

```
Initialization // determine the location of unknown node whose 3 or more than 3
neighbors are anchors and extend the anchor set
For each unknown node u_i in the network:
  u_i looks for anchors in its neighbors
  if there are at least 3 anchors, say a_i1(x_i1, y_i1),a_i2(x_i2,y_i2),a_i3(x_i3,y_i3), then
    calculate the distances between u_i and a_i1,a_i2,a_i3, denoted by d_i1,d_i2,d_i3 separately
    The coordinates of u_i, denoted by (x_i,y_i), are calculated by directed triangulation
    localization algorithm (2) is used to estimate the localization error Δ_i of u_i
    if Δ_i < ε, then u_i is extended to an anchor // ε is a constant, which is the
      maximal tolerant error to extend a node to anchor
Initialization completed
For each unknown node u_j in the network:
  u_j looks for 3 anchors in its neighbors randomly, in which the original anchors are
  selected in priority
if 3 anchors a_j1(x_j1, y_j1), a_j2(x_j2,y_j2) and a_j3(x_j3,y_j3) are found then
    calculate the distances between u_j and a_j1,a_j2,a_j3, denoted by d_j1, d_j2 and d_j3 sepa
    rately
    the coordinates of u_j, denoted by (x_j,y_j), are calculated by directed triangulation
    localization algorithm
    (2) is used to estimate the localization error Δ_j of u_j
    if Δ_j < ε, then u_j is extended to an anchor
 else
    The location of node u_j is determined by Min-Max algorithm
end
```

AELA tries to expand the set of anchors in the networks, which improves the cover rate of anchors, increases the localization time and reduces the power consumption of localization. AELA is executed in every unknown node. Any node can execute the algorithm no matter to extend the node to an anchor or to determine the location of it. AELA is a distributed localization algorithm.

Even though AELA can determine the location of a node almost accurately in general, wrong localization appears in some time. We improves AELA algorithm for wrong localization.

3.3 Improved AELA Algorithm

AELA randomly selects 3 anchors to determine location of a node. The selection of anchors will affect the accuracy of localization and produce significant error. Even the location calculated will be error(for example, 3 anchors are in line).We improve AELA by the following strategies.

(1) Selection of anchors. When determining the location of node *u*, AELA detects its neighbors. If there are 3 original anchors within one hop, the 3 anchors are used to determine the location of node *u*. Otherwise, AELA looks for corresponding ones in the extended anchors.

(2) 3 anchors in line. If 3 anchors are in line, we will get two locations symmetrically lies in the two sides of the line. Obviously only one will be the right location. This situation is called 3 anchors in line. When it occurs, we should select three new anchors and recalculate the location of the unknown node.

Evaluation of the result distance. When the coordinates of unknown node *u* is determined, it is used to calculate distances between *u* and the anchors a_1,a_2 and a_3 separately. The three distances are denoted by d_1,d_2 and d_3. If $\max(d_1,d_2,d_3)$ is more than the longest distance of one hop, the measured distance is thought of wrong and 3 new anchors should be selected and recalculate the distance until get the right one.

4 Experiments and Analysis

A simulative environment of sensor networks is constructed to show the validity of the proposed node localization algorithm. In this environment sensors and proportioned anchors are put randomly in an N*N area. To simplify the testing and analysis, according to real world sensor networks the simulative environment satisfies the following constraints. (1) The communication radius of each sensor is 10. (2) When sending and receiving a packet, each node consumes just one measure unit of power. (3) Each communication sends or receives one packet.

In the experiments, we consider the effects of density and the scale of the network, the distribution of sensors, the ratio and the distribution of anchors on different node localization algorithms. Then we compare and analyze the differences of AELA to typical localization algorithms on such aspects as localization error, power consuming and expansibility of these algorithms. The experiments focus on the effects of density of sensors, distance measure error, ratio of number of anchors to number of whole nodes etc. on localization error. The power consuming of the above aspects and the distribution of localization error of different algorithms are also concerned. We compare Min-Max and DV-hop algorithms with our algorithm AELA in the experiment.

The effects of density of sensors on localization error are shown in figure 1. In this experiment we distribute 400 sensors randomly in an N*N area, where N is between 250 and 500. The distance measure error is 10%. The number of anchors is 5% of the number of whole sensors in the network. The anchors are all randomly put in the area. Figure 1 shows that the localization error of all the three algorithms increasing with the enlarging of the area. It also shows that the error increasing rate of AELA is clearly slower than the other two algorithms, especially when the density of sensors is high. We know that when increasing the density of sensors in the experiment area, the number of sensors that can be extended to anchors increases simultaneously. Thus the ratio of the number of anchors increases and the localization error of the algorithm decreases.

Figure 2 gives the experimental results of the effects of distance measure error on localization error. 400 sensors are randomly distributed in a 400*400 area. The number of anchors is 5% of the number of whole sensors in the network. The distance measure error changes from 5% to 25%. The anchors are also randomly put in the area. Figure 2 shows that the distance measure error has a obvious effect on AELA algorithm. But, the anchor extension strategy adopted in this paper restricts the localization error of AELA to a bound. It is better than the other two algorithms when the distance measure error less than 20%. DV-Hop algorithm is not affected by the distance measure error, but it has higher localization error inherently.

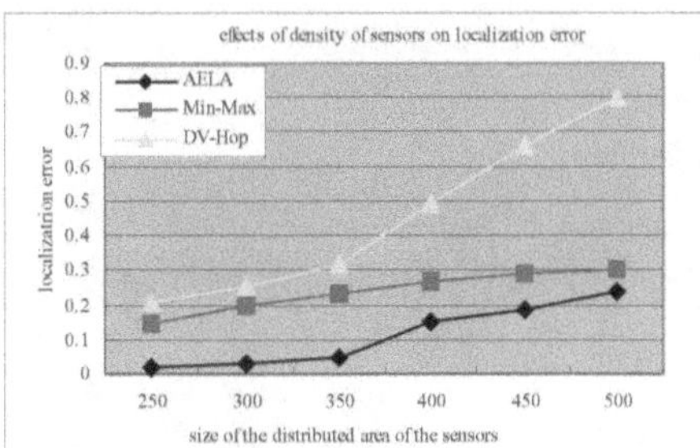

Fig. 1. Effects of density of sensors on localization error

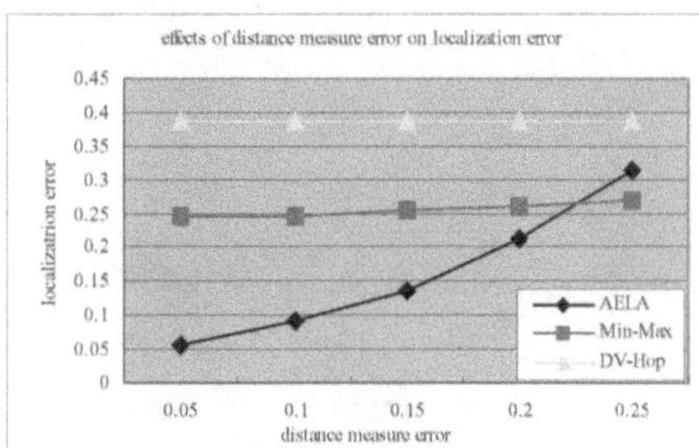

Fig. 2. Effects of distance measure error on localization error

Figure 3 is the comparison with the effects of ratio of number of anchors on the lo calization error. In this experiment we distribute 400 sensors randomly in a 400*400 area. The distance measure error is 10%. The number of anchors is 5%-30% of the number of whole sensors in the network. The anchors are also randomly put in the area. Experiment shows that the change of ratio of anchors has insignificant effects on AELA. If the ratio of anchors reaches a limit, say 5%, AELA can extend sensors to anchors, which is consistent with the experimental result. The experiment also shows that the ratio of anchors has a remarkable effect on Min-Max and DV-Hop. With the increasing of ratio of number of anchors, the localization error of the two algorithms decreases obviously. As long as the percent of anchors reaches 20%, the two algorithms get better results.

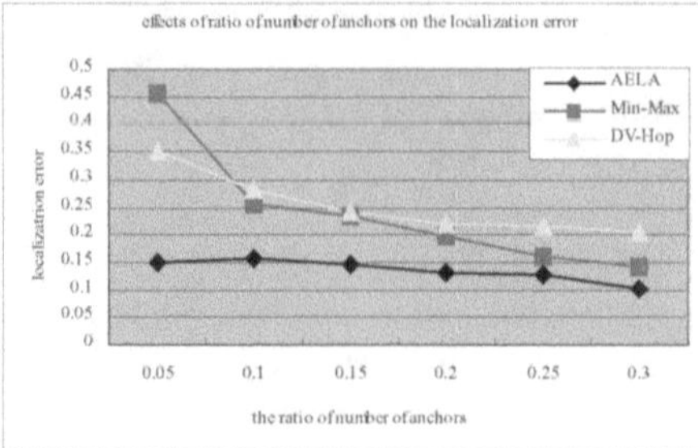

Fig. 3. Effects of ratio of number of anchors on the localization error

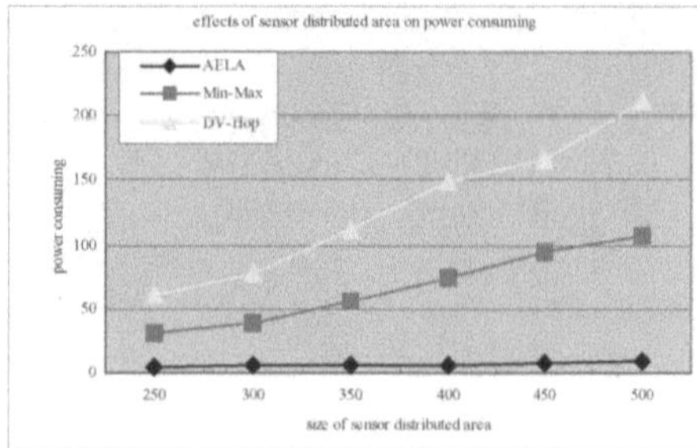

Fig. 4. Effects of density of sensors on power consuming

Figure 4, 5 and 6 are the average power consumed of one localization corresponding to the above three groups of experiments separately. These figures show that AELA is the least power consuming algorithm. The density of nodes, the distance measure error and the ratio of number of anchors have almost no effect on power consuming to determine the location of nodes in AELA. After the extension of anchors, AELA determines the location of a node based on directed triangulation localization algorithm. Communication only occurs between the unknown node and its three anchors. Multi-hop communication is needed only in special case so power is greatly saved.

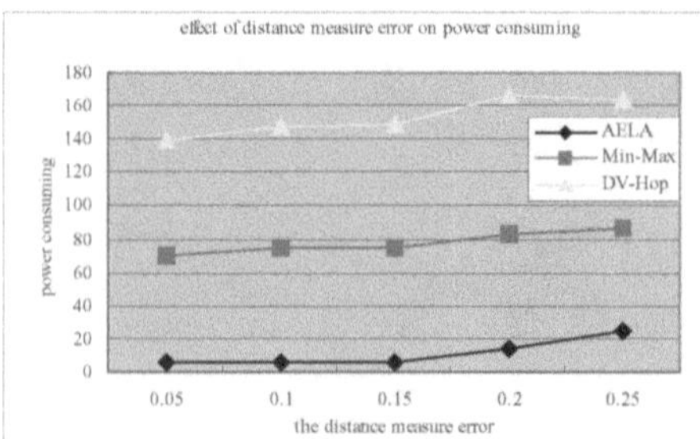

Fig. 5. Effect of distance measure error on power consuming

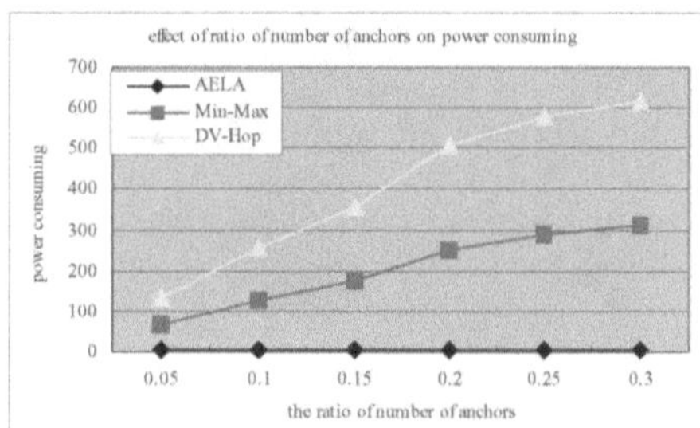

Fig. 6. Effect of coverage of anchors on power consuming

Figure 7 and 8 are experiments on adaptability of the network scale. In these experiments we keep the density of nodes and distribute 100-600 sensors randomly in a rectangle area. The number of anchors is 20. They are also randomly put in the area. The distance measure error is 10%.

Figure 7 shows how the changing of network scale affects the localization error. Figure 8 shows the power consuming in node localization. We can see from the two figures that with the increasing of the network scale, the localization error of AELA increases slowly and the consumed power in node localization is almost changeless. All these experiments indicate AELA has better adaptability for large scale sensor networks. In Min-Max and DV-Hop, the increasing of the network scale results in the increasing of the localization error and the power consumed. The adaptabilities of these two algorithms are not well.

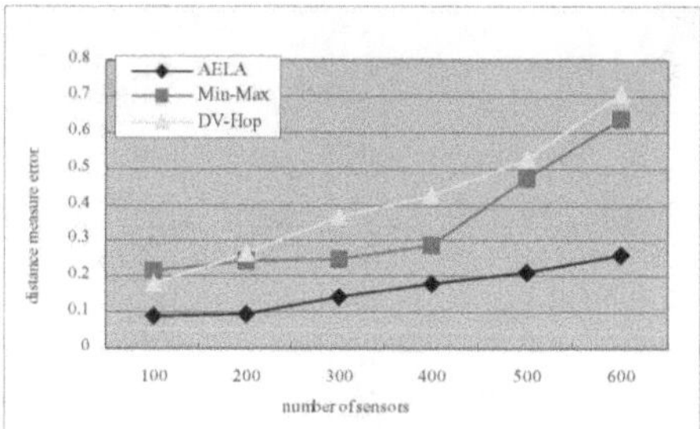

Fig. 7. Effect of network scale on the localization error

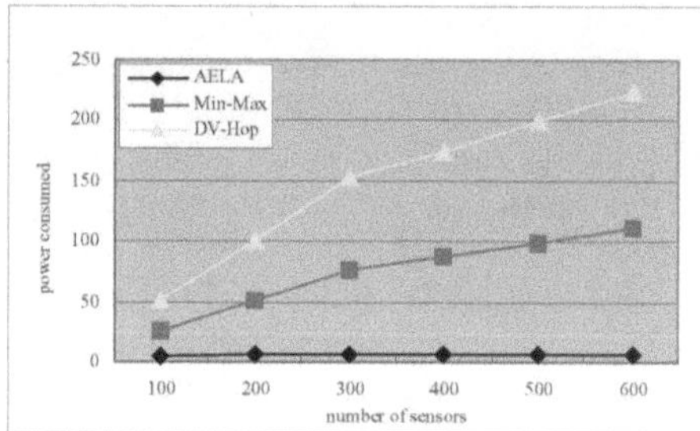

Fig. 8. Effect of network scale on the power consumed in node localization

5 Conclusion

Node localization is very important in sensor networks. This paper analyzes some typical node localization algorithms and proposes AELA, a new power efficient node localization algorithm. In AELA, the communication cost is lower and the localization accuracy is higher. It is adaptive to nodes density and the number and distribution of anchors. Experiments and analysis show that AELA is better than traditional localization algorithms in such aspects as localization accuracy and power consuming. It is independent with the density of nodes, the distribution of nodes and the ratio of number of anchors. At the same time, it is adaptive with the network scale and very suitable for large scale sensor networks.

Till now, there are few research works on localization techniques considering the moving of sensors. In the existing techniques[12], the localization error is obvious. In the future work, we will focus on localization technique of moving sensors.

References

1. Ian F. Akyildiz, Weilian Su, Yogesh Sankarasubramaniam and Erdal Cayirci, A Survey on Sensor Networks, *IEEE Communications Magazine*, vol. 40, no. 8, Page(s): 102 -114.
2. Bulusun, etc. Density-adaptive beacon placement algorithms for localization in Ad hoc wireless networks. IEEE Infocom 2002. New York, USA, 2002.
3. J.Beutel, Geolocation in A Pico radio Environment, Swiss Federal Institute of Technology, Zurich, Switzerland, 1999.
4. BULUSU N, HEIDEMANN J, ESTRIN D. GPS-less low-cost outdoor localization for very small devices. IEEE Personal Communications, 2000,7(5):28-34.
5. C.Savarese, J.Rabay and K.Langendoen, Robust Positioning Algorithms for distributed Ad-Hoc wireless Sensor Networks, USENIX Technical Annual conference, June 2002
6. D. Niculescu and B.Nath. DV-based Positioning in Ad hoc Networks. Telecommunication Systems, 22(1-4):267-280, 2003. 7
7. D.Nicolescu and B.Nath. Ad-hoc positioning system. Proceedings of the Senventh Annual International Conference on Mobile Computing and Networks. Rome, Italy, 2001.
8. Koen Langendoen, Niels Reijers. Distributed Localization in Wireless Sensor Networks: a Quantitative Comparison, Computer Networks (43), 2003: 499-518

9. A. Savvides, etc, The bits and .ops of the N-hop multilateration primitive for node localization problems, First International Workshop on Wireless Sensor Networks and Application, Atlanta, GA, 2002.
10. Y.Shang, etc, Localization from mere connectivity, The Fourth ACM Symposium on mobile Ad-Hoc Networking and Computing, Annapolis, MD June 2003.
11. D.Nicolescu and B.Nath, Ad-hoc Positioning System using AoA, In Proceedings of the IEEE/INFOCOM 2003, San Francisco, CA, April 2003.
12. Lingxuan Hu etc, Localization for mobile sensor networks, Tenth Annual International Conference on Mobile Computing and Networking. 26 September-1 October 2004.

A Residual Energy-Based MAC Protocol for Wireless Sensor Networks*

Long Tan, Jinbao Li, and Jianzhong Li

School of Computer Science and Technology, Heilongjiang University,
150080 Harbin, China
Tanlong01@163.com, Jbli@hit.edu.cn, Lijzh@hit.edu.cn

Abstract. The Residual Energy-Based MAC Protocol (REB MAC) presented in this paper is aimed to solve the problems of how to reduce the collisions from interfering nodes in event-driven wireless sensor networks, how to promote the communication efficiency of the system and how to ensure a balance energy consumption of WSN, etc. We combine node's residual energy with node's orientation in a shared wireless channel, and provide different back-off intervals for nodes having different residual-energy and in different orientation so as to reduce the collisions among neighbor nodes and promote the communication efficiency of the system. In many sensor applications, not all the nodes that sense an event need to report it. Only some of them need to report. So this paper provides a design of using parts of nodes for data transmission so that we can save the energy and balance the energy consumption between neighbor nodes.

1 Introduction

Wireless Sensor Network (WSN) has gained widespread attention in recent years. They can be used for testing, sensing, collecting and processing information of monitored objects and transferring the processed information to users[1]. The network has a wide range applications including health, military, and security.

Since Wireless Sensor Network works in a shared-medium, medium access control (MAC) is an important technique that enables the successful operation of the network. One fundamental task of the MAC protocol is how to avoid collisions among a large number of neighbor nodes which communicate each other at the same time in a share-medium. There are many MAC protocols that have been developed for wireless voice and data communication networks like IEEE802.11[2].

However, sensor nodes are constrained in energy supply and bandwidth[3]. Since WSN node is usually very cheap, charging or recharging the battery is not usually feasible and necessary. Therefore, how to maximize the node's battery lifetime is very important in WSN. Many research works have been finished to solve energy problem in [4,5,6,7,8].These works are mainly focused on MAC layer. Of course, we must

* Supported by key project of the National Natural Science Foundation of China, Grant No.60533110; the National Natural Science Foundation of China under Grant No.60473075; the key project of the Natural Science Foundation of Heilongjiang province under Grant No.ZJG03-05; the research project of Heilongjiang educational office under Grant No.10551246.

H.T. Shen et al. (Eds.): APWeb 2006, LNCS 3842, pp. 431 – 440, 2006.

know challenges necessitate energy-awareness at all layers of networking protocol stack. For example, Network layer protocol, energy aware routing protocol[12], Directed Diffusion Protocol[13] and so on., are all designed for reducing the energy consumption of nodes.

In this paper, the issue of event-driven WSN is put into consideration. It has 3 features [9]. (1) Sensor networks are event-driven and have spatially correlated contention. In most sensor networks, multiple sensors are deployed in the same geographic area. In addition to sending periodic observations, when an event of interest happens, the sensing nodes that observe the event send messages reporting the event. (2) Not all sensing nodes need to report an event. In many sensor applications, not all the nodes that sense an event need to report it. Specifically, we find that many applications are designed to have every sensing node send a message, but it is enough for a subset of these messages to reach the data sink.(3)Time-varying density of sensing nodes. In many sensor networks, the size of the set of sensing nodes changes with time, e.g., when a target enters a field of sensors.

According to these three features, we make the following works: the residual energy of nodes is introduced into the mechanism of data transmission, period sleep ,collision handling in order to ensure a balanced energy consumption, prolong the lifetime of WSN and prevent the network island . The neighbor nodes are classified according to angle of arrival (AOA) so as to ensure the connection of networks. Whether to pass the data or not is up to the node's residual energy so that the energy consumption is balanced. Finally, the protocol of this paper is introduced on the basis of S-MAC and the efficiency is tested through experiments.

The rest of the paper is organized as follows. Section II introduces related work on sensor networks' contention-based MAC protocol, their requirements and our ongoing research project. The protocol that this paper proposed is detailed in Section III. Finally, simulations and results are presented in Section IV, and concluding in Section V.

2 Related Work

The MAC protocol for WSN is often divided into Contention-based MAC and contention-free MAC. The contention-based MAC protocol is also known as random access protocol. Typically, some nodes communicate with each other in a shared-medium, and only one node can use the channel to communicate with others. Colliding nodes back off for a random duration and try to compete the channel again. Distributed coordination function (DCF) is an example of the contention-based protocol in the standardized IEEE 802.11[4].

The contention-free MAC is based on reservation and scheduling, such as TDMA-based protocols[2]. Some examples of the kind of protocol are Time Division Multiple Access (TDMA); Frequency Division Multiple Access (FDMA);Code Division Multiple Access (CDMA).

Since this paper focuses on a distributed protocol , we'd like to introduce some typical distributed MAC protocols for WSN.

S-MAC protocol is based on IEEE802.11 MAC protocol. It is a MAC protocol aiming at reducing energy consumption and support self-configuration . S-MAC protocol assumes that in normal circumstances, data transmission is little in WSN. The nodes coordinate to communication and the network can tolerate some additional message latency.

The idea of T-MAC protocol is to reduce the idle listening time by transmitting all message in burst of variable length m and sleeping between bursts. There are two solutions for the early sleeping problems: future request-to-send, FRTS and full buffer priority. But they are not very effective.

Both S-MAC and T-MAC use periodic sleep/wakeup cycle to reduce energy consumption .But this savings may be offset by decreased throughout and a disadvantage is that the latency of sending a message can be increased. And there is also the problem of data communication pause. That is , the node on sleep have to wait for the active period to transmit data if events are monitored . The nodes have to wait for the next hop nodes change to its active period. This kind of delay will increase with the increase of the path hop.

Sift MAC protocol use a fixed-sized contention window and a carefully-chose, non-uniform probability distribution of transmitting in each slot within the window . Sift only sends the first R of N reports without collisions. But Sift doesn't consider the node's residual energy ,that is, some low energy nodes may run out. The paper presents a new way of solving to send the first R of N reports and fully considered the residual energy.

In above-mentioned MAC layer protocols, in order to reduce the energy consumption ,more is considered to lessen the idle listening period, to use period listening and sleeping , to avoid overhearing and to reduce bit numbers of MAC address of the communication data packet[10]. But none of them has considered the issue of residual energy of nodes .Whereas GAF[14] puts residual energy into consideration , it focuses on using the energy of cluster head in a cluster. Our idea is that the handling of residual energy is important to the lifetime of WSN. If the energy of some node is nearly exhausted , It can't be chose as working node and needs to be replaced by its neighbor node which has more residual energy in case that the network island would appear.

At the same time , we believe that to solve the energy balancing problem at the lower layer has a more performance than higher-layer sensor network protocol .So, how to balance the energy consumption among the network neighbor nodes at MAC layer, and how to reduce the channel competition collision, ensure the effective communication and save energy are the problems that this paper tries to tackle.

The current MAC protocol use traditional binary exponential back off algorithm to tackle the collision problem in the course of communication. But the algorithm is designed for the faire distribution of shared channel. This paper has a revision of the back off mechanism of collision and introduces the idea of nodes residual energy, so that it is feasible to energy is fair usage for all nodes.

3 Residual Energy-Based MAC Protocol (REB-MAC Protocol)

When N neighboring nodes sense an event at the same time , not all nodes need to transmit report of its . Only R of N need to report and the rest can give up transmission. When choosing the first R of N potential reports , two factors are put into consideration. The first is that R nodes are chose according to the residual energy. The second is that the node is chose according to different positions to ensure the representative feature of data. Meanwhile, the collisions avoiding and the collisions handling mechanism are put into consideration among the competing nodes.

3.1 Preliminary Conditions and Assumptions

- In the event-driven WSN, a single event-ID is distributed for every event. The node has an event table (see table 1) which includes event-ID, the number of nodes responding to an event and the event-related neighbor nodes.

Table 1. Event Information Table

Event-ID	Numbers of nodes responding to an event	Event-related neighbor nodes
005050	1	A
005050	1	B
002300	2	C
002100	3	D

- Every node need a neighboring node information table (see table 2) including neighboring Nodes ID, Residual Energy and Orientation. The orientation position is decided by the angle which a node's signal arrives the node. For example, if 4 orientations are divided according to the direction of east ,west ,south and north , then the angle's distribution should be in [0,90], [90,180], [180,270], [270,360].

Table 2. Neighboring Node Information Table

Neighboring Nodes-ID	Residual Energy	Orientation
A	0.55	1
B	0.30	3
C	0.80	2
D	0.10	4

- The proposed protocol is derived from the distributed Coordination Function in the Ieee802.11 stand , which adopts RTS-CTS-DATA-ACK communication mechanism. Such mechanism can solve the problem of Hidden-station and overhearing. The RTS packet need carry Residual Energy, Event-ID and residual Time of channel usage.
- The proposed protocol is based on S-MAC. The nodes are put into periodic listen and sleep . Because of the residual time field of RTS-CTS-DATA-ACK packet, the neighboring nodes of source node and target node sense these packet, record the residual time and get into sleep state. The Sleep time is equal to the residual time, When the sleep time is up, the nodes re-listen the channel.

In order to reduce energy consumption , the nodes must be in sleep of low-level energy consumption . Meanwhile , the idea of residual energy is introduced which can sense collisions of multi-nodes in one event and balance the energy consumption of networks.

Now, we will discuss the MAC protocol Design.

3.2 REB-MAC Protocol Design

3.2.1 Energy Information Transmission Mechanism

The transmission of the node's residual energy information among neighboring nodes is very important for the realization of the proposed protocol.

In this paper, the node's residual energy is picked up by RTS-CTS-DATA-ACK packets. For example, when node X acquires the channel, it'll pass RTS packet which picks up the node's residual energy(say 25%),and X's neighboring nodes can sense and receive this information. When the target node Y has received the RTS packet passed by X, it will pass CTS packet which also carries Y's residual energy. Then Y's neighboring nodes receive the information of Y's residual energy. Every node having received the residual energy information will instantly its local neighboring nodes information chart. It will modify the residual energy information of the existed node and append new information if it doesn't exist in the chart.

Based on S-MAC Protocol, the periodic SYNC packet also carries the information of the node's residual energy to ensure that the user can renew his information chart of the neighboring nodes residual energy. And the transmission of the node's residual energy information lays a foundation for the carry-out of the following mechanism.

3.2.2 Contention Window

We assume that N neighboring nodes in one area sense an event simultaneously. But only R nodes need to pass the data(R/N) because of the redundant nodes. To ensure a balanced consumption of network energy, R nodes which have more residual energy will pass the data, and the rest nodes give up. This is the so-called R/N issue which has been discussed in Sift protocol. But here we propose a different solution.

Our solution is that we assume when one node and all it's neighboring nodes sense a event, according to their residual energy hierarchy, the nodes that have more residual energy have the priority to transmit the information. Based on such assumption, we choose different back off intervals for nodes with different residual energy when they sense the channel. The nodes that have more residual energy are prior to transmit the information, whereas the nodes with less residual energy have longer back off intervals. Hence a balanced energy consumption of network nodes is ensured.

This paper chooses E_i for back off interval B_i of nodes. Different B_i is calculated for different E_i. High E_i value should have low Bi and low E_i should have high B_i.

For each node , It has a E_i and a back-off interval B_i, $E_i \in [0,1]$ is corresponding to $P_i = E_i / \sum E_i$, $P_i \in (0,1)$. Because of the reciprocal relation between E_i and B_i, We define a Q_i with $Q_i = 1 - P_i, Q_i \in (0,1)$; then we set the value of B_i: $B_i = \lfloor B_i \times Q_i \rfloor$.

Despite that B_i may be different chose by different nodes in the first place and value Q_i of residual energy may be different, B_i which is computed according to above formula can be same. In order to solve the problem, random number R_i is generated in [0.9,1.1]. Then the B_i is set: $B_i = \lfloor B_i \times Q_i \times R_i \rfloor$ Hence, transmitting collision is decreased.

3.2.3 Collision Handling

Transmitting collision is unavoidable. For example when a node moves to the neighboring area of another node's wireless signal, it'll pass the information and cause the data collision due to the failure to sensing the signal.

Traditional CSMA/CA uses binary exponential back off algorithm to tackle the collision problem. the mechanism is as the following:

If a collision occurs, then the following procedure is used. Let node i be one of the nodes whose transmission has collided with some other node(s). Node i chooses a new back-off interval as follows: (1) Increment Collision-Counter by 1. (2) Choose new B_i uniformly distributed in [1, $2^{CollisionCounter-1}$ *CW],where Collision Window is a constant parameter.

From above we can see, when collision occurs , contention window will double the size so that communication efficiency is decreased. So, for the second step, we take the same process:

$B_i = \lfloor B_i \times Q_i \times R_i \rfloor$ and the definition of B_i, Q_i and R_i is the same with 3.2.3.The decrease of B_i can increase the throughout of the system.

3.2.4 Message Passing

When an event occurs in WSN, N neighboring nodes sense it simultaneously, but we are interested in the first R of N potential reports because of the redundant nodes. The node will take the information down in its event information chart when it senses an event. At the same time, in order to solve R/N problem, it need to know which neighboring nodes also sense the event and prepare to transmit.

In other words, the RTS packet is passed by the node carries Event-ID. Once the node senses the Event-ID carried by the RTS packet, the number of the nodes responding to the event is added 1 to its counting of the same Event-ID. And the node will go through the periodic listen and sleep. Whenever the node senses the available channel and prepare to transmit the information, it'll check the counting machine first. If the result exceeds R, The node will give up the transmission, and delete the event information. It can also transmit by RTS-CTS-DATA-ACK packets and delete the information from the information chart when the result exceeds R.

The value of R is decided by the distribution density of the nodes , or by the numbers of a node's neighboring nodes .

3.2.5 A Extension of R/N

- **Assumption**

From 3.2.3 and 3.2.4,we can see that different back off intervals are chose for neighboring nodes according to their residual energy so that the priority of the transmission by more residual energy has been ensured. but the problem of not transmitting all-round data will occur. As Figure 1 shows, there are nodes sensing an event. The solid square node is the center node . The hollow circle nodes are ones with low residual energy and the solid circle nodes are ones with high residual energy . The sampling data is only at one orientation and not all orientations. So the orientation of network node must be put into consideration.

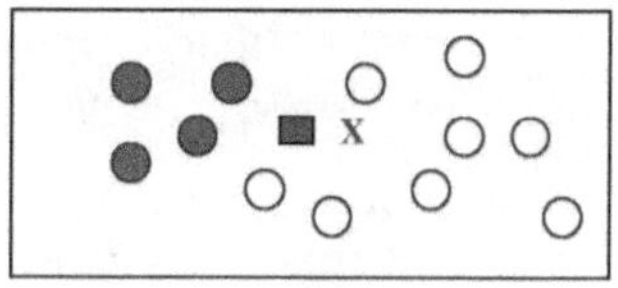

Fig. 1. Several solid square nodes which is at one orientation sending sampling data

- **Solutions**

Our solution is that : A node's neighboring nodes are classified into different area according to their signal's arrival angle . Then the node can be pinned down according to the classified area . Whether to pass the information or not depends on their position.

We use the geographic coordinate, and the node and its neighboring nodes are locate as shown in figure 2.The origin is the node, and the other nodes indicate the neighboring nodes. Located in the area comparing to the origin. From the Figure, we can see in the first 3 cases, the origin node is in the boundary position. The data passing by such nodes has speciality and need to be put into special consideration . In the fourth case , the node is in the key position and play an important role in the wireless network. Because ,when the node's energy runs out, the connectivity will be seriously affected and the network island is easy to occur. In case 5, the node is among the high density distribution of the neighboring nodes , so its important is decrease sharply.

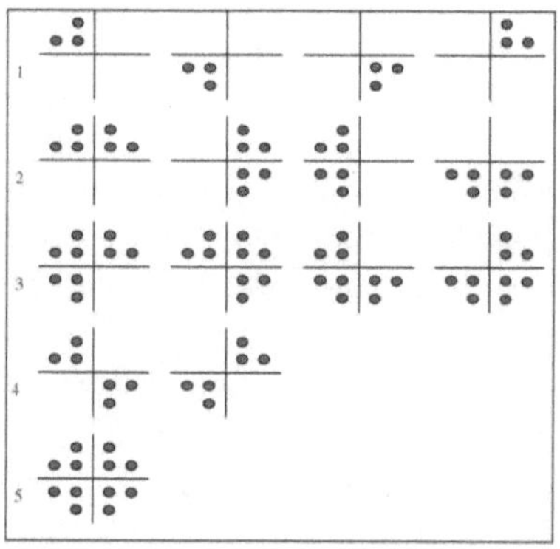

Fig. 2. The orientation information of node

From the analysis ,we have the following 3 solutions.

The first is that: If the node is in the boundary position of the area, it doesn't pass report on according to the itself residual energy. Although R nodes have been monitored, the node still prepares to response for the event. When free channel is sensed, the node will send report when the probability is p ($p \geq 0.5$) and give up the sending when probability is 1-p. So both the energy-saving and the all-round data are ensured.

The second is that: In case 4, the node functions as a relay in WSN. So we will decrease its operation on sending report of a event . When R nodes are monitored, its operation is according to 3.2.4 . Otherwise, When free channel is sensed, the node will send report when the probability is p ($p \leq 0.5$) and give up the sending when probability is 1-p. So both the energy-saving and the all-round data are ensured. When free channel is sensed, the node will send report when the probability is p ($p \leq 0.5$) and give up the sending when probability is 1-p. So both the energy-saving and the all-round data are ensured.

The last one is that: In the case 5, the operation of nodes will be done according to 3.2.4. Furthermore , the node will clear the event in the event information chart.

- **Partitioning Area**

When a node positions its neighboring nodes, the positioning mechanism is based on Angle of Arrival (AOA) described in [11]. AOA provides important assurance for our method. The classification is based on the capability of the nodes to sense the direction from which a signal is received , which is known as angle of arrival. We don't have to position the specific node , we only need to know the angle between the node and its neighboring nodes in the coordinate. Since angle of arrival (AOA) sensing requires an antenna array, or several ultra sound receiver, the hardware cost increases.

The method to classify the area is : When node x is passing the information (which might be any of RTS,CTS,DATA and ACK), because of the broadcast channel , every neighbor node can receive the wireless signal and record the AOA and neighboring node's information. For example,: If 4 areas are divided into according to the orientation of east, west , north and south , then the angle will be located in [0,90],[90,180],[180,270],[270,360].

4 Performance Evaluation

Given the difficulty in performing actual measurements in wireless networking, we first evaluate our system through simulation. We have created a simple simulator capable of creating an arbitrary multi-hop network topology of a group of networked sensors. Each program process represents a networked sensor, and a master process is responsible for synchronizing them to perform bit time simulation. Since our main focus is media access control. The simulator doesn't simulate the actual hardware operating in the TinyOS environment. However, it preserves the event driven semantics.

We assume the value of the original energy is 1. The value of energy consumption is 0.01 for transmitting a RTS/CTS/ACK packet and The value of energy consumption is 0.02 for transmitting a DATA packet.

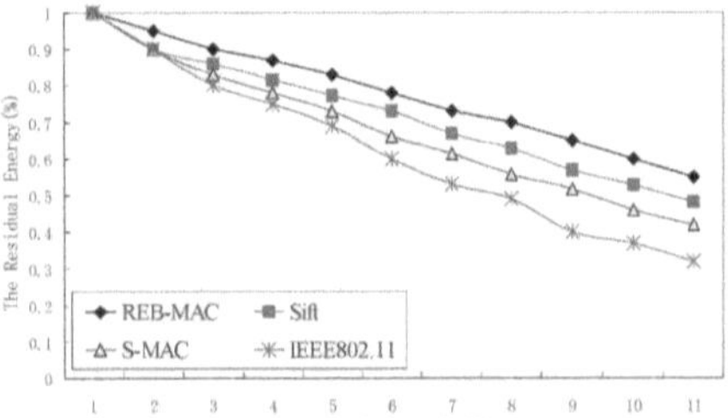

Fig. 3. The different residual energy in different protocols

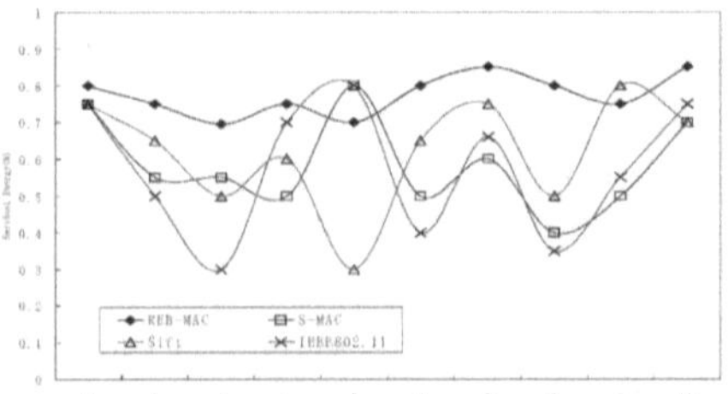

Fig. 4. The different balance of the node's energy in different protocols

First, we compare the network residual energy of 4 protocols of REB-MAC, S-MAC, Sift and IEEE802.11 . The same communication circumstances. The result is shown in Figure 3.

From Figure 3 , we can see REB-MAC shows good features on saving the network nodes energy. REB-MAC introduces the node's residual energy based on S-MAC protocol and choose different back off intervals for nodes of different residual energy so that collisions are decreased and energy is saved.

Figure 4 demonstrate through simulation the balanced the node's energy by REB-MAC , S-MAC , Sift and IEEE802.11 .

Ten neighbor nodes are checked after the node transmits the information. Figure 4 shows the energy consumption of the neighbor nodes . REB-MAC has better performance on balancing neighbor nodes' energy than others.

5 Conclusion

This paper introduces residual energy into the mechanism of data transmission, sleeping and collision handling to enhanced the communication efficiency, ensure the balanced consumption of the node's energy, and present the phenomenon of network island. In the end, the mechanism proposed this paper is on the based of S-MAC protocol and is verified by the simulation.

The distributed handling mechanism used in this protocol adapts the moving nodes better. We also introduce the position information into the method. Due to AOA , hardware cost is increased. We hope this can be improved in our future work.

References

1. Jian-Zhong LI, Jin-Bao LI, Sheng-Fei SHI, Concepts, Issues and Advance of Sensor Networks and Data Management of Sensor, Journal of software, VOL14, No 10, China, 2003
2. LAN MAN Standards Committee of IEEE Computer Society, Wireless LAN medium control (MAC) and physical layer(PHY) specification ,IEEE, New York ,NY,USA,IEEE Std 802.11-1999 edition, 1999.
3. Akyildiz I.F, Su W, Sankarasubramaniam Y, Cayirci E. Wireless sensor network: A survey. Computer Networks. 2002, vol.38, pp.393-422.
4. Wei Ye and John Hedemann, Medium Access Control in Wireless Sensor Networks, USC/ISI technical report ISI-TR-580, OCTOBER 2003.
5. W. Heinzelman, A. Chandrakasan, H. Balakrishnan, Energy-efficient communication protocol for wireless sensor networks, in: The Proceeding of the Hawaii International Conference System Sciences, Hawaii, January 2000.
6. Zhong L, Shah R, Guo C. An ultra-low power and distributed access protocol for broadband wireless sensor networks. IEEE Broadband Wireless Summit[C]. LasVegas, USA, 2001, 3.
7. Ye W, Heidemann J, Estrin D. An Energy Efficient MAC protocol for Wireless Sensor Networks. Proceedings of the 21st International Annual Joint Conference of the IEEE Computer and Communications Societies (INFOCOM 2002). New York, USA, 2002,6.
8. Tijs van Dam, Koen Langendoen, An adaptive energy-efficient MAC protocol for wireless sensor networks, Proceedings of the first international conference on Embedded networked sensor systems, November 2003.

9. Jamieson K,Balakrishnan H, Tay Y C. Sift:A MAC protocol for wireless sensor networks. In : Proc 1st Int'l Conf on Embedded Network Sensor Systems(WenSys),Nov. 5-7,2003,Los Angeles ,CA.
10. Gautam Kulkarni,Curt Schurger,Mani Srivastava, Dynamic Link Labels for Energy Efficient MAC Headers in Wireless networks , IEEE 2002
11. Niculescu D,Nath B. Ad hoc positioning system (APS) using AOA. In : Proc 22nd Annual Joint Conf of the IEEE Computer and Communication Societies(INFOCOM'2003).IEEE, Vol 3,2003
12. R. Shah and J. Rabaey, "Energy Aware Routing for Low Energy Ad Hoc Sensor Networks", in the Proceedings of the IEEE Wireless Communications and Networking Conference (WCNC), Orlando, FL, March 2002.
13. C.Intanagonwiwat, R.Govindan and D. Estrin,"Directed diffusion: A scalable and robust-communication paradigm for sensor networks", in the Proceedings of the 6th Annual ACM/IEEE International Conference on Mobile Computing and Networking (MobiCom'00), Boston, MA, August 2000.
14. Xu Y, Heidemann J Geography-informed energy conservation for ad hoc routing ,In :Proc 7th Annual Int'l conf on MOBILCOMM, Rome, Italy . July 2001. 70~84

Processing Probabilistic Range Query over Imprecise Data Based on Quality of Result*

Wei Zhang and Jianzhong Li

Department of Computer Science, Harbin Institute of Technology, 150001, China
{wzhang74, lijzh}@hit.edu.cn

Abstract. Sensors are employed in many applications to monitor entities such as environment temperature or illumination. Because of limited resources (e.g., battery power and wireless bandwidth), it is impractical for the database to track continuous changing readings from sensors at all times. Consequently, database may produce incorrect query results based on recorded data. However, if the error between the recorded value and the actual value is bounded, probabilistic approach can be applied to process queries over the imprecise data in database. The paper proposes a quality of result based probabilistic range query processing method. Two measures are defined to evaluate the quality of result. A probability model is proposed to estimate the quality of returned results. Based on the model, an algorithm is developed to choose the probability threshold according to user's requirement on the quality of result.

1 Introduction

The applications of sensor networks are received considerable attention recently. Sensors are often employed to monitor entities such as environment temperature, illumination or locations of moving objects, etc. A centralized database tracks the readings of sensors and processes queries about the monitored circumstance. Since resources (e.g., battery power and wireless bandwidth) are limited, it is impractical for the database to record continuous changing data from sensors at all times. As a result, the database may produce incorrect answers based on old data. However, if the error between the database value and the actual value is limited, probabilistic approach can be applied to process queries over this kind of imprecise data. Each probabilistic query answer is returned with a probability to indicate its validity. A predefined minimum probability threshold can be set to filter query answers with probability lower than the threshold.

Given a value range R, the probabilistic range query $PRQ(R, MinC)$ returns a set of tuples (O_i, p_i), where the attribute T of O_i is in R (i.e. $O_i.T \in R$) with probability p_i greater than the probability threshold $MinC$, e.g., PRQ queries ask which sensor(s) return temperature within the value range R, or which object(s) move in to the spatial

* This work was partially funded by the Key Program of the National Natural Science Foundation of China, Grant No. 60533110, by the National Natural Science Foundation of China, Grant No. 60473075, and by the key Natural Science Foundation of Heilongjiang Province, Grant No. zjg03-05.

H.T. Shen et al. (Eds.): APWeb 2006, LNCS 3842, pp. 441 – 449, 2006.

range R with the probability greater than $MinC$. Since the value of object's attribute T is imprecise in above application, two types of errors may be produced while processing probabilistic range queries. (1) Positive error. Object O_i is returned as an answer because p_i is greater than $MinC$, but $O_i.T$ is actually not in V. (2) Negative error. Object O_i is not returned because p_i is less than $MinC$, but O_i actually satisfies queries. Because of the inherited uncertainty of probabilistic method, above errors are often unavoidable in practice. Higher $MinC$ may reduce positive error, but it may increase negative error, on the contrary, smaller $MinC$ may reduce negative error but increase positive error. Therefore, the value of $MinC$ influences the quality of result.

Although the quality of result is an important issue in processing probabilistic queries, little research addresses on this problem. All existing approaches leave users to choose the probability threshold, but most users are concerned more about the quality of result than the value of $MinC$. Moreover, even though the probabilistic result has been filtered by a predefined $MinC$, users still do not know how many objects in the returned results may actually satisfy the given query or how many objects are returned among all objects that are actually satisfy the given query.

The paper proposes a method to process probabilistic range query based on the quality of result. At First, two measures, accuracy and recall, are defined to evaluate the quality of probabilistic result. Then, a probability model is proposed to estimate the quality of result based on the probabilities of objects that possibly satisfy the given query. Finally, an algorithm is developed to choose an appropriate probability threshold according to user's requirement on the quality of result. While querying the imprecise data, users only need to set their requirement on the quality of result. The probability threshold are automatically chosen by the propose method according to users' requirement, e.g. "return the sensors set which contains at least 80% of sensor with readings actually between [70, 90]" or "return the moving objects set containing at least 30% of all objects that will move to region R after 20 minutes".

2 Related Works

Probabilistic queries over imprecise data (e.g., sensor data or location of moving objects) have received growing interests in recent years [1]. Since sensor data is noisy and uncertain by nature, probabilistic approaches are well suited for sensor networks. The probabilistic uncertainty model and a general classification of different types of probabilistic queries for sensor data are discussed in [3]. In [2], Wolfson et al. discuss using probabilistic model to process range queries about moving objects, while Cheng et al. [3] develop probabilistic nearest-neighbor query algorithms. Deshpande et al. [4] proposes an approach using a probabilistic model to answer queries about the attributes in a sensor network. However, little research addresses the quality of probabilistic query result. Different with [2], the quality definitions in this paper are directly related to the percentage of correct answers in the probabilistic result.

3 Query Processing Based on the Quality of Probabilistic Result

For a given probabilistic range query $PRQ(R, MinC)$, let PR_{MinC} denotes the probabilistic result containing all objects that satisfy PRQ with the probability greater than *MinC*, and *TR* denotes the result containing all objects that actually satisfy *PRQ*. The two quality measures are defined as follow:

Definition 1 (*Accuracy*). Accuracy defines the number of correct answers in PR_{MinC} that actually satisfy the given query as a fraction of all answers in PR_{MinC}.

$$Accuracy = \begin{cases} |PR_{MinC} \cap TR| / |PR_{MinC}| & PR_{MinC} \neq \phi \\ 0\% & PR_{MinC} = \phi \text{ and } TR \neq \phi \\ 100\% & PR_{MinC} = \phi \text{ and } TR = \phi \end{cases}$$

Definition 2 (*Recall*). Recall defines the number of correct answers in PR_{MinC} that actually satisfy the given query as a fraction of all answers in *TR*

$$Reall = \begin{cases} |PR_{MinC} \cap TR| / |TR| & TR \neq \phi \\ 100\% & TR = \phi \end{cases}$$

Accuracy represents the effectiveness of *MinC* on eliminating positive errors. Recall represents the effectiveness of *MinC* on eliminating negative errors.

The quality of probabilistic result can be estimated by objects' probabilities in it. Suppose the result of a given probabilistic range query *PRQ*(*R*, *MinC*) is $PR_{MinC} = \{(O_i, p_i) \mid p_i > MinC\}$. Let ξ_i be the indicated random variable that $\xi_i = 1$ represents the object O_i actually satisfies *PRQ*, and $\xi_i = 0$ represents O_i does not satisfy *PRQ*. Let the sample space $\Omega = \{A_k \mid k = 0, 1, \ldots, |PR_{MinC}|\}$, where $|PR_{MinC}|$ is the number of objects in PR_{MinC}. Suppose the discrete random variable η denotes the number of objects in PR_{MinC} that actually satisfy the query. Obviously, $\eta = \Sigma\xi_i$. If event A_k occurs, it means that the number of correct results in PR_{MinC} is *k*, i.e. $P[A_k] = P[\eta = k]$. Although the distribution function of η can be computed by probabilities of objects in PR_{MinC}, the complexity of computation is $O(2^n)$, where $n = |PR_{MinC}|$. Then, we use the expectation of η to estimate $|PR_{MinC} \cap TR|$. When $MinC = 0$, PR_0 contains all objects which satisfy *PRQ* with no-zero probability. Let η_0 denotes number of objects in $\{PR_0 \cap TR\}$. Then, the expectation of η_0 can be used to estimate $|TR|$. Consequently, the accuracy and recall of PR_{MinC} are estimated based on those expectations.

Suppose object O_i and O_j satisfy *PRQ* are independent to each other, i.e. for $\forall i \neq j$, ξ_i and ξ_j are independent random variables. For example, the movements of objects are independent or the readings of sensors are not correlated. Accordingly, $|PR_{MinC}|$ can be estimated by $E\{\eta\}$.

$$E(\eta) = E\left(\sum_{i=1}^{|PR_{MinC}|} \xi_i\right) = \sum_{i=1}^{|PR_{MinC}|} E(\xi_i) = \sum_{i=1}^{|PR_{MinC}|} p_i \tag{1}$$

Therefore, the accuracy of PR_{MinC} can be estimated by

$$E(Accuracy) = E\left(\frac{\eta}{|PR_{MinC}|}\right) = \frac{E(\eta)}{|PR_{MinC}|} = \frac{\sum_{i=1}^{|PR_{MinC}|} p_i}{|PR_{MinC}|} \tag{2}$$

For any given error bound ε, the probability that the estimation error of PR_{MinC}'s accuracy exceeds ε can be estimated according to Chebychev's inequality,

$$P\left[\left|Accuracy - E(Accuracy)\right| \geq \varepsilon\right] \leq \frac{D(Accuracy)}{\varepsilon^2} \tag{3}$$

where the variance of PR_{MinC}'s accuracy is computed by

$$D(Accuracy) = D\left(\frac{\eta}{|PR_{MinC}|}\right) = \frac{D\left(\sum_{i=1}^{|PR|}\xi_i\right)}{|PR_{MinC}|^2} = \frac{\sum_{i=1}^{|PR|}D(\xi_i)}{|PR_{MinC}|^2} = \frac{\sum_{i=1}^{|PR_{MinC}|}p_i\times(1-p_i)}{|PR_{MinC}|^2} \tag{4}$$

Similarly, the recall of probabilistic result PR_{MinC} can also be estimated. Since η_0 denotes the number of results in TR, the recall of PR_{MinC} equals η/η_0 when $\eta_0 > 0$.

$$E(Recall) = E\left(\frac{\eta}{\eta_0}\right) \leq \frac{E(\eta)}{E(\eta_0)} = \sum_{i=1}^{|PR_{MinC}|}p_i \bigg/ \sum_{i=1}^{|PR_0|}p_i \tag{5}$$

We the division of η and η_0's expectations to estimate $E(Recall)$. Due to the correlation between η and η_0, the value of $E(Recall)$ may less than the quotient of expectations. According to Chebychev's inequality,

$$P\left[\left|\eta - E(\eta)\right| \geq \varepsilon\times E(\eta)\right] \leq \frac{D(\eta)}{(\varepsilon\times E(\eta))^2} \Leftrightarrow P\left[E(\eta)\times(1-\varepsilon) \leq \eta \leq E(\eta)\times(1+\varepsilon)\right] \geq \left(1 - \frac{D(\eta)}{(\varepsilon\times E(\eta))^2}\right)$$

then $P\left[\frac{E(\eta)\times(1-\varepsilon)}{E(\eta_0)\times(1+\varepsilon)} \leq Recall \leq \frac{E(\eta)\times(1+\varepsilon)}{E(\eta_0)\times(1-\varepsilon)}\right] \geq \left(1 - \frac{(D(\eta))}{(\varepsilon\times E(\eta))^2}\right)\times\left(1 - \frac{(D(\eta_0))}{(\varepsilon\times E(\eta_0))^2}\right) =$

$$\left(1 - \frac{\left(\sum_{i=1}^{|PR_{MinC}|}p_i\times(1-p_i)\right)}{\varepsilon^2\times\left(\sum_{i=1}^{|PR_{MinC}|}p_i\right)^2}\right)\times\left(1 - \frac{\left(\sum_{i=1}^{|PR_0|}C_i\times(1-p_i)\right)}{\varepsilon^2\times\left(\sum_{i=1}^{|PR_0|}p_i\right)^2}\right) \tag{6}$$

Although Chebychev's inequality can only provide a coarse bound about the estimated accuracy of probabilistic result, theorem 1 given below guarantees that the more objects are there in probabilistic result, the more accurate the estimated value of accuracy is.

Theorem 1. For any given probabilistic range query $PRQ(R, MinC)$, suppose its probabilistic result $PR_{MinC} = \{(O_i, p_i) \mid p_i > MinC, i = 1, \ldots, n\}$, then,

$$\lim_{n\to\infty}[Accuracy - E(Accuracy)] = 0$$

Proof (sketch). Let the indicate random variable $\xi_i = 1$ represents the event that the objects O_i actually satisfies PRQ, then $P[\xi_i = 1] = p_i$. Since $E(\xi_i) < \infty$ and $D(\xi_i) < \infty$, $i = 1, 2, \ldots, n$, and

$$\lim_{n\to\infty}\frac{1}{n^2}D\left(\sum_{i=1}^{n}\xi_i\right) = \lim_{n\to\infty}\frac{1}{n^2}\left(\sum_{i=1}^{n}C_i\times(1-C_i)\right) \leq \lim_{n\to\infty}\frac{1}{n^2}\times\frac{n}{4} = \lim_{n\to\infty}\frac{1}{4n} = 0$$

By *Markov's (Weak) Law of Large Numbers*, the random variable sequence $\{\xi_i\}$ satisfies the weak law of large number. This means

$$\lim_{n\to\infty}\left[\frac{1}{n}\sum_{i=1}^{n}\xi_i - E\left(\frac{1}{n}\sum_{i=1}^{n}\xi_i\right)\right]=0$$

Since $Accuracy=\frac{1}{n}\sum_{i=1}^{n}\xi_i$, theorem 1 holds. ∎

Algorithm. *Choose_MinC* (PR_0, *accuracy* [*recall*], ε, *ep*, N_{Min})
//Choose *MinC* based on user's requirement on quality of probabilistic result
Input: Candidate Probabilistic Result PR_0,
Requirement on the quality of result *accuracy* or *recall*,
Permitted estimation error ε, Error probability threshold *ep*,
Minimum number of objects in PR_{MinC} N_{Min}
Output: Probability threshold *MinC*

1. $PR_{MinC} = PR_0$;
2. Compute current $D(\eta)$, $E(\eta)$ and $E(\eta_0)$;
3. $Last\_MinC = MinC = 0$; //*Last_MinC* records threshold for current max quality
4. $Max\_accu = accu = E(\eta)/|PR_{MinC}|$; // *Max_accu* records current max accuracy
   [$Max\_reca = reca = 1$;] // for choosing *MinC* based on recall
5. Compute current error probability *cur_ep* based on formula (3) or (6);
6. Sort objects in PR_{MinC} based on the increasing order of probability;
7. While ($|PR_{MinC}| > N_{MinC}$) and (($accu < accuracy$) or ($cur\_ep > ep$)) {
   [While ($|PR_{MinC}| > N_{MinC}$) and (($reca < recall$) or ($cur\_ep > ep$))] // for recall
8. $MinC = O_1.p_1$; // PR_{MinC} is sorted, p_1 is the min probability in PR_{MinC}
9. $PR_{MinC} = PR_{MinC} - O_1$; //remove object with $p_i <= MinC$
10. While (($O_i.p_i <= MinC$) and ($|PR_{MinC}| > N_{MinC}$)) {
11. $PR_{MinC} = PR_{MinC} - O_i$; //remove object with $p_i <= MinC$
12. $E(\eta) = E(\eta) - O_i.p_i$;
13. $D(\eta) = D(\eta) - O_i.p_i\times(1 - O_i.p_i)$;
14. Compute current error probability *cur_ep* based on formula
    (3) for accuracy or (6) for recall; }
15. If ($|PR_{MinC}| > 0$)
16. compute current quality of result *accu* and *reca*;
17. If ($accu > Max\_accu$) {
18. [If ($reca > Max\_reca$)] // for recall
19. $Last\_MinC = MinC$;
20. $Max\_accu = accu$; // record current max accuracy
21. [$Max\_reca = reca$;] // for recall }}
22. If formula (2) holds for accuracy [formula (5) holds for recall]
23. return *MinC*;
24. Else if ($|PR_{MinC}| <= N_{MinC}$) // does not find suitable *MinC*
25. If ($accu < Max\_accu$) [($reca < Max\_reca$) //for recall]
26. return *Last_MinC*; // return MinC for max estimated quality

End *Choose_MinC*

Fig. 1. Algorithm *Choose_MinC*

According to above analysis, we propose an algorithm *Choose_MinC* to choose an appropriate probability threshold *MinC* which can let the estimated quality of result meets user's requirement or the highest quality that a PR_{MinC} can reach. After obtaining PR_0 which contains all objects that satisfy the query with non-zero probability, the algorithm first use $E(\eta_0)$ to estimate $|TR|$ based on probabilities in PR_0. Then, the algorithm gradually increases *MinC*. Meanwhile, the accuracy of result is estimated by $E(\eta)/|PR_{MinC}|$ and the recall of result is estimated by $E(\eta)/E(\eta_0)$. Besides the requirement of accuracy or recall, the permitted estimation error ε and the probability threshold *ep* that the error of estimated accuracy or recall exceeds ε also need to be set either by users or query processing method. If formula (2) or (4) is hold under the given parameters, the algorithm terminates and returns current *MinC*. If the algorithm can not find a *MinC* to satisfy the formulas, it returns a *MinC* which maximizes the estimated quality of result. While increasing *MinC*, the accuracy of result is increased and corresponding recall is reduced. Accordingly, the algorithm can only choose *MinC* for user's requirement on accuracy or recall at a time. Since the error of estimated value may be higher while fewer objects are in PR_{MinC}, one can also set a threshold on the minimum number of objects N_{Min} in probabilistic result. If $|PR_{MinC}|$ is equal or fewer than the threshold, the algorithm terminates without considering other parameters. The detail algorithm is given below. The parameters in can be set as default profile except the requirement of accuracy or recall.

4 Experiment Evaluation

This section reports experiment result on the performance of proposed method. The system environment for experiment is a Pentium 4, 2.4GHz processor, 512M memory and 80GB hard disk.

We use the application of monitoring moving objects to evaluate the effectiveness of the proposed approach. Since the future movement of objects is often influenced by many uncertain factors, such as change of velocity, weather condition or traffic condition, the future locations of moving objects are predicted based on their current recorded locations. The predicted locations can be considered as a kind of imprecise data. The uncertainty location range of a moving object is a circle with radius r bounding the current recorded location of the object, where r can be computed by multiplying object's max speed with the predicted time t. This model can be generalized to the interval uncertainty model, which bounds the uncertainty of any continuously changing sensor data. The probabilistic range queries in experiment are predictive range queries about the imprecise locations of moving objects in future instances. Suppose $O.P(t)$ denotes the location of moving objects O at predicted time t. The query $PRQ(R, MinC) = \{(O_i, p_i) \mid$ *the probability that* $O_i.P(t) \in R$ *at the future time* t *is* $p_i\}$. The movements of objects are generated by [5] under the road network of Illinois. The map is normalized to $[0,1]\times[0,1]$. In the experiment, 100,000 moving objects and 200 predictive range queries are generated. All experiment results are the average value of 200 queries result. The initial locations of objects and queries are uniformly distributed in the map. The speed of moving objects is uniformly distributed in [0.06, 0.12]. Each range query covers 1% of the map. At first, all objects that possibly satisfy the queries are retrieved according to predicted time and max speed. Then, two kinds of probability density functions are used to compute the probability that a moving object satisfies a probabilistic range query. One is uniform distribution function denoting as UN in the figures, the other is the probability density functions that are estimated by a trajectory analyze method based on historical trajectories generated in the map [6], denoting as PF in the figures. Finally, the quality of result returned by two probability computation methods is compared.

Fig. 2 and Fig. 3 compare the absolute error and the relative error of estimated |*TR*| computed based on two functions at different predicted times. According to the model proposed in section 0, the number of results in *TR* can be estimated by aggregating the probabilities in PR_0. The accuracy of the estimated values reflects the correctness of the proposed method. The locations of objects become more imprecise as predicted time is increased, since the uncertainty ranges expand. The figures show that the accuracy of estimated values is decreased as the imprecision of data is increased. Since the probabilities computed by estimated distribution functions are more accurate than those computed by uniform distribution functions, PF is more insensitive to the change of data's imprecision. We notice that the outcomes of two methods are similar while predicted time is 10 minutes. Because uncertainty ranges are small at short predicted time, uniform distribution function can work well for probability computation under this condition. However, the correctness of uniform distribution is decreased as the imprecision of data is increased. Accordingly, How to obtain an accurate distribution function is an important issue in processing probabilistic queries over imprecise data.

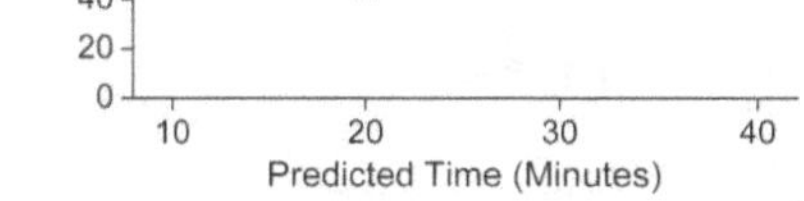

Fig. 2. Absolute error of estimated |*TR*|

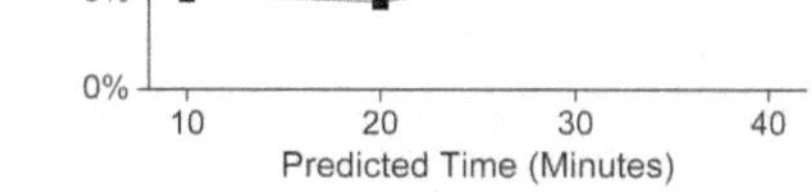

Fig. 3. Relative error of estimated |*TR*|

Fig. 4 compares the actual and estimated quality of result when *MinC* is chosen by algorithm *Choose_MinC* according to user's requirement on accuracy at different predicted times. The settings in the algorithm are ε = 10%, ep = 0.4 and N_{Min} = 30. The requirement on accuracy is 70%. It shows that the algorithm works well when predicted time not greater than 30 minutes. Although the error between the actual and estimated accuracy of the returned answers is more than 10% when predicted time is more than 40 minutes, the algorithm still tries to choose a *MinC* to maximize the accuracy of returned result. The difference between the actual accuracy of returned result and the highest accuracy of the probabilistic result is 4.57% for PF and 3.4% for UN. It also shows that the error of estimated accuracy increases when the imprecision of data increases (as predicted time increases). This is because the uncertain ranges of objects' locations are larger and the error in estimated distribution functions is also increased. In the figure about recall of returned result, the probabilities are average threshold chosen by the algorithm according to the requirement.

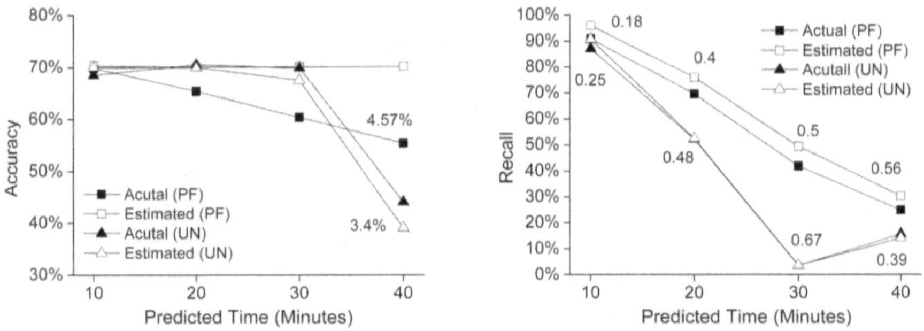

Fig. 4. Actual vs. estimated quality of result at different predicted times

Fig. 5 plots the actual and estimated quality of result when *MinC* is chosen by the proposed algorithm according to different requirement on accuracy when predicted time is 20 minutes. It shows that the proposed algorithm works well under the quality requirements. We notice that the recall of returned result decreases as corresponding accuracy increases. This confirms that the positive and negative error can not be eliminated at the same time. It also shows that the proposed model can accurate estimate the quality of returned probabilistic result.

The estimated and actual quality of results returned by UN is lower than that returned by PF in most cases. This suggests the probabilities computed by PF are more accurate in presenting the validity of probabilistic answer.

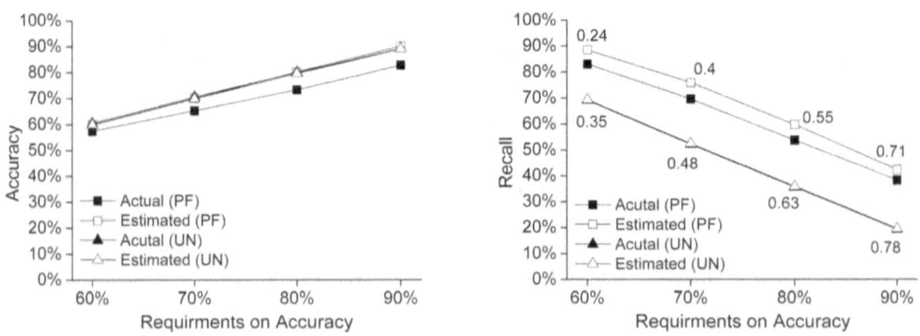

Fig. 5. Actual vs. estimated quality of result at different requirements on accuracy

5 Conclusion

Probabilistic approach is often used to process queries over imprecise data such as readings of sensors and sampling locations of moving objects. The paper defines two measures to evaluate the quality of probabilistic range query result. A probability model is proposed to estimate the values of quality measures about returned result. An algorithm is developed to choose the probability threshold for any given probabilistic range query according to users' requirement on the quality of result.

References

1. Deshpande, A., Guestrin, C., Madden, S.: Using probabilistic models for data management in acquisitional environments. In: CIDR. (2005) 317–328
2. Wolfson, O., Chamberlain, S., Dao, S., Jiang, L., Mendez, G.: Cost and imprecision in modeling the position of moving objects. In: ICDE. (1998) 588-596.
3. Cheng, R., Kalashnikov, D.V., Prabhakar, S.: Evaluating probabilistic queries over imprecise data. In: SIGMOD. (2003) 551-562
4. Deshpande, A., Guestrin, C., Madden, S., Hellerstein, J.M., Hong, W.: Model-driven data acquisition in sensor networks. In: VLDB. (2004) 588–599
5. Hadjieleftheriou, M.: Spatio-temporal generators. (http://www.cs.ucr.edu/~marioh/generators/index.html)
6. Zhang, W, Li, J.Z.: A Probabilistic Approach for Predictive Spatio-Temporal Range Query Processing. Submitted to journal

Dynamic Node Scheduling for Elimination Overlapping Sensing in Sensor Networks with Dense Distribution

Kyungjun Kim[1], Jaemin Son[2], Hoseung Lee[2], Kijun Han[2], and Wonyeul Lee[3]

[1] School of Information & Communication, Daegu University, Korea
kjkim@daegu.ac.kr
[2] Department of Computer Engineering, Kyungpook National University, Korea
{leeho678, jmson}@netopia.knu.ac.kr,
kjhan@bh.knu.ac.kr
[3] Department of Information and communication, Youngsan University, Korea
lumpen@ysu.ac.kr

Abstract. One of the main challenges in wireless sensor networks is to maximize network life time and to minimize power consumption. We propose an energy efficient mechanism for selecting active node which involved in sensing operation in a given dense field. Unlike traditional approaches, this architecture can obtained the complete self-organization of nodes as well as the connectivity of the network. This mechanism can reduce the communication cost by decreasing the number of sensing nodes in highly dense area. Our results show that the dynamic scheduling mechanism of our proposed scheme allows them to outperform existing mechanisms over a variety of scenarios. Our simulation results show that our mechanism reduces the number of transmitted packets in dense sensing area.

1 Introduction

Wireless sensor networks are small, cheap and low power device with a limited battery capacity. The communication procedure that consumes most of the energy in wireless sensor networks is transmission. Hence, low power communication is the most important requirement for a wireless sensor networks, in order to ensure an as long as possible lifetime to the entire network. To accomplish this task, a lot of researchers are devoted to energy-save solutions. Some background material on energy saving subject appears in the previous work [1, 9].

Sensors may be deployed more densely at interesting physical locations. In sensor field all sensor share common sensing tasks. With redundant coverage, multiple sensors cover the same physical area. Therefore, many sensor nodes may report the correlated data related to the same attribute [6].

This implies that not all sensors are required to perform the sensing tasks during the whole system lifetime. Making some nodes sleep does not affect the overall system function as long as there are enough working nodes to assure it [4]. Some literature on this subject appears in the following works [1-3]. In these schemes control packet may be increase in the specific dense area significantly. Thus, network lifetime may be short due to packet overhead. In results, “Sensing Hole” may be incurred.

H.T. Shen et al. (Eds.): APWeb 2006, LNCS 3842, pp. 450 – 459, 2006.

In dense wireless sensor networks with a large number of nodes, a previous dynamic node scheduling scheme is proposed to provide node longevity and connectivity [2, 3]. Also, in these schemes the same event reports and collisions rapidly bring energy consumption in dense area, and then some area can not be sensed at all which causes a sensing hole.

This is the main obstacles confronted for the energy saving in the topology control of wireless sensor networks. If the forwarding nodes located in sparse area, sparse areas rapidly exhaust their remaining energies, the nodes within dense area will be isolated, and then they cannot be involved in data forwarding and sensing operation any more.

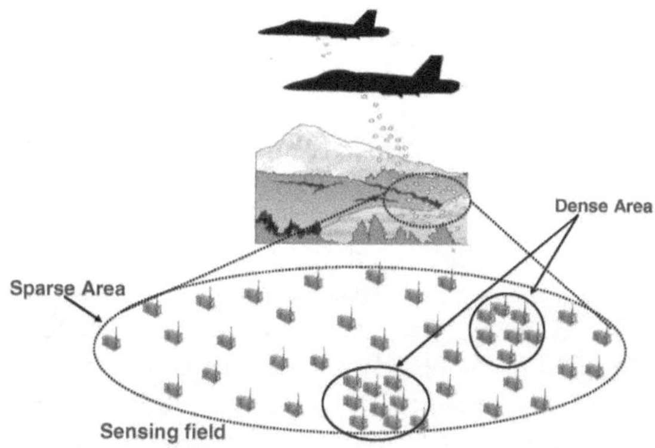

Fig. 1. Sensing hole model

In a result they fail to carry on their missions although their energies are still left. With respect to the simple energy model and node lifetime we can observe that the energy consumption is always less and network lifetime is always prolonged. Fig. 1 illustrates a sensing holes model, e.g. dense area.

This paper proposes a dynamic node scheduling scheme for elimination overlapping sensing in wireless sensor networks with dense distribution to avoid sensing holes problem. This scheme that reduces the number of event packets conveyed through the network are therefore important while also being required for reduce effectively energy consumed by densely deployed sensor nodes. In the second part of the paper we develop a network average operation lifetime and present an example applying, and discuss the example results.

The rest of the paper is organized as follows. In Section 2, we discuss related work from the existing literature, presenting the context for our work. We provide a basic description of the dynamic node scheduling scheme and develop our mathematical model for our scheme in Section 3. Section 4 contains the description of our experiments to evaluate the performance of these strategies, and an analysis of the results presented. Finally, we present concluding remarks in Section 5.

2 Related Works

Various issues in the design of wireless sensor networks have been areas of extensive research in recent years [1-4]. Topology control is an important issue because the only way to save power consumption in the communication system is to completely turn of the node's power, an idle mode is almost as power hungry as the transmit mode [7].

Topology control deals with the problem of computing and maintaining a connected topology among nodes in wireless ad hoc and sensor networks [9]. There exists considerable previous works addressing the topology control problem of minimizing node transmission power, with guarantees of network connectivity.

Liu et al. [8] has been addressing topology control with per-node transmission power adjustment in wireless sensor network. Lin considers the problem of topology control in a network of heterogeneous wireless devices with different maximum transmission ranges.

Cerpa et al. [2] refers to habitat monitoring as a driver for wireless communication technology, and focuses on power-saving by nodes outside regions where interesting changes could be observed, switching themselves off, and being triggered to switch back on only when interesting activity is detected in their vicinity.

Xu et al. [3] focuses on using powered down modes for devices to conserve power, based on whether data traffic is predicted on not, and on the number of equivalent nodes nearby that could be used for alternate routing paths. The assumption here is that the underlying routing will be based on conventional ad hoc routing protocols. Sensor networks, however, typically would require a lighter weight approach to routing, where decisions are based on succinct information from immediate neighbors only.

Chan et al. [11] present an emergent mechanism for highly uniform cluster formation that can achieve a packing efficiency close to hexagonal close-packing.

Simon et al. [10] present three different protocols which, when compared to other approaches, significantly reduce or completely eliminate control message overhead. This scheme provide topology transparent technique for automatic time slotted link management in sensor networks in order to determine transmission schedules between sensor nodes. This scheme leads to additional device unit in sensor nodes.

Schurgers et al. [7, 13] proposed on-demand unicast-based forwarding for achieving energy-efficiency by allowing as many sensors to sleep as possible. However, it is vulnerable to node failure or topology change because packets are dropped until the broken path is required.

Our work is different from all the above studies because we study a scheme which uses general sensor, and need not take into account the costs of the other types of nodes in the overall system design problem.

3 Dynamic Node Scheduling

Proposed scheme controls the network topology by scheduling active nodes to reduce energy consumption. If we initially deploy a large number of sensors and schedule them to work alternatively [4], node lifetime can be prolonged correspondingly. When sensor nodes are randomly deployed, the sensors go to the setup phase to determine active nodes.

We provide detailed pseudo code of dynamic node scheduling in Fig. 2. Our scheme consists of two parts; setup and steady state phases. In setup phase each node is given a random backoff values, and it attempts a transmission of the control packet with its own ID when its backoff timer is expired. If there is a collision of control packets from one or more nodes, nodes are given another backoff values and then repeats the same procedure. At this time the neighbor nodes [4] listen to the control packet from other nodes. The neighbors within sensing area send an ACK packet with its ID when its backoff timer is expired.

```
for all node i ∈ dense area do
  repeat
    setup node i <-backoff_times;
    if setup_times terminates then
      BROADCAST node id to its neighbors;
      if collision occur then
        reject reports received from other nodes;
        resetup node i <-backoff_times;
      else
        its and neighbor's ordering update;
        wait for its neighbor for responding and receiving;
      end if
    end if
  until setup_time ≤ threshold;
  while all node have transmission energy do
    choose active_node from ordering list;
    SEND active_node_duty_cycle to its neighbor;
    sleep node decide l-duty_cycle ; /* l is sleep period */
    repeat
      active node with duty_cycle operation;
    until deplete the entire energy;
  end while
end for
```

Fig. 2. Pseudo-code of algorithm

Upon receiving ACK packet a wakeup order of each node determine. In this way, all nodes perform a setup operation for a given time, t_{setup}. If a node listens to control packet from neighbor sensor but fail to send ACK packet during t_{setup}, and then the sensor executes the mission independently. When setup time was completed, the energy remained in the entire sensors are expressed by

$$E_i = E_i - \left(e_{i,tx} + t_{setup}\left(e_{i,tx} + e_{i,rx}\right)\right)$$

During setup time, t_{setup}, transmitter and receiver circuitry dissipate a power $e_{i,tx}$ and $e_{i,rx}$, respectively. After the setup phase, an active node on the steady phase can be participated in mission of sensing until its energy depletes. On contrary inactive nodes move to the l-duty state where *(l=1, 2, 3,..., m),* they set up wakeup timers and turn off their radios. When the wakeup timer of the sleeping node is expired, neighbor nodes first listen to the transmission signal from the active node. If a valid signal does not heard until a designated time, the wakeup node will be selected as active node by assuming that the current active node drains completely its energy.

Fig. 3 presents a timing chart to illustrate procedure for selecting active nodes. Generally, to forward data in r rate over distance d, the power consumption for node *i* *(i=1,2,..,n)* is

$$e_{i,tx} = r(\varepsilon_0 + \varepsilon_1 d^{\sigma}),$$

where ε_0 is the energy spent by the transceiver electronic circuitry and ε_1 is the energy consumed in the transmitter based on distance. Let the pass loss of exponent σ considers $2 \le \sigma \le 4$ for the free space and short-to-medium radio range.

In this section we provide the operational details of our scheme. Node A, B, and C dropped in the dense area. The actions taken by a node at various stages of its operation are as follows:

Step 1: The nodes initialize in the *BAÇKOFF* state. Concurrently, each node monitors the beacon messages for each backoff time.

Step 2: When node's backoff value is expired, broadcast its own information by using beacon packet to neighbor node. If a collision happens among some nodes, nodes will be re-setup backoff values, and repeat the operation during coordination phase.

Step 3: Receiving node can know the sensing area of node which sent a beacon by received power levels of a beacon reply to acknowledgement message. Neighbor node can know *ID* number of other node by this way. Otherwise, receiving operation is repeated.

Step 4: When initialized coordination phase expired, for the first time first node transmit beacon packet elect to be as an active node.

Step 5: The representative node moves into the *ACTIVE* state. This active node participated in data forwarding, transmitting, and receiving process of the networks until energy drains.

Step 6: Remaining candidate nodes moved to the *SLEEP* state. This nodes turns off radio, set up wakeup timer and go to *SLEEP* state. While designated long sleep time stay in the *SLEEP* state.

Step 7: When listen time coming up, designated nodes are waked up. The nodes start listening of transmitting signal of an active node. If non-valid signal of active node, it will assume that the RS node's energy was to be drained.

Step 8: The candidate node with second *ID* transmits declare message (*DM*) to the neighbor. This node re-elect to the RS.

We use a circular symmetry distribution [6]. Assume that n_{all} all nodes are deployed in the whole sensing field, $\Re$; The average number of neighbor nodes in general cases, $n_{out,}$ can be calculated as $n_{all}\pi R^2/\Re$, where R is transmission range. Using a n_{ou} the number of sensor on duplicated sensing area can be denoted as

$$n_{in} = n_{out}\pi r^2 / R \ ,$$

where r is sensing range. We must ensure that $r \le R$ to reduce overhead.

As shown in Fig. 1, the sensing hole is defined as a circular region with a power range of R, approximately. In this paper, our analysis considers one round that every node transmits its data one times. For proposed scheme, the number of sleep node can be shown as $n_{sleep} = n_{in} - 1$ since we always ensure that an active node is only one.

Firstly, to derive the average setup latency with collision, we need to calculate the probability P_{on} that the number of active users in the sensing area. The probability of an active state in the duty cycle shows as follows,

$$p_{on} = \sum_{n=1}^{a} \binom{u_a}{n} \left(\frac{j_0 + j_1 + j_2}{s} \right)^n \left(\frac{s - (j_0 + j_1 + j_2)}{s} \right)^{u_a - n}$$

$$\begin{aligned} for \quad & j_0 = idle; \\ & j_1 = receive; \\ & j_2 = transmit; \quad respetively. \end{aligned}$$

Assume that there are u_a active users within the transmitting area. The state, S is composed of the four states; idle, receive, transmit, and sleep. In addition, we similarly obtained the probability of a sleep state as follows,

$$p_{off} = u_a \left(\frac{j_0}{s} \right)^n (u_a - n) \left(\frac{s - j_0}{s} \right)^{u_a - n} \quad for \quad j_0 = idle$$

The energy consumed by an active node can be calculated as

$$e_{i,active} = e_{i,tx} \cdot \kappa_i \cdot p_{on} \ ,$$

respectively, where κ_i is the number of transmitted messages by i-th node within sensing area. Therefore, the lifetime of sensor node in terms of transmitting message can be shown as $t_i = E_i / e_{i,active}$. Based on an addressed equation, the expected lifetime of active nodes included in the specific sensing area can be obtained as

$$T = t_1 + t_2 + \cdots + t_{n-1} + t_n \, .$$

However, in the general case of the sensor networks, the total energy consumed by active nodes can be calculated as $e_{tot,active} = \sum_{i=0}^{n_{in}} e_{i,tx} \kappa_i \cdot (p_{on} + p_{off})$ since the numbers of active nodes are n_{in} and all nodes work on concurrently. Therefore, the expected lifetime, T can be obtained as $T = 1 / t_1 + t_2 + \cdots + t_{n-1} + t_n$, approximately.

4 Simulation Results

Simulation compared our scheme with [2] and we also carried out a simulation to evaluate the performance of our scheme in terms of energy consumption and transmitting delay. We simulate 20-100 sensor nodes using network topology of $80m \times 80m$ and a sink randomly deployed. Fig. 4(a) and 4(b) show the network topology in the entire sensor networks provided by without and with node scheduling, respectively.

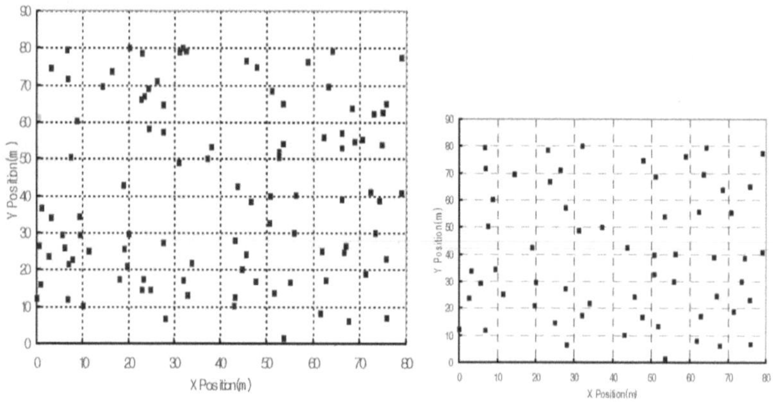

(a) (b)

Fig. 4. Networks topology without, (a) and without the node scheduling mechanism, (b)

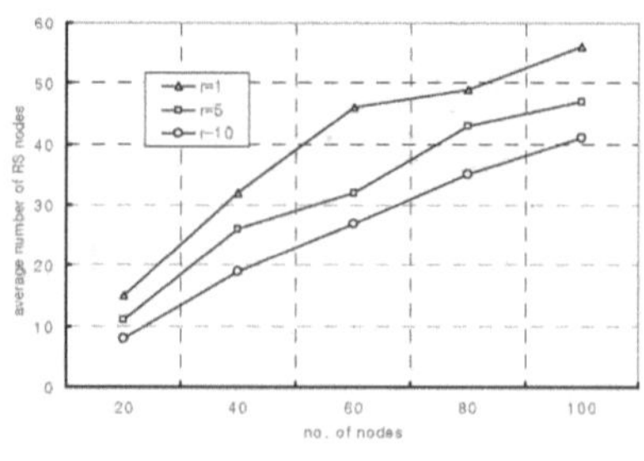

Fig. 5. The number of active nodes versus number of deployed node

In Fig. 5, we present simulation results of our scheduling approach over random topology. We can see that decreasing the number of the original deployed nodes, which is consistent with our expectation. Fig. 5 shows the number of an active node with candidate nodes.

The effects of changing sensing range, e.g. *1m, 5m, and 10m*, in terms of round times is examined. The data interarrival times follow the exponential distribution $(\mu = 0.1 - 0.5\text{sec})$ and data length is 64kbyte. The transmission delay measures the ratio of overall delay to the total number of data received by sink during one round. Here, we define one round as the time when the sink receives sensing data from a sensor node. We also fixed each node's initial energy to $1 \pm 0.2 Jule$. The energy for transmit and forward a packet is $1.5 \mu Jule$, and for receive and listen a packet is $1.3 \mu Jule$. In our simulations, we assume that sensing area is set as *1m, 5m, and 10m.*

Figure 6 illustrates an amount of the energy dissipation per round in our scheme depending on sensing area and GAF [3]. From this illustration, we can see that increasing the node life time of the network since one of the activated nodes inherits the mission of current active node for sensing when current active node wears out remaining energy. In results, the numbers of transmitted packets are decreased.

In Fig. 7 simulation results indicate that packet transmission delay versus the number of rounds.

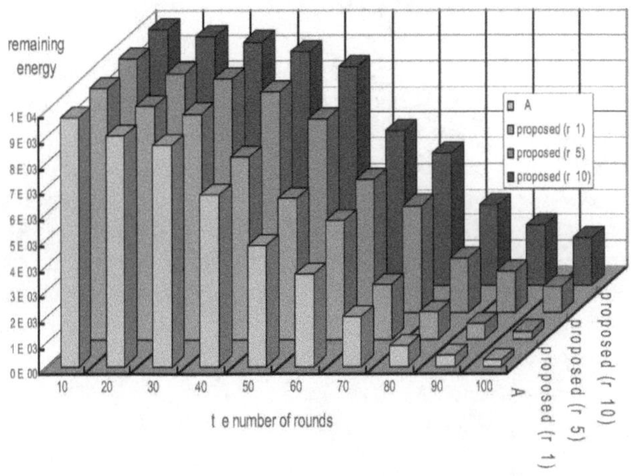

Fig. 6. Compared of the amount of consumed energy versus number of rounds

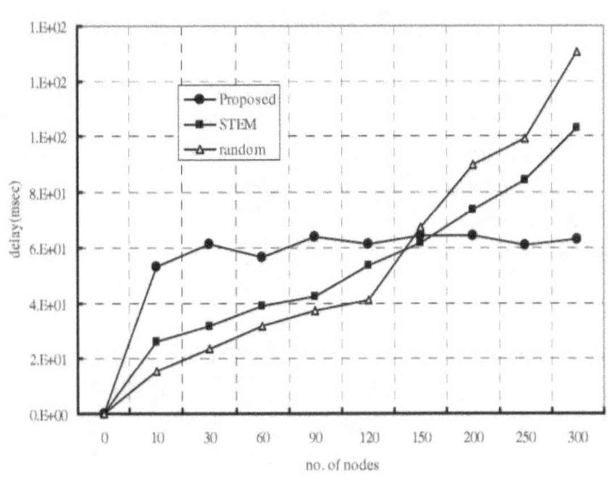

Fig. 7. Effect of delay depending on the number of rounds

Our scheme is always holding forwarding node since node's lifetime prolong within sensing area. Sensing area, *r* is problem to decide a density of sensor and drastically affect the network's communication delay. According to the sensing distance, the percentage of active nodes can observe that decrease around 71%(*1m*), 52%(*5m*), and 40%(*10m*).

In addition, when node density is less than 1 node per 80m, the numbers of active nodes reduce around 40%, therefore packet forwarding reduces 40%. These results indicate that by reducing the number of active node we can dramatically increase the network life time.

The distinguishing advantages of our scheme are a much longer network lifetime through energy conservation and an active sensor node among sensor nodes, and a small communication overhead required to establish a working duty schedule among nodes.

5 Conclusions and Future Work

A way of increasing the network lifetime in wireless sensor network is to activate some nodes while other sleep. When active nodes cover the sameness area, our schemes also can reduces delay and energy consumption, and then increases the lifetime of the network operation lifetime by finding active node. We investigated our results show that our scheme outperforms than existing topology control protocols in terms of minimum energy dissipation, system life time and transmission delay.

Of particular interest is the scenario when entire nodes in the network are deployed sparsely, in this case sensing holes will be scale. The study of delay performance, network lifetime of our scheme with scalability of sensing hole problem are included in our future works.

References

[1] C.Y. Chong and S.P. Kumar, "Sensor Networks: Evolution, Opportunities, and Challenges," *Proceeding of the IEEE*, vol. 91, no. 8, Aug. 2003, pp. 1247-1256.

[2] A. Cerpa and E. Estrin, "ASCENT: Adaptive Self-Configuring sEnsor Networks Topologies," *IEEE Transaction on Mobile Computing*, vol. 3, no. 3, July 2004, pp. 272-284.

[3] Y. Xu, J. Heidemann, and D. Estrin, "Geography-informed Energy Conservation for Ad Hoc Routing," in Proc. of Mobicom 2001, July 2001, pp. 70–84.

[4] D. Tian and N.D. Georganas, "A Node Scheduling Scheme for Energy *Conservation in large Wireless Sensor Networks," Wireless* Communication and Mobile Computing, vol. 3, 2003, pp. 271-289

[5] J. Zhu and S. Papavassiliou, "On the Energy-Efficient Organization and the Lifetime of Multi-Hop Sensor Network," *IEEE Communication Letter*, vol. 7, no. 11, Nov. 2004, pp. 535-539,.

[6] S. Arnon, "Deriving an Upper Bound on the Average Operation Time of a Wireless Sensor Network," *IEEE Communication Letter*, vol. 9, no. 2, Feb. 2005, pp. 535-539.

[7] C. Schurgers, V. Tsiatsis, S. ganeriwal and M. Srivastava, "Topology Management for Sensor Netwroks: Exploiting Latency and Density," in Proc. of International Symposium on Mobile Ad Hoc Networking & Computing (MobiHoc'02), vol. 1, no. 1, June 2002, pp. 135-145.

[8] J. Liu and B. Li, "Distributed Topology Control in Wireless Sensor Networks with Asymmetric Links," in Proc. of IEEE GLOBECOM'03, vol. 3, Dec. 2003, pp. 1257-1262.
[9] P. Goberl, A. Ziviani, P. Todoroval, M. D. Amorim, P. H unerberg , and S. Fdida, " Topology Control and Localization in Wireless Ad Hoc and Sensor Networks," *Ad Hoc & Sensor Wireless Networks,* vol. 1, 2005, pp. 301–321.
[10] R. Simon and E. Farrugia, "Topology Transparent Support for Sensor Networks," in Proc. of 1st European Workshop of Wireless Sensor Networks (EWSN), *LNCS 2920*, Jan. 2004, pp. 122-137.
[11] H. Chan and A. Perrig, "ACE: An Emergent Algorithm for Highly Uniform Cluster Formation," in Proc. of 1st European Workshop of Wireless Sensor Networks (EWSN), *LNCS 2920*, Jan. 2004, pp. 154-171.
[12] S. Arnon, "Deriving an Upper Bound on the Average Operation Time of a Wireless Sensor Network," *IEEE Communication Letter*, vol. 9, no. 2, Feb. 2005, pp. 535-539.
[13] C. Schurgers, V. Tsiatsis, S. Ganerival, and M. Srivastava, "Optimizing Sensor Networks in the Energy-Latency-Density Design Space," IEEE Transactions on mobile Computing, vol. 1, no. 1, January 2002, pp. 70-80.

Grid-Enabled Medical Image Processing Application System Based on OGSA-DAI Techniques*

Xiaoqin Huang, Linpeng Huang, and Minglu Li

Department of Computer Science & Engineering, Shanghai Jiao Tong University,
No.1954, HuaShan Road, Shanghai 200030, China
huangxq@sjtu.edu.cn

Abstract. Grid-enabled Medical Image Processing Application System (MIP-Grid) based on OGSA-DAI techniques aims at providing high performance medical image process services in a large distributed grid computing environment. The MIP-Grid is designed using web services technologies and standards and is based on the test-bed of ShanghaiGrid. It is composed of six modules including user management, image management, medical image management, task schedule, account and monitor. It provides support for authorization, account, schedule and monitor. The various image process algorithms are implemented as web services by Java and are deployed in the nodes of MIP-Grid. OGSA-DAI provides an extension to the OGSA framework by allowing access to and integration of data held in heterogeneous data resources. MIP-Grid is based on OGSA-DAI middleware. The advantage of the MIP-Grid is scalability, flexibility and reusability and is potential to become a mainstream grid application enabling technology.

1 Introduction

The growing popularity of the Internet technologies enable the clustering of a wide variety of geographically distributed resources. This new paradigm is popularly terms as "grid" computing [1] [2]. The computational grid is becoming a new paradigm high performance computing, primarily concerned with large-scale pooling of computational and data resources and aims to provide the infrastructure for integrating computational resources to form a singe virtual machine, or enable solving large-scale problems that cannot be solved on a single system [2]. Grid computing began as a technology for scientific usage but now is developing to be used as e-business.

As a quick response to this worldwide technical tide, several grand fundamental research projects had been launched by Chinese government to face the challenges and capture the opportunities. In parallel with these national grids, a city grid project going by the name of ShanghaiGrid, is supported science and technology commission of Shanghai municipality. The aim of ShanghaiGrid is solving "isolated island of information", shielding the resource heterogeneity, changing from web browsing to resource sharing, and resolving the problems of dispersed resources and establish the uniform standards [2][4].

---

* This paper is supported by ShanghaiGrid grand project of Science and Technology Commission of Shanghai Municipality (No.03DZ15027, 05DZ15005).

H.T. Shen et al. (Eds.): APWeb 2006, LNCS 3842, pp. 460–464, 2006.

Medical image process is very import to improving the health care for all the people in the world. These applications need high performance computing environment to compute and storage bulkiness data. Several grid systems have been proposed in the last few years. But few research groups have focused on offering an environment to combines the application of computational grid and medical image process. So in this paper, we propose an MIP-Grid. The rest of the paper is organized as follows. Section 2 introduces the overview of MIP-Grid. Section 3 is service oriented architecture of MIP-Grid. Section 4 describes OGSA-DAI techniques in MIP-Grid. Section 5 presents medical image processing application with the MIP-Grid. The last section is conclusion.

2 The Overview of MIP-Grid

MIP-Grid is one of the research projects of Shanghai Jiao Tong University Grid Computing Center that aims to create a grid test-bed for medical image computing. MIP-Grid work is based on the test-bed ShanghaiGrid [2] [3]. The grid architecture is designed based on the Grid Service standards and the Open Grid Services Infrastructure and WS-Resource Framework and supposed to meet various requirement from business, legal and social, security, performance, and application aspects. MIP-Grid contains 8 nodes that are connected by 100Mb/s Ethernet LAN and connects to CERNET by a gateway. The primary goal of the MIP-Grid system is to build a medical image processing application platform in grid environment. It provides doctors a completely distributed environment to process medical images to do their health care research and diagnose diseases for patients. Brain cancer surgery simulation is one of the medical service application included in the MIP-Grid test-bed, which provides a virtual try-out space for the pre-operative planning of brain cancer surgery.

The mechanism of the medical image process is described as follows: firstly, user sends his request with specific task information which may contain several subtasks and the description of specific invocation style, such as sequential, parallel and so on to task scheduler through the web portal of MIP-Grid, then task scheduler analyzes the task information and try to find the suitable services available. After careful selection, the lightest load node is chosen to execute the subtask, which involves invoke the web service deployed on it. In the meantime, account management module generates account information for this task. User could query the expense for the task he submitted and the money left in his account. Finally, when the task finished, the system will send an email to inform user of the state of his task. The data management system is based on OGSA-DAI middleware. Heterogeneous databases can be accessed by the same interface transparently.

3 Service Oriented Architecture of MIP-Grid

The MIP-Grid architecture, shown in Fig.1, uses a client/server topology employing a service–oriented architecture. It is composed of five layers: Application, Grid, OGSA-DAI middleware, Databases and hospital digital diagnoses systems. The application layer has realized functions of user management, Image management, account management, resource monitor and system introduction. The Grid layer is the Globus Toolkit and OGSA-DAI layer is OGSA Data Access and Integration middleware. The last layer is Hospital Digital Diagnose Systems that generate the primitive medical data. The MIP-Grid architecture is mainly a pluggable component framework, which aims to provide flexible support to various applications. MIP-Grid system is to be integrated with other heterogeneous systems flexibly in domains. A Service Oriented Architecture (SOA) consists of three primary components: the service provider provides the service, the service requester is the client that requires a service to be performed and the service agency provides registration and discovery services. SOA has dynamic discovery as an additional characteristic [5]: a service requestor uses UDDI [6] to discover registered service providers and does a dynamic binding to a found service provider. So SOA architecture is adapted to MIP-Grid.

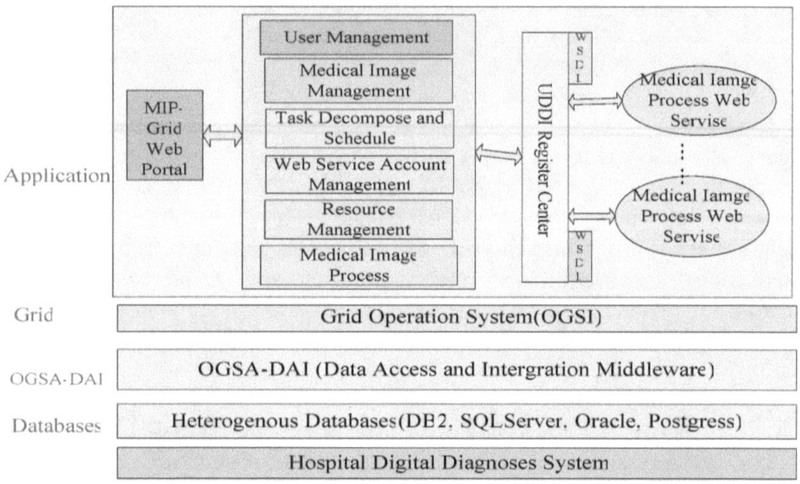

Fig. 1. Medical Image Processing Grid (MIP-Grid) Architecture

4 OGSA-DAI Techniques in MIP-Grid

In this paper we propose a five layer medical image processing grid system architecture MIP-Grid which integrated data access and integration middleware OGSA-DAI (the third layer) as in Fig.1 .OGSA-DAI is a middleware product defines services and interfaces, which extends those defined in the Open Grid Services Infrastructures specification, wrap individual physical data resources so they may be used by higher-level services to provide greater transparency, supports the exposure of data resources, such as relational (MySQL, SQL Server, DB2, Oracle) or XML databases (eg. Xindice) and Files (eg. files and directories) on to Grid. Specifically, the OGSA-DAI software extends the Globus Toolkits with a means of exposing database interfaces to the grid at server sites. An interface is exposed as a set of 'grid data services', which are a specialization of 'grid services'. Grid data services are exposed to the grid through their deployment in a grid services container (such as Globus

Toolkit) running inside a web server. Various interfaces are provided and many popular database management systems are supported see Fig.1. The software can also be extended to provide new functionality [5]. OGSA-DAI uses three main service types, the functions of them can see Fig. 2:

- DAI Grid Service Registry (registry) for discovery
- Grid Service Factory (GDSF) to represent a data resource
- Grid Data Services (GDS) to access a data resource

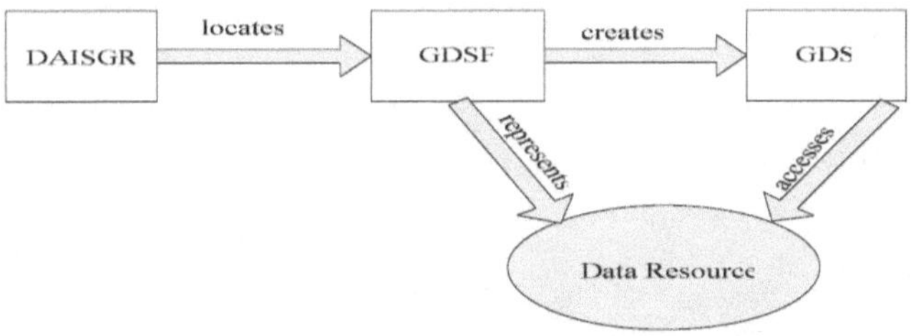

Fig. 2. OGSA-DAI uses three main service types

The MIP-Grid project integrated OGSA-DAI middleware to assist with access and integration of data from separate data sources via the grid. Through the OGSA-DAI middleware, MIP-Grid can organize the different computer resources under grid environment, hides the underground heterogeneous and dynamic, implements the grid interoperability characteristics, enables users to share access and process medial images through secure and transparent grid system. We have developed a client support OGSA-DAI Client Toolkit API to access the underlying heterogeneous data resources without knowing the location and type of the databases.

5 Medical Image Processing Application with the MIP-Grid

Images of various kinds are increasingly important to medical diagnostic processes and difficult problems are encountered in selecting the most appropriate imaging modalities, acquiring optimal quality images, and processing images to obtain the highest quality information. The primary goal of the MIP-Grid system is to build a

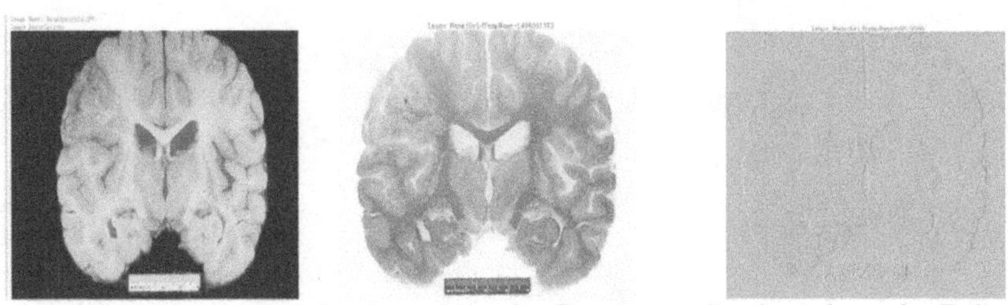

before process after the web service Reverse after the web service Relievo

Fig. 3. Medical image processing results by MIP-Grid

medical image processing application platform in Grid environment. Brain cancer surgery simulation is one of the medical service application included in the MIP-Grid test-bed, which provides a virtual try-out space for the pre-operative planning of brain cancer surgery. Nine various image process algorithms (including Gauss Smooth, Sharpen, Reverse, Box Smooth, Relievo, BorderPull, BorderVertical, Borderlaplace, and BorderHorizon) have been implemented by Java and packaged as web services are deployed in the nodes of MIP-Grid. Fig.3 presents some medical image processing results by MIP-Grid.

6 Conclusions

In this paper, we presented a medical image processing grid system MIP-grid. The goal of the system is to provide high performance medical image processing services in a large distributed Grid computing environment. According to our experiences on integrating OGSA-DAI middleware for building MIP-Grid applications describes in this work, advantages of using OGSA-DAI techniques are evidence. By using OGSA-DAI, heterogeneous disparate resources can be accessed uniformly. Owning to adopt Java and web services, it can run in any software environment that supports web service and provides JVM. The advantage of the MIP-Grid is scalability, flexibility and reusability. It is potential to become a mainstream grid application enabling technology. MIP-Grid successfully combines the application of medical image processing with grid computing technology.

References

1. Foster, I., Kesselman, C., 1999. The Grid: Blueprint for a New Computing Infrastructure. Morgan Kaufmann, Los Altos, CA.
2. Minglu Li, Hui Liu. et al. "Shanghai-Grid in Action: the First Stage Projects Towards Digital City and City Grid". The Second International Workshops on Grid and Cooperative Computing (GCC2003), pp440-447, 2003.
3. Ying Li, MingLu Li., et al. "A workflow services middleware model on ShanghaiGrid". 2004 IEEE International Conference on Services Computing, Shanghai, China 15-18 September 2004, pp. 366-371.
4. Ying Li, Ming Lu li. et al. 2004. "SH- MDS: a ShanghaiGrid Information Service Model". 2004 IEEE International Conference on Services Computing, Shanghai, China 15-18 September 2004, pp. 295-300.
5. http://www.ogsadai.org.uk/docs/docs.php#current
6. T.Andrews et al: Specification of the Business Process Execution Language for Web Services Version 1.1; at: http://ifr.sap.com/bpel4s/

A QOS Evaluating Model for Computational Grid Nodes*

Xing-she Zhou, Liang Liu, Qiu-rang Liu, Wang Tao, and Jian-hua Gu

School of Computer, Northwestern Polytechnic University,
Xi An, Shaanxi, 710072, China
liu_nwpu@263.net

Abstract. Computational Grid is a cooperative computing environment which collects all kinds of high performance software and hardware computing resources distributed in WAN and provides networked computing services. For the sake of improving the self-adaptability of resource management and accelerating the application and development of Computational Grid, an evaluating model of a computational grid node's QOS is put forward which is based on the whole running conditions and the execution results of computational grid jobs on the node. Applied in NPU Campus Computational Grid, this model achieves good effect.

1 Introduction

Computational Grid is a cooperative computing environment which collects all kinds of high performance software and hardware computing resources distributed in WAN and provides networked computing services. Sharing widely, collecting effectively and releasing fully the power of computing resources are the purpose that it pursues. However, compared with traditional Distributed Computing, its run-time environment and application model make it face more difficult technical challenges, among which the resource scheduling is the key one. It will help strengthening the self-adaptability of the resource scheduling if the QOS evaluating for computational grid nodes is introduced into the resource scheduling and considered as an important reference factor.

2 Benefits

Currently, the major projects of typical Computational Grid (such as Globus, Condor Legion and etc) little care the QOS evaluating for computational grid nodes. However, it can bring the following important benefit if as the important reference factor in the resource scheduling.

1) For resource consumers, it helps improving their trust in Computational Grid and better meeting their expectation. Because an evaluating result reflects a computational grid node's historical QOS and is considered as an important reference factor in scheduling, more submitted jobs are scheduled to the nodes which own higher evaluating results and the success rate of the submitted jobs are enhanced.

* This work was supported by HP, Platform and NPU HPC.

H.T. Shen et al. (Eds.): APWeb 2006, LNCS 3842, pp. 465–471, 2006.

2) For resource providers, it helps encouraging them to optimize and update the software/hardware configurations of owned computational grid nodes to provide better computational service because their profits are related to the nodes' QOS evaluating results.
3) For Computational Grid, it helps increasing the availability and reliability of the whole system. As an agency system, Computational Grid can eliminate the nodes which provide poor QOS, reduce the agency risk in the dynamic complicated unknown environment and enhance run-time benefit of the system by the evaluating mechanism.

3 Requirements

As an evaluating mechanism, the QOS evaluating for Computational Grid nodes should meet the following requirements:

- **Fairness**

Because the evaluating has the global important effect, it must base on facts and a single standard to evaluate the QOS of nodes in order that the evaluating results can be both accepted by resource consumers and resource providers.

- **Simpleness**

In order to reflect the actual QOS of nodes in reason, it can integrate multi evaluating factors/indexes and evaluate from multi layers/viewpoints. However, this will bring more challenges and cost to the evaluating decision-making and result in the increase of complex and subjectivity, which will bring side effect to the fairness of the evaluating mechanism. So the evaluating mechanism should have good operability besides easiness.

- **Security**

Because the evaluating results of nodes involve the benefit of resource consumers and resource providers, it should ensure the confidentiality, integrality and authenticity of itself and the evaluating results. From the view of security, the evaluating mechanism should be brought into the management and protection scope of Trusted Computing Environment of Computational Grid.

4 Model

According to the purpose and requirements of the QOS evaluating for Computational Grid nodes, an evaluating model of a computational grid node's QOS is proposed. The details of it are as follows.
Assuming:

$T_{JTotal:}$ the total time that a just finished job, J stays on a computational grid node, C;

$T_{JG\text{-}PEND:}$ the total time that J waits for being scheduled by LRMS (Local Resource Management System) on C;

$T_{JG\text{-}RUN:}$ the total time that J uses the CPU of C;

$T_{mG\text{-}PEND}$: the averaged time that m recently successfully finished jobs waits for being scheduled by LRMS on C。Notice: each of them has the same job type with J and each magnitude is very near to J.

$T_{JG\text{-}RSUSP}$: the total time that J is suspended since it first uses the CPU of C;

E_{JEnd}: the finished status of J (G-DONE or G-EXIT);

C_{JEnd}: the finished cause of J (Success, Global-Migration, Self-Failure, or Other-Failure);

$T_{JTotal} = T_{JG\text{-}RUN} + T_{JG\text{-}RUN} + T_{JG\text{-}RSUSP}$;

Let:

Y_J is the QOS evaluating variable of C.

$X_J =$

$$\frac{T_{JG-PEND}+T_{JG-RSUSP}}{T_{JTotal}}\times 100 \; (T_{JG-PEND}<T_{mG-PEND} \,||\, \text{J has the license restriction})$$

$$\frac{T_{mG-PEND}+T_{JG-RSUSP}}{T_{JTotal}}\times 100 \; (T_{JG-PEND}>T_{mG-PEND} \,\&\&\, \text{J has not the license restriction})$$

(Notice: because the resources which have license restrictions commonly are scarce and Jobs needing such resources have to queue up, the value of X_J is set a smaller one to encourage resource owners to provide more such resources. Obviously, X_J reflects the J's execution efficiency and QOS provided by C. The larger of the value of X_J is, the more J is suspended by LRMS on C.)

Then the function mapping relation between X_J and Y_J is defined as follows:

$Y_J = F(X_J) =$

$$\begin{cases} \dfrac{X_J(2X_J-\alpha)}{\alpha^2}C - \dfrac{4X_J(X_J-\alpha)}{\alpha^2}B + \dfrac{(2X_J-\alpha)(X_J-\alpha)}{\alpha^2}A & (1) \\ C & (2) \\ \dfrac{(X_J-\beta)(X_J-\delta)}{(\varphi-\beta)(\varphi-\delta)}D + \dfrac{(X_J-\delta)(X_J-\varphi)}{(\beta-\varphi)(\beta-\delta)}C & (3) \\ E & (4) \\ F & (5) \\ G & (6) \\ H & (7) \end{cases} \qquad \text{(F1)}$$

Restriction conditions in F1 are defined as follows:

(1): $0 <= X_J <= 100\alpha$ && E_{JEnd} = G-DONE

(2): $100\alpha < X_J <= 100\beta$ && E_{JEnd} = G-DONE

(3): $100\beta < X_J <= 100\varphi$ && E_{JEnd} = G-DONE

(4): $100\varphi < X_J$ && E_{JEnd} = G-DONE

(5): E_{JEnd} = G-EXIT && C_{JEnd} = Global-Migration

(6): E_{JEnd} = G-EXIT && C_{JEnd} = Self-Failure
(7): E_{JEnd} = G-EXIT && C_{JEnd} = Other-Failure

Constant declaration in F1 is defined as follows:

1) $\alpha \in (0, 1)$ & $\beta \in (0, 1)$ & $\delta \in (0, 1)$ & $\varphi \in (0, 1)$ & $\alpha < \beta < \delta < \varphi$: because their values are the decisive factor of fairness, the responding values can commonly be set by Delphi technique to assure their rationality.
2) $A>B>C>0$ & $D<0$ & $A= F_1(0)$ & $B=F_1(50\alpha)$ & $C=F_1(100\alpha)=F_1(100\beta)$ & $0=F_1(100\delta)$ & $D=F_1(100\varphi)$: F_1 uses their appropriate values to construct parabolas with different curvatures and directions.
3) $E<0$: when X_J is larger than 100φ, it is necessary to punish the QOS evaluating value of C because J's execution efficiency is too bad, but $|E|$ should be rational.
4) $F<0$: it is necessary to punish the QOS evaluating value of C because it brings side effect to J that J is migrated from C to other node. However the global migration of jobs is not frequent, so $|F|$ should be rational.
5) $G>0$: it is necessary to compensate the QOS evaluating value of C because it may bring side effect to C that J's exceptions make it exit execution, but $|G|$ should be rational.
6) $H<0$: it is necessary to punish the QOS evaluating value of C because its exceptions make J exit execution, but $| H |$ should be rational. Actually, the values of *H*, *G*, *E*, *F* can be set by Delphi technique to assure their rationality.

According to F_1, the variable scope of the QOS evaluating value caused by J who finishes successfully can be demonstrated as follows:

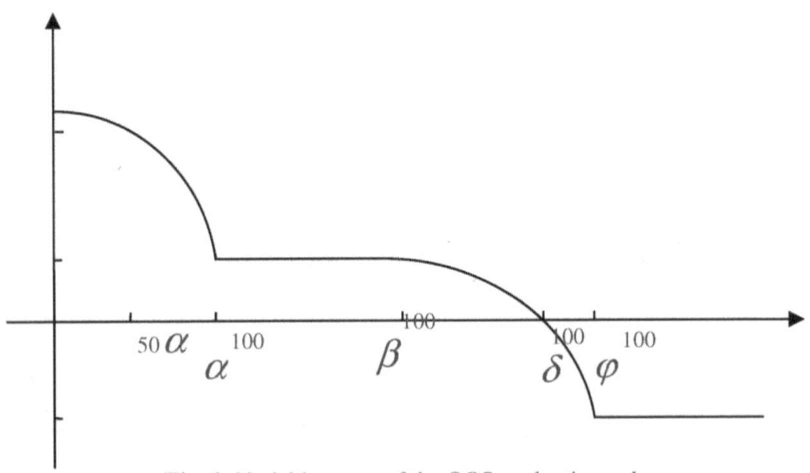

Fig. 1. Variable scope of the QOS evaluating value

Though it is easy to calculate the variance of the QOS evaluating value of C according to J's running condition and execution result, it is not reasonable to update the value just on the ground of just a finished job, J, and such update will violate statistical laws and do harm to the fairness of the QOS evaluation. Based on the formula, F1,

the formula, F2 and the formula, F3 are put forward to assure the fairness. F2 is used to calculate the variance of the QOS evaluating value of C in a QOS evaluation. F3 is used to calculate the newest QOS evaluating value of C.
The definitions of the two formulas are as follows:

Let:
V_{nQOS} is the variance of the QOS evaluating value of C in a QOS evaluation.
Y_i is the variance of the QOS evaluating value of C according to $F(X_i)$. (i=1, 2, …, n)
Then the function mapping relation between Y_i and V_{nQOS} is as follows:

$$\begin{cases} V_{nQOS} = F(Y_1, Y_2, \ldots, Y_n) = \sum_{i=1}^{n} \omega_i Y_i \\ \sum_{i=1}^{n} \omega_i = 1 \\ 0 <= \omega_i <= 1 \end{cases} \quad \text{(F2)}$$

Again let:
V_{QOS} is the QOS evaluating value of C.
Then the function mapping relation between V_{nQOS} and V_{QOS} is as follows:

$$V_{QOS} = V_{QOS} + V_{nQOS} \quad \text{(F3)}$$

Ultimately, F1, F2 and F3 make up of the whole QOS evaluating model. In F2, every value in the weight vector $\omega(\omega_1, \omega_2, \ldots, \omega_n)$ can be self-adaptively adjusted on the ground of the whole analyse of Y_i(i=1, 2, …, n) to better meet the evaluating aim. For example, if the major values of Y_i belong to (A, C], the responding values of ω_i can be set bigger. In general, more encouragement and less punishment is the aim that the evaluating model pursues.

5 Effect

Basing on the QOS evaluating model above, we realize a QOS evaluation service and deploy it in NPU Campus Computational Grid as an important basic service. The QOS evaluating value of each node provided by it is used as an important decision factor in BMQOS, which is a general self-adaptive resource scheduling algorithm. And eight typical computational grid nodes are specially chosen to prove its effect. The eight nodes are HP Cluster, Lenovo Cluster, SGI Numa Server(16 CPUs), IBM Workstation Cluster(10 workstations), SUN Workstation Cluster(6 workstations) and 3 High PC Clusters(20 PCs, 16 PCs and 30 PCs respectively). For convenience, they are named CN1, CN2, CN3, CN4, CN5, CN6, CN7 and CN8 respectively. LRMSs of CN1, CN3, CN4 and CN8 are LSF, CN2's LRMS is PBS improved by Lenovo and LRMSs of the others are OpenPBS. What's more, the working, management and maintenance of CN1, CN2, CN3, CN4 and CN8 are much better than those of the others. The QOS evaluating values of the eight nodes are recorded every three days.

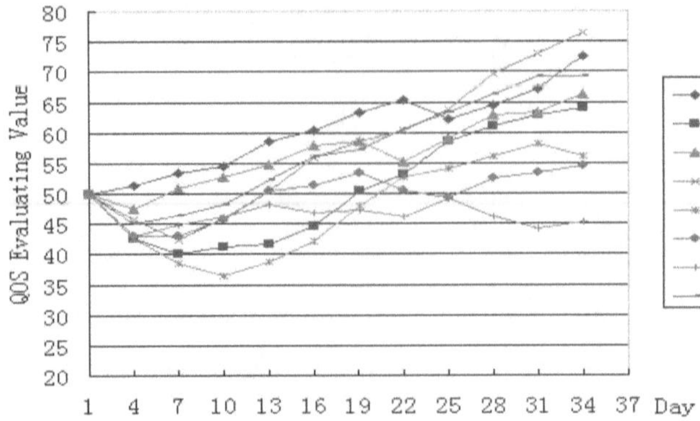

Fig. 2. QOS evaluating values

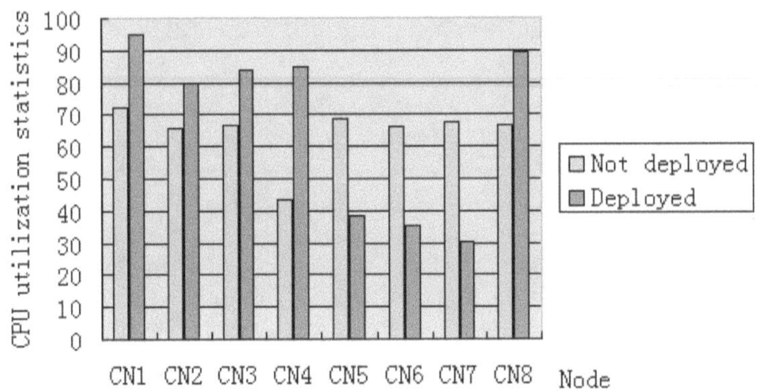

Fig. 3. CPU utilization statistics compare

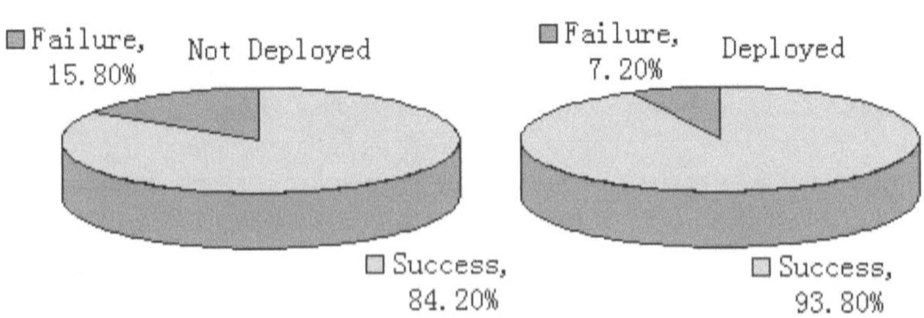

Fig. 4. Job execution result statistics compare

About a month later that the service is deployed, the CPU utilization statistics and the success rate statistics of jobs are calculated. Compared with the responding statistics a month ago that the service is not deployed, the introduction and application of the QOS evaluation service show a very exciting effect.

6 Summary

The QOS evaluating model for computational grid nodes put forward can help greatly improving the self-adaptability of resource management and accelerating the application and development of Computational Grid. Now this model has been applied in NPU Campus Computational Grid. And the good effect brought by it has effectively proved its function.

References

1. Foster, I. and C. Kesselman, eds. The Grid: Blueprint for a New Computing Infrastructure. Morgan Kaufmann, 1999.
2. Liu Liang, Zhou Xing-she, and Gu Jian-hua: A Multi-Agent System for Grid Computing. The Second International Conference on Active Media Technology, 2003
3. Yao Wang, Julita Vassileva: Trust and Reputation Model in Peer-to-Peer Networks. Third International Conference on Peer-to-Peer Computing, IEEE, 2003
4. http://www.xahuading.com/bbs/article.asp?ntypeid=33&titleid=1347&page=2
5. Christophe Diot and Aruna Seneviratne: Quality of Service in Heterogeneous Distributed Systems. Proceedings of The Thirtieth Annual Hawwaii International Conference on System Sciences, IEEE, 1997
6. Farag Azzedin and Muthucumaru Maheswaran: Towards Trust-Aware Resource Management in Grid Computing Systems. Proceedings of the 2nd IEEE/ACM International Symposium on Cluster Computing and the Grid, 2002
7. Farag Azzedin and Muthucumaru Maheswaran: Integrating Trust into Grid Resource Management Systems. Proceedings of the International Conference on Parallel Processing, 2002

An Enterprize Workflow Grid/P2P Architecture for Massively Parallel and Very Large Scale Workflow Systems*

Kwanghoon Kim

Collaboration Technology Research Lab.,
Department of Computer Science,
Kyonggi University
kwang@kyonggi.ac.kr
http://ctrl.kyonggi.ac.kr

Abstract. This paper proposes a layered workflow architecture that is used for not only distributing workflows' information onto Grid or P2P resources but also scheduling the enactment of workflows. The layered architecture proposed in this paper, which we call *Enterprize Workflow Grid Architecture*, is targeting on maximizing the usability of computing facilities in the enterprize as well as the scalability of its underlined workflow management system in coping with massively parallel and very large scale workflow applications.

Keywords: Enterprize Workflow Grid/P2P Architecture, Workflow Models, Massively Parallel and Very large-Scale Workflow.

1 Introduction

In recent, out of the new types of architectural requirements[2], the scalability requirement is the most important and impeccable issue in the workflow and business process management (BPM) technology literature. The scalability issue [1] is for supporting very large scale workflow automation and process-driven collaborative works in a very large-scale enterprize, because almost all conventional workflow and BPM systems are based upon client-server or clustered computing environments, and these environments might be inappropriate for providing the affordable efficiency to a huge amount of process-driven collaborative works and massively parallel and very large-scale workflows as well. So, it is necessary to explore some very feasible and new computing infrastructure satisfying those requirements of the very large scale process-driven collaborative works and systems. Fortunately, Grid and Peer-to-Peer (P2P) computing environments [3] are extensively available in recent, and we need to explore some reasonable approaches for applying Grid/P2P as an infrastructure for very-large scale process-driven collaborative works and systems.

* The research was supported by the research fund of KOSEF (Korea Science and Engineering Foundation), No. R05-2002-000-01431-0.

H.T. Shen et al. (Eds.): APWeb 2006, LNCS 3842, pp. 472–476, 2006.

This paper proposes a special-purpose layered architecture that is called *Enterprize Workflow Grid/P2P Architecture*. The layered architecture means a logical hierarchy of grid's node configuration, and it consists of three layers - Workflow layer, Role layer and Actor layer. The workflow layer maintains ICN-based workflow models that are built by a workflow modeling tool, and the role layer and the actor layer manage role-based workflow models and actor-based workflow models, respectively, that are automatically generated from the ICN-based workflow models trough the corresponding construction algorithms[4]. A serial of methods for configuring, gathering and downloading workflow information based upon the layered architecture is theoretically elucidated by a formal approach in this paper.

2 The Problem Scope and Backgrounds

What we see happening now in the workflow literature is that workflows' complexity is in the stage of a rapid scaling up and that workflows' applicability is just at the point of transition from the end of the pilot test stage to the beginning of the cold reality stage, which is gaining practical benefits. Therefore, we are in the front of *the world of Massively Parallel and Very Large Scale Workflows and Business Processes*[2]. As a consequence of this atmosphere, we need to be concerned about the massively parallel and very large scale workflow and business process management systems. At the same time, it is necessary to make some criteria, which is called the degree of workflow complexity, for effectively characterizing them. So, massively parallel and very large scale workflows and business processes of the main concern of this paper, can be clarified based on the degree of workflow complexity [1] consisting of three perspectives and dimensions— *Workflow Engagement*, *Workflow Structure* and *Workflow Instantiation*. The scope of this paper is to accomplish the highest degree of workflow complexity by supporting the highest levels of services in all three dimensions. Especially, in order to be satisfied with the highest levels of services in all dimensions, it is necessary for the system to be completely renovated by a new fundamental and philosophical spirit as you can easily imagine. So, in this paper, we are focusing on accomplishing the highest level of the workflow complexity by renovating only the software architectural aspect as well as the hardware architectural aspect of a system. In the next sections, we describe the enterprize workflow Grid architecture and give the theoretical details of the architecture.

3 Enterprize Workflow Grid Architecture

By considering the backgrounds and the scope described in the previous section, we design, at first, a workflow architectural framework that can be a generic workflow enactment architecture for handling massively parallel and very large scale workflow models on Grid computing environment. In this section, we describe a reasonable workflow Grid architecture that is named *Enterprize Workflow Grid Architecture* that derived from the framework[4].

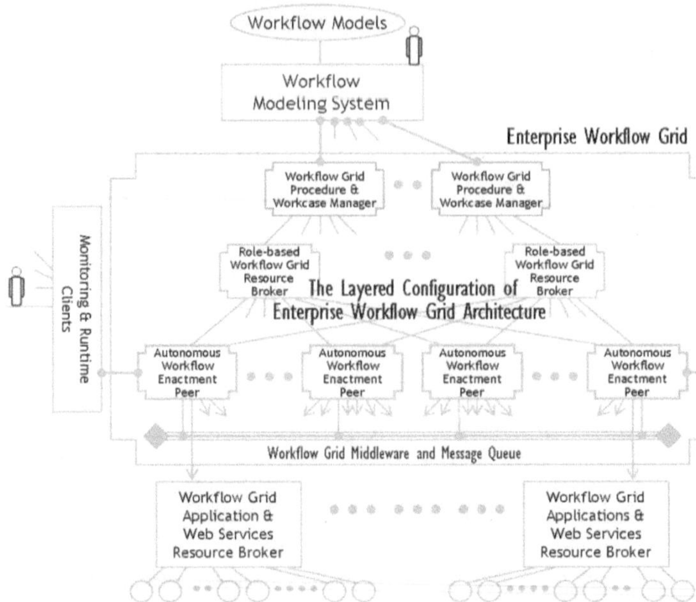

Fig. 1. The Layered Enterprize Workflow Grid Architecture

3.1 The Enterprize Workflow Grid Architecture

In order to accomplish the primary requirement, *Scalability* for massively parallel and very large scale workflows, this paper proposes a conceptual architecture as shown in Fig. 1, which is called Enterprize Workflow Grid Architecture, and describes its functional components. At the same time, the main property of the Enterprize Workflow Grid Architecture is described through a set of workflow models that is the primary theoretical background for distributing workflow information to each of Grid nodes over enterprize-wide network. As shown in Fig. 1, the enterprize workflow Grid enactment service part is configured by the layered approach that provides hierarchical relationships between workflow enactment components, each of which is installed on a workflow Grid node.

The layered architecture reflects the organizational structure in order to efficiently use the physical Grid network structure of the enterprize. So, the workflow enactment modules (workflow Grid procedure and workcase manager) in the top layer handle a set of workflows modeled by the ICN-based workflow modeling methodology, the modules (role-based workflow Grid resource broker) in the middle layer maintain a set of role-based workflow information modeled by the role-based workflow models that are automatically transformed from the ICN-based workflow models through an algorithm designed in this paper, and finally the modules (autonomous workflow Grid enactment peer) in the bottom layer take in charge of activity enactment functionality based on the actor-based workflow information modeled by the actor-based workflow models that are automatically transformed from the ICN-based workflow models through an algorithm designed in this paper, too. Due to the page limitation, the details of the functionality and the transformed workflow models are not described in the paper.

The enterprize workflow Grid enactment service part is surrounded by four different managers: workflow procedure modeling manager, workflow administration and monitoring manager, workflow client manager and workflow Grid application and web service request broker. They support the logical connections (interface-1, interface-2, interface-3 and interface-4) with the enterprize workflow Grid enactment service part.

3.2 A Possible Deployment of the Enterprize Workflow Grid Architecture

Based upon the transformed workflow models, it is able to distribute the corresponding workflow information to the layered nodes of the enterprize workflow Grid architecture, as shown in Fig. 2. The enterprize workflow Grid architecture is based upon a huge enterprise-wide Grid network interconnecting a large number of computing facilities, and each of which installs a Workflow enactment module, through high speed collaboration channels that are called Coupling/Decoupling mechanism.

In Fig. 2, it is assumed that a single workflow modeling manager has connections to a set of workflow enactment modules, and it is, therefore, possible to reside a lot of logical enactment architectures in the enterprize workflow Grid

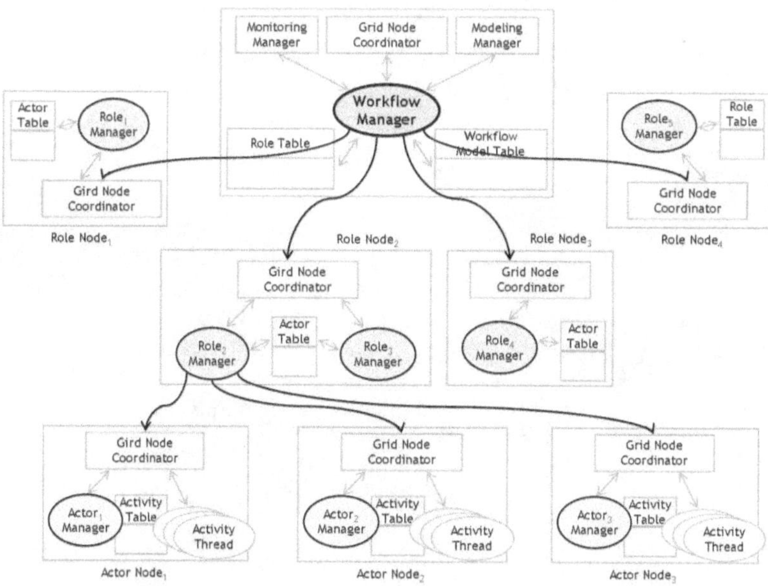

Fig. 2. The Resource Distribution on the Enterprize Workflow Grid

enactment service boundary. The configuration of a logical architecture can be done by layering fashion. This hierarchical configurations among three types of workflow enactment modules are very important for accomplishing scalable workflow architectures. Through this, we can have more flexible and powerful scheduling mechanisms among Grid peers: activity-to-actors mapping, activity-to-roles mapping and activity-to-computing facilities mapping.

4 Conclusion

So far, we have proposed the layered Enterprize Workflow Grid Architecture that is possibly applicable for massively parallel and very large scale workflow systems, and described its functionality and theoretical foundations for constructing the enterprize workflow grid architecture and its resource configuration that is logically connecting a set of workstations and/or PCs used for enacting the massively parallel and very large scale workflow procedures. The three components of the enterprize workflow Grid architecture—the workcase manager, role-based resource broker and the workflow Grid peer—associated with the layered configuration are able to receive and store their related information, such as activity control precedence information, relevant data, invoked applications, role, and so on that are needed for enacting the corresponding workflow procedures. Finally, the research was started from the belief that the nature of Grid computing environment is fitted very well into building a platform for the maximally parallel and very large scale workflow systems. We would say that the belief was not misunderstood through this paper.

Notes and Comments. The research was supported by the research fund of KOSEF (Korea Science and Engineering Foundation), No. R05-2002-000-01431-0.

References

1. Ahn, H., Kim, K.: An EJB-based Very Large Scale Workflow Management System and Its Performance Measurement. To Be Published on Proceedings of the International Conference on Web-Aged Information Management, Hangjou, China (2005)
2. Alonso, G., Schek, H.: Research Issues in Large Workflow Management Systems. Proceedings of NSF Workshop on Workflow and Process Automation in Information Systems: State-of-the-Art and Future Directions (1996)
3. Baker, M., et al.: Grids and Grid Technologies for Wide-area Distributed Computing. SOFTWARE- Practice and Experience (2002)
4. Kim, K., Kim, H.: A Peer-to-Peer Workflow Model for Disributing Large Scale Workflow Data onto Grid/P2P. Journal of Digital Information Management, Vol.3, No. 2 (2005)

Grid-Enabled Metropolis Shared Research Platform*

Yue Chen[1,2], YaQin Wang[1], and Yangyong Zhu[1]

[1] Department of Computing and Information Technology,
Fudan University, Shanghai, China
{yyzhu, 041021067}@fudan.edu.cn
[2] Computer Science and Technology School,
Soochow University, Suzhou 215006, China

Abstract. Scientific and industry research heavily depend on the scientific data and archives. There are lots of different, non-interoperable resources in Metropolis. By using Grid, putting the scientific resources together to form a shared metropolis research platform can facilitate the research processes, which could lead to enhance metropolis technique force and innovation ability, i.e, the integration of various biological databases and the data mining service can greatly help the biologist to search, analyze biological sequences. The architecture of the SRP and its main services are introduced in this paper. The way how to integration of scientific data and archives are discussed in detail.

1 Background

Advances in information technique are changing the way scientists and enterprise doing research. There is an exponential growth of online materials such as archives, electric books, video, audio, and pictures. The structures of such materials are different: some are organized in digital libraries, some are in databases, and some are plaintext. Historically, there exist different systems to manage these materials and can not share information with each other. Today, technology innovation hugely depends on the scientific data and documents, the online materials become an important resource for researchers to do research. For example, when a biologist wants to figure out the genetic factors of one disease, he would first use micro-array methods to find out which gene is abnormal, searching it using BLAST [1] in genome sequence database, returning a BLAST report contain references to records for homologous proteins in the SWISSPROT [2] protein database, then he would turn to SWISSPROT to search that proteins and get the ids of the abstracts describing these proteins in Medline abstract database, using the ids he would search the abstract and full text in Medline database. All these steps hugely depend on different on-line biologic databases or scientific archives. Same thing would happen in making a new production in enterprise.

Today's scientific databases, digital libraries are usually domain-depended, a library usually focus on organize specialist knowledge or information. But the tendency of research is cross-domain; researchers usually turn to different databases, libraries to search resources.

* This paper is supported by national natural science foundation of china (No.60573093).

H.T. Shen et al. (Eds.): APWeb 2006, LNCS 3842, pp. 477–485, 2006.

On other hand, in Metropolis, there may exist hundreds of Universities, Science Research Institute, Digital Libraries which have a lot of on-line resources. For example, there exist 25 national key labs, 30 metropolis key labs, 128 enterprise research centers in Shanghai (one of the biggest city in China), the number of databases is more than 100, and the scientific data are about 10TB and the annual production of scientific data are about 100 GB. How to make full use of those resources for the city to enhance its technique force and innovation ability is a big challenge.

One of the efficient ways to meet this challenge is to put the scientific resources together to form a metropolis shared research platform (SRP), these resources including archives, scientific database, scientific data, digital libraries, patent literature, scientific instruments and so on. The first step of SRP is to integrate scientific data and archives to form a shared research platform to facilitate researchers to search, utility these data. The basic function of SRP is to provide a unified interface to facilitate the discovery of content stored in distributed resources. Meanwhile the SRP also provides value-added services to researchers, such as workflow service, group discuss, online meeting, annotation, document visualization and so on.

There are many approaches to construct SRP such as metadata exchange (typically OAI-PHM [3]) which is used in Digital Library, Federation database system and centralized database. But these approaches can not meet the needs of SRP. First, data and archives have different form, which could be plaintext, xml documents, multimedia, structured data and so on. Second, these data are stored in different systems with different platforms; the biggest obstacle for building SRP is that many systems use different, non-interoperable technologies. Third, we do not want to simply integrate such data, but to provide some value-add services such as data mining, scientific workflow to fully use these data, which could need high computational and storage capabilities. In addition, the policy, resource management, security should be taken into account.

Grid technology has already played very important roles in e-science and lots of projects demonstrate the power of the Grid. So using a Grid as basic infrastructure of SRP is a better choice to meet the tendency of the developing of the e-science.

2 Related Work

Grid as Cyberinfrastructure [4] for e-Science has been accepted by lots of scientists. The UK e-Science Program [4] is one of the most successful Grid projects developed to promote scientific and data-oriented Grid application development for science and industry. The goal of the e-Science project is to develop a Grid e-Utility infrastructure for e-Science applications. It includes a wide variety of projects including genomics, bioscience, particle physics, health and astronomy, environmental science, engineering design, chemistry and material science and social sciences. It focuses on how to manage very large data collections, very large scale computing resources and high performance visualization.

NEESgrid [5] is linking earthquake researchers across the U.S. with leading-edge computing resources and research equipment, allowing collaborative teams to plan, perform, and publish their experiments.

The goal of the Texas Internet Grid for Research and Education (TIGRE) project [6] is to build a computational grid that integrates computing systems, storage systems and databases, visualization laboratories, instruments and sensors across Texas. TIGRE will enhance the computational capabilities for Texas researchers in academia, government and industry massive computing power and by integrating this into a Grid.

There are a lot of other Grid projects helping scientist to do collaborate research by providing distributed computing resources and manage huge experiment data. Little work has been done to organize distributed scientific archives. Data Grid usually maintains one domain-special data, while in SRP, there needs a mechanism to integrate scientific data from different knowledge domains. One of its challenges is how to manage metadata.

3 Architecture of SRP

As we discussed above, the main characteristics of SRP should include:

- Providing a unified way to access distributed information resources such as archives, databases, pictures transparently.
- Providing typical functions, like search, annotation, personalization, visualization, etc al.
- Providing value-add services, like workflow, data mining service
- Allowing information providers dynamically joining or leaving SRP
- Security and policy assurance among different information providers
- Scalability and quality control.

3.1 Architecture

The topology of the Grid-based SRP is shown in Fig.1. The SRP is formed by many autonomy domains, each of them can provide certain information such as biologic database, medicine database, archives. Each domain is controlled by the Global Management Services (GMS) which includes task management service, search management service, resource monitor service, data replica service, etc al. To simplify the security model and QoS, currently we use the global CA and global information service. All users access the SRP through a global portal. The logic view of SRP is shown in Fig.2. The main services are described as following:

- **Certification service**

The security of SRP is based on GSI [7]. There are two types of certification. Every user has a X.509 certification which has associated certain roles indicating user's right. The other is system certification which is used to building trust relationship among domains.

- **Information service**

Information service provides a way to query the real time information about the Grid including storage resources, instrument resources, CPU-static information, CPU-workload information, memory-static information, memory workload,

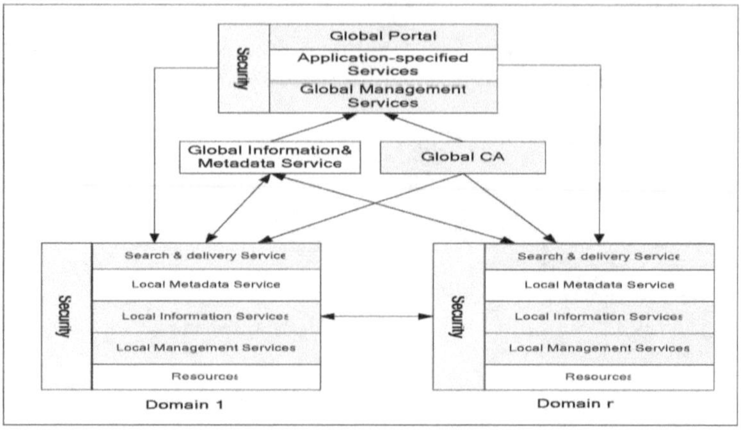

Fig. 1. The topology of SRP

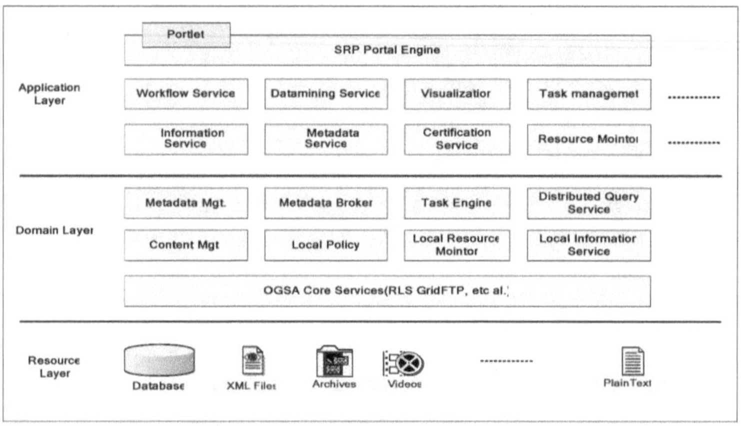

Fig. 2. The logic view of SRP

network information, etc al. Resources must register to information service to be used by Grid. It is organized in tree structure. The global information service is a parent node, every Grid node is a leave node. Some functions such as workload balancing, self-tuning resource usage are heavily depended on information service.

- **Workflow service**

Workflow is defined as "The automation of a business process, in whole or in part, during which information or tasks are passed from one participant to another for action, according to a set of procedural rules"[8]. In SRP, using workflow can bound several steps into one process that facilitate the research processes. The workflow can be stored and re-execute. For some areas, especially in biology, it could reduce the repeated works largely. We use Java CoG Kit [9] to construct workflow.

- **Data mining services**

The amount of scientific data and documents are huge. Some data need to be converted into information and knowledge to become useful for researchers. Data mining is a process to find regulations from very large collections of data—sometimes hundreds of millions of individual records to informs, instructs, answers, or otherwise aids understanding and decision-making. The data mining function includes: association rules, clustering, decision trees, etc al.

- **Task management**

In SRP, task is a key conception, SRP regards users option as a serials of tasks. The task management service is in charge of assigning job to certain domain. It is like the job schedule in the computational Grid.

Integrating distributed databases and archives is an important aspect of the SRP, which will be discussed in detail.

3.2 Scientific Data Integration

The scientific data integration system contains five main components:

(1) Data service broker (DVB)

Every Grid nodes has a DVB which in charges of exchanging data between Grid nodes and other services. Its main functionalities include: providing an interface for query the scientific data; providing an interface for query the local data dictionary; getting the URL of the WSDL [10] document for particular query from the information service; checking the policy and rights.

(2) Data dictionary

Different systems always have their own data dictionary to describe the data structure of its data. In order to sharing data among different systems, there must be a mechanism to associate the names of entities in the universe of terms. Data

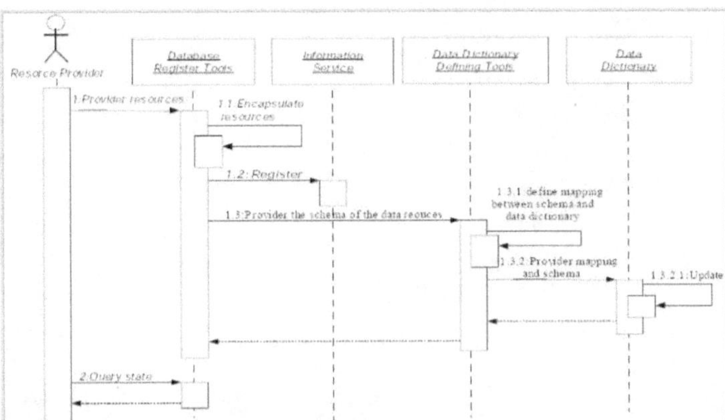

Fig. 3. Steps of register data resources

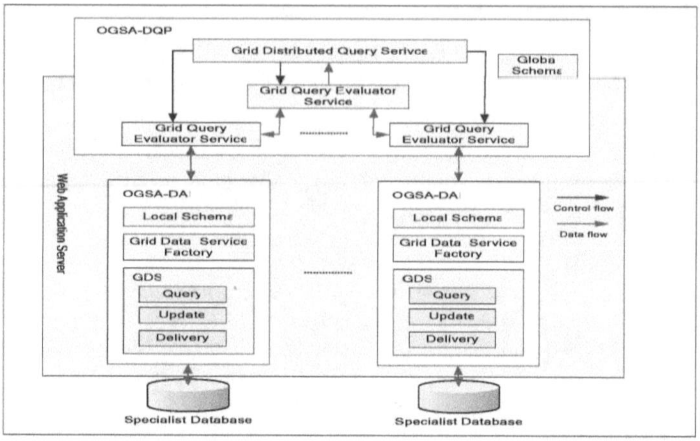

Fig. 4. GDS and DQP

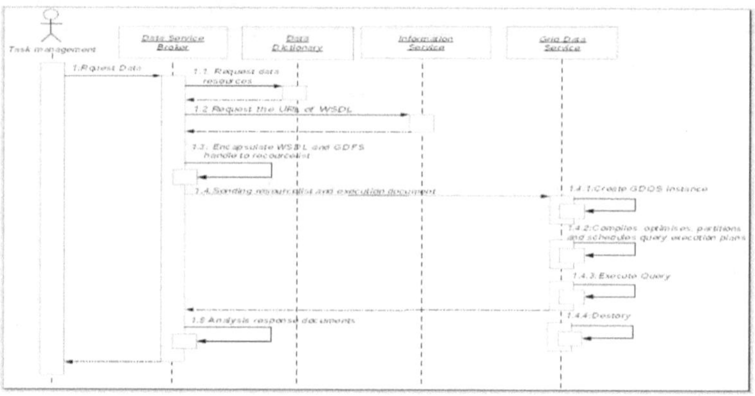

Fig. 5. The general steps of how to get data from distributed data resources

dictionary can map the relation between data resource with certain terms. In some areas, there already exist ontology (such as Gene Ontology [11], GO), it will be selected as data dictionary.

(3) Data dictionary defining tools

Data dictionary is defined by specialists of certain areas, using these tools to maintain the correctness of data dictionary.

(4) Database register tools

Using these tools to add and remove a data source from a Grid node. A database accessed through the grid infrastructure must provide Grid Data Service(GDS) [12], which is created by Grid Data Service Factory (GDSF) [12]. Register tools will encapsulate data resource to GDSF, and send the database scheme to the data dictionary defining tools to define the data dictionary. The steps are shown in Fig.3.

(5) Grid Data Service (GDS)

GDS is a Grid service that allows access to a data resource, which is a core component of Open Grid Service Architecture - Data Access and Integration (OGSA-DAI) [13]. All data resources are wrapped by Database register tools and exported as GDS. Based on GDS, we can use OGSA-DQP (distributed query process)[14] to compile and evaluate queries that combining data obtained from various GDS, as shown in Fig.4. The detail information of DQP would be found in [15].

Fig.5 shows the steps of how to get a scientific data in SRP.

3.3 Scientific Archives Integration

The SRP provides a unified interface to all the scientific archives. As we know, scientific archives usually are stored in digital libraries. Different systems use different non-interoperable technologies, especially the organization of metadata are different. In order to increase the interoperation of different archive systems, OAI has been put forward. But this protocol demands that the metadata descriptions of each archive systems are same, and need metadata harvesting to exchange metadata between each of them, which can not be applied in SRP. Currently we use Query interface and semantic mapping table to do distribute searching among different archives. The main components about the integrated archives system are:

(1) User management. Control the access right and policy of the SRP users.
(2) Query interface. The interface is between existing DL and SRP. Using this interface, the current DL operation does not need to do any change.
(3) Semantic mapping table. For different archive systems, the search options such as search fields are different. The semantic mapping table maps the query fields to the archive systems' acceptable format.
(4) Semantic mapping tools. Define the mapping table.

The search steps are shown in Fig.6.

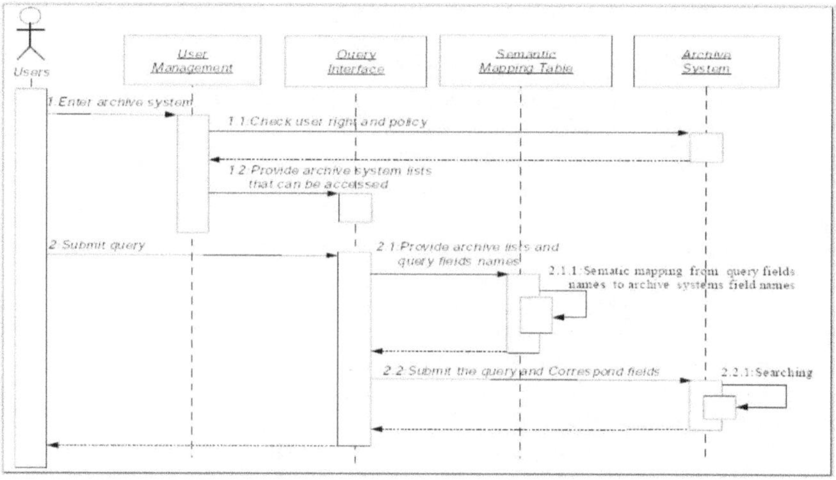

Fig. 6. The general steps of how to search from different archive systems

4 Conclusion

To form a SRP is a hard work, it needs a lot of time to analyze the current systems, define the metadata, mapping the semantic tables. Currently, an integrated biologic data service has been developed and placed in SRP. This Services provide biologist a unify portal for search biologic sequences from various databases such as GenBank [16], EMBL [17], DDBJ [18], SwissProt, PIR [19]. We should know that the formats of the sequences in these databases are not same. Also, a bioinformatics mining service is placed on SRP to provide gene expression similarity analysis service, gene expression path way service, specially gene analysis service and et al.

The developing of SRP heavily depends on Data Grid technology and the current Grid middlewares. The important aspect of building SRP is how to organize metadata. Maybe ontology will be a better choice for knowledge sharing. We hope that the SRP not only integrates data, but also provides knowledge to researchers.

References

1. Altchul SF, et al. Gapped blast and psi-blast: a new generation of protein database search programs. Nucleic Acids Res., 1997,25(17): 3389-3402.
2. Boeckmann B, Bairoch A, Apweiler R, Blatter MC, Estreicher A, Gasteiger E, Martin MJ et al. The SWISSPROT protein knowledgebase and its supplement TrEMBL in 2003. Nucleic Acids Res., 2003, 31(1): 365–370.
3. Nelson, M.L.; Calhoun, J.R.; Mackey, C.E. The OAI-PMH NASA technical report server. Proceedings of the 2004 Joint ACM/IEEE Conference on Digital Libraries, 7-11 June 2004 Page(s):400-408.
4. Hey T and Trefethen A.E. Cyberinfrastructure for e-Science. Science, vol. 308, May 6, 2005.
5. Gullapalli, S.; Dyke, S.; Hubbard, P.; et al. Showcasing the features and capabilities of NEESgrid: a grid based system for the earthquake engineering domain. Proceedings of 13th IEEE International Symposium on High performance Distributed Computing, 4-6 June 2004.Page(s): 268- 269.
6. Texas Internet Grid for Research and Education (TIGRE) project web page, http://www.hipcat.net/Projects/tigre (access date: 10 April 2005)
7. Welch V, Siebenlist F, Foster I, et al.. Security for Grid Services. Proceedings of the 12th IEEE International Symposium on High Performance Distributed Computing (HPDC-12), June 2003.IEEE Computer Society Press: Washington DC, 2003:48–57.
8. The Workow Reference Model web page, http://www.aiim.org/wfmc/standards/docs/tc003v11.pdf. (access date :10 April 2005).
9. G, von Laszewski, I. Foster, J. Gawor, P. Lane. A Java Commodity Grid Toolkit. Concurrency: Practice and Experience, 13, 2001.
10. 10.Christensen E, Curbera F (eds). Web Services Description Language (WSDL) 1.1. W3C Note. http://www.w3.org/TR/wsdl, March 2001.
11. Ashburner M, Ball CA, Blake JA and et al. Gene ontology: tool for the unification of biology. Nature Genet, 2000, 25(1): 25-9.
12. Graham PJ, Sloan TM, et al.. FirstDIG: Data Investigations using OGSA-DAI. OGSA-DAI mini-workshop, AHM2004.
13. OGSA-DAI web page, http://www.ogsadai.org.uk (access date: 10 April 2005).

14. M. Nedim Alpdemir, Arijit Mukherjee, Anastasios Gounaris, et al. OGSA-DQP: A Service for Distributed Querying on the Grid. processdings of 9th International Conference on Extending Database Technology, (Lecture Notes in Computer Science, vol.2992), 2004. pp. 858 – 861.
15. Nedim Alpdemir, Arijit Mukherjee, Anastasios Gounaris, et al. Using OGSA-DQP to Support Scientific Applications for the Grid. processdings of the First International Workshop on Scientific Applications of Grid Computing, SAG 2004, (Lecture Notes in Computer Science, vol.3458),2005.pp.1-13.
16. Benson DA, K.-M. I., Lipman DJ, Ostell J, Rapp BA, Wheeler DL.GenBank. NUCLEIC ACIDS RESEARCH 28 (1), 2000: 15-18.
17. Stoesser G, Sterk P, Tuli MA and et al. The EMBL Nucleotide Sequence Database. Nucl. Acids. Res. 2004 32(1): 27-30.
18. Miyazaki S, Sugawara H, Ikeo K and et al. DDBJ in the stream of various biological data. Nucl. Acids. Res. 2004 32(1): 31-34.
19. Barker WC, Garavelli JS, Huong H and et al. The Protein Information Resource (PIR). Nucl. Acids. Res. 2000 28(1): 41-44.

Toolkits for Ontology Building and Semantic Annotation in UDMGrid*

Xiaowu Chen, Xixi Luo, Haifeng Ou, Mingji Chen, Hui Xiao,
Pin Zhang, and Feng Cheng

The Key Laboratory of Virtual Reality Technology, Ministry of Education,
School of Computer Science and Engineering, Beihang University,
Beijing 100083, P.R. China
chen@buaa.edu.cn

Abstract. University Digital Museum Grid (UDMGrid) has been developed to provide one-stop information services about kinds of digital specimens in the form of grid services. In order to speed up the way to make the digital specimen information resources interoperable based on semantic annotation using ontologies, three toolkits have been exploited to support the ontology building and the semantic annotation about the university digital museum information resources. These include toolkits for ontology editing, web content semantic annotation, and database content semantic annotation.

1 Introduction

Eighteen featured university museums have been digitized mainly relating to Geology & Geography, Archaeology, Humanities & Civilization, and Aeronautics & Astronautics [1]. These digital museums play an important role in the fields of education, scientific research, as well as specimen collection, preservation, exhibition, and intercommunication. However, these digital museums dispersed on different nodes in CERNET (China Education and Research Network) [2] confront a problem that the multi-discipline resources at these digital museums are isolated and dispersed without sufficient interconnection. Hence it is necessary to propose a digital museum resources integration solution, through which these eighteen digital museums would be incorporated as a more comprehensive virtual one.

UDMGrid (University Digital Museum Grid)[3][4][5][6], a typical application of information grid, has been developed to provide one-stop information service about kinds of digital specimens in the form of grid services. From the user's perspective, UDMGrid performs as a virtual digital museum, in which users can browser the digital specimen information in multiple manners on only one UDMGrid portal instead of eighteen separate homepages, without rushing about among these digital museums. However, the information resources of digital museums are constructed by different domain experts, who use special metadata to describe information, thus the heteroge-

* This paper is supported by China Education and Research Grid (ChinaGrid)(CG2003-GA004 & CG004), National 863 Program (2004AA104280), Beijing Science & Technology Program (2004A11).

H.T. Shen et al. (Eds.): APWeb 2006, LNCS 3842, pp. 486 – 495, 2006.

neity among these metadata brings difficulties for semantic inter-operation which is important to mine the latent semantic relation between numerous of digital specimen information resources.

The semantic web brings new ways to make the digital specimen information resource inter-operable, since it envision a world-wide distributed architecture where data and computational resource will easily inter-operate based on semantic marking up of web resources using ontologies [7]. The basic research of semantic web: ontology building and semantic annotation are indispensable to integrate millions of the digital specimen information resource.

In 1993, Ontology was defined by Gruber as "an explicit specification of a conceptualization" [8], which are accepted most by the semantic web community. Ontology defines common vocabularies for people to share information in a domain, including machine-interpretable definitions of basic concepts and relations between them. In recent year, many ontology building toolkits have been developed. These toolkits are aimed at providing support for the ontology building and management process. For example, OilEd [9] is a graphical ontology editor developed by the University of Manchester., which allows the definition and description of classes, slots, individuals and axioms within ontology. Its editing functions are provided by graphical user interface—mouse driven drop-down menus, toolbars and buttons. Protégé-2000[10] is developed by the Stanford Medical Informatics(SMI) of Stanford University . It provides a graphical and interactive ontology-design and knowledge-base–development environment. The Protégé-2000 user interface consists of several tab for editing Classes、Slots、Forms、Instances and Queries. WebOnto [11] is developed by the Knowledge Media Institute (KMI) of the Open University. It is a web-based toolkit for visualization, browsing and development of ontologies and knowledge models written in OCML. Its main advantage over other available toolkits is that it supports editing ontologies collaboratively, allowing synchronous and asynchronous discussions about ontologies development.

Semantic annotation is a process to annotate all sorts of Web resources and their components with concept classes, concept properties and other metadata according to correlative ontology. At present, there are many universities and research organizations researching and developing semantic annotation toolkits for Web content, among which the typical ontology-based ones are the following: SMORE [12] (Semantic Markup, Ontology, and RDF Editor) developed by MIND (Maryland Information and Network Dynamics Lab) SWAP(Semantic Web Agents Project) research group, University of Maryland provides an integrated developing environment (IDE) to support seamless semantic annotation during online Web content creation. It extended the functions of an annotation toolkit by providing functions like E-mail and image annotation, ontology maintenance, screen shooting, etc. OntoMat-Annotiser [13] developed by AIFB academy, University of Karlsruhe in Germany is a module-based ontology-driven toolkit for Web content creation and annotation. Its interactive mode allows free switching between creating and annotating. Annotea [14] developed by W3C is a Web-based shared annotation system based on a general-purpose open RDF infrastructure. It regards Web annotation stored on appropriative (ontology) server as document notes (called XDoc) made by the author or others. COHSE [13] (Conceptual Open Hypermedia Services Environment) developed by Information Management Group (University of Manchester) and Intelligent, Agents, Multimedia

Group (University of Southampton) supports link creation and navigation on semantic Web by using metadata. Metadata describing document content are used to link several documents. SHOE [13] (Simple HTML Ontology Extension) Knowledge Annotator developed by Parallel Understanding System Group, Department of Computer Science, University of Maryland allows using 'select and fill in' mode to add SHOE knowledge to Web pages.

Previously, the work about ontology building and semantic annotation in UDMGrid are done by filling out forms, which is so ineffective that this kind of works occupied too much proportion of the whole integration works. Therefore, a three toolkits have been exploited to support the ontology building and the semantic annotation about the university digital museum, including the toolkit for ontology editing, which makes experts build the domain ontology more conveniently, the toolkits for web and database content semantic annotation, separately for two information resources.

The remainder of this paper is organized as follows. Section 2 is about the ontology building toolkits, including the toolkit for ontology edit. For the reason that there are two resources in UDMGrid: database and web pages, section 3 and 4 are separately elaborate the semantic annotation toolkit for different renounces. Section 5 ends this paper with conclusions and future work.

2 Ontology Editing

The second toolkit is used for ontology editing. At present, the developments of domain ontologies in UDMGrid (University Digital Museum Grid) are done by the developers, which make the work hard and inefficient. For people who are not familiar with the professional field, developing domain ontologies is difficult, fallible and also lack of authority. It is feasible for the domain experts of each digital museum to build domain ontologies for they have better knowledge about each domain. In this way the building process will be more efficient, correctable and authoritative. But the ontology editors used nowadays are mostly universal editor. Its complex functions and lack of translating support not only increase the difficulty of usage but also don't fit the need of our project. Because of foregoing reasons, we have developed an UDMGrid-ontology [15] editing toolkit to assist the domain experts to build domain ontologies collaboratively. This toolkit is aimed at providing a friendly and Human-Computer Interacted interface to support the process of developing, managing and storing of the domain ontology. At the same time, it can provide ontology information for the annotation toolkits.

Domain ontology in UDMGrid-ontology editing toolkit is presented by the hierarchy of trees. As Fig.2 shown, the root of the tree is the General Concept Class in the domain, and the subclasses categorize concepts into more specific fields. Each hierarchy of Concept Class has its concept properties which describe the common vocabularies needed for sharing information in a field. Domain ontologies are stored in an uniform format in the ontology repository. They are built by domain experts of the eighteen featured university museums. In order to prevent the misoperation of domain ontologies, UDMGrid-ontology edit toolkit has access control in the process of the Concept Class editing. For example, the domain expert in archaeology is not able to delete the Concept Class built by a geologist. UDMGrid-ontology edit toolkit also can provide interface for annotation toolkits. The interface offers ontology information including both hierarchy information and Concept Properties of the Concept Classes. The interface also can receive the annotation and store it in the ontology repository.

As Fig.4 shown, UDMGrid ontology editing toolkit is divided into five Modules: Display Module, Ontology-management Module, Data-access Module, Permission-control Module and Ontology-annotation Interface.

Display Module : Display Module is used to present the tree hierarchical representation of domain ontologies. When a Concept Class in the tree is chosen, Display Module will present all the detailed Concept Properties from the Ontology-management Module, and support the editing process. Display Module also can send the tree hierarchical representation model to Ontology-management Module.

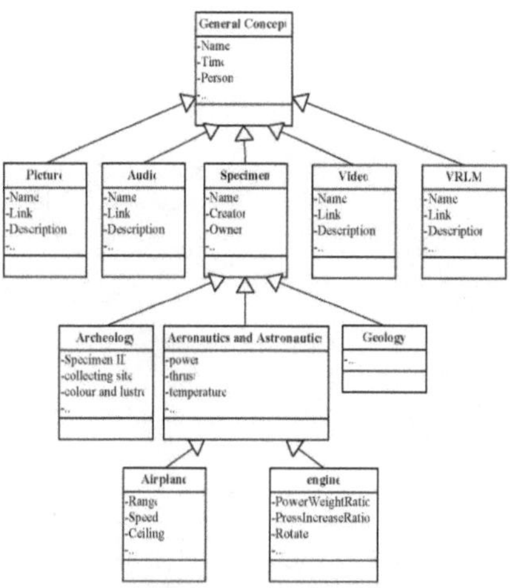

Fig. 1. The hierarchical representation of the domain ontologies

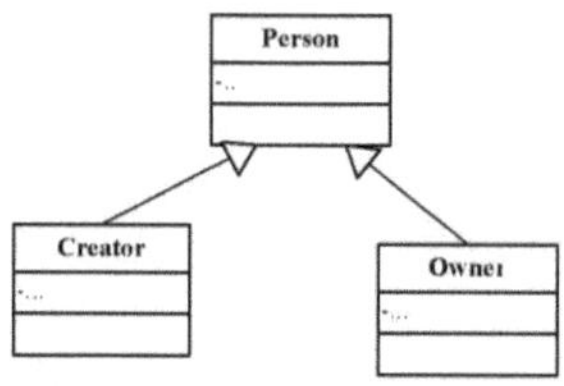

Fig. 2. The inheritance of Concept Properties

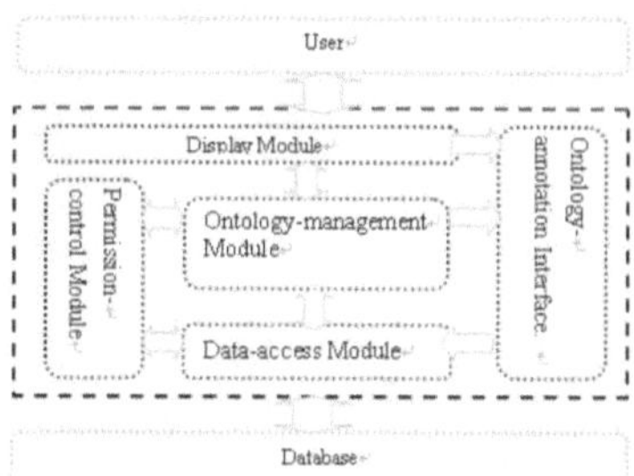

Fig. 3. Architecture of UDMGrid ontology edit toolkit

Ontology-management Module : Ontology-management Module is used to build and manage the Concept Class and the Concept Property from Display Module or Data-access Module. Concept Class has its own Properties and can be inherited by its subclasses. The Concept Properties also can be inherited but it is selective. For example, as Fig.3 shown, "Person" is a Concept Property in "General ", while it is the super class of " Creator" and "Owner" in"Specimen". When "Person" is selected to be the super class, it will not be inherited by "Specimen", so by this way this inheritance is selective.

Data-access Module : Data-access Module provides the ontology repository, including storing the Concept Class and Concept Property from Ontology-management Module, Querying, Inserting, Deleting and Updating information and sends the results to the Ontology-management Module. Data-access Module also can receive the annotations from Ontology-annotation Interface and store them in ontology repository.

Permission-control Module: Permission-control Module constraints the operations of the Concept Class. When Ontology-management Module builds the Class Model, Permission-control Module will add the "Creator" field from its developer's login information. Once people want to delete a Concept Class, it will compare the Creator of the class and its all subclasses with the current user. If they don't match each other, the delete operation will be refused.

Ontology-annotation Interface: Ontology-annotation Interface provides information model of the ontology to annotation toolkits which includes the hierarchy from Display Module and detailed properties from Ontology-management Module. It also gets the annotations from annotation toolkits and stores them in ontology repository.

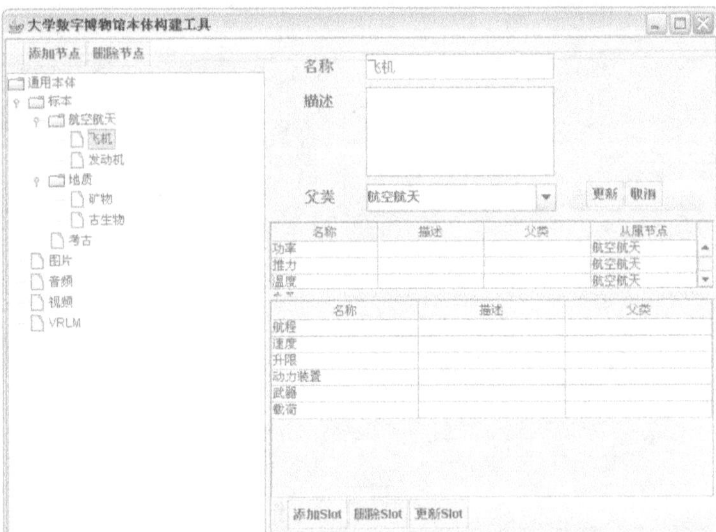

Fig. 4. Main GUI of UDMGrid ontology editing Toolkit

UDMGrid ontology editing toolkit provides a Human-Computer Interacted interface. Editing functions are provided by graphical user interface, which makes users build the domain ontology conveniently.

Starting the toolkit & logging into the database: Once ontology editing toolkit is started, it will get access to the ontology repository. Users need to input the necessary information of the ontology repository as well as the login information. After connection, the toolkit will come into the main interface.

Viewing & rearranging the hierarchy of ontology tree: The Main Interface of UDMGrid is shown as Fig.5. The Concept class hierarchy with selective inheritance is shown in the left pane. Users can use the toolbar to add and delete classes and so to rearrange the hierarchy.

Viewing & editing detailed properties: The right pane shows detailed information for the selected class, including the description of the Concept Class and all the Concept Properties. For example, when the Concept Class "airplane" is chosen, the description information of the concept class will be shown in the form, at the same time, the detailed properties of the concept class will be displayed below. The Concept Property not only include its own property of the "airplane", such as "Range", "Ceiling" ,but also include the properties inherited from the Concept "aeronautics and astronautics", such as "Power", "Thrust", "Temperature" etc. Editing the Concept Properties can be done directly in the table. Users can add several new rows, edit the information of any cell or delete more than one row at a time.

Deleting the concept class: When users want to delete the Concept Class, ontology edit toolkit will ask them to confirm the delete operation, and then it will compare the Creator of the Concept Class and the current user, if they don't match each other, the delete operation will be refused.

3 Web Content Semantic Annotation

The second toolkit is used for web content semantic annotation. In UDMGrid, there are a number of digital specimens resources presented as static Web pages (html files). These kinds of digital specimens need to be classified and indexed by semantic annotating on Web pages when integrating collections of all the university digital museums. The toolkits mentioned above are all general-purpose annotation toolkits and their ontology repositories and other components are not fit for classifying museum collections. Directly using those toolkits to classify digital specimens can hardly be very efficient. Hence we developed UDMGrid Semantic Annotation Toolkit for Web Content. Our toolkit has assimilated the excellence of other semantic annotation toolkits, such as integrated user interface, annotation sharing, form-filling mode annotating, etc. In addition to the primary function of semantic annotation, our toolkit provides extra functions such as user authentication, Website structure detection, batch annotation adding, etc., which improves the accuracy and efficiency of digital specimens classification.

UDMGrid Semantic Annotation Toolkit for Web Content is used to extract the attributes information (regarded as keywords to classify the specimen) of digital specimens from the Web pages of digital museums, create mappings between keywords and the corresponding ontology, and store the annotations (formed by correspondences of keywords, ontology and the Web page URL) in annotation database. The modules architecture of our toolkit is shown in Fig.6.

Website Structure Detection Module: This module detects the layered structure of the page links of digital museums Websites and provides Website structure data for Web Pages Display Module.

Web Pages Display Module: This module gets data from Website Structure Detection Module to display the tree structure of html pages in digital museums Web-sites, calls the embedded Web browser to show the Web page selected from the Website tree structure by the user, and allows the user to browse the page, select and drag texts. It also provides the URL of current opened page when an annotation is being created.

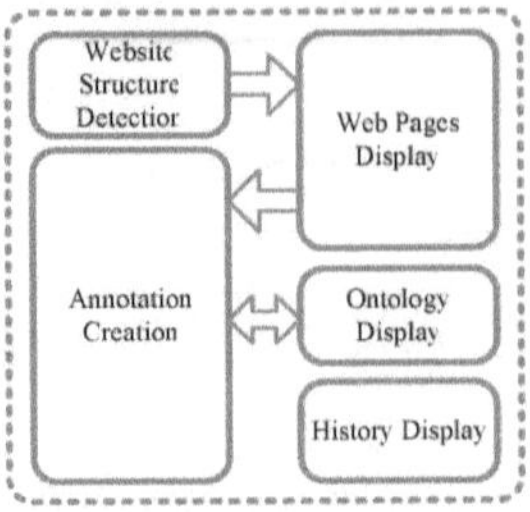

Fig. 5. Architecture of UDMGrid Semantic Annotation Toolkit for Web Content

Fig. 6. Website Structure Detection Dialog

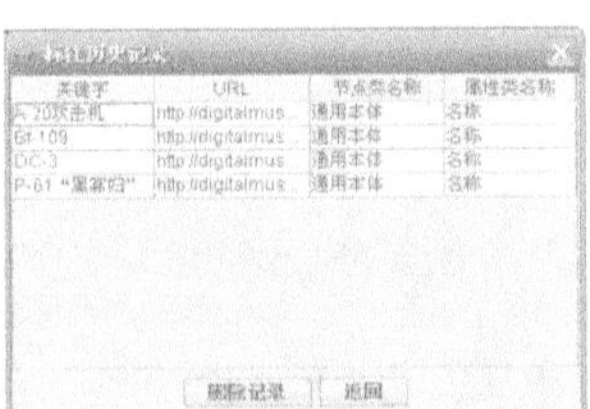

Fig. 7. Annotation History Dialog

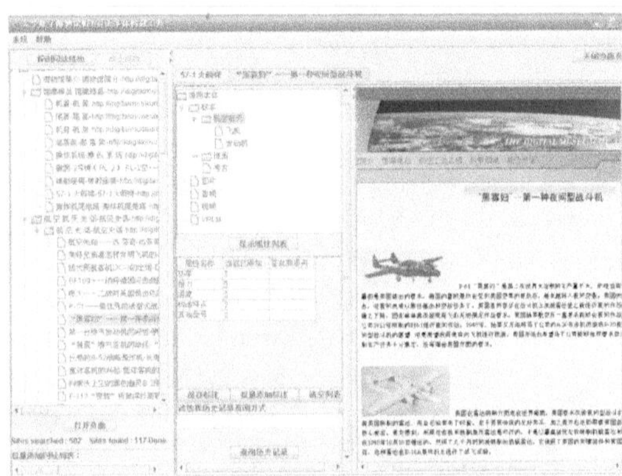

Fig. 8. Main GUI of UDMGrid Semantic Annotation Toolkit for Web Content

Ontology Display Module: This module displays the tree structure of the concept classes and the concept property list of the concept class selected from the tree structure by the user. It allows the user to fill in the property value by dragging and dropping text. It also monitors the change of data in concept property list and calls the Annotation Creation Module to save data when necessary.

Annotation Creation Module: This module gets concept properties of a certain concept class from ontology repository, provides data for ontology display and gets data from Web Pages Display Module and Ontology Display Module to create and save annotations.

History Display Module: This module queries the annotation database in a certain mode (by concept class name, concept property, keyword or URL), lists the annotation records and allows records deleting in both single record mode and multi-record mode.

The toolkit implements an integrated user interface where most user operations can be completed. The work flows of this toolkit are as follows:

Starting the toolkit & logging into the database: After starting the toolkit, the user need to input the IP address, port number, database name, username and password in the database connection dialog. After logging into the database successfully, the main GUI will be displayed (Fig.9).
Detecting Website structure: Clicking on the button "detect Website structure", the user will be asked to input the root URL of the Website to be detected (e.g. http://digitalmuseum.buaa.edu.cn/), the maximum number of pages to be detected and the maximum depth of detection in a dialog (Fig.7). After that, the toolkit begins to detect Website structure and the detection result will show dynamically in the Website structure pane of the main GUI. The page selected from the Website tree structure can be shown in the embedded Web browser (e.g. in Fig.9, a page titled "'Black Widow'-the first night fighter" is opened).
Browsing pages & adding annotations: After the user selects a concept class (e.g. airplane) from the tree structure of concept classes, the toolkit lists all the concept properties of that class. If the user selects a section of text in the Web page opened in the embedded Web browser and drags the text to a certain row of the concept property list, the toolkit will automatically use the text as an annotation to the current page (keyword) and map the text to the corresponding ontology of the row.
Adding annotations in batches: After dragging the selected text to the concept property list, the user may select more than one page from the Website tree structure pane and click on the button "batch annotation adding" to add current annotations to all the selected Web pages.

4 Database Content Semantic Annotation

The third toolkit is used for database content semantic annotation, which provide assist to museum database administrators with database metadata extracting and mapping from database metadata to UDMGrid ontology. Four core functions referred are database metadata extracting, mapping generation and information registration to UDMGrid ontology information center. This toolkit is composed of three modules as shown in Fig.10 which are display module, database metadata extracting module and access agent module.

Display module: contains two parts which are information display and mapping relationship annotation. The interface of the toolkit is divided into four separated part: displaying database information; displaying the relation between tables of different databases (mainly focus on the foreign –key of table); displaying ontology information and displaying mapping relation. Database information, and ontology information are shown as tree structure, and the relation between tables and mapping information will be seen as table structure

Database metadata extracting module: is up to get metadata from heterogenous databases. We use JDBC to connect databases and get all metadata information needed. The information will be sent to display module

Access agent module: is responsible for interacting with UDMGrid ontology information center including getting ontology data from center and send registration data to center

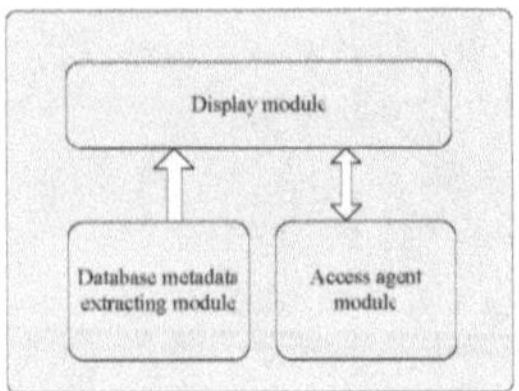

Fig. 9. The module of database resource annotation toolkit

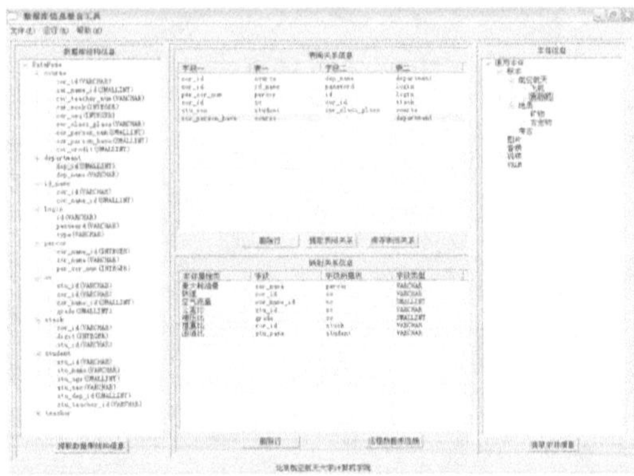

Fig. 10. Main GUI of UDMGrid Semantic Annotation Toolkit for Database Content

The process of registering database is composed of several steps such as getting database metadata, appending the table relation, add mapping relation etc. Let's take the registration of Beihang university digital museum database for example:

- The user who is database administrator chooses the type of database and fill out the form with the information to access the database such as database address, user name and password, then access to the system, Fig.11 shows the main interface of the toolkit
- On the main interface of toolkit, the user can get ontology information from ontology information center, the result will be display on the main interface
- For there are relationships between tables, user adds these relationships on the interface. After that, metadata of the database is submitted to ontology information center
- Finally, user assigns the mappings from database metadata to ontology and submits this information to ontology information center. Now the registration is completed.

5 Conclusion and Future Work

UDMGrid has been developed to provide one-stop information service about kinds of digital specimens in the form of grid services. In order to make the digital specimen interoperable, semantic web technologies: ontology and semantic annotation have been applied. For improving the effect of ontology building and semantic annotation, three toolkits have been exploited, including, the toolkit for ontology building is for ontology editing, which makes experts build the domain ontology more conveniently. Anther two toolkits are about semantic annotation for two information resources, including web resource and database resource. To sum up, these three toolkits speed up the way to make the digital specimen information resource inter-operable based on semantic annotation using ontologies.

Although these three toolkits help the exploiter a lot, however, a great deal of work has to be done by human, therefore, the research for semi-automatic or automatic ontology building and semantic annotation are the key topics of study work in the future.

References

1. University Digital Museums, http://www.edu.cn/20020118/3018035.shtml
2. China Education and Research Network, http://www.edu.cn/
3. Xiaowu Chen, Xixi Luo, Zhangsheng Pan, Qinping Zhao. A CGSP-based Grid Application for University Digital Museums. Third International Symposium on Parallel and Distributed Processing and Applications (ISPA'2005), Nanjing, China, 2005
4. Xiaowu Chen, Zhi Xu, Zhangsheng Pan, Xixi Luo. UDMGrid: A Grid Application for University Digital Museums. Grid and Cooperative Computing (GCC 2004), pp. 720~728, Wuhang, China, 2004
5. 5. Hai Jin. ChinaGrid: Making Grid Computing a Reality. Digital Libraries: International Collaboration and Cross-Fertilization - Lecture Notes in Computer Science, Vol.3334. Springer-Verlag, December 2004, pp.13-24
6. UDMGrid, www.udmgrid.net
7. Marie-Christine Rousset. Small can be beautiful in the semantic web. International Conference on Semantic Web (ISWC 2004), pp.6-16, Springer-Verlag, Berlin Heidelberg New York (2004)
8. GruberTR.A Translation Approach to Portable Ontology Specifications. Knowledge Acquisition, 1993, 5:199~220
9. Bechhofer S, Horrocks I, Goble C, et al. OILEd: A reason-able ontology editor for the semantic web[R].Joint German/Austrian conference on Artificial Intelligence, 2001, 2174:396-408
10. Noy N F, Sintek M, Decker S,et al. Creating semantic web con-tents with protege-2000[J].IEEE Intelligent Systems,2001, 16(2):60-71
11. Domingue J.Tadzebao and WebOnto: Discussing, browsing, and editing ontologies on the web[R]. Proceedings of the 11th Knowledge Acquisition for Knowledge-Based Systems. Workshop, 1998
12. Kalyanpur A, Hendler J, et al. SMORE-Semantic Markup, Ontology and RDF Editor [EB/OL]. http://www.mindswap.org/papers/SMORE.pdf, 2003 - 09
13. OntoWeb: A Survey on Ontology Toolkits. OntoWeb Deliverable1.3 [EB/OL]. http://babage.dia.fi.upm.es/ontoweb/wp1/OntoRoadMap/documents/D13-v1-0.pdf, 2002 - 05
14. Kahan J, Koivunen M, et al. Annotea: An Open RDF Infrastructure for Shared Web Annotations [A]. Proceedings of the WWW10 International Conference [C]. Hong Kong, May 1-5, 2001
15. Xixi Luo, Xiaowu Chen. OOML-Based Ontologies and Its Services for Information Retrieval in UDMGrid. Sixth International Workshop on Advanced Parallel Processing Technologies (APPT 2005). Lecture Notes in Computer Science, Vol 3756. Springer-Verlag, Berlin Heidelberg Hongkong(2005) 342 – 352

DPGS: A Distributed Programmable Grid System*

Yongwei Wu, Qing Wang, Guangwen Yang, and Weiming Zheng

Department of Computer Science and Technology,
Tsinghua University, Beijing, 100084, China

Abstract. Workflow mechanism is used into grid system to combine multiple grid services to implement complex grid application. But the workflow is not programmable, and is not flexible enough for users as well. In this paper, a Distributed Programmable Grid System (DPGS) is put forward. In DPGS, a course-grained parallel programming interface GridPPI is implemented. Through it, user could couple multiple web services in DPGS to completed complicated requests. Based on Globus Toolkit 3.9.3, the DPGS provides a simply organized, extendable and scalable grid environment for grid designer to design and deploy traditional or new applications.

1 Introduction

As the tremendous development in internet and intranet technology, the grid computing technology is put forward for the new requirement in high performance computing. The purpose of grid computing is to utilize high-speed networks to integrate true supercomputers, clusters, storage facilities, and scientific instruments to form a suitable, pervasive and ubiquitous, and potentially infinite scalable meta-computer for parallel and collaborative work [2, 4]. One of the essential point in grid technology is that the grid expand the distribute computing inside an intranet to the whole internet, and thus bring with a series of new problem in data management, job schedule and information monitor and discovery.

To date, many of the grid system uses web service or grid service (based on OGSI [3] or WSRF [1]) to encapsulate one or more computing tools to supply certain professional computing task. But how to use these services coordinately? This means one professional user may want to use more than one of these services to complete a complex task, For example, a CFD(Computational Fluid Dynamics) task may have several steps: build model, create mesh, domain decomposization and at last do CFD resolve. One solution is to supply a workflow mechanism, such as the BPEL[6]. With a job description specification, the workflow mechanism can describe a series of jobs and the topology order of them.

* This Work is supported by ChinaGrid project of Ministry of Education of China, Natural Science Foundation of China under Grant 60373004, 60373005, 90412006, 90412011, and National Key Basic Research Project of China under Grant 2004CB318000.

H.T. Shen et al. (Eds.): APWeb 2006, LNCS 3842, pp. 496–505, 2006.

A standard workflow mechanism can also defines the input and output relation among jobs in a workflow. The workflow executor will then analyze the workflow description and execute the jobs as user's specificity. The famous workflow mechanism supported system, such as UniCore[7], CGSP(China Grid Support Platform)[8] both supplies a graphical interface for user to build and submit a workflow and can support a great many of professional applications.

But the workflow is not programmable, which means the user is limited with the job description specifications and can not communicate with user's own application in an easy way. At the same time, the workflow is controlled by the grid system itself. It is not flexible enough for users.

In this paper, based on Globus Toolkits, a Distributed Programmable Grid System (DPGS) is put forward. In DPGS, user could code his own distributed parallel GridPPI [5] programs to complete complicated grid application. The GridPPI is a coarse-grained/task-level distributed parallel programming interface for grid computing. It provides a group of generic and abstract function prototypes with well-specified semantics. Following a standard interface specification such as GridPPI, users could couple multiple different computing tools distributed over multiple heterogeneous machines to run practical complex computing applications.

The content of this paper includes eight sections, the motivations of DPGS is discussed in detail first in section 2. In section 3, a brief introduce of the GridPPI specification is discussed. From section 4 to section 6, DPGS architecture, three main function modules and communication in it are proposed in detail. At last, programming example and conclusion will be put forward.

2 Motivation

Because of the limitation of bandwidth and latency over Internet, it is still not practical to implement fine-grained parallel computation over grid. Grid is more suitable for the course-grained parallel computation. MPICH-G2 [9] is an exponent grid-enabled extension of the original MPICH for the compliance of grid system. It provides one way for users to integrate multiple machines, potentially of different architectures, to run normal cluster MPI applications. But in order to get little message communication between grid nodes, we must modify the original applications. In fact, this is very difficult and sometimes impossible. So the low-level or fine-grained parallel computation based on frequent massage passing between the grid nodes is still a rather unrealistic, and grid enabled coarse-grained distributed parallel computing, such as the GridPPI, is quite emphasized much more and more at present.

On the other hand, more and more grid applications require the cooperative use of multiple computing tools at the same time, such as sophisticated scientific and engineering computing problems, integration of all sorts of information resources located different places. So the grid system should not only provide the process for specific task of one computing tool but also should give out a mechanism for the coordinate and parallel use of several computing tools. The

GridRPC [10] is a grid-enabled remote procedure call standard for grid programming, but it is procedural and is not designed for parallel process. Workflow is a most popular mechanism for the coordinate use of several computing tools and the system, such as UniCore[7], CGSP[8] has achieved a great success. But the workflow is not programmable for users and thus the capabilities are limited by the specification of the workflow description.

From the programmer's view, DPGS provides an MPI-like program environment which aims at the coarse-grained task-level parallel process. It hides the dynamic, distribution, heterogeneity of grid system for users, and programmers could couple multiple grid services to completed complicated tasks without knowing where the services required by the program are.

3 Parallel Programming Interface for Grid Computing (GridPPI)

The GridPPI defines specification for task-level distributed programming interface. Because its interface definition is similar with the MPI, we call it MPI-like. These interfaces include service discovering and selecting, task submitting and reporting, communication between subtasks, asynchronous waiting functions, etc.. GridPPI is MPI-like, which means it is different with the MPI. MPI is based on message-level communication, and suitable for fine-grained parallel programming, while the GridPPI is defined for coarse-grained task-level program. The GridPPI interfaces can be divided into three groups.

- Service Discovering and Selection
  These interfaces is designed for programmer to customize his strategy in service discovering and selection.
- Task Related
  Programmer uses these interfaces to request a specified service to execute one atom job, send input data and get computing results in his own program.
- Monitoring and Communication
  These interfaces are designed for monitoring the status of each atom job, querying the service and resource information. At the same time, user could complete the communication between different atom tasks and more enable that atom task could communicate with local program directly.

GridPPI is implemented in DPGS to provide a user programming interface. Through it, user could couple multiple grid services deployed in the DPGS to complete complex grid application.

4 Framework of DPGS

The Distributed Programmable Grid System (DPGS) is a grid system, on which programmer or user can run GridPPI programs, and build graph or web based grid service for elementary users. In general, DPGS consists of three modules,

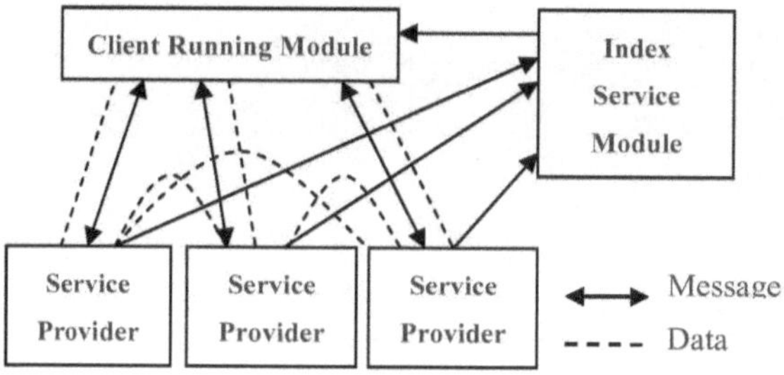

Fig. 1. Framework of DPGS

index service module, service provider module and client running module. The index service module is in charge of making index of all available services in the grid system and allowing the client program to search the specified grid services. The service provider module is running on the supercomputer or cluster, it encapsulate various computing tools and accept client's request for certain tool. Of course, the provider should register all the provided services and their capabilities to the index service node. The client is the core running module for GridPPI programs. It searches the available services it needs via the index module and distributes the job tasks to the service providers. The relation of these three modules is shown in figure 1.

5 Three modules of DPGS

Index Service Module

The index service module is the information center of the whole system. It collects service related information and computing node capabilities of the system. Though it is the center of information, the architecture of index service module can be designed distributed. Mentioned previous, our system is built with the GT and naturally we adopt its MDS (Monitoring and Discovery System) components in our index service module. Currently, the MDS component implemented in GT 3.9.3 is based on WSRF (Web Service Resource Framework) and called MDS4. The topology of MDS4 is show in figure 2 and you can see the nodes in MDS architecture are organized as a multi-branches tree. The IndexService node is a domain center and in charge of collecting all domain resources' information, including physical resource information and web service information. The information in MDS4 is represented as ResourceProperties of Web Service based on WSRF. An IndexService node is composed of two processors: Aggregator Link and Aggregator Source. The Aggregator Source responses web service's subscription and notifications and it collects all subscribed web services' resource properties in a certain strategy. Collected information will then be delivered to the Aggregator Link processor and be either forward to high level IndexService node or deal by local service.

Our index service module utilizes the organization of the MDS4 and supplies our own Aggregator Link for service selection and a WSRF service on each

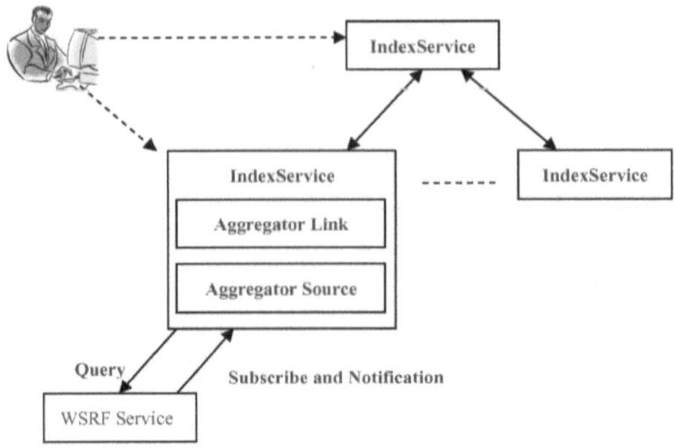

Fig. 2. Architecture of MDS4 in DPGS

real computing node for information collection. The WSRF service collects local service information and report to its domain index service. In the global IndexService node, a web service works as Aggregator Link to deal with resource information and let the client to search information through GridPPI specified interface.

Service Provider Module

In our distributed programmable grid system, programmer can use abundant computing tools to complete his computing task, such as numerical calculation, bio-information processing, graph analyzing, hydromechanical computing and other high performance computing tools. These tools are deployed on the computing resource nodes by the service provider module. The service provider module manages all these computing tools. For the convenience and flexibility of parallel and distributed computing, we encapsulate these tools with the uniform interface as the GridPPI specification. Figure 3 shows the architecture of the service provider module.

As mentioned in previous sections, our system is designed with the globus toolkit. Currently used globus toolkit version is 3.9.3. You can see in the figure that the computing service is deployed on the globus service container and its outer interface is designed as the GridPPI specification.

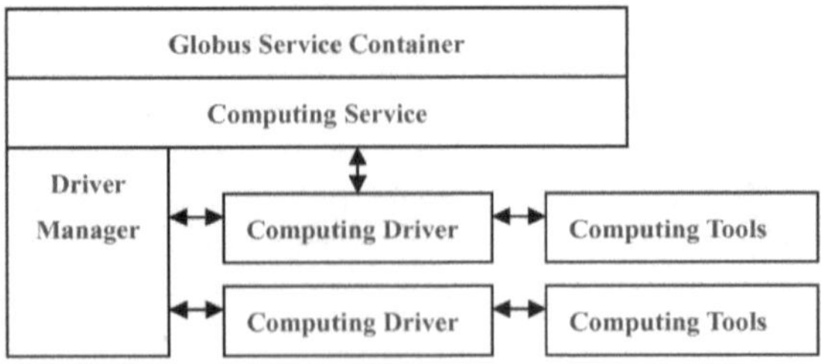

Fig. 3. Architecture of the Service Provider in DPGS

As to the GridPPI specification, there are several computing tools on one computing node and the user put the tool name in the request's parameter to specify which tool he wants to use. In the view of technology, we can implement a grid service for each computing tools. Because each grid service has its own endpoint and thus the client module can call different services for different tools. But this is an awful way, because in grid service specification, each service will have a handler instance in runtime. The more services exist in the container, the more running instance in runtime. It will of course add the burden of the computing node. On the other hand, implement different service for different tools will result in the hardness of managing the running tasks.

So in DPGS, we implement only one computing service in one computing node. For the use of multiple computing tools, we design the computing driver and the driver manager. The computing driver is an encapsulation of the computing tools. In our system, the computing tools are limited to command line program and thus these tools have similar behaviors. Pick out the similarity in characterizes of all computing tools, we get a set of uniform interfaces. We call them computing driver interface. For each computing tool, we will design its own implementation of the computing driver interface, which is called the computing driver. When user requests to use a specific computing tool, the driver manager will call the responding computing driver's constructor to create a new computing driver instance to run the computing tool. The driver manager naturally acts as a manager of all computing driver in the computing node. It is in the responsibility of registering new computing driver, unregister old computing driver and creating computing driver instances for user's request. On the other hand, the driver manager also acts as an information probe for the index service module. It collects all available computing driver's information and reports to the GRIS module and then reports to the GIIS node.

Client Running Module

The client running module is a client library for user to program and submit GridPPI task. It encapsulates the request to the index service module and service provider module as the GridPPI interfaces. It is designed for user to easy design distributed and coordinated parallel programs and with the core running module, user can run his distributed program directly. Figure 4 gives a brief view of the model of the client running module.

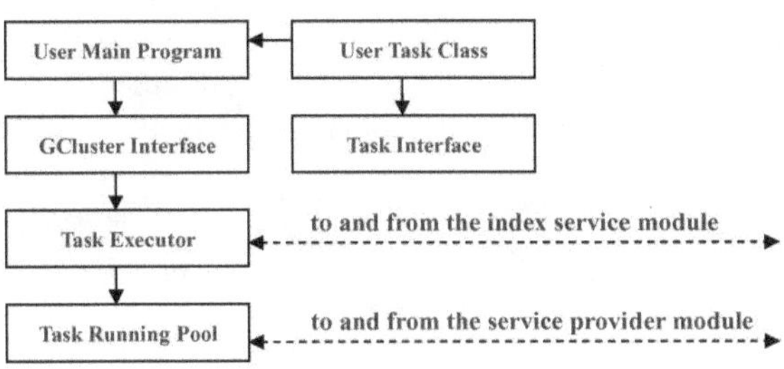

Fig. 4. Architecture of the Client Module in DPGS

The programmer uses the Task Interface to write his own task class, which can be treated as a MPICH program in traditional parallel program. The user's main program is a user customized java program, it can be of any form. To start run user's task, it uses the GCluster Interface to load and run user's task class. The GCluster Interface will then call the core running module to distribute and start the task. The core running module mainly includes the Task Executor which search for available service provider in the system and the Task Running Pool which contains all running tasks and monitor the tasks' status.

6 Communication in DPGS

Large File Transfer
Since the execution of computing tool will sometimes need large files for input or generate large result file, it will be a time consuming procedure to transfer these data files between nodes if they are transferred based on the SOAP. In order to accelerate the file transfer between nodes as well as between client and nodes, we adopt the GridFTP component of globus toolkit. The GridFTP is designed to support a secure and efficient third-party controlled file transfer between multiple ftp servers and as an improvement on normal ftp server, GridFTP is more effective than normal ftp.

And as GridFTP can support third-party transfer, we can control the data transfer between two computing nodes on the client side and this can simplize the data transfer control of our total system.

Communication and Synchronization
As a distributed programmable grid system, it is essential to support the communication between different tasks (nodes) if it wants to enable the user to coordinated use distributed computing resources. The communication between nodes in DPGS is implemented in three aspects.

For simple values, such as the options of command-line tools, are transferred based on the SOAP (Simple Object Access Protocol) and the message exchanging between different tasks is indirect that means the value transferred from one task to another is first transferred to the client and then sent to the target task. Surely, the client has encapsulated these procedures with interface and the procedure is transparent to the programmer.

For large files, as described in previous paragraph, we use GridFTP client to exchange data file between different nodes. Since the transfer time of large file may be very long, we make the data transfer function asynchronous. The task can call waitTransfer function to wait the transfer finished just before it wants to use the data file immediately. This can utilize the time of transfer to start other jobs.

But in some condition, when two tasks are running on the same site, the data transfer between these two tasks can be simplified. We only need to map a file name in one task to filename on another task.

Then how to synchronize between tasks? Firstly, we will tell how the multiple tasks of a job run in our grid system. The atom task in DPGS is the user's task class, when user submits the task class with the GCluster interface, we will instantiate the task class. For distributed program, there will multiple copies of the task's instance with different node identities and each copy of instance will have a corresponded running thread. Since the user has written different codes for different identities, then these copies will work differently. Since the actual computing tools are deployed in the service provider, the task thread will be thin loaded. Now you will see that the synchronization between different tasks is an easy way, because they are all threads and it is many way to synchronize between threads.

7 Example

In this section, we will show you how to solve an actual application with the support of DPGS.

Some application, such as gene sequence comparison, needs to process bulk size data. It is certain that we want to depart the origin data into several blocks and process the blocks distributed. Let us try to solve this problem in three ways.

Firstly, we use the MPICH-G2 to design a parallel program to complete this task. It is easy for MPI to do this job. We can read different blocks based on the process id retrieved from MPINUM variable. But as to reality, we know that MPICH program start one or more progress on each site, and off course the input data will be copied to the target node. When the input data is in bulk size, the copy of input data will take a very long time. On the other hand, the MPICH-g2 needs to know the computing tool's absolute path, but it is sometimes very incontinence in grid system.

For the alternate way, we use the UNICORE grid system to solve the problem. Since UNICORE provides a friendly user interface to create and submit workflows, we can easily to create such a workflow that has several parallel atom jobs which do one block of the input data. But since the workflow is not programmable, we should depart the input data into blocks at first. It reduces the convenience of UNICORE. So the lack of programmable interface makes the workflow mechanism not so universal in high performance computing.

Now you can see how DPGS make all these problems an easy task. Since the DPGS uses MPI-like interface GridPPI, we can design parallel problem just like we design with MPICH-G2. Different with the MPICH-G2, the parallel problem in DPGS runs only on the client machine and it only distributes the needed data to target service provider for data processing. In this way, the time of transferring input data is reduced to the least. More effectively, we can distribute the some blocks on different time, which means we can transfer data when some data is being processed. And we can balance the load of different site with the execution time of it. All this can be done is because the control of the parallel problem is on the client and the input data is one the client. Another, the computing tools is encapsulated in the DPGS, so the program designer does not need to know the absolute path of the computing tool.

From the above problem, we can see the DPGS can solve more universal problems and solve in a more effective way. A sample code for DNA Sequence Assembly (Cap3 is corresponding program) is as followings. We suppose that there are three Cap3 services available in DPGS. In our example, a DNA sequence is divided into three sub-sequences, and for each sub-sequence, corresponding assembly is completed at a real computing node through one Cap3 service call.

```
public class TestApp implements TaskListener {
 public ReceiveMessage(String msg){
  ... //user specified message show; }
 public static void main(String[] args){
  GCluster gcluster=GCluster.getInstance();
String[] hostlist=gcluster.FindService("ComputeService/Cap3");
  //find required service list.
  if (hostlist!=null&&hostlist.size()>0){
   TestApp app=new TestApp
   gcluster.Initialize(hostlist); //initialize the computing pool;
   int hostneeded=3;   //our task needs three real computing nodes;
   gcluster.Submit(hostneeded,"TestTask",app);
   //submit and begin to run the task;
   gcluster.Wait();  //wait until all the subtasks have finished;
   gcluster.Finalize();//finalize connection with the remote nodes;
  }
} class TestTask extends Task {
  public void run(){
  CString block,rblock;
  int sid,rid,eid;
  rid=0;
  int id=GetSubTaskId();  //get the suttask id;
  block=GetBlock(id);    //get the block file with the id;
  sid=AsySendFile(block);
  do{
   WaitTransfer(sid);
   eid=AsyExecute("cap3 "+block); //execute commands in non-blocked model;
   block=GetBlock(id);    //get next block to calculate;
   if (block!=null)
   { sid=AsySendFile(block); } //send file during the execution;
   WaitExecute(eid);//wait the execution to be over.
   rblock=GetResult();
   if (rid!=0)
       WaitTransfer(rid);  //wait the last block is received
   rid=AsyReceiveFile(rblock);
  }while(block!=null);
} }
```

8 Conclusion and Future Work

The DPGS aims at giving out a solution for user to program parallel program in grid system more easily. With this system, the user can coordinate use computing tools distributed over the internet to complete the complex scientific problem. In this paper, we describe how to construct and deploy such a grid system. By the support of GridPPI specification, we encapsulate different computing tools with uniform interface and let the tools can be accessed via grid service mechanism. On the base of globus toolkit, we have build a distributed, practical, high utilizable grid system, and the programmer can run their coarse-grained task-level parallel application over this grid system easily and achieve high performance.

For further work, we will emphases on more efficient resource selection and service selection. Currently, we let user to custom the selection strategy, but it is more reasonable to hide the selection of resource and services. For an expansion to the current system, we will research for more efficient resource selection strategy, for example, select the highest performance or lowest load resource. We will also more human readable resource selection approach, which means programmer can specify a service in a more flexible way.

References

1. Karl Czajkowski, Donald F Ferguson, Ian Foster, Jeffrey Frey. *The WS-Resource Framework*, 2004
2. Foster, I., Kesselman, C., Tuecke, S. *The Anatomy of the Grid: Enabling Scalable Virtual Organization*, International J. Supercomputer Applications, Vol. 15, No. 3, 2001
3. Foster, I., Kesselman, C. *The Physiology of the Grid: An Open Grid Services Architecture for Distributed Systems Integration*, http://www.globus.org/, 2002
4. Foster, I. *What is the Grid? A Three Point Checklist*, Grid Today, Vol. 1, No. 6, 2002
5. Yongwei Wu, Qing Wang, Guangwen Yang, Weiming Zheng. *Coarse-grained DistributedParallel Programming Interface for Grid Computing*, In proc. of Grid and Cooperative Computing, 2003
6. Tony Andrews, Francisco Curbera, Hitesh Dholakia, Yaron Goland, Johannes Klein, Frank Leymann, *Business Process Execution Language for Web Services*, 2003
7. Unicore "http://www.unicore.org/forum.htm"
8. China Grid Support Platform "http://www.chinagrid.edu.cn", 2004
9. Karonis, N., Toonen, B., Foster, I. *MPICH-G2: A Grid-Enabled Implementation of the Message Passing Interface*, Journal of Parallel and Distributed Computing, Vol. 63, No. 5, pp. 551–563, 2003
10. Nakada, H., Matsuoka, S., Seymour, K. *GridRPC: A Remote Procedure Call API for Grid Computing*, Lecture notes in computer science, Vol. 2536, pp. 274–278, 2002

Spatial Reasoning Based Spatial Data Mining for Precision Agriculture

Sheng-sheng Wang, Da-you Liu, Xin-ying Wang, and Jie Liu

Key Laboratory of Symbolic Computing and Knowledge Engineering of Ministry of Education, College of Computer Science and Technology, Institute of Mathematics, Jilin University, 130012 Changchun, China
wss@jlu.edu.cn, dyliu@jlu.edu.cn

Abstract. Knowledge discovery in spatial databases represents a particular case of discovery, allowing the discovery of relationships that exist between spatial and non-spatial data. Spatial reasoning ought to play a very important role in spatial data mining, but the research combined SR and SDM are very few. This paper describes the conception and implementation of SRSDM, the tool for data mining in spatial databases based on spatial reasoning method. Most spatial data mining systems only support topological relation, nearly all previous GIS and AI researches focused on single spatial aspect . Those were quite inadequate for practical applications. We propose a new spatial knowledge representation which integrates topology, direction, distance and size relations. SRSDM includes three parts: extracting spatial relations, frameworks for traditional or new data mining algorithms.

1 Introduction

Spatial Database are database systems for the management of spatial data[1]. Spatial data mining (SDM) is the extraction of interesting spatial patterns and features, general relationships that exist between spatial and non-spatial data, and other data characteristics not explicitly stored in spatial databases[2]. SDM has become one of imminent tasks, which need to be studied currently, because the amount of spatial data obtained from precision farming and other sources has been growing tremendously in recent years[4].

Spatial reasoning (SR) ought to play a very important role in spatial data mining, but the research combined SR and SDM are very few. Spatial reasoning has a wide variety of potential applications in AI and other fields [3][5].

In this paper, we a put forward a spatial reasoning based spatial data mining tool to discovery knowledge in precision agriculture spatial data. The following steps is the data processing flow of the system.

(1) Generating Spatial Relations

All the spatial relations are derived from spatial reasoning theory. There are two ways for generating spatial relations: One way is extracting from the spatial database through Spatial Relation Extract model, another is obtains directly form user interface.

H.T. Shen et al. (Eds.): APWeb 2006, LNCS 3842, pp. 506 – 510, 2006.

(2) Updating Spatial Relations

Using spatial reasoning method, adds new relations which can be deduced from existing relations, and deletes conflicted relations.

(3) Spatial Data Mining

All the spatial relations obtained above together with no-spatial data are sent to traditional data mining algorithms for discovering useful patterns.

Most spatial systems only support topological or direction , distance , size relation respectively. Nearly all previous GIS and AI researches focused on single spatial aspect . Those were quite inadequate for practical applications. Our system integrates four spatial aspects including topology, direction , distance and size.

2 Spatial Relation

Topological Relations

Topological relations are the most important spatial relations which have been studied most. The best known topological theory is Region Connection Calculus (RCC for short)[6]. RCC-8 is well-known in state-of-the-art Geographical Information System, spatial database, visual languages and other applied fields. {DC, EC, PO, TPP, NTPP, TPPI, NTPPI, EQ} are Jointly Exhaustive and Pairwise Disjoint (JEPD) basic relations of RCC-8 deduced by C(x,y).

Direction Relations

To process spatial relations other than topology for objects in a uniform framework, multi-dimensional objects are represented by an abstract point (the geometric center of the object). Space is equivalent divided into four parts by two lines across the reference object. {N,S,W,E,C} are the basic direction relations. Here x {C} y means the geometric centers of object x and y are at the same position, otherwise {N,S,W,E} are the four areas that the object related to the reference object may exist. The two lines expect the point 'C' belong to 'N' and 'S' area.

Distance Relations

Distance is also an important spatial aspect in both qualitative and metric space. Similar to direction our distance model is also depended on the geometric center.

Three basic qualitative distance relations are defined as :

Cnt : x and y are topological connected.

Near: Geometric center distance of x and y is less than or equal to L (a constant value).

Far: Geometric center distance of x and y is more than L.

Size Relations

We assume that all the spatial regions are measurable sets in R^n. The size of an n-dimensional region corresponds to its n-dimensional measure. For example, the size of a sphere in R^2 corresponds to its area. The size relation of two objects can be qualitative represented by three basic relations {<,=,>}, and they could be further extended to {∅ ,<,=,>,≤,≥,≠,*}.

Updating Spatial Relations

All kinds of qualitative spatial relation are some kinds of abstracts of metric geometry interrelations of two objects. So they are inherently interdependent. Considering all the possibility, interdependences of every two spatial aspects are discussed in [9].

3 Spatial Data Mining Tool

Spatial Reasoning Based Spatial Data Mining (SRSDM) is a system based on qualitative spatial reasoning. This section presents its architecture and gives some technical details about its implementation.

After extracting and updating spatial relations, traditional data mining algorithms are performed and applied in precision agriculture. All the spatial relations obtained above together with no-spatial data are sent to traditional data mining algorithms for discovering useful patterns.

Since the spatial relations have been preprocessed , they can be treated as normal data. The core data mining algorithms of SRSDM are the traditional algorithms such as ID3 and STING. The SRSDM also has open interface for adding new algorithms.

The architecture of SRSDM aggregates three main components: Knowledge and Data Repository, Data Analysis and Results Visualization. The Knowledge and Data Repository component stores the data and knowledge needed in the knowledge discovery process. This process is implemented in the Data Analysis component, which allows the discovery of patterns or others relationships implicit in the analyzed geographic and non-geographic data. The discovered patterns can be visualized in a map using the Results Visualization component. These components are afterwards described.

The Knowledge and Data Repository component group three central databases:

1. A Geographic Database (GDB) constructed based on spatial data middleware MapXtreme. The geographic identifiers system was integrated with a spatial schema allowing the definition of the direction, distance ,size and topological spatial relations that exist between the adjacent regions of the municipality level.
2. A Spatial Knowledge Base (SKB) that stores all the composition table and can perform Updating Spatial Relations Algorithm.
3. A non-Geographic Database (nGDB) that is integrated with the GDB and analyzed in the Data Analysis component. This procedure enables the discovery of implicit relationships that exist between the geographic and non-geographic data.

The Data Analysis component is implemented through the knowledge discovery module, and is characterized by six main steps:

1. Data Selection. This step allows the selection of the relevant non-geographic and geo-spatial data needed for the execution of a defined data-mining task.
2. Data Treatment. This phase is concerned with the cleaning of the selected data, allowing the corrupt data treatment and the definition of strategies for dealing with missing data fields.
3. Data Pre-Processing. This step allows the reduction of the sample set to be analyzed.

4. Geo-Spatial Information Processing. This step verifies if the geo-spatial information needed is available in the GDB.
5. Data Mining. Several algorithms , including association rule mining, classification, clustering ,can be used for the execution of a given data mining task. In this step, the several available algorithms are evaluated in order to identify the most appropriate for the defined task. The selected one is applied to the relevant non-geographic and geo-spatial data, in order to find implicit relationships or other interesting patterns that exist between them.
6. Results Interpretation. The interpretation of the discovered patterns aims to evaluate their utility and importance to the application domain.

The Results Visualization component is responsible for the management of the discovered patterns and its visualization in a map. For that, SRSDM uses a Geographic Information System (GIS), integrating the discovered patterns with the cartography of the analyzed region. This component aggregates two main databases:

1. The Patterns Database (PDB) that stores all relevant discoveries. In this database, each discovery is catalogued and associated with the set of rules that represents the discoveries made in a given data mining task.
2. A Cartographic Database (CDB) with the cartography of the region. It aggregates a set of points, lines and polygons with the geometry of the geographical objects.

We perform a spatial data mining tool SRSDM for agricultural practices. SRSDM is applied to agrarian spatial database of Nongan county (located in Jilin Province , China). In Nongan county, soil sampling is performed to gather and manage agrarian in-formation every year from 1997. The soil sample data contains one hundred or so fields including nutrient concentrations (such as nitrogen, phosphor, kalium), meteorologic data(such as rainfall, air temperature, humidity) ,organic matter, agrotype, breed, yield etc. . Each soil sample data was combined with time and location. Mobile GPS devices were used to locate the sample points. This project is supported by Chinese National “863” Project.

4 Conclusion

Contributions of this paper are:

(1) Proposes a new qualitative spatial relation model which compose topology , direction, distance and size.
(2) Describes the conception and implementation of SRSDM, a system for data mining in spatial databases. SRSDM presents a new approach to this process, which is based on qualitative spatial reasoning. SRSDM is applied in precision agriculture.

Acknowledgments

Our work is supported by NSFC of China Major Research Program 60496321, Basic Theory and Core Techniques of Non Canonical Knowledge; National Natural Science

Foundation of China under Grant Nos. 60373098, 60173006, the National High-Tech Research and Development Plan of China under Grant No.2003AA118020, the Major Program of Science and Technology Development Plan of Jilin Province under Grant No. 20020303, the Science and Technology Development Plan of Jilin Province under Grant No. 20030523,Youth Foundation of Jilin University (419070100102).

References

1. Gueting, R.H. 1994. An Introduction to Spatial Database Systems. VLDB Journal 3(4).
2. Koperski, K. and J. Han (1995): Discovery of Spatial Association Rules in Geographic Information Systems, Proceedings. 4th International Symposium on Large Spatial Databases (SSD95), Maine, 47-66.
3. A.G.Cohn and S.M. Hazarika, Qualitative Spatial Representation and Reasoning: An Overview , Fundamental Informatics , 2001,46 (1-2),pages 1-29
4. Brecheisen S., Kriegel H.-P.,Kröger P., Pfeifle M.: Visually Mining Through Cluster Hierarchies, Proc. SIAM Int. Conf. on Data Mining (SDM'04), Lake Buena Vista, FL, 2004, pp. 400-412.
5. M.Teresa Escrig, Francisco Toledo, Qualitative Spatial Reasoning: Theory and Practice, Ohmsha published,1999,pages 17-43
6. Cohn, Z. Cui, and D. Randell, "A spatial logic based on regions and connection," Proc. Third International Conference on Principles of Knowledge Representation and Reasoning(KR '92), 1992
7. Alfonso Gerevini, Jochen Renz, Combining topological and size information for spatial reasoning, Artificial Intelligence 137 (2002) 1–42
8. M. Vilain, H.A. Kautz, P. van Beek, Constraint propagation algorithms for temporal reasoning: A revised report, in: D.SWeld, J. de Kleer (Eds.), Readings in Qualitative Reasoning about Physical Systems, Morgan Kaufmann, San Mateo, CA, 1990, pp. 373–381.
9. Sheng-sheng WANG, Da-you LIU , Spatial Query Preprocessing in Distributed GIS, GCC 2004 LNCS3251, 737~744

Distributed Group Membership Algorithm in Intrusion-Tolerant System

Li-hua Yin, Bin-xing Fang, and Xiang-zhan Yu

Research Center of Computer Network and Information Security Technology,
Harbin Institute of Technology, Harbin 150001
yinlh@hit.edu.cn

Abstract. Intrusion tolerance is capability of Internet systems withstanding attacks and intrusions under unsafe environment. This paper presents the architecture of an intrusion tolerant system using group communication. A distributed group membership algorithm is described which introduces a strategy *detecting failure in local servers and announcing them to remote servers* to avoid the side effects of remote failure detection. The paper also points out that stability of failure detector is a necessary condition but not sufficient condition of algorithm cease. On analyzing the essential of block, block detection and avoidance mechanism is designed. Finally, we have developed a group membership prototype system on WAN condition. Experiment results show the algorithm has well performance in complicated Internet condition.

1 Introduction

Information systems have become distributed including large number of computers interconnected by communication networks. Critical information systems demand to provide continuous service with 7 Day 24 Hours. Once compromises and failures are happened, they will conduce to not only services broken down but also huge losses in financial and time. So systems are required high dependability.

Intrusion tolerance is a capability of keeping systems working correctly despite existing faults (accidental or malicious). It assumes that systems are vulnerable in a certain extent and attacks on components can happen and some will be successful; but ensures the overall system remains secure and operational [1].

Traditional technology separates tolerant process into four steps and the whole process is complicated to actualize and manage. Group communication[2] can provide multicast service with multifarious message and group membership service. That makes multi-communication simple and easy to manage.

Assume process of system accords with request/response model. Clients send requests to servers and servers deal with the requests and send responses to clients. Servers are important components of system that we pay attentions on them to tolerate intrusions. Group membership service provides member management and failure detection[3] and combines resource replication, failure response and recovery together[4]. Considering the characteristic of WAN, we devise a tolerance layer in the

H.T. Shen et al. (Eds.): APWeb 2006, LNCS 3842, pp. 511 – 515, 2006.

system, which separates message communication from group membership completely logically and physically.

Group membership algorithm is implemented in distributed special servers. Each server takes charge of local clients/member's request in LAN and servers exchange member messages among them. Distributed C/S frame is adopted[5] which is *detecting failure in local server and announcing them to remote servers.* executes in every LAN where clients are. Special failure detection servers (FDS) monitor all the local clients and FDSes exchange messages via a special channel.

2 Description of Group Membership Algorithm

View consistency is the most fundamental function and the essence of consistency is consensus. Traditional consensus algorithm requires a three phase commit protocol:

1. Preparation Phase, with an initiator proposes a new proposal to other processes.
2. Ready Phase, all followers respond with the proposal and ready to commit.
3. Commit Phase, all processes commit their proposals. If they agree on the new view, the commit phase is on successful transactions or it fails.

Preparation phase is kernel of consensus. Means of messages dissemination and collection determines actions of subsequent phase. There are three kinds of consensus algorithm, which are broadcast-based and coordinator-based and ring-based.

2.1 Fast Agreement Algorithm

Broadcast-based algorithm is a symmetric distributed algorithm. All processes have equal status that the relation of them is initiators and followers not masters and slaves. Initiator broadcasts its proposal and waits for other processes' proposals. Followers compute their proposals after receiving a proposal and broadcast them. Each process judges by itself whether the proposals are consistent.

Assume communication among servers and FDSes is reliable FIFO order. For example, client A joins into group G, steps are described below (shown by Fig. 1):

1. Client A sends JOIN message to local group membership server 1.
2. Server 1 broadcasts NOTIFY message to server 2 and delivers CHANGE message to client A. Server 2 delivers CHANGE message to its local client B after receiving NOTIFY message.

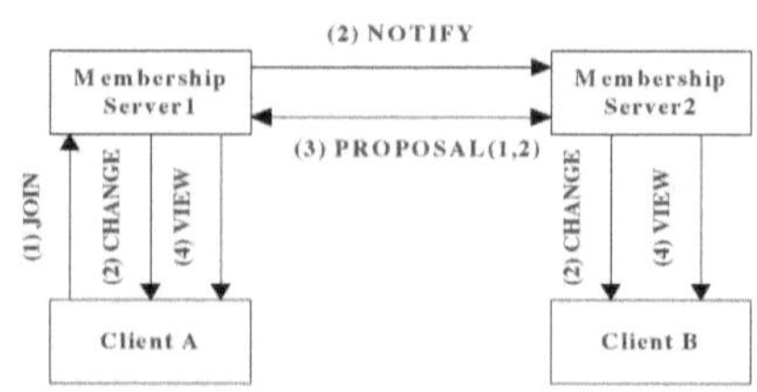

Fig. 1. Sketch map of the group membership service algorithm

3. Server 1 and 2 initiate membership algorithm and broadcast PROPOSAL.
4. Servers deliver VIEW message to client A and B respectively when all servers' PROPOSAL messages are consistent.

Algorithm is event-driven and functions are implemented when messages arrived. Group views, which includes in PROPOSAL messages, are used to check consistency. Each server holds up-to-date proposals of all servers in proposal buffer. Proposal buffer will be emptied after achieving consistency.

The process of member servers receiving NOTIFY message is similar to that of local JOIN event except extracting contents of NOTIFY message firstly. Variable *start_change_num* in PROPOSAL messages is used to compute view ID to assure the sequence of view identifier.

2.2 Cease Condition of Algorithm

The failure detectors are based on time-out mechanism and they monitor local clients and other remote servers at the same time. Algorithm applies trust strategy for local failure detection. As shown in Fig. 1, if Membership Server 1 (MS1) suspects Client A has a failure, the process of MS1 is similar to that of A asks for leaving the group. For remote servers' detection, algorithm applies distrust strategy because stability of links is worse and probability of reporting failure caused by unstable link is large.

Due to the inherent issue of remote failure detector, algorithm only assures that *it will cease and achieve consistency when failure detector is stable*. Stability of failure detector is defined: Failure detector is stable in member set S of group G, if exists time t_0, when $t > t_0$, the local view of all membership servers of G is set S.

Definition above requires failure detector keeping stable after t_0. But failure detector is only required keeping stable long enough to complete algorithm in actual systems. It can be proved that stability of failure detector is a necessary condition but not sufficient condition of algorithm cease.

2.3 Block Detection and Avoidance

Suppose SS is a set of group membership servers, which serve group G, CS is a set of group membership after failure detector was stable. Before stability of failure detector, the last *proposal* produced by s is $last_s$. Then $last_s.members$ = CS. Reliable link assures any server, s' ($s' \in$SS, $s' \neq s$), can receive $last_s$. If all s' use $last_s$ and their own proposal $last_{s'}$, the view achieves consistency and algorithm will not block.

If block has happened, then exist servers s and s' ($s' \in$SS, $s' \neq s$) do not use $last_s$ and $last_{s'}$ synchronously.

- s uses its own $last_s$ before receiving $last_{s'}$, namely s achieves consistency using $last_s$ and a certain proposal before $last_{s'}$. Algorithm is not start when s receives $last_{s'}$, so s' is blocked.
- s uses $last_{s'}$ before sending its own $last_s$, namely s achieves consistency using $last_{s'}$ and a certain proposal before $last_s$. And then s sends $last_s$ and s' achieves consistency using $last_s$, so s is blocked.

That is to say, if proposals are dissynchronous, block is produced and it must happen to the sender. Our attention is only on dissynchronous of proposals which have the same content. Algorithm is divided into two parts: Fast Agreement algorithm (FA) and Slow Agreement algorithm (SA). SA is implemented when a block is detected and it makes servers achieve consistency. After receiving each proposal, servers check whether a block is produced to determine sending proposal or not.

- If server *s* achieves consistency using its own $last_s$ and afterward it receives $last_{s'}$, algorithm is not start when *s* receives $last_{s'}$, so s detects a block.
- If server *s* achieves consistency using $last_{s'}$ and afterward sending its own $last_s$, when s' receives $last_s$, it finds that its proposal ID is the same used by *s* to achieve consistency last time, so s' detects a block.

To avoid block, algorithm resynchronize proposals of servers when a block is detected. If *s* detects a block, it starts SA algorithm sending proposal using a new ID, or it follows. It can be proved that detection mechanism can detect all possible blocks and block avoidance algorithm cease correctly if it is started.

3 Experiment Results and Analysis

We accomplish a prototype of group membership and experiment it on WAN testbed. Algorithm (coded in C++ language) is executed on ShuGuang servers, which has Intel Pentium III 1GHz CPU and 512M Memory. Operate system on it is Red Hat Linux 7.1.2.96-98 with gcc version 2.96. We select three same servers in Heilongjiang, Hainan and Xinjiang named HLJ, HN and XJ respectively.

Clients are simulated with multi-thread program and each thread served as a client in LAN. Each client executes JOIN and LEAVE operation in a group selected from 10 groups. Number of clients is adjustable. The metric of experiments is below:

1. Total number of local events: reveal times of requests that clients send.
2. Total number of views: number of views that algorithm achieves consistency replying external events.
3. Total number of SA views: reveal times of block avoidance algorithm started.
4. Spending time of algorithm: duration of algorithm from unexecuted state to next unexecuted state resulted in local events.

Firstly, gentle test is done that there are 3 clients in each site and duration of requests is 5-10s for each client. Results are shown in Table 1 and Fig. 2(a). Number of SA views all is 0, namely, block avoidance algorithm is not started. For instance with HLJ, local events deliver 1227 views totally. There are 1189 events' spending time between 70ms and 150ms and that is 97.5% of total events.

Table 1. Results of gentle test and stormy test

	Gentle test			Stormy test		
	Local events	Views	SA views	Local events	Views	SA views
HLJ	1227	3664	0	56556	157266	85
XJ	1226	3659	0	56440	156241	88
HN	1226	3661	0	56634	157163	88

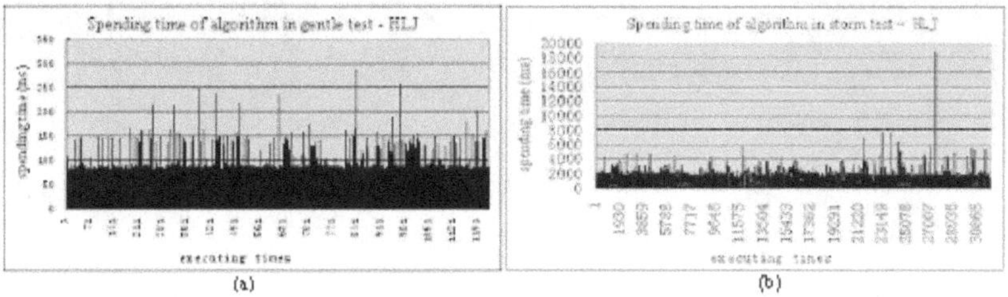

Fig. 2. Spending time of group membership algorithm - HLJ

For network is stable and gentle test cannot examine the capacity of algorithm, stormy test is done that clients' request speed is increased and test time is prolonged. The duration of requests is 1-5s for each client and the test is nearly kept on 15 hours. Results are shown in Table 1 and Fig. 2(b).

Consistent views are increased very quickly in stormy test. And SA views are produced all three servers but they are very small proportion that is less than 0.1% of all. Most of events complete in 2 seconds and few spend more than 4 seconds. As an example with HLJ, algorithm starts 53702 times caused by local events (only shows 32000 times). There are 52954 executions within 2 seconds that is 98.6% of all and 53631 executions within 4 seconds that is 99.9% of all. Analysis of results indicates that algorithm has a well performance even though running in complicated Internet.

4 Conclusion

The paper presents the architecture of an intrusion tolerant system and a distributed group membership algorithm is described which introduces *local failure detection and remote announcement* strategy. The paper also describes cease condition of algorithm in detail and points out that stability of failure detector is a necessary condition but not sufficient condition of algorithm cease. On analyzing the essential of block, we design block detection and avoidance mechanism.

Finally, we have developed a group membership prototype on WAN. Experiment results show that the algorithm has a well performance to implement in complicated Internet condition. It helps to establish intrusion tolerant system in wide area network.

References

1. Pal P, Webber F, Schantz R et al. Survival by Defense- Enabling. Proceedings of the New Security Paradigms Workshop 2001, New Mexico: ACM Press, 2001. 71-78
2. Birman K. The Process Group Approach to Reliable Distributed Computing. Communications of the ACM, 1993, 36 (12): 37-53
3. Défago X, Hayashibara N, Katayama T. On the design of a failure detection service for large scale distributed systems. Proc of the PBit 2003, Japan: A&I Ltd, 2003. 88-95
4. Chockler G V., Keidar I, and Vitenberg R: Group Communication Specifications: A Comprehensive Study. In ACM Computing Surveys 33(4), pages 1-43, December 2001
5. Keidar I, Sussman J, Marzullo K et al. Moshe: A Group Membership Service for WANs. ACM Transactions on Computer Systems (TOCS), 2002, 20(3): 191-238

Radio Frequency Identification (RFID) Based Reliable Applications for Enterprise Grid*

Feilong Tang[1], Minglu Li[1], Xinhua Yang[2], Yi Wang[1], Hongyu Huang[1], and Hongzi Zhu[1]

[1] Department of Computer Science and Engineering, Shanghai Jiao Tong University, Shanghai 200030, China
tang-fl@cs.sjtu.edu.cn
[2] Software Technology Institute, Dalian Jiao Tong University, China

Abstract. Radio frequency identification (RFID) provides a quick, flexible, and reliable electronic means to detect, identify, track, and manage a variety of items. It has the potential to significantly alter how processes occur and how companies operate. Currently, the development of RFID and Grid technologies has opened the door to many new RFID applications, many of which require transaction support. This paper proposes a transaction commit protocol which can ensure reliable execution of RFID applications in Grid environment, and a transaction compensating approach to undo committed sub-transactions. Reliable RFID applications can be realized by the proposed protocol effectively.

1 Introduction

Radio frequency identification (RFID) is becoming a hot spot in wireless industry [1]. Using an RFID tag, it is much easier for companies to track their products from manufacturers to consumers in order to reduce labor levels, enhance visibility and improve inventory management. RFID is a varied collection of technical approaches for many applications across a wide range of industries. For supply chain management (SCM), automatic identification, inventory management and control, and overall business process improvement, RFID has proven to be a powerful solution in both public and private sector projects. RFID technology overcomes the limitations of other automatic identification approaches that use light to communicate, such as bar codes and infrared technology, because a tag may be hidden or invisible to the eye and can be used in harsh or dirty environments. Generally speaking, by comparison with other identification technologies, RFID has following advantages that: (1) it does not require the transponder to

* This paper is supported by 973 Program of China (2002CB312002), National Natural Science Foundation of China(60473092, 60433040), Natural Science Foundation of Shanghai (05ZR14081), ChinaGrid of MOE of China, and ShanghaiGrid grand project of Science and Technology Commission of Shanghai Municipality (03DZ15027, 05DZ15005).

H.T. Shen et al. (Eds.): APWeb 2006, LNCS 3842, pp. 516–524, 2006.

be in line-of-sight so that items do not need to be located at particular orientation for scanning. (2) it can work in bad environments like moisture, dirt, frost etc, and (3) multiple tag identification is possible[2].

Nowadays, enterprises are under the pressure of the competition of the global market. Therefore, it is important to manage business process to achieve the maximum productivity. SCM usually is used to optimize supply chain processes in order to achieve minimal cost and maximal profit for enterprises. In a SCM process, it is essential that participants get item information such as location of items in time and accurately. Traditional methods for inventory and asset management are not well suited to today's evolving supply chain. RFID technology has opened the door to a new era in SCM, unachievable using existing barcode technology, because it allows products to be followed in real-time way by providing accurate and detailed information on all items and allowing organizations to use this information to increase efficiency. Leading corporations have recognized the intrinsic advantages of RFID and recently moved to introduce the technology in SCM by establishing a mandate, forcing suppliers to use RFID as well. Moreover, RFID readers can communicate to tags in milliseconds and have the ability to scan multiple items simultaneously, enabling the automation of many SCM tasks. Thus, the SCM will possibly be one of the most important applications of RFID technology. It is forecasted that by 2005, the SCM will be the most widely adopted application in RFID industry and enjoy the most share in the market [3,4].

The SCM process often requires reliable execution, keeping the system consistency free from failures and other concurrent activities. It is necessary that if some parts of a supply chain fail others have to change their actions accordingly, which can be supported by transaction processing technology because the transaction is an effective means to tolerate faults. In general, a supply chain in Grid environment is a long-lived and complex interaction process, involving multiple autonomic parties and accessing to multiple Grid resources under the control of different organizations and management policies.

This paper proposes a long-lived transaction coordination protocol, whose main advantage is to automate the business process so as to hide users from complex details, to support reliable SCM based on RFID technology in Grid environment.

2 Related Work

2.1 RFID

Recent technological developments have opened the door to many new RFID applications. However, few researches focus on reliable RFID technology in Grid environment. Existing efforts mainly solved how to construct RFID systems and reduce the cost of the RFID tag, and analyzed which features RFID has and to which fields RFID can apply.

A distributed framework for ubiquitous Physical Object Tracking and a new protocol based on RFID tags was proposed in [5]. The architecture harnessed

RFID technology to provide absolute visibility and control over inter-organizational transactions and thereby enable real time tracking. The protocol tracks the location of the physical objects as they pass through transactions. Thus, this ubiquitous deployment of RFID based object tags and automated identification and tracking can circumvent the delays and errors due to human intervention.

[3] introduced the RFID system architecture and components, discussed the application scenarios and standards. It presented that a complete RFID system is composed of three parts: base station, transponder and the communication interfaces.

Li et al. [6] proposed a Mobile Healthcare Service (MHS) System, a platform that uses RFID technologies and mobile devices for positioning and identifying persons and objects both for inside and outside hospital when disease takes place, to shorten the tracking time and increase the accuracy of infection control. Based on the applications for SARS (Severe Acute Respiratory Syndrome) Infection Control Precautions, this system demonstrates how to receive patient's location and bio-information by using RFID technology for hospital and government to react a real-time infection control measures from the auditing mechanism among isolated patients in households or residential settings. Also, this model provides the possibility to bring medicare service becoming ubiquitous crossing geographic barriers and enable medical information technology from e-Medicare to m-Medicare for future development in medical industry.

2.2 Transaction Processing

Distributed transaction processing (DTP) and object transaction service (OTS) are widely used in the traditional distributed environment. DTP defines three kinds of roles, Application Program, Transaction Manager and Resource Manager, and two types of interfaces, TX and XA interfaces. These two models do not release the locked resources until the end of a global transaction, thus are not impracticable to coordinating long-lived transactions.

WS-Coordination (WS-C) and WS-Transaction (WS-T) [7,8] provide a set of transaction specifications for Web Services. WS-C describes a transaction framework comprising Activation Service, Registration Service and Protocol Service. It can accommodate multiple coordination protocols. WS-T classifies transactions in the Web Services environment into atomic transactions and business activities, and defines the corresponding coordination protocols. Business Transaction Protocol (BTP)[9] is another important service-oriented transaction specification that defines a conceptional model and a set of complex messages to be exchanged between a coordinator and participants, specifies how to interact between Web services.

3 A Brief Review of RFID

The RFID system consists of Tag, Reader, Transponder and application systems. The Electronic Product Code (EPC) is stored on the tag. Tags

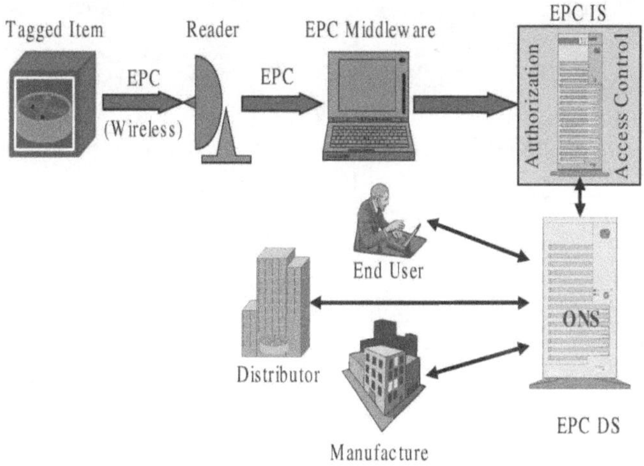

Fig. 1. EPCglobal network based on RFID

communicate their EPCs to Readers using radio frequency identification. Readers communicate with Tags via radio waves and deliver information to local business information systems[10,11].

EPC is the next generation of product identification [12]. Unlike the current numbering schemes used in commerce, the EPC uses an extra set of digits, a serial number, to uniquely identify all items so that it provides the ability to track and trace every item anywhere in the supply chain. An EPC number consists of four parts: (1) header, which identifies the length, type, structure, version and generation of EPC, (2) manager number, which identifies the manufacturer of a product, (3) object class, which identifies the product class, and (4) serial number, which is the specific and unique number to each item.

EPCglobal network built upon a stack of technologies and components is a form of RFID applications. It enables trading partners in the global supply chain to collect and communicate dynamical information about the movement of individual items. Dynamical information conveys data specific to and variable for an individual instance of an object, divided into Instance Data (e.g., serial number of a product) and History Data (e.g., arrival and departure time). EPCglobal network eliminates human errors by reading the EPC of items automatically, and can dramatically improve efficiencies of the supply chain by tracking and tracing every item anywhere securely and in real-time. Fig. 1 depicts the core components of EPC network [13]. The item is tagged with an EPC tag. The reader reads the EPC code of the item remotely and wirelessly. The unique EPC of the tagged item is then transferred through the EPC Middleware to the EPC Information Services (EPC IS) that are used to exchange the EPC-related data with other trading partners. The end user uses the EPC Discovery Services (EPC DS) to track and trace the movement status of the physical goods. The core component of the EPC DS is the Object Naming Services (ONS) that connect the unique EPC to the EPC IS, where the product information of the item can be found.

4 Coordination of Reliable SCM Process Based on RFID

4.1 Problem Presentation

Consider a supply chain process to illustrate what is needed. A client purchases a set of computers so that he simultaneously orders a car for shipment and hires a warehouse for storing these computers. This activity can be represented as three sub-tasks and each sub-task is performed by a Grid service, as shown in Fig. 2. Each computer is attached an unique RFID tag and three service providers have their own RFID readers. Using RFID technology, the client can track the status of the computers: purchased from a manufacturer, shipped by the car or stored in the warehouse, and then confirm or cancel actions taken previously. The essential requirements are

- the activity completes only if all the three sub-tasks successfully execute. If any sub-task fails, the client either contacts with other substitute service to perform missing work or aborts the activity by compensating other committed sub-task(s).
- the three sub-tasks complete independently.

As a result, such an activity can be handled as a long-lived transaction which satisfies above two requirements.

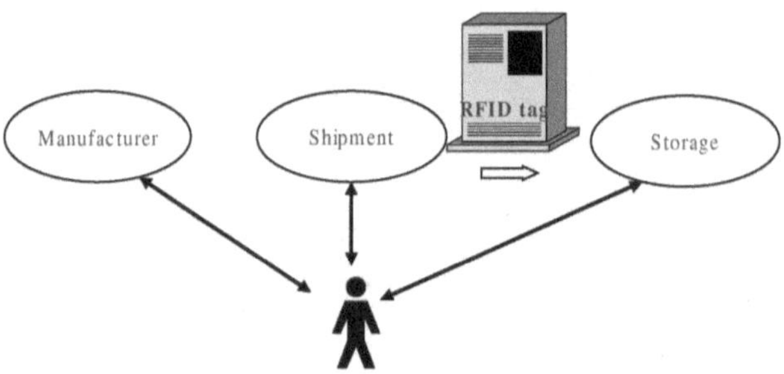

Fig. 2. An supply chain activity based on RFID technology

4.2 Transaction Model

Definition 1. A long-lived Grid transaction (LGT) is a 4-tuple {T,D,S,R}, where T={T_1, T_2,..., T_n} is the set of sub-transactions, D is the set of data operated by the transaction, S is the set of states, and R is the set of the dependency relationship between states [16,17,18].

Sub-transactions T_1, T_2,..., T_n of a LGT may further be divided until they become basic atomic transactions. To adapt to the requirement of loose coupling and the autonomy of Grid services, a long-lived Grid transaction relaxes: (1) atomicity. Instead of discarding all changes, a LGT may commit some sub-transactions and cancel the rest. (2) isolation. In a LGT, each sub-transaction can commit and release accessed resources before the global transaction finishes.

In Grid environment, transaction management is extremely challenging because of following factors:

- long-lived transaction. Execution of a transaction often takes a long time due to business latency or/and user interaction, which makes it infeasible to lock the resources.
- heterogeneity and loosely coupling. Grid technologies focus on sharing dynamic, cross-organizational resources, where their hardware and software may be extremely different from each other. Therefore, resources are coupled in loose way.
- failure. Both network nodes and communication links may fail. Thus, transaction must have the ability to recover from various failures.

Coordination of the LGT adopts following basic policies:

- participants independently commit sub-transactions,
- the coordinator can determine to confirm or cancel some committed sub-transactions within a given time T, and
- if some participants fail to commit or do not join, the global transaction can carry on by locating new participants.

4.3 Commit Protocol

A transaction service that consists of a coordinator and participant performs the following commit protocol.

Initiation of a LGT. For remote Grid services to join in a transaction, the transaction service sends CoordinationContext (CC) messages to them. The CC message includes necessary information to create a transaction, including transaction type, transaction identifier, coordinator address and expires. Each participant returns a Response message to the coordinator.

Participants Commit Independently. A coordinator sends Enroll messages to all participants. The latter reserves and allocates resources, records operations in the log, then directly commits the sub-transaction. If successful, each participant generates compensating transaction and returns a Committed message, which contain execution results, to the coordinator. Otherwise, it automatically rollbacks operations taken previously, returns Aborted message, and is removed from the transaction.

Confirmation of a User. According to returned results, the user may take either action through the coordinator:

- For successfully committed participants, the user confirms some and cancels the others by sending Confirm and Cancel messages to them respectively, within T.
- For failed participants, the user need not reply them and may renew to locate new participants.

Confirmation of Successful Participants. Within T, if a participant receives a Confirm message, it responds a Confirmed message. Otherwise, it executes a compensating transaction to undo the effects of the commit of the sub-transaction.

4.4 Transaction Compensation

Compensating transaction semantically undoes the effects of committed sub-transactions. In the LGT, each sub-transaction associates with a compensating transaction. If a user cancels a committed sub-transaction, the coordination protocol invokes corresponding compensating transaction to recover system to the consistent state before the sub-transaction commits. Compensating transaction may maintain the system integrity, without having to cancel other sub-transactions.

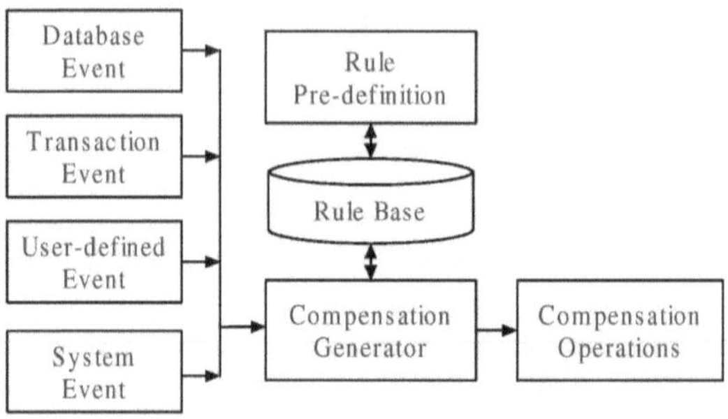

Fig. 3. Generation of compensating transaction

Generation of Compensating Operations. Generation of compensation transaction adopts event-driven mechanism. Only operations that affect data value or states of an application system need to generate corresponding compensating operations. The events include:

- modification of data, such as update, insert and delete operations.
- coordination of transaction, such as Begin, Enroll messages.
- compensating actions defined by a user.
- system event, such as restarting a system.

Compensating operations are generated in the execution process of a sub-transaction. When pre-defined events occur, the transaction service creates compensating operations in a reverse order according to compensation rules. If the sub-transaction fails, all the compensating operations generated previously will be abandoned. When the sub-transaction commits, the Enroll message drives the transaction service to encapsulate all compensating operations into a compensating transaction. As shown in Fig. 3, the Rule Pre-definition interface is used to set compensating rules. It provides following methods:

setCompensatingRule (): set compensating rules for a Grid service.
getCompensatingRule (): get compensating rules of a Grid service.

Generation and Execution of Compensating Transactions. Generation of compensating transaction involves following procedures:

- By Rule Pre-definition interface, providers of Grid services set up the generation rules of compensating operation.
- According to specified rules, which are stored in Rule Base, the transaction service automatically generates compensating operations in the execution of sub-transaction.
- When the sub-transaction commits, the transaction service encapsulates the compensating operations generated previously into a compensating transaction.

In processing a LGT, both Cancel message and timeout signal startup corresponding compensating transaction.

4.5 Security Solution

Different from traditional distributed system, in the Grid environment, a transaction may involve to access to many remote resources, while different resources often are controlled under different organizations and policies. To ensure the security of transaction, it is necessary to implement the mutual authentication in a convenient way, and then determine whether the user is authorized to request the resource based on some local policies. We use GSI [14,15] to address these issues. The security solution works like this:

- Authentication. It first creates a proxy credential signed by user's private key by using a user proxy. The GSI checks the user's identity using its authentication algorithm which is defined by secure socket layer protocol.
- Authorization. The service maps the proxy credential into local user name by using text-based map file, then checks local policy to determine whether the user is allowed to access its local resources. If user is authorized, the service allocates a credential C_p to create a process that accesses the resources.
- Delegation. For user to access other remote resources, process credential C_p is promulgated on behalf of user. By tracing back along the certificate chain to check the original user certificate, processes started on separate sites by the same user can authenticate one another, enabling user to sign once, run anywhere.
- Encryption. It implements communication protection by using SSL.

5 Conclusions and Future Work

RFID is the new trends of technology development and application in the big area of e-logistics and supply chain. Since China has become the world of product manufacturing and supply, adoption of these new technologies is important to upgrade the infrastructure of logistics and supply chain. This paper has presented a long-lived transaction commit protocol which can support for reliable execution of RFID applications in Grid environment. Main advantage of the model is to automate business process so as to hide users from complex details. We can easily foresee that more research effort will be directed to these new directions.

References

1. C. Atock. Where is my stuff. Manufactory Engineer. Vol. 82, 2003. pp. 24-27.
2. K.V.S. Rao. An overview of backscattered radio frequency identification system (RFID). Microwave Conference. Volume: 3 , 30 Nov.-3 Dec. 1999. pp. 746 - 749.
3. T.Flor, W.Niess and G. Vogler. RFID: the integration of contactless identification technology and mobile computing. Proceedings of the 7th International Conference on Telecommunications. Volume: 2 , June 11-13, 2003. pp. 619 - 623.
4. K. Michael, L. McCathie. The Pros and Cons of RFID in Supply Chain Management. Proceedings of International Conference on Mobile Business, July 2005, pp:623 - 629.
5. P. De, K. Basu, and S.K. Das. An ubiquitous architectural framework and protocol for object tracking using RFID tags. The First Annual International Conference on Mobile and Ubiquitous Systems: Networking and Services, Aug. 22-26, 2004. pp. 174 - 182.
6. C. J. Li, L. Liu, S. Z. Chen et al.. Mobile healthcare service system using RFID. IEEE International Conference on Networking, Sensing and Control, Volume 2 , March 21-23, 2004. pp. 1014 - 1019.
7. F. Cabrera, G. Copeland, T. Freund et al., Web Services Coordination(WS- Coordination). August, 2002. http://www.ibm.com/developerworks/library/ws- coor/.
8. F. Cabrera, G. Copeland, B. Cox et al., Web Services Transaction (WS-Transaction). August, 2002. http://www.ibm.com/developerworks/library/wstranspec/.
9. S. Dalal, S. Temel, M. Little, M. Potts and J. Webber, Coordinating Business Transactions on the Web. IEEE Internet Computing, Volume 7, Issue 1 , Jan.-Feb. 2003. pp. 30 - 39.
10. F. Zhou, C. H. Chen, D.W Jin et al.. Evaluating and Optimizing Power Consumption of Anti-Collision Protocols for Applications in RFID Systems. Proceedings of ISLPED'04, California, USA, August 9-11, 2004. pp. 357-362.
11. C.Law, K.Lee, and K. Y.Siu. Efficient Memoryless Protocol for Tag Identification. Proceedings of the 4th International Workshop on Discrete Algorithms and Methods for Mobile Computing and Communications, Boston, Massachusetts, August, 2000. pp. 75-84.
12. EPCglobal Inc. http://www.epcglobalinc.org/.
13. EPCglobal. The EPCglobal Network: Overview of Design, Benefits and Security. September 24, 2004. http://www.epcglobalinc.org/news/EPCglobal
14. R. Butler, V.Welch, D. Engert, I. Foster, S.Tuecke, J. Volmer and C. Kesselman. A national-scale authentication infrastructure. Computer, December, 2000.
15. I. Foster, C. Kesselman, G. Tsudik, and S. Tuecke. A security architecture for computational Grids. ACM Conference on Computer and Communications Security.1998.
16. F. L. Tang, M. L Li, Joshua Z. X Huang et al.. Petri-Net-Based Coordination Algorithms for Grid Transactions. Proceedings of Second International Symposium on Parallel and Distributed Processing and Applications (ISPA'2004). Hong Kong, China, 13-15 Dec. 2004, LNCS 3358: 499-508.
17. M.L. Li, H. Liu, F. L. Tang et al.. ShanghaiGrid in Action: the First Stage Projects Towards Digital City and City Grid. International Journal of Grid and Utility Computing, Vol. 1, No. 1, 2005, pp. 22-31.
18. F. L. Tang, M. L. Li and J. Z. X. Huang. Real-time transaction processing for autonomic Grid applications. Engineering Applications of Artificial Intelligence, 17(7), 2004, pp 799-807.

Predictive Grid Process Scheduling Model in Computational Grid*

Sung Ho Jang and Jong Sik Lee

School of Computer Science and Engineering,
Inha University, Incheon 402-751, South Korea
ho7809@hanmail.net, jslee@inha.ac.kr

Abstract. Importance and need of grid process scheduling have been increased in accordance with development of grid computing. In order to distribute and utilize grid processors efficiently, grid computing system needs scheduling policies that manage and schedule grid process. This paper reviews current scheduling policies and proposes an efficient scheduling model which is called the predictive process scheduling model. For efficient scheduling, this paper presents the processing time prediction algorithm to resolve problems of grid scheduling. The predictive process scheduling model predicts processing times of processors, allocates a job to a processor with minimum processing time, and minimizes overall system execution times. For performance evaluation, this paper measures turn-around time, job loss, throughput, and utilization. Empirical results show that the predictive process scheduling model operates with the less 69.5% of turn-around time and the less 76.4% of job loss and improves the more 119.6 % of throughput and the more 117.8% of utilization than those of existing scheduling models such as random scheduling and round-robin scheduling.

1 Introduction

Grid computing [1], [2] has been noticed as new issue of information technology by prevalence of internet and growth of computer network. Grid computing improves system's computing capability and resolves complex and large-scale computing problems as using geographically dispersed computing resources and services on computer network. As complex and large-scale computing problems that are not solved by clustering system and super computer are being increased, research and development of grid computing is being progressed gradually. Grid computing system connects available computing resources such as computers, applications, and storages to networks for high speed and performance computing and minimizes system execution time.

In grid environment, grid users can use dispersed computing resources of grid computing system as a single system. Grid has to divide a service into several jobs

* This research was supported by the MIC(Ministry of Information and Communication), Korea, under the ITRC(Information Technology Research Center) support program supervised by the IITA(Institute of Information Technology Assessment).

H.T. Shen et al. (Eds.): APWeb 2006, LNCS 3842, pp. 525 – 533, 2006.

and allocate divided jobs to proper processors for efficient distribution of dispersed jobs and guarantee certain job execution. Therefore, grid needs scheduling policies that assign various jobs to processors and decides processing orders of assigned jobs and manages computing resources in order to improve system's computing speed and to disperse throughputs [3], [4]. Scheduling policies are related directly to optimizing overall system performance. Computing resources of grid computing system consist of geographically and systematically independent objects that have individual management policies. Also, grid computing system is characterized by system dynamics that handles a variety of processors and jobs on continues time. For these system dynamics, process scheduling in grid environment is very complex and difficult.

This paper proposes the predictive process scheduling model and presents the processing time prediction algorithm that is applicable for computational grid. The prediction process scheduling model calculates predicted processing times of each processing components by using historical experience data provided from processors and groups all processors into service types. Also, the predictive process scheduling model predicts service types of jobs and distributes jobs to a processing component with minimum processing time in a group suitable for job's service type and finally improves overall system performance. This paper implements the predictive process scheduling model on the DEVS modeling and simulation environment and executes to evaluate its efficiency and reliability compared with existing scheduling models such as the random scheduling model and the round-robin scheduling model.

This paper is organized as follows: Section 2 describes existing grid scheduling policies. Section 3 describes the predictive process scheduling model and the processing time prediction algorithm. Section 4 discusses experiment and its results. The conclusion is in Section 5.

2 Related Works

In order to manage grid computing resources efficiently, we consider four major objectives of grid scheduling problems; overcoming heterogeneousness of grid process, supporting a variety of applications, maximizing overall system performance, improving processor utilization. In a point of job allocation times, grid scheduling policies can be classified to two models that are static scheduling and dynamic scheduling [5].

In static scheduling [6], a compiler in charge of a scheduler determines which jobs should be assigned to which processors at compile time. A complier calculates a processing schedule with using given processors and jobs before execution time. Static scheduling is unnecessary code switching by moving work loads and provides low synchronization and overhead. But, static job scheduling requires that all processors and parameters of grid computing system are known prior to execution time and has low utilization of processors. Also, static scheduling is lacking in ability to deal with problems that are generated at exceptional situation.

Dynamic scheduling [7] moves the focus of scheduling control from a compiler to processors that allocate jobs to themselves and to other processors at execution time. Dynamic scheduling is possible to cope with exceptional situation immediately and minimizes imbalance of work loads. But, dynamic scheduling increases correspondence overheads. Dynamic scheduling can be classified to two models that are centralized scheduling and distributed scheduling depending on where scheduling is executed, where information about scheduling is stored. In centralized scheduling [8], sending or receiving processors contact a designated central processor in charge of a scheduler to send jobs to other processors or to receive jobs from other processors. Centralized scheduling provides simple structure and convenient maintenance. But, a designated central processor is possible to become a bottleneck. In distributed scheduling [9], all processors take charge of scheduling and storing information without a scheduler, idle processors are allocated jobs from a shared global queue at execution time by accessing a queue. Distributed scheduling generates some runtime overhead, but provides improved load balancing.

The predictive process scheduling model predicts processing times of processors by using a historical experience data analysis of static scheduling, also guarantees flexibleness to cope with exceptional situation as providing a real time characteristic of dynamic scheduling. The predictive process scheduling model has a central scheduler like centralized scheduling. But in our model, processors predict processing times and store information to reduce scheduler's work loads on behalf of a scheduler.

3 Predictive Process Scheduling Model

We propose the predictive process scheduling model to resolve scheduling problems of grid. Grid computing system needs the scheduling model that allocates a job suitable for processor capacity to a processor for quick processing time. The predictive process scheduling model predicts the next job processing time of processors and allocates jobs to appropriate processors for solving this problem. The main objective of our model is to reduce overall system execution times by minimizing job losses and maximizing throughput and improving processor utilization. In order to optimize system performance, the predictive process scheduling model has to process jobs to the full. A system execution time is related to processing times of processors that are affected by processor capacity, processor utilization, service size, and service complexity. If all processors on grid have same performance, grid process scheduling is no troubles. But, grid process scheduling and predictions of job processing times are very complex and difficult since performances of processors are actually various. Also, diverseness of service size and service complexity are important factors to be difficult to predict job processing times. To simplify and solve this problem, we provide the processing time prediction algorithm and consolidate processor's historical experiences into databases. The model calculates the next job processing time of a system by using databases before the next job is inputted to grid computing system. As experience data are stored to databases gradually, calculation of predicted job processing times becomes more precise and less an error.

Fig. 1 presents the processing time prediction algorithm [10] by pseudo code. Predict_time_List[1] is the predicted processing time of the first job on grid computing system. Predict_time_List[] indicates an array that accumulates predicted processing times of processors and real_time_List[] indicates an array that accumulates real processing times of processors. These arrays represent databases of experience to execute services on grid computing system during regular times. Predict_time_List[0] and real_time_List [0] can be obtained by experiments. α is learning rate. Before the

```
If (1st job predicted time not exist)
   predict_time_List[1] = ((1-α) * predict_time_List[0])+(α * real_time_List[0]));
Else If (1st job prediction time exist && nth job predicted time not exist)
{
   for (i=1;i<n-1;i++)
   {
      prediction[i] = predict_time_List[i]/ predict_time_List[i-1];
      real[i] = real_time_List[i]/ real_time_List[i-1];
      time = ((1-α) * prediction[i])+(α * real[i] ));
      total_Time * = time;
   }
   predict_time_List[n] = total_Time * predict_time_List[1];
}
```

Fig. 1. Processing time prediction algorithm

first job is inputted to grid computing system, predict_time_List[1] that indicates the first predicted processing time is calculated. When the n-1th job is still processing on a system, it is possible that the nth job of services is inputted to grid computing system. In this case, we can calculate the nth job predicted processing time like the case of first job, but it is impossible that we calculate the nth job predicted processing time precisely. Because, as the number of jobs is increased, an error between real processing times and predicted processing times is increased due to system dynamics. But, prediction[] and real[] can be calculated easily. Prediction[] is the rate of predict_time_List[n]/ predict_time_List[n-1] and real[] is the rate of real_time_List[n]/ real_time_List[n-1]. We can predict the nth job processing time on grid computing system as calculating the predicted 1st~ n-1th job processing times repeatedly as Fig. 1. Then, the nth job is allocated to a processor with the minimum n^{th} job predicted processing time. We can hereby reduce overall system execution times and improve utilization of processors.

Fig. 2 illustrates a sequence of calculating predicted processing times of jobs. In the model, when the nth job is sent to a processor, the n+1th job's predicted processing time is calculated instantaneously by using prediction[] and real[]. The calculated n+1th job's predicted processing time is sent to a scheduler and is used to allocate the n+1th job to a proper processor.

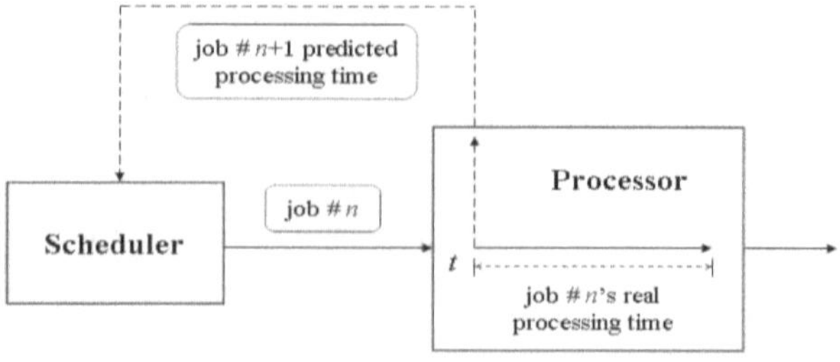

Fig. 2. Sequence of calculating the n+1th job processing time

The predictive process scheduling model consists of five types of components: grid user, coordinator, scheduler, processor, and analyzer. A grid user sends jobs to a coordinator after job generation. A coordinator predicts service type of jobs and then sends jobs to a scheduler of an appropriate group suitable for type of jobs. A scheduler compares predicted processing times of processors in the group and distributes-jobs to a proper processor. A processor processes jobs and stores experience data (name, generating time, processing time, service type, process utilization and job loss) to file and calculates the next job processing time. An analyzer evaluates system performance after receiving jobs and messages from processors. In the predictive process scheduling model, a coordinator in charge of job scheduling is selected in center and grid users and processors are connected to a coordinator through computer networks like centralized scheduling. But, contrary to centralized scheduling, a scheduler only takes charge of allocating jobs, comparing predicted times and searching services of jobs. And processors take charge of storing job information data and calculating predicted times.

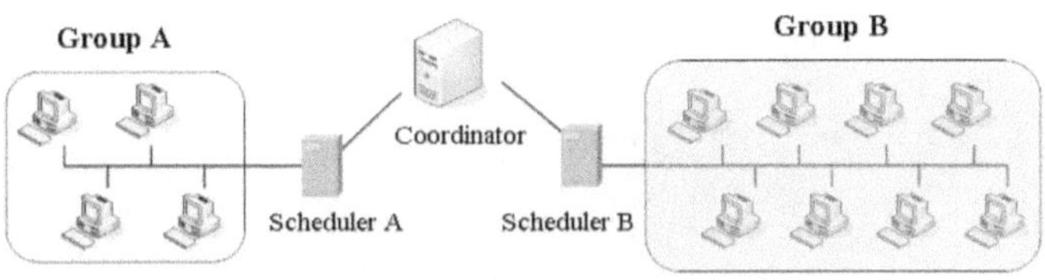

Fig. 3. Grouping for multiple type service

The predictive process scheduling model supports not only a single type service but also various multiple type services. If multiple type service's predicted processing time is calculated as a single type service, an error of predicted processing times increases by the disparity of job execution times of services. Therefore, we apply grouping to our model for solving this problem. To group all processors into service type, we use the rate of average processing times. We assume that services are classified to group A and group B and an average processing time of group A is 10 and an average processing time of group B is 20. At this time, a coordinator groups all processors into group A and group B with 1:2 as shown Fig. 3. The number of groups is consistent with the number of services and the number of processors of groups is related to the rate of average processing times. To prevent that work loads are centralized in a coordinator, we arrange schedulers classified by service types that take charge of management of processors. If a grid user inputs a job to grid computing system, a coordinator predicts service type of a job and sends it to a scheduler of a proper group. Then, a scheduler allocates it to a processor with the minimum predicted processing time in a group. Through this process of grouping, the predictive process scheduling model can get precise predictions and prevent a coordinator from centralization of work loads.

4 Experiments and Performance Evaluation

In order to evaluate usefulness and efficiency of the predictive process scheduling model, we executed the predictive process scheduling model on DEVSJAVA modeling and simulation environment [11] and also conducted two experiments (single type service and multiple type service) to test prototype models and estimated efficacy of our model in comparison with conventional scheduling models such as the random scheduling model and the round-robin scheduling model.

4.1 Experiment 1: Single Type Service

The first experiment is to measure turn-around time and the total number of job loss on assumption that grid only performs a single type service. Turn-around time is calculated by (1) where N is the number of processed jobs. Fig. 4(a) illustrates variations of turn-around time by the number of jobs. The process scheduling model provides reduced processing times compared with other models regardless of the number of jobs. Fig. 4(b) illustrates variations of the total number of job loss by simulation time. In Fig 4(b), the process scheduling model shows minimum job loss. For example, the process scheduling model recorded the 13.75% job loss as losing 1375 jobs while the random scheduling model and the round-robin scheduling model recorded the 38.5% job loss and the 47% job loss when simulation time is 2000.

$$\text{Turn-around time} = \left(\sum_{i=1}^{N}(\text{Processing time of job \#i} + \text{Wating time of job \#i})\right)/N \tag{1}$$
$(N = \text{the number of processed jobs})$

Reduction rate of T_A(turn-around) time =

$$Average\left(\sum\left(1-\frac{\text{T\_A time of Predictive process scheduling}}{\text{Average of T\_A time of Random scheduling \& Round robin scheduling}}\right)\times 100(\%)\right) \tag{2}$$

Reduction rate of job loss =

$$Average\left(\sum\left(1-\frac{\text{Job loss of Predictive process scheduling}}{\text{Average of job loss of Random scheduling \& Round robin scheduling}}\right)\times 100(\%)\right) \tag{3}$$

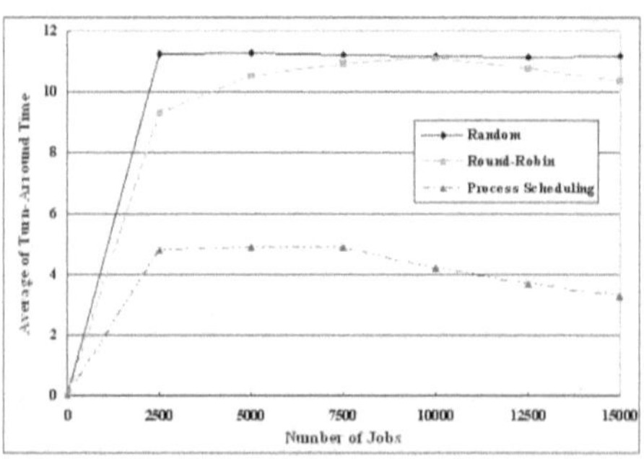

(a)

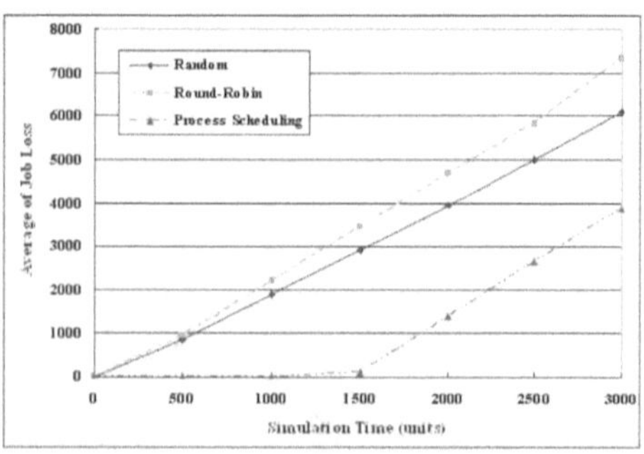

(b)

Fig. 4. (a) Comparison of turn-around time (b) Comparison of job loss (Predictive process scheduling model vs. Random scheduling model vs. Round-robin scheduling model)

We used (2) and (3) to analyze reduction rates of turn-around time and job loss. As a result, reduction rates of turn-around time and job loss for the process scheduling model over other models were 69.5% and 76.4%. These results demonstrate that our model is stable regardless of simulation times and provides reliable transmission of jobs on computer networks.

4.2 Experiment 2: Multiple Type Services

The second experiment is to measure throughput and utilization of multiple type services for system dynamics of grid computing. Throughput and utilization are calculated by (4) and (5).We assume that multiple type services are classified to type A that needs 9~11 processing times and type B that needs 28~32 processing times. Fig. 5(a) illustrates variations of throughput by simulation time. In Fig. 5(a), we can see that the process scheduling model preformed the maximum throughput. It demonstrates that the process scheduling model processes the most jobs by time units. Fig. 5(b) illustrates variations of utilization by simulation time. The process scheduling model recorded utilization more than 90 % that is definitely higher than other models.

$$\text{Throughput} = \text{The total number of processed jobs} / \text{The total execution time} \tag{4}$$

$$\text{Utilization} = \frac{\text{The total processing time of all processors}}{\text{The total processing time of all processors} + \text{The total waiting time of all processors}} \times 100(\%) \tag{5}$$

$$\text{Improvement rate of throughput} = Average\left(\sum \frac{\text{Throughput of Predictive process scheduling}}{\text{Average of throughput of Random scheduling \& Round robin scheduling}} \times 100(\%)\right) \tag{6}$$

$$\text{Improvement rate of utilization} = Average\left(\sum \frac{\text{Utilization of Predictive process scheduling}}{\text{Average of utilization of Random scheduling \& Round robin scheduling}} \times 100(\%)\right) \tag{7}$$

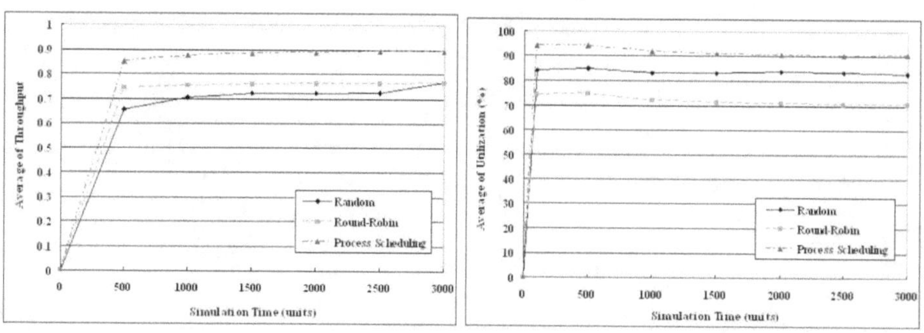

Fig. 5. (a) Comparison of throughput (b) Comparison of utilization (Predictive process scheduling model vs. Random scheduling model vs. Round-robin scheduling model)

We used (6) and (7) to analyze improvement rates of throughput and utilization. As a result, improvement rates of throughput and utilization for the process scheduling model over other models were 119.6% and 117.8%. These results demonstrate that the process scheduling model improves overall system performance and processor utilization by reducing idle processors and increasing throughput.

5 Conclusion

This paper presents the predictive process scheduling model to resolve problems of grid scheduling and specifies a processing time prediction algorithm that calculates job processing time of processor. The predictive process scheduling model provides real-time scheduling and experience data analysis and decentralization of work loads. Also, the predictive process scheduling model groups all processors of grid computing system into a service type to minimize an error of prediction processing time by the imbalance of service execution time and assigns jobs to a processor with minimum processing time in a group suitable for service types of jobs. We can reduce idle processors occurred by wrong job allocation and guarantee high processor utilization because the predictive process scheduling model always checks conditions of processors and gives priority to idle processors. In this paper, we simulated our model to evaluate model's efficiency and reliability. Our experiment results demonstrate that the predictive process scheduling model reduces the more 69.5% of turn-around time and the more 76.4% of job loss and improves the more 119.6 % of throughput and the more 117.8% of utilization than random scheduling and round-robin scheduling. The predictive process scheduling model materializes high speed computing and finally improves entire system performance.

References

1. Berman, F., Fox, G., Hey, T.: Grid computing: making the global infrastructure a reality. J. Wiley, New York (2003)
2. Foster, I., Kesselman, C.: The Grid: Blueprint for a new Computing Infrastructure. Morgan Kaufmann Publishers (1998)
3. Krauter, K., Buyya, R., Maheswaran, M.: A taxonomy and survey of grid resource management systems for distributed computing. Software Practice and Experience (2002) 135–164
4. Buyya, R., Abramson, D., Giddy, J.: Nimrod/G: an architecture for a resource management and scheduling system in a global computational grid. High Performance Computing in the Asia-Pacific Region, 2000. Proceedings, Vol. 1 (2000) 283 -289
5. Hamscher, V., Schwiegelshohn, U., Streit, A., Yahyapour, R.: Evaluation of Job-Scheduling Strategies for Grid Computing. In Proc. Grid '00 (2000) 191–202
6. Dan M. and Wei Z.: A Static Task Scheduling Algorithm in Grid Computing. Lecture Notes in CS, Vol. 3033. Springer-Verlag (2004) 153 - 156
7. Yuanyuan Z., Yasushi I. and Hong S.: A Dynamic Task Scheduling Algorithm for Grid Computing System. Lecture Notes in CS, Vol.3358. Springer-Verlag (2004) 578
8. Lichen Z.: Scheduling Algorithm for Real-Time Applications in Grid Environment. 2002 IEEE International Conference on, Vol. 5 (2002)

9. Wang, Q., Gui, X., et al: De-centralized Job Scheduling on Computational Grids Using Distributed Backfilling. Lecture Notes in CS, Vol. 3251. Springer-Verlag (2004) 285 - 292
10. Gao, Y., Rong, H., Tong F., et al.: Adaptive Job Scheduling for a Service Grid Using a Genetic Algorithm. Lecture Notes in CS, Vol. 3033. Springer-Verlag (2004) 65 - 72
11. Zeigler, B.P., et al: The DEVS Environment for High-Performance Modeling and Simulation. IEEE CS & E, Vol. 4, No3 (1997) 61-71

A Dependable Task Scheduling Strategy for a Fault Tolerant Grid Model*

Yuanzhuo Wang[1,2], Chuang Lin[2], Zhengli Zhai[1], and Yang Yang[1]

[1] School of Information Engineering, University of Science and Technology Beijing, Beijing 100083, China
[2] Department of Computer Science and Technology, Tsinghua University, Beijing 100084, China
{yzwang, chlin}@csnet1.cs.tsinghua.edu.cn

Abstract. Grid provides an integrated computer platform composed of differentiated and distributed systems. In this paper, aiming at the heterogeneity and dynamism of a grid system, a novel fault-tolerant grid-scheduling model is presented based on Stochastic Petri Net. On the other hand, a new grid-scheduling strategy, the united strategy for the availability factor and expected accomplishing time (*USAT*), is put forward, In the end, the performance of the scheduling strategy based on the fault-tolerant grid-scheduling model is analyzed by SPNP software package. The numerical results show that *USAT* strategy can reduce these bad effects of dynamic and autonomic resources to some extent so as to guarantee quality of service (QoS).

1 Introduction

Grid is becoming more attractive and promising platforms for solving large-scale computing intensive problems, which realize a coordinated resource sharing and a problem solving in dynamic, multinstitutional virtual organizations[1], and the resources are highly heterogeneous. Since the resources in grid are heterogeneous and dynamic, the resource organizing and task scheduling become a very complicated problem, in a grid environment.

SPN, stochastic Petri net, is a graphics and mathematics mode and analysis tool. The traits of SPN, such as describing prioritized, concurrent, asynchronous, stochastic, nondeterministic events and resource share, are suitable for research system resource management, task-scheduling model and strategy[2]. From the point of heterogeneity and dynamism of grid, this makes the availability[3] of task accomplished in a grid system as the research goal. Since scheduling mechanism fitting to dynamism is added, the interrupt degree of each server will be explained and then availability evaluation function can be obtained, thereby making the scheduling strategy more adapted to non-dedicated[4] trait of s server states. The work of this paper is a precondition for nontrivial quality of service (QoS).

* This paper is supported by the National Natural Science Foundation of China (No.90412012 and No. 60373013).

H.T. Shen et al. (Eds.): APWeb 2006, LNCS 3842, pp. 534 – 539, 2006.

2 SPN Scheduling Model

In this part, the SPN scheduling model will be given, in which, according to scheduling strategy tasks being dispatched to the servers and the server resource being occupied by resource provider are represented by immediate transitions with zero firing time. The subscript symbols of tasks represent the category of tasks, and the other subscript symbols represent the sequence of servers.

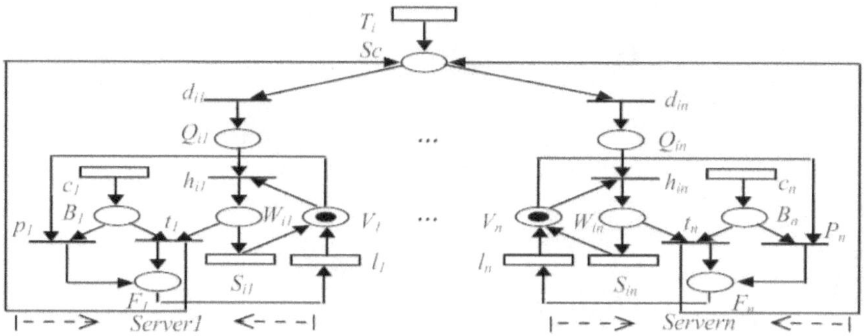

Fig. 1. Fault-tolerant grid Scheduling SPN Model with Dynamic Mechanism

• Transitions ($1 \leq I \leq m$, $1 \leq j \leq n$):

T_i: Arrival of tasks $Task_i$ at rate λ_i. It is submitted according to the Poisson process[5] .
d_{ij}: Models dispatching tasks $Task_i$ to server j (S_j) .
h_j: Models tasks $Task_i$ executed by the server j.
s_{ij}: Executing $Task_i$ by server j, the average rate μ_{ij} is exponentially distributed.
c_j: Request from the provider of server j . The arrival rate η_j is the Poisson process[6] .
t_j: $Task_i$ running in the server j is intermitted and $Task_i$ will be rescheduled.
p_j: Due to arrival of request from provider, resource in V_j will be occupied.
l_j: The provider's own task is running in server j , suppose the service rate is at θ_j.

• Places ($1 \leq i \leq m$, $1 \leq j \leq n$):

Sc: According to the scheduling strategy,it will distribute tasks $Task_i$ to the server j.
Q_{ij}:Models the task of different rank waiting queue for server j with capacity b_j.
W_{ij}: Models a task $Task_i$ being executed by server j.
V_j: Models the position of resource of server j.
B_j: Models the position that provider of server j applies to use the server resource.
F_n: Models the position that the server resource is using by its provider.

3 Scheduling Strategy

3.1 Task-Dispatching Strategy

In this paper, we consider the task scheduling strategy related to the availability and executing time in a server. We present a united strategy for the availability factor and expected accomplishing time($USAT$), according to which, a task will be dispatched tothe server expected to have the shortest completing time and the best availability.

Definition 1. ***EAT*** is the expected accomplishing time of the $Task_i$ in the server j, then

$$EAT(Task_i, S_j) = ((M(Q_{ij})+1)/\mu_{ij}) + \sum_{k=1}^{i-1}(M(Q_{kj})/\mu_{kj}) \tag{1}$$

Where $M(Q_{ij})$ is the quantity of tasks in the waiting queue.

Definition 2. The availability factor, β_j, which is a probability that a task can be executed in a server accurately without interrupt due to the unavailability of resources.

Define the state space S=(0,1,2,3), where'0'denotes when a task arrives, the resource is available, '1'denotes when the resource is unavailable, no tasks arrive,'2' denotes during a task executing, the resource is always available,'3'denotes during a task executing, the resource becomes unavailable. Suppose stochastic processes N_t, and the value of N_t in S denotes state of the Stochastic system in the time t, and $\alpha_j = \sum \alpha_{ij}$, $\mu_j \sum \mu_{ij}/m$, (j=1,…,n).

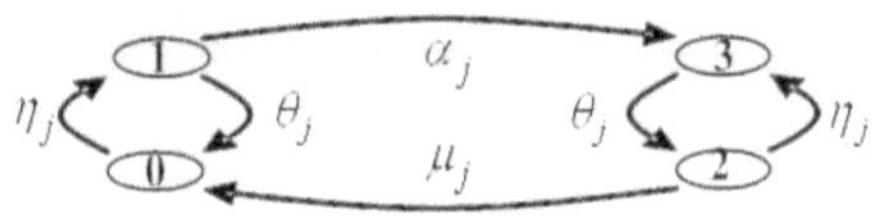

Fig. 2. State transition figure of N_t

From figure 2, we can know N_t is a continuous time Mar-kov Chain (MC), The invariant distribution $\pi=(\pi_0, \pi_1, \pi_2, \pi_3)$ of N_t can be obtained through solving equations $\pi Q=0, 1^T\pi=1$,where Q is the transition rate matrix,$\pi_1=\eta_j\pi_0/(\alpha_j+\theta_j)$, $\pi_2=\eta_j\alpha_j\pi_0/\mu_j(\alpha_j+\theta_j)$, $\pi_3=\eta_j\alpha_j(\eta_j+\mu_j)\pi_0/\theta_j\mu_j(\alpha_j+\theta_j)$,$\pi_0=\mu_j\theta_j(\alpha_j+\theta_j)/(\eta_j\theta_j(\alpha_j+\mu_j)+\eta_j\alpha_j(\eta_j+\mu_j)+\mu_j\theta_j(\alpha_j+\theta_j))$. According to the above description of state space of the availability factor, we can obtain

$$\beta_j=1-\pi_3=(\theta_j\mu_j(\alpha_j+\theta_j)+\eta_j\theta_j(\alpha_j+\mu_j))/(\eta_j\theta_j(\alpha_j+\mu_j)+\eta_j\alpha_j(\eta_j+\mu_j)+\mu_j\theta_j(\alpha_j+\theta_j)) \tag{2}$$

Definition 3. ***USAT*** is the united strategy for the availability factor and expected accomplishing time. The $USAT$ target function of $Task_i$ in server j is as follow.

$$USAT(Task_i, S_j)=\omega_1 Est_j+\omega_2 Ava_j \tag{3}$$

Where Est_j=min($EST(Task_i,S_j)$)/$EST(Tast_i,S_j)$, $Ava_j=\beta_j/\max(\beta_j)$, (j=1,…,n), ω_j is weight of each server. For figuring out the reasonable values of ω_j, we set up the optimal target function, according to multiple attribute decision making.

$$\begin{cases} \max V(\omega) = (\sum_{i=1}^{n}\sum_{k=1}^{n}|Est_i - Est_k| + \sum_{i=1}^{n}\sum_{k=1}^{n}|Ava_i - Ava_k|)\omega_j \\ \quad s.t. \quad \omega_j \geq 0, j=1,2 \quad \omega_1^2+\omega_2^2=1 \end{cases} \tag{4}$$

Let $Est_i=a_{i1}$, $Ava_i=a_{i2}$ and found the Lagrange function, obtain the optimal solutions

$$\omega_j = \sum_{i=1}^{n}\sum_{k=1}^{n}|a_{ij}-a_{kj}| \Big/ \sqrt{\sum_{j=1}^{2}(\sum_{i=1}^{n}\sum_{k=1}^{n}a_{ij}-a_{kj})^2}, (j=1,2) \tag{5}$$

Put ω_j into the formula (3) and find maximal $USAT(Task_i, S_j)$, then dispatched the task to the server that is correlative to the maximal *USAT*. Aiming at above mentioned scheduling strategy, the enabling predicate of the transition d_{ij} is $(M(Q_{ij})<b_{ij}) \cap ((for \forall k \neq j, USAT(Task_i,S_j) \geq USAT(Task_i,S_k)) \cup (for \forall k \neq j, M(Q_{ik})=b_{ik}))$.

3.2 Task-Selecting Strategy

We consider the weighted priority (WP) as task-selecting strategy. In which, each waiting queue can be provided with different priorities. It can be described in the enabling predicate and firing probability of transition h_{ij}. The enabling predicate of h_{ij} is $(M(Q_{ij})>0)$. We use symbol ω_i to denote the weight of $Task_i$. The firing probability of h_{ij} is $P(M(Q_{ij}))=1$, if $i \in RS(M)$, $P(M(Q_{ij}))=\sigma_i$, if $i \in RS(M)$, $P(M(Q_{ij}))=0$, otherwise. where $RS(M)=\{k|M(Q_{kj})> 0$ and $M(Q_{lj})=0$, for $1 \leq k \leq n$, $\forall l \neq k$ $1 \leq l \leq n\}$, $RN(M)=\{k|M(Q_{kj})> 0$ and $M(Q_{lj})=0$, for $1 \leq k \leq n$, $\exists l \neq k$ $1 \leq l \leq n\}$, $\sigma_i = \omega_k/(\omega_k+\Sigma\omega_l)$.

4 Performance Analysis

We will do an experiment to analyze the performances of the task scheduling strategies based on the SPN model in figure 1. In the experiment, *USAT* strategy, *WP* strategy and the software package SPNP (Stochastic Petri Net Package)[7] will be used. To avoid the state space to explode and simplify the model solution, without loss of generality, we only consider two servers and the tasks are assigned to two classes in our example. Class 1 tasks have higher cost and class 2 tasks have lower. We assume $b_{11}=b_{12}=b_{21}=b_{22}=10$; $\mu_{11}=12$, $\mu_{12}=9$, $\mu_{21}=8$, $\mu_{22}=6$ tasks/s; $\lambda_1=\lambda_2$ and $\lambda_1+\lambda_2=\alpha_{11}+\alpha_{12}+\alpha_{21}+\alpha_{22}$, where α_{ij} is $Task_i$ arrival rate for the server j; $\eta_1=4$, $\eta_2=2$ requests/s and $\theta_1=6$, $\theta_2=4$ unit /s.

In figure 3, we analyze the relation between β_j and α_j. We can find the availability factor will decrease when the task arrival rate increase. And when α is so small, β is close to 1. At that time, we can consider the server is very dependable, because the interrupt hardly occurs. All of these accords with the actual condition so well that we think β can denote the availability of servers basically.

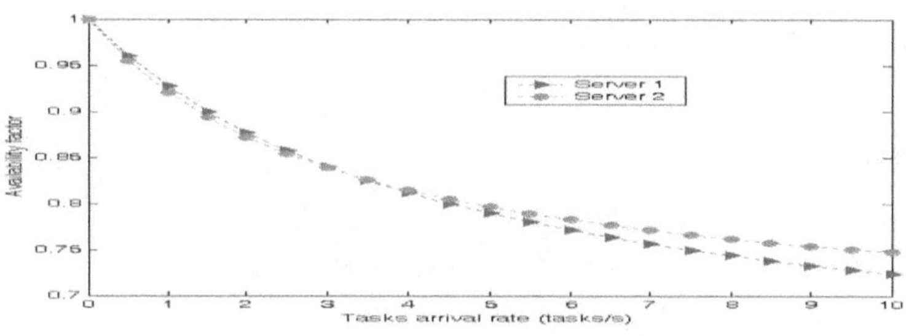

Fig. 3. The relation between the task arrival rate and the dependability factor

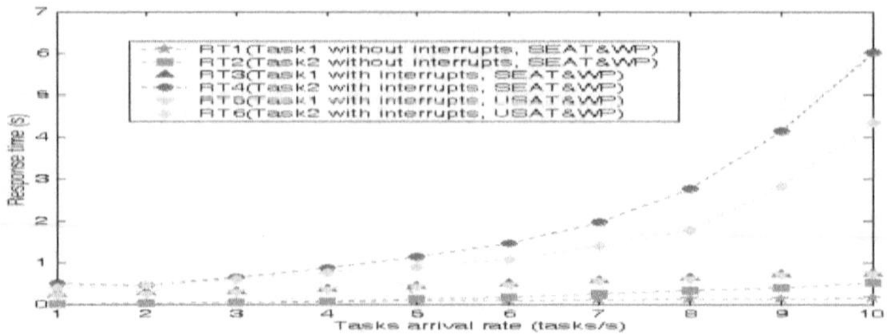

Fig. 4. The effect for task response time of *USAT* strategy

In figure 4, we compare the response time of three instances for two classes tasks. Two groups strategies are adopted, *SEAT* (shortest expected accomplishing time) and *WP*, *USAT* and *WP*. RT1, RT2, RT3, RT4, RT5, RT6 are obtained. We can find the tasks with high higher priority and without interrupts tasks have the short response time. At last, when the interrupts exist, *USAT* and *WP* are adopted. Since the availability factor is added into the scheduling strategy, the response time of *USAT* is shorter than that of *SEAT* for both classes of the tasks. Though it can not attain the level without interrupts, *USAT* can reduce these bad effects in part to guarantee QoS.

5 Conclusion

In this paper, a novel fault-tolerant grid-scheduling SPN model is presented, which describes the heterogeneity and dynamism of a grid system. On the other hand, a new scheduling strategy, *USAT*, is put forward, in which the availability factor is introduced in the grid task dispatching strategy. According to the performance analysis results, we can find that the *USAT* strategy can realize that the tasks of higher priority have shorter response time. And through dynamic updating the value of the availability factor termly, the new task can always be dispatched to the most dependable node of present time to execute, which makes the each-node load dynamic balance.

In the next step, more researches need be done in scheduling strategies based on the SPN model, in which we hope to study the effect degree of an interrupt to different-task performances, analyze more dependability parameter, such as Survivability, performability, maintainability ect, to describe a grid system roundly and make these effects to be embodied well-grounded in the fault-tolerant scheduling strategy.

References

1. Foster, C. Kesselman, and S. Tuecke, The Anatomy of the Grid: Enabling Scalable Virtual Organizations, International J. Supercomputer Applications, 2001.
2. T. Murata, Petri Nets: Properties, Analysis and Applications, Proceedings of the IEEE, 1989, 77(4):541-580.
3. Algirdas A., Jean-Claude Laprie, Brian Randell. Basic Concepts and Taxonomy of Dependable and Secure Computing. IEEE Transactions on Dependable and Secure Computing. 2004,1(1):11-33.

4. Linguo Gong, Xian-He Sun, Senior Member, Performance Modeling and Prediction of Nondedicated Network Computing IEEE Trans on Computers, 2002,51(9):1041-1055.
5. David M., William H., Kishor S. Model-based evaluation: from availability to security[J]. IEEE Transactions on Dependable and Secure Computing. 2004, 1(1):48-65.
6. Zhiguang Shan, Chuang Lin, Fengyuan Ren, Modeling and Performance Analysis of a Multiserver Multiqueue System on the Grid, Distributed Computing Systems, 2003. FTDCS 2003. Proceedings. The Ninth IEEE Workshop on Future Trends, 2003: 337–343.
7. G. Ciaodo, J. Muppala, and K.S. Trivedi, SPNP: Stochastic Petri Net Package, in: Proc. Petri Nets and Performance Models, 1989:142-151.

Multi-agent Web Text Mining on the Grid for Enterprise Decision Support

Kin Keung Lai [1,2,3], Lean Yu [1,3], and Shouyang Wang [1,2]

[1] Institute of Systems Science, Academy of Mathematics and Systems Science, Chinese Academy of Sciences, Beijing 100080, China
{yulean, sywang}@amss.ac.cn
[2] College of Business Administration, Hunan University, Changsha 410082, China
[3] Department of Management Sciences, City University of Hong Kong, Tat Chee Avenue, Kowloon, Hong Kong
{msyulean, mskklai}@cityu.edu.hk

Abstract. In this study, a multi-agent web text mining system on the grid is developed to support enterprise decision-making. First, an individual intelligent learning agent that learns about underlying text documents is presented to discover the useful knowledge for enterprise decision. In order to scale the individual intelligent agent with the large number of text documents on the web, we then provide a multi-agent web text mining system in a parallel way based upon grid technology. Finally, we discuss how the multi-agent web text mining system on the grid can be used to implement text mining services.

1 Introduction

With the development of technology, the enterprises are suffering more pressures than ever. To obtain competitive edges, the utilization of intelligent mining techniques has received more and more attention. Currently, text mining, which can handle non-structured textual data, has becoming a new decision support tool for enterprise decision-makers. Since the most natural form of storing information is as text, text mining is believed to have a higher commercial potential than data mining [1]. A recent study, conducted by Delphi Group (http://www.thedelphigroup.com/), has indicated that 80% of a company's information is contained in textual documents. Thus, it is important to develop a web text mining system for enterprise decision-making.

In the web text mining, one crucial problem is how deal with the large numbers of available text documents over a tolerable limit. For this problem, a multi-agent intelligent learning system based on the grid technology [2] is proposed. The main motivation of this study is to develop a multi-agent web text mining system on the grid that offers valuable knowledge to support enterprise decision-making. The rest of this study is organized as follows. Section 2 presents a framework of the back propagation neural network (BPNN) based intelligent learning agent for text mining. To scale the computational load for the large-scale text mining task, a multi-agent web text mining system on the grid is proposed in Section 3. Section 4 concludes.

H.T. Shen et al. (Eds.): APWeb 2006, LNCS 3842, pp. 540 – 544, 2006.

2 The BPNN-Based Intelligent Agent for Web Text Mining

Web text mining, a new research field in knowledge discovery, refers to the process of using unstructured web-type textual document and examining it in an attempt to discover implicit patterns "hidden" within the web documents using interdisciplinary techniques from data mining, machine learning, and natural language processing [1]. One main goal of web text mining is to help people discover knowledge for decision support from large quantities of semi-structured or unstructured web text documents.

Actually, web text mining consists of a series of tasks and procedures, which involves many interdisciplinary fields mentioned above. Because the final goal of text mining is to support decision, the web text mining must adapt the dynamic change over the time as the web text documents increase rapidly. Thus, web text mining must have learning capability. In this study, the BPNN is used as a computational agent for web text mining. In the environment of our proposed approach, the BPNN agent is first trained with the many related web documents, and then the trained BPNN agent can project to new documents for decision when new web document arrives. Fig. 1 illustrates the main components of a BPNN agent and the control flows among them. Note that the control flows with thin arrow represent learning phase and the control flows with bold arrow represent discovering phase of web text mining system.

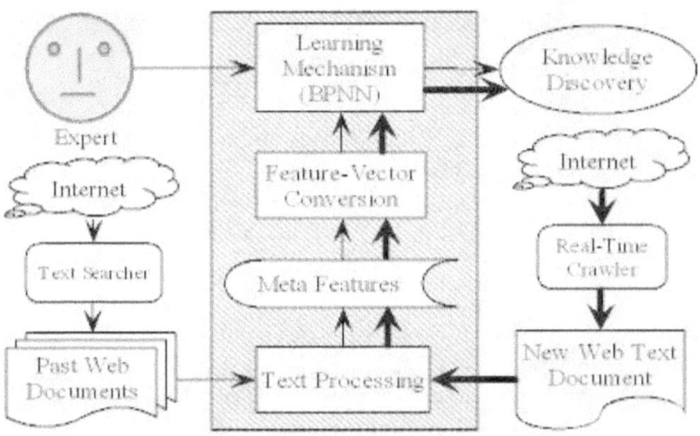

Fig. 1. The framework of a BPNN agent for web text mining

As can be seen from Fig. 1, the framework of the BPNN agent for web text mining consists of four main components: text search and collection, text processing, feature vector conversion, and learning mechanism, which is described in detail as follows.

(1) Text search and collection. Clearly, the first step in web text mining is to collect the text data. Its work is to find related text documents by retrieval tools.
(2) Text processing. When web text documents are collected, the collected text documents are mainly represented by semi- or non-structural information. Its aim is to extract typical features that represent the text contents from these collected texts.
(3) Feature vector conversion. Before using knowledge discovery algorithm, text feature data must be transformed into numerical data. Here we use binary form to

perform conversion. We simply check for the presence "1" or absence "0" of words by comparing with predefined indices to formulate a numerical table with binary form.

(4) BPNN agent learning mechanism. In this study, the BPNN is used as an intelligent agent to explore the hidden patterns. Actually, BPNN agent is a supervised learning mechanism in the form of the neural network associative memory as shown in Fig. 2 as the shaded rectangle. Thus the BPNN agent acts in two phases: a training phase (the top part) and a testing phase (the bottom part), as illustrated in Fig. 2.

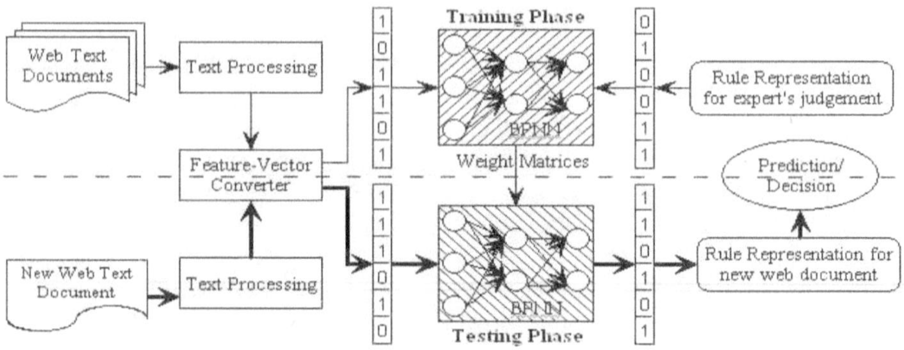

Fig. 2. The learning mechanism of BPNN agent for web text mining

During the training phase, the input and the output layer of the BPNN are set to represent a training pair (x, y) where x is produced by the feature vector converter and y is produced by the expert's judgments. Commonly, $x\in R^n$ is an n-dimensional feature vector containing the independent variable or attributes, and $y\in \{0, 1\}$ is the dependent variable or truth. The goal is to construct a function or a model f,

$$y = f(x) = f_a(x) = f(x; a),\ a\in A, \tag{1}$$

where $f = f_a$ is defined by specifying parameters $a\in A$ from an explicitly parameterized family of models A. To search the optimal parameters a, the BPNN learning procedure is performed for all training pairs. The BPNN procedure repeatedly adjusts the link-weight matrices of BPNN in a way that minimizes the error for each training pair. When the average squared error is acceptably small, the BPNN stops and produces the link-weight matrices, which is stored as the knowledge for the use of testing phase.

During the testing phase, the input layer of the BPNN is activated by the feature vector produced by the feature-vector converter for a new web text document. This activation of the BPNN spreads from the input layer to the output layer using the link-weight matrices stored during the training phase. That is, the model $f = f_a$ determined by training phase is applied to previously unseen feature vectors x to produce the output of BPNN, a vector representation whose components are all between 0 and 1.

In principle, our approach proposed above offers the potential solution to the web text mining problem. But it is infeasible for a single BPNN agent to handle large-scale text documents. For this problem, a multi-agent web text mining system on the grid is proposed in the next section.

3 Multi-agent Web Text Mining on the Grid

3.1 The Structure of Multi-agent Web Text Mining System

Assume that we have a number of BPNN-based intelligent agents, each of which has its own available text documents described in the previous section. For handling the different web text documents with different categories, a two-layer multi-agent web text mining system is constructed, as illustrated in Fig. 3.

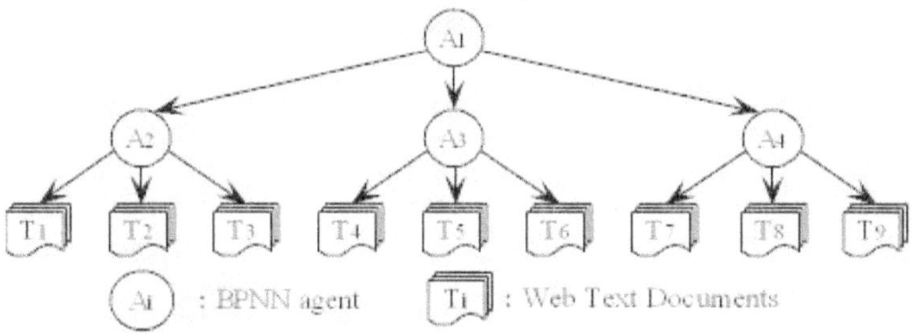

Fig. 3. The structure of multi-agent web text mining system

From Fig. 3, the two-layer multi-agent web text mining system includes one superordinate BPNN agent and several subordinate BPNN agents. Here the superordinate BPNN agent can treat the subordinate BPNN agents in the same way as the subordinate BPNN agents treat their available text documents. Usually, the multi-agent-based web text mining system can be performed by distributed system in a parallel way. However, the operation of multi-agent web text mining system may increase computational requirements, for example, adding some computers to deploy the BPNN agents. For this requirement, the grid technology is applied in this study.

3.2 The Multi-agent Web Text Mining System on the Grid

With the growing demands of computational requirements of the multi-agent web text mining system, grid infrastructures are foreseen to be one of the most critical yet challenging technologies to meet the practical demands for high performance and high efficiency text mining in a large variety of web text documents. In the past few years, many software environments for gaining access to very large distributed computing resources have been made available, such as Globus [3] and Condor [4]. Based upon the previous work, a multi-agent-based web text mining system on the grid is proposed. That is, our BPNN agent can be deployed in different grid and implemented collaboratively. Fig. 4 shows the architecture of the web text mining with three grids.

As a result, the multi-agent-based web text mining system on the grid can collaboratively discover some useful knowledge for enterprise decision support in an efficient way. For further explanation, a simulated study should be provided. Due to space limitation, the simulated experiment is omitted here.

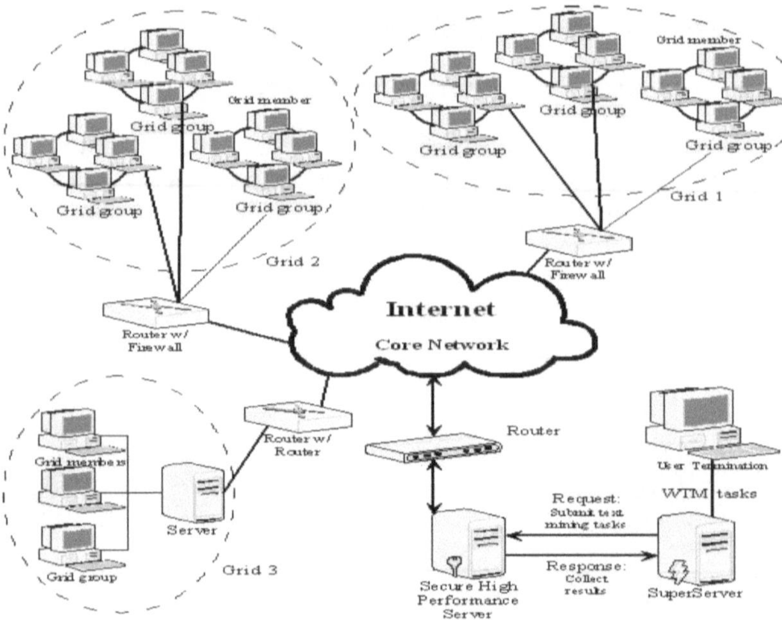

Fig. 4. The architecture of the multi-agent web text mining system on the grid

4 Conclusions

This study proposes a multi-agent web text mining system on the grid to support enterprise decision. In this study, we first propose a single intelligent agent to perform text mining. With the rapid increase of web information, a multi-agent web text mining system on the grid is then constructed for large-scale text mining application.

References

1. Yu, L., Wang, S.Y., Lai, K.K.: A Rough-Set-Refined Text Mining Approach for Crude Oil Market Tendency Forecasting. International Journal of Knowledge and Systems Sciences 2 (2005) 33-46
2. Foster. I., Kesselman, C., Tuecke, S.: The Anatomy of the Grid: Enabling Scalable Virtual Organizations. International Journal of High Performance Computing Applications 15 (2001) 200-223
3. Litzkow, M., Livny, M.: Experience with the Condor Distributed Batch System. Proceedings of the IEEE Workshop on Experimental Distributed Systems (1990) 97-101
4. Foster, I., Kesselman, C., Tuecke, S.: Globus: A Metacomputing Infrastructure Toolkit. International Journal of Supercomputer Applications 11 (1997) 115-128

Semantic Peer-to-Peer Overlay for Efficient Content Locating*

Hanhua Chen, Hai Jin, and Xiaomin Ning

Cluster and Grid Computing Lab,
Huazhong University of Science and Technology, Wuhan, 430074, China
hjin@hust.edu.cn

Abstract. The decentralized structure together with the features of self-organization and fault-tolerance makes peer-to-peer network a promising information-sharing model. However, the efficient content-based location remains a challenge of large scale peer-to-peer network. In this paper we present SemreX, a semantic overlay for desktop literature documents sharing in peer-to-peer networks. We present a semantic overlay algorithm by which peers are locally clustered together according to their semantic similarity and long-range connections are rewired for short-cut in the peer-to-peer networks. Experiment results show that routing in the semantic overlay greatly improves the recall of search as well as reduces routing hops and messages.

1 Introduction

Peer-to-peer network has shown a great potential to become an excellent information sharing way. However, traditional peer-to-peer topology and routing mechanisms fail to locate *content* in large scale peer-to-peer networks efficiently.

Current peer-to-peer search mechanisms can be classified into three types [1][2]. In the first approach, a centralized index is maintained at a server, and all queries are directed to the server. The centralized index server becomes a performance bottleneck and single point of failure in large scale peer-to-peer systems. Another approach of peer-to-peer network is commonly called unstructured overlay. Queries based on file name randomly walk [3] or are flooded across the network. Flooding based approaches may lead to heavy network traffics by generating large number of query messages while random walk methods may reduce the messages at the cost of recall rate. The third approach is the *Distributed Hash Table* (DHT) based scheme, which is efficient for *exact match* lookups. However, if the exact key is not known, the users cannot locate the objects they are looking for. It is commonly believed that structured overlays are more expensive to maintain because their topology and data placement constraints make it harder to adapt to highly dynamical peer-to-peer environment.

SemreX considers the scenario that research participants in computer science share the articles in their desktop file systems and retrieve the scientific articles they want by submitting semantic based queries to the peer-to-peer networks. The main focus of

* This paper is supported by the National 973 Key Basic Research Program under grant No.2003CB317003.

H.T. Shen et al. (Eds.): APWeb 2006, LNCS 3842, pp. 545–554, 2006.

this paper examines the use of semantic overlay for efficient content locating. Peers in SemreX network are organized according to the semantic similarity of the topics that the peers contain. Query messages are routed to the peers who are much more similar with them and mostly like to return the results.

The rest of this paper is organized as follows. Section 2 describes the overview of the system model of the SemreX. We propose the semantic overlay algorithm in section 3. Section 4 introduces the query routing algorithm in semantic overlay. Section 5 simulates the overlay and routing algorithms and analyzes the experiments results. We review some related works in section 6. Section 7 concludes the paper and describes our future work.

2 System Model of SemreX

Fig.1 illustrates the four layers system model of a semantic based peer-to-peer system.

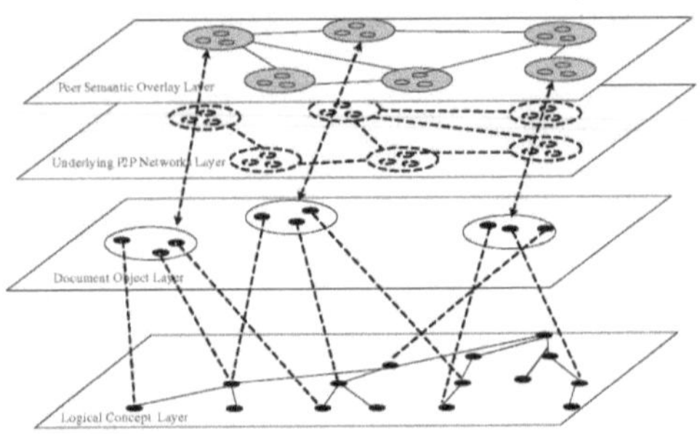

Fig. 1. Four-Layer system model of SemreX

Logical concept layer of SemreX provides the shared concept model over the peer-to-peer network. For computer scientific literature retrieval application, two kinds of ontology are introduced, ACM Topic [4] and SemreX publication metadata. With sub- and super- topic relations, 1287 concepts are associated in the IS-A ACM Topic hierarchy. SemreX publication metadata includes the formal description of the component such as author and publisher.

Here, we mainly focus on the global shared homogeneous ontology. Much effort in the research on how to mapping and emerging heterogeneous ontology has been made in recent years [5].

Document object layer provides the capability to classify and index documents. The local peer is viewed as a set of documents.

$$P = \{d_j, j=1, 2, ..., n\}=\{<T_i, \lambda_i>, i=1, 2, .., m\} \quad (1)$$

Here, n denotes the number of documents distributed in a peer and m denotes the number of topics in the peer. The matrix below describes the document classification:

$$C(P)=(c_{ij});\ 0<i<m, 0<j<n \quad (2)$$

where c_{ij} is defined as below:

$$c_{ij} = \begin{cases} 1/k & \text{if } d_j \in T_i \text{ and } d_j \text{ is classified into } k \text{ topics, } k \geq 1 \\ 0 & \text{if } d_j \notin T_i \end{cases} \quad (3)$$

In our previous work [6], we described the method to classify the documents on a peer into different concept categories. Here, a single document can be classified into at least one topic, and thus $\sum_{i=1}^{m} c_{ij} = 1$. λ_j is the proportion of the statistical occurrence of documents belonging to T_i. It is calculated by the following method:

$$\lambda_i = \frac{\sum_{j=1}^{n} c_{ij}}{n} \quad (4)$$

In order to manage local information, such as keywords and metadata, which can be extracted from documents, each peer maintains an internal indexing model stored in the local repository. This layer also provides the basic functionalities such as information extraction, query processing, and indexing updating.

Our semantic overlay algorithm roots from small world characteristics [7] of peer-to-peer network in the following two aspects. First, each peer in the semantic overlay knows its local neighbors with similar interest at high probability approximating to $p=1$. Second, some nodes know a small number of randomly chosen distant nodes.

The semantic overlay algorithm measures the similarity between peers. We use $P = \{<T_i, \lambda_i>, i=1, 2, .., m\}$ to describe the participant research interests, where T_i denotes a research field the peer's owner interested in, and λ_i shows the degree of interest to T_i. The similarity between two different peers is described as the similarity among the sets of ranked topics, which are concept nodes on the ACM Topic tree, shown in Fig.2.

$$Sim(P^1, P^2)=Sim(\{<T_i, \lambda_i>, i=1, 2, .., m\}, \{<T_j, \lambda_j>, j=1, 2, .., n\}) \quad (5)$$

In our model, the underlying peer communication layer serves as a transport layer for other layers of the system model and hides all low-level communication details

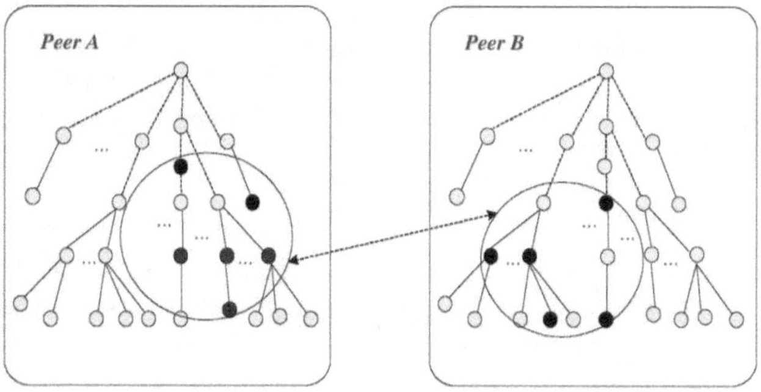

Fig. 2. Semantic similarity between peers

from the rest layers. These functions may include peer discovery, peer grouping, peer advertising, message communicating, peer monitoring, etc.

3 Semantic Similarity Based Overlay

3.1 Semantic Similarity Between Peers

The study of semantic similarity between lexically expressed concepts has been a part of natural language processing for many years. A number of measurement methods have been developed in the previous decade, among which [8] gives the best results.

$$Sim(T_1,T_2)=f_1(l)\cdot f_2(h)=\begin{cases} e^{\alpha l}\cdot\dfrac{e^{\beta h}-e^{-\beta h}}{e^{\beta h}+e^{-\beta h}} & if\,(T_1\neq T_2)\\ 1 & if\,(T_1\neq T_2)\end{cases} \tag{6}$$

Here, l counts the shortest path length between T_1 and T_2 and h counts the hierarchy depth from the leave of T_1 and T_2 to the top of the concept. $\alpha>0$ and $\beta>0$ are parameters scaling the contribution of shortest path length and depth, respectively. The strongest correlation between equation (6) and human similarity judgments is at 0.2 and 0.6. Based on the method, the following equation is proposed to measure the similarity between two peers:

$$Sim(P_1,P_2)=\sum_{j=1}^{|P_2|}\sum_{i=1}^{|P_1|}[Sim(T_i,T_j)\times(\lambda_i\times\lambda_j)] \tag{7}$$

Here, $|P_1|$ and $|P_2|$ are the topic numbers in the two peers. λ is calculated by equation 4. The similarity between the sets of ranked concepts of each other is calculated by summing up products of the similarity value between two topics separately selected from P_1, P_2 and the ranks of both topics.

3.2 Algorithm for Semantic Overlay

Before introducing the overlay algorithm, we specify the neighbors of peer P^k in the semantic overlay network as below:

$$Neighbor_{semantic}(P^k)=\{P^k{}_1, P^k{}_2, \ldots, p^k{}_m\}\ \ m>0 \tag{8}$$

In order to model the semantic overlay of SemreX, we mainly consider two aspects. First, each peer knows its local neighbors, which have the similar interest, at high probability approximating to $p=1$. The following threshold is used to qualify the interest similarity.

$$Sim(P^l, P^k) > Threshold_{semantic\_similarity} \tag{9}$$

Second, each node knows a small number of randomly chosen distant nodes. In [9], the high connectivity nodes play the important role of hubs in communication and networking and can be exploited when designing efficient search algorithms. We intuitively propose the probability as below to create long-range connections among peers in SemreX.

$$p_{long\_distance} = \begin{cases} -\log\frac{h}{TTL_{long}} \bullet e^{-\frac{\tau}{n_1 n_2}} & if\,(\frac{1}{e} < \frac{h}{TTL_{long}} < 1) \\ 0 & if\,(0 < \frac{h}{TTL_{long}} < \frac{1}{e}) \end{cases} \quad (10)$$

Here, h quantifies the actual hops when one peer receives the advertisement for creating long-range contact from the source peer with TTL_{long}. n_1, n_2 quantifies the degree of the two peers, that is the number of neighbors of each peer. τ is the parameter scaling the contribution of the degrees of peers. It is obvious that the long-range rewiring probability is monotonically non-decreasing as degree of peers increases and non-increasing as the real hops between two peers increases.

3.2.1 Clustering Local Peers with Short Distance

Algorithm 1 describes how to cluster the local neighbors. When a peer enters the peer-to-peer network, it advertises its semantic information with a short TTL_{short} to other peers it knows. When any peer receives the advertisement, it decides to accept the new comer as a neighbor or forward it to all his neighbors according to "interest" similarity. If the new comer is accepted as "friendly neighbor", a feedback will be

Algorithm 1. Peer clustering with short distances

//Assume P^k is an entering peer, and P^l is a peer which receives the advertisement of P^k
Input: $SemreX=\{P^1,P^2,\ldots,P^n\}$; $P^k=\{<T^k_i, \lambda^k_i>, i=1,2,\ldots,m^k\}$
Output: $Neighbor_{semantic}(P^k)$ $Neighbor_{semantic}(P^l)$
Procedure for the new comer P^k:
set $Neighbor_{semantic}(P^k)=\Phi$;
set $P^k.TTL=TTL_{short}$;
advertise ($\{<T^k_i, \lambda^k_i>, i=1,2,\ldots,m^k\}$ and $P^k.TTL$);
while(true) do
  listening friendly feedback from other peers ;
  if (receives a friendly feedback from P^l) **then**
    set $Neighbor_{semantic}(P^k)= Neighbor_{semantic}(P^k) \cup \{P^l\}$;
  end if
end do
Procedure for the receiver P^l:
while (true) **do**
  listening advertisement from the network
  if (receives a advertisement from P^k) **then**
    $P^k.TTL= P^k.TTL$ -1.
    if ($Sim(P^l, P^k) > Threshold_{semantic\_similarity}$) **then**
      Set $Neighbor_{semantic}(P^l)= Neighbor_{semantic}(P^l) \cup \{P^k\}$;
      Send friendly feedback to P^k;
    end if
    if ($P^k.TTL>0$) **then**
      Forward advertisement ($\{<T^k_i, \lambda^k_i>, i=1,2,\ldots,m^k\}$ and $P^k.TTL$);
    end if
  end if
end do

Fig. 3. Algorithm for peer clustering with short distances

sent to the new comer to allow it to share the friendship. As this "flooding" like advertising with quite short TTL_{short} only takes place when the peer enters, it will not lead to heavy network traffic in the overlay.

3.2.2 Rewiring Neighbors with Long Distance

Algorithm 2 describes how to create long-range short-cut in the overlay created in algorithm 1. Each peer issues a long-range contact request message with the TTL_{long} to the network at the probability $p=e^{-k/s}$, where s is the number of the neighbors of the source peer and k is the parameter scaling the contribution of the degrees of peers. Apparently, peers with higher degree will have more chances to issue such requests. The message randomly walks around the networks, and long-range connections are created at the probability as equation (10). This long rewiring can be designed to take place at a random time after the peer enters the network or periodically in a rather long interval.

Algorithm 2. Long-range edges form short-cut

//Assume P^k is a source peer, and P^l is a peer which receives the rewiring advertisement of P^k
Input: $SemreX=\{P^1, P^2, \ldots, P^n\}$; $Neighbor_{semantic}(P^k)=\{P^k_1, P^k_2, \ldots, p^k_s\ s>1;\}$
$Neighbor_{semantic}(P^l)=\{P^l_1, P^l_2, \ldots, p^l_t;\ t>1;\}$
Output: updated $Neighbor_{semantic}(P^k)$ $Neighbor_{semantic}(P^l)$
Procedure for the new comer P^k:
set $P^k.TTL=TTL_{long}$;
generate a random number $r\ (0<r<1)$;
if ($r< p=e^{-k/s}$) **then**
advertise ($\{<T^k_i, \lambda^k_i>, i=1,2,\ldots,m^k\}, s, P^k.TTL$) to one random neighbor of P^k;
end if
while(true) do
listening friendly feedback from distant peers ;
if (receives a friendly feedback from P^l) **then**
set $Neighbor_{semantic}(P^k)= Neighbor_{semantic}(P^k) \cup \{ P^l \}$;
end if
end do
Procedure for the receiver P^l:
while (true) **do**
listening advertisement from the network
if (receives a advertisement for rewiring from P^k)
$P^k.TTL= P^k.TTL -1.$
generate a random number $r\ (0<r<1)$;
if ($\frac{1}{e} < \frac{TTL_{long} - P^k.TTL}{TTL_{long}} < 1$ and $r < -\log \frac{TTL_{long} - P^k.TTL}{TTL_{long}} \bullet e^{-\frac{\tau}{st}}$) **then**
Set $Neighbor_{semantic}(P^l)= Neighbor_{semantic}(P^l) \cup \{ P^k \}$;
Send friendly feedback to P^k;
end if
if ($P^k.TTL>0$) **then**
forward ($\{<T^k_i, \lambda^k_i>, i=1,2,\ldots,m^k\}$, s , $P^k.TTL$) to one random neighbors of P^l;
end if
end if
end do

Fig. 4. Algorithm for rewiring long-range edges

4 Query in Semantic Overlay

In SemreX, queries may contain literature metadata, content keyword, topics, and other attributes. The basic idea of query algorithm in semantic overlay is to select similar neighbors to forward the query instead of flooding the query or sending it to a random set of peers. Equation (11) proposes the method for the semantic similarity calculating between a query and a peer.

$$Sim(T_Q, P) = \max_{T_i \in P} \left\{ Sim(T_Q, T_i) \times \lambda_i \right\} \tag{11}$$

Here, T_Q is the topic the query is about to search. P is the neighbor peer to be compared with. λ_i is the rank of topic T_i in the peer P.

The simplest criterion for peer selection is the threshold. In this case the query message will be forwarded to the peers that meet the following criterion.

$$Sim(T_Q, P) > Threshold_{semantic\_similarity} \tag{12}$$

This kind of routing may have a good searching efficiency because every time the most similar peers are selected. However, it has a potential "danger of swamp", that is to say no similar candidates are available and the search process is forced to stop before getting any results. To solve this problem, we introduce a random mechanism for the query to "jump out of the swamp". In this case, the peer P^l is selected at the probability decided by equation (13), where Sim_{max} is the similarity value of the most similar neighbor, and Sim_{min} the least similar neighbor peer.

$$p_{forword}(P^l) = \begin{cases} \dfrac{Sim(T_Q, P^l) - Sim_{\min}}{Sim_{\max} - Sim_{\min}} & if\,(Sim_{\max} - Sim_{\min} \neq 0) \\ 1 & if\,(Sim_{\max} - Sim_{\min} = 0) \end{cases} \tag{13}$$

After a query is routed to the similar peers, the simple keyword matching can be processed by local information retrieval mechanism.

5 Performance Evaluation

We evaluate the recall rate and the message traffic of a query in a semantic overlay through experiments. Recall is a standard measure in information retrieval. It describes the proportion of all relevant documents included in the retrieved set.

$$Recall = \frac{|\, Document_{relevant} \cap Document_{retrieved} \,|}{|\, Document_{relevant} \,|} \tag{14}$$

The most notable overhead in peer-to-peer systems tends to be the processing load that the network imposes on each participant.

$$Message\_traffic = \frac{\sum_{i=1}^{n} Message(P^i)}{n} \tag{15}$$

5.1 Experimental Setup

The simulator generates semantic overlay from the original Gnutella-like network. Eight original graphs with different scales (from 100 nodes to 800 nodes) are used as original Gnutella-like networks in simulation. Each of them accords with a power-law with the exponent $\alpha=3.0$ and the average degree 2.8~3.4. We model the population of document using Zipf distribution, which is followed by Napster, Gnutella and Web Queries. Table 1 summarizes the simulation settings. We compare the efficiency of the semantic overlay and the Gnutella style.

Table 1. Settings for evaluating recalls and traffic

	Descriptions	Values
N	Number of nodes in the network	100 – 800
α	Exponent α of power law	3.0
d	Average degree	2.7-3.4
T	Number of ACM topics in the network	30
D	Max number of documents on each node	2000
Tsd	Threshold of similarity between peers	0.5
Q	Max number of queries by each peer	200
C	Max keywords in each document	25
TTL	Time to Live	2 - 5

5.2 Experiment Results

Fig.5 shows that the recall rates of both our semantic overlay model and Gnutella with the increasing of *TTL*. When *TTL* is small (i.e, *TTL* = 2 or 3) the recall rate of our model outperforms Gnutella apparently, but both recall rates are very close when *TTL* equals 4. The possible reason is that the number of nodes in our experiment is relatively small and the average shortest distance is less than 5. When we set *TTL* = 4, the flooding method of Gnutella can crawl almost all the network but causes very heavy traffic at the same time.

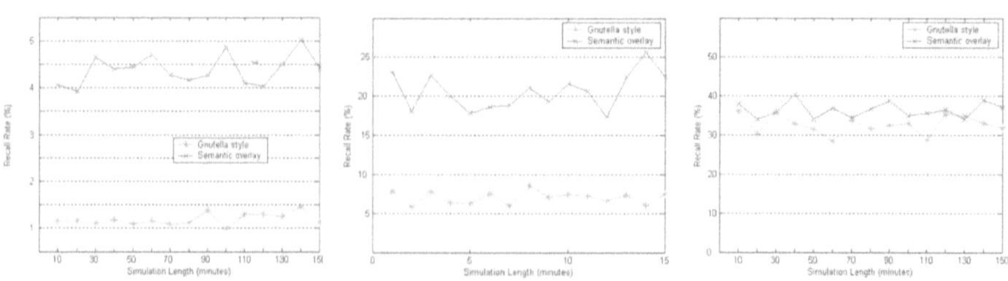

(a) *TTL*=2 (b) *TTL*=3 (c) *TTL*=4

Fig. 5. Comparing recall rates of Gnutella and Semantic overlay model

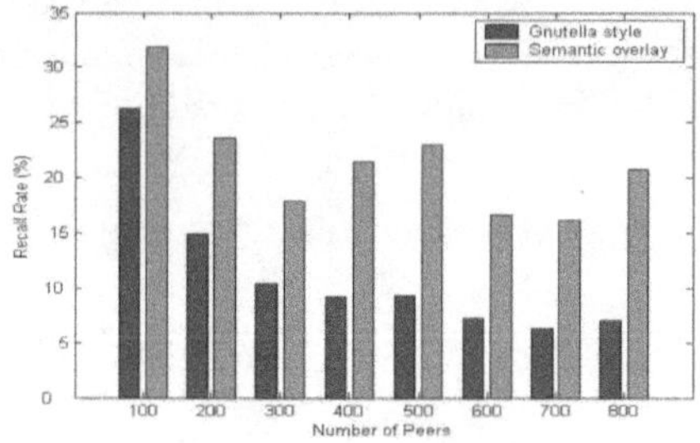

Fig. 6. Comparing recall rates of Gnutella and semantic overlay model

Fig.6 shows the results of recall that when the number of nodes varies from 100 to 800, the recall rate of our model greatly outperforms Gnutella. The advantage of our model increases apparently as the scale of the peer-to-peer network increases.

With fixed scale of 800 nodes, we change *TTL* from 2 to 4. Simulation results show that our model can reduce message traffic dramatically as *TTL* increases, shown in Fig.7.

The simulation results show that semantic overlay model can increase the recall rate as well as reduce message traffic dramatically. The semantic overlay is efficient and may be promising for information sharing peer-to-peer systems.

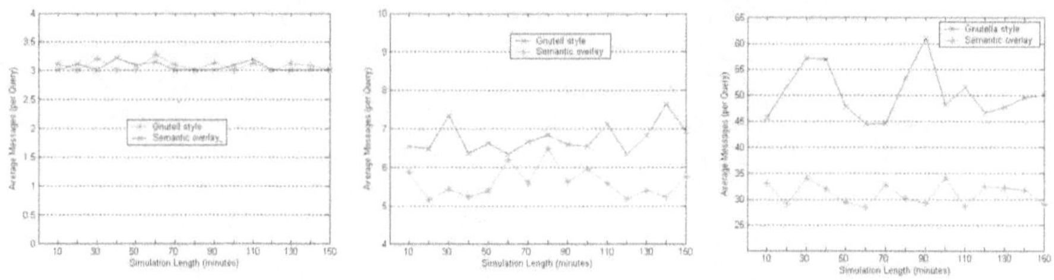

(a) *TTL*=2 (b) *TTL*=3 (c) with *TTL*=4

Fig. 7. Comparing average messages per query request when varying TTL values

6 Related Works

Very limited work in the semantic-based information sharing in peer-to-peer networks has been specifically addressed. Notable exceptions are pSearch [10] and Bibster [11].

pSearch distributes document indices through the P2P network based on document semantics generated by LSI and organized as a CAN. The search cost for a given query is reduced. However its performance under dynamic conditions is unknown.

Bibster, is another model based on semantic overlay. In Bibster, peers advertise their expertise in peer-to-peer networks. The knowledge about the expertise of other peers helps to form a semantic topology.

The main differences of our work are that we propose a statistical way to measure the similarity between any two distributed peers. We also describe a heuristic routing algorithm to achieve better recall rate and less overhead of peer-to-peer networks.

7 Conclusion and Future Works

In this paper we present SemreX, a semantic overlay for desktop literature documents sharing in peer-to-peer network environment. Based on the four-layer system model, we present a semantic overlay algorithm by which peers are locally clustered together according to their semantic similarity and long-range connections are rewired the for short-cut in the peer-to-peer network. Simulation results show that routing in the semantic small world overlay greatly improves the recall of search as well as reduces hops and messages.

In the next step, we will consider evaluating the semantic overlay and querying routing algorithms in a network with much larger scale, and try to find statistical properties of the proposed semantic overlay, such as average path lengths, degree distributions, and cluster coefficient that characterize the structure of the network.

References

[1] H. T. Shen, Y. Shu, and B. Yu, "Efficient Semantic-Based Content Search in P2P Network", *IEEE Transactions on Knowledge and Data Engineering*, Vol.16, No.7, July, 2004, pp.813-826.

[2] D. S. Milojicic, V. Kalogeraki, R. Lukose, K. Nagaraja, J. Pruyne, B. Richard, S. Rollings, and Z. Xu, "Peer-to-Peer Computing", *HP-technique report*, 2002.

[3] C. Gkantsidis, M. Mihail, and A. Saberi, "Random Walks in Peer-to-Peer Networks", *Proceedings of IEEE INFOCOM'04*, Hong Kong, China, March, 2004.

[4] The ACM Topic Hierarchy, http://www.acm.org/class/1998.

[5] Y. Kalfoglou and W. M. Schorlemmer, "Ontology Mapping: The State of the Art", *Proceedings of Dagstuhl Seminar on Semantic Interoperability and Integration*, Germany, 2005.

[6] H. Jin, X. Ning, and H. Chen, "Efficient Query Routing in Semantic Overlays Based on Latent Semantic Indexing", *CGCL technical report*, Huazhong University of Science and Technology, 2005.

[7] D. J. Watts and S. H. Strogatz, "Collective Dynamics of Small-world Networks", *Nature*, Vol.393, June, 1998, pp.440-442.

[8] L. Yuhua, Z. A. Bandar, and D. McLean, "An Approach for Measuring Semantic Similarity Between Words Using Multiple Information Sources", *IEEE Transactions on knowledge and data engineering*, Vol.15, No.4, July/August 2003, pp.871-882.

[9] L. A. Adamic, R. M. Lukose, A. R. Puniyani, and B. A. Huberman, "Search in Power-law Networks", Physical Review E, Vol.64, American Physical Society, 2001.

[10] B. Sujata, Z. Xu, and S. Dwarkadas, "Peer-to-Peer Information Retrieval Using Self-Organizing Semantic Overlay Networks", *Proceedings of ACM SIGCOMM'03*, Karlsruhe, Germany, Aug. 2003, pp.175-186.

[11] P. Haase, J. Broekstra, and et al., "Bibster: A Semantic-Based Bibliographic Peer-to-Peer System", *Proceedings of International Semantic Web Conference*, Nov.2004, pp.122-136.

xDFT: An Extensible Dynamic Fault Tolerance Model for Cooperative System*

Ding Wang, Hai Jin, Pingpeng Yuan, and Li Qi

Cluster and Grid Computing Lab,
Huazhong University of Science and Technology, Wuhan 430074, China
hjin@hust.edu.cn

Abstract. According to the requirement of high-availability, real-time and high performance in cooperative system, an *Extensible Dynamic Fault Tolerance model* (xDFT) is proposed in the paper. xDFT model dynamically sets load quality of server node with variability of system load to change server redundancy. It not only improves the service efficiency, but also implements load balancing in a more efficient and simply way.

1 Introduction

Computer Supported Cooperative Work (CSCW) has been developed to help multi-users accomplish a task cooperatively. Using such systems, groups of geographically distributed users and services can share information that is created and updated dynamically. Collaboration is characterized by a degree of dynamics and flexibility. Thus, it is important for cooperative systems to guarantee reliable and high performance cooperation among participants.

The grid based *Co-Mark Geographical Information System* (CoGIS), which supports the cooperative processing of the widely distributed geographical information by multi-users, is developed. In CoGIS, there are session management, message transferring middleware, marking tools and GIS. The message transferring middleware, which is a *message oriented middleware* (MoM), resides in different nodes. Every operation of clients is processed and transferred by the message transferring middleware. Therefore, to guarantee the high reliability of the message transferring middleware without scarifying performance is the key to the success of CoGIS in the dynamic collaborative environments.

In this paper, we propose an *Extensible Dynamic Fault Tolerance* model to adapt to the above requirements of CSCW applications.

2 Related Works

Fault tolerance [1] is usually implemented by increasing redundant resources, and exponential increment of availability can be achieved. Software fault tolerance is

* This paper is supported by National Science Foundation of China under grant 60273076 and 90412010.

H.T. Shen et al. (Eds.): APWeb 2006, LNCS 3842, pp. 555 – 559, 2006.

often achieved in a manner of software module redundancy [2], which can be divided into two categories: Active Replication [3] and Primary Backup [4].

The mechanisms, such as Active Replication and Primary Backup, can not adapt to the dynamic characteristics of CoGIS. Therefore, we propose an *Extensible Dynamic Fault Tolerance* model (xDFT). This model is made up of two parts. One is the underlying fault tolerant architecture. The other is the fault tolerance mechanism proposed according to the characteristics of the architecture and CoGIS. xDFT model meets the demands of cooperative systems on fault tolerance well. It can alter the load threshold of service node and redundant degree dynamically according to the load status of cooperative system, which improve the utilization rate of system resource and the performance of message transferring middleware.

3 xDFT Architecture

The architecture of xDFT is service ring which can adapt to the dynamic characteristics of cooperative systems very well. Assume that there are n nodes where service objects can been distributed. The pattern that k service nodes form a k-degree service ring is defined as follow:

Definition 1. If k service nodes $\{N(0), N(1), \dots, N(k-1)\}$ construct a service ring, any node $N(i)$ is connected with $N(j)$ and $N(h)$, where $j = (i-1) \bmod k$, $h = (i+1) \bmod k$.

Definition 2. The distance between any two nodes $N(i)$ and $N(j)$ is $d(i, j)$, where $d(i, j)=(i-j) \bmod k$. Any node-task $T(i, t, r)$ has r-1 backup nodes which are adjacent to the

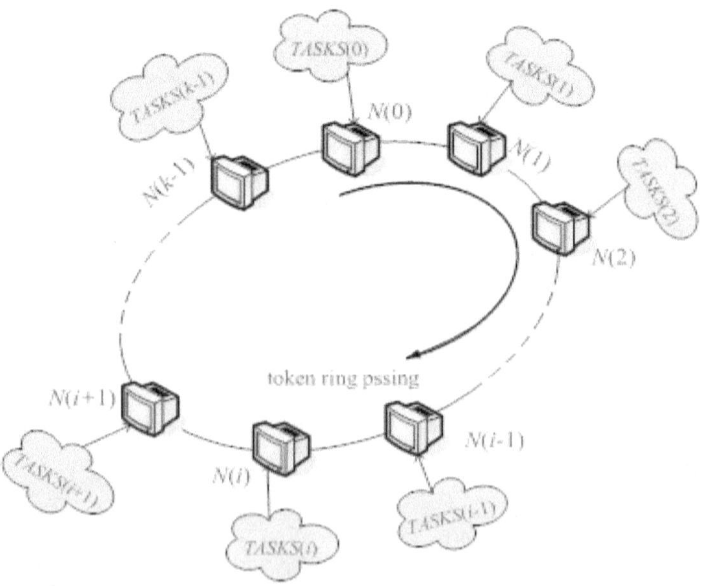

Fig. 1. K-degree Service Ring Architecture

primary node *N(i)*, then the node_id of backup nodes are *(i-m) mod k* and *(i+n) mod k*, *m* and *n* have the following range:

$m \in [1, M]$ and $M = \lfloor r/2 \rfloor \bmod k$;

$n \in [1, N]$ and $N = \lfloor (r-1)/2 \bmod k \rfloor$, where *k* is the quantity of nodes on the current service ring.

According to the definition above, the architecture of k-degree service ring is depicted as Figure 1.

We know that the proper threshold of service node L_{max} and service redundant rate *r* can be chosen according to the number of cooperative task in the system and they decide the number of the nodes on the service ring. The nodes on the service ring serve cooperative tasks in parallel, which not only improve the capacity of message processing, but also utilize the resources effectively. When some nodes on the service ring fail, service ring architecture can have valid service nodes as the substitute immediately and the service ring is automatically repaired to provide the persistent and reliable service to those cooperative tasks, which can ensure the service *non-stop*.

4 Fault Tolerance Mechanism of xDFT

The fault tolerance mechanism of xDFT model includes three algorithms: service nodes assignment algorithm, cooperative tasks deleting algorithm, and service ring restoration algorithm. Assume that the type of service failure is fail-stop, the backup service nodes which are not on the service ring are valid. The followings give the description of three algorithms.

Service Nodes Assignment algorithm. System assigns the light-loaded service node on the service ring to cooperative tasks according to a *Load Share* (LS) strategy, in order to secure the load balance of the nodes on the service ring. If all the nodes on the ring have reached the threshold, then new service nodes will be added into the ring to serve cooperative tasks.

Cooperative Tasks Deleting algorithm. The number of cooperative tasks, which is correlative with the serial numbers of tasks and the loads of nodes, is dynamically changed. But the node_task reflects the current state of cooperative tasks. So when there is a cooperative task which is corresponding to a *T(i, t, r)* exited, the serial numbers of tasks which are served by node *N(i)* should be changed along with it.

Service Ring Restoration algorithm. Fault tolerant system usually tests failure by the means of timeout mechanism. Heartbeat messages are sent to the objects being monitored periodically. If reply is not found in a period of time, the target node is assumed to be failed. Based on this timeout mechanism, our fault tolerance mechanism checks node failure by sending heartbeat messages to two adjacent nodes on the service ring. Assume node *N(i)* fails, firstly transfer the load of *N(i)* to the substitutes and rebuild the service ring. Then check whether *NL(token_id)* exceed the threshold of node *N(token_id)*. If yes, send the token to next valid node whose load is less than threshold of the load of a service node L_{max}.

5 Performance Analysis

We adopt xDFT model in grid based *Co-Mark Geographical Information System*. A user's label actions on GIS are transferred as messages. These messages are processed and distributed to every user within the cooperative group by service nodes, which ensures that the map of every user in the group is identical. In CoGIS, we set the threshold of the load of a service node $L_{max} = 3$, the redundant degree $r = 3$.

Figure 2 shows the curve of average response time when system processes batch messages when there is no failure of service nodes and every fault tolerance mechanism adopts the same redundant rate with the increment of system load. From Figure 2, we can conclude that with the increment of cooperative tasks, Active Replication and Primary Backup experience a harsh performance degradation of message processing due to the exceeded system load. But in xDFT model, though the response time will be increased when nodes join in the service ring, due to the applicable load balance characteristic, the performance of message processing is always good no matter system is light-loaded or heavy-loaded.

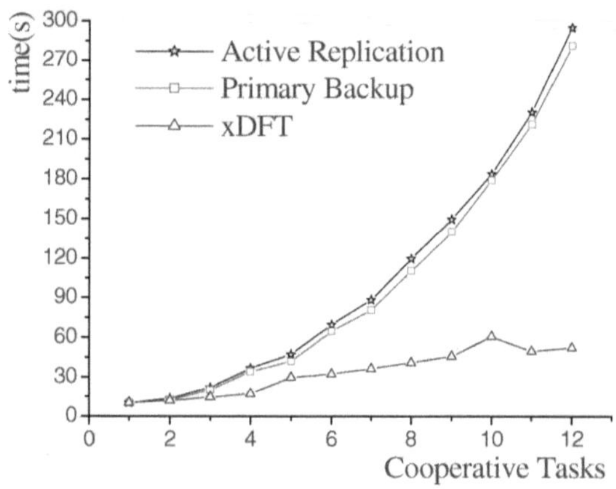

Fig. 2. Average response time without failure

Figure 3 shows the curve of average response time when system processes batch messages when a service node fails. From Figure 3, we can conclude that the fault tolerance performance of xDFT model is still superior to Active Replication and Primary Backup.

According to the above experimental data, xDFT model has the following advantages:

1. The threshold of load is determined by the system load and available service nodes that system can provide. To choose light-loaded node to response system request and the changeable redundant degree not only improves the availability of system and the efficiency of message service, but also costs less system resource.
2. The algorithm is separated from the reliable communication protocol and does not touch the details of message transfer. Hence good scalability can be achieved.

3. Clients participate in fault tolerance positively, which improves the availability and reliability of system. When a failed client restarts and requests for service connect again, it can connect to the valid primary service node correctly and retrieve the identical data information as the other user within the cooperative task.

4. The fault tolerance mechanism is transparent to users. The response to system failure is in time and the restoration is fast with a low cost.

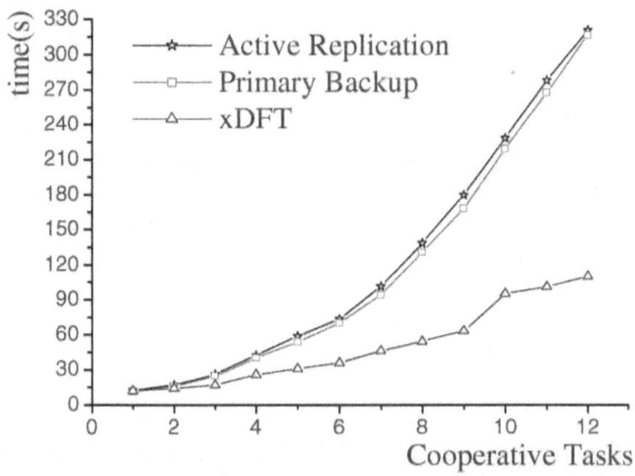

Fig. 3. Average response time with one failure

6 Conclusion

This paper introduces an *Extensible Dynamic Fault Tolerance* model (xDFT). One of the characteristic of this model is the combination of fault tolerance architecture and fault tolerance mechanism. The other characteristic of this model is that service nodes and fault tolerance nodes are allowed to scale dynamically according to the current setting and status of system. By adopting xDFT model, cooperative system can provide high performance and reliable message transfer and process service.

References

[1] A. Bondavalli, S. Chiaradonna, F. Di Giandomenico, and J. Xu, "An adaptive approach to achieving hardware and software fault-tolerance in distributed computing environment", *Journal of Systems Architecture*, March 2002, Vol.47, No.9, pp.763-781.

[2] W. Tang and Y. Zhang, "Replication-based Fault-Tolerant Model in Distribute System", *Computer Engineering and Application*, 2001.23: 130-132.

[3] A. Polze, J. Schwarz, and M. Malek, "Automatic generation of fault-tolerant CORBA service", *Proceedings 34th International Conference on Technology of Object-Oriented Languages and Systems*, Santa Barbara, CA, August 2000, pp.205-213.

[4] R. Giguette and J. Hassell, "Designing a resourceful fault-tolerance system", *Journal of Systems and software*, May 2002, Vol.62, No.1, pp.47-57.

A Grid-Based Programming Environment for Remotely Sensed Data Processing

Chaolin Wu[1,2], Yong Xue[1,3,*], Jianqin Wang[4], and Ying Luo[1,2]

[1] State Key Laboratory of Remote Sensing Science,
Jointly Sponsored by the Institute of Remote Sensing Applications of Chinese,
Academy of Sciences and Beijing Normal University,
Institute of Remote Sensing Applications, Chinese Academy of Sciences,
P.O. Box 9718, Beijing 100101, China
[2] Graduate University of the Chinese Academy of Sciences, Beijing 100049, China
[3] Department of Computing, London Metropolitan University,
166-220 Holloway Road, London N7 8DB, UK
[4] College of Information and Electrical Engineering, China Agricultural University,
Beijing 100083, China
mywuchaolin@163.com, y.xue@londonmet.ac.uk

Abstract. Grid computing can provide significant computational power which can be applied to remotely sensed data processing. But not all the users in the field of remote sensing have the required knowledge of the grid computing. In this paper, we introduce a Grid-based programming environment (GPE) for remotely sensed data processing. User who doesn't have the knowledge of how to deal with transactions of the Grid computing environment can program with it. Although GPE isn't fit for the algorithms in which there exists strong correlation, it works well with the other algorithms and accelerates the computation evidently.

1 Introduction

Grid computing, one of the most important topics in the computing field in the last decade, harnesses a diverse array of machines and other resources to solve problems beyond a single machine's available capacity [1][2]. More and more computing-intensive applications benefit from grid computing. There are several famous grid standard and toolkit today, such as the Globus Project and the Condor Project.

The technology of remote sensing is making rapid progress, too. The huge amount of remotely sensed data and the complexity of the processing algorithms result in the increase of computation time.

Luckily, Grid computing can provide strong computational power to solve the speed problem of remotely sensed data processing [3]. Users should understand the infrastructure of the Grid computing. It restrains the application of grid computing. In this paper, we present a Grid-based programming environment (GPE) to give a

* Corresponding author.

H.T. Shen et al. (Eds.): APWeb Workshops 2006, LNCS 3842, pp. 560 – 564, 2006.

resolution to this problem. We introduce the theory and the construction of GPE. Experiment has been carried out on this environment. At the end, we will give an overview of the environment and discuss the next work.

2 General Introductions to Grid-Based Programming Environment

2.1 Overview

Grid-based Programming Environment (GPE) is a programming tool developed mainly for the remotely sensed data processing. It is developed under WindowsNT, using JAVA, IDL (Interactive Data Language) language and Condor software. So far, GPE is designed for standard c language programmming. Like other programming environment, users can edit, save, compile and execute the programs with it. Fig.1 shows the GUI of GPE. There are three textboxes in Figure 1. The upper left textbox is for codes editing. The upper right one is for the statements of including head files editing. The status information is shown on the lower textbox.

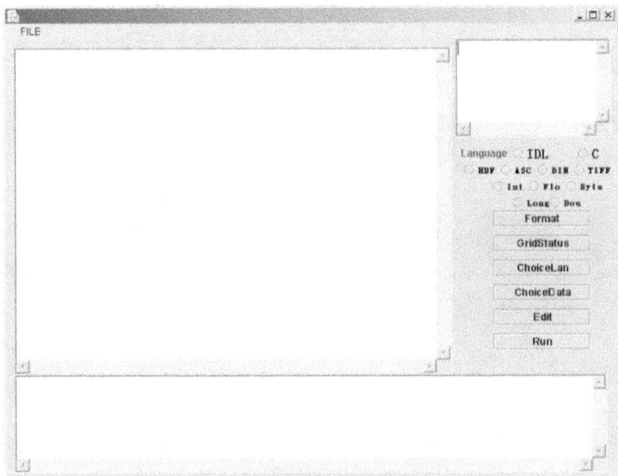

Fig. 1. GUI of Grid-based programming environment

2.2 Basic Principle

According to different processing characteristics, there are three computing task management mechanisms - geometric parallel, algorithm parallel, object-oriented parallel based on Grid computing [4]. The basic principle of GPE is geometric parallel mechanism. In a nutshell, the whole remotely sensed data is distributed among multiple machines to be processed. With the same algorithm, the amount of the remote sensing image data is the most significant one of all the factors of impacting the computation speed. [5] The geometric parallel processing mechanism applied to the remotely sensed data processing means that algorithms run on the different machines are the same and the data to be processed is divided into multiple portions. Theoretically, the time of the whole procedure is less than running the algorithm on one single machine.

3 Some Details in the Development of GPE

GPE is developed using JAVA and IDL (Interactive Data Language) programming language. The workflow of GPE is shown in Fig.2. Some details of GPE development are discussed below.

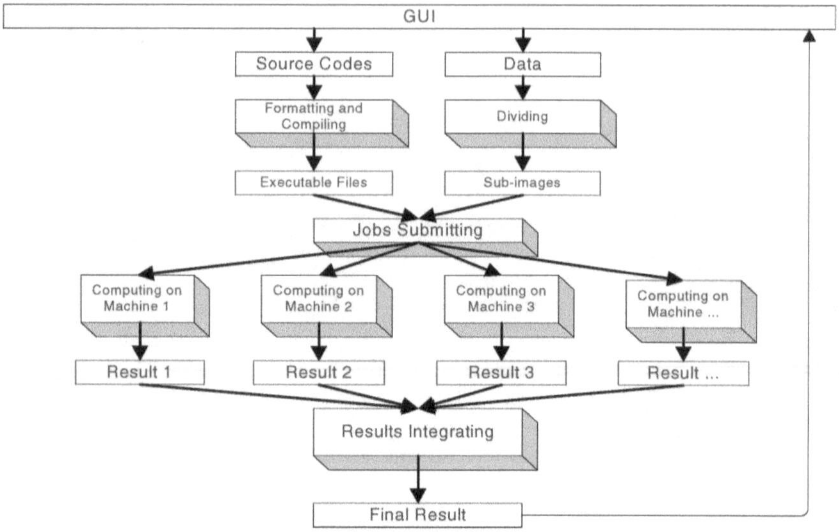

Fig. 2. Workflow of GPE

3.1 Grid Platform

We adopt Condor as the grid platform of the GPE. Condor is a specialized workload management system for compute-intensive jobs. Condor provides a job queuing mechanism, scheduling policy, priority scheme, resource monitoring, and resource management. [6] Taking into account these characteristics, Condor can be used to build Grid computing environment for remotely sensed data processing. Condor helps process the lower-layer transactions such as job scheduling and resource monitoring. Users don't need to interact with Condor directly, so they can ignore the technical details of Condor.

3.2 Dividing Style

Some of the algorithms for remotely sensed data processing require particular image shape. The edge pixels have to be pre-processed in some algorithms, too. One simple example is Laplacian filtering. In this algorithm, the neighbor pixels of each pixel are needed to calculate the result. But some neighbor pixels of edge pixels are null. Therefore, the edge pixels are needed to be pre-processed.

To meet these demands, there are several dividing styles in GPE: row-style, column-style and square-style. Besides these styles, the image data can be divided with overlap-style or non-overlap-style. With the overlap-style dividing, the neighbor sub-images partially overlap with each other. It means that the pixels near the edge of the neighbor sub-images are the same. The size of the overlapping part is adjustable.

3.3 Specifying the Size of the Data

The remotely sensed data processing algorithm often involves circulations. So the size of the image data must be known in program. In Grid computing environment, the data image is divided into multiple parts according to different dividing style. Therefore, size of the sub-image is diverse, which cannot be specified to be constants in programs. In GPE, a size function library is used to specify the size of the data. A series of size functions returning the size of the image data are developed. If the user intends to use the size of the image data, the size function is used in programs without defining by user. Having finished editing the head files editing textbox and the codes textbox, user clicks the Format button to create the final source codes. Actually GPE puts the content of the head files editing textbox, the size function and the content of the codes editing textbox together.

4 Experiments with GPE

Aerosol information is important for many remotely sensing applications. We adopt the aerosol optical thickness retrieval as the experiment with GPE. The algorithm and model we used is SYNTAM [7]. Our Grid computing testbed is composed of five Pentium 4 PCs. The remotely sensed data of 512×512 was used in the experiment. The program of SYNTAM is edited, compiled and executed with GPE. We divide the data into different numbers of parts. The number of parts is smaller or equal to 5. Result of the experiments is shown in Figure 3.

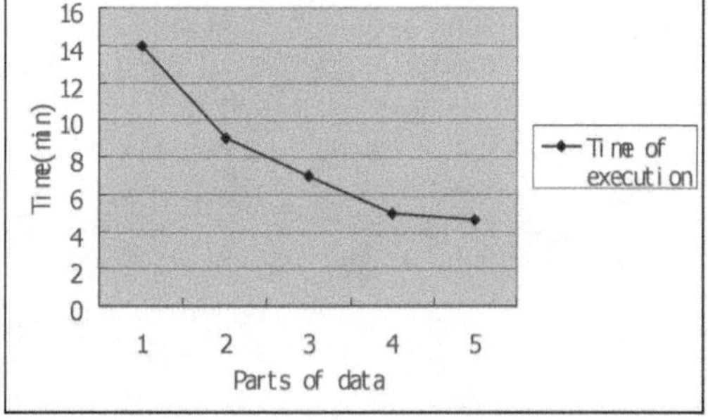

Fig. 3. This shows the relation between the number of the parts of data and the time of execution

The results of the experiment show that GPE can help improve the remotely sensed data processing. There is little difference between the executing time of 4 parts and 5 parts. It may be because of the different speed of the machines. Our computing testbed has three machines with better CPUs than the others. According to condor's resource management mechanism, the other two machines will be used when we have more than three parts of data. Then the low speed of the two machines has impact on the total executing time. The performance of GPE relies on Condor heavily because Condor is responsible for the job execution.

5 Conclusions and Further Development

GPE is a convenient Grid-based programming tool for remotely sensed data processing. It runs the programs on Grid and user can program with it regardless of the Grid environment. GPE isn't suitable for the algorithm in which there exists strong correlation. Even with this restriction, GPE works well for the other algorithms that process the data pixel by pixel. But, by now GPE can compile and execute the programs of standard C language. The future work must focuses on the development of environment for other programming languages.

Acknowledgement

This publication is an output from the research projects "Grid platform based aerosol monitoring modeling using MODIS data and middlewares development" (40471091) funded by NSFC, China, "Dynamic Monitoring of Beijing Olympic Environment Using Remote Sensing" (2002BA904B07-2) and "863 Program - Remote Sensing Information Processing and Service Node" funded by the MOST, China.

References

1. Foster, I., Kesselman, C., Tuecke, S.: The Anatomy of the Grid: Enabling Scalable Virtual Organizations. *International Journal of Super-computer Applications,* vol.15. (2001) 200-222
2. Foster, I. and Kesselman, C. (eds.). The Grid: Blueprint for a New Computing Infrastructure. Morgan Kaufmann (1999)
3. Cai, G., Xue, Y., Tang, J., Wang, J., Wang, Y., Luo, Y., Hu, Y., Zhong, S. and Sun, X.: Experience of Remote Sensing Information Modelling with Grid computing. *Lecture Notes in Computer Science,* Vol. 3039. (2004) 1003-1010
4. Xue, Y., Wang, J.Q., Wang, Y.G., Wu, C.L., and Hu, Y.: Preliminary Study of Grid Computing for Remotely Sensed Information. *International Journal of Remote Sensing*, Vol.26. (2005) 3613-3630
5. Wang, J., Sun, X., Xue, Y., Wang, Y., Luo, Y., Cai, G., Zhong, S. and Tang, J.: Preliminary Study on Unsupervised Classification of Remotely Sensed Images on the Grid. *Lecture Notes in Computer Science,* Vol. 3039. (2004) 995-1002
6. Berman, F., Hey, A. and Fox, G.: Grid Computing – Making the Global Infrastructure a Reality. John Wiley & Sons (2003)
7. Tang, J.K., Xue, Y., Yu, T., Guan, Y.N.: Aerosol Optical Thickness Determination by Exploiting the Synergy of TERRA and AQUA MODIS. *Remote Sensing of Environment*, Vol. 94. (2005) 327-334

Multicast for Multimedia Delivery in Wireless Network

Backhyun Kim, Taejune Hwang, and Iksoo Kim

Department of Information and Telecommunication Engineering,
University of Incheon, Incheon, Korea

Abstract. In this paper we propose a novel technique for multimedia service using multicast delivery in wireless network. It supports seamless multimedia service that uses basic tree and their neighboring mobile nodes (NMNs) in wireless network. The basic trees are generated based on hop-counts from each mobile node (MN) toward base node (BN). Each MN has some NMNs (1-hop away) which are composing the upper, lower or peer MNs within its transmission range and are located at different basic trees. MN joins to a specific multicast (Mcast) group through its basic tree. For protecting seamless service according to mobility of MNs that have already joined Mcast group, those MNs send periodically Mcast join message to their NMNs when they move to the other basic trees, and registers to those basic trees. In this case NMNs that received Mcast join message send it to their upper MN over the same basic tree when they don't join Mcast group just like wired Mcast. But the MNs on the new basic tree do not send Mcast streams until the moved MN registers to a new basic tree for reducing the amount of traffic.

Keywords: Wireless network, Multicast, Multimedia, Routing and Ad-hoc network.

1 Introduction

Ad-hoc networks consist of many mobile hosts connected by wireless links. Each mobile node (MN) operates not only as an end-system, but also as a router to forward packets with the multihop manner in ad-hoc networks. The ad-hoc network topology is dynamic one, so it may be frequently changed due to the nodes' movements. Routing protocols for ad-hoc networks can generally be divided into two categories. One is a proactive routing protocol that attempts to allow each MN using it to always maintain an up-to-date route to each possible destination MN in the mobile wireless network. The other is on-demand routing protocol to establish routing path when a specific MN wants to send data to destination MN [1, 2, 3, 4]. The basic concept of these protocols is flooding that overwhelming amount of packet transmission, most of them unnecessary, can quickly exhaust the battery of hosts and may hang up the entire network as a result of severe packet contention and collision [5, 6, 7].

The conventional multicast technique in mobile ad-hoc networks use routing table, these are severe consume of network bandwidth and power to flood control packet through the network [8, 9].

This paper presents a new technique for multimedia service using multicast delivery in ad-hoc network. It supports seamless multimedia service that uses basic tree

H.T. Shen et al. (Eds.): APWeb 2006, LNCS 3842, pp. 565–572, 2006.

and their neighboring mobile nodes (NMNs) in wireless network. For establishing basic tree, MNs initially send a request packet toward BN, and then some basic trees based on hop-count toward BN are established in ad-hoc network. Also, the each MN has some NMNs which are composing upper, lower or peer MNs on the other basic trees within transmission range and are located different basic trees [10]. The NMNs to a specific MN (hop count(HC) = n) are composed of the upper MN(HC=n-1), peer MN(HC=n) or the lower MN(HC=n+1) MNs toward BN within its transmission range.

For establishing Mcast tree, MN joins to a specific Mcast group through its basic tree and MNs on basic tree maintain their table that NMNs' entry and whether their NMNs are joined Mcast group or not. And to support seamless Mcast service according to mobility of MNs that joined a specific Mcast group, those MNs send periodically Mcast join message to their NMNs when they move to the other basic trees. In this case the lowest hop-counted NMN that received Mcast join message sends it to its upper MN on basic tree when it doesn't have Mcast group just like wired Mcast delivery. But the MNs on the new basic tree do not send Mcast streams until the moved MN is out of range from old basic tree for reducing the amount of traffic. Thus, all MNs in ad-hoc wireless network have a table to manage MNs on their basic tree, their NMNs, their mobility and whether they are joined Mcast group or not. For this, only a few bits are added in a mapping table that logical address is mapped into physical address in wireless network.

The rest of this paper is as follows: Section 2 describes the structure of ad-hoc wireless network, and explains creating basic tree and mapping technique converting physical IP address into logical address. Section 3 shows an algorithm for multimedia service using multicast in wireless network, and Section 4 deals with simulation and analysis of the results. Finally, we discuss our conclusion.

2 The Structure and Creating a Basic Tree in Ad-Hoc Network

The structure of ad-hoc network for supporting seamless multimedia service using Mcast consists of base node (BN) and a number of mobile nodes (MNs). The Fig. 1 shows overall basic trees according to the number of hop-count toward BN from MNs and 1-hop MN's locations, set as {a, z}, in wireless network. The BN may be a MN or fixed node, and the number of BN can be either one per a basic tree or only one in ad-hoc network.

Creating a basic tree is initiated by sending a broadcast packet (request packet; REQ) to BN from all MNs in the ad-hoc network. Some of them receive directly reply packet (REP) from BN, they are the group of the nearest *1- hop* MNs. The MNs which receive it directly from an *1-hop* MN become *2-hop* MNs, and then MNs received it from a *n-1 hop* MN be an *n-hop* MNs.

And neighboring mobile nodes (NMN) of *n-hop* MN on a specific basic tree are consisted of the upper MNs *(n-1 hop)*, lower MNs *(n+1 hop)* and peer MNs *(n-hop)* within its transmission range. The reason of management of NMNs list is that MNs have a characteristic for mobility. Thus MNs can be easily connected on the other basic trees when they move from their basic tree to other one. As a result, the management of NMNs is very important point for handoff in ad-hoc network environment.

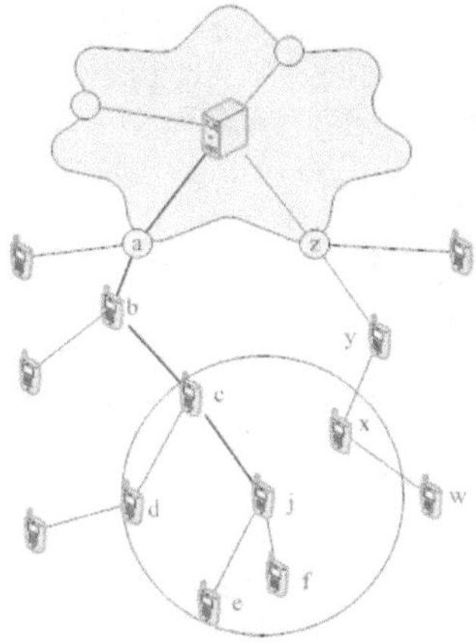

Fig. 1. The delivery tree structure with basic trees

This paper adopts a special bit-field to manage NMNs and whether MNs are join multicast group or not in mapping table that converts logical address into physical IP address. All MNs on the same basic tree have the same location-field (classifying basic trees) and mapping table. Although logical address needs theoretically only k-bit (*log_2 n: n is number of MNs*) in order to assign all MNs, this paper needs more few bits for managing NMNs and indicating whether MNs join Mcast group or not. Fig. 1 shows the delivery tree structure with basic tree that the NMNs of MN *j* is the set as{c, d, e, f, x} within its transmission range. The nearest 1-hop MN of MNs' set {b, c, d, e, f, j} and {w, x, y} are MN *a* and MN *z*, respectively. The hop count (HC) of MN *j* is 4, and its location field and peer-classifying field are 1101 and 10-01-11, respectively.

The structure of mapping table to manage basic tree, NMNs, Mcast group and address conversion is composed of 4-fields; Multicast-field, NMN-field, logical and physical address. And logical address indicates the information of basic tree, and it is divided into location and peer-classifying field of MNs. These address allocation is

Multicast bit 2 bits	Tag 1 bit	Peer-Classifying Field 2n bits	Location Field 4 bits	Physical Address 48 bits

(a) Address structure

11	1	10-01 (MN c)	1101	12AB0CE7
10	1	10-01-10 (MN d)	1101	2357ABCD
01	1	10-01-11-10 (MN e)	1101	15EC03435
11	1	10-01-11-11 (MN f)	1101	345212BC
11	0	01-11 (MN x)	1110	6789CDAB

(b) Mapping Table of MN *j*

Fig. 2. A mapping table with neighboring MNs and join or prune of Mcast groups for MN *j*

self-configured [6, 11, 12]. The location numbers and the peer-classifying numbers of MNs are generated sequentially by the BN and the upper MN, respectively [10].

The Fig. 2 shows a part of mapping table for *MN j* that has *NMNs* {*c, d, e, f, x*}. In Fig. 2, 1-bit Tag-field indicates NMNs of *MN j*. The 2-bits multicast-bit (composing 3-Mcast group; 01, 10 and 11) indicates whether the MNs have already join the specific Mcast groups or not. Thus Fig. 2 shows that *NMNs* {*c, f*} on the same basic tree where the value of their location field is same 1101 have already joined Mcast group 11, also *NMNs* {*d*} and *NMNs* {*e*} have joined 10 and 01, respectively.

The positions of MNs on its basic tree are found from location field of logical address. Thus, a basic tree for *MN j* from Fig. 1 includes {*c, d, e, f*} and NMNs for *MN j* are {*c, d, e, f, x*}. The reason that *NMNs* {*c, d, e, f*} are on the same basic tree is that they have an identical location field, 1101. If the logical address of *MN j* is 27D, *MN d* have an identical hop-count (HC=4), and *MNs* {*e, f*} are MNs that have HC = 5. The method for assigning logical address is no relation to BN except hop-1 MNs, but it depends on upper MN only. Also, Fig. 2 shows *NMNs* {*c, f, x*} have already join Mcast group 3, *MN d* joins Mcast group 2 and *MN e* has already join Mcast group 1. And specific MNs' information in mapping table is modified only when some MNs move to other basic tree or as a result change the relationship with its NMNs, join or prune of Mcast group and send only changed MNs' items to BN.

Logical address on MNs is shown in Fig. 1 and 2, the 1st and 2nd parts of it indicate location of its basic tree in mobile wireless network, the rests of it indicate to classify peer MNs with the same hop-count. Thus peer-classifying field 1 and the location field 2-1-1-2 means that location is the 1st basic tree from BN, the 2nd among hop-2 MNs, the 1st hop-3 and hop-4 MN, and the 2nd among hop-5 MN on its basic tree.

The size of the mapping table for converting logical address into physical IP address is $n(L + P + 32)$ bits, where n is the number of MNs in ad-hoc network and $L+P = l$ is the length of logical address. And each MN has to maintain identifying table for its 3-kinds of NMNs, its size is lx bits, where x is the number of NMNs per a specific MN. And the size of overhead for each MN's managing table is indicated by $l(x + n) + 32n$.

3 Algorithm for Multimedia Service Using Multicast in Ad-Hoc Network

To provide seamless multimedia service using Mcast delivery in ad-hoc network, MNs have to join initially a specific Mcast group through their basic trees. Of course, MNs have to generate basic tree based on hop-count toward BN. MNs may out of range of their initial basic tree because they have a characteristic of mobility. Thus we adopt management of NMNs on the other basic trees to maintain seamless service according to mobility. The reason of this ability is that the NMNs always identify their NMNs including moved MN to their basic tree. For example, we assume MN 1 on basic tree 1 joined Mcast group k and its NMNs are MN a(upper node), MN b(peer) and MN c(lower) on basic tree 3. In this case MN a, b and c identify that MN 1 is located basic tree 1, and know MN 1 is joined Mcast group k. If MN 1 is moving from basic tree 1 to basic tree 3 and there are no MNs on basic tree 3 that joined

Mcast k, they postpone join procedure for Mcast group k until MN 1 registers basic tree 3. The reason of this step is that MN 1 does not deviate the range of basic tree 1. But as soon as deviate from the range of basic tree 1, it requests participation to basic tree 3. At this time one of MN a, b, and c initiates join procedure for Mcast group k. Delaying for join procedure protects duplication Mcast streams to MN 1 and consuming of available bandwidth for MNs on basic tree 3. Before the MN 1 registers to basic tree 3, there is no problem for handoff according to MN 1's mobility if basic tree 3 is already joined Mcast group k.

The procedure for service using Mcast delivery including handoff mechanism explained above is summarized as follows,

i) A specific MN-a broadcasts Mcast group JOIN message on its basic tree and its NMNs on the other basic trees
ii) All MNs received Mcast JOIN packet examine their mapping table whether they have MNs that already joined Mcast group or not
iii) If MNs on its basic tree already have joined Mcast group,,
then MN has sent Mcast join message is serviced through its basic tree
else the requesting MN checks its NMNs whether they joined the Mcast group or not,
and if one of NMNs has already join that group
then it is serviced through that NMN
else its basic tree joins the Mcast group to BN
iv) Then the service starts through its basic tree or NMS on the other basic tree, and periodically sends Mcast join message.
v) If MN that joined Mcast group is moving toward other basic tree,
then MNs on some basic trees within its transmission range check their table whether they joined the Mcast group or not
vi) If a new basic tree already has joined that Mcast group,
then MN that moved to that basic tree registers that tree and receives Mcast streams sequentially
else one of MNs on a new basic tree sends the Mcast group join message to BN as soon as it detects the MN, but after that basic tree joins the group does not send Mcast stream until moved MN has registered to the basic tree.
vii) Moved MN receives Mcast streams from its basic tree until it has registers a new basic tree
viii) As soon as it registers to a new basic tree, MNs sends Mcast streams through their basic tree

4 Simulation and Analysis Performance of Proposed Algorithm in Ad-Hoc Network

In this section, we show simulation results to demonstrate the benefit of proposed mobile ad hoc network with the caching and the location estimation mechanism to support robust streaming service, and analyzes on the results of performance using it. We assume that simulation network is created within a 1000m x 1000m space with

100 MNs that are homogeneous and energy-constrained. The transmission range of nodes is selected from uniform distribution 200m but we set this 100m default. Basically, the proportion of MNs to communicate with BN is 10%. MNs move at maximum speed with 10 m/sec and pause time is 5 seconds. The number of 1'st NMNs that are 1 hop away from BN is 16 identified by location field 4 bits. Each MNs has 4 child MNs identified by peer-classifying field. Thus, NMs away more than 2 hops is identify themselves with peer-classifying field 2n bits where n is the number of hop count to leaf MNs counted from BN. We set this value to 10 to support seamless connection between BN and MNs. So the maximum hop count becomes 10.

The service request rate λ follows Poisson distribution. The service request rate λ follows Poisson distribution and the expression is as follows,

$$f_x(X = k) = \lim_{n \to \infty} \binom{n}{k} P^k (1-P)^{n-k} = \frac{\lambda^k e^{-\lambda}}{k!}$$

Our workload and system parameters are summarized in Table 1. The default values are listed under the *Default* column. We also vary some of these parameters to do sensitivity analysis. The ranges of values used for simulation are given in the third column under the *Range*.

Table 1. Parameters used for the simulation

Parameter	Default	Range
Number of mobile nodes MNs	100	N/A
Request rate λ (requests/min)	5	1 ~ 10
MN mobility (m/second)	10	0 ~ 20
Transmission range R_t (radios: m)	100	0 ~ 200
Number of 1'st NMNs	16	N/A
Number of child MNs	4	N/A

Fig. 3(a) shows the comparison between conventional scheme and proposed scheme in the view of the total network bandwidth consumption in entire network. The X-axis shows the time after simulation starts while the Y-axis shows the total network bandwidth consumption in entire MANET in the unit of bitrate as 128 kbps.

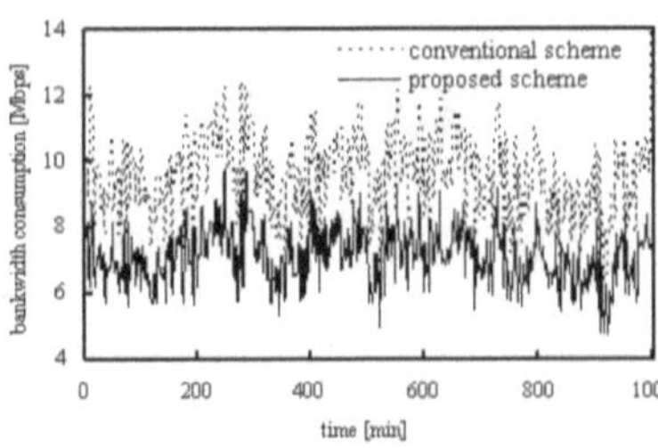

(a) Network bandwidth consumption

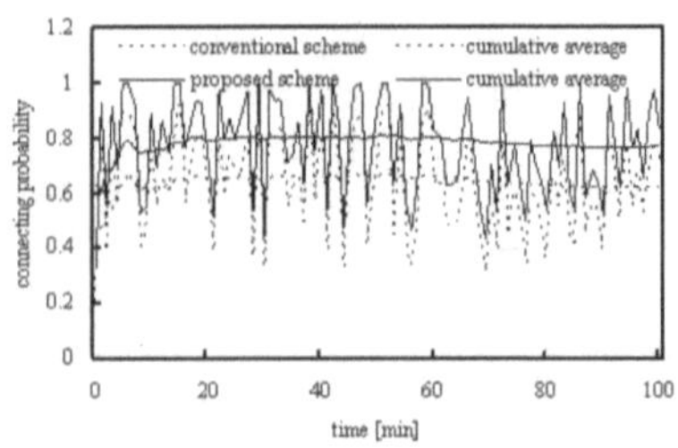

(b) Connecting probabilities in MNs = 100

Fig. 3. Simulation results

Form the result, proposed scheme saves the total network bandwidth consumption compared to the conventional scheme all the time.

Fig. 3(b) shows the variation in the network bandwidth consumption as the number of MNs is changed in conventional scheme and proposed scheme. The X-axis shows the time after simulation starts while the Y-axis shows the connecting probability. The connecting probability means the probability that the ReqMN is continuously served even if the route for BN is broken due to the movement of MNs over delivery tree. Form the result, proposed scheme reduces the duration of service blocking compared to the conventional scheme all the time, where cumulative average indicates the mean connecting probability from time 0 to time t.

5 Conclusion

This paper presents Mcast for multimedia delivery in ad-hoc network. For supporting seamless service using Mcast delivery in wireless ad-hoc network, we adopt the concept of basic trees and neighboring mobile nodes (NMNs). We confirm this technique is very simple and has minimum overhead for adopting NMNs. And the allocation of address according to the number of hop-count toward base node is self-configuration and this technique does not exchange routing table among basic trees, but only a part of mapping table is changed when MNs is moving from their basic tree to the other one. This technique may has a problem that it may not receive a short part of Mcast stream during the MN moves to the other basic tree that there is no MH which joined requesting Mcast group, but it can solve with buffer that provides conventional Real-media and Window media player.

Acknowledgement

This work was supported by the Ministry of Commerce Industry and Energy(MOCIE), the Korea Institute of Industrial Technology Evaluation and Planning(ITEP) through the Multimedia Research Center at University of Incheon.

References

[1] D. Johnson, D. Maltz and Y. Hu, "Dynamic Source Routing Protocol for Mobile Ad-hoc Networks", Internet Draft, draft-ietf-manet-dsr-09.txt, April 2003

[2] C. Perkins, E. Royer and S. Das, "Quality of Service for Ad-hoc On-demand Distance Vector Routing", Internet Draft, draft-ietf-manet-aodvqos-00.txt, July 2000

[3] J. Broch, D. Maltz, D. Johnson, Y. Hu and J. Jetcheva, "A Performance Comparison of Multi-hop Wireless Ad-hoc Network Routing Protocols", In Proc. of the 4th Annual Int'l Conf. On Mobile Computing and Networking (MobiCom 1998), pp85-97, October 1998

[4] P. Johansson, T. Larsson, N. Hedman, B. Mielczar and M. Degermark, "Scenario based Performance Analysis of Routing Protocols for Mobile Ad-hoc Networks", In Proc. of the 5th Annual Int'l Conf. On Mobile Computing and Networking (MobiCom 1999), pp195-206, August 1998

[5] B. Chen, K. Jamieson, H. Balakrishnan, and R. Morris. "Span: An Energy-Efficient Coordination Algorithm for Topology Maintenance in Ad Hoc Wireless Networks", In Proc. of MOBICOM'01, pages 85–96, July 2001.

[6] Santashil PalChaudhuri, Shu Du, Amit K. Saha, and David B. Johnson, "TreeCast: A Stateless Addressing and Routing Architecture for Sensor Networks", In Proceedings of the 4th IPDPS International Workshop on Algorithms for Wireless, Mobile, Ad Hoc and Sensor Networks (WMAN 2004), pp. 221a, IEEE, Santa Fe, NM, April 2004

[7] Brad Karp and H. T. Kung, "GPSR: greedy perimeter stateless routing for wireless networks," in Mobile Computing and Networking, pp243-254, 2000

[8] Mohammad llyas, "The handbook of ad-hoc wireless network," CRC press 2003

[9] L.S.Ji and M.S.Corson, " Differentil Destination Mcast MANET Mcast Routing for Multihop Ad-hoc Network," Proc. Infocom vol. 2, Apr. 2001

[10] Backhyun Kim and Iksoo Kim, "Overlay Multicast Routing Architecture in Mobile Wireless Network" HPCC 2005, Sorrento, Italy Sep. 2005

[11] C. Intanagonwiwat, R. Govindan, and D. Estrin, "Directed diffusion: A scalable and robust communication paradigm for sensor networks," in Proceedings, Sixth Annual Int. Conf. on Mobile Computing and Networking (MobiCOM '00), pp. 56–67 Boston, Massachussetts, USA, 2000

[12] Kai Chen and Klara Nahrstedt , "Effective Location-Guided Overlay Multicast in Mobile Ad Hoc Networks," International Journal of Wireless and Mobile Computing(IJWMC), Special Issue on Group Communications in Ad Hoc Networks, Inderscience Publishers, vol. 3, 2005

Model and Simulation on Enhanced Grid Security and Privacy System

Jiong Yu[1,2], Xianhe Sun[3], Yuanda Cao[1], Yonggang Lin[1], and Changyou Zhang[1]

[1] School of Computer Science and Technology, Beijing Institute of Technology
{yujiong, ydcao, bitailin, zhchy}@bit.edu.cn
[2] College of Information Science and Engineering, Xinjiang University
[3] Department of Computer Science, Illinois Institute of Technology

Abstract. The wide acceptance of the grid technology has created pressure to add some features that were not part of its original design, such as security, privacy, and quality-of-service support. In this paper, we have proposed the enhanced grid security and privacy (EGSP) system architecture including EGSP system model, identity protection system, onion routing system, reputation system, and security technology. We also present a network simulation of the model and analyze its scalability.

1 Introduction

With a promising prospect in recent years, grid technology draws much attention now [1, 2]. Grid applications are designed to allow computers to easily interconnect and to assure that network connections will be maintained. This same versatility makes it rather easy to compromise data privacy in grid applications. In this paper, we present the security and privacy aspects in grid computing system, with emphasis on the expansions and features of the grid security. We have proposed the enhanced grid security and privacy (EGSP) system architecture. The objective of the EGSP system is to show that the privacy of the user may be protected in many kinds of processes by incorporating privacy enhancing technologies embodied within an Intelligent Grid Agent (IGA). Then, we do the further research on the scalability of the models for the EGSP system. We have proposed several models for the different security and privacy protection technologies employed in the EGSP system, and have tested system scalability under the different situations.

2 System Architecture

In order to protect the IGA against privacy intrusion and security attacks, the IGA should have the features: the privacy protection-related functions, the mechanisms (like pseudonym system, identity protector, anonymous communication, authentication, confidentiality, and non-repudiation, etc.).

In the EGSP agent structure, an IGA can be mainly divided into four parts: the functions, the knowledge bases, the mechanisms, and data. Each part consists of general components, privacy protection-related components, and security-related components.

H.T. Shen et al. (Eds.): APWeb 2006, LNCS 3842, pp. 573 – 582, 2006.

- The functions include the general functions, the privacy protection-related functions, and the security-related functions. The general functions will perform the task of the agent using data and its knowledge base. The privacy protection-related functions will protect the user's or the agent's privacy. The security-related functions will show where and what security measures should be taken to protect the agent against other entities' attack.
- The knowledge bases also include the general knowledge bases, the privacy protection-related knowledge bases, and security-related knowledge bases. The general knowledge bases will store the definitions such as what a task means and when the agent needs to perform the task. The privacy protection-related knowledge bases define what privacy means and how to act towards it. The security-related knowledge bases define what security means and when to apply the specific measures like encryption, digital signature, hash function, etc.
- The mechanisms include the privacy protection-related mechanisms and the security-related mechanisms. The privacy protection-related mechanisms include the privacy enhancing technologies such as anonymity systems, pseudonym systems, public-key infrastructure, and anonymous grid communication, etc. The security-related mechanisms include the infrastructure specific security measures that decide in which grid environment and which security measures should be taken, and the security communication aspects to provide the security mechanisms such as confidentiality, authentication, and integrity.

In EGSP, the grid privacy enhancing technologies include the anonymity system, pseudonym system, anonymous communication network, etc. These grid privacy enhancing technologies should be combined and supported by the security, trust, interaction, and reputation environments, e.g. PKI, Certification, SSL, authentication, encryption, and signature, etc. Figure 1 shows the EGSP agent in its environment.

The EGSP system consists of several components: PKI, CA, IGA agent platform, Information management server, Resource management server, and Data management

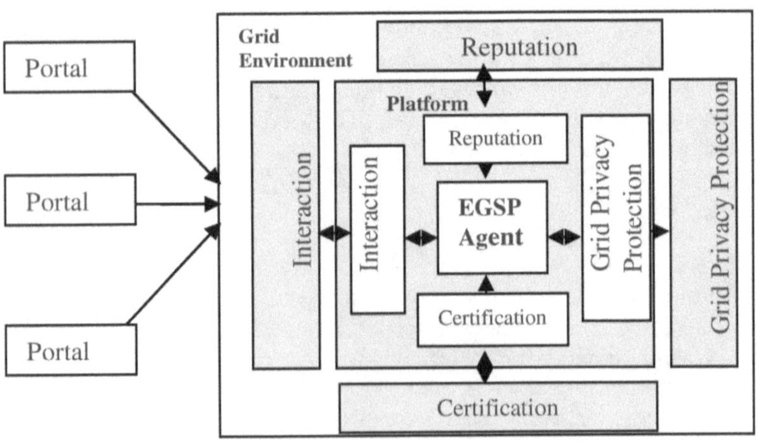

Fig. 1. EGSP agent in its environment

server. The certification authority (CA) will issue the certificates to the user, server, and IGA platform respectively. The PKI provides an infrastructure for security and privacy protection of the whole EGSP system. A secure communication channel will be set up between the user grid portal and application server, the application server and IGA platform, and the IGAs using the security technologies like SSL, HTTPS, Secure XML, etc. The anonymous communication between the IGAs also can be protected with the Onion Routing network.

In the EGSP system, several privacy protection-related technologies like identity protector, onion routing network, and reputation system, will become the important factors that may affect the EGSP system.

3 Identity Protection Systems

In the EGSP system, an identity protection system will control the exchange of the identity between the various system elements, especially between the personal agent and task agent. An important function of the identity protector is to convert a user's identity into a pseudonym and hide the user's identity by a private credential, etc. The pseudonym is an alternate (digital) identity that the user adopts when using the system. Examples of pseudonyms in conventional information systems include account numbers at banks and social security numbers.

A good identity protection system should be able to authenticate users, control abuse by intruders, users, services or applications, and provide accountability measures for users. If so, a private credential may be issued to a user agent known by a pseudonym in the EGSP system since the private credential have the following useful properties.

- *Anonymity:* Anonymity is the state of being not identifiable within a subject set. It serves as the base case for grid privacy protection.
- *Control:* Full anonymity may not be beneficial to anyone, especially in the situation that at least one of the parties in a transaction has a legitimate need to verify previous contacts, the affiliation and eligibility of the other party, and so on.
- *Credential Sharing Implies Secret Key Sharing:* The agents or users who have valid credentials might want to help their friends to obtain whatever privileges the credential brings improperly. They could do so by revealing their secret key to their friends such that their friends could successfully impersonate them in all regards.
- *Unforgeability of Credentials:* A credential may not be issued to an agent or user without the system or credential authority's cooperation.
- *Selective Disclosure:* The holder of private credentials can show the private credentials' attributes without revealing any other information about the private credentials.
- *Re-issuance:* The issuer can refresh a previously issued private credential without knowing the attributes it contains. The attributes can even be updated before the private credential is re-certified.
- *Pseudonym as a Public Key for Signatures and Encryption:* Additionally, there is an optional feature of a pseudonym system: the ability to sign with one's pseudonym, as well as encrypt and decrypt messages.

On the other hand, privacy protection requires that each individual have the power to decide how the personal data is collected and used, how it is modified, and to what extent it can be linked; only in this way can individuals remain in control over their personal data. When using private credentials, organizations cannot learn more about a private credential holder than what he/she voluntarily discloses, even if they conspire and have access to unlimited computing resources. Individuals can ensure the validity, timeliness and relevance of their data.

Private credentials are beneficial in any authentication-based environment in which there is no strict need to identify individuals at each and every occasion. Private credentials do more than protect privacy: they minimize the risk of identity fraud. More generally, private credentials are not complementary to identity certificates, but encompass them as a special case.

The identity protection system is very useful, especially in rental grid service environment. The reason is that the accountability and anonymity are essential properties in a charge system. Clearly, anonymity is intended to hide a user's identity, whereas accountability is intended to expose the user's identity, thereby holding the users responsible for their activities. The identity protection system is an effective solution for that.

In the EGSP system, an identity protector creates two domains within the information system: "identity domain" and "pseudo-domain". The "identity domain" denotes the domain in which the user's identity is known, the domain in which the user's identity is secret is termed "pseudo-domain”.

In addition, the identity protection systems by themselves do not protect against wiretapping and traffic analysis in the EGSP system. On grid systems, one can deploy the anonymous communication services such as MIX network, or Onion Routing network against the traffic analysis attacks.

Based on the EGSP system architecture, the identity protector (IP) can be used in two ways to control the exchange of the user's identity with the EGSP system

- Identity Protector is placed between the agent and the external environment;
- Identity Protector is placed between the user and the agent.

For EGSP system scalability, the important factors are not the above different models but the complexity of the identity protectors since the system may need more computation or network resources to manage and authenticate the users if the system deploys complex mechanisms like private credential system. In order to make the testing simple, we design the following testing models to test its scalability on the EGSP system (see Figure 2).

Based on this model, we will test the EGSP system scalability when the following different mechanisms are deployed on the identity protection system.

- Simple pseudonym system based on password authentication (simple authentication);
- Complex private credential system based on the public-key certificate authentication (strong authentication).

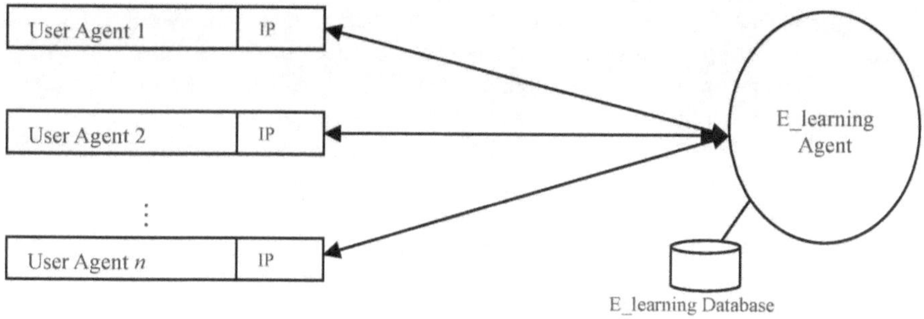

Fig. 2. Testing model for identity protection system

4 Onion Routing

Since traffic analysis also is a serious menace to agent-based applications. An adversary can monitor and compromise certain parts of a distributed agent system by matching a message sender with the receiver. Protecting the disclosure of communication partners or the nature of communication between partners is an important requirement for confidentiality in an e-business context. It is also a property desired by agent users who want to keep their agent lives and relationships private. In order to protect the communications between the agents against the traffic analysis attacks like communication pattern attack, timing attack, etc. [3, 4], Korba proposed an alternate onion routing (OR) approach [5]. We use this onion routing transaction on the grid systems in order to provide anonymous communication for multiple agents in the EGSP system. The primary goal of onion routing is to provide strongly anonymous communications in real time over a public network with reasonable cost and efficiency. A secondary goal is to provide anonymity to the sender and responder, so that the responder may receive messages but be unable to identify the sender, even though the responder may be able to reply to those messages.

5 Reputation Systems

Multi-agent systems have been expected to take an important role in the future information society and especially in grid e-business applications. However, another major weakness of grid e-business applications of multi-agent systems is the raised level of risk associated with the loss of any notion of reputation and trust. This loss of trust and reputation is due to each agent only having limited information about the reliability of others, or the product and service quality during transaction, especially when the agent communicates with a new platform or a new agent, or uses a new service. A reputation system, which could collect, distribute and aggregate a participant's past experiences with the existing services, would be useful to build a level of trust in the agent society, for instance helping other agents choose the reliable services in a multi-agent systems.

In the enhanced grid security and privacy system, we present a reputation evaluation system, which consists of several components: a certificate authority (CA), a reputation evaluation agent, a MIX agent, a service provider agent, and a client agent. Each agent involved in this system, must register and get its identification certificate from the CA after it starts. Each service provider agent must register its services to the reputation evaluation agent. During each term, the client agents evaluate the reputation of the service via their access through the service provider agents according to their past experience. The evaluation results are protected using a nested hybrid encryption algorithm, and sent to a modified MIX cascade consisting of several MIX agents. The final MIX agent sends the last layer ciphers to the reputation evaluation agent. After the reputation evaluation agent gets all of the results, it then calculates and publishes the final reputation evaluation results of the service provider agents.

The reputation evaluation system offers several advantages. First, it would protect the privacy of the client agents during evaluation since the modified MIX cascade outputs the evaluation messages in a randomly permuted order. Second, it prevents the same client agents from repeating the evaluation during the same evaluation term since the first MIX agent could authenticate and record the action of the client agents, and since each MIX agent also has a batch signature for the messages it outputs. Additionally, the MIX agent does not know the evaluation results since the evaluation results are encrypted using the nested encryption algorithm.

Since our reputation system is based on a simple MIX system, the main testing component is the MIXes. But since the different authentication mechanisms deployed in the reputation system may have the different impact on the EGSP system scalability, we compare the scalability of the following two situations -- simple password authentication and complex certificate authentication. Figure 3 depicts the testing model.

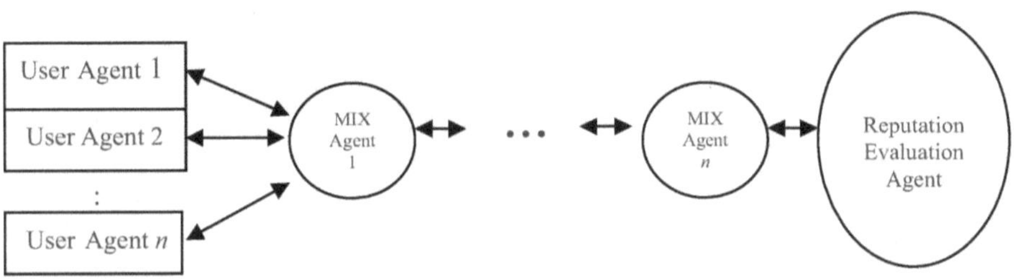

Fig. 3. Testing model for reputation evaluation system

6 Testing Metrics and Results

We mainly focus on the testing of the scalability of the special security and privacy protection technologies (such as identity protector, reputation evaluation system, etc.) in the EGSP system. According to multi-agent communications, multi-agent systems will need to scale in a number of different dimensions as follows.

- The total number of agents involved increasing on a given platform.
- The total number of agents involved increasing across multiple systems or platforms.

- The size of the data upon which the agents are operating is increasing.
- Increasing the diversity of agents.

In order to compare the EGSP system scalability under the different environments, we need to identify metrics for measuring scalability, such as the performance of the privacy protection technologies, the workload of the security functions and algorithms, and communication costs between various elements. The metrics may also be related to conversation and privacy policies, such as:

- The total number of simultaneous conversations supported,
- The response time between conversations,
- The algorithms that will be used for anonymous protection, etc.

In order to obtain the complexity cost for interaction between user agents and E_learning agent when the security and privacy protection technologies are deployed in the EGSP system, we define the following measuring method for the testing metrics (see Figure 4).

$$Complexity = \sum_{k=1}^{n}(a_k\alpha_k + b_k\beta_k + c_k\delta_k + d_k\gamma_k)$$

where a_k, b_k, c_k, $d_k = 0$ *or 1*. If all *a, b, c, d* equal 1, the *complexity* represents the total complexity cost for all agent actions.

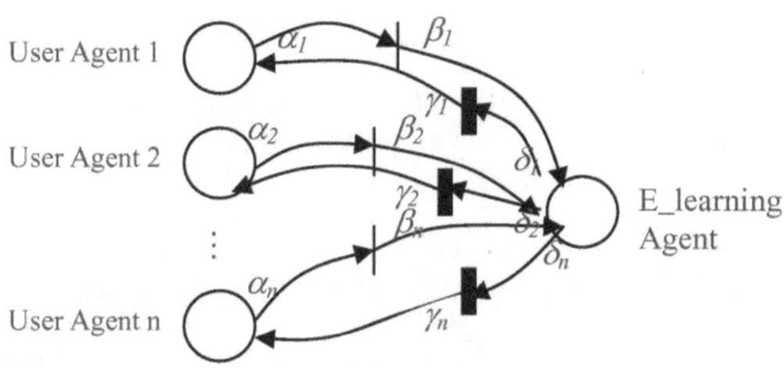

Fig. 4. Measuring method for the EGSP system scalability

The parameters α_1, α_2, …, α_n represent the computing delays of the user agents associated with request-message, security and privacy processing. The parameters β_1, β_2, …, β_n represent messaging delays from the user agents to the E_learning agent associated with the security and privacy processing like onion routing network. The parameters δ_1, δ_2, …, δ_n represent the computing and searching delays of the E_learning agent associated with authentication, decryption, search, and match processing, etc. The parameters γ_1, γ_2, …, γ_n represent messaging delays from the E_learning agent to the user agents also associated with the security and privacy processing. Figure 4 depicts the measuring method for the EGSP system scalability simulation.

In a grid application system, the important scalability parameters should be user size, E_learning size, E_learning search and match speed, response time for a query, computing complexity for privacy and security processing, etc. Thus, in our simulation, the main simulation parameters include user size, total processing time(T_Time) for all request and reply messages in both users' agents and E_learning agent side. The total processing time includes the computing complexity cost for privacy and security processing.

Based on the testing model for identity protection system in Figure 2, the tests are performed. The testing software is JADE (3.0) multi-agent platform. The E_learning agent is run in the main container, and the user agents are run in the other container.

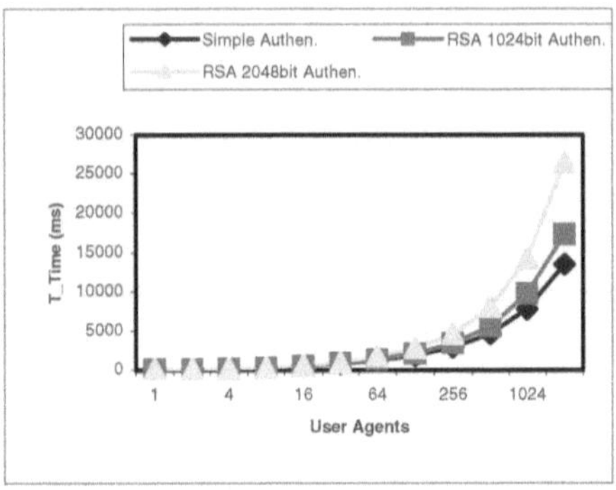

Fig. 5. T_Time for the different identity protection systems

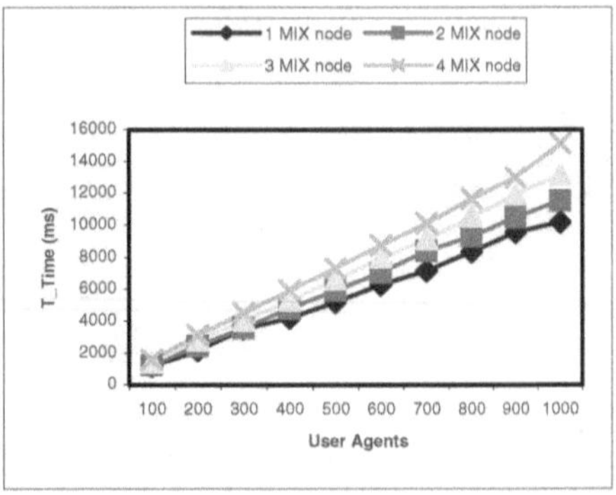

Fig. 6. T_Time for the reputation evaluation system

The simulation testing was done with the user agents using different identity protection technologies for the authentication: simple authentication (based on password) and strong authentication (based on RSA algorithm). We also test the effect of the number of the user agents on the T_Time under the above different authentication situations. We test the user agent scalability from 1 to 2048, where each user agent sends one request-message to the E_learning agent. Figure 5 depicts the total processing time for the request and reply messages under the different authentication processing, where the testing results are based on the one-time simple authentication (using MD5, or SHA), and the one-time strong authentication (using IAIK JCE 1024bit RSA and 2048bit RSA) for the computation and processing.

Since as the authentication systems, the workload usually is in the server side, normally, we use the short key as the verification key for the strong authentication (using public key cryptography) in order to make the server (E_learning agent) more efficiency in the testing and real applications.

From the above testing results, we know that the simple authentication has the best scalability, and the strong authentication (using 1024bit RSA algorithm) also has a good scalability, but the strong authentication (using 2048bit RSA algorithm) has a little bad scalability. On the other hand, as we mentioned, since the verification key (public key) usually is very short (about 14bit) for the strong authentication, its scalability is OK for the real applications. In addition, we also could get a balance between the scalability and the security level for the real applications according to the testing. In the following testing, we will use 2048bit RSA for testing since current e-commerce applications usually use it.

Based on the testing model for reputation evaluation system in Figure 3, the tests are performed. We test the reputation system model under JADE (3.0) multi-agent platform and NS-2 respectively based on the above parameter, where we assume the link delay is about 10ms. The simulation testing is done according to the user agents using the MIX Cascade under the different MIX node size in the model. We test the effect of the number of the user agents on the T_Time under the different MIX node size, and the scalability of the user agents from 100 to 1000. In addition, each user agent only sends one evaluation message to the reputation evaluation agent in the following testing. Figure 6 depicts the testing results.

From the above testing results, we know that the size of the MIX nodes only has a small impact on the scalability of the reputation system. On the other hand, since the reputation system only collects and calculates the reputation values once a period (e.g., one year or one month), it really does not such impact on the scalability of the EGSP system.

7 Conclusion

The goal of this paper is to produce an analysis of the design of EGSP privacy enhancing technologies with a view to improving grid security, privacy and usability of implementations. In the EGSP system, many privacy protection functions, such as identity protection system and onion routing, are supported by basic security technologies like cryptographic technologies, hash functions, and digital signature, etc. These basic security technologies provide the following functions.

- Confidentiality: Confidentiality is a service used to keep information secret from all but those who are authorized to see it. There are many approaches to providing confidentiality. Currently, the mathematical algorithms include the symmetric key cryptography like AES, IDEA, 3-DES, and asymmetric key cryptography like RSA, ElGamal.
- Integrity: Data integrity is the property whereby data has not been altered in an unauthorized manner. The unauthorized data manipulation includes insertion, deletion, and substitution. The methods for providing data integrity include hash function, MAC, digital signature, authenticator.
- Authentication: Authentication includes entity authentication and message authentication in grid applications. The entity authentication is the process whereby one party is assured of the identity of a second party involved actually, i.e. corroborating the identity of an entity. The message authentication provides to one party, which receives a message, assurance of the identity of another party, which originated the message, i.e. corroborating the source of information. The former usually uses the mechanisms like password, or challenge-response identification; the later usually uses the hash functions, MACs, or digital signature, etc.
- Non-repudiation: Non-repudiation is a service, which prevents an entity from denying previous commitments or actions. A digital signature is usually used for this in the grid security applications.

- An identity protection system normally only has a small impact on the EGSP system scalability if the software is designed appropriately whatever it uses the simple or strong authentication.
- A reputation system usually would not have a deleterious impact on EGSP system scalability if the software is designed appropriately and the reputation evaluation has a life cycle.

Acknowledgments

This work is supported by National Natural Science Foundation of China under Grant No. 60563002 and Scientific Research Program of the Higher Education Institution of XinJiang under Grant No. XJEDU2004I03.

References

[1] Chien, A. A., Sun, X. H.. Xu Z. W.: Viewpoints on Grid Standards. Journal of Computer Science & Technology. Vol. 20(1). (2005) 1-4

[2] Foster , Kesselman, C.: Concepts and Architecture. In The Grid 2: Blueprint for a New Computing Infrastructure. Morgan Kaufmann Publishers (2004)

[3] Raymond, J.: Traffic Analysis: Protocols, Attacks, Design Issues, and Open Problems. in H. Federrath, editor, Anonymity (2000)

[4] Song, R. G., and Korba, L.: Review of Network-Based Approaches for Privacy. Proceedings of the 14th Annual Canadian Information Technology Security Symposium. Ottawa, Canada (2002)

[5] Korba, L., Song, R. G., and Yee, G.: Anonymous Communications for Mobile Agents. In Proceeding of the 4th International Workshop on Mobile Agents for Telecommunication Applications (MATA'02). Barcelona, Spain (2002) 171-181

Performance Modeling and Analysis for Centralized Resource Scheduling in Metropolitan-Area Grids*

Gaocai Wang[1], Chuang Lin[2], and Xiaodong Liu[1]

[1] Graduate School at Shenzhen, Tsinghua University, 518055, Shenzhen, Guangdong, P.R. China
{wanggc, liuxd}@sz.tsinghua.edu.cn
[2] Department of Computer Science and Technology, Tsinghua University, 100084 Beijing, P.R. China
chlin@tsinghua.edu.cn

Abstract. Metropolitan-Area Grid (MAG) normally deals with a more limited computation and data-intensive problems on geographically distributed and smaller range resources. Therefore, in a MAG, resource scheduling is distinguished from other Grid. Current research on performance evaluation of resource scheduling in MAG is based on simulation techniques, which can only consider a limited range of scenarios. In this paper, we propose a centralized resource scheduling model in a MAG and give a formal framework via Stochastic Process Algebras (SPA) to deal with this problem. Within this framework, we model and analyze the performance of resource scheduling, allowing for a wide variety of job and data scheduling algorithms. Moreover, we can evaluate the combined effectiveness of job and data scheduling algorithms, rather than study them separately.

1 Introduction

A Metropolitan-Area Grid (MAG) environment connects a collection of more limited computation, data-intensive and information service problems on distributed geographically among multiple sites in a city, and enables users to share these resources. Some infrastructure and software projects have been undertaken to realize various visions of MAG, such as ShanghaiGrid[1], CSAR of Mini-Grid[2] and ChicagoSim[3]. ShanghaiGrid aims at constructing a metropolitan-area information service infrastructure and establishing an open standard for widespread upper-layer applications from both communities and the government. Different from other Grid projects that are designed mainly for larger-scale scientific usage, MAG mainly focuses on computation, data-intensive and information service problems for a small district. Therefore, in a MAG, resource scheduling is obviously distinguished from other Grid projects.

* This work is supported by the National Natural Science Foundation of China (No. 90412012), NSFC and RGC (No. 60218003), the Natural Science Foundation of Guangdong Province and the China Postdoctoral Science Foundation.

H.T. Shen et al. (Eds.): APWeb 2006, LNCS 3842, pp. 583 – 589, 2006.

Resource scheduling is defined as the process of making scheduling decision involving resource over multiple sites. Resource scheduling can be further classified into centralized scheduling and distributed scheduling. A centralized scheduling uses a center for each job to service, while a distributed scheduling may use global information for each job to service. It has been observed that the centralized scheduling scheme is simple and efficient and is used in smaller Grids, such as Metropolitan-Area Grids. Distributed scheduling scheme can provide fault tolerance and scalability for large-scale Grids.

To use a MAG, users typically submit requirements/jobs. In order for a job to be executed, two types of resources are required: computing facilities, data access and storage. The MAG must make scheduling decisions for each job based on the current state of these resources, such as workload of computing elements, and location of data. Different job and data scheduling algorithms may bring different performance for the MAG.

Many research works have been done on the performance evaluation of MAG, but most of which use simulation techniques, which can only analyze a limited range of scenarios. For example, in [3], a discrete event simulator, called ChicagoSim, was constructed to evaluate the performance of different combinations of job and data scheduling algorithms. Furthermore, many related works are based on a single factor of job or data scheduling in other Grids. In [4,5], performance is analyzed with the assumption that jobs have been allocated to certain computing elements. While in [6,7], performance is analyzed with the assumption that data have been accessed. The research to study the combined effectiveness of job and data scheduling strategies has been pointed out to be very complex [8].

We propose a centralized resource scheduling model in MAGs and develop a formal framework via Stochastic Process Algebras (SPA) to addresses the above mentioned issues. Our framework is based on a general scheduling architecture of MAG. In this centralized resource scheduling architecture, there are several servers, each of which can provide computational and data-storage resources for submitted jobs. Each server is composed of a number of processors and storage. Processors provide compute power and can access the local storage at that server. System-level schedulers control the scheduling of jobs to servers. Node-level schedulers are responsible for the scheduling of jobs that have been allocated to servers. It follows the framework that the SPA [10] model can be constructed. In the uniform model, we present different job scheduling algorithms for System-level schedulers and Node-level schedulers, and further evaluate the system performance.

The rest of the paper is organized as follows. Section 2 describes the general and centralized scheduling architecture of MAG that we use for our modeling and analysis. Section 3 presents the SPA model, while Section 4 is dedicated to a description of job scheduling algorithms within the model. We conclude and point to future directions in Section 5.

2 Centralized Scheduling Architecture

MAG system consists of many homogeneous or heterogeneous resource sites. They have different hardware architecture, operation system, file system, local job manager and authentication mechanism. At the same time, they maybe belong to different organizations. Users are authorized to submit jobs from any resource sites. The submitting jobs may implement in local sites or long-distance sites.

Our study is based on a general and centralized scheduling architecture, and depicted in figure 1. The logic of the architecture can be encapsulated in three distinct modules:

(1) **Server.** Each server comprises a number of processors and storage. Due to the heterogeneousness of Grid environments, different server may have a different number of processors. The processors of a server can only access the local storage.
(2) **Queue.** Queue can be classified into system-level queue (*SLQ*) and node-level queue (*NLQ*). Each system-level queue receives jobs from user and submits to system-level schedulers. Node-level queue receives jobs from system-level scheduler and submit to servers. Each job can be allocated to any of the servers and further dispatched to any of the processors of a server. Each job requires some specific data be available at the local storage before it can be executed.
(3) **Scheduler.** It is the core of the system and can be classified into two schedulers: system-level scheduler (*SLS*) and node-level scheduler (*NLS*).

- **System-level scheduler.** *SLS* is regarded as the first-level scheduler of the whole system and control on the scheduling of all incoming jobs. In the system, jobs can be classified depending on their different priority levels. *SLS* can consider many factors for job dispatching, such as the requirements and preferences of the users or jobs, status of the resources, current load of the server, location of the resource server, etc. Each job is submitted to some *SLS* in terms of its priority. Once an *SLS* receives a job, it immediately makes a decision on which *NLQ* the job should be assigned to, according to some scheduling algorithm. It may use the global information, such as load of each server, and/or location of the data required by a job, as input to its decisions.
- **Node-level scheduler.** *NLS* is the local scheduler of a server and is responsible for selecting a waiting job from the multiple queues of the server according to a task-selecting policy. When a job is delivered to *NLS* from *SLS*, it is managed by

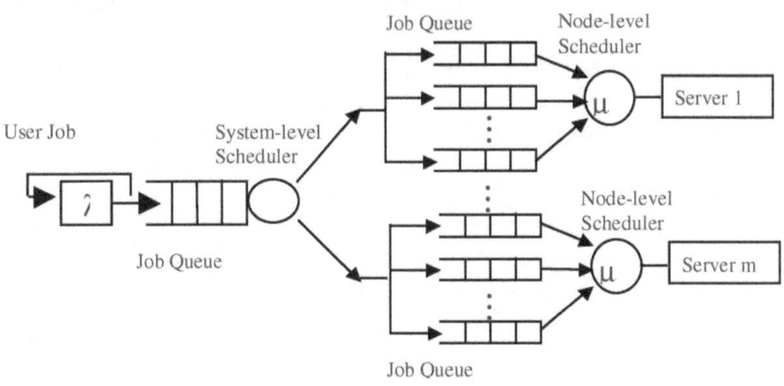

Fig. 1. A MAG Centralized Scheduling Architecture

the *NLS* of that server. The *NLS* determines how to schedule the jobs allocated to it, according to its associated scheduling algorithm. It only uses the local information, such as load of each local processor, to guide its decisions.

From the system description, we can see that the MAG scheduling system is distinct from traditional Grid schedule systems, because we use a centralized resource scheduling approach.

3 SPA Model

To study the performance of centralized resource scheduling in MAG, we adopt the modeling and analysis method, which allows for the performance evaluation in various scenarios.

We choose the SPA as the base for our study, since it is a powerful formal tool that is able to handle prioritized, concurrent, asynchronous, stochastic and nondeterministic events. The mainly advantages of SPA is that they allow the creation of highly modular model description. Process algebras offer several attractive features, such as compositionality, formality and abstraction. In the existing performance modeling paradigms, these features are not necessarily available. Queuing networks offer compositionality but not formality. Stochastic Petri nets offer formality but not compositionality; neither queuing networks nor stochastic Petri net offers abstraction mechanisms.

Suppose there are q classes of jobs, the jobs in each class have the same priority level. The priority level values range from 1 (the highest priority) to q (the lowest one). Jobs with priority level i are denoted by r_i. In accordance, the jobs in the system are classified into q categories. Each class i submits jobs r_i to *SLS* according to a Poisson distribution with the same mean arrival rate.

The system consists of m servers, each of which contains a depository with an infinite capacity for storing data, and may have different compute power. To consider a general case, we assume that server comprises several processors, and each processor provides the exponential distributed service durations with different mean rates for different priority-level jobs. In each server, there are n waiting queues of jobs, each for one priority level and with a finite capacity. Jobs in the same waiting queue are managed in FIFO (First-In-First-Out) order. If a job is in the turn to be scheduled, it can be executed only when the processor is free and its required data is available. Each processor can provide service for at most one job at any time, and the jobs from different waiting queues are selected for service according to their priorities, i.e., jobs with higher priorities have higher priorities to be executed.

There is only one system-level scheduler in the system. And one node-level scheduler in each distributed one server.

In the following, we propose a SPA model of the MAG centralized scheduling system. We first consider the scheduling system as the parallel composition of the following components or process: load process (the user's jobs, process requirements and system operative procedure) (*Load*), the system-level schedulers (*SLS*), the n node-level schedulers (*NLS*) and the m servers (*Proc*).

$$GridS := Load \parallel_A SLS \parallel_B \parallel \underbrace{(NLQ_0 \parallel NLQ_0 \parallel \ldots \parallel NLQ_0)}_{q}$$

$$\parallel_C \underbrace{(NLS \parallel NLS \parallel \ldots \parallel NLS)}_{n} \parallel_D \underbrace{(\mathrm{Pr}\,oc \parallel \mathrm{Pr}\,oc \parallel \ldots \parallel \mathrm{Pr}\,oc)}_{m}$$

Here, *A*, *B*, *C* and D denote action sets between these process. *A*={*a*}, B={*d*}, *C*={*c*} and *D*={*dd*}.

The *Load* can be refined to two components: An arrival process (*Arr*) and a system-level queue (*SLQ*).

$$Load := Arr \parallel_a SLQ$$

The *Arr* submits jobs to *SLQ* according to a Poisson distribution with the same mean arrival rate. The arrival process is modeled as a Poisson stream with an infinite sequence of incoming requests, creating jobs a with rate λ, (a, λ). (a, λ). $(a, \lambda)\ldots(a, \lambda)$. Which can be formulated recursively.

$$Arr := (a, \lambda)$$

The *SLQ* waits for the arrival of a job with action (*a*, -), or alternatively deliver a job to the *SLS*, if it is requested to do so and it is not empty, with action (*d*, -). In order to get finite models, the queue is bound to a maximum number of jobs, and $0< i < maxQ$.

Modeling the *SLQ* is a simple task. The *SLQ* schedule all arrival user's jobs to the *NLQ* in terms of different scheduling policies, and satisfied with different user's requirements, action (d, ∞), or alternatively carries out action (c, ∞) when the queue isn't empty, or do not anything action (*empty*, -) when the queue is empty.

$$SLQ_0 := (a,-).SLQ_1$$
$$SLQ_i := (a,-).SLQ_{i+1} + (d,-).SLQ_{i-1}$$
$$SLQ_{\max Q+1} := (a,-).SLQ_{\max Q} + (d,-).SLQ_{\max Q-1}$$

The *SLS* schedule all arrival jobs in terms of scheduling policies, such as the requirements and preferences of users or jobs, status of resources, current load of servers, location of resource servers, etc. The *SLS* satisfied with different user's requirements, action (d, ∞), or alternatively carries out action (*c*, -) when the *SLQ* isn't empty. Or do not anything action when the *SLQ* is empty.

$$SLS := (d,\infty).(c,-).SLS + (empty,-).SLS$$

Similarity, the jobs arrive the *NLQ* of server, action (*c*, -). The *NLQ* delivers a job to server, if it is requested to do so and it is not empty, action (*dd*, -). The *NLQ* is bound to a maximum number of job, and $0< i < maxQ$. The *NLQ* is described as the following.

$$NLQ_0 := (c,-).NLQ_1$$
$$NLQ_i := (c,-).NLQ_{i+1} + (dd,-).NLQ_{i-1}$$
$$NLQ_{\max Q} := (c,-).NLQ_{\max Q} + (dd,-).NLQ_{\max Q-1}$$

The *NLS* receives jobs repeatedly from the *NLQ* and submits to server according to different scheduling policies, scheduling action (dd, ∞), and processes it with rate μ, action (p, μ).

$$NLS := (dd,\infty).NLS + (empty,-).NLS$$
$$\Pr oc := (dd,\infty).(p,\mu).\Pr oc$$

Where all component processes are specified as above, we can see that the expressive power of SPA is outlined.

4 Different Scheduling Algorithms for Scheduler

System-level scheduling and node-level scheduling are the core of the MAG scheduling system, and for each there is a set of different algorithms. In the section, we give these algorithms respectively.

4.1 *SLS* Algorithms

SLS algorithms are used to decide the destination *NLQ* for a given job. Four sophisticated algorithms are presented below.

(1) **Random.** This algorithm randomly selects a *NLQ*.

(2) **Least Load.** This algorithm selects the *NLQ* that has the least load. Here, load is assumed to be the number of jobs in the waiting queues.

(3) **Minimum Predicted Response Time.** This algorithm selects the *NLQ* with the minimum predicted response time. More precisely, predicted response time is the delay the job spent in this system, from when a *Arr* starts to submit the job until the job execution is completed.

(4) **Minimum Expected Overall Waiting Delay.** This algorithm selects the *NLQ* with the minimum expected overall waiting delay. More precisely, expected overall waiting delay is the delay the job spent at a server, which takes all local processors of the server into consideration.

4.2 *NLS* Algorithms

NLS algorithms are implemented at the node-level scheduler of a server to select the optimal destination processor for a given job if the job is already assigned to *NLS*. Three sophisticated algorithms are presented below.

(1) **Random.** This algorithm randomly selects a processor.

(2) **Least Load.** This algorithm selects the processor that has the least load, i.e. of which the waiting queue possesses the minimum number of jobs.

(3) **Minimum Expected Waiting Delay.** This algorithm selects the processor with the minimum expected waiting delay. More precisely, expected waiting delay of a job is the delay the job spent at a processor.

5 Conclusions and Future Work

A MAG enables geographically distributed smaller range user to collaborate and share computer, data and information resources. The sheer volume of the data and computation calls for sophisticated data management and resource allocation. This paper is one step to developing a formal framework, instead of a simulator, to investigate the performance of such a system.

In this paper, we construct the SPA model based on a general and centralized scheduling architecture of MAG. In the uniform model, we can model and analyze the performance of scheduling system based on SPA. We present different job scheduling algorithms. In future work, we want to develop an analysis tool to evaluate the performance of practical MAG. Particularly, this tool is planned to be able to plug in different algorithms for selecting the best server, the best processor, and the best replication.

References

1. Minglu Li, Min-You Wu, Ying Li, et.al. ShanghaiGrid: A Grid Prototype for Metropolis Information Services. APWeb 2005, LNCS 3399, pp. 1033-1036.
2. John Brooke, Martyn Foster, Stephen Pickles, et. al. Mini-Grids: Effective test-beds for GRID application. http://www.csar.cfs.ac.uk
3. K. Ranganathan and I. Foster. Simulation Studies of Computation and Data Scheduling Algorithms for Data Grids. Journal of Grid Computing, 1(1): 53-62, 2003.
4. William H. Bell, David G. Cameron, Luigi Capozza, A. Paul Millar, Kurt Stockinger, and Floriano Zini. Simulation of Dynamic Grid Replication Strategies in OptorSim. Proceedings of the 3rd Int'l. IEEE Workshop on Grid Computing (Grid'2002), Baltimore, USA. Springer Verlag, Lecture Notes in Computer Science.
5. S. Venugopal, R. Buyya, and Lyle J. Winton. A Grid Service Broker for Scheduling Distributed Data-oriented Applications on Global Grids. Middleware for Grid Computing 2004: 75-80.
6. V. Hamscher, U. Schwiegelshohn, A. Streit and R. Yahyapour. Evaluation of Job-Scheduling Strategies for Grid Computing. Proceedings of the Seventh International Conference of High Performance Computing. 2000.
7. H.A. James, K.A. Hawick and P.D. Coddington. Scheduling Independent Tasks on Metacomputing Systems. Proceedings of Conference on Parallel and Distributed Computing Systems. 1999.
8. Frédéric Desprez and Antoine Vernois. Simultaneous Scheduling of Replication and Computation for Data-Intensive Applications on the Grid. Technical Report. 2005. http://www.ens-lyon.fr/LIP/Pub/Rapports/RR/RR2005/RR2005-01.pdf.
9. Stephen Gilmore, Valentin Haenel, Jane Hillston, and Leï la Kloul. PEPA nets in practice: Modelling a decentralised peer-to-peer emergency medial application. In M. Núñez *et al*, editor, Applying Formal Methods: Testing, Performance, and M/E-Commerce (EPEW 2004), volume 3236 of *LNCS*, pp262-277. Springer-Verlag, October 2004.

AGrIP: An Agent Grid Intelligent Platform for Distributed System Integration

Jiewen Luo[1,2], Zhongzhi Shi[1], Maoguang Wang[1,2], and Jun Hu[1]

[1] Institute of Computing Technology, Chinese Academy of Sciences,
P.O. Box 2704, Beijing 100080, China
luojw@ics.ict.ac.cn
http://www.intsci.ac.cn/en/index.html
[2] Graduate School of Chinese Academy of Sciences,
Beijing 100080, China

Abstract. Grid and agent communities both develop concepts and mechanisms for open distributed systems, albeit from different perspectives. How to apply the agent technology in Grid infrastructure to facilitate distributed system integration (virtual organization formation) becomes an interest topic in recent years. In this paper, we investigate the issue and present an agent grid intelligent platform, called AGrIP, from the implementation point of view. AGrIP is based on the FIPA-compliant multi-agent environment MAGE and has four different layers, which apply the agent interface services for interaction and communication. It can integrate legacy systems and enables interoperability between distributed heterogeneous systems (organizations), expedite dissemination and retrieval of data, automate operator tasks and support the decision-making process. Up to date, it has been applied to several practice projects as the robust infrastructure. We will expound its recent application in Agent Grid Based City Emergency Inter-Act Project as an illustration.

1 Introduction

Grids are a distributed computing technology whose objective is to provide the basic mechanisms for forming and operating dynamic distributed collaborations, or virtual organizations as they are sometimes called [1]. While Grid infrastructure has focused on such things as the means for discovering and monitoring dynamic services, managing faults and failures, creating and managing service level agreements, creating and enforcing dynamic policy, to name a few – to date, only limited progress has been made on creating the higher level reactive behaviors that would enable truly dynamic formation of virtual organizations (VOs). Hence, we need the basic intelligent platform that facilitates to form VOs and enables independently operating entities to interact with one another with partial knowledge and emerge a robust desirable behavior. This is exactly the range of problems that are being addressed by intelligent agent technologies. Under this view, we have built the agent grid intelligent platform AGrIP. From our experiments and applications, it truly provides a robust and ideal platform for distributed system integration.

H.T. Shen et al. (Eds.): APWeb 2006, LNCS 3842, pp. 590–594, 2006.

2 Platform Architecture

We propose a four-layer model in AGrIP for agent grid platform from the implementation point of view, as illustrated in figure 1:

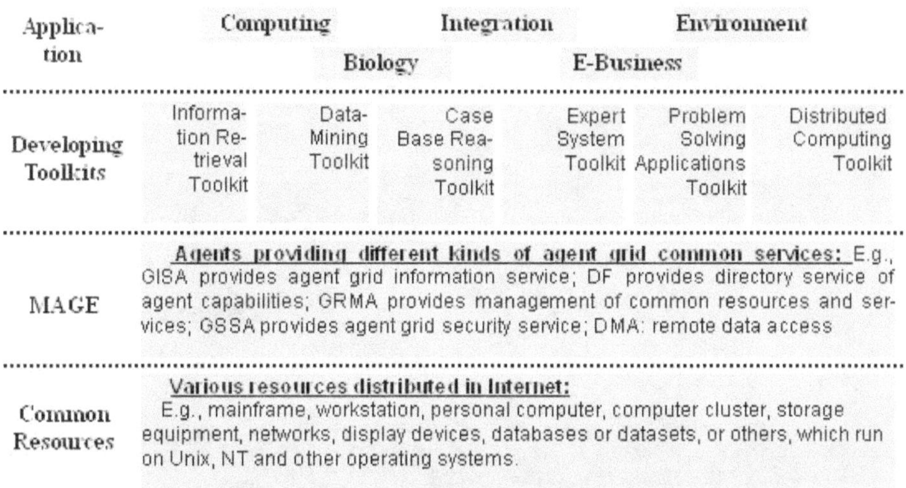

Fig. 1. Architecture of Intelligent Platform AGrIP

1. Common resources: consist of various resources distributed in Internet, such as mainframe, workstation, personal computer, computer cluster, storage equipment, databases or datasets, or others, which run on Unix, NT and other operating systems.
2. Agent environment: it is the kernel of Grid computing which is responsible to resources location and allocation, authentication, unified information access, communication, task assignment, agent library and others.
3. Developing toolkit: provide developing environment, containing agent creation, information retrieval, data mining, case base reasoning, expert system etc, to let users effectively use grid resources.
4. Application service: organize certain agents automatically for specific purpose application, such as power supply, oil supply e-business, distance education, e-government.

3 Multi-agent Environment

As shown in figure 1,the most important module in the AGrIP platform is MAGE (http://www.intsci.ac.cn/en/research/mage.html). It is a multi-agent environment with a collection of tools supporting the entire process of agent-oriented software engineering and programming. It is designed to facilitate the rapid design and development of new multi-agent applications by abstracting into a toolkit the common principles and components underlying many multi-agent systems. The idea was to create a relatively general and customizable toolkit that could be used by software users with only basic competence in agent technology to analyze, design, implement and deploy multi-agent systems [5].

It mainly consists of four subsystems: Agent Management System, Directory Facilitator, Agent, and Message Transport System.

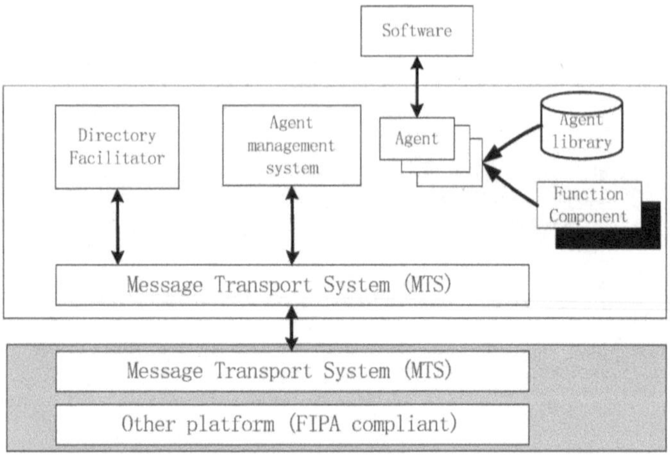

Fig. 2. The Architecture of MAGE

1) **Agent Management System** is a mandatory component of MAGE. It maintains a directory of AIDs (Agent Identifiers), which contain transport addresses for agents registered in MAGE and offer white pages services to other agents.
2) **Directory Facilitator (DF)** is an indispensable component of MAGE. It provides yellow page services to other agents. Yellow page service allows agents to publish one or more services they provide so that other agents can find and successively exploit them. Agents may register their services with the DF or query the DF to find out which services are offered by other agents.
3) **Message Transport Service (MTS)** is the default communication approach between agents on different FIPA-Compliant agent platforms. It uses FIPA ACL as the standard communication language.
4) **Agent** is the fundamental actor in MAGE, which combines one or more service capabilities into a unified and integrated execution model that may include access to external software, human users and communications facilities.
5) **Software** in figure 2 represents all non-agent, external components accessible to an agent. For example, Agents may add new services or acquire new communication/negotiation protocols, etc.

4 Agent Interface Services

We need a powerful agent environment to provider interfaces for the hierarchical architecture of the AGrIP platform. MAGE is a distributed agent environment and has many advantageous features. Hence, we build the agent interface services based on it.

4.1 Directory Service

Directory services are a vital part of any grid software or infrastructure, providing fundamental mechanisms for discovery and monitoring, and hence for planning and adapting application behavior. In AGrIP, there are two types of directory service. Correspondingly, there are two types of agent: **DF** agent and **GISA** agent.

As we can see from the architecture of MAGE, **DF** (Directory Facilitator) is a mandatory component that provides a yellow pages directory service to agents. It is the trusted, benign custodian of the agent directory. MAGE may support any number of DFs and DFs may register with each other to form federations. Every agent that wishes to publicize its services to other agents, should *register* its service description with DF. Also an agent can *deregister* itself form DF, which has the consequence that there is no longer a commitment on behalf of the DF to broker information relating to this agent. At any time, and for any reason, the agent may request the DF to *modify* its service description. An agent may *search* in order to request information from a DF.

GISA (Grid Information Service Agent) contains static and dynamic information about compute resources, as well as static and dynamic information about the network performance between compute resources. It provides information directory service. You query GISA to discover the properties of the machines, computers and networks or other common resources that you want to use.

4.2 Resources Management

We build the **GRMA** (Grid Resource Management Agent) in MAGE platform, which is an important agent that provides capabilities to do remote-submission job start up. **GRMA** unites Common Resources and services, providing a common user interface so that you can finish a job with any common resource or service. **GRMA** is a general, ubiquitous service, with specific application toolkit commands built on top of it.

The GRMA processes the requests for resources for remote application execution, allocates the required resources, and manages the active jobs. It also returns updated information regarding the capabilities and availability of the computing resources to GISA and DF.

Furthermore, GRMA provides an API for submitting and canceling a job request, as well as checking the status of a submitted job. We extend Globus Resource Specification Language (RSL) to describe request. Users write request in ERSL and then request is processed by GRAM as part of the job request.

4.3 Data Management

DMA (Data Management Agent) is built in MAGE as an agent mainly aiming at access remote data and avoid useless data transfer. Specifically, when a client submits only one problem, it is possible to optimize the overall computation time when several servers can perform the computation or when data needed are already stored on storage elements. Using this service, clients will submit their problems with data identifiers as parameters instead of full data.

5 Conclusion

Establishing grids is an important undertaking in developing scalable infrastructures. Although Grid and agent communities both develop concepts and mechanisms for open distributed systems, they focus different perspectives historically. How to combine these two technologies and make them benefit from each other is the direct motivation for our recent work. In this paper, based on our past work on multi-agent system, we have presented an agent grid intelligent platform from the implementation point of view. AGrIP focuses on service-oriented layer in terms of current existing running environment and applies the agent interface services for interaction between different layers, which make it convenient to access data resource and integrate heterogeneous legacy systems. Because of its stable performance, it has been applied to several real projects such as Agent Grid Based City Emergency Inter-Act Project mentioned above.

Acknowledgments

This work is supported by the National High-Tech Programme of China (Grant No. 2003AA115220), the National Basic Research and Development Plan of China (Grant No. 2003CB317000) and the Youth Research Fund of CUMT (Grant No. 0D4489).

References

1. Ian Foster. and Kesselman. The Grid: Blueprint for a New Computing Infrastructure (2nd Edition). Morgan Kaufmann, 2004.
2. Ian Foster, Carl Kesselman, Nicholas Jennings. Brain Meets Brawn: Why Grid and Agents Need Each Other. AAMAS2004, New York
3. http://www.objs.com/agility/tech-reports/990623-characterizing-the-agent-grid.html
4. Keith G. Jeffery, Knowledge, Information and Data, A briefing to the Office of Science and Technology, UK, February 2000.
5. Zhongzhi Shi, Haijun Zhang, Yong Cheng, Yuncheng Jiang, Qiujian Sheng, Zhikung Zhao: MAGE: An Agent-Oriented Programming Environment. IEEE ICCI 2004: 250-257
6. http://www.intsci.ac.cn/en/
7. Zhongzhi Shi, Youping Huang, Qing He, Lida Xu, Shaohui Liu, Liangxi Qin, Ziyan Jia, Jiayou Li. MSMiner-A Developing Platform for OLAP. Decision Support Systems, 2005
8. Foster, I. Internet computing and the emerging grid. *Nature* 408, 6815 (2000).

Scalable Backbone for Wireless Metropolitan Grid

Lin Chen, Minglu Li, and Min-You Wu

School of Computer Science and Engineering,
Shanghai Jiao Tong University, Shanghai 200030, P.R. China
chen.lin@sjtu.edu.cn, li-ml@cs.sjtu.edu.cn, mwu@sjtu.edu.cn

Abstract. Wireless metropolitan grid promises to offer various broadband services to citizens anywhere with low cost. The problem of throughput and scalability are still critical challenges for the success. In this paper, we propose and evaluate scalable backbone architecture which employs super nodes with asymmetric capability to reduce the hop count as well as increase the scalability. Multi-channel multi-radio approach is utilized to increase the throughput. A detailed performance evaluation shows that the deployment of about 20% super nodes can increase the network throughput by a factor of up to 5 compared with the conventional single channel multi hop architecture.

1 Introduction

As complementary part of wired network in metro area, wireless metropolitan grid makes it easier to extend grid computing to large numbers of devices that would otherwise be unable to participate and share resources [1]. Once more or less complete grid of access points are put up around a city, grid participants could wirelessly connect into the metro grid anywhere, anytime, to access numerous services with low cost, including VoIP, video-on-demand, information distribution for city services and so on.

Most of these applications have high bandwidth requirements. However, currently popular multi hop architecture is not scalable for large scale network such as wireless metropolitan grid. Thus improving network scalability and throughput becomes critical requirements for the success of wireless metro grid.

In this paper, we propose scalable backbone architecture for the wireless metropolitan grid. Since throughput decreases sharply with the increase of hops [2], this result gives us a clue of improving the throughput by decreasing the average hop count between source and destination nodes. So we construct a backbone composed by super nodes and router nodes. The purpose of the construction of backbone is to improve the network's reliability and scalability. They are usually less stationary. Super nodes have larger transmission ranges than router nodes. When two distant nodes communicate, the hops between them can be reduced by the aid of neighboring super nodes. However, the increase of transmission range may cause more interference between neighboring nodes. To avoid this, we utilize multi-radio multi-channel approach. In our architecture, we equipped each super node with two radios, one for communication with router nodes, the other one for the communication between super nodes. They are tuned on different channels. In this way, multiple parallel transmissions can take place without interfering.

H.T. Shen et al. (Eds.): APWeb 2006, LNCS 3842, pp. 595–599, 2006.

We evaluate the performance of our backbone architecture with NS-2. Simulation shows that with the deployment of a backbone with about 20% super nodes the network throughput is increased by a factor of up to 5 compared with conventional single channel multi hop architecture.

The remainder of this paper is structured as follows. Related work is addressed in Section 2. After that, we will introduce the scalable backbone architecture in Section 3. In section 4, we will present simulation evaluations. Finally, Section 5 closes this paper with some brief concluding remarks and future research directions.

2 Related Work

There are quite a few works related to wireless backbone. Backbone has been used extensively in various aspects (e.g., routing, broadcast, scheduling) for wireless networks. Methods on how to minimize the cost of backbone, how to select nodes to form a backbone in distributed way, and how to maintain backbone in mobile environments is introduced in [4] [5]. A key distinction between our backbone and previous work is that our backbone nodes are stationary which are used only for the relay of traffic. So our focus is on improving the network capacity, instead of coping with mobility or minimizing power usage.

There are also a lot of works related to using multiple radios. In [3], two radios are utilized to improve network performance and a routing metric called WCETT which considers expected packet transmission time and channel diversity for a path is proposed. A routing and interface assignment algorithms for static multi channel network with the assumption that all the traffic is directed toward specific gateway nodes is proposed in [6]. Compared with [6], our proposal is designed for more general scenario, where any nodes can communicate with each other. In [6], by equipping each node with two radios, the network throughput can be improved by a factor of 6 to 7. In our system, we deploy 20% randomly selected super nodes with two radios. Though the throughput may be improved by a factor of 5, it's certainly more cost effective and easy to implement.

3 System Model

As shown in Figure 1, the scalable backbone architecture consists of router nodes, super nodes and access points. Router node denotes the ordinary stationary wireless node which is used to relay traffic between mobile hosts in wireless metro grid. Access points serve as gateways between wireless metro grid and a wired grid. All the grid resources such as file servers, Internet gateways, application servers that reside on the wired grid can be accessed through any of the access points. Super nodes dispersed in wireless metro grid are used to relay traffic among router nodes or between router nodes and access points.

Since the transmission range of a node can be tuned by adjusting the transmission power of source node or changing the antenna gains. In this paper, we suppose the transmission power is fixed for all nodes except that super nodes are equipped with higher-gain antennas. Hence, the super nodes can transmit much longer distance than router nodes.

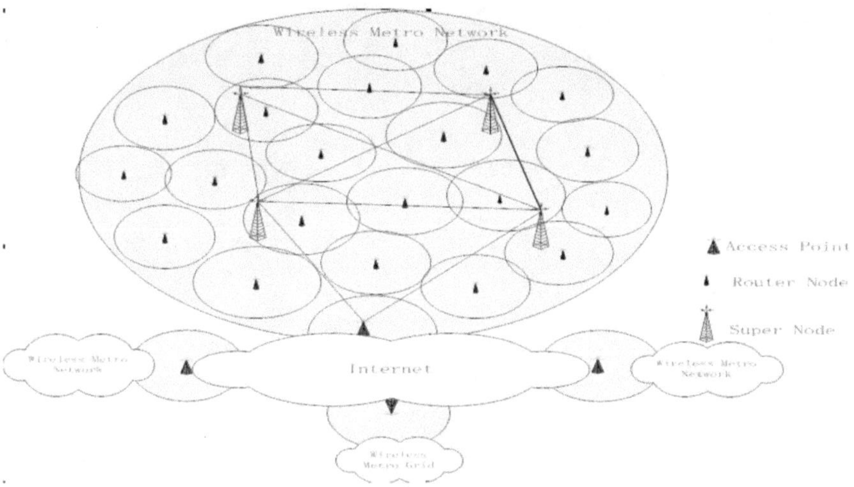

Fig. 1. Scalable backbone architecture for wireless metropolitan grid

However, the increase of transmission range may cause more interference between neighboring nodes. To alleviate this, we employ multi-radio multi-channel approach. Each super node in the backbone is equipped with two 802.11-compliant radios, each of which is tuned to a particular channel. One radio is used to communicate with router nodes, so the channel should be tuned to the same channel with router nodes. Another radio is used to communicate between super nodes.

As to the routing, we propose a shortest path routing based on DSDV for multi channel environment. Compared with traditional table-driven routing, routing table contains not only the next hop node, hop count but also specific radio information. When a super node relays packet, it search the routing table to get the radio information. Then it uses this radio to transmit this packet. This routing and channel assignment protocol is simple to use and proved to be effective.

4 Performance Evaluations

To study the overall performance of the proposed backbone architecture, we perform an extensive simulation study using NS-2. In this section, we present the simulation results demonstrating the performance improvement of deploying super nodes and the contribution of multi-channel.

4.1 Grid Topology

Now let us consider the grid backbone scenario. One hundred nodes are regularly placed in 1000m*1000m area. Super node is dispersed regularly in the grid. Each node is a packet source, sending packet to a randomly selected destination. Super node two channels denote that it is equipped with two radios with different channel and transmission range. Super node one channel means that it is equipped with only one radio whose transmission range is three times of that of router nodes on the same channel. As shown in the left hand of Fig. 2, the throughput of super node two radios

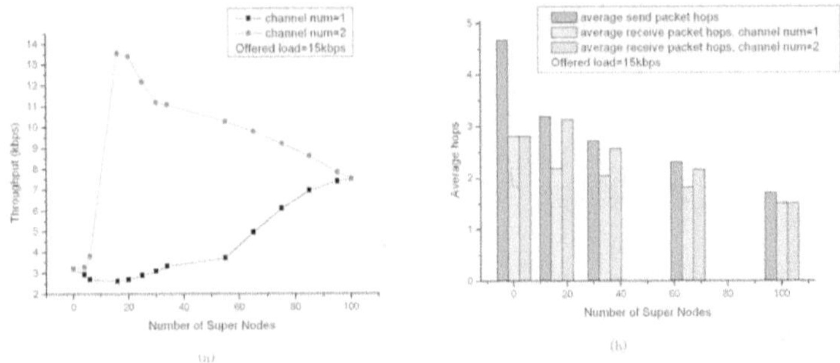

Fig. 2. (a) Throughput in grid networks with one or two channel. (b) Average packet send hop count and the received packet count for channel number one or two respectively, as a function of super node number in the grid.

increase almost linearly with the increase of super nodes until it reaches to 20 % of all backbone nodes. The optimal point of throughput denotes that the network reaches an optimal traffic allocation pattern between the two channels. After that, the channel used by the communication among super nodes become congested which induce the drop of throughput.

Due to the interference caused by the larger transmission range, the throughput of super node one channel scenario is even dropped a litter compared with that of the pure router node scenario. However, the throughput begin to increase when super node increase to a certain level. In the right hand of Fig 2, we can see that the average packet hop count reduce as super nodes increases. So the increase of throughput when the number of super node becomes larger is due to the reduction of average hop count.

4.2 Random Setting

We relax the regularity of node placement. Instead, assume that nodes are placed uniformly at random on a square area. The result as shown in Fig. 3 is similar to the

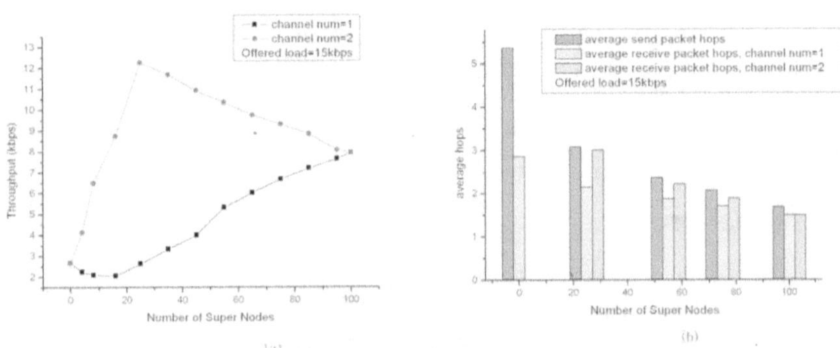

Fig. 3. (a) Throughput with different number of super nodes. (b) Average packet send hop count and the received packet count for channel number one or two respectively, as a function of super node number in the grid.

grid setting. The throughput of super node with two radios increases linearly with the increase of super nodes until it reaches to an optimal point. Once again, the throughput of super node one channel is dropped a litter compared with that of the pure router node scenario and then it increases when super node increase to a certain level. To sum up, we draw the conclusion that when super nodes number reach about 20% of the total backbone node number, the throughput improvement can reach an optimal point whose throughput is five times than that of the original pure router node setting. Besides, reducing average packet hop count can improve system throughput even through it may cause more interference.

5 Conclusions and Future Work

This paper describes a scalable backbone architecture for wireless metro grid. The goal is to solve the problem of improving network throughput as well as scalability by exploiting the multi-radio multi-channel and hierarchical structure.

The performance evaluation based on this architecture demonstrates that the scalable backbone architecture is quite promising. In the future, we plan to apply directional antenna technologies to further increase range as well as scalability.

References

[1] L. McKnight, S. Bradner, "Wireless grids: distributed resource sharing by mobile, nomadic, and fixed devices," IEEE Internet Computing, July-August, 2004.
[2] J. Li, C. Blake, D. De Couto, H. Lee, R. Morris, "Capacity of ad hoc wireless networks," in Proceedings of Mobicom 2001.
[3] R. Draves, J. Padhye, B. Zill, "Routing in multi radio, multi hop wireless mesh networks," In Proceedings of Mobicom 2004.
[4] Y. Wang, W. Wang, X. Li, "Distributed low-cost backbone formation for wireless ad hoc networks," in Proceedings of Mobihoc 2005.
[5] U. Kozat, G. Kondylis, B. Ryu, M. Marina, "Virtual dynamic backbone for mobile ad hoc networks," in Proceedings of IEEE ICC 2001.
[6] A. Raniwala and T. Chiueh, "Architecture and Algorithms for an IEEE 802.11 based multi channel wireless mesh network," in Proceedings of Infocom 2005.

Research on Innovative Web Information System Based on Grid Environment*

FuFang Li[1], DeYu Qi[1], and WenGuang Zhao[2]

[1] School of Computer Sci. & Tech., South China Univ. of Tech., GuangZhou 510640, China
lifuf@mail.csu.edu.cn

[2] Campus Network Center, Renmin Univ. of China, Beijing 100872, China
zwg@ruc.edu.cn

Abstract. An innovative WIS (Web Information System) based on grid environment is presented in this paper. At first, we talk about related technologies using in the area. Then, we give out the detailed design and implementation of an experimental WIS system. Finally, we sum up our work and point out future work we are preparing to do.

1 Introduction and Related Work

Web Information System (WIS) has been spanned across many industrial and commercial sectors especially in Internet-based applications for its good scalability, flexibility, reliability, robustness, etc [6]. WIS is traditionally designed and implemented using html, cgi, scripts, asp (.net), JSP (Servlet), and web service technology. For years, web services have been a major technology on constructing complex web-based applications. Paper [7][8] talk about web service technology, application experiences, and models. But web service technology has limitation which cannot meet with user's needs in many occasions, such as complex data processing, complex business data analyzing, and decision making, etc, for it is lack of security, flexible interoperability and state management of itself, etc [8].

Today, significant progress has been made on Grid technology [1][4][5]. Globus Toolkit [5](GT for abbr.), one of the most important grid computing platform, has now provided "*grid service*" as the upgrade of web service. Grid service provide new mechanism to help developers construct applications in scenarios that web services may not easy to perform, such as complex data processing, complex business data analyzing and decision making, etc. Compared with web services, the key concept of Grid service is that it provides stateful and transient services, with Service Data, Notifications, Service Groups, portType extension, lifecycle management, GSH & GSR, while web service doesn't provide [2][1].

Recently, grid technology and its application has been a hot spot. Many large projects are being carried out one after another [1], but they are mainly in scientific research area. In this paper, we try to present a new type of WIS for commercial business application based on grid technology. In the following part of this paper, we give out the design and implementation of an experimental project -- a grid-based WIS. At first, we present out our detailed design and implementation of the grid-

* This paper was supported in part by NSFC under Grant 60475040, and the Provincial Key Sci. & Tech. Program of GuangDong, China, under Grants 20034310,2003A1030404.

H.T. Shen et al. (Eds.): APWeb 2006, LNCS 3842, pp. 600 – 604, 2006.

based WIS in succession. Then, we put forward the conclusion of our work. And at last we point out the work that we are preparing to do in the future.

2 Design of the WIS Based on Grid Environment

The overall structure of the proposed WIS is described in Figure 1. It consists of three parts: the WIS-Grid environment based on Globus Toolkit, a web server with Servlet engine, and the end user's web browser. Besides these three main parts, there's a credential server, which issues various types of credentials for various entities (such as Globus server hosts, users, etc) of the system, and thus provides security mechanics for system by establishing trusts between the system's entities.

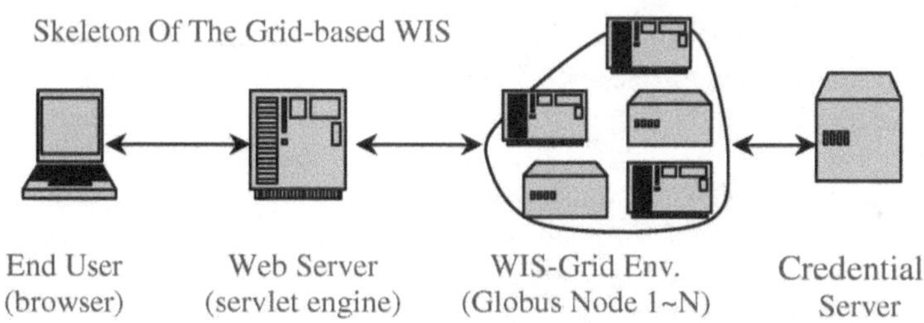

Fig. 1. Skeleton of the Grid-based WIS (Construction of the grid-based WIS)

Working scene of the system is: an end user uses his browser to send a specific request to the web server to do certain work. Then, the web server sends the request to a Servlet. Finally, the Servlet submit the job to grid service(s) deployed on the servers using APIs provided by Java CoG Kit (Java Commodity Grid Kits) [3].

2.1 The WIS-Grid Environment

The WIS-Grid Environment consists of various types of nodes linked by LAN or WAN. The nodes are servers with different hardware and software platform, with Globus server and grid service container. The Globus servers are responsible for resource allocation and management, job scheduling and management, grid Meta information management, security management, and so on. In each grid service container, there are grid services for certain purpose use, such as accessing database, business data analyzing, decision making, and transferring data, etc.

2.2 The Web Server

The Web Server is the portal for the WIS system. It's an ordinary web server, with JSP (Java Server Pages) and Servlet engine. In order to develop Java Servlets, beans, and other applications that can access Globus servers from the web server, Java CoG Kits must be deployed on it. By this way, we can access WIS-Grid Environment from the web server.

2.3 The Credential Server

The Credential Server (i.e. CA for the system) is responsible for issuing and managing X.509 based identity certificates for various entities of the system. Any entity, such as users and resources, of the system should use its identity certificate or its proxy to authenticate itself to other Grid entities, so as to established trusts between them.

3 Implementation of Grid-based WIS

The grid-based WIS is an experimental WIS for a bookseller who owns two or more large wholesale centers and many distribution centers in the country.

3.1 Construction of Grid-based WIS System

Core part of the system is the WIS-Grid Environment, and is shown in figure 2. The WIS-Grid Environment consists of eight Intel Pentium Ⅳ PC servers distributed on LAN and WAN, five of them with Red Hat Linux platform, the other three with Windows 2000 server. They are divided into two groups linked by WAN, and 100M Ethernet links servers in each group. We install GT3.2.1 all service package in Linux platform servers, while GT3.2.1 WS Core package in the Windows 2000 servers.

We set up a simple CA for the system, using the simpleCA package that is included in the GT3.2.1 package. Then we install the distribution package of the CA on other Globus servers, so as to set up authentication mechanism for the system. By signing credentials for various entities, trusts could be established for the system.

The web server of the system is the portal for both applications(Servlets, beans, etc) to use grid services deployed in the system, and for end users to use the system. We use Apache Tomcat as the web server, and with Java CoG Kits installed, so that Java Servlets and beans can access grid services deployed in Globus servers.

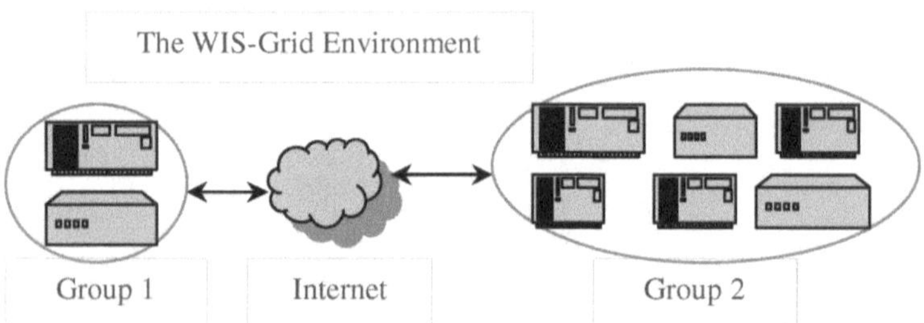

Fig. 2. Core part of the system: the WIS-Grid Environment

3.2 Implementation of Grid Services in the WIS-Grid Environment

By now, we've implemented eight grid services using Java with CoG Kits APIs for our system. The grid services and their descriptions are shown in table 1.

As an example, let's look at the grid services: *gs_get_Sale*. Its function is to collect and calculate the total sale of a certain period of time, such as a day, a month, etc. It is deployed on all Globus servers, and each one on the very server is responsible for it's local sale processing and also cooperatively calculate the company's total sale. When one needs to get the sum of a day's sale, he just call the servlet that responsible for this function, the servlet then use APIs of CoG Kit to submit the job to *gs_get_Sale* to fulfill the task and fetch back the result. In order to obtain good performance and

Table 1. Table of system's grid services and their descriptions

Name	Description
gs_get_sysInfo	Obtain system information of memory size, CPU load and frequency, active threads, etc.
gs_db_conn	To establish connection to the database of the system.
gs_proc_deal	To process a single deal.
gs_get_storage	Get book storage of the whole distributed system.
gs_get_daySells	Get a day's detailed book sell information.
gs_get_Sale	Collect and calculate total sale of a certain period of time.
gs_create_orderAdvice	Create advice on order plan for decision makers.
gs_create_sellAdvice	Generate an advice on market strategy.

efficiency, we use an algorithm (see section 3.3) to schedule related grid services to cooperatively complete the task efficiently. In our experimental system, the grid services we've implemented have been proved to work well.

3.3 Algorithm of Job Scheduling for the System

Currently, the algorithm only considers the computer's CPU frequency and available memory as the primary indication of server's available processing ability, we'll try to find out better measurement in the future. We use *gs_get_sysInfo* (see Table 1) to obtain server's available memory (MEN_a), CPU load (CPU_l) and CPU main frequency (CPU_f), and we use expressions (1) to measure the server's available processing ability. The value of "*ability*" is used as the computer's available capability for job schedule in our current experimental system.

$$\text{ability} = MEN_a * (1 - CPU_l) * CPU_f \tag{1}$$

The end user uses a Servlet to submit job to related grid services. Then related grid services do their local part of job respectively, and cooperatively fulfill the whole task in succession. When the first one of this grid services finishes it's local job, it should find out the server whose available computational ability is the largest, and let this server (namely "*total server*") to collect and calculate the total result. In the meantime, it informs other related grid services to send their local results to the total server to calculate the final result. After all related grid services have finished their local job and sent their results to the total server, it begin to calculate the total result and return it to the request user. Algorithm of job scheduling is as following:

(1) A Servlet submit the job to grid services deployed on the correlative servers;
(2) Each related grid service does its local part of the job;
(3) If (one grid service finished its local job and no one else finished before) {
Call *gs_get_sysInfo* to obtain the servers' current condition, and calculate each server's available computational ability by (1), and chose the one whose available computational ability is the largest as the "*total server*";
Send local result to the total server to collect and calculate the total result;
Inform all other related grid services where is the "total server";
} else if (one of the grid services had finished its local part of job before) {
Send local result to the "total server" to collect and calculate the total result; }

(4) If (all of the related grid service have finished their local job) and (the "total server" has finished)

Return the result to the user who sends the request.

(5) End.

3.4 Using Grid Services in the Web Server

First of all, the Java CoG Kits class files must be added to server's environment variable CLASS_PATH, otherwise you can't compile and use the Java Servlets to access system's grid services; Then, we implemented Java Servlets for our grid-based WIS system by using APIs of Java CoG Kits to schedule related grid services to fulfill certain function; Finally, the way to use Servlet in JSP pages are the same as ordinary Java Servlet.

4 Conclusions

We've tried to present out the design and implementation of an innovative new type of WIS based on grid environment. The experimental WIS system has been running successfully for a period of time, it shows good performance, reliability, robustness, flexibility, and scalability. Our work has proved the design and implementation of the system are rational and effective. The experimental project we'd done presents a reference for those who want to use grid-computing technology in their application systems in commercial business fields.

Although we've constructed an experimental WIS system based on grid technology, there's still many works should be done in the future. In succession, we'll try to find better way to measure available computational capability of the server machine in the grid environment, and to find better strategy of job distribution to optimize the job schedule algorithm. And we'll continue doing more research work on performance, reliability, architecture and protocol for Grid-based WIS.

Acknowledgements. Thanks to the colleagues of school of computer sci. and tech. of SCUT and campus network center of Renmin University, China. They gave us much more help while their names are not listed in the authors.

References

1. Ian Foster and Carl Kesselman; The Grid: Blueprint for a New Computing Infrastructure. Elsevier Inc., Singapore, Second Edition, 2004.
2. Open Grid Services Infrastructure(OGSI) web page: http://www.ggf.org/ogsi-wg.
3. Java CoG Kits(Java Commodity Grid Kits) web page: http://www.cogkit.org.
4. Foster I., Kesselman C., Nick, etc; Grid services for distributed systems integation. IEEE Computer 35(6), 37-46, 2002.
5. The Globus ToolKit web page: http://www.globus.org.
6. Nor Adnan Yahaya, Goh Poh Gin, etc; Developing InnovativeWeb Information Systems Through the Use of Web Data Extraction Technology. Proceedings of (AINA'05), 2005.
7. Steve Vinoski; Integration with Web Services. IEEE Internet Computing 1089-7801/03 November-December 2003 p75-77
8. Clark, D.; Next-generation web services, Internet Computing, IEEE, Volume 6, Issue 2, March-April 2002 Page(s):12 - 14

A Framework and Survey of Knowledge Discovery Services on the OGSA-DAI

Jian Zhan and Lian Li

Computer Science Department, Lanzhou University, Lanzhou 730000, China
flysmart@lzu.edu.cn

Abstract. In the past few years, Knowledge discovery communities have contributed a rich set of methods and tools that had been used for the analysis of large data sets. On the other hand, Grids are increasingly being used for collaborative work. Grid users would similarly benefit from having access to databases, mainly, those involved in collaborative data analysis of large datasets and those requiring sharing of data. OGSA-DAI provides an extension to the OGSA framework by allowing access to and integration of data held in heterogeneous data resources. In this paper we survey some issues, which focus on the extension of the Grid technology to Knowledge Discovery Services that are designed and being implemented on top of OGSA-DAI Grid Services. The proposed architecture defines a set of additional layers to implement the services of distributed knowledge discovery process.

1 Introduction

In this paper, we survey the structure and components of Grid knowledge discovery processes and their mapping onto appropriate Grid services. The Grid will represent in a near future an effective infrastructure for managing very large data sources and providing high-level mechanisms for extracting valuable knowledge from them [1]. To solve this class of applications, we need advanced tools and services for knowledge discovery. Here we will discuss the Knowledge Discovery Grid: a Grid-based software environment that implements Grid-enabled knowledge discovery services [2, 3]. The Knowledge Grid can be used as a high-level system for providing knowledge discovery services on dispersed resources connected through a Grid. These services allow professionals and scientists to create and manage complex knowledge discovery applications composed as workflows integrating data sets and mining tools provided as distributed services on a Grid. To application developers these services can be viewed simply as an OGSA-compliant Grid service. Further, we address the challenge of integrating these services and describing the various interactions between them and how to dynamically compose new services out of existing ones.

1.1 Grid Services and OGSA-DAI

Today many public organizations, industries, and scientific labs produce and manage large amounts of complex data and information. Unfortunately,

H.T. Shen et al. (Eds.): APWeb 2006, LNCS 3842, pp. 605–609, 2006.

high-level tools to support the knowledge discovery and management in distributed environments are lacking. Grid technologies have been developed with a view to easing the efficient sharing of resources within a heterogeneous and distributed environment. Grid services extend standard web services by providing support for associating state with services, managing the lifetime of service instances, and standard mechanisms for subscription and notification of state changes. Grid service interfaces are being standardized as part of an overall Open Grid Services Architecture (OGSA).

The main Grid services for Knowledge Discovery Grid offered are the following [4]: Monitoring and Discovery Service, Resource Allocation Manager, Grid Security Infrastructure, Dynamically-Updated Resource Online Co-allocator, Heartbeat Monitor, GridFTP, Replica Catalog and Management.

The goal of OGSA-DAI is to provide a uniform service interface for data access and integration to databases exposed to the Grid[5], hiding differences such as database driver, data formatting and delivery mechanisms. The DAI service has three main components: a service registry for discovery of service instances, a data factory service for representing a data resource and a data service for accessing a data resource, such as a relational database. The OGSA-DAI service uses an extensible activity framework. These services will therefore provide the basic operations that can be used by higher-level services to offer greater functionality, such as data federation and distributed queries.

The OGSA-DAI architecture also aims to encourage the design of efficient applications and evolvable services. To address the former, there is support for grouping multiple requests on an OGSA-DAI service into a single message sent to a service.To support service evolution, request messages are self-describing in which they identify the specific operation to be called, so allowing a service to evolve to support new operations without requiring existing applications to be modified.

We have suggested extending the free available OGSA-DAI Grid Data Service reference implementation to provide a virtual table. Offering the same metadata as a normal Grid data source, it can be used and integrated in existing applications quite easily to hide the distribution and heterogeneity of the participating data sources by reformulating requests against the logical schema.

1.2 The Knowledge Discovery Process

Knowledge Discovery concerns with applying appropriate algorithms to extract knowledge from a prepared dataset [6]. The overall process involves the repeated application of the following steps:

- Understanding the problem domain. This step includes relevant prior knowledge and goals of the application.
- Data cleaning. Data from real-world sources are often erroneous, incomplete, and inconsistent, perhaps due to operation error or system implementation. Such low quality data need to be cleaned prior to data mining, including removal of noise or outliers, collecting necessary information to model or

account for noise, strategies for handling missing data fields, and accounting for time sequence information and known changes, etc.
- Data Preprocessing and Transformation. This step will create a target data set, select a data set, or focus on a subset of variables, or data samples, from multiple, heterogeneous data sources. Many data mining algorithms work only on special transformed data, so some conversion must be done.
- Knowledge mining. This step describes the application and parameterization of a concrete knowledge discovery algorithm, to search for patterns within the dataset, like a classification, association,sequence and cluster analysis.
- Data Presentation. The last step will present the results of Knowledge Discovery with distinct measures. Knowledge discovery algorithms deliver a set of patterns. Often these patterns are not interesting to the end-user. Hence, the results of Knowledge Discovery have to be prepared in some appropriate ways to user. Various presentation forms exist, like tables, charts or more sophisticated presentation mechanisms.

2 The Architecture of Knowledge Grid

2.1 Requirement in Grid Services for Knowledge Discovery

Some issues about Knowledge Discovery Grid architecture design are listed [7]:

Data heterogeneity and large size. The system must be able to cope with very large data sets that are geographically distributed and stored in different types of repositories as structured data in DBMS, text in files or semi-structured and unstructured data.

Data Security. Since the Grid involves different organizations that share their resources, it is important to establish a certain level of security mechanism. Only authorized people are allowed to access the data through Grid. WS-Security is a good starting point for exploring the Grid service security issues.

Asynchronous Grid Services. A Knowledge Discovery task could be long running. Asynchronous operations should be considered. Otherwise, a client application may be undesirably blocked until the service results are returned.

*Flexibility.*The application should allow the integration of components that are optimized for different platforms. This heterogeneity is however hidden behind well-defined service interfaces. The services shall support heterogeneous environments and shall be extensible with ease.

Compatibility with existing Grid infrastructure. A high degree of compatibility with existing Grid infrastructures and tools is mandatory.

Openness to tools and algorithms. The system architecture must be open to the integration of new knowledge discovery packages. Analysis models will be added to extend the knowledge discovery services without affecting the lower levels.

Service transparency. Users should be able to run their applications on the Grid in an easy and transparent way, without needing to know details of the Grid structure and operation, network features and physical location of data sources.

Dynamic Service Composition Language, which is specially designed to support highly dynamic and complex workflows.

Of course, the most important Knowledge Discovery Grid architecture design issue is the design of an appropriate data access and integration model and, consequently, specification of the services implementing this model. The Knowledge Discovery Grid may be organized in two levels: the Core-Layer Services and the Application-Layer Services [8, 9].

2.2 The Core-Layer Services

The core-layer is a view over the Knowledge Discovery Grid base.

1. The Knowledge Directory Service that manages metadata describing Knowledge Grid resources. Such resources comprise hosts, repositories of data to be mined, tools and algorithms used to extract, analyze, and manipulate data, distributed knowledge discovery execution plans and knowledge obtained as result of the mining process.
2. Resource Broker Service is used for matchmaking of requests and available resources. It might be used to find best-fitting resources, e.g. a cluster with efficient network access to the dataset.
3. The Data and Algorithms Access Service allows for the search, selection, transfer, transformation, and delivery of data and algorithms.
4. The Data Presentation Service offers facilities for presenting and visualizing the knowledge models extracted (e.g., association rules, clustering models, classifications).

2.3 The Application-Layer Services

The Application-Layer Services are a set of OGSA services with well-defined interfaces that are used as needed to assemble applications on top of them.

1. *Information and Monitoring Service.* Information services maintain knowledge about the resources available on the Grid, their capacity and current utilization. Monitoring of the involved software and hardware resources prior to and continuously during job execution is furthermore of general importance.
2. *Replication and Caching Service.* The difference between replication and caching is not clearly defined.usually without control of users and administrators, Cached copies often have shorter lifetimes than replicas . Replication is usually a more sophisticated technique, providing control mechanisms for system administrators, hierarchical layouts, enhanced synchronization, etc.
3. *Data Integration and OLAP Service.* Data integration refers to transferring data subsets from multiple data sources into usually one data source. OLAP Service provides algorithms to perform Knowledge Discovery on cubes.
4. *Dynamic Service Composition Engine.* This service allows a user to specify long-running jobs, and then submit this description to a workflow engine that takes care of the execution of this process. Additionally support for interactive use and control of the complete knowledge discovery process and their individual steps are required.

3 Conclusions

In this paper we have discussed some issues, which focus on the application and extension of the Grid technology to knowledge discovery in Grid databases. We believe that such an approach holds great promise. We have presented here a general framework that is capable of combining data analysis with data integration on OGSA-DAI. There are many topics that we have not touched upon such as knowledge maintenance, the exact nature of knowledge-based decision support and how inference services will be supported under the OGSA architecture. This is work for the future.

References

1. Foster, I., Kesselman, C., Tuecke, S.: The anatomy of the Grid: Enabling scalable virtual organizations. Intl. J. Supercomputer Applications, 15(3), 2001.
2. A. Congiusta, C. Mastroianni, A. Pugliese, D. Talia, P. Trunfio. Enabling knowledge discovery services on Grids. European Across Grids Conference (AxGrids), 2004. LNCS 3165, pp. 250-259, Springer-Verlag, Berlin, Germany, 2004.
3. Mario Cannataro, Knowledge Discovery and Ontology-based services on the Grid, Ninth Global Grid Forum, Semantic Grid Research Group Workshop, October 5-8,Chicago,2003.
4. Towards Open Grid Services Architecture (OGSA), http://www.globus.org/ogsa/
5. Open Grid Services Architecture Data Access and Integration (OGSA-DAI), http://www.ogsadai.org
6. Brezany, P., Hofer, J., Tjoa, A Min, Wöhrer, A.: Towards an Open Service Architecture for DataMining on the Grid. Submitted to Dexa 2003, September 2003, Prague, Czech Republic.
7. Mario Cannataro, Domenico Talia GRID: High Performance Knowledge Discovery Services on the Grid:Workshop on Grid Computing, LNCS 2242, Springer Verlag,2001.
8. A.Congiusta, A.Pugliese, D.Talia, P.Trunfio, Designing Grid services for distributed knowledge discovery. Web Intelligence and Agent Systems (WIAS), vol.1, n.2, pp.91-104, IOS Press, 2003.
9. Guenter Kickinger, Peter Brezany, A Min Tjoa, and Juergen Hofer.Grid Knowledge Discovery Processes and an Architecture for Their Composition. IASTED 2004, Innsbruck, Austria, February 17-19, 2004.

A New Heartbeat Mechanism for Large-Scale Cluster*

Yutong Lu, Min Wang, and Nong Xiao

School of Computer, National University of Defense Technology,
410073 Changsha, HuNan, China
ytlu@nudt.edu.cn, kingminmail@126.com, xiao-n@vip.sina.com

Abstract. Distributed managed clusters have appeared in recent years, and computing intensive scientific problems request large-scale clusters. However, many of the traditional heartbeat mechanisms do not fit large-scale distributed managed clusters. In this paper, we propose a switch-based heartbeat mechanism named *heartbeat ring*, which adapts to large-scale distributed managed clusters. Heartbeat ring mechanism has the prominent advantages in simplicity, scalability and adaptability, and so on. Finally, based on a prototype implemented on Linux platform, experiment evaluation is presented.

1 Introduction

Heartbeat mechanism is the most common method to achieve high availability in a cluster. A heartbeat subsystem consist of a set of daemons, which monitor the running state of the cluster nodes through a series of heartbeat messages. According to the management approach, clusters can be classified into two types: centralized managed cluster and distributed managed cluster. Most of the traditional clusters belong to centralized managed cluster. In these clusters, a specific node takes charge of the heartbeat management. It periodically sends inquiry messages to other nodes. An active node then sends a heartbeat message back to the heartbeat management node as its response to the inquiry. In such case, the heartbeat management node becomes the bottleneck of the cluster. If there are no standby nodes for heartbeat management, once the management node fails, the whole heartbeat subsystem of the cluster will fail. In addition, in a small cluster it is a waste to use a specific node for heartbeat management. In a distributed managed cluster, such as openMosix [10], Kerrighed [11] and so on, all nodes in the cluster are equivalent. There are neither master nodes nor slave nodes, thereby none of the nodes can take charge of the heartbeat management in these clusters.

To improve the availability of large-scale distributed managed clusters, a distributed heartbeat mechanism should be designed to monitor the running state of nodes. This makes single point failures transparent to applications with the cluster reconfiguration mechanism. The two main objectives of heartbeat mechanism are as follows:(1)To use resources as little as possible;(2)To detect node failure as soon as possible. However, these two objectives are somewhat contradictory. Any heartbeat mechanism is a compromise between the two objectives. In this paper, we present a

* This research is supported by NFS of China (NO.60573135) and 973-2003CB317008.

H.T. Shen et al. (Eds.): ADWeb 2006, LNCS 3842, pp. 610 – 619, 2006.

new heartbeat mechanism named heartbeat ring, which can effectively conciliate the contradiction in large-scale distributed managed clusters.

2 Heartbeat Ring Mechanism

We assume that there are N nodes in system, to each of which we assign an unique logical number Ni ($0 \le Ni \le N-1$), the communication subsystem can guarantee messages be transferred reliably and in order among nodes.

Nodes are divided into groups, nodes in the same group constitute a heartbeat ring (We assume that there are m nodes in a ring). The notation <Na, Nb> represents that node Na and node Nb is logical neighbor nodes in a heartbeat ring. We call Na is the prior neighbor of Nb, and Nb is the next neighbor of Na. For the convenience of discussion, we assume N % m = = 0. We can then obtain the number of heartbeat rings (denoted as M) in system is M = N / m.

The set of heartbeat ring in the system is $R = \{R_0, R_1, \ldots, R_{M-1}\}$, where each heartbeat ring is

$R_i = \{ N_{m*i}, N_{m*i+1}, N_{m*i+2}, \ldots, N_{m*i+(m-1)} \} (0 \leq i \leq M-1)$

We can follow the above scheme to partition all the nodes into M heartbeat rings. The partition scheme is also depicted in Fig.1.

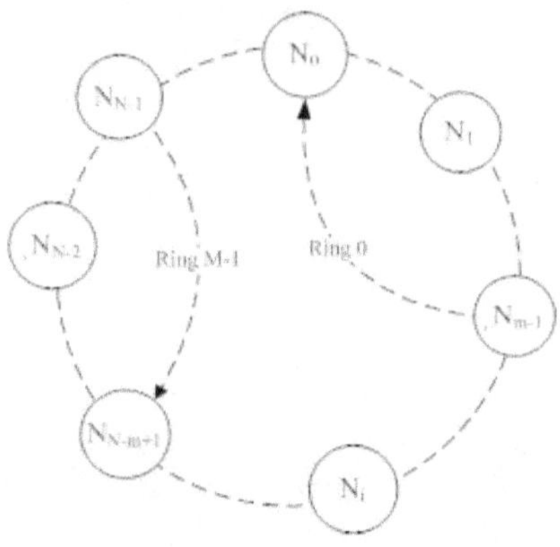

Fig. 1. A partition scheme for heartbeat ring mechanism

In the heartbeat ring mechanism two kinds of heartbeat messages are defined: HB1 message and HB2 message. For a node pair <Na, Nb> in the heartbeat ring, node Na should deliver a HB1 message to its next neighbor Nb after it receives a HB1 message from its prior neighbor. If all nodes in the heartbeat ring are active, HB1 heartbeat message is transferred circularly along the heartbeat ring. Each node in a heartbeat ring maintains a timer, if the timer (for HB1 heartbeat message) of node Nb is over a threshold, Nb will send a HB2 message to Na to check the running state. If node Na receives a HB2 message from its next neighbor Nb, Na should send back an acknowledgement message immediately, which represents its active state. If node Nb does not receive any response message from node Na during a specified interval (denoted as $T_{timeout}$), Node Na is considered to be failure.

We introduce the concept of coordinator node and vice coordinator node in the heartbeat ring. There is one and only one coordinator node in a heartbeat ring. The next neighbor node of the coordinator node is the vice coordinator node. At the initialization stage each node computes a function to determine that if it is the coordinator (for example, we can use the modulo function. If the logical number of a node satisfies the condition n % m = 0, it will be the coordinator of a heartbeat ring). The function should guarantee that there is one and only one coordinator in a heartbeat ring. The coordinator of a heartbeat ring will send a message to its next neighbor node to notify it of being appointed to be the vice coordinator. After that, the message is delivered along the heartbeat ring until it is passed back to the coordinator. Such that all the other nodes in the ring know their coordinator and the coordinator learn the configuration of the ring.

We use T_{circle} to denote the time for a HB1 heartbeat message to be transferred a circle around a heartbeat ring. If each node in the ring receives a HB1 message during the period of T_{circle}, all the member nodes in the heartbeat ring are regarded to be active. If node Nb finds that its timer is over T_{circle}, it suspects that its prior node Na might be failed, so it sends a HB2 message to check if Na is still active or not. If Na is active, it should immediately send an acknowledgement message back to Nb. Otherwise if Nb does not receive any message from Na during a specified interval $T_{timeout}$, Na is considered to be failure.

Coordinators take charge of the construction of heartbeat rings. The logical numbers of nodes in a heartbeat ring should be in clockwise order (or counterclockwise order). The heartbeat rings' configuration information (a subset of the global configuration information) are managed by coordinators. The vice coordinators also have a copy of that configuration information. The configuration information is updated when the heartbeat ring's configuration changes. A new coordinator should multicast a message about its appointment to other coordinators, any coordinator that receives this message should update their configuration information about the coordinators.

If a coordinator fails, its next neighbor node, which is the vice coordinator node, will detect the failure according to the heartbeat ring algorithm. The vice coordinator will be the new coordinator, other coordinators will be notified and a new vice coordinator node will be designated. Any non-coordinator node that detects a failure will report to the coordinator, and then the coordinator will reconstruct the heartbeat ring.

3 Analysis of Heartbeat Ring Mechanism

3.1 Parameters Configuration

Before discussing this question, we introduce some parameters first:

T_{circle}: The time required for a HB1 message to be transferred a circle around the heartbeat ring. Since T_{circle} is not a constant, the value we use in practice for the heartbeat daemon's timer is a little larger than the average of T_{circle}.

D_i: The interval between node Ni sends out a HB1 message and the message is handled by the heartbeat daemon on the next neighbor node, including the transmission delay, queue delay in the buffer and process scheduling time. D_i is related to the interconnect network, the load of the network and the corresponding node.

T_{sleep}: This parameter is introduced to decrease the bandwidth usage of the heartbeat subsystem. After a node in a ring receives a HB1 message, it delays a period of time (denoted as T_{sleep}) before delivering it to its next neighbor node.

$T_{timeout}$: If the timer of a node is timeout, the node will send a HB2 message to its prior neighbor node in the ring and wait for the response message. If it does not receive any response message during a period of time (denoted as $T_{timeout}$), its prior neighbor is considered to be failure.

If a heartbeat ring is composed of m nodes, the following equation holds:

$$T_{circle} = \sum_{i=1}^{m} D_i + mT_{sleep} \tag{1}$$

From the equation above, we learn that T_{circle} is a function of m and T_{sleep}. Note that m = N / M, where N is the number of nodes in the system while M is the number of heartbeat rings. To obtain an appropriate value of T_{circle}, we should partition the nodes into a proper number of heartbeat rings and adopt a proper T_{sleep}.

Now we can compute the delay of node failure detection, which is shown in Fig.2:

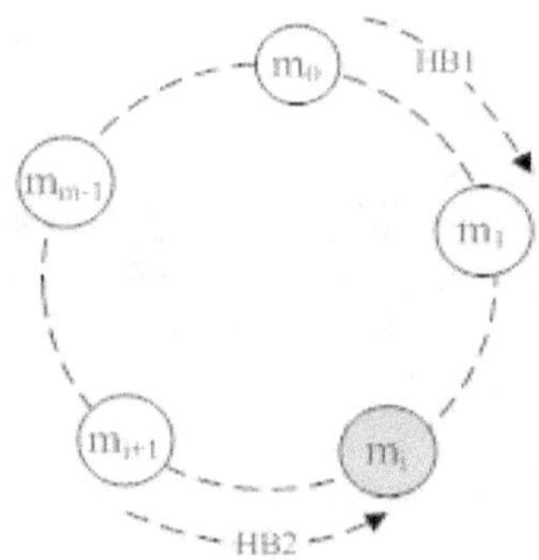

Fig. 2. Node failure detection

If node m_i in a heartbeat ring fails, node m_{i+1} can not receive the HB1 heartbeat message due to the failure of node m_i. When the HB1 message arrives Node m_i, the timer of node m_{i+1} is (m-1) T_{circle}/m, the timer of node m_{i+2} is (m-2)T_{circle}/m, and so on. The timer of node m_{i+1} will be the first to become timeout. After the timer is timeout, node m_{i+1} will send a HB2 message to node m_i and wait for the response message from m_i. After an interval of $T_{timeout}$, node m_i will be considered to be failure. We assume that node m_i fails equiprobably at any time in a T_{circle}. The maximum delay of node failure detection can be written as $T_{max} = T_{circle} + T_{timeout}$ (Node m_i fails at the moment after it successfully delivers a HB1 message to node m_{i+1}). On the other hand, the minimum delay of node failure detection is $T_{min} = T_{timeout}$ (Node m_i fails at the moment when it is about to deliver a HB1 message to node m_{i+1}). Therefore, the average delay of node failure detection is as follows:

$$T_{avg} = T_{circle}/2 + T_{timeout} \tag{2}$$

From the equation (1) and (2), we learn that to reduce the delay of node failure detection, we should decrease the parameter of T_{sleep} and $T_{timeout}$.

We can also compute the bandwidth used by the heartbeat subsystem. HB1 heartbeat messages deliver in one direction along the heartbeat ring, and do not need acknowledge messages, so they use less network bandwidth than other heartbeat mechanisms that require acknowledge messages. If each HB1 message has L bytes, the bandwidth used by the heartbeat subsystem can be calculated as follows:

$$B = 8 * L * m / T_{circle} \tag{3}$$

From equation (3) and also referring to equation (1), we learn that to reduce the network bandwidth usage, we should increase the value of T_{sleep}.

From the discussions above, we know that T_{sleep} is a compromise between the usage of network bandwidth and the delay of node failure detection.

$T_{timeout}$ is another parameter to set. Referring to equation (2), the delay of node failure detection goes up with the increasing $T_{timeout}$. On the other hand, too small $T_{timeout}$ will result in mistaking an active node for a failure node in the case that the network or the node is too busy to response in time. Thus, $T_{timeout}$ is a compromise of the delay of node failure detection and the mistaking of node failures.

3.2 Message Complexity Analysis

During the initialization stage, each node computes a function to determine if it is a coordinator. A coordinator will send a message to its next neighbor in the ring to announce its appointment, then the message is delivered along the heartbeat ring. Node that receives the message will attach its configuration information to the message and delivers it to its next neighbor until the message reaches the coordinator again, which requires N messages (m * M = N). In this way, nodes know their coordinator and coordinators learn the configuration of the rings. Each coordinator will broadcast a message of its appointment, other coordinators that receive the message will update their configuration information about coordinators in the system, which requires M * N messages. In this way, every coordinator can get a global consistent view of all coordinators. From the discussion above, the total number of messages sent during the initialization stage is (M+1)*N.

If there is no node failure, each heartbeat ring is an autonomous system, only HB1 messages are delivered in the heartbeat rings (m messages in a ring for each round of a circle). There is no other message in the heartbeat rings. So during a heartbeat circle, N messages are delivered among nodes.

When a non-coordinator node fails, each node except the failure node in the heartbeat ring will send a HB2 message to its prior neighbor to check the running state, each active node will send back a HB2 acknowledgement message, which requires 2*(m-1)-1 messages(the failure node will not respond). The node that detects the failure will report to the coordinator, one message is required for the failure report. The coordinator will reconstruct the heartbeat ring, then it will notify the prior neighbor and the next neighbor of the failure node to update their configuration, which requires 2 messages. Additionally, the coordinator will notify the vice coordinator about the configuration change. As above, we learn that the total number of messages for handling a non-coordinator node failure is 2m+1.

When a coordinator fails, the coordinator failure will be detected by the vice coordinator according to the heartbeat ring algorithm, then the number of messages for failure detection (HB2 message and the corresponding acknowledgement message) message is 2*(m-1)-1(the failure coordinator will not respond).The vice coordinator will notify the coordinator's prior neighbor of the failure (to reconstruct the heartbeat ring), which requires one message. The vice coordinator will be appointed the new coordinator, the new coordinator will announce its appointment in the ring and designate a new vice coordinator, which requires m-1 messages. We know that the total number of messages be transferred in the ring for failure handling is 3*(m-1).In addition, the new coordinator will notify other coordinators of its appointment (other coordinators will notify their vice coordinators), which requires 2*(M-1) messages. From the discussion above, we learn that the total number of messages for coordinator failure handling is 3*(m-1) +2*(M-1).

We assume that every node fails equiprobably, then the probability of a coordinator failure is 1/m and that of a non-coordinator node failure is (m-1)/m, therefore the average number of messages required (denoted as $f(m)$) for failure handing can be computed as follows (note that M = N / m):

$$f(m) = \frac{m-1}{m}(2m+1) + \frac{1}{m}[3(m-1) + 2(M-1)] = 2(m+1) + \frac{2M-6}{m}$$
$$= \frac{2N}{m^2} - \frac{6}{m} + 2m + 2 \qquad (4)$$

To get the minimum value of $f(m)$, we compute the derivative of $f(m)$ as follows:

$$f'(m) = -\frac{4N}{m^3} + \frac{6}{m^2} + 2 \qquad (5)$$

We let $f'(m)=0$, and then get the following equation:

$$-\frac{4N}{m^3} + \frac{6}{m^2} + 2 = 0 \qquad (6)$$

Equation (6) is equivalent to the following equation:

$$m^3 + 3m - 2N = 0 \qquad (7)$$

According to the Cardan formula, the real root of equation (7) can be calculated as follows:

$$m = \sqrt[3]{-\frac{-2N}{2} + \sqrt{(\frac{-2N}{2})^2 + (\frac{3}{3})^3}} + \sqrt[3]{-\frac{-2N}{2} - \sqrt{(\frac{-2N}{2})^2 + (\frac{3}{3})^3}}$$
$$= \sqrt[3]{N + \sqrt{N^2+1}} + \sqrt[3]{N - \sqrt{N^2+1}} \approx \sqrt[3]{2N} \quad (N \to \infty) \qquad (8)$$

From equation (8), we learn that in the case that N is large enough, if the number of nodes in a ring is approximate to $\sqrt[3]{2N}$ (For m is an integer, the round-off of $\sqrt[3]{2N}$ is a recommendation), messages required for failure handling will be the minimum.

3.3 Characteristic of Heartbeat Ring Mechanism

1. Complexity
As discussed in section 3.2, if there are no node failures, the number of messages exchanged in a heartbeat circle T_{circle} is N (where N is the number of nodes in the cluster). The message complexity is O (n), better than other mechanisms with O (n^2) message complexity;
2. Scalability
Since the message complexity of the heartbeat ring algorithm is O (n), the number of heartbeat messages exchanged in the cluster increases linearly with the increasing scale of the cluster. So it has good scalability.
3. Adaptability
The heartbeat ring mechanism not only fits large-scale clusters, but also fits small-scale clusters. If the cluster is small-scale (for example only 4 nodes in cluster), we can organize all the nodes in one heartbeat ring. On the other hand if the cluster is large, we can partition the cluster into multiple heartbeat rings.
4. Parallelism
Multiple heartbeat rings may exist in the same cluster. If all nodes in the cluster are alive, HB1 heartbeat messages are delivered in the heartbeat rings simultaneously. Hence the running state of nodes that belong to different heartbeat rings can be monitored in parallel, and the efficiency of node failure detection is also improved in this way. If multiple nodes that belong to different heartbeat rings fails in the same heartbeat circle, all the failures can be detected.

4 Implementation and Evaluation

We have implemented a prototype of the heartbeat ring algorithm on Linux platform. The heartbeat message format that we adopt in the heartbeat ring algorithm is a set of ASCII (name, value) pairs [9]. New message formats can be added as new (name, value) pairs. This message format has the advantage of being very simple, easy to understand, and yet very flexible. However, it has a few disadvantages. ASCII data is bulky, and having names in every message makes it more so. This can be made a little less problematic by choosing short field names for the fields found in heartbeat messages [9].

Our experimental cluster consists of 64 PCs (Pentium Ⅳ 2.4G CPU, 512M RAM). Nodes are connected by 100M switched Ethernet and all the nodes are in one subnet. We partition the cluster into 8 heartbeat rings, each is composed of 8 nodes (From the conclusion of section 3.2, we learn that 5 nodes in a ring will lead to the minimum messages required for failure handling. For the sake of simplicity, we adopt the scheme of 8 nodes per ring). A heartbeat daemon runs on every node, each maintains a timer of its own and listens to a specified port for heartbeat messages. Heartbeat daemons communicate with each other by UDP socket or using UDP broadcast for broadcasting.

The parameters we use in our experiment for the heartbeat ring algorithm are listed in Table 1.

Table 1. Parameters used in the heartbeat ring prototype experiment

Parameter	Nodes In Cluster	Nodes In a Ring	HB1 Message Size(Byte)	$T_{timeout}$ (ms)
Value	64	8	150	4000

Since T_{circle} is not a constant, the timer of each heartbeat daemons is set to a value (denoted as T) larger than the average of T_{circle}. In our experiment, we use the following function to compute T: $T = T_{circle}+200$ (ms).Note that T_{circle} is the average value obtained from the experiment. For T_{sleep}, we use different values (from 200ms to 1000ms) in our experiment.

We let the heartbeat daemon on one of the nodes terminate at some random time between 0 to T (a heartbeat circle) after it delivers a HB1 heartbeat message to its next neighbor node. In this way we can simulate a node failure. In order to compute the delay of node failure detection, the heartbeat daemon that simulates the node failure will send a message to its next neighbor node to notice the time it terminates (before it terminates). Its next neighbor node will detect the failure and report to the coordinator node using the heartbeat ring algorithm. To obtain the average delay of node failure detection, we do the experiment 20 times for each T_{sleep}. According to the

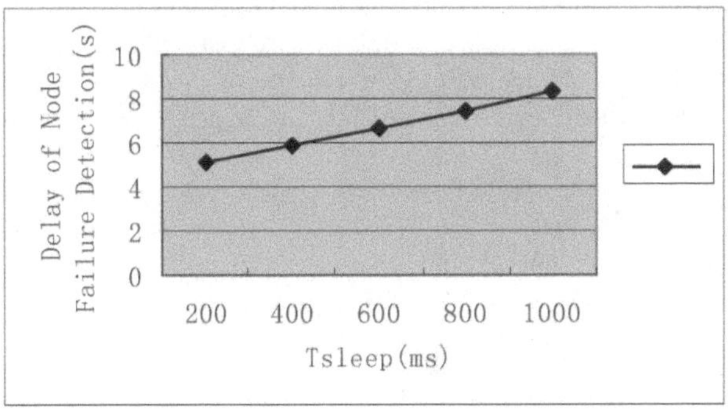

Fig. 3. The relation between T_{sleep} and the delay of node failure detection

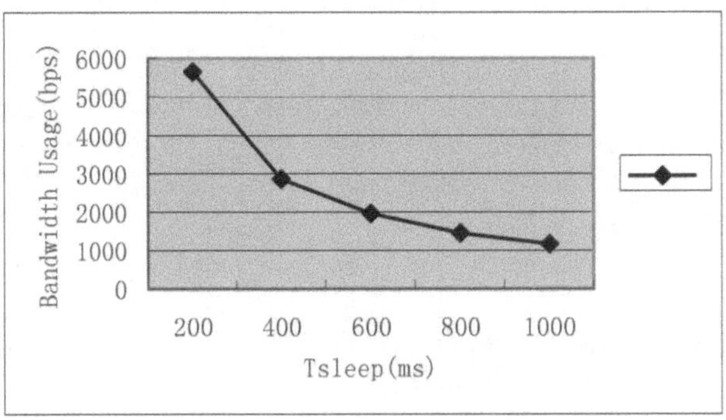

Fig. 4. The relation between T_{sleep} and the bandwidth usage

experiment results, the relation between the parameter T_{sleep} and the delay of node failure detection is depicted in Fig.3.

We obtain the average value of T_{circle} by experiments, then use the formula $B = 8 * L * m / T_{circle}$ to compute the network bandwidth usage for the heartbeat subsystem. According to the experiment results, the relation between the parameter T_{sleep} and the bandwidth usage is depicted as Fig.4.

5 Related Work

Heartbeat is a fundamental mechanism for fault-tolerance computer systems, it is widely used in many fields, such as system diagnosis [3], mobile computing [5] or network fault detection [6]. Takizawa *et al* analyzed a family of four heartbeat protocols [1]. The first three of these protocols have the same disadvantage of poor scalability, the fourth protocol defines the first node to be the master node, which takes charge of transferring the heartbeat message among the system and maintaining the timer. This decreases the availability of the whole cluster because the master node becomes a critical node of the heartbeat subsystem. Hou *et al* presents a distributed heartbeat mechanism, in which one master node and multiple standby nodes are running the same heartbeat daemons but in different states [2]. In this model, the master node has to frequently exchange heartbeat messages with standby nodes, so it becomes the bottleneck and do not fit for the large-scale clusters.

Linux FailSafe [12] is well-known open-source software for high-availability, which is originally developed by SGI. In a cluster which adopts FailSafe for heartbeat, each node periodically multicast heartbeat messages to other nodes, if the heartbeat of a node can not be listened by other nodes, the node is considered to be failure. In a heartbeat period, the number of messages transferred among nodes is $N*(N-1)$, the message complexity is $O(n^2)$. Linux FailSafe has poor scalability and only fits small-scale cluster.

6 Conclusion and Future Work

Heartbeat ring is a heartbeat mechanism for large-scale distributed managed clusters. It has the advantage of simplicity, scalability and adaptability, and so on. However, it doesn't consider internal network failure and assumes the communication subsystem guarantees messages be transferred reliably. In fact the network is always unreliable and dual network is always used for high availability clusters. Heartbeat ring mechanism should be adapted to unreliable internal network cluster. In addition, how to efficiently recover the cluster from failure and make single point failure transparent to applications is also another future work for improving the availability of cluster.

References

1. Gouda, M.G.; McGuire, T.M. Proceedings of the 18th International Conference on Distributed Computing Systems (1998) 202 - 209
2. Zonghao Hou, Yongxiang Huang, Shouqi Zheng. Design and Implementation of Heartbeat in Multi-machine Environment. Proceedings of the 17th International Conference on Advanced Information Networking and Applications (2003) 583-586

3. Barborak,M., M. Malek, and A. Dahbura, The Consensus Problem in Fault-Tolerant Computing, ACM Computing Surveys, Vol. 25 (1993) 171-220
4. Tseng, Y. C., Detecting Termination By Weight Throwing in a Faulty Distributed System, Journal of Parallel and Distributed Computing, Vol. 25, No. 1(1995)
5. Pradhan, D. K. et. al.,Recoverable Mobile Environment Design and Trade-off Analysis, Proceedings of Annual Symposium on Fault Tolerant Computing (1996.) 16-25
6. Vogels, W.,World Wide Failures, ACM SIGOPS European Workshop(1996)
7. Alan Robertson. Linux-HA Heartbeat System Design. Proceedings of the 4th Annual Linux Showcase & Conference (2000)
8. Hwang K, Xu Z W. Scalable Parallel Computing: technology, architecture, programming, McGraw-Hill (1998)
9. The Linux-HA project, http://linux-ha.org (2005)
10. The openMosix project, http://www.openMosix.org (2005)
11. The Kerrighed project, http://www.kerrighed.org (2005)
12. The Linux FailSafe Project. http://oss.sgi.com/projects/failsafe (2005)

Parallel Implementing of Road Situation Modeling with Floating GPS Data*

Zhaohui Zhang[1,2], Youqun Shi[3], and Changjun Jiang[1]

[1] Department of Computer Science & Technology of Tongji University, Shanghai 200092, P.R. China
[2] Department of Computer Science & Technology of Anhui Normal University, Wuhu 241000, P.R. China
[3] School of Computer Science & Technology of Donghua University, Shanghai 200051, P.R. China
zhzhang@163.com

Abstract. Most traffic flow models are based on the traffic data from inductive loops. However, this paper is to model the road situation with GPS data of floating vehicles. The relationship of the time and the passing velocity through a road segment is presented in the models which can reflect urban traffic situation. Moreover, a parallel algorithm is proposed to build the models and its task scheduling policy can make the efficiency of CPUs be about 75% in the heterogeneous computing platform. The experimental results also indicate it.

1 Introduction

Finding out the rules of the traffic situation to guide the vehicles or provide the reasonable travel lines for drivers is one of the key issues in intelligent transportation systems [1]. Generally, the traffic flow models are built with the data from inductive loops [2][4]. These models, however, reflect the traffic situation of few main roads and that of most other roads are vacant. In fact, there are many vehicles with GPS devices in large cities now. The GPS data are originally used in vehicle scheduling for each running company. But the GPS data may be used to model the road situation because the vehicles run everywhere in the urban road net. So the models built with the GPS data maybe reflect the traffic situation of most roads.

This paper is to model the road situation with GPS data and implement it with a parallel algorithm because of massive GPS data. The models will be used in Urban Traffic information Service Grid [3] to support the services of real-time road situation and dynamic travel guidance.

* This work was supported in part by the Shanghai Science & Technology Research Plan of China under Grant No. 03DZ15029,05DZ15005, the National Natural Science Foundation of China under Grant No. 90412013, the National High Technology Development 863 Program of China under Grant No.2004AA104340, and the Natural Science Research of Anhui Universities(2004KJ167).

H.T. Shen et al. (Eds.): APWeb 2006, LNCS 3842, pp. 620–624, 2006.

2 Road Situation Modeling

The longitude and the latitude in a piece of GPS data are mapped onto a road segment id by deviation correcting. And the direction is transformed to two directions of a road segment as 0 or 1. So a GPS record is presented as road segment id, direction, velocity, and time.

The road situation in a direction of a road segment for a day is presented as the relationship of velocity and time, that is $v = f(t)$. Given n data points $(t_i, v_i), i = 0,1,...,n-1$, we can use the least square method to complete data fitting. The approximating polynomial with degree m-1 is $f(t) = \sum_{i=0}^{m-1} a_i t^i, (m \le n)$.

To determine above polynomial, we construct a new polynomial which is linearly composed of orthogonal polynomials $P_i(t)$, i.e. $f(t) = \sum_{i=1}^{m-1} C_i P_i(t)$, where $\{P_i(t)\}$ is constructed with Gram-Schmidt method[4] by

$$P_0(t) = 1,$$
$$P_1(t) = t - \alpha_1,$$
$$\cdots\cdots$$
$$P_i(t) = (t - \alpha_i)P_{i-1}(t) - \beta_{i-1}P_{i-2}(t),\ i = 2,3,...,m-1.$$

Let $d_i = \sum_{j=0}^{n-1} P_i^2(t_j), i = 0,1,...,m-1$, then according to Gram-Schmidt theorem, we can get $\alpha_{i+1} = \frac{1}{d_i}\sum_{j=0}^{n-1} t_j P_i^2(t_j)$ and $\beta_i = d_i / d_{i-1}$, $i = 0,1,...,m-2$. And the polynomials in $\{P_i(t)\}$ are orthogonal with each other. Using the least-square method, we can get $C_i = \frac{1}{d_i}\sum_{j=0}^{n-1} v_j P_i(t_j),\ i = 0,1,...,m-1$.

In fact, curve fitting with an approximating polynomial is to work out C_i. And a time-velocity model of road situation comes out correspondingly, i.e.

$$v = f(t) = \sum_{i=0}^{m-1} a_i t^i, (m \le n).$$

Fig.1 and fig.2 are curves of the data fitting with above method. In the figures, a point presents the mean velocity of all vehicles in a direction of a road segment for an interval of 15 minutes. From these figures, we can get the change trend of the velocity in a road segment. Obviously, at about 8 a.m. and at about 5 p.m., the velocity is very small. Actually, the two periods of time are justly in rush hour.

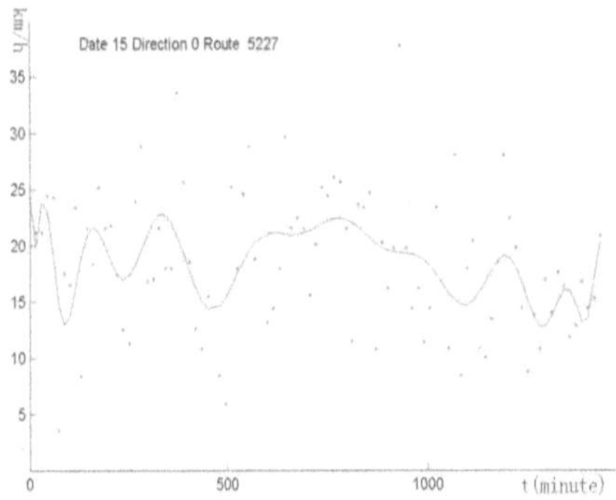

Fig. 1. The Fitting Curve in Direction 0 of Road Segment

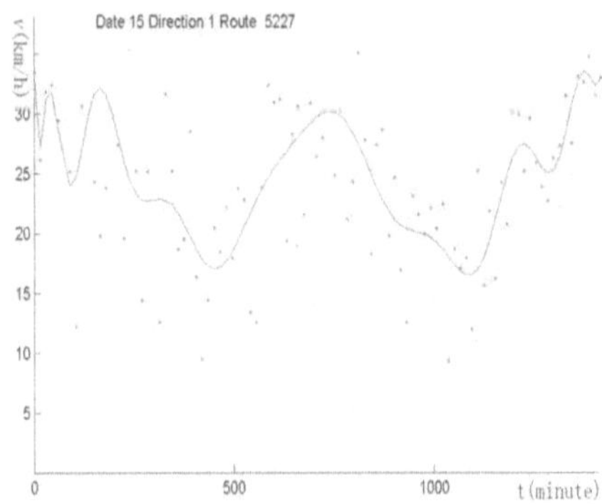

Fig. 2. The Fitting Curve in Direction 1 of Road Segment

3 Parallel Algorithm of Modeling the Road Situation

3.1 The Architecture of Parallel Computers

In this paper, we process data and build the models of road situation with heterogeneous computers including a master computer and some distributed slave ones. The job scheduling machine is the master for distribute the computational task to the slave node. The distributed computers are computational nodes which slave to the job scheduling machine. The GPS data are stored in the GPS database from which the job scheduling machine gets data. The computational resource monitor takes charge of the resource information of the distributed computers and provides it to the master machine.

3.2 Designing of the Parallel Algorithm

According to the architecture, the basic designing thought of the parallel algorithm is that the job scheduler in the master gets the information of the idle computers, partition the task to subtasks, and distributes each of them to the respective computer for processing. The key point of the algorithm is how to partition the task to the subtasks rationally so that the computational resources are used enough.

Given n CPUs denoted by $c_1,\ c_2, \cdots, c_n$ and the speed of them is respectively $s_1,\ s_2, \cdots, s_n$, let $r_i = s_i \Big/ \sum_{j=1}^{n} s_j , i = 1,2,...,n$. It is the proportion of computational ability of c_i to n CPUs.

Suppose the computational quantity of the task is N. So the task can be partition n subtasks and the computational quantity of each subtask is $N \times r_i$.

Proposition: Based on above policy of the task partitioning, the computing time of every CPU is equal to each other and the time is minimum.

The proof is omitted.

According to that policy of task partition, the algorithm is described as below.

The scheduling algorithm of the job scheduling machine:

STEP 0: Get the resource information of n idle computers and computes r_i.

STEP 1: Compute the size of each subtask $q_i = N \times r_i$ and record the amount of road segments for every process, denoted by $d_i, i = 1, 2, ..., n$.

STEP 2: Read the GPS data of k road segments so that the amount of them not less than $q_i, i = 1, 2, ..., n$. Then dispatch these data to c_i.

STEP 3: When all tasks are dispatched, begin to wait and receive the results from the distributed computers.

STEP 4: If the quantity of road segments in c_i is more than $q_i, i = 1, 2, ..., n$, receive the redundant data. Compute the total of the received road segments.

STEP 5: Let $d_i = d_i - q_i, i = 1, 2, ..., n$. If d_i<0, transfer $d_i \times 14$ pieces of received data to c_i.

STEP 6: Wait and receive the results from the distributed computers, and put them into the models library of road situation.

The algorithm of every distributed computer:

STEP 0: Receive the amount of road segments denoted by d, q_i and GPS data. Divide a day into n discrete intervals.

STEP 1: Compute the mean velocity of every interval in every direction of every road segment for every day of 7 days.

STEP 2: Let $d = d - q_i$. If d>0, send d pieces of data to the job scheduling machine.

STEP 3: If d<0, receive d pieces of data from the job scheduling machine.

STEP 4: For every road segment, every day of 7 days and every direction, compute all C_i and a_i according to the formulas in section 2.

STEP 5: Send the results to the job scheduling machine.

3.3 The Experiment

The experiment data come from Shanghai Urban Transportation Information Center, which include the road information of more than 25000 road segments and the GPS data from more than 2000 taxies and buses for last 3 months. And the experiment platform is Traffic Information Grid[3].

In the experiment, the algorithm is done by 1 processor, 4 processors, 8processors and 16 processors. The running time is shown in Fig.3, and the speedup and CPU efficiency are in Fig.4. The figures show that the running time of the algorithm will reduce with the increasing amount of CPUs. The increasing multiple of the speedup is about equal to the increasing multiple of the CPUs. And the efficiency of the CPUs is about 75%.

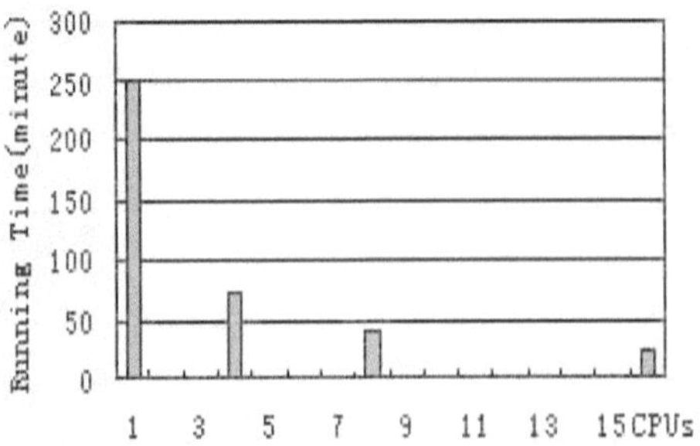

Fig. 3. The Running Time of the Algorithm for Different Amount of CPUs

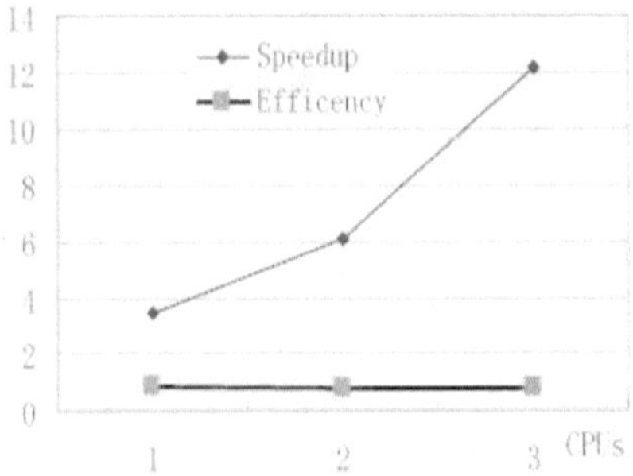

Fig. 4. The Speedup of the algorithm and Efficiency of CPUs for Different Amount of CPUs

4 Conclusions

In this paper, we conclude that the models of road situation built with GPS data of floating vehicles can reflect the urban traffic situation. The precision of the models are determined by the acquisition frequency of GPS devices and the distributed density of the vehicles. Moreover, modeling the road situation must be computed with parallel algorithm for massive data. The algorithm presented in this paper can get the good running effect and its task scheduling policy can make the efficiency of CPUs be about 75% in the heterogeneous computing platform.

References

1. Z.S. Yang: The theory and model of inducement system of city traffic flow (in Chinese). Beijing：People Traffic Press, 1999.
2. D.W Chen, J.P. Zhang: Freeway Traffic Stream Modeling based on Principle Curves, IEEE Intelligent Transportation Systems Proceedings, China, October 12-15,2003, pp.368-371
3. C.J. Jiang, Z.H. Zhang, et al. Urban Traffic Information Service Application Grid. J. Computer Science & Technology. Vol20(1):134-140,2005
4. D. H. Wang, D.Y: Qu, A study of a Real-time Dynamic Prediction Method for Traffic Volume, China Journal of Highway and Transport, Vol 11, pp 102-107

Research on a Generalized Die CAD System Architecture Based on SOA and Web Service

Xinhua Yang[1], Feilong Tang[2], and Wu Deng[1]

[1] Software Technology Institute, Dalian Jiaotong University, Dalian 116028, China
xhyang@263.net
[2] Department of Computer Science and Engineering, Shanghai Jiao Tong University, Shanghai 200030, China
tang-fl@cs.sjtu.edu.cn

Abstract. First of all, the factors that cause difficulty in CAD/CAE/CAM/PDM integrating are analyzed, and a Web Service-based service-oriented architecture (SOA) is introduced in this paper. Besides, based on the special requirement, characteristic of die design and the analysis, a new approach for integrating CAD/CAE/CAM/PDM by adopting Web Service is presented. Furthermore, a service-oriented architecture of generalized Die CAD system is given based on Web Service. The advantage of the architecture is finally expatiated.

1 Introduction

The design of mechanical product is an iterative and complicated decision-making process accompanied by excessive factors. In order to reduce the developing period and improve design quality, people ceaselessly seek Hi-Technology centered by CAD as the platform for modern mechanical produce and design. Traditional geometry-based CAD system can not meet the demand of integrating and intelligent of CAD system. People have begun to apply themselves to the research of new generation of intelligent and integrated CAX (CAD/CAM/CAE) system. But the traditional CAX system has many problems: tight coupling, un-reusable, no united standard, limited by the special development language and operating system. Because of so many defects, many problems arise when integrating CAD/CAM/CAE/PDM. In addition, any change will affect the whole integrated system, and even result in system collapse. With the emergence of the Web Service technology, especially Web Service-based SOA, a new approach for integrating CAD/CAM/CAE/PDM is introduced. Based on the Web Service, this paper will present a SOA-based architecture of generalized Die CAD system.

2 Service-Oriented Architecture and Web Service

2.1 Service-Oriented Architecture

Service-Oriented Architecture (SOA) is a solution for designing and setting up the loosing coupling software system, it can publish business functions in the manner of

H.T. Shen et al. (Eds.): APWeb 2006, LNCS 3842, pp. 625–631, 2006.

programmable and accessible service, and the other application can use these services by using the published and findable interface. So, the key conception of SOA is SERVICE, and any application of SOA is regarded as a service to be called and administrated. W3C defined SOA as follows: the service provider delivers ultimately request results to service user by the aid of accomplishing a set of work. The ultimately results usually change the status of user, provider or both. To some extent, SOA is a model which is used for designing, developing, deploying and administrate discrete logic units under computer environment.

There are three roles in SOA, shown as Fig.1. Service provider publishes its own service, and also makes response to the request; Service broker registers and makes classifications of the published service providers, it also provides search service; Service requester seeks requisite service by using service broker, and make use of the service. The components of SOA must have one or more of the above mentioned roles. These roles carry out such operations as publish, find and bind. Publish operation helps service provider to register its own function and interface; Find operation helps service requester to find special service aided by service broker; Binding operation helps service requester to use the provided services in deed.

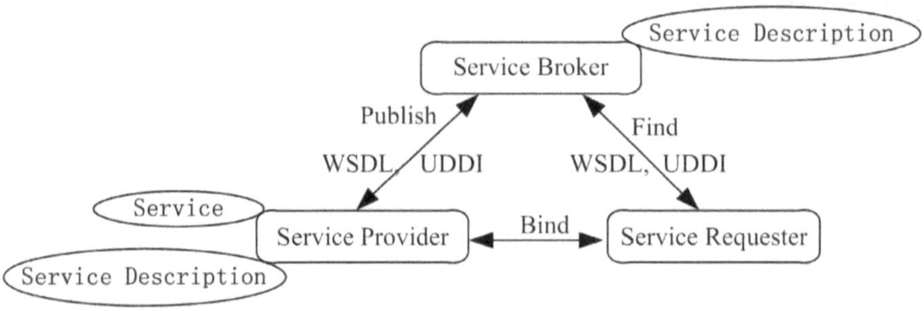

Fig. 1. Web service-based SOA

2.2 Web Service-Based SOA

Web service is a new generation of web application. It combines the advantage of component-oriented and web technologies, and they can describe its own service. It can also publish, locate and transfer modularized application in web. The functions provided by web service may be simple, but it also contains extraordinary complicated business logic. Once web services are deployed, the other applications can find and request them.

From the structural aspects, the core of web service is service. Web service represents a kind of implementation of SOA, and it is the most popular one. In addition, the three operations of SOA can only process when the components of SOA interact. Therefore some standardized technologies are used in web service, including UDDI, WSDL, HTTP, SOAP, XML and so on. Among them, SOAP is used to define how to request service, UDDI to publish and find service, WSDL is for the self-description of service information, XML is a consolidated format of data information. Web service becomes the best choice for developing SOA application.

The web service-based SOA has some specialties such as communication over firewall, loose coupling, platform independent and Reusable of data and software. These specialties have many advantages, for instance, it can greatly improve the function of Web service; make real of inter-operation; employ and enlarge different kinds of data and service resources; and dynamic binding different services to accomplish specified functions. All of these will help find comparatively ideal solutions to deal with the existing and potential problems in the process of integrating CAD/CAE/CAM/PDM.

3 A Service-Oriented Die CAD System Architecture Based on Web Service

3.1 A Structure Pattern of Traditional Generalized Die CAD System

In a broad sense, a generalized Die CAD system is referred to an integrated system of CAD/CAE/CAM/PDM, most of which are built on workstation. Their system structure pattern is shown as Fig.2. The functions include:

- Geometry modeling system

The system is used to modeling for work piece and die set geometry structure. Besides, die materials selecting and technology parameters setting are also done in this system.

- Emulate and analysis system

This system processes dynamics, kinematics, yawp and machining process emulation. The result is the basis for edit the design results. Emulate and analysis system is kernel of whole generalized Die CAD system, it determined whether the design solution is rational or not. However, it is the most complicate, time-consuming, and resource-consuming part in the whole system.

- Data management system

This part is in charge of managing standard parts/components base, design knowledge base, design case base and other product data.

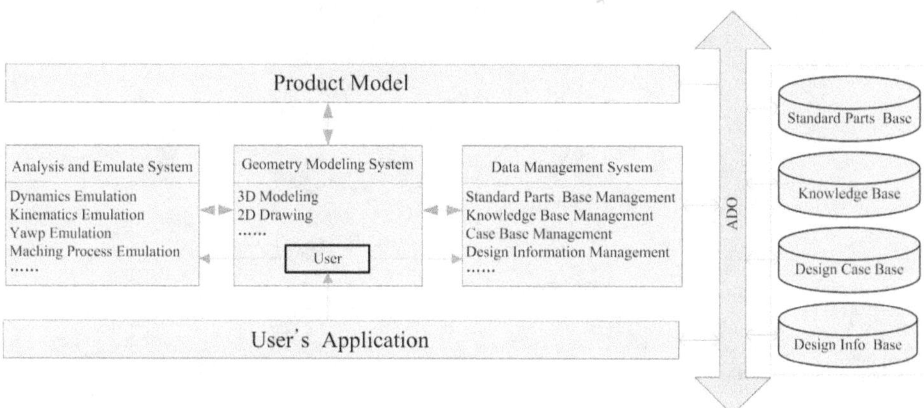

Fig. 2. Traditional generalized CAD system architecture pattern

Different parts of the CAD system under such structure are comparatively independent and easy to handle. But there are still some disadvantages; for instance, the investment is very big, the share capacity is poor, system upgrading and data exchanging is not very convenient, and it does not support long-range design. Aside from that, the tight coupling structure makes it impossible to realize distributing and opening application. What's more, the problems like development language and platform dependent are unavoidable, since the system is usually developed in a special program language under special operating system.

3.2 A Service-Oriented Die CAD System Architecture Based on Web Service

With the development of network and virtual manufacture technology, Internet/Intranet-based CAD system appears, shown as Fig.3. The idea of this system is to make the best of advantage of network bandwidth to separate user interface and background analysis module. The user interface can provide I/O function. Emulate analysis and data management systems are deployed on a server. This is an embryonic form of web-based integrated CAX system.

It is a great progress to put emulate and analysis system alone in server. Its specialties are as follows: first of all, there is no need for users to configure for every CAD system with a computer of a high capability while using the system. It is because that such time and resource consuming emulate and analysis system is placed in a special server to work, if necessary, groups of servers can work together and analysis in order to speed up analysis; second, it is convenient to realize data share if all data are put in the end of the server and operated together; what's more, such mechanism is fit for long-distance development, for if a corporation put CAE system server in a place, any long-distance server can carry out long-distance analysis and see about the results as long as they are authorized. However, as for implementation and maintenance of such configuration, it is far from better than the above mentioned framework which is from web service to service. So a logic model of Generalized Die CAD System structure based on SOA and Web Service is proposed, shown as Fig.4.

The model is comprised of three levels: data level, service lever, and client level. Data level includes design knowledge base, 3D standard parts base, design case base, as well as providing product data management of the whole life cycle of the product;

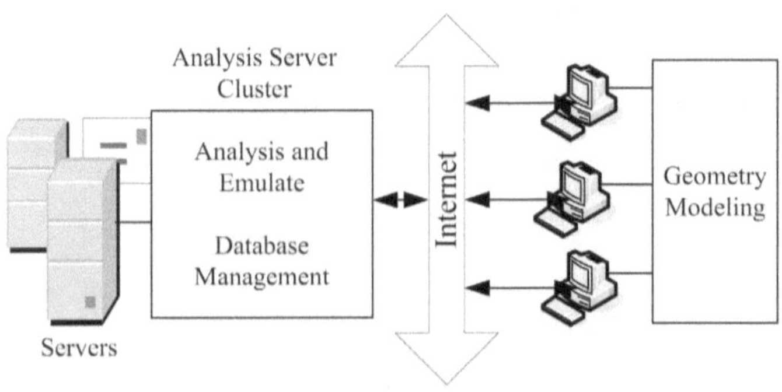

Fig. 3. Generalized CAD system structure based on Internet/Intranet

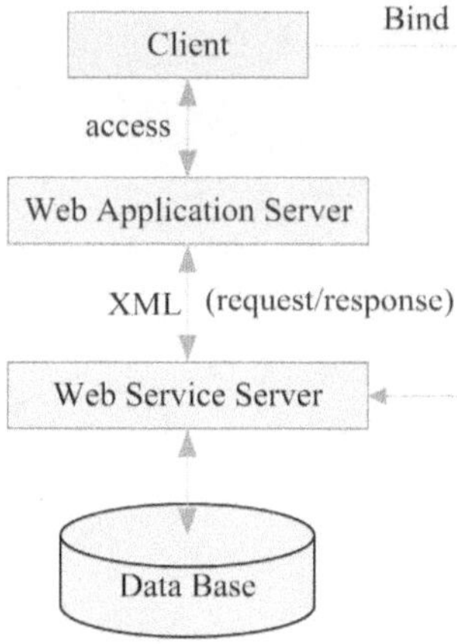

Fig. 4. Logic model of CAX System based on SOA and web service

service level provides services to the outer applications, it is comprised of two parts: one is web service server; the other is web application server. Web application server receive request from clients and then send to the related web service. At last, the application server sends result back to the clients. It is the Web services server who deals with the assignment. Client includes website explorer and other demanded application. With the needs of such die deign, based on Fig.4, a Generalized Die CAD System Architecture Based on SOA and Web Service is proposed, shown as Fig.5. The architecture has such characteristics:

- Easy implementation

It results from the specialty of the web service. Because of the promotion by Microsoft, Sun, and IBM corporations, there are lots of free instruments which can quickly help generate and deploy web service. Also they can easily change the original application to web service. In doing so, it is not necessary to rewrite the existed system - analysis module- and reduce the cost of development. It is especially important to those companies who have already invested much time and money. We developed a prototype by using Microsoft Windows. NET Framework. It support more than 20 programming languages; can administrate many software development related work. It is convenient to help set up, deploy and administrate a safe, reliable application of high safety and high capacity.

- Easy integration with other system

Once a web service is published, it will be found and used by requested application according to its illuminate. Even if the service is changed, the application does not have to change, which makes the integration with other system, such as CAD, CAM, and PDM, easier.

- System being independent from developing language and operating system

Due to adopting HTTP and XML, the restriction from special developing language and operating system is avoided. Therefore, the service such as analysis and material selection service can provide service for any application which is developed under any platform and in any language.

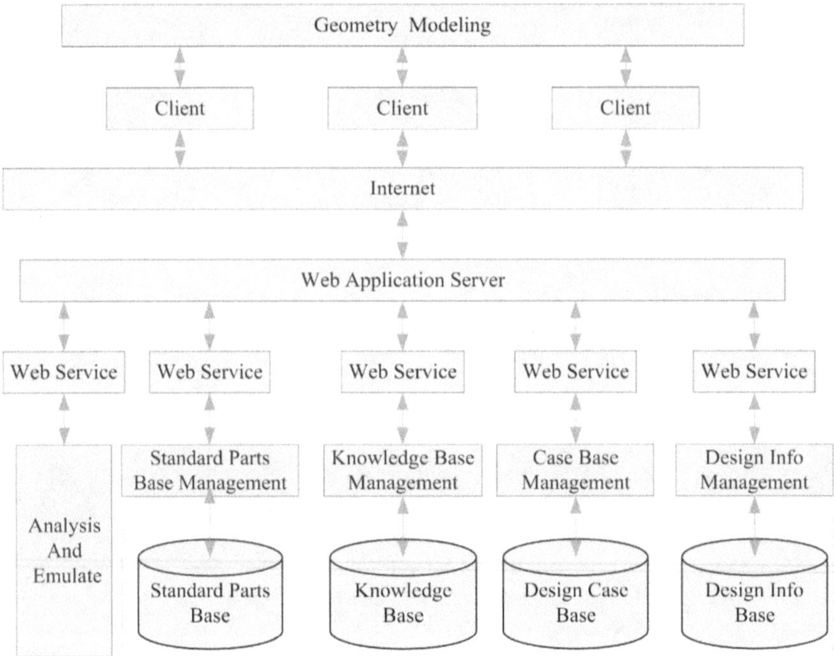

Fig. 5. A generalized die CAD system architecture based on SOA and web service

4 Conclusions

An integrated architecture of generalized Die CAD system is presented based on web service and SOA. The main difference from the traditional CAX is that this system employs web service as its integrating standard, and act as an integrating point between applications. Web service enhances its ability of agility, integrating, and reusability while building up system. As a result, developing efficiency of CAD system is improved, and cost of development and maintenance is reduced. Since many problems of web service, such as slow response, poor safety, still exist, problems of CAX system which is developed on the basis of web service and SOA are also inevitable. However, the author is confident that with the development of web service technology, these problems will surely be resolved in the near future.

References

1. Mechael S. Pallos.: Service-Oriented Architecture: A Primer[J]. eAI Journal, 2001(9): 32-35
2. Zhang Ming-bai, Xia An-bang.: Agile information system framework based on service-orient architecture in virtual enterprise. Computer Integrated Manufacturing System. Vol.10. 2004(8):985-990

3. Aoyama M, Weerawaran S, Mruyama H, et al. Web services engineering: promises and challenges[A]. Proceedings of the 24th International Conference on Software Engineerin[C]. Los Alamitos, CA, USA: IEEE Computer Society, 2002. 647-648.
4. CHEN Ke, Zhang Yi-sheng, LIANG Shu-yun, LI De-qun: Research and application of mould injecting CAE system based on web service. Research on Computer Application. 2004(4):42-44
5. Thomas J P., Thomas M, Chinea G.: Modeling of web services flow [A]. Proceeding of 2003 IEEE International Conference on E-Commerce [C]. Los Alamitos, CA, USA: IEEE Computer Society. 2003. 391-398.

Towards Building Intelligent Transportation Information Service System on Grid*

Ying Li[1,2], Minglu Li[1], Jiao Cao[1], Xinhong Wu[3], Linpeng Huang[1], Ruonan Rao[1], Xinhua Lin[1], Changjun Jiang[4], and Min-You Wu[1]

[1] Department of Computer Science and Engineering, Shanghai Jiao Tong University, Shanghai, China
[2] Computer Science and Technology School, Soochow University, Suzhou, China
[3] Shanghai Urban Transportation Information Center
[4] Tongji University, Shanghai, China
{liying, li-ml, cao-jian}@cs.sjtu.edu.cn

Abstract. Poor interpretability of current transportation systems has become an obstacle to further develop the intelligent transportation systems (ITS). Our design and implementation of intelligent transportation information service systems (ITIS) focuses on integrating heterogeneous data, transportation systems, and resources by using the grid technique. The ITIS project will refine and summarize the business model in Shanghai transportation information service system, design and set up open standards for intelligent transportation information service and simulation, develop grid supporting platform for transportation information service, integrate and fuse massive dynamic transportation data and legacy transportation systems, construct high performance computing (HPC) platform and dynamic parallel transportation simulation platform. ITIS will provide various high-level transportation information services for both citizens and government, which include optimal dynamic bus riding planning service, dynamic on-board navigation service, bus arrival-time prediction service, network optimization and simulation system, large-scale traffic-flow simulation system. Using these services will help to reduce the traffic congestion and other traffic problems, enhancing the transportation intelligence.

1 Introduction

Shanghai is a municipality of eastern China at the mouth of the Yangtze River. Today, it has become the largest economic center and an important port city in China, with a land area covering 6340 km^2 and a population of 16 million people. It is the host city of the 2010 Shanghai World Expo. With the rapid development of economic and the increasing number of automobiles, the problem of urban traffic congestion has become more and more serious. To solve such problems, Shanghai government puts its focus not only on road infrastructure construction, but also on transportation intelligence

* This paper is supported by ShanghaiGrid grand project of Science and Technology Commission of Shanghai Municipality (No.03DZ15027, 05DZ15005).

H.T. Shen et al. (Eds.): APWeb 2006, LNCS 3842, pp. 632–642, 2006.

development for higher performance and better service. Recent years, the government has made tremendous effort toward solving traffic problems such as traffic congestion, air pollution, traffic guidance and et al, therefore, some transportation information management systems have been put into use or are under developing, i.e., taxi dispatch system, public transportation management system, traffic signal-control system, incident-detection system. These systems play important roles in solving the traffic problems in Shanghai, acting as subsystems of ITS.

In using these systems, one problem has emerged gradually. The design of these sytems does not consider the interoperation among each other. These systems belong to different government agencies, use different technologies and the traffic data cannot be shared among them. In order to provide satisfactory service to users, transportation systems have to work together intimately. For example, to analyze and forecast traffic status, we need massive amounts of information from different systems, which includes weather conditions, digital maps, historic data, GPS systems, traffic-light information. But unfortunately, due to the management, security and technique issues, these data can not be access in real-time. And the heart of ITS lies in gathering and using system information in real time to improve real-time control [1].

Another problem is how to store, fuse, and utilize the transportation information data (TID) in these systems. TID is fundamental to ITS, as a big city, the amount of TID of Shanghai in each system are huge. Even more, different systems use different ways to store their data. It is difficult to provide a good way to interoperate among these systems.

Shanghai government has already noticed the weakness of the non-interoperation of these systems. In order to provide better services to citizen, further reduce the traffic congestion, provide real-time traffic information to decision makers, it launches the ITIS project, which aims to build a platform to integrate various transportation systems as a whole. ITIS will be based on previous successful closed ShanghaiGrid [2] [3] research project, which has already developed a set of software and tools called ShanghaiGrid Operating System (SGOS) to construct information service grid (ISG). It provides sophisticated tools to implement the ITIS.

2 ShanghaiGrid and SGOS

ShanghaiGrid aims to construct a metropolitan-area Information Service Grid (ISG) and establish an open standard for widespread upper-layer applications from both communities and the government. It is one of five top grand Grid projects in China. It is based on the current four major computational aggregates and networks in Shanghai, including Shanghai Supercomputing Center (SSC), and various campus supercomputer centers in Shanghai Jiao Tong University (SJTU), Tongji University (TJU) and Shanghai University (SHU). It is planned to enable the heterogeneous and distributed resources to collaborate in an information fountain and computational environment for Grid services, seamlessly and transparently. ShanghaiGrid has connected several major Grid nodes to form a 0.6 Tflops aggregate computing power and a 4 TB aggregate storage power, sophisticated information environment [3].

Shanghai government wants to use the Grid technology to construct a basic infrastructure for e-science, e-business, e-education, e-government and e-life, as the basic facilities of the city, similar to transportation and communication systems, water and power lines. So ShanghaiGrid as an infrastructure will fully use the existing techniques and resources to provide rich functionality of information services. Currently, several applications have been developed and put into use in the ShanghaiGrid, such as computational fluid dynamics, medicine image processing, drug discovery Grid, et al. The core of ShanghaiGrid is the SGOS, which provides middlewares, services and tools to satisfy the needs of building the ISG. Moreover, the SGOS hides the complexity of the Grid techniques for developers building Grid applications. The main components of SGOS are brief introduced as following:

- ShanghaiGrid information service (SGIS) [4]. SGIS provides a standard way to register, publish, update and unregister information such as computation resources, web services, grid services and user-defined information. Different from the MDS [5] that used in GT [6], it puts focus on how to organize self-defined information such as workflow.
- ECA (Event-Condition-Action)-rule-based workflow management system (EWMS) [7]. It is important for ISG to build a collaborative workflow infrastructure that allows users to describe the interactions between services and compose new workflow out of existing services to build complex applications consisting of thousands of tasks and services. However, the existing approaches do not provide enough functionality to support flexible service composition, workflow modeling and enactment. Our EWMS combines graphical process representation and ECA rules in controlling Grid workflow process, using integration adapter to facilitate the composition of all possible services, supporting hierarchical graph definition that allows workflow coursing and refinement. In this way, EWMS extends the scope of resource sharing and offers a well-layered view for complicated workflow.
- Grid transaction service (GridTS) [8]. GridTS is used to ensure system consistency in Grid services while handling different types of transactions represents. The GridTS has three main components: The service discovery component is used to search for appropriate Grid services to execute specified sub-transactions, and uses a two-level registry mechanism to adopt the transient Grid services. The transaction component coordinates the atomic and coherent transactions. The latter is defined to satisfy the requirements of long-lived Grid transactions by automatically generating and executing compensation transactions. The real-time transaction component is responsible for managing transactions with a strict time restriction. The ratio of successful real-time transactions can be improved significantly by executing functional, alternative services in parallel. These components enable the GridTS to intelligently handle various transactions in the service Grid environment.
- Grid monitor service (M-Grid). M-Grid is a resource monitoring and analysis system in grid. M-Grid provides an infrastructure for conducting online monitoring and performance analysis of a variety of grid resources distributed environments.
- Data integration service. The Open Grid Services Architecture Data Access and Integration (OGSA-DAI) [9] provides a common interface that can be used to

access remote databases and XML files. Currently, we use it to integration data from various systems.

- Protocols adaptive file transfer (PAFTP). PAFTP is core middleware for data transport, which supports various protocols such as GridFTP, bbFTP, HTTP, FTP. User can transport files either from client software named SHGridFTP, or from browser.
- Application delivery toolkit (ADT) [10]. ISG uses the Java Network Launching Protocol (JNLP) [11] client to support the ubiquitous computing. ADT is used here to develop a JNLP-enabled application (a jar file) and store it with a delivery service for mobile device to download and execute.

Other services or middlewares include: Accounting Service [12], Security service, Grid portal [13], et al.

3 Architecture of ITIS

3.1 Overview

The ITIS project will refine and summarize the business model in Shanghai transportation information service field, design and set up standards, assessments for Intelligent transportation information service and simulation, develop a set of protocols and standards to connect resources such as storage, computing, network to form an ITIS grid environment based on ShanghaiGrid, integrate and fuse massive dynamic transportation data and legacy transportation management systems, construct HPC platform and dynamic parallel transportation simulation platform, and provide high-level transportation information services for both citizen and government.

The main reasons that ITIS needs Grid technology are based on following facts:

- Integration of computational resources and various transportation systems. There exits dozens of transportation systems in Shanghai. These systems are independent, autonomic and none-interoperated. Grid can share computation, storage and other resources among these systems, cooperate among different transportation systems and provide huge computational power. Grid services provide an approach to build distributed systems that deliver application functionality as services to end-user applications or to build other services. The existing transportation systems can be wrapped with web Services or grid services, thus individual exiting systems become the building blocks, which could be easily used to develop ITIS.
- Massive transportation data fusion. Transportation data are distributed, dynamic and of great volume, and could be collected by various kinds of sensors, GPS systems, video cameras, etc, from different systems. Shanghai is the biggest city in China, the production of daily transportation data is huge, which could accumulate to several PB a year. Table 1 shows the amount of GPS data in Shanghai, it reaches 17GB per day. So the massive transportation data must be fused and handled by high preference computers and networks, Grid is an ideal way.

Table 1. The amount of GPS data in Shanghai

Year	Automobie type	count	Daily(GB)	Yearly(TB)
2004	Public bus	3000	1.690	0.602
	Taxi	5000	2.816	1.004
	special vehicle	1000	0.563	0.201
	total	9000	5.069	**1.807**
2005	Public bus	7000	3.943	1.405
	Taxi	20000	11.265	4.015
	special vehicle	3400	1.915	0.638
	total	30400	17.123	**6.103**
2006 (estimated)	Public bus	8000	4.506	1.606
	Taxi	30000	16.898	6.023
	special vehicle	4000	2.253	0.803
	total	42000	23.657	**8.432**

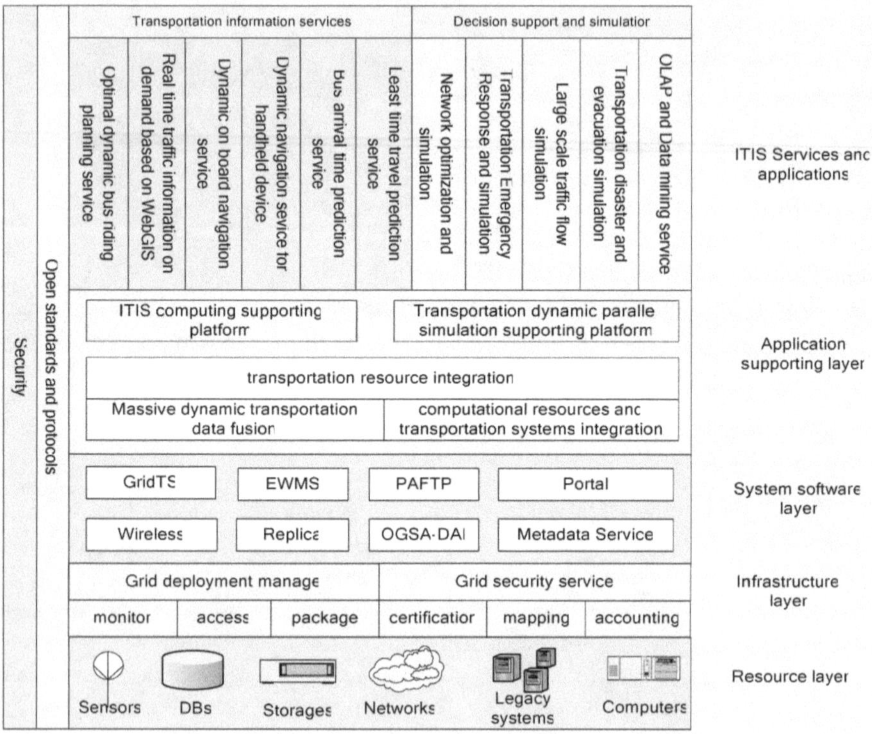

Fig. 1. Architecture of ITIS

- Large-scale and complex traffic-flow simulation. Simulation of traffic-flow is a key approach to study, evaluate, and better understand traffic condition in certain area. It is playing an increasingly important role as a problem solving tool for transportation system analysis. Traditionally, PC server can only simulate several intersections simultaneously, while Shanghai has about 14000 intersections and 21000 road sections, it needs huge computational power to do such simulation.

Grid can provide the computational power by dynamically allocate the computation resources from several supercomputer centers, such as Shanghai supercomputer center, or PC clusters. On another hand, simulation of real traffic-flow demands on integration of various transportation systems to provide traffic data, which include road-sensors, traffic light systems, GPS systems et al.

3.2 Architecture

As shown in Fig.1, ITIS consists of five parts. The bottom is resource layer, which contains various resources, i.e. road sensors, databases, storages. These resources are distributed and have various types. We treat the legacy transportation systems as a type of resources that can offer certain services.

Infrastructure layer is on the top of the resource layer which is used to construct the grid nodes. On the top of infrastructure layer is system software layer, which provides high level services such as workflow, transaction support.

Application supporting layer integrates computational resources, data resources and business logical as a whole. Upper-layer applications can use these resources transparently and easily.

Application layer is the top layer of ITIS Grid. It provides various transportation information services and simulations to satisfy the needs of citizens and decision makers.

4 Sub-projects of ITIS

ITIS comprises five sub-projects, including

1) Development of open protocols and standards for transportation information service applications.
2) Research on Grid supporting platform
3) Transportation resources integration.
4) Dynamic parallel transportation simulation.
5) Implementation of intelligent traffic information services.

The detail information about these projects is discussed as follows.

4.1 Protocols and Standards

In ITS, there exist several standards to describe traffic data, such as ISO-GDF [14], SDAL [15] and various standards developed by different governments. This became an obstacle for integrating different transportation management systems. Meanwhile, open standards and protocols must be applied to construct Grid nodes, grid services, web services and simulations to ensure the interoperation among them. These protocols and standards include:

- Protocols for connecting grid nodes.
- Standards for grid security.
- Standards for grid metadata. Metadata service plays important roles in grid. It is heavily used by services, protocols, workflow, security, data access and data

integration. Different systems have their own metadata. The standards give a semantic definition of the grid resources. The research topics include: how to encode the different information in a uniformed way? How to define the metadata? How to query, update, and map the metadata?
- Protocols for data exchanging.
- Protocols for service invoking.
- Standards for building the parallel transportation simulation platform.
- Standards for transportation information services.

4.2 Grid Supporting Platform

The design of ITIS grid supporting system is based on the idea that grid kernel should be minimized and the functionality should be provided as plug-in services. The architecture of the platform is shown in Fig.2.

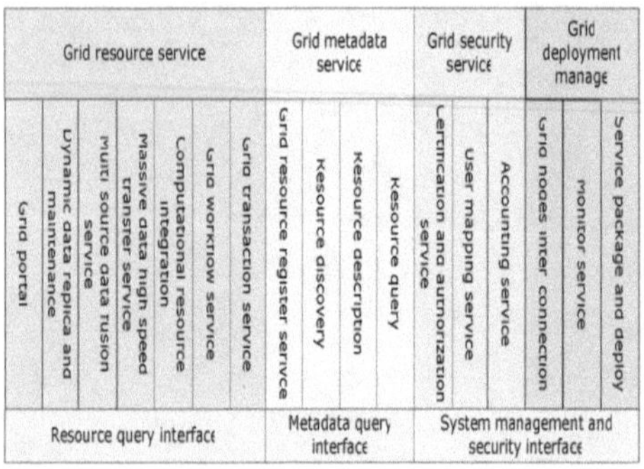

Fig. 2. Architecture of the ITIS grid supporting platform

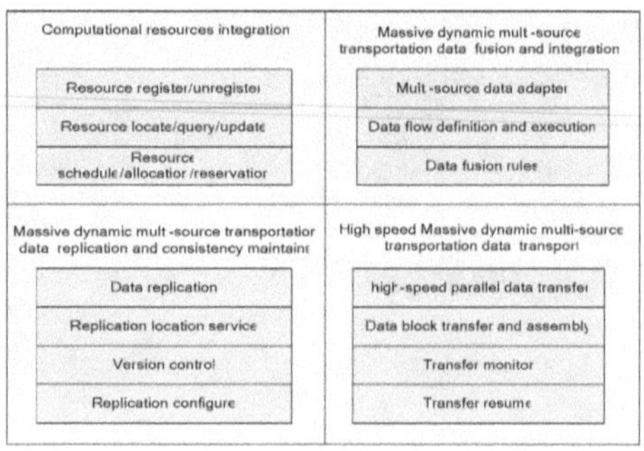

Fig. 3. Transportation resource integration

The main researches are:

- Design the micro grid kernel based on SOA
- Refine the existing middlewares in SGOS and design new middlewares such as high-speed data transfer service, massive data fusion service to meet the requirements of ITIS.
- Make it compatible with Web Service, OGSI and WSRF.

4.3 Transportation Resource Integration

Transportation resource integration includes computational resources integration and data integration. Fig.3 shows the main research topics.

The purpose of computational resources integration is to connect several supercomputers and clusters to form high performance distributed computing environment mainly for transportation simulation and real-time data processing.

The massive dynamic multi-source transportation data integration mainly uses the Data Grid technique. For every data source, there are one or more corresponding data adapters providing data services to other grid application. By using Data flow, ITIS can handle data in an automatic way.

Another aspect of data resource integration is data fusion. For example, the GPS data are collected by taxi, public bus, and special vehicle. These GPS data should be merged for further process. This kind of data fusion is heavily needed in ITIS. Data fusion needs high speed data transport, i.e. parallel data transfer, third-part data transfer, fault-detected and automatic transfer resuming.

Legacy transportation management systems integration is high level business logical integration. The legacy systems export their business logical as web or Grid services by using grid supporting platform, i.e., taxi location service, parking information service, as shown in Fig.4.

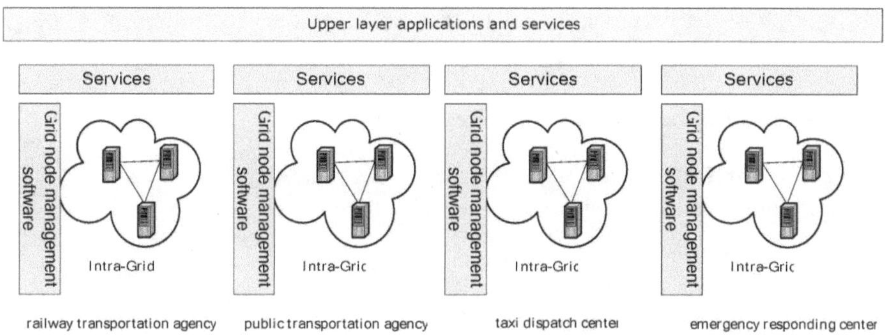

Fig. 4. Legacy transportation management systems export their business logical as services

4.4 Transportation Simulation

Transportation simulation as a basic problem simulating and solving tool is widely used in ITS. Due to the computational power limitation, traditional simulation tools can only simulate small-scale to middle-scale traffic condition, and usually not real-time simulation. Based on ITIS, we want to construct a transportation simulation platform for large-scale real-time dynamic traffic flow.

There exist some similarities between traffic flow and fluid dynamics. In traffic dynamics, vehicle is treated as fluid flow. But in fact, traffic flow is much more complex than fluid dynamics. In Shanghai, tens of thousands of automobiles, bicycles, pedestrians each have their own trait and mobility form a complex mixed traffic flow. In order to provide accurate, real-time traffic prediction, high performance computing power is needed to satisfy the requirement of complexity problem solving. Generally speaking, a simulation process has four steps: modeling, meshing, domain decomposition and solution. The study focuses on following aspects:

- Architecture of parallel simulation system. It defines the standards, protocols and implementation details of simulation system in Grid.
- Domain decomposition for transportation simulation. Domain decomposition divides input mesh into several small meshes that are used in solution process. The strategy of decomposition will affect the efficiency of solution greatly.
- Workflow based simulation scheduling. It is used to schedule the parallel solution according to the complexity of problems and the computational resources of Grid.
- Agent based traffic flow simulation. Classical mathematical simulation methods are hard to simulation the interaction among different transportation entities while the interaction is important aspect of realistic environment. In real world, an entity has several properties such as reaction, autonomy, decision, etc al. We can regard entity as an agent with these properties, thus the essential of simulation will turn into the study of the behavior among a collection of autonomous agents, with each agent has its goals, decisions, rules, et al. The nature property of the distribution of the agent is suitable for parallel process.
- Visualization of simulation results. Through various visualization tools, traffic information and condition can be clearly presented to decision makers.

4.5 Transportation Information Services

The design and implementation of transportation information services can be divided into two catalogs: services for decision maker and services for public.

Based on transportation simulation, ITIS provides several simulations as decision support systems:

- Network optimization and simulation system
- Transportation emergency response and simulation system
- Large-scale traffic-flow simulation system
- Transportation disaster and evacuation simulation system

Different from real-time analysis of traffic data, OLAP and Data mining service will help decision makers to further study the historic data and find knowledge or useful patterns among these data, which include:

- Grid-enabled OLAP service
- Cluster Analysis service
- Association rules service
- Decision tree service
- Outlier analysis service

Traditional approach of traffic information forecast used in Shanghai is semiautomatic adjust the traffic congestion level and show it in the display at the entrance of some important roads, or forecast it through radio. Some web sites provide traffic congestion information, but this information is neither real-time nor serviceable. Based on transportation data and systems integration, one key feature of ITIS is that it can provide real-time dynamic traffic information services, which include:

- Real-time traffic information on demand based on WebGIS. WebGIS has provided a new efficient means for traffic information publishing through browsers. With the graphic interface, traffic congestion and other information would be easily acquired by citizen.
- Optimal dynamic bus riding planning service. This service calculate least-time riding schedule by giving the start and end point according to the predict modeling based on the real-time traffic data.
- Dynamic on-board navigation service and dynamic navigation service for handheld device. These services provide an approach to access the traffic information by mobile devices.
- Bus-arrival-time prediction service. E-display is equipped at several bus stops in Shanghai to show citizen when the next bus will arrive by using this service. It uses the real-time data from GPS, traffic light system and road sensors to predict arrival time of public bus.
- Least-time travel prediction service. This service gives user a least-time travel schema according to the real-time traffic condition.

Through these traffic information services, citizen could use various ways to gain the traffic condition and make their own travel plan avoiding traffic congestion. Fig.5 shows user get traffic information through PDA, fig.6 shows that user get bus-arrival-time information from E-display at bus stop.

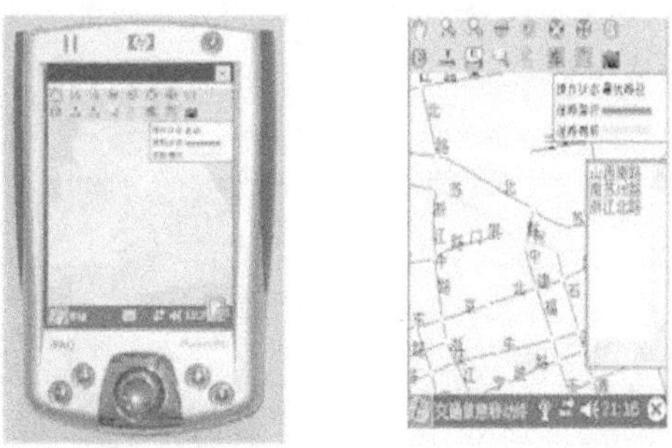

Fig. 5. User get traffic information through PDA

Fig. 6. E-display used to forecast the bus arrival time

5 Conclusion

Transportation intelligence is one of practical approach to lessen the traffic problems by using limited money and effort compared with building road infrastructure. With the development of ITS, the non-interoperation of each systems and non-exchangeability of transportation data became an obstacle to further reduce the traffic congestion and solve other traffic problems. ITIS wants integration various transportation systems and data to provide real-time, dynamic transportation information services to avoid these problems by using Grid. Citizens and decision makers will gain better services from ITIS.

This paper introduces the architecture of the ITIS and its main components. It uses SGOS to integrate transportation data, existing transportation systems and supercomputers to form a sophisticated Grid environment for hosting information services. Under this environment, traffic simulation systems could simulate large-scaled real-time dynamic traffic flow to analyze and forecast traffic condition. The Real-time traffic information on demand service and other information services could help citizens to be aware of the traffic condition and avoid traffic congestion.

The research and development of ITIS will construct a production Grid and bring better transportation information services to the public.

References

1. B. Abdulhai, "ITS, eh! Meet Canada's flagship ITS centre and testbed". IEEE Intelligent Systems 18 (2003), pp. 86-89.
2. Li ML, Wu MY, Li Y, et al. "ShanghaiGrid: an Information Service Grid". Concurrency Computat.: Pract. Exper. Accepted.
3. Li ML, Liu Hui, Jiang CJ, et al. "Shanghai-Grid in Action: The First Stage Projects towards Digital City and City Grid", LECT NOTES COMPUT SC 3032: 2004, pp.616-623.
4. Li Y, Li ML, Yu JD, Cao L. "SH-MDS: a ShanghaiGrid information service model". Proceedings of 2004 IEEE International Conference on Services Computing, (SCC 2004). pp. 295- 300.
5. Czajkowski K, Kesselman C, Fitzgerald S, Foster I. "Grid information services for distributed resource sharing". Proceedings of the 10th IEEE International Symposium on High-Performance Distributed Computing (HPDC-10), August 2001.
6. Foster I, Kesselman C. "Globus: A metacomputing infrastructure toolkit". International Journal of Supercomputer Applications 1997; 11(2):115–128.
7. Chen Lin, Li ML, Cao J. "An ECA Rule-based Workflow Design Tool for ShanghaiGrid". Processdings of WWW2005.
8. Tang FL et al. "Real-time transaction processing for autonomic Grid applications". Engineering Applications of Artificial Intelligence 2004; 17(7):799–807.
9. OGSA-DAI Web page. http://www.ogsadai.org.uk [1 Nov. 2005].
10. Li BY et al. "A Grid-based application delivery toolkit for ubiquitous computing". Proceedings of Grid and Cooperative Computing: Second International Workshop (GCC 2003) (Lecture Notes in Computer Science, vol. 3032),pp.786–793
11. JSR-000056 JavaTM Network Launching Protocol and API Web page. http://www.jcp.org/aboutJava/communityprocess/final/jsr056/ [1 Nov. 2005].
12. Yu JD, Qian Q, Li ML. "An Accounting Services Model for ShanghaiGrid". Parallel and Distributed Processing and Applications: Third International Symposium, ISPA 2005. pp. 620 – 629.
13. LI Y, Li ML, Yu JD. "ShanghaiGrid Portal: The Current Stage of Building Information Grid Portal". LECT NOTES COMPUT SC 3307: 2004, pp.82-86.
14. The Geographic World Standard for ITS web page, http://roadmap.teleatlas.com/ROADMAP_Pres_Rve_GDF_5_Sep_2002.pdf [1 Nov. 2005].
15. SDAL Format web page, http://www.sdalformat.com/ [1 Nov. 2005].

Design and Implementation of a Service-Oriented Manufacturing Grid System

Shijun Liu, Xiangxu Meng, Ruyue Ma, Lei Wu, and Shuhui Zhang

School of Computer Science and Technology, Shandong University, Jinan 250100, China
{lsj, mxx}@sdu.edu.cn

Abstract. A Service-oriented Manufacturing Grid (MG) System according to OGSA named MGRID is presented and discussed in detail. In MGRID, various manufacturing resources compose the foundation of applications above it. To virtualize the resources, we present an encapsulation model based on Web Service Resource Framework (WSRF) specification. To solve the problem of dynamic organization of manufacturing job, we design a job management system, which accomplishes dynamic composition of manufacturing services. At last, a prototype is given to demonstrate our method.

1 Introduction

The term "the Grid" was coined in the mid 1990s to denote a proposed distributed computing infrastructure for advanced science and engineering [1]. The real and specific problem that underlies the Grid concept is coordinated resource sharing and problem solving in dynamic, multi-institutional virtual organizations [2]. Grid technology improves the performance of networked manufacturing system in resource sharing, cooperation, network security, transparent of using, and so on, which makes the base of networked manufacturing system [3].

MG is a cooperation platform and resource sharing system among manufacturing enterprises. Several special problems related to modern manufacturing that must be considered in MG architecture design: How to manage distributed, heterogeneous and autonomy manufacturing resources in a networked-based manufacturing pattern? How to organize manufacturing services for easily finding and invoking? How to dynamically organize a manufacturing job from manufacturing services? Aimed at solving these problems, MGRID, A Service Oriented Manufacturing Grid is presented in the paper, the architecture of MGRID and its two important issues, resource virtualization and dynamic job management, are discussed respectively.

2 Related Works

Before the "Manufacturing Grid" is coined, there are many advanced manufacturing patterns have been presented such as Networked manufacturing, e-manufacturing, agile manufacturing, virtual supply chain, holonic manufacturing systems, etc. In our view, MG was developed by integrated the distillates of these patterns, and be a new manufacturing pattern by combined Grid computing technology.

H.T. Shen et al. (Eds.): APWeb 2006, LNCS 3842, pp. 643 – 647, 2006.

The first Grid application in manufacturing field is the Information Power Grid (IPG) supported by NASA and NSF in America [4]. With the increasing application in many fields and the development of Grid technology, researchers in industry and academe pay more attention to the applying grid technology to manufacturing. Enterprise Grid, a new concept means supporting grid computing or grid technologies, architectures and ideas utilized in an Enterprise [5]. These applications apply gird computing technologies on enterprise work and supporting manufacturing process, but not establish a new manufacturing pattern at all.

There are many concepts express MG as new manufacturing models. A MG is the harnessing of distributed manufacturing resources to satisfy emerging business requirements, which would enable spare production or distribution capacity in one company to be available to other organizations, maximize the efficiency of the whole network [6]. MG eliminates the heterogeneousness of resources and shortens the distance between them by encapsulating the resources as standard services, provides these manufacturing services for the customers so transparently that the enterprises/individuals can obtain all the services easily, just like using the remote resources as conveniently as using local ones [3].

A SOA (Service-Oriented Architecture) is a component model that interrelates the different functional units of an application, services, through well-defined interfaces and contracts between these services [7]. Some research works introduced services into Grid system such as JISGA in "e-science" of UK [8]. Web Services Resource Framework (WSRF), a specification developed by OASIS, is a joint effort by the Grid and Web Services communities, so it fits pretty nicely inside the whole Web Services Architecture. WSRF provides the stateful services what OGSA needs [9].

3 The Architecture of MGRID

MGRID is a virtual organization of manufacturing unit who is interconnected by many services. To avoid misunderstanding, some terms used in this paper is defined first:

Manufacturing Resource: The manufacturing resource is material or facility involved in the entire product lifecycle, which ranges from CAD, CAPP, CAE and CAM to various kinds of machine tools. In MGRID, manufacturing resources are virtualized as web services.

Manufacturing Service: Special services facilitate manufacturing procession registered in MG, which e often provided by third-party and shared by MG users, such as 3D design service, analysis service, simulation service, machining service and so on.

Manufacturing Job: An integral manufacturing procession could implement special manufacturing task. In MGRID, it can be combined by several services and executed under the control of workflow system.

The main of MGRID is middleware supporting the applications of manufacturing which indicated by the dash line rectangle in figure 1. The middleware is composed of three layers, the resource virtualization layer, the kernel layer and the shell layer.

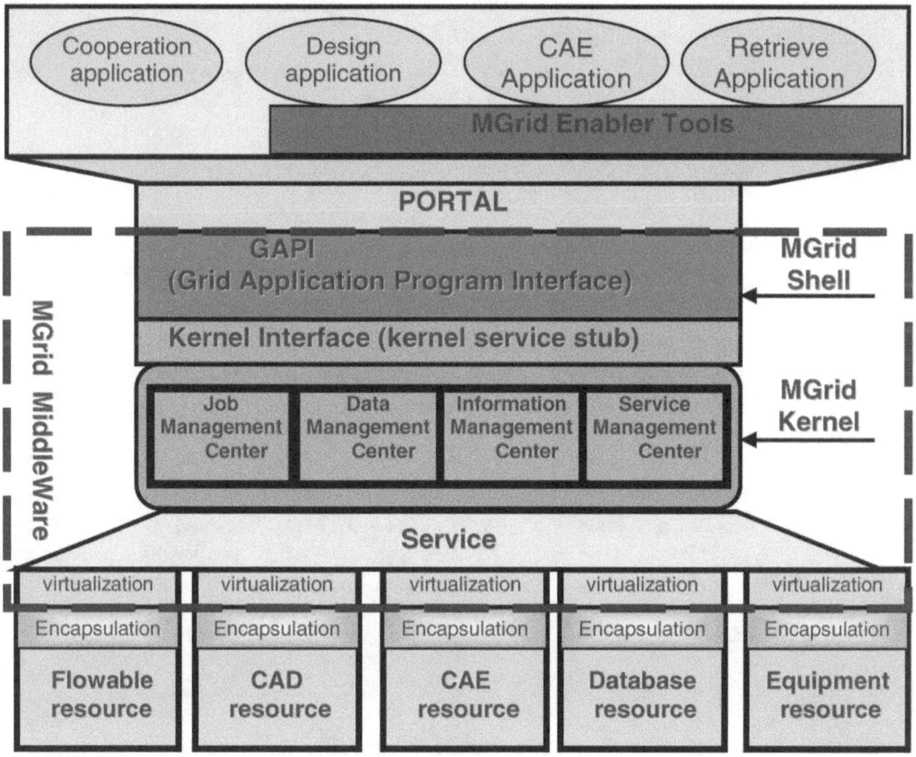

Fig. 1. The architecture of MGRID

Resource virtualization is performed by developing a WSRF service and encapsulating the manufacturing resources as the resource of WSRF service. Then the service should be registered into the MGRID.

The kernel layer, which performs the main functions of MGRID, is composed of four control centers: job management center, data management center, information management center and service registration center.

The shell layer provides interfaces for users to invoke the kernel of MGRID. Two kinds of interfaces are provided. The first is GAPI, namely Grid Application Program Interface, which allows the user to develop applications by invoking the kernel services of MGRID. Another is the portal, where users can invoke the kernel services or manufacturing services provided by other providers to accomplish specific work.

3.1 Virtualization of Manufacturing Resource

The organizing of manufacturing services is a main functionality of MGRID, which includes publishing, storing and retrieving of manufacturing services.

For many resources are physical resources themselves like equipments, the various manufacturing resources must be expressed in an accessible way. By encapsulated the attributes and operations of the resources, they can be invoked as web services, which be called resource virtualization.

The resource encapsulation template is actually a WSRF service deployed into GT4 Java Core, which acts as a resource container. The users can encapsulate and deploy resources with it, then provide resources with the service to users.

3.2 Dynamic Manufacturing Job Management

In the job management, an executable job is a invoking to plain web services, WSRF services and composite services. According to the different modes of invoking, the job management has three invoking engines: composite service invoking engine, general web service invoking engine and OGSA-DAI [10] service invoking engine. In practice, every service encapsulates a specific resource module (functional logic of the manufacture resource) and makes it virtual.

Composite service invoking engine accomplishes the composite service which be described by BPEL [11]. Composite service is used to invoking flows composed by several manufacturing services. The following is the design of Composite service engine. A BPEL engine (ActiveBPEL) is integrated and a flow design tool for BPEL compatible flow is provided to organize web services to a composite service, the composite service could be deployed to execute and be inspected in the system.

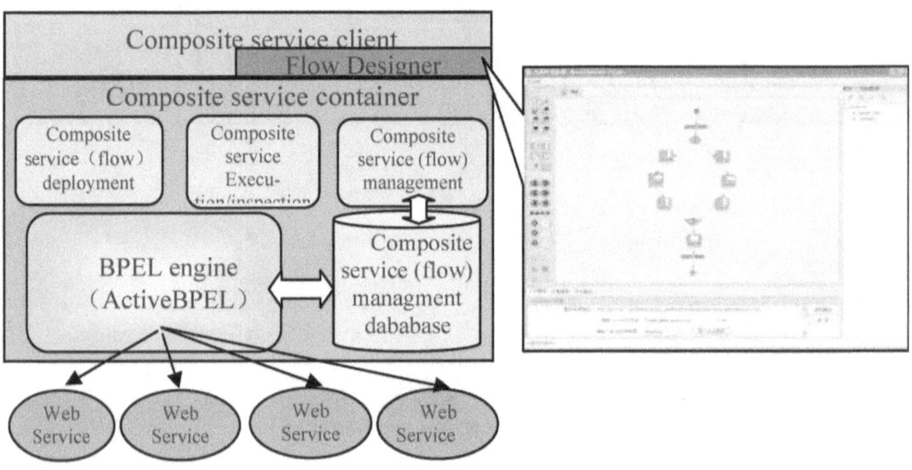

Fig. 2. Composite service management system and the flow design tool

4 Implementation and Conclusion

We have developed the middleware to support establishing manufacturing grid system. A prototype platform have been deployed, the portal (www.MGRID.cn) can be visited now. From the portal, the users can encapsulate their resources to service and register into the MGRID. These services can be requested by others or be composed to composition service which performing manufacturing job. The flow design tool is provided to generate BPEL file and other ActiveBPEL compatible files, which help the dynamic manufacturing job organizing.

In this paper, the whole architecture of MGRID is presented with several important issues be discussed, especially manufacturing resources virtualization and dynamic organization of manufacturing job. These approaches improve the performance in resources sharing, manufacturing services requesting and support applications such as dynamic enterprise alliance establishing on the MG system. However, researching on manufacturing grid is far from mature with lots of new problems left to study. But undoubtedly, grid could bring significant advantages to the industry by making better use of existing manufacturing capacity and capabilities.

Acknowledgements

The authors would like to acknowledge the support provided for the project by the ChinaGrid Project (CG03-GF012) and the Science & Technology Development Projects of Shandong Province (2004GG1104011, 2004GG1104017).

References

[1] Foster, I. and Kesselman, C. (eds.), *The Grid: Blueprint for a New Computing Infrastructure*, Morgan Kaufmann, 1999.
[2] Ian Foster, Carl Kesselman, and Steve Tuecke, "The anatomy of the grid: Enabling scalable virtual organizations", *International Journal of Supercomputer Applications*, http://citeseer.nj.nec.com/foster01anatomy.html, 2001.
[3] FAN Yu-shun, LIU Fei, QI Guo-ning, *Networked manufacturing System and its applications*, China Machine Press, 2003, Beijing. p258.
[4] William E. Johnston, Dennis Gannon, and Bill Nitzberg "Grids as Production Computing Environments:The Engineering Aspects of NASA's Information Power Grid", *Presented at the Eighth IEEE International Symposium on High Performance Distributed Computing*, Aug. 3-6, 1999, Redondo Beach, California.
[5] http://www.gridalliance.org/en/index.asp April, 2004
[6] Institute for Manufacturing, University of Cambridge, "lastminute.manufacturing Turning ideas round fast with an intelligent manufacturing grid", *Cambridge Manufacturing Review*, Spring 2004, http://www.ifm.eng.cam.ac.uk/service/cmr/04cmrspring/allspring04.pdf
[7] Mark Endrei, etc. Patterns: Service-Oriented Architecture and Web Services, ibm.com/redbooks, April 2004
[8] Yan Huang, "JISGA: A Jini-Based Web Service-Oriented Grid Architecture", *The International Journal of High Performance Computing Applications*, vol. 17, no. 3, pages 317-327, Fall 2003.
[9] Borja Sotomayor, The Globus Toolkit 4 Programmer's Tutorial, Version 0.1.1, http://gdp.globus.org/gt4-tutorial/, 2005
[10] Open Grid Services Architecture Data Access and Integration, http://www.ogsadai.org.uk/
[11] Business Process Execution Language for Web Services version 1.1, http://www-128.ibm.com/developerworks/library/specification/ws-bpel/

The Research of a Semantic Architecture in Meteorology Grid Computing

Ren Kaijun[1,2], Xiao Nong[1], Song Junqiang[1], Zhang Weimin[1], and Wang Peng[3]

[1] National Laboratory for Parallel & Distributed Processing,
National University of Defense Technology, Changsha, Hunan 410073, P.R. China
cn_renkaijun@hotmail.com, xiao-n@vip.sina.com
[2] Science College, National University of Defense Technology,
Changsha, Hunan 410073, P.R. China
[3] Southwest Inst.of Electron&Telecom.Tech., Shanghai 200434, P.R. China

Abstract. Meteorology is a complex, interdisciplinary area. Meteorology Grid Computing tries to offer a flexible, secure, coordinated resource sharing and problem-resolving environment by making good use of semantic grid ideas. In this paper, a semantic architecture in Meteorology Grid Computing is presented. With the architecture, we firstly discussed the Semantic Computing Service according to the semantic descriptions of grid computing resource. Then Semantic Data Access Service is illuminated by constructing automatic metadata mapping, which provides users with the convenience to quickly access data storage facilities in on-demand manner. Finally, Meteorology Grid Expert System is presented, and it will offer meteorology knowledge environments to facilitate the forecasters and scientists with analyzing the future weather situation.

1 Introduction

Meteorology Grid Computing aims to provide scientist with seamless, reliable, secure and inexpensive access to resources, and help Scientists efficiently search and retrieve information, analyze meteorological data and predict the future weather situation. In the research, we make good use of the Semantic Grid ideas[1]. Semantic Grid try to integrate the Semantic Web and Grid technologies and it can be defined as "an extension of the current Grid in which information and services are given well-defined meaning, better enabling computers and people to work in cooperation[2, 3]."

A semantic architecture in Meteorology Grid Computing primarily refers to the Semantic Grid ideas. For example, by the help of the semantic description of grid computing resource, searching and scheduling of resource become simple and more efficient; by ontology mapping, many kinds of highly diverse, distributed datasets can be accessed in a uniform way independent of format and physical location. Additionally, meteorology Grid Computing also integrates meteorology grid expert system, which provides forecaster with support of assistant intelligent decision. In section 2 we present with semantic architecture view and in section 3 semantic computing service is discussed. Section 4 illustrates semantic data access service, and in section 5

H.T. Shen et al. (Eds.): APWeb 2006, LNCS 3842, pp. 648 – 652, 2006.

we highlight meteorology grid expert system. Finally experiments and summary are given in section 6.

2 Meteorology Semantic Grid Architecture (MSGA)

In this section, we give an overview on the Meteorology Semantic Grid Architecture (MSGA). As shown in figure 1, **Meteorology Grid Portal** is similar to a general website, which offers a uniform entry and makes all kinds of users directly to access Meteorology Grid Resource through browser. Generally, portal will provide different users with different view according to theirs roles. **Semantic Basic Service** is comprised of a series of web services, which themselves consist of web services and can be used as standalone appli- cations. For example, Grid Monitoring, Workflow Management, Job Management, Resource Scheduling, and Ontology Management can supply services for semantic computing. **Meteorology Grid Computing Middleware** mainly refers to series of toolkits and protocols, which aim to shield the heterogeneous and distributed properties of Grid Resources. **Meteorology Grid Computing Fabric** is a layer that includes computational resources, valuable instruments, storage systems, network resources, knowledge resources, mapping information, ontologies, visualizing devices and so on.

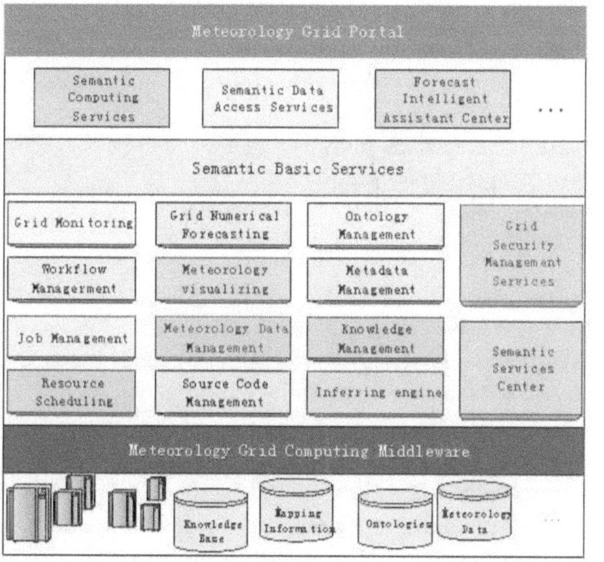

Fig. 1. Meteorology Semantic Grid Architecture

3 Semantic Computing Service

Semantic Computing Service plays a key part in MSGA because modern weather numerical forecasting model and data assimilation system demand a huge computing power. Although the accuracy of weather forecasting depends on many factors, quickly acquiring the experiment result is frequently becoming critical. In developing Semantic Computing Service, we use the presentation of semantic web resources to describe grid computing resource, and build up general ontology vocabularies of Grid Computing Resource in MSGA. By using shared ontologies, people can share a common language and a common understanding of what the terms mean[4]. Figure 2 illustrates these standpoints.

As shown in figure 2, **Job Running Demand Description** can help people select parameters or describe their demands of job running, such as Operation System Type, Memory Size, Cpu Level, Max Latency, Job's Priority; Although different users may have different description of their jobs, **Semantic Translation Service** can translate these descriptions to standard formats according to the General Resource Ontologies; **Job queue Management** takes charge of the sequences of job's running in order of their priorities and time; **Description Update Service** dynamically collects state information of grid resource transferred by Grid Monitoring Service, and modifies RDF State List in time(RDF State List records the value of grid node properties)[5]. **Semantic Resource Scheduling** can acquire state information of Grid resource from RDF State List for Real-Time, process the request of Job queue Management, and select some suitable jobs to run on the suitable grid nodes.

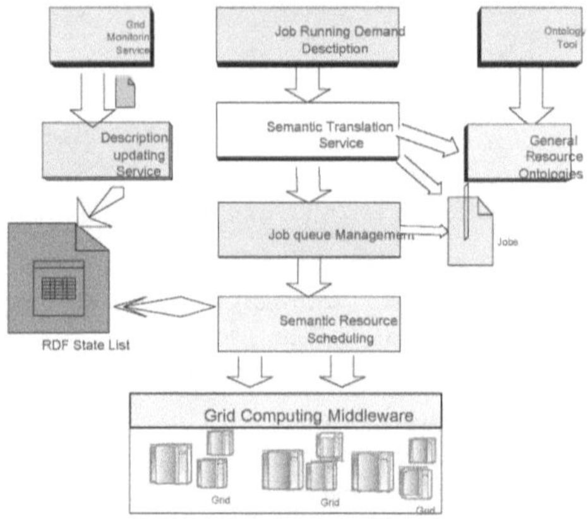

Fig. 2. Semantic Computing Service

4 Semantic Data Access Service

As the development of modern weather forecasting technology, digit observation devices are generating a wealth of highly diverse, widely distributed, autonomously data resources. Simultaneously, more and more simulations and experiments produce amount of result data. The data produced and the knowledge derived from them will lose value in the future if the mechanisms for sharing, integration, cataloging, searching, viewing, and retrieving are not quickly improved. Therefore, how to integrate the diverse, distributed, autonomic data resources is becoming a key challenge in the research of Meteorology Grid Computing[6].

Semantic Data Access Service aims to provide users with the convenience to quickly access data storage facilities in on-demand manner, and quickly share the

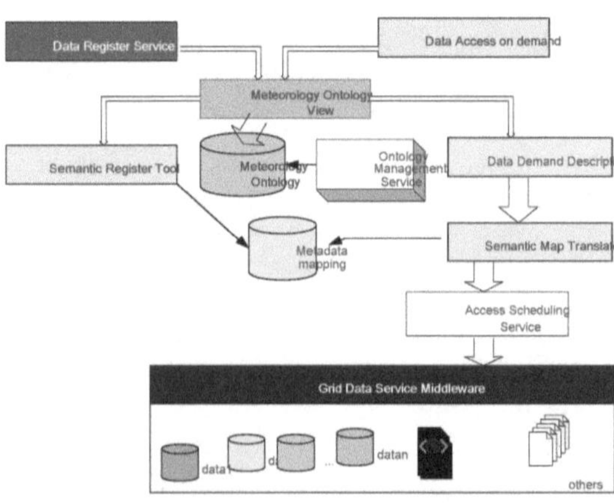

Fig. 3. Semantic Data Access Service

experiment results among the geographically distributed teams of researchers. Semantic Data Access Service will incorporate ontologies, interchange technologies, and other concepts being explored in the Semantic Web and Semantic Grid. Figure 3 shows the clear idea of Semantic Data Access Service. In figure3, **Meteorology Ontology View** can offer users to browse the ontology vocabularies, and users can select cared vocabularies to see detailed information. Ontology Management Service facilitates the creation, management, and maintenance of ontology vocabularies for administrator and experts. **Data Register Service** can help data providers visually browse the key ontology vocabularies like normal user, and facilitate them specifying the mapping between a relational schema and ontology vocabularies. **Semantic Register Tool** gives the response for the request from Data Register Service, and answers for writing the mapping relation information to mapping database. **Data Demand Description** facilitates user to describe what data they real want to get by referring to ontology vocabularies in on-demand manner. The description information is ultimately translated into some key ontology vocabularies, which will be sent to Semantic Map Translator. **Semantic Map Translator** searches the Metadata mapping database to find mapped information so that it can decide which correlation data resources to participate in the next specific grid data scheduling. **Access Scheduling Service** generates a distributed access plan and delivers it to specific Grid Data Service Middleware. Simultaneously it arranges and trims the return results to end-users.

5 Meteorology Grid Expert System(MGES)

MGES is an important part in Meteorology Grid Computing, and it provides an assistant intelligent platform for forecasters or scientists to analyze and predict the future weather situation basing the meteorology expert's knowledge. MGES is closely associated with the other components in MSGA, such as Semantic computing Service, Semantic Data Access Service. Figure 4 conveys the idea. **Knowledge Acquiring** can provide a serial of tools to make expert's knowledge symbolization, formalization and regularization, which are finally expressed exactly and stored in the knowledge base. We also offer a set of maintenance tools including Knowledge Adding, Knowledge Querying, Knowledge Deleting, and Knowledge Arranging, etc. **Inferring Computing** is

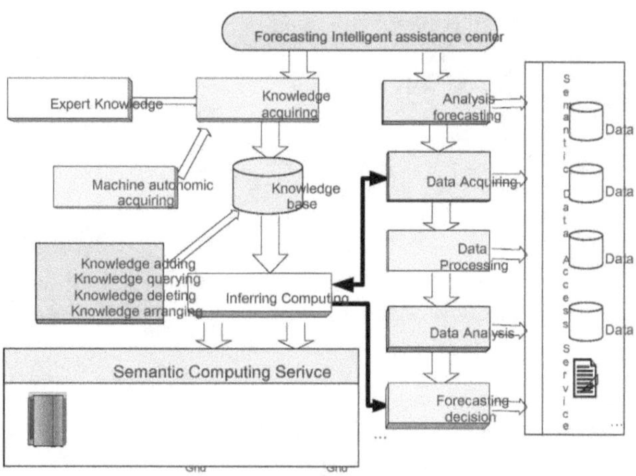

Fig. 4. Meteorology Grid Expert System

a control center with inferring technique. It use specific data information concerned with forecasting problem from the component of Data Acquiring, select available knowledge to form a inferring computing job, and send the request of inferring computing to Semantic Computing Service. Finally, it accepts the returned inferring result and passes the result to Forecasting Decision for forecaster to offer a forecasting reference. **Data Acquiring** provides the media between Inferring Computing and accessing concerned data facts. **Forecasting Decision** can facilitate forecasters to analyze and forecast the future weather situation basing on the inferring result.

6 Experiments and Summary

Currently, a team is contributing to the research and development of MSGA, and a basic prototype has been implemented and deployed in Chinese Meteorology Administration (http://grid.cma.gov.cn:8080). However, there is a major distance to achieve our goal. For example, many functions and services haven't yet finished; some arithmetic need to be further proved to be validated; the establishment of ontologies demands more meteorology experts and knowledge engineers to cooperate. At present, the research team are divided into two groups, one group are taking active part in the research of Semantic Grid besides tracking national experiences, the other group are doing experiments to consummate our system.

Acknowledgements

This research is supported partially by National "973" Foundation Research Plan of China (No.2003CB317008) and National Natural Science Foundation of China (No.60573135).

References

1. David De Roure, N.R.J., Nigel R.Shadbolt, The Semantic Grid:Past,Present and Future. Procedings of the IEEE, 2004. 93(3): p. 669-181.
2. De Roure, D.a.H., J.A, E-Science: the Grid and the Semantic Web. IEEE Intelligent Systems, 2004. 19(1): p. 65-71.
3. T.Berners-Lee, J.H., The Semantic Web. Scientific American, 2001. 279(5): p. 34-43.
4. N, G., Understanding,Building,and Using Ontologies. International Journal of Human computer Studies, 1997. 46: p. 293-310.
5. P.Hayes, RDF model theory. http://www.w3.org/TR/rdf-mt, 2004.
6. Fox, G., Data and metadata on the semantic grid. Computing in Science and Engineering, 2003. 5(5): p. 76-78.

The Design Method of a Video Delivery Grid

Zhuoying Luo and Huadong Ma

Beijing Key Lab of Intelligent Telecommunications Software and Multimedia,
School of Computer Science and Technology,
Beijing University of Posts and Telecommunications, Beijing 100876, China

Abstract. How to improve the reliability and quality of video delivery has great influence on the extensible and high-quality video services. Grid computing, for dynamic share and collaboration among all kinds of resources, can provide a solution for optimizing video delivery. This paper proposes a conceptual system of video delivery grid. First, the paper provides the model of video delivery grid, and discusses how to select distributed services and create a service flow dynamically. Then, the paper describes the design of video delivery grid based on Globus. Moreover, the prototype of video delivery grid is implemented. The efficiency of this solution was shown by the experiments in the video conference system.

1 Introduction

Now grid computing is spring up. Globus [2] and Condor make grid sophisticated and practical. Moreover, multimedia applications are so booming that single media server or conventional transmission ways become bottlenecks because of mass real-time data. So it is worth studying how to optimize video transmission by grid technology.

Meanwhile, Access grid [4] manages lots of resources, and served for large-scale distributed, collaborative work. Kontiki [5] grid delivery technology securely delivers high quality video, software and all digital content over existing corporate networks.

Herein we propose a model of video delivery grid, and design and implement a system prototype based on Globus. The rest of this paper is organized as follows. Section 2 discusses the conceptual model of video delivery grid. Section 3 decribes the system of video delivery grid based on Globus. Section 4 studies a case in video conference. Finnally, some conclusion is made in Section 5.

2 Conceptual Model of Video Delivery Grid

Now service integration is a hot topic in acadamic and industry. Reference [6] proposed some models to monitor and control the process of the service integration. Reference [7] proposed CAFISE, a mode of software service integration. These methods provide us with the idea of service reuse and integration, but pay litte attention to dynamic resource environment. Grid computing with dynamic resource management can help to maintain a reliable environment for service integration.

H.T. Shen et al. (Eds.): APWeb 2006, LNCS 3842, pp. 653–658, 2006.

2.1 Definitions

First, we give some definitions relative to our model. In [8], resource and service are defined according to OGSA [3], and we also inherit these definitions.

Definition 1. Resource is a kind of entity, which can be operated by managable interfaces and other mechanism in the designed way in the grid environment.

Definition 2. Node is a kind of resource composed of the resources with the same IP address.

Definition 3. Service is a component in service oriented archtecture. It can provide some functions or have some ability to implement software system.

Moreover, services need to be integrated with each other by service computing policy. Therefore we define some concepts relative to service computing as follows.

Definition 4. Service s_1 is the predecessor of service s_2, denoted as s_1=pred(s_2), only if s_2 doesn't execute until s_1 is finished and no other services are executed between s_1 and s_2. Service s_2 is called as the successor of s_1, denoted as s_2=succ(s_1). Pr(s) and Su(s) are the sets of predecessors and successors for the service s, respectively.

Definition 5. Service computing policy is the controlling relationship between services, and it can be described as P={SEQUENCE, SPLIT, JOIN, REPEAT}.

- SEQUENCE means that Su(s) execute once the service s is finished.
- SPLIT means that Su(s) don't be called until the service s is finished.
- JOIN means that the service s doesn't execute until Pr(s) are finished.
- REPEAT means the repeated execution of the service s.

Definition 6. An action is defined as a group of operations which can perform services in the given order, to implement complex distributed businesses.

We can define the model of video delivery service grid based on above concepts.

Definition 7. Video delivery service grid is defined as M= (A, S, R, f_{AS}, f_{SR}, P), $A \cap S = \Phi$, $S \cap R = \Phi$, where A is the set of finite actions, S is the set of finite services, R is the set of finite resources.

$f_{AS} \subseteq A \times S$ denotes the relationship between actions and services, that is, an action is implemented by some services.

$f_{SR} \subseteq S \times R$ denotes the relationship between services and resources, that is, executing of a service need use some resources.

P is a set of service computing policies.

2.2 Design Policies

Based on our model, for an action, the involved services are dynamically selected and the service flow is also temporarily built in a dynamic resource environment as shown in Figure 1.

First, we need select out specific services for an action. After the type of service is decided by action requirement, the performance of the node running the service is considered as the selection criterion. Because the impact that the same service has on different kinds of resource vary by type of the service, the performance of the node relative to the service can be decided by the sum of all impact of resources on it. We introduce a cost function to measure the dependence $R_{(n,\,s)}$ as follows.

$$R_{(n,\,s)} = \sum \frac{C_i}{A_i} \times w_{(i,\,s)}, \quad 0 \le C_i \le A_i, \; 0 < w_{(i,\,s)} < 1 \text{ and } \sum w_{(i,\,s)} = 1 \tag{1}$$

C_i is the quantity of consumed resource of the type i in the node n; A_i is the quantity of all resource of the type i in the node n; $w_{(n,\,i)}$ is the weight decided by the type of service (s) and the type of resource (i) on the node n. In video delivery service grid, the more the impact or dependence is, the larger the relative value of $w_{(n,\,i)}$ is.

Then the process of selecting node is described as follows:

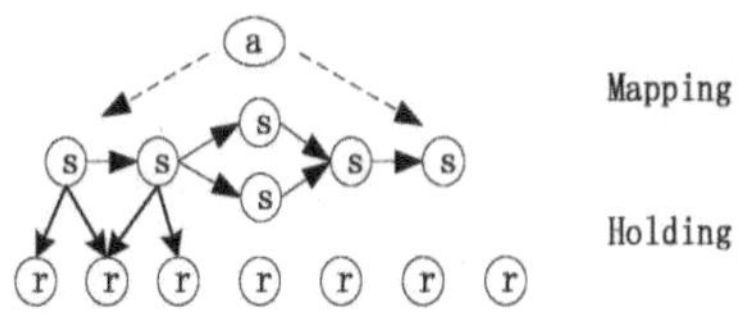

Fig. 1. An action can be mapped into a service flow (a-action, s-service, r-resource)

Step 1. Find St, the type of video forwarding service by video delivery action a;
Step 2. Create V_{St}, the set of all nodes providing such services with the type St.
Step 3. Calculate the relative performance of all nodes in V_{St} according to (1), that is, $R_{(n,St)}$ ($n \in V_{St}$). Then sort all nodes in the ascending order.
Step 4. Decide N, the number of available nodes at most by the rank of the applicant, where rank is Common, VIP or Supper. That is, the higher the rank is, the bigger N is. Then select out the first N nodes from V_{St}.

Second, how to build a service flow depends on creating a data route among the selected nodes because video is directly transferred among video forwarding service on these nodes. We design the process of creating a data route based on graph theory.

Assume that P is the video sender, Q is the video receiver, and V_N is the set made of N selected nodes.

The distribution of video nodes can be viewed as an undirected graph $G = \{V, E, W\}$, where $V = \{g \mid g \in V_N \vee \{P\} \vee \{Q\}\}$; $E = \{(x, y) \mid x \in V, y \in V\}$ is the set of undirected edges, that is, the path between two nodes. $w(x, y) \in W$ is the weight of undirected edge (x, y), e.g. the latency, in undirected graph G.

Therefore the data routing problem can be solved by Dijkstra shortest path algorithm from P to Q in undirected graph G. Then we can find the least-weight data route from the sender P to the receiver Q.

3 Video Delivery Service Grid

We design a video delivery service grid based on above methods. The hierarchical structure of system is illustrated in Figure 2. The system can be divided into four layers from bottom to top.

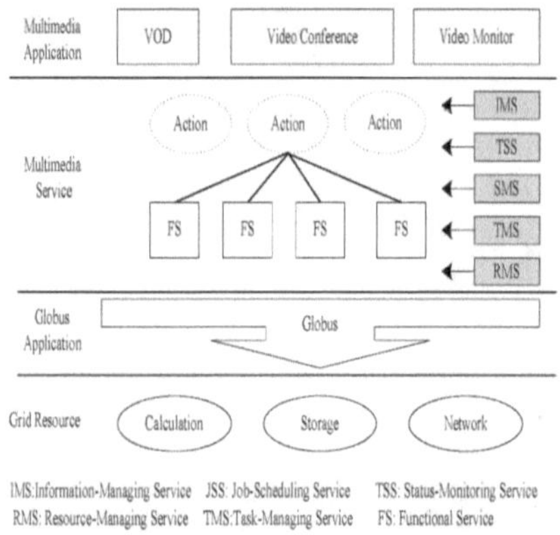

Fig. 2. Hierarchical structure of system

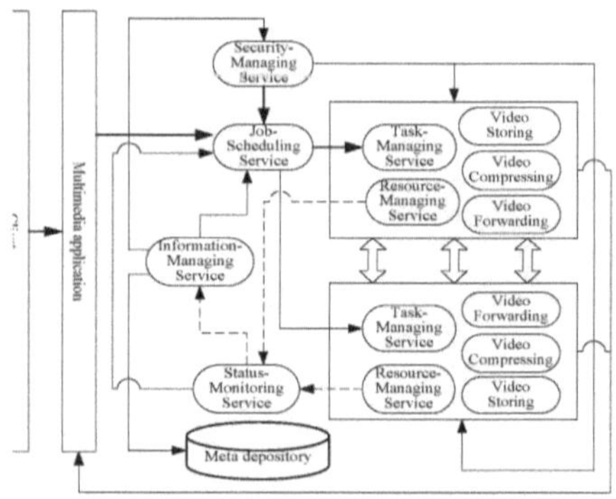

Fig. 3. Functional structure of system

- Grid Resource layer is made of calculation, storage, network and other resource.
- Globus Application encapsulates heterogeneous resources and provides uniform access entry of resources.
- Multimedia Service makes several grid services integrate into a video delivery action according to the given policy or flow.
- Multimedia Application performs lower video delivery actions to implement complex multimedia applications, such as video conference and remote teaching.

Herein, we focus on multimedia service as Figure 3. These grid services can be divided into two classes: systemic services and functional services

Systemic services are all permanent services and also killer services because they help to maintain a running environment for system.

Information Managing Service (IMS) manages static and dynamic information of all resources and services, and updates their status in real time.

Job Scheduling Service (JSS) parses out multimedia actions, decides the service policy, distributes tasks by negotiation, and resumes failure tasks.

Task Managing Service (TMS) accepts task distribution by negotiation, creates and destroys instances of local functional services.

Resource Managing Service (RMS) manages all local resources and reports status of local resources to SMS periodically.

Status Monitoring Service (SMS) collects status reports and commits them to IMS periodically. It alerts JSS to resume failure tasks when fail to receive any reports.

Security Managing Service performs user identification authentication and so on.

Functional services, e.g., video forwarding, implement the specific functions of multimedia actions. They may be permanent or temporary services, and are hot-plug.

4 A Case Study in Video Conference System

Video delivery action plays an important role in mass video data. So we test the prototype of video delivery service grid on the video conference system of our lab, see Table 1. In a video conference, sender client is at 59.64.159.209 and receiver client is at 59.64.156.218. We designed experimental steps as follows:

Table 1. Deployment of service in video delivery service grid

Grid Service	IP Address of Nodes
Information management service	59.64.156.185
Job scheduling service	59.64.159.190
Status monitoring service	59.64.156.182
Video forwarding service	59.64.156.222, 59.64.158.175
Task management service	59.64.156.13, 59.64.158.251
Resource management service	

Step 1. The video delivery service grid was asked to create a route from sender to receiver through several grid nodes. Video flow was delivered successfully.
Step 2. We closed some grid node (59.64.158.175) in the created route in order to check the self-active mechanism. Thus, the video flow was shut off.
Step 3. Self-adapted mechanism of video delivery service grid found the node (59.64.158.175) was disable, and resumed those undone tasks on other node (59.64.156.13). Therefore video flow continued.

The experimental results show video delivery service grid can implement remote video data transmission and find faults and resume tasks by self-adapted mechanism.

5 Conclusion

The paper proposes a service integration solution on video transmission in multimedia applications by dynamic distributed resource share and service integration, and self-adapted mechanism. A prototype system is developed based on our solution, and the experimental results show our design is reasonable and efficient. In the future we will make more effort to the security policy among services from different providers, and study how to make a reasonable and practical criterion to measure the quality of services.

Acknowledgement. The work is supported by the Co-sponsored Project of Beijing Committee of Education (SYS100130422), the National Natural Science Foundation of China (60242002) and the NCET Program of MOE, China.

References

[1] Ian Foster, Carl Kesselman, Steven Tuecke, "The anatomy of the grid: enabling scalable virtual organizations", *CCGRID2001*, pp: 6–7.
[2] http://www.globus.org.
[3] Ian Foster, Jeffrey M. Nick, Steven Tuecke, "The Physiology of the Grid: An Open Grid Services Architecture for Distributed Systems Integration", *Global Grid Forum*, 2002.6.
[4] http://www.accessgrid.com
[5] http://www.kontiki.com

[6] F. Casati, E. Shan, U. Dayal, and M.C. Shan. "Business-oriented management of Web services". *Communications of the ACM*, 46(10):55-60, October 2003.
[7] HAN Yanbo, ZHAO Zhuofeng, LI Gang, "CAFISE: An Approach to Enabling Adaptive Configuration of Service Grid Applications", *Journal of Computer Science and Technology*, July 2003, 18(4):484-494.
[8] "Open Grid Services Architecture Glossary of Terms", http://forge. gridforum.org/ projects/ ogsa-wg.

A Secure Password-Authenticated Key Exchange Between Clients with Different Passwords

Eun-Jun Yoon and Kee-Young Yoo*

Department of Computer Engineering, Kyungpook National University,
Daegu 702-701, Republic of Korea
Tel.: +82-53-950-5553; Fax: +82-53-957-4846
ejyoon@infosec.knu.ac.kr, yook@knu.ac.kr

Abstract. In 2004, Kim et al. proposed an improvement to Byun et al.'s client to client password-authenticated key exchange(C2C-PAKE) protocol in a cross-realm setting. However, the current paper demonstrates that Kim et al.'s C2C-PAKE protocol is susceptible to a one-way man-in-the-middle attack and a password-compromise impersonation attack. Also, we presents an enhancement to resolve such problems.

Keywords: Cryptography, Security, Kerberus, Key agreement, C2C-PAKE.

1 Introduction

In 2002, Byun et al. [1] presented a new password-authenticated key exchange protocol between two clients with different passwords, which they call the Client-to-Client Password-Authenticated Key Exchange (C2C-PAKE) protocol. The goal of their protocol is that two clients can establish a shared secret key based on the condition that they pre-shared their passwords either with a single server (a single-server setting) or respectively with two servers (a cross-realm setting). However, Chen [2] has shown the C2C-PAKE protocol in a cross-realm setting is not secure against dictionary attack from a malicious server in a different realm. Recently, Kim et al. [3] have also shown that the C2C-PAKE protocol is vulnerable to the Denning-Sacco attack [4] by an insider adversary. Furthermore, they proposed the modified protocol, which repairs the problem of the Denning-Sacco attack by an insider adversary and is secure against dictionary attack from a malicious server. Nevertheless, this improved scheme is still susceptible to a one-way man-in-the-middle attack [5], where an attacker can easily impersonate a client to establish a shared secret key with another client, and a password-compromise impersonation attack, where the compromise of an entity Alice's long-term password *pwa* will allow an adversary to impersonate Alice. Accordingly, the current paper demonstrates the vulnerabilities of Kim et al.'s modified C2C-PAKE protocol and presents an enhancement to resolve such problems. The proposed C2C-PAKE protocol resists such attacks, while also providing greater

* Corresponding author.

H.T. Shen et al. (Eds.): APWeb 2006, LNCS 3842, pp. 659–663, 2006.

efficiency because it can reduce the number of round, message transmission costs and computation costs.

2 Review of Kim et al.'s C2C-PAKE Protocol

This section briefly reviews Kim et al.'s C2C-PAKE [3]. Notations used in Kim et al.'s protocol and proposed protocol are defined as follows:

- Alice, Bob: honest user or client.
- $ID(A)$, $ID(B)$: Alice's identity and Bob's identity.
- Eve: attacker.
- pwa, pwb: passwords memorized by Alice and Bob.
- E_X: symmetric encryption with secret value X.
- KDC_A, KDC_B: key distribution centers which store $ID(A)$, pwa, $ID(B)$, pwb.
- K: symmetric key shared between KDC_A and KDC_B.
- $Ticket_B$; Kerberos ticket issued to Alice for service from Bob.
- L: lifetime of $Ticket_B$.
- p, q: sufficiently large primes such that $q|p-1$.
- G: subgroup of Z_p^* of order q.
- $g \in G$: generator.
- H, H_1, H_2: secure one-way hash functions.

We will omit 'mod$p$' from expressions for simplicity. Kim et al.'s protocol proceeds with 9 Steps as follows:

(1) Alice chooses a random number $x \in_R Z_p^*$, computes g^x and $M_1 = E_{pwb}(g^x)$. Then she sends M_1, $ID(A)$ and $ID(B)$ to KDC_A.
(2) KDC_A obtains g^x by decrypting M_1. KDC_A chooses a random number $r \in_R Z_p^*$ and makes $Ticket_B = E_K(g^{x \cdot r}, g^r, ID(A), ID(B), L)$. Finally KDC_A sends $ID(A)$, $ID(B)$, $Ticket_B$ and L to Alice.
(3) Upon receiving the message from KDC_A, Alice forwards $ID(A)$ and $Ticket_B$ to Bob.
(4) Bob chooses a random number $y \in_R Z_p^*$, computes g^x and $M_2 = E_{pwb}(g^y)$. Then he sends M_2, $ID(A)$, $ID(B)$ and $Ticket_B$ to KDC_B.
(5) KDC_B obtains $g^{x \cdot r}$ and g^r by decrypting $Ticket_B$. Then KDC_B chooses a random number $r' \in_R Z_p^*$, and computes $g^{x \cdot r \cdot r'}$ and $g^{r \cdot r'}$. Finally KDC_B sends $g^{x \cdot r \cdot r'}$ and $g^{r \cdot r'}$ to Bob.
(6) Bob computes $cs = H_1(g^{x \cdot y \cdot r \cdot r'})$ using $g^{x \cdot r \cdot r'}$ and y. Then Bob chooses a random number $a \in_R Z_p^*$, and computes $M_3 = E_{cs}(g^a)$ and $g^{r \cdot r' \cdot y}$. Bob sends M_3 and $g^{r \cdot r' \cdot y}$ to Alice.
(7) After receiving M_3 and $g^{r \cdot r' \cdot y}$, Alice also can compute cs using $g^{r \cdot r' \cdot y}$ and x. Next, Alice chooses a random number $b \in_R Z_p^*$, computes the session key $sk = H_2(g^{ab})$, $M_4 = E_{sk}(g^a)$ and $M_5 = E_{cs}(g^b)$. Finally she sends M_4 and M_5 to Bob for session key confirmation.
(8) After receiving M_4 and M_5, Bob gets g^b by decrypting M_5 with cs, and computes sk with g^b and a. Bob verifies g^a by decrypting M_4 with sk. Finally, Bob sends $M_6 = E_{sk}(g^b)$ to Alice for session key confirmation.
(9) Alice verifies g^b by decrypting M_6 with sk.

3 Cryptanalysis of Kim et al.'s C2C-PAKE Protocol

This section demonstrates that Kim et al.'s C2C-PAKE protocol is vulnerable to a one-way man-in-the-middle attack and a password-compromise impersonation attack.

A One-Way Man-in-the-Middle Attack. Kim et al.'s protocol is vulnerable to a one-way man-in-the-middle attack, where an attacker Eve can easily impersonate Bob to establish a common secret session key cs' with Alice. Suppose that Eve interposes the communication between Alice and Bob. Then, Eve can perform the one-way man-in-the-middle attack as follows:

(1)* Upon intercepting $g^{x \cdot r \cdot r'}$ and $g^{r \cdot r'}$ sent by KDC_B in Step 5, Eve chooses a random number $y' \in_R Z_p^*$, and computes modified $cs' = H_1(g^{x \cdot r \cdot r' \cdot y'})$ by using $g^{x \cdot r \cdot r'}$ and y'. Then Eve chooses another random number, $a' \in_R Z_p^*$, and computes $E_{cs'}(g^{a'})$ and $g^{r \cdot r' \cdot y'}$. Eve sends modified messages $E_{cs'}(g^{a'})$ and $g^{r \cdot r' \cdot y'}$ to Alice.

(2)* After receiving Eve's modified message $E_{cs'}(g^{a'})$ and $g^{r \cdot r' \cdot y'}$, Alice also will compute cs' by using modified value $g^{r \cdot r' \cdot y'}$ and her selected random number x in Step 1. Alice will choose a random number $b \in_R Z_p^*$, and compute the session key $sk = H_2(g^{a'b})$, $M_4' = E_{sk}(g^{a'})$ and $M_5' = E_{cs'}(g^b)$. Finally, she will send M_4' and M_5' to Bob for session key confirmation.

(3)* Upon intercepting M_4' and M_5' sent by Alice, Eve obtains g^b by decrypting M_5' with cs', and computes sk with g^b and a'. Then Eve verifies $g^{a'}$ by decrypting M_4' with sk. Finally, Eve sends $M_6' = E_{sk'}(g^b)$ to Alice to confirm the forged session key.

(4)* After receiving M_6', Alice will verify g^b by decrypting M_6' with sk. It is easy to check whether Alice will accept this modified key confirm message M_6', as $D_{sk'}(M_6) = D_{sk'}(E_{sk'}(g^b)) = g^b$. Finally, Alice will accept modified session key cs', and then will use cs' as a session key, making Kim et al.'s protocol insecure.

A Password-Compromise Impersonation Attack. Kim et al.'s protocol is vulnerable to a password-compromise impersonation attack as follows:

(1)* When Eve comprises pwa of Alice, she is able to get g^x form intercepted M_1 in Step 1, she then can send Alice a forged g^y and M_3 in Step 6, where $cs = H_1(g^{xy})$.

(2)* Alice can not distinguish between this message is from Bob (knowing pwb) or Eve (knowing pwa).

4 Proposed C2C-PAKE Protocol

This section proposes a secure C2C-PAKE protocol that, unlike Kim et al.'s C2C-PAKE protocol, can withstand the above mentioned attack. The proposed C2C-PAKE protocol proceeds with 8 Steps of the followings:

(1) Alice chooses a random number $x \in_R Z_p^*$, and computes g^x and $M_1 = E_{pwa}(g^x)$. Then, she sends M_1, $ID(A)$ and $ID(B)$ to KDC_A.
(2) KDC_A obtains g^x by decrypting $E_{pwa}(g^x)$. KDC_A chooses a random number, $r \in_R Z_p^*$, computes $g^{x \cdot r}$ and $M_2 = E_{pwa}(g^r)$, and makes Kerberos ticket $Ticket_B = E_K(g^{x \cdot r}, g^r, ID(A), ID(B), L)$. Finally, KDC_A sends M_2, $Ticket_B$ and L to Alice.
(3) Upon receiving the message from KDC_A, Alice obtains g^r by decrypting M_2 and computes $g^{x \cdot r}$. Then, Alice stores $g^{x \cdot r}$ and L, and forwards $ID(A)$ and $Ticket_B$ to Bob.
(4) Bob chooses a random number, $y \in_R Z_p^*$, and computes $M_2 = E_{pwb}(g^y)$. Then, he sends $ID(A)$, $ID(B)$, M_2, and $Ticket_B$ to KDC_B.
(5) KDC_B obtains g^y, $g^{x \cdot r}$ and g^r by decrypting M_2 and $Ticket_B$, respectively. Then, KDC_B chooses a random number $r' \in_R Z_p^*$, computes $g^{r'}$, $g^{y \cdot r'}$, $g^{x \cdot r \cdot r'}$ and $g^{r \cdot r'}$, and makes $M_3 = E_{R'}(g^{x \cdot r}, g^{x \cdot r \cdot r'}, g^{r \cdot r'})$, where $R' = H(g^{y \cdot r'})$. Finally, KDC_B sends $g^{r'}$ and M_3 to Bob.
(6) Upon receiving the message from KDC_B, Bob computes $R' = H(g^{r' \cdot y})$, and obtains $g^{x \cdot r}$, $g^{x \cdot r \cdot r'}$, and $g^{r \cdot r'}$ by decrypting M_3. If it contains $ID(B)$, then Bob computes $cs = g^{x \cdot y \cdot r \cdot r'}$, $M_4 = g^{r \cdot r' \cdot y}$, and $M_5 = H(ID(B), ID(A), cs, g^{x \cdot r})$. Finally, Bob sends M_4 and M_5 to Alice for session key confirmation.
(7) After receiving M_4 and M_5, Alice computes $cs = g^{x \cdot y \cdot r \cdot r'}$. Then, Alice computes $H(ID(B), ID(A), cs, g^{x \cdot r})$ and verifies it with M_5. If it holds, Alice authenticates Bob. Finally, Alice computes $M_6 = H(ID(A), ID(B), cs, g^{x \cdot r})$, and sends it to Bob for session key confirmation.
(8) After receiving M_6, Bob computes $H(ID(B), ID(A), cs, g^{x \cdot r})$ and verifies it with M_6. If it holds, Bob authenticates Alice. After the Step 8, $SK = H(g^{x \cdot y \cdot r \cdot r'})$ is used as Alice and Bob's common secret session key.

5 Security Analysis and Performance Comparison

This section discusses the security and efficiency of the proposed C2C-PAKE protocol.

Security Analysis. In this subsection, we shall only discuss the enhanced security features. The rest are the same as original Kim et al.'s protocol as described in literature [3].

(1) The proposed C2C-PAKE protocol can resist a one-way man-in-the-middle attack unlike the Kim et al.'s C2C-PAKE protocol. Our protocol uses a shared Diffie-Hellman Key $g^{y \cdot r'}$ between Bob and KDC_B to protecting the two values $g^{x \cdot r \cdot r'}$ and $g^{r \cdot r'}$ that will send by KDC_B in Step 5.
(2) Unlike the Kim et al.'s C2C-PAKE protocol, the proposed C2C-PAKE protocol can resist a password-compromise impersonation attack. Our protocol shares Diffie-Hellman Key $g^{x \cdot r}$ between Alice and KDC_A to avoid a password-compromise impersonation attack.

Table 1. Comparisons of computational costs

	Kim et al.'s C2C PAKE				Proposed C2C PAKE			
	KDC_A	Alice	Bob	KDC_B	KDC_A	Alice	Bob	KDC_B
Exponent operation	2	4	4	2	2	3	4	4
Symmetric operation	2	5	5	2	3	2	2	2
Hash operation	0	2	2	0	0	3	3	1
Number of rounds	8				7			

Performance Comparison. The computational costs of Kim et al.'s C2C-PAKE protocol and the proposed C2C-PAKE protocol are summarized in Table 1. Obviously, the proposed protocol is more efficient than Kim et al.'s protocol.

6 Conclusions

The current study demonstrated that Kim et al.'s C2C-PAKE protocol is vulnerable to one-way man-in-the-middle attacks and password-compromise impersonation attacks. Thus, an enhancement to Kim et al.'s C2C-PAKE protocol was proposed. The proposed C2C-PAKE protocol resists those attacks, while also providing greater efficiency because it can reduce the number of round, message transmission costs and computation costs.

Acknowledgements

This research was supported by the MIC(Ministry of Information and Communication), Korea, under the ITRC(Information Technology Research Center) support program supervised by the IITA(Institute of Information Technology Assessment.

References

1. Byun, J.W., Jeong, I.R., Lee, D.H., Park, C.S.: Password-Authenticated Key Exchange between Clients with Different Passwords. ICICS 2002. LNCS 2513. (2002) 134-146
2. Chen, L.: A Weakness of the Password-Authenticated Key Agreement between Clients with Different Passwords Scheme. The document was being circulated for consideration at the 27th the SC27/WG2 meeting in Paris, France, 2003-10-20/24. (2003)
3. Kim, J.Y., Kim, S.J., Kwak, J., Won, D.H.: Cryptanalysis and Improvement of Password Authenticated Key Exchange between Clients with Different Passwords. ICCSA 2004. LNCS 3043. (2004) 895-902
4. Denning, D., Sacco, G.: Timestamps in Key Distribution Protocols. Communications of the ACM. Vol. 24. No. 8. (1981) 533-536
5. Schneier, B.: Applied Cryptography-Protocols, Algorithms, and Source Code in C. 2nd edi.. John Wiley & Sons, Inc.. (1995)
6. Diffie, W., Hellman, M.: New Directions in Cryptography. IEEE Transaction on Information Theory. Vol. IT-22. No. 6. (1976) 644-654

A Fault-Tolerant Web Services Architecture

Lingxia Liu[1,2], Yuming Meng[3], Bin Zhou[1], and Quanyuan Wu[1]

[1] School of Computer Science, National University of Defense Technology,
Changsha 410073, China
lingxia_liu@tom.com
[2] The Telecommunication Engineering Institute, Air Force Engineering University,
Xi'an 710077, China
[3] College of Information Science and Engineering, Central South University,
Changsha 410083, China

Abstract. Web services have been enjoying great popularities in recent years. The high usability of the Web service is becoming a new focus for research. According to the demands of Web services, we present a fault-tolerant Web services architecture named FTWS based on the service approach and the reflection approach. Its characteristics are: (1) The fault-tolerant mechanisms are transparent, easy to use and also flexibly customized; (2) The fault-tolerant properties are flexibly configured; (3) The target service programmers almost needn't to care the fault-tolerant mechanisms. The Architecture is set forth in detail in the article. The workflow of the system is narrated by three states of a fault-tolerant Web service.

1 Introduction

Web service is a new application model for decentralized computing. The use of Web services on the World Wide Web is expanding rapidly as the need for application-to-application communication and interoperability grows. It will become the mainstream technology of e-business.

As Web services start to be deployed across enterprise boundaries and for collaborative e-business and e-transaction scenarios, availability becomes a critical issue [1] [2].

A lots of standards (such as UDDI, WSFL) are provided for Web service discovery, Web service composition etc. But now, none of the existing technology supports how to ensure high usability of the Web service. The WS-Reliability and WS Reliable Messaging (WSRM) only address reliable messaging [3].

Fault-tolerant technology is one of the best solutions of providing high useable services. There are three conventional approaches to integrating fault tolerance mechanisms within distributed systems, mainly, the system approach [4], the service approach [5] and the reflection approach [6]. The characteristics of Web services bring the new challenges to the traditional fault-tolerant technology. All the three approaches can't fully satisfy the characteristics of Web services.

According to the demands of Web services, we propose a new fault-tolerant architecture based on the service approach and the reflection approach. The architecture is shown in figure 1.

H.T. Shen et al. (Eds.): APWeb 2006, LNCS 3842, pp. 664 – 671, 2006.

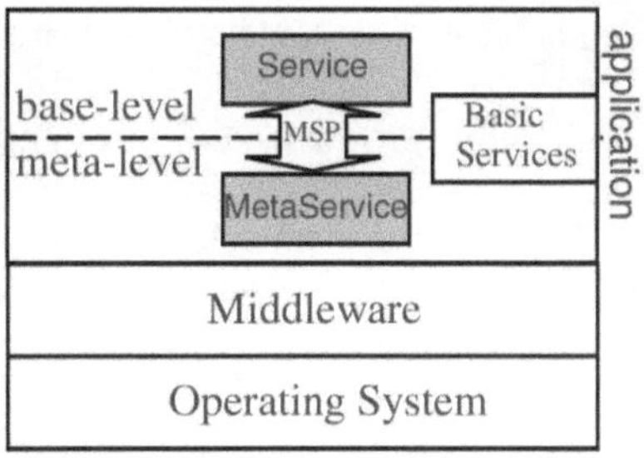

Fig. 1. The fault-tolerant architecture

The Basic Services provides the services required in fault-tolerant computing. Application is composed of two sub-layers. The service sub-layer implements the functional part of the application and the metaService sub-layer implements the non-functional part of the application. The service and the metaService are bound dynamically (at run time) using MetaService Protocol (MSP). The event model is used to implement MSP mechanism. Events specify interaction between services and metaServices.

The remainder of this paper is organized as follows. In section 2, the related works are reviewed and outlined in Section 2. In section 3, the architecture of FTWS is introduced in detail. Next, the workflow of FTWS is set forth with an example. In section 5, the prototype implementation is briefly introduced. Finally, in section 6, we conclude the paper.

2 Related Works

There are some works addressing available Web services in recently years.

Liang [7] proposes a fault-tolerant web service on SOAP (called FT-SOAP) using the service approach. It extends the standard WSDL by proposing a new <WSG/> element to describe the replicated web services. The client side SOAP engine searches for the next available backup from the group WSDL and redirects the request to the replica in the case that the primary server has failed. The efficiency is very low. Moreover, the service requester needs to use the custom FT-SOAP engine and it destroys the interoperability of the Web services.

Artix [8] is IONA's Web services integration product. It provides a WSDL-based naming service by Artix Locator. Multiple instances of the same service can be registered under the same name with an Artix Locator. When service consumers request a service, the Artix Locator selects the service instance based on a load-balancing algorithm from the pool of service instances. To a certain degree, it provides high useable services for the service consumers.

[9] proposes a mechanism termed active UDDI, which allows the extension of UDDI's invocation API in order to enable fault-tolerant and dynamic service invocation. Its function is similar to the Artix Locator.

[10] proposes a dependable Web services framework named DeW. Once a failure for one specific service occurs, the proxy raises a "WebServiceNotFound" exception and downloads its handler from DeW. The result of handling the exception is

choosing another location that hosts the same service and re-invoking the method automatically. The main goal of DeW is to realize physical-location-independence. Only the stateless target services can use the framework to guarantee usability.

There are also some works addressing providing fault-tolerant capability for composite Web service [11] [12] [13]. The fault-tolerant composite Web service is requester-oriented and the fault-tolerant Web service is provider-oriented. It's the main difference between them.

3 Architecture of FTWS

According to the fault-tolerant architecture put forward above, we present a fault-tolerant Web services architecture named FTWS (Fault-tolerant Web services) shown in figure 2.

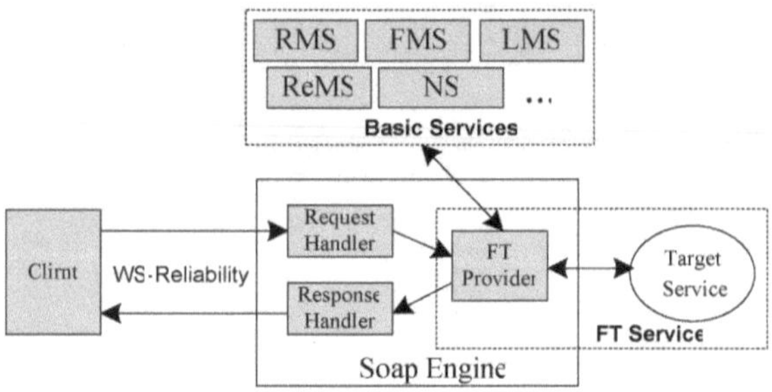

Fig. 2. The architecture of FTWS

In the architecture, the Basic Services provide services required in fault-tolerant computing. A FT (Fault-tolerant) service is implemented by the FT Provider part and the Target Service part. The FT Provider is in charge of fault-tolerant logic (corresponding to the meta-level shown in figure 1) and the Target Service is responsible for the business logic (corresponding to the base-level shown in figure 1).

3.1 Basic Services

Every basic service is published as a Web service and deployed to the platform. The interactions among the basic services comply with WS-notification [14] specification. Note that the flexible interaction mode permits users to add or remove every basic service provided by the system or developed by the users themselves.

3.1.1 Replication Management Service

The RMS (replication management service) performs the replication management including group constitution, membership management and coordinating a fault recovery process. The RMS is similar to a naming service, but its function is stronger than a naming service's. The service is implemented by the RM (replication manager) and individual service factories if need.

3.1.2 Fault Management Service

The FMS (fault management service) takes charge of detecting the fault of the services in the system. The service is implemented by the FN (Fault Notifier) and Fault Detectors. The FD (Fault Detector) detects faults in the system and reports faults to the FN. The FN then propagates the reports to the RM.

The fault management model is shown in figure 3. The FD sends the fault event to the RM via the FN when it detects a failure and then the RM decides whether a recovery process should be started according to the fault-tolerant properties.

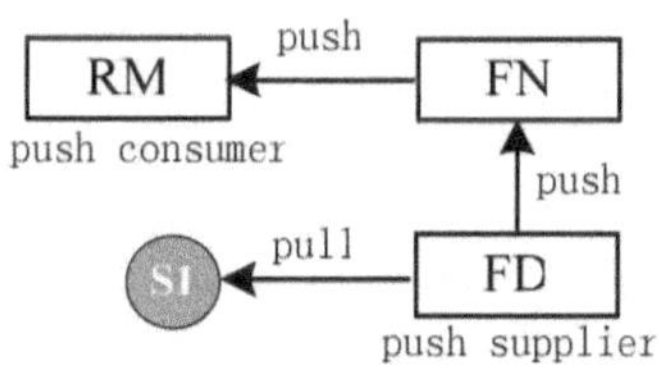

Fig. 3. The Fault Management Model of FTWS

3.1.3 Logging Management Service

The LMS (logging management service) records the state and actions of the members of a service group in a log. The log preserves the order in which messages were received by the members of the service group, so that they can be replayed in the correct order during recovery.

3.1.4 Recovery Management Service

The main purpose of log is for setting the state of a new member. During normal operation, the LMS records the state and actions of the members in a log. The ReMS (Recovery Management Service) sets the state of a member, either after a fault when a backup member of a service group is promoted to the primary member, or alternatively when a new member is introduced into a service group. It applies messages from the log to the member to bring that member to the correct current state, so that it can start to work normally.

3.1.5 Notification Service

The NS (Notification Service) is responsible for the interaction between the FT Provider and the Basic Services and among the Basic Services. The service comply WS-notification specification.

We point out and classify the major event kinds needed in the service. We classify these events into three categories: message-related events, method-related events and management-related events.

3.2 FT Service

A FT Service is composed of two sub-layers, including the FT Provider layer and the Target Service layer. In the system, the FT Provider has many implementations. Users can develop their own FT Provider implementations for their services. Each FT Provider implementation is for corresponding target service.

3.2.1 FT Provider

From analyzing the generic phases of the replication protocols, we conclude that FT Provider should implement these functions:

- setting and getting the state of the target service;
- controlling the client invocations
- exchanging protocol information between participants of an algorithm(such as appointing the new primary service)
- creating or deleting a service replica

In addition, the FT Provider should provide different bridge connection with the diversity types of the target services.

3.2.2 Target Service

The target service implements the functional part of the FT service. The target service needs to implement interface depending on characteristics of the service for fault-tolerant logic, such as Checkpointable interface, Factory interface and PullMonitorable interface. Except these, the target service doesn't need care other fault-tolerant logic.

4 Workflow

We will illustrate the workflow of the FT service with a service using passive replication style and infrastructure-controlled membership style.

4.1 Deploy-Time

The system administrator deploys the FT service to FTWS system via management interface. The flow of deploying the FT service is shown in figure 4:

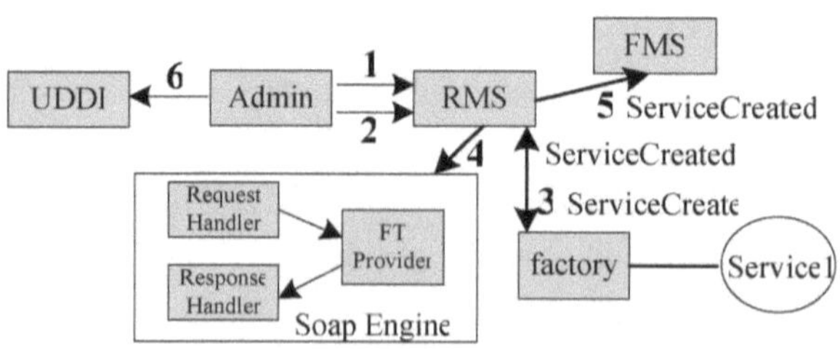

Fig. 4. The flow of deploying the FT service

(1) First, the administrator invokes the RMS to constitute a service group; (2) Then the administrator sets the fault-tolerant properties of the service group; (3) The RMS invokes the factories on the different hosts to create the members according the fault tolerance properties (ServiceCreate event). The factories return the URL of the member to the RMS after creating the member (ServiceCreated event); (4) The RMS activates fault detectors to monitor the members in the service group (ServiceCreated

event). The failure detectors then start to monitor the members in the service group; (5) The RMS registers the service group information to the SOAP engine. The SOAP engine creates the WSDL of the FT service according to the registered information. Note that the WSDL document is regular. It doesn't include the redundancy information. The binding URL of the FT service is the URL of the SOAP engine and the name of the FT service is the name of the service group; (6) Finally the administrator or the client of the UDDI will publish the deployed FT service to the UDDI.

4.2 Run-Time

In run-time, the FD monitors the members and the LMS logs the request and response information in reliable storage and periodically log the states of the primary member.

The flow of invoking the FT service is shown in figure 5:

(1) The service requester retrieves the WSDL of the FT service via UDDI's database and creates request according to the WSDL; (2) The SOAP engine receives the request message and analyzes the message to get the target service name, the method name, the parameter types and the parameter values. It then transmits the information to the FT Provider. The FT Provider notifies the LMS to log the request after receiving the request (MessageReceived event); (3) The FT Provider orientates the request to the primary service according to the service group information in the SOAP engine; (4) The primary service processes the request and returns the response to the FT Provider; (5) The FT Provider receives the response and notifies the LMS again to log the response (MethodDone event); (6) The FT Provider returns the response to the SOAP engine and the SOAP engine returns the response to the requester.

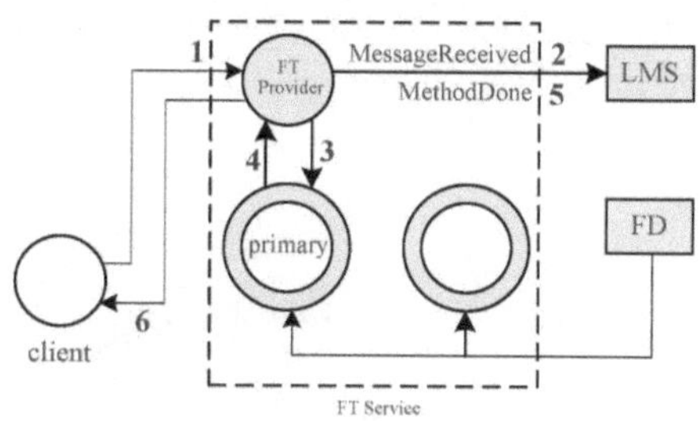

Fig. 5. The flow of invoking the FT service

4.3 Recover-Time

The FD reports the fault event to the FN after it detects a failure and then the FN notifies the RM (replication manager). The RM coordinates the fault recovery process according to the fault event. The RM is responsible for notifying the SOAP engine to update the service group information if a new member is created.

The flow of processing the failure of the primary member is shown in figure 6:

(1) The fault event is delivered to the RM through the FN (ServiceFailure event); (2)The RM then starts the recovery process according the fault properties. The RM (a) first invokes the ReMS to promote the backup member as the new primary member

(SetState event). The ReMS will invoke the LMS to get the state information (GetState event); (b) then creates a new member according to the factory information and invokes the ReMS to set the state of the new member (SetState event); (3) The RM notifies the SOAP engine to update the service group information.

Note that the SOAP engine saves the request messages after the primary member fails and sends these messages to the new primary one.

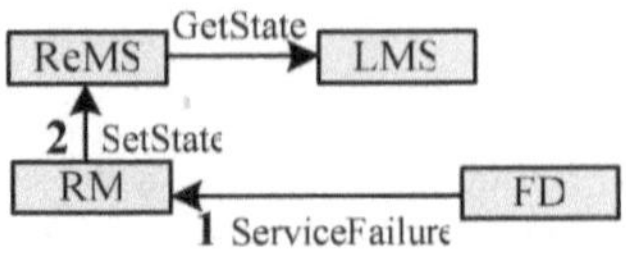

Fig. 6. The flow of processing the failure

5 Conclusion

In this paper, we presented a new fault-tolerant Web services architecture. In the architecture, the fault-tolerant mechanisms are transparent, easy to use and also flexibly customized. The fault-tolerant properties are flexibly configured and the target service programmers almost needn't to care the fault-tolerant mechanisms. We developed a prototype of the fault-tolerant Web services platform based on StarWebService [15].

Acknowledgements. This work is supported by the National High-Tech Research and Development Plan of China ("863" plan) under Grant No. 2004AA112020, 2003AA115210, 2003AA111020 and 2003AA115410 and the National Natural Science Foundation of China under Grant No.90412011.

References

1. Web Services Architecture Requirements. Available online at http://www.w3.org/TR/wsa-reqs (2004)
2. Leavitt, N.: Are Web services finally ready to deliver? IEEE Computer, 11 (2004) 14–18
3. Web Services Architecture. Available online at http://www.w3.org/TR/ws-arch/ (2003)
4. Powell, D.: Distributed Fault Tolerance-Lessons Learnt from Delta-4. In: Banatre, M., Lee, P.A. (eds.): Hardware and Software Architecture for Fault Tolerance: Experiences and Perspectives. Lecture Notes in Computer Science, Vol. 774. Springer-Verlag, Berlin Heidelberg New York (1994) 199–217
5. Birman, K.J.: Replication and Fault tolerance in the Isis System. ACM Operating Systems Review. 5 (1985) 79–86
6. Fabre, J.C., Perennou, T.: A Metaobject Architecture for Fault-tolerant Distributed Systems: The FRIENDS Approach. IEEE Transactions on Computers. 1(1998) 78–95.
7. Liang, D., Fang, C.L., Chen, C., Lin, F.X.: Fault-tolerant web service. Proceedings of the Tenth Asia-Pacific Software Engineering Conference, Thailand (2003)
8. Artix Technical Brief. Available online at http://www.iona.com/artix (2004)

9. Jeckle, M., Zengler, B.: Active UDDI-An Extension to UDDI for Dynamic and Fault-tolerant Service Invocation. 2nd Annual International Workshop of the Working Group on Web and Databases of the German Informatics Society, Germany (2002)
10. Alwagait, E., Ghandeharizadeh, S.: DeW: A Dependable Web Services Framework. 14th International Workshop on Research Issues on Data Engineering, USA (2004)
11. Wei, X., Hong, J.B., Jing, L., Nong, C.J.: A Mobile Agent-Based Fault-tolerant Model for Composite Web Service. Chinese Journal of Computers. 4(2005) 558–567
12. Pleisch, S., Schiper, A.: Approaches to fault-tolerant and transactional mobile agent execution-An algorithmic view. ACM Computing Surveys. 3 (2004) 219–262
13. Dialani, V., Miles, S., Moreau, L., Roure, D.D., Dialani M.L.: Transparent fault tolerance for web services based architectures. Eighth International 12 Europar Conference, Germany (2002)
14. WS-Notification. Available online at http://ifr.sap.com/ws-notification/ws-notification.pdf (2004)
15. StarWebServices2.0. Available online at http://sourceforge.net/projects/starws (2004)

A Grid-Based System for the Multi-reservoir Optimal Scheduling in Huaihe River Basin

Bing Liu[1], Huaping Chen[1], Guoyi Zhang[2], and Shijin Xu[3]

[1] School of Management,
University of Science and Technology of China, Hefei, Anhui, China
liubing@mail.ustc.edu.cn, hpchen@ustc.edu.cn
[2] Department of Computer Science and Technology,
University of Science and Technology of China, Hefei, Anhui, China
National High Performance Computing Center, Hefei, Anhui, China
zgyustc@ustc.edu.cn
[3] Huaihe River Commission, Ministry of Water Resources,
Bengbu, Anhui, China
xsj@hrc.gov.cn

Abstract. The up- and mid-stream of Huaihe River Basin is a complex system of reservoirs and river-ways. It is difficult for flood control and reservoir scheduling. It is ineffective to perform sequential computations for optimal scheduling of multi-reservoir due to the system complexity. In this paper, we implemented the multi-reservoir optimal scheduling algorithm in a Grid environment. Key components as multiple Protocols were developed within the layers of Grid architecture. The proposed Grid computing architecture provides an innovative design of multi-reservoir optimal scheduling system for increasing the accuracy of flood control and speedup of computing.

1 Introduction

The Huaihe River Basin is geographically located in Eastern China. The basin occupies 27×10^4 km^2 with a population of 150 millions. The up- and mid-stream of the river is a complex system of many reservoirs, and sub-rivers or steams (See Fig.1.). It was a poorly flooding region in a worst environmental condition until a centralized reservoirs schedule system was developed. To make better control flooding, we integrate the nine biggest reservoirs as a whole system together by introducing a multi-reservoir optimal scheduling algorithm. The algorithm is implemented in a Grid environment for the consideration computing efficiency.

This paper is organized as follows. Section 2 presents the background about the project, reporting what we have accomplished recently. Section 3 introduces the Grid portals and the core components associated with our proposed Grid system. In Section 4, a mathematical model and related scheduling algorithms are addressed in detail. Section 5 presents the preliminary results of the system. In Section 6 gives a conclusion and future work.

H.T. Shen et al. (Eds.): APWeb 2006, LNCS 3842, pp. 672–677, 2006.

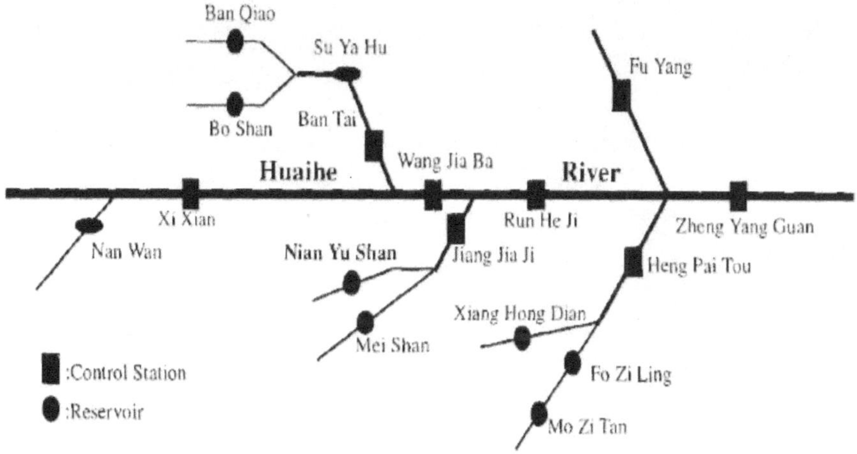

Fig. 1. The reservoirs and control stations of up- and mid-stream of Huaihe River Basin

2 Background

The hydrological situation in Huaihe River Basin is a very complex environment. In the last decade, especially after 1991, many projects of water conservancy have been constructed, integrating various anti-flooding facilities with water-logging drainage, irrigation networks, and navigational channels. The projects changed the hydrological boundary conditions of the river, and it is urgent to develop a feasible and applicable scheduling model with a high efficiency.

With the supports from China Government's, the project of developing a large-scale scheduling model started in 2004. The project is built upon the previous work of flood predicting and scheduling system for covering the whole basin using the new scheme [5, 6]. The nine biggest reservoirs are integrated into the scheduling procedure at the first time in a cooperated manner. With the supports from National High Performance Computing Center (NHPCC) in Hefei and Grid Computing Group [4] at University of Science and Technology of China (USTC), we successfully deployed our system in USTC developed Grid Portals.

3 System Design

Our Grid test-bed is consisted of three Grid nodes; two are located in USTC at Hefei, and one in ICT at Beijing. The main storages maintained at the first two nodes, while the third one serves as the computing service.

With the consideration of the reusability of the protocol components and the reduction of the application complexity, a layered Protocol architecture [9] is proposed, as showed in Fig.2. The Protocols are addressed in the following.

Basic Protocol is responsible for the interoperation with basic Grid services. It contains some fundamental functions for accessing the Grid system in a component

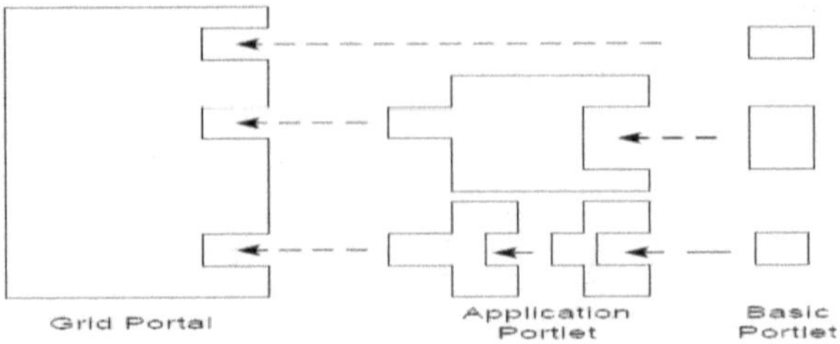

Fig. 2. Layered Protocol Architecture

manner, such as information discovery, single sign-on (authentication and user profile management), file/data management, job submission etc. Application Protocol is designed for specific applications that have core logic issues. The Protocol has multiple interfaces for high level application layer like Basic Protocols and lower-level layered Grid portals. The Basic Protocol can be invoked by one or more Application Protocols, vice versa; an Application Protocol can also invoke several Basic Protocols. Thus, for the purpose of building an application Portal, we can compose the Basic Protocols and the Application Protocols, moreover, the protocols come from different Grid nodes.

A multi-reservoir scheduling is an iterative, adjusting procedure. First, the scheduling system needs end-users to submit predicting results of flooding. These data can be acquired from the executions in flood prediction systems. Once a scheduling system gains the data, it starts to operation the monitoring module to check whether the control nodes (17 main control nodes in Huaihe River Basin) are in a safe state without any parameter adjustment. If not, a computation with properly adjustable parameters begins to execute, and the scheduling procedure operates. This process will repeat until the maximal runoffs and water-levels are under a controllable situation. After the iterative process is accomplished, the final computing results are fetched back to the users.

The necessary developments of the scheduling system in terms of Grid portals are cataloged as follows.

Forecast_data_process. This basic protocol is used to receive and process the prediction data submitted by the end users. This data process is related to the flood prediction system. It also plays a function of converting data format from input to output.
Parameter_process. This basic protocol is similar to the previous one, except it invokes the file/data transformation and communication of parameters that are relevant to each reservoir project.
Single_reservoir_schedule. This is an application protocol designed for single reservoir optimal scheduling process. Different reservoir has different process of charging and discharging runoff.
Multi_reservoir_schedule. This is also an application protocol responsible for the co-scheduling of the nine reservoirs.
Result_data_process. This protocol deals with the scheduling result data, desirable formats required by the end-users for extendable flood scheduling process.

The two application protocols are the key components in the system. Our effort is focused in the scheduling algorithms and their implementations in the Grid portal environment.

4 Scheduling Model and Algorithms

Multi-reservoir scheduling is a kind of multi-variable and multi-step decision. There are m (where m is number of reservoirs) variables to be decided each step, and each variable have S (where S is interval number of capacity separated) possible values. Hence the amount of computing work will increase tremendously with the growth of S because a best scheme needs to be selected from S^m possible schemes in each decision step.

4.1 Mathematical Model

We use the Maxim Decreasing Flood Peak Principle to the multi-reservoir optimal scheduling process. That means we should minimize the integral of the square of runoff to time at each control nodes. The scheduling process is to find the output runoff process of the reservoirs with the known conditions such as charging runoff process, waterlevel-capacity relation curve, initial waterlevel, the desired waterlevel of each reservoir. According to the principle of the dynamic programming, we regard the up- and mid-stream of Huaihe River Basin as a global system and each reservoir as a subsystem. The system's optimization can be separated into two steps: one is to separate the system by carrying out optimal computing to each subsystem; another is get the global optimal scheme based on the optimization of subsystem by establishing relation between subsystems. According to the requirements of the system, we carried out the concordant optimal computing between the subsystems.

Therefore, we took the up-stream of Zheng Yang Guan station as first-level system (Sysl). It consists of two parts: the up-stream of Run He Ji station (Sys21) and the up-stream of Heng Pai Tou station (Sys22), which are second-level systems. The second-level system Sys21 includes the up-stream of Wang Jia Ba station (Sys3 1) and the up-stream of Jiang Jia Ji station (Sys32), which are third-level systems. The third-level system Sys31 includes the up-stream of Xi Xian station (Sys41) and the up-stream of Ban Tai station (Sys42), which are fourth-level systems.

According to the level of system, the objective functions are defined as follows [1]:

- The forth-level system:

$$Sys41 = \min \int_{t0}^{td} (q_{nwo} + q_{xxo})^2 dt \tag{1}$$

$$Sys42 = \min \int_{t0}^{td} [(q_{bqo} + q_{bso} + q_{bbo})^2 + (q_{syho} + q_{bto})^2] dt \tag{2}$$

- The third-level system:

$$Sys31 = \min \int_{t0}^{td} (Sys41 + Sys42 + q_{wjbo})^2 dt \tag{3}$$

$$Sys32 = \min \int_{t0}^{td} (q_{mso} + q_{nyso} + q_{jjjo})^2 dt \tag{4}$$

- The second-level system:

$$Sys21 = \min \int_{t0}^{td} (Sys31 + Sys32 + q_{rhjo})^2 dt \tag{5}$$

$$Sys22 = \min \int_{t0}^{td} [\int_{t0}^{td} (q_{mzto}^2 + q_{fzlo}^2) dt + q_{xhd0} + q_{hpto}]^2 dt \tag{6}$$

- The first-level system:

$$Sys1 = \min \int_{t0}^{td} (Sys21 + Sys22)^2 dt \tag{7}$$

Where q is hydrological process, the *t0* and *td* are the start and end time respectively when the flood exceeds the secure discharge in the downstream of reservoirs, which are also called optimal operation time.

4.2 Single Reservoir Optimal Scheduling Algorithm

Single reservoir optimal scheduling algorithm [2] is the base of multi-reservoir optimal scheduling algorithm. First, divide the reservoir capacity and time range into small units, thus we get a volume-time mesh. Second, with area forecasting results and the outflow of up-stream reservoirs, generate the original scheduling scheme of the reservoir. Third, expand the original scheme to get an expanded area, and then, generate a better scheme in this area. After the better scheme is made, expand it again and get a new better scheme. Repeating all the steps above, the best scheduling scheme can be generated finally.

4.3 Multi-reservoir Optimal Scheduling Algorithm

From above we can see that the single reservoir scheduling algorithm is iterative and time-consuming if executed in a sequential manner. In the Grid Portal environment, we can develop one protocol instance for one reservoir. Every protocol is instantiated respectively to compute out the local optimal scheduling scheme, and the results are broadcasted to every other node. The co-scheduling protocol is responsible for monitoring and controlling the generation of a new best scheme. The algorithm will end when none of the nodes get a new best scheduling scheme after broadcasting. The algorithm is as follows [3]:

```
forall node do sk-init(); //Generate the original
scheduling scheme
deltav=3000000; //The scheduling step length
while (deltav>10) do {
    repeat =1;
    while ( repeat = 1) do {
    forall node do broadcast();//broadcast the results
    forall node do {
```

```
        single(); //every nodes compute respectively
        calculate();
        }
        if (no nodes get a new best scheme) repeat=0;
        }
        deltav = deltav * rew;
    }
    output(); //Output the result
```

Theoretically speaking, the algorithm above may not give a global optimal scheme but a partial optimal scheme. So we set a recycling attenuation factor *rew* to extend *deltav* in the single reservoir scheduling process. After getting the best scheme, set *deltav* to a new value with multiplying *rew*. Thus we can make sure the result is the best scheme from the engineering's perspective.

5 Conclusion and Future Work

In this paper, we discussed the multi-reservoir optimal scheduling algorithm and its deployment in USTC Grid Portal. Using the layered protocol architecture, the development of the core logic is independent and the reusability of common function component is possible. Taking advantage of Grid computing environment, we can get better precision of the results and cutting down the computing time, which is valuable in practical flood control work.

This effort is only a part of the whole scheduling system, yet it is the most computing intensive part. We would deploy the flood-run area and the flood-store area scheduling subsystems in the future, thus we can get the whole scheduling system for the Huaihe River Basin.

References

1. Xu, S.J, Xu, .H, Xin, J.B.: the Application the algorithm of Dawning-1000 in Optimal Flood Decision Making of Clustered Reservoirs in the Huaihe River Basin. In Proceeding of the High Performance Computing Conference, Singapore, Sept. (1998)
2. Ye., B.R, Lu, Z.L.: Optimal Decision Making for Reservoir. In the Press of Hehai University, Feb. (1990)
3. He, B.F, Ding, D.F, Ma, X.X.: the Model and Method of Multi-reservoir Multi-objective Optimum Control Operation. Journal of Hydraulic Engineering, Beijing, No.3 (1995)
4. http://www.gridchina.org/.
5. Xu, H., Chen, H., etc.: Solution of Dynamic plan model of Joint Optimal Decision Making of Large Reservoirs in the Huaihe River Basin. Hydrology, Vol. 1. (in Chinese) (2000)
6. Mao R.: the Reservoir Cluster Optimal Scheduling Algorithm of Huaihe River and Its Parallel Implementation. In The Fourth International Conference/Exhibition on High Performance Computing in Asia-Pacific Region, May, Beijing (2000)

A Logic Foundation of Web Component*

Yukui Fei[1,2], Xiaofeng Zhou[2], and Zhijian Wang[2]

[1] College of Information Science and Engineering Shandong Agricultural University, Taian 271018, China
[2] College of Computer and Information Engineering, Hohai University, Nanjing 210098, China
feiyukui1@sina.com

Abstract. Web component supports service-oriented development. This paper presents a logic foundation of Web Component and its rational inference capability. After the role of Web Component is analyzed, a semantic framework to describe Web Component with a modal logic is explored. The dynamic and intelligence of Web Component is addressed.

1 Introduction

Web service aims to provide the interoperability between diverse applications. The platform independence of Web services interfaces allows the easy integration of heterogeneous systems. Much work has been done to achieve this aim, such as Web Services Description Language (WSDL) [1], Universal Description, Discovery and Integration (UDDI) [2], Semantic Web Services [3], Ontology Web Language for Services (OWL-S) [4] etc. However, little attention has been devoted to the properties of Web service itself. A common problem is that a service is a passive entity rather than a free-will and goal-direction entity. When an environment changes, a service can not adjust its pertinence.

In order to solve this problem, we use Web Component introduced in [5] which discussed the properties and structure of Web Component. Comparing with traditional software component technology, Web Component is dynamic and intelligently-adjustable. In this paper, we present a rational model of Web Component by the means of a logic system- VS-BWI. Section 1 introduces the term of Web Component. Section 2 presents a semantic framework illustrating the relationship between environment and Web component. After a logic system- VS-BWI is given in Section 3, the rational mechanism of Web Component is address, followed by a summary.

2 Semantic Framework

A semantic model of Web Component and the model environment can be given based on the following definitions.

* Supported by the National Grand Fundamental Research 973 Program of China under Grant No. 2002CB312002.

H.T. Shen et al. (Eds.): APWeb 2006, LNCS 3842, pp. 678 – 681, 2006.

Definition 1 (Environments): A *environment* is a tuple *Env* = <*E, vis, fe,* e_0>, where the *E = (e*1*, e*2*,...)* is a set of instantaneous local states for the environment; *vis*: $E \rightarrow 2^E$ is the *visibility function of the VS-BWI* system. It assumes that the function *vis* partitions *E* into mutually disjoint sets and that $e \in vis(e)$, for any $e \in E$. Elements of the co-domain of the function *vis* are called *visibility sets*. The *vis* is *transparent*, if for any $e \in E$; we have $vis(e) = \{e\}$.

$f_{e:}$: $E \times Act \rightarrow E$ is a total *state transformer function* for the environment, where the *Act* is the set of *actions* for the Web Component. The function *fe* is assumed to be an injection, with the $e_0 \in E$ is the *initial state* of *Env*.

Definition 2 (Web Component): Given an environment, a Web Component is a tuple *Wc* = *{L, Act, see, do, fa;* l_0*}* where:

$L = \{l_1, l_2, ...\}$ is a set of *instantaneous local states (mental states)* for the Web Component.

Act = *{a,a'...}* is a set of *actions*.

see : *vis*(*E*)→*Perc* is the *perception function*, mapping visibility sets to *percepts*.

do : *L*→*Act* is the *action selection function*, mapping local states to actions.

fa : *L*×*Perc*→*L* is the state transformer function for the Web Component.

$L_0 \in L$ is the *initial state* for the Web Component.

Definition 3 (Global states for a *VS-BWI* system): A set of *global states G* = {g, g', g'', ...} for a *VS-BWI* system is a subset of *E*×*L*.

Definition 4 (*VS-BWI* systems): A *VS-BWI system* is a pair *S =(Env, Wc)*, where the *Env* is an environment, and *Wc* is a Web Component. The class of *VS-BWI* systems is denoted by *S*.

3 VS-BWI Logic

Define a language $L_{VS\text{-}BWI}$. Assume a set A of atomic actions and a set P of atomic propositions. Then the language $L_{VS\text{-}BWI}$ is given by the BNF grammar:

$\phi ::= p(\in P) \mid \neg\phi \mid \phi_1 \wedge \phi_2 \mid \ldots$

$V\phi \mid S\phi \mid B\phi \mid W\phi \mid I\phi \mid [\alpha] \mid A\alpha$

$\alpha ::= a(\in A) \mid \alpha_1 ; \alpha_2 \mid \phi? \mid$

if ϕ then α_1 else α_2 fi|

while ϕ do α od

Definition 5 (Generated Kripke structures): Given a VS-BWI system S, S=< Env, Wc>, the Kripke frame M=(W, π,R_X)(X stand for V, S, B, W, I) generated by S is defined as follows:

W = G, where G is the set of global states reachable by the system S;

π is a truth assignment to the primitive propositions of states.

The class of frames generated by the class of *VS-BWI* **S** system will be denoted by M; Similarly, M will denote the frame generated by the system S. As might be expected, the generated frames are equivalence frames.

With Definition 5 we have effectively built a bridge between systems and Kripke frames. In order to determine whether a formula $\phi \in L_{VS\text{-}BWI}$ is true in a model/state pair (M, w) (if so, we write $(M, w) \models \phi$), we stipulate:

M, w $\models$ p iff $\pi(w)(p)$ = true, for $p \in L_{VS\text{-}BWI}$
The logical connectives are interpreted as usual.
M, w $\models B\phi$ iff M, w' $\models \phi$ for all w' with $R_B(w,w')$
M, w $\models W\phi$ iff M, w' $\models \phi$ for all w' with $R_W(w, w')$
M, w $\models I\phi$ iff M, w' $\models \phi$ for all w' with $R_I(w, w')$
M, w $\models V\phi$ iff M, w' $\models \phi$ for all w' with $R_V(w, w')$
M, w $\models S\phi$ iff M, w' $\models \phi$ for all w' with $R_S(w, w')$
M, w $\models [\alpha]\phi$ iif M', w' $\models \phi$ for all M', w' with $R\alpha((M, w); (M', w'))$.

Here $R\alpha$ is defined as usual in dynamic logic by induction from the basic case Ra.

4 Rational Inference of VS-BWI Logic

With the *VS-BWI* logic, we can reason how Web Component works. It help us to comprehend the intelligent and dynamic properties of Web Component.

4.1 Gathering Information

The relationship between Web Component perceives and the one pre-known. Def. 2 indicates complete transformer functions characterize Web Component. It never lose information, when a system keep updating their internal state; the following holds.

$\models S\phi \Rightarrow B\phi$ iif *the state transformer function fa is complete;*
$\models B\phi \Rightarrow S\phi$ iif *the state transformer function fa is local.*

4.2 Setting Goals

With the consideration of wishes to be the most primitive and motivational attitudes, and represented by a plain normal modal operator, the Wi operator can be interpreted as: $M,s \models Wi\phi \Leftrightarrow \forall s' \in W((s, s') \in Wi \Rightarrow M, s' \models \phi)$.

In order to transform the wishes to goals, a Web Component needs to select candidate goals based on the criteria of unfulfilledness and implement ability. This requires a Web Component choose a wish if it is (as yet) unfulfilled and realizable. Unfulfilled-ness of a formula ϕ is easily expressed by a classical negation $\neg\phi$. The notion of realization is somewhat more involved. For this purpose we introduce an realizable operator $\Diamond_i\phi$ which we interpret as follows:

$$M, s \models \Diamond_i\phi \Leftrightarrow \exists k \in IN \exists a_1,\ldots, a_k \in At(M, s \models PracPoss_i(a1,\ldots, ak,\phi))$$

Where the ϕ is realizable by i , if i has the practical possibility to perform a finite sequence of atomic actions yielding ϕ.

Having defined wishes and selections, one may straightforward to define goals. The goals can then be accoomplished.

Definition 6: For $i \in A$ and $\phi \in L_{VS\text{-}BWI}$, we define: $\mathbf{G_i}\phi \leftrightarrow \neg\phi \wedge W_i\phi \wedge \Diamond_i\phi$.

4.3 Making Plans

Having formed goals, an implement is needed. For convenience's sake an Intend predication, we plan a Web Component which can perform an action to achieve the goal.

Definition 7: For $\alpha\in Act, i\in A$ and $\phi\in L_{VS\text{-}BWI}$, $Intend_i(\alpha,\phi)=^{def}Can_i(\alpha,\phi)\wedge B_iGoal_i\phi$.

5 Conclusion

The concept of Web component integrates individual elementary or complex services together. This paper considers Web component as a dynamic and intelligently-adjustable software component. The adaptive mechanism of Web component provide a feasibility for self automatic adjustment to the behavior responding to the environment change.

References

1. Christensen, E., Curbera, F., Meredith, G., Weerawarana, S.: Web Services Description Language (WSDL) 1.1 (2001)
2. The Universal Description, Discovery and Integration (UDDI) protocol. Version 3, 2003. At http://www.uddi.org/.
3. McIlraith, S., Son, T.C., Zeng, H: Semantic Web Services. IEEE Intelligent Systems, Special Issue on the Semantic Web, 16(2) (2001) 46--53
4. OWL-S Coalition. OWL-S 1.0 Release. at http://www.daml.org/services/owl-s/1.0/
5. Fei, Y.K., Wang, Z.J.: A Concept Model of Web Component. In Proc. of IEEE International Conference on Services Computing (2004) 159-164
6. DePalma, N., Laumay, P., Bellissard L.: On the Emergence of a Web Services Component Model. In the Proceeding of WCOP, Budapest, Hungary (2001) (http://www.research.microsoft.com/~cszypers/events/ WCOP2001/Curbera.pdf).
7. Yang, J. Papazoglou, M. P.: Web Component: A Substrate for Web Service Reuse and Composition. CAiSE (2002) 21-36

A Public Grid Computing Framework Based on a Hierarchical Combination of Middleware

Yingjie Xia, Yao Zheng, and Yudang Li

College of Computer Science, and Center for Engineering and Scientific Computation, Zhejiang University, Hangzhou 310027, P.R. China
{xiayingjie, yao.zheng}@zju.edu.cn, adangs@163.com

Abstract. Grids, as one implementation of public computing, can be deployed by some middleware to integrate all kinds of resources across institutional boundaries, to tackle complex problems in scientific and engineering computation, data storage, scientific visualization, etc. In this paper, we propose a public computing grid framework built upon the hierarchical combination of two popular middleware products, Globus Toolkit (GT) and Sun Grid Engine (SGE). The communication between them can be conducted by Transfer-queue Over Globus (TOG). We discuss issues related to the deployment and the usage of this kind of hybrid grids. We examine it using serial programs and parallel program codes, and compare it with the grids deployed by only GT or SGE, respectively. The case studies imply that this hybrid grid is suitable for loosely coupled applications with high computational complexity.

1 Introduction

Public computing is an architecture designed to harness not only the idle cycles of participating nodes but also memory and secondary storage. It can potentially utilize the idle cycles distributed in the hundreds of millions of personal computers all over the world, instead of supercomputers and clusters [12, 13].

The term "Grid", emerged in the mid1990s, denotes a distributed computing infrastructure for coordinated resource sharing and problem solving in dynamic, multi-institutional domain [1]. After its emergence, many substantial projects based on grid applications in different areas came out, like DataGrid (CERN), IPG (Information Power Grid, NASA), Butterfly Grid, etc. As one implementation of public computing, the grid shares many issues with it, such as the data transfer and resource scheduling, which can be optimized by using the appropriate middleware products, e.g. Globus Toolkit (GT) [3], the most popular one to set up the grid platform, and Sun Grid Engine (SGE) [4], a specified tool for cluster grid proposed by Sun Microsystems, Inc.

The choice of the middleware commonly depends on the grid resources, computing environment and specific tasks. Based on personal computers, compared with deploying the grid by only SGE or GT separately, we can make a combination of the both products, which can be called a hybrid grid. Since this new framework can bring together the advantages of both SGE and GT in data transfer, resource management,

H.T. Shen et al. (Eds.): APWeb 2006, LNCS 3842, pp. 682–689, 2006.

etc., we will be able to create more efficient, more independent and even more inexpensive grids than before.

In this paper, we present the design and implementation of the new public computing grid framework. The software, Transfer-queue Over Globus (TOG), is used to transfer the tasks from GT to SGE [9]. We also use some test cases to compare the performance of the hybrid grids with the grids deployed by the sole GT. As designed for cluster grids, SGE is not available for common use. However, we can use it on personal computers by NFS or NIS, and utilize the SGE schedule policy to assist GT to construct a better grid environment.

This paper is organized as follows. Section 2 introduces background information and related work in the grid deployment with Globus Toolkit and SGE. In Section 3, we describe the design and implementation of the hybrid grid framework. Test cases and discussions with the hybrid grid and a single personal computer are presented in Section 4. Finally, conclusions and future work are addressed in Section 5.

2 Background and Related Work

We are to review two middleware products, Globus Toolkit and Sun Grid Engine, by which we build the public computing grid environments. Globus Toolkit has been widely adopted by most projects in scientific computing, bioinformatics, game, etc., while Sun Grid Engine is a product developed to build cluster grids, campus grids and global grids.

2.1 Globus Toolkit

The Globus Toolkit is an open source software toolkit used for building Grid systems and applications. It is being developed by the Globus Alliance, which is a community of organizations and individuals developing fundamental technologies behind the "Grid", that lets people share computing power, databases, instruments, and other on-line tools securely across corporate, institutional, and geographic boundaries without sacrificing local autonomy. The toolkit includes software for security, information infrastructure, resource management, data management, communication, fault detection, and portability [2]. The latest version of GT is 4.0, which bases on Open Grid Service Architecture (OGSA), while the earlier version before 3.0 written in C language has no character in web service.

After Globus Toolkit developed, the project spurred a revolution in the way science is conducted. It facilitated the application of the concept "grid", like European Data Grid, Earthquake Engineering and Simulation (NEES), FusionGrid, the Earth System Grid (ESG), etc. After the version 3.0, which introduces the web service, many enterprises deployed GT that brings the grid into more practical business.

2.2 Sun Grid Engine

Sun grid strategy puts forward three evolution steps: cluster grid, campus grid, and global grid [4]. Sun develop its own middleware to deploy grid, Sun Grid Engine, which is also an open source community effort to facilitate the adoption of distributed computing solutions. Actually, Sun Grid Engine is developed specifically for cluster grids which don't need any credential, authentication and authorization. We can also install SGE on personal computers by simulating the cluster environment with Network File System (NFS). The grid deployed with SGE has one master node, which supervises all resources in the network to allow full control and achieve optimal utilization of the resources available, and all other execution nodes, which execute the distributed tasks.

SGE has been used in some grid projects, such as White Rose Grid, which is conducted by Leeds University, York University, and Sheffield University, delivering stable, well-managed HPC resources supporting multi-disciplinary research, and a Metropolitan Grid across the Universities [10]. NTU Campus Grid, which is built by Nanyang Technical University, connects four research centers within the university and 3 external sites to provide a larger scale grid computing environment [11].

3 Design and Implementation

We create two personal computer groups, either of which is constituted by six personal computers. We install SGE "Master" program and GT on two Master hosts, and SGE "Exec" program on all the hosts. The SGE "admin users" of the both master hosts applies for the signed certificates from the same Certificate Authorization. The products of SGE and GT that we use are SGE6.0 and GT2.4.

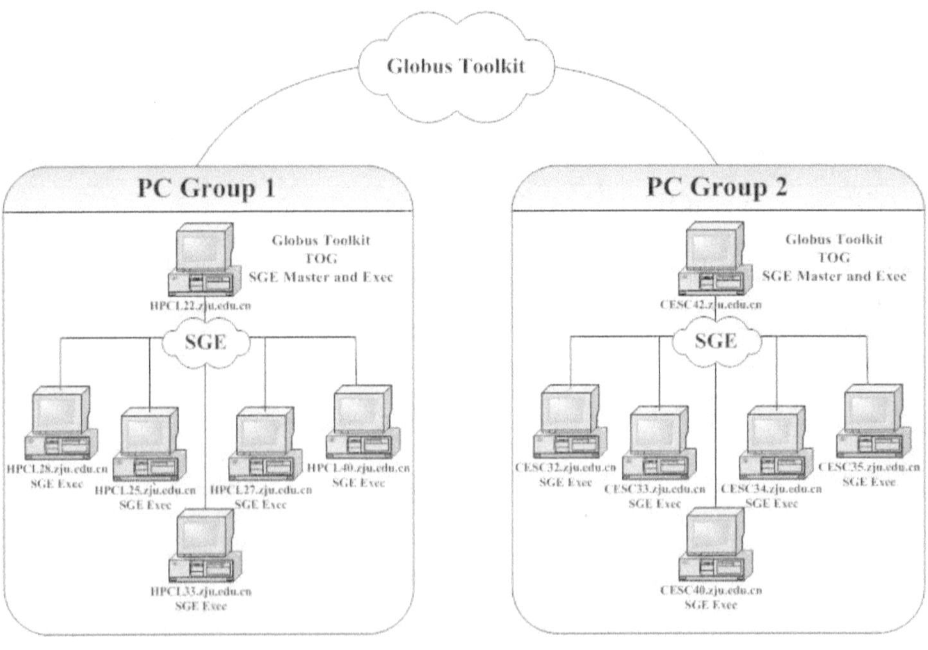

Fig. 1. The grid framework built on personal computers in our laboratory

The installation of both SGE "Master" program and GT are not explained here, referring to their detailed documentation. The SGE "Exec" program can be installed in such a way of first exporting the SGE directory of master hosts using NFS, then mounting the directory on the execute hosts and running the install program.

We connect SGE and GT by using the TOG, modifying the two key files tge.pm and jobmanager-tge of TOG bundle to set the correct paths to SGE and GT, and copying them to the corresponding locations [9].

The tasks, written in a RSL file, can specify which job manager to use. If tge.pm is selected, its function "submit" is used to parse the RSL file, rewrite the task to a temporary script, and finally call the SGE to submit this script. Another important function "poll", defined also in tge.pm, monitors the status of the submitted job, and takes corresponding actions.

In order to run an MPI-based program code on our grid platform, the TOG must be modified to transfer the code, and the SGE has to supply an environment for execution. The file "tge.pm" adds the MPI option, so that the field "jobtype" of the RSL file, which is submitted by the GT and managed by jobmanager-tge file, can support "mpi" value. SGE configures a Parallel Environment (PE) to integrate with the software LAM/MPI, which is used to run the MPI-based program code.

Until now, we have built the whole framework of a personal computer grid using SGE6.0 and GT2.4, as shown in Figure 1.

4 Case Analyses

4.1 Case Tests

We submit a RSL file specifying three serial jobs to the master hosts, respectively, using the GT, and it will call the SGE to distribute each job to one Exec node, following the schedule policy customized by the SGE. The result will be returned to the submit host with no copy left on local hosts. The TOG plays a bridging role in the whole process by getting the job script from the GASS cache in master hosts, submitting to SGE master host, and returning the results to the same cache.

Compared with serial jobs, an MPI-based program code takes a more important position in the application of the grids, because such kind of programs can distribute their processes to each grid node, pass messages between them and gather the returns to achieve a final result. We make use of three MPI-based program codes as test cases, including the computation of $\prod$, looking for prime numbers, and the implementation of the finite difference method to solve a Poisson equation. We have also made a comparison of program execution between cases on the grid and on a single personal computer. The snapshot of running an MPI-based program is shown in Figure 2.

We compute the value of $\prod$ by numerical integration, $\pi = \int_0^1 \frac{4}{1+x^2}dx$. It can be approximated by dividing the interval [0, 1] into some number of subintervals, assigning part of them to each process and finally computing the total area of the rectangles. In our experiment, there are 2,000,000,000 subintervals in [0, 1]. The search of prime number between 1 and 20,000,000 is much easier. We also divide the whole

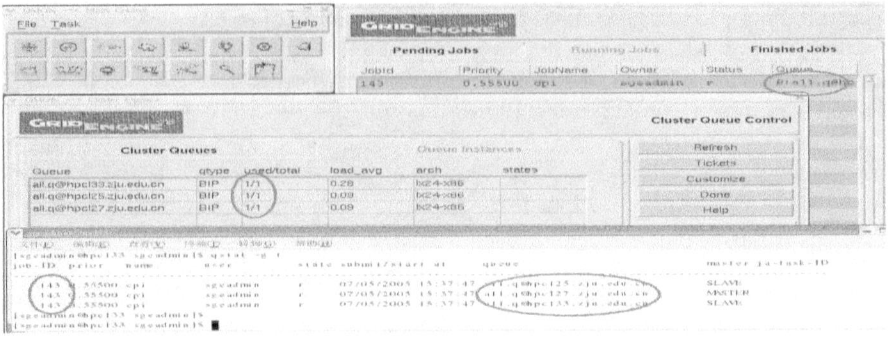

Fig. 2. Submitting a RSL file specifying an MPI-based program, where the SGE uses a PE to run it. The program is specified in three processes, which execute on different hosts, with the same job-ID.

interval into many subintervals, which have the length of 100, and distribute them to each process by Round Robin method. Another test case is the MPI-based program code to solve the 2D Poisson equation by means of the finite difference method with a mesh of 1200*1200. It has large amount of message passing between each process during the computation, while the other two cases only distribute the intervals and gather the results in the end.

(a) Geometrical model (b) A mesh and 16 domains concerned (b) Displacement contour

Fig. 3. Simulation of a crank and the result visualized by ParaView

Figure 3 shows the corresponding geometrical model, discretization of the model, and the simulation result of a structure analysis for a crank. The simulation is carried out by the Finite Element Method in our grid framework, which consists of four personal computers and a network of speed 100-Megabytes per second. The resulting data is visualized by ParaView.

The execution time of the test cases on our grid, which is deployed on different number of nodes, is listed in Table 1. The corresponding performance ratios, measured by the reciprocals of the execution time, are shown in Figure 4.

Table 1. The execution time of the test cases on our grid, deployed on different number of nodes. The unit of the time is second.

	1 node	2 nodes	3 nodes	4 nodes	5 nodes	6 nodes
Pi	106.3822	53.4733	36.2582	26.9114	21.6224	18.1084
Prime	72.6589	36.5495	24.5040	18.3640	14.7603	12.3718
Poisson	372.8538	195.0383	130.5143	99.9352	81.8654	70.1519
Crank Simulation	51509	27535	22462	14342	14051	12973

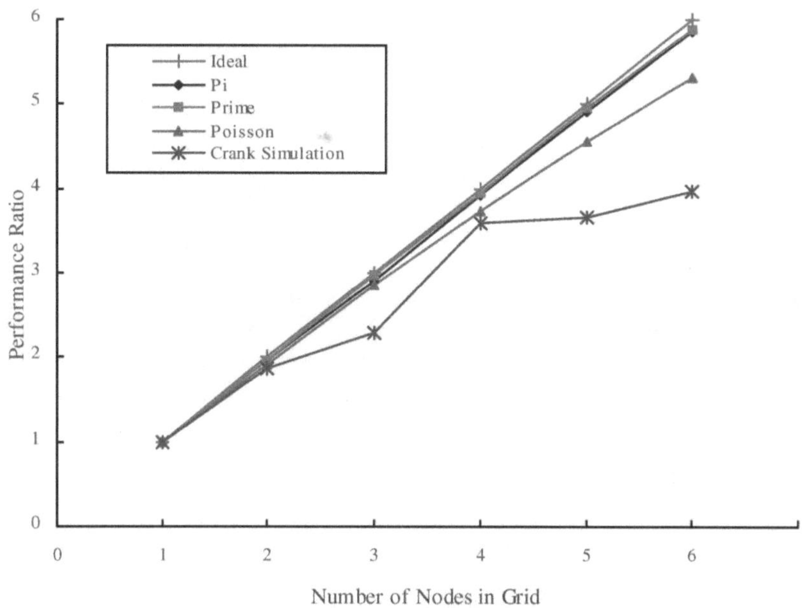

Fig. 4. Performance ratios for different numbers of nodes on our grid

4.2 Discussions

The results of the test cases show that our hybrid grid is a powerful vehicle to support computation-intensive applications. From Figure 4 the performance ratios of the benchmarks Pi and Prime are very close to the ideal values, while the other two cases fall away much farther, due to the overhead of mass data communication between nodes. It indicates that this grid framework is suitable for loosely coupled applications with high computational complexity, for the sake of network bottleneck.

Compared with the grid deployed by GT or SGE separately, our framework allows nodes to join or leave freely, while the other part of the grid keeps stable. It also combines the schedule policy of the local part, which is organized by SGE, and the global management that is conducted by GT. This hybrid grid migrates SGE from a cluster to personal computers, which makes the whole cost drop much. The use of the

SGE fills a gap in the GT for its lack of efficient schedule policy, and the GT can support data transfer between SGE masters by its tool, gridftp.

5 Conclusions and Future Works

In this paper, we propose a new method to build a public computing grid on personal computers by using a hierarchical combination of Globus Toolkit and SGE. It can incorporate the advantages of both grid middleware products, and build an efficient, stable, simple and inexpensive grid framework. The construction of the environment simulates the cluster grid, which comes from Sun grid strategy, with the hand of GT and TOG, transferring data between cluster grids, and connecting GT with SGE, respectively. We take some serial programs and parallel program codes as benchmarks, to estimate the performance of our grid framework. The results represent some significant improvement for the high computational complexity and low communication applications. Therefore, we could claim that our new framework gives a better solution to deploy a public computing grid on personal computers, which blazes a new path to tackle a certain kind of complex problems in the area of scientific and engineering computation.

At the present time, we only apply the framework in our lab, of which the network belongs to a local area network. Therefore, we plan, firstly to deploy our grid in a different subnet of the campus network, then to extend to a wide area network, and thirdly to increase the number of nodes on our grid to compare with the real cluster grid.

Acknowledgements

The authors wish to thank the National Natural Science Foundation of China for the National Science Fund for Distinguished Young Scholars under grant Number 60225009. We appreciate helpful discussions among the members of the Grid Computing Group at the CESC, Zhejiang University, and would like to thank them for their input in the project.

References

1. Foster, I., Kesselman C., Tuecke S.: The Anatomy of the Grid: Enabling Scalable Virtual Organizations. *International Journal of High Performance Computing Applications*, 15 (3): (2001) 200-222
2. Foster, I., Kesselman, C., Nick, J. M., et al., The Physiology of the Grid: An Open Grid Service Architecture for Distributed System Integration. URL: http://www.globus.org/research/papers/ogsa.pdf/ (February, 2002)
3. Foster, I., Kesselman, C.: Globus: A Metacomputing Infrastructure Toolkit. *Int. J. Supercomputer Applications*, 11(2) (1997) 115-128
4. Sloan, T. M., Abrol R., Cawood, G., et al.: Sun Data and Compute Grids. *Proceedings of the 2nd UK e-Science All Hands Meeting*, 2-4 September, Nottingham, UK (2003)
5. Sloan, T.: Going Global with Globus and Grid Engine. *EPCC News, Issue 48*, Spring (2003)

6. Jing, T., Lim, M. H., Ong Y. S.: A Parallel Hybrid GA for Combinatorial Optimization Using Grid Technology. *IEEE Congress on Evolutionary Computation*, December 8-12, 2003, Canberra, Australia
7. Lai, C.L., Yang, C.T.: Construct a Grid Computing Environment on Multiple Linux PC Clusters. *Tunghai Science, Vol. 5*, July (2003) 107–124 107
8. Foster, I., Karonis, N.,: A Grid-Enabled MPI: Message Passing in Heterogeneous Distributed Computing Systems. Proc. *1998 SC Conference*, November, 1998
9. Abrol, R., Seed, T.: Transfer-queue Over Globus (TOG): How To. URL: http://gridengine.sunsource.net/download/TOG/tog-howto.pdf/ (July, 2003)
10. Austin, J., What is the White Rose Grid? URL: http://www.wrgrid.org.uk/workshop2005/JimAustin-Introduction.pdf.
11. Nanyang Technical University Campus Grid. URL: http://ntu-cg.ntu.edu.sg
12. Anderson, D.: Public Computing: Reconnecting People to Science, *Conference on Shared Knowledge and the Web*, November 2003
13. Pellicer, S., Ahmed, N., Pan, Y., et al., Gene Sequence Alignment on a Public Computing Platform, *The 7th International Workshop on High Performance Scientific and Engineering Computing*, Oslo, Norway, June 15, 2005

A Workflow-Oriented Scripting Language Based on BPEL4WS*

Dejun Wang[1], Linpeng Huang[1], and Qinglei Zhang[2]

[1] Dept. of Computer Science and Engineering, Shanghai Jiao Tong University, Shanghai 200030, P.R. China
{wangdejun, lphuang}@sjtu.edu.cn
[2] Dept. of Mechanical and Power Engineering, Shanghai Jiao Tong University, Shanghai 200030, P.R. China
{qingleizhang}@sjtu.edu.cn

Abstract. This paper proposes a high-level scripting language, which can be used to express workflow for scientific and engineering tasks running on Computing Grid. Since it is difficult for common computing users to explore the grid computing resource successfully without computer-experts' help; it is feasible that computing users should be presented an easy-study-and-use language to express their workflow and it is up to computer-expert to realize an interpreter to translate the scripting-language file into XML scripting language file. Furthermore, this destination file should conform to specification of BPEL4WS such that the prototype system realized will hold good expansibility.

1 Introduction

Computing Grid in research has been able to provide a high-performance, relatively safe, and credible computing environment based on shared heterogeneous computer resources. It can balance the relation between the holding of high performance computer nodes and expensive analysis software and resource-thirsty of computing users.

However, it is discouraging for users including engineers and scientists to have to spend much time on studying how to use Grid since it often provides command-line method to submit computing work requirement; meanwhile this also takes the Grid professionals a lot of time to teach users. It is necessary to realize a friendly user-interface which makes users study and use easily grid resource without much knowledge of service environment. By this, users can specialize in computing task and computer professionals can offer more and better computing service.

Accordingly, computer experts have done much R&D work and many kinds of high-level scripting language have been defined and supported, such as language like C shell [5], BPEL4WS or other language like BPEL4WS based on XML [6,8,9,10]; some researchers are working hard to realize a visual client-control-workflow interface for users to describe their tasks visually [7,11].

In this paper, we give the whole definition of scripting language syntax presented by production-formula-rules according to context-independent grammar. Meantime,

* This paper is supported by key project (No.025115033) of the Science and Technology Commission of Shanghai Municipality.

H.T. Shen et al. (Eds.): APWeb Workshops 2006, LNCS 3842, pp. 690–697, 2006.

we give an abbreviated introduction about our system architecture including workflow manager and manager's running mechanism based on agents.

The paper will be organized as follows: the next section introduces workflow-control system architecture supporting scripting language including workflow manager and illustrates scripting interpreter's running mechanism. Section 3 will give a detailed specification about scripting. Section 4 will present a study-case to clear our idea. Section 5 overviews other researchers' achievement having enlightened us, conclude this paper and propose some idea about future work.

2 Script Language Running Mechanism

2.1 System Architecture

To make common users use our grid resources transparently and conveniently, we absorb merit of portals [3] and workflow mechanism into our grid system. Fig 1. illustrates our destination system architecture[10,11]. System includes four main components: Workflow-Service-Interface (WSI), Script-Decomposition-Agent (SDA), Script-Interpreter (SI), and Workflow-Manager (WM). WSI accepts and manages user's workflow scripting files and sends files to SDA; SDA reads user's scripting file and automatically obtains calculated data resource files, registers this task in work-list including users' result file saving path, and uses task-stack data structure to record tasks subfile; SI reads tasks subfile and translates them into file according to BPEL4WS, which will be read by WM. WM includes Workflow Monitor and Scheduler Services(WMSS), Workflow Admin Services(WAS), and Workflow Engine Service (WES) components. WM takes part on controlling when and which agents will be scheduled, which node they will be executed on and how to map user's simple computing command to grid service so on. WES accepts messages from control-agent

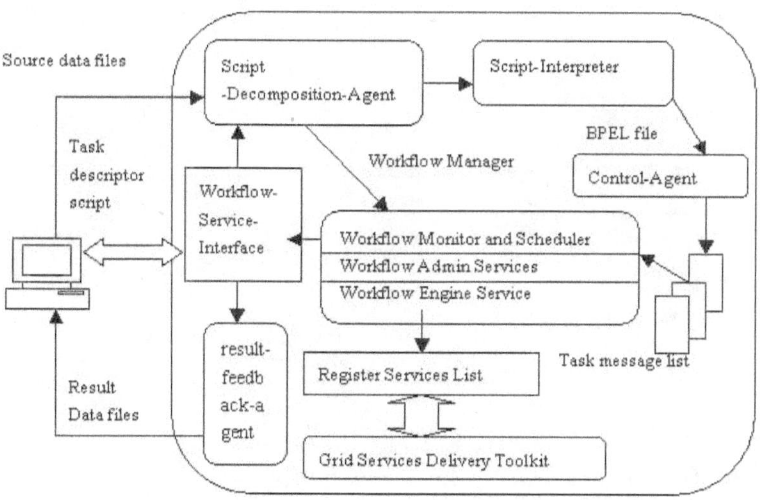

Fig. 1. System architecture

and looks up Grid Services in Grid Services Delivery Toolkit (GSDT) and creates task-agents. (Control-agent controls task-agents' hierarchy to control subtasks' sequent and concurrent execution); WMSS can query the instance currently running and return the status to the GSDT and send finish-message to WSI to send back result data files; WAS mainly takes on role management, audit management and so on.

2.2 Workflow Execution Mechanism

As expressed in Fig1, computing users can submit workflow description scripting through web portal. This scripting file will be accepted by WSI running on Grid Access Node and be passed to SDA. SDA will analyze, get data source files from client-end, and register one workflow running information in work-list and send message to SI. Next, SI will bring out workflow file conforming to BPEL4WS based on task-stack. Meanwhile, WMSS creates control-agent according to work-list information, and control-agent will produce the hierarchy of sequent and concurrent subtasks' execution messages. And when all computing subtasks have been achieved, control-agent will send a successful message to WSI through WMSS, which will send message to GSDT and save result files through GSDT. WSI will create result-feedback-agent, which will take charge of interaction with client-end, including saving result data files to client-end. Since we focus on description of scripting, we will pass over agents' mechanism. Fig.2 gives workflow's execution flowchart.

3 Script Specification

In this section, we will give detailed specification of scripting language illustrated in Fig.3. We will omit relatively simple lex rules and only focus on syntax rules. According to context-independently grammar, we give scripting language's syntax specification formally by production-formula-rules. Grammar G is a tuple (Vt, Vn, S, ρ); Vt expresses a set of end-symbols; Vn expresses a set of middle-symbols; S

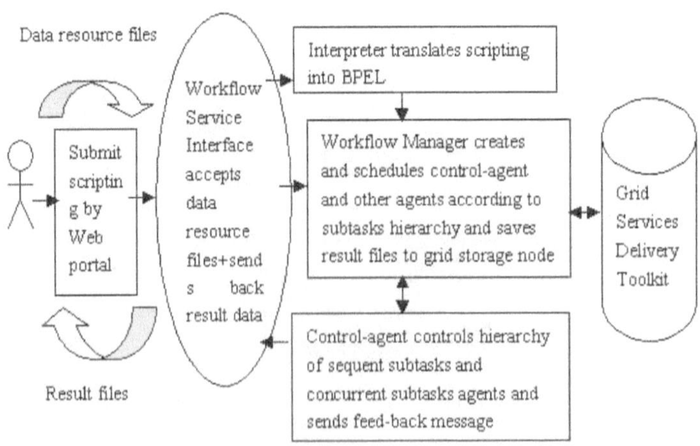

Fig. 2. Workflow running flowchart

```
Program —> { Identify; wait(PremiseFiles); DataFiles;ResultFilesPath;SentenceBlock; }
Identify —> groupid = Identifiers; selfid= Identifiers; fromid= IdList;toid= IdList;
IdList —> Identifiers; IdList| ε
SentenceBlock —> Sentence;SentenceBlock| ε
PremiseFiles —> FileList;
DataFiles —> Data=(FileList);
ResultFilesPath —> Result=(FilePath);
FileList —> FileName; FileList| ε
Sentence —> TaskGroup | SwitchSentence | WhileSentence
TaskGroup —> sequent(TaskList) | concurrent (TaskList) | TaskList
TaskList —> Task; TaskList| ε
Task —> exec(ServiceName ParameterList);
ServiceName —> Identifiers
ParameterList —> ParameterItem; ParameterList | ε
ParameterItem —> Identifiers |Number | FileName
SwitchSentence —> switch {ConditionOpList;default:SentenceBlock; }
WhileSentence —> while Condition{ SentenceBlock;}
ConditionOpList —> ConditionOp ;ConditionOpList| ε
ConditionOp —> Condition: SentenceBlock; break;
Condition —> LogicExpr
LogicExpr —> (Expr CompOper Expr) |(LogicExpr) and (LogicExpr) |(LogicExpr) or
(LogicExpr) | not(LogicExpr)
Expr —> Number | Identifers | (Expr) CalOper (Expr)
```

Fig. 3. Production-formula-rules of syntax

expresses a set of start-symbols and equals to {Program}; ρ expresses a set of production-formula-rules. Each detailed definition is explained as follows:

Vt={Identifiers, Number, CalOper, CompOper, LogicOper, Keywords, Divider, FileName, FilePath, ExtName};
Vn={Program, Identify, IdList, SentenceBlock, PremiseFiles, DataFiles, ResultFilesPath, FileList, TaskGroup, TaskList, Task, ServiceName, Sentence, ParameterList, ParameterItem, SwitchSentence, WhileSentence, ConditionOpList, ConditionOp, Condition, LogicExpr, Expr}.

4 A Case-Study

To analyze diesel-engine-shaft vibration, each part design team should first analyze the part's vibration character data and then submit analysis result to analyze mutual effect and the whole shaft vibration character. Among these, some analysis work can be made concurrently by each team and some analysis depends on other analysis and needs to be executed sequentially. For example, shaft's inherence frequency analysis and frequency response analysis also may be finished without waiting other nodes but only after getting above correlative parts' analysis data (for example, pedestal's transverse and fore-and-aft vibration, brace-linker's transverse and fore-and-aft vibration, propeller's torsional vibration and so on), the shaft's torsional, fore-and-aft, and random vibration analysis may be continued concurrently, and at last coupled vibration.

4.1 Workflow Description by Pedestal Designer Nodes

Scripting submitted by pedestal designer team to analyze pedestal's vibration as follows(the analysis requirement scripting of other parts like brace linker, propeller is similar as this; to save space, we use related parts' first 3 letters to name data files):

4.1.1 Workflow Description Scripting About Pedestal Vibration Analysis

```
groupid=shaft123456; selfid=pedestal; toid=shaft;
Data=(ped1.bdf; ped2.bdf;);
Result=(D:\shaft-pedestal\);
...
concurrent(...
   exec(transverse ped1.bdf; ped1.f06;);
   exec(fore-aft ped2.bdf; ped2.f06;);
    );
...
```

4.1.2 Scripting After Translating

```
<links>
 <link name="pedestal-to-shaft"/>
</links>
<sequence>
 <flow>
  <invoke operation="transverse" portType="FEM:bdf".../>
  <invoke operation="fore-aft" portType="FEM:bdf".../>
  <target linkName="pedestal-to-shaft"/></invoke>
 </flow>
</sequence>
```

4.2 Workflow Description by Shaft Analysis Nodes

According to the first paragraph in this section, coupled vibration analysis about shaft should be put after inherence frequency, frequency response, torsional vibration, random vibration and fore-and-aft vibration analysis. Inherence frequency character should be analyzed before frequency response analysis. Analysis of torsional vibration, fore-and-aft-vibration, random vibration may be concurrent.

4.2.1 Workflow Description Scripting About Shaft Vibration Analysis

```
groupid=shaft123456; selfid=shaft;
fromid=pedestal; bracelinker; propeller;...  toid=shaft;
wait(ped2.f06; bra2.f06; pro2.f06;);
Data=(sha1.bdf; sha2.bdf; sha3.bdf; sha4.bdf;
sha5.bdf;);
Result=(D:\shaft\);
...
sequent(...
  exec(inhere-freq sha1.bdf; sha1.f06;);
```

```
  exec(freq-resp sha2.bdf; sha2.f06;);
  ...
  concurrent(
   exec(torsional sha1.f06; sha4.bdf; sha4.f06;);
   exec(fore-aft sha5.bdf; sha5.f06;);
   exec(random sha3.bdf; sha3.f06;);
  );
  ...
  exec(coupled unitedata.f06);
  )
...
```

4.2.2 Translated Sentences from Groupid to Toid Lines

```
<links>
   <link name="pedestal-to-shaft"/>
   <link name="bracelinker-to-shaft"/>
   <link name="propeller-to-shaft"/>
</links>
```

4.2.3 Translated Wait Sentence Lines

```
<flow>
  <receive partnerLink="pedestal" portType="FEM:f06"
     operation="copy" variable="file" value="ped2.f06">
  <receive partnerLink="bracelinker" portType="FEM:f06"
     operation="copy" variable="file" value="bra2.f06">
  <receive partnerLink="propeller" portType="FEM:f06"
     operation="copy" variable="file" value="pro2.f06">
</flow>
```

4.2.4 Translated Sequent(concurrent…) Sentences

```
<sequence>
 <invoke operation="inhere-freq" portType="FEM:bdf".../>
 <invoke operation="freq-resp" portType="FEM:bdf".../>
 <flow>
 <invoke operation="torsional" portType="FEM:flist".../>
 <invoke operation="fore-aft" portType="FEM:bdf".../>
 <invoke operation="random" portType="FEM:bdf".../>
 </flow>
 <invoke operation="coupled" portType="FEM:f06".../>
   <source linkName="bracelinker-to-shaft">
   <source linkName="pedestal-to-shaft">
   <source linkName="propeller-to-shaft">
 </invoke>
</sequence>
```

5 Conclusion and Future Work

About workflow description on Grid, many researchers have made amount of work and got great achievement. Walker et al. define a scripting like C Shell in [5], which supports users to invoke computing service conveniently on Grid, but it can't deal with nodes' interaction, sequent and concurrent execution. C.S. Hunt et al design a scripting JXPL based on XML. However, JXPL's coordination and concurrency expression capability is relatively weaker than BPEL4WS. Amin et al's work [7] realizes a client-controllable workflow system, which is friendly to users. However, this software's running needs enough bandwidth support and requires users' high level computer-using-ability. Mahon et al realize a system supporting BPEL4WS. However, it isn't a piece of cake to study and use BPEL4WS for common users. Yu et al [9] and Baldridge et al [10] have proposed a language based on XML respectively and implemented a Grid Service Environment to support scripting language's execution.

We propose a scripting language easy to study and use, and an architecture to support it's execution. We think that it is feasible that users describe workflow by a simple scripting and it will be interpreted by an interpreter into BPEL4WS, and then executed on GSDT. Our GSDT includes many engineering computing modules having been wrapped up beforehand. Why BPEL4WS is selected as destination language is that it is relatively comprehensive in description of workflow, has good interaction, coordination, concurrency description ability, and has become an actual standard for business workflow description.

However, we still need to do amount of research work to build an easy, safe, convenient, trusty workflow running environment for computing users: first, we need more discussion and learning from computing experts to complement our scripting language and extend our computing service toolkits; secondly, our scripting language description ability is a subset of BPEL4WS and still is in the process of perfection; thirdly, We need to use formal method to strictly, not empirically verify our scripting language's description ability to perfect it with the evolving of BPEL4WS; fourthly, the communication and coordination between our tasks still depend on simple messages and files on storage nodes, namely, we still hasn't implemented true real-time cooperation design; fifthly, presently, we must take proper measures to keep data's secret and secure in addition to existing Grid Security Architecture; sixthly, it is better to provide error-tolerance means for users to write scripting more easily without too much care.

References

1. Chao, K.M., Younas, M., et al.: Analysis of Grid Service Composition with BPEL4WS. AINA, Vol.01, no.1, 18th (2004) 284-289
2. Specification: Business Process Execution Language for Web Services. Version 1.1 (2003) http://www-106.ibm.com/developerworks/library/ws-bpel/
3. Gannon, D.,et al.: Building Grid Portal Applications From a Web Service Component Architecture. In Proc. of the IEEE, Vol.93, No.3 (2005) 551-563
4. Wu, Y.W. et al.: Grid Computing Pool and Its Framework. ICPPW (2003) 271-277
5. Walker, E., Minyard, T.: Orchestrating and Coordinating Scientific Engineering Workflows using Gridshell. IEEE (2004) 270-271
6. Hunt, C.S. et al.: JXPL: An XML-based Scripting Language for Workflow Execution in a Grid Environment", IEEE.2005,pp.345-350
7. Amin, K., et al., "GridAnt: A client-Controllable Grid Workflow System. In Proc. of the 37th Hawaii International Conference on System Sciences (2004) 1-10

8. Mahon, R.: Cooperative Design in Grid Services. In The 8th International Conference on Computer Supported Cooperative Work in Design Proceeding (2003) 406-412
9. Yu, J., Buyya, R.: A Novel Architecture for Realizing Grid Workflow Using Tuple Spaces. In Proc. of the Fifth IEEE/ACM International Workshop on Grid Computing (2004) 1-10
10. Baldridge, K.K. et al.: The Computational Chemistry Prototyping Environment. In Proc. of The IEEE, Vol.93, No.3 (2005) 510-521
11. Li, Y., et al.: A Workflow Services Middleware Model on ShanghaiGrid. IEEE SCC (2004) 366-371

Comments on Order-Based Deadlock Prevention Protocol with Parallel Requests in "A Deadlock and Livelock Free Protocol for Decentralized Internet Resource Co-allocation"

Chuanfu Zhang, Yunsheng Liu, Tong Zhang, Yabing Zha, and Wei Zhang

College of Mechaeronics Engineering and Automation,
National University of Defense, Technology, Changsha 410073, China
zhangchuanfu@yahoo.com.cn libertylys@hotmail.com
{zw, childzt}@hotmail.com, zhayabing@sina.com

Abstract. This paper discusses the order-based deadlock prevention protocol with parallel requests (ODP^3) [1]. From the analysis of theorems about ODP^3, we found that the conclusions of paper [1] are not correct. The ODP^3 method is not free from deadlock and live-lock. An example is given to illustrate our deduction.

Keywords: Co-allocation, Deadlock, Livelock, ODP^3.

1 Introduction

Grid-based applications on Internet frequently require a simultaneous co-allocation of multiple resources for performance computation. A mechanism for co-allocation is needed avoid the deadlock and live-lock, if multiple applications request the common co-allocation at the same time. A deadlock is defined as a undesirable phenomenon that the common recourses are blocked, while multiple applications simultaneously process the allocation within a working group [3][4].

The papers [1][2] presented a protocol of order-based deadlock prevention with parallel requests (ODP^3) for co-allocation of Internet resources. They concluded that applications powered by the implementation of ODP^3 and deployed on Internet are free from deadlock. However, our recent study based on our theoretical deduction indicates that they are not free from deadlock; hence, the conclusion in the papers [1][2] may be incorrect. This paper presents our proof though a rigorous derivation. Section 2 briefly introduces the ODP algorithm and deadlock and livelock.

2 ODP^3 Algorithm and Deadlock and Livelock

The ODP^3 algorithm with relevant definitions and theorems was introduced by [1][2]. For the description of ODP^3, an application on Internet α is considered. Let $g_\alpha = \{g_\alpha^1, g_\alpha^2, \ldots, g_\alpha^{n\alpha}\}$ be the set of states of α which requests co-allocation resources, and $R_\alpha = \{R_1, R_2, \ldots, R_{m\alpha}\}$ the set of resource types defined in g_α, and o the order of each Internet resource.

H.T. Shen et al. (Eds.): APWeb 2006, LNCS 3842, pp. 698–701, 2006.

In the papers [1][2], the resource allocation behavior of α is defined as a finite state machine, M_α, which describes all possible sequences of resource acquisitions. α can fulfill all resource allocation requirement. Each state, s_α^i, $i=0,1,\ldots,L_\alpha$, in M_α represents a state of resource allocation defined by a specific composition of allocated resources, where L_α is the number of states of states of M_α.

Definition 1[1]: Let α be an Internet application. A path of finite length in M_α, $\langle S_\alpha^{i_1},\ldots,S_\alpha^{i_n}\rangle$, such that $0<i_l\le L_\alpha$, $\forall l=1,\ldots n$, is safe, if (i) $S_\alpha^{i_n}\in g_\alpha$, and (ii) $S_\alpha^{i_l}(R_j)\ge S_\alpha^{i_{l+1}}(R_j)$, $\forall l=1,\ldots n-1$, $\forall R_j\in R_\alpha$ such that $o_j\ge\pi_\alpha^{i_l}$, where $\pi_\alpha^{i_l}=\min\{o_k \mid S_\alpha^{i_l}(R_k)>0, R_k\in R_\alpha\}$.

Definition 2[1]: Given Internet application α, its local resource allocation state, $S_\alpha^i\notin g_\alpha$ such that $0<i\le L_\alpha$, is safe if there exists a safe path starting form S_α^i.

Lemma 1[1]: For Internet application α, its local resources allocation state, S_α^i, such that $0<i\le L_\alpha$ and $S_\alpha^i\notin g_\alpha$, is safe if there exists a goal state $S_\alpha^j\in g_\alpha$ such that $S_\alpha^i(R_k)\ge S_\alpha^j(R_k)$, $\forall R_k\in R_\alpha$ satisfying $o_k\ge\pi_\alpha^i$.

Lemma 1 is a criterion to ensure an effective computation with state safety. However, the Lemma 1 may not always be correct. If the set of goal states of α has a single goal state, i.e. $g_\alpha=\{g_\alpha^1\}$, the Lemma 1 holds well. In this case, a resource cannot be allocated unless the co-allocated resources are of the same or higher order. If the set of goal states of α has multiple goal states, i.e. $g_\alpha=\{g_\alpha^1,g_\alpha^2,\ldots\ldots,g_\alpha^{n_\alpha}\}$ and $n_\alpha>1$, the Lemma 1 may not hold correctly. The safety states cannot ensure the resource collocated, unless the co-allocated resources are of same or higher order. Section 3 will explain this case with an example.

ODP[3] utilizes an optimistic approach. It requires application α to start by multicasting parallel requests for all the resources. The associated amount of allocations are defined in $g_\alpha^+=\overset{+}{\cup}_{i=1}^{n\alpha} g_\alpha^i$ [1]. Let Q_α be a multi-set that maintains the co-allocated resource types successfully. Initially the set is empty. After the multicast requests for resources are received, the successfully allocated are temporarily recorded in a multiset T_α. Any goal state in g_α can then be covered by the allocated resources in $Q_\alpha\overset{+}{\cup}T_\alpha$, until the procedure terminates.

Otherwise, ODP[3] makes a progress toward the goal states by retaining some of the allocated resources based on the safety of the state represented by $Q_\alpha\overset{+}{\cup}T_\alpha$. If $Q_\alpha\overset{+}{\cup}T_\alpha$ is safe upon Lemma 1, it is desirable to remian all the resources defined in $Q_\alpha\overset{+}{\cup}T_\alpha$, and sets the application's current resource allocation state Q_α to $Q_\alpha\overset{+}{\cup}T_\alpha$. On the other hand, if $Q_\alpha\overset{+}{\cup}T_\alpha$ is not safe, it is necessary to drop out some of the resources in T_α for safety consideration. Therefore, the objective is to construct the subset Q_α^* of $Q_\alpha\overset{+}{\cup}T_\alpha$ in such a way that Q_α^* is safe and drop out the fewest resources among all the proper subsets of $Q_\alpha \overset{+}{\cup} T_\alpha$. Once Q_α^* is computed, the next step is to cancel all the surplus resources in T_α that are not selected in Q_α^*, and then set Q_α to Q_α^*. Subsequently, the procedure repeats for the remaining resources defined by $g_\alpha^+ \backslash Q_\alpha$, until one of the goal states in g_α is reached.

Theorem 1[1]: Consider Internet application α, which co-allocates resources in ODP^3 algorithm. Let M_α be the finite state machine that represents the resource allocation behavior of α. There is no a cycle existing in M_α. Furthermore, $S_\alpha^i(R_k) \le S_\alpha^j(R_k)$, $\forall R_k \in R_\alpha$, $\forall i, j (i \ne j)$ such that $\langle S_\alpha^i, S_\alpha^j \rangle$ is a direct path in M_α and $o \le i, j \le L_\alpha$.

In paper [1], the proof of Theorem 1 indicates that application α is not allowed to de-allocate resources form Q_α. Only the resources in T_α can be de-allocated from the ODP^3. That means α is allowed to make a transition to the next resources allocation state, only if additional resources are allocated. The result from [1] granted that the resource allocation amount is monotonically increasing.

The conclusion is correct, if each request of resources makes a state transition. The question is what happens if the resources allocation state transit from one to another?

The resource providers are determinants. If the multiset T_α is empty due to two facts that any resources can't be allocated and that the allocated resources are released again due to states safety, the application α will not be allowed perform a transition to the next allocation resources state. The amount of allocation resource increases (but not monotonically). If each request of resource cannot operate the state transition, the deadlock may arise. The main reason is that the safety sates, according to Lemma 1[1], cannot avoid the existence of above case. Therefore, the Theorem 1[1] given in ODP^3 seems reasonable, although it is not correct.

3 An Example of Deadlock in ODP^3

Let us consider an Internet application set that requires co-allocation of resources. If the applications implement ODP^3, the applications are not free from deadlock and livelock arises.

We suppose the Internet applications compete for the 5 different resource types that are geographically distributed. The maximum capacity of each resource type is set to 5. Each application may require up to three different resource types. Each application has two alternative co-allocation schemes. We arbitrarily assume $o_1 > o_2 > o_3 > o_4 > o_5$.

The application set A has six application, $A = \{\alpha_1, \alpha_2, \alpha_3, \alpha_4, \alpha_5, \alpha_6\}$. Each application's goal states can be given as:

$g_{\alpha 1} = \{R_0 + 4R_1 + 3R_3, 3R_1 + 2R_2 + 3R_4\}$, $g_{\alpha 2} = \{R_0 + 3R_2 + 2R_3, 2R_1 + 2R_2 + 3R_4\}$,

$g_{\alpha 3} = \{R_2 + 4R_3 + 3R_4, 2R_0 + 2R_2 + R_4\}$, $g_{\alpha 4} = \{4R_0 + 3R_2 + R_3, R_0 + 4R_1 + R_4\}$,

$g_{\alpha 5} = \{R_0 + 2R_1 + R_3, 2R_1 + R_2 + R_3\}$, $g_{\alpha 6} = \{2R_1 + 2R_2 + 4R_3, 2R_1 + 3R_3 + 2R_4\}$

According the multiset union definition [1], the application's union multiset of their goal states can be computed as

$g^+_{\alpha 1}=\{R_0+4R_1+2R_2+3R_3+3R_4\}$, $g^+_{\alpha 2}=\{R_0+2R_1+3R_2+2R_3+3R_4\}$, $g^+_{\alpha 3}=\{2R_0+2R_2+4R_3+3R_4\}$, $g^+_{\alpha 4}=\{4R_0+4R_1+3R_2+R_3+R_4\}$, $g^+_{\alpha 5}=\{R_0+2R_1+R_2+R_3\}$, $g^+_{\alpha 6}=\{2R_1+2R_2+4R_3+2R_4\}$

The ODP[3] is used in all applications to request and co-allocate the resources. After certain times of resource requests, each application successfully allocates some resources; but not enough to execute on Internet. The application's resource allocation states are as follows: $S_{\alpha 1}=\{R_0\}$, $S_{\alpha 2}=\{2R_1+2R_3\}$, $S_{\alpha 3}=\{2R_2\}$, $S_{\alpha 4}=\{3R_0+R_3\}$, $S_{\alpha 5}=\{R_0\}$, $S_{\alpha 6}=\{2R_1+2R_2\}$

According to Lemma 1[1], we can find all the application's resource allocation states are safe. Unfortunatley, the six applications have deadlock and livelock. After each application requests resource, the resource allocation states do not make a transition, because the temporarily-recorded multiset T_α will be de-allocated to be empty set according to Lemma 1[1]. So each application's resources allocation states keep unchangeable, regardless of the applications requesisition. Moreover, the remainder of resources, $\{R_1+R_2+2R_3+5R_4\}$, are allocated and de-allocated repetitively. Therefore, the livelock is not avoidable.

4 Conclusion

This paper explains why the ODP[3] are not free from deadlock and livelock in resource co-allocation on Internet. It gives a proof that lemma and theorem of paper [1] is not sufficient. Insufficiency may lead to the improper conclusion. From the resource co-allocation simulations, we found that the ODP[3] resource allocation method can not help to improve the performance of resource co-allocation.

References

1. Park, J.,: A Deadlock and Livelock Free Protocol for Decentralized Internet Resource Co-allocation, IEEE Transactions on systems, man and cybernetics –Part A: systems and humans, Vol. 34, No. 1, pp. 123, January (2004)
2. Park, J.: A Scalable Protocol for Deadlock and Livelock Free Co-Allocation of Resources in Internet Computing, Proceedings of the 2003 Symposium on Applications and the Internet (SAINT'03), IEEE Press (2003)
3. Czajkowski, K., Foster, I., and Kesselman, C.: Resource co-allocation in computational grids, 7th IEEE Symposium on High Performance Distributed Computing, pp. 219-228 (1999)
4. Foster, I., Kesselman, C., Lee, C., Lindell, B., Nahrstedt, K., Roy, A. A distributed resource management architecture that support advance reservations and co-allocation, Intl. Workshop on Quality of Service (1999)

Dynamic Workshop Scheduling and Control Based on a Rule-Restrained Colored Petri Net and System Development Adopting Extended B/S/D Mode*

Cao Yan[1], Liu Ning[2], Guo Yanjun[3], Chen Hua[1], and Zhao Rujia[4,5]

[1] Xi'an Institute of Technology, Xi'an, Shaanxi 710032
jantonyz@163.com
[2] China First Heavy Industries, Fularji, Heilongjiang, 161042, P.R. China
[3] Shaanxi Qinchuan Machinery Development Co., Ltd.
[4] Xi'an Jiaotong University, Xi'an, Shaanxi 710049
[5] Jiangsu Teachers University of Technology, Changzhou, Jiangsu 213001, P.R. China

Abstract. Because of the dynamic characteristics of a manufacturing system, long-term production plan and schedule are not feasible, neither is complete analysis of the manufacturing system and process in advance. In the paper, after the gap between theoretic researches and practical applications of workshop scheduling is analyzed, the hierarchical framework of agile manufacturing oriented workshop scheduling and control based on MAS is put forward. According to practical application requirements, traditional Petri net is expanded and RCPN is put forward to model workshop activities. Then, the architecture of workshop scheduling system based on RCPN is presented. Finally, the scheduling system that adopts 3-layer B/S/D mode is developed on Internet/Intranet by using Web database and Java The application of the system developed has been used at machine tool large parts workshop of Shaanxi Qinchuan Machinery Development Co., Ltd and the system has been proved to be effective.

1 Introduction

Workshop scheduling is how to plan and control various production activities in a workshop to fulfill given production tasks under resource and time restriction. Efficient workshop scheduling is a crucial way to increase operation efficiency and management [1-2]. To pursue quality at short time and low cost, it is sound emphasized by manufacturing and management departments. Because of the dynamic characteristics of manufacturing tasks, workshop states and so on of a manufacturing system [3-4], long-term production plan and schedule are not feasible, neither is complete analysis of the manufacturing system and process in advance. In addition, the reciprocity of various manufacturing resources is dynamic and unpredictable. Condequently, almost every manufacturing entity in the manufacturing system has to make its own decision independently. And its decision-making appears particularly important in distributed manufacturing environment. In order to solve the workshop scheduling problem, dynamic workshop scheduling based on MAS [5-7] is adopted in the paper. Thus, the

* The paper is supported by Project 50405029 of National Natural Science Foundation of China.

H.T. Shen et al. (Eds.): APWeb 2006, LNCS 3842, pp. 702–708, 2006.

manufacturing system is divided into cooperative agents that are in communication with each other. As a result, the multi-objective optimization problem of workshop scheduling and control is translated into the problem of competition, cooperation and cooperative resolution among agents.

As a visual and intuitionistic modeling tool for distributed event dynamic system (DEDS), Petri net is widely applied to workshop scheduling of manufacturing systems. Based on the analysis of the theories of workshop scheduling and Petri nets as well as some extended Petri nets, this paper puts forward Rule-restrained Colored Petri Net (RCPN) and provides a set of scheduling rules and decision-making rules. Then, the architecture of workshop scheduling system based on RCPN is presented. Finally, the shop scheduling prototype system based on RCPN is developed for the machine tool large parts workshop of Shaanxi Qinchuan Machinery Development Co., Ltd.

2 Dynamic Workshop Scheduling and Control Framework Based on MAS

According to the analysis of workshop functions, the hierarchical framework of dynamic workshop scheduling and control is divided into four levels, namely production planning, manufacturing task decomposition and assignment, scheduling and control, and resource management, as shown in Fig. 1. The activities on the four levels are executed iteratively and dynamically according to the state changes of a workshop. Its advantages are as follows.

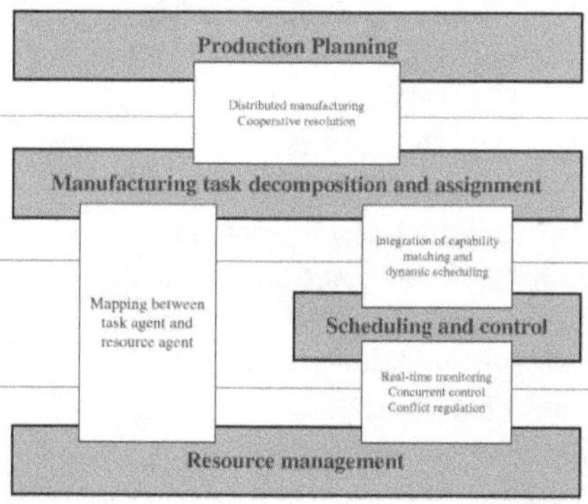

Fig. 1. Dynamic workshop scheduling and control framework

- Based on manufacturing task decomposition and assignment, the mechanisms of cooperative work and decision-making among different levels are established.
- Negotiated bidding approach is introduced to accomplish manufacturing task decomposition and assignment in distributed manufacturing environment.
- Capability matching and dynamic scheduling are integrated to realize dynamic task assignment and control.

- According to manufacturing task demands, agent granularity and MAS model are determined dynamically.
- Dynamic reconfiguration of manufacturing tasks is supported to adapt to the dynamic changes of the manufacturing system.

3 Rule-Restrained Colored Petri Net (RCPN)

Petri net is widely used in manufacturing system modeling and control [8-9]. But there also exist many serious problems when it is applied to complex manufacturing systems because of its inherent characteristics. Therefore, Rule-restrained Colored Petri Net (RCPN) is put forward, as shown in Fig. 2.

RCPN is the extension of traditional Petri net, and is defined as: N=(P, T, F, μ, R). The meaning of P, T, F and μ is the same as that of traditional Petri net. $R=\{r^1,r^2,\ldots\ldots,r^i\}$, r^i (i=1,2,……, n, n is the number of rules). They represent the control, logical, and mathematical constraints that activate corresponding transitions.

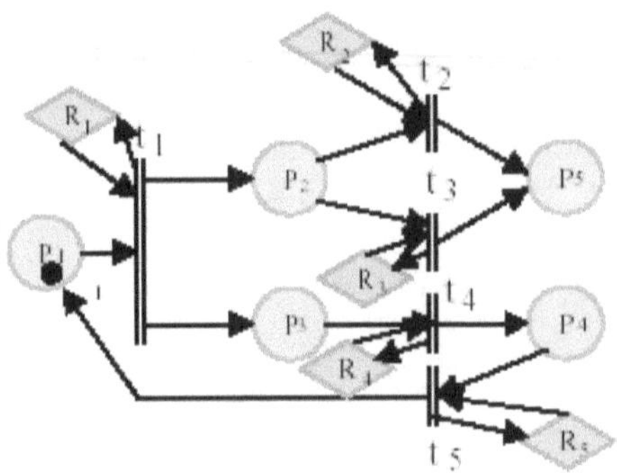

Fig. 2. A Rule-restrained Colored Petri Net

It is due to the introduction of knowledge-based constraint rules that the RCPN model established can be more legible and intuitionistic. What is more important, the number of nodes is reduced and the model is simplified. This facilitates the analysis and computation based on the model. At the same time, the RCPN model becomes more rigorous and compact to some degree and the possibility of deadlock is also reduced. Consequently, the reality, integrality, logicality, and terseness of complex manufacturing system models, especially discrete event dynamic system models, can be improved.

4 RCPN's Decision-Making Rules

RCPN rule library is composed of decision-making rules, knowledge items, and decision-making algorithms that are realized by programs. Dispatches and key workpieces are always of the highest priority. Decision-making rules can be divided into three categories:

- Simple rules are used to make decisions direct based on workpiece data, operation requirements, and equipment parameters, such as shortest machining time, etc.
- Complex rules are formed by the combination of simple rules. They take the form of *rule 1→rule 2→⋯*.
- Heuristic rules are used to deal with complex situations, such as timing scheduling, responding to transition activation, etc.

5 System Modules

According to functional requirements, the system includes main control module, input module, scheduling module, and output module that are integrated into a whole through information share and message mechanism, as shown in Fig. 3.

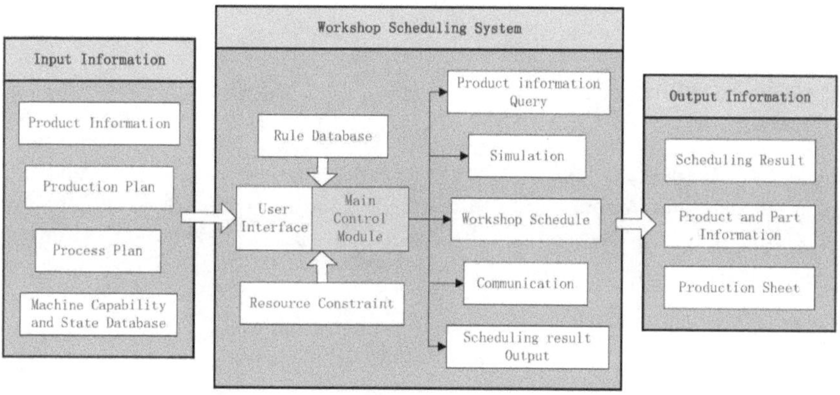

Fig. 3. System modules

6 System Development

6.1 Functional Objectives

The main functional objectives are:

- Support dynamic scheduling to adapt to the changes of manufacturing environment.
- Browse and query workshop production plans, product information, part data, etc.
- Trace the state of production tasks according to workshop production plans.
- Browse the RCPN model of the manufacturing workshop.
- Output scheduling results as Gantt charts.

6.2 System Architecture----Extended B/S/D Mode

The factors affecting system performance are appropriate architecture, self-governed functional modules, extensibility and maintainability. Based on above consideration and existing infrastructure, extended B/S/D mode is adopted [10], as shown in Fig. 4.

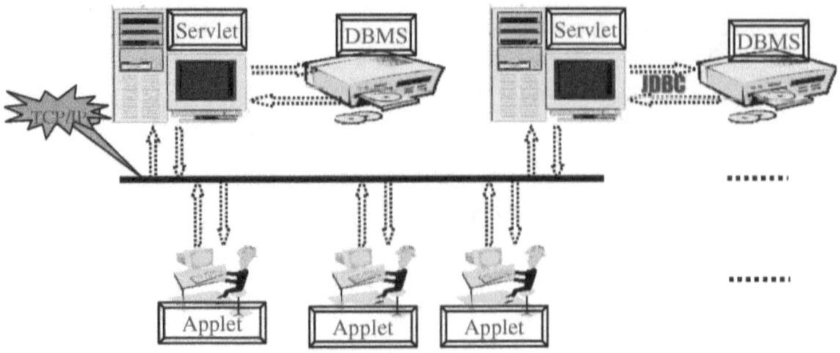

Fig. 4. 3-Layer B/S/D system architecture using Java

Java servlets are used to extend the functions of web server, and Java applets are used to extend the functions of web browser. Workshop scheduling is realized through the communication between the applets and servlets.

6.3 System Workflow

Java applets running at client browser act as the interface between users and the system. Furthermore, they can take on some computation capability. Java servlets mainly receive input data and commands from clients and call corresponding modules to accomplish the commands, such as part data scan, data query, workshop scheduling, etc. In the system, JDBC (Java Database Connection) is chosen to access Web database.

7 Application

The system developed has been used at machine tool large parts workshop of Shaanxi Qinchuan Machinery Development Co., Ltd, the layout of which is shown in Fig. 5.

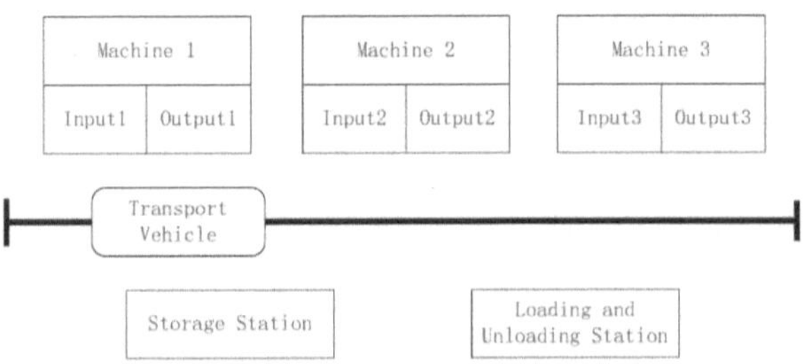

Fig. 5. Workshop layout

After Java API-enabled web server is started, run the browser on a client and browse URL that contains the scheduling system. The main window of RCPN based scheduling system is shown in Fig. 6. Click *Production Plan→Connection* step by step to connect to web database, and then other functions are all set. After input *User*

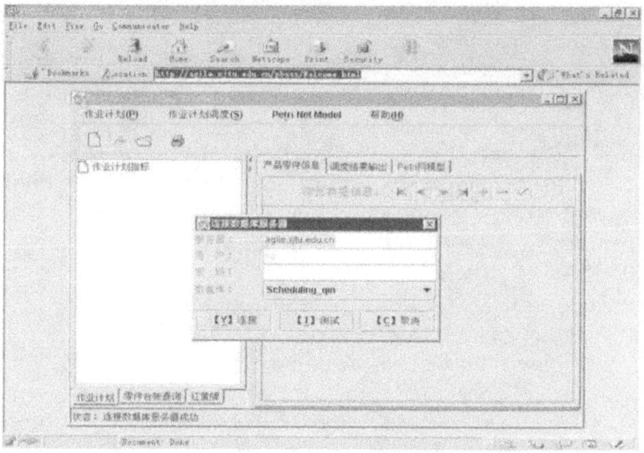

Fig. 6. System main window

and *Password* that is needed to log in web database, choose the corresponding web database where production plans are recorded to accomplish database server connection and system initialization.

After web database server is connected, production plan data can be browsed and queried. Workshop scheduling is divided into two phases. Firstly, preliminary scheduling is carried out to sequence the order by which the workpieces enter into the manufacturing system. This order is a preliminary one. Secondly, according to their manufacturing requirements and equipments' state and capability, re-scheduling is carried out to match the workpieces with corresponding resources of the manufacturing system. Constraints and scheduling rules are applied to the matching procedure. The scheduling results are shown in Gantt charts in detail. If production plans are changed, the same operations can be used to carry out re-scheduling again. The RCPN model can be browsed at any time when the system is running.

8 Conclusions

In the paper, the hierarchical framework of agile manufacturing oriented production scheduling and control based on MAS is put forward. Aiming at the problems of traditional Petri net in modeling manufacturing processes, traditional Petri Net is expanded and RCPN is put forward according to practical requirements. To respond market requirements rapidly, the architecture of workshop scheduling system based on RCPN is presented. And the scheduling system that adopts 3-layer B/S/D pattern is developed on Internet/Intranet by using web database and Java. The application of the system developed has been applied to machine tool large parts workshop of Shaanxi Qinchuan Machinery Development Co., Ltd. And the system has been proved to be effective. According to the application results, other functional modules, such as personal information, financial service (cost and bill, etc.), etc, are under development and will be integrated into the system to improve its capability.

References

1. Wu, S.-Y.D., Richard, A.W.: An Application of Discrete-event Simulation to On-line Control and Scheduling in Flexible Manufacturing. Int. J. Prod. Res. 27(1989) 1603-1623
2. Xiong, R., Wu, C.: Current Status and Developing Trend of Job Shop Scheduling Research. Journal of Tsinghua University (Science and Technology) 38(1998) 55-60
3. Brennan, R.W.: Performance Comparison and Analysis of Reactive and Planning-based Control Architectures for Manufacturing. Robotics and Computer Integrated Manufacturing 16(2000) 191-200
4. Bongaerts, L., Monostori, L., McFarlane, D., Kádár, B.: Hierarchy in Distributed Shop Floor Control. Computers in Industry 43(2000) 123-137
5. Fischer, K.: Agent-based Design of Holonic Manufacturing Systems. Robotics and Autonomous Systems 27(1999) 3-13
6. Cantamessa, M.: Hierarchical and Heterarchical Behaviour in Agent-based Manufacturing Systems. Computers in Indusry 33(1999) 305-316
7. Rabelo, R.J., Camarinha-Matos, L.M., Afsarmanesh, H.: Multi-agent-based Agile Scheduling. Robotics and Autonomous Systems 27(1999) 15-28
8. Zuberek, W.M.: Time Petri Nets in Modeling and Analysis of the Simple Scheduling for Manufacturing Cells. Computers and Mathematics with Applications 37(1999) 191-206
9. Champagnat, R., Esteban, P., Pingaud, H., Valette, R.: Petri Net Based Modeling of Hybrid Systems. Computers in Industry 36(1998) 139-146
10. Wu, P., Chen, W., Li, W.: Java Technology for Application System Development Based on Web. Application Research of Computers 17(2000) 84-86

A Dynamic Web Service Composite Platform Based on QoS of Services*

Lei Yang, Yu Dai, Bin Zhang, and Yan Gao

School of Information and Engineering, Northeastern University, P.R. China 110004
qwe_yanglei@163.com, zhangbin@mail.neu.edu.cn

Abstract. In this paper, a web service composite platform is introduced which aims to compose the services dynamically. And more importantly, in order to get a most qualified composite service, a selection task needs to be done. And after carefully study on the special features of composite service, a relatively new QoS model is proposed in this paper based on which we also give the way of how to use this model to select the most appropriate composite service among several potential composite services.

Keywords: Web services, Web service composition, QoS.

1 Introduction

Web Services, with XML based standards like UDDI [1], WSDL [2] SOAP[3], are touted as tools for universal connectivity and interoperability of applications and services. However, sometimes only a single service can not satisfy user's requirement. Thus, composing available services into a value-added one is needed.

While when discussing web service composition, lots of issues needed to consider. First, the composed one must start from the user's giving condition and end up with implement user's desire effect. Then how to find a series of services which can implement this is an essential problem for the composition. Second, services with same function may be large. Thus, a selection is needed in order to choose the most qualified services for the composition. Then, a selection between these services is needed. Thus, another problem needed to solve is how to establish a selecting criteria-QoS and how to use it to do the selection.

In this paper, a service composite platform is introduced which illustrates the whole life of how to compose a composite service dynamically and for the selection problem, an appropriate QoS model is established which is a revolution to prevailing ones [4-6] and a selection algorithm based on such model is also given.

This paper is organized as follows: section 2 summarizes the related works in this field; then, the service composite platform is introduced in section 3; section 4 introduces how to compose available services, what QoS model is to adopt and how to select the most qualified composite service based on such model; section 5 through experimentation, proves the usefulness of proposed model and selection approach; finally, we summarize the contribution of this paper and our future work.

---

* This work is supported by the National Key Technologies Research and Development programming in the 10th Five-year (2004BA721A05) of PRC.

H.T. Shen et al. (Eds.): APWeb 2006, LNCS 3842, pp. 709 – 716, 2006.

2 Related Works

Some related works [4-6] proposed idea about using QoS to evaluate Web Services. [4] suggested that the evaluating factors of QoS for Web services should include performance, reliability, integrity, accessibility, availability. The QoS template presented in [5], includes cost, time. Jorge Cardoso proposed the factors used in a comprehensive QoS model [6], which include cost, time, reliability and fidelity.

In the proposed QoS model, we not only consider basic QoS factor as [4-6], but also take consideration of relation degree between services. Relation degree between services can be an important factor to evaluate how the compatibility of composite service. Although several QoS models have been proposed recently, how to apply such model into selection is addressed few. The most similar work to us is [4], but because of QoS model it takes not considering relation degree between services, then [4] applies integer programming for selection. In this paper, besides proposing a new QoS model, we also show how to use this model to do the selection.

3 Service Design Oriented Platform

We will discuss the whole lifetime of dynamic composition of Web services and highlight how to use QoS to make the platform generate a qualified service. Architecture of this platform can be seen in Fig. 1.

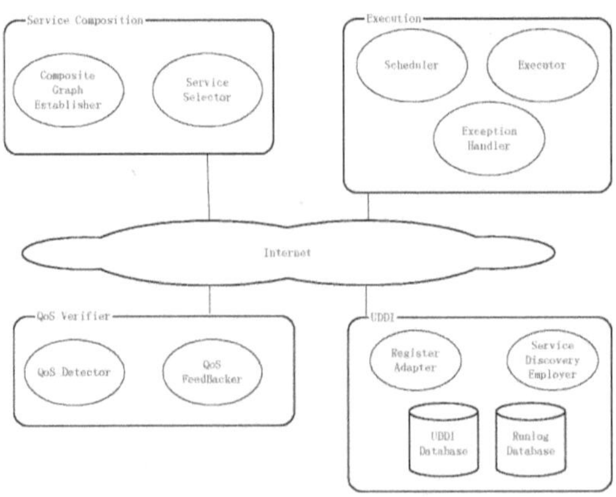

Fig. 1. Architecture of Dynamic Web Services Composite Platform

There are 4 parts: UDDI is a storage of services which is a base for the whole composition; QoS verifier is used to test the QoS of services and returns the results to UDDI; service composition which is a core in the whole life will compose a composite service whose performance is better than others; Execution is responsible to execute composite service. In theses parts, the core one is service composition for that if the establisher can not draw a proper process then the composition is a failure; and if the selector fails to find proper services, then the composition can not execute properly which also is a failure. Thus, here, we will discuss this issue in detail.

4 QoS-Driven Composite Service

4.1 QoS Evaluation Model

4.1.1 Single Path Composite Service and DAG Composite Service

There are two types of composite service: single path one and complex one.

Definition 1: Single Path Composite Service. A single path composite service is one composite service that from the initial node to the final node, there is only one path.

Definition 2: Complex Composite Service. A complex composite service is one composite service that from the initial node to the final node, there are several paths.

A complex service is composed by several single path services. Then, when discussing QoS for composite service, we just mention single path composite service.

4.1.2 QoS Evaluation Model for Single Service

For each single service, we define a QoS evaluation model which follows the traditional QoS evaluation model just as paper [4-6] proposed. In the following a QoS vector of service s is given: $QoS(s)=<Q_{pr}(s), Q_{du}(s), Q_{av}(s), Q_{rat}(s), Q_{rep}(s)>$, where $Q_{pr}(s)$ indicates the fee that a service requester has to pay for invoking the service s, $Q_{du}(s)$ measures the expected delay in seconds between the moment when a request is sent and the moment when the results are received, $Q_{av}(s)$ is the probability that the service s is accessible, $Q_{rat}(s)$ is the probability that a request is correctly responded, and $Q_{rep}(s)$ is a measure of trustworthiness of the service s.

4.1.3 QoS Evaluation Model for Composite Service

We propose a different QoS vector for composite Web Services as followings: $QoS(S)=<Q_{pr}(S), Q_{du}(S), Q_{av}(S), Q_{rat}(S), Q_{rep}(S), Q_{md}(S)>$, Where S is a single path composite service; $Q_{pr}(S)$ to $Q_{rep}(S)$ has the same meaning to QoS of single service s (we summarize them in table 1) and as for $Q_{md}(S)$ we give its definition as follows:

Definition 3: Matching Degree QoS. A matching degree QoS reflects the matching degree between participated services. It can be expressed as follows: $Q_{MD}(S)=< Q_{IO}(S), Q_{ST}(S) >$, where $Q_{IO}(S)$ indicates how the services can be operate properly with each other and $Q_{ST}(S)$ is the statistical relationship between services.

Definition 4: Input/Output Matching Degree. $\forall s_i \in S \wedge s'_{i-1}$ is the set of services which are invoked before s_i, $Q_{IO}(s'_{i-1}\Delta s_i)$ indicates the relation degree of the overall parameters of s'_{i-1} and the input parameters of s_i. We use p to signify the number of parameters of s'_{i-1} and q to signify the number of input parameters of s_i. In the following, we give a formula of $Q_{IO}(s'_{i-1}\Delta s_i)$:

$$\begin{cases} Q_{IO}(s'_{i-1}\Delta s_i)=\left(\sum_{k=1}^{q}\sum_{l=1}^{p}\frac{\mathrm{IO}(s_{i,k}, s_{i-1,l})}{q}\right)\times\left(\sum_{l=1}^{p}\sum_{k=1}^{q}\frac{\mathrm{IO}(s_{i-1,l}, s_{i,k})}{q}\right) \\ \mathrm{IO}(x,y)=\frac{1}{1+\alpha} \end{cases} \quad (1)$$

where, $s_{i-1,l}$ signifies the parameter numbered l in s'_{i-1} and $s_{i,k}$ signifies the input parameter numbered k of s_i. IO(x,y) is the function to calculate the concept matching degree of such two parameters. If parameter x and y is the same semantic concept, then $\alpha=0$; else, α can be a number above 0.

Then the Input/Output parameter matching degree of S can be calculated as (3).

$$Q_{IO} = \sum_i \frac{Q_{IO}(s'_{i-1}\Delta s_i)}{n} \tag{2}$$

where, n is the total number of tasks involved in service S.

Definition 5: Statistical Relation Degree. $\forall s_i \in S \wedge s'_{i-1}$ is the set of services which are invoked before s_i, $Q_{ST}(s'_{i-1}\Delta s_i)$ indicates the statistical relation degree between service of s'_{i-1} and s_i. It can be calculated as follows:

$$\begin{cases} Q_{ST}(s'_{i-1}\Delta s_i) = \prod_p ST(s'_{i-1,p}, s_i) \\ ST(s'_{i-1,p}, s_i) = \dfrac{2}{1+e^{-\gamma}} \end{cases} \tag{3}$$

where γ is the time that service $s'_{i-1,p}$ and s_i are bound together. In fact, γ is obtained from run log database. The more frequently $s'_{i-1,p}$ and s_i are bound together, the higher γ is and also the higher $ST(s'_{i-1}\Delta s_i)$ is. Then S's Q_{ST} can be computed as:

$$Q_{ST}(S) = \frac{\sum_i -\log_2^{Q_{ST}(s'_{i-1}\Delta s_i)}}{n} \tag{4}$$

Table 1. Aggregation Function for computing the basic QoS of composite service S

Criteria	AggregationFunction1	Function Score	AggregationFunction2
Price	$Q_{pr}(S)=\sum Q_{pr}(s_i)$	$Score(Q_{pr}(s_i))=1/Q_{pr}(s_i)$	$Q_{pr}(S)=\sum Score(Q_{pr}(s_i))$
Duration	$Q_{du}(S)=\sum Q_{du}(s_i)$	$Score(Q_{du}(s_i))=1/Q_{du}(s_i)$	$Q_{du}(S)=\sum Score(Q_{du}(s_i))$
Reputation	$Q_{re}(S)=\sum Q_{re}(s_i)$	$Score(Q_{re}(s_i))=Q_{re}(s_i)$	$Q_{re}(S)=\sum Score(Q_{re}(s_i))$
SuccessRate	$Q_{rat}(S)=\prod Q_{rat}(s_i)$	$Score(Q_{rat}(s_i))=\ln(Q_{rat}(s_i))$	$Q_{rat}(S)=\sum Score(Q_{rat}(s_i))$
Availability	$Q_{av}(S)=\prod Q_{av}(s_i)$	$Score(Q_{av}(s_i))=\ln(Q_{av}(s_i))$	$Q_{av}(S)=\sum Score(Q_{av}(s_i))$

In order to use a uniform model to express elements in the QoS vector, we use function Score, which turns each element to a form following the ascent property, and makes the problem a linear one. Table 1 illustrates Score. Then we can use a MCDM [7] technique to give an overall evaluation for S as follows:

$$QoS(S) = \frac{(Q_{pr}(S)*W_{pr} + Q_{du}(S)*W_{du} + Q_{av}(S)*W_{av} + Q_{rat}(S)*W_{rat} + Q_{rep}(S)*W_{rep} + Q_{IO}(S)*W_{IO} + Q_{ST}(S)*W_{ST})}{(W_{pr} + W_{du} + W_{av} + W_{rat} + W_{rep} + W_{IO} + W_{ST})} \tag{5}$$

where W are the *weights* assigned by the users or a system.

After put aggregation function2 and (3)(4) into (5), (5) can be expressed as (6):

$$QoS(S) = \frac{\sum_i \left(\begin{array}{l} Score(Q_{pr}(s_i))*W_{pr} + Score(Q_{du}(s_i))*W_{du} + Score(Q_{av}(s_i))*W_{av} + Score(Q_{rat}(s_i))*W_{rat} \\ + Score(Q_{rep}(s_i))*W_{rep} + \dfrac{Q_{IO}(s'_{i-1}\Delta s_i)*W_{IO} + Q_{ST}(s'_{i-1}\Delta s_i)*W_{ST}}{n} \end{array} \right)}{(W_{pr} + W_{du} + W_{av} + W_{rat} + W_{rep} + W_{IO} + W_{ST})} \tag{6}$$

where n is the total number of tasks involved in service S. The purpose of selection is to find a set of services for S which makes (6) gets the max value.

4.2 Composite Algorithm

4.2.1 Forming Composite Process

Composite service can be formed according to users' requirement. Several approaches [8-10] have been focused on this issue. These approaches ultimately form a composite process where tasks and dependencies between tasks are identified.

A composite process of "Travel Planner" is shown in Fig.2. And such composite services just identify composite process while does not refer to any detail of concrete services. How to map tasks to concrete services, it is a selection which aims to find appropriate service for each task and make the whole composed one have best QoS.

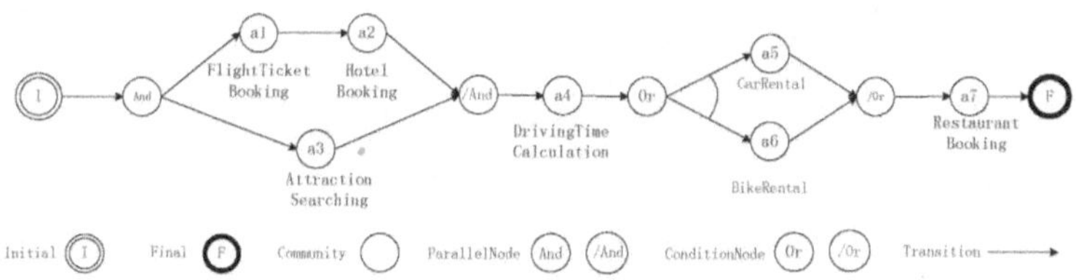

Fig. 2. A composite process of "Travel Planner" expressed by statechart

4.2.2 QoS-Driven Composite Service Selection Algorithm

As discussed above, when doing the selection, a work of transformation from complex composite service to single path one is needed. And any path from the initial node to the final node is a single path composite service. Then for each path we can do the selection. That is to say, for Fig.2, we can do the selection on one of its paths, like Fig.3 shows. We must admit that after the selection, there exists a combination job. For this paper mainly focus on selection, we will not discuss the combination.

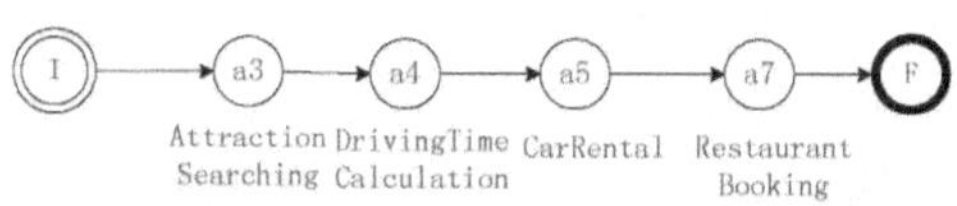

Fig. 3. A Single Path of Fig.2

For each task in Fig.3, there exist a large number of services which can perform desired task. Then a selection job needs to be done which aims to find the most qualified composite service. In order to do this selection, for each service we must calculate the QoS value of it. Then for the whole composite service process, the QoS calculating algorithm can be viewed as Algorithm 1 shows.

```
  Procedure Calulating_QoS;
  Begin
    T=next_Task_of(Initial);
    While T is not Final node do
    begin
        For each service s in T do
          Calculate s's QoS using (2)(4) Table 1;
          Depose next Task;
    End;
End;
```

Algorithm 1

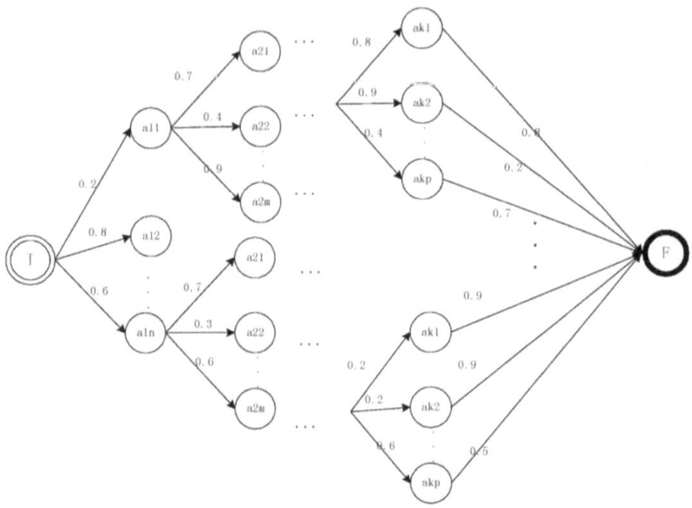

Fig. 4. Service Graph after Calculated QoS

Then using Algorithm 1, for each service, the needed QoS can be calculated which ultimately forms a graph as Fig.4 which is a weighted graph. The weight from $a_{i,k}$ to $a_{i+1,l}$ signifies the QoS values calculated by Algorithm 1.

Then, the selection is a multistage decision-making problem where for each task find a service to make composite service *S* have most satisfied QoS. Dynamic Programming Algorithm can be used to solve such problem as Algorithm 2 shows.

```
procedure DynamicProgramming;
Begin
 F_max[E]:=0;
    for i:=number of service tasks is S downto 1 do
        for each service u • task i do
        Begin
          F_i[u]:=0;
          for each service v • task i+1 • v is linked with u do
          if F_i[u]<weight(u•v)+F_i+1[v] then
            F_i[u]:=w(u, v)+F_i+1[v];
        End;
 output F_1[I];
End;
```

Algorithm 2

5 Experimentation

The experiments are run with a PC of Intel PentiumIV 2.4G and 1GB RAM. The operation system is WinServer 2000. And the algorithms involved in are written by Java. Because there is limited number of Web services in hand of us, we simulated data of services and relation degree to be samples.

We do the experimentation, where only one Input/Output relation degree is considered in order to testify how the quality of composite service changed and how the interoperability of the composite service is. The experimentation result is shown in Table 2. The interoperability can be calculated by (2).

From the results, we can know that with the increase of weight of IO, the interoperability of composite services based on proposed QoS will be greater which indicates the better performance of the composite service. And when the weight reaches a value, the interoperability remains the same. While if only taking account of non-relation QoS, the interoperability cannot be assured.

Table 2. Comparison of Interoperability of Composite Service between Two QoS Model

W_{pr}	W_{du}	W_{re}	W_{av}	W_{ST}	W_{IO}	InterOperability of Composite Services Selected Based on Proposed QoS	InterOperability of Composite Services Selected Based on non Relation QoS [4-6]
0.1	0.1	0.1	0.1	0	0	0.377	0.377
0.1	0.1	0.1	0.1	0	0.1	0.412	0.377
0.1	0.1	0.1	0.1	0	0.2	0.659	0.377
0.1	0.1	0.1	0.1	0	0.3	0.887	0.377
0.1	0.1	0.1	0.1	0	0.4	0.913	0.377
0.1	0.1	0.1	0.1	0	0.5	0.913	0.377
0.1	0.1	0.1	0.1	0	0.6	0.933	0.377
0.1	0.1	0.1	0.1	0	0.7	0.933	0.377
0.1	0.1	0.1	0.1	0	0.8	0.933	0.377
0.1	0.1	0.1	0.1	0	0.9	0.933	0.377
0.1	0.1	0.1	0.1	0	1	0.933	0.377

6 Conclusions

In summary, we give a service oriented design platform in which we discuss whole life a composite service. In order to get a most qualified composite service, QoS has been used through out the composition. The QoS model we proposed, compared with current popular QoS ones, takes account of matching degree in order to find services which have best operability. Also, we put such model into composition reality and show how to use dynamic programming algorithm to solve it. Finally, we envision the future work of us: Optimize the QoS evaluation model; Study on a new approach to do the global optimization.

References

1. IBM Corp., Microsoft Corp., UDDI Technical White Paper. *http:// www.uddi.org* (2000)
2. Christensen. E., Curbera. F., Meredith, G.: Web Services Description Language (WSDL) 1.1. http://www.w3.org/TR/2001/NOTE-wsdl-20010315 (2001)
3. Box. D., Ehnebuske, D., Layman, A., Mendelsohn, N.: Simple Object Access Protocol (SOAP) 1.1. *http://www.w3.org/TR/2000/NOTE-SOAP-20000508* (2001)
4. Liangzhao, Z., Boualem, B.: QoS-Aware Middleware for Web Services Composition. *IEEE Transactions on Software Engineering*, No.5, May (2004) 311-327

5. Fengjin, W., Zhoufeng, Z.: A Dynamic Matching and Binding Mechanism for Business Services Integration. *In Proc. of the EDCIS 2002,* September (2002) 17-20
6. Cardoso, J., Bussler, C.: Semantic Web Services and Processes: Semantic Composition and Quality of Service. *On the Move to Meaningful Internet Computing and Ubiquitous Computer 2002*, Irvine CA (2002).
7. H.C.-L and Yoon K.. Multiple Criteria Decision Making. *Lecture Notes in Economics and Mathematical Systems*. Springer-Verlag (1981)
8. Drew, M.: Estimated-regression Planning for Interactions with Web Services. *In Pro. of the 6th International Conference on AI Planning and Scheduling*, Toulouse, France, 2002.
9. Brahim M. Athman B. and Ahmed K. E. Composing web services on the semantic web. *The VLDB Journal*, 12(4), November (2003)
10. Dan,. W., Evren, S., James, H., Dana, N. and Bijan, P.: Automatic Web Services Composition Using Shop2. *In workshop on planning for web services*, Trento, Italy, June (2003)

Modeling Fetch-at-Most-Once Behavior in Peer-to-Peer File-Sharing Systems

Ziqian Liu and Changjia Chen

School of Electronics and Information Engineering, Beijing Jiaotong University, Shangyuancun, Haidian District, Beijing 100044, China
liu_ziqian@yahoo.com.cn, changjiachen@sina.com

Abstract. Recent measurement studies show that the object popularity distribution in Kazaa file sharing systems deviates significantly from the Zipf distribution which is commonly seen for the World Wide Web. We measure a real BitTorrent network and we figure its object popularity distribution, which also shows, on a log-log scale, a non-Zipf curve with flattened head. The fetch-at-most-once behavior of peer-to-peer (P2P) client is responsible for such a non-Zipf distribution and we propose two mathematical models to describe this. The models are based on different probability assumptions, though both indicate flatter heads in object popularity distribution curves than Zipf would predict. Our models provide theoretic tools to analyze differences between P2P file-sharing system and Web systems.

1 Introduction

Peer-to-peer (P2P) file-sharing systems have been developing dramatically in recent years and have evolved into the most popular applications in the terms of user numbers and generated traffic as well. The fact is that Internet has witnessed a dramatic shrift of its traffic from the http traffic to the multi-media traffic caused by P2P file-sharing applications [1-4].

When comparing P2P file-sharing systems with the Web-based content distribution systems, three aspects should be considered:

1. Web-based systems adopt the client-server mode. Web servers are responsible for publishing contents. In a P2P-based system, each client can be viewed as a server and a client at the same time, i.e., the client shares what it has with other clients; meanwhile, it gets resources from other clients.
2. Typical Web contents are small size of HTML text pages and images at about several KBs, while P2P systems are especially used for delivering large files from tens of MBs up to GBs, which are usually audios/videos and large software.
3. Authors in [3] point out the fact that files, or the so-called objects, shared in P2P systems are *immutable*, and most of the objects are fetched at most once per client; however, Web pages are *mutable* and can be fetched thousands of times per client. Indeed, you usually download the same movie only once but you may check the same website (e.g., Google) thousands of times.

Our work is enlightened and motivated by [3] based on the third point listed above. In [3], the authors point out the particular *fetch-at-most-once* user behavior in P2P

H.T. Shen et al. (Eds.): APWeb 2006, LNCS 3842, pp. 717 – 724, 2006.

file-sharing systems, and they propose a *simulation model* to demonstrate that it is just the fetch-at-most-once that causes the popularity distribution of P2P objects deviates substantially from the Zipf distribution which is commonly seen for the Web. However, they did not give any *mathematical analysis* to clarify why it is so. We want to take a further step here.

The main contribution of this paper is the proposal of two probability models to show how the fetch-at-most-once behavior of P2P client impacts the object popularity distribution in P2P systems. The models provide succinct representations to describe the fetch-at-most-once phenomenon, and the models help to better understand the difference in user behavior between P2P systems and Web systems. Besides, we measure a real BitTorrent network and obtain its object popularity distribution which is very similar to that of Kazaa in [3].

The paper is organized as follows. In Section 2, we give the BitTorrent object popularity distribution by real measurement data to see how the fetch-at-most-once behavior impacts the popularity distribution curves. In Section 3, we propose our models to mathematically represent a client's fetch-at-most-once process. We list related work in Section 4 and conclude in Section 5.

2 Object Popularity Distribution

It has been shown that the Web demonstrates quite a number of Zipf distributions [5,6,7,8]. The Zipf property of Web access patterns exhibits such a fact that a very few of objects are extremely popular, while there is a long tail of unpopular objects. Specifically, the popularity of the ith-most popular object is proportional to $i^{-\alpha}$, where α is the Zipf exponent. Obviously when plotted on a log-log scale, Zipf distribution should show linear. In contrast, a 2002-year measurement studies [3] of the well-known P2P system, Kazaa [9], show that the object popularity distribution is not Zipf but a curve with much flatter heads than Zip would predict on a log-log scale.

Today, BitTorrent (BT) [10] has surpassed Kazza and evolved into the most popular P2P network [4]. To our best knowledge, no one has ever studied the object popularity distribution in BT networks. We believe that the fetch-at-most-once behavior still holds for BT clients, and we implement a measurement to obtain the object popularity distribution in BT systems. In our university, we have a campus BT network. We collect and record, from March 23 to April 3 2005, a set of movie-fetching data from this P2P network. Taking the download frequency of each movie by different clients as a metric of the movie's popularity, we get the popularity distribution shown in Fig. 1.

From Fig.1 (b), we see that the BT object popularity curve has an obviously *flatter head* than the Zipf-fit curve, indicating that the most popular movies are significantly less popular than Zipf would predict. This observation is very similar to what was found in Kazaa systems in [3]. In contrast, WWW object popularity curves usually do not have such an obvious flattened region, though sometimes they may have a slightly flattened heads because of the Web proxy cache [5,8]. Fetch-at-most-once behavior of P2P clients is shown *by simulation* to be the cause of such a flattened head in [3], but no mathematical explanations are provided. In the next section, we will propose probability models to describe this.

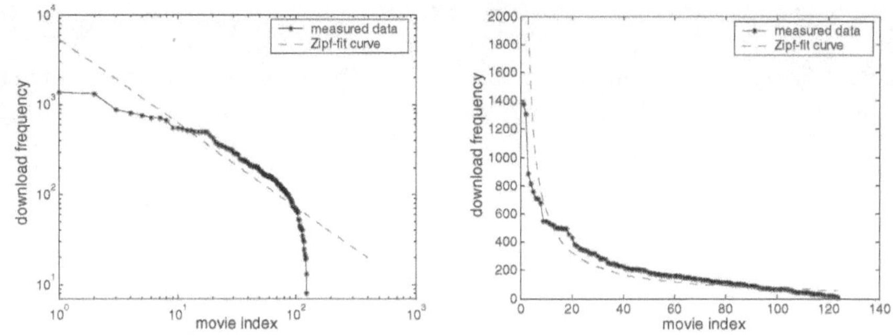

(a) (b)

Fig. 1. The movie popularity distribution of our campus BitTorrent network from March 23 to April 3, 2005, along with the Zipf curve fit with Zipf exponent $\alpha = 0.93$. (a) linear scale. (b) log-log scale.

3 Models

In this section, we propose two probability models, namely the *Rescaling Model* and the *Phase-Type Model*, to give mathematical analysis of the fetch-at-most-once behavior per client. Both models have a common hypothesis, i.e., the underlying popularity of objects in the file-sharing systems is driven by Zipf's law, even though the observed object popularity distribution becomes non-Zipf because of the fetch-at-most-once clients. This hypothesis is the same as in [3]. However, the two models have different probability assumptions on the objects' popularity variation when one of the objects is fetched out from the candidate object set. Our models focus on how a fetch-at-most-once client will impact the original underlying Zipf curves, and both models indicate flatter heads of object popularity curves (log-log plots) in contrast with Zipf curves.

3.1 Rescaling Model

Remember a client only request the same object once (in this paper, to be requested means the same as to be fetched, we just use these two words interchangeably.). So in this model, we assume that the subsequent requests from the client follow the distribution obtained by removing already fetched objects from the candidate object set and rescaling so the total probability is 1.0. Specifically, assume there are I candidate objects to be fetched in the system, and they are ranked by the underlying popularity, and so they follow Zipf(α), i.e., the probability of object i to be fetched is $P_i \sim i^{-\alpha}$. After object i has been requested, the probability of the rest objects (i.e. object j, $j = 1, \ldots, I$ and $j \neq i$) to be fetched is changed to be

$$P_j' = \frac{P_j}{1 - P_i}, \qquad j = 1, \ldots, I \text{ and } j \neq i \tag{1}$$

Still, we have $\sum_{j \neq i} P_j' = \sum_{j \neq i} P_j / (1 - P_i) = (1 - P_i)/(1 - P_i) = 1$. Under such an assumption, given two previously unfetched objects, the ratio of the probabilities that the client will fetch these objects next is identical to their ratio in the original Zipf distribution.

Apparently, when the client fetches object i in his first request, it will follow the Zipf distribution: $P_i^{(1)} = P_i \sim i^{-\alpha}$. When the client fetches object i in his second request, which means before fetching object i, the client already fetches object j_1, $j_1 \neq i$, in his first request. Then the probability of fetching object i in his second request is

$$P_i^{(2)} = \phi_2 \sum_{j_1 \neq i} P_{j_1} \frac{P_i}{1-P_{j_1}}, \quad i = 1,\ldots,I$$

where ϕ_2 is the normalization factor to make sure that $\Sigma_i P_i^{(2)} = 1$, and $\phi_2 = (\Sigma_i \Sigma_{j_1 \neq i} P_{j_1}(P_i/(1-P_{j_1})))^{-1}$.

If the client fetches object j_1 and j_2, $j_1 \neq j_2$, in turn in his first two requests, , then the probability for the left object i, $i \neq j_1 \neq j_2$, to be fetched subsequently is

$$P_i'' = \frac{\dfrac{P_i}{1-P_{j_1}}}{1-\dfrac{P_{j_2}}{1-P_{j_1}}} = \frac{P_i}{1-P_{j_1}-P_{j_2}}$$

Hence, the probability of fetching object i in the third request is

$$P_i^{(3)} = \phi_3 \sum_{j_1 \neq i} \sum_{j_2 \neq j_1 \neq i} P_{j_1} \frac{P_{j_2}}{1-P_{j_1}} \frac{P_i}{1-P_{j_1}-P_{j_2}}, \quad i = 1,\ldots,I$$

Deducing by analogy, we obtain the probability of fetching object i in the kth request:

$$P_i^{(k)} = \phi_k \sum_{j_1 \neq i} \cdots \sum_{j_{k-1} \neq \cdots \neq j_2 \neq j_1 \neq i} \frac{P_{j_1} P_{j_2} \cdots P_{j_{k-1}}}{(1-P_{j_1})(1-P_{j_1}-P_{j_2})\cdots(1-P_{j_1}-P_{j_2}-\cdots-P_{j_{k-1}})} P_i, \quad k \geq 2, i = 1,\ldots,I \quad (2)$$

With Equation (2), we can examine how the client's fetch-at-most-once behavior impacts the underlying Zipf curves of the object popularity distribution. We plot in Fig. 2 the object popularity distribution curves with different request time k. We can see

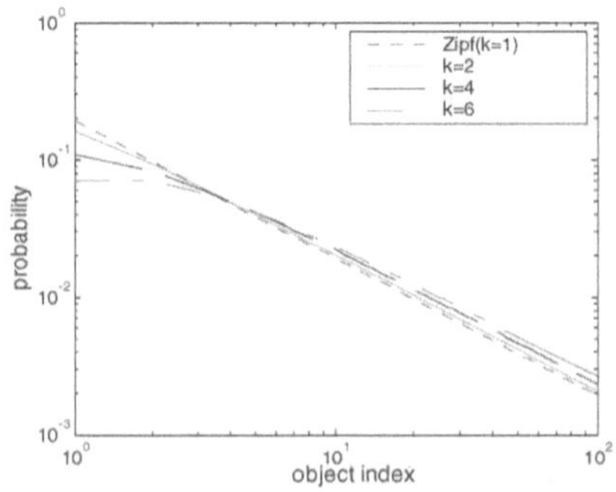

Fig. 2. Object popularity curves of different request time k computed by Rescaling Model with 100 candidate objects. The *dotted line* is the underlying Zipf popularity distribution, implying k=1. The *solid line*, the *dashed line* and the *dash-dotted line* correspond to k=2,4,6 respectively.

that the fetch-at-most-once behavior of the client leads to the most popular objects to be less popular than Zipf would predict, which is similar to what we have see in our real data set (Fig.1(b)) and in [3]. In addition, as the request times k increase, the head of the probability curve becomes flatter and flatter.

3.2 Phase-Type Model

In the above rescaling model, *all* the probabilities of the subsequent requests from the same client will be changed no matter which object has been fetched. However, another reasonable hypothesis is that only *part of* the probabilities of the subsequent requests will be affected by the previous fetch. Specifically, when object i (here i is also the rank of the object) is fetched out from the candidate object set, the probabilities of the subsequent requests for the objects whose ranks are higher than i remain the same; for those objects whose ranks are lower than i, they just upgrade their ranks for one position, and the probabilities correspondingly change to what they are at the new ranks. Equation (3) gives the mathematical expression, where the smaller the subscript j is, the higher the rank is.

$$P_j' = \begin{cases} P_j, & \text{for } j < i \\ P_{j-1}, & \text{for } j > i \end{cases} \tag{3}$$

The above hypothesis maintains the original sequence of object popularity, i.e., the originally higher (lower)-ranked objects still have higher (lower) probabilities after other objects being requested. Although it seems to be unfair in that the probabilities of the subsequent requests for those objects ranked higher than i will not change but those ranked lower than i will increase their absolute probabilities to be requested subsequently. However, given a large number of candidate objects, such a probability increase can be very limited so that the unfairness can be neglected. Under such a hypothesis, the whole fetching process of a client until he gets object i can be modeled by a discrete phase-type (PH) distribution [11]. The state transition diagram is given in Fig. 3. It is an $(i+1)$-state discrete Markov chain, among which states $\{1, 2, \dots, i\}$ are transition states, and state $i+1$ is the absorbing state representing that object i is fetched finally by the client.

We take transition state 1 as an example to explain how this diagram works: when a client start to fetch objects (first request) in the system, he starts at state 1; if object i is fetched right at this request (with a probability $P(i)$), the Markov chain enters into absorbing state $i+1$; otherwise either (1) the rank of the fetched object is lower than i (i.e., $j>i$, which happens with probability $P(j>i)$), and the Markov chain stays at state 1, or (2) the rank of the fetched object is higher than i (i.e., $j<i$), the Markov chain enters into state 2, which happens with probability $P(j<i)$. An extreme instance happens when the client has fetched i-1 times, and those i-1 objects are all higher-ranked than object i, the Markov chain enters into state i. Now object i has upgraded its rank for i-1 positions and becomes highest-ranked, namely rank 1, in candidate object set, which indicates the probability of object i being fetched in the subsequent request is changes to be P_1. Then, in the upcoming request, either object i is fetched with probability P_1 and the Markov chain enters into the absorbing state or the Markov chain stays at state i with probability $P(j>1)$.

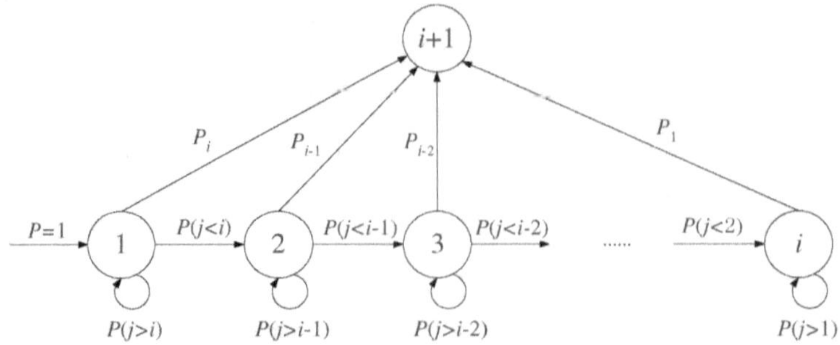

Fig. 3. Discrete PH distribution of the fetching process of a client

The transition probability matrix $\boldsymbol{P}$ of the Markov chain can be written as

$$\boldsymbol{P} = \begin{bmatrix} \boldsymbol{T} & \boldsymbol{T}^0 \\ \boldsymbol{0} & 1 \end{bmatrix} \tag{4}$$

where $\boldsymbol{T}$ is a substochastic matrix [11], such that $\boldsymbol{I}$-$\boldsymbol{T}$ is nonsingular, and it records the one-step transition probabilities between all the transition states; $\boldsymbol{T}^0$ records the transition probabilities from all the transition states to the absorbing state. They can be expressed respectively as

$$\boldsymbol{T} = \begin{bmatrix} P(j>i) & P(j<i) & & & & \boldsymbol{0} & \\ & P(j>i-1) & P(j<i-1) & & & & \\ & & P(j>i-2) & P(j<i-2) & & & \\ & & & \ddots & & & \\ & \boldsymbol{0} & & & & P(j>2) & P(j<2) \\ & & & & & & P(j>1) \end{bmatrix}, \quad \boldsymbol{T}^0 = \begin{bmatrix} P_i \\ P_{i-1} \\ P_{i-2} \\ \vdots \\ P_2 \\ P_1 \end{bmatrix}$$

The transition times k for the Markov chain to enter the absorbing state, namely the total number of request times for the client to at last fetch object i, obey the PH distribution, and the probability density of phase type is:

$$P_i^{(k)} = \boldsymbol{\alpha} \boldsymbol{T}^{k-1} \boldsymbol{T}^0, \quad k \geq 1, i = 1, \ldots, I \tag{5}$$

where $\boldsymbol{\alpha} = \underbrace{(1\ 0\ \ldots\ 0)}_{i}$ is the initial probability vector, and $\alpha_n, n = 1, \ldots, i$ specifies the initial probability for the Markov chain to start transition from state n. The corresponding probability generating function is $f(z) = z\boldsymbol{\alpha}(\boldsymbol{I} - z\boldsymbol{T})^{-1}\boldsymbol{T}^0$.

With Equation (5), we can examine how the client's fetch-at-most-once behavior impacts the underlying Zipf curves of the object popularity distribution. Fig. 4 plots the results computed by Equation (5). It is clear that the heads of the object population distribution curve becomes flatter as k increases, which is similar to Fig. 2.

Both the Rescaling Model and the PH Model show that the fetch-at-most-once user behavior will change the underlying Zipf distribution. The fact is that not all the P2P users will fetch the most popular objects in their very first requests, which will decrease

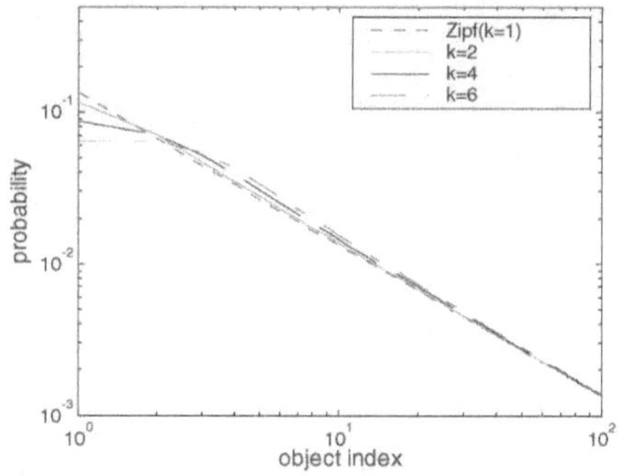

Fig. 4. Object popularity curves of different request time *k* computed by PH Model with 1000 candidate objects. Only the top 100 objects are shown here for clarity. The *dotted line* is the underlying Zipf object popularity distribution, implying *k*=1. The *solid line*, the *dashed line* and the *dash-dotted* line correspond to *k*=2, 4, 6 respectively.

the probabilities (lower than Zipf probabilities) for these users to fetch the most popular objects in their subsequent requests. Thus the popularities of these most popular objects are lower than Zipf would predict. The law of large numbers also ensures this. In contrast, the "fetch-repeatedly" behavior of Web users will not impact the underlying Zipf distribution, so the object popularity distribution fits Zipf well.

4 Related Work

Much has been studied on Zipf distributions in the Web [5,6,7,8]. Some studies [5,8] have shown that the use of Web proxy caches will lead a Zipf load to be a non-Zipf popularity distribution with a flattened head. Comparing with the Web popularity distribution which has been extensively studied, the relevant research in P2P networks has been very limited. Gummadi et al. [3] observed non-Zipf property in Kazaa object popularity distribution, and they also revisited and showed that the data set from a video rental store [12], which had been said to be Zipf, is non-Zip. [3] pointed out that the client's fetch-at-most-once behavior, distinct from the "fetch-repeatedly" behavior of Web users, is the cause of the non-Zipf property. They proposed a simulation model to prove their statements.

5 Conclusion

We measured a real BitTorrent network, from which we obtained its object popularity distribution. Although BitTorrent is a different P2P application to Kazaa, the client's fetch-at-most-once behavior is the same. We see the measured object popularity distribution is obviously different from a Zipf curve in that the most popular objects are significantly less popular than Zipf would predict. We mathematically modeled a client's fetch-at-most-once behavior based on two different probability hypotheses, namely the Rescale Model and the PH model. Both models demonstrate non-Zipf object popularity distribution curves with flattened heads in log-log plots. In the future, we plan to consider the updates of the P2P objects into our models because we are thinking that the comparatively shorter lifetime of a P2P file than a Web site will be another reason that causes the P2P object popularity distribution to be non-Zipf.

Acknowledgments. We thank Yongxiang Zhao for discussion on PH distribution. This work was supported by the National Natural Science Foundation of China (NSFC) grant 60132030, 60202001.

References

1. Plonka, D.: Napster Traffic Measurement, March 2000. Available at http://net.doit. wisc. edu/data/Napster, March (2000)
2. Saroiu, S., Gummadi K. P., Dunn R. J., Gribble S. D., Levy H. M.: An Analysis of Internet Content Delivery Systems. In OSDI (2002)
3. Gummadi, K. P., Dunn, R. J., Saroiu S., Gribble, S. D., Levy H. M., Zahorjari J.: Measurement, Modeling, and Analysis of a Peer-to-Peer File-Sharing Workload. In SOSP'03 (2003)
4. Karagiannis, T., Broido A., Brownlee, N., Claffy, K.C, Faloutsos M.: Is p2p dying or just hiding? In Globecom (2004)
5. Breslau, L., Cao, P., Fan, L., Phillips, G., Shenker S.: Web Caching and Zipf-like Distributions: Evidence and implications. In Proc. of IEEE INFOCOM (1999)
6. Gadde S., Chase J., and Rabinovich M.: Web Caching and Content Distribution: A view from the interior. In Proc. of the 5th International Web Caching and Content Delivery Workshop, May (2000)
7. Padmanabhan V. N. and Qiu L.: The Content and Access Dynamics of a Busy Web site: Findings and Implications. In Proc. of ACM SIGCOMM (2000)
8. Doyle, R. P., Chase, J. S., Gadde, S., Vahdat A. M.: The Trickle-down Effect: Web Caching and Server Request Distribution. In Proceedings of the Sixth International Workshop on Web Caching and Content Delivery (2000)
9. Kazaa. http://www.kazaa.com
10. Cohen, B.: Incentives Build Robustness in Bittorrent. In Workshop on Economics of Peer-to-Peer System. Berkeley, USA, May (2003) http://www.bittorrent.com/
11. Neuts, M. F.: Matrix-geometric Solutions in Stochastic Models: An Algorithmic Approach. The Johns Hopkins University Press (1981)
12. Video Store Magazine, Published by Avanstar Communications, March (2000) http://www.videostoremag.com.

Application of a Modified Fuzzy ART Network to User Classification for Internet Content Provider

Yukun Cao, Zhengyu Zhu, and Chengliang Wang

Department of Computer Science, Chongqing University,
Chongqing 400044, China
marilyn_cao@163.com

Abstract. Internet has entered the age led by ICP (Internet Content Provider). Helping users to locate relevant information in an efficient manner is very important both to users and to ICP services. This paper presents a new approach that employs a modified fuzzy ART network to group users dynamically based on their Web access patterns. Such a user clustering method should be performed prior to ICPs as the basis to provide personalized service. The experimental results of this clustering technique show the promise of our system.

1 Introduction

With the advent of the Internet and the Web, the amount of information available grows daily. Internet has entered the age led by ICP (internet content provider), which is defined to highly depend on creativity, having enthusiasm and technological capacity, and fast bandwidth as well. ICPs can implement online service; hence fostering e-business. However, having too much information at one's fingertips does not always guarantee high quality information. One solution is an individual's recommendation that helps users to find the information they would interest in by producing a list of recommended information for each user. However, with a great number of users, how it is impossible for ICPs identify their interests; unless to build a customer Internet service. In such custom-oriented service system, user classification is one of the most important entities.

We employ a modified fuzzy ART system that dynamically groups users according to their Web access and behaviors. The remainder of the paper is organized as follows. In Section 2, the framework to automatically extract user preference and recommend personalized information is expatiated in detail. Implementation issues and the results of empirical studies are presented in Section 3, followed by a conclusion section.

2 A User Cluster Framework

In this section, an on-line user cluster framework is presented, which is performed as prior to an Internet bookstore in our experiment. The framework includes three modules: user behavior recording, user profile generating and user grouping.

H.T. Shen et al. (Eds.): APWeb 2006, LNCS 3842, pp. 725 – 732, 2006.

2.1 User Behavior Recording

Most personalization systems gather user preference through asking visitors a series of questions or needing visitors rating those browsed web pages. Although relevance feedback obtained directly from users may make sense, it is troublesome to users and seldom done. In the paper, we present a user behavior recording module to collect the training data without user intervention through tracking the users behavior on a e-commerce web site. The user behavior includes the browsing time, the view frequency, saving, booking, clicking hyperlinks, scrolling and so on.

According to some relate works, visiting duration of a product pages or images is a good candidate to measure the preference. Hence, in our work, each product page or image, whose visiting time is longer than a preset threshold (e.g. 30 seconds), is analyzed and rated. Periodically (e.g. every day), the module analyzes the activities of the previous period, whose algorithm is shown as follows:

```
BEGIN
If (page category Pi doesn't exist in user log file)
{favorite(Pi)=0;}
For each page a user browsed in page category Pi
  { if (page browsing time) > threshold
      { switch (happened operation)
          { case  (saving, booking operation happened):
                    favorite(Pi)= favorite(Pi)+0.03;break;
            case  (page-view frequency>threshold):
                    favorite(Pi)= favorite(Pi)+0.02;break;
            case  (clicking, scrolling operation hap-
pened):
                    favorite(Pi)= favorite(Pi)+0.01;break; }
      }
  }
updating favorite(Pi) in User Log file;
END
```

where the function *favorite*(P_i) measures the favorite degree of a certain page category in a ICP web site, and the record in user log file is shown as follows: *page-id, category, favorite*. The *category* element is the category path of a resource, what is a path from the root to the assigned category according the hierarchical structure of Internet bookstore. For example, in a Internet bookstore, "JavaBean" category is a subclass of "Java" category, "Java" category is a subclass of "Programming" category, and "Programming" category is a subclass of "Computer & Internet" category, then the category path of the pages or images belonging to "JavaBean" is "/JavaBean/Java/Programming/Computer&Internet".

2.2 User Profile Generate (Generator)

In this approach, we employ a tree-structured scheme to represent user profile, with which users specify their preference. Generator could organize user preference in a hierarchical structure according the result of Recorder and adjust the structure to the changes of user interests. User profile is a category hierarchy where each category represents the knowledge of a domain of user interests, which could easily and precisely express user's preference. The profile enhances the semantic of user interests and is much closer to a human conception. The logical structure of the preference tree is shown as follows:

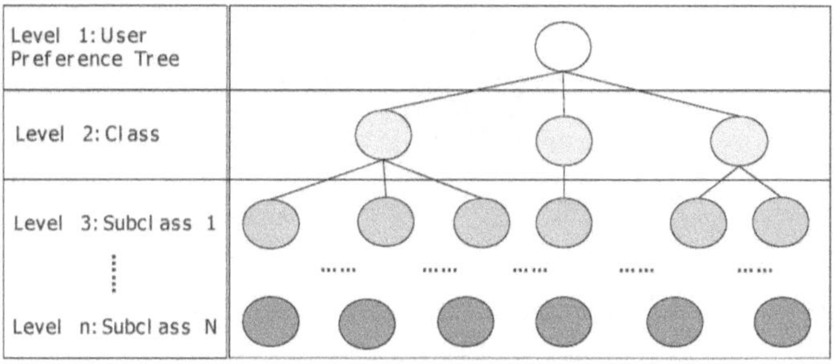

Fig. 1. The logical structure of user profile

User profile is established according the hierarchical structure of a certain e-commerce web site. Each node in the tree, representing a category might be interested in, is described by an energy value E_i what indicates the favorableness of a page category. E_i controls the life cycle of a category in a profile. The energy increases when users show interest in the page category, and it decreases for a constant value for a period of time. Relatively, categories that receive few interest will be abstracted gradually and finally die out. Based on the energy values of categories, the structure of user profile can be modulated as users interests change. The algorithm is shown as follows:

```
  BEGIN
  for each (page cagetory Pi in user log file f)
  { inserting(Pi);
    if ( Energy Ei of Pi) >1 { Ei =1; }
  }
  if (the days from the last updating) > threshold {up-
dating(f)}
  END
```

To construct user profile, we employ two Functions: *inserting* and *updating*. The inserting operation is utilized to insert new categories into a profile and adjust the energy values of existing categories. The updating operation is utilized to remove those categories users don't interest anymore. And the energy value must be in [0,1] what is expected by the modified fuzzy ART neural network.

2.2.1 Inserting

The User Log File mentioned in section 3.1 is considered as the basis of inserting operation to construct the user profile. For each page in a log file, we first check if the category of the product exists in the preference tree. If the category exists, the *energy* value of the category should be refreshed. If the category does not exist, we will create the category in user profile, whose *energy* is the value of *favorite*. Then the *energy* value of the new node should be calculated. The following method is used to calculate the new energy value of each category:

$$E_i = \frac{\sum_{p \in P_i^{new}} W_{p,i}}{\left|P_i^{new}\right|} + \lambda \times E_i \quad (1)$$

where E_i is the energy value of page category C_i, P_i^{new} is the set of the pages assigned to the category C_i in user log file , the absolute value $\left|P_i^{new}\right|$ is the number of products in P_i^{new} , and $W_{p,i}$ is the *favorite* of the product *p*. The parameter λ, called *decaying factor*, is set from 0 to 1, hence the older records have less effects to the representation of category. In our experiment, λ is assigned to 0.98.

2.2.2 Updating

Since user interests often change, it is important to adjust the user profile incrementally, in order to represent user interests accurately. In discussion of the changes of user interests, it is found that there are two types of the user interests. One is the long-term interest and the other is the short-term interest. The long-term interest often reflects a real user interest. Relatively, the short-term interest is usually caused by a hot products event and vanishes quickly. The updating operation is designed to adjust the part reflecting user short-term interests.

In contrast to the inserting operation that adds the new interesting categories into user profile, the updating operation is the mechanism to remove the out-of-favor categories. Categories with a continual attention can continuously live, otherwise, they will become weak and finally die out. In user preference, every category's energy value should be reduced a predefined value ψ periodically (e.g. 15 days). The parameter ψ, called *aging factor*, is used to control the reduction rate. In the experiment, ψ is assigned to 0.90.

When no or few products browsed in a category, its energy value will decline gradually. If a category's energy value is less than (or equal to) a pre-defined threshold, we remove the category from user preference tree. To keep a personal view on part to the trend of user interest, categories with low energy value are removed.

2.3 User Cluster (Cluster)

User cluster could group users into different teams according their profiles using adaptive neural network. Nowadays, there are various approaches to cluster analysis, including multivariate statistical method, artificial neural network, and other algorithms. However, some of the methods like self-organizing map algorithm implies some constraints: the need to choose the number of clusters a priori, heavier computational complexity and merging the groups representing the same cluster, because the SOM, by approximating the distribution patterns, finds more than one group representing the same cluster. Moreover, successive SOM results depend on the training phase and this implies the choice of representative training examples. For this reason, we employ a modified fuzzy ART, one of the clustering methods using neural network, for cluster analysis.

The Fuzzy ART [8] network is an unsupervised neural network with ART architecture for performing both continuous-valued vectors and binary-valued vectors. It is a pure winner-takes-all architecture able to instance output nodes whenever necessary and to handle both binary and analog patterns. Using a 'Vigilance parameter' as a threshold of similarity, Fuzzy ART can determine when to form a new cluster. This algorithm uses an unsupervised learning and feedback network. It accepts and input vector and classifies it into one of a number of clusters depending upon which it best resembles. The single recognition layer that fires indicates its classification decision. It the input vector does not match any stored pattern, it creates a pattern that is like the input vector as a new category. Once a stored pattern is found that matches the input vector within a specified threshold (the vigilance $\rho \in [0,1]$), that pattern is adjusted to make it accommodate the new input vector. The adjective fuzzy derives from the functions it uses, although it is not actually fuzzy. To perform data clustering, fuzzy ART instances the first cluster coinciding with the first input and allocating new groups when necessary (in particular, each output node represents a cluster from a group). In the paper, we employ a modified Fuzzy ART proposed by Cinque al. [9] to solve some problems of the origin fuzzy ART. The algorithm is shown as follows:

```
BEGIN
For each (input vector Vi)
{ for each (exist cluster Ci) {C*=argmax(choice(Ci, Vi));}
  if match(C*, Vi)≥ρ {adaptation(C*, Vi);}
  else { Instance a new cluster; }
}
END
```

Function *choice* used in the algorithm is the following:

$$choice\ (C_j, V_i) = \frac{(|C_j \wedge V_i|)^2}{|C_j| \cdot |V_i|} = \frac{(\sum_{r=1}^{n} z_r)^2}{\sum_{r=1}^{n} c_r \cdot \sum_{r=1}^{n} v_r} \tag{2}$$

It computes the compatibility between a cluster and an input to find a cluster with greatest compatibility. The input pattern V_i is an n-elements vector transposed, C_j is the weight vector of cluster J (both are n-dimensional vectors). "$\wedge$" is fuzzy set intersection operator, which is defined by:

$$\begin{aligned} x \wedge y &= \min\{x, y\} \\ X \wedge Y &= (x_1 \wedge y_1, \cdots, x_n \wedge y_n) = (z_1, z_2, \cdots, z_n) \end{aligned} \tag{3}$$

Function *match* is the following:

$$match\ (C^*, V_i) = \frac{|C^* \wedge V_i|}{|C^*|} = \frac{\sum_{r=1}^{n} z_r}{\sum_{r=1}^{n} c_r^*} \tag{4}$$

This computes the similarity between the input and the selected cluster. The *match* process is passed if this value is greater than, or equal to, the vigilance parameter $\rho \in [0,1]$. Intuitively, ρ indicates how similar the input has to be to the selected cluster to allow it to be associated with the user group the cluster represents. As a consequence, a greater value of ρ implies smaller clusters, a lower value means wider clusters. Function *adaptation* is the selected cluster adjusting function, which algorithm is shown as following:

$$adaptation\ (C^*, V_i) = C^*_{new} = \beta(C^*_{old} \wedge V_i) + (1-\beta)C^*_{old} \tag{5}$$

Where the learning parameter $\beta \in [0,1]$, weights the new and old knowledge respectively. It is worth observing that this function is not increasing, that is $C^*_{new} < C^*_{old}$. In the study, the energy values of all leaf nodes in a user profile consist an *n-elements* vector representing a user pattern. Each element of the vector represents a product category. If a certain product category doesn't include in user profile, the corresponding element in the vector is assigned to 0. Pre-processing is required to ensure the pattern values in the space [0,1], as expected by the fuzzy ART.

The origin fuzzy ART is similar with modified fuzzy ART mentioned before, but the origin one employs different *choice* function. The choice function utilized in the origin fuzzy ART is as following:

$$choice\ (C_j, V_i) = \frac{|C_j \wedge V_i|}{\alpha + |V_i|} = \frac{(\sum_{r=1}^{n} z_r)}{\alpha + \sum_{r=1}^{n} v_r} \tag{6}$$

Where α is choice parameter providing a floating point overflow. Simulations in this paper are performed with a value of $\alpha \approx 0$.

3 Experiment

To verify our proposed system, we built origin fuzzy ART, *k*-means, and SOM classifier. In this section, these classifiers are briefly described.

3.1 Other Classifiers Used in Our Experiments

K-means is one of the simplest unsupervised learning algorithms that solve the well known clustering problem. The main idea is to partition (or clustering) *N* data points into *K* disjoint subsets S_j containing N_j data points so as to minimize the sum-of-squares criterion as the following equation:

$$J = \sum_{j=1}^{k} \sum_{n \in S_j} \left\| x_n - \mu_j \right\|^2 \tag{7}$$

where x_n is a vector representing the nth data point and μ_j is the geometric centroid of the data points in s_j. In general, the algorithm does not achieve a global minimum of J over the assignments.

The self-organizing maps or Kohonen's feature maps are feedforward, competitive ANN that employ a layer of input neurons and a single computational layer. Let us denote by *y* the set of vector-valued observations, $y = [y_1, y_2, ..., y_m]^T$, the weight vector of the neuron *j* in SOM is $w_j = [w_{j1}, w_{j2}, ..., w_{jm}]^T$. Due to its competitive nature, the SOM algorithm identifies the best-matching, winning reference vector w_i (or winner for short), to a specific feature vector y with respect to a certain distance metric. The index i of the winning reference vector is given by:

$$i(y) = \arg\min_j \{ \| y - w_j \| \},\ j = 1, 2, \ldots, n \tag{8}$$

where n is the number of neurons in the SOM, $\|\cdot\|$ denotes the Euclidean distance. The reference vector of the winner as well as the reference vectors of the neurons in its neighborhood are modified using:

$$w_i(t+1) = w_i(n) + \Lambda_{i,j}(t)[x(t) - w_i(t)]\ ,\ t = 1,2,3,\ldots \tag{9}$$

Where $\Lambda_{i,j}(t)$ is a neighborhood function, and t is a discrete time constant.

3.2 Experiment Result

In the experiment, we construct an experimental web site and the proposed framework utilizing Java servlet and Java bean. The trial simulated 45 users behavior on an experiment Internet bookstore over a 30-day period, and they were pre-grouped 15 groups. The experimental web site is organized in a 4-level hierarchy that consists of 4 classes and 50 subclasses, including 5847 book pages and images obtained from www. Amazon.com. As performance measures, we employed the standard information retrieval measures of recall (r), precision (p), and F1($F1=2rp/(r+p)$). Origin fuzzy ART was simulated by an original implementation. It was used in the fast learning asset (with $\beta=1$) with α set to zero. Values for the vigilance parameter ρ were found by trials. In the simulation of k-means, parameter K representing the number of clusters is assigned to 7 by trials. In particular, we used a rectangular map with two training stages: the first was made in 750 steps, with 0.93 as a learning parameter and a half map as a neighborhood, and the second in 300 steps, with 0.011 as a learning parameter and three units as a neighborhood. Map size was chosen by experiments. In the proposed system, decaying factor λ is assigned to 0.95, aging factor ψ is set to 0.03, β is set to 1, and vigilance parameter ρ is assigned to 0.96 by trials. With the growth of vigilance parameter, the amount of clusters is increased too.

Figure 2 illustrates the comparisons of three algorithms mentioned before, including precision, recall and F1. The average for precision, recall and F1 measures using

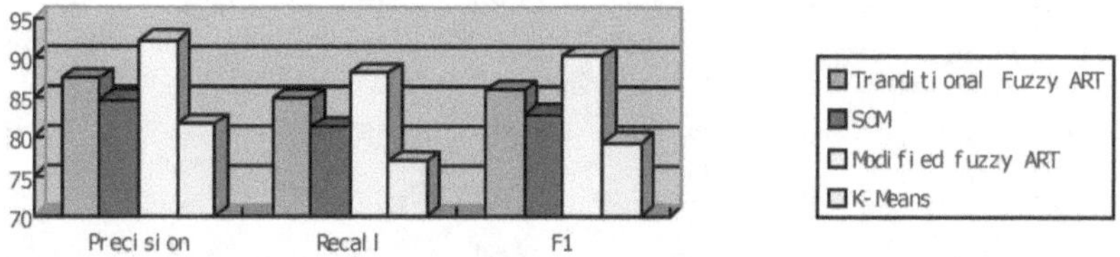

Fig. 2. The comparison of SOM, origin ART and modified fuzzy ART algorithm

the SOM classifier are 81.7%, 78.3%, 79.9%, respectively. The average for precision, recall and F1 measures using the origin fuzzy ART classifier are 87.3%, 84.8%, 86%, respectively. The average for precision, recall and F1 measures using the k-means classifier are81.6%, 76.9%, 79.2%, respectively. In comparison with the proposed system, the precision, recall, and F1 measures are 92.3%, 88.1%, 90.15%, respectively. This indicates that if the parameters are selected carefully, the proposed framework could group users' pattern accurately.

4 Conclusions

This paper presents a new framework to automatically track user access patterns on Internet through commerce Web site and group users using an adaptive neural network. Our approach, essentially based on neural network computation, i.e., learning capacity, satisfies some of its main requirements: fast results, fault and noise tolerance. A pattern grouping module totally independent of the application was also proposed. The cluster system, made up of the modified fuzzy ART and the user pattern track module, was very simple to use. Such system does not use specific knowledge as adopted in the most proper operators. It becomes possible to customize it to different scenarios.

References

1. Chen. C.H., Khoo, L.P.: Multicultural factors evaluation on elicited user requirements for product concept development, Proceedings of 16th Interneational Conference for Production Research (ICPR-16), July 29-August 3 (2001) 15-23
2. Yan, W., Chen, C.H,: A radial basis function neural network multicultural factors evaluation engine for product concept development, Expert System, Vol. 18(5), (2001) 219-232
3. Cotrell M, Girard B: Forcasting of curves using a Kohonen classification. J Forecast, Vol. 17, (1998) 429-439
4. Curry, B., Davies, F.: The Kohonen self-organizing map: an application to the study of strategic groups in the UK hotel industry, Expert System, Vol. 18(1) (2002) 19-30
5. Lee, S.C., Yung, H.S.: A cross-national market segmentation of online game industry using SOM, Expert Systems with Application, Vol. 27 (2004) 559-570
6. Santos, K. Rangarajan, Pboba, V.: Adaptive Neural Network Clustering of Web Users, Computer, Vol. 4, (2004) 34-40
7. Hu, T.L., Sheu, J.B.: A Fuzzy-based user classification method for demand-responsive logistical distribution operations, Fuzzy Sets and System, Vol. 139 (2003). 431-450
8. Carpenter, G.A.: Fuzzy ART: fast stable learning and categorization of analog patterns by an adaptive resonance system, Neural Networks, Vol. 4 (1991) 759-771
9. Cinque, L., Foresti, G.: A clustering fuzzy approach for image segmentation, Pattern Recognition, Vol. 37 (2004) 1797-1807

IRIOS: Interactive News Announcer Robot System

Satoru Satake[1], Hideyuki Kawashima[2], Michita Imai[2,3],
Kenshiro Hirose[1], and Yuichiro Anzai[2]

[1] Open Environmental Systems, Graduate School of Keio University,
3-14-1 Hiyoshi, Yokohama, Japan
[2] Information and Computer Science, Keio University,
3-14-1 Hiyoshi, Yokohama, Japan
[3] JST PRESTO

Abstract. This paper presents an interactive news announcer robot system IRIOS that performs on the humanoid robot, Robovie. IRIOS satisfies the interest trend requirement and the topic change requirement for a capricious user by Time Conscious(TC)-TfIdf vector. The results of experiments showed that TC-TfIdf strategy satisfied both requirements while other strategies did not.

1 Introduction

News is one of the most informative information in our daily lives. It is provided by newspapers, radios and TVs. Among them, the most effective way to inform news is by TV programs that uses announcers. If announcers perform their presentations solely for us and choose news contents interactively estimating our interests, we would receive interesting news more efficiently, leading us to enjoy it even further. This paper presents such an interactive news demonstration system using a communication robot and news documents on the web. In the rest of this paper we denote the ith demonstrated news document as nd_i for simplicity.

Through our researches on human-robot interactions[1, 2, 3], we have studied that human changes his/her interest gradually in the process of interactions. Therefore to realize an interactive news announcer robot system for human, we think both **interest trend requirement** (R_{trend}) and **topic change requirement** (R_{topic}) should be satisfied.

- R_{trend} is the requirement to detect capricious human's interest. If the current news article is attractive for a user, the subsequent news should be in a similar genre, and also similar to past attractive nd_i. Generally speaking, users have stronger interests to the current topic compared with older ones. Therefore, a nd_i should be prioritized over $nd_k (i > k)$.
- R_{topic} is the requirement to change demonstration topic. If the current news is not attractive for a user, the subsequent news should be not only dissimilar to it, but also similar to past attractive nd_is.

In previous work, toward the development of an interactive information providing system such as software agents that perform with web browsers, researches have been conducted deeply and widely [4, 5, 6, 7]. These agents hold a set of words as a feature vector to represent user interests. The feature vector is generated by analyzing words in

H.T. Shen et al. (Eds.): APWeb 2006, LNCS 3842, pp. 733–740, 2006.

documents and browsed time. Unfortunately these agents cannot satisfy both requirements. These agents do not pay attention to the gradual change in interests, because these target application, such as a survey of markets and researches, suppose the user interests are static in the process of interaction.

To satisfy the above two requirements, we newly present **time conscious (TC)-TfIdf vector** that is based on TfIdf vector. TC-TfIdf vector is composed of TfIdf vectors of demonstrated nd_is, a time decreasing function, and a sign function. To satisfy R_{trend}, TC-TfIdf vector multiplies the time decreasing function by the conventional TfIdf vector. The function reduces the weight of a nd_i in accordance with time, and hence it prioritizes the current nd_i over past nd_is. To satisfy R_{topic}, TC-TfIdf vector times the sign function to the conventional TfIdf vector. The function reflects whether each demonstrated nd_i attracted a user or not. It emphasizes attractive nd_is and diminishes boring nd_is by controlling the sign for each nd_i.

Furthermore, we present an interactive news announcer robot system **IRIOS** that continually provides nd_is by estimating human interest using TC-TfIdf vector and a communication robot called Robovie[8]. IRIOS provides nd_is with utterances and gestures. For example, for sad news IRIOS makes Robovie to execute sad looking motions.

The paper is organized as follows. In section 2, we formalize requirements that should be satisfied for interactive news demonstrations. In section 3, we present the first contribution of this paper, TC-TfIdf vector that satisfies both the requirements. In section 4, we present the second contribution of this paper, the interactive news demonstrations robot announcer system IRIOS. In section 5, we show the results of experiments with IRIOS. In section 6 we discuss about some related work. Finally in section 7, we conclude this paper.

2 Problem Formulation

The purpose of this paper is to develop a system that interactively provides nd_is for human considering his/her interest. To achieve the purpose, we should tackle on the following two problems.

2.1 Interest Trend Requirement (R_{trend})

While enjoying news, our interest gradually changes as time goes on. We are more interested in recently demonstrated nd_is, and less interested in nd_is that was presented previously.

In summary, nd_i should be prioritized over nd_{i-1}.

This nature should be modeled on an interactive news announcer robot. We refer it as R_{trend} in this paper.

2.2 Topic Change Requirement (R_{topic})

An interactive news announcer robot should demonstrate attractive nd_is. Therefore, if nd_2 was not attractive, the robot should choose a subsequent nd_3 that is dissimilar to

nd_2. Furthermore, if nd_1(which was demonstrated before nd_2) was attractive, the nd_3 should be similar to nd_1.

In summary, an interactive news announcer robot should choose a nd_k that
be not only similar to attractive $nd_i(i < k)$,
but also be dissimilar to unattractive $nd_j(j < k)$.

This requirement should be satisfied on an interactive news announcer robot system. We refer it as R_{topic} in this paper.

3 Satisfying Two Requirements: TC-TfIdf Vector

3.1 Algorithm Design

To satisfy two requirements, we incorporate two weighted functions into the well-known TfIdf vector.

For R_{trend}, TC-TfIdf vector incorporates a time decreasing function $TD(t)$ as shown in the equation (1).

$$TD(t) = e^{-\alpha t} \tag{1}$$

In this paper, we coordinates α as $TD(60sec) = \frac{1}{4}$.

For R_{topic}, TC-TfIdf introduces a sign function shown in the equation (2). If nd_i does not attract a user, $s(nd_i)$ gives negative weight, or $s(nd_i)$ gives positive weight.

$$s(nd_i) = \begin{cases} 1 \textbf{ when } nd_i \textit{ is attractive} \\ -1 \textbf{ when } nd_i \textit{ is unattractive} \end{cases} \tag{2}$$

Here we present TC-TfIdf vector that satisfies two requirements. Suppose a robot executed demonstrations n times, and t_i represents the demonstrated time for each nd_i. Now we give the formula of TC-TfIdf vector in equation (3). In equation (3), $\boldsymbol{V}_{TCTI}(t_{n+1})$ indicates TC-TfIdf vector at time t_{n+1}, and $\boldsymbol{V}_{TI}(nd_i)$ indicates TfIdf vector of nd_i demonstrated on t_i.

$$\boldsymbol{V}_{TCTI}(t_{n+1}) = \sum_{i=1}^{n} s(nd_i) \times TD(t_{n+1} - t_i) \times \boldsymbol{V}_{TI}(nd_i) \tag{3}$$

$\boldsymbol{V}_{TCTI}(t_{n+1})$ selects the nd_{n+1} from **a set of candidates for the** nd_{n+1} **and it is represented as** $SC(nd_{n+1})$. The nd_{n+1} has the highest dot product between $\boldsymbol{V}_{TCTI}(t_{n+1})$ and $\boldsymbol{V}_{TI}(c)$ in $SC(nd_{n+1})$.

Calculation of TfIdf Vector. At first, words in a nd_i are extracted by using ChaSen[9]. We extract only the types of "verb", "noun", "adjective" and "unknown words" because they mainly characterize documents. Then using the extracted words, TfIdf vectors are calculated.

After that, top thirty words in descending order of TfIdf Value are selected as vector dimensions for each $\boldsymbol{V}_{TI}(nd_i)$. The reason why we limits the number of vector dimensions to thirty is the acceleration of computation. We found out the limitation number thirty is appropriate under our observation that most of news sites are characterized by using from twenty to thirty words.

3.2 Behavior of TC-TfIdf

Here we explain the behaviors of $\boldsymbol{V}_{TCTI}(t_n)$ through an interaction in Fig. 1. In the interaction, IRIOS firstly selects unattractive nd_i and secondly selects attractive nd_i. Four states of the interaction are shown in Fig. 1, which are denoted from (A) to (D). Through the four states, left rectangles show $\boldsymbol{V}_{TCTI}(t_n)$s, and right rectangles show $\boldsymbol{V}_{TI}(nd_n)$s. In a rectangle, a word is assigned a signed amplitude. The length of an arrow indicates an amplitude, and the direction of an arrow indicates sign of vector value: upper arrow is positive and downward arrow is negative. In the rest of this subsection, we refer "Fig. 1 (α)" to simply "(α)" for succinctness.

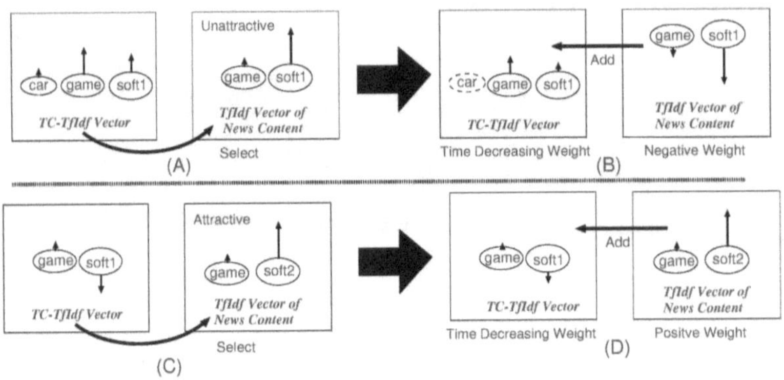

Fig. 1. Behavior of $\boldsymbol{V}_{TCTI}(t_n)$

We explain the detail of the interaction from (A) to (D). (A) and (C) shows the selection of nd_i, and (B) and (D) shows the calculation of $\boldsymbol{V}_{TCTI}(t_n)$. (A) shows that $\boldsymbol{V}_{TCTI}(t_n)$ selects nd_n from $SC(nd_n)$. After the selection of nd_n, $\boldsymbol{V}_{TCTI}(t_n)$ should be recalculated. (B) shows the calculation of the effect of R_{topic} and R_{trend}. To satisfy R_{topic}, sign function gives -1 to nd_n(the right rectangles of (B)). To satisfy R_{trend}, $\boldsymbol{V}_{TCTI}(t_n)$ are decreased by $TD(t)$, and the amplitude for "car" is decreased to 0 by $TD(t)$. Consequently the amplitude for "car" is deleted from $\boldsymbol{V}_{TCTI}(t_{n+1})$. (C) shows the calculation result of $\boldsymbol{V}_{TCTI}(t_{n+1})$ and the selection of attractive nd_{n+1}. By the effect of R_{topic} in (B), nd_{n+1} does not include word "soft1". (D) shows a new word "soft2" of nd_{n+1} is added to $\boldsymbol{V}_{TCTI}(t_{n+2})$.

4 Interactive News Announcer Robot System: IRIOS

IRIOS consists of a server on a dedicated computer and a client on Robovie.

4.1 IRIOS Server

Fig. 2 shows IRIOS server that consists of client manager, page exchanger, TC-TfIdf manager, and candidate collector. We explain the behaviors of IRIOS server by describing the process of searching the next nd_i.

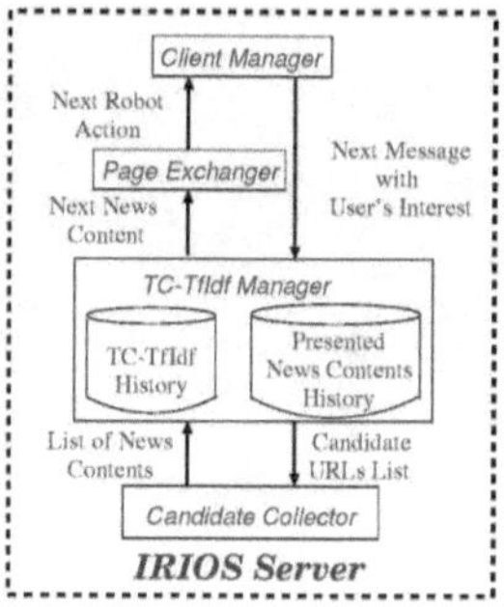

Fig. 2. IRIOS Server

ID	Format	Motion
0	<0>	Interesting
1	<1>	Surprising
2	<2>	Pity

Fig. 3. Motion Control Tag

1: <0>
2: **IRIOS company takes great strides**
3: **on the Web for the Year 2006.**
4: **The portal site of IRIOS**
5: **is selected as one of the top 10 cool sites.**
6: **For the top remarkable topic,**
7: **the 50TH story from the public BB**
8: **was selected**
9: <1>

Fig. 4. Sample of Robot Behaviour

Searching the Next nd_i. The next nd_i request is sent by IRIOS client with the result of interest recognition whether the current nd_i attracts a user. Client manager passes it to TC-TfIdf manager. Then it calculates a new TC-TfIdf vector by using the result of interest recognition and TC-TfIdf history shown in section 3. TC-TfIdf manager selects the URLs of $SC(nd_i)$ and passes them to candidate collector. It downloads $SC(nd_i)$ and passes them to TC-TfIdf manager. TC-TfIdf manager selects the nd_i as shown in section 3.1 and passes it to page exchanger. Page exchanger generates behaviors of Robovie from the nd_i as described in the next paragraph. We denote them as rb_i. And it sends both nd_i and rb_i to IRIOS client on Robovie. **In the rest of this paper we denote the set of nd_i and rb_i as $ndrb_i$.**

Generation of Robot Behaviors. rb_i consists of motion control tags and utterance texts as shown in Fig. 3. Motion control tags have three kinds of motions such as interesting motions, surprising motions, and pity motions. Utterance texts are only plain texts that describe uttered contents.

An example of rb_i is shown in Fig. 4. In the example, the first and ninth lines show motion control tags. The first line shows the execution of an interesting motion, and the ninth line shows the execution of a pity motion. The other lines show utterance texts, and the change of lines in a sentence shows the stop of utterance for a few seconds.

4.2 IRIOS Client

IRIOS client software consists of three modules as shown in Fig. 6. Connection manager communicates with IRIOS server. Contents executor demonstrates $ndrb_i$ by using motors and a speaker on Robovie, executes interest detector, and finally sends the result of the interest detector to the connection manager with a message to search for the next $ndrb_i$. Interest detector recognizes whether the current demonstrated $ndrb_i$ attracted a user or not. To show interest to the current demonstrated $ndrb_i$, the user should touch Robovie's shoulder.

IRIOS client performs on Robovie shown in Fig. 5. Robovie is a humanoid type robot. It has 11 degrees of freedom and a variety of sensors such as 24 ultrasonic range sensors, 1 omni-directional camera, 2 temperature sensors, 2 infrared sensors, 10 tactile sensors, and 16 touch sensors.

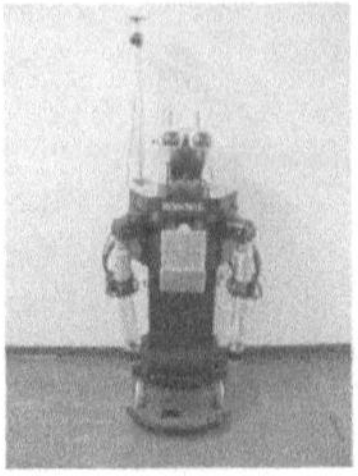

Fig. 5. Robovie

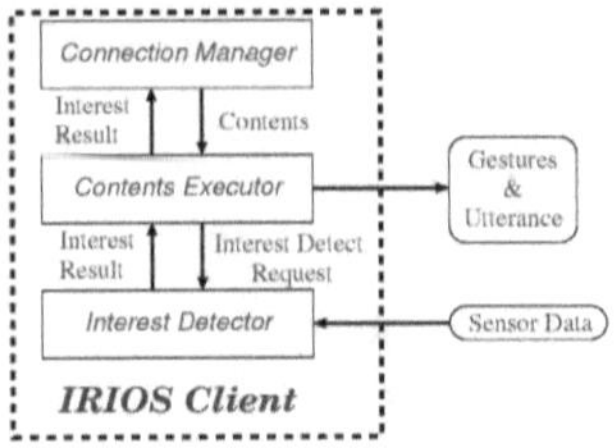

Fig. 6. IRIOS Client

5 Evaluation

5.1 Environment

We developed IRIOS by using C++ with more than 8500 lines. IRIOS client performs on Robovie and IRIOS server performs on a dedicated machine of which specifications are: pentium4 3.0GHz CPU, 4 GB RAM, 1 Gbps Ethernet N/W, and RedHat Enterprise OS. In this evaluation, the source of nd_i was set to only IT Media news site[10], and all of nd_i were obtained from there.

5.2 Strategies

In our experiments, we adopted the following three strategies. The first strategy is "considering all TC-TfIdf records (**TCR**)". The TCR is the method we proposed in section 3. TCR uses all of TC-TfIdf records, and therefore a nd_i selected by the strategy is not only similar to the preferred nd_i for a user, but also dissimilar to the unpreferred nd_i for the user throughout the interactions. The second strategy is "considering only the last TfIdf record(**LTR**)". LTR uses only the last nd_i. Therefore a nd_i selected by LTR is similar to the last nd_i if it is preferred by a user, or is dissimilar to the last nd_i if it is not. The third strategy is "considering all TfIdf records (**TR**)". TR has been used in related works. TR uses all of TfIdf records and therefore a nd_i selected by TR is not only similar to the preferred nd_is, but also dissimilar to the unpreferred nd_is for a user throughout the interactions.

5.3 Interaction Scenario

For each strategy mentioned above, we conducted two interactions between a user and the Robovie. An interaction was executed as follows.

(1) The user shows an interest to the first three $ndrb_i$s ($ndrb_{1,2,3}$).
(2) The user does not show any interest to a consecutive demonstration($ndrb_4$).

To satisfy R_{trend}, an attractive $ndrb_i$ after an attractive $ndrb_{i-1}$ should be more attractive than $ndrb_{i-1}$. For example, $ndrb_5$ should be the most similar to $ndrb_3$, and $ndrb_2$ should be more similar to $ndrb_5$ than $ndrb_1$.

To satisfy R_{topic}, $ndrb_5$ should be not only similar to $ndrb_{1,2,3}$, but also dissimilar to $ndrb_4$ because $ndrb_{1,2,3}$ attracted the user, while $ndrb_4$ did not.

5.4 Results

Fig. 7 shows the results of experiments. We denote the similarity between $ndrb_5$ and $ndrb_n$ as $sim(5,n)$ that is calculated as follows.

$$sim(5,n) = \boldsymbol{v}_{TI}(nd_5) \cdot \boldsymbol{v}_{TI}(nd_n). \quad (4)$$

For example, $sim(5,4)$ shows a dot product between $ndrb_5$ and $ndrb_4$.

To satisfy R_{trend}, the following conditions should hold:
(1) $sim(5,3) > sim(5,2)$, (2) $sim(5,2) > sim(5,1)$.

To satisfy R_{topic}, the following conditions should hold:
(1) $sim(5,4) < sim(5,3)$, (2) $sim(5,4) < sim(5,2)$, (3) $sim(5,4) < sim(5,1)$.

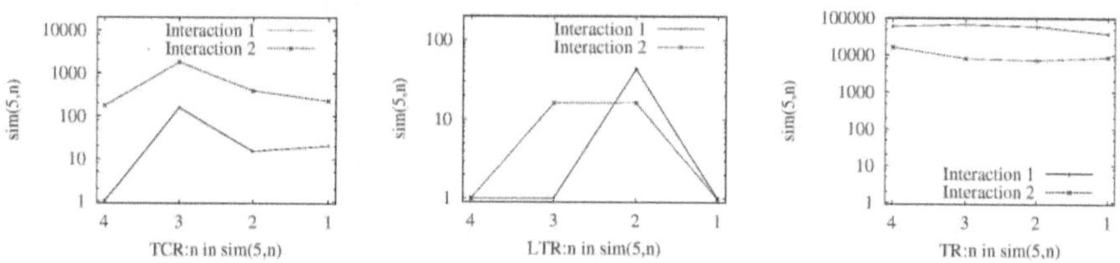

Fig. 7. $sim(5,n)$ with TCR, LTR, TR

The results of TCR shows that on each interaction $sim(5,3)$ is the largest value. The interaction 1 satisfied $sim(5,2) > sim(5,1)$. Although the interaction 2 did not satisfy the condition, the difference between $sim(5,2)$ and $sim(5,1)$ on interaction 2 was quite small (lower than 10). Therefore we argue TCR could satisfy the R_{trend}. Furthermore, $sim(5,4)$ shows the smallest value. It shows that the TCR could satisfy the R_{topic}. In summary, the results of experiments showed that the TCR could realize both the R_{trend} and R_{topic}.

On the other hand, LT and TR did not satisfy R_{trend} or R_{topic}. As for LT, all of $sim(5,4)$, $sim(5,3)$, $sim(5,2)$, and $sim(5,1)$ showed very low values (please note that max Y axis is only 100 in this graph), and all $ndri_{4,3,2,1}$ were dissimilar to $ndri_5$ that expressed that $ndri_5$ was not similar to past attractive $ndri_i$s. This shows both the R_{trend} and the R_{topic} were not satisfied properly. As for TR, we cannot observe the change between $sim(5,4)$ and $sim(5,3)$. Therefore the R_{topic} was not satisfied by the TR strategy.

We summarize that our proposed TCR strategy satisfied for both R_{trend} and R_{topic} while other strategies did not.

6 Relation Works

TDT(**T**opic **D**etection and **T**racking) systems [11, 12, 13] can track news contents in which a user is interested. Especially [13] considers time-ordering of news contents.

However [11, 12, 13] do not pay attention to the gradual change in interest. [11, 12, 13] suppose user interests are static in interaction, therefore they tracks the news contents which a user explicitly orders to track at the beginning. [13] only consider the time when the news contents is issued, but does not consider the time when a user expresses.

7 Conclusion

This paper presented IRIOS, an interactive news announcer robot system. IRIOS satisfies two requirements. (1) Searching news considering interest trend of a user. (2) Actively changing a current topic to attract a user if the current news is not attractive for the user. To satisfy requirements, IRIOS provided TC-TfIdf vector that is a time conscious extension of TfIdf vector. The results of experiments showed that IRIOS selected appropriate news contents not only dissimilar to unattractive one, but also similar to attractive one. Hence IRIOS could satisfy two requirements, and we conclude that IRIOS can perform as an interactive news announcer robot system.

We plan to have two future works. (1) Extending the evaluation method of user interest. IRIOS uses very simple interaction. To realize richer interaction, we should use utterance of user. To evaluate user interest in the rich interaction, the word of the user utterance and its timing are important. (2) Extending the generation algorithm of robot utterance and motions. The current IRIOS uses very simple generation algorithm, so we must extend more attractive one.

References

1. Yuichiro Anzai. Human-Robot-Computer Interaction: A New Paradigm of Research in Robotics. *Advanced Robotics*, 8(4):357–369, 1994.
2. Michita Imai, Tetsuo Ono, Hiroshi Ishiguro, and Yuichiro Anzai. Attention Mechanism for Utterance Generation. In *Proc. of 9th IEEE ROMAN*, pages 1–6, 2000.
3. Michita Imai and Mariko Narumi. Generating common quality of sense by directed interaction. In *Proceedings of the 12th IEEE International Workshop on Robot and Human Intaractive Communication(RO-MAN 2003)*, pages 199–204, 2003.
4. S. Zabala, G. Loerincs, Y. Bello, and V. Dias. Calvin: A personalized web-search agent based on monitoring user actions. In *GI Jahrestaung (1)*, pages 353–357, 2001.
5. T. Bauer and D. B. Leake. Real time user context modeling for information retrieval agents. In *10th Intl. Conf. on Information and Knowledge Mangement(CIKM)*, pages 568–570, 2001.
6. J.C. Bottraud, G. Bisson, and M.F. Bruander. An adaptive information research personal assistant. In *Proc. of Workshop Artificial Intelligence, Information Access and Mobile Computing IJCAI*, 2003.
7. Liren Chen and Katia Sycara. Webmate: A personal agent for browsing and searching. In *Proc. of the 2nd Intl. Conf. on Autonomous Agent*, pages 132–139, 1998.
8. Takayuki Kanda, Hiroshi Ishiguro, Tetsuo Ono, Michita Imai, and Ryohei Nakatsu. Development and Evaluation of an Interactive Humanoid Robot "Robovie". In *Proceedings of IEEE International Conference On Robotics and Automation*, pages 1848–1855, 2002.
9. ChaSen's Wiki FrontPage. http://chasen.naist.jp/hiki/chasen.
10. ITmedia News. http://www.itmedia.co.jp/news.
11. Yuen-Yee Lo and Jean-Luc Gauvain. The LIMSI Topic Tracking System for TDT2001. In *Proc. of 2001 Topic Detection and Tracking(TDT) Workshop*, 2001.
12. M. Connel, A. Feng, G. Kumaran, H. Raghavan, C. Shah, and J. Allan. UMass at TDT 2004. In *Working Notes of the TDT-2004 Evaluation*, 2004.
13. Ramesh Nallapati, Ao Feng, Fuchun Peng, and James Allan. Event threading within new topics. In *Proc. of 2004 ACM CIKM International Conference on Information and Knowledge Management*, pages 446–453, 2004.

WIPI Mobile Platform with Secure Service for Mobile RFID Network Environment

Namje Park[1], Jin Kwak[1,*], Seungjoo Kim[1,*], Dongho Won[1,*], and Howon Kim[2]

[1] School of Information and Communication Engineering, Sungkyunkwan University, 300 Chunchun-dong, Jangan-gu, Suwon-si, Gyeonggi-do, 440-746, Korea
{njpark, jkwak}@dosan.skku.ac.kr, skim@ece.skku.ac.kr, dhwon@dosan.skku.ac.kr
[2] Information Security Research Division, ETRI, 161 Gajeong-dong, Yuseong-gu, Daejeon, 305-350, Korea
khw@etri.re.kr

Abstract. Recently, RFID (Radio Frequency Identification) technology is practically applied to a number of logistics processes as well as asset management, and RFID is also expected to be permeated in our daily life with the name of 'Ubiquitous Computing' or 'Ubiquitous Network' within the near future. The R&D groups in global now have paid attention to integrate RFID with mobile devices as well as to associate with the existing mobile telecommunication network. Such a converged technology and services would lead to make new markets and research challenges. However, the privacy violation on tagged products has become stumbling block. We propose light-weight security mechanism which is constructed by mobile RFID security mechanism based on WIPI (Wireless Internet Platform for Interoperability). WIPI-based light-weight mobile RFID security platform can be applicable to various mobile RFID services that required secure business applications in mobile environment.

1 Introduction

Due to rapid development of information technology, handheld terminal is evolving into a low-power, ultra-light, integrated, and intellectual terminal to support various information service and ubiquitous environment, and it will develop to a more advanced form current services. The wireless internet infrastructure integrated with the mobile communication system and RFID gave birth to mobile RFID to provide new services to users, and the standardization of mobile RFID information protection technology such as the protection and verification of personal information, authorization, and key management and its technological development are being progressed along the way.

RFID reader has been mainly used as RFID tag recognizable unattended information production terminal, and now it is expanding into the mobile RFID service providing useful information to users by reading various RFID tag information through RFID tag

* This work was supported by the University IT Research Center Project funded by the Korean Ministry of Information and Communication.

H.T. Shen et al. (Eds.): APWeb 2006, LNCS 3842, pp. 741 – 748, 2006.

chip and RFID reader chip installed to cellular phone. Mobile RFID service is defined as to provide personalized secure services such as searching the product information, purchasing, verifying and paying for the product while on the move through the wireless internet network by building the RFID reader chip into the mobile terminal[4]. The service infrastructure required for providing such RFID based mobile service is composed of RFID reader, handset, communication network and protocol, information protection, application server, RFID code interpretation, and contents development.

In this paper, the light-weight mobile RFID middleware of WIPI-based environment is presented. The proposed platform, the ETRI (Electronics and Telecommunications Research Institute) mobile RFID security middleware platform, is composed of AAL (Application Adaptation Layer) and RFID-WIPI HAL (Handset Adaptation Layer). The proposed AAL is the core component of the security middleware platform.) Security platform is a building block for the extended security API (Application Programming Interface) for secure mobile RFID and it has to be integrated with WIPI and mobile RFID security mechanism for phone-based RFID service to provide more secure mobile business. It enables business to provide new services to mobile customers by securing services and transactions from the end-user to a company's existing e-commerce and IT systems.

2 Overview of Mobile RFID

2.1 Mobile RFID Technology

RFID is expected to be the base technology for ubiquitous network or computing, and to be associated with other technology such as telemetric, and sensors. Meanwhile Korea is widely known that it has established one of the most robust mobile telecommunication networks. In particular, about 78% of the population uses mobile phones and more than 95% among their phones have Internet-enabled function. Currently, Korea has recognized the potential of RFID technology and has tried to converge with mobile phone. Mobile phone integrated with RFID can activate new markets and end-user services, and can be considered as an exemplary technology fusion. Furthermore, it may evolve its functions as end-user terminal device, or 'u-device (ubiquitous device)', in the world of ubiquitous information technology[11].

Actually, mobile RFID phone may represent two types of mobile phone devices; one is RFID reader equipped mobile phone, and the other is RFID tag attached mobile phone. Each type of mobile phone has different application domains, for example, the RFID tag attached one can be used as a device for payment, entry control, and identity authentication, and the feature of this application is that RFID readers exist in the fixed positions and they recognize each phone to give user specific services like door opening. In the other hand, the RFID reader equipped mobile phone, which Korea is paying much attention now, can be utilized for providing end-users detailed information about the tagged object through accessing mobile network.

Korea's mobile RFID technology is focusing on the UHF range (860~960MHz), since UHF range may enable longer reading range and moderate data rates as well as relatively small tag size and cost. Then, as a kind of handheld RFID reader, in the selected service domain the UHF RFID phone device can be used for providing object information directly to the end-user using the same UHF RFID tags which have widely spread.

2.2 Mobile RFID Services

Mobile RFID service structure is defined to support ISO/IEC 18000-6 A/B/C through the wireless access communication between RFID tag and RFID reader, but there is no RFID reader chip supporting all three wireless connection access specifications yet that the communication specification for the cellular phone will be determined by the mobile communication companies[11,12]. It will be also possible to mount the RF communication function to the Reader Chip using SDR technology and develop ISO/IEC 18000-6 A/B/C communication protocol in software to choose from protocols when needed.

Mobile RFID terminal's function is concerned with the recognition distance to the RFID reader chip built into the cellular phone, transmission power, frequency, interface, technological standard, PIN specification, UART communication interface, WIPI API and WIPI-HAL API extended specification to control reader chip. RFID reader chip middleware functions are provided to the application program in the form of WIPI API as in figure 1. Here, 'Mobile RFID Device Driver' is the device driver software provided by the reader chip manufacturer.

Mobile RFID network function is concerned with the communication protocols such as the ODS (Object Directory Service) communication for code interpretation, the message transmission for the transmission and reception of contents between the cellular phone terminal and the application server, contents negotiation that supports Mobile RFID service environment and ensures the optimum contents transfer between the cellular phone terminal and the application server, and session management that enables the application to create and mange required status information while transmitting the message and the WIPI extended specification which supports these communication services[2,3,8].

The service model, as shown in figure 1, is a RFID tag, reader, middleware and information server. In the view of information protection, the serious problem for the RFID service is a threat of privacy. Here, the damage of privacy is of exposing the information stored in the tag and the leakage of information includes all data of the

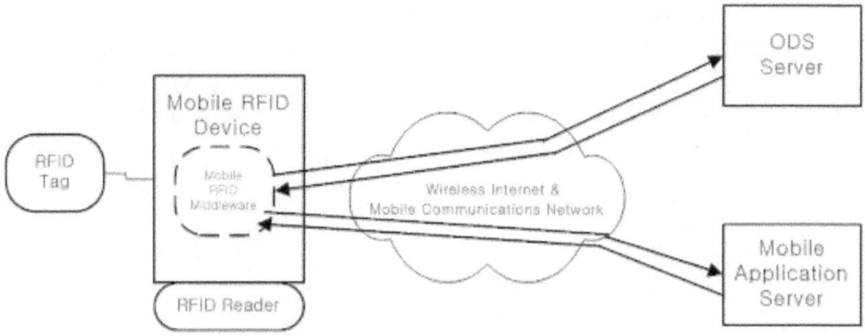

Fig. 1. Architecture of Mobile RFID Services

personal possessing the tag, tagged products and location. The privacy protection on RFID system can be considered in two points of view. One is the privacy protection between the tag and the reader, which takes advantage of ID encryption, prevention of location tracking and the countermeasure of tag being forged. The other is of the exposure of what the information server contains along with tagged items. First of all, we will have a look about the exposure of information caused between the tag and the reader, and then discuss about the solution proposing on this paper.

3 Security Requirements for Secure Mobile RFID Services

Mobile RFID service structure provides its services by associating the mobile communication network and the RFID application service network based on the RFID tag. The area to consider the security basically is the RFID tag, reader terminal area, mobile communication network area, RFID application service network area, and security issues like the confidentiality/integrity/authentication/permission/non-repudiation shall be considered in each network area. Especially, as the mobile RFID service is the end user service, the issue of privacy protection must inevitably become a serious issue to consider, and as the contents accessibility increases due to the off-line hypertext property of RFID, the authentication for adult service must also become another important issue to consider.

1) Mobile RFID service based on the user's ownership of tagged products, needs to guarantee the confidentiality on the tag code information or user data information for personal privacy protection. In this case, mobile RFID application service provider shall provide the confidentiality to the said information or other means to prevent personal privacy infringement.
2) The integrity of the data shall be guaranteed in order to check counterfeiting/falsification of the data transmitted through the communication path in each section of the mobile RFID service network reference structure. However additional code based data integrity other than the least method (for example, CRC) specified in the air interface specification is not required in the communication section between tag and reader terminal considering the limit of the calculation capacity of the tag. However, it is necessary to develop a method to secure the data integrity in the tag for special mobile RFID application service where the personal information is stored in the user data information of the tag and transmitted.
3) Mobile RFID application service including the processes like bill payment between the reader terminal user and the application server requires the non-repudiation for the data transmitted by the reader terminal user and the application server. In this case, the reader terminal and the application server must be able to execute non-repudiation.
4) Mobile RFID application service that uses the password for halting the tag or authorizing the access to the tag shall be able to safely manage such passwords and safely authorize the key to the reader terminal, and such functions shall be provided by the mobile RFID service infrastructure; for example, the application server or separate key management server.

5) Since mobile RFID service is a B2C service using RFID tag for end users, it inevitably accompanies the issues of personal privacy infringement that it must provide solutions for such issues.

4 WIPI Platform-Based Mobile RFID Security Model

4.1 Architecture of Mobile RFID Middleware System

Extracting the core specifications from the full specifications of the Wireless Internet Platform (WIP), the functions of handset hardware, native system software, hanset adaption module, run time engine, APIs, and application programs are the areas of the core functional specifications of WIP. Actually, in the WIP specifications, only the handset adaptation and APIs are included and the other parts of functions of the wireless Internet platform are considered as the requirements to the handset vendors whether they accept it or not. For example, the run time engine part is required as the mode of down load of binary code for its maximum performance.

The core functions of the WIP are the handset adaptation and APIs which are called 'Handset Adaptation Layer (HAL) ' and 'Application Adaptation Layer (AAL)', respectively. The HAL defines the specifications for supporting the hardware independent on platform porting as an abstract layer. And the AAL defines the specifications for application programming interface (API) of the wireless Internet platform. The AAL supports the C/C++ and Java programming languages.

Figure 2 depicts the mobile RFID middleware platform based on WIPI layers. The mobile RFID middleware platform concerns three layers of the common wireless Internet layers, mobile RFID API layer, RFID engine, and handset adaptation layer. The RFID engine is defined as a requirement to the implementations. The native system software defines the operating system of handset device.

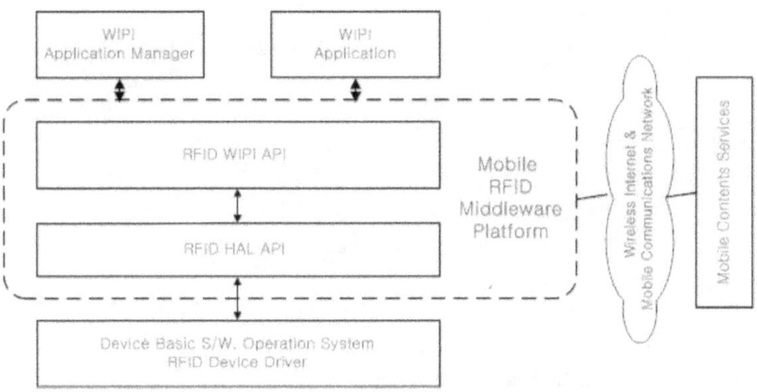

Fig. 2. Proposed Architecture of WIPI-based Mobile RFID Middleware

The RFID device handler provides the definitions for functions of starting the platform and transferring the events from the upper layer of HAL to the RFID H/W Reader. The categories of RFID device handler API cover call, RFID device, network, serial communication, short message service, sound, time, code conversion, file system, vocoder, input method, font, frame buffer, and virtual key. The AAL provides the definitions for functions of adaptive functions for RFID engine, C/Java API, and crypto library, and RFID security components[5].

The detailed structure is made as RFID reader module/chip, RFID reader device driver, RFID reader HAL, RFID reader control API, RFID code-support API, Network API (Embedded for RFID), Security API (Embedded for RFID), RFID reader control APP, RFID custom application.

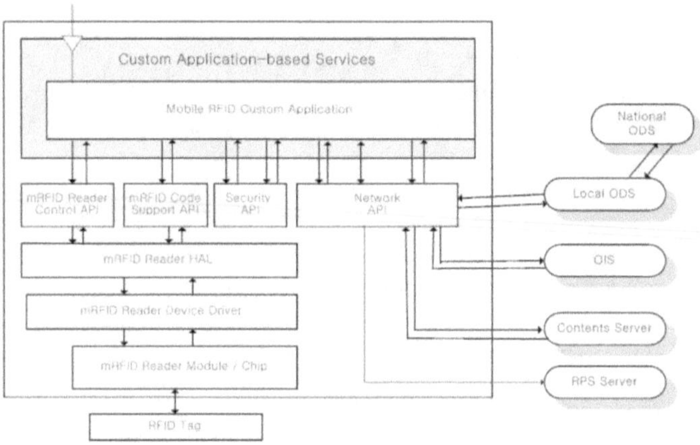

Fig. 3. Mobile RFID Security Services based on WIPI Platform

4.2 Proposed Security Enhanced Mobile RFID Middleware System

In this section, we design a security enhanced RFID middleware to support trust and secure m-business based on RFID. Mobile RFID terminal's function is concerned with the recognition distance to the RFID reader chip built into the cellular phone, transmission power, frequency, interface, technological standard, PIN specification, UART communication interface, WIPI API and WIPI-HAL API extended specification to control reader chip. RFID reader chip middleware functions are provided to the application program in the form of WIPI API as in figure 4. Here, 'Mobile RFID Device Driver' is the device driver software provided by the reader chip manufacturer.

Mobile RFID network function is concerned with the communication protocols such as the ODS communication for code interpretation, the message transmission for the transmission and reception of contents between the cellular phone terminal and the application server, contents negotiation that supports mobile RFID service environment and ensures the optimum contents transfer between the cellular phone terminal and the application server, and session management that enables the application to create and mange required status information while transmitting the message and the WIPI extended specification which supports these communication services.

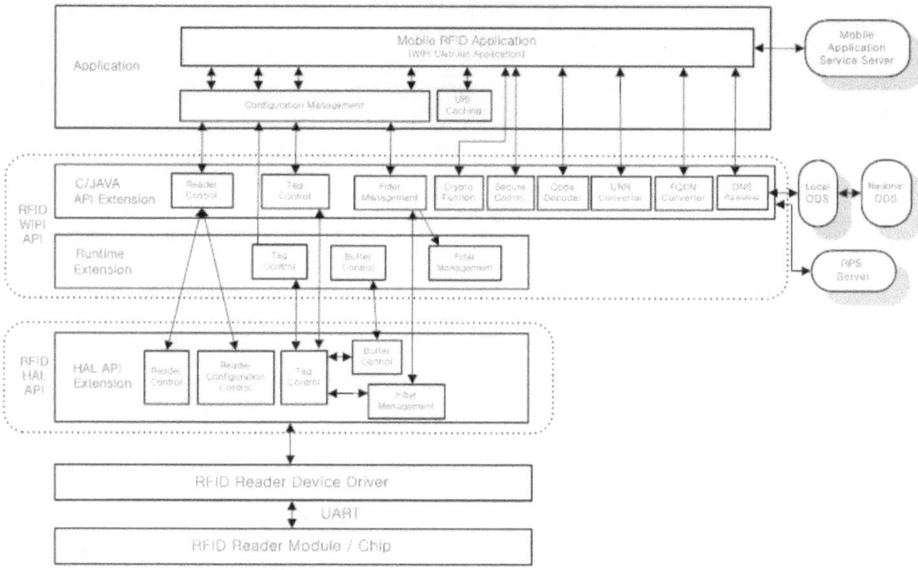

Fig. 4. Security Enhanced Mobile RFID Middleware System

5 Conclusion

In this paper, the WIPI-based mobile RFID security middleware platform is proposed. With this propose, the application areas of this platform is also presented briefly. The current status, problems, and issues in mobile communication service as well as the requirement analysis, the recommended domestic standard of the WIPI, and its profile are discussed in this paper. From the discussion, the motivation and necessity of proposing the security middleware platform is derived. Although the WIPI-based mobile RFID platform is the recommended domestic standards in Korea at present, it will be able to refer and consider as one of the proposed draft international standards in mobile communication service. The merits of the platform are common API for diverse types of multimedia contents, more effective in function and performance than conventional platforms do, and standards for handset layer porting. As the platform is recommended as a domestic standard for mobile RFID application service in Korea, the most beneficial parts will be content provider and mobile user. In this paper, the application areas of the proposed platform are discussed briefly in the fields of RFID-based LBS (Location Based Service), RFID-based mobile payment, RFID-based mobile CRM (Customer Relationship Management), and mobile ASP (Applications Service Provider).

For further study of this area, the verification and validation of the light-weight security middleware model by design and implementing some pilot-scale service system is necessary. It is also required to develop evaluation and authentication methodologies with the assistance of toolkits for the granularity of the QoS (Quality of Service) of the pilot-scale service system.

Acknowledgement

The first author is a Ph.D. Student (part-time) at Sungkyunkwan University. Currently, He is working as a member of the engineering staff at Electronics and Telecommunications Research Institute (ETRI), Korea.

References

1. Tsuji T. Kouno S. Noguchi J. Iguchi M. Misu N. and Kawamura M.: Asset management solution based on RFID. NEC Journal of Advanced Technology. vol.1, no.3, Summer. (2004) 188-193
2. Sullivan L.: Middleware enables RFID tests. Informationweek, no.991 (2004)
3. Seunghun Jin, et. Al.: Cluster-based Trust Evaluation Scheme in Ad Hoc Network. ETRI Journal, Vol.27, No.4 (2005) 465-468
4. Woo Yong Han, et. Al.: A Gateway and Framework for Telematics Systems Independent on Mobile Networks. ETRI Journal, Vol.27, No.1 (2005) 106-109
5. S. E. Sarma, S. A. Weis, and D.W. Engels.: RFID systems, security and privacy implications. Technical Report MIT-AUTOID-WH-014, AutoID Center, MIT, (2002)
6. Weis, S. et al.: Security and Privacy Aspects of Low-Cost Radio Frequency identification Systems. First Intern. Conference on Security in Pervasive Computing, SPC (2003)
7. M. Ohkubo, K. Suzuki and S. Kinoshita: Cryptographic Approach to "Privacy-Friendly" Tags, RFID Privacy Work-shop, (2003)
8. Jan E. Hennig, Peter B. Ladkin, Bern sieker: Privacy Enhancing Technology Concepts for RFID Technology Scrutinised, RVS-RR-04-02, 28 October (2004)
9. Ari Juels, Ronald L Rivest, Michael Szydlo: The Blocker Tag: Selective Blocking of RFIDTags for Consumer Privacy. 10th ACM Conference on Computer and Communications Security, (2003)
10. Ari Juels, Ravikanth Pappu: Squealing RFID-Enabled Banknotes. In R. Wright, ed., Financial Cryptography, (2003)
11. Se-Won OH, Jong-Suk CHAE: Information Report on Mobile RFID in Korea. ISO/IEC JTC1 SC31 WG4, Report (2005)
12. Kyung Won Min, Suk Byung Chai, Shiho Kim: An Analog Front-End Circuit for ISO/IEC 14443-compatible RFID Interrogators. ETRI Journal, Vol.26, No.6 (2004) 560-564

Tourism Guided Information System for Location-Based Services

Chang-Won Jeong[1], Yeong-Jee Chung[2], Su-Chong Joo,[2] and Joon-whoan Lee[1]

[1] Research Center for Advanced LBS Technology of Chonbuk National University, Korea
[2] College of Electrical, Electronic and Information Engineering, Wonkwang University, Korea
{mediblue, chlee}@chonbuk.ac.kr,
{yjchung, scjoo}@wonkwang.ac.kr

Abstract. Mobile information community develops quickly, as mobile telecommunication technology matches to the third generation. XML-based GIS becomes a global standard and the foundation. Recent developed Geography Markup Language (GML) allows integration of GIS location-based services, telematics, and intelligent transportation systems. In this paper, we propose a tourism information system for supporting the location based service of GIS applications. The system implements thin-client/server technology for mobile Web mapping service. The system includes traditional GIS system for navigation service and location finder POI services. The system for location and POI determination with design concerns are presented. An experimental user interface of PDA within the system is illustrated for the system procedures.

Keywords: GML, LBS, Mobile tourism service, GIS, SVG.

1 Introduction

Web becomes a popular tool for information distribution and Web based geographic Information Systems (GIS) are rapidly deployed to applications [1]. Since wireless networks enable new infrastructure for mobile services, Location Based Service (LBS) for mobile users begin to track and measure the user position for providing better service performance [2,3]. Therefore, the LBS urgently need a mapping information system, together with conventional GIS services and infrastructures. LBS based tourism information system may contain tour planning, navigation support to yellow page services, and commerce [4]. To generate interactive maps is an important component in today's tourism information system.

Since existing GIS services were developed independently, there is no interoperability to support diverse map formats. Recently developed GML is a new methodology to deal with geographic information sharing. GML is an XML encoding for transport and storage of geographic information, including both spatial and non-spatial properties of geographic feature [5-7]. GML is important to draw some clear distinctions between geographic data and graphic interpretations of the data, as it appears on a map or other form of visualization. To generate a map with GML data, one must follow GML standards and coded into a suitable graphical presentation. In

H.T. Shen et al. (Eds.): APWeb 2006, LNCS 3842, pp. 749 – 755, 2006.

general, GML data are coded into an XML graphical format using SVG (Scalable Vector Graphics), VML (Vector Markup Language), X3D technologies. In the past, people developed some prototype for distributing vector data on Internet. These protocols are complementarily based on GML and SVG. GML is used for string and distributing geographic data, while SVG is for presenting data [8, 9]. When a request to a map is performed, a GML file is created and to be translated into an SVG file. This step may also perform some generalization transformations.

Portable devices, such as cellular phones, GPS devices, PDAs, and Palm, geo-referenced information (GRI) are undergoing a significant change. The change is driven by software systems such as ESRI [10], MapInfo [11], Intergraph [12] and AutoDesk [13] which allow us publish geographical data online. However, the data and software systems are proprietary and completely controlled by vendors. The maps in image formats or in embedded objects are not interoperable; hence forming an obstacle of integrating searched results from different systems together.

The LBS is an integrated technology in telecommunication and GIS. LBS was developed based on that a portable device sends its location information to a gateway; the gateway search through its database to find the most relevant information near the location and sends it back to the client for further use. However, a problem in this technology is that the gateway must maintain a centralized GRI database to support queries.

XML-based data integration architectures become popular since XML is a kind of text-based protocol that is easily processed and exchanged between users. GML, an extension of XML and proposed by OGC is to solve the GRI interoperability problem. Several spatial data types, such as points, poly-lines and polygons, as well as earth projection types are defined in GML DTD. Any software that supports GML can use geographical data in a GML document. An XML-based spatial data mediation infrastructure for global interoperability study is conducted in San Diego Supercomputer Center [13].

This paper suggests a thin client/server information system for LBS. It was experimented in within a small region. Section 2 describes a general overview of the information system. Section 3 shows the servicing procedures respectively. The proposed prototype implementation is described in Section 4; followed by a conclusion and future works.

2 Proposed System Architecture

The overall architecture of our proposed system is illustrated in Fig. 1. The system architecture is structured by the following. The architecture serves as a generic infrastructure that can be applied to other LBS applications. Therefore, a well-formed interface has to be provided that allows the appropriate use of the services for the different applications. The system adopts a three-tier architecture.

The first is a client tier. Each client has two components: GPS and Service agents. GPS agent provides the physical location of a user to the TM (Transverse Mercator) [14]. GPS receiver with deferential correction (DGPS) is used to determine location and to track the path of travel. Position information is provided for mapping. The Service agent supports geographical view utilities based on Map and POI.

The second is a mediator. Whenever the mediator receives a request from a client, it first determines which service manager is related to map and divided a query into a sub-queries. The mediator then finds the corresponding map in its database. Mediator has a service manager which consists of four modules (in Fig.1); mainly a GIS-based solution; DXF to SVG/GML translating, collecting, storing, and searching and retrieving maps.

The third is the database tier. It supports data management of spatial or non-spatial data. For a POI service, database contains object identification, name for map presentation, coordination system, and additional information entities. The roles of each component in the thin client and server are described like below.

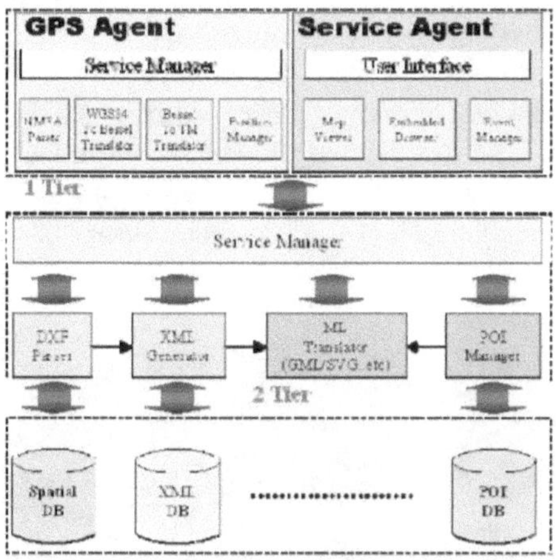

Fig. 1. Proposed System Architecture

Thin client side

- Service Manager: total management services invoked by a Web service, controlling the process of response message, and monitoring each component.
- NMEA Parser: extracting valid information fetched from NMEA information of GPS receiver.
- WGS84 to Bessel Translator: translating Bessel to WGS84 (using Molodensky-Badekas model).
- Bessel to TM Translator: translating Transverse Mercator.
- Position Manager: managing with log file and user position tracking.
- User Interface: providing two-way communication between GPS agent and users.
- Map Viewer: supporting SVG and GML displays
- Embedded Browser: providing additional POI information based on HTML
- Event Manager: managing all layer controls and POI events.

Server side

- Service Manager: managing service modules; receiving the service requests from client, and then returns the information of the created XML byte stream to service agents.
- DXF Parser: translating DXF file into Tag Tree.
- XML Generator: generating well-formed XML document in a tag tree.

- ML Translator: translating markup language using XSLT schema which is suitable for client GIS environments (SVG, GML, etc.).
- POI Manager: extracting a POI information requested from client.

3 Service Procedure

The workflow of both control commands and information contents are described in Fig. 2. Step 1 performs an acquisition of location information; Step 2 request from the client reaches a service manager by the means of the XML soap/http protocol through the communication layer. Selected position information is sent to the service manager. Steps 3-5 are executed under POI environments using client's selection, upon the given position information in Step 2. This step filters a map of service area. In Step 6, the response information with the XML byte stream is collected from the Service manager. The generated data is passed to the communication layer for further transformation to an appropriate format. Figure 3 shows a Message Flow for representing the whole management procedures mentioned above.

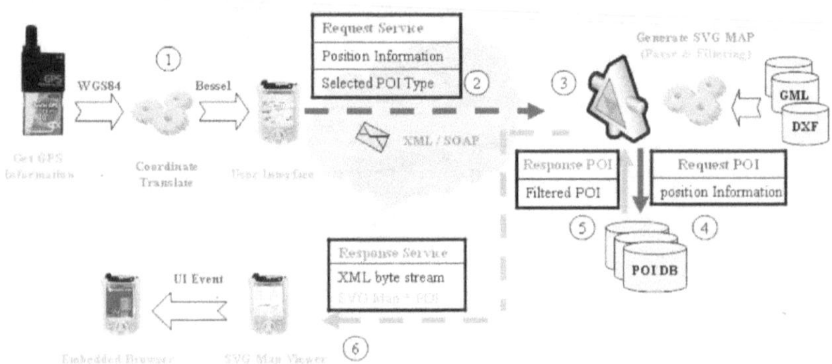

Fig. 2. Service Flow

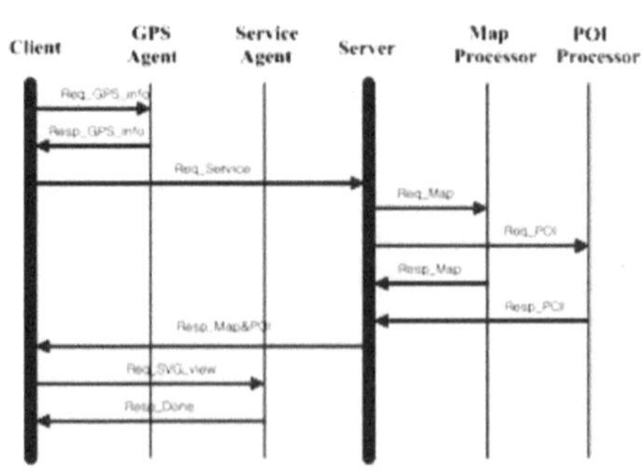

Fig. 3. Message Flow

4 Implementation of the Tourism Information System for LBS

A prototyped implementation of the Tourism information system for LBS is implemented for the explanation of the system mechanism. The main implementation goal is to process spatial data, and to handle both the geometry and the properties of the geographical elements; this allows the various data providers to share heterogeneous datasets and the users to access the data in a completely transparent way. The processing of XML/GML documents and their visualizations in a graphical way with the interaction of the user is depicted. Since the GML data structure is XML compliant, it can be transformed in a SVG format for easily to be displayed on a Web browser with SVG viewing utility.

The physical environment for implementation is shown in Figure 4. We constructed a Web service using a computer with Windows 2003 server. Net framework for interacting among components and/or service objects. The model components of the client and the server are implemented by C# language. Information of the POI is constructed to a relational database. These databases are managed by the MS SQL 2000. The Prototyped Implementation Environment as shown in Figure 4 presents the executing results of the navigation service and an example of the POI services in the system are provided. For displaying the procedures and the executing results of services on our system, a GUI-window interface is designed.

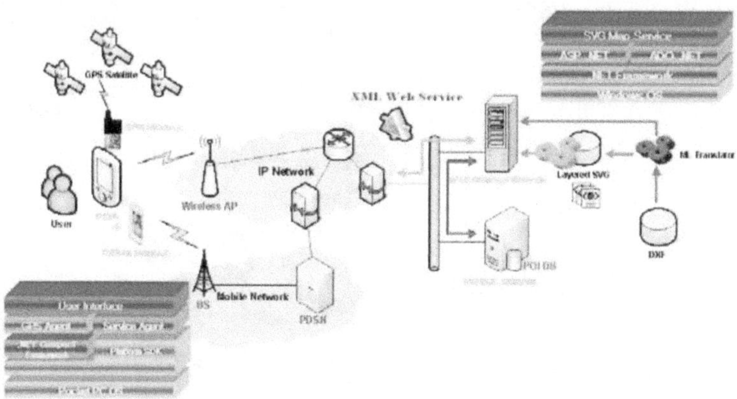

Fig. 4. Service Configuration

To demonstrate the operation of the service, a small part of Jeonju-City was selected and spatial data and POI information were converted from a GIS format of DXF to SVG.

The client side supported zoom in/zoom out and full extent of geometric data for visualization and POI listing of textural data. Selected POI results were overlapped on base maps that were given from the other GML data, or directly from flat geographical data files as well as spatial databases.

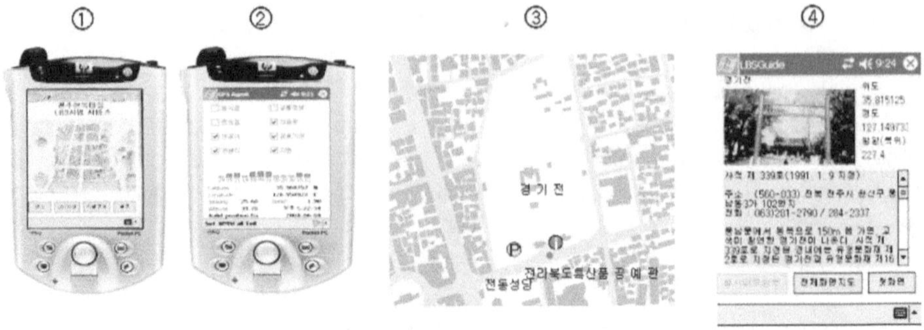

Fig. 5. The map of Han-Ok Village with the Korean traditional houses in Jeonju-city and POI information

Figure 5 illustrates the screens displayed on the PDA. Click setting button of first phase of Figure 5, after pointing which one you like, you fill the choosing POI out in check space, and then click WMSCall button. One can see the map and POI information corresponding to a given service. These GUI is displaying user position by red dot on the base map in PDA, and then, selecting the POI displayed on the map. And these screens are displayed in first page and user can browse the map and select the POI to be displayed in GUI. And then it shows the related information with the position information as results executed by the UI event.

As mentioned before, all processes in this system, either spatial analysis or invoking XML-based map contents are carried out in the server side and just a response in XML form is sent to client. XML parsers in client side interpret the XML contents and a service agent displays the spatial data and/or POI information's in the form of image and texts. Fig. 6 shows the map of small area query results returned from server.

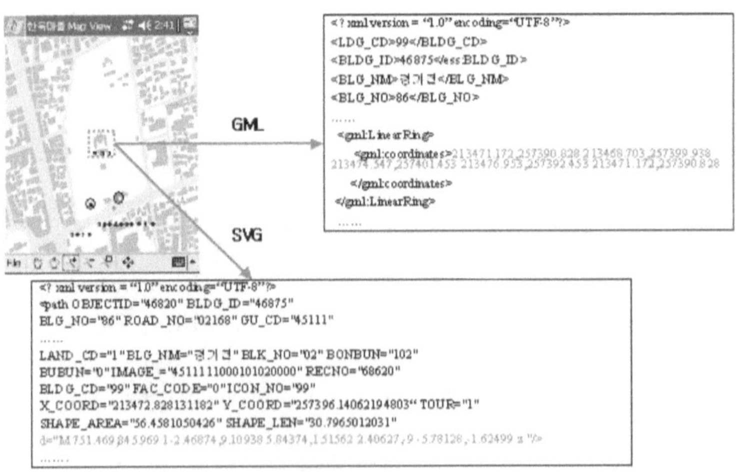

Fig. 6. Map of area showing GML and SVG

5 Conclusions and Future Work

Many WMS (Web Mapping Services) and POI (Point of Interest) based services begin to function in mobile GIS with the fast development of wireless devices. Location based services play a signification part in wireless application. With increasing the bandwidth of wireless communication, LBS systems are feasible for wireless users want to gain more. This paper described a thin client/server information system for location based service. System was implemented in a small area. This paper serves as a case study tries to expose the potential of wireless technology to serve LBSs. The future study focuses on an object-oriented database system capable for large spatial dataset.

Acknowledgments

This research was supported by University IT Research Center Project.

References

1. Shekhar, S., Vatasavi, R.R., Sahay, N., Burk, T. E., Lime, S.: WMS and GML based Interoperable Web Mapping System. In proceedings of the 9th ACM International Symposium on Advances in Geographic Information Systems. ACMGIS 2001 (Nov. 2001), ISBN 1-58113-443-6.
2. Zipf, A., Malaka, R.: Developing "Location Based Services" (LBS) for tourism –The service providers view. In: Sheldon, P., Wober, K. and Fesenmaier D. (Eds.): Information and Communication Technologies in TOURISM 2001. Proceedings of ENTER 2001, 8th International Conference. Montreal. Springer Computer Science. Wien, NewYork. 83-92
3. Schmidt-Belz, B., Makelainen, M., Nick, A., Poslad, S.: Intelligent Brokering of Tourism Services for Mobile Users. ENTER 2002. January 23-25 (2002) Innsbruck
4. Stephanidis, C., Paramythis, A., Sfyrakis, M., Stergou, A., Maou, N., Leventis, A., Paparoulis, G., & Kaagiannidis, C., (1998). Adaptable and Adaptive User Interfaces for Disabled Users in the AVANTI Project. In S. Trigila, A. Mullery, M. Campolargo, H. Vanderstraeten & M. Mampaey(Eds.), Intelligence in Services and Network: Technology for Ubiquitous Telecommunications Services – Proceedings of the 5th International Conference on Intelligence in Services and Networks (IS&N '98), Antwerp, Belgium, 153-166
5. OpenGIS Consortium, Geography Markup Language, http://www.opengis.net/gml/
6. Open GIS Consortium, Simple Feature Specification, http://www.opengis .org/ specs/ ?page=specs
7. W3Consortium, XML, http://www.w3.org/xml/
8. SVG Explorer of GML Data, Bonati L. P., Fortunati L., Fresta G. (2003)
9. Making maps with Geography Markup Language(GML), Lake R., Galdos Systems Inc, October (2000)
10. MapInfo, http://www.mapinfo.com
11. InterGraph, http://www.intergraph.com
12. AutoDesk, http://www.autodesk.com
13. GML3.0 specification, http://www.opengis.org/docs/02-023r4.pdf
14. Welcome to CommLinx Solutions - GPS Tracking Systems, http://www. commlinx. com.au/default.htm
15. Lehto L., Standards-Based Service Architecture for Mobile Map Applications, 5th AGILE Conference on Geographical Information Science, Palma (Balearic Islands, Spain) April 25-27 (2002)

A New Bio-inspired Model for Network Security and Its Application

Hui-qiang Wang, Jian Wang, and Guo-sheng Zhao

Department of Computer Science and Technology,
Harbin Engineering University, Harbin, 150001, China
hqwang@hrbeu.edu.cn, wangjianlydia@163.com

Abstract. Bio-inspired approach for network security is appealing because of the obvious analogies between the security of network systems and the survival of biological species. However, nearly all the existing researches only focus on some facets of network security using partial security mechanisms of biosystem. In this paper, a comprehensive bio-inspired model for network security is proposed to fully exhibit the performances by which the biology achieves security. The analysis shows that the model can not only provide a framework for researchers but also offer some new research angles for pursuers in the field.

1 Introduction

Computer network is an important infrastructure of a country, so its security receives more attention widely in the academia, industry and government. On the other hand, hacker attacks are more frequent than ever before and computer viruses spread even quickly. These factors make it increasingly difficult for the existing network security methods to keep pace with threat proliferation. In response to this situation, some efforts have been made on developing new methods for building efficient network security systems.

Bio-inspired is a new kind of theory and method developing rapidly in recent years. It emphasizes on "inspired", the ongoing research is not to completely copy the nature but to explore and learn valuable security mechanisms that can be used for computer systems. Researchers have taken several bio-inspired approaches and applied them to network security realm, such as artificial immune system[1], diversity[2], virus propagation[3] and feedback control loop[4] etc. Nevertheless, the existing researches mostly focus on borrowing partial ideas from biological systems to resolve some facets of network security problems, for instance intrusion detection[5], anti-viruses[6], fault-tolerance[7] and so on. It is more significant to consider the biological security mechanisms as a whole. Hence this paper aims to combine the biological security mechanisms with network security problems systematically, and then attempts to present a holistic bio-inspired model which can help the researchers to build an effective network security system.

2 A New Bio-inspired Model

We know that biological system is extremely large and complex, so it holds a whole suit of security mechanisms. If we can borrow these mechanisms and apply them to

H.T. Shen et al. (Eds.): APWeb 2006, LNCS 3842, pp. 756 – 759, 2006.

the design of network security mechanisms systematically, it would certainly pave a new way for the work.

2.1 The Nature of Bio-inspired Network Security

Unlike the traditional computer and network systems, in the nature, biology especially for human realizes security by a set of completely different ways. Distinguished from the security level, it would be labeled for organism organization security, the individual security, the group security, the social security and the species security; We can also summarize from the means which biology takes, classified as: prevention, detection and response, tolerance (fault-tolerance, intrusion-tolerance, disaster-tolerance) together with recovery; According to the attribute by which the biology achieves security guarantee, there may prominently display for diversity (heredity), the evolution (learning, memory and self-adaptation), the autonomic characteristic (self-adjustment, self-protection, self-repair), the redundancy and distributability, the reconfiguration and regeneration, the sociality (credit system, deterrent mechanism, force method) and so on. All the above mentions constitute the holistic security mechanisms for biology, which are highly desired for network security system and greatly appropriate to it.

Network security is an all-around technology and a systematic engineering. In order to maintain network security effectively, we can also consider the security problem from different levels, such as a computer component, an individual computer, a local area network, the Internet, the global network etc. For accessing various network applications, the primary concern should be certain attributes of the security. These attributes define the qualities relevant to the network security. The network system security concerns itself with provision of the following six attributes: diversity, evolution, autonomy, redundancy & distributability, reconfiguration & regeneration and society etc. By building a matrix with the security levels positioned along the horizontal axis and the security attributes aligned down the vertical, we have the foundation for the model. We have now outlined a matrix which provides us with the theoretical basis for our model. What it lacks at this stage is the means that we take to insure the security attributes can be maintained in every security level. The means may differentiate from the scheduling, listing for prevention, detection and response, tolerance, together with recovery, and it is the third dimension of our model.

2.2 The Model Overview

The completed model appears as figure 1, inspired by the foregoing analyses. This is a three-dimensional model. And in every dimension, it has several layers. Examining the intersections of the three dimensions gives researchers a needed multidimensional view of the scope of bio-inspired approach for network security. Any "cube" in the three-dimensional space may represent a certain security level is provided with some or other characteristic by such means. All aspects of bio-inspired approach for network security can be viewed within the framework of the model. For example, we may cite a cryptographic module as prevention measure which insures security in the individual level. But each measure is not enough for the application of prevention. Other layers such as detection and response etc. then function as the complementarities for proper application and use of the security means. Not every security mean begins with a specific prevention measure. It may also be solely a tolerance security control. The model helps us to understand the overall nature of biological security mechanisms that a partial perspective cannot define. Based on it, we can attempt to build a more effective bio-inspired network security system.

It is noticeable that the process is continuous and recursive. Simultaneously, every axis may extend infinitely from both directions, which makes it unnecessary to alter the premise even as the means, attributes and human understanding evolve. More important, there exist interactions among the levels, the means and the attributes, fully exhibiting the integrity of security systems.

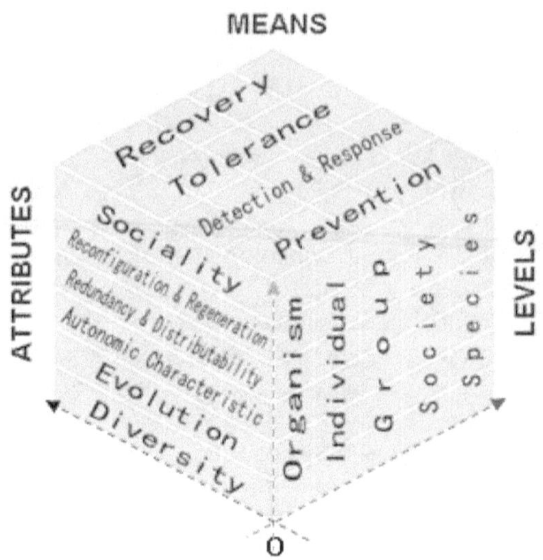

Fig. 1. A comprehensive bio-inspired model for network security system. This is a three-dimensional model, and there are several layers in each dimension.

2.3 Applications of the Model

The model has several significant applications. Initially, the two-dimensional matrix is used to identify security levels and system vulnerabilities. Then, the four layers of security means can be employed to minimize these vulnerabilities based on the knowledge of the threat to the network system. Let us take a brief look at these applications.

A developer may begin using the model with defining different security levels within the system. When a security level is identified, then they will work down the vertical path to address all the critical security attributes. Once vulnerabilities are emerged in this fashion, it becomes a simple matter to work down through the four layers of security means orderly. If prevention is available, the designer knows that detection and response, tolerance as well as recovery will be logical follow-on aspects of that control. If prevention cannot be identified, then detection and response must be viewed as the next likely avenue, and so on.

Another important application is realized when the model is used as an evaluation tool. More important, the one hundred and twenty individual "cubes" created by the model can be extracted and examined individually. This key aspect can be useful in categorizing and analyzing countermeasures. It is also a tool for defining organizational responsibility for network security. By considering all 120 such "cubes", the analyst is assured of a complete security standards and criteria, this model connotes a true "system" viewpoint.

3 Conclusion

We develop this model to respond to the need for a theoretical foundation for modeling the bio-inspired approach for network security. And the comprehensive bio-inspired model for network security acts as a guide for the researchers who are concerned about it. The subjects of future research include how to realize the network system structure corresponding to the model that we put forward and test the feasibility in simulation environments.

References

1. Forrest, S. Perelson, A.S.: Self-Nonself Discrimination in a Computer. In Proceedings of IEEE Symposium on Research in Security and Privacy, Oakland, 5 (1994)
2. Forrest, S., Somayaji, A. Ackley, D.H.: Building Diverse Computer Systems. In Workshop on Hot Topics in Operating Systems, (1997) 67-72
3. Kephart, J.O., White, S. R.: Directed Graph Epidemiological models of Computer Viruses. Proceedings of the 1991 IEEE Computer Security Symposium on Research in Security and Privacy, Oakland California, 5 (1991) 343-359
4. Somayaji, A., Forrest, S.: Automated Response using System-call Delays. In proceedings of the 9th USENIX Security Symposium, (2000) 185-197
5. Dasgupta, D.: An Immune-based Technique to Characterize Intrusions in Computer Networks. In IEEE Transactions on Evolutionary Computation, 6 (2002)
6. Williamson, M. M., Léveillé, J.: An Epidemiological Model of Virus Spread and Cleanup. Hewlett-Packard, 12 (2003)
7. Bradley, D., Tyrrell, A.: Embryonics+Immunotronics: A Bio-inspired Approach to Fault Tolerance. http://www.amp.york.ac.uk/external/media.

Partner Selection System Development for an Agile Virtual Enterprise Based on Gray Relation Analysis*

Chen Hua[1], Cao Yan[1], Laihong Du[2], and Zhao Rujia[3]

[1] Xi'an Institute of Technology, Xi'an, Shaanxi 710032
chenhua126@163.com
[2] Xi'an University of Finance and Economics, Xi'an, Shaanxi 710061
[3] School of Mechanical Engineering, Xi'an Jiaotong University, Xi'an, Shaanxi 710049

Abstract. The paper analyzes the state of the art of partner selection and enumerates the advantage of partner selection based on gray relation analysis comparing to the other algorithms of partner selection. Furthermore, partner selection system based on gray relation for an Agile Virtual Enterprise (AVE) is analyzed and designed based on the definition and characteristics of the AVE. According to J2EE mode, the architecture of partner selection system is put forward and the system is developed using JSP, EJB and SQL Server.

1 Introduction

An Agile Virtual Enterprise (AVE) is a provisional network organization that is composed of several independent enterprises that are connected by information technology for the purpose of seizing rapidly changing market opportunities [1-3]. Aiming at some market demand, various resources of the enterprises in the AVE are optimized and deployed along the increment direction of value chain. Thus, each enterprise can take full advantage of its core competence and the AVE is able to respond to market changes rapidly.

After the characteristics of candidate partners are analyzed and evaluated, the optimal partner constitution of the AVE is determined [4-6]. Then, the cooperative mode between the partners is also determined that is one of the key elements to estimate whether an AVE can succeed or not. At present, partner selection of the AVE usually adopts integer programming, fuzzy evaluation, synthetic analysis and comparison, multi-objective decision-making, and so on [7-12] in domestic and oversea researches. These methods make evaluation indices nondimensional in order to eliminate the difference between them. This leads to large difference of evaluation structure. Sometimes, many indices are incomparable or qualitative, this makes it more difficult to evaluate various indices synthetically. Gray relation theory makes up the deficiency of the aforementioned approaches. It can change incomparable indices into comparable ones. Thereby, it is suitable for multi-objective decision-making. Accordingly, gray relation theory is adopted to select partners of the AVE in the paper.

---

* The paper is supported by Project 50405029 of National Natural Science Foundation of China and Project 2003K03-G20 of Shaanxi Science and Technology Foundation.

H.T. Shen et al. (Eds.): APWeb 2006, LNCS 3842, pp. 760 – 766, 2006.

2 Analysis and Design of the AVE Partner Selection System

The core enterprise of the AVE is called an alliance leader that is responsible for managing the running and coordination of the whole AVE. Every enterprise that provides its core competence for the AVE is called an alliance leaguer. Confronted with a market opportunity, the alliance leader analyzes the opportunity and breaks a project down into smaller ones that are released on Internet. Then, after candidate partners balance their own capabilities and possible profit that can be achieved through cooperation in the AVE, they decide whether they bid for the projects or not. Finally, the alliance leader evaluates the bids according to predefined evaluation system and selects the optimal partners to form the AVE.

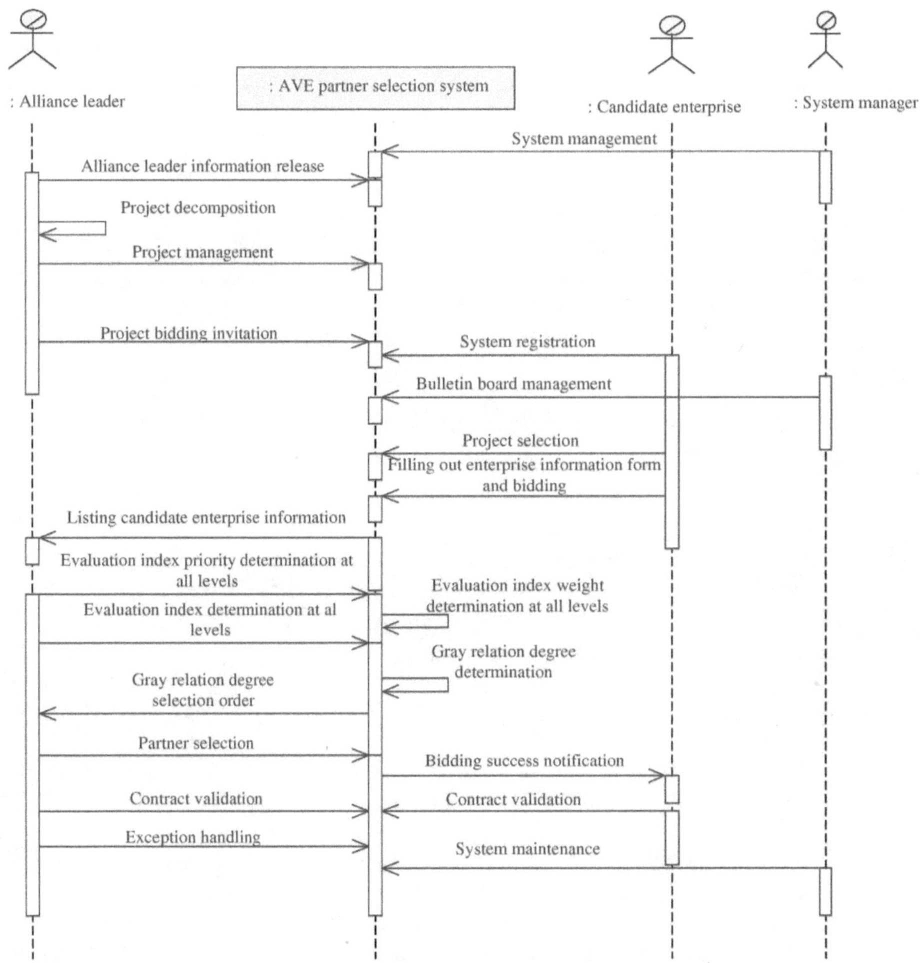

Fig. 1. Partner selection workflow in the AVE

Adopting object oriented ideas and UML modeling tool, partner selection in the AVE is modeled.The partner selection workflow and realization sequence of functional modules in the AVE are shown in Fig. 1.

The functional modules related to a system manager include alliance leader management, partner management, candidate enterprise management, system maintenance, bulletin board management, etc. The functional modules related to the candidate enterprise include project browse, system registration, project bidding, enterprise information release, etc. The functional modules related to the alliance leader include exception handling, project management (project creation, modification, deletion, release, and so on), partner selection based on gray relation analysis that is carried out based on the evaluation indices and weights extracted from the information provided by candidate enterprises.

First, the system manager authorizes the corresponding authority to the alliance leader, candidate enterprises, common users, and so on. Then, the leader releases the basic information of the AVE and decomposes the project into smaller ones that form a series of items. And then, the succedent work of the leader is to manage the whole project. It mainly includes project creation, modification, deletion, release, etc. Especially, once a project is released, it cannot be modified or deleted. After the candidate enterprises are registered in the system, they can look over the information that they are concerned about on the bulletin board. If they find the project they need, they can fill out the information form that the leader requires. The forms are submitted to the leader who selects the partners based on gray relation algorithm after the evaluating indices and their priorities at all levels are determined. Finally, the contract is validated by the leader and partners, and the AVE is formed.

3 Architecture of Partner Selection Based on Gray Relation Analysis in the AVE

After the functions of partner selection system are analyzed and determined, the multi-level partner selection system architecture is constructed using Web technology and database technology, as shown in Fig. 2. It adopts B/W/D mode where client browser provides operation interface for users and Web server carries out data access, information decomposition, service transaction, etc based on database and XML files. The system is divided into four levels, namely user interface level, request receiving level, transaction level and data storage level.

- User interface level adopts Web-based HTML and XML pattern. A user accesses data through the interface provided by Web server and EJB server to guarantee background data security.
- Request receiving level mainly receives requests from the browser and transfers them to service transaction level. At the same time, it transfers transaction results back to the browser. The process is achieved through JSP pages and servlets. This level can accomplish some simple logic handling, such as data verification, client browser inspection, etc. But it is not recommended to accomplish complex logic handling at this level.

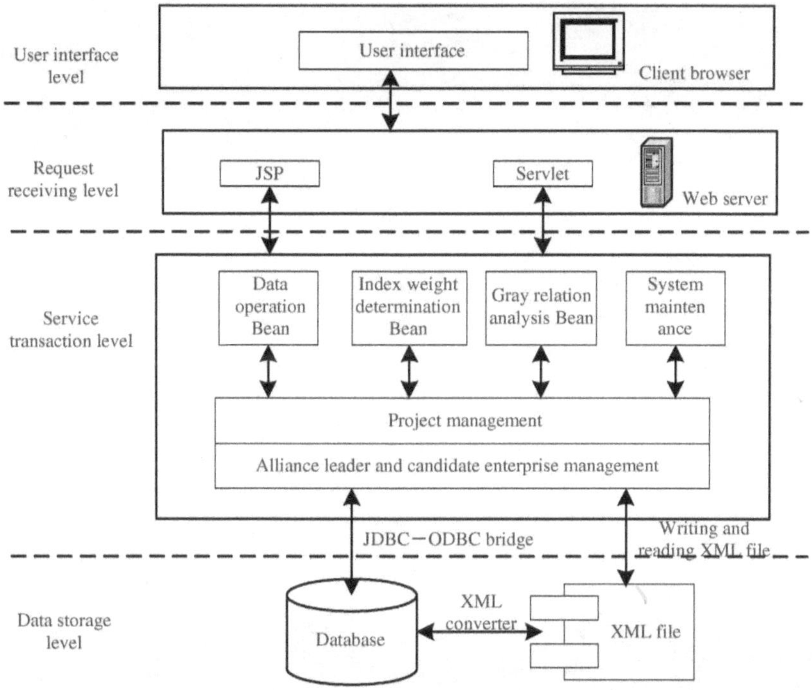

Fig. 2. The partner selection architecture based on gray relation analysis of the AVE

- Service transaction level is the core of the system. At this level, based on alliance leader management, candidate enterprise management and general user management according to different roles and their authorities, project creation, modification, deletion and release are realized. Then, database manipulation, evaluation index weights determination, and partner selection based on gray relation analysis are accomplished. This level is responsible for handling client requests from request receiving level and returning results to request receiving level. If it is necessary, the results are transferred to data storage level to store or update data or XML files. This level runs on Java application server where all transaction logics are encapslated in EJB (Enterprise Java Beans) modules.
- Data storage level includes database and XML file management. Data of resources and clients are stored in the database that provides data service for sevice transction level, such as storing the results from service transaction level, returning searched data to service transaction level. XML files are used to share information with systems outside the AVE. Bidirectional translation between XML files and relational database can be realized through XML converters.

4 Evaluation Index System and Index Quntification Model of Partner Selection

The goal of partner selection in the AVE is to make it possible to quickly produce the products that satisfy market requirements at right time. In the paper, the indices

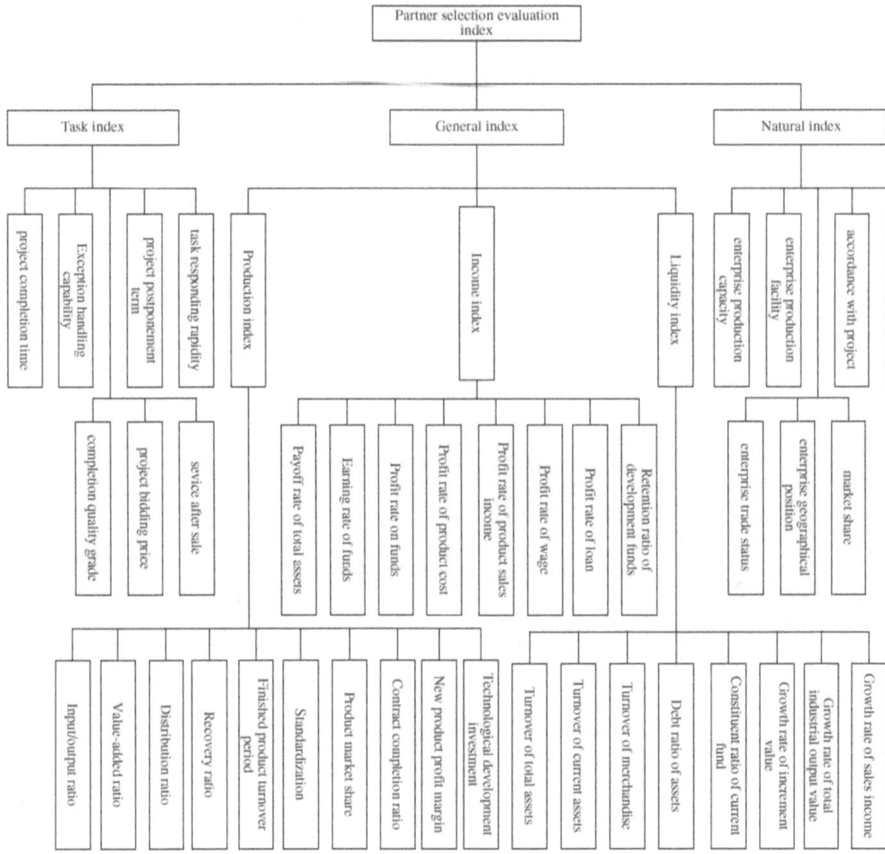

Fig. 3. Partner selection evaluation system of the AVE

of partner selection in the AVE can be divided into three categories, namely task indices, natural indices, and general indices, as shown in Fig. 3.

In the process of partner selection in the AVE, the first step to realize gray relation selection is to quantify evaluating indices that form the sequence to be compared. This work facilitates the realization of the algorithm. The process to quantify various indices is as follows.

- General indices are percentage numbers and quantified that need be normalized to be used in gray relation analysis.
- Task indices mainly include project completion time L_{221}, completion quality grade L_{222}, project bidding price L_{223}, service after sale L_{224}, project postponement term L_{225}, task responding rapidity L_{226}, and exception handling capability L_{227}. Their quantification standard is shown in table 1.
- Natural indices mainly include enterprise production capacity L_{211}, enterprise production facility L_{212}, accordance with project L_{213}, enterprise credit standing L_{214}, enterprise trade status L_{215}, enterprise geographical position L_{216}, market share L_{217}. Their quantification standard is shown in table 2.

5 Partner Selection System Implementation of the AVE

According to system architecture and gray relation selection algorithm, following J2EE mode, JSP and EJB are used to develop client programs and server programs. The database adoped is SQL Server 2000. Network sever is Apach Tomcat4.1.12. The system developed is illustrated as follows according to different user roles.

- System manager space mainly includes alliance leader management, candidate enterprise management, bulletin board management, etc. Alliance leader management includes information management of leader enterprises, such as leader enterprise authority, project information, general data, etc. Candidate enterprise management is similar to alliance leader management. Bulletin board management includes bulletin release, management of the information released by alliance leaders and candidate enterprises, etc.
- Alliance leader space includes project management, bulletin board management, partner selection, manufacturing resource optimazation, allocation and evaluation, etc. Project management mainly includes project creation, modification, deletion, release, etc. One can look over detailed project information by clicking detailed information icon and a project status can not be changed if it has already been released. Bulletin board management mainly includes the management of project bid invitation, project bidding information, bulletin information, and so on. Partner selection module is used to choose the optimal cooperative enterprises from candidate enterprises based on gray relation algorithm.
- Candidate enterprise space includes bid invitation information browse, project bidding, etc. During the process of bidding, a candidate enterprise is asked to fill out the information form required by the alliance leader that introduces the candidate enterprise itself in detail.

6 Conclusions

The core of an AVE is how to produce high-grade products at righ time and place and by right enterprises through reasonably choosing appropriate partners and optimizing resource utilization. In the paper, UML is used to analyze and design the functions and workflow of partner selection in the AVE. After the evaluation indices system is determined, gray theory is used to solve the partner selection problem. The system developed provides tools for enterprises to respond to market demands quickly. The architecture of partner selection system is put forward according to J2EE mode and JSP, EJB and SQL Server are adopted to develop the system. The future researches are optimal resource allocation, process control, and so on in the AVE according to given manufacturing tasks after the partners have been selected based on gray relation analysis.

References

1. Yang, S.L., Li, T.F.: Agility Evaluation of Mass Customization Product Manufacturing. Journal of Materials Processing Technology 129 (2002) 640-644
2. Noaker, P.M.: The Search for Agile Manufacturing. Manufacturing Engineering 11 (1994) 40-43
3. Ellram, L.M.: Total Cost of Ownership: An Analysis Approach for Purchasing. International Journal of Physical Distribution and Logistics Management 25 (1995) 4-23
4. Narasimban, R., Talluri, S., Mendez, D.: Supplier Evaluation and Rationalization via Data Envelopment Analysis: An Empirical Examination. Journal of Supply Chain Management 37 (2001) 28-37
5. Jayaraman, V., Srivastava, R., Benton, W.C.: Supplier Selection and Order Quantity Allocation: A Comprehensive Model. Journal of Supply Chain Management 35 (1999) 50-58
6. Cachon, G.P., Zipkin, P.H.: Competitive Inventory Policies in a Two-Stage Supply Chain. Management Science 45 (1999) 936-953
7. Kasilingam, R.G., Lee, C.P.: Selection of Vendors - A Mixed-Integer Programming Approach. Computers & Industrial Engineering 31 (1996) 347-351
8. Hinkle, C.L., Robinson, P.J., Green, P.E.: Vendor Evaluation Using Cluster Analysis. Journal of Purchasing 29 (1996) 49-58
9. Weber, C.A., Ellram, L.M.: Supplier Selection Using Multi-Objective Programming: A Decision Support Systems Approach. International Journal of Physical Distribution and Logistics Management 23 (1993) 3-14
10. Petroni, A., Braglia, M.: Vendor Selection Using Principal Component Analysis. The Journal of Supply Chain Management 36 (2000) 63-69
11. Wang, S.Y., Xu, W.M., Wang, J.G.: A Fuzzy Sets Model and its Application in Evaluation. Journal of Mathematics for Technology 14 (1998) 88-91
12. Mikhailov, L.: Fuzzy Analytical Approach to Partnership Selection in Formation of Virtual Enterprises. The International Journal of Management Science 30 (2002) 393-401

RealTime-BestPoint-Based Compiler Optimization Algorithm

Jing Wu and Guo-chang Gu

College of Computer Science and Technology, Harbin Engineering University, Harbin 150001, China
99061632@163.com

Abstract. Static single assignment (SSA) is a key technique in compiler optimization. Lengauer-Tarjan is a fast algorithm for finding dominators in a flow-graph during the implementation of SSA. There are many useless calls to the recursive function EVAL in Lengauer-Tarjan, and it causes to execute many calls and returns. To solve these problems, an algorithm searching for real-time best-point, which is called RTBP (Real-Time Best-Point), is presented. The criterions related to RTBP are introduced. The causes of capacity differences between RTBP-based Lengauer-Tarjan and EVAL-based Lengauer-Tarjan are comparatively analyzed in theory. Then a static experiment is projected for illustration. Being used in Lengauer-Tarjan, RTBP can save a great deal of runtime and storage space. In a good many circumstances, the Lengauer-Tarjan based on RTBP is more efficient than EVAL-based Lengauer-Tarjan.

Keywords: Real-time best-point, live-vertex, semilive-vertex, complete semilive-vertex.

1 Introduction

In 1979, Lengauer and Tarjan proposed the Lengauer-Tarjan algorithm together. In 1998, Buchsbaum et al presented a linear-time algorithm based on Lengauer-Tarjan. However, they stated that their algorithm run ten to twenty percent slower than Lengauer-Tarjan on "real flowgraphs". In 2001, Keith D.Cooper, Timothy J.Harvey and Ken Kennedy proposed a simple, fast algorithm for finding dominators together. EVAL function is used to search for best-point in most of the algorithms mentioned above. However, since EVAL adopts a recursive call method, it needs to execute many calls and returns, and there are a lot of useless calls to EVAL during the implementation of these algorithms, which waste a great deal of runtime and storage space. In order to solve the problems mentioned above, this paper proposes an algorithm searching for real-time best-point (RTBP) which can be applied to Web-base computing in optimization in the future with its real-time character.

2 Problem Description

Lengauer-Tarjan is a fast algorithm for finding dominators in a flowgraph during the implementation of SSA which is an optimization compiler technique. It is described in

H.T. Shen et al. (Eds.): APWeb 2006, LNCS 3842, pp. 767 – 774, 2006.

[7] that Lengauer-Tarjan uses one function to construct the forest and another to extract information from it:

Link(p, n): Add edge(p, n) to the forest.

EVAL(v): If v is the root of a tree in the forest, return v. Otherwise, let r be the root of the tree in the forest which contains v. Return the non-root ancestor u of v that has the lowest-numbered semidominator on the path $r \xrightarrow{*} v$, u is the best-point of v on the path $r \xrightarrow{*} v$.

EVAL searches for the best-point of a vertex on some path with a recursive call method. When searching upwards, it compresses the path by setting *ancestor*[v]←*ancestor*[*ancestor*[v]], and modifies the best-point best[v] of v.

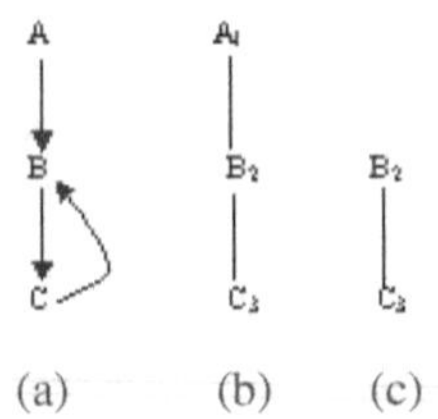

Fig. 1. A control flowgraph and its DFS tree. (a) is a control flow graph (CFG). (b) is the DFS tree of (a). (c) is a spanning tree before A_1 is linked into the forest.

As shown in Fig.1, the best-point of C_3 must be itself. Since the initialization best[C_3]←C_3 has already been done in Link(B_2, C_3), it's not necessary to call EVAL(C_3) to find the best-point of C_3. But EVAL(C_3) is called during the implementation when we compute the dominator of C_3 and the semidominator of B_2.

There are many similar useless calls to the recursive function EVAL during the implementation of Lengauer-Tarjan. From the aspect of time, when the best-point of some vertex on some path is needed, EVAL is called even if it doesn't need to, and many calls and returns are executed, thereby it wastes a lot of time. From the aspect of space, it needs a great deal of space to store data. Thus a new algorithm is needed to solve these problems.

3 Formalized Description of Concepts and Theorems

It is described in [8] that Lengauer-Tarjan for finding dominators is based on the DFS tree of CFG (control flow graph). For convenience, we shall assume in this paper that all vertices are identified by number. Lengauer-Tarjan visits the vertices from the biggest number to the smallest number.

3.1 Correlative Concepts

Definition 1 (dominator). Let $G = (V, E, r)$ be a flowgraph with start vertex r. A vertex v dominates another vertex $w \neq v$ in G if every path from r to w contains v. Vertex v is the immediate dominator of w, denoted $v = idom[w]$.

Definition 2 (semidominator). A vertex s is the semidominator of another vertex n if there is a path that begins to separate from the tree at the possible highest ancestor s and links the tree again at vertex n.

Theorem 1 (semidominator theorem). For any vertex $w \in V$ and $w \neq r$, $sdom[w] = min$ ($\{v \mid$ there is a path $v \rightarrow w$ and $v<w\} \cup \{sdom[u] \mid u>w$ and there is a path such that $u \overset{*}{\dashrightarrow} v \rightarrow w\}$).

Theorem 2 (dominator theorem). Let $w \neq r$ and let u be a vertex for which $sdom[u]$ is minimum among vertices u satisfying $sdom[w] \overset{+}{\rightarrow} u \overset{*}{\dashrightarrow} w$ on a DFS tree. Then

$$idom[w] = \begin{cases} sdom[w], & sdom[u] = sdom[w] \\ idom[u], & else \end{cases}$$

3.2 Some New Concepts and Theorems in RTBP

samedom[n]: *Idom*[n] can be computed through $idom[n] \leftarrow idom[samedom[n]] = idom[y]$ where y satisfies $y<n$ and $idom[y] = idom[n]$. But $idom[y]$ is an unknown quantity, so y is recorded in *samedom*[n].

" $visit(n, t)$ = true " describes that vertex n is being visited at the time t; otherwise, $visit(n, t)$ = false.

" $empty(n)$ = true " describes that set n can be emptied; otherwise, $empty(n)$ = false.

Definition 3 (live-vertex). A vertex n is a live-vertex if the best-point of vertex n is judged to be used later at the time t, denoted $live(n, t)$ = true; otherwise, denoted $live(n, t)$ = false. A vertex n is a live-vertex during a span of time T, denoted $live(n, T)$ = true; otherwise, denoted $live(n, T)$ = false.

Definition 4 (real-time best-point). A vertex v is a real-time best-point if the best-point v of live-vertex n makes a necessary and timing update according to the change of the forest structure, which synchronizes the best-point v of live-vertex n with the forest structure, denoted v = best[n].

Definition 5 (all-live-vertex). A live-vertex n is a all-live-vertex if the best-point of vertex n needs to be searched for at the time t, denoted $alive(n, t)$ = true; otherwise denoted $alive(n, t)$ = false.

Definition 6 (semilive-vertex). A live-vertex n is a semilive-vertex during a span of time T if the best-point of vertex n doesn't need to be searched for at the time t (T is a span of time from t to the time when n becomes not alive), denoted $blive(n, T)$ = true; otherwise, denoted $blive(n, T)$ = false.

Definition 7 (complete semilive-vertex). Let T be the entire span of time during vertex n keeps alive, then $live(n, T)$ = true. If the best point of n is itself or can be looked as itself during every time segment T' of T, then the best point of n isn't needed to be searched for during T for the initialization $best[n] \leftarrow n$ has been done in LinkChild(*parent*[n], n). Such vertex n is called complete semilive-vertex, denoted $cblive(n, T)$ = true; otherwise, denoted $cblive(n, T)$ = false.

$W[n]$: The set of live-vertices in a spanning tree below and contain vertex n when n is being visited.

W: The set of live-vertices in a spanning tree below vertex n before n is visited.

Definition 8 (minimum successor of *n*). In CFG, a vertex *v* is the minimum successor of vertex *n* if *v* is the smallest successor among these successors *u* satisfying *u*∈*succ*(*n*) and *u*<*n*. The minimum successor of vertex *n* doesn't exist if *n* have no successor or all successors are bigger than *n*, denoted *succmin*[*n*]←*n*.

4 RTBP Algorithm Description

The thinking of RTBP: making the best-point *v* of live-vertex *n* real-time brings *v* with a necessary and timing update according to the change of the forest structure, which synchronizes *v* with the forest structure. RTBP-based Lengauer-Tarjan can use the best-point of *n* directly in implementation, and doesn't need to call recursively to search for the best-point of *n* every time, which solves the problems during the implementation of EVAL-based Lengauer-Tarjan discussed above.

First, for each vertex *n*, let *W*[*n*]←*child*[*n*]←{} and let *idom*[*n*]←*sdom*[*n*]←*samedom*[*n*]←0 during the initialization. Then declare a set *W* and an integer array *succmin*[*N*], where *N* is the number of vertices in CFG. RTBP is described as follows:

```
(1) if (child[n] = {})  W←{};
(2) else {
(3)  W←∪W[m], m∈child[n];
(4)  for each element u of W {
(5)   if ((idom[u]=0&&samedom[u]=0)||(succmin[u]≠u
        &&succmin[u]<n)){
(6)    if (sdom[n]<sdom[best[u]]) best[u]←n;
(7)   }
(8)   else remove element u from W;
(9)  }
(10)}
(11)if (sdom[n]≠1&&n≠3&&n≠1) {
(12) succmin[n]←n;
(13) for each successor v of n {
(14)  if (v<succmin[n]) succmin[n]←v;
(15) }
(16) if (sdom[n] = parent[n]&&succmin[n]≥sdom[n]) W[n]←W;
(17) else W[n]←W ∪ {n};
(18)}
```

LinkChild(*p*, *n*) is described as follows:

```
(1)LinkChild(p, n){
(2)  child[p]←child[p]∪{n};
(3)  best[n]←n;}
```

RTBP needs to make Lengauer-Tarjan correspondingly change from four places.

(1) Let *N* be the number of vertices in CFG and delete array *ancestorr*[*N*];

(2) Declare a set *W* and an integer array *succmin*[*N*]; add set array *W*[*N*] and *child*[*N*] and Let *W*[*n*]←{} and *child*[*n*]←{} for each vertex *n*.

(3) Substitute LinkChild(*parent*[*n*], *n*) for Link(*parent*[*n*], *n*) in Lengauer-Tarjan.

(4) Substitute *best*[*v*] for the two calls to EVAL(*v*) in Lengauer-Tarjan and embed RTBP after LinkChild(*parent*[*n*], *n*).

5 Criterions Related to RTBP

5.1 Live-Vertex Criterion

If *visit*(*n*, *t*) = true and a vertex *u* satisfies one of the following conditions, then *live*(*u*, *t*) = true.

(a) $idom[u] = 0$ and $samedom[u] = 0$; (b) $succmin[u] \neq u$ and $succmin[u] < n$

5.2 Complete Semilive-Vertex Criterion

If a vertex *n* satisfies one of the following conditions, then *cblive*(*n*, *T*) = true , where *T* is the entire span of time during *n* keeps alive.

(a) $n=1$; (b) $sdom[n] = 1$; (c) $n = 3$; (d) $sdom[n] = parent[n]$ and $succmin[n] \geqslant sdom[n]$

5.3 Empty *W*[*n*] Criterion

If vertex *n* satisfies one of the conditions (a), (b) and (c) of complete semilive-vertex criterion, *empty*(*W*[*n*]) = true. If vertex *n* satisfies the condition (d) of complete semilive-vertex criterion, *empty*(*W*[*n*]) = false.

6 An Analysis of Capability Differences

6.1 A Static Experiment

This static experiment is to get two groups of different experimental data during the executions of RTBP-based and EVAL-based Lengauer-Tarjan, and the experimental data are analyzed elementarily. Choose a CFG randomly which is shown in Fig.2(a).

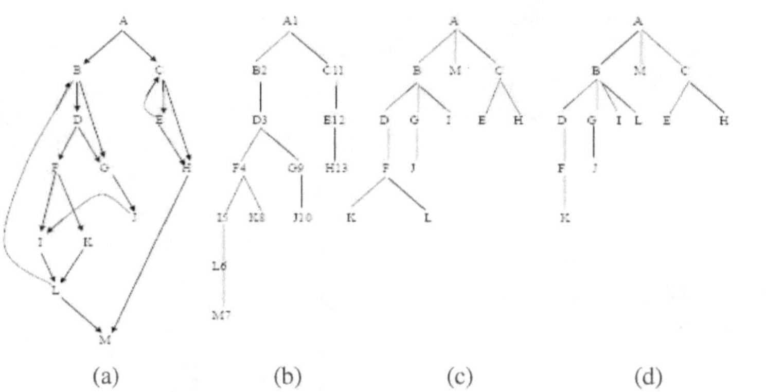

Fig. 2. A control flow graph and its DFS tree. Number labels in (b) is the vertex number

For convenience, all vertices are identified with number here. The experimental data are shown in Table 1 and Table 2 respectively.

Table 1. The experimental data record of RTBP-based Lengauer-Tarjan

<table>
<tr><th>n</th><th>child[n]</th><th>sdom[n]</th><th>best[n]</th><th>W</th><th>succmin[n]</th><th>W[n]</th><th>idom[n]</th><th>samedom[n]</th><th>best using</th></tr>
<tr><td>13</td><td></td><td>11</td><td>13× 11</td><td>{}</td><td>7</td><td>{13}</td><td>0× 11</td><td>0</td><td></td></tr>
<tr><td>12</td><td>{13}</td><td>11</td><td>12</td><td>{13}</td><td>11</td><td>{13}</td><td>11</td><td>0</td><td>|12, 13</td></tr>
<tr><td>11</td><td>{12}</td><td>1</td><td>11</td><td>{13}</td><td></td><td></td><td>1</td><td>0</td><td>12|11</td></tr>
<tr><td>10</td><td></td><td>9</td><td>10× 9</td><td>{}</td><td>5</td><td>{10}</td><td>9</td><td>0</td><td>|10</td></tr>
<tr><td>9</td><td>{10}</td><td>2</td><td>9</td><td>{10}</td><td>9</td><td>{10,9}</td><td>0× 2</td><td>0</td><td></td></tr>
<tr><td>8</td><td></td><td>4</td><td>8</td><td>{}</td><td>6</td><td>{}</td><td>4</td><td>0</td><td>|8</td></tr>
<tr><td>7</td><td></td><td>1</td><td>7</td><td>{}</td><td></td><td></td><td>0× 1</td><td>0</td><td>13|</td></tr>
<tr><td>6</td><td>{7}</td><td>4</td><td>6× 5</td><td>{}</td><td>2</td><td>{6}</td><td>0</td><td>0× 5</td><td>8|</td></tr>
<tr><td>5</td><td>{6}</td><td>2</td><td>5</td><td>{6}</td><td>5</td><td>{6,5}</td><td>0× 2</td><td>0</td><td>10|6</td></tr>
<tr><td>4</td><td>{8,5}</td><td>3</td><td>4</td><td>{6,5}</td><td>4</td><td>{6,5}</td><td>3</td><td>0</td><td>|4</td></tr>
<tr><td>3</td><td>{9,4}</td><td>2</td><td>3</td><td>{10×,9,6,5}</td><td></td><td></td><td>2</td><td>0</td><td>|9,5,3</td></tr>
<tr><td>2</td><td>{3}</td><td>1</td><td>2</td><td>{}</td><td></td><td></td><td>1</td><td>0</td><td>6|7,2</td></tr>
<tr><td>1</td><td>{11,2}</td><td>0</td><td>1</td><td>{}</td><td></td><td></td><td>0</td><td>0</td><td>|1</td></tr>
<tr><td>0</td><td>{1}</td><td></td><td></td><td></td><td></td><td></td><td></td><td></td><td></td></tr>
</table>

Table 2. The experimental data record of EVAL-based Lengauer-Tarjan

<table>
<tr><th>n</th><th>sdom[n]</th><th>ancestor[n]</th><th>best[n]</th><th>idom[n]</th><th>samedom[n]</th><th>EVAL calling</th></tr>
<tr><td>13</td><td>11</td><td>12× 11× 1</td><td>13× 11</td><td>0× 11</td><td>0</td><td></td></tr>
<tr><td>12</td><td>11</td><td>11× 1</td><td>12× 11</td><td>11</td><td>0</td><td>|12, 13(12)</td></tr>
<tr><td>11</td><td>1</td><td>1</td><td>11</td><td>1</td><td>0</td><td>12(11)|11</td></tr>
<tr><td>10</td><td>9</td><td>9× 3</td><td>10× 9</td><td>9</td><td>0</td><td>|10</td></tr>
<tr><td>9</td><td>2</td><td>3× 2</td><td>9</td><td>0× 2</td><td>0</td><td></td></tr>
<tr><td>8</td><td>4</td><td>4</td><td>8</td><td>4</td><td>0</td><td>|8</td></tr>
<tr><td>7</td><td>1</td><td>6× 1</td><td>7</td><td>0× 1</td><td>0</td><td>13(11)|</td></tr>
<tr><td>6</td><td>4</td><td>5× 4× 2× 1</td><td>6× 5× 2</td><td>0</td><td>0× 5</td><td>8|</td></tr>
<tr><td>5</td><td>2</td><td>4× 2</td><td>5</td><td>0× 2</td><td>0</td><td>10(9)|6(5)</td></tr>
<tr><td>4</td><td>3</td><td>3× 2</td><td>4× 3</td><td>3</td><td>0</td><td>|4</td></tr>
<tr><td>3</td><td>2</td><td>2</td><td>3</td><td>2</td><td>0</td><td>|9(3), 5(4(3)), 3</td></tr>
<tr><td>2</td><td>1</td><td>1</td><td>2</td><td>1</td><td>0</td><td>6(4(3))|7(6(2)), 2</td></tr>
<tr><td>1</td><td>0</td><td>0</td><td>1</td><td>0</td><td>0</td><td>|1</td></tr>
</table>

Experimental data analysis:

The total executive statements of all best-point searches in RTBP-based Lengauer-Tarjan (including additional initialization statements): $S_1 = 293$;

The total executive statements of all best-point searches in the EVAL-based Lengauer-Tarjan (including call and return executive statements): $S_2 = 354$;

The additional executive statements in the EVAL-based Lengauer-Tarjan:

$\Delta S = S_2 - S_1 = 61$;

The proportion between ΔS and S_2: $\Delta S / S_2 = 17.2\%$.

6.2 Causes of Capability Differences

There are some capability differences between RTBP-based Lengauer-Tarjan and EVAL-based Lengauer-Tarjan. We will analyze the causes at length in theory in the following text:

(1) When RTBP is adopted, it doesn't need to search for the real-time best-point of a complete semilive-vertex satisfying one of the following conditions, while these operations are still to be done when EVAL is adopted:
(a) n=1; (b) $sdom[n]$=1; (c) n=3; (d) $sdom[n] = parent[n]$ and $succmin[n] \geqslant sdom[n]$.

(2) In RTBP, when the best-point of a vertex u needs to be updated, it is directly turned into n that is being visited, while it needs to recursively call EVAL(u) if the best-point of u needs to be searched for in EVAL. If the root of a spanning tree containing u is the parent of n at this time, it must call EVAL(n) in the implementation, which is a useless call and can be replaced with n actually.

(3) If the parent of n is the same with the semidominator of n, the dominator of n can be computed when n is visited. When RTBP is adopted, $idom[n]$ is directly turned into $best[n]$ which is initialized in LinkChild($parent[n]$, n); when EVAL is adopted, it needs to recursively call EVAL(n) which is a useless call and can be replaced with n.

(4) When EVAL with a recursive method is adopted, it needs to use a great deal of time to execute calls and returns, and it needs to use a lot of space to save data; RTBP is embedded in Lengauer-Tarjan, so it doesn't need to execute calling procedures.

(5) Many branch statements are used in RTBP, which increase many short jump statements when it is compiled, while there are few branch statements in EVAL. In RTBP, there are additional variables: $child[n]$, W, $W[n]$, $succmin[n]$ and several operations: adding, deletion, assignment, finding for the minimum successor which keeps updated real-time data, while the problem doesn't exist in EVAL.

7 Conclusion

In this paper, a compiler optimization algorithm RTBP based on real-time best-point is presented, and it makes four changes to the former Lengauer-Tarjan. A criteria used in RTBP is introduced. We comparatively analyzed the causes of capacity differences between RTBP-based Lengauer-Tarjan and EVAL-based Lengauer-Tarjan in theory , and a static experiment is designed as an explanation. The theoretical analysis shows that RTBP can stop searching in time after the dominator of a vertex n and the semidominator of the minimum successor of n are computed. When RTBP is adopted, it can save a lot of searches for real-time best-point ,and it avoids many executions of calls and returns, thereby it saves a great deal of runtime and storage space. However, RTBP needs to add several variables and operations to keep updated real-time data, so it occupies some space and runtime. Actually, many flowgraph have the characters described in this paper, so RTBP-based Lengauer-Tarjan is more efficient than the former Lengauer-Tarjan in many circumstances.

In the following work, we will make further improvement and experimental analysis to RTBP-based Lengauer-Tarjan. Secondly, we want to replace EVAL with RTBP in other optimization algorithms based on EVAL, and to test their capabilities, which can make RTBP more widely used in the future. Thirdly, since RTBP is a real-time tool, we will try to apply RTBP to Web-based computing in optimization in order to make RTBP more applicable.

References

1. Cooper, K. D., Harvey T.J., Kennedy K.: A Simple, Fast Dominance Algorithm. Software Practice and Expereince (2001)
2. Buchsbaum, A. L. et al. A New, Simpler Linear-Time Dominators Algorithm. AT & TLabs-Research (1998)
3. Alstrup, S., W.Lauridsen P., Thorup M.: Dominators in Linear Time. http://www. it-c. dk/people/stephen/newpapers. html (1997)
4. Muchnick, S. S.: Advanced Compiler Design and Implementation. China Machine Press (2003)
5. Bilardi, G., Pingali K.: Algorithms for Computing the Static Single Assignment Form. ACM Transactions on Computational Logic, January (2003)
6. Pineo, P.P.: An Efficient Algorithm for the Creation of Single Assignment Forms. Proceedings of the 29th Annual Hawaii International Conference on System Sciences (1996)
7. Lengauer T., Tarjan R.E.: A Fast Algorithm for Finding Dominators in a Flowgraph. ACM Transactions on Programming Languages and Systems (1979) 1(1):121-141
8. Appel, A. W. et al. Modern Compiler Implementation in Java. 2nd Edition, Publishing House of Electronics Industry (2004)

A Framework of XML-Based Geospatial Metadata System

Song Yu, Huangzhi Qiang, and Sunwen Jing

School of Computer Science, North China Electric Power University, Baoding, China
syu1999@163.com

Abstract. This paper presents the study of a XML-based geospatial metadata system. After a brief review about relevant XML technology, a data structure of XML document is introduced. The conversion between relational database and XML document are discussed, with emphasis on the algorithm of function form, XML file, and the algorithm appraisement. The deployment of the XML technology system on the geospatial metadata system with public traffic transfer algorithm is given.

Keywords: Metadata, geospatial metadata system, XML technology.

1 Introduction

Metadata is dataset which contains the description, entity, and process on the data itself. Metadata is efficient for people to manage service-oriented data and composes of attributes which allow discrepancy. Geospatial metadata[1] is geography space related metadata with descriptive information resources. The standardization of geospatial metadata is urgently needed to solve various problems. The standardization is built on the foundation of novel geographic information systems (GIS), and today's XML technology provides a standard data format for such sharing. XML technology plays an important role in supporting geospatial metadata [2, 3], and provides the definition the international identification of geography rule in information encoding. XML technology is applicable to geographic spatial information management systems and their relevant network applications.

When a XML data steam to the interfaces of DOM and SAX systems, the system application must read the XML data file. The definition in DOM interface in terms of series of objects will recognize the data entity of the XML file and then convert the file format into a hierarchically-structured data. The conversion re-expresses the relations among each element defined in the XML data. A SAX based system uses a unidirectional, traversal structured file as events driving. When a XML analyzer finds an incident, it uses a special function to handle the conversion. A DOM interface can, on the other hand, recognize a random search for document element. However, it has to store the whole data structure into a memory. Especially, when a XML data file has a very complex structure, it requires considerable memory space and resource; hence the conversion process very costs. Although a SAX interface does not need to buffer the

H.T. Shen et al. (Eds.): APWeb 2006, LNCS 3842, pp. 775–778, 2006.

data, it must pre-recognize a pre-ordered visitation which may not randomly read the elements within the data file. A XML schema has more built-in XML's DTDs [5], and supports various user-oriented data type, suitable to descriptive relation database model. A XML schema itself is a XML data with data structure can be processed in DOM technical transformation. The conversion between the XML data and the one in relational database must be developed upon the common DTD[3-4]. This paper aims at developing a XML schema for the improvement of efficiency in data conversion [6]. This paper also presents the implementation of such schema to a public transit system.

2 Conversion Between Relational Database and Geographical Space Metadata

After a XML data file is converted to an entity or a table in the relational database of a public transit system, The XML schema can be illustrated in Fig.1. The system was programmed in ASP.

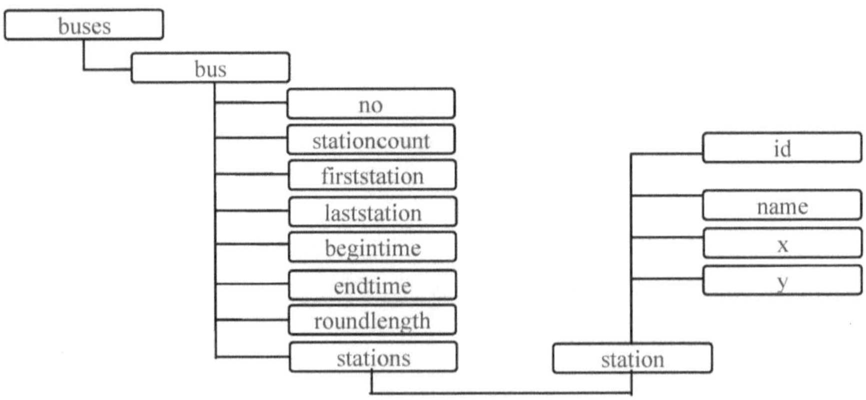

Fig. 1. The XML schema of public transit system

Following is automatically export XML file.

```
<?xml version='1.0' encoding='GB2312'?>
     <buses>
       <bus>
          <no>1</no>
          <stationcount>11</stationcount>
          <firststation> Smoke factory </firststation>
          <laststation> Railway station </laststation>
          <begintime>6:00</begintime>
          <endtime>21:00</endtime>
          <roundlength>11 kilometers </roundlength>
```

```
        <stations>
           <station>
             <id>253</id>
             <name> Smoke factory </name>
             <x>115.50812300</x>
             <y>38.84309100</y>
           </station>
           ......
        </stations>
   </bus>
   ......
   </buses>
```

Traditionally a database of metadata must has logic synthesis and if a system contains a component to convert between data in a N-independent database, one has to install N(N − 1)/2 exchange modules, and its complex degree is $O(N^2/2)$. Our proposed system with careful implementation of XML technology may tremendously decrease the operations, hence increase an efficacy. If one intends to perform it on N databases, only N conversion modules needed; thus complex degree is O(N).

3 A XML-Based Space Metadata Application[6,7]—The Transit Exchange Algorithm

If a public transit network can be described by an adjacency matrix $(a_{ij})_{n\times n}$, defined as $a_{ij} = 1$ for a bus Stop i which can reach to Stop j and 0 for a bus stop i which can't reach to stop j. The algorithm is given as follows

(a) For a direct condition, one can judge whether a_{xy} is 1 in $(a_{ij})_{n\times n}$;
(b) For switching another bus, a double cycles can be used with $O(n^2)$.
(c) For transits exchange, one upper level of cycle is used with $O(n^3)$; With an increase of n, the complex degree will increase significantly;

For obtaining exchanged bus number, an optimal process is needed, which leads a compound adjacency matrix $(a_{ij})_{n\times n}$: $a_{ij} = A$ for a bus which can directly drive from Stop i to Stop j directly; while 0 doesn't. The matrix A is a linear chain table with a complex data structure. It contains necessary information such as bus number, and the distance between Stops i and j. For a compound adjacency matrix, one only needs to join the operation for the structure of data in algorithm. The following is the descriptive algorithm description of two exchange transits.

```
for i=1 to n
 for j=1 to n
  if a_xi≠0 and a_jy≠0 then
   if a_ji≠0 then
```

```
        {returns bust stop i, bust stop j;
         Handle the data structure in A; get information;
         Returning to the shortest distance;}
```

Set up a compound matrix XML-DOM[7], the buses algorithm for exchange transit can be processed as:

```
(a) Find corresponding "item" to station x;
(b) For each "reach" do
     {Get name of station i;
       Find corresponding "item" to station i;
       For each "reach" do
     {If has name of station y then
     {Record corresponding "bus no" and "distance";
      Return true;}
      }
      If true then
        Record corresponding "bus no" and "distance";}
  {c} Find the shortest distance
```

4 Conclusion

The advantage of converting an entity in a relational database to XML based system may provide an efficient and user-end approach. The model was implemented to a bus transit system to demonstrate the feasibility.

References

1. Suresh, R, Shukla P., SchWenke.G.: XML-Based Data Systems for Earth Science Applications. Geoscience and Remote Sensing Symposium (2000)1214-1216
2. Sun, Y.: XML technology is newest to trail: The campaign of W3C concerning XML. http://www.xml.org.cn/
3. Wan, C.X., Liu Y.: XML data management based on relational database. Computer Science (8) (2003) 64-68
4. Chai, X. L.: Metadata system and data exchange based on the open Web architecture of XML. Master Thesis, Fudan University, Shanghai (2000)
5. Zhou, J.T., Wang M.L.: Analysis and the technical comparison of XML Schema and XML DTD. http://www-900.ibm.com/developerWorks/cn/xml/x-sd/index.shtml (2002)
6. Sun, W.J.: The research and implementation of the spatial metadata system based on XML. Master Thesis, Baoding, North China Electric Power University (2004)
7. Sun, W.J., Song Y., Zheng C.Y.: Research on public traffic transfer algorithm based on XML technology. Journal of Electronics & Information Technology, supple (2003) 431－435

Deployment of Web Services for Enterprise Application Integration (EAI) System

Jie Liu, Er-peng Zhang, Jin-fen Xiong, and Zhi-yong Lv

School of Computer Science and Technology,
Harbin Engineering University, Harbin, China
zhangep@163.com

Abstract. The process to explore application integration for enterprise information system is called Enterprise Application Integration (EAI). Generally, EAI that based on the peer-to-peer has many limitations, such as poor extensibility, difficulty of management, and high-cost etc. These disadvantages can be overcome by Web services technology which helps to integrate large-scale, distributed enterprise applications together. This paper presents a framework of EAI which based on Web services, and gives discussions on its major functional modules.

1 Introduction

Every enterprise has its own application environment on which many applications (such as Enterprise Resources Planning (ERP), Customer Relationship Management (CRM), Supply Chain Management (SCM) and Enterprise Portal etc.) are independent each other. The environment lacks of communications among applications and maintaining cost is very high. With the exponential expansion of real-time information of customers' need and merchant partners' supplies, the enterprise application integration (EAI) on a heterogeneous system become urgently needed. How to integrate the existing multiple software systems together without modifying applications efficiently is a bag challenge. Thanks to middleware technology, some EAI systems powered by the existing enterprise software tools such as DCOM, CORBA, Java RML, and EJB, to perform application integration. Although the middleware technology becomes more mature, many technical issues should be studied in developing financial system, telecommunication, and other software systems: (1) the requirement of homogeneity : DCOM technology mainly depends on Microsoft platform. Although the CORBA issued by Object Management Group (OMG) is used to solve the integration of inhomogeneous systems, objectively speaking, it should deploy the same ORB(Object Request Broker) products within a CORBA plant; (2) the security of firewall : Under the thinking of security, it always deploys firewall between the application systems and the outside systems, generally the 80 port opened only. While it is too complex to solve the problems in firewall with the traditional groupware models technologies; (3) the inter-work among different groupware models : It lacks effective data communications and standard protocols

H.T. Shen et al. (Eds.): APWeb 2006, LNCS 3842, pp. 779 – 782, 2006.

between different groupware models. Fortunately Web services technology provides solutions to the above problems, hence, it bridges different application systems. Web services served as a medium to communicate applications. Each Web service provider not only maintains its own function, but also presents the communication with others. In addition, a Web services-based system can reduce the cost significantly.

This paper reports our recent study on how to apply Web services technology to EAI system. Section 2 outlines the Web services for software integration. Section 3 presents a framework of EAI which based on Web services, and gives discussions on its major functional modules, followed by a conclusion section.

2 Related Work

The target of Web Services is to fulfill the cooperation among cross-platform applications and the communications among procedural modules. Web Services may be referred as a service-oriented collection of functional components on Web, utilizing standard protocols and exchangeable data format, such as HTTP, XML, and SOAP etc. Web Services play three roles, services provider, services register and services applicant. Web Services includes three major cores, SOAP (Simple Object Access Protocol), WSDL (Web Service Description Language), and UDDI (Universal Description Discovery and Integration). The communications among different applications is realized by SOAP protocol in Web Services, while the WSDL which based on XML describes message format, data type, operation, communication protocol binding, and service address, and offers uniform standard for the service provider to describe the service and service information, which helps users to understand and invoke Web Services. UDDI is used to maintain information integrity. It supplies a set of standard methods with services providers to register the relevant information, to search services, and to shares information distributed globally.

3 Web Services-Based EAI

Web services-based EAI integrates multiple individual applications together, while each application still maintains its own business functionally. According to the Meta Group, most Global 2000 enterprises have more than 40 applications. Although it is unnecessary to integrate all applications, a scalable integration system is demanded to extend additional functions at a lower cost if it needed. The traditional technology based point-to-point integration can not meet the need. The design of an EAI solution system contains many objects such as defining and cataloging business processes, business events, IT components, process rules and messages, and message content. Each object can be a components or application (shown in Figure 1).

In a Web services-based EAI system, each application is a service-oriented, distributed component module. The EAI system can integrate applications from multiple enterprises. The Web services-based EAI framework can be seen in Fig.2.

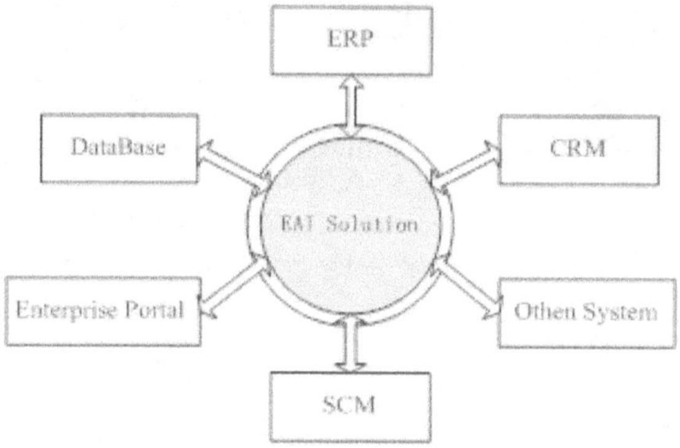

Fig. 1. A EAI-solution system which integrates multiple software components

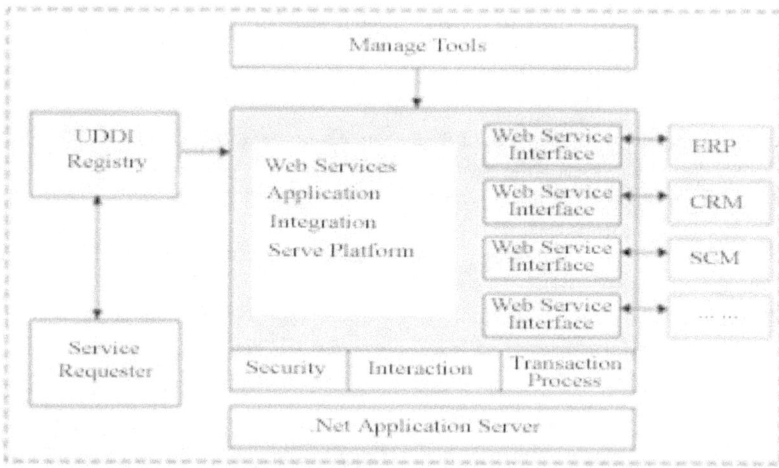

Fig. 2. EAI framework based on Web Services

The system contains many functional modules described in the following words. An application-integration module within the system provides multiple W-S interfaces to link to subsystems (applications such as ERP, CRM etc.). This module must be registered in UDDI through SOAP protocol to become recognized service applicants; it also provides an interface for end-users (enterprise's user, supplier, etc.). Management tools module configures and manages the service such as monitoring service execution, security status, and management of application integrations and service resources. The development tools module plays roles in (1) Create Web Services application integration service platform; (2) Reconstruct all subsystems and plug to the Web Services; (3) Set up private UDDI registry server; (4) Publish all sealed Web Services in subsystem to UDDI register server; (5) Invoke the intercommunication between two relevant services, as long as the information of interface of Web services is found in the UDDI Register server and bond it to service platform.

4 Conclusions

This paper presents a framework of Web services-based EAI system which can realize flexible integration of applications. The communications between applications and EAI solution are W-S interfaces. Based on the proposed W-S EAI system, enterprises can share information of different departments, applications, platforms and systems in a real-time mode; thus it increases the efficiency of enterprise operation and reduces redundant costs.

References

1. Samtani, G., Sadhwani D.: EAI and web services easier enterprise application integration? 2002, available at: http://www.webservicesarchitect.com/content/articles/samtani01.asp
2. Eshel, E.: Enterprise application integration in financial services, in: J. Keyes (Ed.), Financial Services Information Systems, Auerbach Publications, New York (2000), pp. 469– 483; B. Gilmer, High-speed networking topologies, Broadcast Engineering 40 (7) (1998, June) 42–46
3. Linthicum, D.S.: Enterprise Application Integration, Addision-Wesley Longman, Reading, MA, 2000
4. Orenstein, D.: Enterprise application integration, Computerworld, 1999 (Oct. 4), available at: http://www.computerworld.com
5. Sealey, R.: E-business integration drives EAI: interview with Aberdeen's Tom Dwyer, EAI Journal, 2000 (July–August) (Dallas, TX) available at: http://www.EAjournal.com
6. Urlocker, Z.: Return on e-business integration, EAI Journal, (Dallas, TX) available at: http://www.EAjournal.com
7. Lublinsky, B.: Achieving the ultimate EAI implementation, EAI Journal, (2001, February) 26–31

A Distributed Information System for Healthcare Web Services

Joan Lu[1], Tahir Naeem[1], and John B. Stav[2]

[1] School of Computing and Engineering, University of Huddersfield, HD1 3DH, UK
j.lu@hud.ac.uk
[2] Department of Technology, Sor-Trondelag University College, Trondheim, Norway
John.B.Stav@hist.no

Abstract. This paper introduces the reader to the design considerations and implementation in the development of a client server system for GE Healthcare Technologies (GEHT). It assesses the viability of using new technology to implement a secure reliable distributed system. It also discusses the advantages of the new Microsoft.Net platform over established technologies. Finally, it concludes that the new system can provide data capture and retrieval functionality using a mobile computing device to pass data to an information system for GEHT employees across the globe. Throughout the report the design documentation is represented in the form UML documents to enable the reader to comprehend the workflow and lines of communication of the proposed system.

1 Introduction

There is little doubt the extent to which computer technology has revolutionised modern business practices. The information needs of organisations have driven the development of information systems into the new world of mobile computing to provide on-demand information retrieval and capture.

Healthcare information system is always a hot topic to the scientists from both computing and healthcare communities, such as Electronic Health Records (HER), Patient management Systems (PMS) [7]. As part of its information needs, GE Healthcare, a world known company in healthcare information systems, maintains a master database of all its successful product installations across the world [2]. The current system uses Microsoft Access technology to maintain locally stored caches of the master database. All data is entered off-line and then synchronised with the master database periodically. The user interacts with the database using forms developed in Access and further functionality is added by VB macros.

The users of the old system have highlighted the following flaws [1, 2]. As the master database has grown, the task of synchronizing locally cached copies of the data takes longer and is inherently prone to errors. The user interfaces are poorly designed and only perform basic validation upon submission to the master database.

The objective of this project is to investigate a possibility to migrate the existing system to a new system that is able to retrieve and manipulate data using a mobile device, such as Personal Digital Assistant (PDA).

H.T. Shen et al. (Eds.): APWeb 2006, LNCS 3842, pp. 783 – 790, 2006.

The software to be developed will be called as the Global Integration Software Tool (GIST). The developed software will be tested by General Electric Healthcare, which is a division of General Electric, one of the world foremost technology implementation companies. GE Healthcare is a $14 billion unit of the GE with 42,500 employees in UK [2].

2 Mobile Healthcare Devices

We expect that health care organizations soon will ultimately use a wide variety of mobile hardware solutions in order to offer flexible and improved communication solutions for various staff groups. This include mobile devices like Medical Tablet PCs [6], Figure 1, that are convenient for users such as physicians and nurses who are highly mobile and need quick, unobstructed access to data and information. Medical Tablet PCs are well suited for clinicians who want a single portable device, e.g. at the range of 10.4 - 16 inches, offering for instance free-text data capture, e-mail, clinical data sheets etc. Job functions that quickly need to be hands free may select Mini-Medical Tablet PCs that have just been introduced to the market, with screen sizes down to 8 inches. However, as many organizations already have a portfolio with mixed deployment of mobile devices, user preference will pick away wild points.

Fig. 1. ThinkPad Medical Tablet PC applications in the system [6]

Many Tablet PC users have already requested devoices that is smaller and more portable than most traditional tablet computers. The Mini-Medical Table PC, that has a size that is comparable to a paperback book, runs on the Microsoft Windows XP Tablet PC operating system (see fig. 1). They use Intel Pentium M processors, embedded Bluetooth for peripheral connections, and 802.11 a, b and g wireless network technologies. Other features include an eraser that can be used on screen. They also include several security features. During the fall Nokia Inc. will begin selling a mini tablet computer measuring 5.6 by 2.6 inches, i.e. slightly larger than a PDA. It will contain a 4.13 inches high-resolution screen. It runs on an open source, Linux based operating system specifically developed for the device. It will come with embedded Wi-Fi, Bluetooth wireless technology, handwriting recognition and an on screen keyboard. Operating systems update beginning in 2006 is expected to support additional voice and messaging capabilities.

3 Analysis

It is generally accepted that the new challenge in developing for modern enterprise system is to achieve platform independence and interoperability. Thus, using multi-platform programming languages, such as JAVA and XML, is a current trend. With the advent of the Java programming language and its new rival the .Net suite of programming languages, platform independent solutions are relatively straightforward to construct. The reason for choosing XML is that its format can be read by different systems. Justification about using these languages has been intensively discussed in numerous literatures [3, 4].

For the development platform, Microsoft.Net is taken into consideration because it is an open programming platform, which can be utilized by multiple languages [5].

.NET programs execute on a virtual machine called the Common Language Runtime (CLR). All .Net language code is first translated into a common language called the Intermediate Language (IL). This is so that a .NET program can be run on any computer provided a version of CLR is implemented for it. All IL files are packaged into units called assemblies. These assemblies are loaded into the common language run-time (part of the .Net framework) and compiled by the just- in-time IL compiler and executed within the Common Language Runtime.

The stakeholders expressed early in the design process that the new system must be scalable. By adopting the .net platform, it is envisaged that future developers could write new clients that would integrate with the server in a language of their choice.

The .net framework is shipped with a powerful Integrated Development Environment (IDE) called Visual Studio. This development environment aids fast application development and prototyping. Hence, the .net platform will help realize a prototype at an earlier stage.

Currently the .Net platform offers an advanced platform with which to integrate web services. A web service is an application or block of executable code that is hosted on a web server. Web services are re-useable components that are based on standard software protocols. Web Services can be consumed by any application that understands how to parse an XML-formatted stream.

Microsoft .NET Web Services currently supports three protocols: HTTP GET, HTTPPOST, and SOAP (Simple Object Access Protocol), as these protocols are standard protocols for the Web, it is very easy for client applications to use the services provided by the server.

SOAP serves as a mechanism for passing messages between the clients and servers. In this context, the clients are Web Services consumers, and the server is the Web Service. The clients simply send an XML-formatted request message to the server to get the service. The server responds by sending back yet another XML-formatted message. The SOAP specification describes the format of these XML requests and responses. It is simple, yet it is extensible, because it is based on XML.

4 System Design

A client server system built upon the .Net framework is proposed as shown in figure 2. It is a two-tier system, i.e. client - web service container - backend system. Within web

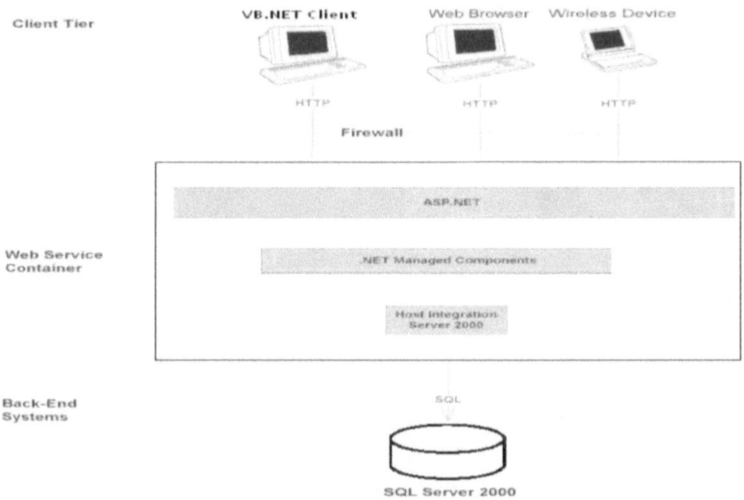

Fig. 2. System architecture of proposed system

service container, security issue - firewall is considered. At the back end, a suitable commercial relational database is to be used. As SQL Server 2000 is used extensively within the organisation presently it is the first choice as the data logic component.

The proposed system will incorporate three disparate clients. The first client to be developed will be a stand-alone VB.net client on client machines using windows based operating system. The second client will be a C# client running on a Hewlett Packard iPaq running the Pocket PC 2003 operating system.

The final client to be developed will be a Java client running on a mobile phone device. The overview of the system is presented as a deployment diagram in figure 3 for the reader's consideration.

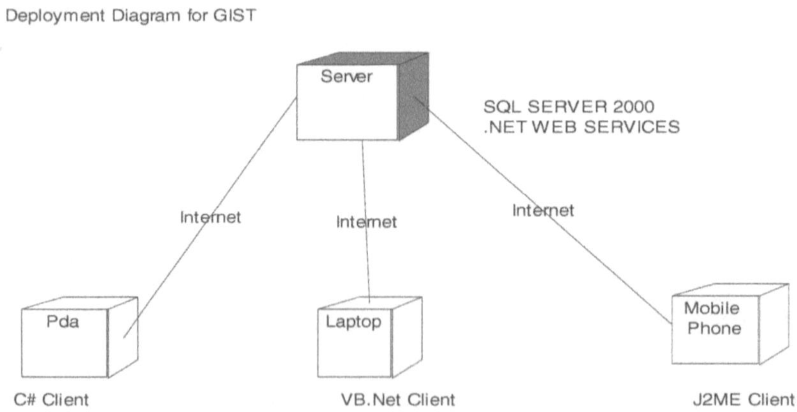

Fig. 3. Deployment diagram

5 Implementation and Results

The current system has been deployed using an Intel based server running the Windows 2003 server operating system. The server contains both the data logic layer and web service container. The existing database structure has been normalized and is presented in [8].

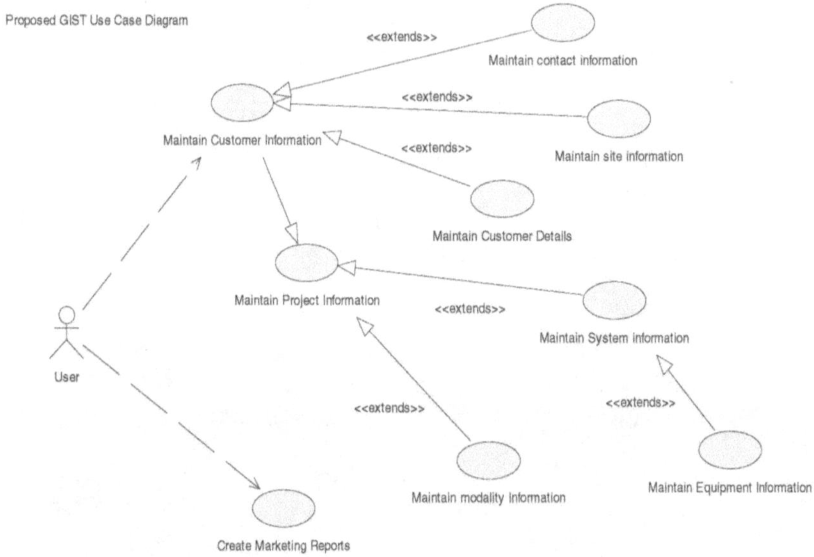

Fig. 4. User case diagrams for proposed system

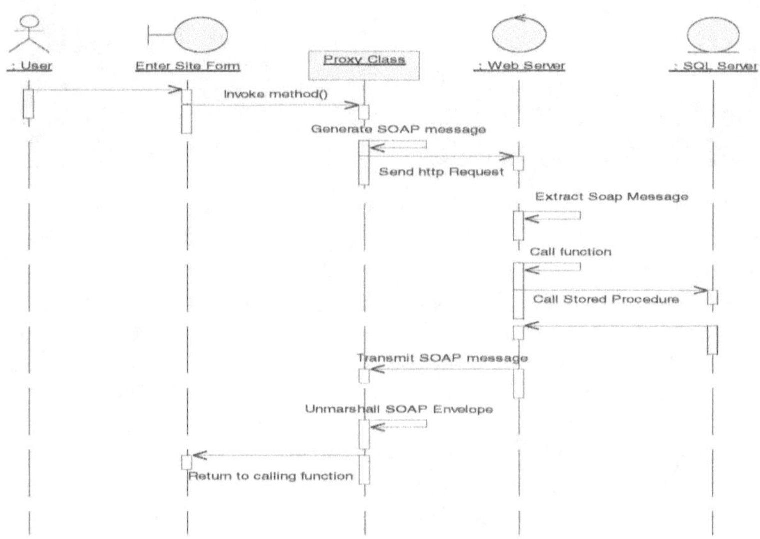

Fig. 5. Sequence diagram depicting web service interaction

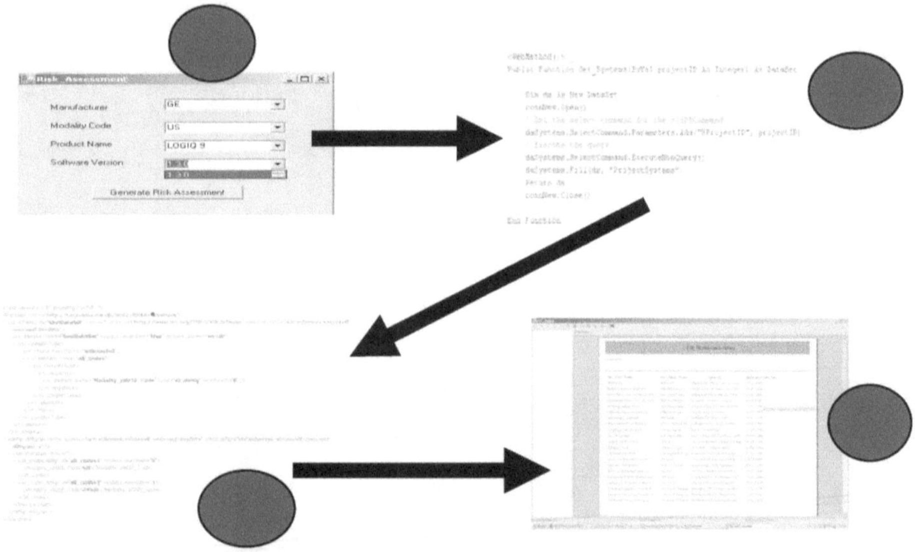

Fig. 6. Client – Web Service call

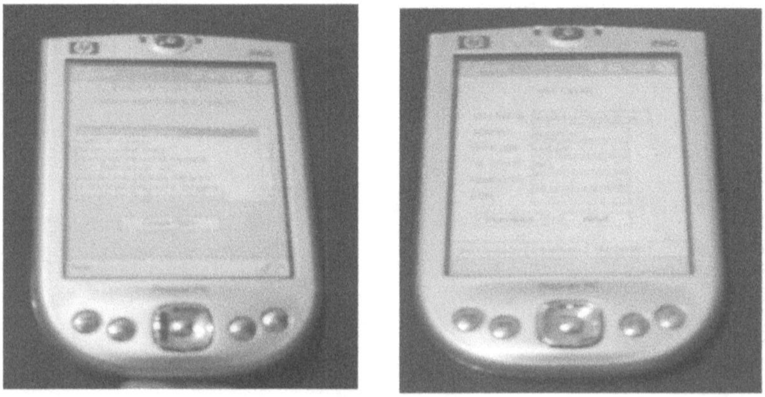

Fig. 7. PDA applications in the system

In the proposed system web services will be defined and the procedures and functions will be invoked using TCP/IP calls. The web service will marshal data to and from clients using XML embedded within SOAP envelopes. Once the method is invoked it calls a stored procedure that extracts the dataset and returns it in the form of an XML document. The major functional components of the proposed system are depicted in a use case diagram as shown in fig. 4. Fig. 5 shows the interactions between the various entities in the systems in the form of a sequence diagram.

The Microsoft.net platform has been adopted to implement the middleware solution. In respect to product development, Microsoft.Net web services are easier to develop and implement. Web services also allow a greater range of client to access their interfaces, as any client that can marshal http requests can communicate with a web service. Figs. 4 and 5 depict the interaction between the communication between the internal classes and the entities within the proposed system. It is hoped the reader will gain an appreciation of the communication the internal communication within the proposed system. A sample web service method and its return value are demonstrated in Figure 6.

The client applications reside on two different hardware devices. The most sophisticated client has been implemented using the VB.net and can run on any Windows operating system. A sample screenshot of the PDA client is given in fig. 7.

The smaller PDA client represents the mobile aspect of the solution. It was developed to provide GE management with evidence to the mobile computing features of the new system.

6 Conclusion and Future Work

Migration of the traditional system to a distributed system using mobile computing devices has been achieved. Although the current software is still a prototype, the following functionalities, which match the initial requirements, are generally achieved after investigation.

- On-line clients for users to interact with the database
  The solution provided here offers the functionality that once connected the Internet the clients can interact with the database in real-time.
- Handling concurrent users
  It has been tested for multiple connections to the middle-tier and also simultaneous connections to the database with multi-users.
- Scalable and extensible system
  By adopting the web services platform, architecture has been selected to allow clients on multiple devices and multiple platforms to communicate with data logic layer.
- The ability to retrieve and manipulate data using a mobile device
  The PDA client is, though simple, serves as a proof of solution for wireless connectivity.

The next phase of the project is the development of a java client running on a j2me enabled mobile phone device. The j2me client will provide further evidence to the integration of non-windows based clients with the .Net web service platform.

References

1. Papazoglou, M.P., Henderik, Proper, A., Yang J.: Landscaping the information space of large multi-database networks, Data & Knowledge Engineering, Volume 36, Issue 3, March 2001, Pages 251-281
2. Naeem, T.: Internal report, School of Computing and Engineering, University of Huddersfield, 2005
3. Sergio, R., Elisa, V.: Object-oriented algorithm analysis and design with Java Science of Computer Programming, Volume 54, Issue 1, January 2005, Pages 25-47

4. Lu, Z, A Survey of XML Applications on Science and Technology, the International Journal of Software Engineering and Knowledge Engineering, Vol-1, page 1-33, 2005.
5. Heasman, J.: Migrating to the .NET platform: an introduction, Network Security, Volume 2004, Issue 4, April 2004, Pages 6-7 "in press"
6. Medical Tablet PC, URL: http://www.medicaltabletpc.com/
7. Piggott, D., Teljeur, C., Kelly, A.: Exploring the potential for using the grid to support health impact assessment modelling, *Parallel Computing, Volume 30, Issues 9-10, September-October 2004, Pages 1073-1091*
8. Lu, Z., Naeem, T.: Mobile Computing in Healthcare Information Systems, The 11th UK-Chinese Conference in Automation and Computing Science, September, 2005, Sheffield, UK.

The Research of Scientific Computing Environment on Scilab

Zhili Zhang[1,2], Zhenyu Wang[1], Deyu Qi[1], Weiwei Lin[1], Dong Zhang[1], and Yongjun Li[1]

[1] College of Computer Science and Engineering, South China University of Technology, Guangzhou 510640, P.R. China
[2] Computer Network Center, Xuchang University, Xuchang 461000, P.R. China
zzl@xctc.edu.cn

Abstract. The paper focuses on the implements of distributed parallel computing on Scilab, a wide-used Grid environment. Netbutterfly Grid Computing System (NGCS) is designed , Some of key issues, such as the architecture of NGCS ,job distributing, system communications, fault tolerance and security problem are analyzed and discussed. And a new science computing method is advanced. Finally, an example on Grid computing environments is presented. The experiment shows that it's the results are satisfying.

Keywords: Distributed parallel computing, Grid computing, Scilab, globus toolkit.

1 Introduction

With the appearances and developing rapidly of the computer and Internet technology, science and engineering calculation have found extensive application, it has already become an important direction of scientific research. Moreover, it is of greatly potential value to explore distributed parallel computation system by utilizing the existing computing resource on the Internet. The implementation of current parallel computation has two ways mainly: The first is parallel computer way, in which parallel computers can be classified as tight coupling computers and loose coupling computers. However, it costs too much to implement this traditional parallel computation, thus cannot meet the needs of the general application. The second way is network parallel computation system, made up of a set of interconnecting isomorphic or isomerous computing units and the related resource, which can be used by the user as a single computing environment to complete the parallel computation [1]. The typical network parallel computation system is PVM, and the hardest nut concerning these systems is that they only have the isomer capability of the processors but are unable to solve problems concerning the isomer of operation system and protocol.

Grid has recently arisen as a computation environment. It supports high performance computation and extensive resource sharing [2]. However, the current Grid environments, such as OGSA/Globus, are still far away from directly supporting

H.T. Shen et al. (Eds.): APWeb 2006, LNCS 3842, pp. 791 – 798, 2006.

distributed parallel computation. As for common users, cheap and easy distributed parallel computation environment is the most effective implementation platform for carrying on large-scale scientific computation. Thereby, it is necessary to discuss and achieve distributed parallel computation under existing Grid environment.

This paper is structured as follows. The second section introduces the network computation platform of Netbutterfly Grid Computing System (NGCS) based on the operation engine of Scilab [3] and OGSA/Globus, key problems are analyzed and several related solutions are suggested. Then the third section discusses the test example of NGCS. Finally, the fourth section draws a conclusion.

2 Distributed Parallel Computation Based on the Scilab

2.1 NGCS Distributed Parallel Computing Architecture

As Fig.1 shows, NGCS system is a virtual parallel computer made up of several Grid computing nodes. It can perform parallel computing task submitted by users. Each Grid computing node is a parallel one, it provides Grid service to execute sub-tasks of parallel job and uses the Scilab to describe the algorithm.So NGCS makes the description of problems easier. Computing service layer makes the computing process abstract. When the task is accepted, computing service layer will find proper resources to perform the task. Application layer is designed to use and manage the computing service efficiently. It can coordinate multiple applications and use Grid middle ware — Globus Toolkit to call the Grid service instance coordinately. Compared with the traditional parallel computer and network parallel computing, this architecture has an evident advantage, that is, it fully make use of resource on Internet to realize large-scale parallel computing and it can resolve the problem in the isomerous environment such as different processing unit and operating system. It can utilize the network infrastructure as the programming environment of distributing parallel computation. Also, it is easy to realize this architecture.

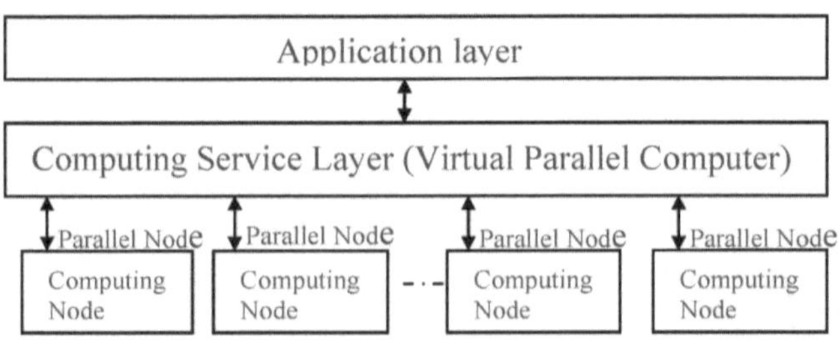

Fig. 1. NGCS Architecture

2.2 NCGS Design Framework

Figure 2 shows that data container stores parallel program and application data; computing container contains N-number of resource nodes to provide computation service. Resource directory includes computation resource and data resource services.

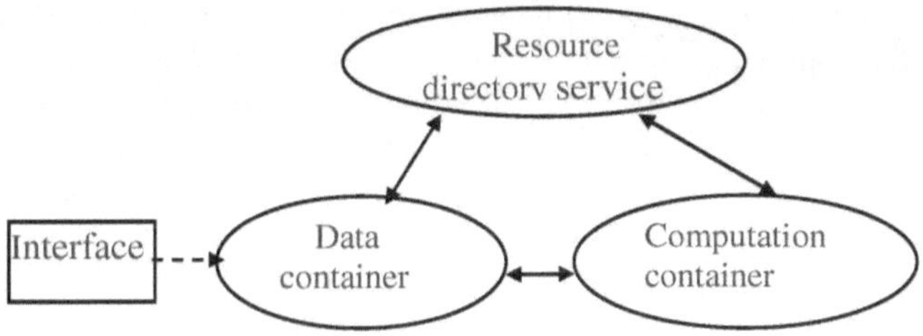

Fig. 2. NGCS Application architecture model

When NGCS begin to run, it sends tasks to the data container. And then, the data container and the computation container cooperate with each other to finish the task. During this process, both containers try to find resources from directory service to work until the task is finished.

In physical implementation, NGCS adopts the core server-group structure, and the client is the resource provider and also the resource consumer. The internal computing resources is an effective aggregation of the client resources. NGCS server adopts the design of extendable clusters, and each module can run respectively. The server-group structure as Fig.3 shows. Its merits are: extendable, heavy in workload, redundant and highly reliable. The server is responsible for the organization and Scheduling of the resource and tasks.

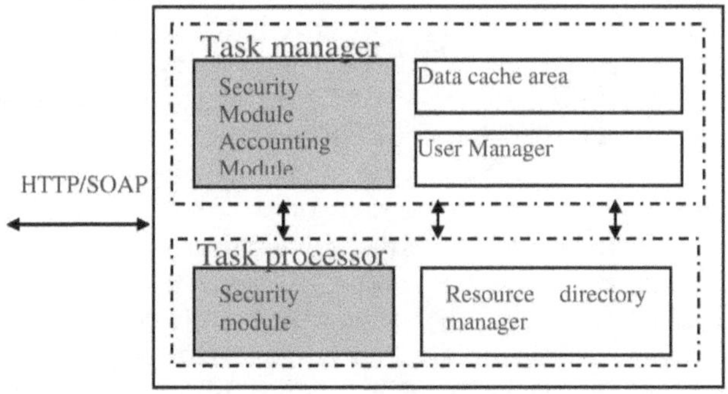

Fig. 3. NGCS Server Group

NGCS client includes task-connecting interface and Scilab Grid computing virtual machining. Task-connecting interface is the interface for user's application to enter the NGCS. Users send their tasks to NGCS through the task-connecting interface. Scilab Grid computing virtual machining is the NGCS computing node and it provides computing capability. Figure 4 shows that client node is classified into task model and computing model. In the task model, a client sends a computing task to the system and waits for it to complete computing. In the computing model, a client is a computing node and provides computation service to the system. Since every client node is a Globus Toolkit-made Grid node, It can work on all kinds of computer from microcomputer to supercomputer and support all operation system such as Windows, Unix, Linux and the coming systems, Which makes it convenient to achieve the network parallelism among the heterogeneous computers and take good use of the existing network resource to implement distributed parallel computation.

The task of NGCS is submitted to the system through the task-connecting interface of client node, and the system assign computing resource to the task dynamically until the task is finished. During the process of the task, the use of the computing node is decided by the system in dynamic style. The system makes the computing process transparent to users. In order to get the right result, the system needs at lease one usable resource node.

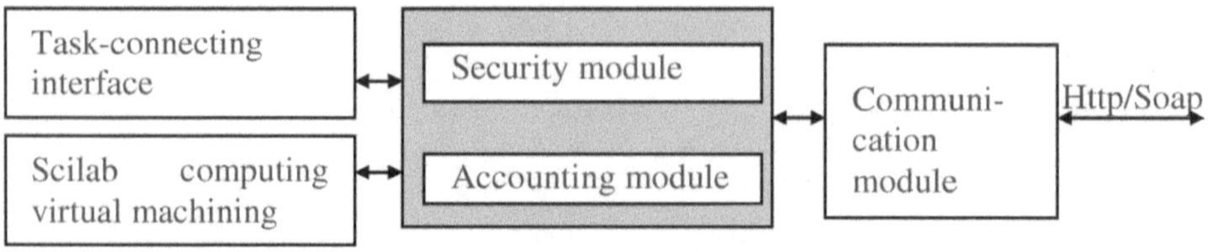

Fig. 4. NGCS client node structure

2.3 System Code Design

This system uses the Scilab script language to describe science computing tasks. The Scilab is an open source project sponsored by INRIA.Its syntax is like the science computing language Matlab. So it is easy to describe the tasks and for users to master the way of describing tasks more efficiently. It has rich data type and can be used in science computing, mathematic modeling, decision optimization, linear and non-linear control, etc. Since the NGCS chooses interpreting execution, the script can be executed directly on different NGCS node and different operate system together.

For the sake of making the Scilab suitable to parallel computation on the net, the system adds distant data read/write instructions of NGCS_RD and NGCS_WR, and deletes dangerous instructions such as diskette operation which might harm client computers. The entrance of the whole operation program is the file of main.ngcs, and other programs are transferred as process. Main.ngcs is a file describing the task flow, and its syntax has only two keywords NGCS_CX and NGCS_END.

NGCS_CX indicates the conditional execution of the program. When the expression of X is true, the system would execute equally all the functions in the NGCS_CX sentence.

NGCS_END indicates the end of the program. This instruction generally is used to end the system missions. When the system is executing this sentence, this instruction would release all the allocated resources and means quitting the system. When the expression of X is true, the whole operation task is over, and the system notifies the task-provider with the sign and logouts the buffer area of the resource node.

2.4 Discussion About Key Techniques

2.4.1 Parallel Task

Traditional parallel computing model is based on data parallel. Data-based parallel has a high parallel degree, but it is hard to resolve irregular problems. It is better to use function-based parallel in resolving irregular problems. NGCS parallel scheduling language describes the relationships between tasks, and decomposes the problems naturally into all levels of sub-tasks in the program. Because task parallelism integrates data parallelism and function parallelism, so it could cope with the anomalous problems effectively before it could support rather high parallelism degree. Furthermore, program designer can also translate the serial program into parallel program conveniently. NGCS encapsulates the data and operation, and implements them concurrently. There needs data parallelism when several tasks have the same operation and different datum. There needs function parallelism when several tasks have different operations [4]. Since distributed parallel computation based on Scilab could extend the parallel computation environment to metropolitan network using GLOBUS Grid nodes as parallel computation nodes, tasks computed concurrently can be distributed to the computation resource in the Grid to finish, which would improve the NGCS' performance. In addition, NGCS achieves data parallelism and function parallelism, and realizes the distributed parallel computation based on Internet.

2.4.2 System Communication

In order to realize NGCS communication on the Internet, NGCS chooses SOAP 1.2[5] standard as the encapsulation protocol and maps the function call to system program. NGCS extends the Scilab, encapsulates SOAP and adds SOAP_SEG operator NGCS_SOAPEG in the Scilab, which enables clients to have access to data in the system data cache, thus realizing the data transparency to clients. NGCS_SOAPEG([Type],[Name]) operator has two arguments: *Type* and *Name*. *Type* determines the system operation type, such as *read* or *write*. *Name* refers to the name of the variable needing to be processed, presented by strings headed by letters. When these is a "*" in front of the name of the variable, it means data pointer operation. Otherwise it means value operation..

2.4.3 Fault Tolerance Mechanism and Security Problem

In ideal status, the network should have these characteristics: short latency, wide bandwidth, low error rate, remarkable scalability. Current internet is not a ideal net, it has unacceptable latency, limited bandwidth, random and unpredictable errors. So there should be a suit of fault tolerance mechanism that can used to solve these problems on the internet based parallel computing system. This parallel computing environment is made up of several computers connected by internet and these computers are self-governing. So the system is more reliable. Any fault in a single computer of this parallel computing environment will not affect the functionality of others computing resources. These feasible and practice way to realize fault tolerance is to implement this mechanism by the application program itself. NGCS system is based on Grid computing middleware Globus toolkit, which can used heartbeat technique to tracking faults in this system and gain the purpose of error tolerance.

NGCS use SOAP to implement the bottom communication, so it can deploy in a wide range on internet. But it is hard to avoid the exposure of computing nodes, data security and node safety are the problem that may restrict the deployment. NGCS use an strategy that follow the theory of limited non-transferable trust to gain security of the system. The task that the control system dispatched to the nodes is smallest trust unit, task scripts can not access local file system of the nodes and can only access to assigned memory.

3 Test of Example

To verify the validity of NGCS system, a data-coupled computation task is designed: N Queen's problem is a classic problem. One such problem can be divided into N N-1-grain size problems, namely, N parallel computation tasks. The computing task is described using NGCS and deployed to a LAN, which establishes a scientific computing environment to perform parallel computing. We compare the speedup rate of running tasks obtained from the cases with various number of effective nodes. Here are the algorithm implementation and application program of simplified N Queen's problem using NGCS(omitter).

It is feasible and easy to deal with the parallel problems in NGCS. When a task is running, the system would send out all the parallelizable sub-tasks, each of which can be deployed in a computer and becomes an executable parallel computation node. After previous task completes execution and obtains related data, system would judge whether the parallelizable conditions of the remained code is mature or not. Computation tasks utilize the NGCS parallel macro language to describe the coupling relationship of the code, so there is no need of analyzing the coupling relationship with manual work. The followings are the simplified Grid service implementation algorithm complied with Scilab, and Grid client application algorithm (omitter).

3.1 Test Environment and Result

There are two prerequisites to using NGCS to carry on distributed parallel computation: (1) NGCS server system has at least two usable client nodes. (2) Task coding of NGCS application is reasonable. A small application system is designed to verify the validity. Five computers consists of the isomerous network environment. Host 1 is deployed the resource catalog service and collaborative service of NGCS. Host 2 is the accessing node of custom application. Hosts 3, 4 and 5 are operation resource nodes. The following is the problem solving and test results. Table 1 shows the practical and theoretic running time. Figure 5 shows the practical and theoretic test results of speedup rate.

Table 1. Running timetable of the N empress' problem (Unit:second)

Host number	Actual test process	Practical(theoretic) running time.
Single machine environment	NGCS.MAIN runs in the host 2 Computed node: Host3	5.422 (3)
Two nodes	NGCS.MAIN runs in the host 2 Computed node: Host3,Host4	3.661 (2)
Three nodes	NGCS.MAIN runs in the host 2 Computed node:Host3,Host4,Host5	1.812 (1)

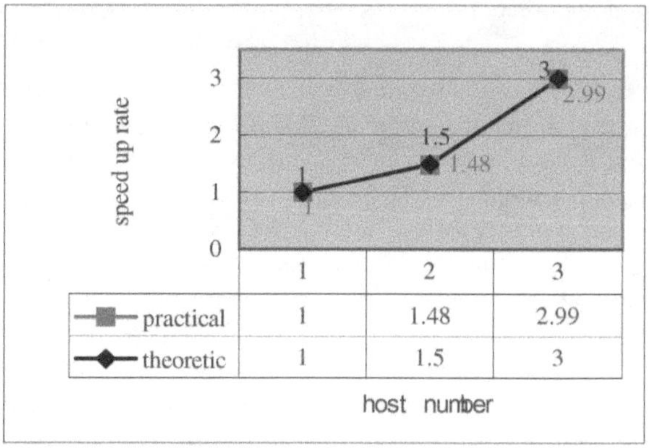

Fig. 5. The practical (theoretic)test results of speedup rate

Experiment result expresses that with the increase of effective operation nodes, the speed of solving the system tasks is becoming higher and higher. Because of the brand width and transmission delay on network, the relationship between the increase of operation nodes and the speedup of tasks solving does not rigidly conform to the theoretic value. In fact, with the increase of operation nodes, the acceleration of the tasks solving is less than the sum of single computation ability of the new add nodes.

3.2 Comparison Between NGCS and Other Parallel System

Table 2 is a comparison between NGCS and other parallel system. NGCS provides a friendly user interface, which is useful to reduce the difficulty for users to build cluster system application and developing period. As for the broad users, cheap resources and easy coding method is driving them to choose NGCS to carry on large-scale scientific computation.

Table 2. The comparison between NGCS and other parallel system

Name	Apply platform	Run way	Run platform	Usage difficulty	APP language	Efficiency
PVM	Cluster	compile	Cross-platform	difficult	Fortran /C++	High
MPI	Cluster	compile	Cross-platform	difficult	Fortran /C++	High
Linda	Cluster	compile	Cross-platform	moderate	C++	High
Lily-Task [6]	Cluster	compile	Windows Linux	easy	C++	High
Ngcs	Internet	Explain to carry out	Windows Linux	easier	Java /Scilab	middle

4 Conclusions

This paper puts forward a new distributed parallel computation method based on Grid computation environment, which achieves Scilab scientific computation task under Internet environment. The newly presented method takes good use of the scattered unused and isomerous resource to acquire computation ability, shields the user service details, simplifies the difficulty of use, and automatically allocates and transfers the tasks on working nodes. So the programmer does not pay attention to the corresponding relationship between task and disposing node, which reduces the programming details of users. Moreover, NGCS implements the system dynamic load balance, enhances the executing efficiency of program, simplifies the implementation of parallel computation, and provides a new approach for achieving large-scale distribute parallel computation. Finally, an example verifies the validity of the distributed parallel computation, and result turns out to be good.

Acknowledgements

Supported by the National Natural Science Foundation of China, Grant No. 60475040, the Provincial High-tech Program of Henan, Grant No. 0524480010.

References

1. Gregory, F.P.: In Search of cluster, Second Edition, Prentice Hall PTR Upper Saddle River Nj (1998)
2. Foster, I., Kesselman, C., Tuecke S.: The Anatomy of the Grid, International Journal of Supercomputer Applications, 15(3) (2001) 200~222
3. Scilab, INRIA, http://www.scilab.org/
4. Gui, X.L., Qian, D.P., He, G.: Design and Implementation of a campus-wide Meta computting system(WADE), Journal of Computer Research and Development (in Chinese) 39(7) (2002) 888~894
5. SOAP Version 1.2 http://www.w3.org/TR/soap12/.
6. Tao, W., Li X.: LilyTask - A Task-Oriented Parallel Computation Model, APPT 2003, LNCS 2834, pp.157~161,Springer-Verlag Berlin (2003)

A Model of XML Access Control with Dual-Level Security Views

Wei Sun, Da-xin Liu, and Tong Wang

College of Computer Science and Technology, Harbin Engineering University,
Harbin, Heilongjiang Province, China
sunwei78@hrbeu.edu.cn

Abstract. XML becomes a standard format for data interchanges on Internet, especially in E-commerce. Although XML technology has been widely used, the research and development on XML security is still at the early stage. The control of XML access is important for protecting XML documents from being illegally modified or accessed. Most of available models utilize a single level check point. In this paper, we proposed an access control model with dual level access control: file-level and element-level (or attribute-level). The model allows adopt the XBLP policy with file-level security, while employs Hide-Node View for element-level security. The architecture framework of the access control model and implementation are briefly described.

1 Introduction

As a large number of corporations and organizations increasingly deploy their services on Internet for increasing the efficiency of business-transaction and productivity, how to efficiently access XML-based data with different user privileges become an important security issue. Considerable efforts have been made to develop access control models for managing XML data in Internet. Oasis [6], and Hada and Kudo [5] proposed the standards for the access control police of XML documents. Dimiani et al. [4] discussed the access control based on the DTD of XML specifications, and proposed a fine-grained access control model that is based on element-level and attribute-level access control. Their model is suitable to a large security system. Li et al. [11] proposed a model of access control based on mandatory access control (MAC). The model also implements the fine-grained access control. However, the MAC policy is not suitable to the hierarchy of XML documents. In [12], a role based access control (RBAC) is proposed. Fan et al. [9] proposed the idea of security view, and security views based on DTD of XML implement to revaluate query on XML documents. However, the schema information is unknown by some low-level access. Fundulaki, and Marx [10] recently provided a comparison of above models using XPath and specified their access control policies.

This paper contributes a new approach by introducing a dual level security views. Given an XML data with documental DTD, our model allows an access control policies to pledge to security access of XML file at both file- and element levels. Our

H.T. Shen et al. (Eds.): APWeb 2006, LNCS 3842, pp. 799–802, 2006.

security specification model supports MAC policy; hence it is very suitable for high security system. At the element-level access control, our access control policy is based on the novel notion of *hide-node views* whose mechanism guarantees that unauthorized user from accessing sensitive data; hence protecting the schema information.

2 File-Level Access Control Based on XBLP

BLP model is a widely used MAC model proposed by Bell and LaPadula in 1976. The BLP Model describes access by active entities (called subjects) and passive entities (called objects). One entity can, depending on type of access, be in both roles. The three properties lead to the following rules for access control decisions. A current access (S[i], O[j], p) is granted, only if the following conditions are met:

(a) ss-property: λ(S[i]) dominates λ (O[j]), if p = read.
*(b) *-property*: λ(O[j]) dominates λ (S[i]), if p = write.
(c) ds-property: x is in cell *M[i,j]* of matrix *M* of authorized accesses.

All properties and security levels must be enforced by the system. Each property is added to the other ones without ever reducing system security. A state that fulfils all properties is called a secured state.

The ss-property and *- property ensure the information exchanges between ones at two same levels, or from low level to high level. XBLP model prompts us use restrict *-property to replace of *-property, and not used *ds-property.*

*(b) restrict *-property:* λ*(O[j]) =* λ *(S[i]), if p = write.*

3 Element-Level Access Control Based on Hide-Node Views

Abstractly, a hide-node view defines a mapping from an instance of document DTD D to instances of a marker-view DTD D_v . Let S=(D, acl) be an access specification. A hide-node view $V : S \rightarrow D_v$ can be defined as a pair $V = (D_v, \sigma)$, where σ stands for XPath annotations used to extract accessible data from an instance of D. Specifically, each element B in D_v , $\sigma(B, op)$ is an XPath set defined over document instance of D. If a document is accessible, $\sigma(r_v, op) = r$, where the r_v and r are the root types of D_v and D, respectively. That is the σ maps the root of T to the root of its view.

We now present a novel algorithm that derivates Hide-node Views, given an access specification S=(D, acl), a hide-node view $V = (D_v, \sigma)$ can be computed. The computational algorithm is shown in Fig.1.

4 Access Control Model Based on Views

An Access Control Model is illustrated in Fig. 2. In order to manage different documents in XML database, an authentication server component in introduced, which plays an administrator role in XML database. Two other components for operating the

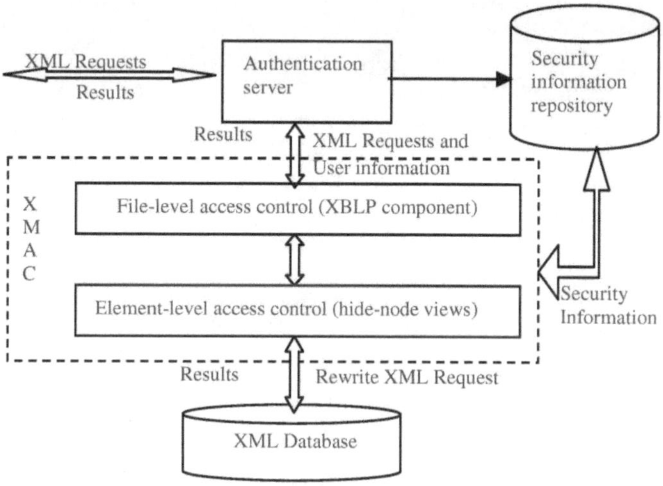

Fig. 1. Hide-node Views Derivation Algorithm

Procedure build_view(S, A)
Input: specification S=(D, acl) and an element type A in D
Output: hide-node view $V = (D_v, \sigma)$ for A and its descendants in D
If visited[A] then return else visited[A]:=true;
Case the A-production $A \rightarrow \alpha$ in the document DTD D of
  (1) $A \rightarrow B_1, \ldots, B_n$:
    for i from 1 to n do
      if acl(B_i ,op)=Y then $\sigma(B_i, op) = \sigma(A, op)$; build_view(S, B_i);
      else if acl(B_i ,op)= $[q]$ then $\sigma(B_i, op) = \sigma(A, op) \cup [q]$; build_view(S, B_i);
      else $\sigma(B_i, op) = \phi$; build_view(S, B_i);
  (2) $A \rightarrow B_1 + \ldots + B_n$: /*similar to (1)*/
  (3) $A \rightarrow B*$: /*similar to (1)*/
  (4) $A \rightarrow str$ /* do null */
  for i from 1 to n do
    reduce_path($\sigma(B_i, op)$); //expression $\sigma(B_i, op)$ reduction
  return;

Fig. 2. Access Control Model

dual level checks are the XBLP component for file-level access control and element-level access control with hide-node views. The security information is achieved as repository in a security information repository system, basically a database system. Such system on the other hand can provide security access information for system monitoring and security management. After the dual check points, the XML data is subject to be rewritten in to permanent XML database system.

5 Conclusions

We propose a new model for high securing XML data based on the file-level control and element-level control using hide-node views. This XML security model provides both content access control and schema availability. The two access controls implement XBLP and Hide-node Views respectively. The model can be implemented on a query engine for XML query rewriting and optimization. We validate these techniques yield substantial reductions in processing time through our experimental studies. Nevertheless, this model provides not only the fine-grained access controls of XML data at file-level and element-level, but also the high flexibility, compared to the transitional access control systems.

References

1. Bertino, E., Ferrari, E.: Secure and Selective dissemination of XML documents. *ACM Transactions on Information and System Security*, 5(3) (2003) 290-331
2. Cho, S., Amer-Yahia, S., Lakshmanan, L., Srivastav D.: Optimizing the Secure Evaluation of Twig Queries. *In Proc. of 28th VLDB* (2002) 490-501
3. Damiani, E., Vimercati, S. di, Paraboschi, S., Samarati P.: Securing XML Documents. *In Proc. of 7th EDBT* (2000) 121-135
4. Damiani, E., Vimercati, S., Paraboschi, S., Samarati, P.: A Fine-grained Access Control System for XML Documents. *ACM Transactions on Information and System Security*, 5(2) (2002) 69-202
5. Hada, S., Kudo M.: XML Access Control Language: Provisional Authorization for XML Documents. http://www.trl.ibm.com/projects/xml/xacl/xacl-spec.html.
6. Oasis: eXtensible Access Control Markup Language (XACML). http://www.oasis-open.org/committees/xcaml
7. Miklau, G., Suciu, D.: Controlling Access to Published Data Using Cryptography. *In Proc. of 29th VLDB* (2003) 898-909
8. Murata, M., Tozawa, A., Kudo, M., Hada, S.: XML Access Control Using Static Analysis. *In Proc. of Computer and Communications Security* (2003) 73-84
9. Fan, W., Chan, C.Y., and Garofalakis, M.: Secure XML Querying with Security Views. *In Proc. of the 2004 ACM SIGMOD*, (2004) 587 -598
10. Fundulaki I., and Marx, M.: Specifying Access Control Policies for XML Documents with XPath. *In Proc. of 9th SACMAT*, ACM Press, (2004) 61-69
11. Li, L., He, Y.Z., Feng, D.G.: A Fine-Grained Mandatory Access Control Model for XML Documents. *Journal of Software*, 15(10) (2004) 1528-1537
12. Sandhu, R., Coyne, E.J., Feinstein, H.L.: Role Based Access Control Models. *IEEE Computer*, 29(2) (1996) 38-47

A Web-Based System for Adaptive Data Transfer in Grid

Jiafan Ou, Linpeng Huang, and Minglu Li

Department of Computer Science, Shanghai Jiao Tong University,
Shanghai, China
wonderow@sjtu.edu.cn

Abstract. Appearance of GridFTP in Grid won't substitute the old data transfer protocols, however, existing data servers confuse the users and applications. There is no unified data accessing approach. This paper proposes an implementation of web based adaptive Grid data transfer solution over multiple protocols. The system is made up of three tiers: a transfer core named PAFTP, transfer service based on WSRF, and portlet application. The core hides diversity of various protocols and provides a universal interface to higher level data access. This solution not only offers multi-protocol reliable data transfer, simple file operation and monitoring on transfer status, but also emphasizes performance of mass file transfer.

1 Introduction

The goal of the Grid is to share computing, storing and other resources in wide area or distributed environments [1]. Globus Project is a research on developing fundamental technologies to build computational Grid. Globus Toolkit (GT), their product, has become de facto standard of the Grid. In computational Grids but data Grids and service Grids access to distributed data is a component of consequence. It is typically as important as access to distributed computational resources [5]. As a number of storage systems are being used in the Grid community, users who wish to access different storage systems (e.g. HPSS, DPSS and so on) are forced to use multiple protocols or APIs. A common protocol would be established to unify data transfer in different storage systems. On the other hand, distributed scientific and engineering applications always require large amounts of data (always gigabytes to petabytes) transfer and access. GridFTP protocol [5] and family of tools were born out of a realization that the Grid environment needed a fast, secure, efficient, and reliable transport mechanism.

However, a lot of Internet data transfer protocols remain in the Grid. It puts us in trouble to determine many kinds of data servers (such as GridFTP server, FTP server, Web server and so on) and use varied tools to get data or even transfer data between these servers. Meanwhile in certain field, such as scientific experiments, large amounts of data are generated and need to transfer. GridFTP does not qualify for bulk data transfer so far. Instead bbFTP [6] is usually applied in such field, e.g. AMS project in CERN. What's the worse, lazy administrator won't change his data server when migrating to the Grid. It lacks a universal interface to manage the data from different server. An approach is called to meet the "broad" data management. Moreover, traditional ways require rich client to transfer data which is lack of flexibility. Users must always prepare and get a client tool with them.

H.T. Shen et al. (Eds.): APWeb 2006, LNCS 3842, pp. 803 – 810, 2006.

In this paper we describe an implementation of web based protocol-adaptive data transfer solution including: transfer core called PAFTP, PAFT service that offer reliable data transfer and monitoring. Using the APIs provided by GT and CoG kits we successfully developed web data transfer application in the Grid. With the solution, we can submit transfer tasks on the browser and query status anywhere. In section 2 we take a look at the different familiar protocols, then analysis the necessity of adaptive data transfer, also the core architecture and improvement. In section 3 we introduce the WSRF based data transfer service, overall architecture and portlet application. In section 4 we will give a little detail on implementation and performance comparison. Finally in section 5 conclusions.

2 Enhanced Adaptive Data Transfer over Multi-protocol

2.1 Different Protocols

There are so many data transfer approaches on daily bases. It is also true in the Grid. Since the Grid doesn't intend to replace the existent protocols in the present network, the various data transfer protocols will remain and play important roles.

FTP is the most commonly used file transfer method. This is the simplest way to exchange files between computers. SCP and SFTP are more secure replacements for the common FTP. They are always used to transfer small files containing sensitive data. bbFTP [6] is a FTP-like system that supports parallel TCP streams for data transfers. It is the preferred method for transferring large data files thanks to its implemented "big window" defined in RFC1323. From the popularities of World Wide Web, we are also commonly using HTTP as a choice for transferring files.

GridFTP protocol, which extends the standard FTP, includes several exciting features, such as Grid Security Infrastructure (GSI) and Kerberos support, third-party control of data transfer, parallel/striped/partial data transfer, automatic negotiation of TCP buffer/window sizes, and so on. The table below shows the comparison of different mechanisms are shown in Table 1.

Table 1. Comparison of different file transfer mechanisms

	GridFTP	**FTP**	**SFTP**	**bbFTP**	**HTTP**
Streams	Multiple	Single	Single	Multiple	Single
TCP Window	Negotiated	Fixed	Fixed	Big Window	Fixed
Encryption	GSI and Kerberos	SFTP	SSH	Only Username and Password	HTTP S
3rd-Party Transfer	Supported	Supported	Supported	N/A	No
Resuming supported	Yes	Yes	Yes	Yes	Yes
Others	N/A	N/A	Slow.Used for small files	Optimized for large files	N/A

Although GridFTP takes many advantages of other protocols, it can't satisfy different purpose -- each protocol has his strong point.

2.2 Available Clients and APIs

It takes GridFTP server and a command line client (globus-url-copy) along within GT, but no interactive client for GridFTP [2]. UberFTP, developed at the NCSA under the auspices of NMI and TeraGrid, acts as an interactive client tool like common "ftp" command. All of them work in console mode and support only GridFTP or part of above protocols.

GT provides client library to access files on remote server (mainly GridFTP server) for programming that is constituted of two parts: globus_ftp_control and globus_ftp_client. However, the rapid development of the next generation Grid service requires the ability to reuse commodity frameworks, technologies, and toolkits in cooperation with Grid technologies [3]. Commodity Grid (CoG) Kits is a tool accomplished the motivation. The CoG package "jglobus" contained in GT, is very one to develop Grid applications. It includes AXIS, data transfer, GRAM, MDS, security and other components.

2.3 PAFTP Core and Enhanced Transfer

Similar to DSI (Data Storage Interface) in GridFTP server, we are about to build a transfer core called PAFTP. There are many data storage systems other than common file system that it might be useful to access data from, for instance HPSS, SRB, a database, non-standard file systems, etc. DSI intends to provide an interface to those storage systems, just like our system wants to integrate formerly referred protocols and provides a unified interface. In addition, user can flexibly implement the interface for new protocol for his particular application. The interface includes many features: authorization, listing, files operation, files transfer and transfer mode, type, process and so on. Some of them are optional and user can choose to implement with requirement. It works across multiple protocols; judges the type of data servers; determines the transfer mechanism automatically, so that we call it PAFTP, short for "protocol-adaptive file transfer protocol".

Figure 1 is hierarchy model of the core architecture. There are three layers. Base level is data storage system, while data server in the second level lays on it. Previous data server runs over simple file system. GridFTP server supports more storage system by DSI and allows user to extend the driver. Our PAFTP is working on the third level, i.e. application interface layer. In PAFTP, File access and operation (including authentication, etc.) are wrapped over multiple protocols. Data exchange between different protocols, e.g. third-party transfer over different data servers, is well implemented. The PAFT service which we will discuss later is also designed on it.

Traditional data access client doesn't concern performance of mass file transfer. Although the protocol pays much attention in multiple streams (parallel) or servers (striped) of single file transfer, transfer rate gains limited increment in multiple files task. Here we propose an enhanced mass data transfer in two phases.

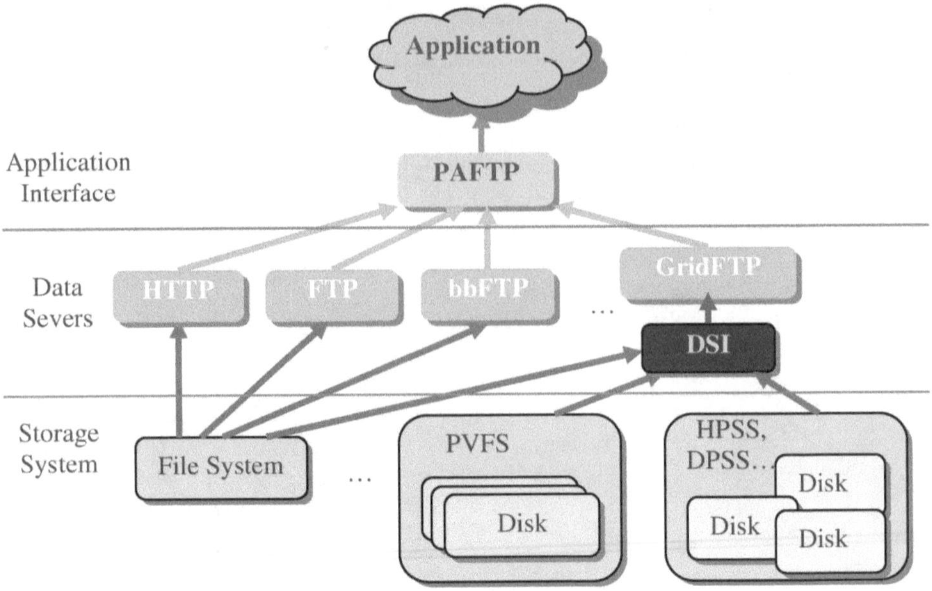

Fig. 1. Architecture of PAFTP core

Study implies that the transfer parameters of GridFTP affect each other. The optimal number of streams strongly depends on the type of connection particularly on the latency value, while optimal TCP buffer size depends on the network connection (latency and bandwidth), the file size, and the number of streams [9]. The regular streams number can be selected from 1 to 32 and TCP buffer size 2KB to 32KB. In a mass file transfer task we can detect and decide the value by experiment. To estimate the network condition, a small set of files was transferred primarily. Since the file size varies and does relatively small effect in determining the other parameters, we can choose files randomly in foregoing transfer. However, a file of too small or large size should not be chosen in order to avoid inaccurate statistic or loss of performance. By changing the limited value of parameter in transfer, we can depict the network characteristics somewhat exactly. The rest of files can be transferred with the right optimal parameters.

Ordinary transfer always uses single thread. It doesn't take advantage of the multiple sockets and slows down totally transfer rate of mass files. All the protocols support multiple concurrent connections, so we can divide files into several batches to achieve maximum bandwidth each of which use a separated connection. The number of batches also depends on various factors, such as network connection, actually allowed connections and so forth. It is more complex than pervious parameters choosing so that we usually use 2 to 4 or a fixed percent of tasks number concurrencies practically. Concurrent batch are scheduled by optimized algorithm. Besides that we maintain a "connection pool" for storing available connections. Alive connections are held in the pool and can be taken when client requires one. That saves plenty of time because it passes over socket connecting, authenticating and authorizing and other burdened process. But we must take care of concurrent problem like security issues and load balancing.

Experiment result shows that it gains considerable enhancement by using above means. Holistic performance is elevated in mass file transfer.

3 PAFT and Portlet Web Application

3.1 PAFT

PAFT (Protocol-Adaptive File Transfer) is an improved Grid service, which lies on PAFTP core, based on WSRF and supports third-party data transfer and simple file operation over multi-protocol and dynamic monitoring. The WSRF (Web Service Resource Framework) specifications [2] define a generic and open framework for modeling and accessing stateful resources using Web services. This framework comprises mechanisms to describe views on the state (WS-ResourceProperties), to support management of the state through properties associated with the Web service (WS-ResourceLifetime), to describe how these mechanisms are extensible to groups of Web services (WS-ServiceGroup), and to deal with faults (WS-BaseFaults). PAFT is a WSRF-based, permanent, easy-call, reliable file transfer service.

GT has already provided a service that performs reliable file transfer by using the RFT (Reliable File Transfer) service [1, 10]. RFT is developed with automatic failure recovery while overcoming the limitation of its predecessor technology, GridFTP. Analogously, PAFT is introducing as a Grid service extending RFT. Most properties of RFT is remained in PAFT, such as managing third-party data transfer, deleting files, failure detection (auto-recovery from dropped connections and temporary network outage by retrying), status and performance querying. Right part of figure 2 demonstrates how an instance of PAFT service is created and started (by portlet), and then controls the transfer between two data server regardless of different protocols.

As referred above, PAFT is built on PAFTP core so it can deal with data transfer over multiple protocols. User can put in a set of transfers between two data servers, which can be any GridFTP servers, bbFTP servers, FTP servers, HTTP servers. Once the request is submitted, the transfer state is stored in a persistent manner (i.e. in database). And it returns a unique handle that will be used to query the status further and recover transfer when failure occurs. When several requests submitted, intelligent parameters tuning and connection pool will work. Both of them could enhance the multiple transfer tasks.

3.2 Portlet Empowered Application

A portal is a web application which typically provides content aggregation from different sources, and hosts the presentation layer of different backend systems. It also has sophisticated personalization features which provide customized content to users. Porlets are visible active components users see within their portal pages. They act as information presentation and broker in multiple tiers web application.

Figure 2 depicts the overall architecture of data transfer solution. A client request is processed by the portal web application, which retrieves the portlets on the current

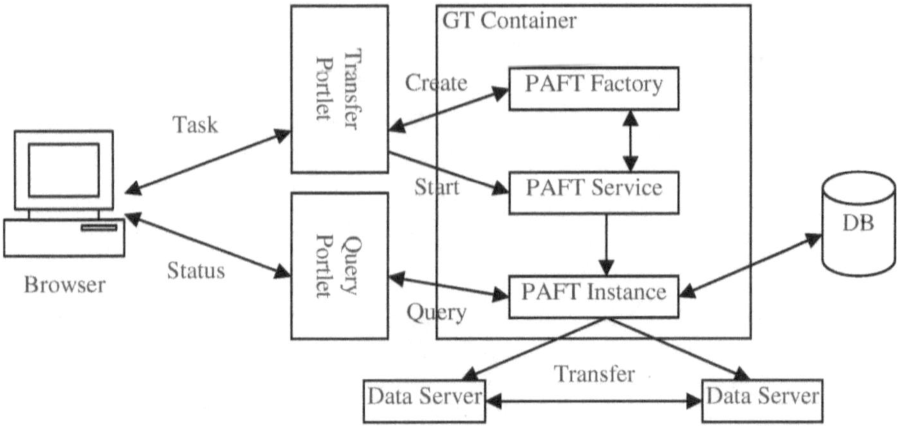

Fig. 2. Overall architecture

page for the current user. Each portlet is in charge of its own responsibility. For example, transfer portlet accepts the submitted transfer task and then interacts with the PAFT service. It creates and starts a PAFT instance, and delivers transfer task to PAFT service in background. Query portlet invokes query function of PAFT to inquire about the transfer status and information wanted. In this way user can submit and query transfers anywhere a browser is installed, so client tools are never needed in a third party data transfer. Portlets can be easily deployed in other containers.

4 Implementation

On the foundation of CoG we intend to design the core of data transfer interface over multi-protocol. First of all, we need an interface "PAFTP" used in the core (which can be used in PAFT service) that could provide a universal access to different data servers. We use the "Bridge" pattern to address design problems by putting the "PAFTP" abstraction and its implementation in separate class hierarchies.

Thus PAFTP support many data system and servers including GridFTP, FTP, bbFTP, SFTP and HTTP and so on. Local and network file system are even treated as a server type for convenience and compatibility. What's more, the client can judge the type of data server automatically without telling what protocol used. It is not difficult to do this. We can either use regular server port (e.g. 2811 is always GridFTP server, 21 stands for FTP server and so forth) or decide by the responding message returned by the server, or both of them.

The web administration system (Figure 3) allows users to perform third-party transfer across data servers and to specify the transfer parameters, CA subjects (if necessary) and pairs of URL. Integrated modules and friendly graphical user interface enable people playing more conveniently and intuitively. Two portlets are in their "view" mode and ready for action. After transfer task submitted, an instance of PAFT service was created by portlet. Potential transfers were performed by PAFTP core used in the service. An instance ID and temporary state report can be retrieved. The instance ID can be used in the status querying farther.

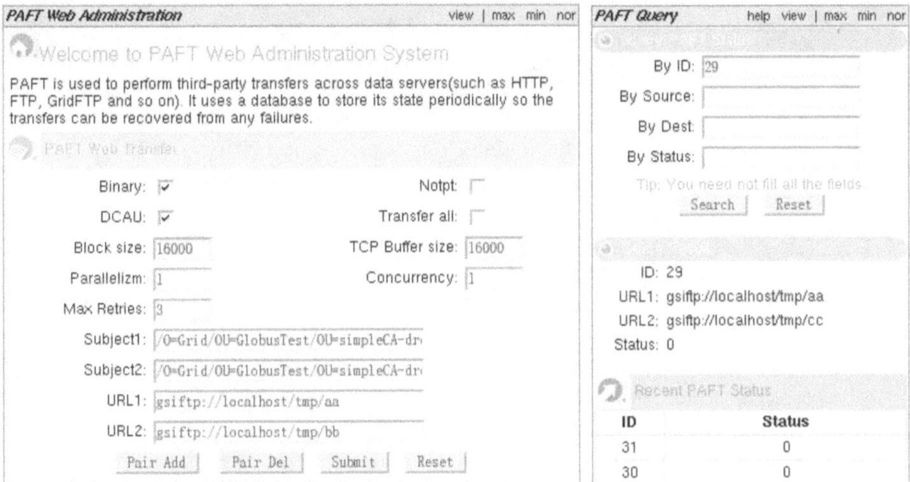

Fig. 3. Portlets of PAFT web administration and query

The bar chart below (Figure 4) shows our testing results of mass third-party file transfer using Grid service in gigabyte Ethernet environment. Each file in transfer is of 1MB size. Test was going with 5 to 60 files transfer by both PAFT and RFT. It cost so much time because the process included spending of Java program starting, service creation, server authorization, and even transfer status displaying. All environments were same for PAFT and RFT to ensure the accurate comparison results between them. We used fixed two concurrencies (i.e. two connections) in the mass file transfer.

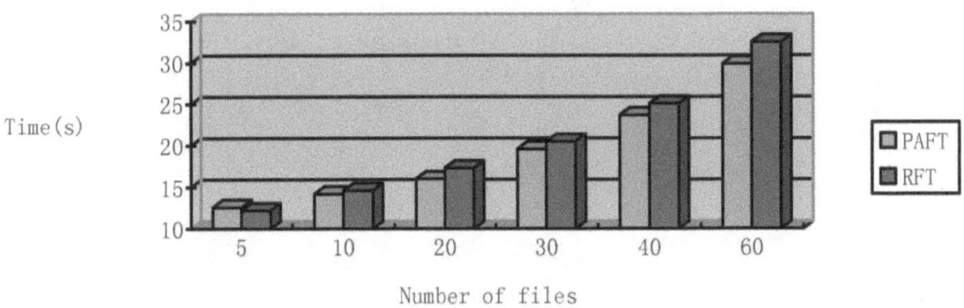

Fig. 4. Performance of PAFT and RFT

We can conclude from the figure that increasing disparity becomes more clearly while number of files rises. There is 8% performance increment in 60 files transfer of PAFT comparing to RFT. By tuning parameters, such as TCP buffers, number of streams, etc. in our enhanced algorithms, PAFT gets a totally improvement comparing to RFT.

5 Conclusion

In this paper we proposed a web based protocol-adaptive data transfer solution including data transfer core, service and web application. This idea was enlightened by "globus-url-copy" command in GT and promoted by our project. That command supports a subset of protocols our system introduced, but user must manually specify the right protocol nevertheless.

Reliable Grid service PAFT supports simple file operation and transfer between data servers of different protocols. Portlets represent user interface in the web in order to provide convenient interaction and invoke PAFT service. Corresponding PAFTP core is introduced, which is a transfer interface over multiple protocols. We do nice schedule and parameters adjustment in mass file transfer and reasonably improve the performance. All results have been tested in our Grid computing lab centered with IBM P690, a Grid-oriented high performance computer.

References

1. Foster, I., Kesselman, C.: *The Grid 2: Blueprint for a New Computing Infrastructure*, 2004
2. The Globus Alliance. http://www.globus.org. 2003-2005
3. The CoG Kits. http://www.cogkits.org. 2003-2005
4. Silva, V.: Transferring files with GridFTP. April 2003
5. Allcock B., et al.: GridFTP: A Data Transfer Protocol for the Grid. 2001
6. The bbFTP – Large Files Transfer Protocols. http://doc.in2p3.fr/bbftp. 2003-2005
7. Lim, S., Fox, G., et al.: Web Service Robust GridFTP. PDPTA 2004
8. Cao, L., et al.: Design and Implementation of Grid File Management System Hotfile. GCC 2004
9. Cannataro, M., Mastroianni, C., Talia, D., and Trunfio, P.: Evaluating and Enhancing the Use of the GridFTP Protocol for Efficient Data Transfer on the Grid. Euro PVM/MPI (2003)
10. Madduri, R.K., Hood, C.S., Allcock, W.E.: Reliable File Transfer in Grid Environments. LCN'02 (2002)

Optimal Search Strategy for Web-Based 3D Model Retrieval

Qingxin Zhu* and Bo Peng

School of Computer Science and Engineering,
University of Electronic Science and Tech. of China,
Chengdu 610054, China
qxzhu@uestc.edu.cn

Abstract. In this paper we propose an optimal search strategy for web-based 3D model retrieval. Special considerations are given to the determination of the target's initial probability distributions. Two optimal search strategies are derived by using Lagrange multiplier method. Experimental results shows that this approach is more efficient than random search.

Keywords: Search theory, 3D model retrieval, mobile agent, Lagrange multiplier.

1 Introduction

The structures of 3D shapes can be easily acquired by the advanced modeling and visualizing techniques. This led to an exponentially growth of 3D models in the Internet. However, search the web for a model is a hard task just like search a needle in a pile of hay. Many search engines have been designed to help indexing large portions of the web. Some popular text-based search engines are Google Image Search[1] and AltaVista[2]. The traditional method of indexing is not suitable for this case anymore. Since 1990's many content-based methods for similarity retrieval of multimedia objects have been proposed. A number of Content Based Retrieval (CBR) systems have already been developed. The main idea here is to create a set of features that will efficiently describe a 3D model. Content-based methods provide us a more flexible and precise way to describe 3D shapes, and thus make non-textual data searching possible. Smith et al.[3] developed a CBR system for the World Wide Web. Scarloff et al.[5] developed a content-based image query system including a gatherer, which collects images from the Web. Beigi et al.[4] applied the principle of meta-searching to a number of available image search engines. Since an exhaustive search of the Internet is infeasible, it is a big challenge to find an efficient way to search 3D models for a limited resource allocation.

Recently, a new technique called mobile agents is developed. Mobile agents are programs that migrate from host to host in the network, the initial state of the program is saved when transporting to a new host, and restored to allow the

* corresponding author.

H.T. Shen et al. (Eds.): APWeb 2006, LNCS 3842, pp. 811–818, 2006.

program to continue from where it left off. This technique is efficient for content-based 3D model searching over Internet. When search engine receives a client's request, some agents are created. They move automatically among web-sites to perform 3D model retrieval. When target is found the result is returned to the client.

Usually, a feature vector is used when performing similarity retrieval, which maps the essential features of a 3D model to a point of high-dimensional space[6][7]. Consequently, the original task is equivalent to finding a nearest point from the given point in a subset of the high-dimensional space. However, most of the existing algorithms for similarity retrieval do not consider the limitation of resources (time and money) which is assigned to the search task. These algorithms assume that the resources allocated for search is unlimited, thus they search each class of 3D objects sequentially in an exhausted manner, i.e., extracting features for each model and matching them one by one in databases. When the number of models in the databases and the dimension of the feature vectors of objects increases, the running time of the algorithms will increase exponentially, causing the retrieval process failure for a given amount of resource.

In this paper, we study the 3D model retrieval issue under a limited time restraint. We assume that the total search time is bounded and hence the retrieval task will not succeed for sure. In this case, we derive the optimal strategy with which the task will succeed with the highest probability. The remainder of this paper is organized as follows: in section 2, we introduce the optimal search theory and design the mathematical model for 3D model retrieval. In section 3, we derive an optimal search strategy for 3D model retrieval in the web. In section 4 we give some experimental results. In section 5 we summarize and give some suggestions for the future work.

2 Optimal Search Model

Pioneered by G. Kimball and B. Koopman in 1940's, optimal search theory is developed from the statistical decision theory in Operations Research. Optimal search theory is the theory of finding the "best" way to detect a pre-claimed object, usually called the "target". Now it has been widely used in military, industrial, agriculture, criminology, market investigation, census, medical research, and so on. [8][9] [10][11][12][13]

We may categorize optimal search problems according to whether the space and time are discrete or continuous, and whether the target is stationary or mobile. The problem considered in this paper falls into the category of stationary target in discrete spaces. This kind of optimal search problems has three basic elements defined below.

- Initial probability distribution of the target location. Suppose the target is located in some subset A of space R^n, it's position is given by $y = (y_1, \cdots, y_n)$, the initial probability density function is denoted by $p(x)$ and defined by:

$$p(x) = \text{Prob } [x = y], \forall x \in A$$

$$p(x) \geq 0, \qquad \sum_{x \in A} p(x) = 1$$

- Detection function. The detection function relates the amount of resource utilized in searching an area to the probability of detecting the target given that it is located in that area. In discrete space $\{C_1, \cdots, C_n\}$ it becomes:

$$b(i,t) = \text{Prob}[\text{detect target at } t | \text{ target is in } C_i].$$

- Resources constraint. Typically, the searcher only has a limited amount of resources available to conduct the search. Usually, the resource is represented by the time used to do a search.

Let K denote the upper bound of total searching time, the optimal search strategy under this constraint will be a time allocation sequence

$$(k_1, k_2, \cdots, k_m), \qquad \sum_{j=1}^{m} k_j \leq K$$

which can maximize the probability of detecting the target. (Other formulation of the optimal search problem is to minimize the expected resources consumption for detecting the target.) Given the initial probability distribution function of the target location and the detection function, we can compute the optimal resource allocation, i.e., the optimal search strategy by Lagrange multiplier method.

To perform a retrieval task, the client submits a retrieval request that may be an example model or a feature vector extracted from it. A Searching Service Provider (SSP) receives the client's request and estimates the initial distribution of the target (the matching object) based on the information stored in the local database in form of an index. Then it computes the optimal search strategy for each mobile agent under pre-assigned resource constraint and dispatches the searching agent to travel along a set of web-sites, where it runs a CBR program and returns a list of 3D models that match the target. Since every web-site updates its models, the index kept by SSP should be updated as well. This can also be done with the help of the updating agents, called the crawlers by some authors, which transport the feature vectors of updated models to SSP. In both cases, mobile agents perform the retrieval task on web-sites' local database until the allocated resource is used out.

3 Optimal Search Strategy

Before we can compute an optimal search strategy, it is necessary to decide the initial probability distribution of the target and the detection function. In most domain-specific databases, 3D models are classified according to their functions and shapes. For instance, there may be classes named by "tables", "cars", "buildings" and so on. The models in the same class shares a high level similarities comparing with those in different classes. Feature vectors extracted by shape-based retrieval algorithms serve as good descriptions for the member of each class, thus can be used to derive the initial probability distribution of target. Assume the feature vector of a 3D model is v, $v \in R^d$. Thus, v is a mapping from the set of 3D models into a subspace of d-dimensional vector space. Define the distance in this vector space as follows:

$$\|\vec{v} - \vec{w}\| = (\sum_{1 \leq i \leq d} |v_i - w_i|^2)^{1/2}.$$

Let $\{C_1, \cdots, C_n\}$ be the set of 3D models. for each class C_i, let

$$\bar{x}_i = \frac{\sum_j x_j}{m_i}, \quad 1 \leq j \leq m_i,$$

where m_i is the total number of models in C_i. Suppose the target is mapped to a point y in the d-dimensional vector space R_d, and the i-th member of C_i is mapped to a point x_i in R_d. We then define the target's initial probability distribution as follows:

$$p(i) = \frac{\|\bar{x}_i - y\|^{-1}}{\sum_{j=1}^{N} \|\bar{x}_j - y\|^{-1}}, \quad i = 1, \cdots, N$$

where N is the total number of 3D model classes in the whole database.

If the target indeed locates in the class C_i, we should have a higher detection probability if searching time is longer. Therefore we assume the detection function $b((i,t)$ is regular. That is, for each i, $b((i,t)$ is continuously differentiable and the derivative $b'(i,t)$ is decreasing with $b'(i,0) > 0$ and $b'(i,\infty) = 0$. Furthermore, we assume

$$b(i,t) = 1 - e^{-q_i t}, \quad (i = 1, \cdots, N),$$

where parameter q_i is a constant satisfying $q_i > 0$. The value of q_i depends on the complexity of models involving the number and type of models in the current search class. Intuitively we may choose bigger q_i for easier models and smaller q_i for more complex models.

Assume K is the total time allowed for searching. Now we can compute the optimal search strategy f^* as follows[13]. Define:

$$\ell(i, \lambda, t) = p(i)b(i,t) - \lambda t, \quad 1 \leq i \leq N.$$

Consider

$$\frac{\partial \ell}{\partial t} = p(i) q_i e^{-q_i t} - \lambda = 0, \tag{1}$$

Solve the equation to yield the optimal time allocations

$$t_i = (1/q_i) \ln(q_i p(i)/\lambda).$$

From the constraint condition we have

$$\sum_{i=1}^{N} t_i = \sum_{i=1}^{N} \frac{1}{q_i} \ln \frac{q_i p(i)}{\lambda} \leq K. \tag{2}$$

The equality is achieved in the boundary. The detection probability $P[f^*]$ of the optimal search plan is given by

$$P[f^*] = \sum_{i=1}^{N} p(i)(1 - e^{-q_i t_i}) = \sum_{i=1}^{N} p(i)(1 - e^{-\ln \frac{q_i p(i)}{\lambda}}) = 1 - \sum_{i=1}^{N} \frac{\lambda}{q_i}.$$

When all q_i's are equal, i.e. $q_i = q(i = 1, 2, \cdots, N)$, we can easily derive the upper bound of t_i^* in terms of $p(i)$ and q. From (2) we see that

$$\lambda \geq q[\prod_{i=1}^{N} p(i)]^{1/N} e^{-qK/N},$$

hence

$$t_i^* = \frac{1}{q} \ln \frac{qp(i)}{\lambda} \leq \frac{a}{q} + b,$$

where

$$a = \ln \frac{p(i)}{(p(1) \cdots p(N))^{\frac{1}{N}}}, \quad b = \frac{K}{N}$$

Since b is the average value of the search resource allocated in each class, This result shows that the extra resources assigned to a class can not exceed a/q.

The regularity property of the detection function implies that a higher detection probability can be attained if searching time is longer. However, sometime this assumption may not be true. For example, a 3D model may be removed or protected (hidden) in a web-site, in this case assigning more search time will not increase the probability of detecting the target since the agent can never detect the target in this web-site. Therefore when the time spent on a web-site goes beyond some constant, the detection probability is going to drop. In this situation, a "bell shape" form of detection function (such as normal distribution) is more applicable.

Consider the following detection function:

$$b(i,t) = e^{-(t-t_i)^2}, \quad t > 0, \quad i = 1, 2, \cdots, N \tag{3}$$

$$b(i,t) = 0, \qquad t = 0 \tag{4}$$

t_i is a constant. Consider the following Langrangian function:

$$\ell(i, \lambda, t) = p(i)e^{-(t-t_i)^2} - \lambda t, \quad t > 0$$

Hence

$$\frac{\partial \ell}{\partial t} = p(i)[-2(t - t_i)]e^{-(t-t_i)^2} - \lambda, \tag{5}$$

Obviously, when $t \geq t_i$,

$$\frac{\partial \ell}{\partial t} < 0$$

the maximum value of ℓ is attained in the area of $[0, t_i]$. Assume $z \in [0, t_i]$, let

$$\frac{\partial \ell}{\partial t} = 0$$

we have

$$t_i - t = \frac{\lambda}{2p(i)} e^{(t_i - t)^2}.$$

we can get the optimal resource allocation by solving the following equations:

$$\begin{cases} \beta_i e^{\alpha_i \xi_i^2} - \xi_i & = 0, \qquad (i = 1, 2, \cdots, N) \\ \sum_{i=1}^{N} (t_i - \xi_i) - K = & 0. \end{cases}$$

Where

$$\xi_i = t_i - t, \qquad \beta_i = \frac{\lambda}{2p(i)\alpha_i}.$$

4 Experiment Results

In order to evaluate our method we design a simulation experiment based on the optimal search algorithm described above. The simulation is performed on a Pentium4-1G PC with 256MB RAM. 3D models in different web-sites are stored in their local database. There are 1,000 web-sites and 8800 3D models randomly (uniformly) distributed among them. An incomplete and out-of-date list of the index of these models is kept in SSP. The feature retrieval program used to search 3D models is carried by agents, which will transfer to the web-sites to perform the feature extraction, compare with the feature vector of the target model.

We can see a significant improvement of the detection probability comparing to the sequential search method. Without using optimal search strategy, the whole search process costs about 500s to go through all the web-sites. With the

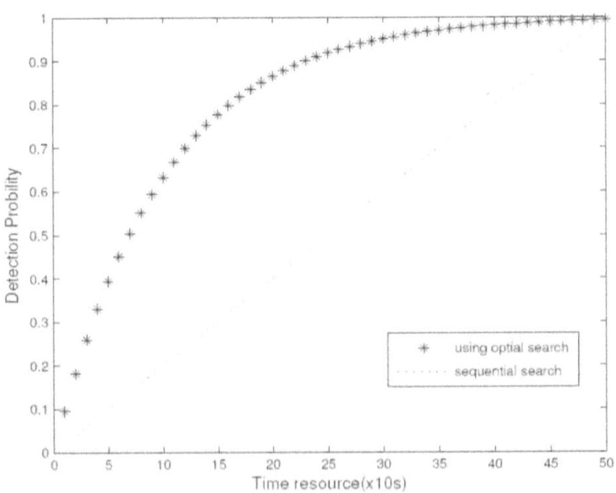

Fig. 1. Detection probabilities vs resource bound

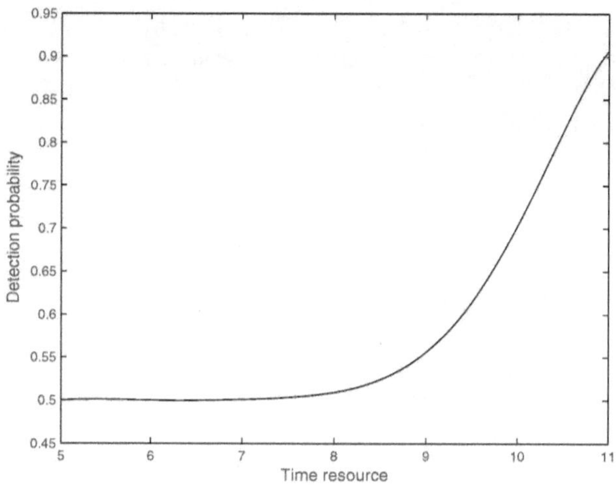

Fig. 2. Detection probabilities for $b(i,t) = e^{-(t-4)^2}$

time constraint setting to 50-500, the detection probability is proportional to the time allocated. When the optimal search strategy is employed, the detection probability is increased, especially for the small time limit.

Fig. 1 shows the detection probability of sequential search and optimal search strategy.

Fig. 2 illustrates the changes of detection probability with a "bell-shaped" detection function $b(i,t) = e^{-(t-t_i)^2}$. The total time bound K varies from 5 minutes to 11 minutes. According to the formula (3), t_i is the maximum point of the detection probability for the i-th web-site. Hence for the time limit K, the average value of t_i is 4. Now let $t_i = 4$, we can see that the detection probability increases very slowly when time bound K is less than $2 \times t_i$, after that value the detection probability increases quickly.

5 Conclusion

In this paper we discuss a novel method for web-based 3D model retrieval based on optimal search theory. The main contribution of this paper is the methodology proposed for model retrieval under limited time resource. In particular, we give the method to compute the initial probability distribution of target's location and the form of detection function, thus formulate the original problem as an optimal search problem. Our experimental results show that the optimal search strategy is more efficient comparing to the sequential search.

Our work also suggests several directions for future research. First, we may use better method to estimate initial probability distribution precisely. In ref.[[14] we discussed the criterion for choosing initial probability distributions and the error estimation for optimal search plan. These results can also be reformed here Second, when detection function is regular, how to choose a suitable parameter

q_i is a difficult task that requires carefully analysis of models, such as modelling errors, number of models and complexity of models in the current class.

To conclude, the application of optimal search strategy to 3D model retrieval will demonstrate advantages over other techniques, especially when the number of models is huge and their location changes randomly.

References

1. Google Image search. http://www.google.com/images.
2. AltaVista. Altavista search engine. http://www.altavista.com.
3. J.R. Smith, S.F. Chang. An image and video search engine for the world-wide web. In Proc. Storage and Retrieval for Image and Video Databases V (SPIE V) (San Jose, CA, USA, February 1997).
4. M. Beigi, A.B. Benitez, S.F. Chang. MetaSeek: A content-based meta-search engine for images. In Proc. SPIE VI (San Jose, CA,USA, January 1998).
5. S. Sclaroff, L. Taycher, M.L. Cascia. Image Rover: A content-based image browser for the world wide web. In Proc. IEEE Work shop on Content-based Access of Image and Video Libraries(San Juan, Puerto Rico), June1997.
6. S. Loncaric. A survey of shape analysis techniques. Pattern Recognition, 31(8):983-1001, 1998.
7. M. Kazhdan, T. Funkhouser, and S. Rusinkiewicz. Rotation invariant spherical harmonic representation of 3D shape descriptors. In Symposium on Geometry Processing, June 2003.
8. O. Benichou, M. Coppey, M. Moreau, P.H. Suet, R. Voituriez. Optimal search strategies for hidden targets, submitted to Phys. Rev. Lett. 2005
9. Bhaskar DasGupta, JoãoP. Hespanha and Eduardo Sontag, Computational Complexities of Honey-pot Searching with Local Sensory Information, 2004 American Control Conference (ACC 2004), 2134-2138, 2004.
10. R. Chandramouli. Web search steganalysis: Some challenges and approaches. Proc. IEEE ISCAS, Special session on Information Hiding 2004.
11. Douglas W. Gage. Many-Robot MCM search systems. Proceedings of the autonomous vehicles in mine countermeasures symposium, Monterey CA. 4-7 April 1995.
12. Ramin Rezaiifar and Armand M. Makowski, "From Optimal Search Theory to Sequential Paging in Cellular Networks," IEEE Journal on Selected Areas in Communications, Vol. 15, No. 7, p. 1253-1264, September 1997.
13. L.D. Stone, Theory of Optimal Search, Mathematics in Science and Engineering, Vol. 118, Academic Press, 2nd Ed. New York, 1980
14. Zhu Qingxin, Zhou Mingtian, John Oommen. Some Results on Optimal Search in Discreate Spaces. Chinese Journal of Software. 12(12):1748-1751, December 2001

ParaView-Based Collaborative Visualization for the Grid

Guanghua Song, Yao Zheng, and Hao Shen

College of Computer Science, and Center for Engineering and Scientific Computation, Zhejiang University, 310027, P.R. China
ghsong@cs.zju.edu.cn, yao.zheng@zju.edu.cn

Abstract. This paper describes our efforts to develop visualization service on the Grid. The focus of this paper is our work on grid-enabling the ParaView, a widely used parallel visualization software package. Upon the analysis of the ParaView source code, the architecture as well as the implementation of ParaView-based client side cooperation of object visualization has been presented. Furthermore, the deployment of the collaborative ParaView as a visualization service in the Grid has been addressed.

1 Introduction

The computation simulations of nature generate mass amounts of numeric information far more than what human beings could process. Scientific visualization emerges to help solve this problem by taking all the data and transferring them into images, enabling us to have a better insight of the scientific information that would be otherwise impossible. Collaborative visualization software puts teamwork into action using electronic communication between people or groups to increase the productivity.

There have been works focusing on providing visualization capabilities in the Grid. Jason Wood et al [1] presented works on Grid-enabling the IRIS explorer. Peng Liu et al [2] proposed a Java-based Java 3D as a visualization environment in the Grid. Charles Moad et al [3] focused on devising an effective solution to view large data sets in the Grid at a visually pleasing frame rate.

This paper reports on the research aimed at adding the collaboration functionality into ParaView [4], a widely-used, open-source parallel visualization software, and deploying it in the Grid as a visualization service.

Important aspects of our work include understanding the architecture of ParaView and its underlying library Visualization Toolkit (VTK) [6], which will be discussed in Section 2. Detailed source code level analysis is also performed in Section 3 in order to make the necessary structural modifications. A client-to-client collaboration implementation is presented in Section 4. In Section 5, the deployment of the modified client-to-client collaborative ParaView as a visualization service in the MASSIVE Grid [8] is reported. In Section 6 we list the conclusions and future work.

H.T. Shen et al. (Eds.): APWeb 2006, LNCS 3842, pp. 819–826, 2006.

2 Overview of VTK and ParaView

VTK is an open source, freely available software system for 3D computer graphics, image processing, and visualization [7]. VTK consists of a C++ class library, and several interpreted interface layers including Tcl/Tk, Java, and Python. VTK has two major subsystems - the graphics model and the visualization pipeline. The graphics model forms an abstract layer above the graphics language (for example, OpenGL) to insure cross-platform portability. VTK data processing pipeline transforms data into forms that can be displayed by the graphics subsystem or into other data formats that the pipeline can further process.

ParaView is a key application built on VTK. It uses VTK as the data processing and rendering engine and has a user interface written in a blend of Tcl/Tk and C++. The relationship between VTK and ParaView can be illustrated by Fig. 1.

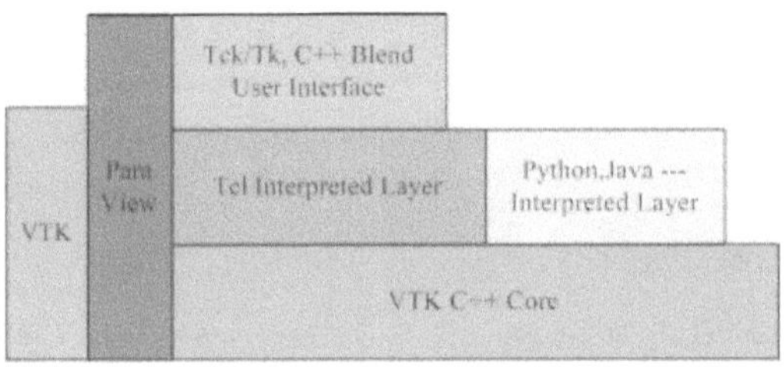

Fig. 1. VTK, ParaView and their relation

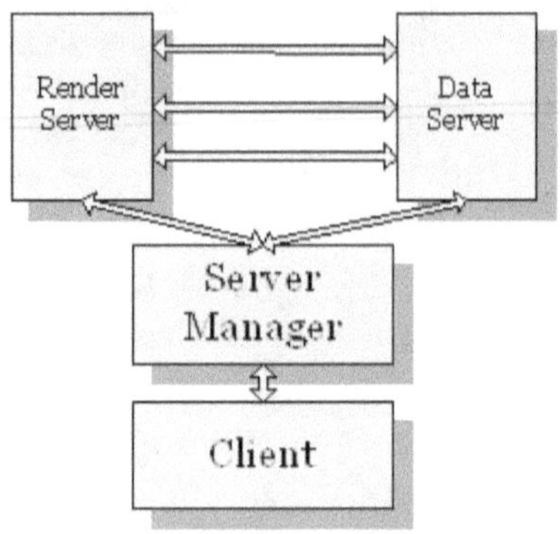

Fig. 2. Major components of Para View

ParaView supports all the functionality that VTK has, such as distributed execution and parallel processing, which makes it a scalable application to carry out various scientific visualization tasks.

ParaView can be divided into four major components: Client, Server Manager, Data Server and Render Server, as shown in Fig. 2 [5]. The servers support running of MPI applications. Client-to-Server communication is carried out through TCP/IP sockets. The architecture of ParaView is also quite flexible, each component can be running on different node and some components could be merged – in extreme, ParaView could be running as a standalone application on a single machine.

The programming language used in ParaView is a blend of C++ and Tcl/Tk. Tcl is an interpreted language based on an interpreter written in C. Tk is a library of basic elements (called widgets) for building graphical user interface built on top of Tcl.

The VTK Kernel is written in C++, it provides a Tcl/Tk Interpreted Layer. A layer of wrapper is also provided so that Tcl/Tk could call the underlying library in an object-oriented way.

3 Analysis of ParaView

Our analysis is based on ParaView 1.8.0. The main focus of the analysis is more on the add-on functionalities of the user interface and less on VTK itself, as the collaboration process relies heavily on user actions.

The research of collaboration does not have much to do with the parallel method of execution, nor with the batch running mode. Therefore the running mode this paper looks into is the standalone mode and the client/server mode.

In the main classes of ParaView, vtkPVApplication is a representative, which manages all the sub-windows and is in charge of interpretation of all Tcl commands. vtkProcessModuleGUIHelper can be used to provide GUI without forcing the processing module to link to a GUI, especially when ParaView is running in the client/server mode and the server side doesn't have a GUI attached. vtkProcessModule is in charge of process execution according to the running mode specified, particularly when ParaView is running as a standalone application or as client/server distributed mode.

3.1 Widgets and Wrappers

As mentioned above, every basic element in Tk is called a widget, ParaView encapsulates every Tk widget in a corresponding C++ class so that ParaView could control and manipulate the Tcl/Tk graphical interface through C++. The interpreted layer VTK provides is written in C, not C++, therefore a wrapper is needed to fill the gap. ParaView contains a program to read the C++ header files and automatically generate the wrapper codes. These wrapper codes not only settle the problem of dynamic callback from Tcl to C++, but also handle the differentiations between C++ and Tcl and make necessary conversions, they even provide some extra methods that are unavailable in C++.

3.2 Server Manager and Client

The Server Manager in ParaView is an intermediary among the data, the render servers and the user interface. It provides an interface to create and manage objects in parallel. The server manager runs on a single processor – either the client (when running ParaView in client/server mode) or the first process (when running in distributed stand-alone mode). The server manager sends commands to the server, and the server is responsible for executing them. The ParaView GUI has access to the server manager, and this is the only way for the GUI to access the server objects.

The server manager controls all the servers and has a simple interface the client(s) can access. The server manager is responsible for creating VTK objects on the server, changing the settings of these objects, and obtaining information about these objects. The client will tell the Server manager to create or change a VTK object, and it will ask for information about existing objects.

The ParaView client contains the user interface and is responsible for passing the values from the user interface to the server manager. It also updates the user interface exploiting information gained from the servers.

The ParaView server manager is also responsible for handling communication between the client and the server(s) as well as maintaining a copy of the state of the server(s). It is created to simplify the development of distributed visualization applications.

4 Extending ParaView

ParaView is designed for easy extension in many aspects. The Tcl/Tk graphical user interface is intrinsically flexible, additional file formats support can be further added by either writing a simple XML configuration file (if the VTK reader already exists) or by first implementing a VTK reader in C++ and then adding it to the XML file for ParaView readers.

4.1 Ways to Implement Collaboration

After analyzing the main structure of ParaView, two modifying proposals could be made: the first one is to make two independent ParaView applications (either standalone or Client/Server) interact through sending information of what is being done at the client side (as shown in Fig. 3). This could be implemented through hacking into the trace file (mentioned later), since actions that will affect the data model will be logged into the trace file.

The second way is to break the one-to-one client/server mode so that multi clients could connect to the same server manager. This eliminates the problem of redundant calculation. But the implementation will alter the client's behavior completely. Currently, when the user invokes an action, the client will send information to the server, which in turn will retrieve the geometry model, and will transform it to a 2-D image to present to the user. However, if multi-clients were working, every client's action will have effects on other clients. That is, there should be a mechanism that tells the client when to get the geometry model and update their user interfaces.

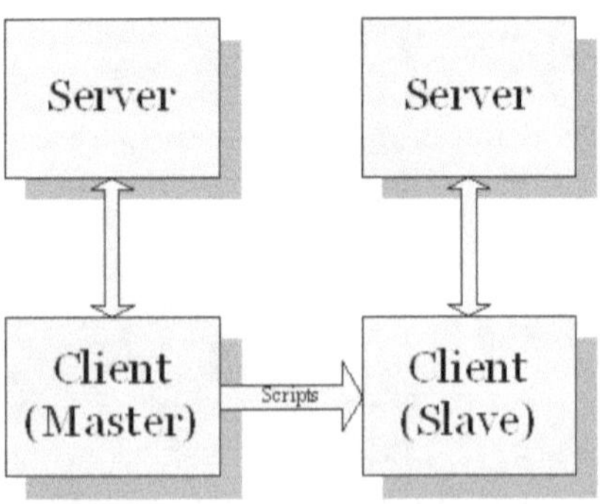

Fig. 3. Client-to-client collaboration

4.2 Implementation of Collaboration through Trace Files in ParaView

ParaView keeps track of whatever it does to the data model in a trace file. The trace file is created on the client side when the GUI has completed loading. There are generally two categories of traces: the first is the trace of the application, through vtkPVApplication, it keeps track of the creation and destruction of the sources and filters (Data Objects); the second series is the traces of various types of data objects, changes of parameters of the data objects will be stored in the corresponding trace files.

As the traces that ParaView keeps constitute the exact Tcl/Tk commands that could be executed, the communication code is written in Tcl.

```
namespace export
proc serverOpen {channel addr port} {
    fileevent $channel readable "readLine $channel"
    puts "OPENED - addr $addr, port $port"
}
proc readLine {channel} {
    variable ::Application
    variable ::kw
    if {[gets $channel line]<0} {
    } else {
            eval $line
    }
}
set server [socket -server serverOpen 33000]
```

At the slave client, a server socket is created waiting for the master to connect. Once connected, the slave client will receive commands from the master and evaluate dynamically at the same namespace as the main interpreter has.

```
set sock [socket 127.0.0.1 33000]
proc writeLine {channel line} {
  puts $channel $line
  flush $channel
}
```

At the master client, a function named "writeLine" is provided for the traces to be transferred to the other client. Wherever traces take place, check the mode and send the trace to the other client in the following way:

```
*(this->TraceFile) << buffer << endl;
if (this->GetCollborateMasterMode())
this->Script("writeLine $sock {%s}", buffer);
```

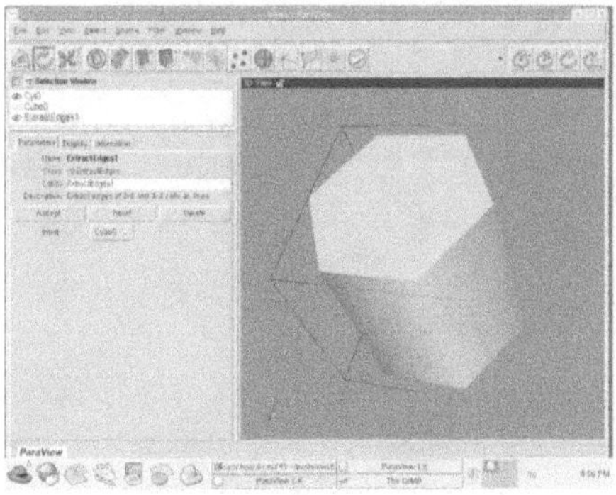

(a) Master

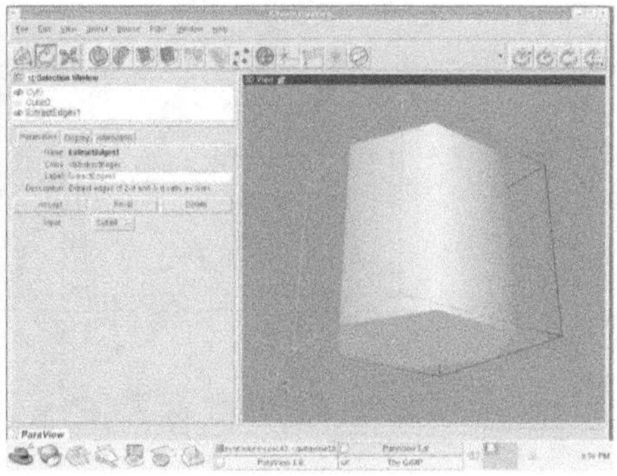

(b) Slave

Fig. 4. Snapshot of Master and Slave in Collaboration Mode

The source code modified skipped the positional data that determine the camera position so that each client can rotate in its own model without affecting the other. However, the data models for the two clients are the same. Collaboration snapshots of the master and the slave, as shown in Fig. 4(a) and Fig.4(b) respectively, illustrate this feature.

5 Deployment of the Modified ParaView on the Grid

Our primary goal of studying the ParaView is to deploy it as a parallel and collaborative visualization service in the MASSIVE Grid. By this kind of service, users will be allowed to visualize large data sets (such as large volume geometry and mesh data sets) by making use of powerful rendering capabilities of the PC clusters in the Grid, which is a key enabler for engineering and scientific computation, no matter how weak there desktop computers' rendering capabilities are.

It is anticipated that two types of collaborative visualization will be supported in MASSIVE. Firstly, one participant will be designated as the leader and will be able to navigate the data by selecting the viewpoint, lighting conditions, and other related attributes. In this mode all participants will see the same scene as the leader, and will be able to interact via audio links. In the second approach each participant will be able to navigate the data independently. The idea here is that when a participant discovers something of interest, other participants can subscribe to that participant's view. In effect, this forms a sub-group of participants with a leader, as in the first mode.

We have implemented the first type of collaborative visualization by deploying the modified collaborative ParaView as one kind of visualization service in the MASSIVE grid, which is constructed on the basis of the Globus toolkit. ParaView is deployed on two PC Clusters: Cluster A is the Dawning PC cluster with 9 rendering nodes, and cluster B is a simulated PC Cluster consisting of 3 compatible PCs. Fig. 5 demonstrates the deployment framework of the modified ParaView on the Globus-based Grid environment.

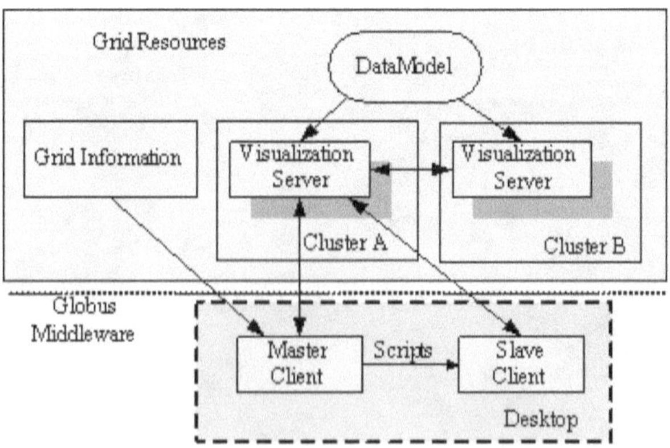

Fig. 5. Deployment of collaborative ParaView on the grid

In the deployment experiment, we exploit 3 nodes of both Cluster A and Cluster B, to make use of the parallelism of the ParaView. However, as each cluster manages its nodes internally, i.e., with local IPs, it is impossible to implement the parallelism among different PC cluster nodes by means of Globus JobManager and MPICH-G2. We have implemented it by designing a dedicated transfer agent [9] in the master node of each cluster. The RSL (Resource Specification Language) file for submitting the ParaView server is as follows:

```
+(&(resourceManagerContact="cesc12.zju.edu.cn/jobmanager-cluster_fork ")
(label="subjob 0")
(count = 3)
(environment=( GLOBUS_DUROC_SUBJOB_INDEX 0)
(LD_LIBRARY_PATH /usr/local/globus/lib )
( GLOBUS_LAN_ID lan1))
(executable="./bin/paraview"))
((resourceManagerContact=" cesc41.zju.edu.cn/jobmanager-cluster_fork ")
(label="subjob 3")
(count = 3)
(environment=( GLOBUS_DUROC_SUBJOB_INDEX 1)
(LD_LIBRARY_PATH /usr/local/globus/lib )
(GLOBUS_LAN_ID lan2))
(executable="./bin/paraview"))
```

Where "cesc12.zju.edu.cn" is the hostname of the master node of the DAWNING PC Cluster (Cluster A), and "cesc41.zju.edu.cn" is the hostname of the master node of Cluster B.

6 Conclusions and Future Work

This paper analyzes the front-end architecture of ParaView and presents a way to achieve collaboration through client-to-client message passing. The implementation of collaboration utilized the embedded tracing mechanism in ParaView.

In addition to the trace file based client side collaboration, we have deployed the modified ParaView as a kind of visualization service in the MASSIVE grid.

The implementation provided in this paper is an inter-client one-to-one model, one act as master and the other as slave. The slave is literally unable to perform any action or else the result is unpredictable. A mechanism for multi-client synchronization should be provided to help eliminate the possible inconsistency between clients.

The client-server model could be further extended to support multiple users. The clients should all connect to a central controller; the controller receives information from any client and broadcasts them to other clients. The support of synchronization is of much importance.

In many cases, the data model would become too large to be visualized by a single computer. In this case, the model of a single server should be used, where every client should connect to its corresponding server. It is much easier for synchronization as the data model is consistent, but the clients should be notified when the server is updated. In this case, the client/server model should be converted to a subscriber/listener model.

The analysis of the Server Manager is a good start, as it is an interface between clients and servers.

Acknowledgements

This work is supported by the National Natural Science Foundation of China under grant Number 90412014. We would like to thank the Center for Engineering and Scientific Computation, Zhejiang University, for its computational resources, with which the research project has been carried out. We should give special thanks to researchers from the Department of Computer Science, South East University, China, for their productive contributions.

References

1. Wood, J., Brodlie, K.,: gViz: Visualization and Computational Steering on the Grid, Proceedings of the UK e-Science All Hands Meeting, Editor Simon J. Cox (2004) 54-60
2. Liu, P., Li, S., Du, Z.: Visualization of High Performance Computation under Network Environment, Mini-Micro Systems, 23(10) (2002) 1209-1213
3. Moad, C., Plale, B.: Portal Access to Parallel Visualization of Scientific Data on the Grid, Technical Report TR593, Computer Science Department, Indiana University, Bloomington, IN., http://www.cs.indiana.edu/pub/techreports/TR593.pdf/ (2005)
4. Henderson, A.: The ParaView Guide: A Parallel Visualization Application, ISBN 1-930934-14-9, Kitware, Inc. (2004)
5. ParaView – All You Need for Parallel Visualization. Martin K., Kitware Inc., http://www.paraview.org/ (2005)
6. Schroeder, W. J., Avila, L.S., Hoffman W.: Visualizing with VTK, Kitware Inc., http://www.vtk.org/ (2005)
7. The Visualization Toolkit – An Object-Oriented Approach to 3D Graphics, http://public.kitware.com/pipermail/vtkusers/2002-September/062597.html/ (2005)
8. Zheng, Y., Song, G., Zhang, J., Chen, J.: An Enabling Environment for Distributed Simulation and Visualization, Proceedings of the 5th IEEE/ACM International Workshop on Grid Computing (Grid 2004), Pittsburgh, USA (2004)
9. Huang, X., Song, G.: Running Globus Parallel Jobs on PC Clusters with Local IP Addresses, Journal of Southern Yangtze University (Science Edition) (accepted)

ServiceBSP Model with QoS Considerations in Grids*

Jiong Song[1,2], Weiqin Tong[1], and Xiaoli Zhi[1]

[1] School of Computer Engineering and Science, Shanghai University, Shanghai 200072, China
[2] School of Information Science and Engineering, Zhejiang Normal University, Jinhua 321004, China
songjiong_cs@163.com, {wqtong, xlzhi}@mail.shu.edu.cn

Abstract. Grid computing is the cutting-edge computing technology which is promising to aggregate large-scale and geographically-distributed computing resources for next generation of computing. Though the Grid computing is popular in today's IT infrastructure, the concrete service-oriented Grid environment (system) is difficult to develop. Quality of Grid Services (QoGS) shields the heterogeneity of available resources. Such a QoGS requires interoperability between Grid resources and a consistent developer's interface, which must be specified by feasible and applicable virtual organizations (VO). In addition, an economic model of Grid community may also be considered. With the consideration of the behaviors and characteristics of such desirable Grid systems, an architecture and model of service-based BSP or ServiceBSP (service-based Bulk-Synchronous Parallelism) is proposed, at the aim at establishing a high interoperation and high quality cooperation between each Grid service, while developing an efficient mechanism to evaluate the performances of Grid applications.

1 Introduction

Grid computing is the high-end computing technology and infrastructure that foster and promote the cooperative uses of distributed resources, crossing organizational boundaries and operated by "virtual organizations" (VOs) [1]. It is the state-of-the-art of large-scale, parallel and distributed computing. Due to the heterogeneity and uncertainty of Grid resources, the system implementation and programming interface are more complex than on conventional computing systems. How to deploy application on Grids still remains a challenging problem, although lots research efforts have been devoted.

Recently, the combination of Grid computing (mainly promoted by academies) and Web services (mainly developed by IT industrials) technologies prompts people to develop Grid services [2], which defined as services-oriented Grids. Such marriage is based on the technical emergence of Open Grid Services Architecture (OGSA) [2]

* This work is supported in part by National Natural Science Foundation of China under grant number 60573109, Shanghai Municipal Committee of Science and Technology under grant number 05dz15005, Shanghai High Institution Grid Project and Zhejiang Normal University Foundation.

H.T. Shen et al. (Eds.): APWeb 2006, LNCS 3842, pp. 827–834, 2006.

and Web Services Resource Framework (WSRF) [3] which promotes the rapid development of the service-oriented Grid computing technologies.

Since Grid computing becomes a service-based technology, the quality of service (QoS) obviously plays an important role in developing a cotemporary Grid. Traditional QoS refers to non-functional properties such as performance, availability, etc [4]. Although the QoS has different meanings for resources, it is important for Grid customers to select their desired services. On the other hand, Grid resource providers can price their existing Grid services based on the evaluation of the corresponding QoS value. Therefore, a stabilized quantitative QoS is the precondition of Grid applications with a predictable performance in service-oriented Grid computing.

This paper briefly reviews a Bulk-Synchronous Parallelism (BSP) model with an emphasis on how and why the BSP can be introduced to Grid computing. Based on BSP model, ServiceBSP for Grids is proposed and presented. The ServicBSP model not only provides an innovative architecture and creative paradigm for constructing feasible Grid developer's programming interface, but also features the organizational function for the cooperation in parallel processes. Programs' cost models in terms of performance time and cost are addressed to evaluate the proposed model. The paper is structured in the following. Section 2 presents the relevant previous research work. Section 3 depicts ServiceBSP in detail. Conclusion and future work are presented in last section.

2 Previous and Related Works

The concept of BSP model and its contributions to both parallel computing and Grid computing are depicted as follows.

2.1 BSP Model

The BSP model was initially proposed as a bridging model [5] for parallel computation. Much work on BSP algorithms, architectures and languages has demonstrated convincingly that BSP provides a robust model for parallel computation, which offers the prospect of both scalable parallel performance and architecture independent parallel software.

BSP programs have both a horizontal structure and a vertical structure [6]. The horizontal structure arises from concurrency, and consists of a fixed number of virtual processes. These processes are not regarded as having a particular linear order, and may be mapped to processors randomly.

The vertical structure arises from the progress of a computation through time. For BSP, this is a sequential composition of global supersteps, which conceptually occupy the full width of the executing architecture. Each superstep is further subdivided into three ordered phases consisting of:

- Computation locally in each process, using only values stored in local memory of each processor,

- Communication actions amongst the processes, involving movement of data between processors,
- Barrier synchronization.

Each end of barrier synchronization is the start of next superstep. It iterates during the execution of BSP program. Structuring programs in this way enables their costs to be accurately determined from a few simple architectural parameters.

Most message-passing libraries, such as MPI (Message Passing Interface), are based on pairwise send-receive operations, which are likely to cause deadlocks. Deadlocks do not occur in a BSP program, which is partitioned into phases or supersteps, because explicit send and receive operations are no longer necessary.

2.2 The Integration of BSP Model and Grid

BSP model is such an attractive parallel programming model that much work is done to consider whether it can be adapted for use in Grid environment. Two aspects of work are presented in the public literature mainly:

1. Constructing platform to support BSP programs run in Grid environment, e.g. BSP-G. BSP-G [7] is an implementation of BSP model that allows users to run a BSP program on Computational Grid. It uses services provided by the Globus Toolkit for authentication, authorization, resource allocation, executable staging, and I/O, as well as for process creation, monitoring, and control. BSP-G implements the core BSPlib according to the BSP standard proposed by BSP worldwide using Globus Toolkit services to support efficient and transparent execution in heterogeneous Grid environments.
2. Modifying BSP model and adapting it to Grid environment. BSP model was originally intended for use within a reliable, homogeneous, dedicated parallel computing environment, rather than with the unpredictable and variable resources that are associated with Grid computing. Some new models such as HBSP and Dynamic BSP, which are extensions to BSP model, were presented for adapting BSP model to Grid environment.

The goal of HBSP (Heterogeneous BSP) [8] is to provide a framework that makes parallel computing a viable option for heterogeneous systems. HBSP enhances the applicability of BSP by incorporating parameters that reflect the relative speeds of the heterogeneous computing components. Dynamic BSP [9] is a significant modification to the BSPGRID [10] approach, which addresses the heterogeneity issues, as well as fault-tolerance. It will also offer a more flexible programming model, with the ability to spawn additional processes within supersteps as and when required. The essence of Dynamic BSP is to use the task-farm model to implement BSP supersteps, where the individual tasks correspond to virtual processors.

3 ServiceBSP Programming

Although there has clearly been substantial progress concerning Grid implementation of BSP, service-oriented computing which is the trend of Grid computing was hardly mentioned in above work. A programming method in Service Grid is imperative. ServiceBSP programming in Service Grid is proposed as follows, which consists of ServiceBSP programming model and programs' cost models.

3.1 ServiceBSP Programming Model

Before a new programming model is presented, let us consider some characteristics of Grid applications:

1. Grid computing has parallelism in nature and Grid applications are loose coupled to some extent, which coincide with the characteristic that BSP model is one of coarse grained parallel computing models. A representative Grid application consists of many services which are distributed in different localities of Grid. For completing the application task, cooperative work and communications between services are imperative. The dependency and communication relations between services may cause deadlock to some extent.
2. The Grid computing environment is dynamic in nature. Considering that Grid resource providers join in or leave Grid community freely, QoS of many services are unstable. Many Grid applications demand high QoS, such as tele-immersion, distributed real-time computing, multi-media applications, and so on. These applications are sensitive to the changes of QoS, which cannot accept those services whose QoS are unstable.
3. Grid community is an economic community. Application developers hope to evaluate the costs of their applications in terms of time and economy before these applications run in Grid environment.

Based on above factors and BSP model, ServiceBSP programming model is presented now, which uses both job-parallel and task-parallel mechanisms. A Grid application is firstly divided into several jobs because of its loose coupled characteristic. Jobs execute in parallelism and a little communication occurs between jobs. A user agent negotiates with Grid Services Information Center (GSIC) and reserves a suitable service which meets application developer's requirements in terms of QoS and price for every job.

In Grid community, all Grid services register their information in GSIC, but most of them provide unstable QoS. GSIC should provide services with stable QoS to meet application requirements. Some self-configuring regulation methods are proposed in [11] to improve and stabilize Grid services' QoS when the runtime environment changes. Here, GSIC provides some regulated services to applications via dispatching Grid agents which carry jobs' data and requirements to those local domains where there exist a lot of source services which provide same or similar capability. Local domain means that these source services communicate rapidly and controlled by same authority, which makes it easy to integrate services. The Grid agents arrive at those domains and create corresponding regulated services for jobs. The main task for a regulated service is to delegate job request to some appropriate source services according to its regulation algorithm. Although source services have unstable and low QoS, from the user's view, a regulated service is a single service with high and stable

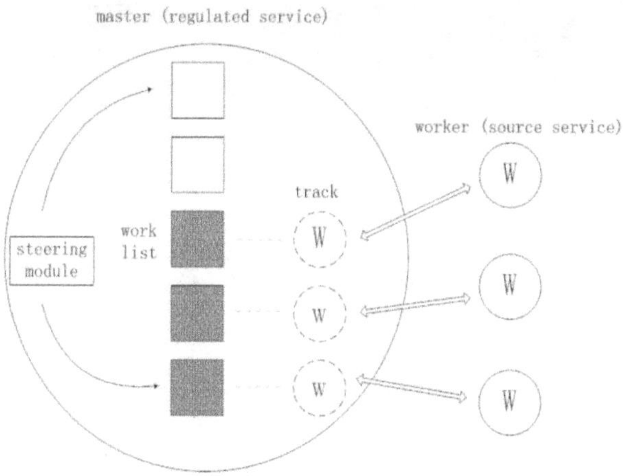

Fig. 1. Master-worker framework

QoS. Regulated services provide stable QoS to applications by shielding the unstable factors of source services (e.g., the failures and changes of source services). A regulated service appears nothing externally special compared with a real one for a Grid management middleware.

In this paper, a regulated service organizes many source services by task-parallel mechanism. An excellent paradigm of task-parallel mechanism is master-worker (i.e., task-farms) model (Fig. 1). There has been considerable success in utilizing the internet to solve embarrassingly parallel problems using task-farms, for instance by the application of screen savers performing drug-protein docking simulations on vast numbers of personal computers [12]. Task-farming has also been proposed as a general programming paradigm for Grid computing [13].

A regulated service (i.e., master) consists of three parts, which are work list, tracking module and steering module. Work list records only all uncompleted work units. Tracking module records remote worker services and uncompleted works, and dispatch uncompleted work units to worker services. Steering module drives computation via assigning work, checking result and modifying work list, which is in charge of providing stable QoS to users.

After above phases, some regulated services with stable and high QoS which execute corresponding job are obtained. Considering the good characteristic of BSP model, these regulated services are organized in BSP style. A superstep (Fig. 2) in ServiceBSP programs consists of three ordered phases as following:

1. Local computations phase

A representative Grid job usually communicates with others continually. But in a superstep of ServiceBSP program, any data sent by other jobs are not need in local computations phase of every job. All communications occur in local computations phase are not executed until next phase. In this phase, every regulated service works locally for corresponding job, without any communications between regulated services. The next phase commences until all regulated services complete the local computations phase.

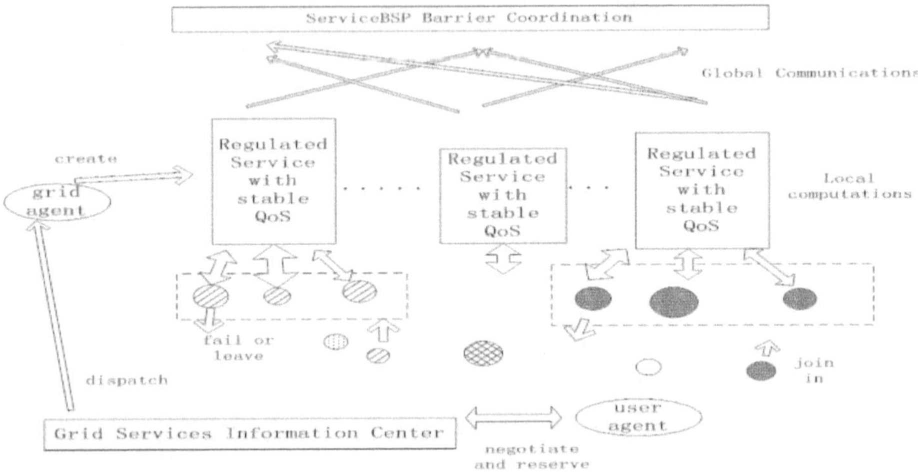

Fig. 2. A superstep in ServiceBSP program

2. Global communications phase

All communication operations would execute in global communications phase. ServiceBSP model divides computation and communication into different phases, which brings three advantages:

- Possible deadlock is avoided. Considering all communications into a whole eliminates possible deadlock between services, and this work would completed by the system. It would alleviate the burden of application developers,
- Communication cost is alleviated. System could incorporate several communication services which occur in a pair of services into a "big" communication service, which alleviates communication cost. When computation and communication as a whole, application developers expect that good QoS of networking exists in whole computation phase because of intermittent communication. This cost is expensive and wasteful. Processing all communication operations in a concentrated phase will minimize the cost of networking services,
- Dividing computation and communication into different phases makes it easier to predict the cost of programs.

3. Barrier coordination phase

For the sake of ensuring all communications completed and commencing next superstep, a barrier coordination phase is needed following global communications phase, which is communications between regulated services in essence.

Each end of barrier coordination is a global consistent status, when all services obtain synchronization. It is excellent time to set checkpoint for fault tolerance.

3.2 ServiceBSP Programs' Cost Models in Terms of Time and Economy

Application developers hope to evaluate their applications' costs in terms of time and economy when programming. Here, two cost models are presented.

1. A ServiceBSP program's time cost in a superstep is:

$$T = T_{\text{local computations}} + T_{\text{global communications}} + L \,. \tag{1}$$

Here, the time cost of local computations is the maximum among all local computations' time costs in a superstep. An application developer can predict the time cost of a service's local computations by the workload of a job and the QoS of the service that performs the job. Global communications time is function of the traffic of communication and QoS of networking. L is time cost for barrier coordination, which is function of job number and QoS of networking. A program's time cost is the sum of all supersteps' time costs.

2. According to the economic model of Grid community, Grid resource providers provide Grid services, and services with different QoS charge different prices. User agents should negotiate with GSIC for the benefit of the user, and reserves suitable services with stable QoS and endurable price.

In local computations phase of a superstep, some jobs are completed earlier than others. But these jobs could not enter into communications phase until all services' local computations complete. For these services, a little time is wasted because of synchronization.

A ServiceBSP program's economic cost in a superstep is:

$$M = M_{\text{local computations}} + M_{\text{global communications}} + M_{\text{barrier}} \,. \tag{2}$$

$$M_{\text{local computations}} = T_{\text{local computations}} \times \sum Mj \,. \tag{3}$$

$\sum Mj$ is the sum of all regulated services' local computations prices. The communication cost is the product of communication time and the price of networking service, which consists global communications cost and barrier coordination cost. A program's economic cost is the sum of all supersteps' economic costs. Application developers should distribute suitable workload and require proper QoS for every job for the purpose of reducing the costs in terms of time and economy. But it is a tradeoff between time and money in some occasions.

4 Conclusion and Future Work

In this paper, ServiceBSP programming in Grid environment is proposed for the purpose of helping application developers develop programs with high performance/ price. ServiceBSP model builds on Valiant's BSP model, and retains its key element: the superstep structure. Considering the Grid community is an economic community, program's cost models in terms of time and economy are presented.

The next logical step is implementing our model and testing it in real-life system. In addition to that, here are some issues that would be worthy of further consideration.

- Security. Commercial enterprises have to be extremely careful about data security, and this tends to be the main barrier to the uptake of Grid computing in industry. A ServiceBSP implementation offering data encryption could help to solve this problem,
- Debug. Service is unit in service-oriented Grid computing. How to debug services is worthy of consideration when programming in Grid environment.

References

1. Foster, I., Kesselman, C., Tuecke, S.: The Anatomy of the Grid: Enabling Scalable Virtual Organizations. Int. J. Supercomputer Applications, Vol. 15(3) (2001) 200-222
2. Foster, I., Kesselman, C., Nick, J.M., Tuecke, S.: The Physiology of the Grid: An Open Grid Services Architecture for Distributed Systems Integration. http://www.globus.org/-alliance/publications/papers/ogsa.pdf (2002)
3. Czajkowski, K., Ferguson, D.F., Foster, I., et al.: The WS-Resource Framework. http://-www.globus.org/wsrf/ (2004)
4. Farkas, P., Charaf, H.: Web services planning concepts. Proceedings of First International Workshop on C(number) and (dot)Net Technologies on Algorithm, Computer Graphics and Visualization, Plzen, Czech Republic 2 (2003) 9-12
5. Valiant, L.G.: A bridging model for parallel computation. Communications of the ACM, 33 (8) (1990) 103–111
6. Skillicorn, D.B., Hill, J.M.D., McColl, W.F.: Questions and Answers about BSP. Scientific Programming, Vol. 6(3) (1997) 249-274
7. Tong, W.Q., Ding, J.B., and Cai, L.Z.: A Parallel Programming Environment on Grid. Proc. of ICCS2003. Lecture Notes in Computer Science, Vol. 2658(1) (2003) 225-234
8. Williams, T.L., Parsons, R.J.: The Heterogeneous Bulk Synchronous Parallel Model. Parallel and Distributed Processing. Lecture Note in Computer Science, Vol. 1800, Springer-Verlag, Cancun, Mexico (2000) 102-108
9. Martin, J.M.R., Tiskin, A.V.: Dynamic BSP: Towards a Flexible Approach to Parallel Computing over the Grid. In: East, I., et al. (eds.): Communication Process Architecture 2004. IOS Press (2004) 219-226
10. Vasilev, V.: BSPGRID: Variable resources parallel computation and multiprogrammed parallelism. Parallel Processing Letters, Vol. 13(3) (2003) 329–340
11. Zhi, X.L., Rong, L., Tong, W.Q.: Improving grid service's QoS through self-configuring regulation. Engineering Applications of Artificial Intelligence 17 (2004) 701-710
12. Davies, E.K., Glick, M., Harrison, K.N., and Richards, W.G.: Pattern recognition and massively distributed computing. Journal of Computational Chemistry, Vol. 23(16) (2002) 1544–1550
13. Goux, J.P., Kulkarni, S., Yoder, M., and Linderoth, J.: Master-worker: An enabling framework for applications on the computational grid. Cluster Computing, 4(2001) 63–70

An Efficient SVM-Based Method to Detect Malicious Attacks for Web Servers

Wu Yang[1], Xiao-Chun Yun[1,2], and Jian-Hua Li[1,3]

[1] Information Security Research Center, Harbin Engineering University, Harbin 150001, China
yangwu@hrbeu.edu.cn
[2] Computer Network and Information Security Technique Research Center, Harbin Institute of Technology, Harbin 150001, China
yxc@hit.edu.cn
[3] College of Information Security Engineering, Shanghai Jiao Tong University,
lijh888@sjtu.edu.cn

Abstract. In recent years, with the rapid development of network technique and network bandwidth, the network attacking events for web servers such as DOS/PROBE are becoming more and more frequent. In order to detect these types of intrusions in the new network environment more efficiently, this paper applies new machine learning methods to intrusion detection and proposes an efficient algorithm based on vector quantization and support vector machine for intrusion detection (VQ-SVM). The algorithm firstly reduces the network auditing dataset by using VQ techniques, produces a codebook as the training example set, and then adopts fast training algorithm for SVM to build intrusion detection model on the codebook. The experiment results indicate that the combined algorithm of VQ-SVM can greatly improve the learning and detecting efficiency of the traditional SVM-based intrusion detection model.

1 Introduction

With the rapidly growing connectivity of the Internet, networked computer systems are increasingly playing vital roles in our modern society. While the Internet has brought great benefits to this society, it has also made critical systems such as web servers vulnerable to malicious attacks (e.g. DOS/DDOS, Probe Scanning etc.). Since a preventive approach such as firewall is not sufficient to provide sufficient security for a computer system, intrusion detection systems (IDS) are introduced as a second line of defense and become a research hotspot in the fields of network security.

At present, intrusion detection techniques can be categorized into misuse detection and anomaly detection. Misuse detection systems, for example [1], use patterns of well-known attacks or weak spots of the system to identify intrusions; Anomaly detection systems, such as [2], firstly establish normal user behavior patterns (profiles) and then try to determine whether deviation from the established normal profiles can be flagged as intrusions. In recent years, the continual emergence of new attacking methods like Nimda and Slammer etc has caused great loss to the whole society. So,

H.T. Shen et al. (Eds.): APWeb 2006, LNCS 3842, pp. 835 – 841, 2006.

the advantage of detecting future attacks has specially led to an increasing interest in anomaly detection techniques. Current anomaly detection methods are mainly classified by statistical anomaly detection [3], anomaly detection based on neural network [4] and anomaly detection based on data mining [5], etc. In network intrusion detection application, network auditing dataset usually includes much noise data. On such dataset, the detecting effect of the intrusion detection methods above is not highly desirable and the false positive rate of the model is comparatively high, which restricts the practicability of intrusion detection on a certain degree. So it is necessary to study the method to improve detection rate of intrusion detection model.

Statistical learning theory (SLT) [6] has recently emerged as a general mathematical framework for estimating dependencies from finite samples, which is arguably the best available theory for predictive learning. In the beginning, SLT was a purely theoretical analysis of the function estimation from a given collection of data. Afterward, a new type of learning algorithm (called SVM) based on the statistical learning theory was proposed. SVM algorithm has good generalization performance even in the case of finite samples, so some researchers begin exploring its applications to intrusion detection [7]. Intrusion detection model based on SVM still has better detection performance even in the case of finite samples. In practical applications, it is often the case that the size of the intrusion detection training dataset is very large (e.g. KDD-99 dataset). Since the training method for SVM is fundamentally a quadratic programming (QP) problem with a constraint, the computing cost of SVM algorithm is very high and very big memory size is needed when SVM algorithm is trained on much more training samples. In addition, the intrusion detection model leaned by SVM on a large-scale training dataset includes many support vectors (SV), which causes that the classifying speed of detecting model is slightly slow at the detecting stage. So it is necessary that the traditional SVM algorithm be optimized and improved to reduce the number of support vectors in order to enhance the running efficiency of network intrusion detection method based on SVM without degrading the detecting rate.

2 An Improved Algorithm Based on GSAVQ and SVM for Intrusion Detection

For the case that the computing efficiency of intrusion detection method based on standard SVM is inferior on the large-scale training dataset, we propose an improved efficient algorithm based on vector quantization and support vector machine for intrusion detection (VQ-SVM). This algorithm includes two stages: 1. Vector quantization stage: an efficient vector quantization algorithm based on genetic simulated annealing (GSAVQ) is adopted to preprocess the intrusion detection training dataset, thus a reduced training codebook is produced. 2. SVM training stage: a fast training algorithm of improved SMO is used to train SVM on the codebook to construct the decision function for intrusion detection model. VQ-SVM algorithm reduces the number of support vectors, eliminates the influence of the noise data on the optimal hyperplane and greatly improves the learning and detecting speed of the SVM-based intrusion detection model.

2.1 Genetic Simulated Annealing Vector Quantization (GSAVQ)

Vector Quantization and Codebook Design Algorithm [8]. Vector quantization (VQ) is an efficient technique for data compression. A vector quantizer can be defined as a mapping Q from a k-dimensional space R^k into a certain finite subnet C, namely $Q: R^k \rightarrow C$, $C = \{Y_0, Y_1, \ldots Y_{N-1} \mid Y_i \in R^k\}$. The subnet C is called a codebook and its elements C_i are called codewords. Given one codeword $Y_p = (y_{p0}, y_{p1}, \ldots y_{p(k-1)})$ and the test vector $X = (x_0, x_1, \ldots x_{k-1})$, the following formula is satisfied:

$$d(X, Y_p) = \min_{0 \le j \le N-1} d(X, Y_j) \qquad (1)$$

Of which $d(X, Y_j)$ is the square Euclidean distortion measure between vector X and codeword Y_j. Each vector X can find its nearest codeword $Y_p = Q(X \mid X \in R^k)$ from codebook C.

One of the key problems for vector quantization is to design good performance codebook. Assume the training vector set $X = \{X_0, X_1, \ldots X_{M-1}\}$, the codebook to be produced is $C = \{Y_0, Y_1, \ldots Y_{N-1}\}$, $X_i = \{x_{i0}, x_{i1}, \ldots x_{i(k-1)}\}$, $Y_j = \{y_{j0}, y_{j1}, \ldots y_{j(k-1)}\}$, $0 \le i \le M-1$, $0 \le j \le N-1$. So the process of codebook design is to look for an optimal clustering scheme that the training vector set X is partitioned into N subsets $S_j (j = 0, 1, \ldots N-1)$. The centroid vector Y_j of the subset S_j is used as codeword. The aim of the codebook design is to find the best classification of training vectors. Given the number of the training vectors M and the number of codewords N, codebook design problem is an NP-hard problem to classify M training vectors into N clusters.

Codebook Design Algorithm Based on Genetic Simulated Annealing. VQ-SVM algorithm adopts a codebook design algorithm based on genetic simulated annealing (GSAVQ- Genetic Simulated Annealing Vector Quantization) [9] for pre-processing training dataset. Based on the training vector set partition, genetic algorithm (GA) is firstly used to design codebook (Called GVQ). As an efficient, parallel and near global optimum search method, GA can automatically achieve and accumulate the knowledge about the search space, and adaptively control the search process to approach the global optimal solution. However, the convergence speed of GA is a little slower because of its poor local optimum search ability. Simulated annealing (SA) is a near global optimum search method based on the idea of physical annealing, whose operation object is not a group of approximate solutions like GA but a single approximate solution. The convergence speed of SA is affected by a lot of factors and it is not so easy to approach the global optimal solution. In order to improve the local optimum search ability of GA and avoid the "premature phenomena" of GA, SA is introduced in genetic vector quantization (GVQ) algorithm, which is called GSAVQ algorithm. GSAVQ makes full use of the virtues of GA and SA, further reduces the opportunities of the algorithm getting into the local minimum and obtains a near global optimum codebook in a much shorter time.

2.2 Fast SMO Training Algorithm for SVM

For small training sets (typically less than a few hundred vectors), the QP problem solution for SVM algorithm is straightforward using standard QP packages such as Newton and MINOS. When the training data set is too large, the memory required to store the kernel matrix becomes large and therefore may not fit in this memory. Consequently, it is necessary to use methods based on the decomposition of the QP problem. The Sequential Minimal Optimization (SMO) [10] is an efficient decomposition method for solving the problem of training SVM on the large-scale dataset.

The SMO breaks the large QP problems into a series of the smallest possible QP subproblems, which can be solved analytically. The SMO algorithm generally selects a working set B of fixed size, and then solves the QP subproblem on the working set B. It inspects all the samples which are not satisfied with the condition of Karush-Kuhn-Tucker (KKT), and heuristically selects some samples to exchange with those whose λ_i is equal to zero in working set B. This iteration proceeds until all samples meet KKT condition. SMO algorithm only processes optimization problem consisting of two Lagrange multipliers at each iteration, allowing an analytical solution for the two Lagrange multipliers, which avoids iterative numerical methods for QP subproblem. The efficiency of the decomposition methods for SVM training is a tradeoff between iterative times and subproblem optimization. Although the time spending of SMO algorithm is a little at each subproblem optimization, iterative times of SMO is so much as to influence the efficiency. In addition, in selecting samples for working set, the efficiency of choosing strategy is not high. Therefore, VQ-SVM algorithm adopts an improved SMO algorithm [11] as the training algorithm for standard SVM, which firstly supposes an even q and is simply shown as follows:

Step1. Select q samples to construct the working set B_i according to some one strategy. Other $n-q$ samples constitute the free set N_i and keep fixed;

Step2. Decompose original problem and solve a QP subproblem on the working set B_i in term of B_i and N_i;

Step3. Check the termination condition. If the condition is met, the training process ends; otherwise, go to step 1.

It is well known that the optimal hyperplane of the SVM is affected greatly by the noise near the boundary of the two classes [12]. Thus the decision functions obtained by SVM are sensitive to noises close to the decision boundary. The classical minimizing square error in vector quantization will reduce or even eliminate the influence of noises when using VQ method to preprocess training dataset because VQ is an averaged algorithm and a specific sample in the large training set has little effect on the final result. VQ-SVM algorithm can reduce the number of support vectors, not only improve the training and detecting speed but also guarantee not to degrade the generalization performance somewhat.

When making vector quantization on the whole training dataset, sometimes it will spend longer time. A method is adopted to reduce the preprocessing time cost at the VQ stage: Firstly, divide all the original training dataset into many subsets according to the number of the training data set in each class. Secondly, make vector quantization on each subset. At last, train the SVM using the new dataset coming from the codebook produced on each subset.

3 Experiment Tests

Experiments have been carried out on a subset of the dataset created by DARPA in the framework of the 1998 Intrusion Detection Evaluation Program. This subset have been pre-processed by the Columbia University and distributed as part of the UCI KDD Archive [13]. The available dataset is made up of a large number of network connections related to normal and malicious traffic. Each connection is represented as a 41-dimension feature vector. Connections are also labeled as belonging to one out of five classes, i.e. Normal, Denial of Service (DOS) attacks, Remote to Local (R2L) attacks, User to Root (U2R) attacks, and Probing attacks (Probe). In the original dataset, all classes of attack examples mix up together, which makes the original dataset include much noise. So, in order to acquire accurate experiment results, the original dataset should be partitioned into four types of attacking datasets and one normal dataset according to types of examples. Because the attacking datasets of DOS type and PROBE type include large numbers of examples, they are separately mixed with normal dataset into two mixed datasets and used for testing VQ-SVM algorithm.

We separately test the standard SVM and VQ-SVM algorithm on the mixed datasets of DOS type and PROBE type to compare their performances. The training dataset of DOS type includes 19 feature attributes, and 48873 connection records, while the testing dataset of DOS type consists of 29044 connections. The training dataset of PROBE type includes 29 feature attributes and 10138 connection records, while the testing dataset of PROBE type consists of 6475 connections. For GSAVQ algorithm, the experiment parameters are set as follows: the crossover probability p_c is 0.9 and the mutation probability p_m is 0.01, the population size is 40, the number of iterations is limited to 150. The initial temperature T_0 is 50 and the temperature is decreased by 0.6% after each iteration until the number of iterations reaches 150, $\varepsilon = 0.001$. For fast training algorithm of improved SMO, the size of working q is 6, $C = 5$, and the RBF kernel function is used where $1/\sigma^2 = 0.01$. We compare the performances of SVM algorithm and VQ-SVM algorithm with different number of training subsets k and size of codebook N. The experiment results are shown in Table 1 and Table 2.

Table 1. Performance comparison for SVM and VQ-SVM on sample set of DOS attack

	k	N	Training Time(s) (VQ+SVM)	Detecting Rate (%)	Number of SV
Traditional SVM			1948.37	95.68	7112
	100	100	258.42(84.36+174.06)	94.86	2476
VQ-SVM	150	150	530.33(52.14+478.19)	95.21	4492
	200	150	775.68(43.67+732.01)	96.53	4542

Table 2. Performance comparison for SVM and VQ-SVM on sample set of PROBE attack

	k	N	Training Time (s) (VQ+SVM)	Detecting Rate (%)	Number of SV
Traditional SVM			429.15	84.37	8109
	100	20	10.56(4.11+6.45)	82.53	1733
VQ-SVM	100	40	42.62(8.43+34.19)	83.96	3717
	150	50	246.18(13.52+232.66)	84.72	6617

It can be seen from these tables that, when appropriate values for parameter k and N are set, VQ-SVM algorithm can simplify the classification boundary, greatly reduce the training time and the number of support vectors without degrading or even slightly increasing detecting accuracy. After being trained on the same training dataset, the detecting time of SVM and VQ-SVM is tested on the different testing datasets. The results are shown in Fig. 1. Compared with the traditional SVM algorithm, VQ-SVM algorithm greatly reduces the detecting time of the intrusion detection model and improves the running efficiency of the model.

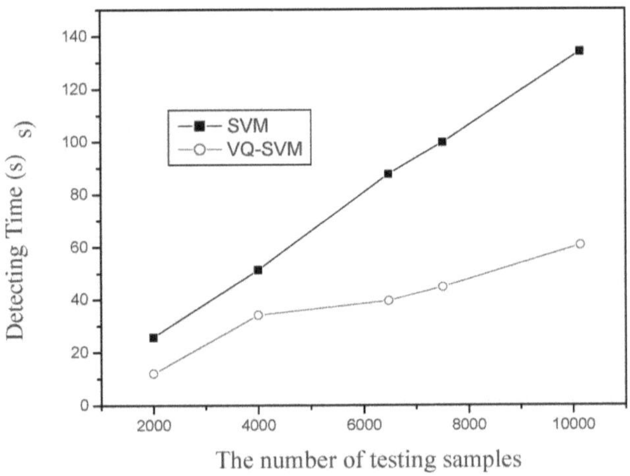

Fig. 1. Detecting time of SVM and VQ-SVM in contrast

4 Conclusion

We discuss intrusion detection method based on SVM algorithm for web environment in this paper. For the case that the computing complexity of standard SVM algorithm is high and the learning (or detecting) efficiency is inferior when the size of training dataset for intrusion detection is very large, an efficient intrusion detection algorithm based on VQ and SVM is proposed. VQ-SVM algorithm combines fast GSAVQ algorithm and training algorithm of SMO. The experiment results validate the effectivity of the presented VQ-SVM method to detect DOS-like attacks for web servers.

References

1. Illgun, K., Kemmerer, R., Philips, A.: State Transition Analysis: A Rule-based Intrusion Detection Approach. IEEE Transactions on Software Engineering. 2 (1995) 181-199
2. Karlton, S., Mohammed, Z.: ADMIT: Anomaly-based Data Mining for Intrusions. In Proceedings of the 8th ACM SIGKDD International Conference on Knowledge Discovery and Data Mining. ACM Press, Edmonton Alberta Canada (2002) 386–395
3. Anderson, J. P., et al.: Detecting Unusual Program Behavior Using the Statistical Components of NIDES. http://www.sdl.sri.com/papers/5sri/5sri.pdf (1995)
4. Debar, H., Becker, M., Siboni, D.: A Neural Network Component for an Intrusion Detection System. In Proceedings of 1992 IEEE Symposium on Security and Privacy. Oakland CA (1992) 240-251
5. Taylor, C., Foss, J. A.: NATE: Network Analysis of Anomalous Traffic Events, A Low-cost Approach. In Proceedings of New Security Paradigms Workshop, New Mexico USA (2002) 89-96
6. Vapnik, V.: The Nature of Statistical Learning Theory. NY: Springer-Verlag (1995)
7. Mukkamala, S., Janowski, G., Sung, A. H.: Intrusion Detection Using Neural Networks and Support Vector Machines. In Proceedings of the IEEE International Joint Conference on Neural Networks, Hawaii (2002) 1702-1707
8. Linde, Y., Buzo, A., Gray R.: An Algorithm for Vector Quantizer Design. IEEE Transactions on Communications, 1(1980) 84-96
9. Pan J. S., Lu Z. M., Sun S. H.: Vector Quantization Based on Genetic Simulated Annealing. Signal Processing, 7(2000) 1513-1524
10. Platt J.: Fast Training of Support Vector Machines using Sequential Minimal Optimization, Advances in Kernel Methods-Support Vector Learning. MA: MIT Press, Cambridge (1999)
11. Yang, J. Y., Wei, X. G., et al.: A Fast SVM Learning Algorithm. Journal of Nanjing University of Science and Technology, 5(2003) 530-536
12. Zhang, X.: Using Class-center Vectors to Build Support Vector Machine. In Proceedings of the 1999 IEEE Signal Processing Society Workshop. New York (1999) 3-11
13. KDD CUP 1999. http://kdd.ics.uci.edu/database/kddcup99/kddcup99.html (1999)

Design and Implementation of a Workflow-Based Message-Oriented Middleware

Yue-zhu Xu[1], Da-xin Liu[1], and Feng Huang[2]

[1] College of Computer Science and Technology, Harbin Engineering University, Harbin Heilongjiang Province, China
xuyuezhu@hrbeu.edu.cn

[2] School of Mechanical and Electrical Engineering, Harbin Engineering University, Harbin Heilongjiang Province, China
waspxyz@sina.com

Abstract. The rapid growth of data exchange on the networks has brought on many critical problems that require an answer. Generally, Internet data exchange systems are based on traditional client/server architecture, which models are less scalable and bring on especially high maintenance cost in the data exchange domain. For these reasons, we present a workflow-based message-oriented middleware (WMOM) system model for asynchronous communication platforms. The model combines workflow mechanism and message-oriented middleware. It not only makes applications to be isolated from communication network, but also improve the flexibility and scalability.

1 Introduction

Data exchange between applications in computer networks has become more and more popular, but such exchange on the rapidly expanding Internet has brought to light many unsolved issues. Generally, Internet data exchange systems are based on traditional client/server architecture, which models are less scalable and incur especially high maintenance cost in the data exchange domain. For these reasons, we present a new middleware-mediated transaction model for asynchronous communication platforms. The transaction model combines workflow mechanism and message-oriented middleware, especially exception management. The transaction model extends distributed object transactions to include message-oriented transaction.

In this paper, we will first provide messaging paradigms, some critical technologies used currently in MOM, and workflow schedule theory. We will then describe function design to WMOM system. We will also discuss the basic idea, internal structure and implementing techniques. Finally, we will give a real-world example to illustrate how this model can improve the flexibility and scalability.

2 Related Works

2.1 Message-Oriented Middleware

Traditionally, data exchange is organized hierarchically with a network framework.

Middleware is a class of software technologies designed to help manage the complexity and heterogeneity inherent in distributed systems. It is defined as a layer of

H.T. Shen et al. (Eds.): APWeb 2006, LNCS 3842, pp. 842 – 845, 2006.

soft-ware above the operating system but below the application program that provides a common programming abstraction across a distributed system, as shown in Figure 1. [1]

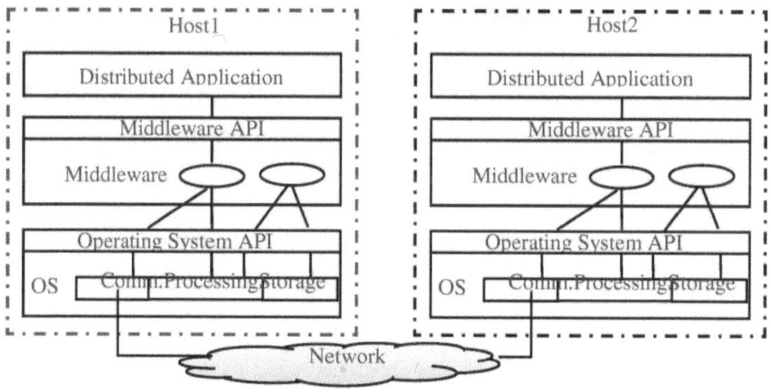

Fig. 1. Middleware Layer in Context

Middleware have been proposed to solve the distributed communication, improve the asynchronous communication. In Ref.[2], Message-Oriented Message(MOM) is be introduced, which promotes an asynchronous, decoupled, data-driven communication style. MOM provides the abstraction of a message queue that can be accessed a network, and provides the credible and reparable massages communication between heterogeneous environment and applications. MOM does not need real-time send massage to recipient, but send massage to right destination once. It is very flexible in how it can be configured with the topology of programs that deposit and withdraw messages from a given queue.

2.2 Workflow Mechanism

Workflows have been introduced to support the modeling, execution, and monitoring of business processes. The workflow technology provides a flexible and appropriate environment to develop and maintain next generation of component-oriented enterprise-wide information systems. The production workflow applications are built upon business processes that are generally quite complex and involve a large number of activities and associated coordination constraints.

Workflow model can be read, operated, and controlled by certain workflow management systems. Workflow schedule depends on the process what is definition of the activities and the logic relationships between activities. In this paper, we only introduce the schedule theory, and default that the process which be defined. [3]

3 WMOM Architecture

Consider an application that implements a middleware-mediated transaction which includes messages that sent out with schedule message. The application wants the simplicity to "send and forget" when sending out a message. But the problem is brought out when the transaction is failure. So, this flow will be compelled to interrupt.

Ideally, the application would create a corresponding compensation message at the same time the primary message is sent, and have the delivery be predicated on the failure of the transaction. However, standard middleware does no support this type of message send. Therefore, the application typically will

a) Create some data structure for a compensating message;
b) Add application data for compensation and schedule data such as timestamps and the id of the primary message that it compensates, and;
c) Store the data persistently.[4]

For this purpose, a WMOM system model extending the function of standard middleware is implemented for asynchronous communication platforms and a persistent message queue that is used to temporarily store compensating messages is built, as shown in Figure 2.

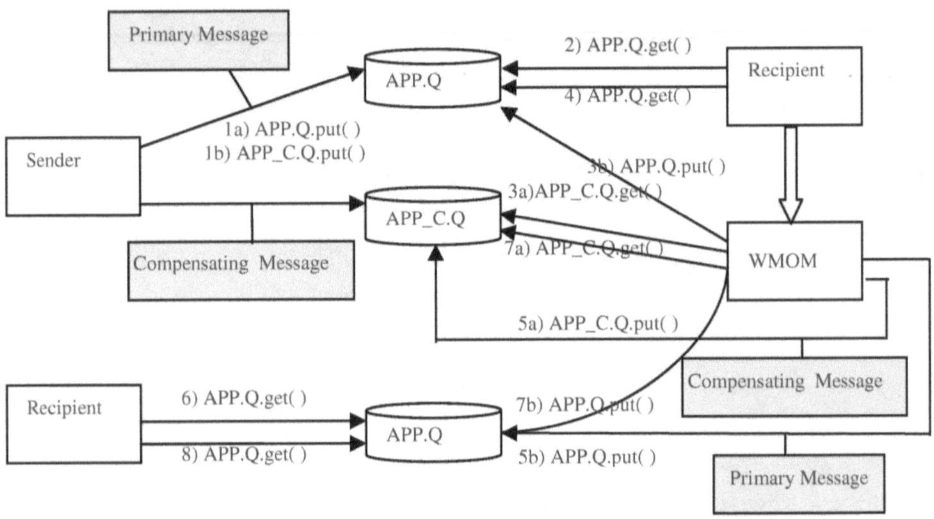

Fig. 2. WMOM architecture

The WMOM system model observes the sender's message which is data of application, and once a message sent:

a) The primary message which includes the id of workflow and the corresponding compensating message which includes the address of destination in addition are wrote into APP.Q and APP_C.Q queue separately;
b) The WMOM system observes the sent transaction, and once a transaction;
c) The corresponding compensating message are read from the APP_C.Q queue by WMOM;
d) The actual message recipient addressed and the information of workflow are extracted from the message;

e) The information of workflow is analyzed, when the recipient is the right next activity in the workflow, and

f) The message which distribute to the scheduled application in the workflow are forwarded to their designated destinations.[5]

The WMOM system uses an agreed message property field to associate compensating message to a transaction. The WMOM system further encodes which action to take should the transaction succeed.

4 Conclusion

To provide a method to resolve asynchronous communication platforms, the WMOM system model has been described in this paper. The WMOM system combines workflow mechanism and MOM. It not only makes applications to be isolated from communication network, but also improve the flexibility and scalability. It is a very simple and inexpensive solution that can easily be implemented. The WMOM system model helps to significantly reduce application code and application programming complexity, as most of the required functions are now provided by the middleware.

Further work could extend the workflow-oriented middleware to be able to determine the transaction status of the sender application, register itself with the transaction monitor as a participant of the transaction, although the impact of such extensions on the portability and credibility of the models needs to be investigated.

References

1. Bakken, D. E.: MIDDLEWAE. Encyclopedia of Distributed Computing, Kluwer Academic Press (2003)
2. Tai, S., Totok, A., Mikalsen, T., Rouvellou, I.: Message Queuing Patterns for Middleware-MediatedTransactions [M]. http://www.research.ibm.com/AEM/pubs/mqpatternsSEM2002.pdf
3. Zhuge, H.: A Process Matching Approach for Flexible Workflow Process Reuse. Information and Software Technology, (44) (2002) 445-450
4. Tai, S., Mikalsen, T., Rouvellou, I., Sutton, S.: Conditional Messaging: Extending Reliable Messaging with Application Condition. In Proc.22nd International Conference on Distributed Computing System, IEEE (2002)
5. Xu, Y.Z., Liu, D.X., Huang, F.: A Flexible Workflow Model Based On ECA Rules. Web Information System and Application (2005)

Consistency of User Interface Based on Petri-Net

Haibo Li[1,2] and Dechen Zhan[1]

[1] Center of Intelligent Computing of Enterprises,
School of Computer Science & Technology, Harbin Institute of Technology,
P.O. Box 315, 150001 Harbin, China
[2] Engineering Institute, Northeast Agricultural University,
150030 Harbin, China
{Lihaibo, dechen}@hit.edu.cn

Abstract. There exists a difference between traditional control mode and Web interface based one. Operation consistency of Web interfaces is not guaranteed by the traditional control mode. This paper presents a Petri-net based approach to analyze the design of Web interface. The proposed method can be used to identify interface inconsistency and convert interface operation model featured by Petri-net for increase the coverage ability of graph; hence improving the graph. Finally, the paper describes the consistency rules for various operations using XML protocol with the aim at achieving standardize operations of user interface.

1 Introduction

Comparing with tools for graphical interfaces (such as AWT), today's Web-based graphic user interface (GUI) in HTML always adopts new methods and their implementations. The interfaces become more dynamic, maintained on Web server. They can be edited by UIMS like FrontPage. The content a Web page on a Web server is requested and displayed on client system through a Web browser. On the other hand, Web applications are server oriented and most of the contents of Web applications are pre-compiled. They can be maintained easily with lower cost in Web management system [1,2]. However, one of disadvantages in Web applications is its inflexible operation. Unlike traditional interfaces developed by either VB or VC, the web application interface has less controllability. For example, to make a button disabled or hidden is tricky. During a process of business logic, events to modify data or to click hyperlinks are triggered by manipulating the pages. Developers deal with a sequence to operate an operational flow. However, users may not following developers' expectation driven by the logic flow, especially for the graphic interfaces that have semantic and redundant operations. For developers, it is easy to keep consistency of operations on a simple interface rather than complicated one. Therefore, an effective analysis on graphic interface is needed to guarantee consistency of operations.

Recently many research focus on the configurability of interface [3,4,5] and the property of multi-interface[6]. An information system always deals with simple

H.T. Shen et al. (Eds.): APWeb 2006, LNCS 3842, pp. 846 – 852, 2006.

business logic, such as adding, deleting, and modifying. This paper proposes a Petri-net based analysis method. A generalized operation process on graphic interface is described by Petri-net, before study the Coverability of Graph (CG) [7]. Introducing a simplified CG, erroneous operational sequences can be fixed, before expressed in term of XML format, as a rule to control operation on graphic interface. In addition, the simplified CG helps to identify semantic redundant operations; hence further improve interface design.

The rest of the paper is organized as follows. In Section 2, an abstract pattern of interface is given and described by Petri-net. Sectiôn 3 analyzes the soundness of operation flow on the interface pattern. Section 4 describes the operation rule in XML format. Section 5 presents examples of applications to demonstrate how the rules can be used. Section 6 presents a summary with conclusions and future work.

2 Abstract Pattern of User Interface

2.1 User Interface Pattern

In order to discuss the consistency of Web-based interface expediently an interface style, or interface pattern given As mentioned above, data processed by an business information system are information entities, such as customer orders, products, business analysis and reports, facility resources, vendor invoices, and employee information as well. These entities can be referred as 'business objects", a descriptive abstracts in the domain of business information system. The business attribute can be defined as

Definition 1. A business object is a triple $bo=(id, A, M)$, where *id* is an identifier assigned to the business object.*A* is a set of attributes a_i $(i=1,2,\ldots, n)$ of *bo, M* is a set of methods m_i $(i=1,2,\ldots, p)$ which acts on *bo*.

Definition 2. A business operation is a triple $op=(r, bo, A)$. It is an atomic action put on *bo* by a specical role *r* and changes the attribute set *A* of business object. Let $d_j(bo) \in A$ be the *j*th category of attributes accessed by *r*.

Being triggered continuously by a series of events, the attributes of business objects can be changed correspondingly to achieve the final goal of business mission and activities. An interface pattern (style) presents a mode in which business objects are processed. For example, one can create a pattern which has three major attributes: basic, running and fixed-assets attributes respectively. Based on the Definition 1 and 2, all attributes of a business object can be divided into many areas. A typical interface pattern can be given as a master-detail pattern, which contains query, card, and detail areas upon one the user functions. The pattern illustrated in Fig. 1 is used to discuss our study of interface consistency hereby.

Definition 3. User Interface (UI) can be expressed as *UI*= (*area, op, s*), where the *area* is a set of sub-areas. The *op stands for operations* acted on d_j, which can be divided into two steps: step of producing non-persistent data and step of persistent operating. *s*, The $s=\{n, p\}$ refers as the state of business object, where the *n* and *p* are non-persistent and persistent states respectively.

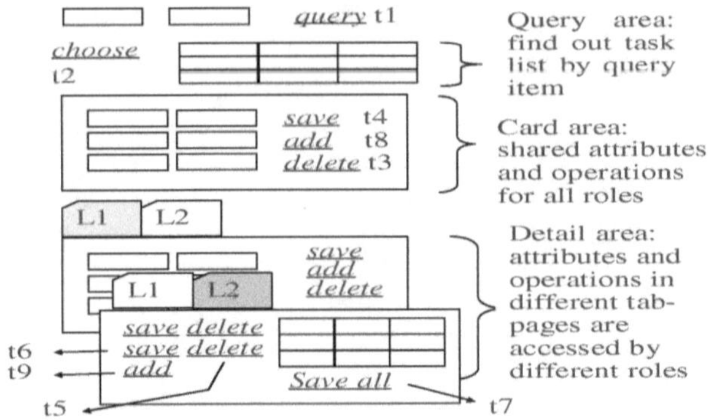

Fig. 1. A typical interface pattern

A persistent object is a business object that is pre-stored in permanent memory, while a non-persistent object represents a business object that is to be modified on interface and yet being stored in permanent memory. Modifying data on interface generates non-persistent object. This way, one can define a persistency rule that the state of non-persistent object produced is held before being processed by a persistent operation.

2.2 Describing Interface Pattern Using Petri-Nets

The Petri-nets (PN) [8] is a modeling tool that can be used to describe a process of interface design. The Petri-nets has two components: transition and placing, related by a directed arc. Hereby, the basic definitions of Petri net is given

Definition 4. A Petri-net N is a triple $N=(P,T,F)$. P is a finite set of the places; T is the finite set of the transitions with $P \cap T = \varnothing$. The flow relation F can be defined by $F \in (P \times T) \cup (T \times P)$.

Petri-net deploys many stochastic discrete event systems. There are several characristics to describe an interface pattern in Petri-net. A Petri-net is graphical and has rich mathematical foundations built in. It can reflect the dynamic characteristic of a system. However, the number of operations on UI can not be increased infinitely, although Petri-net theoretically explodes the number of states from the point of view. Despite of that operations on an interface are standard sequences, from the user point of view, their hyperlinks are clickable in any sequences; whereas it is difficult to control an operational flow when refreshing.

To analyze the consistency of interface, a 'standard' operation flow can be described by a PN, as shown in Fig.2. The 'standard' hereby means expectation demanded by a developer. Unfortunately, users may not follow developers' desirable flow, and operate differently.

Data and control places are employed within a PN to identify the data and control flow. In Fig.2 data places d1, d2, d3, d3', d4, and d4' and their relationships are expressed by the arrow, dash lines, while the control flow is illustrated through solid lines. Semantic interpretation can be given in the following. The execution of an

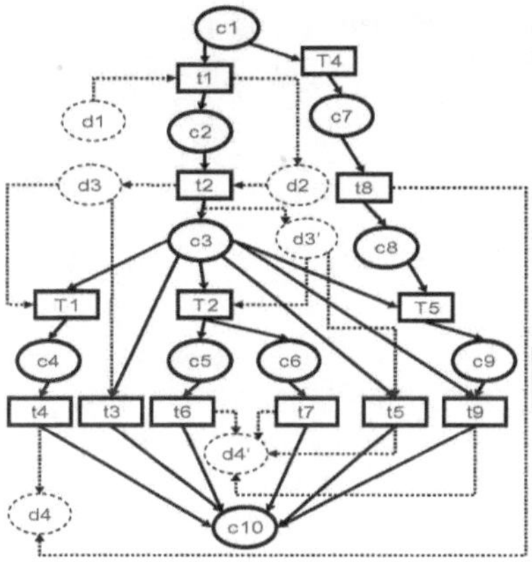

Fig. 2. Master-detail pattern's PN graph

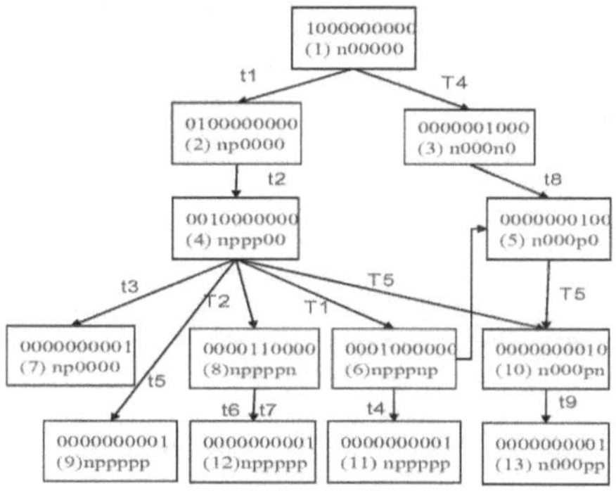

Fig. 3. CG of master-detail interface pattern

operation *t* requires data tokens on the data input places of t and produces tokens on the data output places of *t*. The places data d1, d2, d3, d3', d4, and d4' represent query, task, card area data, detail area data, target data in card area, and target data in detail area, respectively. Without lose the generality, we suppose that there is only one detail area. Transitions t1, t2, …, and t9 refer 9 operations on an interface; their physical interpretations can be seen in Fig.1. T1, T2, T3 and T5 are added; hence to describe non-persistent data produced by card and detail areas, respectively.

At this point, the relationship between a business object and operation in the master-detail pattern is only described by PN. To analyze the consistency of interface, one has to analyze finite operation states, data states, and reachable marking in PN for the identification of incorrect operation flow and design.

3 Analyzing Consistency of Operations on Interface

Now let's discuss the operation state on interface by Coverability Graph (CG) of PN. A converting algorithm of CG was proposed by [7] and lately improved by [9,10]. The CG is introduced to check reachability from one marking (state) to another. The transformation from a PN to CG is necessary. Fig. 3 is a converted CG from PN (Fig.2), which addresses all states and their changes in life cycle of a business object.

The explanation of Fig.3 can be given as follows. The graph consists of 13 nodes which represent the possible markings of the operation flow. The entries of each node in the first line represent the markings of the control places c1,…, and c10; the entries in the second line represent the markings of the data places d1,d2,d3,d3',d4, and d4' with the corresponding states of the tokens. For example, the node (8) has two control tokens (c5 and c6), two non-persistent data (d1, and d4'), and four persistent data (d2, d3, d3', and d4). Since the syntax of PN must be satisfied with that there exists only one start marking and one end marking in graph; thus implicitly indicating the CG needs to be improved.

How to improve CG needs two strategies: (1) get ride of states without linking to persistent object, and (2) pay attention to those states which change from n to p (i.e. these related nodes need persistent operations). Data place d1,d2, d3, and d3' should be masked, because the only states of data place d4 and d4' are changed from n to p. Node (7) is the cutting point, whose state is out of business object's life cycle. The improved CG and corresponding PN graph can be found in Fig.4. From Fig.3, one can see that there are two problems need to be solved. First, one should realize that an arrow from node (6) to node (5) is changeable; but no corresponding operation. As a result, users intend to modify data in card area; but unconsciously produce another new business object. An operation of empty area changing state from p to 0 is needed. That is the empty data d4' on the interface may be changed to T6. Second, the semantic explanation for t7 in Fig.3 is 'save one row' and 'save all row' respectively. They cause the same state node (12), and have semantic redundancy. The solution to reduce semantic redundancy is to distinguish d4' from non-persistent operation T2 and T3 whose semantic explanations are 'catch event of modifying one row' and 'catch event of modifying many rows' respectively.

4 Consistency XML-Based Interface

Considerable applications can be implemented on XML-based systems [11]. Fig.5 is a segment of such system with an innovative CG.

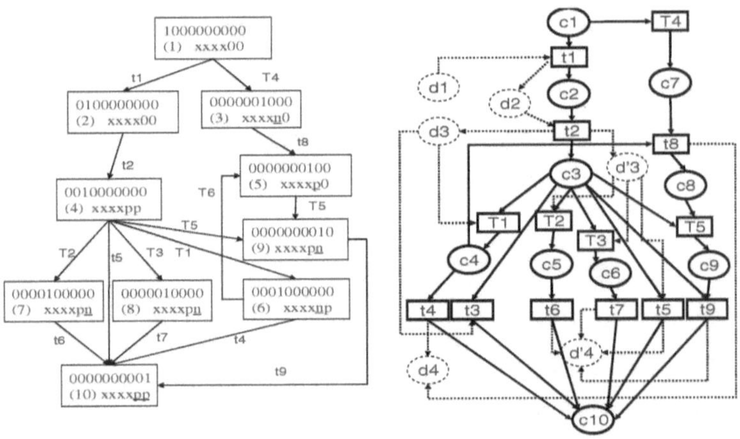

Fig. 4. Improved CG (left) and corresponding PN graph (right)

```
<operation >
< preoperation name="cardarea_modified" succoperation ="cardsave" defaultop ="cardsave" >
        <errmsg>modified data have not been saved!</errmsg></predecessor >
< preoperation name="cardarea_added " succoperation ="cardadd" defaultop ="cardadd">
        <errmsg>added data have not been persisted!</errmsg></predecessor >
< preoperation name=" cardarea_modified " succoperation ="cardadd" defaultop ="reset"></predecessor >
< preoperation name=" row_modified" succoperation ="saverow" defaultop =" saverow ">
        <errmsg>modified data of current row have not saved!</errmsg></predecessor >
< preoperation name=" many_rows_modified " succoperation ="saveall" defaultop =" saveall ">
        <errmsg>modified data of rows have not saved!</errmsg></predecessor >
< preoperation name=" detailarea_added " succoperation ="add " defaultop =" add ">
        <errmsg>modified data of rows have not saved!</errmsg></predecessor >
</ operation>
```

Fig. 5. Specification of interface consistency

Obeying the consistency specification, if a conflicting operation happens, software system can prompt some directive information, or execute default operation, or function directly.

5 Development and Application

As an example, an equipment management with an interface of master-detail pattern (see Fig.6) is programmed. Modifying data in card area produces non-persistent business object, and operation 'save' or 'update' can produce persistent business object. The consistency of all these operations depends on operation specification in terms of in XML expression.

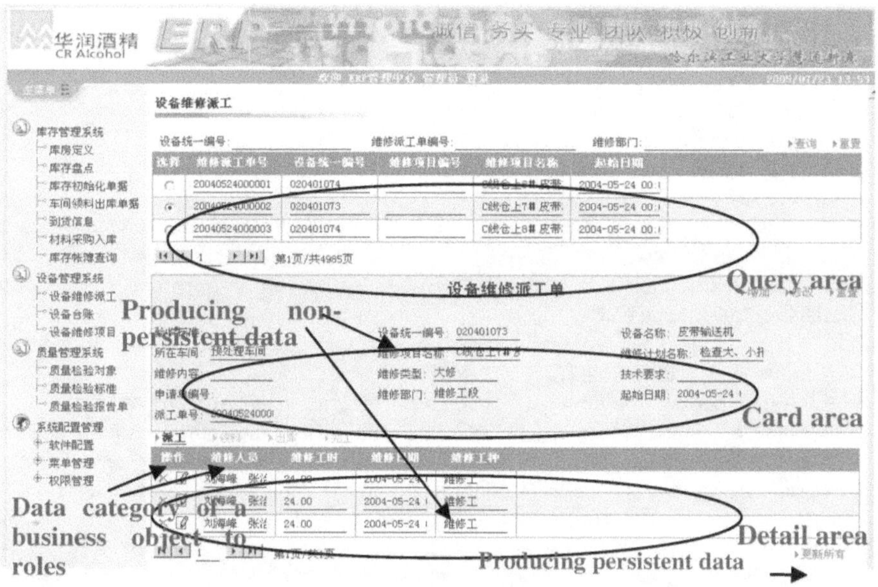

Fig. 6. A case of master-detail interface pattern – dispatching

6 Conclusion and Future Work

Current ERP systems are built on software component and integrated middleware. The consistency of operation on interface may not be guaranteed. An operation flow with an interface pattern built in Web-based application in manufacturing enterprises is described in Petri-net. A transformation from Petri net graph to CG is presented. Incorrect states can be identified after improving the CG; followed by a proposal that a consistency specification in XML format is needed. After giving a consistency rule upon strict theory, even defect about interface design, semantic redundancy can be avoid. The paper does not discuss the case that an asynchronous operation may appear on some interface. In the future, we will focus on other issues such as time-consumed operation in equipment maintenance plan, background operation, and parallel business process etc.

Acknowledgments

This work was supported by the National Natural Science Foundation of China No. 60573086.

References

1. Kasik, D.J., Lund, M.A., Ramsey, H.W1: Reflections on using a UIMS for complex applications, Vol. 6, IEEE Software, (1989) 54-61
2. Brad, A.M.: User Interface Software Tools. Vol. 2, ACM Transactions on CHI, (1995) 64-103
3. Liu. J.I., Zhang, S., Hu, T.: An Integrated Interface Based on Web and XML for Interoperability between Enterprises. Vol. 5 High Technology Letters, (2002) 71-75
4. Wang, Y., Lei, Y., Huang, S.: User Interface Management with XML, Vol. 4, Journal of Computer0aided Design –Computer Graphics, (2004) 566-571
5. John, G., John, H.: Developing Adaptable User Interfaces for Component-based Systems. Vol. 14, Interacting with Computers, (2002) 175-194
6. Zhu, J., Zhang, G., The Formal Specification and Property Verification of Interactive User Interface, Software Journal, (11) (1999) 1163-1168
7. Kaep, R.M., Miller, R.E, Parallel Program Schemata, Journal of Computer and System Sciences 3 (1969) 147-195
8. Petri C.A., Kommunikation, M.A.: PhD Thesis, Institue fur Instrumentelle Mathematik der Universitat Bonn, (1962)
9. Ye, X., etc.: On Reachability Graphs of Petri Nets. Computers and Electrical Engineering Vol.29, Issue: 2, (2003) 263-272
10. Giua, A., Seatzu C.: The Observer Coverability Graph for the Analysis of Observability Properties of Place/Transitions Nets, Proceedings of the 6th European Control Conference, Porto, Portugal, (2001) 1339-1344
11. Elmasri, R., etc.: Conceptual Modeling for Customized XML. Schemas Data & Knowledge Engineering. Vol. 54, Issue: 1, July, (2005) 57-76

Research of Multilevel Transaction Schedule Algorithm Based on Transaction Segments

Hongbin Wang, Daxin Liu, and Binge Cui

College of Computer Science and Technology,
Harbin Engineering University, Harbin, Heilongjiang, China
wanghongbin@hrbeu.edu.cn

Abstract. A new multilevel transaction schedule algorithm based on transaction segments is proposed as a high-ready-wait algorithm. A multilevel transaction is divided into several transaction segments. High security level transaction segments are executed if there aren't any conflicted low security level transaction segments. Transaction segments are committed in an increasing order of security levels in multilevel transactions. This algorithm eliminates the read-firstly semantic dependency and write-firstly semantic dependency in multilevel transactions without using multi-version, so it can be implemented using un-trusted codes. The algorithm is described and proved that it is A-CIS-correct in this paper.

1 Introduction

Most of the work to date on transaction management for multilevel secure (MLS) DBMSs focuses on single-level transactions (which can read data at multiple sensitivity levels but write data only at a single level). In some applications, users need to read or write data at different security levels. However it is impossible for a single level transaction to finish the task. Therefore, multilevel transaction algorithm is promising to solve the problem [1] [2]. Previous multilevel transaction schedule algorithm includes low-first and high-ready-wait algorithms [3]. In this paper, a new multilevel transaction schedule algorithm based on multiple transaction segments is proposed. It can be serves as a fundamental high-ready-wait algorithm.

2 Basic Concept

The concepts of transaction are introduced before the presentation of proposed algorithm.

Definition 1(Transaction Segment): Intuitively, we define a transaction segment of a multilevel transaction as a sequence of consecutive read and write operations labeled at same security level, where write operations must a last operation, such that:

(1) Each S_i consists of a sequence of read operations and only one write operation.
(2) For each write operation w[x] in S_i, $L(x)=L(S_i)$.

H.T. Shen et al. (Eds.): APWeb 2006, LNCS 3842, pp. 853 – 856, 2006.

(3) Every read operation r[x] in S_i is such that $L(x) \leq L(S_i)$.
(4) Each S_i consists of a sequence of operations that should range from the operation that is the first operation after the end of previous transaction segment operations to the next write operation.

Definition 2 (Transaction segment Read or Write Set): A read set (or a write set) of a transaction segments S_i, denotes as R-set $_{Ti}$ (or W-set $_{Ti}$), consists of the data objects that will be read (or written) by S_i. When S_i is submitted to the scheduler, the scheduler receives R-set $_{Ti}$ and W-set $_{Ti}$. If there is intersection between the read set of the previous transaction and the write set of the latter transaction, and the level of previous transaction totally dominates the level of the latter transaction; there is the read-firstly semantic dependencies between the previous transaction and the latter. If there exits an intersection between the write set of the previous transaction and the read set of the latter transaction, the level of latter transaction dominates the level of the previous transaction; there exists a write-firstly semantic dependency between the previous transaction and the latter transaction.

3 The Description of Algorithm

The multilevel transaction schedule algorithm remains its atomicity and security [4][5]. Blaustein and Jajodia [4] proposed three atomicity rules, i.e. basic ML-atomicity, L-atomicity, and complete atomicity, respectively.

A new multilevel transaction schedule algorithm based on transaction segments is proposed hereby. The algorithm is developed from basic the high-ready-wait algorithm that adjusts the execution order of the multilevel transaction operations. The basic idea is to execute the high-level transaction segment precedent over the others in the multilevel transaction. If there is the read-firstly semantic dependency between certain transaction segments S_H and preceding transaction segment S_L, S_L must be executed before S_H; thus eliminating read-firstly semantic dependencies. The algorithm can be implemented using un-trusted codes. The following is the concrete description of the algorithm:

Algorithm1: multilevel transaction schedule algorithm based on transaction segments.

Input: a multilevel transaction T_i.

Output: a total ordering of operations of multilevel transaction T_i, at the same time relative order of conflict operations remain the same.

Step 1: T_i is first analyzed before being divided into several transaction segments, and each transaction segment is designated a unique serial number, the security level of transaction segment is the same as the one of the write operation.

Step 2: For each transaction segment S_i of the multilevel transaction T_i, move it to the front as possible. The move procedure can be described as follows:

If the security level of S_j doesn't dominate the security of S_i and if the intersection is not empty between the write set of S_j and the read set of S_i, there exist the write-firstly semantic dependencies between S_i and S_j. If the execution order of S_i and S_j is un-exchangeable, stop moving S_i. If the intersection is empty between the write set of

S_j and the read set of S_i, there doesn't exist the write-firstly semantic dependencies between S_i and S_j. S_i moves before S_j. S_i can be compared with the preceding transaction segment. Repeat the above procedure until S_i can't be moved forward anymore.

Step 3: Each transaction segment in T_i is sequentially executed and each transaction segment is committed to the single-level DBMS at the same security level. If there are several sequences of consecutive transaction segments at the same security level, these transaction segments are committed to the same single-level DBMS. Each transaction segment is accomplished without commitment.

Step 4: Each transaction segment at the same security level is committed in increasing order of security levels, the ability of high-level transaction segments to commit at each security level is determined before the transaction segments with the next lower security level are committed, and all transaction segments at each security level must be committed in a condition that the atomicity is maintained.

4 Analysis of the Algorithm

The multilevel transaction schedule algorithm meets the L-atomicity, C-correction, I-correction, and S-correction, i.e. the ACIS criteria. Let's verify this algorithm according to the correctness criteria stated in [3].

(1) Correctness
First let's prove that the multilevel transaction schedule algorithm based on transaction segments proposed in the previous section is correct. A multilevel transaction is divided into several transaction segments with the same execution order of transaction operations. This way, the result of transaction execution is the same, no matter the transaction is accomplished in one time or in several times. This algorithm only exchanges the execution order of transaction segments without conflicts at different security levels. Therefore the result of the exchange don't influence read and write operations, and consequently the result of this schedule algorithm is correct.

(2) Atomicity
Only executing transaction segments with a dominating security level is committed when all dominated transaction segments have committed. Therefore, transaction segments have to be committed in an increasing order of security levels. Because it requires that all transaction segments within the each level must have confirmed commitment, the algorithm maintains the basic ML-atomicity, although some transactions are not complete atomicity owing to the particularity of transaction itself. For these transactions, user may designate special transactions to be executed from specified security levels. Therefore this algorithm is L-atomic.

(3) Security
This algorithm commits transaction segments in an increasing order of security levels. No matter high level transaction segment is committed or not, it doesn't influence the commitment of transaction segments at lower security levels, and the algorithm

restricts information flows from higher security level to lower security level.Therefore it is secure.

(4) Consistency
Each transaction segment in a schedule is conflict-equivalent to its original order. Therefore, the result of read or write operations is equivalent to original result.

(5) Isolation
The algorithm is dedicated in a multilevel environment. In such manner at the same time isolation and security of multilevel is achieved. [3]

The algorithm based on transaction segments can be used in a multilevel transaction, whereas multi-version timestamp ordering scheduler can be utilized between multilevel transactions.

5 Conclusion

A new multilevel transaction schedule algorithm based on transaction segments is proposed in this paper, and this algorithm proposes the concept of transaction segment, and defines the read set, the write set of transaction segments. Due to the definition of the transaction segment, we know the transaction segments are the smaller unit than the transaction sections, it increases the flexibility of the multilevel transaction schedule algorithm based on transaction segments. This algorithm proposed in this paper describes two major approaches, Low-first algorithm and High-ready-wait algorithm, along with a hybrid approach using each algorithm, and eliminates the read-firstly semantic dependency and write-firstly semantic dependency in multilevel transactions without using multi-version, so it can be implemented using untrusted codes. In this paper, we describe the algorithm and prove its correctness and it is accord with A-CIS-criteria.

References

1. Jojodia, S., Smith, K. P., Blaustein, B. T.: Securely Executing Multilevel Transaction. Database Systems Security, 7 (1997) 259-269
2. Aluri, V. etc: Transaction Processing in Multilevel Secure Databases with Kernelized Architecture: Challenges and Solutions. IEEE Transactions on Knowledge and Data Engineering, 9(5) (1997) 697-708
3. Smith, K. P. etc: Correctness Criteria for Multilevel Secure Transactions. IEEE Transactions on Knowledge and Data Engineering, 8(1) (1996) 32-45
4. Blaustein, B. etc: A Model of Atomicity for Multilevel Transactions. IEEE Symposium on Security and Privacy 5 (1993) 120-134
5. Costich, O., Jajodia, S.: Maintaining Multilevel Transaction Atomity in MLS Database System with Kernelized Architecture. Database Security 5 (1993) 249-265

Web Navigation Patterns Mining Based on Clustering of Paths and Pages Content

Feng Gang, Guang-Sheng Ma, and Hu Jing

College of Computer Science & Technology,
Harbin Engineering University, Harbin 150001, China
{fenggang, maguangsheng}@hrbeu.edu.cn

Abstract. Combining the paths similarity and the pages content similarity, a novel clustering algorithm is presented. The actions character of users is revealed more exactly by clustering. The data scale is reduced by a long way during clustering. Based on the clusters, the user navigation patterns are generated by mining the Web log. The experiment result shows that the user navigation interest conversion patterns mined from Web log are typical and intuitionistic.

1 Introduction

At present, the methods mining user navigation patterns concentrate on analyzing the navigation paths[1-3]. The mining results do not consider the pages content similarity. So it can not reveal the actions character of users efficaciously, but only indicate the related pages[4]. The meanings of user navigation patterns is not obvious.

Aiming at above problems, a novel clustering algorithm based on the paths similarity and the pages content similarity is presented in this paper. It reveals the actions character of users more exactly. The user navigation interest sequences are generated by mining the user sessions in Web log. The typical and intuitionistic user navigation patterns could be mined from the user navigation interest sequences.

2 The Analysis of Similarity

We can computing the similarity of two navigation paths as follows.

Definition 1. The similarity between C_i and C_j is

$$S_1^{ij} = \frac{|C_i \cap C_j|^{\alpha+\beta}}{\max(|C_i|,|C_j|)^{\alpha} \cdot |C_i \cup C_j|^{\beta}} \quad (0 \le \alpha, \beta \le 1) \tag{1}$$

where α and β is the adjusting factors, $|C_i|$ is the path length of C_i.

Basing on relation degree between theme and document, we can analyze the pages content similarity.

H.T. Shen et al. (Eds.): APWeb Workshops 2006, LNCS 3842, pp. 857 – 860, 2006.

Definition 2. The relation degree between document D_j and theme T_i is denoted as:

$$R_{ij} = \sum_{m=1}^{N} \frac{\left|k_{i,m}^{D_j}\right|}{\left|D_j\right|} \times w_{i,m} \tag{2}$$

where $k_{i,j}$ is the *j*th keyword of T_i, $w_{i,j}$ is the weight of $k_{i,j}$, $\sum_{j=1}^{N} w_{i,j} = 1$, N is the number of keywords in T_i, $|k_{i,m}^{D_j}|$ is the appearance times of $k_{i,m}$ in D_j, $|D_j|$ is the sum of the words in D_j.

Definition 3. The similarity between page P_i and P_j can be denoted as:

$$S_2^{ij} = \frac{\sum_{k=1}^{n} R_{ki} R_{kj}}{\sqrt{[\sum_{k=1}^{n} R_{ki}^2][\sum_{k=1}^{n} R_{kj}^2]}} \tag{3}$$

where n is the number of themes.

3 Clustering Algorithm

In the clustering algorithm, we cluster the paths according to the similarity of user navigation paths at first. Then the pages content similarity of clustering result is analyzed. If the similarity do not meet the requirement, then we cluster the paths newly. Above process is repeated until the similarity meet the requirement.

The similarity between arbitrary two users navigation paths form the enormous similarity coefficient matrix, so a lot of memory are consumed during clustering. But many small similarity coefficient are ineffectual for clustering. So we filter them by specifying the threshold value θ.

Clustering algorithm must aforehand specify the threshold value δ of pages similarity. While the average of pages similarity in cluster is above or equal to δ, the clustering result can be accepted, otherwise we must increase θ and cluster the paths again. If the pages similarity do not meet the requirement and θ=1, then we reduce δ and execute the clustering algorithm newly.

Clustering Algorithm :

```
Input : the Web log file without repeated paths (WLF),
δ and θ
 Output: pages cluster C
 Steps :
  AV = 0;
  While ( AV < δ and θ < 1 )
        θ = θ + 0.01;
```

```
    C = {Φ};
    While (WLF is not end )
        Getting a record;
        While (WLF is not end )
            Getting a record;
            Computing the similarity of paths S1;
            If S1 > θ then reserving the path number;
        EndWhile
        Forming the temporary cluster Ct;
        If Ct ⊄ C  then  Ct joining C ;
    EndWhile
    Computing the subjection of common subset in
    arbitrary two clusters in C to two clusters,
    eliminating repeated subset by subjection;
    AV = the average of S2 in C;
EndWhile
If AV ≥ δ  then output C ;
```

4 Mining the User Navigation Patterns

There are four Web pages clusters:{P1, P2, P3, P4},{P5, P6},{P7, P8, P9} and {P10, P11, P12, P13}. Their clusters No. are 1, 2, 3 and 4, corresponding intuitionistic descriptions (Themes) are CD1, CD2, CD3 and CD4 respectively.

The user sessions are obtained by analyzing the Web log. Substituting corresponding clusters No. for the pages in user sessions, user sessions can be transformed into the navigation interest sequences.

Definition 4. The user navigation interest sequence is defined as:

$$UIS_t = < l_k^t.IP, l_k^t.UID, \{(l^t.cluster, l^t.time)\}^m > \qquad (l^t \in N,\ 1 \le k \le m) \qquad (4)$$

Subject to

$$\begin{cases} if \quad l_k^t.time - l_{k-1}^t.time \le \tau & then \quad 2 \le k \le m-1 \\ if \quad l_k^t.time - l_{k-1}^t.time > \tau & then \quad k = m \\ l_m^t.time - l_1^t.time \le W_M \end{cases} \qquad (5)$$

where m is the number of Web documents, τ is the threshold value of navigation time, W_M is the length of time window.

There are six user sessions: P2→P7→P8, P3→P10→P13, P12→P8→P13, P3→P4→P11→P12, P4→P6 and P8→P7→P13. Corresponding navigation interest sequences are 1→3→3, 1→4→4, 4→3→4, 1→1→4→4, 1→2 and 3→3→4.

We utilize GSP algorithm[5] to mine user navigation patterns. The conversion patterns of user navigation interest are obtained by mining the navigation interest sequences. Substituting corresponding themes for clusters No., we can get the intuitionistic descriptions of user navigation patterns: CD1→CD4→CD3, CD1→CD4 →CD2, CD3→CD4→CD3, CD3→CD4→CD4.

5 Experiment Result

The experiment data is a week log of Microsoft homepage in Jan. 2000. It contains 496 pages and 42766 records. We specify $\delta = 0.4$ in clustering algorithm. The requirement of pages content similarity is met while θ is adjusted to 0.27. The number of clusters is 61. According to the referenced length method[6], specifying $\tau = 40$s, 1873 user sessions are generated. Utilizing GSP algorithm ($minsup = 10$), we got 205 typical and intuitionistic conversion patterns of user navigation interest.

6 Conclusion

This paper estimates the similarity of user actions on the basis of the navigation paths and pages content, presents a more effectual clustering algorithm. By mining the user sessions in Web log, typical and intuitionistic user navigation patterns are obtained. The method in this paper can help Web administrators grasp the character of user actions and arrange the structure of sites reasonably.

References

1. Wang S., Gao W., et al: Path clustering: Discovering the Knowledge in the Web Site. Journal of Computer Research & Development, Vol.38. Science Press, Beijing (2001) 482-486
2. Mobasher B., Cooley R. and Srivastava J.: Creating Adaptive Web Sites through Usage-Based Clustering of URLs. In: IEEE Knowledge and Data Engineering Workshop (KDEX'99), IEEE Press, New York (1999) 32-37
3. Larsen B., Aone C.: Fast and Effective Text Mining Using Linear-Time Document Clustering. In: Proc. of the 5th ACM SIGKDD Int'l Conf. on Knowledge Discovery & Data Mining (KDD-99), San Diego (1999) 16-22
4. Büchner A. G., Mulvenna M. D.: Discovering Behavioral Patterns in Internet Log Files: Playing the Devil'S Advocate. In: Proc. of the 12th Biennial Int'l Telecommunications Society Conf.(ITS-98), Stockholm (1998)
5. Han J., Pei J., et al.: Prefix Span: Mining Sequential Patterns Efficiently by Prefix-Projected Pattern Growth. In: Proc. 2001 Int'l Conf. on Data Engineering (ICDE'01), Heidelberg (2001) 215-224
6. Cooley R., Mobasher B., Srivastava J.: Data Preparation for Mining World Wide Web Browsing Patterns. Knowledge and Information Systems, Vol.1. Springer-Verlag, London (1999) 5-32

Using Abstract State Machine in Architecture Design of Distributed Software Component Repository*

Yunjiao Xue, Leqiu Qian, Xin Peng, Yijian Wu, and Ruzhi Xu

Department of Computer Science and Engineering, Fudan University,
Shanghai Key Laboratory of Intelligent Information Processing, Fudan University,
PO Box 200433, 220 Handan Road, Shanghai, China
{yjxue, lqqian, pengxin, wuyijian, rzxu}@fudan.edu.cn

Abstract. Recently many enterprises have established their own software component repositories. Because of the physical isolation to each other and independent decision on the classifying and specification mechanisms, the repositories form a distributed and heterogeneous system, hindering the reusability of component resource. Due to the infeasibility of integrating all the repositories physically, it is necessary to use a collaborative way to integrate such repositories and form a logically uniform architecture with consistent user interface and retrieval mechanism, to improve the reuse of software components. In this paper we propose an architecture of integrated system based on intelligent agent, and make use of ASM in its architecture design, which can be validated formally. This architecture implements the required fundamental functionality.

1 Introduction

The increase of software components has led to a remarkable amount of enterprise repositories [1-3][5]. For sharing software components among enterprises, a high level, regional repository beyond enterprises is needed, such as a city- or country-level ones, which is named as a centralized, integrated component repository.

In general, enterprises tend to forbid the external access due to security. The direct access is inaccessible, which needs a middle layer. Ideally, distributed enterprises can easily submit their queries to the centralized repository through a uniform portal. However, there exist some problems, which are outlined in the following.

(1) When numerous retrieval requests are sent to the centralized one, they will form remarkable workload to the server (due to the bottleneck of the system performance), thus significantly decreases the efficiency.
(2) In reality, the enterprises are not directly access to avoid secret-keeping due to high business competition.
(3) To achieve requested information on the centralized server and their own systems could influence data integrity and redundant work.

Therefore, a system with a collaboration mechanism is urgently needed to integrate the distributed information available at various enterprise repositories, while

* Partially supported by NSFC Grant No. 60473062; National 863 High-Tech Research and Development Program of Chin, a under Grant No. 2002AA114010.

H.T. Shen et al. (Eds.): APWeb 2006, LNCS 3842, pp. 861 – 868, 2006.

sustaining data isolation. Such a system should provide a uniform logical view and retrieval interface to the outer world. The retrieval requests sent to the system will be transferred to the inner repositories, and ultimately a single set of results upon on each request can be fetched to the end users.

Unfortunately, a distributed architecture is very complicated. During the constructing process of each repository, the enterprises may employ different specification mechanisms, leading to many heterogeneous systems. This tremendously increases the complexity of the overall system. The intelligent agent-based technique introduced in [13-16] can be an alternative solution. It is beneficial to the integration of component repositories.

This paper reviews the related work on component repository. It presents a general idea of the Abstract State Machines (ASM) method and its architecture design. A discussion of its validations is also presented, followed by a conclusion.

2 Related Work

The major topics in repository construction include types of reusable software components, classification methods, storage, and search and retrieval mechanisms [6]. People are still working hard to develop the theory of component repository. For example, some systems use REBOOT (Reuse Based on Object-Oriented Techniques) [7] and PCTE (Portable Common Tool Environment) in Europe [8], STARS program in the USA that proposes a reference model of component repository, and an instance named ALOAF (Asset Library Open Architecture Framework) [9]. These programs focus on the component models and specification paradigms. The JBird project at Beijing University [3] deployed the component repository concept to come up with a long time, and advised a facet model for the component specification. The government office of Shanghai in China also started a project of component repository research to explore its application for enterprises [4]. Other projects, such as ComponentRank [10], Codebroker [11], and the Ohsugi et al's system [12] dedicated to the exploration of component retrieval in a repositary system. Tangsripairoj et al [6] introduced an interesting attempt, SOM (Self-Organizing Map) to construct component repositories.

3 Abstract State Machines

3.1 Introduction

The terminology of Abstract State Machines (ASM) was defined in [17], captures in mathematically rigorous yet transparent form of some fundamental operational intuitions of computing. This allows the practitioner to work with ASMs without any further explanation, viewing them as "pseudocode over abstract data" which comes with a well defined semantics supporting the intuitive understanding. Based on Börger's work, ASM is a practical design method that can solve the fundamental problems in software development [19]. With ASMs, one can elaborate the informally presented requirements of a desired system, and turn them into a satisfactory ground model, i.e. a functionally complete with abstract description of sufficient but not more than necessary rigor. The model can (a) be read and understood by and justified to the customer as solving his problem, (b) defines relevant system features for user expectation, and (c) only contains the logic of the problem requirements for the system behavior (i.e. does not rely upon any further design decision belonging to the system implementation).

3.2 Basic Definition

ASMs are systems with transition rules.

if *Condition* **then** *Updates*

which transforms abstract states. The *Condition* (so called guard) under which a rule is applied is an arbitrary first-order formula without free variables. *Updates* is a finite set of function updates (containing only variable free terms) of form

$$f(t_1, \ldots, t_n) := t$$

whose execution is to be understood as *changing* (or defining, if there was none) the value of the (location represented by the) function *f* at the given parameters. Hereby we employ Gurevich abstract state machine theory, which was formerly known as *evolving algebras* or *ealgebras* and introduced in [18], as our approach's fundation. In its definition, the states of an ASM are simply the structures of first-order logic, except that relations are treated as Boolean-valued functions.

We introduce rules for describing changes to states. At a given state *S* whose vocabulary includes that of a rule *R*, *R* gives rise to a set of updates; to execute *R* at *S*, fire all the updates in the corresponding update set. An *update instruction R* has the form

$$f(t_l, t_l, \ldots, t_r) := t$$

where the *f* is an *r*-ary function name and each t_i is a term. A *block rule R* is a sequence R_1, ..., R_n of transition rules. To execute *R* at *S*, execute all the R_i at *S* simultaneously. A *conditional rule R* has the form

if *g* then R_0 else R_1 endif,

where *g* (the *guard*) is a term and R_0, R_1 are rules. The meaning of *R* is the obvious one: if *g* evaluates to *true* in *S*, then the update set for *R* at *S* is the same as that for R_0 at *S*; otherwise, the update set for *R* at *S* is the same as that for R_1 at *S*. A *choice rule R* has the form

choose *v* satisfying *c(v)*
  R_0 (*v*)
end choose

where *v* is a variable, *c*(*v*) is a term involving variable *v*, and *R*(*v*) is a rule with free variable *v*. This rule is nondeterministic. To execute *R* in state *S*, choose some element of *a* of *S* such that *c*(*a*) evaluates to *true* in *S*, and execute rule R_0, interpreting *v* as *a*. If no such element exists, do nothing.

4 Architecture Design

4.1 Integration Requirements

In the Internet computing environment, the following requirements must be satisfied to integrate various component repositories. They are: (1) It is unnecessary to explicitly integrate all available repositories into a physically centralized repository; thus avoiding the great cost of integration and performance bottleneck in a central server. (2) It must support at least one central portal, while most of independent enterprise repositories are responsible for their own components management. (3) The retrieval requests from users must be sent to the central portal, such as via a Web site; thus the end users do not need to know the existence of other repositories. (4) Each repository must access retrieval requests consistently with maintaining interoperability and compatibility. The retrieving results must be sent to the end users in a unified format.

4.2 Overall Design

To implement the collaboration among enterprises, a collaboration model with a formal framework is developed to represent the interactions of agents. The top-level view of the whole architecture is shown in Fig. 1.

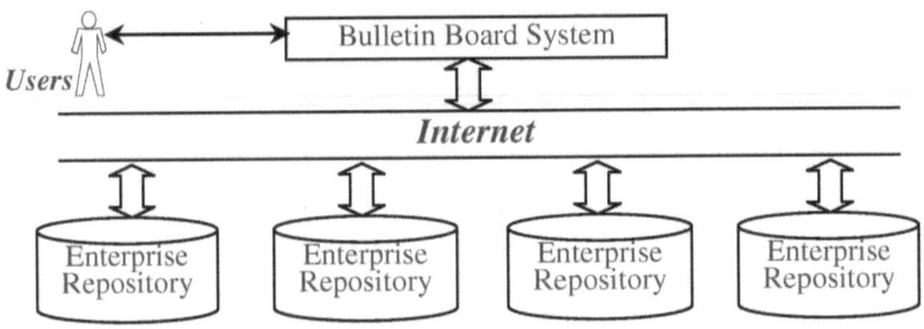

Fig. 1. The top-level view of the architecture

In the architecture, many enterprise repositories can be connected to Internet, and a centralized Bulletin Board System (BBS) acts as a mediator of the integrated behavior. The users will interact with BBS, for sending their retrieval requests and receiving the retrieving result from the same board. Each repository runs several agents that take charge of getting requests from the board, retrieving the object component in a local repository, and of returning the results to the board (if find some).

The BBS can be further partitioned into three regions. Some sharable component specifications that the enterprises do not want to keep secret can be submitted to the *Region of Sharable Component Specifications* of the Bulletin Board System. User retrieval requests are pooled in the *Region of Component Retrieval Requests*. After each request is performed, if there are any satisfied results, they will be sent to the *Region of Returned Retrieval Results*. Users observe the results of their requests from the *Region of Returned Retrieval Results* of the Bulletin Board System.

For each region, there is an intelligent agent running on an enterprise repository that takes charge of interacting with it.

4.3 ASM Design

As an abstracted machine, the state of the system is a 4-arity tuple $\Sigma = (S, R, A, U)$, where S, R, A and U respectively abstracts the state of the whole system, the retrieval requests, the agents running on the enterprise repositories, and the results of the agent performing the requests. Here the sharable component specifications are not mentioned because they are not involved in the parallel retrieving process.

To simulate the architecture, we abstract the system into a set **S** of states,

S = {*WaitingforRequest, WaitingforAgent, RequestPerformed*}, with the meaning of each state as follows,

- *WaitingforRequest*: No any request in *the Region of Component Retrieval Requests* is un-performed.
- *WaitingforAgent*: A new request is sent to the system by some user, but there is no any agent from the enterprise repository that fetches it. So the system is waiting for some agent to perform the new one.
- *RequestPerformed*: A new request is performed by at least one agent and there is no any request keeping un-performed.

A denotes the set of all agents, $A = \{a_1, a_2, \ldots, a_n\}$, where each a_i is an agent and n is the amount of the repositories that join this system. n will increase if there are new repositories becoming the members of the system, making the system extensible.

R is a finite set of all the requests, notated as *r*. $R = \{r_1, r_2, \ldots r_{max}\}$, where *max* denotes the maximal amount of the requests that the region could contain (the expired requests will be archived). The state of each request is defined as a tuple *rs* with an indefinite arity. A mapping function *Ret*: $R \times A \rightarrow 2^A$ will compute the new state of each request and change its state into a new one, denoting which of all the agents have performed it. Correspondingly, the state of each agent is defined as a tuple with an indefinite arity. A mapping function *Fet*: $A \times R \rightarrow 2^R$ will compute the new state of each agent and change its state into a new one, denoting which of all the requests it has performed.

U is a finite set of all the results returned after the requests were performed by some agents, together with corresponding requests. $U = \{u_1, u_2, \ldots u_{max}\}$, where u_i is a result and *max* is the maximal amount of the results that the region could contain. In the same way, the expired results or the results that users have accessed could be archived. Each u_i has the form of (*r*, *a*, *c*), where *r* means a retrieval request, *a* means an agent that has performed *r*, and *c* is a set of the component specifications that match the request according to *a*. That is, *a* may find one or more component which specification(s) are compatible with the one(s) appearing in the request *r*.

The ASM of the system is a set *T* of transition rules, including the following ones,

Rule 0*: *SysStat := WaitingforRequest

This rule defines the system an initial state specification.

***Rule 1*:**

```
if newrequestcreated(r) & SysStat = WaitingforRequest
   then
    SysStat := WaitingforAgent
    R := AddReq(R, r)
end if
```

Note: *newrequestcreated* is an external event with a parameter *r* denoting a new retrieval request. *SysStat* is the system controlling state variable. The function *AddReq*(*R*, *r*) will append the new request *r* to *R*, thus making *R* changed.

***Rule 2*:**

```
choose r in R and a in A with rs(r) =∅ or a∉rs(r)
   do fetchedbyagent(a, r)
end choose
```

That is, if some request *r* is not performed by any agent, or *r* is not performed by some agent *a*, then *a* will have a chance to perform *r*.

***Rule 3*:**

```
if fetchedbyagent(a,r)& SysStat=WaitingforAgent
  then
    SysStat := RequestPerformed
    rs(r) := Ret(r, a)
end if
```

Note: *fetchedbyagent* is an external event with two parameter *a* and *r* denoting that some agent *a* fetches the request *r*. The function *Ret*(*r*, *a*) will add *a* into *r*'s state *rs*, specifying that *r* is performed by a new agent *a*.

***Rule 4*:**

```
choose a satisfying retrieve(a, r) ≠ ∅
   U := AddRes(r, a,  retrieve(a, r))
end choose
```

That is, for some request *r*, if an agent *a* performs it and finds some results, then returns this information to the server by appending it to the corresponding region.

***Rule 5*:**

```
for all r do
  if rs(r)≠∅ then SysStat := WaitingforReques end if
end for
```

When there is no any unperformed request, *Rule 5* will reset the state of the system to the initial one.

Validation: We will give an abbreviated validation to the system's functionality. When there is no any user sending retrieval requests, the system will stay in a static state, with *Rule 0* establishing an initial state. If there is any new request, with *Rule 1* the system will change its state and some agent could be activated to perform the new request. With *Rule* 2, an agent will merely perform those requests that it didn't touched before, so the unnecessary repetition and confliction is avoid. Also, a request will not be always neglected by any agent. Through *Rule 3*, for any request, at least one agent will perform it (as we do not require that each agent must perform each request). A distributed retrieval mechanism is implemented in this way. *Rule 4* insures the satisfying results could be sent to the server, and then users may find them via the server's interface. *Rule 5* lets the transitions to be closed and form a cycle. For further elaboration of the design, more rules could be complemented. Figure 2 demonstrates the transition of the system's state under the given rules.

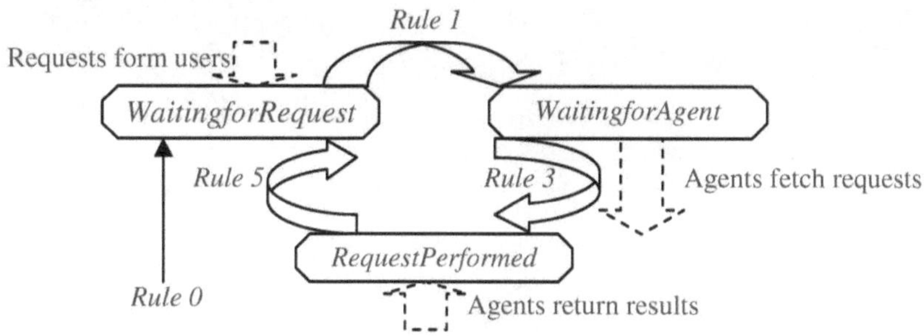

Fig. 2. State transition diagram of the system

5 Conclusion

External processes are forbidden to access an enterprise's internal information because of the security requirements. So, when we fail to find a desired component in current repository, we could not get direct help from other repositories. Otherwise, common users cannot access most of the enterprise repositories due to the unawareness of the address or the access protection. It is the reason that we propose the project of distributed heterogeneous software component repository.

Intelligent agent is an appropriate way to achieve the integration of distributed heterogeneous repositories. In this paper we propose an architecture of the system, and introduce a detailed design based on ASM, which is a good way to simulate the architecture and validate it.

The research issues introduced in this paper are the beginning of an on-going work. Even if the basic results and the main investigation direction have been given, much effort, both theoretical and practical, is needed to achieve a complete treatment of the problem. The future work includes the more detailed design of the structure of 4 or maybe more kinds of agents. The new retrieval methods in the distributed environment will be explored. Most of all, the exchanging of component specification between heterogeneous classifying mechanisms is a vital topic to achieve the integration.

References

1. Basili, V. R., Briand, L C., Melo, W.L.: How Reuse Influences Productivity in Object-Oriented Systems. Communications of the ACM 39 (10) (1996) 104-116
2. Bellinzona, R., Gugini, M.G., Pernici, B.: Reusing Specifications in OO Applications. IEEE Software, March Volume 12, Issue 2, (1995) 65-75
3. Yang, F.Q., Mei, H., and Li,K.Q.: Software Reuse and Software Component Technology. Acta Electronica Sinica, Vol. 27, No.2 (1999)
4. The Web site of Shanghai Component Repository. http://www.sstc.org.cn/. Accessed 5 Aug. (2005)

5. Henninger, Scott: An Evolutionary Approach to Constructing Effective Software Reuse Repositories. ACM Transactions on Software Engineering and Methodology, Vol. 6, No. 2, April, (1997) 111-140
6. Tangsripairoj, S., Mansur, S., Samadzadeh, H..: Application of Self-Organizing Maps to Software Repositories in Reuse-Based Software Development. Proceedings of the 2004 International Conference on Software Engineering Research and Practice (SERP'04), Las Vegas, Nevada, June 2004, Vol. II, (2004) 741-747
7. Faget, J., Morel, J.M.: The REBOOT Environment. Proc. of 2nd International Workshop on Software Reusability (Reuse'93), Lucca, Italy, March (1993)
8. Long, F., Morris, E.: An Overview of PCTE: A Basis for a Portable Common Tool Environment. Technical Report CMU/SEI-93-TR-1, ESC-TR-93-175, Software Engineering Institute, Carnegie Mellon University, March (1993)
9. STARS Technical Committee. Asset Library Open Architecture Framework: Version 1.2, Informal Technology Report, STARS-TC-04041/001/02, August (1992)
10. Inoue, K., et al.: Component Rank: Relative Significance Rank for Software Component Search. In Proceedings of the 25th international conference on software engineering, Portland, Oregon, USA, May 6-8 (2003)
11. Yunwen, Y., Fischer, G.: Information Delivery in Support of Learning Reusable Software Components on Demand. In the Proceedings of the 7th international Conference on Intelligent User Interfaces, California, USA, 2002, ACM Press
12. Ohsugi, N., et al.: Recommendation System for Software Function Discovery. In Proceedings of the 9th Asia-Pacific Software Engineering Conference (2002)
13. Etzioni, O., Lesh, N., Segal, R.: Building Softbots for UNIX. In Etzioni, O., ed., Software Agents — Papers from the 1994 Spring Symposium (Technical Report SS–94–03), AAAI Press, (1994) 9–16.
14. Roesler, M., Hawkins D.T.: Intelligent agents. Online, vol. 18, no. 4 (1994) 18-32
15. Linda Rosen.: MIT Media Lab Presents the Interface Agents Symposium: Intelligent Agents in Your Computer? Information Today, Vol. 10, No. 3 (1993) 9-10
16. Maes, P.: Agents that reduce work and information overload. Communications of the ACM, Vol. 37, No. 7 (1994) 30-40
17. Börger, E., Stärk R.: Abstract State Machines. USA, Springer, 2003.
18. Gurevich, Y., Algebras, E.: An Attempt to Discover Semantics", Current Trends in Theoretical Computer Science, eds. G. Rozenberg and A. Salomaa, World Scienti_c, 266-292, 1993.
19. Börger, E.: High Level System Design and Analysis Using Abstract State Machines. In Hutter, D., Stephan, W., Traverso, P., Ullman, M., eds., Current Trends in Applied Formal Methods (FM-Trends 98). Springer LNCS 1641 (1998) 1-43

An Information Audit System Based on Bayes Algorithm*

Fei Yu[1,2], Yue Shen[1], Huang Huang[1], Cheng Xu[3], and Xia-peng Dai[1]

[1] School of Computer & Information Engineering,
Hunan Agricultural University Changsha, 410128, China
{yufei, shenyue, huangh}@hunau.net
[2] State Key Laboratory of Information Security,
Graduate School of Chinese Academy of Sciences, Beijing, 100049, China
hunanyufei@163.com
[3] College of Computer and Communication, Hunan University,
Changsha, 410082, China
cheng_xu@yeah.net

Abstract. It is difficult to collect information over Gigabit networks for information audit. In the paper, the information audit system adopts the network processor to collect and analyze the date in the low level of network. Through taking an advanced research on current algorithm, some improvements of the Bayes categorization algorithm have been made as well as the proposal of a text categorization model of the minimal risk Bayes decision. In addition, it considers the risk probability of mistaking the related text for unrelated text during the text categorization. The experiments results show that it promotes the precision of text categorization.

1 Introduction

Along with the network to extend continuously, the amount of Internet user increases quickly, the Information Foundation Facilities has become an important degree of the national economy. By way of an important composing part of Information Foundation Facilities, the information security relates to the national alive or dead, economic development, social stability. Every kind of badness information, retroactive information and the information referred to national security and secret recur to Internet more and more to spread through this kind of open communication method of the multi region and multinational field. To resolve this problem of security, except that there would attack these irregularity and criminal offence through lawmaking, it is also a kind of important means to audit network information[1][2].

At present, network information audit system realizes information filtering function mostly through capturing and analyzing text information[3]. Comparing with network filtering technique that depends purely on IP address and URL access control list, based text information filtering technique may filter real-time badness in the network, such as network information in some e-mail,chat-room etc.

* Supported by Hunan Provincial Natural Science Foundation of China(03JJY3103).

H.T. Shen et al. (Eds.): APWeb 2006, LNCS 3842, pp. 869 – 876, 2006.

In the paper, we introduce some key technologies on Information Audit firstly, and then an analysis has been done about text categorization using Bayes algorithm. In addition to that, we have made an improvement on the Bayes categorization algorithm. At last, a performance analysis has been done aimed at the improved Information Audit model.

2 Key Technology

Computer does not have intelligence of people. After reading an article, people can bring a blurry cognition to the content of article according to their self ability of understanding, while computer can hardly "spell over" the article. From radically saying, computer can only recognize 0 and 1, so the text must be transformed to the format which computer can read[4].

2.1 Expressing of Text

According to Bayes categorization[5], if the words or vocables which composed the text can ascertain the type of text absolutely, the text can be replaced by the set constituted by these words or vocables. In spite of losing much information related to the context of article, this promise can formalize the expressing and disposing of the text and can get a better effect in information audit.

In the information searches, the way of expressing of text is using the vector space model. The model regard the text as the out-of-order sequence which composed by the inner vocables and the appearance frequency of this words. In other words, the text can be expressed by using the set of the vocables and their degrees. Indeed, it is not all the vocables in text that participate in expressing the text. Otherwise, the set is probably very big, and some conjunctions and popular vocables in text(for example, "if", "because", "main", "relate to" and so on) also need not be regarded as the vocables which express the text. In addition, the etyma need be picked up from the word in the English text. In this article, we named the vocables which participate in expressing the text as the key words.

2.2 The Technology of Message Disposal

2.2.1 The Technology of WWW Message Disposal

The text information of www is mostly proclaimed in writing, and its message can be searched and checked directly[6]. If the message which includes the "key words" is found, we can get some information such asthe destination MAC address, the source MAC address, the source IP address, the destination IP address, the IP proto col, the transport layer protocol, the source port number, the destination port number, the original application message and so on according to the head of WWW meassge, and then send the content of text to the central controller to analyze and dispose after it is encapsulated to the original socket message.

2.2.2 The Technology of BBS and FTP Message Disposal

The existent format of the most message information of BBS and FTP is text file or binary file. If it is the text file, we can search and check the whole-length message; if it is the binary file, we can do it after transforming the binary file to the text file. If the message which includes the "key words" is found, we can get some information such asthe destination MAC address, the source MAC address, the source IP address, the destination IP address, the IP protocol, the transport layer protocol, the source port number, the destination port number, the original application message and so on according to the head of BBS and FTP message, and then send the content of text to the central controller to analyze and dispose after it is encapsulated to the original socket message.

2.2.3 The Technology of E-Mail Content Disposal

Presently, the audit based on mail content can deal with the information package which is expressed with the either of the four kinds of coding: the 7BIT coding, the 8BIT coding, the Base64 coding and the Qouted-Printable coding. In these four kinds of coding, the 7BIT coding and the 8BIT coding are proclaimed in writing, but the Qouted-Printable coding and the Base64 coding are not. MIME means Multipurpose Internet Mail Extension. By using the way of MIME, the mail which include the voice, the video, the image and the voice code of the different nation can be transformed to the character set named ASCII subset of Base64. After Opening a file coded with MIME by using WORDPAD, we can say this file adopt the MIME coding only if the string "This is a multi-part message format" is in it. Base64 coding has a symbol with "Content-T ransfer-Encoding:base64". Quoted-Printable is another coding format of MIME, and has a symbol with "Content-Transfer-Encoding: quoted-printable". The former two kinds of coding are expressed and transited with the format of proclaimed in writing. So firstly, we search the content of the mail information package by using the "key words" matching technology. If the content of information package include the given "key words", we can capture this information package and send it to the central controller server to secondary analysis and statistics. While the latter two kinds of coding is expressed and transited with non-proclaimed in writing. At first, audit system switches the "key words" according to the correlative coding format, then matching the mail message with the switched "key words", and to some mail message which include the "key words", the information package need to be translated dynamic to proclaimed in writing. After that, the information package need to be send to central controller to analyze and dispose.

2.3 Draw-Out of the Special Item

The vocables, constituting the text, are abundance, and the dimension numbers of the vector space which express the text are also great, probably reaches above ten thousand. Therefore, we need compress the dimension numbers. Firstly, increase the running speed to improve the effect of the program. Secondly, all vocables, about several ten thousand, have different meanings to information audit. Some general and popular vocables, of all kinds, take small contribution to the classifying, while some vocables, taking great part in some class, but small part in other classes, take great contribution to the information audit. In order to improve the precision of the classifying, for each class, we should remove the vocables which their expressive force are weak, and pick out the special item set in allusion to this class[7].

In our system, the judge standard, draw-out of special item to the information of vocables and classes has been adopted. The realizing progress as follows:

1) In the original cases, the special item set include all the emerged vocables in the class.
2) To each vocable, calculate the information quantity of vocables and classes.
3) To all the vocables of this class, sort the information quantity according to the above calculation.
4) Choose some vocables as special items.

According to the draw-out of the special item, for all the training text of each class, their vector dimension numbers should be compressed so that the vector express can be reduced.

3 The Improvement of Bayes Categorization Algorithm

Bayes algorithm is also used widely in text categorization[8]. The mathematic method describes as follows :

1) Calculate the probability vector $(w_1, w_2, w_3 ......w_n)$ as characteristic word belongs to every class:

$$w_k = P(W_k \mid C_j) = \frac{1+\sum_{i=1}^{|D|} N(W_k, d_i)}{|V| + \sum_{s=1}^{|V|} \sum_{i=1}^{|D|} N(W_s, d_i)} \tag{1}$$

2) Partition words according to characteristic word as new text comes, then calculate the probability of text d_i belonging to class C_j:

$$P(C_j \mid d_i; \hat{\theta}) = \frac{P(C_j \mid \hat{\theta}) \prod_{k=1}^{n} P(W_k \mid C_j; \hat{\theta})^{N(W_k, d_i)}}{\sum_{r=1}^{|C|} P(C_r \mid \hat{\theta}) \prod_{k=1}^{n} P(W_k \mid C_r; \hat{\theta})^{N(W_k, d_i)}} \tag{2}$$

$P(C_r \mid \hat{\theta})$ act as resemble meanings, $|C|$ act as the sum of class, $N(W_k, d_i)$ act as the word frequency of W_k in d_i, n act as the sum of characteristic word.

3) Compare probability of new text belongs to all classes and distribute text to the class with maximal probability.

On the basis of Bayes probability formula[6], the probability of given vectors $d(\omega_1, \omega_2, \cdots \omega_n)$ belonging to class $C_k(k = 1,2,\cdots m)$ is as follows:

$$P(C_k \mid d) = P(C_k) \times P(d \mid C_k) \;/\; P(d) \tag{3}$$

$$P(d) = \sum_{k'=1}^{m} P(d \mid C_{k'}) \times P(C_{k'}) \tag{4}$$

To judge the categories of unrecongnise text, it can calculate $P(C_k \mid d)$ from previous formula, which denotes the matching between words in the text and category in vector space model, to decide the probability of whether the text belongs to class C_k. Back check probability $P(C_k \mid d)$ can be obtained by earlier check probability $P(C_k)$ and condition probability $P(d \mid C_k)$.

Suppose w_j is the j category, probability of word arisen in text is independence relatively, there is:

$$P(d \mid C_k) = P(w_1, w_2, \cdots w_n \mid C_k) = \prod_{j=1}^{n} P(w_j \mid C_k) \tag{5}$$

Suppose N_k represent the text sum which belongings to the class C_k in the training swatch volume, N is the text sum of training swatch volume. The earlier probability $P(C_k)$ of the formula (3)is:

$$P(C_k) = N_k / N \tag{6}$$

Bayes algorithm should modified in order to avoid numerator or denominator to be 0 when counting condition probability. Suppose $N(w_t, d_i)$ is the sum of word w_t arising in text d_i; $P(C_j \mid d_i) = \{0,1\}$, if the text d_i in training volume belongs to class C_j, then get 1, otherwise get 0; $\mid V \mid$ denote the sum of category in vector space model, the condition probability $P(w_t \mid C_k)$ is modified as:

$$P(w_t \mid C_k) = \frac{1 + \sum_{i=1}^{|V|} N(w_t, d_i) \times P(C_j \mid d_i)}{\mid V \mid + \sum_{s=1}^{|V|} \sum_{i=1}^{|D|} N(w_s, d_i) \times P(C_j \mid d_i)} \tag{7}$$

Because uncorrelated text will be fault judged as correlated text in formula (7), it should introduce risk or loss factor from fault judge uncorrelated text. Suppose that:

Observe ω is d dimension random vectors $w = [\omega_1, \omega_2, ..., \omega_d]^T$;

State space Q is make up of m states(class), $Q = \{C_1, C_2, ..., C_m\}$;

Decision-making space is make up of decision-making a_i, i=1,2,..., a ;

Loss gene is λ (a_i, C_j), λ denote the loss of decision-making a_i as the state is C_j;

When the loss from fault judge is taken into account, The decision is not made according to back check probability. How to get the least loss at decision-making should be considered, therefore if decision-making is a_i for given text d, then corresponding to the condition expect loss is as follows:

$$R(\alpha_i \mid d) = \sum_{j=1}^{m} \lambda(\alpha_i, C_j) \times P(C_j \mid d) \ , \qquad i = 1,2,\cdots,\alpha \tag{8}$$

At the consider of text fault judgement, we hope it should have the least loss . So the distinguish rules of least risk Bayes is:

If $R(\alpha_i \mid d) = \min R(\alpha_j \mid d)$, $j = 1, 2, \cdots, m$, then d belongs to class a_i. (9)

Bayes text categorization machine divided text into two classes: related and unrelated text. We construct a group of eigenvector $d(\omega_1, \omega_2, \cdots \omega_n)$ related text to match every swatch, and obtain back check probability $P(C_k \mid d)$ with Bayes categorization algorithm by earlier check probability $P(C_k)$ and condition probability $P(d \mid C_k)$. Training swatch volume comes by description of text source file of pretreatment to make up of categorization machine, which classify test swatch on the back check probability of test swatch volume. We divide text categorization into training phase and categorization phase. In the training phase, classified knowledge is from training swatch volume to build categorization machine; In the categorization phase, current text is distributed to possible classes according to categorization machine.

4 System Architecture

Based network processor information audit system model consists of network interface module, network processor module, intelligent coprocessor module and storage module. The network processor presides over process and transfer of data, and deliver to the some information of the data, such as the source IP address, destination IP address to intelligent coprocessor module. The intelligent coprocessor module proceeds analytical matching for the network data packet, according to information gained it makes out judgment how to process data packet, and assigns network processor module how to do. The storage module uses for buffer storage.

Intel IXP 1200 has the powerful function of packet processing and programming. Every I/O bus can process the packet with the peak value of 6.6Gbps. In our information audit system, we use Intel IXP 1200 to simulate real-time data collection and processing [9].

IXP 1200 is composed of 7 RISC processors, secondary storage interface. IX bus interface and PCI bus interface. In the 7 RISC processor, 6 are the packet processing engines and the rest one, called “StrongARM”, is used to manage/control the packet processing engine. IXF1002 has 2 full duplex Gbytes MAC interfaces. The speed of data collection can reach 5.12Gbps. IXF440 has 8 full duplex 10/100M MAC interface. IXF1002 and IXF440 are connected with IXP1200 by a IX bus. They transmit the collected data packets to network processor through the IX bus.

5 Performance Simulation and Test of System

For researcher and developer about information audit system, they usually test performance of every kind of information audit system, can help themselves understand status that technique have developed and these shortage, thereby would study those key and difficult technique problem weightily; Moreover, for information audit system user, they can choose the product that may suit for them via by testing performance of information audit system.

5.1 Simulation of Network Traffic

It's objective and complete for information audit system's testing results no other than using the real network traffic. The packets created by general network traffic simulation don't consider the packets' contents at all, which will lead lots of misinformation in the information audit system. To solve this problem, the network traffic simulation in the information audit system experiment environment must simulate different protocol. By analyzing the real network traffic in different time segments and then calculating, we will get the protocol's traffic probability distribution respectively. Based on this model, we design a stream generator which simulate high speed stream (total stream > 1000gbps), the realization please see another thesis of our team.

5.2 Design of Test and Analysis of Result

The two standard performance of evaluating text categorization system is Precision and integrity. Precision is the inosculate ratio of manual categorization results with all judged text. Recall is the inosculate ratio of text in categorization system with text of manual categorization result.

We collect 600 texts as training swatch volumes in Internet, including violence, eroticism, reaction and mediocrity. There are 500 texts related with mediocrity topic, 45 texts with violence topic, 35 texts with eroticism topic and 20 texts with reaction topic. We divide all texts into 4 groups, select 100 texts as training swatch randomly, repeat 5 times, take the average value, and then take weighted average according to all sorts of swatches. To avoid chanciness of test, it should recombine training swatch volume after testing categorization one time.

From test result Fig.1 and Fig.2, we know that the Precision and Recall will be increase as importing loss gene, and have better performance compare to traditional Bayes categorization algorithm.

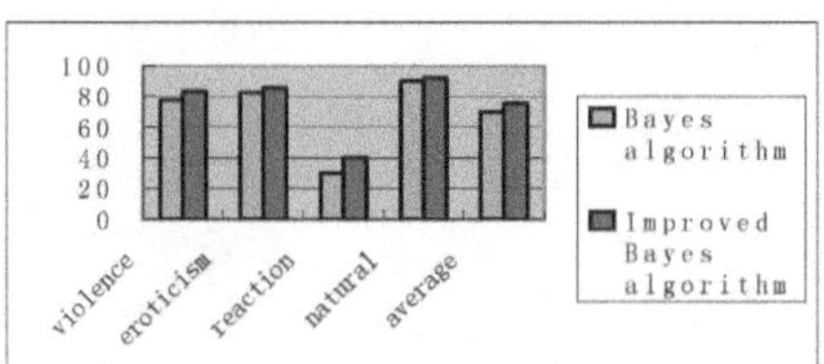

Fig. 1. Precision

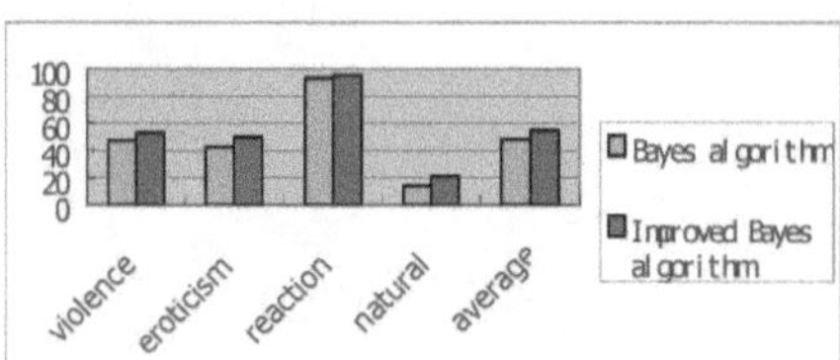

Fig. 2. Recall

6 Conclusion

Based on text information filtering technique exists itself in obvious limitation: some badness information providers transfer their badness information which are embedded to another image file or formed directly as image file, in order to avoid audit of network information audit system. Along with the development of multimedia technology and obviously advance of network bandwidth, image and video information increase more and more in the Internet. Pictures added newly to the Internet each year have exceeded 80 billion pages in which there have respectable harmful information. A research in Carnegie Mellon University shows that there has 83.5% picture information contain pornographic content stored in USENET newsgroup. It is a non-disputed fact that there has a great deal of badness information spread in the Internet. Thereby, it is very necessary to audit image content in the network. There need us to take into the research hard.

References

1. Huang. Yangcheng, Chen Ying, Li Shenglei, et al. Research on network secure auditing system using distributed agents[C]. *IEEE Region 10 Annual International Conference,* 2002:391-395
2. Guenther, Kim. Conducting an information audit on your intranet[J]. *Journal of Research and Practice in Information Technology,* 2002, 34(1):47-64
3. Yu Fei, Hunag Huang, Xu Cheng, et al. Badness Information Audit Based on Image Character Filtering, *ISPA Workshops 2005,* LNCS 3759,2005:647-656
4. Cohen W W,Singer Y. Context-sensitive learning methods for text categorization[C] *In: Proc of the 19th Int'l ACM SIGIR Conf on research and development in information Retrieval. Zurich,*1996,307-315
5. Wu Xiu-Qing The organization of Web Pages Based on Bayes Algorithm[J]. Computer Enginerring,2000,03:6-7
6. Lin Hong-fei. The Mechanism of Text Title Classif Ication Based on Exam Ples[J]. *Computer Research and Development*,2001,38(9):1132-1136
7. Sun Jian□Wang Wei□Zhong Yi-xin. Automatic Text Categorization Based on K-Nearest Neighbor[J]. *Journalof Beijing Univeersity of Posts and Telecommunications*.2001,24(1):42-46
8. Yan Mao-song. The Project of Venture Decision based on Bayes[M]. *Tsinghua University Press* ,1998
9. Fei Yu, Zhu Miaoliang, Yufeng Chen, et al. An Intrusion Alarming System Based on Self-Similarity of Network Traffic[J]. *Wuhan University Journal of Natural Sciences,* 2005, 23(1):169-173

Distortion Analysis of Component Composition and Web Service Composition

Min Song, Changsong Sun, and Liping Qu

College of Computer Science and Technology, Harbin Engineering University, Harbin, Heilongjiang Province 150001, China
soongmin04@163.com,
{sunchangsong, quliping}@hrbeu.edu.cn

Abstract. This paper discusses the consistency of component composition and Web service composition, therefore all kinds of distortions during component composition are defined and analyzed, and then some distortion cases are discussed, and from the view of the semantic of function behavior qualitative analysis is conducted of the possible distortion cases that several composition modes may lead to, in order to evaluate the system distortion and provide a evaluate model for distortion testing.

1 Introduction

With the development of component technology, internet technology, Web service technology and grid technology, the formation of the open network application and the idea of "software as service" will certainly cause the main form, running, producing and using pattern of the software system to arise great change[1]. Up till now, the way of software development is shifting from Function-Oriented to Service-Oriented, Flowing-Oriented method; from module-based to component (service)-based method [2]. And, all the service-oriented, component-based development methods are the service provided by independent components or COTS from different developers which form software application system thought dynamic composition, gradually stableness. This method can effectively support the software reuse in the network environment, and has become the important research in software industry.

However, this method also has some faults. Firstly, because of the separation of the software (component) developer and its user, the component developer cannot know the using environment of components completely, while the component user cannot understand the details of the internal implementation [3]; secondly, the software architecture, function of system decompose integration method and using environment and so on that components depended on during the development phase may be totally different from their using phase. Although the component has been described in detail by the developer, the combination between component (service), that is the components software system is not necessarily the best, thus resulting in some system error --- distortion, when the component composition or service composition form the application system. The purpose of this paper is to research the distortions of component composition, by first introducing the component composition and Web service

H.T. Shen et al. (Eds.): APWeb 2006, Workshops LNCS 3842, pp. 877 – 884, 2006.

composition. Web service is viewed as software development component-based on Internet, and this paper conducts qualitative analysis of the possible component distortions that may appear during component composition based on the method of component and Web service composition.

2 Composition of Component and Web Service

The main purpose of component development is reuse. When a new system in the same domain is developed, it can determine a newly-applied requirement regulation based on domain model, and then select suitable system architecture. Based on this, components are selected and composed, thus forming new application system. Composition of component is the process that connects, configures and composes unit components to form component or system that has stronger function, and is the operation in which unit component becomes in harmony with the environment of component. Composition of component is the core technology of component-based development which researches the component composition mechanism based on component model. Components will form application system and realize its reuse value only after they are composed. The essence of component composition is to establish correlation between components, and based on this correlation to coordinate their functional behavior and organize them into an organic entity. Through the interface or connector, the component matches, coordinates and composes the function requirement and service of the component and others , thus shaping the integrated function and service with new, larger granularity, supporting the reasoning of the attributes and behavior of integration function and service, and determining the effect that integration function and service have on the system.

Web service is one of the composite service-oriented architecture distributed computing technology [4], which provides an idea of service supply and consumption, therefore the provider can publish the service that can realize special task, and the consumers of the service can select and buy different kinds of service base on service requirement, and integrate the basic service from different providers, platforms and systems in order to realize the applied system of the complex service system. In the recent years, theory and technology in the field of Web service have made rapid progress in every aspect, and composition of Web service is one of the key research goals. Composition of Web service is the elementary service communicate and cooperate with each other so as to realize the composition service function of larger granularity; developer can resolve the complex problems by effectively uniting the Web service of various kinds of functions[5]. Complex Web service consists of elementary service, and service consists of service component. Compared with the service component, service can be quoted by the external users[6], however, the service component encapsulation corresponding service functions and appropriate data, thus making them relatively independent, and their attributes include the information of the component function description and operation series, the operational limitation and dependence information among the components. Dynamic Web service composition means the process that when dynamic establishes a new service that can satisfy specific application needs from a series of service components[7]. Therefore, from the procedure and result of Web service composition, Web service composition agrees with components composition. From the aspect of software reuse, when Web service is viewed as reusable software composition entity, Web service composition can also be viewed as the software development component -based on the Internet[8]. Therefore, during the process of distortion study, this paper will view Web service composition as component composition.

3 Distortion Analysis of Component Composition

3.1 Several Relevant Definitions

According to the performance of components during the testing, the distortions of component during the process of composition mainly include function distortion and performance distortion. This paper discusses the function distortion, especially implicit distortion, giving some relevant definitions about component distortion firstly.

Definition 1. Function distortion refers to the disagreement between the work ability that software entity is expected to perform and the work ability that can be really achieved. According to the forms of component at different stage, component distortion can be divided into explicit distortion and implicit distortion.

Definition 2. Explicit distortion refers to the function that what the component unit (single component) shows in testing incompatible with the component requirement. For the software testing, explicit distortion can be thought of as function bug.

Definition 3. Implicit distortion refers to the situation that the component unit does not show any function distortion in testing, but when two or more components that do not have explicit distortion form into larger component or software system, the function that shows does not totally match the anticipated function.

As far as the current component development or component testing is concerned, explicit distortion is easy to be tested, and its characteristics are very obvious, but implicit distortion is not easy to be triggered or appear in the component unit testing. When two components are composed, distortion may not appear, while when component No. n ($n > 2$) is composed distortion appears (here it is called model distortion, or system distortion). And this phenomenon can be called distortion accumulation or manifestation of distortion. But it is very difficult to locate the position (component) where the system distortion occurs.

3.2 The Analysis of Component Compose Behavior

During component composition, functionally there will be the following situations:

1. Component A and component B merge into component C, and the function of component C is equal to that of component A and component B combined, is given by func(C)= func(A)+ func(B);

2. Component A and component B merge into component C, and the function of component C is bigger than that of component A and component B combined. As is shown in Fig. 1, the shadowy part is the overlapping function of A and B, and the part with horizontal lines is the function that A and B both have but component C does not need. That is, the function realized by component C is bigger than the expected

function of component C, and it is called function redundancy, is given by func(C)> func(A)+ func(B);

3. Component A and component B merge into component C, and the function of component C is smaller than that of component A and component B combined. As is shown in Fig. 2, the dotted frame part is the absent function, and the shadowy part is the overlapping function. That is, the function realized by component C is smaller than the expected function of component C, and it is also called function omission, is given by func(C)<func(A)+ func(B).

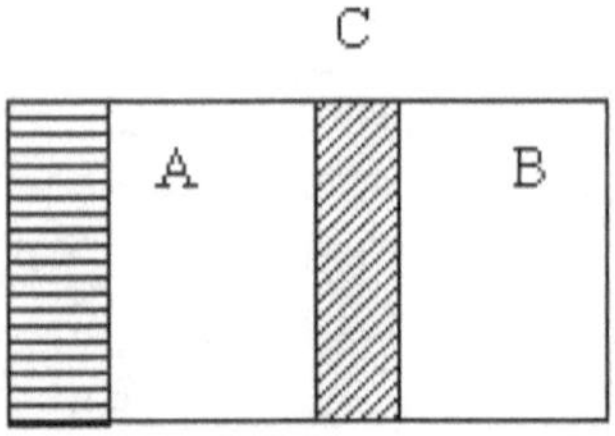

Fig. 1. Component function redundancy

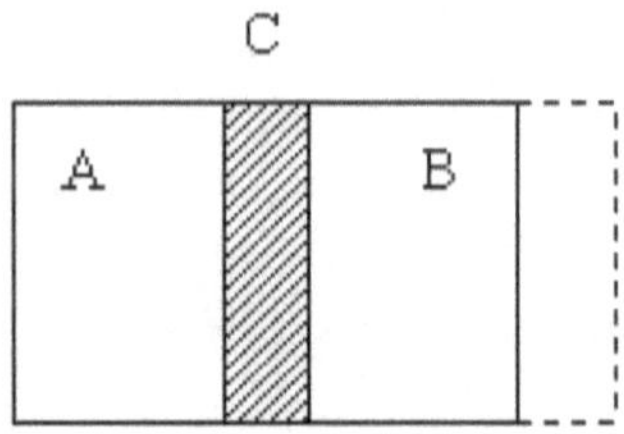

Fig. 2. Component function omission

For the component composition, the most ideal case is the situation described in No.1, but during the process of component composition, redundancy of function or omission of function always occurs, or both cases exist, which are all considered function distortion.

3.3 Component Composition Mechanism and Distortion Analysis

When a programmer is developing components and testing the units, explicit distortion is easy to be detected and corrected, but the component implicit distortion is really difficult to be discovered during the phase of component developing and unit testing, while not until the process of component composition (integral testing) will the component distortion (implicit distortion) gradually appear. Accordingly, in order to discover implicit distortion in the early phase of the development, which is of considerable significance to the schedule, cost and maintenance of the software development, the research on the distortion in this paper mainly aims at the implicit distortion.

To facilitate the research on component distortion, this paper introduces the following definitions:

Definition 4. Function behavior semantics($func_{sem}$) : It is the abstract form and description of the component function behavior, and it is composed of the definition space set, the domain space set and the environment space set of function behavior, is given by:

$$func_{sem} = \Omega_{def} \times \Omega_{dom} \times \Omega_{env}$$

where, Ω_{def} : definition space, means the set of the characteristics and their relationship of the component semantics.

Ω_{dom} : domain space, means the set of the characteristics and their relationship of the domain knowledge.

Ω_{env} : environment space, means the set of the characteristics and their relationship of the semantics restriction.[9]

Definition 5. Unit function behavior semantics ($func_{sem}{}^{cond}$): that is, the function behavior semantics has definite boundary, and the component implementation of this semantics is to accomplish the components of specified function, is given by:

$$func_{sem}{}^{cond} = \Omega_{def'} \times \Omega_{dom'} \times \Omega_{env'}$$

where: $\Omega_{def'} \subset \Omega_{def}$, $\Omega_{dom'} \subset \Omega_{dom}$, $\Omega_{env'} \subset \Omega_{env}$.

Definition 6. Atom function behavior semantics ($func_{sem}{}^{atom}$): It is the semantics that can no longer be divided. It is composed of a definition space set element $\Omega_{def''}$, a domain space set element $\Omega_{dom''}$, and an environment space set element $\Omega_{env''}$, is given by:

$$func_{sem}{}^{atom} = \Omega_{def''} \times \Omega_{dom''} \times \Omega_{env''}$$

where: $\Omega_{def''} \in \Omega_{def'}$, $\Omega_{dom''} \in \Omega_{dom'}$, $\Omega_{env''} \in \Omega_{env'}$.

Based on the above-mentioned definitions, the composition of atom function behavior forms unit function behavior, the integration of unit function behavior forms the component function behavior, composed component forms software system, the integration of component behavior forms the software that can fulfill a certain function. Therefore, in this sense, component composition and function integration are consistent.

Definition 7. Function behavior integration operation: Function behavior integration operation is the "action" taken to integrally compose the atom function behavior or unit function behavior as a larger granularity function behavior or function system.

According to the degree of complexity of component function behavior integration operation, it can be divided into an operation of more than two levels; one is atom integration operation, and the other is unit integration mode. Atom integration operation cannot be further divided, and its integration object is the realization method and interface of function. Unit integration mode is the integration operation that aims at atom function behavior or unit function behavior operation.

From the view of integration pattern, atom integration operation can be divided into two major types - "and" operation and "or" operation. Component is the object of system composition, and the common component composition is composed by the connectors. Therefore, based on the document [10], the implicit distortion of several kinds of composition methods is analyzed. During the process, it is supposed that the explicit distortion of every atom component has been rectified in the process of the component development.

1. The distortion analysis of component connection composition, concurrent composition and sequence composition

Connect component A with B, thus composing component C. The function behavior of component C is the parallel running of every component function behavior, while it is coordinated and restricted by connector at the same time. Components A and B are composed component C through parallel composition mechanism, and the function behavior of C is running the function behavior of A and B in parallel. Components A and B are composed component C through sequence composition mechanism, and the function behavior of C is to run function behavior A firstly, and then run function behavior B.

During the component connect composition, concurrent composition and sequence composition, the function behavior of component C is the operation result of component A's and component B's behavior "and". The function match requires the following relationship:

$$C(\Omega_{def}) = A(\Omega_{def}) \cup B(\Omega_{def})$$
$$C(\Omega_{dom}) = A(\Omega_{dom}) \cup B(\Omega_{dom})$$
$$C_{env}(x) = A_{env}(x) \wedge B_{env}(x), \text{ where, } x \in \Omega_{env}.$$

If $C(\Omega_{def}) \subset (A(\Omega_{def}) \cup B(\Omega_{def}))$, or $C(\Omega_{dom}) \subset (A(\Omega_{dom}) \cup B(\Omega_{dom}))$, or $C_{env}(x) \neq A_{env}(x) \wedge B_{env}(x)$, then it is likely that function absence (distortion) would emerge; if $(A(\Omega_{def}) \cup B(\Omega_{def})) \subset C(\Omega_{def})$ or $(A(\Omega_{dom}) \cup B(\Omega_{dom})) \subset C(\Omega_{dom})$, then function redundancy may appear.

2. The distortion analysis of component select composition

Component A and B select composition component C, the function behavior of C is to execute the function of A or B based on the exterior environment requirement. Select composition to get a more powerful composite component, and this composite component can provide the function of the two components, but within a certain period of time, only one of those can be executed.

During the component select composition, the function behavior of component C is the result of the operation of component A's and component B's behavior "or". The function match requires the following relationship:

$$C(\Omega_{def}) = A(\Omega_{def}) \cup B(\Omega_{def})$$
$$C(\Omega_{dom}) = A(\Omega_{dom}) \cup B(\Omega_{dom})$$
$$C_{env}(x) = \neg (A_{env}(x) \rightleftarrows B_{env}(x)) \text{ , where, } x \in \Omega_{env}.$$

From the formula mentioned above, because the components A and B can only execute one of them at a certain time, then component C does not produce function distortion.

3. The distortion analysis of component duplicate composition

Component A duplicate as component C, the function behavior of component C is collateral execution n of component A function behavior. The duplicate composition can get a more powerful complex component, and it provides the same type of components collateral execution at the same time, which is used to increase the performance or reliability.

During the process of component duplicate composition, the function behavior of component C is the result of the behavior "or" operation of n component. The function match requires the following relationship:

$$C(\Omega_{def}) = A(\Omega_{def})$$
$$C(\Omega_{dom}) = A(\Omega_{dom})$$
$$C_{env}(x) = A_{env}(x), \text{ where, } x \in \Omega_{env}.$$

From the formula mentioned above, we can see that if component A does not produce function distortion, then component C does not produce function distortion either.

4. The distortion analysis of component interruption composition
Component A and B interruption composition component C, and the function behavior of component C is to execute the function behavior of component A first; once component B begins to work, then interrupt the function behavior of A, and then execute B. Interruption composition is used to deal with fault or recovery.

During the component interrupt composition, the function behavior of component C is the operation result of component A's and component B's behavior "and". The function match requires the following relationship:

$$C(\Omega_{def}) = A(\Omega_{def}) \cup B(\Omega_{def})$$
$$C(\Omega_{dom}) = A(\Omega_{dom}) \cup B(\Omega_{dom})$$
$$C_{env}(x) = (A_{env}(x) \wedge \neg B_{env}(x)) \vee (\neg A_{env}(x) \wedge B_{env}(x)), \text{where, } x \in \Omega_{env}.$$

If $C(\Omega_{def}) \subset (A(\Omega_{def}) \cup B(\Omega_{def}))$ or $C(\Omega_{dom}) \subset (A(\Omega_{dom}) \cup B(\Omega_{dom}))$, or $C_{env}(x) \neq (A_{env}(x) \wedge \neg B_{env}(x)) \vee (\neg A_{env}(x) \wedge B_{env}(x))$, then it is likely that function absence (distortion) would emerge; if $(A(\Omega_{def}) \cup B(\Omega_{def})) \subset C(\Omega_{def})$ or $(A(\Omega_{dom}) \cup B(\Omega_{dom})) \subset C(\Omega_{dom})$, then function redundancy may appear.

Based on the component composition form, the paper carries out the qualitative analysis of whether component distortion will appear during the component composition process, in order to discover and prevent distortion in the earliest development phase, especially to prevent the emergence of implicit distortion, so as to improve the quality of software development, and reduce the cost of development and maintenance.

4 Summary

Web service is a self-contain, self-describe, loose-coupling soft component that can be described and published, discovered and transferred via the network[11]. The Web service combines the virtue of with component-oriented method and Web technology, Essentially, the Web service and component composition agree with each other, and defines the related concepts of component composition distortion and analyzes several cases of distortion. Through analyzing the 6 composition methods of atom composition set of operation, this paper supplies the theoretical basis of the qualitative analysis of whether component distortion appears during the process of component composition.

The research of Web service composition and component composition still remains in the developmental stage. To further probe into this field, we can carry out the following research: the research on the algorithm of component's distortion degree; how the component distortion degree is restricted; the locating and the improvement of the component distortion.

References

[1] Hu Jianqiang, Zou Peng, Wang Huaimin, Zhou Bin. Research on Web service description language QWSDL and service matching model. Chinese Journal of Computer, Vol.28.(2005): 505-513

[2] Xu Gang, Huang Tao, Liu Shaohua, Ye Dan. Survey on the core techniques of distributed application integration Chinese Journal of Computer, Vol.28.(2005):433-444

[3] Mao Xiaoguang, Deng Yongjing. A general model for component-based software reliability. Journal of Software, Vol.15.(2004):27-32

[4] Yang Shengwen, Shi Meilin. A model for Web service discovery with Qos constraints. Chinese Journal of Computer, Vol.28.(2005):589-594

[5] Liao Jun, Tan Hao, Liu Jinde. Describing and Verifying Web service using Pi-Calculus. Chinese Journal of Computer, Vol.28.(2005): 635-643

[6] Tosic V, Mennie D, Pagurek B. Dynamic service composition and its applicability to business software systems. Workshop on Object-Oriented Business Solutions (WOOBS 2001), 2001

[7] Yue Kun, Wang Xiaoling, Zhou Aoying. Underlying techniques for Web services: A survey. Journal of software, Wol.15.3.(2004): 428-442

[8] Zhao Junfeng, Xie Bing, Zhang Lu, Yang Fuqing. A Web services composition method supporting domain feature. Chinese Journal of Computer, Vol.15.(2005):731-738

[9] Jia Yu, Gu Yuqing. Domain Feature Space-Based Component Semantics Express Method Journal of Software, Vol.13. (2002): 311-316

[10] Ren Hongmin, Qian Leqiu. Research on Component Composition and Its Formal Reasoning . Journal of Software , Vol.14.(2003): 1066-1074

[11] Wang Zhijian, Fei Yukui, Lou Yuanqing. Component technology and application. Science Press (2005)

A Semantic Web Approach to "Request for Quote" in E-Commerce

Wen-ying Guo[1,2], De-ren Chen[1], and Xiao-lin Zheng[1]

[1] College of Computer Science, Zhejiang University,
Hangzhou, 310027, China
gwy@hz.cn
[2] College of Computer & Information Engineering,
Zhejiang Gongshang University, Hangzhou,
310035, China
drchen@zj.edu.cn, xlzheng@cs.zju.edu.cn

Abstract. It is challenge for an interoperable multi-agent system (MAS) to understand the communications among software agents. With the standardization of ontology, the semantic Web services can make the communication more flexible and automated. This paper presents an ontology-based, runtime semantic solution for solving the interacting problem between two agents. The paper demonstrates how to employ the OWL description and service ontology to a Request for Quote (RFQ) scenario, and how to develop a methodology for runtime semantics.

Keywords: Semantic, matchmaking, ontology, RFQ.

1 Introduction

Semantic Web has great potentials in the E-commerce. Current online shopping by a key word searching is tedious and time consuming. The searching results strongly rely on no descriptive product name and picture. A keyword search often results in large amounts of irrelevant information. Attentions have been pain to look for an alternative solution: semantic Web services [1], with an aim at utilizing resources available at more accessible and automated agents. According to a semantic specification in ontology, a commercial infrastructure can be featured for a better communication between buyer and seller through agent services.

Communication among software agents has long been recognized as a challenge to interoperable multi-agent systems (MAS). A simplest way to achieve such communication is to require all agents use common vocabularies. Either this approach or inter-ontology translation is impractical. The recent solution to this problem is to use semantic Web initiated by W3C [2, 3], the DARPA Agent Markup Language Project [4], and EU's Information Science and Technology Program [5]. A specification called DAML+O1L (Ontology Inference Layer) was created as a standard, ontology-based language for definition, manipulation, and reasoning [11]. Current solutions for agent interaction problems as outlined as follows.

H.T. Shen et al. (Eds.): APWeb 2006, LNCS 3842, pp. 885 – 888, 2006.

One is that agents share with same knowledge with vocabularies in a single base ontology. Such solution is more general and stable. They can be constructed in some ontology specification languages [6] or in some other forms (e.g., WordNet, a natural language-based taxonomy [7]). The other is that agents use different ontology defined on top of the base ontology, which allows each agent to develop its own inherited vocabularies. Usually, the agent-specific ontology is changed more frequently than the base ontology [8]. We intend to provide an alternative different from the above two. Instead, we develop a runtime agent interaction method that is based on the second solution; but has more flexibilities.

In this paper, we propose a new runtime semantic solution for heterogeneous agents. It is organized as follows: Section 2 reviews related work in the study of agent interaction. Section 3 describes RFQ (Request for Quote) scenario. Section 4 shows our framework of RFQ ontology. Section 5 addresses the deployment of our RFQ ontology to the matchmaking algorithms, and demonstrates the performance analysis. Section 6 gives a conclusion and outline of future works.

2 RFQ (Request for Quote) Scenario

Considering the E-Commerce scenario of RFQ [9], a buyer agent broadcasts its requirements to all agents. Those agents who are able to meet the demand reply with their services with product information. For example, let A1 the shirt wholesaler, and A2 the shirt vendor. They share a common ontology ONT-0, which gives details for shirt parameter such as color, size and texture. Each has its own specialized ontology. ONT-1 defines semantics of products to order for A1, while ONT-2 defines items in the product catalog for A2 based on its own system (see Figure 1).

During negotiation, A1 sends a RFQ to A2 a message "shirt_for_younger", a term defined in ONT-1. Before A2 determines a quote, it needs to understand what A1 means and if there exits a semantically similar term in its catalog as defined in ONT-2. The process can be accomplished by identifying the meaning of terms defined in different ontology and matching these terms semantically. Therefore, we give the following class definition in OWL

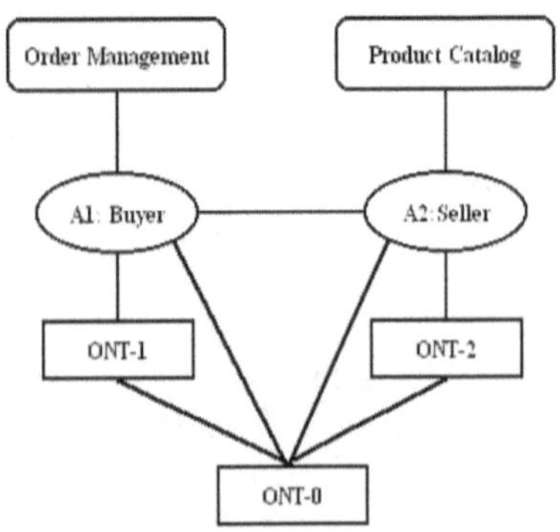

Fig. 1. RFQ scenario involving two agents

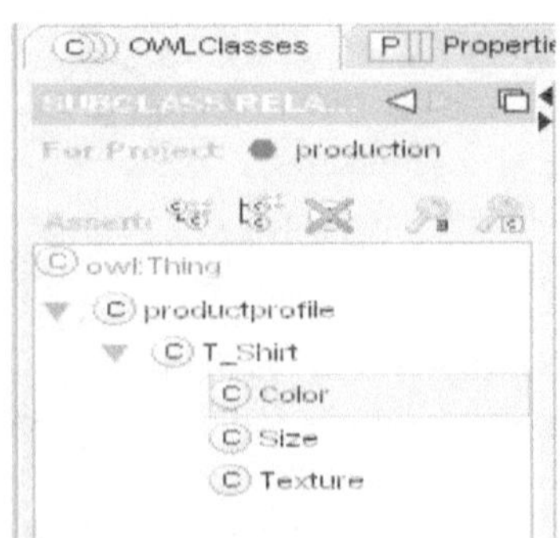

Fig. 2. Define the T-Shirt classes and the its class hierarchy

```
<?xml version="1.0"?>
<rdf:RDF xmlns:rdf=
"http://www.w3.org/1999/02/22-rdf-syntax-ns#"
    xmlns:rdfs="http://www.w3.org/2000/01/rdf-schema#"
    xmlns:owl="http://www.w3.org/2002/07/owl#"
    xmlns="http://www.owl-ontologies.com/unnamed.owl#"
  xml:base="http://www.owl-ontologies.com/unnamed.owl">
  <owl:Ontology rdf:about=""/><owl:Class rdf:ID="Size">
    <rdfs:subClassOf><owl:Class rdf:ID="T_Shirt"/>
    </rdfs:subClassOf></owl:Class>
  <owl:Class rdf:ID="Texture"><rdfs:subClassOf>
      <owl:Class rdf:about="#T_Shirt"/></rdfs:subClassOf>
  </owl:Class>
  <owl:Class rdf:ID="Color"><rdfs:subClassOf>
      <owl:Class rdf:about="#T_Shirt"/></rdfs:subClassOf>
  </owl:Class><owl:Class rdf:ID="productprofile"/>
  <owl:Class rdf:about="#T_Shirt">
    <rdfs:subClassOf rdf:resource="#productprofile"/>
  </owl:Class>
  <owl:ObjectProperty rdf:ID="isBlueColor"/>
  <owl:ObjectProperty rdf:ID="isCottonTexture"/>
  <owl:ObjectProperty rdf:ID="hasName"/>
  <owl:ObjectProperty rdf:ID="is40Size"/>
  <Size rdf:ID="S40"/>
  <Texture rdf:ID="Cotton"/><Size rdf:ID="S30"/>
  <Texture rdf:ID="Silk"/><Color rdf:ID="Red"/>
   <Color rdf:ID="Blue"/><Color rdf:ID="green"/>
  <Size rdf:ID="S50"/></rdf:RDF>
```


3 Matchmaking Algorithms and Performance Analysis

Since A2 only understands ONT-0 and ONT-2, but not the "shirt_for_younger" from A1's RFQ, it asks A1 by using agent communication language. After obtaining the description of the term from different ontology, A2 starts its matchmaking process.

The process of matchmaking results in a buyer who has a list of potential trade partners, each with an associated partially specified service description. This description defines the set of possible services interested to the buyer. The following is the demonstration about how to implement the RFQ case.

The extended "shirt-for-younger" in a semantic querying provides a rich information to A2. However, in order to let A2 truly understand this concept, it is necessary to map or re-classify this description into one or more concepts defined in its own ontology ONT-2. This can be accomplished by introducing different ontology likely to match. All partially matched target concepts are considered as candidate maps of the source concept. If the best candidate is found, a quote is generated by A2 and then sent to A1. Otherwise, additional steps may be needed.

Using ns1 and ns2 as namespaces for ontology ONT-1 and ONT-2, we programmed in Protégé project. Figure 3 and 4 show the class definitions and its hierarchy in order management (ONT-1) and running reasoning under RacerPro respectively.

Let α the set of all agents. Given query Q, the matchmaking algorithm returns the set of agents that are compatible matches(Q): matches(Q) = $\{A \in / \alpha \text{ compatible}(A, Q)\}$.

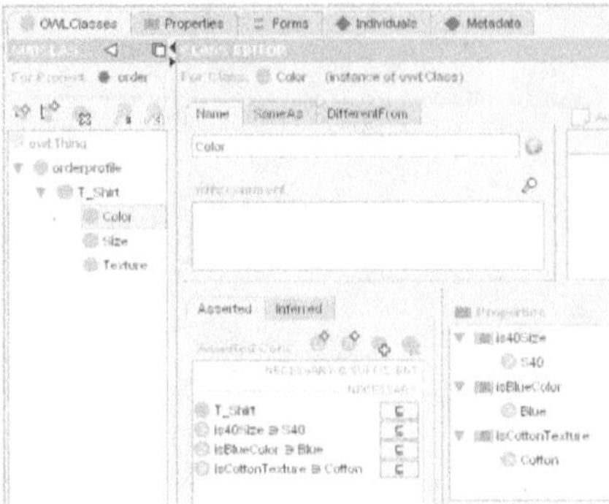

Fig. 3. Class definition and its hierarchy in ONT-1

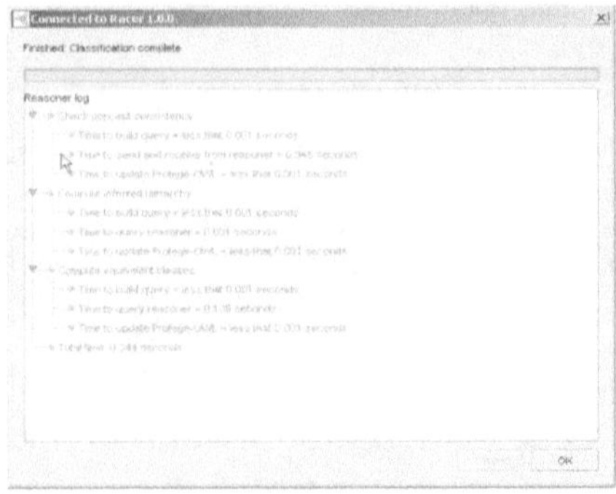

Fig. 4. Running reasoning under RacerPro

Two descriptions are compatible if their intersection is satisfied: for above RFQ, the query from the buyer = (product profile(items$\sqcap$hasname.{T-shirt} $\sqcap$Color.{blue} $\sqcap$Size.{40} $\sqcap$texture.{cottontexture})). The intersection of the query with the provider is satisfied. Finally, matchmaking$\in$matches(Query) in RacerPro.

4 Conclusions and Future Work

This paper develops an algorithm for runtime agent interaction, setting up our ontology in protégé 3.0 and run it in RacerPro. The only concern is that a service is represented by input and output properties of the service profile. In the future, we will work on e-commerce interactions, such as negotiation, proposals, and agreements.

References

1. Domingue J., Stutt A., Martins M., and Tan J., Petursson H., and Motta E.: Supporting Online Shopping through a Combination of Ontologies and Interface Metaphors. Int. J. Human-Computer Studies 59 (2003) 699–723
2. Bemers-Lee, T: What the Semantic Web Can Represent. http://www.w3.org/ DesignIssues/ RDFnot.html (1998)
3. Semantic Web page: http://www.w3.org/2001/sw/
4. DAML Web page: http://www.daml.org/
5. OIL Web page: http://www.ontoknowledge.org/oil/
6. Farquhar, A., Fikes, R., and Rice, J.: The Ontolingua Server: a Tool for Collaborative Ontology Construction. Int. J. of Human-Computer Studies 46(6) (1997) 707-727
7. MacGregor, R.M: The Evolving Technology of Classification-based Knowledge Representation Systems. in Principles of Semantic Networks: Explorations in the Representation of Knowledge, J. Sowa (ed.), Morgan Kaufmann (1991)
8. Weinstein, P. and Birmingham, W.P: Comparing Concepts in Differentiated Ontologies. In Proceedings of the 12th Workshop on Knowledge Acquisition, Modeling and Management (KAW'99)
9. Peng Y., Zou Y., Luan X., Ivezic N., Gruninger M., and Jones A.: Semantic Resolution for e-Commerce. Proceedings of the Int. Conf. on Autonomous Agents, n3, (2002) 1037-1038

An Effective XML Filtering Method for High-Performance Publish/Subscribe System

Tong Wang, Da-Xin Liu, Wei Sun, and Wan-song Zhang

Department of Computer Science and Technology,
Harbin Engineering University, China
{Wangtong, daxinliu1, weisun1, wansongzh}@hrbeu.edu.cn

Abstract. During the process large-scale XPath queries against fast XML streams on Internet, a bottleneck occurs due to the lack of memory for filtering. This paper presents an effective automaton method to reduce the memory need by diminishing the tedious operators (such as "//" and "*") in XPath expressions. The method contains a product automata to convert XPath to the actual path; thus to reduce the complexity in search space. The proposed method was implemented in MFSA (**M**ulti- **F**inite **S**tates **A**utomata) system for filtering queries of subscribers. The empirical evidence shows its efficiency and stability when the scale of queries is large.

1 Introduction

XML becomes the de facto standard for data interchange on Internet. There exit many Web-based, high performance publish/subscribe systems, in which the entities of data must stream fast cross networks. Besides, these systems need a fast determination of user interests.

The challenge of XML-based publish/subscribe system is how to publish fast incoming streams of messages for subscribers with XPath queries. A XML filtering technique is needed. In the past, people used Finite State Automaton and SAX parser [1-4] to filter the XML data. Diao et al proposed YFilter technique [2], a extension of XFilter [1], to pre-compute multiple queries and combine them as a single NFA (Nondeterministic Finite Automaton). The drawback of theYFilter is that NFA has more state tracks, which influences the performance. Alternatively, deterministic, finite-transducers are more promising, since the whole procedure only requires have one state track [2]. However, for multiple XPath expressions (XPE), the DFA states converted from NFA grows very fast, which causes a bottleneck due to computer' memory lacks. For example, an ancestor-descendant operator "//" can possibly result in an exponential increase of the size of data with the structure of DFA [4]. In order to solve this problem, we offer an effective and optimal approach to diminish the unnecessary operators such as "*" and "//" within XPEs; thus reduce the search space consequently and improve the performance.

Different from YFilter [2] and XPush [3] methods, we utilized the constraints of DTD to remove the indeterminacy in a single XPE. We observed that the XML message streams in our application, unlike the document-oriented XML data used for

H.T. Shen et al. (Eds.): APWeb 2006, LNCS 3842, pp. 889 – 896, 2006.

document exchange, are almost data-oriented XML data which are well structured without recursive path, and have the DTD to validate the XML message. Most of the research extracts the information from DTD information and use the information as an index [5,6]. The extraction concurrently gives a time increase due to additional expense for indices. Since the space is deficient while processing high-volume XPEs, we abandoned the index techniques in our current work. Hartmut [7] concentrated on the horizontal information in DTD to optimize queries using automata. Inspired by Hartmut's work, we focused on the product automaton using DTD. Kim [8] also constructs a DTD Finite State Automaton for each regular expression respectively and obtains the Classifying Tree (CT) to reduce the search space. Instead, we constructed a holistic DTD automaton.

With the motivation for solving computational problems in search space, this paper introduces an effective and optimal method for XML filtering. Our method contains three components of contribution, mainly (1) a binary operation of automata is proposed for optimizing query plans by diminishing the ancestor-descendant "//"and "*"; (2) an efficient filtering scheme is applied in MFSA system; and (3) experiment testbeds is designed and implemented to shows the stability of performance in MFSA with large XPEs.

The reminder of the paper is organized as follows: the optimizing method in logical query is presented in Section 2. MFSA architecture and filter engine are depicted in Section 3. An evaluation of performance is given for discussion, followed by a conclusion section.

2 Logical Query Rewriting

XML can be viewed as a labeled-edge tree in nature [9] and same does XPath. XPath is composed of some regular path expressions, although a subset {/(child), //(descendant), [](branching), *(wildcard)} is commonly used for path navigation. Adding "/" and "*" for the flexibility to expressions, the indeterminacy of expressions makes the query more complex. In the following, after briefly reviewing DTD and its automaton, we define the product between XPE and DTD automatons at an aim to reduce unnecessary "//"and "*", followed by an analysis the complexity of the product automaton.

2.1 DTD and Automata

A DTD consists of a series of elements and attributes. Only the child relation of the context helps the navigation in a XML document. Therefore, the elemental numbers and sibling relations can be ignored. During the process of query deterministic rewriting, recursions in DTD constrain lead to an exponential increase of the states. In the present study only XML with non-recursive DTDs are considered. The recursive DTD refers to either the tree-like DTD or directed acyclic graph (DAG) DTD. A simple DTD can be defined as follows.

Definition 1 (Simple DTD). Simple DTD is upon two assumptions (1) the element cardinality, the sibling order, and the attributive values are ignored; (2) there are no recursions in DTD.

```
Algorithm DTD Automaton
Input: Simple DTD
Output: DTD automaton D(Q_d, Σ_d, δ_d, B_d, F_d)
1.Initial D to a null automata;
2.For each rule {m → n|p}
3.  replace{m → n|p} with {m → n; m → p};
4.For each rule {m → np}
5  replace{m → np} with {m → n; m → p};
6.For each rule {m → n}
7  { If m is NOT in Σ
8    then { Q_d = Q_d ∪ {state(m)}
9           Σ_d = Σ_d ∪ {m}
10          δ_d = δ_d ∪ {δ_d((state(m), n) = state(n))}}}
```

Fig. 1. Algorithm DTD Automaton

Figure 1 shows the construction of a holistic DTD automaton, where Σ is the set of nodes occurring in DTD; $m \rightarrow n$ is a rule expression for the children relation. Each node $n \in \Sigma$ corresponds to a state in the automaton, which is depicted as state (n). Since we have changed the "|" relation in the DTD definitions and the number of the nodes is ignored; the automaton we construct is a deterministic finite automaton.

2.2 Optimization by Product Automaton

Different from other product operation of automaton [10][11], we express the product automaton for XPEs as follows:

Definition 2 (product operation of automaton). given two automata: $M(Q_m, \Sigma_m, \delta_m, B_m, F_m), N(Q_n, \Sigma_n, \delta_n, B_n, F_n)$, we construct a new automaton product$(Q_p, \Sigma_p, \delta_p, B_p, F_p)$ of M and N, let $Q_p = Q_m \times Q_n$, $Q_p = F_m \times F_n$, $B_p = B_m \times B_n$, $\delta_p = \delta_m \times \delta_n$, where $\delta_m \times \delta_n = \{ f((q_{m1}, q_{n1}), e_p) \rightarrow (q_m, q_n) \mid f(q_{m1}, e_p) = q_m, f(q_{n1}, e_p) = q_n, e_p = e_m \cap e_n, (q_m, q_n) \subseteq Q_p,$ $e_m \in \Sigma_m, e_n \in \Sigma_n, e_p \in \Sigma_p, \}$ *written* Product =M $\otimes$ N.

The resulting automaton is composed of states labeled by the pairs of states: each state corresponding to each automaton. If a normal dot product without contains is used for a pair of states (q_m, q_n) (where $q_m \in Q_m, q_n \in Q_n$), there generates many invalid states. Therefore we chosen a pairs followed by a cross product like $\delta_m \times \delta_n$. Figure 2 shows the procedure to construct product automatons. Giving the initial states of P from line1 to 3, one can check the rules in line 5. The reptilian of executing line 6 to line 8 will terminate, until the pair states of line5 is no longer found.

During the optimization, the turning points (including root, branching nodes and leaves) in the XML tree are taken into special consideration. The path within the two turning points is defined as *turning path*. Compared with the Location Steps method depicted in [2], *turning path* is a much more efficient unit with a greater granularity in processing XPEs. The optimized logical query by the product automaton is demonstrated as follows.

Algorithm *Product Automaton*

Input: automaton M,N

Output: product of automaton P=M⊗N

1 Initial P to a null automaton;

2 $F_p = \{(f_m, f_n) \mid f_m \in F_m, f_n \in F_n\}$;

3 $B_p = \{(b_m, b_n) \mid b_m \in B_m, b_n \in B_n\}$;

4 do while

5 if $f((q_{m1}, q_{n1}), e_p) \to (q_m, q_n) \mid f(q_{m1}, e_p) = q_m, f(q_{n1}, e_p) = q_n, e_p = e_m \cap e_n, (q_m, q_n) \subseteq Q_p$

6 then { $\delta_p = \delta_p \cup f((q_{m1}, q_{n1}), e_p) \to (q_m, q_n)$;

7 $Q_p = Q_p \cup \{(q_m, q_n)\}$;

8 $\Sigma_p = \Sigma_p \cup \{a\}$; }

9 until the pair states of in line5 can't be found

Fig. 2. Algorithm of product automaton in optimal logical query

Given an XPath expression xp, XPath automaton X, and DTD automaton D, one can obtain the product $P_{X\otimes D}$=X⊗D. The turning path in xp between turning points t_1, and t_2 corresponds to the states in the automaton. Buneman et al. [12] presented and proved that a database DB conforms to a schema S, if a simulation from DB to S appears. If DB conforms to S and S is deterministic, there always exists a minimal simulation. Ignored the numeric constrains of the elements the proposed DTD is deterministic. The simulation takes place from the XPE to DTD constrains. In other words, the DTD can be viewed as a graph and any XPE is the sub-graph of DTD graph.

Turning points t_1 and t_2 in xp correspond the states x_1 , $x_2 \in X$, while x_1 and x_2 correspond to the state-pair set $p_1 :(x_1 , d_i) \subset P_{X\otimes D}$, $p_2 :(x_2 , d_j) \subset P_{X\otimes D}$, respectively, where $d_i, d_j \in D$. If there exists a reachable element sequence between t_1 and t_2, one can least find a simulation from p_1 to p_2 in the $P_{X\otimes D}$, or vice versa. Furthermore, because there is no other turning point between t_1 and t_2 corresponding to state sets p_1 and $p_2 \subset P_{X\otimes D}$, the disjunction of these deterministic paths from p_1 to p_2 is the optimizing logical query plan. The whole process is iterative in order to handle other *turning paths* in xp.

Example 1. Let DTD G be { $a \to y, y \to ctn \mid g, t \to ke, c \to f, n \to g$ }, given XPath expression xp= //g, what is the deterministic query path xp' ?

The xp is a regular path expression and the corresponding automaton is easily built; The DTD automaton is shown in Figure3. The $P_{X\otimes D}$ can be obtained using Algorithm *Product Automaton, where* Q_p ={ $(x_1,d_1),(x_1,d_3),(x_2,d_7)$ }. As discussed above, $x_1, x_2 \in Q_x$ correspond to the vertices (turning points) of xp, all the paths between p_1 : (x_1, d_1) and $p_2 :(x_2 , d_7)$ are actual deterministic paths being optimized. The deterministic path can be expressed as xp' =/y/n/g| /y/g.

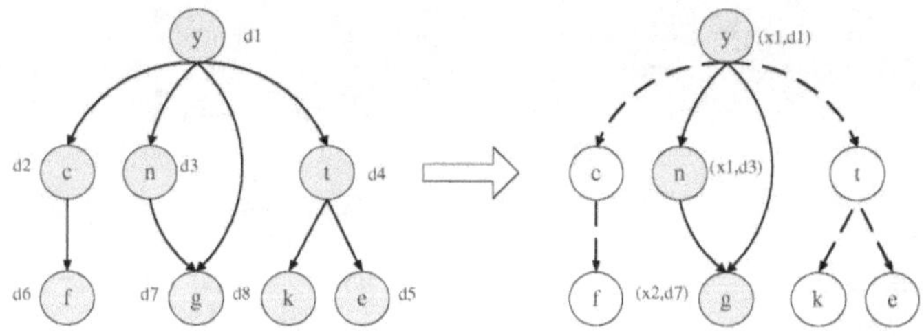

Fig. 3. DTD automaton and $P_{X \otimes D}$ of Example 1; the states of Q_p are filled in deeper color and the transitions are drawn with bold lines

The rewriting process consists of two steps: (1) the product and (2) the optimization. The states pairs of product automaton can be obtained by scanning the XPath and DTD. The deterministic paths between the *turning points* can then be obtained. The *Simple DTD* is only addressed hereby, because the process of product automaton is polynomial. Besides, the recursion in automata is also polynomial.

3 MFSA Architecture and Implementation

The MFSA (**M**ulti- **F**inite **S**tates **A**utomata) architecture (see Figure 4) has five components (1) the XPath parser for user profiles; (2) the DTD Parser to convert a non-recursive DTD to a simple DTD and leave the recursive one along;(3) an event-based parser SAX for incoming XML data; (4) the message factory for processing query results and send to the appropriate users; and (5) filter engine, the center of the system.

When a user profile comes, our system parses it into logical query expressions and rewritten by DTD constrains. The optimized XPEs are aggregated to build the CombFA (representing all these queries), which can evaluate XML publishing incoming message streams. The final query results are disseminated to the correlative subscribers by the message factory. During the processes of two XML message streams, CombFA can be reconstructed or updated (delete or add XPEs).

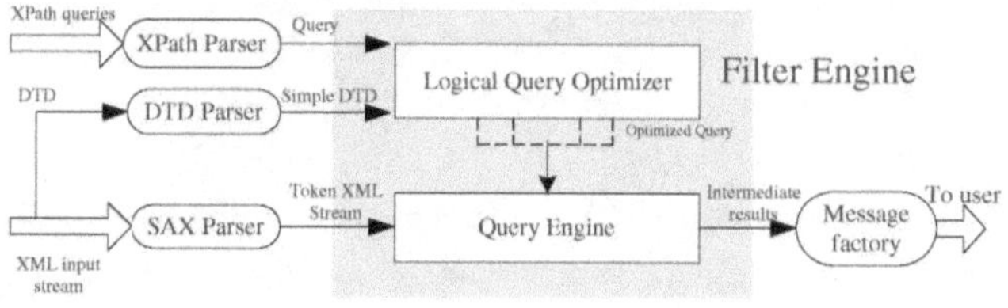

Fig. 4. MFSA Architecture

3.1 Query Engine

The query engine has two basic functions: merging the XPEs and evaluating the input XML streams. Firstly, we combine these optimized queries into one single finite automaton. To build a finite automaton is an incremental process according to location step [2] (abbr. step), like appending a string to a trie index. The cost of the construction is under polynomial time. We called the combined Finite Automaton CombFA, and supposed a new XPE xp to be appended into the CombFA. We constructed CombFA by traversing the CombFA step by step until both two conditions are satisfied. They are (1) the accepting state of xp is reached and (2) a state is reached when no transition matches the corresponding transition of xp. In the first case, we labeled the final state as an accepting state and added the query ID to the query set associated with the accepting state. In the second case, we created a new branch from the last state reached in the CombFA. This branch consists of the mismatched transition and the remainder steps of xp. Under the condition that the step in xp has branches, we considered the state corresponding to the transition current state and call this procedure recursively.

Now the CombFA as our query engine starts. The matching process is driven by a series of SAX events generated by XML stream message. Since the matching engine CombFA is a Deterministic Finite Automaton, the matching is an explicit process. Hereby, we only present the main idea: *start of document* event triggers a new XML stream. When *start of element* event comes to the engine, it triggers a state transition in the automaton. When *end of element* event occurs, the automaton backtracks to the previous state. A runtime stack is used to keep track of the current and previously visited states. Upon *end of document* event, the system checks if any accepting state are reached. The message factory processes the query results and disseminates the profiles to the end-users.

4 Experiments

We implemented MFSA using Java 1.4. All experiments were conducted on a workstation with 1.5GHz Intel P4 CPU and 512 MB memory. To compare with the YFilter method, we chosen the same SAX1.0 of Xerces toolkit as the YFilter did; We also implemented a simplified form in YFilter mehtod for comparison.

The dataset used in our experiments is the integrated collection of functionally annotated protein sequences available at the Georgetown Protein Information Resource (GPIR) (http://pir.georgetown.edu). The DTD of this is a tree containing 66 elements. We generated the synthetic XPath queries using a similar version of XPath generator like [4]. The modified generator can generate XPath queries based on our input parameters including number of queries n, with "*" occurring probability $w \in (0,1)$, and "//" occurring probability $d \in (0,1)$. We measured performance time as metrics. The time is defined as the one between *start of Document* and *end of Document* events of the XML stream.

Our experimental studies had two goals. One is to test the efficiency of the XPath deterministic optimization based on test sets of $D_{d=0.2,n=50000}$ and $D_{d=0.4,n=50000}$. The evaluations are performed based on the XML fragments of the Protein dataset using YFilter and MFSA, respectively. The results show the DFA gets ahead of NFA, while CombFA outperforms YFilter. Furthermore for $D_{d=0.2,n=50000}$ and $D_{d=0.4,n=50000}$, the

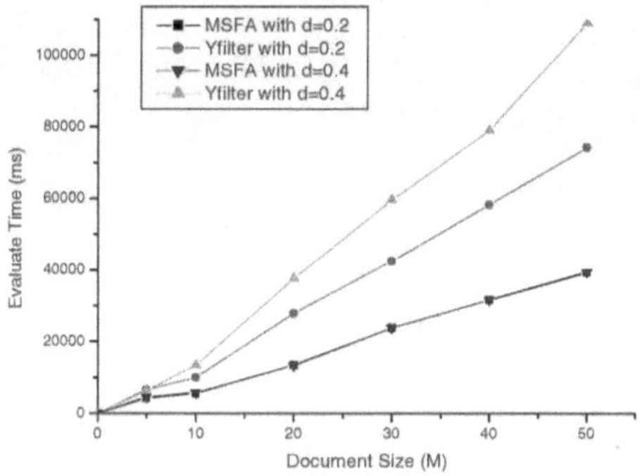

Fig. 5. Query rewriting test (n=50000) on functionally annotated protein sequences available at GPIR

MFSA shares the same respond time with YFilter. In contrast, YFilter does pay a large performance penalty if the uncertain operation "//" increases. However, the construction time of CombFA is a much longer than the one of NFA. It has less influence, because the construction is complexity polynomial, which can be performed at the intervals between two XML streams.

The other is to evaluate the performance if the number of XPEs is large. Our experiments show MFSA performs with a stable running time of 4500 ms (n=250,000) after a linear increase. It is due to the fact that CombFA with 250,000 XPEs already take the whole protein DTD, if and only if the simulation of the XPEs reaches the DTD graph (the space bound), as we discussed in Section 2.2. With the n increasing, the performance of MFSA is stable.

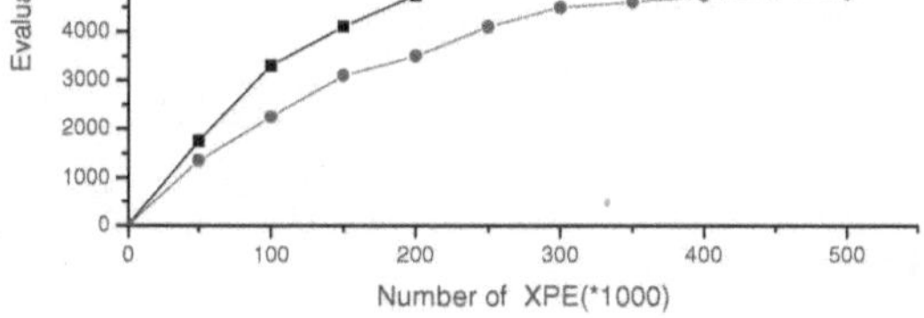

Fig. 6. Influence by XPE number (5M file)

5 Conclusions

This paper introduces an effective and novel optimizing method for converting XPath to actual deterministic path by a product automaton. This method is implemented on a

MFSA system for filtering large scale XPEs. The conducted experiments show that the proposed system is not sensitive to "//" of XPE; perfect performance can be achieved if the number of XPEs is large. The limit of the system is that it only fits for dataset with non-recursive DTD. We continue investigate the filtering of XML message of dataset with recursive DTD as our future research plan.

References

1. M. Altinel, M.J. Franklin: Efficient filtering of XML documents for selective dissemination of information. In Proceedings of VLDB Conference (2000)
2. Y. Diao, P. Fischer, M. Franklin, and R. To: YFilter: Efficient and scalable filtering of XML documents. In Proceedings of ICDE (2002)
3. Ashish Gupta, Dan Suciu, Stream Processing of XPath Queries with Predicates, In Proceeding of ACM SIGMOD Conference on Management of Data (2003)
4. T. J. Green, G..Miklau, M. Onizuka, D. Suciu: Processing XML streams with deterministic automata. In Proceedings of ICDT, Springer-Verlag, Berlin, Germany (2003)
5. Yannis Papakonstantinou, Victor Vianu: DTD Inference for Views of XML Data. In Proceedings of PODS (2000)
6. J. McHugh, J. Widom: Query optimization for XML, in Proceedings of the Conference on VLDB, Edinburgh, Scotland (1999)
7. Hartmut Liefke: Horizontal Query Optimization on Ordered Semistructured Data, in Proceedings of WebDB (1999)
8. T. S. Chung and H. J. Kim: Extracting Indexing Information from XML DTDs. Information Processing Letters, 81(2) (2002)
9. E. R. Harold and W.S. Means: XML in a Nutshell. O'Reilly (2001)
10. Christoph Koch: Optimizing Queries Using a Meta-level Database.CoRR cs. DB/0205060: 7 (2002)
11. O. Benjelloun, F. Dang Ngoc: Exchanging Intentional Xml Data. In Proceedings of the ACM Sigmod San Diego, California, USA (2003)
12. P. Buneman, S. Davidson, M. Fernandez, D. Suciu: Adding structure to unstructured data. In Proceedings of ICDT, Springer-Verlag, Deplhi, Greece (1997)

A New Method for the Design of Stateless Transitive Signature Schemes

Chunguang Ma[1,2], Peng Wu[2], and Guochang Gu[2]

[1] Information Security Research Center,
Harbin Engineering University, 150001 Harbin, China
[2] College of Computer Science and Technology,
Harbin Engineering University, 150001 Harbin, China
{Machunguang, Wupeng, Guguochang}@hrbeu.edu.cn

Abstract. Transitive signature is a new and useful cryptology tool for information security, Internet security, and e-commercial security. Most of the current transitive signature schemes are stateful, which increases the store cost and impacts the computing efficiency of signing algorithm. In this paper, a new practical method is introduced to transform the state transitive signature schemes to the stateless ones without loss their security. According to the proposed method, three concrete stateless transitive signature schemes based on Factoring and RSA are presented respectively. Under the moderate assumption, two schemes are secure against the adaptive chosen-message attacks in random oracle model.

Keywords: Cryptography, digital signature, stateless signature, transitive signature.

1 Introduction

Transitive Signature Scheme. The notation of transitive signature scheme, introduced by Micali and Rivest [1], is a way to digitally sign vertices and edges of a dynamically growing transitively closed graph, in order to guarantee two properties as

Compose-ability: Given the signatures of edges and, anyone can easily derive the signature of edge.

Transitively unforgeable: It is computationally hard for any adversary to forge the digital signature of any edge that is not in the transitive closure of a graph , even the adversary can request the legitimate signer to digitally sign any number of vertices and edges of in the adaptive chosen-message fashion.

Related Works. In 2002, Micali and Rivest [1] first introduced the concept of transitive signatures, and present a (non-trivial) transitive signature scheme, called MRTS, that was proven to be transitively un-forgeable under adaptive chose-message attack, assuming that the DLP is hard in an underlying prime-order group and assuming the security of an underlying standard signature scheme. They also presented a natural RSA-based transitive signature scheme indicating that even

H.T. Shen et al. (Eds.): APWeb 2006, LNCS 3842, pp. 897 – 904, 2006.

though the scheme seems secure, it could be proved that un-forgeable under non-adaptive chosen-message attacks may happen. However, a proof of unforgeable under adaptive chosen-message attacks was not available. Followed the works by Micali and Rivest [1], Bellare and Neven [2] presented a novel realizations of the transitive signature primitive called the FBTS-1 scheme. It was proven transitively un-forgeable under adaptive chosen-message attack assuming the factoring problem is difficult. However, the RSATS-1 scheme was proven transitively unforgeable under adaptive chosen-message attack, by realizing one-more RSA-inversion could not the problem when concerning the security of RSA based scheme. In their paper, the FBTS-2 and RSATS-2 were proposed which based on the hash-based modifications of FBTS-1 and RSATS-1, respectively, achieving shorter signature by eliminating the need for node certificates. The methods were proven to be more secure under the same assumptions in random oracle model. Zhu, Feng and Deng [3] addressed a problem related to transitive signature schemes, namely, how to construct a transitive signature scheme so that the representation structures of the signature scheme, nodes and edges in the graph can be implemented compactly. To solve this problem, they defined an algebraic structure for representation of vertices and edges in an undirected graph that is coincident with the one of signature schemes constructed latter. A realization of a transitive signature scheme based on DLP was then proposed to be proven as unforgeable under adaptive chosen-message attack. The concept of transitive signature can be extended for generality; namely the signature schemes that admit forgery of signatures can be derived by some special operation upon the previous signatures while resisting other forgeries. Johnson et al. [4] formalized a notion of hommorphic signature schemes. Context Extraction Signatures by Stenfeld et al. [5] is a redactable signature scheme with set-homomorphic signatures. The scheme was addressed within our framework. Alternatively, a signature scheme that is homomorphic with respect to the prefix operation was developed by Chari et al. [6].

Except RSATS-2 [2], which is transitive signature schemes whose signer is naturally stateless, all of the transitive signature schemes are stateful. That means a transitive signing algorithm must maintain the state information for each queried node of graph. It is important for the composition that the signer associates with a single public label to node, and for the security that associates with a single secret label. However, the scheme increases store cost and reduces the computing efficiency. How to make signing algorithm stateless is consequently an issue need to be considered in developing more efficient transitive signature schemes.

In this paper, we introduce a practical transformation that makes the signer stateless without loss of security. Conventionally a transformation from the stateful to stateless cases in RASTS-2 is based on the natural trapdoorness of the RSA function. Different from that of RASTS-2, we propose a transformation upon any given function (not necessary use trapdoor-function). Let the signer's secret key include a secret key, and use a pseudorandom hash function as the underlying coins (randomness) for all choices made by the signer related to node. This way enables the signer to re-compute quantities as need rather than store the data which may cause data inconsistency (same quantities for a given node). The above idea promote us to develop two concrete, stateless transitive signature schemes, TS-FB and TS-RSA, respectively. These schemes are modifications of stateful transitive signature schemes FBTS-1 and RSATS-1, respectively. They are more secure under the underlying cryptographic assumptions in random oracle model.

2 Notions and Definitions

We let || denote the concatenation on strings. We let $\mathbb{N} = \{1, 2, \cdots\}$ be the set of positive integers. The notation $x \overset{R}{\leftarrow} S$ denotes that x is selected randomly from set S. If A is a possibly randomized algorithm then the notation $x \overset{R}{\leftarrow} A(a_1, a_2, \cdots)$ denotes that x is assigned the outcome of the experiment of running A on input $a_1, a_2, \cdots$. The notation $H(\cdot,\cdot)$ denotes a public hash function that maps an arbitrary string to an element of a given set.

Graph and Transitive Closure. All graphs in this paper are undirected. A graph $G^* = (V^*, E^*)$ with two finite sets V^* of vertices and $E^* \subseteq V^* \times V^*$ of edges is said to be *transitively closed* if for all nodes $i, j, k \in V^*$ such that $\{i, j\} \in E^*$ and $\{j, k\} \in E^*$, it also holds that $\{i, k\} \in E^*$. The *transitive closure* of the graph $G^* = (V^*, E^*)$ is the graph $\tilde{G} = (V^*, \tilde{E})$ where $\{i, j\} \in \tilde{E}$ if and only if there is a path from i to j in G^*. Note that the transitive closure of any graph is a transitively closed graph.

Definition 1. A *transitive signature scheme TS=(TKG,TSign,TVf,Comp)* is specified by four polynomial-time algorithms, and the functionality is as follows:

1) The randomized *key generation algorithm TKG* takes input 1^k, where is the security parameter, and return a pair (tpk, tsk) consisting of a public key and matching secret key.
2) The *signing algorithm TSign*, which could be stateful or randomized (or both), takes input the secret key *tsk* and *nodes* $i, j \in \mathbb{N}$, and returns a value called an *original signature* of edge $\{i, j\}$ relative to *tsk*. If stateful, it maintains state that it updates upon each invocation.
3) The deterministic *verification algorithm TVF*, given *tpk*, nodes $i, j \in \mathbb{N}$ and a candidate signature σ, returns either 1 or 0. In the former case we say that σ is a valid signature of edge $\{i, j\}$ relative to *tpk*.
4) The deterministic *composition algorithm Comp* takes *tpk*, nodes $i, j, k \in \mathbb{N}$ and values σ_1, σ_2 to return either a value σ or a symbol $\perp$ to indicate failure.

Especially, the transitive signature scheme is called *stateful,* if the signing algorithm needs to maintain some state information; otherelse it is called stateless.

3 Stateless Transitive Signature Schemes

3.1 A Stateless Transitive Signature Scheme Based on Factoring

Factoring Problem. A *modulus generator* is a randomized, polynomial-time algorithm that on input 1^k return a triple (N, p, q) where $N = pq$, $2^{k-1} \le N < 2^k$ and p, q are distinct, odd primes. Formally, for any modulus generator MG and security parameter $k \in \mathbb{N}$, we define the advantage of an adversary A via

$$Adv_{MG,A}^{fac}(k) = \Pr\left[r \in \{p,q\} : (N,p,q) \xleftarrow{R} MG(1^k); r \xleftarrow{R} A(k,N) \right].$$

We say that factoring is hard relative to MG if the function $Adv_{MG,A}^{fac}(\cdot)$ is negligible for any A whose running time is polynomial in k.

The Scheme. We are given a modulus generator MG and a standard digital signature scheme $SDS = (SKG, SSign, SVf)$. We associate to them a transitive signature scheme $TS-FB = (TKG, TSign, TVf, Comp)$ defined as follows:

- Given input 1^k, the key generation algorithm TKG first runs SKG on input 1^k to generate a key pair (spk, ssk) for the standard signature scheme SDS. It then runs the modulus generator MG on input 1^k to get a triple (N, p, q). It randomly selects a number $hk \xleftarrow{R} \mathbb{Z}_N^*$. Finally, it outputs $tpk = (N, spk)$ as the public key of the transitive signature scheme and $tsk = (N, ssk, hk)$ as the matching secret key.
- Let $V \in \mathbb{N}$ is the set of all queried nodes. The signature algorithm $TSign$ does the following:
  - I. $TSign$ assigns each node $i \in V$ to a *secret label* $l(i) \leftarrow H(hk, i)$ by running a public hash function $H(\cdot,\cdot):(0,1)^* \to \mathbb{Z}_N^*$ whose first parameter is the secret key hk known only by the signer.
  - II. It then assigns to each node $i \in V$ a *public label* $L(i) = l(i)^2 \bmod N$.
  - III. It assigns each node $i \in V$ a *node certification* $C(i) = (i, L(i), \Sigma(i))$, where $\Sigma(i) = SSign(ssk, i \,\|\, L(i))$ is a standard signature on $i \,\|\, L(i)$ under ssk by running the standard signature algorithm $SSign$.
  - IV. When invoked on inputs (tsk, i, j), meaning when asked produce a signature on edge $\{i, j\}$, it does the following:

    If $j < i$ then swap them.

If $i \notin V$ then $V \leftarrow V \cup \{i\}$, and generates the node certification $C(i)$.

If $j \notin V$ then $V \leftarrow V \cup \{j\}$, and generates the node certification $C(j)$.

$l(i) \leftarrow H(hk,i), l(j) \leftarrow H(hk,j)$; $\delta(i,j) \leftarrow l(i)l(j)^{-1} \bmod N$.

Return $\sigma(i,j) \leftarrow (C(i), C(j), \delta(i,j))$ as the signature of $\{i,j\}$.

- The verification algorithm *TVf*, on input $tpk = (N, spk)$, nodes i, j and a candidate signature σ, proceeds as following:

  If $j < i$ then swap them.

  Parse σ as $(C(i), C(j), \delta)$, parse $C(i)$ as $(i, L(i), \Sigma(i))$ and parse $C(j)$ as $(j, L(j), \Sigma(j))$.

  If $SVf(spk, i \,\|\, L(i), \Sigma(i)) = 0$ or $SVf(spk, j \,\|\, L(j), \Sigma(j)) = 0$ then return 0.

  If $L(i) \equiv \delta L(j) \bmod N$ then return 1 else return 0.

- The composition algorithm *Comp* takes nodes i, j, k, a signature $\sigma_1 = (C_1, C_2, \delta_1)$ of $\{i, j\}$ and a signature $\sigma_2 = (C_3, C_4, \delta_2)$ of $\{j, k\}$, and proceeds as follows:

  Let $C_i \in \{C_1, C_2\}$ be such that C_i parse as $(i, L(i), \Sigma(i))$.

  Let $C_j \in \{C_1, C_2\}$ be such that C_j parse as $(j, L(j), \Sigma(j))$.

  If $C_j \notin \{C_3, C_4\}$ then return $\perp$.

  Let $C_k \in \{C_3, C_4\}$ be such that C_k parse as $(k, L(k), \Sigma(k))$.

  If $j < i$ then $\delta_1 \leftarrow \delta_1^{-1} \bmod N$.

  If $k < j$ then $\delta_2 \leftarrow \delta_2^{-1} \bmod N$.

  $\delta \leftarrow \delta_1 \delta_2^{-1}$, Return $\sigma(i,k) = (C_i, C_k, \delta)$.

Theorem 1. Let *MG* be a modulus generator; $SDS = (SKG, SSign, SVf)$ be a standard signature scheme, and *H* is a cryptographic hash function. Let *TS-FB* be the transitive signature scheme corresponding to the above definitions. If the factoring problem associated to *MG* is difficult, and *SDS* is secure against forgery under adaptive chosen-message attack; then *TS-FB* is transitively unforgeable under adaptive chosen-message attack in the random oracle model.

3.2 A Stateless Transitive Signature Scheme Based on RSA

One-more RSA-inversion Problem. The RSA key generator *RG* is a randomized, polynomial-time algorithm that on input 1^k outputs a triple (N, e, d) where

$2^{k-1} \le N < 2^k$ and $ed \equiv 1 \bmod \varphi(N)$. *N*, *e* and *d* are called the public modulus, the encryption exponent and the decryption respectively. The RSA function and its RSA-inverse associated (N, e, d) are defined by

$$RSA_{N,e}(x) = x^e \bmod N \text{ and } RSA_{N,e}^{-1}(y) = y^d \bmod N$$

where $x, y \in \mathbb{Z}_N^*$. To invert RSA at a point $y \in \mathbb{Z}_N^*$ means to compute $x = RSA_{N,e}^{-1}(y)$. The one-more RSA-inversion problem introduced by Bellare, Namprempre, Pointcheval and Semanko [7] is a natural extension of RSA-inversion problem underlying the notion of one-wayness to a setting where the adversary has access to a decryption oracle. Security under one-more-inversion considers an adversary given input an RSA public key N, e and two oracles. The *challenge* oracle, denoted by $ChO(\ )$, takes no inputs and returns a random target point in $\mathbb{Z}_N^*$, chosen a new each time the oracle is invoked. The *inversion* oracle, denoted by $InvO(\cdot)$, given $y \in \mathbb{Z}_N^*$ returns $x = RSA_{N,e}^{-1}(y)$. Let $k \in \mathbb{N}$ be the security parameter, and let $m : \mathbb{N} \to \mathbb{N}$ be a function of *k*. Let *A* be an adversary with access to two oracles $ChO(\ )$ and $InvO(\cdot)$. Consider the following experiment:

Experiment $Exp_{RG,A,m}^{rsa}(k)$

$(N, e, d) \overset{R}{\leftarrow} RG(k)$

For $i = 1$ to $m(k)+1$ do $y_i \leftarrow ChO(\ )$

$(x_1, \cdots, x_{m(k)+1}) \leftarrow A^{InvO(\cdot)}(N, e, k, y_1, \cdots, y_{m(k)+1})$

If the following are both true then return 1 else return 0

$\forall i \in \{1, \cdots, m(k)+1\} : x_i^e \equiv y_i \pmod N$

A made at most $m(k)$ oracle queries

We define the advantage of A via

$$Adv_{RG,A,m}^{rsa}(k) = \Pr\left[Exp_{RG,A,m}^{rsa}(k) = 1\right].$$

The one-more RSA-inversion problem is said to be *hard* if for any adversary *A* whose time-complexity is polynomial in the security parameter *k*, the function $Adv_{RG,A,m}^{rsa}(\cdot)$ is negligible for all polynomially-bound $m(\cdot)$.

Intuitively, the assumption of hardness of the one-more RSA-inversion problem states that it is computationally infeasible for the adversary to output correct inverse of all the target points if the number of queries it makes to its challenge oracle. When the adversary makes one challenge query and no inversion queries, this reduces to the standard one-wayness assumption.

The Scheme. We associate to any RSA key generator *RG* and to any standard digital signature scheme $SDS = (SKG, SSign, SVf)$ a transitive signature scheme $TS - RSA(TKG, TSign, SVf, Comp)$ defined as the following:

- TKG runs $SKG(1^k)$ to generate a key pair (spk, ssk) for *SDS*, runs the $RG(1^k)$ to generate an RSA key (N, e, d), and randomly selects a number $hk \overset{R}{\leftarrow} \mathbb{Z}_N^*$. It outputs $tpk = (N, e, spk)$ as the public key of the transitive signature scheme and $tsk = (N, ssk, hk)$ as the matching secret key.
- The signing algorithm *TSign* is identical to that of the *TS-FB* scheme except that now the public label $L(i)$ is computed as $L(i) \equiv l(i)^e \bmod N$, where the secret label $l(i)$ is computed as $l(i) \leftarrow H(hk, i)$ by running a public hash function $H(\cdot,\cdot)$.
- The verification algorithm *TVf* is also very similar to that of *TS-FB*, the only difference is the test on the edge label, which now consists of checking that $L(i) \equiv \delta^e L(j) \bmod N$.
- The *Comp* algorithm is perfectly identical to the composition algorithm of *TS-FB*.

Theorem 2. Let *RG* be a RSA key generator, let $SDS = (SKG, SSign, SVf)$ be a standard signature scheme, and *H* is a cryptographic Hash function. Let *TS-RSA* be the transitive signature scheme associated to them as defined above. If the one-more RSA-inversion problem associated to *RG* is difficult, and *SDS* is secure against forgery under adaptive chosen-message attack; then *TS-RSA* is transitively unforgeable under adaptive chosen-message attack in the random oracle model.

4 Conclusion

Transitive signature is a new concept and some open problems are unsolved. A practical approach to modify a stateful transitive signature schemes to stateless without loss of security is presented. Two concrete stateless transitive signature schemes, TS-FB and TS-RSA are unforgeable under adaptive chosen-message attacks in random oracle model. The proofs of the schemes with consideration of their securities are ignored due to the similar derivations of FBTS-1 [2], and RSATS-1 [2]. The main contribution of our schemes are for the random oracle models; but not for FBTS-1, RSATS-1, and MRTS based models. Using our appraoch, a stateless transitive signature scheme based on DLP can be constructed by modifying the stateful signature scheme MRTS [1].

The problem of finding a directed transitive signature scheme remains a very interesting open problem. How to develop a transitive signature scheme without node certification based on DLP will be our future project.

Acknowledgement. This work was partially supported by the National Natural Science Foundation of China under Grant No. 60372094.

References

1. Micali S. and Rivest L.: Transitive Signature Schemes. Topic in Cryptology – CT-RSA'02, Lecture Notes in Computer Science Vol. 2271, , B. Preneel ed. Springer-Verlag (2002) 236-243
2. Bellare M. and Neven G.: Transitive Signatures Based on Factoring and RSA. Advances in Cryptology – ASIACRYPT'02, Lecture Notes in Computer Science Vol. 2501, Y. Zheng ed., Springer-Verlag (2002) 397-414
3. Zhu H., Feng B., and Deng R. H.: A Transitive Signature Scheme Provably Secure against Adaptive Chosen-message Attack. Cryptology ePrint Archive: Report 2003/059 (available via http://eprint.iacr.org/2003/059/).
4. Johnson R., Molnar D., Song D., and Wagner D.: Homomorphic Signature Schemes. Topic in Cryptology – CT-RSA'02, Lecture Notes in Computer Science Vol. 2271, B. Preneel ed., Springer-Verlag (2002) 244-262
5. Steinfeld R., L. Bull and Y. Zheng. Content Extraction Signatures. Information Security and Cryptology – ICISC'01, Lecture Notes in Computer Science Vol. 2288, K. Kim ed. Springer-Verlag (2002)
6. Chair S., Rabin T., and Rivest R.: An Efficient Signature Scheme for Route Aggregation. Manuscript, February (2002) (available via http://theroy.lcs.mit.edu/~rivest/publications.html).
7. Bellare M., Namprempre C., Pointcheval D., and Semanko M.: The One-More RSA-Inversion Problems and the Security of Chaum's Blind Signature Scheme. Cryptology ePrint Archive: Report 2001/002 (available via http://eprint.iacr.org/2001/002/).

A Web Service Composition Modeling and Evaluation Method Used Petri Net

Xiao-Ning Feng, Qun Liu, and Zhuo Wang

Department of Computer Science & Technology,
Harbin Engineering University, 150001,
Harbin, Heilongjiang, China
fengxiaoning@hrbeu.edu.cn
fengxiaoning@hotmail.com

Abstract. The emergence of Web services opens a new way of Web application design and development. It has led to more interest into Web service composition, which is an active area of research. The formidable problem of efficient and effective composition of existing Web services is the subject of much current attention. The study of modeling is one of the most important parts and a key layer of Web service composition. Therefore, there is a need for modeling techniques and tools for reliable Web services composition. In this paper, we propose a method used an Advanced Object-Oriented Petri Net (AOOPN) to model and evaluation the process of Web services composition. This method is expressive enough to capture the semantics of complex Web services combinations.

1 Introduction

In order to survive the massive competition created by the new online economy, many organizations are rushing to put their core business competencies on the Internet as a collection of Web services for more automation and global visibility. The concept of Web service has become recently very popular, however, there is no clear agreed upon definition yet. Typical examples of Web services include on-line travel reservations, procurement, customer relationship management (CRM), billing accounting, and supply chain. In this paper, by Web services (or simply services) we mean an autonomous software application or component i.e., a semantically well defined functionality, uniquely identified by a Uniform Resource Locator(URL)[1].

This paper mainly talks about the modeling method of the Web Services Composition. In one direction, Web service processes can be simulated for the purpose of correcting/improving the design or even for making adaptive changes at runtime. The success of an organization depends greatly on the efficiency and effectiveness of its business processes. The advent of Web services and Web processes (composition of Web services) enables organizations to easily collaborate in their business processes.

When composing a Web process it is useful to analyze and compute overall operational properties. This allows organizations to translate their vision into their

H.T. Shen et al. (Eds.): APWeb 2006, LNCS 3842, pp. 905–911, 2006.

business processes more efficiently, since Web process can be designed according to operational metrics. Operational metrics can be described using a suitable Quality of Service (QoS) model. Such a model makes possible the description of Web services and Web processes according to their timeliness, cost of service, and reliability.

The analysis of Web processes according to their QoS can be carried out using several methods. While mathematical methods have been effectively used, another alternative is to utilize simulation analysis. Simulation plays an important role by exploring "what-if" questions during the process composition phase. Our earlier work on workflows and simulation enables us to perceive how simulation can serve as a tool for the Web process composition problem. The analysis of the QoS of Web processes differs from the analysis of workflows due to the distribution, autonomy, and heterogeneity of its components.

Our current work on using simulation for Web services focuses on extending JSIM and integrating it with Web process design tools, as well as Web process enactment engines. The designer, Web Process Design Tool (WPDT), allows composition to be done graphically. To aid the user in this composition task, our system is enhanced with enactment and simulation features. Enactment of a process helps in evaluating the performance of the individual services and simulation is done to study the process in action, before enactment. In the other direction, using Web services for simulation, simulation models/components can be built out of Web services. Well tested simulation models may be placed on the Web for others to use. Resources and tools used in simulation environments make excellent candidates for Web services. If this vision can be realized, future development can be done on a higher plane, allowing better and more comprehensive solutions to be developed. The rest of the paper is organized as follows. In Section 2, we talk about Web Services Composition while Section 3 introduces the visualized modeling technique Petri Net, mainly related to model Web services, and composition of Web services. Section 4 we explain our performance evaluation approach for evaluating/comparing the invoked Web services composition.

2 Web Services Composition

A Web service has a specific task to perform and may depend on other Web services, hence being composite. For example, a company that is interested in selling books could focus on this aspect while outsourcing other aspects such as payment as shipment. The composition of two or more services generates a new service providing both the original individual behavioral logic and a new collaborative behavior for carrying out a new composite task. This means that existing services are able to cooperate although the cooperation was not designed in advanced. Service composition could be static(service components interact with each other in a pre-negotiated manner) or dynamic(they discover each other and negotiate on the fly).

In this section we talks about the Web services using existing ones as building blocks. Sequence, alternative, iterations, and arbitrary sequence are typical constructs specified in the control flow. More elaborate operators, dealt with in this paper, are parallel with communication, discriminator, selection, and refinement. We also give a formal semantics to the proposed algebra in terms of Petri nets as well as some nice algebraic properties.

Some work has begun on the use of simulation to study Web service composition and Web processes, but little work has been done on the use of Web services to build simulation environments. Web service composition is an active area of research, with many concepts and languages being proposed by different research groups. IBM has proposed WSFL (Web Service Flow Language), an XML based language developed to describe complex service compositions. WSFL supports a flow model and a global model specification for each Web process. The flow model defines the structure of the Web process, while the global model specifies the Web services, which implement the activities in the process. Microsoft's Web service composition language, XLANG, extends the WSDL (Web Service Description Language) to provide a model for orchestration of services. XL, another portable W3C compliant XML programming language, is designed for the implementation of Web Services. In contrast to these XML based standards, researchers are developing DAML-S, which aims to automate Web service tasks (discovery, composition, invocation, and monitoring) using specifications based on onto logies. DAML-S, unlike the earlier XML based languages, is capable of describing the semantics of Web services. Issues such as searching for services and interoperability of selected services arise when a Web service composition is done. Cardoso and Sheth explore semantic searching for Web services and their interoperability. An ontology based solution is proposed in that paper. Though use of simulation to test processes has been carried out earlier for workflow models, simulation of composite Web services represents a new direction. The work that most closely relates to ours is described in Narayanan and McIlraith. In their work, DAML-S service descriptions of composite services are encoded in a Petri Net formalism, providing decision procedures for Web services simulation, verification, and composition [2].

A Web service behavior is basically a partially ordered set of operations. Therefore, it is straight-forward to map it into a Petri net. Operations are modeled by transitions and the state of the service is modeld by places. The arrows between places and transitions are used to specify causal relations.

We can categorize Web services into material services(e.g., delivery of physical products), information services(create, process, manager, and provide information), and material/information services, the mixture of both.

3 Object-Oriented Petri Net(OOPN)

The use of visual modeling techniques such as Petri nets in the design of complex Web services is justified by many reasons. For example, visual representations provide a high level yet precise language which allows to express and reason about concepts at their natural level of abstraction.

Petri net is a well-founded process modeling technique that have formal semantics. They have been used to model and analyze many types of processes including protocols, manufacturing systems, and business processes and etc. A basic Petri net is a directed, connected, and bipartite graph in which each node is either a *place* or a *transition. Tokens* occupy *places*. When there is at least one token in every place connected to a transition, we say that the transition is *enabled*. Any enabled transition may *fire* removing one token from every input place, and depositing one token in each output place.

There are also many High-level Petri Nets, such as Colored Petri Net(CPN), Timed Petri Net(TPN), Fuzzy Petri Nets(FPN), Object-Oriented Petri Net(OOPN) and etc. These Petri Nets extended the application of the Basic Petri Net.

The basic idea of OOPN is to mapping the target system as the collaborate objects. And using the Petri Net to describe the behavior and their communications of each objects. In order to increase the maintainability and reusable of the model. OOPN use the information concealment to keep the each objects unseen from the environment. And only represent its interface to the outside.

Definition 1. *The system in the OOPN constitutes with the reaction objects and their relation. It can be defined as*:

$$S = (O, \ R)$$

where:

O represents a group of objects;

R represents the message relations of the objects;

Definition 2. *The objects* O_i *model in the OOPN can be defined as a hexahydric group:*

$$O_i = (H_i, \ IG_i, \ OG_i, \ IM_i, \ OM_i, \ F_i)$$

where:

H_i *represents the level of the objects;*

IG_i *represents input gate transitions aggregation of objects* O_i ;

OG_i *represents output gate transitions aggregation of objects* O_i ;

IM_i *represents input message places aggregation of objects* O_i ;

OM_i *represents output message places aggregation of objects* O_i ;

F_i *represents a group of flow relation of objects* O_i ;

In the OOPN, the communications of each objects is accomplished by the message places and gate transitions.

Definition 3. *The communication* R_{ij} *between the message sender object* O_i *and the message receiver object* O_j *can be defined as:*

$$R_{ij} = (OM_i, \ G_{ij}, \ IM_j)$$

where:

G_{ij} *represents a special type of transitions, called gate transitions.*

Gate transitions are the switches putting on the message communication way which we can use them to control the state of the OOPN model.

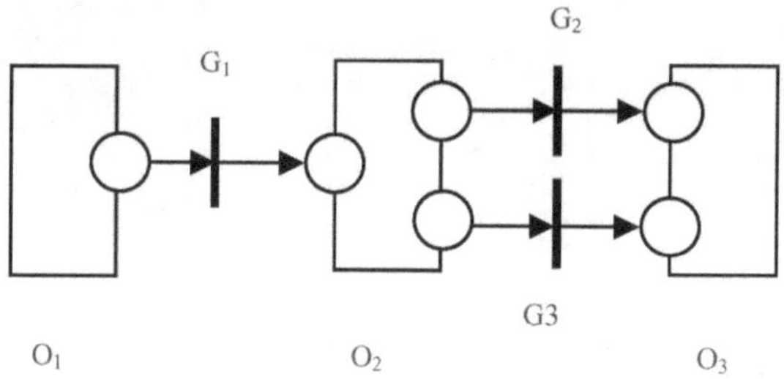

Fig. 1. A simply OOPN model

Graphically, given a simply OOPN model(see Figure 1). It includes 3 objects and 3 gate transitions.

4 Modeling for Web Service Composition

According to the Web services Composition and referred to the OOPN modeling method, a Improved Object-Oriented Petri Net(IOOPN) modeling method was put forward.

Definition 4. *The object Ob_i in the IOOPN can be defined as a hexahydric group* :

$$Ob_i = \{ SP_i, AT_i, IM_i, OM_i, I_i, O_i \}$$

where:

Ob_i represents the object of the system;

SP_i represents a finite State Place aggregation of the object Ob_i ;

AT_i represents a finite Activity Transition aggregation of the object Obi ;

IM_i represents a finite input message places aggregation of the object Ob_i ;

OM_i represents a finite output message places aggregation of the object Ob_i ;

$I_i(P,T)$ represents the input function from places P to transition T : $P \times T \rightarrow N$ (non-negative integer), corresponding to the arcs from P to T,' here $P = SP_i \cup IM_i, T = AT_i$, I(P,T) is matrix ;

$O_i(P,T)$—represents the output function from transition T to places P : $T \times P \rightarrow N$ (non-negative integer) , corresponding to the arcs from T to P , here $P = SP_i \cup OM_i, T = AT_i$, O(P,T) is matrix。

Graphically, given an IOOPN model (see Figure 2). It includes 3objects and 3 game transitions. The object Ob_1 includes one State Place SP_1 , tow Activity Transition AT_1, AT_2, one input message place IM_1, one output message place OM_1。

The Ob_i can be a Web Service or a group of Web Services that accomplishes a function.

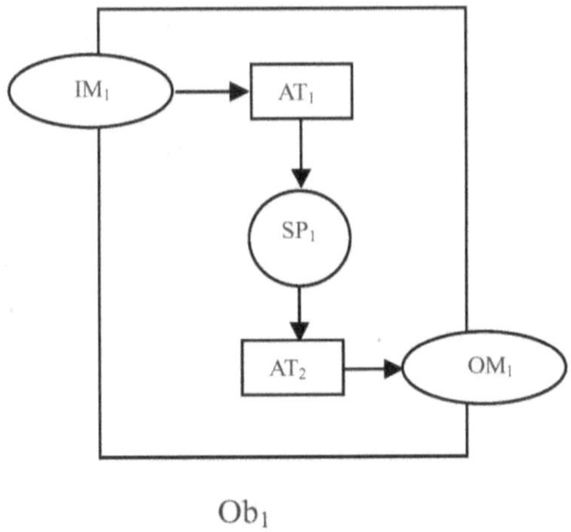

Fig. 2. An IOOPN model

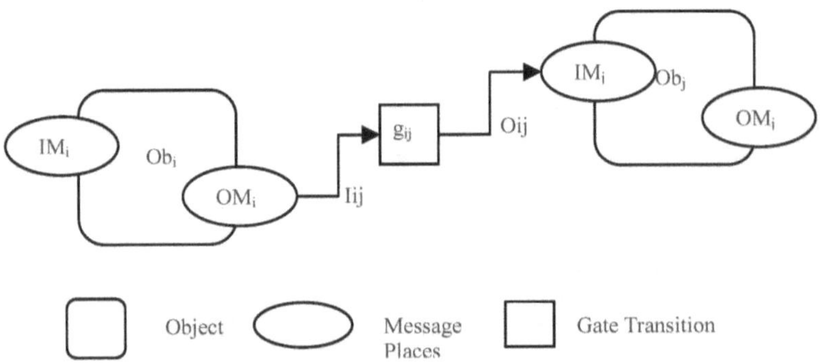

Fig. 3. Objects Information Transfer Relation

Definition 5. *The Information Transfer Relation from object Ob_i to object Ob_j can be defined*:

$$R_{ij}=\{OM_i,g_{ij},IM_j,I_{ij},O_{ij}\}$$

where:

OM_i *represents finite output message places aggregation of the object* Ob_i ;

IM_j *represents finite intput message places aggregation of the object* Ob_j ;

g_{ij}—*represents finite information transfer gate aggregation from the object* Ob_i *to the object* Ob_j ;

$I_{ij}(OM_i,g_{ij})$ *represents input function from output message place* OM_i *to gate* g_{ij}: $OM_i \times g_{ij} \rightarrow N$ (*non-negative integer*), corresponding to the arcs from OM_i to g_{ij};

$O_{ij}(IM_j, g_{ij})$—*represents output function from gate* g_{ij} *to input message place* IM_j: $g_{ij} \times IM_j \rightarrow N$ (*non-negative integer*), corresponding to the arcs from g_{ij} to IM_j.

Graphically, given Objects Information Transfer Relation model (see Figure 3),it shows two objects change information through the Gate Transition.

5 Analysis and Evaluation the Model

We can use the Petri Net to analysis and evaluation the model established by the method talked above. Thus we can analysis the safeness, liveness, reachablity, boundedness and etc. There is many theories in the Petri Net areas. Here we don't discuss it particularly.

In addition, an exactitude model established by the IOOPN or Petri Net should have no deadlocks and any instability. Through the Petri theories, we can analysis the safeness, boundedness, liveness, reachableness and other performances with the reachable graph, reachable tree and state equation. Thus get the evaluation of the composition of the Web services.

References

1. Stephen J. H. Yang, James S. F. Hsieh, Blue C. W. Lan, Jen-Yao Chung:Composition and evaluation of trustworthy Web Services.Proceedings of the IEEE EEE05 international workshop on Business services networks BSN '05. March 2005
2. Yu Tang, Luo Chen, Kai-Tao He, Ning Jing: SRN: An Extended Petri-Net-Based Workflow Model for Web Service Composition. Proceedings of the IEEE International Conference on Web Services (ICWS'04) - Volume 00. June 2004
3. Rachid Hamadi, Boualem Benatallah: A Petri Net-Based Model for Web Service Composition.
4. Sun Jian, Zhang Peng. Modeling and Analysis of Web Services Flow Language (WSFL) Based Petri Nets. MINI-MICRO SYSTEMS. 2004 Vol.25 No.7 P.1382-1386

Multi-agent Negotiation Model for Resource Allocation in Grid Environment*

Xiaoqin Huang , LinPeng Huang, and MingLu Li

Department of Computer Science and Engineering,
Shanghai Jiao Tong University, 200030 Shanghai, China
{huangxq}@sjtu.edu.cn

Abstract. Due to the resources in the Grid are heterogeneous and geographically distributed, the management of resources and application scheduling in large-scale distributed Grid environment is a complex undertaking. Intelligent agents can play an important role in solving these problems. In this paper we formulated this problem as a multi-agent game with the players being agents purchasing service from a common server. We strive to highlight major challenges in managing resources in a Grid computing environment and present some of our recent works on multi-agent negotiation strategies for resource management and scheduling in grid environment. The proposed approach is to realize multiple negotiation models/protocols/strategies that can be selected by the system automatically to adapt to computation needs as well as changing computing resource environment.

1 Introduction

Grid [2] based computational infrastructure is a promising next generation computing platform for solving large-scale resource intensive problems [1]. However, resource management, application development and usage models in these environments is a complex undertaking. Most of the related work in Grid computing dedicated to resource management and scheduling problems adopt a conventional style where a scheduling component decides which jobs are to be executed at which site based on certain cost functions (Legion [8], condor [9], etc). They treat resource as if they all cost the same price and the results of all application have the same value even though this may not be the case in reality. Due to the complexity in constructing successful Grid environments, it is important to find a novel management mechanism and strategies to solve resource management and scheduling in Grid. In [4] Rajkunar Buyya et.al proposed and explored the usage of an economics based paradigm for managing resource allocation in Grid computing environments. For the market to be competitive and healthy, coordination mechanisms are required that help the market reach an equilibrium price - the price at which the supply of a service equals the quantity demanded [4]. Multi-agent Systems have addressed issues of coordination among autonomous, distributed agents for many years. A wide variety of networked computer systems

* This paper is supported by ShanghaiGrid grand project of Science and Technology Commission of Shanghai Municipality (No.03DZ15027, 05DZ15005).

H.T. Shen et al. (Eds.): APWeb 2006, LNCS 3842, pp. 912–918, 2006.

(such as the Grid, the Semantic Web, and peer-to-peer systems) can be viewed as multi-agent systems [3]. Agents with distinct interests or knowledge can benefit by engaging in negotiation whenever their activities potentially affect each other. Through negotiation, agents make joint decisions, involving allocation of resources, adoption of policies, or any issue of mutual concern.

To enhance information coordination, highlight major challenges in resource management and scheduling in Grid environment. In this paper, we proposed and explored models, protocols and strategies for multi-agent negotiation framework to grid computing. The multi-agent approach provided a fair basis in successfully managing decentralization and heterogeneity that is present in human society and human economies. The remainder of the paper is organized as follows. Section 2 introduces multi-agent negotiation framework for resource allocation. Section 3 discusses single issue negotiation model. Section 4 describes multi-issue negotiation. Section 5 gives the conclusion.

2 Multi-agent Negotiation Framework for Resource Allocation

The multi-agent system architecture follows that presented in [5]. See Fig.1. In our project the Grid is viewed as multi-agent systems in which the individual components act in an autonomous and flexible manner in order to achieve their objectives. The multi-agent middleware makes use of agent technology as the main mechanism for grid resource negotiation in the job submission process. It consists of negotiation, migration, and interface modules. In the negotiation module are agents and functions involved in the negotiation process. The migration module completes the negotiation module by matching the Service Level Agreements (SLAs) established by agents, by deciding the place to run the job, and by submitting the job. The OGSA interface module has functions that allow integrating agents into the grid environment. The agent technology has features well fitting for distributed communication, and is particularly robust for the negotiation and migration processes.

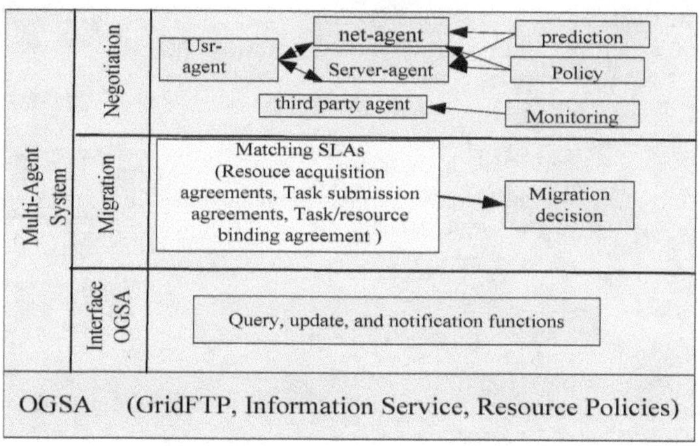

Fig. 1. Multi-Agent System Architecture for Resource Allocation [5]

3 Single-Issue Negotiation Model

We propose the single issue negotiation model and the optimal strategy bring forward by Shaheen S.Fatiam as describe in [8] [9].

The Negotiation Protocol. This is basically an alternating offers protocol [8]. Consider two agents negotiating over a single issue A, the price of an object. Let *b* denote the buyer (user), *s* the seller (server) and [P^a_{min}, p^a_{max}] denote the range of values for price that are acceptable to agent a, where a∈ $\{b, s\}$. A value for price that is acceptable to both b and s, lies between their reservation prices, i.e., the zone of agreement, is the interval [P^s_{min}, P^b_{max}]. (p^b_{max} - p^s_{min}) is the price-surplus. Let T^a denote agent a's deadline by when it must have completed its negotiation. Let $p^t_{b\to s}$ denote the price offered by agent b at time t. Negotiation starts when the first offer is made by an agent. When an agent *s* receives an offer from agent *b* at time t, i.e., $p^t_{b\to s}$, it rates the offer using its utility function U^s. If the value of U^s for $p^t_{b\to s}$ at time t is greater than the value of the counter-offer agent *s* is ready to send at time t', i.e., $p^{t'}_{b\to s}$ with t' >t then agent s accepts. Otherwise a counter-offer is made. Thus the action A that agent s takes at time t is defined as [8]:

$$A^s(t', p^{t'}_{b\to s}) = \text{Quit if } t > T^s \tag{1.1}$$

$$A^s(t', p^{t'}_{b\to s}) = \text{Accept if } U^s(p^t_{b\to s}) \geq U^s(p^{t'}_{b\to s}) \tag{1.2}$$

$$A^s(t', p^{t'}_{b\to s}) = p^{t'}_{b\to s} \quad \text{otherwise} \tag{1.3}$$

Agents' Utility. The Utility derived by agents depends on the final agreement on the price *P* and the duration of negotiation *T*. However, utility from price to an agent is independent of its utility from time, i.e., the buyer always prefers a low price and the seller always prefers a high price. Thus:

$$U^a : P \times T \to \Re \qquad a \in (b,s) \tag{2}$$

We consider the following two von Neumann-Morgenstern utility functions [10] [9] as they incorporate the effects of discounting and bargaining costs:

(1) Adaptive form:

$$U^a(P, T) = U^a_p(P) + U^a_t(T) \tag{3}$$

Where U^a_p and U^a_t are unidimensional utility functions. This form is adequate when the only effect of time is a bargaining cost which is independent of the final outcome.

We defined U_p^a as U_p^a(P) = (P_{max}^b -P) for the buyer and and U_p^s(p) = (P- P_{min}^s) for the seller. U_t^a was defined as U_t^a(T) = c^a T. Thus when (c^a >0) the agent gains utility with time and when (c^a <0) the agent loses utility with time.

(2) Multiplicative form:

$$U^a(P,T) = U_p^a(P)\,U_t^a(T) \tag{4}$$

Where as before, U_p^a and U_t^a are unidimensional utility functions. Here preferences for attribute P, given the other attribute T, do not depend on the level of T. This form is adequate when the effects of time are bargaining cost and discounting. U_p^a was defined as before and U_t^a was defined as U_t^a(T) = $(c^a)^T$. Thus when (c^a >1) the agent gains utility with time and when (c^a <1) the agent loses utility with time.

Agent a's utility from conflict is defined as U^a (C) =0.

Counter-offer Generation. Given the fact that both agents have (different) deadlines, we assume that both agents use a strategy that varies their negotiation behavior with respect to the passage of time. This, time *t* is the predominant factor used to decide which value to offer in the next negotiation move. Here such strategies (e.g. Linear, Boulware, or Conceder) are called time-dependent (from [9]). The strategies vary the value of price depending on the remaining negotiation time modeled as the above defined constant T^a. The initial offer is a point in the interval [P_{min}^a, P_{max}^a]. The constant K^a multiplied by the size of interval determines the price to be offered in the first proposal by agent a [11]. The offer made by agent a to agent b at time t (0<t≤ T^a) is modeled as a function

$$p_{a\to b}^t = P_{min}^a + \phi^a(t)(P_{max}^a - P_{min}^a) \quad \text{for the buyer} \tag{5.1}$$

$$p_{a\to b}^t = P_{min}^a + (1-\phi^a(t))(P_{max}^a - P_{min}^a) \quad \text{for the seller} \tag{5.2}$$

A wide range of time dependent functions can be defined by varying the way in which ϕ^a(t) is computed (see [11] for more details). However, functions must ensure that 0≤ ϕ^a(t) ≤1, ϕ^a(0)= k^a and $\phi^a(T^a)$ =1. That is, the offer will always be between the ranges [P_{max}^a - P_{min}^a], at the beginning it will give the initial constant and when the deadline is reached it will offer the reservation vale. Function ϕ^a(t) is defined as follows [8] [9] [11]:

$$\phi^a(t) = k^a + (1-k^a)\left(\frac{\min(t,T^a)}{T^a}\right)^{\frac{1}{\Psi}} \quad 6)$$

These families of negotiation decision functions represent an infinite number of possible strategies, one for each value of Ψ, two extreme sets show clearly different patters of behavior：(1)*Boulware* [12] - For this strategy Ψ <1 and close to zero. The initial offer is maintained till time is almost exhausted, when the agent concedes up to its reservation value. (2) *Conceder* [13]- For this strategy Ψ >1 and is high. The agent goes to its reservation value very quickly and maintains the same offer till the deadline. (3) *Linear* - when Ψ =1 the price is increased linearly.

4 Mutli-issue Negotiation

We now discuss the multi-issue bargaining model where the issues are independent of each other. Assume that buyer b and seller s, that have an unequal deadlines, bargain over the price of two distinct goods (servers), X and Y, negotiation on all the issues must end before the deadline. We consider two goods (servers) in order to simplify the discussion but this is a general framework that works for more than two goods (services) [8].

Agents' information state: let the buyer's reservation prices for X and Y be P_x^b and P_y^b the seller's reservation prices be P_x^s and P_y^s respectively. The buyer's information state is:

$$I^b =< P_x^b, P_y^b, T^b, U^b, S^b, L_x^s, L_y^s, L_t^s > \qquad (7)$$

Where $P_x^b, P_y^b, T^b, U^b, S^b$ are the information about its own parameters and L_x^s, L_y^s and L_t^s are three lotteries that denotes its beliefs about the opponent's parameters. L_x^s=[α^b, P_{xL}^s ; 1-α^b, P_{xH}^s] is the lottery on the seller's reservation price for X such that $P_{xL}^s < P_{xH}^s$, L_y^s=[β^b, P_{yL}^s; 1-β^b, P_{yH}^s] is the lottery on the seller's reservation price for Y such that $P_{yL}^s < P_{yH}^s$ and L_t^s=[γ^b, T_l^s;1-γ^b, T_h^s] is the lottery on the seller's deadline such that $T_l^s < T_h^s$. Similarly, the seller's information state is defined as [8]

$$I^s =< P_x^s, P_y^s, T^s, U^s, S^s, L_x^b, L_y^b, L_t^b > \qquad (8)$$

An agent's information state is its private knowledge. The agent's utility functions are defined as [8]:

$$U^a(p_x, p_y, t)=(p_x^b - p_x)(\delta_x^b)^t + (p_y^b - p_y)(\delta_y^b)^t \quad \text{for buyer} \qquad (9.1)$$

$$U^a(p_x, p_y, t)=(p_x - p_x^s)(\delta_x^s)^t + (p_y - p_y^s)(\delta_y^s)^t \quad \text{for seller} \qquad (9.2)$$

Note that the discounting factors are different for different issues. This allows agent's attitudes toward time to be different for different issues [8].

Multi-issue Negotiation Protocol. In multi-issue negotiation also use an alternating offers negotiation protocol. There are two types of offers. An offer on just one good is referred to as a single offer and an offer on two goods is referred to as a combined offer. One of the agents starts by making a combined offer. The other agent can accept or reject part of the offer (single offer) or the complete offer. If it rejects the complete offer, then it sends a combined counter-offer. This process of making combined offers continues till agreement is reached on one of the issues. Thereafter agents make offer only on the remaining issue (i.e., once agreement is reached on an issue, it cannot be renegotiated). Negotiation ends when agreement is reached on both the issues or a deadline is reached. Thus the action A that agent s takes at time t on a single offer is as defined in function 5.1. Its action on a combined offer, $A^s(t', X^t_{b\to s}, Y^t_{b\to s})$, is defined as [8]:

1. Quit if $t > T^s$
2. Accept $X^t_{b\to s}$ if $U^s(X^t_{b\to s}, t) \geq U^s(X^{t'}_{b\to s}, t')$
3. Accept $Y^t_{b\to s}$ if $U^s(Y^t_{b\to s}, t) \geq U^s(Y^{t'}_{b\to s}, t')$
4. Offer $X^{t'}_{b\to s}$ if $X^t_{b\to s}$ not accepted
5. Offer $Y^{t'}_{b\to s}$ if $Y^t_{b\to s}$ not accepted

A counter-offer for an issue is generated using the method described in section 3 (Counter-offer Generation). Although agents initially make offers on both issues, there is no restriction on the price they offer. Thus by initially offering a price that lies outside the zone of agreement, an agent can effectively delay the time of agreement for that issue [8]. For example, *b* can offer a very low price which will not be acceptable to *s* and *s* can offer a price which will not be acceptable to *b*. In this way, the order in which the issues are bargained over and agreements are reached is determined endogenously as part of the bargaining equilibrium rather than imposed exogenously as part of the game tree [8].

5 Conclusions

Computational grids are often used for computationally intensive applications. Management issues, including task allocation and resource management, become very import issues. Intelligent resource allocation is still a challenge in the Grid middleware. The problem can be viewed as seeking a concurrent allocation of different resources for every job. Agents can always negotiate to increase their mutual benefits by negotiation despite conflicting interests. Multi-agent based approaches may facilitate the management of these large-scale grids. We present a multi-agent negotiation system base on game theory that aim to decide the best place to run a job in a grid environment. Our main contribution is concerning the selection of grid resources using a multi-agent negotiation process. Due to scalability and performance of multi-agent system, multi-agent negotiation approaches can improve the efficiency of resource allocation in grid. In this negotiation process, we identified and modeled the bilateral, multi-issue negotiation. Our future work is to measure the percentage of improvement our system brings to the resource allocation problem in grid.

References

1. R. Buyya, D. Abramson, and J. Giddy, Nimrod/G: An Architecture for a Resource Management and Scheduling System in a Global Computational Grid, Proceedings of the 4th International Conference and Exhibition on High Performance Computing in Asia-Pacific Region (HPC ASIA 2000), May 14-17, 2000, Beijing, China, IEEE CS Press, USA (2000).
2. Foster, I., and kesselman, C. (editors), The Grid: Blueprint for a New Computing Infrastructure, Morgan Kaufmann Publishers, USA (1999).
3. N.R. Jennings. An agent-based approach for building complex software systems. Communications of the ACM, 44(4): 35-42, April 2001.
4. Rajkumar Buyya et al. Economic Models for Resource Management and Scheduling in Grid Computing.
5. L.Nassif, J. M. Nogueira, M.Ahmed et.al, Agent-based Negotiation for Resource Allocation in Grid, http://wcga05.lncc.br/text/7500.pdf.
6. S. Chapin, J. Karpovich, and A. Grimshaw, The Legion Resource Management 1 Proceedings of the 8th International Conference of Distributed Computing Systems (ICDCS 1988), January 1988, San Jose, CA, IEEE CS Press, USA, 1988.
7. M. Litzkow, M. Livny, and M.Mutka, Condor – A Hunter of Idle Workstations, Proceedings of the 8th International Conference of Distributed Computing Systems (ICDCS 1998), San Jose, CA, IEEE CS Press, USA, 1988.
8. S. S. Fatima, M. Wooldridge, N.R. Jennings, Multi-issue Negotiation Under Time Constraints, AAMAS'02, July 15-19, Bologna, Italy.
9. S. S. Fatima, M.J.Wooldridge, and N.R.Jennings. Optimal negotiation strategies for agents with incomplete information. In ATAL-2001, page 53-68, Seattle, USA, 2001.
10. R.Keeney and H.Raiffa. Decisions with multiple Objectives: Preferences and Value Tradeoffs. New York: John Wiley, 1976.
11. P. Faratin, C.Sierra, and N.R.Jennings. Negotiation decision functions for autonomous agents. International Journal of Robotics and Autonomous Systems, 24(3-40:159-182, 1998.
12. H.Raiffa.The Art and Science of Negotiation. Harvard University Press, Cambridge,USA, 1982.
13. M.J. Osborne and A. Rubinstein. A course in Game Theory. The MIT press, Cambridge, England, 1998.

Discovery of Web Services Applied to Scientific Computations Based on QOS

Han Cao[1], Daxin Liu[1], and Rui Fu[2,3]

[1] School of Computer Science & Technology,
Harbin Engineering University, Harbin 150001, China
caotingquan@sohu.com
[2] School of Economics & Management,
Harbin Engineering University, Harbin 150001, China
[3] Harbin Guoyuan Land-building Evaluation and Consultation Co. ltd,
Harbin 150010, China

Abstract. Computational science is an important and urgent field with multi-disciplinary research. Many science and engineering explorations rely on mature, efficient computational algorithms and implementations, practical and reliable numerical methods, and large-scale computation systems. Since scientific computation consumes many computer resources. And some function quality parameter such as error or max loop times, impact much on function executing. Applying Web services to scientific computation differs from other usage situation of Web services. This paper described the service template as the data structure to discover services, and discuss the algorithm of the similarity degree between ST and SO based on QOS of Web service.

1 Introduction

Computational science focuses on algorithms development and implementations of computing for scientists and engineers. Its impact is already being felt in many science disciplines. Many science and engineering explorations rely on mature, efficient computational algorithms and implementations, practical and reliable numerical methods, and large-scale computation systems. Now more and more systems and infrastructures are developed to support Web services. It is normal to expect Web services to be applied to scientific computations. Scientific computation consumes many computer resources. And some function quality parameter such as error or max loop times, impact much on function executing. So applying Web services to scientific computation differs from other usage situation of Web services, in terms of the importance of the quality of Web services, which includes their response time, cost of service and other application relative quality parameter such as error or max loop times. The quality of service (QOS) is an important issue for Web services based application. Web services QOS represents the quantitative and qualitative characteristics of a Web services based application necessary to achieve a set of initial requirements. Web services QOS addresses the non-functional issues of Web services rather than Web services operations. Quantitative characteristics can be evaluated in terms of concrete measures such as execution time, cost, etc. QOS should be seen as an integral

H.T. Shen et al. (Eds.): APWeb 2006, LNCS 3842, pp. 919 – 922, 2006.

aspect of Web services; therefore, it should be integrated with Web services specifications. Thus computing QOS of Web service allows for the selection and execution of Web service based on their QOS, to better fulfill customer expectations.

2 Specification of Web Service for Scientific Computation

Using Web service in general include four fundamental steps.

(1) The Web service requester and provider entities become known to each other. Normally the requester entity may use a discovery service to locate a suitable service description (which contains the provider agent's invocation address) via an associated functional description, either through manual discovery or autonomous selection. The discovery service is implemented as a registry (such as UDDI). This step is called Web service discovery.

(2) The requester and provider entities somehow agree on the service description and semantics that will govern the interaction between the requester and provider agents;

(3) The service description and semantics are realized by the requester and provider agents; and

(4) The requester and provider agents exchange messages, thus performing some task on behalf of the requester and provider entities.

The functional description is a machine-processable description of the functionality (or partial semantics) of the service that the provider entity is offering. In our work, we use OWL-S specification language to describe Web services. More precisely, we use the OWL-S ServiceProfile. An OWL-S ServiceProfile describes a service as a function of three basic types of information: what organization provides the service, what function the service computes, and a host of features that specify characteristics of the service. The provider information consists of contact information that refers to the entity that provides the service. The functional description of the service is expressed in terms of the transformation produced by the service. Specifically, it specific the inputs required by the service and the outputs generated; furthermore, the profile describes the preconditions required by the service and the expected effects that result from the execution of the service. Finally, the profile allows the description of a host of properties that are used to describe features of the service. The first type of information specifies the category of a given service, for example, the category of the service within the UNSPSC classification system. The second type of information is quality rating of the service. We define QOS of the service here.

In this paper we only provides a simple simulation and classification on the service domains and will focus on the scientific computation service as described in Figure 1. To accomplish such a huge task, computer scientists have to cooperate with specialists in all other domains who can contribute to build the domain specific service ontologies in order to integrate each section into a whole system.

To advertise Web services in a registry, we use a structure, called SO, that holds the description of a real Web service. A SO has five sections that need to be specified:

first the name of the Web service, second the textual description of the Web service, third the QOS of the Web service, forth the set of input parameters of the Web service, last the set of output parameters of the Web service.

QOS should be seen as an integral aspect of Web services; therefore, it should be integrated with Web services specifications. [1] suggests a QOS model that have four dimensions include time, cost, fidelity and reliability. For scientific computation, time and cost must be also as QOS dimensions. For different function, it is must have different QOS dimensions, for example fidelity is a QOS dimensions subject to judgments and perceptions in DNA Sequencing, and a max loop times is a QOS dimensions of NN. So we can use OWL-S ServiceProfile ontology for the specification of QOS metrics. This information will allow for the discovery of Web services based on QOS metrics.

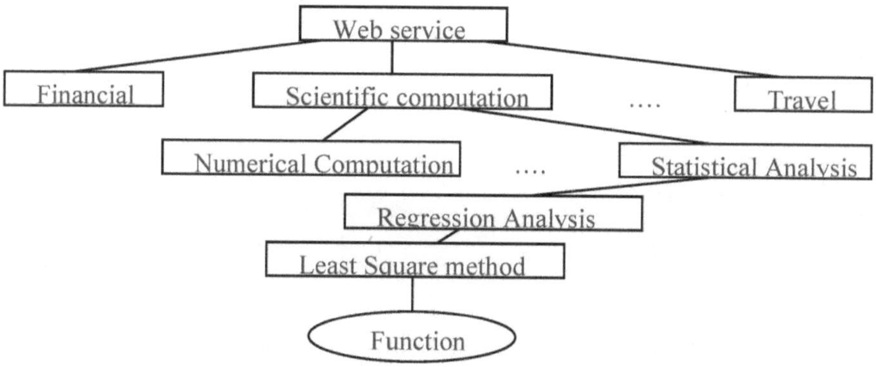

Fig. 1

3 Discovery of Web Service Based on QOS

First the suppliers access the registry service to advertise their Web services. To make an advertisement, a supplier registers a service object (SO) with the system. Clients and customers typically access the system to find Web services registered. This is achieved by sending a service template (ST) to the system. The ST specifies the requirements about the service to discover using OWL-S. When the system receives a discovery message (i.e., a ST) from a workflow system, it is parsed and matched against the set of SOs registered. Then return a SO reference that has the most similarity degree with the ST.

A ST has five sections that need to be specified: first the name of the Web service to be found, second the textual description of the Web service, third the QOS of the Web service, forth the set of input parameters of the Web service, last the set of output parameters of the Web service.

The fields of a ST have the same meaning as the ones defined in a SO. This makes sense because SOs will be matched against STs.

During the discovery phase, system look up in the registry try to find similarities between ST and SO. This is done using syntactic, semantic information and Qos information.

The syntactic similarity of a ST and a SO is based on their service names and service descriptions. In our work, we use "string matching" as a way to calculate how closely service names and service descriptions resemble each other.

The semantic similarity of a ST and a SO is based on their concepts and properties. Similarly, these Web services all come from the same ontology, so the semantic similarity is also easy to compute.

The QOS similarity of a ST and a SO is calculated with the function QSimilarity(ST, SO). The binary function QSimilarity computes the geometric distance of the QoS dimensions specified in the ST and the ones specified in the SO. The function returns a real value between 0 and 1, indicating the similarity of the operational metrics of its arguments. The closer to the value 1 the result is, the more similar a SO is to a ST

$$\text{QSimilarity(ST, SO)}=(\Sigma r_i Qd_i)/n, \qquad \Sigma r_i=1. \tag{1}$$

In (1), n is the number of Qos dimension, r_i the right of the number i dimension. r_i is defined by user.

The Qd is a function to computer a dimension difference between ST and SO.

$$\text{Qd(ST, SO,dim)}=1-|\text{ST.Qos(dim)} - \text{ST.Qos(dim)}| / \text{ST.Qos(dimension)} \tag{2}$$

This dim is a dimension.

4 Conclusions

In this paper, we have presented a simple solution to use Web service in scientific computation. We described the service template as the data structure to discover services, and discuss the algorithm of the similarity degree between ST and SO based on QOS of Web service.

References

1. Cardoso, J., Miller J.: Implementing QOS Management for Workflow Systems. Technical Report, LSDIS Lab, Computer Science, University of Georgia, July, 2002.
2. Jena (2002): The jena semantic web toolkit, http://www.hpl.hp.com/semweb/jenatop.html. Hewlett-Packard Company.
3. Verma K., Sivashanmugam K.: METEOR–S WSDI A Scalable P2P Infrastructure of Registries for Semantic Publication and Discovery of Web Services. Information Technology and Management. Vol. 6, No. 1 (2005) 17-39
4. Klingeman, J. etc: Deriving Service Models in Cross-Organizational Workflows□In Proceedings of RIDE-Information Technology for Virtual Enterprisea (RIDE-VE99), Sydney, 1999
5. Web Services Architecture Requirements, W3C Working Group Note 11 February 2004, http://www.w3.org/TR/2004/NOTE-wsa-reqs-20040211/
6. Borst, W.N.: Construction of Engineering Ontologies for Knowledge Sharing and Reuse. PhD thesis, University of Twente, Enschede, 1997

Common Program Analysis of Two-Party Security Protocols Using SMV*

Yuqing Zhang and Suping Jia

State Key Laboratory of Information Security, Graduate University of Chinese Academy of Sciences, Beijing 100039, P.R. China
zhangyq@gscas.ac.cn,
jiasp@nipc.org.cn

Abstract. A common framework, which can be used to analyze the two-party security protocols, is proposed in this paper. With the common framework, a common program is developed in order that any two-party security protocol can be automatically analyzed through SMV with slight modification of the common program. Finally, we illustrate the feasibility and efficiency of the common program analysis with the SSL 3.0 protocol as a case study.

1 Introduction

Model checking [2] has proved to be a very successful approach to analyzing security protocols. Encouraged by the success of Lowe in analyzing the Needham-Schroeder public-key authentication protocol [3], since 1997, many researchers have attempted to analyze the security of protocols by using model checking technique. Now many security protocols□such as Needham-Schroeder public-key protocol, TMN, Kerberos and so on, have been successfully analyzed with model checkers.

Model checking tools, including FDR, MurΦ, SPIN, SMV used as general purpose model checkers, and NRL, Interrogator used as special purpose model checkers, can verify whether certain conditions are satisfied by building a state graph in the model. Among these model checkers, SMV [4] is not only a powerful analyzing and verifying tool, but also an easy-to-learn and easy-to-use tool.

In previous work [5, 6], for every protocol, the authors had to develop a program when analyzing it with SMV. In this paper, we further study the common character of the two-party security protocols and try to obtain a common framework. With this framework, we can develop a common program, so that we can automatically analyze any two-party protocol only through slightly modification of the common program.

2 SMV System

The SMV (Symbolic Model Verifier) [4] system (see Fig.1.), developed by school of computer science of Carnegie Mellon University, is a tool for checking finite state

* This work is supported by National Natural Science Foundation of China (Grant Nos. 60102004, 60373040 and 60573048).

H.T. Shen et al. (Eds.): APWeb 2006, LNCS 3842, pp. 923 – 930, 2006.

systems against specifications in the temporal logic CTL (Computation Tree Logic). So far, SMV has become a popularly-used model checker for security protocols. The input language of SMV system is designed to allow the description of finite state systems that range from completely synchronous to completely asynchronous and from the detailed to the abstract. The logic CTL allows a rich class of temporal properties. SMV uses the OBDD (Ordered Binary Decision Diagram)-based symbolic model checking algorithm to efficiently determine whether specifications expressed in CTL are satisfied, so it is a powerful analyzing and verifying tool, which is also the reason why we chose SMV as our model checking tool for the analysis of security protocols.

SMV takes a finite state system and a property Φ expressed in CTL as input and outputs true if the finite state system satisfies Φ or false otherwise. If the outcome is false SMV will output a counterexample. In the analysis of security protocols, the counterexample is the possible attack upon the protocol.

Fig. 1. Model checker SMV software

3 Two-Party Security Protocols

The security protocol is an intercommunicating protocol based on the cryptographic system. Two-party security protocols have only two principals, one is initiator and the other is responder, and the running of the protocol is to transmit messages between the two principals. To analyze the two-party security protocols, one should produce a small system running the protocol, together with a model of the most general intruder who can interact with the protocol, and to use a state exploration tool to discover if the system can enter an insecure state, that is, whether there is an attack upon the protocol. The basic analysis framework of the two-party security protocols is as follows (A represents initiator, B represents responder and I represents intruder).

4 The Common Framework Design

4.1 Data Structure for the Messages of the Protocol

In SMV, we integrate the network with the intruder as one module in the sense that the intruder will control the network and each participant communicates with others via the intruder (see Fig.2). Thus, the intruder can overhear, delete, or store every message and generate new messages by using his knowledge of overheard messages.

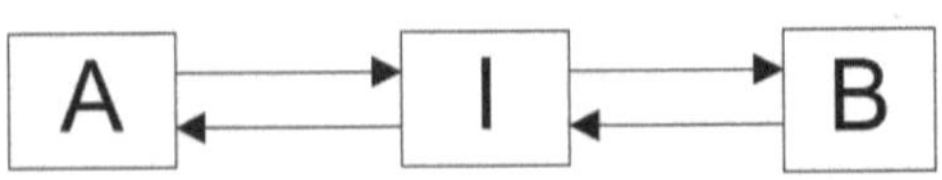

Fig. 2. The analysis framework of two-party security protocols

In a common two-party security protocol, which has n messages, the SMV characterization of the message format must have enough fields for all kinds of information that occur in any of the n intended messages. We use a module to define the data structure "message" that contains the following fields:

```
MODULE message
 VAR
 mtype : {none,msg1,msg2...msgn}; --type of messages. none denotes no message
                                   --n is the number of messages in the protocol;
 source: {A, B, I};                --source of message
 dest: {A, B, I};                  --intended destination
 key: {none,key1, key2, ...keyi};  --encryption key; i denotes the number of
                                   --possible keys used in the protocol.
 data1: { };                       --the first data items of messages. data2: { };
                                   --the second data items of messages
  ...
 datam:{ };                        --the m_th data items of messages
```

4.2 The Finite State System

We define a finite state system, which has 1 initiator *A*, 1 responder *B*, and 1 intruder *I*. Initiator *A* and responder *B* are honest participants, while intruder *I* is not, which can impersonate initiator and responder.

The sets of the system are as follows:

(1) The set of initiators is {A, I, I (A)};
(2) The set of responders is {B, I, I (B)}.

We formulate each participant in the two-party security protocol as a SMV module instance, which consists of honest participants and intruder. According to the analysis framework (Fig.2), in SMV program, the input of initiator A and responder B comes only from intruder I, and the output of A and B is also passed to I.

```
MODULE main
  VAR
  A: initiator (I.outMA);  --initiator. I.outMA is an input formal parameter
  B: responder (I.outMB); --responder. I.outMB is an input formal parameter
  I: intruder (A.outM, B.outM); --intruder I.
```

4.3 The State Transition Graph

A common two-party security protocol has two honest participants: initiator A and responder B. To run a protocol, initiator A sends the first message of the protocol to responder B, after receiving the message, responder B automatically sends the next message to initiator A, then they will in turn send messages between them all through the protocol run. For a protocol of n messages, if n is an even number, then a complete protocol run ends up with the initiator A receiving the last message of the protocol; if n is an odd number, then a complete protocol run ends up with the responder B receiving

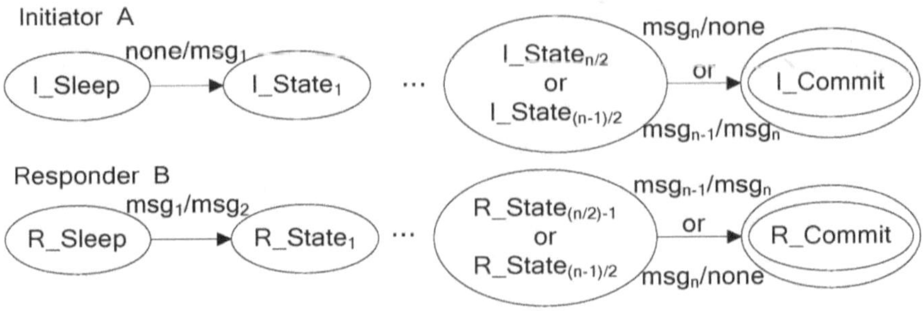

Fig. 3. State transition graphs of initiator A and responder B

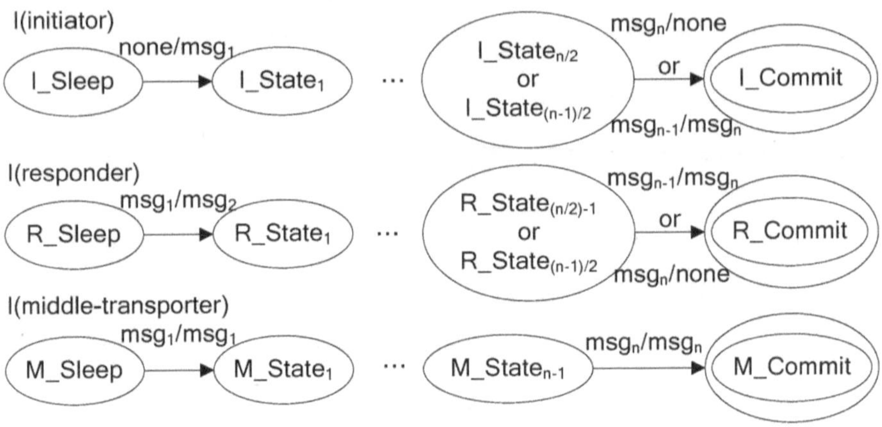

Fig. 4. State transition graphs of intruder I

the last message of the protocol. The state sets of initiator *A* and responder *B* are {I_Sleep,I_State$_1$,...I_State$_{n/2}$(n is even, or I_State$_{(n-1)/2}$ if n is an odd number), I_Commit}and {R_Sleep,R_State$_1$,...R_State$_{(n/2)-1}$(n is even, or R_State$_{(n-1)/2}$ if n is an odd number), R_Commit}.

There are *n* steps in a run of the protocol, which corresponds to the states in A's and B's state transition graphs (Fig.3). Initiator A begins in I_Sleep state and sends msg_1 to responder in the same state, then requests msg_2 from responder in I_state$_1$ state, switches to the next state after receiving msg_2 from responder and sending msg_3 to responder. In this way, initiator A ends in I_commit after receiving msg_n, if *n* is even; otherwise, ends in I_commit after receiving msg_{n-1} and sending out msg_n. Similarly, responder B begins in R_Sleep state and requests msg_1 from initiator in the same state, and then sends msg_2 to initiator, ends in R_commit state after receiving msg_{n-1} from initiator and sending out msg_n in R_State$_{(n/2)-1}$ state if n is even; otherwise, responder B ends in R_commit state after receiving msg_n. Note that responder B uses a variable B.ini to remember who the initiator of the protocol is after receiving msg_1 from initiator.

Since intruder *I* can impersonate initiator *A* and responder *B*, and as a middle-transporter he can also just pass messages between initiator and responder, the state transition graphs of intruder *I* are more complex. Fig.4 gives the state transition graphs of intruder *I* as initiator, responder and middle-transporter.

4.4 System Property

Considering different points of view, we give the properties of the finite state system in logic CTL as follows:

AG(((A.state=I_sleep)&(A.resp=B))->AF((A.state=I_commit)&(B.State=R_Commit) &(B.ini=A)&(I.IA=0)&(I.IB=0))) (1)

Here, A, G, F, ->, and & are CTL symbols. **AG** represents all states of all the paths; **AF** represents the final states of all paths ;**->** represents logic implication; **&**represents logic *and.*

The meaning of the CTL formula (1) is that If initiator A runs the protocol once with B and begins in I_Sleep state, then the system will eventually end in a state which A is in I_Commit state and responder B is in R_Commit state and B believes that the initiator of the protocol is A and intruder I doesn't impersonate A and B.

Responder B may not participant in the protocol, so we give the system property :

AG(((A.state=I_sleep)&(A.resp=B))->AF((A.state=I_commit)&(I.IA=0)&(I.IB=0))) (2)

Initiator A may not participant in the protocol, we give the system property:

AG (((B.state=R_sleep)&(B.ini=A))->AF((B.state=R_commit)&(I.IA=0)&(I.IB=0)) (3)

Model checkers explore the state space of the system when analyzing security protocols and they will stop exploring when a counterexample is found. To explore more efficiently, we should properly modify the CTL description of the system properties when analyzing specific protocols. For example, in the key-establishment protocols, we should also ensure that the intruder will not know the shared key established by initiator and responder at the end of the protocol run,, so we should add (I.knowkey = 0) to the end of each CTL formula.

5 A Case Study: SSL Protocol

We will refer to [7] and analyze a close approximation of the basic SSL 3.0 handshake protocol as a case study. The simplified protocol that closely resembles SSL 3.0 is as follows.

C->S : C, Ver_C, $Suite_C$
S->C : Ver_S, $Suite_S$, $Sign_{CA}\{S, Ks^{+}\}$
C->S : $Sign_{CA}\{C,V_C\}$, $\{Secret_C\}_{Ks+}$, $Sign_C\{Hash(Secret_C)\}$

5.1 Common Program Analysis of SSL 3.0 Handshake Protocol

In the simplified SSL 3.0 handshake protocol, there are three messages, and each of the messages has three data items. So both ***n*** and ***m*** are equal to 3; Keys used in the protocol may be Ks and Ki (intruder *I* may run the protocol and send out the second message with key Ki), so ***i*** equals 2. To be clear, notation C and S instead of A and B are used in the SMV program for the analysis of SSL handshake protocol to denote initiator and responder.

Intruder *I* can run the protocol, so the first message may be like this: I, Ver_i, $Suite_i$; the second message maybe like this: Ver_i, $Suite_i$, $Sign_{CA}\{I, Ki^+\}$; and the third message may be: $Sign_{CA}\{I,V_i\}$, $\{Secret_i\}_{Ks+}$, $Sign_i\{Hash(Secret_i)\}$. For the analysis of SSL 3.0 handshake protocol, we only need to substitute the above message data for the corresponding fields of the module message in section 4.1.

The finite state system is similar to that defined in section 4.2; we only need to substitute C and S for *A* and *B* in module *main*.

According to section 4, the state transition graphs should be like Fig.5 and Fig.6.

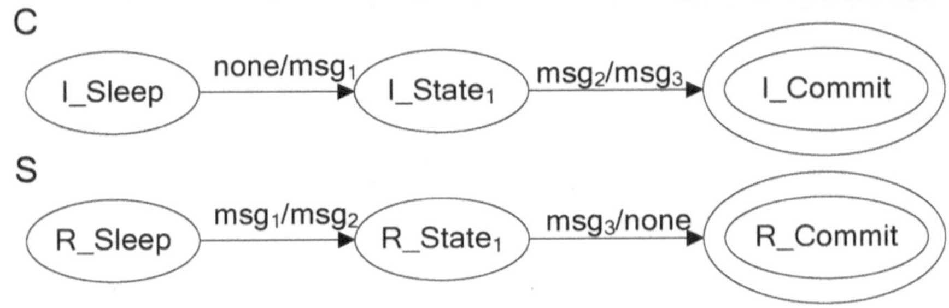

Fig. 5. State transition graphs of initiator C and responder S

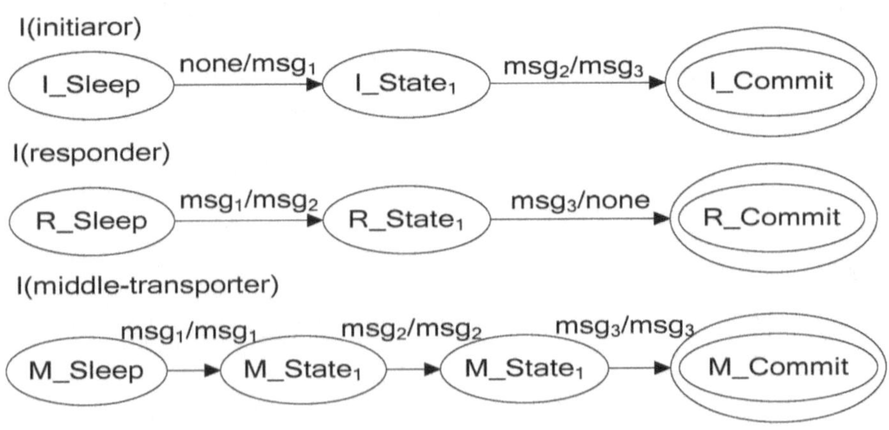

Fig. 6. State transition graphs of intruder I

According to the common framework, besides the module *message* there are three modules in SMV program, namely initiator, responder and intruder. To analyze SSL, we only need to modify the data fields of each module according to module *message* and the state transition according to the state transition graph of each participant.

5.2 System Property

Considering different point of view, we give the properties of the finite state system in logic CTL as follows:

AG (((C.state=I_sleep) &(C.resp=S)) ->AF((C.state=I_commit)&(S.state=R_commit) &(S.ini=C)&(I.IC=0)&(I.IS=0))) (1)
AG (((C.state=I_sleep)&(C.resp=S))->AF((C.state=I_commit)&(I.IC=0)&(I.IS=0))) (2)
AG(((S.state=R_sleep)&(S.ini=C))->AF((S.state=R_commit)&(I.IC=0)&(I.IS=0)) (3)

The meanings of these CTL formulas can refer to section 4.4.

5.3 Checking Results

Our SMV program discovers that the simplified version of SSL 3.0 handshake protocol does not satisfy the properties. Against each property, SMV outputs a counterexample. These counterexamples are the attacks on the basic SSL handshake protocol. We find three attacks by analyzing the outputs.

Attack1: 1.1 C->I : C, Ver_C, $Suite_C$
2.1 I(C)->S : C, $\underline{Ver_i}$, $\underline{Suite_i}$
2.2 S->I(C) : Ver_s, $Suite_S$, $Sign_{CA}\{S, Ks^+\}$
1.2 I->C : Ver_i, $Suite_i$, $Sign_{CA}\{I, K_i^+\}$
1.3 C->I : $Sign_{CA}\{C,V_C\}$, $\{Secret_C\}K_i^+$, $Sign_C\{Hash(Secret_C)\}$
2.3 I(C)->S : $Sign_{CA}\{C,V_C\}$, $\{Secret_C\}Ks^+$, $Sign_C\{Hash(Secret_C)\}$

Attack2: 1.1 C->I(S) : C, Ver_C, $Suitec$
2.1 I->S : I, $\underline{Ver_i}$, $\underline{Suite_i}$
2.2 S->I : Ver_s, $Suite_s$, $Sign_{CA}\{S, Ks^+\}$
1.2 I(S)->C : Ver_i, $Suite_i$, $Sign_{CA}\{S, Ks^+\}$
1.3 C->I(S) : $Sign_{CA}\{C,V_c\}$, $\{Secret_c\}Ks^+$, $Sign_C\{Hash(Secret_c)\}$
2.3 I->S : $Sign_{CA}\{I,V_i\}$, $\{Secret_c\}Ks^+$, $Sign_I\{Hash(Secret_c)\}$

Attack3: 1.1 C->I(S) : C, Ver_c, $Suite_c$
2.1 I(C)->S : C, $\underline{Ver_i}$, $\underline{Suite_i}$
2.2 S->I(C) : Ver_s, $Suite_s$, $Sign_{CA}\{S, Ks^+\}$
1.2 I(S)->C : Ver_i, $Suite_i$, $Sign_{CA}\{S, Ks^+\}$
1.3 C->I(S) : $Sign_{CA}\{C,V_c\}$, $\{Secret_c\}Ks^+$, $Sign_C\{Hash(Secret_c)\}$
2.3 (C)->S : $Sign_{CA}\{C,V_c\}$, $\{Secret_c\}Ks^+$, $Sign_C\{Hash(Secret_c)\}$

So far, we have analyzed SSL and successfully uncovered the attacks on the protocol, which demonstrates the feasibility of our common program analysis.

6 Conclusions

SMV is a powerful analyzing and verifying tool for security protocols. From this paper, we can find that SMV is also an easy-to-learn and easy-to-use tool. Previously, when we analyze a security protocol with a new tool, we have to spend much time learning the programming language and then have to develop a completely new program for every specific protocol. Now with SMV, we only need to modify the data fields and the number of states of the common program instead of developing a completely new SMV program for every specific two-party security protocol.

Our proposed common framework is an efficient method for the analysis of two-party security protocols. But for the multi-party security protocols, it does not work well, so in the future we would like to investigate the feasibility of common program analysis for the multi-party security protocols.

References

[1] Panti.M., Spalazzi.L., Tacconi.S., Valent.S.: Automatic Verification of Security in Payment Protocols for Electronic Commerce. Proceedings of the 4th International Conference on Enterprise Information Systems (ICEIS 2002),Ciudad Real, Spain (2002) 968–974

[2] Lowe G.: Towards a completeness result for model checking of security protocols. Technical Report 1998/6, Department of Mathematics and Computer Science, University of Leicester, 1998. Available from http://www.mcs.le.ac.uk/~glowe/Security/Papers/completeness.ps.gz.

[3] Lowe G.: Breaking and fixing the Needham-Schroeder public-key protocol using FDR. In Proceedings of TACAS. Lecture Notes in Computer Science, Vol. 1055. Springer-Verlag, 147–166 (1996)

[4] SMV. School of Computer Science of Carnegie Mellon University, 1998. Available via URL: http://www.cs.cmu.edu/~modelcheck/

[5] Zhang Y. and Xiao G.: Breaking and fixing the Helsinki protocol using SMV. ELECTRONICS LETTERS, 35(15) (1999) 1239~1240

[6] Zhangn Y., Chen K., and Xiao G.: Automated Analysis of Cryptographic Protocol Using SMV. In Proceedings of International Workshop on Cryptographic Techniques and E-Commerce (CrypTEC '99), July (1999)

[7] Mitchell J. C., Mitchell M., and Stern U.: Automated analysis of cryptographic protocols using Murφ. In Proceedings of the IEEE Symposium on Security and Privacy. IEEE Computer Society Press, 141-151 (1997)

[8] Zhang Y. and Liu, X.: An approach to the formal verification of the three-principal cryptographic protocols. ACM Operating Systems Review 38 (1) (2004) 35–42.

An Integrated Web-Based Model for Management, Analysis and Retrieval of EST Biological Information

Youping Deng[1], Yinghua Dong[2], Susan J. Brown[2], and Chaoyang Zhang[3]

[1] Department of Biological Sciences, University of Southern Mississippi, Hattiesburg, Mississippi 39406, USA
Youping.Deng@usm.edu
[2] Division of Biology, Kansas State University, Manhattan, Kansas 66506, USA
{Yinghua.Dong, Susan.Brown}@ksu.edu
[3] School of Computing, University of Southern Mississippi, Hattiesburg, Mississippi 39406, USA
Chaoyang.Zhang@usm.edu

Abstract. In this work, an integrated Web-based model integrating a number of components has been proposed to analyze, manage and retrieve biological information. In particular, we deal with Expressed Sequence Tags (EST) data that is an important resource for gene identification, genome annotation and comparative genomics. A high-performance and user-friendly three-tier Web application consisting of EST modeling and database (ESTMD) has been developed to facilitate the retrieval and analysis of EST information. It provides a variety of Web services and tools for searching raw, cleaned and assembled EST sequences, genes and Gene Ontology, as well as pathway information. It can be accessed at http://129.130.115.72:8080/estweb/index.html.

1 Introduction

Computer science and information technologies have made a tremendous contribution to the development of bioinformatics in recent years. One of the main areas of bioinformatics is to design and develop Web-based applications consisting of biological database management, information retrieval, data mining and analysis tools, and a variety of genetic Web services to speed up and enhance biological research. In this work, an integrated Web-based model is proposed and developed to manage, analyze and retrieve Expressed Sequence Tags (ESTs) data that are partial sequences of randomly chosen cDNA obtained from the results of a single DNA sequencing reaction.

EST is an important resource for gene identification, genome annotation and comparative genomics. ESTs are used to identify transcribed regions in genomic sequence and to characterize patterns of gene expression in the tissue. Typically, processing ESTs includes original (raw) sequence cleaning such as low quality, vector and adaptor sequence removing, cleaned sequence assembly to become unique sequences, and unique sequence annotation and functional assignment. Keeping track

H.T. Shen et al. (Eds.): APWeb 2006, LNCS 3842, pp. 931 – 938, 2006.

of and managing the information is a critical issue for many labs. Currently available EST database software, e.g. ESTAP [1] has many limitations. ESTAP mainly focuses on data processing and analysis, and does not support Gene Ontology search. RED [2] provides only two simple search tools, by keyword and by Gene Ontology. ESTIMA, a tool for EST management in a multi-project environment [3], provides limited services for detailed EST information search. Other tools such as StackPACK [4], ESTWeb [5] and PipeOnline2.0 [6] mainly focus on developing EST processing pipelines other than EST information management and presentation. None of them provides pathway search so far.

In this article, we introduce a new high-performance Web-based application consisting of EST modeling and database (ESTMD) to facilitate and enhance the retrieval and analysis of EST information. It provides a number of comprehensive search tools for mining EST raw, cleaned and unique sequences, Gene Ontology, pathway information and a variety of genetic Web services such as BLAST search, data submission and sequence download pages. The software is developed using advanced Java technology and it supports portability, extensibility and data recovery. It can be accessed at http://129.130.115.72:8080/estweb/index.html.

2 Software Architecture

ESTMD is an integrated Web-based application consisting of client, sever and backend database, as shown in Fig. 1. The work process is as follows: users input some keywords or IDs from the Web interface and then submit them to the server. The server processes the query and retrieves date from the backend database through the database connection interface. The results are processed and sent to the users in proper format.

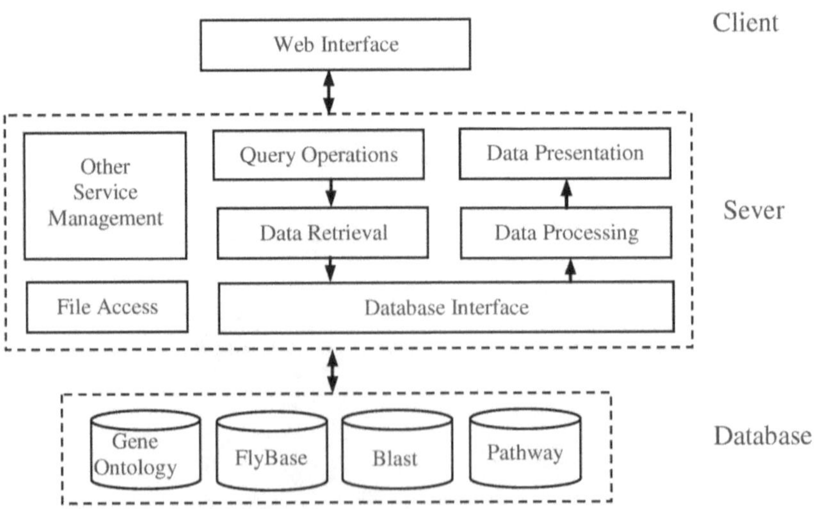

Fig. 1. The software architecture of ESTMD

3 Web Services

The Web application provides a number of search tools and Web services, including search in detail, search by keyword, Gene Ontology search, Gene Ontology classification, and pathway search. Users may search the database by several methods. Users are also allowed to download data from or submit data to the database.

3.1 General Search

Users may search database by gene symbol, gene name, or any type of ID (such as unique sequence ID, clone ID, FlyBase ID, Genbank ID or accession ID). The Web search interface is given in Fig. 2. The keyword search returns results in a table, rather than plain text. The results include clone ID, raw sequence length, cleaned sequence length, unique sequence ID, unique sequence length, gene name and gene symbol. It has a hyperlink to contig view which uses color bars to show the alignment between contig and singlet sequences, as shown in Fig. 3.

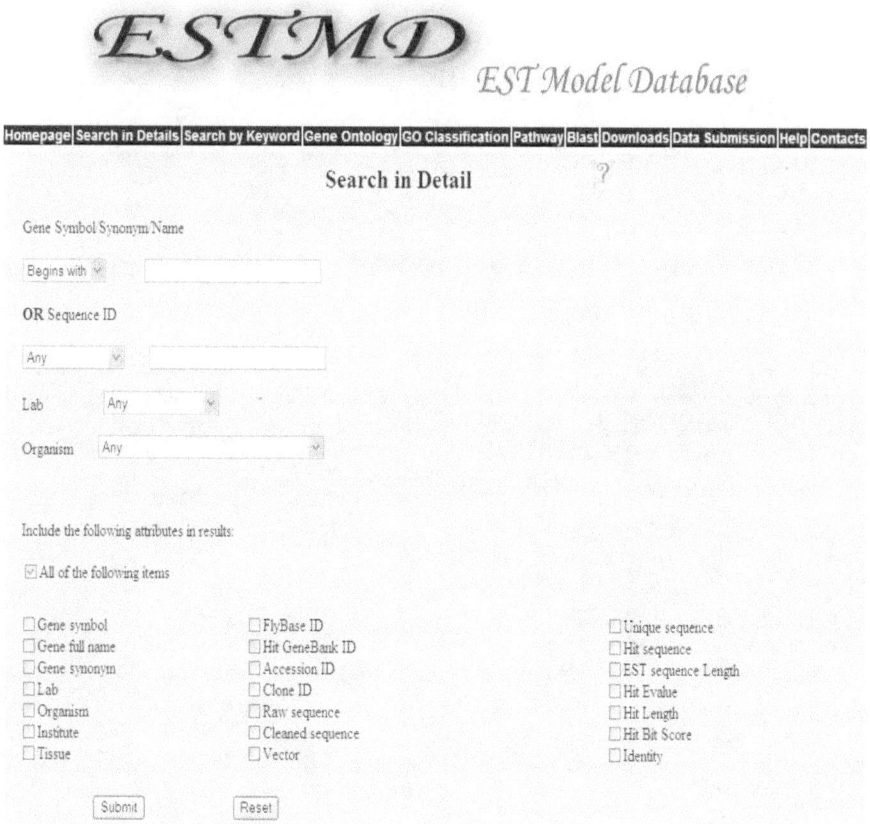

Fig. 2. Web search interface showing fields for user input and attributes of results

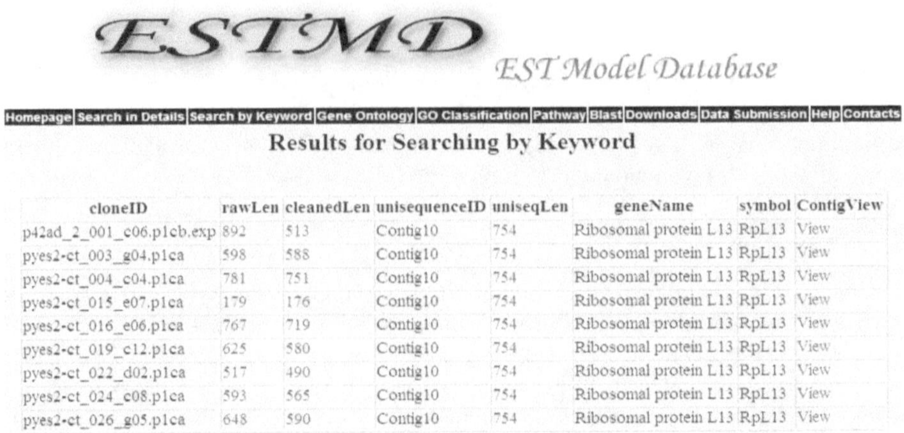

cloneID	rawLen	cleanedLen	unisequenceID	uniseqLen	geneName	symbol	ContigView
p42ad_2_001_c06.p1cb.exp	892	513	Contig10	754	Ribosomal protein L13	RpL13	View
pyes2-ct_003_g04.p1ca	598	588	Contig10	754	Ribosomal protein L13	RpL13	View
pyes2-ct_004_c04.p1ca	781	751	Contig10	754	Ribosomal protein L13	RpL13	View
pyes2-ct_015_e07.p1ca	179	176	Contig10	754	Ribosomal protein L13	RpL13	View
pyes2-ct_016_e06.p1ca	767	719	Contig10	754	Ribosomal protein L13	RpL13	View
pyes2-ct_019_c12.p1ca	625	580	Contig10	754	Ribosomal protein L13	RpL13	View
pyes2-ct_022_d02.p1ca	517	490	Contig10	754	Ribosomal protein L13	RpL13	View
pyes2-ct_024_c08.p1ca	593	565	Contig10	754	Ribosomal protein L13	RpL13	View
pyes2-ct_026_g05.p1ca	648	590	Contig10	754	Ribosomal protein L13	RpL13	View

(a)

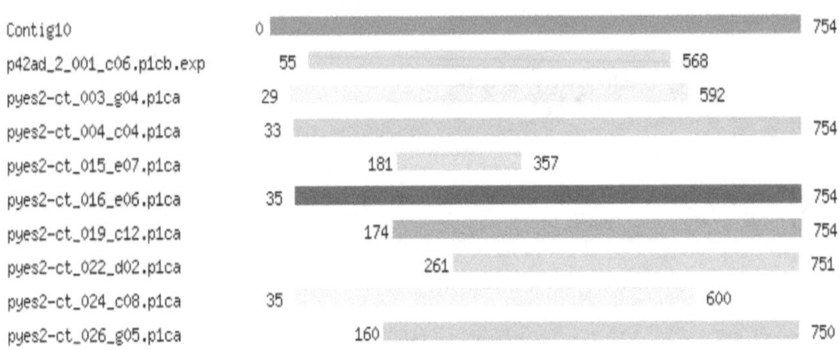

(b)

Fig. 3. An example result of "Search by Keyword". Contig10 is used as keyword to search. **(a)** Standard HTML table presents clone ID, raw sequence length, cleaned sequence length, unique sequence ID, unique sequence length, gene name, and gene symbol. The blue texts mark hyperlinks on the items. **(b)** Contig View of Contig10. The contig bar is shown in red, and the singlet bars are shown in orange, yellow, green, cyan, blue and purple separately.

3.2 Gene Ontology Search and Classification

The Gene Ontology describes the molecular functions, biological processes and cellular components of gene products [7][8]. One interest for scientists who have the EST sequences is to know the functions of these sequences. Searching Gene Ontology (GO) is a good way to quickly find the functions of these sequences and their corresponding genes. ESTMD allows users to search Gene Ontology not only by a single gene name, symbol or ID, but also by a file containing a batch of sequence IDs or FlyBase IDs. The file search capability in ESTMD allows users to get function information of many EST sequences or genes at one time instead of searching one by one. Users can search all the GO terms by selecting one of molecular function, biological process or cellular component to submit their search. The result table includes GO ID, term, type, sequence ID, hit ID (FlyBase ID), and gene symbol. The hyperlinks on terms can show Gene Ontology tree structure, as shown in Fig. 4.

- Gene_Ontology
  - biological_process
    - cell growth and/or maintenance
      - metabolism
        - biosynthesis
          - macromolecule biosynthesis
            - protein biosynthesis
  - biological_process
    - cell growth and/or maintenance
      - metabolism
        - protein metabolism
          - protein biosynthesis

Fig. 4. Gene Ontology Tree Structure View of protein biosynthesis

Classifying genes into different function groups is a good way to know the gene function relationship. Another important feature of ESTMD is Gene Ontology Classification search. ESTMD defines a series of functional categories according to molecular function, biological process and cellular component. Users can classify Gene Ontology of a batch of sequences. The result shows type, subtype, how many sequences and percentage of sequences in this subtype (Fig. 5). This feature is very useful for cDNA microarray gene function analysis. In this type of array, ESTs are printed on slides. Therefore, the Gene Ontology Classification tool in ESTMD can help automatically divide these ESTs into different functional groups.

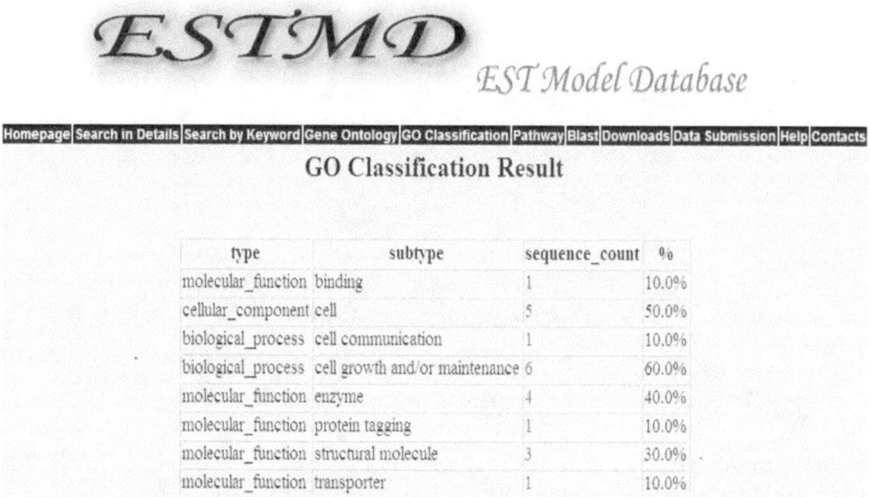

type	subtype	sequence_count	%
molecular_function	binding	1	10.0%
cellular_component	cell	5	50.0%
biological_process	cell communication	1	10.0%
biological_process	cell growth and/or maintenance	6	60.0%
molecular_function	enzyme	4	40.0%
molecular_function	protein tagging	1	10.0%
molecular_function	structural molecule	3	30.0%
molecular_function	transporter	1	10.0%

Fig. 5. The results of classifying Gene Ontology from a text file which contains 10 sequence IDs. Standard HTML table presents types, subtypes, sequence count and percentages.

3.3 Pathway Search

Pathway page allows searching pathway by single or multiple gene names, IDs, EC numbers, enzyme names, or pathway names. File search is also provided in this page. The scope of the search may be the whole pathway or just our database. The results show pathway name, category, unique sequence ID, EC number, and enzyme count (Fig. 6). The pathway information comes from KEGG metabolic pathway [9]. We have downloaded, reorganized and integrated it into our database.

Pathway Search Result

Pathway_name	Category	unisequenceID	ECnumber	Enzyme_count
Arginine and proline metabolism	Amino Acid Metabolism	pyes2-ct_026_h11.p1ca	2.7.3.3	4
Carbon fixation	Carbohydrate Metabolism	Contig97	2.7.1.40	7
Cysteine metabolism	Carbohydrate Metabolism	Contig35	1.1.1.27	10
Glycolysis / Gluconeogenesis	Carbohydrate Metabolism	Contig35	1.1.1.27	10
Glycolysis / Gluconeogenesis	Carbohydrate Metabolism	Contig97	2.7.1.40	7
Propanoate metabolism	Carbohydrate Metabolism	Contig35	1.1.1.27	10
Purine metabolism	Carbohydrate Metabolism	Contig97	2.7.1.40	7
Pyruvate metabolism	Carbohydrate Metabolism	Contig97	2.7.1.40	7
Pyruvate metabolism	Carbohydrate Metabolism	Contig35	1.1.1.27	10
Selenoamino acid metabolism	Metabolism of Other Amino Acids	pyes2-ct_021_f10.p1ca	2.7.9.3	2

Fig. 6. The results of pathway search from a text file, ordered by Pathway, are shown. Standard HTML table presents pathway names, categories, sequence IDs, EC numbers and Enzyme name counts. The blue texts mark hyperlinks on the items.

3.4 Contig View

Users may input contig sequence ID to see the alignments of the contig and all of the singlet sequences contained. This feature allows users to check if the contig is correct (Fig. 3b).

3.5 BLAST

BLAST program [10] is used to search and annotate EST sequences. BLAST page allows users to do BLAST search by choosing different databases. The databases contain raw EST sequences, cleaned EST sequences and assembled unique sequences, as well as NCBI GenBank nr (non-redundant), Swissprot amino acid, gadfly nucleotide and amino acid sequences from FlyBase [11]. As we use insect EST sequences as sample sequences, we have put gadfly sequences into our database for searching. Users can install different databases into the program.

3.6 Downloads and Data Submissions

Users may download our raw sequences, cleaned sequences, and unique sequences. All of the files are in plain text format, and the items are separated by tab. Users may submit data to the database. After submission, the date and user information are stored in the database and a confirmation is sent to the users by email.

4 Development Environments

Apache2.0 acts as HTTP server. Tomcat4.1 is the servlet container used. Both of them can run on UNIX, Linux and Windows NT. It ensures that ESTMD is platform-independent. The server-side programs are implemented using Java technologies. Java Servlets and JSP (Java Server Pages) are used as interface between users and database. XML and XSLT technologies are used to describe, generate and express Gene Ontology tree. Data mining programs are written using Perl. Java, XML, and XSLT are used to generate and express Gene Ontology tree. The user interface of the database is created using HTML and JavaScript. JavaScript can check the validation of the users' input on client side, which reduces some burden on server side.

ESTMD is currently hosted on Red Hat 9 with MySQL4.0. There are more than 20 tables in the database, such as clone, EST, uniSequence, uniHit, FlyBase, FlyBaseDetails, and so on.

5 Conclusion

ESTMD is a new integrated Web-based model that is comprised of (1) front-end user interface for accessing the system and displaying results, (2) middle layer for providing a variety of Web services such as data processing, task analysis, search tools and so on, and (3) back-end relational database system for storing and managing biological data. It provides a wide range of search tools to retrieve original (raw), cleaned and unique EST sequences and their detailed annotated information. Users can search not only the sequence, gene function and pathway information using single sequence ID, gene name or term, but also the function and pathway information using a file including a batch of sequence IDs. Moreover, users can quickly assign the sequences into different functional groups using the Gene Ontology Classification search tool. ESTMD provides a useful tool for biological scientists to manage EST sequences and their annotated information.

Acknowledgements

This work was supported by Dean's Research Initiative award of the University of Southern Mississippi to Youping Deng and the Mississippi Functional Genomics Network (DHHS/NIH/NCRR Grant# 2P20RR016476-04) and NIH grant P20

RR16475 from the Kansas BRIN Program of the National Center for Research Resources, National Institute of Health. The authors sincerely thank Phaneendra Vanka for reading the manuscript and giving suggestions.

References

1. Mao, C., Cushman, J.C., May, G.D. and Weller, J.W.: ESTAP-An Automated System for the Analysis of EST Data. Bioinformatics. 19 (2003) 1720-1722
2. Everitt, R., Minnema, S.E., Wride, M.A., Koster, C.S., Hance, J.E., Mansergh, F.C. and Rancourt, D.E.: RED: The Analysis, Management and Dissemination of Expressed Sequence Tags. Bioinformatics. 18 (2002) 1692-1693
3. Kumar, C. G., LeDuc, R., Gong, G., Roinishivili, L., Lewin, H. A., & Liu, L.: ESTIMA, a tool for EST management in a multi-project environment. BMC. Bioinformatics, 5(2004) 176
4. Christoffels, A., van, G. A., Greyling, G., Miller, R., Hide, T., & Hide, W.: STACK: Sequence Tag Alignment and Consensus Knowledgebase. Nucleic Acids Res., 29(2001) 234-238
5. Paquola, A. C., Nishyiama, M. Y., Jr., Reis, E. M., da Silva, A. M., & Verjovski-Almeida, S.: ESTWeb: bioinformatics services for EST sequencing projects. Bioinformatics, 19(2003) 1587-1588
6. Ayoubi, P., Jin, X., Leite, S., Liu, X., Martajaja, J., Abduraham, A., Wan, Q., Yan, W., Misawa, E., & Prade, R. A.: PipeOnline 2.0: automated EST processing and functional data sorting. Nucleic Acids Res., 30(2002) 4761-4769
7. Ashburner, M., Ball, C.A., Blake, J.A., Botstein, D., Butler, H., Cherry, J.M., Davis, A.P., Dolinski, K., Dwight, S.S., Eppig, J.T., Harris, M.A., Hill, D.P., Issel-Tarver, L., Kasarskis, A., Lewis, S., Matese, J.C., Richardson, J.E., Ringwald, M., Rubin, G.M. and Sherlock, G.: Gene Ontology: Tool for the Unification of Biology. The Gene Ontology Consortium. Nature Genet., 25 (2000) 25-29
8. Gene Ontology Consortium. Creating the Gene Ontology Resource: Design and Implementation. Genome Res. 11 (2001) 1425-1433
9. Ogata, H., Goto, S., Sato, K., Fujibuchi, W., Bono, H. and Kanehisa, M.: KEGG: Kyoto Encyclopedia of Genes and Genomes. Nucleic Acids Res. 27 (1999) 29-34
10. Altschul, S. F., Gish, W., Miller, W., Myers, E.W. and Lipman, D. J.: Basic Local Alignment Search Tool. J. Mol. Biol. 215 (1990) 403-410
11. FlyBase Consortium. The FlyBase Database of the Drosophila Genome Projects and Community Literature. Nucleic Acids Res., 31 (2003) 172-175

A Category on the Cache Invalidation for Wireless Mobile Environments

Jianpei Zhang, Yan Chu, and Jing Yang

College of Computer Science and Technology,
Harbin Engineering University, Harbin, China
chu_yan5@hotmail.com

Abstract. Wireless computing becomes most popular with the development of mobile computers. Cache technique in wireless computing is crucial because it facilitates the data access at clients for reducing servers' loading, hence improve the performance. However, conventional cache technique requires coherence between servers and clients because of frequent disconnection. The cache invalidation strategy becomes an ideal method. In this paper, a category on the cache invalidation is proposed. To evaluate system performance, a mathematical model is proposed. It will develop high performance cache technique for practical wireless mobile computing.

1 Introduction

Caching of frequently accessed data items will be an important technique that will reduce contention on the narrow bandwidth, wireless channel. [1, 2] In the cache invalidation strategies, how to evaluate the performance is a hotspot. In this paper, a taxonomy of cache invalidation strategies is proposed. And according to this, we establish a mathematical model to weigh its performance.

The remainder of this paper is organized as follows. In section 2, we carry on classification on the cache invalidation algorithms. A mathematical model is proposed in section 3. A detail discussion is given in section 4. In section 5, we give conclusions of this paper.

2 Taxonomy of Cache Invalidation Algorithms

2.1 No-Checking Caching Scheme

In [1], Broadcasting Timestamps (*TS*), Amnesic Terminals (*AT*) and Signatures (*SIG*) are effective only for clients which have not been disconnected for a period that exceeds an algorithm specified parameter (e.g. broadcast window *w* and broadcast period *L*) or if the number of updated items during the period is not greater than an algorithm-specified parameter. However, it is possible in these methods that some of

H.T. Shen et al. (Eds.): APWeb 2006, LNCS 3842, pp. 939–942, 2006.

the cached objects are still valid after a long disconnection period or a large number of updates at the server. Thus, these methods don't utilize the bandwidth efficiently.

Bit-sequences (*BS*) algorithm [3] improves the finite limitation. The *BS* algorithm can approach the "optimal" effectiveness for all data items indicated in the report regardless of the duration of disconnection of the clients. *BS* also is applied to optimize other broadcast-based cache invalidation algorithms in which the dynamic bit mapping has to be included explicitly. The optimization reduces the size of the report by about one half while maintaining the same level of effectiveness for cache invalidation. However, compared to *TS* and *AT*, the *BS* algorithm actually wastes downlink broadcast bandwidth and causes clients to spend more time in awake mode.

2.2 Checking Caching Scheme

In order to retain valid data items in the cache, we must identify which part of the cache is still valid. There are several approaches to this problem with different trade-offs. Such as Simple-checking caching scheme, Simple-grouping caching scheme and Grouping with cold update-set report .The third solution presented in [4] is that the mobile host sends back to the server the ids of all the cached data items and their corresponding timestamps. Then the server identifies which data items are valid and returns a validity report to the client. However, this requires a lot of uplink bandwidth and is not power efficient.

2.3 Adaptive Invalidation Report Scheme

This scheme contains two parts, adaptive invalidation report with fixed window and adaptive invalidation report with adjusting window [5]. The former method guarantees that *BS* is broadcast as the next invalidation report The uplink bandwidth required by this method is much smaller than that of checking caching schemes. The latter method integrates *TS*, varying window size and *BS*. The adaptive methods make use of workload information form both clients and server so that the system workload has less impact on the system performance while maintaining low uplink and downlink bandwidth requirement. Furthermore, they achieve good balance between throughout and uplink bandwidth required.

2.4 Selective Cache Invalidation Scheme

There are there methods, group-based cache invalidation, hybrid cache invalidation and selective cache invalidation [6]. The group-based cache invalidation scheme broadcasts a group invalidation report while the hybrid cache invalidation scheme and selective cache invalidation scheme broadcast a pair of invalidation reports. All the schemes allow clients to selectively tune to the portion of the invalidation reports. Thus, the clients can minimize the power consumption when invalidating their cache content. The schemes proposed are efficient both in salvaging the valid cache content and in energy utilization.

3 A Mathematical Model for Cache Invalidation Strategy

As so many cache invalidation strategies are proposed to improve the performance, there should be a method to evaluate its superiority. So we propose a mathematical model: event A denotes "no queries in an interval", event B denotes "mobile client is awake during the interval" and event C denotes "no updates during an interval".

When the mobile client is awake and no queries in the internal, the probability q is

$$q = P(AB) = P(B)\ P(A \mid B) = (1-s)\ e^{-\lambda L} \tag{1}$$

We divide A into A_1 "no query in disconnection" and A_2 "no query in connection". According to addition theorem, we get

$$p = P(\overline{A}) = 1 - P(A) = 1 - P(A_1) - P(A_2) = (1-s)(1-e^{-\lambda L}) \tag{2}$$

$$u = P(C) = e^{-\mu L} \tag{3}$$

As the performance of the scheme is evaluated by many factors such as cache hit ratio and throughput, there should be a method to accomplish it. The throughput is just the total number of queries that can be answered. The traffic in bits due to queries that did not hit the caches is $T(1-h)\ (b_q+b_a)$. Since this amount has to be equal to $LW-B_c$, we have the throughout:

$$T = (1-h)(b_q+b_a)/(\ LW-B_c) \tag{4}$$

We should define the effectiveness of a strategy as

$$e = T/T_{max} \tag{5}$$

4 Model Analysis

The equations above are the basic ones that evaluate the performance of the invalidation reports proposed. T_{max} is the throughput given by an unattainable strategy in which the caches are invalidated instantaneously, and without incurring any cost. Because there are no invalidation reports, B_c would be equal to 0. So, the maximal throughout should be

$$T_{max} = \frac{LW}{\left(b_q + b_a\right)\left(1 - h_{max}\right)} \tag{6}$$

To get the maximum hit radio, we assume that a query occur at some particular instant of time. If the last query on this item occurred exactly τ seconds ago, and there have been no updates during the two queries, the query will "hit" the cache.

$$h_{max} = \int_0^{\infty} \lambda\mu e^{-\lambda\tau} e^{-\mu\tau} d\tau = \frac{\lambda}{\lambda - \mu} \tag{7}$$

Now, we use *AT* scheme as an example to evaluate the performance. We call this value of the number of items that have changed during the windows *L*

$$n_L = n \ (1 - e^{-\mu L}) \tag{8}$$

So, the throughout of the AT is computed

$$T_{AT} = \frac{LW - n_L log(n)}{(b_q + b_a)(1 - h_{at})} \tag{9}$$

And the other parameter is its hit radio, to compute the hit radio for *AT*, it should consider the event in the last query, and there can not be updates in the last intervals.

$$h_{AT} = (1-p) \sum_{i=1}^{\infty} q^{i-1} \mu^i = \frac{(1-p) \ \mu}{1 - q \ \mu} \tag{10}$$

5 Conclusion

Caching is necessary to frequently access objects in mobile clients. It can reduce the contention of channel bandwidth, minimize energy consumption, and cost. However, the process to copy at the client's cache which should be consistent with that of the server is very expensive. We intend to make the process easy and efficient. In so many different cache invalidation algorithms, how to evaluate their performance is becoming a hotspot. We propose a category on the cache invalidation and a mathematical model to evaluate the system performance. It has a light perspective and practical usage in future wireless mobile computing.

References

1. Barbara D. and Imielinksi. T.: Sleepers and workaholics: Caching strategies for mobile environments. In Proceedings of the ACM SIGMOD Conference on Management of Data, (1994) 1-12
2. Barbara D.: Mobile Computing and Database-A Survey. IEEE transactions on Knowledge and Data Engineering, vol. 11, No.1 January/February 1999
3. Jing J., Elmagarmid A., Helal A., and Alonso R.: Bit-Sequences: An adaptive cache invalidation method in mobile client/server environments. Technical Report CSD-TR-94-074, Computer Sciences Department, Purdue University, May 1995
4. Wu K.L., Yu P.S., and Chen M.S.: Energy-Efficient Caching for Wireless Mobile Computing. In the 12th International Conference on Data Engineering, (1996) 336-345
5. Hu O. and Lee D.L.: Adaptive Cache Invalidation Methods in Mobile Environments. In Proceedings of the 6th IEEE International Symposium on High Performance Distributed Computing (1997) 264-273
6. Cai J. and Tan K.L.: Energy-efficient selective cache invalidation. Wireless Networks 5, (1999) 489-502

ESD: The Enterprise Semantic Desktop

Jingtao Zhou and Mingwei Wang

The Key Laboratory of Contemporary Design and Integrated Manufacturing Technology, Ministry of Education, Northwestern Polytechnical University, Xi'an, China 710072
zhoujt@mail.nwpu.edu.cn, Wangmv@nwpu.edu.cn
http://zhoujt.hostrocket.com/index.html

Abstract. The continuous blending of boundaries between personal and corporate data leads to overall enterprise information and knowledge pervading not only common but personal data sources. To fully sharing potentially useful information within entire enterprise, there are growing needs of a generic, interoperable, and flexible infrastructure to integrate and coordinate information across corporate and individual desktops on semantic or knowledge level. In this context, we introduce ESD, a desktop information sharing infrastructure based on Semantic Grid vision to achieve adaptive and intelligence information sharing across enterprise corporate and personal desktops. A primary framework for ESD is introduced based on the analysis of key criteria in realizing the vision of an infrastructure for information sharing, management, searching, and navigating on desktop grid. Focuses of this position paper are placed on the background, vision and the outline of ESD approach.

1 Introduction

Recent advances in Information Technology (IT) have revolutionized the paradigms of information searching, sharing and using. Today's enterprise information and knowledge pervade everywhere of the enterprise rather than enterprise-wide databases. This is especially true for that more and more knowledge achieved by individual may be stored into personal desktop besides common data sources in enterprise. To accomplish a complex task, knowledge workers need achieve any relative information not only from common data sources but also individual data sources by any possible way. However, the continuously increasing information and knowledge in personal computers managed by individual employees is neglected although enterprises have tackled information sharing inside their specific domains for more than a decade. Integrating and sharing all potentially useful information within entire enterprise, it must be of great benefit to both individual and group in collaborative work, research, even business decision and action. Unfortunately, current enterprise information infrastructure is poorly suited for dealing with the continuing, rapid explosion in data both in common and personal information sources.

Meanwhile, emerging new technologies including Semantic Web[1], P2P[2], and Grid[3] are concerned with the organization of resource sharing in large-scale societies. Undertaking the intersection fulfillment of these technologies on desktop environment in enterprise enables new integrative and collaborative use of distributed,

H.T. Shen et al. (Eds.): APWeb 2006, LNCS 3842, pp. 943 – 946, 2006.

autonomous personal and corporate data on intranet even internet. In this context, we propose an enterprise semantic desktop (ESD) based on the undertaking research at the intersection of the Semantic Web and Grid, i.e. Semantic Grid[4], to achieve adaptive and intelligence information sharing across enterprise corporate and personal desktops. Intuitively, ESD can be applied to any networked personal desktops but, here, we only consider its application in an enterprise or virtual enterprise scenario because large-scale and pervasive deployment still requires substantial research on both technology and non-technology problems, such as incentives and obligations.

Differently with proposed semantic desktop based on semantic web (e.g. Gnowsis[5]) or network semantic desktop based on both Semantic Web and P2P (e.g. [6]), ESD focuses on not only organizing and managing information on personal computers but also sharing and integrating information between personal and organizational data sources. In particular, since some data on personal computers inevitably involves some specific organizational domains of an enterprise, not all information on personal computers is symmetric. In other words, there exist, from logic perspective, some hierarchically arranged personal data sources in ESD environment. Likewise, since some information on personal computers in an enterprise may also includes some sensitive individual or group data, corresponding structured robust security services are needed in ESD besides intuitive trust mechanisms as used in P2P networks. Hence, ESD is currently built on top of Semantic Grid although data coordination way of P2P paradigms is also considered in ESD. By inheriting the infrastructure from Grid, Semantic Grid could provide a persistent and standardized infrastructure for ESD. By reflecting principles of Semantic Web and Semantic Web service in grid environment, Semantic Grid enables not only loosely-coupled interoperability but also semantic or knowledge level information coordination for ESD. Accordingly, Semantic Grid could provide a competently basic infrastructure for ensuring the personal information sharing and coordination both on system and semantic level in entire enterprise environment.

2 Vision and Criteria

As shown in Fig.1, the vision of ESD focuses on changing the traditional point-to-point way of personal information sharing into a pervasive sharing way by creating a semantic interconnection environment for personal information sources.

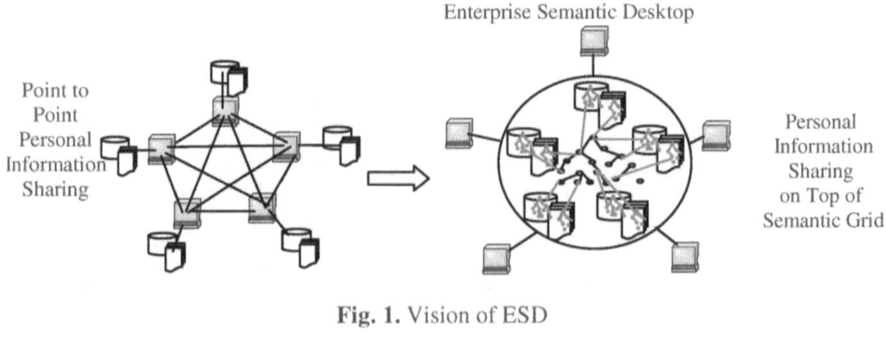

Fig. 1. Vision of ESD

To enable the vision of ESD, following key criteria to meet:

- For infrastructure

Flexibility — ESD should be able to fit into relative existing architectures including Grid, Semantic Web and Semantic Grid Services, and handle new technologies without massive rewrites and without involvement from the supplier. Each information resource on desktop should be capable of participating in the architecture of ESD by configuration.

Loosely-Coupled —Information sources in ESD should be loosely-coupled both on data and system (or service) level to solve the classic "n-squared" problem. Furthermore, it is also a fundamental aspect for efficient, dynamic, and automated information sharing.

Semantic grid services—ESD should support semantic grid services naturally and have the ability to find and access a wide variety of intra- and extra-desktop data sources that these services promise both on system and semantic level.

- For data sources on personal desktop

Flexible and effective access control — As discussed in section 1, some data in personal desktop may need strict access restriction; hence, security and authorization are important issues for desktop data sharing and integration. ESD should provide flexible mechanism for access control, such as fine-grained control over the granularity of the data, the granting and revoking of access permissions, etc.

Automatic or semi-automatic semantic annotating of data sources — Laborious manual construction of semantic mappings or annotations has been a bottleneck of semantic enriching for data sources since semantic finding is an intellectual process. In this context, ESD should provide or support some automatic or semi-automatic tools (e.g. Google desktop search tool) to facilitate this task.

- For user

Desktop client — ESD should provide ubiquitous desktop client for users to not only manage and share information on his/her desktop, but search and navigate information on the whole desktop grid. Furthermore, the desktop client should support general browsers, such as IE, Netscape, FireFox.

3 Primary Framework

Based on the Open Grid Service Architecture (OGSA), ESD provides a generic architecture for semantic sharing of personal information on desktop. Every function in ESD is independently realized as a grid service on top of the Open Grid Service Infrastructure (OGSI) and will be a semantic grid services by semantic enrichment.

As shown in Fig. 2, the architecture consists of three spaces or layers: *basic service space*, *mediation service space* and *desktop client service space.*

Basic service space constructs common and basic services for ESD by providing *access control services* and *semantic enrichment services*. The access control services are responsible for the guarantee of flexible information access control with the support of OGSA-DAI, OGSI common services (e.g. information and logging services), and other specific data access services. Semantic enrichment services deal with relative topics of semantic enriching.

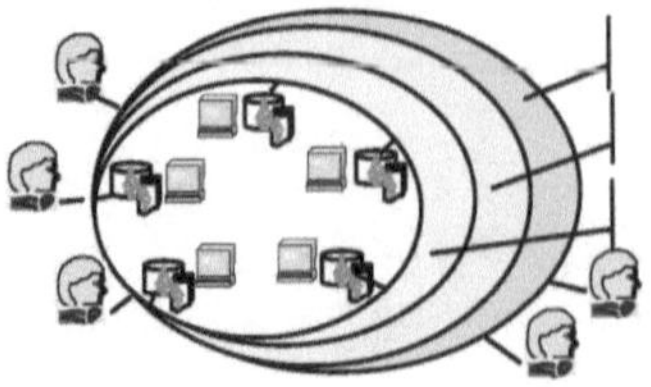

Fig. 2. Primary Framework

Mediation service space provides services to mediate conflicting processes, semantics, and information without custom written programs for the purposes of information sharing by operationalizing system, ontology and data sources.

Desktop client service space provides services called portal services including information management, sharing, searching, and navigating services for front end desktop users. In order to ensure that relative services in ESD can get in desktop grid, ESD builds portal services on top of OGSA.

4 Conclusions

By fitting into existing Grid, Semantic Web and Semantic Grid Services architectures, ESD obtains more flexible and open characteristics. However, many relevant aspects of a complete ESD environment are not addressed in this paper so far. We will show more details in our further work.

References

1. Berners-Lee, T., Hendler, J. and Lassila, O.: The semantic web. Scientific American, Vol. 284, No.5,(2001) 34–43
2. Oram, A. (ed.): Peer-to-Peer: Harnessing the Power of Disruptive Technologies. Sebastapol, California: O'Reilly (2001)
3. Foster I. and Kesselman, C. (eds): The Grid: Blueprint for a New Computing Infrastructure. San Francisco, CA: Morgan Kaufmann Publishers (1998)
4. Roure, D., Jennings, N. R. and Shadbolt, N. R.: Research Agenda for the Semantic Grid: A Future e-Science Infrastructure, UKeS-2002-02 (2001)
5. Sauermann L.: The Gnowsis Semantic Desktop for Information Integration. the 3rd Conference Professional Knowledge Management - Experiences and Visions(2005) 39-42
6. Decker S. and Frank M. R: The Networked Semantic Desktop. In Proc.WWW Workshop on Application Design, Development and Implementation Issues in the Semantic Web, Net York City, NY (2004)

System Architecture of a Body Area Network and Its Web Service Based Data Publishing

Hongliang Ren[1], Max Q.-H. Meng[1], Xijun Chen[1], Haibin Sun[2], Bin Fan[2], and Yawen Chan[1]

[1] Department of Electronic Engineering,
The Chinese University of Hong Kong,
Hong Kong, China
{hlren, max, xjchen, ywchan}@ee.cuhk.edu.hk
[2] Department of Computer Science & Engineering,
The Chinese University of Hong Kong,
Hong Kong, China
{hbsun, bfan}@cse.cuhk.edu.hk

Abstract. Wireless Sensor Networks (WSN) is a research hotspot in recent years and has yielded many fruitful results. However, the biomedical applications of WSN haven't received significant development due to its many unique challenges for the engineers and physicians. In this paper, a system architecture solution of body area network (BAN), our so called project "MediMesh", is presented. A biomedical dedicated BAN node hardware platform is devised to fit the medical monitoring application. The sensor node is built up especially for healthcare monitoring while the biocompatibility and portability are considered. A light weight network protocol is designed considering the radiation effect and communication overhead. After data acquisition from sink stations, a data publishing system based on web service technology is implemented for typical hospital environment. The publishing of biomedical data is realized through 3 phases: first storing the data automatically in a database, then creating information sharing service by using Web Service technology, and finally allowing data access by the physicians and end users.

1 Introduction

As a research hotspot, Wireless Sensor Networks [1] (WSN) has achieved fruitful results, such as node platform manufacturing, embedded operation system development and network protocol algorithms etc. However, the biomedical applications of WSN haven't received significant development due to its many unique challenges for the engineers and physicians. Wireless Biomedical Sensor Networks [2] (WBSN, for short), consists of a collective of wireless networked low-power biosensor devices, which integrate an embedded microprocessor, radio and a limited amount of storage. With the development of miniature, lightweight sensor technologies, many physiological signals such as EEG, ECG, GSR, blood pressure, blood flow, pulse-oxymeter, glucose level, etc., can be monitored by individual node or pill that is worn, carried or

H.T. Shen et al. (Eds.): APWeb Workshops 2006, LNCS 3842, pp. 947–954, 2006.

swallowed. The sensor networks are typically carried or worn by the patients and composed many BANs. BAN provides an efficient way to monitoring the physiological signals of the patients with high performance, particularly in the hospital environment.

The significance of BAN is self-explaining. It allows long-term wireless health monitoring even sometimes the patients or the elders roam in the building. This is especially useful to avoid personal contact when nursing contagious patients in a large hospital. The health information collected is then stored in a database as a health record and can be retrieved through web database by the end users such as patients themselves or the physicians concerned. It then alerts the healthcare professionals with the abnormal changes of patients' health condition. It will reduce the time of routine checkup by the health care professionals, which reduces the cost of medical care. Its real-time monitoring also allows emergency situation to be handled immediately. In addition, higher level medical tasks can be operated because of the coordination of networked nodes. As the aging population is growing in many countries, the needs of real-time and continuous health monitoring of the elderly will continue to increase. The typical application scenarios may be Smart home health monitoring [3], Smart ward [2], Athletic performance monitoring [4], and emergency medical care [5].

Comparing to the generic wireless sensor networks, BAN have to solve some unique challenges as it is related to the health problem of human body. Practically, the major requirement and concerns [2] of BAN in terms of medical care include reliability, biocompatibility of the materials, portability of the sensor nodes, privacy and security [6] consideration, light weight protocols, ability to adjust transmission power dynamically to reduce the RF radiation, and prioritized traffic to ensure the vital signal transmission. Some researchers have been engaged on the challenges. CodeBlue project [5], is trying to build up a wireless infrastructure intended for deployment in emergency medical care, and coping with the communication, computational and programming challenges. They currently are using Mica2 Motes and Telos Motes, connected to a pulse oxymeter and are working on connecting to an ECG. The UbiMon [7] project, which is aimed at investigating healthcare delivery by combining wearable and implantable sensors, proposed body sensor network system architecture. The project MobiHealth [8] is a mobile healthcare project funded by the European Commission, which allows patients to be fully mobile whilst undergoing health monitoring. MobiHealth integrates the BAN (Body Area Network) with public mobile network and aims at developing and trying new mobile value-added services in the area of healthcare. Most of the research work are still under development and have a long way to go.

The project developed by our research group, MediMesh, is a kind of BAN for the purpose of healthcare monitoring in a hospital environment. The wearable or embedded biosensors keep sensing the vital signals of the patients and transmitting them wirelessly to the BAN-Head which maybe also a node or even PDA. In order to get data from an ambulatory patient no matter where they are in a hospital, we are still developing and testing routing schemes that the BAN-Heads can behave as a router to relay others' information to the data sink. Then the physiological data are delivered to a backend archival system for long-term storage and diagnosis analysis. Finally, by using Web Service technology, we create a biomedical data publishing service to retrieve, organize and process data in the database according user's requirement. The system construction is illustrated in Fig.1.

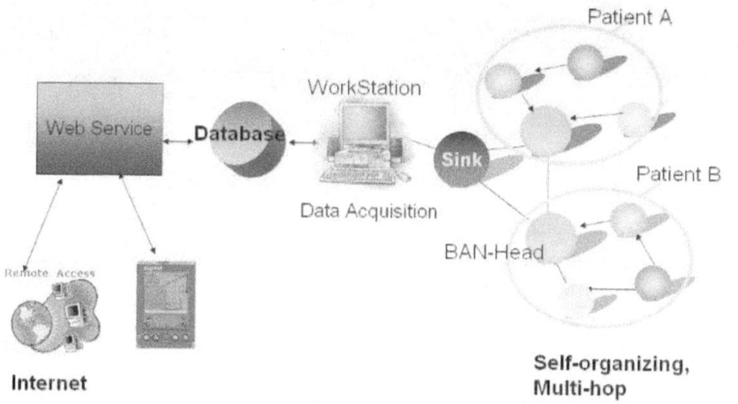

Fig. 1. System Construction of MediMesh

This paper investigates the system architecture of MediMesh project and presents the current research results. The rest of the paper is constructed as following: Section II describes our design of sensor node platform and a prototype of 3-lead ECG sensor; Section III illustrates the network communication protocol implemented on the sensor node and summarizes the principle of the protocol; Section IV provides an inside view of the data publishing system which is the application level design; and then presents the preliminary results from the project implementation; Section VI concludes the paper.

2 Sensor Node Platform

The proposed wireless senor network consists of lots of biomedical sensor nodes. Currently, some sensor node platforms have already been developed for research experiment or habitat survey, such as Telos [9], Mica [10], and SmartDust [11]. While considering the biocompatibility and portability of the node platform for health monitoring, a medical oriented node platform is desired and necessary. As shown in Fig.2, the typical application scenarios [2] of biosensor nodes may be wearable wireless ECG, swallowed sensors that can detect enzymes, intestinal acidity, or embedded glucose level monitor. Therefore, a dedicated miniature medical sensor node, MediMesh node [12], is introduced in this paper.

The appearance of the MediMesh sensor node is shown in Fig.3. With the size of 26*23*mm*, it's portable to serve as a biosensor platform. The MediMesh BAN node provides extra interface to interact with different biosensors. As indicated in [12], the node mainly consists of ultra low power Texas Instruments MSP430F1611 microcontroller, Chipcon CC2420 transceiver, M25P40 4 Mb Serial Flash Memory, and peripheral circuits.

Currently, many microcontrollers integrate non-volatile memory and interfaces, such as ADCs, UART, SPI, counters and timers, into a single chip. In this way, it can interact with sensors and communication devices such as short-range radio to compose a sensor node. TI MSP430F1611 is chosen as the central processing unit mainly

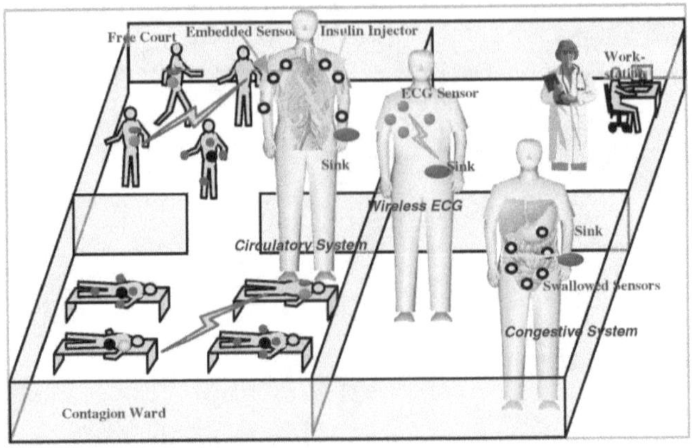

Fig. 2. Application Scenarios of Biosensor Networks

because of its ultra-low computational power consumption. Moreover, it is equipped with a full set of analog and digital processors and has embedded debugging and in-system flash programming through JTAG interface.

The CC2420 [13], IEEE 802.15.4 Zigbee ready transceiver, is ideal for low power, low transmission speed and short range applications with up to several-year battery life. Considering RF safety problem, human body is composed mostly of water that may be heated by excessive radiation. Hence, the radio transmission power should be reduced as low as possible. Herein, CC2420 provides the ability to dynamically adjust transmission power for more than 30 levels. The physical specifications of CC2420 [14] are desirable for healthcare. It operate in unlicensed ISM band with 16 channels in the 2.4 GHz band, 10 channels in the 915 MHz band, and 1 channel in the 868 MHz band. In addition, it offers DSSS (direct sequence spread spectrum) techniques, the wideband less likely to be corrupted by the interference, due to its inherent processing gain.

A 3-lead ECG sensor [12] and a pulse oxymeter are designed for the purpose of research experiment thereafter, as shown in figure 4.

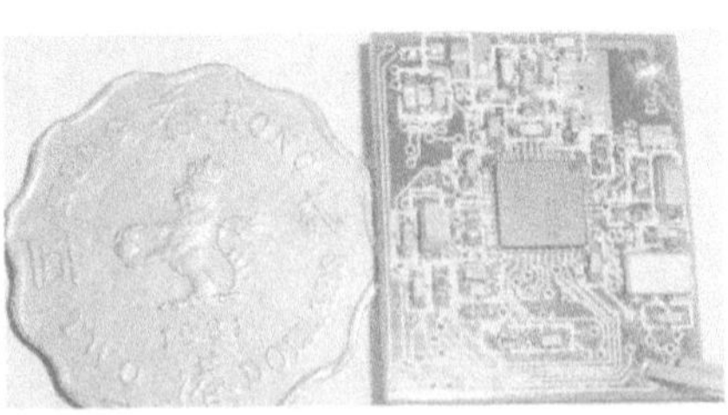

Fig. 3. MediMesh Node Comparing With a Coin

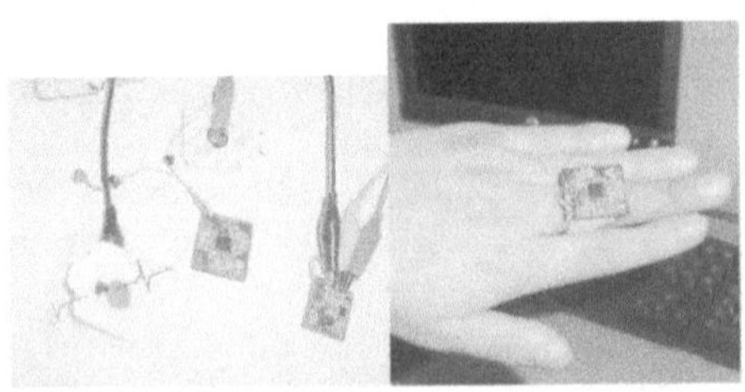

Fig. 4. 3-lead ECG Sensor and Pulse oxymeter

3 Network Protocol

In a hospital environment, a very likely scenario would be many patients that carry multiple physical sensors, as shown in figure 2. Therefore, a flat tree topology model (figure 5) is desirable since each patient branch node only collects data from its group of physical sensors and avoids interference with other patient body area networks. Moreover, all the patient nodes are fully interconnected to allow the patient roaming by relaying messages to each other.

In order to achieve sufficient reliability by using a light weight protocol stack, we build the communication protocol based on TinyOS [15], which is an event-based operating system with all system functions broken down into individual components. The component-based structure of TinyOS allows for an application designer to select from a variety of system components in order to meet application specific goals.

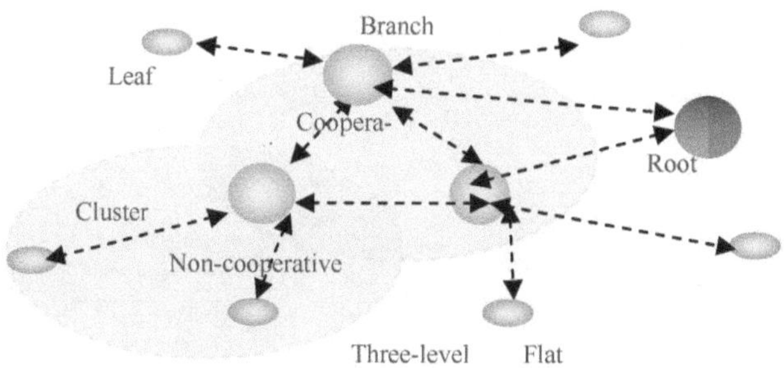

Fig. 5. Networks Logical Architecture

According to the system requirements, multi-hop routing protocol is implemented to relay the information among BAN-heads. Meanwhile, to reduce the impact of RF radiation on human body, a power aware MAC layer mechanism is realised in a BAN to dynamically adjust the transmission power and maintain the wireless link at the same time. Additionally, transmission power control has the potential to increase a network's traffic carrying capacity, reduce energy consumption, and reduce the end-to-end delay.

The principle of the power aware mechanism is described as following. First we got the empirical relationship between packet loss rate and transmission power in a BAN range from a lot of experiment data on MediMesh node. Then, the BAN-head exchange the receive signal strength indication (RSSI) messages and link quality indication (LQI) messages with the BAN-leaves. Once the transmission nodes get the response messages from the receiver by piggybacking packets, they can dynamically adjust the transmission power according to the empirical steps.

Due to the strict requirement of packet loss rate and energy constraints, contention free MAC layer is desirable for BAN. We state a centralized scheduling algorithm, in which link demands are to be satisfied under signal-to-interference-and-noise-ratio (SINR) constraints.

4 Data Publishing System

The publishing of biomedical data is realized through 3 steps, as shown in Fig.6. First of all, all the data collected from the patients' BAN should be stored automatically in a database. Then, by using Web Service technology, we create an information sharing service to retrieve, organize and process data in the database according user's requirement. Finally the end users such as patients themselves or the physicians concerned could access the data through internet by user interface on PCs or Pocket PCs.

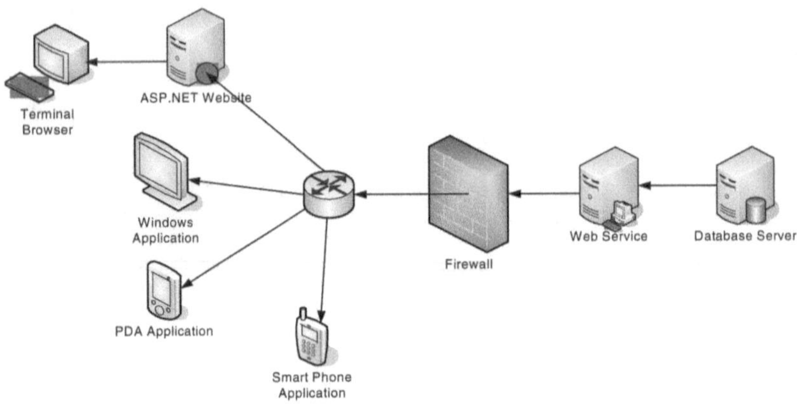

Fig. 6. Architecture of Data Publishing System

4.1 Web Service Technology

The web database service [16] is facile to cooperate with other computer systems or database in the hospital due to its clear interface and low deployment cost. Web service, as defined by the W3C Web Services Architecture Working Group [17], is an interface that describes a collection of operations that are network accessible through standardized XML messaging. They are self-contained, modular units of application logic which provide functionalities to other applications via an Internet connection. The benefits of Web services include the Service decoupling of service interfaces from implementations and platform considerations and an increase in cross-language, cross-platform interoperability. Due to privacy and security consideration, the medical data of the patients are well protected and encrypted behind the firewall. Therefore, Web Service is ideal for biomedical data publishing herein because of its ability to pass the firewall, open standard, platform independent, and ease of integration.

Up to now, we have already realized the functionalities of database server and web service data publishing system. Meanwhile, the user interfaces in the webpage format on PCs and Pocket PC are illustrated in Fig.8.

4.2 Data Acquisition and Network Monitoring

As stated before, all the vital data are gathered from the wireless biomedical sensor networks by the sink nodes connected with the workstation PC. The workstation not only takes the responsibility of data acquisition, but also serves the purpose of real time network monitoring. As Fig.7 shows, the left half plane presents the real time data, while the right plane illustrates the network topology and routing information.

4.3 Data Publishing and Remote Access

Section 4.1 describes the data publishing system in the MediMesh project. Fig. 8 shows the end user interface in a PC and PDA. Patients and doctors can remote access these data via Internet through these application programs.

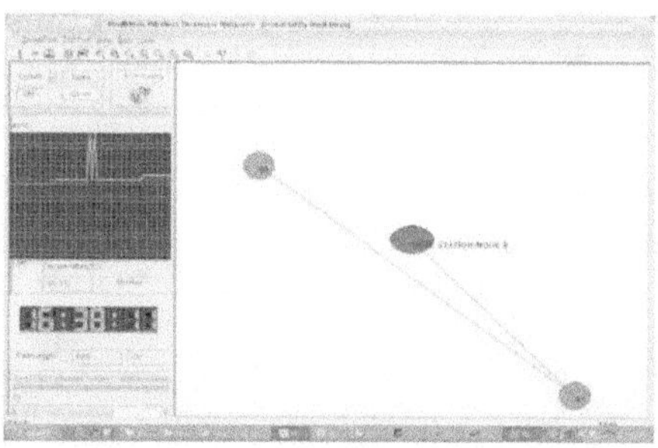

Fig. 7. User Interface of Workstation

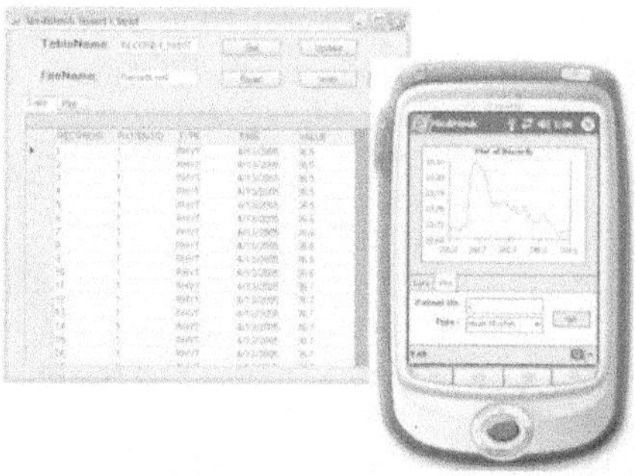

Fig. 8. Remote Access Interface of PC and PDA

5 Conclusions

Wireless biomedical sensor networks exhibit great strength to enhance the medical performance by integrating smart sensors, wireless communication and network technologies. This paper introduces our research project MediMesh and yields some preliminary results. First, the MediMesh sensor node platform is developed while considering the healthcare requirements and biocompatibility. At the same time, several biosensors are designed for research experiment. Then the network protocols are established based on IEEE 802.15.4 Standard and TinyOS, according to the unique challenges and requirements. The introduction of the flat tree topology architecture and network protocols implies our solutions proposed for the BAN in a hospital environment. Finally, data acquisition and data publishing biomedical data are realized for data retrieval and network monitoring. Web service technology is introduced to realize the publishing of physiological data. Our aim is to provide a feasible solution and motivate future R&D activities in this area. Once the technology is refined, medical costs for collecting chronic medical information and long term monitoring will be reduced. With the quickly developed technologies, we wish that BAN will provide a safe and convenient environment for the patients. Meanwhile, the fast developing Internet and web service techniques enable the patients and physician to retrieve the data anywhere at anytime.

Acknowledgment

This project is supported by RGC Competitive Earmarked Research Grant #CUHK4213/04E of the Hong Kong government, awarded to Max Meng.

References

1. I. F. Akyildiz, W. L. Su, Y. Sankarasubramaniam, and E. Cayirci.: A survey on sensor networks. IEEE Communications Magazine vol. 40. no.8. (Aug. 2002)102-114.
2. Ren Hongliang, Max Q.-H.Meng, and Chen Xijun.: Physiological Information Acquisition through Wireless Biomedical Sensor Networks. IEEE ICIA Proceeding (2005).
3. P. E. Ross.: Managing care through the air. IEEE Spectrum (Dec.2004) vol.41, no.12 26-31.
4. Edgar Callaway.: Wireless Sensor Networks: Architectures and Protocols. CRC Press LLC,BocaRaton,FL. (2004).
5. D. Malan, T.F.Jones, M.Welsh, and S. Moulton.: CodeBlue: An Ad Hoc Sensor Network Infrastructure for Emergency Medical Care. International Workshop on Wearable and Implantable Body Sensor Networks (2004)
6. M. Miyazaki.: The Future of e-Health Wired or not Wired. Science of Computer Programming (2003)
7. K.Van Laerhoven, P.L.Lo, and Jason W.P.Ng.: Medical Healthcare Monitoring with Wearable and Implantable Sensors. (2004).
8. "Website:http://www.mobihealth.org/".
9. J. Polastre, R. Szewczyk, and D.Culler.:Telos Enabling UltraLow Power Wireless Research. Int. Workshop on Ubiquitous Computing for Pervasive Healthcare Applications (2005)
10. J. L. Hill and D. E. Culler.: MICA: A wireless platform for deeply embedded networks. IEEE Micro, vol. 22, no. 6, (Nov.2002) 12-24,.
11. B. Warneke, M. Last, B. Liebowitz, and K. S. J. Pister.: Smart dust: Communicating with a cubic-millimeter computer. Computer, vol. 34, no. 1 (Jan.2001)
12. Chen Xijun, Max Q.-H.Meng, and Ren Hongliang.: Design of Sensor Node Platform for Wireless Biomedical Sensor Networks. Proceeding of EMBC (2005)
13. Anon.: Chipcon figure 8 wireless merger to provide ultimate ZigBee solution. Microwave Journal, vol. 48, no. 3. (Mar.2005)
14. IEEE StandardPart 15.4: Wireless Medium Access Control (MAC) and Physical Layer (PHY) Specifications for Low-Rate Wireless Personal Area Networks (LR-WPANs) (2004)
15. D. Gay, P. Levis, R. von Behren, M. Welsh, E. Brewer, and D. Culler, "The nesC language: A holistic approach to networked embedded systems," Acm Sigplan Notices, vol. 38, no. 5. (May 2003) 1-11
16. N. Bassiliades, D. Anagnostopoulos, and I. Vlahavas.: Web Service composition using a deductive XML rule language. Distributed and Parallel Databases, vol. 17, no. 2(Mar.2005) 135-178
17. B. Medjahed, A. Bouguettaya, and A. K. Elmagarmid.: Composing Web services on the Semantic Web. Vldb Journal , vol. 12, no. 4.(Nov.2003) 333-351

A Feature-Based Semantics Model of Reusable Component

Jin Li[1], Dechen Zhan[2], and Zhongjie Wang[2]

[1] School of Computer Science & Technology, Harbin Engineering University, Harbin 150001, Heilongjiang, China
[2] School of Computer Science & Technology, Harbin Institute of Technology, Harbin 150001, Heilongjiang, China
lijin-hrbeu@163.com

Abstract. Component technology plays a key role in the field of software reuse. Components can be reused under various business environments through its changeability .This paper proposes a feature-based semantics model of reusable component, which describes semantics of components by using domain feature space and expresses changeability of components through five kinds of changeable mechanisms of domain features. In addition, this study proposes a self-contained classification of features according to enterprise business model, divides semantics structure and hierarchical relation of three kinds of components, and sets up mapping relations between semantics model of component and business model. The model is verified through the case study of a Web-based information platform for logistics enterprise.

Keywords: Component; Feature; Semantics.

1 Introduction

In object-oriented software engineering, software components are developed to speedup software manufacturing process. Their reuse improves product efficiency, reduces cost, and shortens design cycle. Constructing and designing applicable components becomes a key in software development. Recently people develop some models such as 3C model [1], EVA [2], component model based on automation [3], formalized model [4] based on Petri Net, etc. Most of them are feature-oriented model sbeing widely used in software engineering [5-6]. Therefore, the expressing semantics of component based on feature and feature space becomes important [7].

Current research usually focuses on two topics: (1) grammar and implementation by ignoring semantics; and (2) semantics of component by ignoring realistic applications. Both areas lack the considerations of association and mapping between model of component and domain business model [8]. Thus, existing models are not capable to high efficient components for use and reuse.

This paper outlines the concepts of feature, feature dependent relations, and the mapping between the feature-based model of component and the enterprise's business

H.T. Shen et al. (Eds.): APWeb 2006, LNCS 3842, pp. 955 – 964, 2006.

model. We develop a domain feature –based model. Components are classified upon the characteristics of business elements described by feature. Implementation mechanism of component changeability and classification are studied to understand the reusability of components. The model's methodology is verified through a case study of a Web-based information platform for logistics enterprise.

2 Feature-Based Model

2.1 Feature's Dependent Relations

Domain feature models and associate concepts are introduced as a unified tool to abstract feature-base business model. The feature is defined as a ontological description of the knowledge about objective world. Feature space is defined as a set of field-specific features and a semantics space consists of dependent relations between these features. It can be denoted as Ω=<F, R>, where the F is the set of features and the R is the set of dependent relations between the features. The feature space is usually expressed in terms of a feature tree.

Many semantics dependent relations exist for interaction among features. In traditional model two structural dependent relations, i.e. aggregation and instance, have been considered. We extend these relations to gain the third relation-semantics constraint. Aggregation describes the "whole - part" relation among features. There exist four feature aggregation relations: essential, optional, single-selective, and multiple-selective. Instance relations describe the "general- special" relationship among features. Since each feature behaves differently due to its encapsulation, it has different values called feature items. They are instances of a feature that is an abstract. Feature items also can be viewed as the characteristic of the feature. There is a constraint relation that is implicit semantics dependent relations among features. A constrain relation has sequence relation, functional coupling relation, and transaction logic relation, etc. Generally the constraint relations exist among features of the same type. Different types of constraint relations exist in different domain. Hereby, we describe some constraint relations among $f_1, f_2, \ldots$, and f_n in a unified form $\mathbf{P}(f_1, f_2, \ldots, f_n)$.

Two mechanisms describing changeability are provided in traditional feature models: selectivity and changeability.

(1) Selectivity: expressed as child feature are selective for parent feature. It describes the changeability of semantics structure among features and can be denoted by the four types of aggregation mentioned above.

(2) Changeability: expressed as feature items are changeable for a feature. It describes that feature values different under different business environments. For feature f, changeability exists only value domain of f is greater than 1.

In fact, selectivity of features and changeability of feature items reflect the changeability of aggregation relations and instance relations. Changeability also exists in the constraint relations among features.

(3) Changeability of constraint relations: expressed as constraint relations vary under different business environments.

All the three kind of changeability can be unified defined as changeable points of feature space, *vp*(*vp_body*, *vp_dom*, *vp_type*),in which:

- *vp* is the identification of changeable point.
- *vp_body* is the changeable body, which can be a feature or a feature dependent relation in feature space.
- *vp_dom* is the value domain of changeable point. *Vp_dom* can be a not null set or a null set, meaning that the value domain of this changeable point is uncertainty and only can be determined by specific business environment.
- vp_type is the type of changeable point. There are five types, i.e. selective, single-selective, multiple-selective, feature item selective and constraint relations' changeability , expressed as $vp\_type \in \{V\_O, V\_SS, V\_MS, V\_I, V\_R\}$,

If feature f has changeability (1) or (2), feature f is a changeable feature. Every changeability of a changeable feature is called self-changeable point of feature. direct_vp(f) is used to denote the set of self-changeable points of feature f. all_vp(f) is used to denote the sets of self-changeable points of feature f and all its offspring features, i.e.

$$\text{all\_vp}(f) = \text{direct\_vp}(f) \cup \left(\cup_{g \in \text{decendant}(f)} \text{direct\_vp}(g) \right)$$

The set of all the changeable points in the feature space with the root of f. if all_vp(f)=Φ, f is a fixed feature. If some feature dependent relation **P has** changeability (2), **P** is changeable feature dependent relation, denoted as vp(**P**). vp(Ω) is the set of all the changeable points in the feature space Ω.

$$\text{vp}(\Omega) = \left(\cup_{f \in \Omega} \text{all\_vp}(f) \right) \cup \left(\cup_{P \in \Omega} \text{vp}(P) \right)$$

Concretion of changeable point is that selecting specific value from *vp_dom* according to the type of changeable point and thus eliminating the changeable point.

(a) Expressing component by feature space

Components provide services to the external world. They realize part or full of business goal demanded by single or multiple business models through logical linkage and assemble among each other and reflect specific semantics. Reconfiguration of business model can be realized through increasing, deleting, adjusting and assembling the semantics of the components in the enterprise application domain. So semantics model of component is the software expression of the reconfigurable requirements in the future.

By expressing it in unified feature-based form, a component, in fact, defines a sub feature space of specific business domain. So, semantics model of component is denoted as $fc\langle f_{root}, F, R, PS, RS\rangle$.

- *fc* is the unique identification of the component.
- f_{root} is the root feature in the feature space of the component. Also it is the feature with maximum granularity of which component can implement.
- *F* is the set of features in the component and basic elements constituting the component.
- *R* is the set of feature dependent relations of the component through which features are connected.
- *PS* is the set of services in the form of features provided by the component. $PS \subseteq \{f_{root}\} \cup F$. This demonstrates that the component can not only provide services described by the root feature, but also the ones described by internal features.
- *RS* is the set of services in the form of features required by the component. *F-RS* is the features implemented by itself.

Semantics model of component is demonstrated in figure 1. $\forall f \in fc(F)$, component *fc* covers feature *f*, denoted as cover(*fc*, *f*). Granularity of component is defined as the number of features covered by component, etc, granularity (*fc*)=|*fc*(*F*)|.

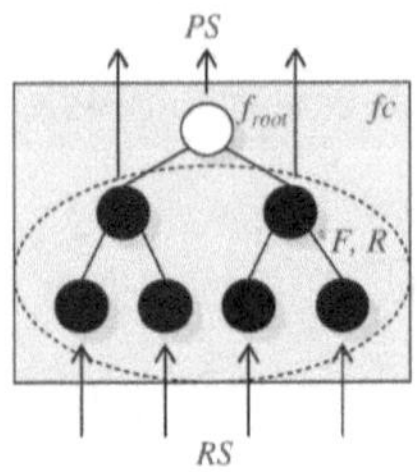

Fig. 1. Semantics model of component

Changeability mechanisms of component. Changeability of components is an important method of component reuse. If a component has changeable points, it can be applied to various business environments. System reconfiguration can be realized through the reconfiguration of changeable points of components. Changeable points of a component are defined as union of the changeable point set in the feature space Ω_{fc} which is composed of the features covered by the component, i.e., vp(*fc*)=vp(Ω_{fc}). If vp(*fc*)=Φ, *fc* is called as fixed component. Otherwise, *fc* is called as reconfigurable component. According to the classification of the feature changeable points, changeable points of component are also classified into five types: *V_O* | *V_SS* | *V_MS* | *V_I* | *V_R*.. Changeable points of multiple types can be contained in a component concurrently.

If a component has changeable points in type of *V_O*、*V_SS*、*V_MS* , features in *fc* has selectivity. Thus components can realize different business functions by selecting features. If *fc* has changeable points in type of *V_I* , *fc* can realize the functions of the feature in various strategies through selecting the feature items. If *fc* has changeable points in type of *V_R* , *fc* can realize different interactive behaviors among features through configuration of constraint relations.

In fact, changeable point of component is a kind of abstraction mechanism. By the abstraction of changeable conditions existing in the feature space of the component and construction of changeable point, suitability, i.e. reusability of the component is raised. The number of the changeable points of component |vp(*fc*)| and value domains of every changeable point dom(*vp*) determine the reusability of the component.

When using a component to construct business model of information systems, it is essential to concrete the changeable points of the component. By eliminating the uncertain factors according to concrete application environment, a reconfigurable component becomes a fixed component.

Changeable point mechanisms of component is demonstrated in figure 2. Hollow points denote internal features covered by the component. Features covered by the component and dependent relations among them have the capability to be changeable points of the component. Every changeable point has corresponding value domain. By selecting specific values in these value domains, components behave differently and can be reused to reconfiguration of the information systems.

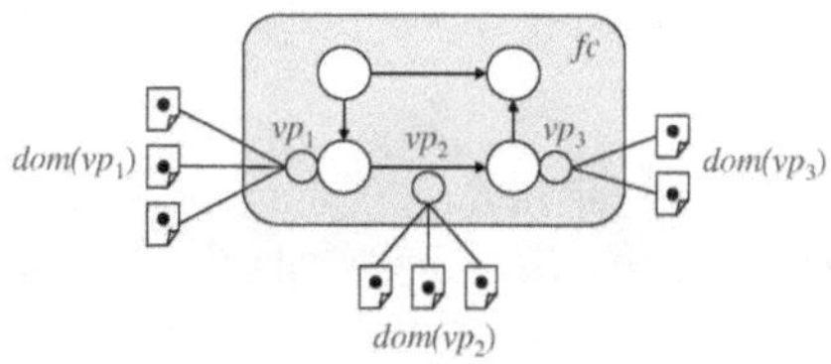

Fig. 2. Changeable points mechanisms of component

So, feature space of a component can be divided into two parts: fixed part composed of features and dependent relations of non-changeable point and variable part composed of changeable point, denoted as

fc<FIXED_PART, VARIABLE_PART>, FIXED_PART(fc) = <F_{fixed}, R_{fixed}>, VARIABLE_PART(fc)=<$F_{variable}$, $R_{variable}$>.

Fixed part of the component represents basic functions which are general for all the application domains and must be reused. Null is not permitted for this part. Variable part of component represents variable functions and is dissimilar in different domain. This part may be null.

Mapping relations between model of component and business. Enterprise business model of ERP domain is composed of basic business elements, such as business object, business operation, business activity, business process and business process across domains, as shown in the left of figure 3. This paper views these business elements as feature and divides them into two classes: entity feature (role feature, business object feature, object's property feature and object's state feature) and behavior feature (business process feature, business activity feature, business operation feature). Business rules, which reflect dependent relations among business elements, are expressed in the form of feature dependent relations.

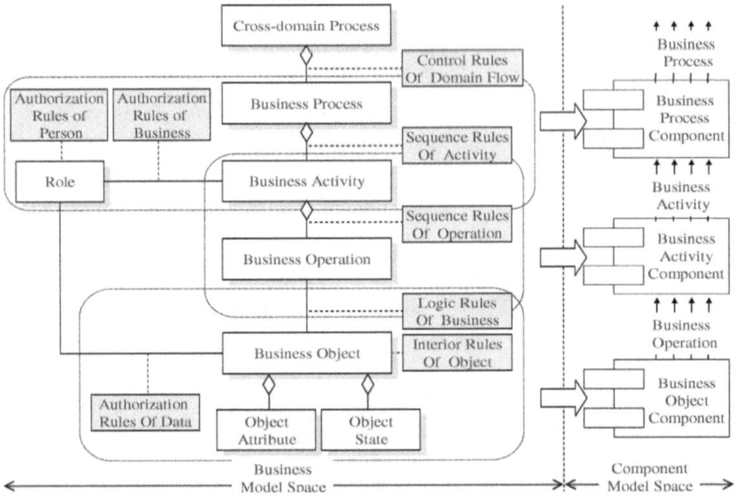

Fig. 3. Mapping relations between the business model and these three kinds of component

According to the types of features in them, components are classified into business process components, business activity components and business object components. Mapping relations between the business model and these three kinds of components are demonstrated in figure 3.

Hierarchical structure exists among these three kinds of components. Business process components are composed of the features provided by business activity components, while business activity components realize business logic by invoking the features provided by business object components. According to this design rule, there are no complex interactive relations among components of the same kind. They are raised into higher level components in the form of business rules and thus the complexity of system is reduced. Interactive behaviors of components are changed by the configuration of business rules and agility of reconfiguration of systems is improved.

3 Information Platform for Logistics Enterprise

3.1 Web-Based Information Platform for Logistics Enterprise

Information platform for logistics enterprise is an integrative information platform maintained by supply chain integrator, which can assemble, organize the resources, capability and technologies of complementary service providers and provide a total solution for supply chain. In addition of providing service for enterprise logistics, it can solve the problem of mutual sharing of logistics information and efficiently utilization of social logistics resources.

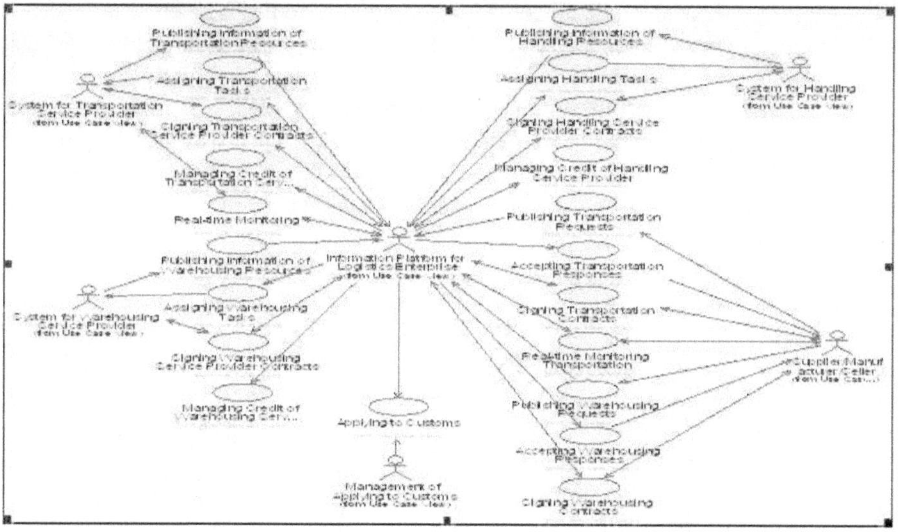

Fig. 4. Information platform for logistics enterprise

Various kinds of service providers publish and exchange logistics information, monitor and control the execution of logistics activities to serve customers through the information platform. Information platform for logistics enterprise is demonstrated in figure 4.

Every service provider publishes information of its resource through the information platform and searches for the demand information that customers released. Every customer publishes demand information of logistics service through the information platform and searches for the information of resources that has already been released. Actual business activities can be carried on when supply and demand matches.

3.2 Feature-Based Reusable Component for Contract Management

Contract is an agreement about commodity, price, payment, delivery etc between enterprise and customer. Any confirmed purpose can be incorporated into contract management. Contract business in information platform for logistics is composed of management of transportation contracts, warehousing contracts and handling contracts. After suppliers publish demand for transportation to the information platform, if the platform finds a transportation service provider who meets the conditions and they match, it is time to manage the contract. It is similar for warehousing contract management and handling contract management except that the contents of contract distinguish because of different purposes.

The concrete steps of contract management includes: inputting provisional contract, generating bill of contract approval, approving contract, contract coming into force and assigning formal contract to production division. If revision is needed, bill of contract alteration is generated and contract is inputted again.

This paper regards business processes like inputting contract, evaluating contract etc. as features and uses business rules to express dependent relations among business elements, which also reflects dependent relations among features. Firstly information of confirmed purpose is inputted to the bill of contract, and then it is time to evaluate the contract. Different contracts distinguish in content and emphases which should be evaluated under various application environments, so relations between contract evaluation and contracts alteration are changeable. This reflects changeability of constraint relations of features.

3.2.1 Reusable Component for Contract Management and Analysis of Its Reusability

Based on analysis of major business in the information platform, analysis and abstraction of the functions, operations of business and information flow, some reusable components are proposed. As mentioned above, transportation service providers, warehousing service providers and handling service providers all contract with the information platform and do their business through contract management, so business related to contract management is design to be a reusable component, which usually is general or incomplete and should be concreted before used.

Component for contract business process is composed of business activity such of inputting contract, alternating contract, inputting bill of contract approval and approving contract. According to the model described above, it is defined as below:

- *fc* is the unique identification of the component for contract business process.
- *froot* is the feature with maximum granularity of which component for contract business process can implement.
- *F* is the set of features in the component for contract business process and is composed of basic activity elements such as inputting contract, inputting bill of contract approval, changing contract and approving contract.
- *R* is the set of feature dependent relations of the component for contract business process, including sequence relation between inputting contract and inputting bill of contract approval. If something about contract changes when business of inputting contract has been finished while bill of contract approval hasn't been inputted, it is necessary to deal these changes by invoking component for contract alteration.
- *PS* is the set of services provided by the component for contract business process. By invoking this component, business related to contract can be handled well even if contract changes. After bill of contract approval has been inputted, it is possible to approve the contract. If finishing the approval, logistics business can be carried on.
- *RS* is the set of services required by the component for contract business process. There are some jobs which should be done before inputting contract. For example, transportation task must exist and has been assigned by the platform before system for transportation service provider executes

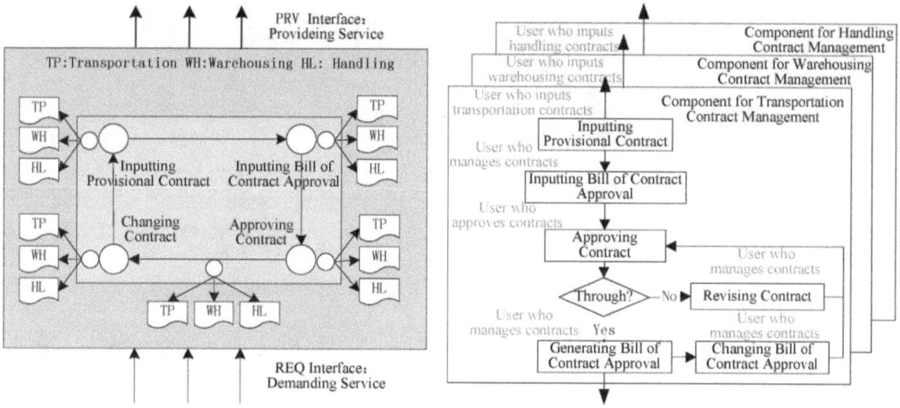

Fig. 5. Denoting changeable points of Component for Contract Management and its instantiation

the component for contract business process. If transportation service provider has capability to do this job, it will contract with platform and invoke component for contract business process. It is similar for warehousing service provider and handling service provider.

Setting changeable points is critical to realize reusability of components for contract business, activity and business object. Five points are set in this mapping. They are including inputting contracts, inputting bill of contract approval, approving contract, alternating contract and association relation between approving contract and changing contract. All these are shown in Figure 5.

When service requirement exist, the component for contract business process is invoked through interface REQ. After finishing its business activities, it provides service of contract management through interface PRV.

As demonstrated in the right of figure 5, business related to contract management for transportation, warehousing and handling service provider can be realized by instancing the changeable points of the component for contract management.

4 Conclusion

Based on the theory of feature modeling, this paper proposes a feature-based semantics model of reusable component, which constructs mapping relations between feature semantics space of component and feature semantics space of enterprise business model. In doing so, it is more practical than traditional models, which only focus formalization theoretically. Changeability of component plays a key role in this model and has been extended from changeability mechanism of existing theory. The model is verified through the case study of business related to contract in a Web-based information platform for logistics enterprise. Component design of enterprise application system can be enhanced with the guide of the model and methodology proposed in this paper.

References

1. Edwards, S.H.: A Formal Model of Software Subsystems. Columbus, USA, The Ohio State University (1995)
2. Weber, H., Padberg, J., Sünbül, A.: Petri Net Based Components for Evolvable Architectures. Transactions of the SDPS, Journal of Integrated Design & Process Science, 6(1) (2002) 1-10
3. Ping, A.I.: Research on the Formal Method of Description for the Flexible Component Composition and its Application to the Water Resources Domain. Nanjing: Hohai University (2002)
4. Daniel, K.: Towards Formal Verification in a Component-based Reuse Methodology. Sweden: Linköping University (2003)
5. Zhang, G.W., Mei, Hong: A Feature-Oriented Domain Model and Its Modeling Process. Journal of Software, 14(8) (2003) 1345-1356
6. Mili, H., Mili, A., Yacoub, S., Addy E.: Reuse-Based Software Engineering: Techniques, Organization, and Controls. New York: John Wiley & Sons, 2002.
7. Jia, Y.: The Evolutionary Component-based Software Reuse Approach. Beijing: Graduation School of Chinese Academy of Sciences (2002)
8. Mei H.: A Component Model for Perspective Management of Enterprise Software Reuse. Annals of Software Engineering. 11 (200) 219–236

Mobile Agents for Network Intrusion Resistance

H.Q. Wang[1], Z.Q. Wang[1,2], Q. Zhao[1], G.F. Wang[1], R.J. Zheng[1], and Da-Xin Liu[1]

[1] College of Computer Science and Technology,
Harbin Engineering University,
Harbin 150001, Heilongjiang Province, China
wanghuiqiang@hrbeu.edu.cn
[2] Herbin Real Estate Trade Center,
Harbin 150001, Heilongjiang Province, China
wang_zengquan@yahoo.com.cn

Abstract. In this paper a distributed IDS systematic model based on mobile agents is proposed and the functions of key modules are described in detail. Then the key modules are implemented in mobile agent platform-IBM Aglets and the results of experiments are discussed and analyzed quantitatively.

1 Introduction

With the development of computer network, network security is becoming more and more serious. The concept of security is important to network itself. Intrusion Detection technology, as the reasonable supplement of firewall, has been a hot topic for more than two decades from the publication of John Anderson's paper. Now, lots of new intrusion detection technologies have been invented to be applied in various domains. There is an exigent requirement for computers to connect to network. With the popularization of network, traditional intrusion detection system can't meet the users' needs because of the increasing complexity and concealment of intrusions [1].

For the reason that current IDS (Intrusion Detection Systems) has one or more defects, the developers hope to use new technologies to get more accurate detection. But the architecture of current IDS has the inherent defects itself; some familiar defects are described as follows:

(1) Delay of time. One of the requirements of the IDS is to deal with events in time. However, current IDSs can't meet this, especially when facing a large number of data, which lead to the result that the functions of IDSs will be declined. For example, the host based IDS may reduce the processing speed of the whole system, and network based IDS may abandon a lot of network packets can't be disposed in time.

(2) A single point of failure. As the central data analyzer is the key entity of the whole system, the network can't be protected if an attacker destroys it in some way.

(3) Limited scalability. All information is controlled by one computer implies the scale of the network will be limited.

(4) Hard to communicate mutually between Different IDSs. Most IDSs are developed for special environment, which make it difficult to be adapted to other environment, even if the latter environment has the same policy and intention as the former one [2].

H.T. Shen et al. (Eds.): APWeb 2006, LNCS 3842, pp. 965–970, 2006.

2 Mobile Agents and Aglet

General Magic Company came up with the concept of mobile agent by carrying out the business system of Telescript at the beginning of 1990s[3]. In short, mobile agent is a program can be moved from one host to another and can mutually operate with other agents or resources. The merits of mobile agent can be described as follows:

(1) Intelligence. Mobile agent collects appropriate information automatically by moving itself to the place where the resources are in. As mobile agent has its own state, so it can move at anytime and anywhere when needed.
(2) Low network traffic. As the mobile agent system may move the request agent to the destination, which make the agent rely on the network transmission less and access needed resource directly. It avoids transmission of large quantities of data and reduces the reliance on the network bandwidth.
(3) Good ability of cooperation. Because of the predefined common communication language and the unified interface, different IDSs can cooperate with others.
(4) Good portability. Current IDS adopts the newest technology of mobile agent and a lot of platforms take Java as the program language. Furthermore, Java is a transplantable language, so it makes IDS to be transplantable.

Aglet is a mobile agent technique that was exploited by IBM in Japan with pure Java, and the company provided the practical platform- Aglet Workbench, which allowed people to develop and move mobile agents on the platform. By far, Aglet is the most successful and comprehensive system [4]. The system framework of Aglet is showed in Fig. 1.

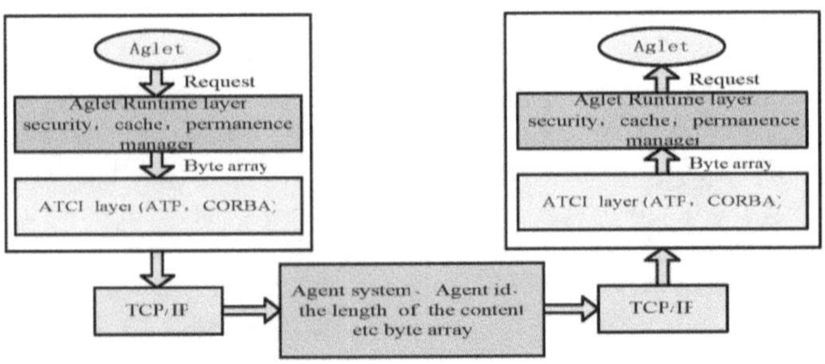

Fig. 1. The system framework of Aglet

3 An IDS Framework Based on Mobile Agents

In order to remedy the actual defects of current IDS, we propose a framework based on mobile agents. The intrusion detection system based on the mobile agents designed in this paper utilizes the IBM Aglet as the platform of mobile agents. The system framework includes the following components: manager, data gathering MA(Mobile Agent) , intrusion analysis MA and intrusion response MA, host monitor MA, database of agent、database of configuration and log document. Fig. 2 shows the system framework.

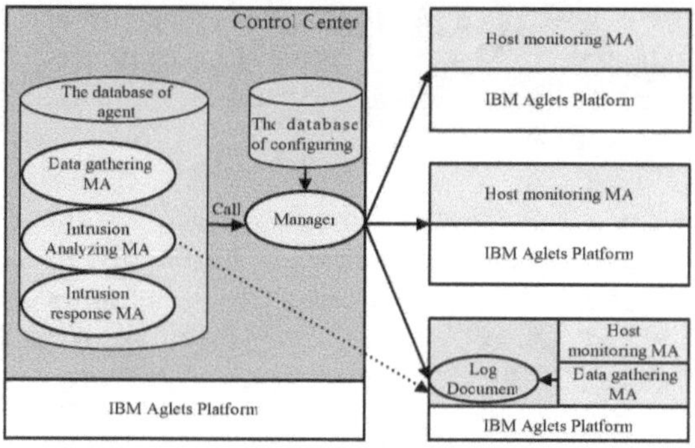

Fig. 2. The framework of the system based on the mobile agents

The data source of IDS can be divided into two parts: host-based data and network-based data. The gathering part of network data source is to record 、 filter and format the connection information of the monitored host, and write them into the log. The data source of the host includes system log and some conserved audit records. To implement the monitor on every host, a host monitor MA is established on every monitored host in the network. If intrusions to some monitored host occur confirmatively, the host monitor MA will report the event to manager directly. Otherwise, the host monitor MA will appeal to the manager and report the suspicious activity directly. After receiving the appeal, the manager distributes a date gathering MA patrolling other hosts in the network to gather information. If a distributed intrusion can be found from the integrated susceptible activities on different hosts, the manager judges whether it's a distributed intrusion by analysis the information collected by data gathering MA. If a distributed intrusion is found, the manager will assign an intrusion response MA to respond intelligently to every monitored host. The database of configuration stores the node configuration information of detecting system.

In the implementation, it can be stored in every node or stored centrally according the scale of the database. The database of agent is the place to store the agent codes. The diversity of algorithms leads to the variety of the agent. So, the scale of the database is possible very big. To avoid of being deceived maliciously, the agent codes had better to be stored in the control center, and the manager can send them to other hosts by the way of agent dispatch.

3.1 Mobile Agents

For the purpose of high adaptability and security of the system, most components described in this paper are packed as mobile agents. The mobile agent is implemented by Aglet in this system, and every monitored host must establish a mobile agent platform-IBM Aglets, which can offer circumstance for the migration and running of the mobile agent. There are four kinds of mobile agents in this model: data gathering MA, intrusion analysis MA, intrusion response MA and host monitor MA. They can be called and sent to other hosts by the manager.

Data gathering MA is implemented by Jpcap. Though there are many IP package-gathering tools, such as Sniffer, Tcpdump and Snoop, they generally run in the UNIX system. As this system is developed in the Windows platform and the programming language is Java, data gathering MA uses the interface offered by Jpcap to intercept the message (including TCP connection, UDP connection and ICMP package information) in the network. After the course of filtration and formatting, the message will be written into the log file.

AS a Java package can access the data link layer directly, Jpcap offers the ability of capturing raw data package for application layer real-time. The intrusion analysis MA mainly analyses the log files in the monitored host system and compares them with the characters of known attack activities to find abnormal activity combined with different detection measures. The intrusion response MA responds to the intrusion events occurred, which can include tracking the intrusion trace to find the intrusion fountain, recording the intrusion events into database, etc. The host monitor MA has three sub-agents to answer respectively for monitor network connection, file operation and privilege operation, so it can complete the intrusion detection function by assisting the intrusion analysis MA.

3.2 Manager

In our system, manager is the centre of controlling and adjusting other components and it maintains theirs configuration information. When any component above is added to the system, it must to register itself in the component list of the manager. The manager also establishes, distributes, incepts and destroys mobile agents according to the requests of the host and the needs of the circumstance. In addition, the manager detects the security of all the mobile agents in the system. At last, the manager receives intrusion alarms from host monitor MA and executes intrusion response using intrusion response MA.

In the implementation of this model, the security of the Aglet is vital because it is authorized to run on every monitored host. If an Aglet in the network is maliciously tampered or an imitative malicious Aglet enters into the running system, the security of the system will be enormously threatened. So, the security regulation of the Aglet system is needed to be set strictly. The Tahiti of the Aglets platform has many kinds of security measures itself, in which the most topic ones include two kinds: the virtual machine certification and the Aglet authority controlling [5].

4 Experiments and Numeral Results

The test and evaluation of an intrusion detection system are extremely difficult, which is because of that many aspects need to be considered, such as operating system and the network circumstance simulation. In our test, we select three hosts established with Win 2000 operating system in a LAN to construct a distributed intrusion detection system platform based on Aglets. The first host acts as monitor host, and the second one as the monitored host, and the last one is for attack. To the recording of the data package flowing through the whole LAN of the data gathering MA, the monitored host should select the machine at the entrance of the network or on the agent server. We select three typical attacks to test, which are Land attack, Winnuke attack and Ping of Death attack respectively. The test results of false negatives rate is showed in table 1.

Table 1. Test of systematic false negatives rate

The number of package	The number of warring that received	False negatives rate
81	78	3.70%
204	190	6.86%
707	652	9.07%

From above analysis we can see that system false negatives rate increase obviously with the increase of the number of packages. The reason can be divided into two parts. One hand, it may has direct relation with the system, because of Jpcap that we use in snatching the network packages itself has time delay in some way, so it may result in losing a small amount of packages; on the other hand, the most important thing is that we send packages through high speed instrument of sending package, it may cause the losing packages that can not be snatched by having no enough time.

In system function test, it examines mainly the situation of CPU and memory utilization rate through Windows mission management in normal network circumstance. We examine console in monitor host end and the situation of CPU and memory took up of data gathering device in monitored host through Windows mission management, and the situation of CPU and memory took up of detectors in detectors end. From the test, we may see that the resource taken up by this system is not higher than traditional system.

Consider the transit time, transit time constitutes the time required for a mobile agent to travel from one host to another. In the test, with the different traffic of packets, transit time has different value. With 50% traffic, the transit time is 0.0831 seconds. With 75% traffic, transit time is 0.3342 seconds. With 95% traffic, transit time is 1.134 seconds.

Due to above all kinds of test, the system can satisfy the flux request of the mini local network.

5 Conclusions

A framework of Intrusion Detection System based on mobile agents is proposed in this paper, and a prototype system based on IBM's ASDK (Aglets Software Development Kit) is implemented and some experiment results are presented. It is based on the mature intrusion detection technology at present, and combines the special advantage of mobile agent technology and distributed system. The design of the model changes the hierarchical system structure of traditional distributed IDS, and uses the system structure of having no control center and regarding the mobile agent as the organize unit, which shows the unique superiority. Mobile agent technology is effective in raising the security of distributed IDSs and the ability of adaptability and cooperate detection. The following is the advantages of the model that we proposed:

(1) IDS can still keep normal run, even some mobile agents have failed. Moreover, mobile agents in the system can evade intrusion, and they can recover by themselves if they suffer from intrusion.

(2) Data relativity, the measure of cooperate detection and the movement of mobile agent make the detection of distributed intrusion become possible. Detect MA can correlate the susceptible events in different monitored mainframe. Response MA can add/reduce dynamically the susceptible level of certain mainframe or registered users, they can enhance the ability of response of result of intrusion detection.

However, some questions still exist. IDS will be in a very dangerous state if invader discovers location of manager, and mobile agent may spend more time in the moving stage. Though the structure was proved that could be well utilized, it still needs to be improved before it is deployed in real circumstance.

References

1. Chunsheng Li, Qingfeng Song, Chengqi Zhang: MA-IDS Architecture for Distributed Intrusion Detection using Mobile Agents [A]. In:Proceedings of the 2nd ICITA, Harbin, China, January (2004)
2. Xiaoli Shangguan: Distributed Intrusion Detection System Based on Mobile Agents. Dissertation for Master`s degree of Taiyuan University of Technology (2003) 1-2
3. JANSEN W: Intrusion Detection with Mobile Agents [A]. Comput Commun, (2002) 25: 1392-1401
4. IBM:Aglets.http://www.trl.ibm.com/aglets/. (2002)
5. Yunyong Zhang, Jinde Liu: Mobile agent technology (M). Pekin Publishing company of TsingHua University (2003) 9, 44-50, 148-152
6. Dengyun Sun.:Study and Implementation of Mobile Agents-Based Distributed Intrusion Detection Systerm .Dissertation for Master`s degree of XiDian University(2004) 43-46
7. C. Krügel, T. Toth: Applying Mobile Agent Technology to Intrusion Detection. ICSE Workshop on Software Engineering and Mobility, Toronto (2001)
8. Eugene H.Spafford, Diego Zamboni: Intrusion Detection Using Autonomous Agents. Computer Networks, (2000) 34: 547-570
9. Steven R.Snapp, James Brentano, Gihan V.Dias, etc: A System for Distributed Intrusion Detection. IEEE (1999):234-236
10. Mobile Computing: http://latte.cs.iastate.edu/research/research.jsp.(2004)

Grid Service Based Parallel Debugging Environment

Wei Wang[1] and Binxing Fang[2]

[1] Information Security Research Center,
Computer Science Department, Harbin Engineering University, China
wwei@hrbeu.edu.cn
[2] Computer Network and Information Security Research Center,
Computer Science Department, Harbin Institute of Technology, China
bxfang@pact518.hit.edu.cn

Abstract. Debugging can help programmers to locate the reasons for incorrect program behaviors. The dynamic and heterogeneous characteristics of computational grid make it much harder to utilize the traditional parallel debuggers to debug grid applications for their defects in architecture. In this paper, we propose a new parallel debugging environment based on grid services, which support the information sharing and resource interoperation. Some new debugging functionalities oriented to Grid applications are appended. The architecture of the proposed debugging environment has high portability and scalability.

1 Introduction

Any programmer will want to know what has gone wrong when a program exposes incorrect behavior or terminates abnormally. Debugging is accepted as a very important activity for achieving a certain level of program quality in terms of reliability. At the same time it is recognized as one of the most difficult phases of the software life-cycle and is often underestimated in software development project. Traditional sequential debugging techniques offer the following typical functionalities: cyclic interactive debugging, memory dumps, tracing and breakpoints. However, these techniques cannot be directly applied in a parallel and distributed environment. The most immediate approach to support debugging functionalities in a parallel and distributed environment is through the collection of multiple sequential debuggers, each is attached to an application process. This may provide similar commands as available in conventional debuggers, possibly extended to deal with parallelism and communication. State-based traditional debugging architecture usually consists of a root debugger and several serial debugger. Many state changes occur that have to be observed, transferred, stored, and processed by the debugging tool. In the worst case, debugging a supercomputer may require another supercomputer to perform the analysis task.

In order to face the rapidly increasing need for computational resources of various scientific and engineering applications, additional impetus is enforced by so-called Grid infrastructure, which increases the available computing power by enabling the integrated and collaborative use of distributed high-end computers and networks. Grid

H.T. Shen et al. (Eds.): APWeb Workshops 2006, LNCS 3842, pp. 971 – 978, 2006.

computing[1] is rapidly gaining in functionality, performance, robustness, and consequently finds acceptance as standard platform for High Performance Computing(HPC). Middleware such as Globus Toolkit provides common abstractions which allow a heterogeneous set of resources to appear as a logical supercomputer. However, debugging grid applications executing on diverse computational platforms and heterogeneous communication networks continues to remain a cumbersome and tedious process for a number of reasons, including:

- Heterogeneity
- Large amount of computational resources
- Dynamic behavior of computational environment
- Authorization/Authentication on different administration domains
- Nondeterministic execution of grid applications.

In this paper, we identified several key capabilities that need to be added to a traditional parallel debugger in order to construct a useful grid-enables parallel debugging environment. These capabilities are listed below:

- Launching grid applications
- Debugging related grid resources management
- Debugging data management

Based on Grid services, we proposed a conceptual designation of parallel debugging environment, called Grid Service Based Parallel Debugging Environment (GSBPDE), a dynamic and reconfigurable software infrastructure for debugging grid applications. We attempts to overcome the limited flexibility of traditional software systems by defining a simple but powerful architectural model based on the concept of Grid services. We are particularly interested in an approach that models the debugger as an event-based system. It uses a previously recorded event trace, in order to analyze the execution history, and to guide program replay with reproducible behavior.

This paper is organized as followings: We review some relate works in section 2. Section 3 will give the overview of GSBPDE, more designation details about GSBPDE are given in section 4, and section 5 gives the conclusion.

2 Related Works

During the development of parallel computing technology, the parallel software has lagged behind the parallel hardware. Parallel debugger is just one case, and parallel debugging techniques are less mature than parallel programming. One main reason which result in this situation is that standardization process is slow in parallel computing field.

In order to impel parallel debugging development, several researchers tried to propose the standard architecture of parallel debuggers. OMIS (Online Morning Interface Specification)(1996)[2], Ptools (Parallel Tools Consortium) and HPDF(High Performance Debugging Forum)(1997)[3] have obtained some results. In OMIS, the uniform parallel program instrumentation interface is provided, and an integrated

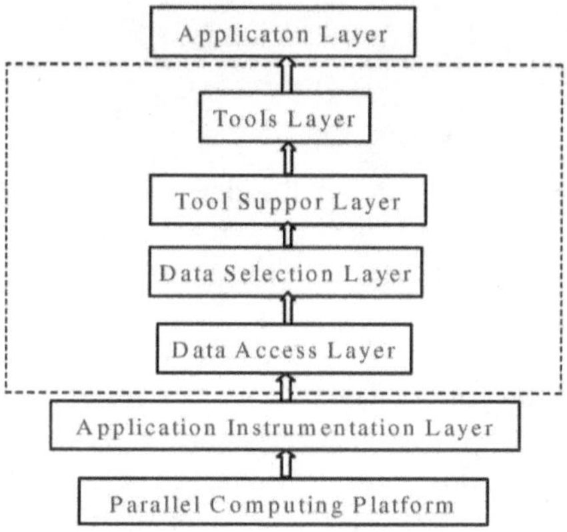

Fig. 1. A general six-layer model of parallel program analysis tools

parallel analysis and debugging environment called TOOLSET is constructed. In TOOLSET, the data format transferred between components is consistent. Ptools is a consortium composed by several universities and institutes, supporting software tools research and development. HPDF is sponsored by Ptools. It tried to define a set of standards relevant to debugging tools for high performance computing. The final result of HPDF is based on command line interface, and it is just on paper, not available. In [4], a general six-layer model of parallel program analysis tools is presented, as shown in Fig.1.Most parallel debuggers adapt to this model. Some instances include fiddle [5],DDBG [6], etc.

All these parallel debuggers are designed oriented to conventional parallel and distributed computing platform. When Grid is concerned, some defects will be exposed, such as:

(1) The network characteristic is high latency, low bandwidth. The command line interface can not be assured to work.
(2) In Grid, a portable parallel debugging environment is needed.
(3) In the six-layer model, the interfaces between layers are tightly coupled, which affect their scalability with deployed in Grid, a large-scale, complex computing platform.
(4) The dynamic characteristic of Grid needs a special resource management module to provide a on-demand computing and debugging platform.
(5) As a shared resource set in Grid, the security strategy should be added, for some detail about the resource will be involved during the program debugging and analysis.

All these defects should be addressed when a new parallel debugging environment is designed in Grid. Obviously those traditional parallel debuggers will not work in Grid, so the new architecture of parallel debugging environment should be proposed, just as follows, a Grid Service Based Parallel Debugging Environment, GSBPDE.

3 GSBPDE Overview

3.1 Grid Service

Globus project was initiated in 1995. For the defects on programming language and architecture, the development of GT2 was delayed. In 2000, some leading companies, including IBM, Microsoft, IBM, BEA System, and Intel, defined Web services together for developing B2B applications. At last, W3C and OASIS proposed the final version.

Globus project noticed the potentiality of Web services, and turned to Web services in 2002. In June the Open Grid Service Architecture, OGSA [7], is proposed. In July, 2003, GGF proposed Open Grid Service Infrastructure, OGSI. The concept of Grid service is presented. In essence, Grid service originates from Web services, and owns some extension functionalities. The most important property is the service state management. Since OGSA/OGSI is constructed on Web services, Grid service can be a standard when Grid application and middleware is developed. This condition provides a chance for parallel debugging environment deployed in Grid.

3.2 GSBPDE Architecture

From the introduction above, a new parallel environment architecture in Grid is proposed, that is GSBPDE. Fig.2 shows the architecture of GSBPDE. Fig.2 shows that GSBPDE breaks through the traditional six-layer model of parallel program analysis tools. Each functionality is a Grid service, loosely coupled from each other, which is adapt to Grid environment. Fig.3 illustrates the relationship of grid services in GSBPDE.

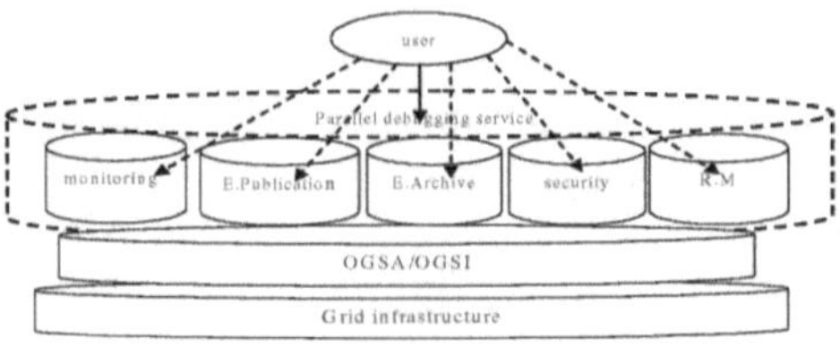

Fig. 2. The architecture of GSBPDE

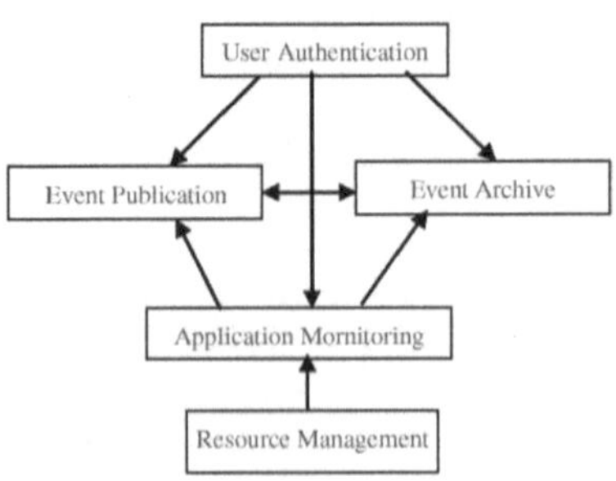

Fig. 3. Relationship between service modules in GSBPDE

3.3 Parallel Debugging Functionality

In addition to support some conventional parallel debugging functionalities, some new special components oriented to Grid are included in GSBPDE, listed below:

(1) Cooperative Debugging. The essence of Grid is resource sharing and cooperation. Grid applications are large-scale and hard to debug by individuals. GSBPDE provides a platform to realize the cooperation in debugging. Through event archive and event publication services, any authenticated user can attend to debug Grid applications.

(2) Multi-history Data Analysis. As traditional parallel applications, Grid applications may be nondeterministic. Only analyzing data generated in one execution is not enough. Multi-history data analysis is necessary for debugging Grid applications. The volume of data may be very large, so this functionality can not be taken into effect in some conventional parallel computing environment. Grid has great storage capacity to support this module.

(3) Resource Management. Cyclic debugging is an effective method for debugging applications, but the dynamic characteristic of Grid makes it difficult to put cyclic debugging into practice. The resource may join in or exit Grid atany time, and the state of the resource will vary with time. So the dedicated resource management module will be add into GSBPDE for selecting, filtering and reserving resource to construct on-demand parallel debugging environment.Fig.4 provides a use case view of GSBPDE.

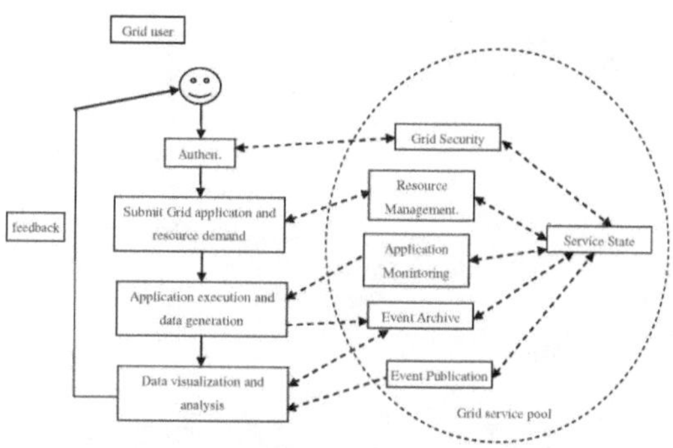

Fig. 4. A use case of GSBPDE

4 GSBPDE Implementation

4.1 Service Interface Description

GSBPDE can be viewed as a Grid service group to support debugging Grid applications. This service group includes the Grid services listed below:

- EventArchive
- EventPublication
- EventVisualization
- UserAuthentication

In order to let user to interact with GSBPDE, the service interface definition should be given first. We use GWSDL to describe the interface. EventArchive is used as an example and the detail is shown in Fig.5. For other services, the interface definition framework is same.

```
<gwsdl:portType name = "factoryGSBPDE" extends = "ServiceGroup"/>
<sd:staticServiceDataValues>
  <ogsi:EntryType>
    <serviceGroupEntryLocator nil = "true"/>
    <memberServiceLoctor>
       <ogsi:handle>
         http://localhost/ogsi/crm/GSBPDE
       </ogsi:handle>
    <memberServiceLocator>
    <content>
      <ogsi:CreateServiceExtensibilityType>
      <createsInterface>EventArchive</createsInterface>
      <createsInterface>GridService</createsInterface>
      </ogsi:CreateServiceExtensibilityType>
    </content>
</ogsi:EntryType>
```

Fig. 5. GWSDL description of EventArchive service interface

4.2 Event Data Description

Heterogeneous resource will generate data with different format. This situation will affect the information share and resource interoperation in Grid. In order to support cooperative debugging in GSBPDE, the monitoring service uses the XML document to represent the debugging data. Fig.6 illustrates the XML Schema of message passing events, and Fig.7 is a specific example.

4.3 Practical Case Illustration

GBSPDE use Globus Tookit3 as the Grid software infrastructure to implement each Grid service module. The following several diagram is the snapshot of GBSPDE working process.Fig.8 is the GBSPDE portal and Grid application and resource demand submission interface.

```
  <xs:schema  xmlns:xsd = http://www.w3.org/1999/XMLSchema
              Xmlns:xhtml = "http://www.w3.org/1999/xhtml">
  <xsd:element name='SourceProcessID' type='xsd: integer'/>
  <xsd:element name='Operation' type='xsd:string'/>
  < xsd:element name='DestProcessID' type='xsd: integer'/>
  < xsd:element name='LogicalClock' type='xsd: string'/>
  < xsd:element name='PhysicalClock' type='xsd: float'/>
</xs:schema>
```

Fig. 6. XML Schema document of message passing event

```
<?xml version = "1.0" encoding = "GB2312" standalone = "no"?>
<Debugging Envent>
  <SourceProcessID>1</SourceProcessID>
  <Operation> "send" </SourceProcessID>
  <DestProcessID>2</DestProcessID>
  <LogicalClock> "1,0,0,4,5" </ LogicalClock >
  <PhysicalClock> 1110107139.804210</ PhysicalClock >
<Debugging Envent>
```

Fig. 7. A XML Document Example of a message sending event

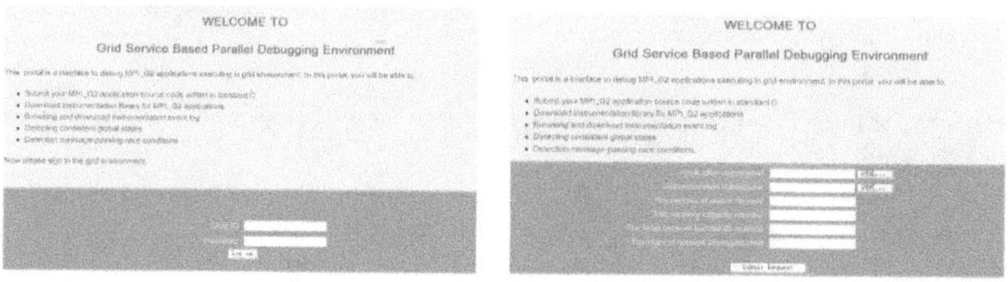

Fig. 8. GBSPDE portal (left) and Grid application and resource demand submission interface (right)

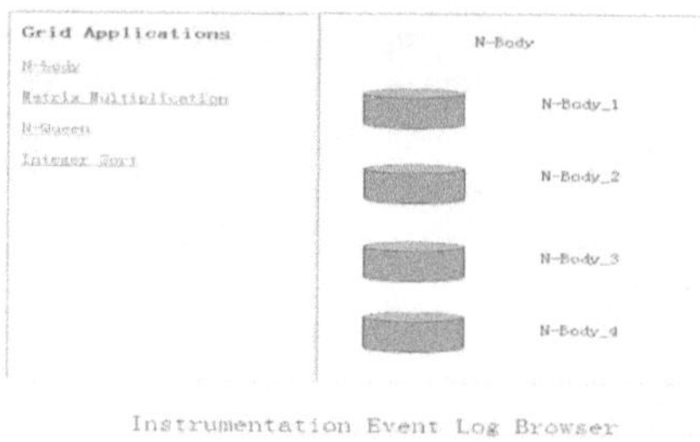

Fig. 9. Grid application monitoring log event browser

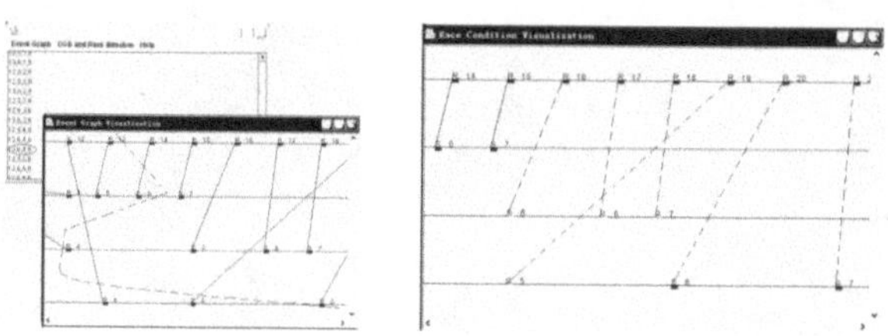

Fig. 10. Global consistent state detection (left) and race message detection (right)

Fig.9 is a browser for Grid user to browse, select and download monitoring the monitoring data corresponding to a specific Grid application. Fig.10 is two debugging functionalities, which are global consistent state detection and message race detection.

5 Conclusion

Debugging is a tedious work when developing software. Parallel debugging can cope with the defects in parallel and distributed applications. In Grid environment, dynamic configuration and heterogeneity make great obstacle for debugging grid applications. This paper presents a Grid service based parallel debugging environment, which provides a good platform for debugging grid applications. Compared with traditional ones, this new environment is more scalable, portable and easy to be standardized.

References

1. Foster, I.,Kesselman,C.: The Grid : Blueprint for a New Computing Infrstruture,Morgan-Kaufmann (1999)
2. Ludwig, T., Wismller, R: OMIS 2.0 A Universal Interface for Monitoring Systems, Proc. 4th European PVM/MPI Users' Group Meeting, (1997) 267-276
3. Francioni, J., Pancake, C. M: High Performance Debugging Standards Effort, Scientific Programming, 8(2000)95-108
4. Klar, R., Dauphin, P., Hartleb, F., Hofmann, R., Mohr, B., Quick, A., Siegle, M: Messung und Modellierung paralleler und verteilter Rechensysteme, B.G. Teubner, Stuttgart, Germany (1995) [in German]
5. Lourenco,J, Cunha,JC: Fiddle: A Flexible Distributed Debugging Architectur eLecture Notes In Computer Science; Proceedings of the International Conferenceon Computational Science.(2003)821-830
6. Neophytou, N,. and Evripidou, Paraskevas: Net-dbx: A Web-Based Debugger of MPIPrograms Over Low-Bandwidth Lines, IEEE Tansaction On Parallel and Distributed Systems, 9(2001)986-995
7. Foster, I., Kesselman, C., Nick, J. and Tuecke, S: The Physiology of the Grid:An Open Grid Services Architecture for Distributed Systems Integration. Globus Project, 2002 omputing. Future Generation Computer Systems. 5(1999) 757-768

Web-Based Three-Dimension E-Mail Traffic Visualization

Xiang-hui Wang and Guo-yin Zhang

College of Computer Science and Technology,
Harbin Engineering University,
150001 Harbin, China
Wangxianghui@hrbeu.edu.cn

Abstract. E-mail pervades many aspects of our lives and is becoming indispensable communication method in areas such as commerce, government, production and general information dissemination. To maintain the security and usability of the e-mail system, every effort must be made to efficient monitoring e-mail traffic and protecting against various types of spam maker. In this paper, we design and implement a web-based 3D visualization system, monitoring the e-mail traffic and providing based on statistic suspicious activities analysis. Our system also provides convenient interactive user interface for selecting interest watching object and different type of analysis method. Our results indicate that analysts can efficient examine the e-mail traffic and rapidly discover abnormal user activities.

Keywords: Web-based visualization, E-mail traffic, Security, Spam, Java3D.

1 Introduction

E-Mail is an important method of the people's communication, and widely used in education, science research, commerce and other areas. Maintaining e-mail system is a hard work, and administrators have to pay attention to e-mail system all the time in order to keep it working order. How to efficient monitoring the e-mail system, it is a tough challenge to the e-mail system administrator. At the same time, some bad guys use e-mail system sending spam, which would reduce security and usability of the e-mail system. So we need to discover the abnormal activities in time, and stop spam delivering.

At present, administrator of e-mail system has to read the log files to check the security event, or receive statistic report at interval sent by the log watcher software. They can not near-real-time monitor the e-mail traffic, efficiently analyze the user activity, and discover the spam maker. Previous security visualization tool almost visualize IP layer information, such as IP address, port and protocol type, to discover attacks and abnormal activities. These security visualization tools are lack of the understanding to the application layer information, and do not have the ability to monitor and analyze the application layer security events.

H.T. Shen et al. (Eds.): APWeb 2006, LNCS 3842, pp. 979–986, 2006.

In this paper, we design a web-based 3D visualization system using Java3D technology, which provides the capability to understand application layer information, efficiently monitor the e-mail traffic and analyze malicious activities.

2 Related Work

Information visualization is a mature field with a wide range of techniques that has been successfully applied to many domains. SeeNet [1] uses an abstract representation of network destinations and displays a colored grid. PortVis [2] produces images of network traffic representation the network activity. NVisionIP [3] uses network flow traffic and axes that correspond to IP addresses; each point on the grid represents the interaction between the corresponding net-work hosts. Tudumi [4] is a visualization system designed to monitor and audit computer logs to help detect anomalous user activities. StarClass [5] is a interactive visual classification method, which maps multi-dimensional data to the visual display using star coordinates, allowing the user to interact with the display to create a decision tree.

Java3D API is a program interface that is used to develop 3D graphics and web-based 3D applications. There has been some work used Java3D techniques to implement real-time or Internet 3D visualization system. Li Xiang [6] designs a Java3D-based terrain 3D visualization system, and M.Emoto [7] develops a Java-based real-time monitoring system to make operation more easily find the malfunctioning parts of complex instruments. During the design of our system, we relied upon the work by Fink [8] and Seven Krasser [9].

3 System Design and Implementation

3.1 Visualization Design

Fig.1 shows an overview of the visualization. The bottom base line denotes the IP address (0.0.0.0 – 255.255.255.255) of the users or the e-mail servers who send emails to our e-mail system. The right base line represent the destination email account (0 - 8191) in our e-mail system where account 0 is at the bottom and account 8191 is at the top. There is a colored line linked the bottom base line and right base line, which means authentication result, yellow for authentication failure, green for success and purple for no authentication. The left base line represent the IP address (0.0.0.0 – 255.255.255.255) of the relaying destination, and the colored line linked right base line and left base line represent the email relaying from our email system to other email system, red for connecting failure, orange for delivering success.

The color lines fade to black over times when the delivering mission is accomplished so that the old delivering activities become less visible. Each email message triggers one glyph that represented by vertical lines in the 3D view, moving from the right or the left base line over time. The height of glyph represents the size of the mail, including the attachments. The distance of the glyph from base line represents age of the email message, when a new email arrived, the glyph moves away from the base line as the email message gets older. The color of the glyph denote more information for the email

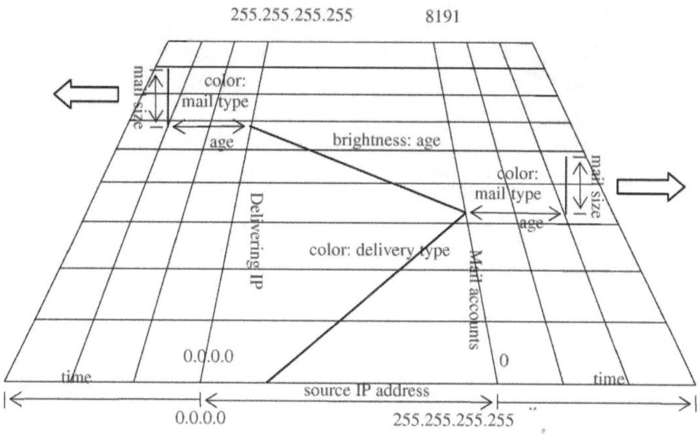

Fig. 1. Visualization Overview

message, green for normal email, red for the email that contains virus, yellow for delivering failure and blue for spam.

3.2 Interaction and Display Controlling

The user can navigate with the mouse through the web-based visualization. When clicking into the browser, some brief information regarding the email message or delivering message closest to the mouse is displayed. For example, if user click the glyphs, the head information of the email, such as 'from', 'to', 'subject' and 'date', are displayed in a popup browser. So the analysts could use this brief information quickly giving a judgment of the e-mail.

The user can use Control Panel (see Fig.2) to control the display of our visualization system. There are four parts of the Control Panel: Mail Display, Link Line Display, Playback Display and SPAM Display.

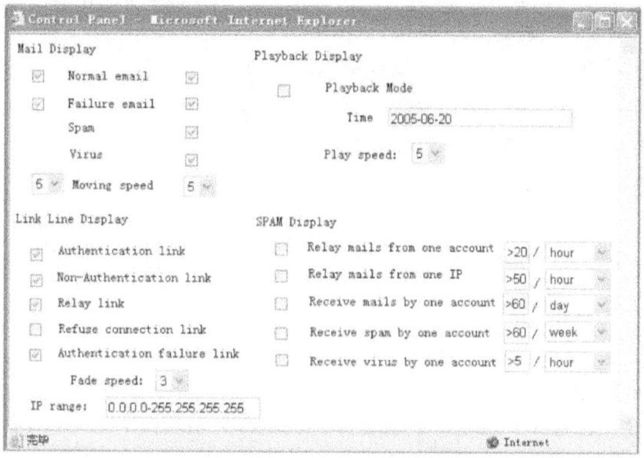

Fig. 2. Control Panel

Mail Display options can be used to choose which type of the email should be display. 'Moving speed' is used to speed up or gear down the moving speed of the glyphs from the base line. Link Line Display options are used to choose which link line should be displayed. 'Fading speed' represents the time of link line fading from its own color to the black. Playback Display options provides a mode that allows use go back to a certain time to monitor the email system. In playback mode, the speed of playback can be adjusted. SPAM is used to monitor the suspicious email account or IP address by gathering statistic information from database.

3.3 System Modules

There are three components (see Fig.3) in our system: Data Collector (DC), Server Center (SC) and Interactive Visualization Client (IVC). DC gathers useful data from e-mail system, and sends the data to the SC. The SC is a database and web server, receives data, store them into the database for playback mode, and respond the requests from IVC. IVC has the ability to request and receive data from SC, and visualize the data in web browser using Java3D technology.

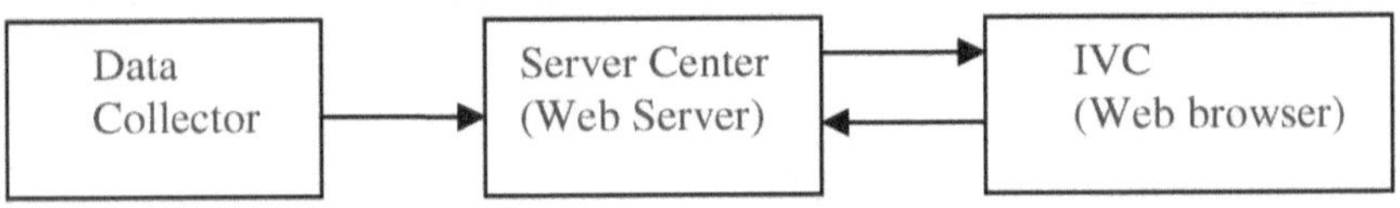

Fig. 3. System Modules

4 Results and Evaluation

4.1 Suspicious Normal Email

To quickly discover who is sending spam to our email system, we just need to adjust the display options to only show the spam in our visualization system. We find that a single IP address sends a lot of spam to our e-mail system. Generally, we should block the e-mail from this IP address, but more useful information can be get using our visualization system. We adjust the display options to show all types of e-mails form this IP address, and some suspicious 'normal emails' are discovered (see Fig.4). It implied that these emails have the ability to avoid our anti-spam system and key work filter system. So these 'normal emails' could help us to improve our filter system, to prevent other spam maker.

4.2 Relayed Spam

Fig.5 show us who is using our email system to send spam to other email system. To find out this type of spam sender, we should display the 'relay mail from one account' (in the Control Panel) and adjust the frequency of the sending emails to '> 20/day'. Then, we find that 2 email accounts are sending more than 20 emails in 24 hours. We also discover that the two accounts are authenticated from the same IP address, which implied that some one maybe use tow accounts in our email system to send spam. Finally, to confirm

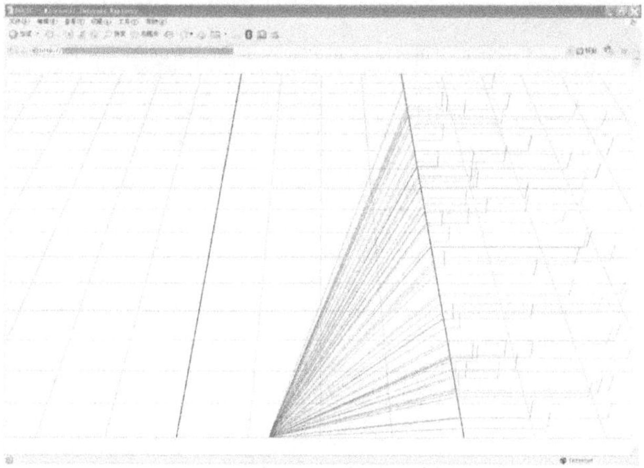

Fig. 4. More Hidden Information

our conclusion, we check the head information of the e-mails, and it shows that all the emails sending from these two accounts are the commercial advertising.

Additionally, there is a red link line between the left base line and right base line, and it shows that our email system is already in the backlist because of the user who sends spam. We double click the 'refuse connection link line' (red line) to check the information, and it shows that this account already has sent more than 150 emails in one week.

4.3 Slow Spam Maker

Fig.6 focus on the suspicious IP address to prevent the person who slowly sending spam and using more email accounts to hide himself. We use 'receive all type of email'

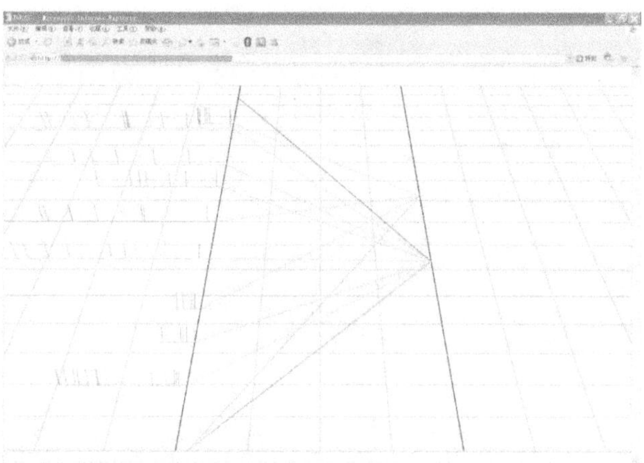

Fig. 5. Spam relayed by our E-mail system

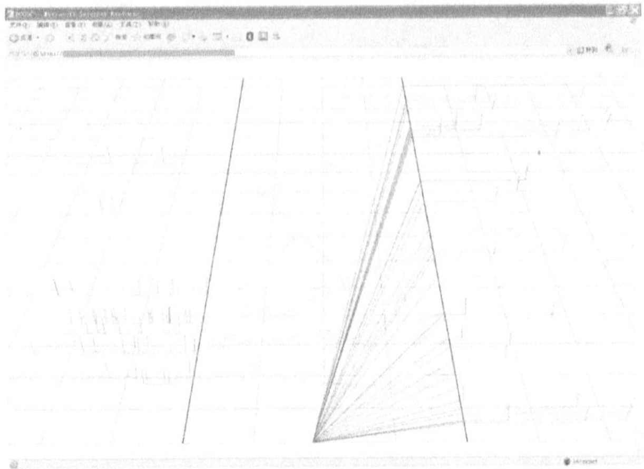

Fig. 6. Slow Spam Maker

option to display who send more than 300 emails in one week. We find a single IP address, which sends a lot of email to our email system and redelivery those to other email systems. After checking the head information of the email, another spam maker is discovered. If only use the 'relay mail from one account' option, we may not discover the spam sender. Because each account do not sending too much emails in a short time.

4.4 Suspicious Accounts Discovery

There are some accounts that are not always receive spam (maybe our anti-spam system does not discover the spam), but they receive too much normal mail, and it is abnormal. Maybe the account is published in forum or web, and the spam makers know their account. For one hand, although there accounts do not receive spam, maybe they

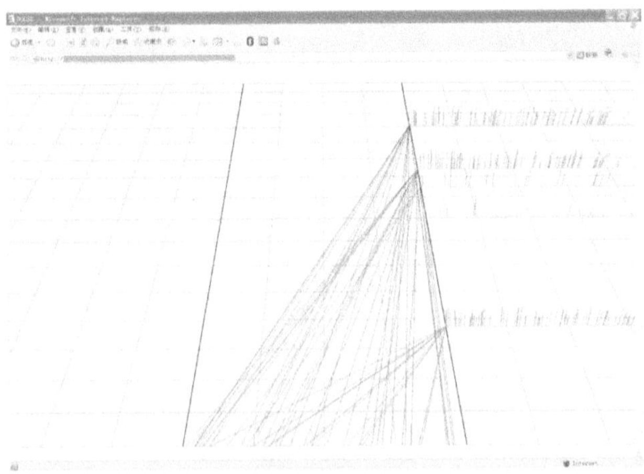

Fig. 7. Suspicious Accounts

are just busy accounts, but there accounts' activities are suspicious, may become 'spam receiver' soon. For another hand, these email accounts receiving so much emails will be filled up quickly and decrease the usability of the email system.

To find these accounts, we adjust display options to show the 'non-authentication link line' (the purple line) and decrease the speed of the fading and moving. Then we choose to display the 'receive all type of mail' and adjust the frequency of the receiving to '> 7/day', which means that our system will show all the accounts receiving more than 7 emails in 24 hours.

Fig.7 shows that those 5 accounts receive more than 7 emails in 24 hours. Especially there are 3 accounts which receive more than 40 emails in 24 hours, and they are the most suspicious and dangerous accounts.

5 Further Work

Although we made key discoveries using our visualization system, we believe there are some areas where our system can be further improved. First, we plan to add zoom capabilities so that mouse can be used to zoom in to a point of interest or zoom out to an overview of all the email traffic. Moreover, we would like to add a controller module to control the email system and restrict email users' activities, such as warning the spam sender, blocking certain emails delivering, creating or deleting email accounts and so on. Finally, we plan to improve our system user interface to make it easier for configuration and display controlling.

6 Conclusion

We have demonstrated how visualization made it easier to monitor e-mail traffic and analyze suspicious activities. Non-visual Internet methods would have much greater difficulty in discovering the abnormal activities, distinguishing between different types of email and monitoring email system. With web-based visualization technology, the analysts could get useful information at a glance, and know what has happened in the e-mail system, or find out that which account is most suspicious and dangerous. Additionally, the system has proven to be a useful tool for anti-spam purpose. We effectively used it in analyzing spam maker activities and their strategy.

We believe that our web-based visualization system is a practical and effective e-mail traffic monitoring and activities analyzing system. The idea of using web-based visualization for email traffic monitoring is an important contribution. Further features built on our system may make it an even more powerful system.

Acknowledgements

This work has been sponsored in part by the Heilongjiang Province Science Foundation under contracts F2004-06. The authors would like to thank Shen Jie for her helpful suggestions and Ye Zai-wei for the implementation.

References

1. Richard A. Becker, Stephen G. Eick, Allan R.Wilks: Visualizing Network Data. IEEE Transactions on Visualization and Computer Graphics, Vol. 1(1), (1995) 16–28
2. Jonathan McPherson, Kwan-Liu Ma, Paul Krbystosek, Tony Bartoletti, Marvin Christensen: PortVis: A Tool for Port-Based Detection of Security Events. The Institute of Data Analysis and Visualization, (2004)
3. Kiran Lakkaraju, Ratna Bearavolu, William Yurcik: NVisionIP—A Traffic Visualiza- tion Tool for Security Analysis of Large and Complex Networks. In International Multiconference on Measurement, Modelling, and Evaluation of Computer-Communications Systems, (2003)
4. Tetsuji Takada, Hideki Koike: Tudumi--Information Visualization System for Monitoring and Auditing. Proceedings of 6th International Conference on Information Visualization, IEEE CS Press, (2002) 570--576
5. Soon Tee Teoh, Kwan-Liu Ma: StarClass--Interactive Visual Classification Using Star Coordinats. Proceeding of the CPSC Conference on Information Visualization (2003)
6. LI Xiang, LI Cheng-ming, WANG Ji-zhou: Java3D-based Terrain 3D Visualization Technique. Bulletin of Surveying and Mapping (2003)
7. M. Emoto, M. Shoji, S. Yamaguchi: Java Based Data Monitoring and Management System for LHD. Proceeding of KEY Conference, Japan (2002)
8. Fink, Ball, Jawalkar N, North, Correa: Network Eye: End-to-End Computer Security Visualization. Submitted for Consideration at ACM CCS Workshop on Visualization and Data Mining for Computer Security (VizSec/DMSec) (2004)
9. Sven Krasser, Gregory Conti, Julian Grizzard, Jeff Gribschaw, Henry Oven, Senior: Real-Time and Forensic Network Data Analysis Using Animated and Coordinated Visualization. Proceeding of the 2005 IEEE, Work Shop on Information Assurance, (2005)
10. Stephen Lau: The Spinning Cube of Potential Doom. Communications of the ACM, Vol. 47(6), (2004) 25–26
11. Shih Dong-Her, Chiang Hsiu-Sen, Yen C. David: Classification Methods in the Detection of New Malicious emails. Information Sciences, Volume 172, Issue 1-2, (2005)241-261
12. T. Okamoto, Y. Ishida: An Analysis of A Model of Computer Viruses Spreading via Electronicmail. Systems and Computers in Japan 33 (14) (2002) 81–90
13. Lin Hui, Gong Jianhua, Wang Freeman: Web-based Three-Dimensional Geo-referenced Visualization. Computers & Geosciences, 25(10), (1999)1177-1185
14. Emoto M., Narlo J., Kaneko O., Komori A., Iima M.:3D Real-Time Monitoring System for LHD Plasma Heating Experiment. Fusion Engineering and Design, Volume 56-57, (2001)1017 – 1021
15. Ma, K.-L.:Visualizing visualizations, User interfaces for managing and exploring scientific visualization data.Computer Graphics and Applications, IEEE,Vol.20(5),(2000)16-19
16. Mandic, M. Kerne, A.:faMailiar & Intimacy-Based Email Visualization. Information Visualization. INFOVIS 2004. IEEE Symposium on, (2004)14

Component Composition Based on Web Service and Software Architecture

Xin Wang, Changsong Sun, Xiaojian Liu, and Bo Xu

Department of Computer Science and Technology, Harbin Engineering University, China
cindychinesewangxin@hotmail.com

Abstract. Software composition is one of major technologies in component-based software engineering. The combination of Internet computing and software engineering prompts great potentials for future software industrials, and extend the scope of software applications. For example, Web service-based software development becomes the next generation software to be used in distributed systems. In this paper, presents a newly-developed software architecture using Web service based composition technique.

1 Introduction

Since the middle of 1990's, object-oriented programming becomes a key component in software engineering. Many research in software development focus on software reuse [1], while the software composition becomes an important component in software engineering. A software system is based on its architecture which contains multiple software components. The architecture establishes the relationships among the components. The architecture also provides the basis and context of software composition. The model of software composition using both Web service and SA is proposed. Section 2 review Web services and Section 3 outline the software composition. Section 3 presents a new composition model Web services, followed by a short summary.

2 Software Component of Composition

The contemporary software development uses the concept of software component. Each component plays a specific function, while their integration features large-scale applications with efficient communications. Gartner Group [3] reports that at least 70% of new software is based on composition modules in software framework and infrastructure. Generally speaking, components are the program modules that function specifically with a set of stipulations of user interfaces; such architecture will be found in today's standardized software enterprises. Before we depict our model, we would like to review couple terminologies in this domain.

2.1 Web Service

Web service is the one of technologies which has been deployed in software engineering. Through Web service protocols, one can promote an existing service to

H.T. Shen et al. (Eds.): APWeb 2006, LNCS 3842, pp. 987 – 990, 2006.

distributed environments; Web Service Description Language (WSDL) as a specification for universal software description, discovery, and integration. The technology promises to combine various software components together to form an integrated software system. Although distributed computing on network is not new, service-oriented integrated software run on network is a cutting edge technology [2-6].

2.2 Software Architecture

An intelligent or smart connector-based software architecture (SCBSA) can be designated to divide the connections among switch, router, and bridge into three parts. Such division generate makes multiple components. The SCBSA is an absolute component which has the following outstanding features: (1) raising system reusability; (2) supporting various kinds of logic architectures; (3) containing system maintainability; (4) remains high efficiency in operation; and (5) design convenience [5].

```
<?xml version="1.0" encoding="UTF-8"?><xsd:schema
xmlns:xsd="http://www.w3.org/2001/XMLSchema" elementFormDe-
fault="qualified"><xsd:element name="Para-list"
type="xsd:string"/><xsd:element name="Ret-Type"
type="xsd:string"/><xsd:element name="Direction"
type="xsd:string"/><xsd:element name="InterfaceIdentifier"
type="xsd:string"/><xsd:element
name="InteriorProcessLogicDescription"
type="xsd:string"/><xsd:complexType name="function-
nameType"><xsd:sequence><xsd:element ref="Para-
list"/></xsd:sequence></xsd:complexType
name="InterfaceBodyType"><xsd:complexType><xsd:sequence><xsd:element
ref="Direction"/><xsd:element ref="Ret-Type"/>
<xsd:element name="function-name" type="function-
nameType"/></xsd:sequence></xsd:complexType><xsd:complexType
name="InterfaceDescriptionType" minOccurs="1" maxOc-
curs="unbounded"><xsd:sequence><xsd:element
ref="InterfaceIdentifier"/><xsd:element name="InterfaceBody"
type="InterfaceBodyType"/></xsd:sequence></xsd:complexType><xsd:compl
exType
name="SetOfInterfaceDescriptionsType"><xsd:sequence><xsd:element
name="InterfaceDescription"type="InterfaceDescriptionType"/></xsd:seq
uence></xsd:complexType><xsd:element
name="Component"><xsd:complexType><xsd:sequence><xsd:element
name="SetOfInterfaceDescriptions"
type="SetOfInterfaceDescriptionsType"/><xsd:element
ref="InteriorProcessLogicDescription"></xsd:sequence></xsd:complexTyp
e></xsd:element></xsd:schema>
```

Fig. 1. XML-based component definition

2.3 Software Component

One can classify the components into infrastructure components, middleware components, and top-layer application components. Infrastructure components are the ones supporting platform systems, data fabric, and other date and hardware resources. The middleware components are generally introduced for supporting software management, cooperation, and administration. It serves the medium bridge between infrastructure components and application-layer components. Application-layer components are the topmost ones which are mainly designed for specific software application functions [4]. All the components used in the paper are unit components, which are preliminarily sampled shown in Fig. 1.

3 Web Service-Based Software Composition Architecture

3.1 Component Searching

A Web Service-based software composition requires have a search component. Since a remote even triggering should be an efficient method to search the UDDI registry, which is a logical unified entity.

In a distributed system with a point-to-point communication, access the information or data through different Web servers is basically operating the UDDI registry. Obviously the UDDI registry becomes the first component. Once the Register is generated, one can initiate a search command by JAXR to search for other components we may need. The JAXR uses JAXM to send message at the background. A service provider system sends XML data using SOAP protocol to the client who request the information. The client's UDDI registry receives the XML data. The UDDI registry in the meanwhile provides the requested information about the components need. Through the JAX-RPC protocol, a Services Description Language (WSDL) based document can be obtained. The WSDL itself is a XML file, which gives all the information about the corresponding Web service. The returned information tells us service kind, service content, and the procedure to access the services. After gaining the WSDL documentation, one can make decision which components are selected.

3.2 Components Composition

Once the components is searched and gained, one can composite the available components for the SCBSA. The role of a switch component is to connect communicational interfaces. For example, an Interface F of Component B is connected to the interface H of Component A, illustrated in Fig. 2. The Component B calls its own Interface F. Router component is used to process the logic inside system. It can be used to control the behavior of switch component through Interface L, M, and N. The function of a bridge component is to map a SCS into another functional component of another SCS. The interior process logic of bridge component can be described by the following function. $\{\{f \mid f(i)=j\},\{g \mid g(k)=m\}\}$, i, $m \in Ia$; $j,k \in Ib$; I, k belongs to exporting type; where J, and m belongs to import types. According to SCBSA, one can composite the instantiated components on a local computer to perform integration.

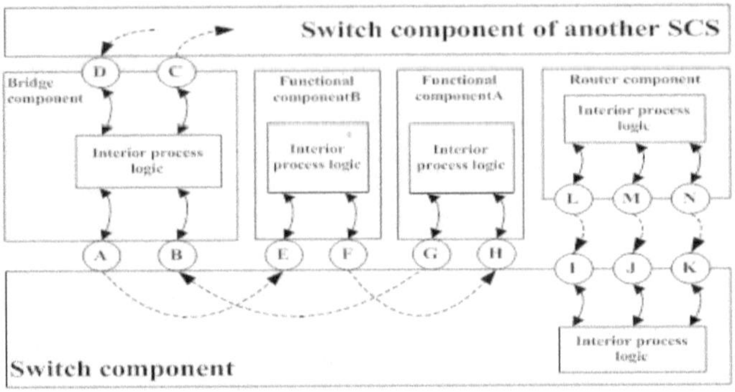

Fig. 2. Architecture of SCBSA

4 Conclusion

This paper proposes a Web services-based software composition model on software components. The description of the model architecture is depicted. The model can be used immigrate existing software components to a distributed system with a high scalability. Our future work is conduct experiments; hence to modify the method and carry out dynamic composition study.

References

1. Yang F.: Thinking on the development of Software engineering technology. Journal of Software, vol. 16(1).(2005) 1-7 (Chinese)
2. Feng C., Jiang H., and Feng J.F.: Theory and practice of software architecture. Post & Telecom Press (2004) (Chinese)
3. Zhao H. and Shen J.: OWL based Web service component. Computer Application. Vol-25(3) (2005) 634-636 (Chinese)
4. Library of Software Component of Shanghai. http://www.sstc.org.cn
5. Gu Y., Sang N., Xiong G.: A Smart-Connector-based software architecture. Computer Science, vol.31 (2004) 151-156 (Chinese)
6. Jasnowski M. Java XML, and Web Services Bible. Publishing House of Electronics Industry (2002)

Evaluation of Network Dependability Using Event Injection

Huiqiang Wang[1], Yonggang Pang[1], Ye Du[2], Dong Xu[1], and Daxin Liu[1]

[1] College of Computer Science and Technology,
Harbin Engineering University, 150001 Harbin, China
wanghuiqiang@hrbeu.edu.cn,
pangarm@yahoo.com.cn
[2] College of Computer, Beijing Jiaotong University, 100044 Beijing, China
mail_dy@163.com

Abstract. Event injection is a new technique for evaluating dependability of target system, and it's developed on the basis of fault injection techniques. This paper proposed an event injection system for assessing dependability of computer network system, analyzed the event injection in details, and described the course of event injection and the key techniques. Finally, the testing results of the response time and average flow speed of network server by DoS attack experiments are given.

1 Introduction

Computer network technique develops rapidly and its application fields expand continuously. The failure of computer system will lead to inestimable loss, especially in key departments. So how to entirely and objectively analyze and evaluate dependability of this kind of computer networks so as to present advanced scheme has been an important topic.

Fault injection [1] has been an active topic to study the dependability of computer for about 20 years, which plays an important role in the domain of hardware detection and fault tolerance design, and also the theory and application of it are still developing.

However, there are some limitations lies in fault injection [2] technology. According to the definition in IFTP and IEEE, dependability is the ability of a system to offer prescriptive services to users, especially the offering service ability in the case of fault and service level being threatened. So, the concept of network dependability here includes the following aspects [3] --reliability, availability, security and safety, and it's an integrated criterion to weigh the service ability of a computer. In computer network system, the reason causing users' satisfaction degree with computer service to descend includes the system fault, the decline of network service ability as well as the latent threats in the computer system security [4]. Fault injection technology mainly focuses on the instance when the target system fail and can't detect the later two instances. As a result, we present event injection technology based on fault injection technology. This paper discusses the concept, basic principle and keys technology of event injection technology in different sections; at last, a part event injection experiment aimed at server in network is discussed.

H.T. Shen et al. (Eds.): APWeb 2006, LNCS 3842, pp. 991–998, 2006.

2 Concepts of Event Injection

Event injection technology[5],[6] is an experiment process by injecting different kinds of system events to target system and observing, calling back and analyzing the response information contraposition injected events from system.

We consider computer system and the computer system environment as a whole system [7], in which all the behaviors can be defined as events, such as electronic component fault, system software fault, malicious code, inclement environment. Event injection technology mainly researches all the events causing the decline of service ability of computer system.

The process of event injection is described by 7 sets that can be called property of event injection .see figure 1:

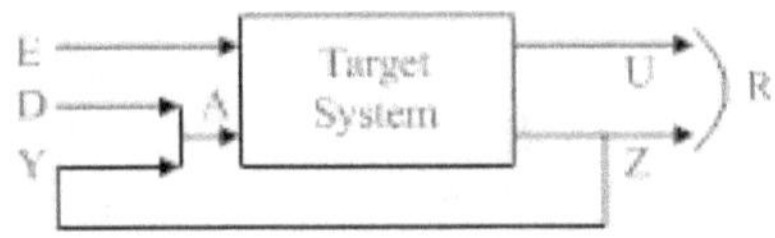

Fig. 1. Properties of event injection

- **E** is event space made up of events that can make the target system failure and make the service ability of target system decline.
- **A** is action space that is composed of standard programs run in target system, expressing the behavior of target system.
- **Z** is the inner state space of target system.
- **U** is user service space offered by target system.
- **D** is outer input data space.
- **Y** is current inner state space of target system.
- **R** is read space collecting the behavior response of target system.

Work process of event injection system is generally divided into 4 steps, which can be described as follows:

1. Choosing event model
   This step decides the event injection strategy according to the experiment target. Controller decides the type, number, occurrence time, persistence time, and injection position of to be injected event and sends control instructions to event injector so as to complete the choice of event sets and event models at last.
2. Executing event injection
   This step accepts event model generated in last step and transforms it into event that can be used in event injection. Then, event injector injects this event into target system according to the injection time, triggering condition, persistence time, and injection place specified by controller.
3. Collecting data, system recovery
   Event injection system injects events into target system, in which the fault tolerant ones detect the effect of events and call corresponding disposal algorithm to recover the effect caused by events. The fault tolerance algorithm of the target system can recover moment fault; to permanence fault, the failure disposal algorithm

needs deciding reconstruction project of system and selecting spare server or spare bus to recover system; to the case in which the offering service ability of system declines, the target system also has corresponding fault tolerance measure. To the failure that can't be recovered by target system, the controller injects reconstruction event into experiment environment to ensure proceeding of the experiment.

4. Analysis, presenting the determination results
   When every individual event injection proceeds the analyzing and examining result stage, this step judges whether the experiment can end. The judging reference can be whether the confidence interval is satisfied, whether the expected probability distribution is steady or whether the parameter gets to a destined threshold, etc. If the injection experiment can't finish, the event injection will go on execute.

After all the event injections have been accomplished in the experiment, data analyzer statistics the case of event detection and recovery of the target system and analyses all the data off line. This step analyses and integrates the results gained from several individual event injections using probability statistics method and gains analysis result by calculating at last.

The result of event injection experiment includes the research of analyzing how the injected event affects invalidation class of the behaviors of target system, the research of analyzing how the failure of some event affects the error diffusion of other components and the research of dependability or the operating load relativity of the relation between events and calculation load characteristic.

3 The Key Techniques of Event Injection System

3.1 Selection of Event Model Library

The event model library should include the event model that can decline the service ability of target system. If the event model that is selected to be injected is more similar to the events occurred during the actual running of the system and covers them to the greatest extent [8],[9], the result of the experiment will be more accurate. Some usual events causing the network system to fail are listed in table 1.

A proper event model library should follow two principles: First, It should include most of event model that can cause the target computer system to fail or decline its server ability. Second, the event model in the event model library should be can detect most of the vulnerabilities of target system that will cause the target system to fail or decline its server ability.

According to different effects on target system caused by event[12], the event models in the model library can be divided into event model causing target system to fail and event model declining the service ability of target system.

The events affecting the service ability of target system mainly include two classes. One is the events that make the system response time extend, the other is the events that threaten the security of the system. The events that are usual in computer system affecting the service ability of target system and the effects are showed in table 2.

Table 1. Usual events causing fault computer network system

Events causing fault hardware	Events causing fault indirect environment	Events causing fault direct environment
fault address	fault user input command	fault file property
fault data line	fault filename of environment variable + path name	fault file authority
fault controller & accumulator	fault executing path of environment variable +library path	fault symbol link, file content
fault memory	fault authority of environment variable mask	fault filename
fault reception & sending of I/O	fault input filename of file system + path name	fault work path, message factuality
fault network transmission	fault file extension input by file system	fault protocol
——	fault network input IP address	fault port
——	fault network input data packet	fault service availability
——	fault network input host name	fault entity
——	fault network input DNS response	fault message
——	fault process input message	fault process
——	——	fault service usability

Table 2. Usual events affecting the service ability of computer network system

Type of event	Event	Effect caused by event
Events making system response time extend	Too many processes dispute CPU	Operation speed of computer declines
	Transport protocol flaw	Packet loss rate rises and transmission speed declines
	Light DoS attack	Response speed of computer decline
Events threatening system security	Attain root authority illegally	System leak, attain root authority, threaten system security
	Network capsulated package eavesdropping	Steal, desterilize other's network capsulated package, attain information illegally

3.2 Users' Degree of Satisfaction

In the injection experiment, event injection system needs to judge whether the target system has recovered to users' satisfaction degree. To the events causing the target system to failure and the ones threatening security of target system, if the target system can't finish them and recover these faults or state threatening the security of target system, it can be considered that the users aren't satisfied. Otherwise, we consider that the users are satisfied. There are many factors may affect users' satisfaction degree, such as system response time, calculating ability and network security problems. In different conditions, the importance of different factors varies. For example, generally the users applying server are sensitive to response time, while security problems in finance network are especially standout. So the users' satisfaction degree problem needs to be synthetically considered.

A general user's satisfaction degree can be considered as an arbitrary value in (0, 1). The larger the value is, the more users' satisfaction degree is; otherwise, the result is less, the less satisfied the user is. Here, we take response time as an example and prescribe the relationship between users' satisfaction degree S and response time T as following:

$$S = \begin{cases} t_0^{\alpha} \cdot T^{-\alpha} & T \geq t_0 \\ 1 & T < t_0 \end{cases} \tag{1}$$

In this relation, α is a constant and α>1.The value of α is determined by the structure and properties of target system. t_0 is a short enough response time. When the response time of target system is shorter than t_0, we consider that users' satisfaction degree gets to 1. Other factors can consult last formula and end users' satisfaction degree must consider all of the factors.

3.3 Statistical Event Coverage

The event coverage estimations obtained through event injection experiments are estimates of conditional probabilistic measure characterizing dependability. The coverage is defined as the probability of system recovery given that a event exits.

For a given event space *G*, coverage is defined as the cumulative distribution of the time interval between the occurrence of a event and it's correcting handling by a system. The coverage factor is defined using the asymptotic value of the distribution.

$$C_a(t \mid G) = P(T_a \leq t \mid G) \tag{2}$$

Where α denotes the action to which the coverage is related.

Y is a random variable that can take the value 0 or 1 for each element of the event space *G*, the coverage factor *C(G)* can be views as *E*[*Y*|*G*], the expected value of *Y* for the population *G*. In term of each event pair $g \in G$, let *Y*(*g*)=1 if *Y*=1 when the system is submitted to g(0 otherwise), and let *P*(*g*|*G*) be the relative probability of occurrence of *g*. Then we get the event coverage:

$$C_a = P(Y_a = 1 \mid G) = E[Y_a \mid G] = \sum_{g \in G} Y_a(g) \cdot P(g \mid G) \tag{3}$$

4 DoS Attack Event Injection Experiments

DoS attack that is called attack of denial service makes the web server fill with large quantities of information to be replied and consumes the network bandwidth or system resource, which leads to the result that the overloaded network or system cannot offer normal network service.

Here we analyze running state and response time by Dos attack experiment, in which we select an experiment server to be tested and analyze the result.

The input parameters of Web server are as follows: attack flow respectively is 23450 bytes, 46900 bytes, 93800 bytes, 234500 bytes and 469000 bytes; and attack lasting time respectively is 1s, 5s and 10s. The output results are average response time and average flow rate, and the experiment whose result is the arithmetic mean value will be carried on three times under the condition of each attack flow and attack lasting time.

The input parameters and testing results of the experiment server are as follows:

Table 3. Data of DoS attack experiment

Attack persis-tence time		DoS attack flow(average attack times per second)									
		23450(5)		46900(10)		93800(20)		234500(50)		469000(100)	
		Response time (ms)	Flow speed (B/s)	Response time(ms)	Flow speed (B/s)	Response time(ms)	Flow speed (B/s)	Response time(ms)	Flow speed (B/s)	Response time (ms)	Flow speed (B/s)
1	1	70	65729	70	65729	80	57513	333	13800	2951	1559
	2	70	65729	70	65729	83	55069	350	13123	3219	1429
	3	70	65541	80	57513	81	56767	332	13857	3708	1241
5	1	70	66581	70	65597	145	31531	2870	1603	15083	246
	2	80	57987	80	56929	151	30326	3021	1523	14901	309
	3	70	65729	80	57426	119	38367	3607	1275	16978	271
10	1	70	66943	82	55729	187	24542	8125	566	31173	148
	2	81	56468	81	56544	153	30036	6668	690	20788	221
	3	80	58596	82	55804	197	23274	7844	587	30909	149

The output result is average response time and average flow speed. The experiment will be repeated 3 times in the condition of each set attack flow and attack persistence time .The testing result is the arithmetical mean.

The testing results are showed in figure 2. It's easy to see that with the increasing of attacking time and data flow, the response time and flow of network server worsen.

Last experiment is a DoS attack to one server. We can carry on the contrast experiments to several servers and to different configurations of servers.

In order to inspect the state of attack flow persisting 5s, formula（1）can be applied to gain the relation curve of attack flow and users' satisfaction degree. Here, supposing$\alpha=1.1$, $t_0=70$ms, as showed in figure 3.

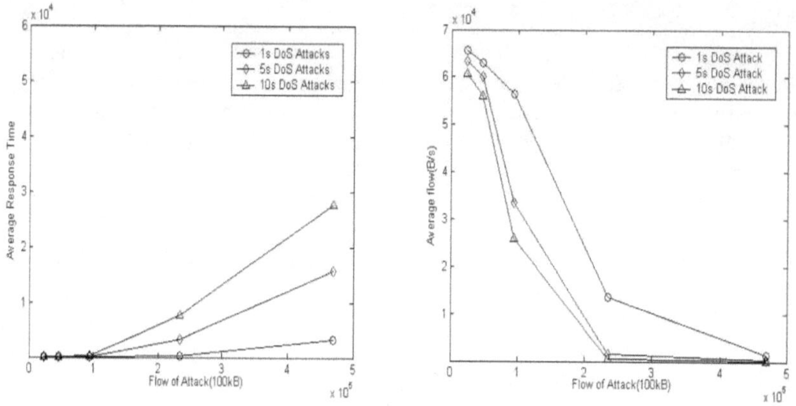

Fig. 2. The average response time and flow speed curve of server

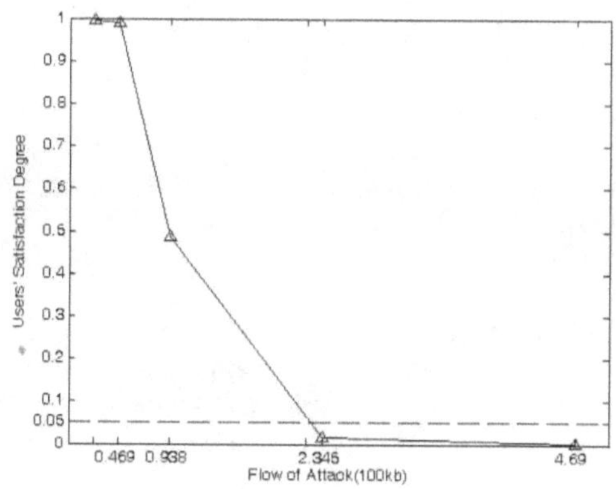

Fig. 3. The relation curve between users' satisfaction degree and attack flow

Supposing that the server service is satisfactory if satisfaction degree is 0.05, we can see that the satisfaction degree is critical value when the attack flow is about 220kb. Also, we can compare the response time of satisfaction degree by experiment on other servers.

5 Conclusions

Dependability evaluation is different from reliability. The dependability of network is a complex problem, and in the simulation method, event injection technology can preferably solve the problems of network dependability evaluation. Event injection technology can not only analyze the cases when the target system fail but also analyze the cases when the capability of target system declines and the system can't offer satisfying services to users. Since event injection technology is a new approach, there are many aspects to be explored in event injection theory and event selection.

References

1. Saurabh Bagchi, Gautam Kar, Joe Hellerstein: Dependency Analysis in Distributed Systems using Fault Injection: Application to Problem Determination in an e-commerce Environment. In Proceedings of Dependable Systems and Networks (DSN). New York, (2000)1-3
2. Huiqiang Wang: Several Key Indexes of Event Injection for Network Dependability Evaluation. Computer Engineering & science Press, 4(2005)54-56
3. M. C. Hsubh, T. Tsai, R.K.Iybr: Fault injection techniques and tools. IEEE Computer. 30, 4(1997)75–82
4. J. C. Laprie: Dependability of Software-Based Critical Systems. Dependable Network Computing. Kluwer Academic Publishers, Amsterdam, the Netherlands, (2000)3-19
5. David Powell, Robert Stroud: Malicious and Accidental- Fault Tolerance for Internet Applications [J]. LAAS-CNRS, Toulouse University, 5(2001)14-17
6. D. T. Stott, B. Floering, Z. Kalbarczyk: Dependability Assessment in Distributed Systems with Lightweight Fault Injectors in NFTAPE, Proc. IEEE Int'l Computer Performance and Dependability Symp (IPDS), (2000)91-100
7. Xiaoyan Li, Richard Martin, Kiran Nagaraja, Thu D.Nguyen, Bin Zhang: A SAN-Based Fault-Injection Test-Bed for the Construction of Highly Available Network Services. In Proceedings of the First Workshop on Novel Uses of System Area Networks (SAN-1),(2002)
8. J. L. Pistole: Loki--An empirical evaluation tool for distributed systems: The run-time experiment framework [M]. Urbana: University of Illinois, (1998)
9. Yangyang Yu: A Perspective on the State of Research on Fault Injection Techniques. Research Report, (2001)7-17
10. Ana Maria Ambrosio, Eliane Martins: A methodology for Designing Fault Injection Experiments as an Addition to Communication Systems Conformance Testing. In Proceedings of Workshop on Dependable Software Tools and Methods (DSN-2005)
11. S.Jha, J.M.Wing: Survivability Analysis of Networked Systems. In Proceedings of Software Engineering, Toronto, (2001)
12. T. Heath, R. Martin, T. D. Nguyen: The Shape of Failure. In Proceedings of the First Workshop on Evaluating and Architecting System dependability (EASY), (2001)
13. Volkmar Sieh, Kerstin Buchacker: Testing the Fault-Tolerance of Networked Systems. In Proceedings of Workshop on Architecture of Computing System (ARCS), (2002)95-105

A New Automatic Intrusion Response Taxonomy and Its Application

Huiqiang Wang, Gaofei Wang, Ying Lan, Ke Wang, and Daxin Liu

College of Computer Science and Technology,
Harbin Engineering University,
Harbin 150001, Heilongjiang Province, China
wanghuiqiang@hrbeu.edu.cn

Abstract. The response taxonomy is a key to realizing automatic an intrusion response system as it provides theoretical framework for responding coherently to attacks. This paper presents a new taxonomy called 5W2H on the basis of analyzing the taxonomies, and the application prototype running over IBM Aglet is given.

1 Introduction

As the development and overreach of computer network, network security becomes more and more serious. Annual reports from the Computer Emergency Response Team (CERT) indicate a significant increase in the number of computer security incidents from six reports in 1988 to 137,529 reported in 2003 [1]. Not only are these attacks becoming more numerous, they are also becoming more sophisticated. Unfortunately, intrusion detection and response systems have not kept up with the increasing threats.

Automatic Intrusion Response System (AIRS) can employ many responses to an intrusion, but not all responses are appropriate for all intrusions. For example, terminating the attacker's session after the attacker has already logged out will have no effect. As such, there is a need to categorize responses so that they are appropriate to the attack. Intrusion response taxonomy is needed for automatic intrusion response as it provides the necessary theoretical framework for responding coherently to attacks. How to classify the responses concerns the efficiency and accuracy of an AIRS.

This paper presents a new taxonomy of 5W2H and discusses its use with an intrusion response system, section 2 describes related work in security flaw and intrusion response taxonomies. Section 3 presents 5W2H taxonomy. Section 4 examines the taxonomy on the IBM Aglet platform. Section 5 shows the discussions and future work.

2 Related Work

Usage of taxonomy in security domain was mainly concentrated on security flaws in early days. It includes the Protection Analysis (PA) taxonomy, Landwehr's taxonomies, Bishop's taxonomy, and the Lindqvist taxonomy. The earliest intrusion response taxonomy is Fisch DC&A taxonomy.

H.T. Shen et al. (Eds.): APWeb 2006, LNCS 3842, pp. 999 – 1003, 2006.

PA taxonomy is the first taxonomy, undertaken at the Information Sciences Institute, its goal was to derive and discover the patterns of errors that would enable the automatic detection of security flaws [5]. It categorized flaws into four different global categories: improper protection; improper validation; improper synchronization; improper choice of operand or operation.

Landwehr's taxonomy classifies vulnerabilities according to genesis, time of introduction, and location [5]. Its goal was to describe how security flaws are introduced, when they are introduced, and where the security flaws can be found, also helping software programmers and system administrators to focus their efforts to remove and eventually prevent the introduction of security flaws.

While this taxonomy was a breakthrough, it was ambiguous. For example, we can't clearly distinguish development phase and operation phase when developing software.

Bishop taxonomy studied flaws in the UNIX operating system and proposed a taxonomy using six axes, and vulnerability is classified on each axis [4]. The first axis is the nature of the flaws; the second axis is the time of introduction. The third is the exploitation domain of the vulnerability and the fourth is the effect domain. The fifth axis is the minimum number of components needed to exploit the vulnerability. The sixth axis is the source of the identification of t vulnerabilities.

Lindqvist taxonomy presented a classification of intrusions with respect to techniques as well as to results [6]. Its goal was to establish taxonomy of intrusions for using in incident reporting, statistics, warning bulletins, and intrusion detection systems.

Using the CIA model provides a good theoretical foundation for the classification of intrusion results, and it based on data from a realistic intrusion experiment, and took a viewpoint of system owner, so it was generally applicable.

The Fisch DC&A taxonomy classified the intrusion response according to: when the intrusion was detected (during the attack or after the attack); the response goal (active damage control, passive damage control, damage assessment, or damage recovery) [7].

As the earliest Intrusion Response Taxonomy it offered an extensive foundation. But additional components are needed to provide more details for intrusion responses.

3 5W2H Taxonomy

We provide the details of an incident base on incident course. There are two different angles of view to the same intrusion incident: the attacker, and the defender. As IRS is a defender, so here we considering from the defender, see Fig. 1, the proposed taxonomy is composed of seven dimensions. The first dimension is the time (When). Different responses can categorize as before attack, during attack, after attack. The second dimension we can estimate how serious the potential of destruction is (How serious). The responses to high destruction should much urgent than low destruction. The third dimension is location of attacker (Where). The responses to an insider must more cautious than outsider. The fourth dimension is type of attack (How to). The response should be different if is a distribute denial of service attack as compared to IP scan. The fifth dimension is the target attacked (What). The response to an attack

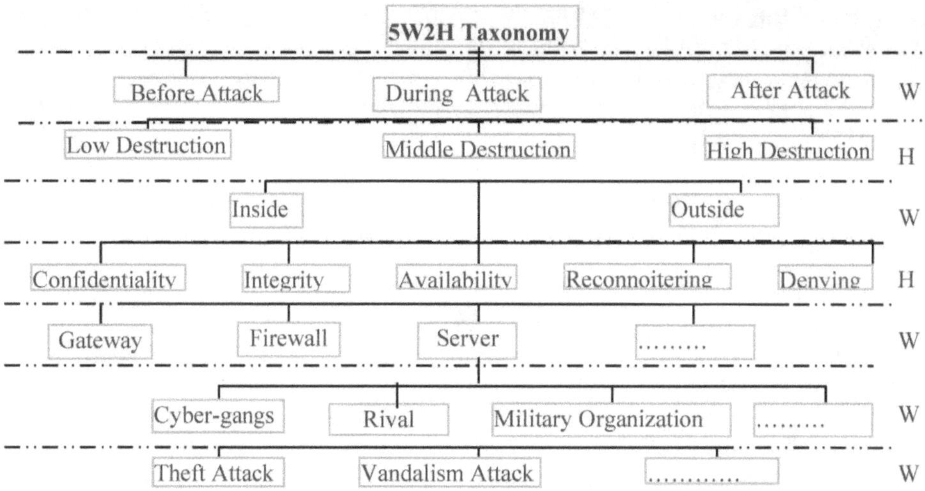

Fig. 1. 5W2H Taxonomy

against a firewall is different than an attack against server. The sixth dimension is the type of attacker. There is a different in responding to rival as opposed to military organization. The last dimension of the taxonomy is plan of attack (Why). Responses to theft attack must quit different from vandalism attack.

Time of response is the pivotal factor to make a correct response, so it's the first key element that should be considered. Trying one's best to push time to the response's border can avoid intrusion while there is sign of invading and really attack not to begin yet. When the attack has been detected and is ongoing, damage control responses should bring into effect. This is the first dimension of W describing time of response.

Potential destruction has an important influence on optimizing response. It can consult data from damage assessment responses. Here we suggest using the Cost-Sensitive Model to sustain response [3]. For example, if Damage Cost (Dcost) > Response Cost (Rcost), it needn't respond; if Dcost = Rcost, we can exploit tolerating intrusion or part resuming to respond on a small scale. These responses attempt to avoid the waste of resources. This is the second dimension of H describing potential destruction.

Location of Attack. Intrusion tracing can divide into active tracing and passive tracing: active tracing prepares tracing information when passing the packet, while passive tracing initiate tracing after having detected the attack. Wang X Y proposed a mechanism to address the problem of tracing [9]. The inside investigating response applies to the attacker who comes from intranet. When an attack to an intranet is detected, it means some systems of the intranet have been breached by the attacker and used to initiate new attacks, or the attack itself is an insider. As the former we can isolate the injured host computer; as the latter we can implement responsibility through inside investigating to respond in more humanized way. This is the third dimension of W to describe location of an attacker.

Type of Attack. Lindqvist taxonomy provides the penetrating classification to type of attacks. But with the development of the ways of attacks, lots of new attack types do not comply with CIA model. Some attacks, such as reconnoitering attacks and denying attacks need to be added to CIA model. This is the forth dimension of H to describe type of attacks.

Target is an important characterization in determining an appropriate response. For example, a Dos attack must correspond different treatment ways between workstation and DNS. We divide the targets of attacks into following categories according to their function: Gateway, Firewall, Workstation, and Server, etc. This is the fifth dimension of W to describe targets of attack.

Type of attackers is also an important characterization in determining an appropriate response. An attacker who uses a well-know tool needn't be considered as serious as the one who distributes and coordinates to attack a system. This classification lets the system absorbed in more complicated attacks. This is the sixth dimension of W to describe type of attackers.

Plan of Attackers. The last dimension is plan of attacks because plan recognition is very intricate, immature, but very useful. IRS can predict the action of attackers, and, automatically and correctly respond to attacks in a timely manner. For example, the response should be different between theft attack and vandalism attack.

4 An Application Prototype

Our application prototype using 5W2H taxonomy scheme is given in Fig. 2. It runs over IBM Aglet platform. When intrusion detection system (here we adopt snort 2.0) provides the detecting results, AIRS takes it as its input and processes into an incident report. Interface maintains a confidence metric that gets by calculating the number of false positives and negatives previously generated. It passes to this metric along with the incident report to the response decision-making model. The response decision-making model utilizes decision-making technology (Cost-Sensitive Model, Response

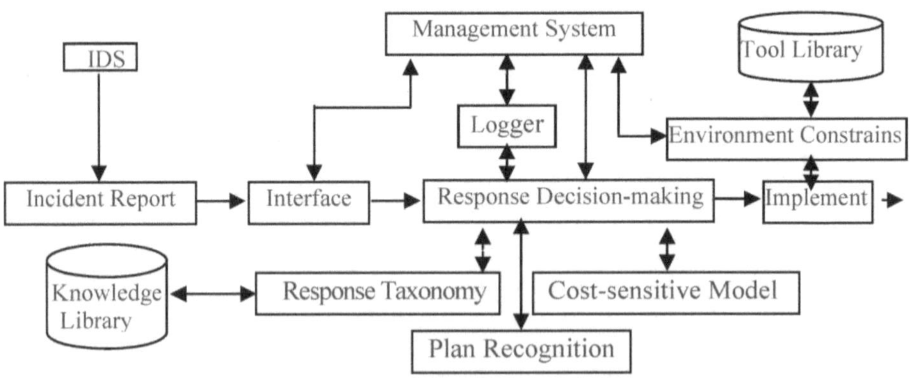

Fig. 2. Application Model of 5W2H Response Taxonomy

Taxonomy, Plan Recognition) to produce tactics of responses. Response taxonomy is used to maintain the Knowledge Library and classify the attack to make response decision-making more pertinent. Implement model decomposes the tactics of responses into concrete actions that can get from the tool library under the control of Environment constrains model, and the concrete actions then are initiated by Aglet as mobile agents to run on goal host. The log record is used for system administrator review. The Management System operates mutually with Interface, Response Decision-making and Environment Constrains model.

5 Discussions and Future Work

This paper carries on thorough classification and description of intrusion incidents, So, 5W2H provides strong support to IRS in determining an appropriate response. Although we have finished a prototype system, Cost-Sensitive Model and Plan Recognition are not perfect since the problem is simplified at the beginning. Future work includes some improvement on them, and that, to make responses much more appropriate, some other techniques are needed to be developed also.

References

1. CERT Coordination Center.: CERT/CC Statistics 1988-2003. http://www.cert.org/stats/cert_stats.ht ml.(2004)
2. Fred Cohen.: Simulating Cyber Attack, Defenses, and Consequence. http://all.net/journal / ntb/ simul ate/simulate.html. (1999)
3. Wenke Lee, Wei Fan, et al.: Toward Cost-Sensitive Modeling for Intrusion Detection and Response. In 1st ACM Workshop on Intrusion Detection Systems. (2000)
4. M.Bishop.: A Taxonomy of UNIX System and Network Vulnerabilities. Tech. Rep. CSE-95-10, Purdue University (1995)
5. C.E. Landwehr, A. R. Bull, et al.: A taxonomy of computer program security flaws. Vol.26 (3), ACM Computing Surveys (1994) 211-254
6. U. Lindqvist and E. Jonsson.: How to Systematically Classify Computer Security Intrusions. Proc.1997 IEEE Symp. on Security and Privacy. Oakland, CA (1997)154-163.
7. E. A. Fisch.: Intrusion Damage Control and Assessment: A Taxonomy and Implementation of Automated Responses to Intrusive Behavior. Ph. D. Dissertation, Texas A&M University, College Station, TX (1996)
8. Geib C W, Goldman R P.: Plan Recognition in Intrusion Detection Systems. In DARPA Information Survivability Conference and Exposition (DISCEX) (2001)
9. Wang X Y, Reeves D S, Wu S F, et al.: Sleepy Watermark Tracing: An Active Intrusion Response Framework. Paris, France: the proceedings of 16th International Conference of Information Security (2001)

Hierarchical Web Structuring from the Web as a Graph Approach with Repetitive Cycle Proof

Wookey Lee

Computer Science, Sungkyul University, Anyang, Korea 430-742
wook@sungkyul.edu

Abstract. The WWW can be viewed as digraph with Web nodes and arcs, where the Web nodes correspond to HTML files having page contents and the arcs correspond to hypertext links interconnected with the Web pages. The Web cycle resolution is one of the problems to derive a meaningful structure out of the complex WWW graphs. We formalize our view of the Web structure from Web as a graph approach to an algorithm in terms of proofing the repetitive cycles. We formalize the Web model that prevents the Web structuring algorithm from being bewildered by the repetitive cycles. The complexity of the corresponding algorithm has been addressed fairly enhanced than the previous approaches.

1 Introduction

Structuring the WWW yields significant insights into Web algorithms for searching, discovering, mining, and revealing Web information. The WWW can be viewed as digraph with Web nodes and arcs, where the Web nodes correspond to HTML files having page contents and the arcs correspond to hypertext links interconnected with the Web pages. The Web-as-a-graph approach can be a starting point to generate a structure of the WWW that can be used for Web site designers, search engines, Web crawling robots, and Web marketers and analysts [3, 13].

The Web-as-a-graph, however, has weaknesses such as Unreachable paths, Circuits, Repetitive cycles. The unreachable path is that a Web page sometimes can not be accessed from the usual path or a hub mode. The circuit as a cycle is that a client visits the same page again and again periodically. In order to generate a Web structure, the circuits and repetitive cycles should be detected and removed, without which a Web client may be lost in Cyber space through the complex cycles [6] or may inevitably gather information with swallow depths from the root node [5].

Why are we interested in the hierarchical structure? One reason is that a Web site consists of a home page (e.g., default.html) that can be the root node from which a hierarchical structure can correspondingly be derived. The other reason is that the hierarchical structure can conceive very simple data structure so that the crawling performance to search the Web on the fly can be highly enhanced.

The typical hierarchical examples are breadth first search and depth first search with which Web catalogues, site maps, and usage mining can be pertained [4, 5, 6]. The breadth first approach, including *backlink* count method [5, 11, 13], has some advantages so that an 'important' Web page can be accessed within relatively fewer

H.T. Shen et al. (Eds.): APWeb 2006, LNCS 3842, pp. 1004 – 1011, 2006.

steps from its root node. It can statistically minimize the total number of depths. In the Web environment, however, the tree by breadth first approach may result extremely flat so that almost all the pages stick to the root node. On the other hand, the depth first approach is popularly adopted for practitioners to exploit a structure with a stack data format [10, 12]. In structuring the Web, the approach is not appropriate because it may result in a long series of Web pages. It means that the series of pages entail mouse clicks, so that as much time consumption to access each page is required. The worst thing on the derived structures by these two approaches is that no measures or values, even no semantics can be endowed.

There are approaches that come from the usage based structuring or Web usage mining that result a Web structure with respect to the popularity of a Web page [2, 19]. The basic notion of the approach is that the more frequent clients visit a Web page, the higher in the hierarchical structure the corresponding Web page will be located. There are two intrinsic weaknesses of the approach: (1) it is very difficult to identify how many a client really accessed or just passed by, and (2) the structure is too fragile to cope with dynamic Web changes.

A topological ordering algorithm [1, 8] converted a Web site to an unbiased hierarchical structure; this can minimize the average distance from the root node to a specific Web page. They also considered the semantic relevance between the Web nodes. The weakness is on the Web changes so that, when there are minor changes in the Web page's weight or in the link weight, then the entire structure needs to be completely reorganized.

In this paper, we formalize the Web model that prevents the Web structuring algorithm from being bewildered by the complex Web cycles and repetitive circuits. Then the discussion on the performance and complexity of the corresponding algorithm will be followed.

This paper is organized as follows: In Section 2, we present the graph theoretic notations and a motivating example. In Section 3, we discuss basic measures. In Section 4, we will discuss the algorithm and experimental results. Finally, we conclude the paper.

2 Web as a Graph and Motivating Example

A Web directed graph $G = (N, E)$, with an arc function $x_{ij} : N^k \rightarrow \{0, 1\}$, $\forall i, j \in N$ consists of a finite Web node set N, a finite Web arc set E of ordered pairs of Web nodes, and the Web arc elements (i, j) respectively, where $i, j \in N = \{0, 1, 2, 3, \ldots, n\text{-}1\}$, and $n = |N|$ the cardinality of Web pages. There is a mapping for the nodes corresponding to Web pages and the arcs to Uniform Resource Identifiers [4, 5].

On investigating the Web digraph domain, there are three approaches: (1) the whole Web [2, 6, 9], (2) a set of strongly coupled components [11], (3) set of a Web site [8, 7]. The first one is utilized to measure the whole size or growing ratio, but it is not appropriate to derive a Web structure. The second focuses a mathematical model, and the third is inclined to practical side. We adopt the third case for implementation perspective, where the homepage is defined as a default page predetermined by the Web server and the other pages are interconnected each other.

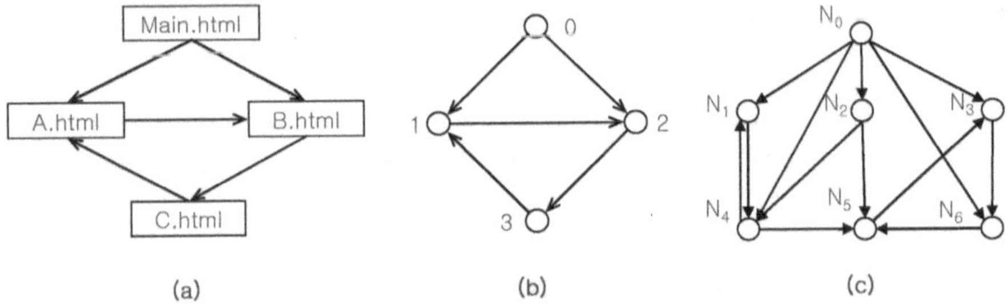

Fig. 2.1. (a) a Web Schema, (b) the corresponding graph, and (c) Example schema

For example, a Web site consists of four Web pages with several links as in Fig. 2.1 (a), which can be mapped to the graph as (b). So we make a small Web site example as (c), which will be used in the following sections.

3 Basic Measures on the Web

In order to determine the topological structure, the *PageRank* measure [11] is introduced in this paper, where the measure is not limited. In the *PageRank*, if source page, *i*, has a link to target page, *j*, then the author of source page, *i*, is implicitly conferring some importance to page, *j*. Let *Rank*(*p*) represent the importance of page *p*. Then, the link (*i*, *j*) confers a certain number of units of rank to, *j*. This notion leads to the following iterative fix-point computation that yields the rank vector over all of the pages on the Web. If, *n*, is the number of pages, assign all pages the initial value 1/n. Let, B_j represent the set of pages pointing to *j*. Links between Web pages propagate the ranks [6]. This vector is computed only once after each crawl of the Web; the values can then be used to influence the ranking of search results [6]. Guaranteeing the rank vector to converge, the matrix of link (*i*, *j*) should be ergodic that includes non-negative and irreducible with primitive transition as well as aperiodic [11]. *PageRank* algorithm uses the following equation with a damping factor (*d*). In Google, the value of the damping factor is set to 0.85 [3, 13], so that the vector converges either slowly or quickly in terms of the magnitude of the damping factor.

$$\forall i, Rank^{(k+1)}(i) = (1-d)E + d(\sum_{i \in B_j} Rank^{(k)}(j) / N_j) \quad where,\ E = \left[\frac{1}{n}\right]_{n \times 1} \tag{3.1}$$

For example, by equation (3.1) we can get the weights of the nodes in the example Fig 2.1(c). The node weights by *PageRank* can be: <R(0), R(1), R(2), R(3), R(4), R(5), R(6)> = <0.865, 0.479, 0.50, 2.25, 0.64, 1.00, 1.25>. See the end row of Table 3.1, that are the converged values by eq. (3.1).

In order to generate a structure from the Web, a node measure is not enough and a link measure should be introduced. In other words, without a link measure, structuring the Web can be a trivial problem. If the nodes only have significant values, then any structures (e.g., a tree or the complete graph) with the node values results in the same total weight sum. Thus we use a Euclidean distance based link measure as in the following equation (3.2) such that both sides of the nodes can be taken into consideration. Where the *Weight(i)* can be a node measure such as PageRank on Web node *i* that can be extended to other measures.

$$x_{ij} = \frac{Weight(i) + Weight(j)}{2} \quad for\ i, j \in N \tag{3.2}$$

The link weights by eq. (3.2) are generated as follows, where x_{ij} represents a link weight from node *i* to *j*: $<x_{01}, x_{02}, x_{14}, x_{41}, x_{04}, x_{24}, x_{25}, x_{45}, x_{03}, x_{53}, x_{06}, x_{36}, x_{65}>$ = <0.8000, 0.664, 0.777, 0.777, 0.984, 0.640, 0.846, 1.166, 1.220, 1.402, 1.161, 1.374, 1.343>.

Table 3.1. *PageRank* values for Fig. 2.1 (c)

N0	N1	N2	N3	N4	N5	N6
1.000	1.000	1.000	1.000	1.000	1.000	1.000
0.858	0.603	0.745	1.878	1.028	1.141	0.745
0.757	0.587	0.552	2.275	0.763	0.969	1.094
0.831	0.495	0.528	2.226	0.684	0.987	1.245
0.873	0.485	0.501	2.226	0.651	1.023	1.237
0.860	0.483	0.504	2.256	0.646	1.002	1.244
0.862	0.479	0.501	2.250	0.644	1.005	1.255
0.866	0.479	0.500	2.249	0.642	1.008	1.253
0.864	0.479	0.500	2.252	0.642	1.006	1.253
0.864	0.479	0.500	2.251	0.642	1.006	1.254
0.865	0.479	0.500	2.251	0.642	1.006	1.253

4 Web Structuring Algorithm and Experimental Results

Now, a repetitive cycle proofing algorithm should be considered as follows. The algorithm visits each node in terms of depth first search where the nodes values are recorded according to the order of visits. Missing cycles can be identified on which the search restarts to find a cycle. Given the Web graph $G = (N, E)$ where the number of node *N*, edges *E*, the edge search time is $O(|E|)$ and the cycle detection time is $O(|N|\cdot|E|)$, thus the complexity will be $O(|N|\cdot|C|\cdot|(E+1)|)$. The detailed complexity analysis is omitted by space limitation.

Even with the Link Measure, the semantic structuring algorithm [8] may generate wrong solutions such that each node has only one parent, but it is not a hierarchical structure anymore. See Fig. 4.2 (a), in that the degenerate case, the more this path may be followed, the more the weight total will increase, which can be called "white hole." If the weights are negative, it can be called a "black hole." It is a cycle, and there are so many cycles in the Web environment. Therefore a cycle proof algorithm should be required to generate a structure.

On the other hand, there is another problem called "repetitive cycles" in the Web graphs. The repetitive cycle is that the identical cycles derived from the same cycles to have the order of the nodes appearing different permutations. For example, the repetitive cycles appear as Fig. 4.2 (a): $N_1 \rightarrow N_2 \rightarrow N_3$, $N_2 \rightarrow N_3 \rightarrow N_1$, $N_3 \rightarrow N_1 \rightarrow$

N_2, or generally (b) $N_1 \rightarrow N_2 \rightarrow \ldots N_n$, $N_2 \rightarrow N_3 \rightarrow \ldots N_n \rightarrow N_1$, etc. The repetitive cycles can make search performance drastically low, because the system has to remember all visited nodes and to analyze whether the node sequences are identical with permutations. In this paper, we solved the problem with a polynomial time algorithm.

Algorithm. CylEnm(integer value n ∈ *N*, integer value s)

```
s = 0
begin
  mark (n) := true;
  for w ∈ A(n) do
    if(w ≠ s) then
      begin
        if(mark (w) = false) then
         begin
           place w on stack;
           CylEnm(w, s);
         end
      end
    else if
      output circuit from s to n to s given by stack;
  u := top of stack;
  delete u from stack;
  mark (u) := false;
end
for s := 1 until n do
      place s on stack;
      CyclEnm(s, s);  u := top of stack;
end
```

Fig. 4.1. Algorithm for removing repetitive cycles from a Web site

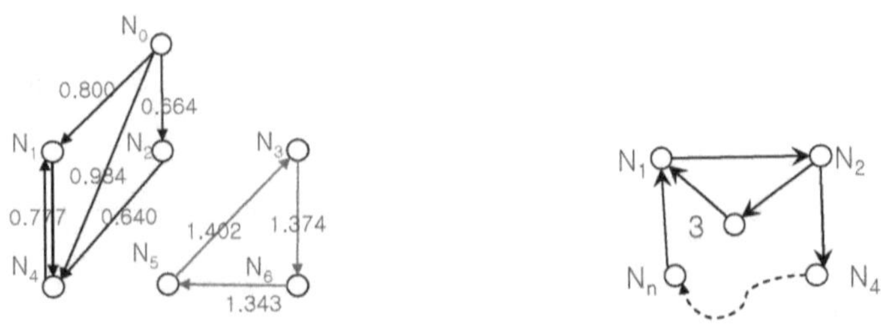

(a) **(b)**

Fig. 4.2. Local solution (a) degenerate case, and (b) repetitive cycles

Therefore, in order to generate the structure for a given Web site, the algorithm 4.3 is described as follows:

1 Initial Domain: input a Web site with homepage (node $i = 0$)
2 Problem Formulation
  2.1 Input: Web nodes and links on the given domain.
  2.2 Cycle proofing by Algorithm in Fig. 4.1.
  2.3 Derive the object function by link weights by equation (3.4)
3 Solve the problem in Step 2 by the mathematical model (See [7])
  3.1 Generate the hierarchical structure
  3.2 Change detection and Sensitivity Analysis

Fig. 4.3. Algorithm 4.3 for structuring a Web site with cycle proofing

The Algorithm can be applied to transform a digraph into a tree. At first, all cycles which may exist in a graph should be removed. Cycle proofing is implemented by depth first approach with stack based algorithm. Except for the root node, the tree node's indegree should be 1. And last, duplicate paths between two adjacent nodes in a graph should be removed.

By the structuring algorithm, the Web site example in Fig. 2.1 (c) can be applied. When the number of nodes increases from N_0 to N_6, the algorithm, then the corresponding procedure can produce the hierarchical structure as Fig. 4.4 and 4.5, respectively. Total weight sum for algorithm 4.3, semantic distance [8], depth first, and breadth first approaches are summarized in Table 4.1 with respect to the increasing number of nodes.

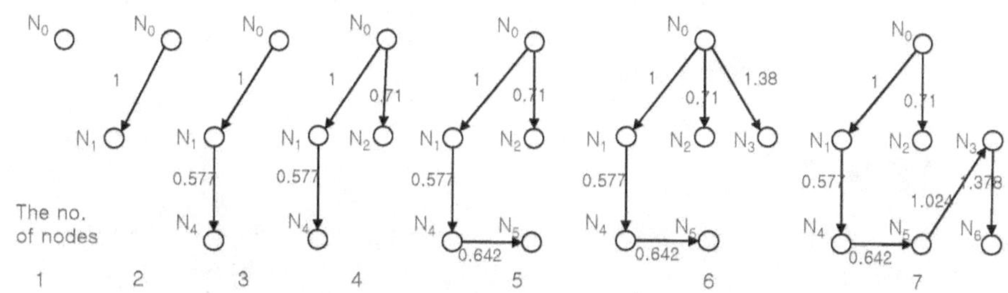

Fig. 4.4. Results by the depth first approach w.r.t the number of nodes

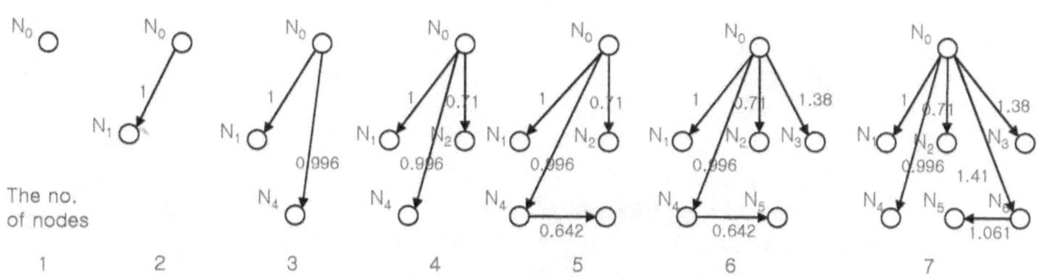

Fig. 4.5. Results by the algorithm 4.3 in Fig. 4.3 w.r.t the number of nodes

Table 4.1. Weight sum for algorithm 4.3, semantic distance, depth first, and breadth first approaches w.r.t the number of nodes

	the number of Nodes						
	1	2	3	4	5	6	7
Algorithm 4.3	1.410	1.000	1.996	2.706	3.348	4.728	6.557
semantic distance	1.410	1.000	1.577	2.287	2.929	4.309	5.719
depth first	1.410	1.000	1.577	2.287	2.929	4.309	5.331
breadth first	1.410	1.000	1.996	2.706	3.348	4.728	6.138

As a result, each hierarchical structure with corresponding topology can be generated w.r.t the increasing number of Web nodes. We can see that the Algorithm 4.3 gives the best weight sum among those four approaches in every stage of the experiment.

5 Conclusions

This paper has been to generate the hierarchical structure of a Web site from directed graphs with removing repetitive cycles. The structure also shows using significant similarity measures PageRank measure generates the corresponding solution, and topological structure. It implies that the model can easily be adapted by and integrated into the current Web search robots as well as the Web site managers. Under the circumstances of frequent Web contents change, the algorithm can be effective for developing an advanced search engine schematic.

Acknowledgement

This work was supported by the Ministry of Science and Technology (MOST)/ Korea Science and Engineering Foundation (KOSEF) through the Advanced Information Technology Research Center (AITrc).

References

1. Barabasi A., Albert R., and Jeong H.: Scale-free Characteristics of Random Networks: the Topology of the World-Wide Web. Physica A 281 (2000) 69-77.
2. Garofalakis, M., Kappos, P. and Mourloukos, D.: Web Site Optimization Using Page Popularity, IEEE Internet Computing, 3(4) (1999) 22-29.
3. Glover, E. J., Tsioutsiouliklis, C., Lawrence, S., Pennock, D., and Flake, G.: Using Web Structure for Classifying and Describing Web Pages. In: Proc. WWW (2002) 562-569.
4. Gurrin, C., and Smeaton, A. F.: Replicating Web Structure in Small-Scale Test Collections, Information Retrieval, 7(3) (2004) 239-263.
5. Henzinger, M. R., Heydon, A., Mitzenmacher, M. and Najork, M.: On near-uniform URL sampling, Computer Networks, 33(1) (2000) 295-308.

6. Kumar R., Raghavan P., Rajagopalan S., Tomkins A.: Crawling the Web for cyber communities in the Web, In: Proc. 8th WWW (1999) 403–415
7. Lee, W., Kim, S., Kang, S.: Dynamic Hierarchical Website Structuring Using Linear Programming, In: Proc. Ec-Web, LNCS Vol. 3182, (2004) 328-337.
8. Lee, W., Geller J.: Semantic Hierarchical Abstraction of Web Site Structures for Web Searchers. Journal of Research and Practice in Information Technology, 36 (1) (2004) 71-82.
9. Mendelzon, A. O. and Milo, T.: Formal Model of Web Queries, ACM PODS (1997) 134-143.
10. Nivasch, G.: Cycle detection using a stack," Information Processing Letters. 90(3) (2004) 135-140.
11. Pandurangan, G., Raghavan, P. and Upfal, E.: Using PageRank to Characterize Web Structure. In: Proc. COCOON (2002) 330-339.
12. Shmueli, O.: Dynamic Cycle Detection. Information Processing Letters. 17(4) (1983) 185-188.
13. Thom, L. H., and Iochpe, C.: Integrating a Pattern Catalogue in a Business Process Model, In: Proc. ICEIS 3 (2004) 651-654.

The Vehicle Tracking System for Analyzing Transportation Vehicle Information

Young Jin Jung and Keun Ho Ryu

Database/Bioinformatics Laboratory, Chungbuk National University, Korea
{yjjeong, khryu}@dblab.chungbuk.ac.kr

Abstract. The several moving object query languages have been designed to deal with moving objects effectively. However most of them are not enough to manage vehicles in transportation system. So, to analyze vehicle information in transportation effectively, we propose the web-based transportation vehicle management system supporting a Moving Object Structured Query Language. The developed system can manage vehicles through examining the history data of vehicles such as departure time, overlapped trajectories, and the distance among vehicles and provide the vehicle information on the internet and a PDA through concurrently processing the query language transmitted from clients.

Keywords: Moving Objects, MOSQL, Moving Object Query Language, Transportation Management System, Location Based Services.

1 Introduction

Nowadays, it is actively researched to deal with and utilize positions of objects relying on the progress of location management technologies and a wireless communication network, the miniaturization of terminal devices. Specially, it is becoming important issues to track the objects such as a vehicle and an aircraft and to provide suitable services to mobile users depending on changed locations in LBS[1].

Moving objects are spatial ones to change their locations over time[2, 3]. Managing the location information of moving objects is very important in LBS, because the quality of the services closely depends on the locations in mobile environment. However, most of existing moving object query languages[4, 5, 6] and management systems[4, 8, 9, 10] are only designed through utilizing the general data model organizing a point, a line, a polygon, not implemented. The utility of previous works could not be evaluated in real world. Besides the designed query languages are not enough to analyze the vehicle trajectories for examining the transportation cost and assisting the manager in making transportation schedule with little cost.

Therefore, to solve this problem, we design and implement the vehicle tracking system for effective transportation vehicle management. The proposed system consists of the MOSQL[11] based query processor for analyzing the history and current information of vehicle, an uncertainty processor[12] for predict near future positions with probability, a moving object index[13, 14, 15] to search data rapidly, an index manager, etc. Besides, it is confirmed for the system to analyze the trajectories through utilizing real vehicle data in the test.

H.T. Shen et al. (Eds.): APWeb Workshops 2006, LNCS 3842, pp. 1012 – 1020, 2006.

The remainder of the paper is organized as follows. Section 2 briefly describes the existing query languages of moving objects. Section 3 introduces the system structure. Section 4 presents MOSQL. Section 5 illustrates the implemented system and test results. Section 6 concludes.

2 Related Works

Moving objects changing their spatial information continuously are divided into moving points considering only locations and moving regions containing shapes and positions[16]. The vehicle location management system monitors the location and state of the moving vehicle in real-time, and displays to client system using map data for checking operation status of vehicle. The representative vehicle location management systems are Commercial Vehicle Operations(CVO)[17], Advance Public Transport System(APTS)[18], and vehicle management and control system of EuroBus[19].

There are several researches on vehicle managing system such as DOMINO[4, 20] CHOROCHRONOS[8, 9], Battle Field Analysis[10]. The MOST in the DOMINO project deals with moving objects through utilizing dynamic attributes considering speed and direction of a moving object, uncertainty processing operators, and Future Temporal Logic, etc. However this prototype is not implemented and does not support history information of past movement of moving objects. CHOROCHRONOS project researches the modeling of moving object, indexing method, query processing, and vehicle management system. However this project did not make a prototype. The battlefield analysis system copes with the movements of enemy and map out a strategy through grasping the positions of our forces and enemy in a war. But it could not support real-time query processing in mobile environment.

When combining space and time, new query types emerge in the moving object database. Moving object queries are divided into coordinate-based queries and trajectory-based queries[9]. Coordinate-based queries consider an object's coordinates such as point queries, range queries, and nearest-neighbor queries. Trajectory-based queries considering object's movements are diversified into topological queries which search object's movement information and navigational queries which search and predict the information derived from object's movement such as speed and direction. To process these moving object queries needs vast amount of data approach since it is required to store temporal, spatial, and spatiotemporal changes. These queries are processed by utilizing the moving object operator. The query language using the operator are FTL(Future Temporal Logic)[4] containing uncertainty operator such as 'may', 'must', STQL(Spatio-Temporal Query Language)[5]. In addition, SQL^{ST} combing SQL^{S} and SQL^{T} is proposed in [21]. The distance based query language using CQL(Constraint Query Language) is designed in [22]. The query language for describing trajectories is studied[11, 12, 13]. However, most of existing moving object query languages are only designed, not implemented. So, the utility of previous works could not be evaluated in real world. Besides the designed query language is not enough to analyze the vehicle information for examining the transportation cost.

3 Transportation Vehicle Management System

The proposed System deals with the history and current vehicle information under the assumption that moving object data are continuously transmitted to a mobile object management server over time. In addition, the only moving point's movement is considered, moving region is not. This section describes the structure of the vehicle management system for controlling the positions of vehicles and providing various services related their locations.

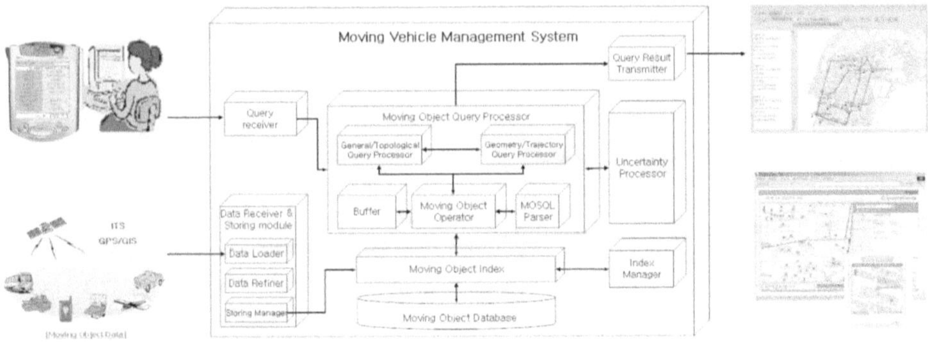

Fig. 1. The structure of the mobile data management system

Figure 1 shows the structure of transportation management system. The system consists of the data receiver & storing module to collect and store the transmitted vehicle locations, the moving object index to search the locations rapidly, the index manager to keep the performance of the index high through updating the index with new data per a specific period such as a day, a week etc., the query processor supporting general, topological, and geometry queries with moving object operators such as the buffer, the section, the trajectory in the MOSQL and an uncertainty processor using the probability about locations, and the searched result can be transmitted to the web client and PDA users through the query result transmitter.

4 Moving Object Structured Query Language

In order to reduce the cost of transportation service, the transportation company managing various vehicles to convey goods plan an optimal schedule with low cost through analyzing the waste of services from checking the count of the duplicated routes of vehicles, the vehicle list visiting a specific spot in a week. Then, the manager has to collect the locations and trajectories of vehicles, recognize the waste of motion. The moving object query language is described for effective management form analyzing the vehicle information.

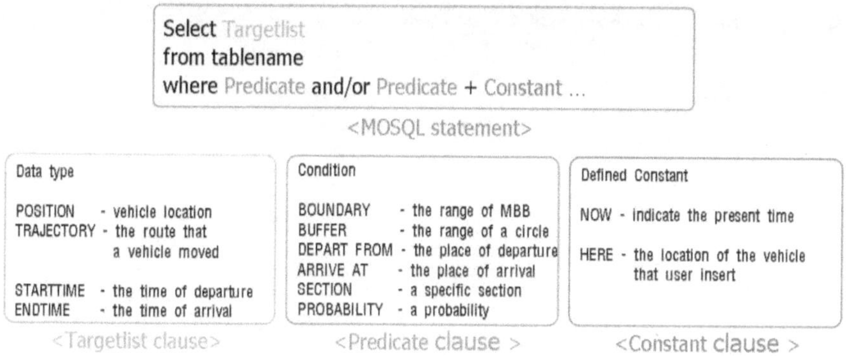

Fig. 2. The structure of the MOSQL statement

Figure 2 describes the organization of the MOSQL statement containing the targetlist, predicate, and constant construction. The target construction describes data values required form the moving object query language. It is used as an attribute name after 'SELECT' in the SQL. The predicate is the construction for describing the conditions to get information user want to know. It is similar to condition clauses after 'WHERE' of the SQL.

The constant having a fixed meaning in the moving object query language is defined by a word like a constant such as € and π. Two reserved constant is utilized in the system. Table 1 describes the defined statement elements of the MOSQL such as a target, a predicate, and a constant written by the MOSQL wizard as well as a user. Table 1 describes the moving object operators to analyze the transportation vehicle information.

Table 1. The operators of the MOSQL

Clause	Construction	Description
Targetlist	POSITION	The position of a moving vehicle at specific time point defined at 'VALID AT' in the MOSQL.
	TRAJECTORY	The moving route of a transportation vehicle through some time period. To search and analyze this trajectory is essential in the moving object applications.
	STARTTIME	The time point for a moving vehicle to depart from a specific place defined at 'DEPART FROM' in the MOSQL.
	ENDTIME	The time point for a moving vehicle to arrive in a specific place defined at 'ARRIVE AT' in the MOSQL.
Predicate	BOUNDARY	The condition clause which gets the trajectories of moving vehicles included in the range of the MBB.
	BUFFER	The conditions to get location information contained in a defined circle.
	DEPART FROM	The specific spot to search the time point for a moving object to depart from the spot.
	ARRIVE AT	This specific spot to search the time point for a moving object to arrive in the spot.
	PROBABILITY	The probability of vehicle existence at a specific time point. it defines the scope of the probability to calculate the predicted location
	SECTION	The condition clause to obtain the trajectories of moving vehicles through describing two spatial points.
Constant	HERE	The current position of a specific vehicle.
	NOW	The current time as the query is issued. It is useful to describe and utilize the temporal information in a query processor and a database.

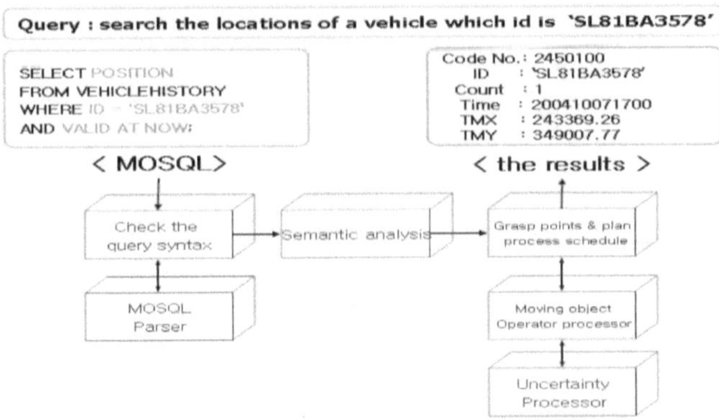

Fig. 3. The MOSQL query processing

Figure 3 show the process step of the MOSQL query. First, the query processor analyzes the syntax of the query through utilizing the MOSQL parser. Next, the vehicle data are searched and refined through the semantic analysis, the moving object operator, and the uncertainty processing. Finally the results of the query are returned to the user.

The section query to search the movement of vehicles visited through two spots shown in table 2 returns the trajectory as a result of this query after inputting vehicle id, time period, two spatial points. The spot in query statement can be presented by a spatial coordinate as well as a building name such as a printing museum and a public garden.

Figure 4 show the trajectory of vehicles passed through A and B spots. The solid line presents the trajectory from the A spot to the B spot, and the dotted line illustrates the other line. The query in table 2 finding the solid line of figure 4 is utilized for the vehicle manager to recognize the number of vehicles passed through a specific spot, to examine whether some vehicles' trajectories are overlapped.

Table 2. The trajectory query passed through two specific spots

	Contents
Query	Find the trajectory of "CB81BA3578" vehicles passed through a start point (243461, 349089), a end point(244032, 350806)
MOSQL	SELECT TRAJECTORY FROM VEHICLEHISTORY WHERE ID= 'CB81BA3578' AND VALID FROM '200312200900' TO NOW AND SECTION FROM (243461,349089) TO (244032, 350806);

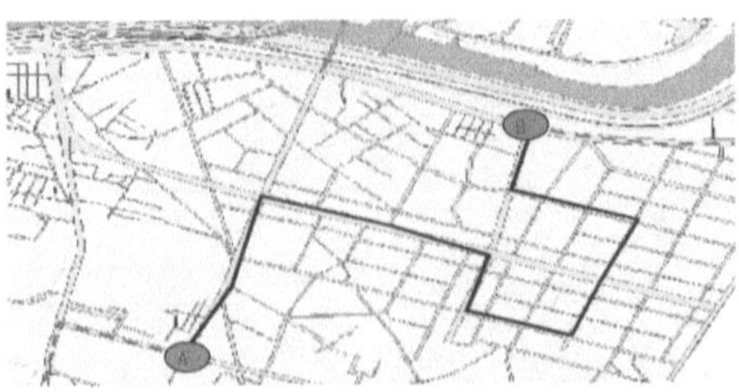

Fig. 4. The trajectory of vehicles passed through two spots – A and B

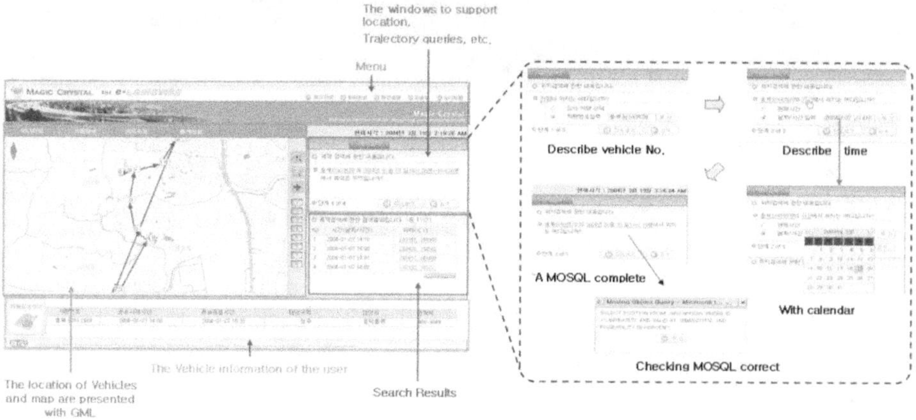

Fig. 5. User Interface utilizing the MOSQL wizard

5 Implementation

The query language for processing moving object information effectively can help the manager analyze the vehicle information, and make a transportation plan with low cost through supporting a moving object operator to process some parts which is difficult to write using the existing SQL.

The query language used in the implemented system is based on the SQL. The MOSQL can be written by a user as well as by a MOSQL wizard in figure 5. The MOSQL wizard helps users create the query language without an error, because the possibility for typing wrong vehicle id, time information, the coordinates of spots is high.

Figure 6 illustrates the steps to processing the MOSQL query. When the MOSQL is transmitted from a client to the server, the server can process the queries with 3 steps: checking the MOSQL syntax, searching data in a moving object index or database, processing the query through utilizing moving object operators according to the query types. After processing these steps, the results is transmitted to the clients and shown in a web browser or a PDA like figure 7.

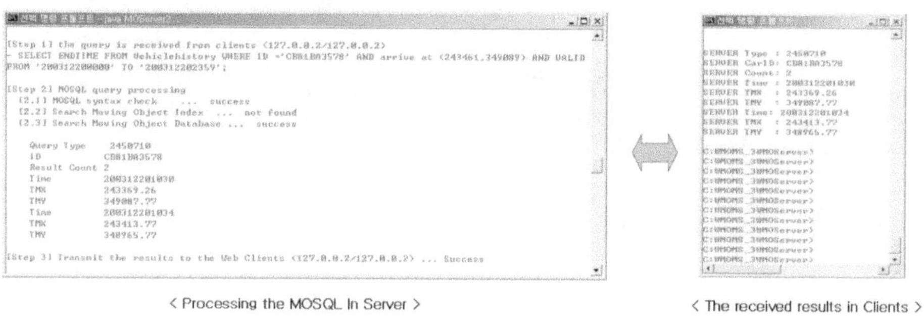

Fig. 6. Processing and transmitting the MOSQL between the server and clients

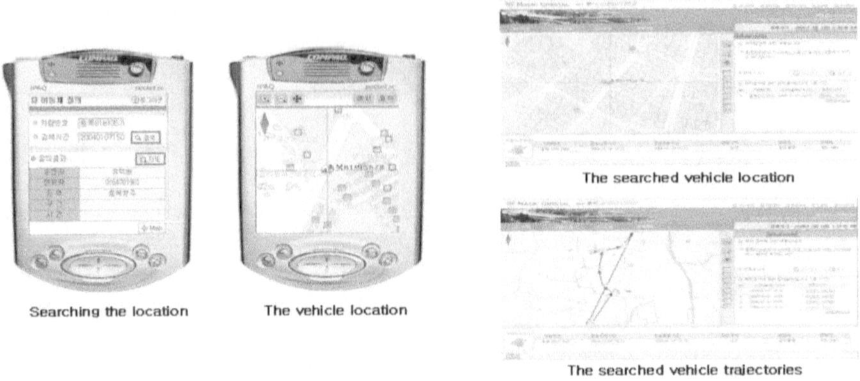

Fig. 7. Vehicle location data converted to transmit to the server

The results searching the location and trajectories of the vehicles is transmitted to Web Clients and PDA users through the wireless communication. Figure 7 presents the trajectories of moving vehicles in a PDA and a web browser. In the browser, the movement of a vehicle is illustrated by arrows and numbers in a left window. The map size can be changed. The right window shows the MOSQL creation wizard and the result of trajectory query. In addition the lower part provides the general information such as vehicle no, the time period, the area of transportation, phone number.

The proposed query language provides moving object operators to search the trajectories between two specific spots, departure/arrival time to check the cost for smooth transportation services. Besides the developed system supports concurrency control to rapidly process a variety of queries transmitted from many clients. The Query processing time is tested with 1 server and 5 client simulators to transmit random query types to the server. Figure 8 describe the analyzed results after processing the random queries transmitted from clients. The cost to process the query in the server is about 1 seconds, however the cost to transmit the query requirement and results is 2 ~ 8 seconds. Therefore the research to reduce the transmission time as well as data processing time is also required. In addition, the research for interface like the MOSQL wizard is needed for dealing with the complex query language. Besides, the developed system supports to processing vehicle information in real time.

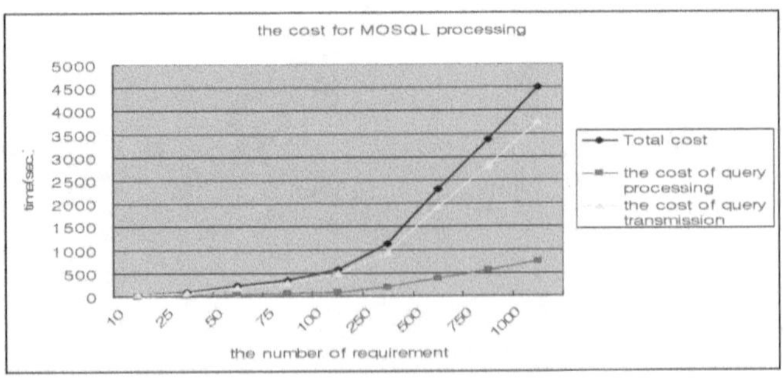

Fig. 8. The analysis of query processing

6 Conclusion

Recently, it is rapidly increasing interest on location-based services in mobile environment. In this paper, we proposed transportation vehicle management system supporting the MOSQL to provide the suitable services depending on the location of vehicle in real-time. The MOSQL is confirmed for the system to analyze the trajectories through utilizing real vehicle data. The implemented system would be useful to process various requirements in the transportation. Currently we are focusing on the extending the MOSQL to satisfy user various requirements in query processor.

Acknowledgement

This work was supported by RRC program of MOCIE and ITEP. The corresponding author is Keun Ho Ryu.

References

1. J. H. Reed, K. J. Krizman, B. D. Woerner, T. S. Rappaport, "An Overview of the Challenges and Progress in Meeting the E-911 Requirement for Location Service," IEEE Communication Magazine, pp. 33-37, 1998.
2. M. F. Mokbel, T. M. Ghanem, W. G. Aref, "Spatio-temporal Access Methods," IEEE Data Engineering Bulletin, Vol. 26, No. 2, pp. 40-49, 2003.
3. R. H. Guting, M. H. Bohlen, M. Erwig, C. S. Jensen, N. A. Lorentzos, M. Schneider, M. Vazirgiannis, "A Foundation for Representing and Querying Moving Objects," ACM Transactions on Database Systems, Vol. 25, No. 1, pp. 1-42, 2000.
4. O. Wolfson, B. Xu, S. Chamberlain, and L. Jiang, "Moving Objects Databases: Issues and Solutions", Proc. Of the 10th Intl. Conf. on Scientific and Statistical Database Management(SSDBM'98), Capri, Italy, 1998.
5. Martin Erwig, Markus Schneider, "STQL: A Spatio-Temporal Query Language," Chapter 6 of Mining Spatio-Temporal Information Systems, Kluwer Academic Publishers, pp.105-126, 2002.
6. H. M. O. Mokhtar and J. Su. "A Query Language for Moving Object Trajectories," Proceedings of the International Scientific and Statistical Database Management Conference, June 2005.
7. H. Mokhtar and J. Su. "Universal Trajectory Queries for Moving Object Databases," Proceedings of IEEE International Conference on Mobile Data Management, Berkeley, CA, January, 2004.
8. S. Saltenis, C. S. Jensen, S. Leutenegger, and M. Lopez, "Indexing the Positions of Continuously Moving Objects", Proc. of the ACM SIGMOD Conf., 2000.
9. D. Pfoser, C. S. Jensen, Y. Theodoridis, "Novel Approaches in Query Processing for Moving Objects," CHOROCHRONOS TECHNICAL REPORT CH-00-03, 2000.
10. K. H. Ryu, and Y. A. Ahn, "Application of Moving Objects and Spatiotemporal Reasoning", Time Center TR-58, 2001.
11. Lee, Hyun Ah, Lee, Hye Jin, Kim, Dong Ho, Kim, Jin Suk, Moving Object Query Language Design for Mov-ing Object Management System," Korea Information Science Symposium 2003, vol 30(2)(II), 2003.

12. D. H. Kim, J. S. Kim, "Development of Advanced Vehicle Tracking System Using the Uncertainty Processing of Past and Future Locations," 7th ICEIC, Hanoi in Vietnam, August, 2004.
13. Y. J. Jung, K. H. Ryu, "A Group Based Insert Manner for Storing Enormous Data Rapidly in Intelligent Transportation System", ICIC, pp. 296-305, August 2005.
14. E. J. Lee, Y. J. Jung, K. H. Ryu, "A Moving Point Indexing Using Projection Operation for Location Based Services", 9th DASFAA, pp. 775~786, March, 2004.
15. E. J. Lee, K. H. Ryu, K. W. Nam, "Indexing for Efficient Managing Current and Past Trajectory of Moving Object," Apweb 2004, pp. 781-787, Hangzhou, 2004.
16. L. Forlizzi, R. H. Guting, E. Nardelli, M. Schneider, "A Data Model and Data Structures for Moving Objects Databases," ACM SIGMOD, pp. 319-330, 2000.
17. IVHS America, Strategic Plan for Intelligent Vehicle-Highway Systems, Report No:IVHS-AMER-92-3, U.S. DOT, 1992.
18. Federal Transit Administration, "Advanced Public Transportation Systems: The State of the Art Update '96", U.S. Department of Transportation FTA-MA-26-7007-96-1, January 1996.
19. EUROBUS, "Case Study on Public Transport Contribution to Solving Traffic Problems", EUROBUS Project, Deliverable 18(version 2.0), 1994.
20. P. Sistla, O. Wolfson, S. Chamberlain, and S. Dao, "Modeling and Querying Moving Objects", Proc. Of the 13th Intl. Conf. on Data Engineering(ICDE'97), Birmingham, UK, April 1997.
21. Cindy Xinmin Chen, Carlo Zaniolo, "SQLST: A Spatio-Temporal Data Model and Query Language," Proc. ER 2000, pp.96-111, 2000.
22. H. Mokhtar, J. Su, and O. Ibarra. "On Moving Object Queries," Proceedings of the 21st ACM SIGACT-SIGMOD-SIGART Symposium on Principles of Database Systems (PODS), Madison, WI, pp.188-198, June 2002.

Web-Based Cooperative Design for SoC and Improved Architecture Exploration Algorithm*

Guangsheng Ma[1], Xiuqin Wang[2], and Hao Wang[3]

[1] Computer Science and Technology Institute, Harbin Engineering University, Harbin, postcode 150001, China
maguangsheng@hrbeu.edu.cn
[2] Computer Science and Technology Institute, Harbin Engineering University, Harbin, postcode 150001, China
sd_wxq@sina.com
[3] Department of Computer and Information Engineering, Heilongjiang Institute of Science and Technology, postcode 150027, Harbin, China
Wanghao_1976@sina.com

Abstract. This paper discusses issues in web-based cooperative design for SoC and gives the web-based design flow. Good partitioning is the precondition of web-based cooperative design. Then the paper focuses on the issue of architecture exploration, improved a partitioning algorithm. The proposed greedy partitioning algorithm introduces a guiding function which is decided by four factors: criticality, saved time, frequency and area of tasks. It stresses the tasks on the critical path, and can improve the resource use efficiency and maximize the system performance.

1 Introduction

With the help of networks and CSCW (Computer Supported Cooperative Work) technology, cooperative design is becoming a comprehensive and effective working method. Cooperative work is widely used in science computing and engineering design [1-3]. The development of web-based cooperative design technique makes more design work can be done on Internet.

Complex SoC (System-on-Chip) system includes both software and hardware. In embedded system, software account for the most part. Many sub-systems can be designed parallel at different homes or companies in distributed areas. But at present, there are no tools support cooperative design on Internet for SoC. Web-based SoC design can not only reduce the time of design but also share some high cost devices such as hardware emulators.

Today SoC design often uses HW/SW (hardware/software) co-design method. The critical step of co-design is the architecture exploration, which by HW/SW partitioning decides which parts of the system should be implemented with software and

* This work is supported by National Science Foundation (60273081) of China.

H.T. Shen et al. (Eds.): APWeb 2006, LNCS 3842, pp. 1021 – 1028, 2006.

which be implemented with hardware, the partitioning result has direct effect on the performance and cost of a system.

The object of HW/SW partitioning is to meet the system requirements in time, cost, area, power consumption etc. This kind of limited optimum problem has been proved to be a NP-difficult problem. There has been much research work on partitioning algorithms. In [4], a iterative partitioning algorithm for re-configurable logic architecture was presented. In [5] proposed a partitioning algorithm with DAG (directed acyclic graph), in which the tasks on critical path was stressed, but the aim was to parallelize the tasks. [6] is a partitioning targeting multi-speed non-period real-time system, this algorithm emphasized real-time, had a strict requirement on time and paid little attention to area. In [7], a PMG (process model graph) was used in the partitioning. In this paper, the hardware area use efficiency was also neglected, besides, it not considered whether the task was on the critical path or not. [8] put forward a dynamic partitioning algorithm, which pointed out that much time of most systems is spent on limited circulations. The author also gave the configurable architecture in [9] to fit this kind of partitioning. While above work succeed in some area, hardware had not been used efficiently and they are not target web-based cooperative design.

This paper first discusses the problem of design SoC system with web-based technology and gives the design flow in section 2 and 3, and then focuses on the issue of architecture exploration, improves the greedy partitioning algorithm in the area of use efficiency of hardware resource. The algorithm is proved correct.

2 Web-Based SoC System Design Platform

On Internet, the traditional platforms need several improvements. After HW/SW partitioning, the whole system needs be divided into several sub-systems to design. Designers in different areas need communicate with each other to discuss and interaction. Communication tools such as chatting tools, electronic whiteboard, and audio tools. Another function is to validate the sub-systems. The platform is similar to platform in [1]. In this platform, there are master side and slave sides. Slave sides are those designer or groups in different area. The master manages the whole design flow and own expensive devices.

3 Design Flow

On Internet, the system design flow will make some change. As show in **Fig. 1**, first, after coarse specification, the system needs to explore the system architecture. The architecture exploration products a HW/SW partitioning that satisfy the system requirement. Then the master assigns tasks to every designer group. The designer will carry on web-based cooperative design. During this process, the designers communicate with each other. Each task is simulated separately before submit to the master. The master will integrate the well-designed tasks, then synthesize and verify the system and finish the whole design. The expensive devices which the master owned can be used many times.

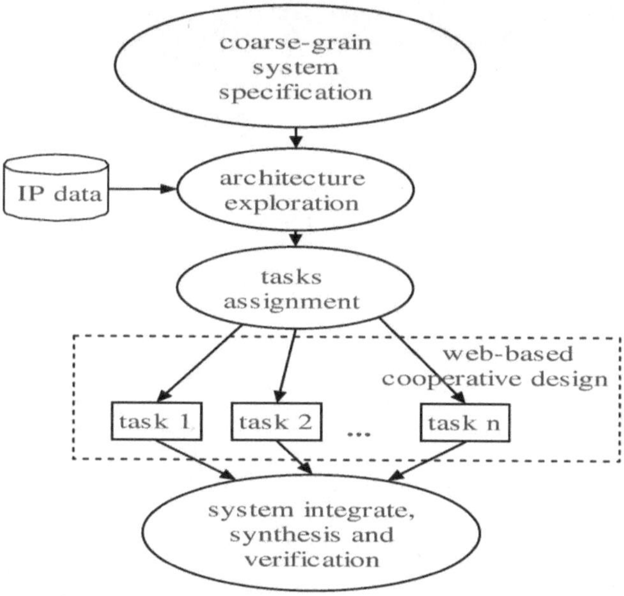

Fig. 1. Web-based design flow

In the design flow, the architecture exploration is one of the critical steps. In the following, I will mainly discuss the architecture exploration issue under given hardware source restricts.

4 Formal Specification of Architecture

FPGA (field-programmable gate arrays) is used to accelerator microprocessor in two ways: one is to act as a coprocessor, another is used in ISA architecture to extend instructions. These two architectures have different requirements on HW/SW partitioning. We only discuss the coprocessor architecture here. This architecture is usually consisted of microprocessor, FPGA and some memory. In which, the FPGA can be general configurable which permits static reconfigure or dynamically configurable. The dynamically configurable FPGA can be fully dynamical configurable or partly dynamical configurable.

The main strategy of greedy partitioning algorithm is to move tasks from software to hardware according to certain principle until it violates the area restricts. This partitioning algorithms can be used for the above coprocessor architecture, which can be specified in a unified formation (A_{constr} , m, A_{DRP}, t_{DRP} , A_{Dmem}) . A_{constr} is the area of general configurable logic; m is the number of dynamically configurable contexts; A_{DRP} , t_{DRP} both are m dimension vectors, $A_{DRP}[i]$ is the area of the i th dynamical configurable context and $t_{DRP}[i]$ is its dynamical configure time; A_{Dmem} is the area of the memory to store dynamically configure codes. For general configurable system, all the parameters except the first one are 0; for partly dynamical configurable system, the first parameters is the its static configurable logic contexts, and others are dynamical configurable parts. For fully dynamical configurable system, the first parameter is 0.

5 Computing Model

Computing model is an abstract of system specification. This paper uses PMG as the computing model , which was used in [4]. Process is the basic unit in system specification, so PMG can be easily obtained from system specification.

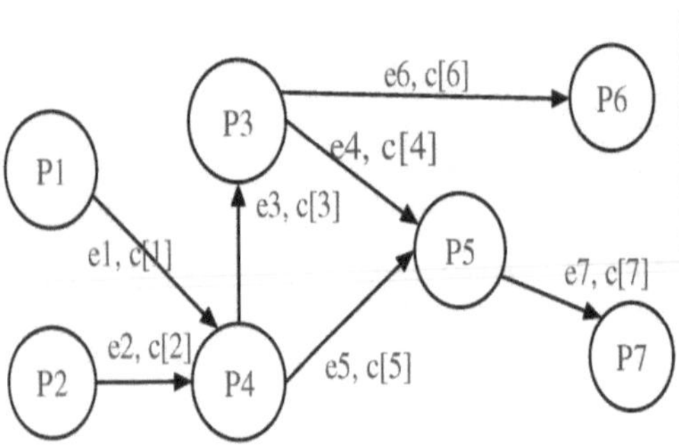

Fig. 2. PMG

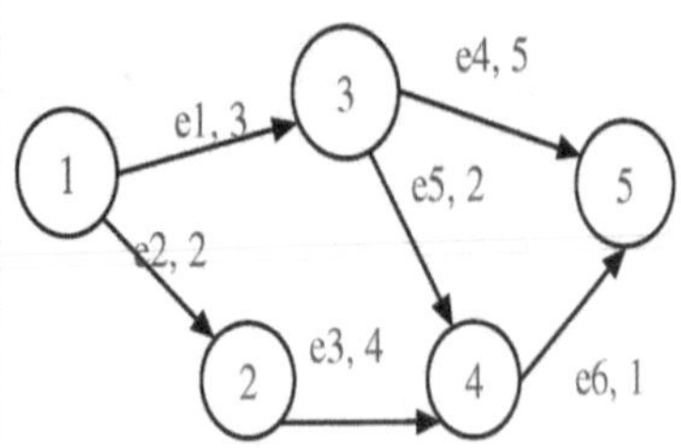

Fig. 3. Example

In this paper, PMG is presented as $G=(V,E,C,H,S,X,\mathrm{r})$. Where V is the set of vertexes, each vertex is a task, $|V|=N$ is the number of vertexes; E is the set of graph edges, each edge is labeled with communication time C; S,H are separately the time of vertexes implemented in software and hardware; the vector X presents a certain partition and r is the execute probability of vertexes. PMG is shown in **Fig. 2**:

$$E[i,j]=\begin{cases}-1,\text{edge i begin at vertex j}\\ 1,\ \text{edge i end at vertex j}\\ 0,\ \text{edge i has no relationship with vertex j}\end{cases};\ X[i]=\begin{cases}1,\ \text{vertex j is in hardware}\\ 0,\ \text{vertex j is in software}\end{cases}.$$

$C[k]$ is the communication time on the edge k while its two vertexes are implemented in different parts, one with software and another with hardware, it's value has relationship with the number and speed of data transmitted on the bus.

Define: for a certain partition X, $C|EX|$ is the communication time between software and hardware of the whole system.

Example 1: as shown in **Fig. 3**, the edges is denoted with communication time, C=(3 2 4 5 2 1). Suppose the vertexes 3 and 4 are implemented in hardware, and others in software. Then the partitioning result is

$X = \begin{bmatrix} 0 \\ 0 \\ 1 \\ 1 \\ 0 \end{bmatrix}$, the communication time between software and hardware of the system should be the sum (13) of communication time on edges $e1, e3, e4, e6$. while $C \mid EX \mid =$

$$(3\,2\,4\,5\,2\,1) \times \left| \begin{bmatrix} 1 & 0 & -1 & 0 & 0 \\ 1 & -1 & 0 & 0 & 0 \\ 0 & 1 & 0 & -1 & 0 \\ 0 & 0 & 1 & 0 & -1 \\ 0 & 0 & 1 & -1 & 0 \\ 0 & 0 & 0 & 1 & -1 \end{bmatrix} \times \begin{bmatrix} 0 \\ 0 \\ 1 \\ 1 \\ 0 \end{bmatrix} \right| = (3\,2\,4\,5\,2\,1) \left| \begin{bmatrix} -1 \\ 0 \\ -1 \\ 1 \\ 0 \\ 1 \end{bmatrix} \right| = (3\,2\,4\,5\,2\,1) \begin{bmatrix} 1 \\ 0 \\ 1 \\ 1 \\ 0 \\ 1 \end{bmatrix}$$

= 13, which is exactly the sum of communication time on the four edges.

When the 4th vertex is implemented in hardware, the additional communication time is the edges of $e3, e5, e6$, then

$$C \mid EX_4 \mid = C \left| \begin{bmatrix} 1 & 0 & -1 & 0 & 0 \\ 1 & -1 & 0 & 0 & 0 \\ 0 & 1 & 0 & -1 & 0 \\ 0 & 0 & 1 & 0 & -1 \\ 0 & 0 & 1 & -1 & 0 \\ 0 & 0 & 0 & 1 & -1 \end{bmatrix} \begin{bmatrix} 0 \\ 0 \\ 0 \\ 1 \\ 0 \end{bmatrix} \right| = C \left| \begin{bmatrix} 0 \\ 0 \\ -1 \\ 0 \\ -1 \\ 1 \end{bmatrix} \right| = C \begin{bmatrix} 0 \\ 0 \\ 1 \\ 0 \\ 1 \\ 1 \end{bmatrix},$$

X_i presents the vertex i is implemented with hardware.

In this model, we can only store the communication time on each edge with its two vertexes. The store complex degree is two sizes of the edges number, and need not a matrix to record each edge relationship with all the vertexes which has a store complex degree of N sizes of the edges number. This can greatly saved the access place.

6 HW/SW Automatically Partitioning Flow

Fig. 4 is the HW/SW partitioning flow graph. Firstly, abstract PMG model from system specification and limited requirement. Profiler profiles the PMG model, evaluate the execute time of every process in software and hardware, the execute probability of each process, and the communication time between two connected process. Each software execute time of each process is given by instruction simulator ISS.

After evaluating all the parameters in the compute mode, the algorithm explores the design space targeting the given architecture. The result of the partitioning is

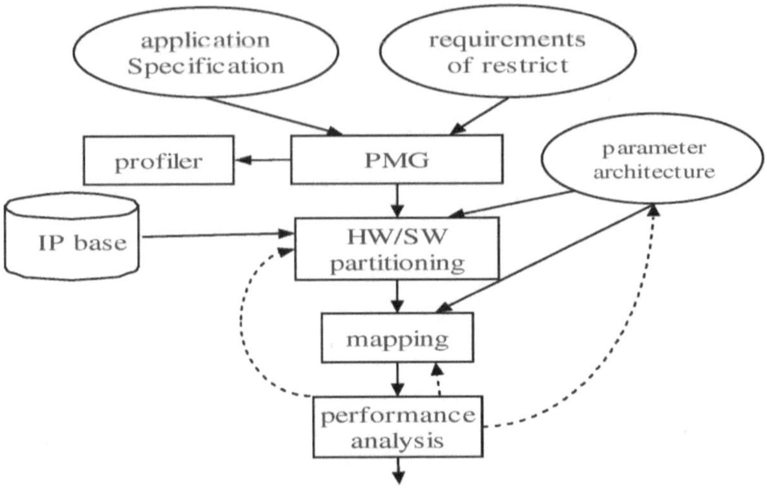

Fig. 4. HW/SW partitioning flow

mapping the nodes in the PMG into software or hardware. Performance analysis judges whether the partitioning can meet the system requirement, if not, then return and do the partitioning again.

7 Guiding Function Based Greedy Partitioning Algorithm

Generally, HW/SW partitioning algorithms move critical part of the system into hardware to improve system performance, while the critical function may be or not on the critical path; and it may be a task of less complex on the critical path or a task of high compute complex off critical path. Besides, the task with high compute complex may have a low execute probability and cannot improve system performance as obvious as a less complex task. Under the limited area resource, we should care four factors: criticality (whether the task is on the critical path), saved time, area and execute probability of a task.

Table 1. Properties of Task

	Criticality $CP[i]$	saved time	Execute probability	Area (number of gates)	weight
T1	0	5	0.2	1007	0.001
T2	1	3	0.3	906	$0.001+\alpha$
T3	0	5	0.5	498	0.005

In this paper, we introduce a guiding function—weight, which is decided by the following properties in **Table 1**. In which, hardware implement saves time ST and weight are separately given in formula (1) and (2):

$$ST[i] = S[i] - H[i] \quad (1)$$

$$weight[i] = \frac{ST[i]}{A[i]} \times r[i] + \alpha \times CP[i] \quad (2)$$

CP (critical path) is n dimension vector, $CP[i]$ records node i is on or not on the critical path; α is a constant, which is small and can be decided by experiment to ensure task under equal circumstances have a higher priority.

According to the guiding function value, the nodes are sort in decreasing order and put in a list, travel each node orderly and explore the design space of the given architecture.

If the move of a node can improve the system performance then the move is accept. In general coprocessor architecture, because the microprocessor and hardware run serially, moving a node form software to hardware can add to communication time of HW-SW communication. For dynamically re-configurable contexts, the reconfigure time is also should be considered. For multi-contexts dynamically reconfigurable architecture, schedule pre-fetch instruction technique is used to reduce reconfigure execute time. With this technique, the reconfigure time of a context is supposed to be overlap with the execute time of other contexts, thus the whole execute time of system includes hardware execute time, software execute time and the communication time between software and hardware.

Mapping a node i of a partitioning X into hardware obtains a new partitioning X^i with the worst system execute time:

$$T^{X^i} = S(1 - X^i) + HX^i + C\,|EX^i| \quad (3)$$

where X^i denotes the node i implemented in hardware.

The change of the whole system execute time is:

$$\Delta T = T^{X^i} - T^X = H[i] - S[i] + C(|EX^i| - |EX|) \quad (4)$$

For dynamically re-configurable logic resource, if move a node from software to hardware, the change of the whole system execute time is:

$$\Delta T = T^{X^i} - T^X = H[i] - S[i] + C(|EX^i| - |EX|) + t_{DRP}/W \quad (5)$$

where W is the size of pre-fetch instruction window in dynamically re-configurable context[9].

8 Results and Conclusions

We have done some experiments about the algorithm proposed in this paper. In this experiment, random numbers was given to the parameters of G and of the architecture, and **Table 2** is the results we got. From this table, we can see the improved algorithm can decrease hardware area and reduce the worst-case time of a system at the same time. But more experiments should be done with real system parameters.

Table 2. The experiment results

experiment	area		Worst-case time		improvement	
	Original algorithm	Improved algorithm	Original algorithm	Improved algorithm	area	time
1	550	525	135	118	4.5%	12.6%
2	443	415	322	298	7.3%	7.5%
3	804	655	345	328	15.4%	5.9%

This paper discussed the problems exist in design SoC on Internet and gives the design flow. Web-based SoC design can reduce the time to market and optimal expensive hardware resource efficiency. There is l much work to do in this area in future.

Another job of this paper is architecture exploration (by HW/SW partitioning), which is the precondition of web-based cooperative design for SoC. The improved algorithm enhanced hardware area efficiency and reduced the system execute time, additionally, the proposed algorithm can explore the design space according to the parameters of the given architecture and maximize the system performance.

References

1. Yuchu Tong, Dongming Lu: A Flexible Multimedia Cooperative Product Design Platform Framework. Proceedings of the Seventh International Conference on CSCW, (2002)198–204
2. Mei liu, Dazhi Liu:Virtual Prototype Based Architecture of Cooperative Design and Simulation for Complex Products. The 8th International Conference on Computer Supported Cooperative Work in Design Proceedings.(2003)546–551
3. Zhao Jianhua, Kanji AKAHORI: Web-based collaborative learning Methods and Strategies in Higher Education. www.eecs.kumamoto-u.ac.jp/ITHET01/proc
4. Juanjo Noguera, Rosa M. Badia: A HW/SW Partitioning Algorithm for Dynamically Reconfigurable Architectures*. Proceedings of the Design, Automation and Test in Europe (DATE), (2001) 729
5. Matthew Jin and Gul N. Khan: Heterogeneous Hardware-Software System partitioning using Extended Directed Acyclic Graph. 16th Int. Conference on Parallel and Distributed Systems.(2003) 181–186
6. Abdenour Azzedine, JeanPhilippe Diguet and JeanLuc Pillippe: Large Exploration for HW/SW partitioning of Multirate and Aperiodic Real□Time Systems. 10th International Workshop on Hardware/Software Co-Design (CODES), (2002) 85-90
7. Pradeep Adhipathi. Model based approach to Hardware/Software Partitioning of SOC Designs. Blacksburg, Virginia. Master thesis. (2004) 12–15
8. Greg Stitt, Roman Lysecky and Frank Vahid*. Dynamic Hardware/Software Partitioning: A First Approach. DAC. (2003) 250–255
9. Roman L. Lysecky and Frank Vahid*. A Configurable Logic Architecture for Dynamic Hardware/Software Partitioning. Proceedings of the Design Automation and Test in Europe Conference (DATE), (2004) 480–485

Research on Web Application of Struts Framework Based on MVC Pattern

Jing-Mei Li, Guang-Sheng Ma, Gang Feng, and Yu-Qing Ma

College of Computer Science & Technology,
Harbin Engineering University, Harbin, China 150001
{lijingmei, maguangsheng, fenggang}@hrbeu.edu.cn

Abstract. The paper introduces MVC design pattern briefly, then discusses the Struts framework based on J2EE MVC pattern and finally gives the development procedure of how to design Web application with Struts framework. From this we can see that software framework and component reuse can enhance the efficiency of software development, offer clear responsibilities between Web page designers and software developers and improve system maintainability and extensibility.

1 Introduction

At present, J2EE has already become the standard of enterprise development of Web application gradually. The SERVLET/JSP technology, which is one important part of J2EE, is widely used in numerous Websites too, However, if only JSP technology is used in Web application development, the business logic, java code and dynamic html would be mixed together, which results in low reusable degree of the program, makes maintenance tedious and difficult, and brings weak adaptability to changes. Since the responsibilities of Webpage designers and software developers are not separated, the software development may be inefficient. Whereas, applying MVC pattern to design Web application can solve problems mentioned above generally.

MVC pattern comes from Smalltalk, and it includes Model, View and the Controller[1]. Among them, the Model means the business logic of the application and is the core of the application. The View implements the appearance of the Model, and it is the external presentation of the application. The Controller accepts client requests, transmits the request data to the corresponding business logic module for processing, and then invokes the corresponding view module to generate result page back to the browser in the way wanted by user. It links the Model and the View together. The advantage of the pattern is as follows: 1) Design components interact in a flexible way; 2) System functionalities are divided into different components so that developers can work concurrently, and the system will be easy to integrate and maintain; 3) The Controller and the View can be easily extend with the extension of the Model; 4) Encapsulation for the business rule can improve the reuse of modules.

H.T. Shen et al. (Eds.): APWeb 2006, LNCS 3842, pp. 1029 – 1032, 2006.

2 Struts Framework

Struts framework is an open source framework[2], and is used to develop Web applications with SERVLET and JSP technology. It has realized a good software design idea in a practical and expansible way, and has advantages of modularization, flexibility and reuse of components. Struts framework is an implementation of the MVC pattern, and includes the SERVLET and JSP tag libraries. It inherits each feature of MVC, and makes corresponding changes and expansions according to the J2EE[3].

Model is used to design and implement system business logic in a form of Java Bean. The concrete Action object is derived from the base Class Action according to different requests and completes the task of "what to do" by invoking the business component made by Bean.

In Struts, the Servlet called ActionServlet plays the role of the Controller. This control component is the entrance of all HTTP requests sent to Struts. It accepts all the requests and distributes them to the corresponding Action classes. The control component also is responsible with filling in ActionForm with the corresponding request parameters, and sends the ActionForm to the corresponding Action class. The Finally the Action class passes the control to a JSP file and the latter produces the View. All these control logics are configured by the XML file Struts-config.xml.

The View, mainly implemented by the JSP result page, separates the application logic and the presentation logic by coding user interface using the user-defined tag libraries provided by Struts. The Struts framework has established relationship between the View and the Model through the user-defined tags.

3 Application Based on Struts Framework

Software development procedure of Web application based on the Struts framework is explained by taking a user registration information system of a bookstore system for an example[4]. Its structure drawing sees Fig. 1.

JSP has the ability to custom tag libraries and include the Web component so it can implement custom-made component, containers and layout managers. Thus the Web

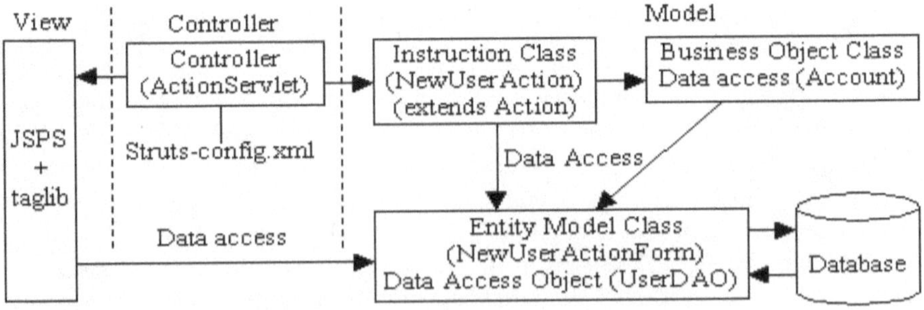

Fig. 1. Structure of the user registration system

application interface, which is easy to extend, reuse and maintain can be implemented. Tag libraries the Struts framework provides can enhance the development efficiency greatly. Therefore, according to demands, Struts bean, html, logic, template tags are quoted separately in the JSP files. In the user registration system, the user needs to fill in the detailed information and submit the form.

Building the Model component is a key task, because it includes business logic of the entire application. System status component (FormBean), also named entity model class, inherits from the ActionForm Class and is used to save form data. The bean Class used to save form data of registration page is:

```
package edu.hrbeu.ebookstore.action;
import org.apache.struts.action.*;
import javax.servlet.http.*;
public Class NewUserActionForm extends ActionForm
{private String userID;
private String password; …
public void setPassword(String password)
{this.password = password;}
public String getPassword()
{return password;}
public void setUserID(String userID)
{this.userID = userID;}
public String getUserID()
{return userID;} … }
```

Instruction component (ActionBean) which extends Action Class is mainly used to control the procedure of the application. After the registering user clicked "OK" button, the request from user would be transmitted by the servlet (Controller) to a ActionBean, "NewUserActon", which invokes the corresponding business logic component Account for processing, and later the request would be forwarded to the related JSP files. The program outline is listed below:

```
package edu.hrbeu.ebookstore.action;
public Class NewUserAction extends Action
{public ActionForward perform(ActionMapping
actionMapping, ActionForm actionForm,
HttpServletRequest httpServletRequest,
HttpServletResponse httpServletResponse)
{ … Account account = new Account();
Account.newAccount();
return new ActionForward("/index.jsp");}}
```

The Controller class need not be redesigned but uses the ActionServlet Class from Struts directly. The core of Struts framework is the Controller Class ActionServlet whose core is struts-config.xml, which is a configuration file containing the whole business procedure of application. During user registering, the newAccount.jsp can be used to implement the registering page; and the NewUserActionForm encapsulates the form data; the NewUserAction implements user registering (the business logic) and controls the procedure of application; the struts-config.xml configuration file implements the relationship among the registering page (newAccount.jsp), data bean (NewUserForm) and logic bean (NewUserAction), its configuration content is :

```
<form-beans>
<form-bean name ="newUserActionForm"
type="edu.hrbeu.ebookstore.action.NewUserActionForm"/>
… </form-beans>
<action-mappings>
<action name ="newUserActionForm"
type ="edu.hrbeu.ebookstore.action.NewUserAction"
validate ="true"
input ="/newAccount.jsp"
path ="/newUserAction"/> …
</action-mappings>
```

When the "OK" button on the registering page is clicked, user request will be submitted to the ActionServlet, which will map the URI of /newUserAction.do to com.hrbeu.ebookstore.NewUserAction, encapsulate the information of user registering to NewUserForm, and eventually invoke the NewUserAction to finish the registering and redirect to the page "index.jsp". Thus the Controller relates the View and Model through struts-config.xml containing the whole logic procedure of application, which is very important for both the early developing and the later maintaining and updating.

4 Conclusion

The adopting of Struts framework based on MVC design pattern to implement Web applications can make full use of the powerful functionalities and the platform-independent feature of J2EE. Struts is a excellent framework for J2EE MVC architecture, which separates the user interfaces and business logic, enable the proper cooperation between Web page designers and java programmers, and thus enhance the flexibility of application; meanwhile it uses ActionServlet with struts-config.xml to implement the navigation for the whole system, thus help developer to strengthen the whole control of system, and makes the system developing regular, easy to integrate, maintain and update.

References

1. Sun Microsystems, Inc.: Model-View-Controller. http://java.sun.com/blueprints/patterns/MVC.html, (2002)
2. J Wang, Fang Liu: JSP Programming Guide. Electronics Industry Publishing Press, Beijing (2002) 78-94
3. Holloway T.: Struts: a Solid Web-App Framework. http://www.fawcette.com/javapro/2002-04/magazine/features/tholloway/default.asp, (2002)
4. The Apache Software Foundation: http://struts.apache.org/struts-doc-1.0.2/userGuide/introduction.html, (2002)

Grid-Based Multi-scale PCA Method for Face Recognition in the Large Face Database

Haiyang Zhang, Huadong Ma, and Anlong Ming

Beijing Key Lab of Intelligent Telecommunications Software and Multimedia,
School of Computer Science & Technology,
Beijing University of Posts and Telecommunications, Beijing 100876, China
Zhhy_bupt@tom.com, mhd@bupt.edu.cn

Abstract. In this paper, we propose an efficient grid-based multi-scale PCA method in the large face database. This method divides the large face database into some small sub-face databases by maximizing the variance in the face sub-database and minimizing the variance between the face sub-databases, then it segments the recognition process into the local coarse profile recognition process and accurate detailed geometric sub-component analysis process, and assigns the local coarse profile recognition process to the nodes of the multimedia service grid to reduce the recognition time. Our experimental results show that with the increase of the face database, this method not only reduces the recognition time, but also remarkably increases the recognition precision, compared with other PCA methods.

1 Introduction

The multimedia service grid is an extensible architecture supporting multimedia processing and multimedia services in a grid computing environment [1, 2]. It can effectively supports traditional multimedia applications including VoD, video conference, graphic processing, and also easily expands new multimedia applications, for example, distributed graphic information processing and graphic information retrieving [3].

In the multimedia service grid, information, computing and storage resources in nodes can be shared with other nodes, so a client accepts a service from many heterogeneous nodes which are with different performances and located dispersedly, and the client may also provide this multimedia service to other clients as a server. So, the service model of the multimedia service grid is that many heterogeneous servers provide the clients with a multimedia service synchronously.

Face recognition is a very important task with great applications, such as identity authentication, access control, counter-strike, surveillance, content-based indexing, and video retrieval system [4]. PCA is to find a set of mutual orthogonal basis functions that capture the directions of maximum variance in the data and for which the coefficients are pairwise decorrelated. Independent Component Analysis (ICA) [5], Nonlinear PCA (NLPCA) [6], and Kernel PCA (KPCA) [7] are all the generalizations of PCA to address high order statistical dependencies. Kernel-based Fisher Discriminant Analysis (KFDA) [12] extracts nonlinear discriminating features.

H.T. Shen et al. (Eds.): APWeb 2006, LNCS 3842, pp. 1033 – 1040, 2006.

It is well known that the larger the face database growing, the smaller the variance between the faces becomes, and the harder distinguishing a face from other faces becomes. Because PCA method utilizes the statistical regularities of pixel intension variations, it is impressible to the number of the faces. So if the number of the face database is beyond a limit, the recognition accuracy of PCA remarkably reduces with the increase of the number of the face database.

So, we propose an efficient Grid-based Multi-scale PCA face recognition (GMPCA) method which divides the large face database into some sub-databases by maximizing the variance in the sub-databases and minimizing the variance between sub-databases. For reducing the recognition time in the sub-databases, this method segments the recognition process into the Local Coarse Profile Recognition (LCPR) process and the accurately detailed Geometric Sub-Component Analysis (DGSCA) process, and assigns LCPR process with sub-databases to multimedia service grid nodes. In LCPR, we compress photos by the Gabor wavelet, and adopt principal component analysis method in sub-face databases to reduce the complexity of LCPR process. Eventually, we construct the face database with the recognition results of LCPR process, and in this database, accurately recognize the face by accurately DGSCA algorithm.

The paper is organized as follows. In the next section, we briefly describe the grid-based multi-scale method in large face database. Section 3 shows the experimental results. The conclusion and future work are presented in section 4.

2 Grid-Based Multi-scale PCA Method

In the large face database, the whole PCA method has large computing complexity, and need renewedly compute the primary eigenvectors and all projections on them of all images in the database when adding a face image into the database. So in GMPCA method, we firstly adopt LCPR algorithm which locally independently extracts primary eigenvectors in every sub-database. This algorithm reduces the computing complexity of the extracting primary eigenvectors process which exponentially increases with the number of samples augmenting, and decreases the scale of modification when a new face image is inserted into the sub-database, and improves the distance between classes which belong to different persons.

For the face images filtered by LCPR process, we adopt detailed DGSCA algorithm which accurately recognizes the face image by integrating the profile information, the detailed information and geometric features information.

2.1 Gabor-Wavelet Transformation

Wavelet transformation is an increasingly popular tool in the image processing and the computer vision. Wavelet transformation has the nice features of space-frequency localization and multi-resolutions. The main reasons for the popularity of wavelet lie in its complete theoretical framework, the great flexibility for choosing bases and the low computational complexity.

Gabor wavelets were introduced to image analysis due to their biological relevance and computational properties. The Gabor wavelets, whose kernels are similar to the 2D receptive field profiles of the mammalian cortical simple cells, exhibit desirable characteristics of spatial locality and orientation selectivity, and are optimally localized in the space and frequency domains. The Gabor wavelets (kernels, filters) can be defined as follows:

$$\psi_{u,v}(z) = \frac{\|k_{u,v}\|^2}{\sigma^2} e^{-\frac{\|k_{u,v}\|^2 \|z\|^2}{2\sigma^2}} [e^{ik_{u,v}z} - e^{-\frac{\sigma^2}{2}}] \tag{1}$$

Where u and v define the orientation and scale of the Gabor kernel, $z=(x, y)$, $\|.\|$ denotes the norm operator, and the wave vector $k_{u,v}$ is defined as follow:

$$k_{u,v} = k_v e^{i\phi_u} \tag{2}$$

Where $k_v=k_{max}/f^v$ and $\phi_u=\pi u/8$, k_{max} is the maximum frequency, and f is the spacing factor between kernels in the frequency domain.

In our experiments, input images are convolved with the Gabor wavelets given as Fig.1.

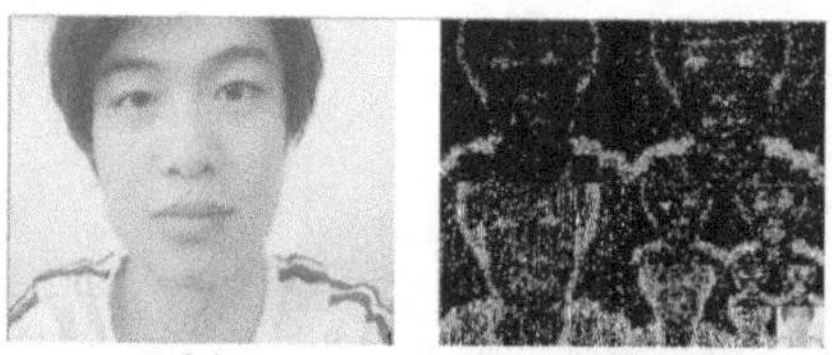

(a) (b)

Fig. 1. (a) the original image, (b) the three-level wavelet decomposition

2.2 Face Database Segmenting Policy

The sample face images firstly are transformed by PCA, and we represent all of the vectors in a set of n d-dimensional samples $x_1,x_2,\ldots\ldots,x_n$, with zero mean, by a single vector $y=\{y_1,y_2,\ldots,y_n\}$. Specifically, we find a linear mapping from the d-dimensional space to a line. Without loss of generality, we denote the transformation vector as w. That is, $w^T x_i=y_i$. Actually, the magnitude of w is of no real significance because it merely scales y_i.. PCA aims to extract a subspace in which the variance is maximized. Its objective function is as follows:

$$\delta_y = \sum_{i=1}^{n}(y_i - \overline{y})^2 \, , \; \overline{y} \equiv \frac{1}{n}\sum_{i=1}^{n} y_i \tag{3}$$

Because the larger the variance of y_i is, the greater the distance between the face images is. D_1, D_2 ..., D_n represent sub-databases, the set of images in which have the maximum average of variance in them, and the minimum variance between them.

We study the set D_1, D_2... D_n, which meet the condition as follows:

$$D_i = \{\, y_j \in D_i \mid \max \frac{w^T S_B w}{w^T S_W w} \,\} \tag{4}$$

where S_B is the between-class diverse matrix, $S_B=(m_1-m_2)(m_1-m_2)^T$. S_W is the within-class diverse matrix,

$$S_w=\sum_{j=1}^{2}\sum_{i=1}^{N_j}(x_i^j-m_j)(x_i^j-m_j)^T \tag{5}$$

where m_j is the average of x_i in the D.

The face database which includes the images transformed by three-level wavelet decomposing is divided into several sub-databases. We initialize these databases by the method mentioned above. If a new face image needs to be added to the face database, we firstly insert the image into the sub-database with the maximum variance. In this sub-database, we compute the primary eigenvectors of local images and the projections of every image on these primary eigenvectors. If the new variance is less than precious variance to a limited value decided by experiment, then we must select other sub-database including the maximum variance excluding the first one to be inserted the face image in.

2.3 Local Coarse Profile Recognition Algorithm

For improving the recognition rapidity, we adopt the LCPR algorithm, which synchronously executes the recognition process with probe T on every sub-database. In j^{th} sub-database, we compute the N_j primary eigenvectors on the local images transformed by Gabor-wavelet, where $N_j=n\delta_y$, n is the coefficient obtained from experiment. Then, we compute the projections of every face image and the probe image T on the eigenvectors, and the distances between the sample face x and the probe face T. The distance is represented as follows:

$$s_x=\|\bar{y}_x-\bar{y}_T\|=\frac{y_x^T y_T}{\|y_x\|\|y_T\|}=\frac{\sum_{i=1}^{N_{Dj}}(y_{xi}\times y_{Ti})}{\sqrt{\sum_{i=1}^{N_{Dj}}y_{xi}^2\times\sum_{i=1}^{N_{Dj}}y_{Ti}^2}} \tag{6}$$

where y_x, y_T represent the projection vector of x and T, respectively,

At last, we select a set of the face images $\{x\,|\,s_x>s_L\}$ from every sub-database as the result of this sub-process, where s_L is the limited value, we can alter the recognition accuracy by adjusting s_L , and the larger s_L is, the lower the recognition accuracy is, and the lower the false recognition accuracy is.

2.4 Detailed Geometric Sub-component Analysis Algorithm

We construct the original face database with the images filtered by LCPR algorithm, and in this database, we compute the fifty primary eigenvectors of the whole face which can approximately distinguish the face image from others and compute the projections on these eigenvectors of every image. The eigenfaces are shown in Fig.2.

Fig. 2. The Eigenface of the sample face in face database

For improving the recognition accuracy, we obtain the geometric features of these images, as example, nose, eyes and mouth, and compute the distributing size including the distance of the two eyes d_e, the distance between the midpoint of the two eyes and the noise d_{en}, the distance of the midpoint of the two eyes and the mouth d_{em}. These features denote the profile of the face. Then, we locate the rectangle areas of the eyes, the nose, and the mouth, and extract the fifty primary eigenvectors of every rectangle area which represent the detailed information of every face image. Then we compute the projections on these eigenvectors of every image.

Eventually, we compute the distance between the sample face x_i and the probe face T by integrating the projections on the whole primary eigenvectors, the geometric features of the profile, and the projection on primary eigenvectors of the every five sense organs rectangle area.

We define the match degree between the sample face x and the probe face T as follows:

$$M = aS_x + \sum_{i=1}^{4} b_i S_{xi} + c(d_{emx}\frac{d_{eT}}{d_{ex}} - d_{emT}) + d(d_{enx}\frac{d_{eT}}{d_{ex}} - d_{enT}) \quad (7)$$

where a, b_i, c, d are the coefficients decided by experiment, S_{xi} denotes the distance about the projection on primary eigenvectors of the every five sense organs rectangle area, d_{emx} and d_{emT}, represent the distance of the midpoint of the two eyes and the mouth on x and T, respectively, d_{enx} and d_{enT} represent the distance between the midpoint of the two eyes and the noise on x and T, respectively, d_{ex} and d_{eT} represent the distance of the two eyes on x and T, respectively.

Finally, we select the face image x with the maximum M as the recognition result.

2.5 Scheduling Policy for Multimedia Service Grid

If the face image database is very large, we need divide it into many sub-databases. So, we could assign these sub-databases on the multimedia service grid nodes to reduce the recognition time and enhance the robustness and flexibility of the recognition process by adequately utilizing storage resources and computing resources of nodes.

We distribute all original face images of persons in many grid nodes, which have enough storage ability to keep these images. The face images transformed by Gabor-wavelet are divided into many sub-databases by the face database segmenting policy, and the original images are divided in accordance with the transformed images. The database of eigenvalues, eigenvectors and the projection of the face images on these eigenvectors in every sub-database, are entirely distributed into all multimedia service grid nodes.

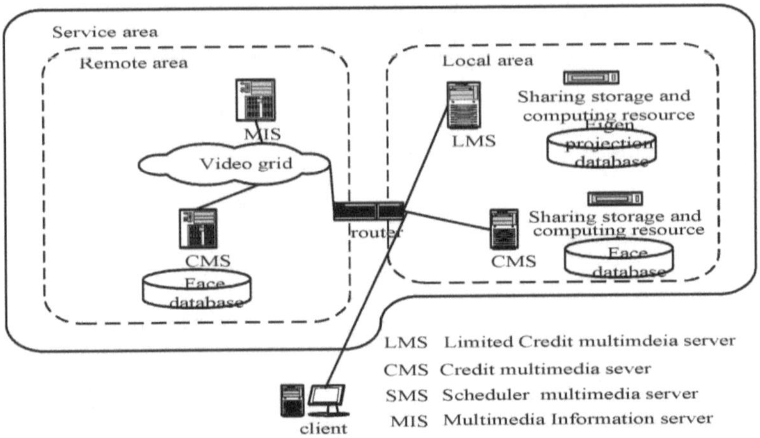

Fig. 3. Multimedia grid service framework of the face recognition

So, the framework of the face recognition service on the multimedia service grid includes the LMS (Limited credit Multimedia Server), CMS (Credit Multimedia Server), SMS (Scheduler Multimedia Server) and MIS (Multimedia Information Server). The framework is shown in Fig.3.

In the framework, LMS nodes denote the distrust nodes which only storage the eigenvalues, eigenvectors and the projection of the face images, and execute the LCFR policy; CMS nodes not only work as the LMS, but also storage the original face image sub-databases and execute the DGSCA policy; SMS node analyses the recognition request, and decomposes the recognition task, assigns the sub-tasks on the nodes, and keeps the validity of the face images database; MIS node is the access of the multimedia grid service, by which the client can interact with multimedia grid service.

When recognition process begins, the probe face image is sent to every node with the feature database of the transformed images. It is projected on the primary eigenvectors, and then every node can obtain the aggregate of similar images with probe image. And these nodes send the identity of these similar images to the node including the all original face images. And this node computes the match result by DGSCA algorithm, and sent it to MIS via SMS

3 Experiments

In experiments, we adopt two sample databases: one is the special face database involving the chromophotographs shot in our system, which can not guarantee the quality of the face images, such as the horizontal and vertical angle of the face and the distance between the face and the camera, and the illumination on the face. This database contains 1000 face images from 50 individuals. Another is the HMMC photo database including many kinds of black-and-white photographes, in which the face has very large proportion, and has very well illumination. It is a common test face database, and includes many expression face images of same person. This database contains 1000 face images from 100 individuals.

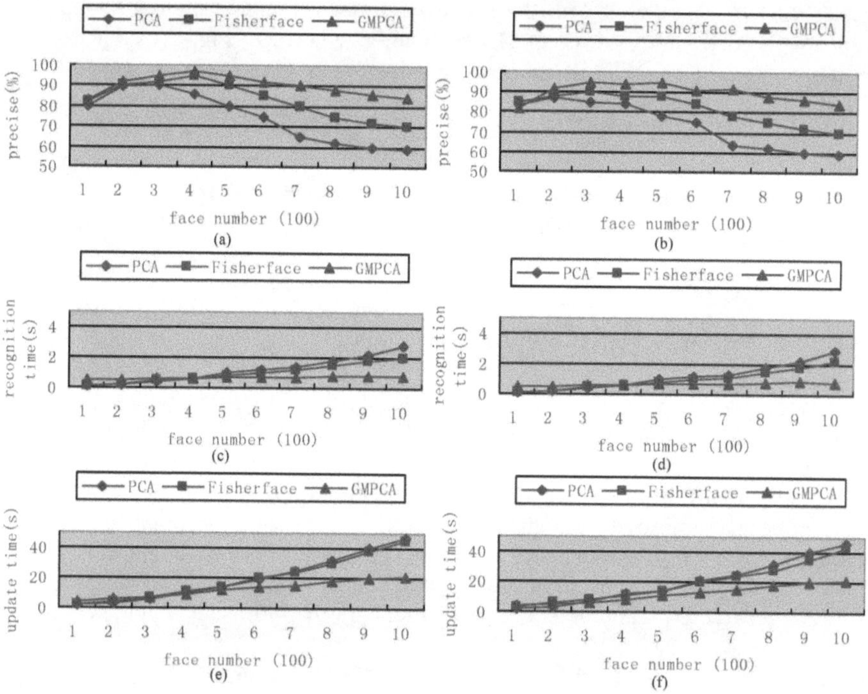

Fig. 4. (a) the comparison of the recognition accuracy in the special face database, (b) the comparison of the recognition accuracy in the HMMC face database, (c) the comparison of the recognition time in the special face database, (d) the comparison of recognition time in the HMMC face database, (e) the comparison of the update time in the special face database, (f) the comparison of the update time in the HMMC face database

We compare the recognition accuracy, the recognition time, and the time of updating database of our system (GMPCA) with PCA method and Fisherface method, respectively in the special face database and the HMCC face database.

The hardware of experiment includes the twenty nodes, each is CPU: P4 3.2G, memory: 512M, hard disk: 200G and the 1000M star network connecting them together. These nodes are constructed as a multimedia grid by Globus 3.2, and we deploy the scheduling service and the recognition services on it.

Fig.4 (a) compares the recognition accuracy with the increase of the scale of the database in the special face database; Fig.4 (b) compares the recognition accuracy with the increase of the scale of the database in the HMMC face database; Fig.4 (c) and Fig.4 (d) respectively compare the recognition time in the special face database and the HMMC face database; the update time is compared in Fig.4 (e) and Fig.4 (f).

Fig.4 (a) shows that the recognition accuracy of GMPCA, PCA, and Fisherface methods reach the maximum approximately at the 400, this could be attributed to the fact that the increase of the number of the primary component could improves the recognition accuracy of GMPCA, PCA, and Fisherface methods. When the number of the databases increases beyond 400, the recognition accuracy of PCA and the Fisherface rapidly deteriorate, and the recognition accuracy of GMPCA smoothly reduces. Fig.4 (b) represents that the expression and illumination of the face would greatly affect PCA, and less affect GMPCA and Fisherface. Fig.4 (c) and Fig.4 (d) show that when the number of the database less than 400, the recognition time of GMPCA is larger than that of PCA and Fisherface, because of the delay of transformation in network and the time cost of scheduling process, and when the number of the database is beyond 400, the time cost of PCA and Fisherface is remarkable larger than that of GMPCA. Fig.4 (e) and Fig.4 (f) represent that the update time of PCA and Fisherface are larger than that of GMPCA in a large face database.

4 Conclusion and Future Work

In this paper, we propose an efficient face recognition algorithm which divides the recognition process into local coarse profile recognition process and accurately detailed geometric sub-component analysis process, and it assigns the recognition process to the nodes of multimedia service grid. Our experiment results show that this method not only improves recognition speed, but also remarkably increases the recognition precision in a large face database, compared with other PCA method. In the future, we need to improve the efficiency of the scheduling algorithm on multimedia service grid, and do some experiments in the large face database.

Acknowledgement. The work is supported by the Co-sponsored Project of Beijing Committee of Education (SYS100130422), the NGI Demo Project of National Development and Reform Committee, the Specialized Research Fund for the Doctoral Program of Higher Education (20050013010) and the NCET Program of MOE,China.

References

[1] I. Foster, C. Kesselman, and S. Tuecke. "The Anatomy of the Grid: Enabling Scalable Virtual Organizations", *International Journal of Supercomputer Applications*, 15(3), 2001.

[2] H. Zhang, H. Ma, "Virtual Semantic Resource Routing Algorithm for Multimedia Information Grid", *GCC2004*, LNCS 3252, pp. 173-181.

[3] S. Basu, S. Adhikari, etc, "mmGrid: distributed resource management infrastructure for multimedia applications", *Parallel and Distributed Processing Symposium International Proceedings*, pp. 8, 2003.

[4] X. Wang, X. Tang, "Unified Subspace Analysis for Face Recognition", *Proc. Int'l Conf. Computer Vision*, pp. 679-686, 2003.

[5] P.C. Yunen, J.H. Lai, "Face Representation Using Independent Component Analysis", *Pattern Recognition,* vol. 35, pp. 1247-1257, 2002.

[6] M.A. Kramer, "Nonlinear Principle Components Analysis Using Autoassociative Neural Networks," *Am. Instit. Chemical Eng. J.*, 32(2), pp. 1010, 1991.

[7] M. Yang, N. Ahuja, and D. Kriegman, "Face Recognition Using Kernel Eigenfaces", *Proc. Int'l Conf. Image Processing*, vol. 1, pp. 37-40, 2000.

[8] Q. Liu, R. Huang, H. Lu, and S. Ma, "Kernel-Based Optimized Feature Vectors Selection and Discriminant Analysis for Face Recognition," *Proc. Int'l Conf. Pattern Recognition*, pp. 362-365, 2002.

Grid-Based Parallel Elastic Graph Matching Face Recognition Method

Haiyang Zhang and Huadong Ma

Beijing Key Lab of Intelligent Telecommunications Software and Multimedia, School of Computer Science & Technology, Beijing University of Posts and Telecommunications, Beijing 100876, China
zhhy_bupt@tom.com, mhd@bupt.edu.cn

Abstract. This paper presents a grid-based parallel elastic graph matching face recognition method. We firstly divide the face into several sub-regions by geometric features decomposing algorithm, and match the sub-regions of probe face image with the corresponding sub-regions of the sample faces by sub-region elastic graph matching algorithm, and these matching processes can be assigned onto a lot of nodes in the multimedia service grid and scheduled by the optimal costs algorithm. Eventually, we obtain the match degrees between the probe face and the sample faces by integrating the weighted matched results of sub-regions. We carried out extensive experiments on the special face database and HMMC standard face recognition database. Compared with the previous algorithms, our algorithm offers better recognition accuracy and more rapid recognition speed.

1 Introduction

Multimedia service grid is an extensible architecture supporting multimedia processing and services in a grid computing environment [1, 2]. Its applications involve graphics, visualization, multimedia streaming. It can effectively support the traditional multimedia applications including VoD, video conference, graphic processing, and also easily expand the new multimedia application, for example, distributed graphic information processing and graphic information retrieving [3, 4].

In the multimedia service grid, information, computing and storage resources in a node can be shared with other nodes. So heterogeneous grid nodes with different performances are located dispersedly, and they can provide the clients with multimedia services and the clients may also provide the multimedia services to other clients as a server. Thus, the network and these servers have very large irrelevance, and the probability that all these servers are not fault is vary little. So, the service model of multimedia service grid is that many heterogeneous servers provide the clients with a multimedia service synchronously. There are more flexible resource scheduling algorithms and available resources in grid than those in traditional network, so the multimedia service grid can guarantee the QoS and efficiency of multimedia service.

Face recognition is a very important task with great applications, such as identity authentication, access control, surveillance, content-based indexing and video

H.T. Shen et al. (Eds.): APWeb 2006, LNCS 3842, pp. 1041 – 1048, 2006.

retrieval systems [5]. Compared to classical pattern recognition problems, face recognition is much more difficult because there are usually many individuals (classes), only a few images per person, so a face recognition system must recognize faces by extrapolating from the training samples. Various changes in face images also present great challenge, and a face recognition system must be robust with respect to much variability of face images such as viewpoint, illumination, and facial expression conditions.

Eigenface, elastic matching, geometric features are three most representative face recognition approaches. Geometric features method based on the relative positions of eyes, nose, and mouth [6]. The prerequisite for the success of this approach is an accurate facial feature detection scheme, which, however, remains a very difficult problem. Eigenface analysis methods, such as PCA, LDA, and Bayes, have been extensively studied for face recognition in recent years. The Eigenface method, such as PCA, uses the Karhunen-Loeve transform to produce the most expressive subspace for the face representation and recognition, and PCA usually gives high similarities indiscriminately for two images from a single person or from two different persons [7]. Elastic graph matching approach has a great success on face recognition. Vertices are labeled with collections of features to describe the gray-level distribution locally with high precision and globally with lower precision, providing for great robustness with respect to deformation. This approach has high time complexity, so it can hardly be applied into the practical system [8].

In this paper, we firstly decompose the face as several sub-regions by some geometrics features of the face and compare the sub-regions of probe face image with the corresponding sub-regions of the face samples by Sub-region Elastic Graph Matching (SEGM) algorithm, and these processes are assigned onto a lot of nodes in the multimedia service grid and scheduled by the optimal costs algorithm. Eventually, we get the match agrees between the probe face and the sample faces by integrating these weighted match results of SEGM algorithm.

The paper is organized as follows. In the next section, we briefly describe grid-based parallel elastic matching face recognition method. Section 3 shows the experimental results. The conclusion and future work are presented in section 4.

2 Grid-Based Parallel Elastic Graph Matching Method

The elastic matching method has large computing complexity, so for reducing the recognition time in the large face databases, Grid-based Parallel Elastic Graph Matching (GPEGM) method standardizes the every face by defining the inner of the eyes as fixed, and filters many faces by comparing the stable features distance and the rigid matching distance with the probe face, and then, decompose the recognition process as several sub-processes, and assigns the parallel recognition sub-processes with the sub-region databases to the multimedia service grid nodes by the optimal scheduler algorithm. In the sub-region elastic graph matching process, we segment the face into sub-regions according to the geometric features.

2.1 Geometric Features Decomposing Algorithm

We adopt face dynamic model to detect the location of the face, and get the location of eyes. When the eyes are located, we roughly frame the rectangle areas of two eyes by their distance. Then, we must search the coordination of the inner and the outer canthus of two eyes by examining the horizontal and vertical intensity signature, and we can obtain the axis of the face, which crosses the middle of the two inner canthuses, and is upright with the joint lines of the inner and the outer canthus of one eye. The joint line of the two corners of mouth is upright with the axis of face, so we can obtain the rough rectangle of mouth and get the two corners of the mouth by examining the horizontal and vertical intensity signature.

The quadratic derivative has the maximum value in the cheekbone of the face, so we can obtain the coordinates of two cheekbones, and the quadratic derivative can be computed by Laplacian. The nose point locates at the axis, and the simple derivative of the grads at the direction of the axis has the maximum value. Then we obtain the features of the inner and outer canthus of two eyes, two corners of the mouth, two cheekbones, and the nose point, which are shown in Fig.1 (a).

We can get some triangles which do not transform with the varieties of the facial expression, and are distinguished between different individuals, such as the triangle constructing with the inner canthus of the two eyes and the nose point, the triangle constructing with the inner and the outer canthus of the left eye and the nose point, the triangle constructing with the inner and the outer canthus of the right eye and the nose point, the triangle constructing with the two cheekbones and the nose point. These triangles are shown as Fig.1 (b).

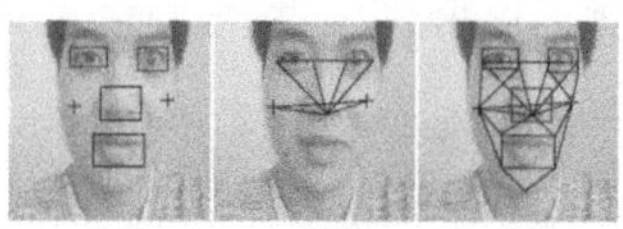

(a) (b) (c)

Fig. 1. (a) the location of the features on the face; (b) the location of the stable triangles on the face; (c) the sub-regions on the face

So, we can decompose the face into some sub-regions shown in Fig.1(c). Every sub-region has different weight in recognition process, because the two eyes, the mouth, and the nose are the facial features, so these sub-regions have larger weight than others, and because these stable triangles have little variations, so these sub-regions have larger weight than others excluding the facial features. The upper face has less variation than the lower face, so the upper sub-regions have larger weight than the lower sub-regions.

2.2 Sub-region Elastic Graph Matching Algorithm

In SEGM algorithm, a face is segmented into sub-regions according to the geometric features, and then the elastic graph matching sub-processes are synchronously executed on every sub-region, and the match results of sub-regions are integrated into the final match result.

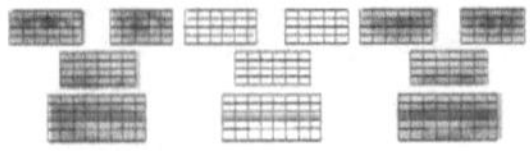

(a) (b) (c)

Fig. 2. (a) the sub-regions of the probe face and the elastic temples of the sub-regions; (b) the elastic temples of the sub-regions; (c) the rigid matching result on detected elastic sub-regions

The SEGM algorithm can be divided into two stages, that is, rigid matching and deformation matching respectively. For rigid matching, the elastic template of the sub-region moves rigidly in the detected elastic sub-region to make the right-up point of the sub-region superposition, and select this point as the match point. This process can be seen in Fig.2.

The second stage is deformation matching. In this process, we change the position of every key-point in the elastic template dynamically and perform matching repeatedly on every sub-region. The deformation of every grid point is limited in the area constructed by the eight grid points around this point to improve the rapidity of the deformation matching process. The energy function is applied to measure the best matching. It is defined as follow:

$$E(M) = \sum_i -\alpha_i \left| \frac{\langle c_i, x_j \rangle}{\|c_i\| \|x_j\|} \right| + \beta \sqrt{\Delta i_x^2 + \Delta i_y^2} \tag{1}$$

This energy function is composed of two parts. The first part indicates the similarity between them, where c_i is the feature vector at the ith key-point in the elastic template, x_i is the feature vector at the corresponding point in the detected elastic graph, a_i is the matching weight of the ith key-point that can be modified dynamically through learning to obtain better recognition results; the second part stands for the deformation of the elastic template, where Δi_x, Δi_y is the deformation of the ith key-point in x and y coordinate respectively. The further the template deforms, the higher this value is. β is the weight showing how template deformation affects the whole energy function.

Procedure 2.1. Deformation matching process of the sub-regions

Input: the elastic template G_t, the detected elastic sub-regions G_d;

Initial: $E=\infty$;

(1) select the right-up point g_x of the elastic temple G_t as the initial point;

(2) g_x moves to the right-up point among the rectangle constructing by the eight points of G_d around it and compute the $Ex(M)$, if $Ex(M)< E$ then $E=Ex(M)$;

(3) g_x moves to the left or down point among the rectangle constructing by the eight points of G_d around it, if this point is not null, then compute the $Ex(M)$, if $Ex(M)< E$ then $E=Ex(M)$ and goto(3), else goto (4);

(4) select the points g_x left to or down to the former point. If this point is not null then Goto(2) else goto(5);

(5) end.

Output: E

If obtaining the matching result of all sub-regions, we integrate them as follow:

$$E(SA) = a[E(M_{el}) + E(M_{er})] + bE(M_m) + cE(M_n) + d[\sum_{i=1}^{tn} E(M_{ti})] + e[\sum_{i=1}^{ln} E(M_{li})] \quad (2)$$

where a, b, c, d, e are respectively the weight of the corresponding sub-regions, and $a>c>b>d>e$, $E(M_{el})$ and $E(M_{er})$ denote the match degree of the left eye and the right eye sub-region, $E(M_m)$ is the match degree of the mouth sub-region, $E(M_{ti})$ denotes the match degree of the stable triangle sub-region, and $E(M_{li})$ is the match degree of the other sub-regions. tn represents the number of the stable triangle sub-regions, and ln represents the number of other sub-regions.

2.3 Optimal Cost Scheduling Algorithm on the Multimedia Service Grid

The GPEGM algorithm has high computing complexity, so we assign the parallel recognition sub-processes with the sub-region databases to the multimedia grid nodes by the optimal scheduling algorithm to improve the recognition speed.

The databases of sub-regions for the face images with the SEGM sub-process are entirely distributed into all grid nodes, and the integrating process of all sub-region matching results is assigned onto the grid node, which has enough storage ability and computing ability to accomplish the integrating process rapidly.

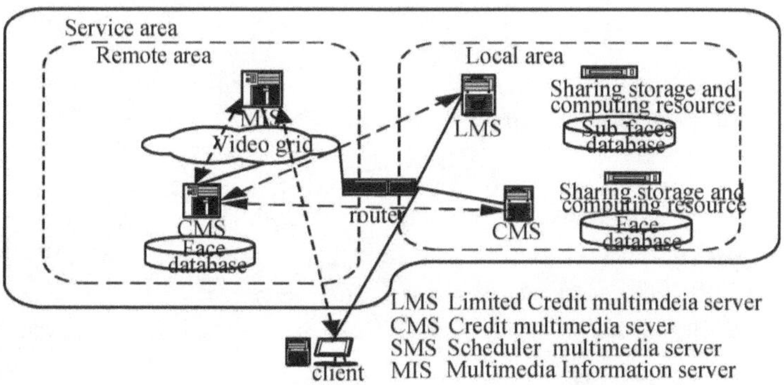

Fig. 3. Multimedia grid service framework of the face recognition

So, the framework of the face recognition service on the multimedia service grid involves the LMS (Limited credit Multimedia Server), CMS (Credit Multimedia Server), SMS (Scheduler Multimedia Server) and MIS (Multimedia Information Server). The framework is shown in Fig.3.

In the framework, LMS nodes denote the distrust nodes which only storage the database of sub-regions, and execute the SEGM sub-process; CMS nodes not only work as the LMS but also storage the original face images and execute the SEGM sub-process, and the segmenting process of sub-regions and integrating the matching result of all sub-regions process; SMS node analyzes the recognition request, and decomposes the recognition task, and assigns the sub-tasks to the nodes, and keeps the validity of the face images database; MIS node is the access of the multimedia grid service, by which the client can interact with multimedia grid service.

Definition 2.1. The ability of a set of LMSs and CMSs is defined as $\Omega_A = \{A_1, A_2, \ldots A_n\}$, $A_i = (A_{i,s}, A_{i,m}, A_{i,n}, A_{i,r}, A_{i,c})$, where $A_{i,s}, A_{i,m}, A_{i,n}$ *and* $A_{i,r}$ denote the storage ability, the computing ability, the network ability, and the credit ability of the grid node, respectively. $A_{i,c}$ is the cost of getting service from this grid node.

Definition 2.2. The recognition requirements of a set of face sub-database can be defined as $\Omega_R = \{R_1, R_2 \ldots R_m\}$, $R_i = (R_{i,s}, R_{i,m})$, where $R_{i,s}$ and $R_{i,m}$ denote the storage requirement, the computing requirement of the node, respectively.

Definition 2.3. The cost of ith LMS or CMS is defined as:

$$C_i = \frac{\alpha A_{i,c}}{\beta A_{i,m} + \gamma A_{i,s}} \tag{3}$$

where α, β, γ are the coefficients and decided by experiment, for the LMS, $\beta >> \gamma$, because the node mainly executes the computing function, for the CMS, $\beta \approx \gamma$, because the node executes the storage function and computing function.

Procedure 2.2. The optimal cost scheduling algorithm

Input: Probe face x, Ω_R, Ω_A, Ω_R initialized by face database segmenting policy;

Initial: Ω_S =null, $C_t = \infty$;

(1) if Ω_R <>Null then select the largest sub-database R_i from Ω_R, delete it from Ω_R and goto (2), else goto (6);

(2) if Ω_A <>Null then select the A_i from Ω_A, delete it from Ω_A, and goto (3), else goto (5), A_i in the local area has high priority;

(3) if $A_{i,s} > R_{i,s}$, and $A_{i,r}$ =*TRUE* then goto (4) else goto (2);

(4) compute C_i, and if $C_i < C_t$ then $C_t = C_i$, goto (2);

(5) assign the sub-database with R_i to the node with A_i, and segment the faces in this sub-database as some sub-region databases Ω_S, $\Omega_R = \{R_{i1}, R_{i2} \ldots R_{il}\}$, $R_{ij} = (R_{ij,s}, R_{ij,m})$ by the geometric features, and initialize the Ω_A, and goto (1);

(6) if Ω_S<>Null then select the largest R_{ij} from Ω_S, delete it from Ω_S, and goto (7), else goto (11);

(7) if Ω_A <>Null then select A_i from Ω_A, delete it from Ω_A, goto (8), else goto (10);

(8) if $A_{i,s} > R_{ij,s}$ then goto (9), else goto (7);

(9) compute C_i, and if $C_i < C_t$ then $C_t = C_i$ goto (7);

(10) assign the sub-database with R_{ij} to the node with A_i, execute the recognition sub-process on it, initialize Ω_A, and goto (6);

(11) end.

3 Experiments

The recognition precision is decided by the precision of the feature comparing process, and rigid matching and deformation matching process, and the integrating process. In the deformation matching process, the grid nodes near the boundary of sub-regions can not move to other sub-regions, so this may reduce the recognition precise, but the matching process in sub-regions become accurate to get optimal matching result.

In experiments, we adopt two sample databases: one is the special face database involving the chromophotographs shot in our system, which can not guarantee the quality of the face images, such as the horizontal and vertical angle of the face and the distance between the face and the camera, and the illumination on the face. This database contains 1000 face images from 50 individuals. Another is the HMMC photo database including many kinds of black-and-white photographes, in which the face has very large proportion and very well illumination. It is a common test face database, and involves many expression face images of same person. This database contains 1000 face images from 100 individuals.

In experiment, we compare the recognition accuracy and the recognition time of our algorithm with the PCA algorithm and Fisherface method, respectively in the special face database and the HMCC face database. The hardware of experiment includes the twenty nodes, each is CPU: P4 3.2G, memory: 512M, hard disk: 200G and the 1000M star network connecting them together. These nodes are constructed as a multimedia service grid by Globus 3.2, and we deploy the scheduling service and the recognition services on it.

Fig.4 (a) describes the comparison of the recognition accuracy with the increase of the scale of the database in the special face database; Fig.4 (b) shows the recognition accuracy with the increase of the scale of the database in the HMMC face database; Fig.4 (c) and Fig.4 (d) respectively compare the recognition time in the special face database and the HMMC face database.

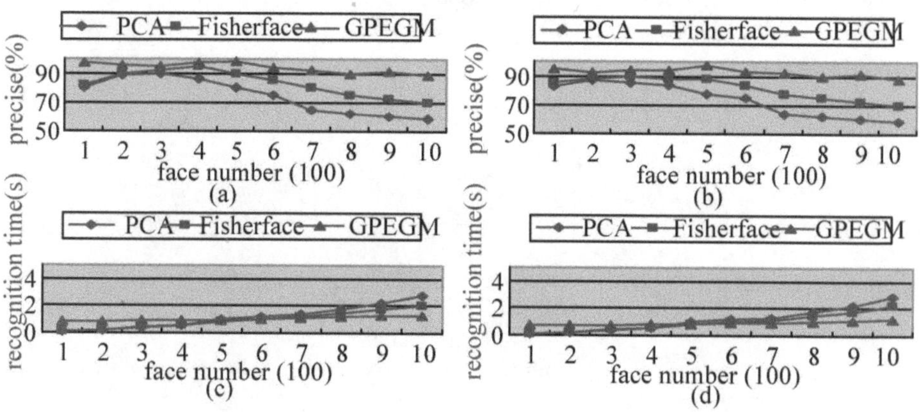

Fig. 4. (a) the comparison of the recognition accuracy in the special face database; (b) the comparison of the recognition accuracy in the HMMC face database; (c) the comparison of the recognition time in the special face database; (d) the comparison of the recognition time in the HMMC face database

Fig.4 (a) shows that the recognition accuracy of PCA and Fisherface methods reach the maximum approximately at the 400 images, this could be attributed to the fact that the increase of the number of the primary component could improves the recognition accuracy of PCA, and Fisherface methods. When the number of the databases increases beyond 400, the recognition accuracy of PCA and the Fisherface rapidly deteriorate. The recognition accuracy of GPEGM smoothly changes with the increase of the number of the face database. Fig.4 (b) represents that the expression of the face would greatly affect PCA, and less affect GPEGM and Fisherface.

Fig.4 (c) and Fig.4 (d) show that when the number of the database is less than 500, the recognition time of GPEGM is larger than that of PCA and Fisherface, because of the transmission delay in network and time cost of the scheduling process, and when the number of the database is beyond 500, the time cost of PCA and Fisherface is remarkably larger than that of GPEGM.

4 Conclusion

This paper presents a grid-based parallel elastic graph matching face recognition method. We decompose the face into several sub-regions by some geometric features of the face, and match the sub-regions of probe face image with the corresponding sub-regions of the face image samples by sub-region elastic graph matching algorithm, and these matching processes can be assigned onto a lot of nodes in multimedia service grid and scheduled by the optimal cost algorithm. In the future, we will modify the segmenting, the deforming matching and the scheduling algorithm to improve the recognition accuracy and reduce the recognition time.

Acknowledgement. The work is supported by the Co-sponsored Project of Beijing Committee of Education (SYS100130422), the NGI Demo Project of National Development and Reform Committee, the Specialized Research Fund for the Doctoral Program of Higher Education (20050013010) and the NCET Program of MOE, China.

References

[1] I. Foster, C. Kesselman, and S. Tuecke, "The anatomy of the grid: Enabling scalable virtual organizations", *International Journal of Supercomputer Applications,* 15(3), 2001.
[2] H. Zhang, H. Ma, "Virtual Semantic Resource Routing Algorithm for Multimedia Information Grid", *GCC2004*, LNCS 3252, pp. 173-181.
[3] A. Zaia, D. Bruneo, A. Puliafito, "A scalable grid-based multimedia server", *13th IEEE International Workshops on Infrastructure for Collaborative Enterprises*, pp:337 – 342,2004.
[4] S. Basu, S. Adhikari, R. Kumar, "mmGrid: distributed resource management infrastructure for multimedia applications", *International Conference on Parallel and Distributed Processing Symposium*, 2003.
[5] X. Wang, X. Tang, "Unified Subspace Analysis for Face Recognition", *Proc. Int'l Conf. Computer Vision,* pp. 679-686, 2003.
[6] T. Kanada, "Picture Processing by Computer Complex and Recognition of Human Faces", Dept. Inform. Sci., Kyoto Univ., Tech. Rep., 1973.
[7] H. Kim, D. Kim, and S.Y. Bang, "Face Recognition Using LDA Mixture Model," *Proc. Int'l Conf. Pattern Recognition,* pp. 486-489, 2002.
[8] Zhan Yongzhao, Ye Jingfu, Niu Dejiao, Cao Peng, "Facial expression recognition based on Gabor wavelet transformation and elastic templates matching", *Third International Conference on Image and Graphics,* pp: 254 – 257, 2004.

Web Service-Based Study on BPM Integrated Application for Aero-Manufacturing

Zhi-qiang Jiang[1,2], Xi-lan Feng[1], Jin-fa Shi[1], and Xue-wen Zong[2]

[1] Department of Industrial Engineering, Zhengzhou Institute of Aeronautics,
Zhengzhou 450015, Henan Province, China
{newroom, CAD}@zzia.edu.cn
[2] School of Mechanical Engineering, Xi'an Jiaotong University,
Xi'an 710049, Shaanxi Province, China
zongw@mailst.xjtu.edu.cn

Abstract. The paper expatiated the practical demands of information resource and technology with modern manufacturing enterprise, and analyzed the causation forming islands of information in allusion to information system construction of enterprise. And adopting the enterprise application an integrated application framework of enterprise Business Process Management (e-BPM) based on Web service with distributed network is introduced. It will promote the enterprise integration effectively of all kinds of legacy systems and new application systems, and more accelerated the information project implement of Aero manufacturing.

1 Introduction

Knowledge and information have replaced the position of capital and energy in economy, and is becoming the important and inexhaustible resource [1]. Information resource is not only includes info data, but also include decision-making model and the management of aeronautical manufacturing. As the info islands have been formed in aero manufacturing and obstructed the overall process of informative construction badly. Enterprise needs a tool to build the information resource center frame urgently, which not only can control the information of customer, supplier project, order and asset; but also the finance, human resource, production and minute sell etc. These can control the information in time and realize the total control for the value chains of aero manufacturing enterprise.

With the appearance of enterprise application integration (EAI), the application integration is possible for different platform and different scheme. The key problem to solve the islands of information is not only software technique, but also more important in process management and standard have related technology. In this paper, the practice requirement of information resource and technology is discussed and many problems to build information system are focused in modern aero manufacturing. A solving method and reaction approach of operation process integrates management base on the distribution network web service is put forward. These promote the integration of legacy system and new application in aero manufacturing, and also accelerate the building of project in the reaction of information.

H.T. Shen et al. (Eds.): APWeb 2006, LNCS 3842, pp. 1049 – 1052, 2006.

2 Business Process Management Architecture

A business process is the combination of the little unit called sub process, shown as in Figure 1. Sub-process is a reusable service. As an absolute unit, every sub process has its input and out put. For example, an order sub process may need the user's name and do some operation. The input information is the details of the order and user's information. Many business processes can reuse a sub process. A sub-process is an integration that can run many applications. It can be seemed as sequence combination on the information flow. Every nod on information flow needs adapter or connector from information flow to back application, database or end user. The founder and actor of business process may be customer, employee cooperator, supplier or application.

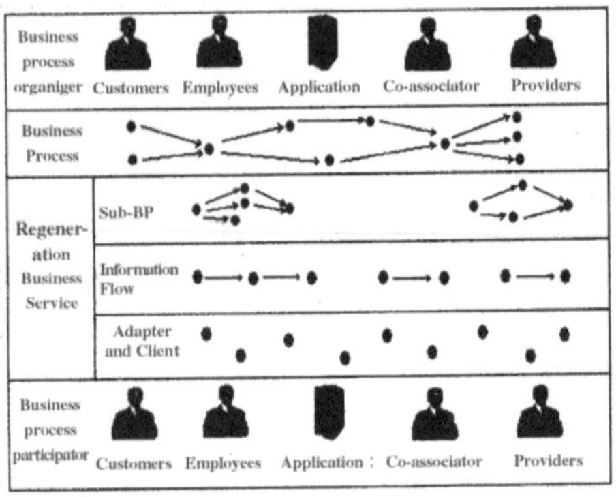

Fig. 1. The business process management (BPM) architecture

Business processing management (BPM) is a kind of tech to understand, define, automation and improve the company business. BPM can build the integer of application on business process degree, which is the combination of work process and enterprise application. These can optimize the business process and improve the flex of process to integrate the inside and outside resource of the enterprise. The acquirement of BPM product includes: *The graphic design tools on BPM, Adapter, Easy configuration interface, The runtime state engine and The process manage engine.*

3 Web Service-Based BPM Integration

3.1 Application Frame for Web Service

Web service is a distributed compute tech, which release and access the business app service by the standard XML protocol in internet/intranet. Web service is a kind of loose bounded integrate service type, that can rapid develop, distribute, find and dynamic bound app service. It uses the open Internet standard-Web Script Definition Language, Unscripted and UDDI, SOAP. The programmed element can be placed in the web, the online application service to meet the special function and other groups can be distributed, and also can access the online service by Internet. Shown in Fig.2.

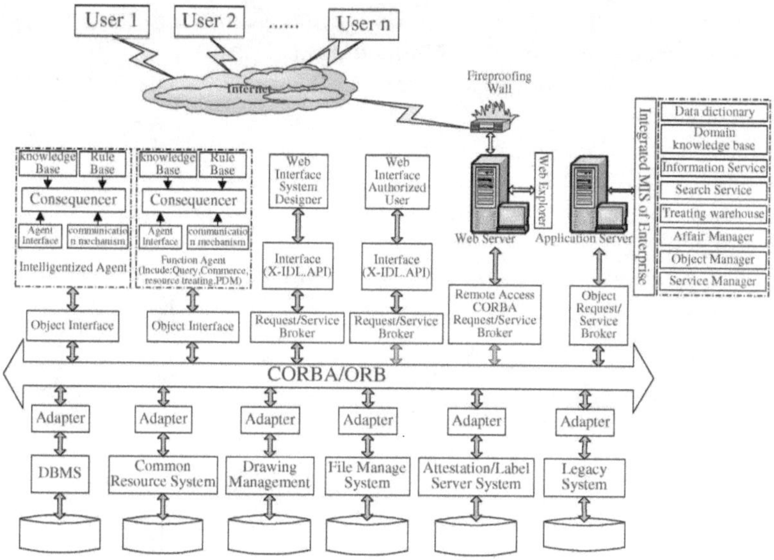

Fig. 2. Web service-based implement framework of BPM integration

3.2 Internet/Web-Based Integrating Method and Implement

User interface integration is integration for user. It replaces the terminal of left system and PC graphic interface with a standard one such as browser. Generally speaking, the function of the app terminal can be mapped one by one to a browser-based user interface. Its express layer must integrate with Legacy System or some packed app as ERP, CRM and SCM. It use the enterprise portal to realize some complex interface reform and design a perfect, customs browser-based interface, that make the unite of many enterprise app come to true.

Method Integration, include the directly and distributed network environment integration across the different platform and application. It contains common code programmed, API, RPC, TP Monitors, CORBA, RMI, MOM and web service software tech. It uses SOAP, that is between c/s acquire and response interactive. The user can access the app server information by web browser. App server can access the web service in the enterprise as SOAP.

BPM model, in the application of Process Collaboration, enterprise app is integrated by B2B protocol and outside system. The inside process is hidden to outside system. So when there is some change in the inside process, it cannot touch the outside mate. These acquire a media service to transform the B2B protocol to enterprise inside process and data language. UML is a language to script, construct, visualize and documentary the software system. It uses the unit model or UML model group to finish the model among the enterprise.

Business Process Integration, uses middle ware to solve the unite model in the distributed environment, what is insure the single stream between app and realize intelligence integration, management, and decision-making support of BPM. When the enterprise adapts this construction, it can peel off the business process logic from the application and concentrate to the BPM, which forms a new layer of BPM. This integration have better process design, test and redesign ability, and make it easier to integrate other system.

Data Integration, is the degree of data source and database inside the company. The integration is finished by transform data from a data source to anther. By just in time or batch method, it can do data transform, data unite, data copy, data access, reload and so on using the tools of middle ware.

Web service provides a new method to EAI. It is an open standard method for definition, distribute and access in local and remote service. After the developer builder a service standard, they can visit the app service in different system, platform and language. The characteristic based on web service includes: *Simple and practicality, Opening, Flexibility, Economy, High efficiency and Dynamic, etc.*

4 Conclusions

With the grown up of middle ware and proxy technology, the P2P mode of EAI and structure of EAI are widely used in the enterprise. The EAI with middle ware and face to web service on business process is not maturity, which needs deeper search and discuss. This paper bring out a web service based solution with distributed network environment to provide a method of improve the integration of legacy system with new enterprise application. And adopting the enterprise application an integrated application framework of enterprise Business Process Management (e-BPM) based on Web service with distributed network is introduced. It will promote the enterprise integration effectively of all kinds of legacy systems and new application systems, and more accelerated the information project implement of Aeronautical manufacturing.

References

1. Xie Youbai. *Journal of Chinese Mechanical Engineering*, 2002, 13(4): 1-4. (In Chinese)
2. Gunjan Samtani, Dimple Sadhwani. [EBPOL] http://www.webservicearchitect.com/2001.
3. E.Box, D. Ehnebuske, et al. [EBPOL] http://www.w3.org/PTRPSOAP, May 2000.
4. Li Huabiao. *Computer World*, 2002, (24) Special B. (In Chinese)
5. Yu Haibing, Zhu Yunlong. *J of Chinese Mechanical Engineering*, 2002, 13(1): 67-71.
6. Smith R.G., Davis R. *IEEE Tans. on System*, 1998, SMCII(1), pp 61-69.
7. Dongdong Hu and Xiaofeng Meng. DASFAA 2005, Beijing, 2005,4.
8. J. Wang, X F Meng, S Wang. *Journal of Software*, Vol15(5):720-729,2004,5.
9. Wang Yun. Nanjing: Southeast Univ. Press, 1998, pp: 30-60.
10. Meng X F, Lu H J, et al. *J of Computer Science and Technology*, 2002, 17 (4): 377-388.
11. Zhang X, Meng X F, Wang S. *Journal of Software*, 2002, 13 (5): 937-945. (In Chinese)
12. Meng Xiaofeng. *Computer Application and Software*, 2003. 20 (11): 30-36. (In Chinese)
13. Zhang Hong. *Computer Applications and Software*, 2004, 21 (10): 35-37. (In Chinese)
14. Luo Rongliang. *Computer Applications and Software*, 2004, 21(11): 110-112. (In Chinese)
15. Xu You-jun, Wang Li-sheng. *Computer Applications and Software*, 2004, 21 (16): 106-108.

Author Index

Lecture Notes in Computer Science

For information about Vols. 1–3754

please contact your bookseller or Springer

Vol. 3860: D. Pointcheval (Ed.), Topics in Cryptology – CT-RSA 2006. XI, 365 pages. 2006.

Vol. 3855: E. A. Emerson, K.S. Namjoshi (Eds.), Verification, Model Checking, and Abstract Interpretation. XI, 443 pages. 2006.

Vol. 3850: R. Freund, G. Păun, G. Rozenberg, A. Salomaa (Eds.), Membrane Computing. IX, 371 pages. 2006.

Vol. 3842: H.T. Shen, J. Li, M. Li, J. Ni, W. Wang (Eds.), Advanced Web and Network Technologies, and Applications. XXVII, 1057 pages. 2006.

Vol. 3840: M. Li, B. Boehm, L.J. Osterweil (Eds.), Unifying the Software Process Spectrum. XVI, 522 pages. 2006.

Vol. 3838: A. Middeldorp, V. van Oostrom, F. van Raamsdonk, R. de Vrijer (Eds.), Processes, Terms and Cycles: Steps on the Road to Infinity. XVIII, 639 pages. 2005.

Vol. 3837: K. Cho, P. Jacquet (Eds.), Technologies for Advanced Heterogeneous Networks. IX, 307 pages. 2005.

Vol. 3835: G. Sutcliffe, A. Voronkov (Eds.), Logic for Programming, Artificial Intelligence, and Reasoning. XIV, 744 pages. 2005. (Sublibrary LNAI).

Vol. 3834: D. Feitelson, E. Frachtenberg, L. Rudolph, U. Schwiegelshohn (Eds.), Job Scheduling Strategies for Parallel Processing. VIII, 283 pages. 2005.

Vol. 3833: K.-J. Li, C. Vangenot (Eds.), Web and Wireless Geographical Information Systems. XI, 309 pages. 2005.

Vol. 3832: D. Zhang, A.K. Jain (Eds.), Advances in Biometrics. XX, 796 pages. 2005.

Vol. 3831: J. Wiedermann, G. Tel, J. Pokorný, M. Bieliková, J. Štuller (Eds.), SOFSEM 2006: Theory and Practice of Computer Science. XV, 576 pages. 2006.

Vol. 3829: P. Pettersson, W. Yi (Eds.), Formal Modeling and Analysis of Timed Systems. IX, 305 pages. 2005.

Vol. 3828: X. Deng, Y. Ye (Eds.), Internet and Network Economics. XVII, 1106 pages. 2005.

Vol. 3827: X. Deng, D. Du (Eds.), Algorithms and Computation. XX, 1190 pages. 2005.

Vol. 3826: B. Benatallah, F. Casati, P. Traverso (Eds.), Service-Oriented Computing - ICSOC 2005. XVIII, 597 pages. 2005.

Vol. 3824: L.T. Yang, M. Amamiya, Z. Liu, M. Guo, F.J. Rammig (Eds.), Embedded and Ubiquitous Computing – EUC 2005. XXIII, 1204 pages. 2005.

Vol. 3823: T. Enokido, L. Yan, B. Xiao, D. Kim, Y. Dai, L.T. Yang (Eds.), Embedded and Ubiquitous Computing – EUC 2005 Workshops. XXXII, 1317 pages. 2005.

Vol. 3822: D. Feng, D. Lin, M. Yung (Eds.), Information Security and Cryptology. XII, 420 pages. 2005.

Vol. 3821: R. Ramanujam, S. Sen (Eds.), FSTTCS 2005: Foundations of Software Technology and Theoretical Computer Science. XIV, 566 pages. 2005.

Vol. 3820: L.T. Yang, X. Zhou, W. Zhao, Z. Wu, Y. Zhu, M. Lin (Eds.), Embedded Software and Systems. XXVIII, 779 pages. 2005.

Vol. 3819: P. Van Hentenryck (Ed.), Practical Aspects of Declarative Languages. X, 231 pages. 2005.

Vol. 3818: S. Grumbach, L. Sui, V. Vianu (Eds.), Advances in Computer Science – ASIAN 2005. XIII, 294 pages. 2005.

Vol. 3816: G. Chakraborty (Ed.), Distributed Computing and Internet Technology. XXI, 606 pages. 2005.

Vol. 3815: E.A. Fox, E.J. Neuhold, P. Premsmit, V. Wuwongse (Eds.), Digital Libraries: Implementing Strategies and Sharing Experiences. XVII, 529 pages. 2005.

Vol. 3814: M. Maybury, O. Stock, W. Wahlster (Eds.), Intelligent Technologies for Interactive Entertainment. XV, 342 pages. 2005. (Sublibrary LNAI).

Vol. 3813: R. Molva, G. Tsudik, D. Westhoff (Eds.), Security and Privacy in Ad-hoc and Sensor Networks. VIII, 219 pages. 2005.

Vol. 3810: Y.G. Desmedt, H. Wang, Y. Mu, Y. Li (Eds.), Cryptology and Network Security. XI, 349 pages. 2005.

Vol. 3809: S. Zhang, R. Jarvis (Eds.), AI 2005: Advances in Artificial Intelligence. XXVII, 1344 pages. 2005. (Sublibrary LNAI).

Vol. 3808: C. Bento, A. Cardoso, G. Dias (Eds.), Progress in Artificial Intelligence. XVIII, 704 pages. 2005. (Sublibrary LNAI).

Vol. 3807: M. Dean, Y. Guo, W. Jun, R. Kaschek, S. Krishnaswamy, Z. Pan, Q.Z. Sheng (Eds.), Web Information Systems Engineering – WISE 2005 Workshops. XV, 275 pages. 2005.

Vol. 3806: A.H. H. Ngu, M. Kitsuregawa, E.J. Neuhold, J.-Y. Chung, Q.Z. Sheng (Eds.), Web Information Systems Engineering – WISE 2005. XXI, 771 pages. 2005.

Vol. 3805: G. Subsol (Ed.), Virtual Storytelling. XII, 289 pages. 2005.

Vol. 3804: G. Bebis, R. Boyle, D. Koracin, B. Parvin (Eds.), Advances in Visual Computing. XX, 755 pages. 2005.

Vol. 3803: S. Jajodia, C. Mazumdar (Eds.), Information Systems Security. XI, 342 pages. 2005.

Vol. 3802: Y. Hao, J. Liu, Y.-P. Wang, Y.-m. Cheung, H. Yin, L. Jiao, J. Ma, Y.-C. Jiao (Eds.), Computational Intelligence and Security, Part II. XLII, 1166 pages. 2005. (Sublibrary LNAI).

Vol. 3801: Y. Hao, J. Liu, Y.-P. Wang, Y.-m. Cheung, H. Yin, L. Jiao, J. Ma, Y.-C. Jiao (Eds.), Computational Intelligence and Security, Part I. XLI, 1122 pages. 2005. (Sublibrary LNAI).

Vol. 3799: M. A. Rodríguez, I.F. Cruz, S. Levashkin, M.J. Egenhofer (Eds.), GeoSpatial Semantics. X, 259 pages. 2005.

Vol. 3798: A. Dearle, S. Eisenbach (Eds.), Component Deployment. X, 197 pages. 2005.

Vol. 3797: S. Maitra, C. E. V. Madhavan, R. Venkatesan (Eds.), Progress in Cryptology - INDOCRYPT 2005. XIV, 417 pages. 2005.

Vol. 3796: N.P. Smart (Ed.), Cryptography and Coding. XI, 461 pages. 2005.

Vol. 3795: H. Zhuge, G.C. Fox (Eds.), Grid and Cooperative Computing - GCC 2005. XXI, 1203 pages. 2005.

Vol. 3794: X. Jia, J. Wu, Y. He (Eds.), Mobile Ad-hoc and Sensor Networks. XX, 1136 pages. 2005.

Vol. 3793: T. Conte, N. Navarro, W.-m.W. Hwu, M. Valero, T. Ungerer (Eds.), High Performance Embedded Architectures and Compilers. XIII, 317 pages. 2005.

Vol. 3792: I. Richardson, P. Abrahamsson, R. Messnarz (Eds.), Software Process Improvement. VIII, 215 pages. 2005.

Vol. 3791: A. Adi, S. Stoutenburg, S. Tabet (Eds.), Rules and Rule Markup Languages for the Semantic Web. X, 225 pages. 2005.

Vol. 3790: G. Alonso (Ed.), Middleware 2005. XIII, 443 pages. 2005.

Vol. 3789: A. Gelbukh, Á. de Albornoz, H. Terashima-Marín (Eds.), MICAI 2005: Advances in Artificial Intelligence. XXVI, 1198 pages. 2005. (Sublibrary LNAI).

Vol. 3788: B. Roy (Ed.), Advances in Cryptology - ASIACRYPT 2005. XIV, 703 pages. 2005.

Vol. 3787: D. Kratsch (Ed.), Graph-Theoretic Concepts in Computer Science. XIV, 470 pages. 2005.

Vol. 3785: K.-K. Lau, R. Banach (Eds.), Formal Methods and Software Engineering. XIV, 496 pages. 2005.

Vol. 3784: J. Tao, T. Tan, R.W. Picard (Eds.), Affective Computing and Intelligent Interaction. XIX, 1008 pages. 2005.

Vol. 3783: S. Qing, W. Mao, J. Lopez, G. Wang (Eds.), Information and Communications Security. XIV, 492 pages. 2005.

Vol. 3782: K.-D. Althoff, A. Dengel, R. Bergmann, M. Nick, T. Roth-Berghofer (Eds.), Professional Knowledge Management. XXIII, 739 pages. 2005. (Sublibrary LNAI).

Vol. 3781: S.Z. Li, Z. Sun, T. Tan, S. Pankanti, G. Chollet, D. Zhang (Eds.), Advances in Biometric Person Authentication. XI, 250 pages. 2005.

Vol. 3780: K. Yi (Ed.), Programming Languages and Systems. XI, 435 pages. 2005.

Vol. 3779: H. Jin, D. Reed, W. Jiang (Eds.), Network and Parallel Computing. XV, 513 pages. 2005.

Vol. 3778: C. Atkinson, C. Bunse, H.-G. Gross, C. Peper (Eds.), Component-Based Software Development for Embedded Systems. VIII, 345 pages. 2005.

Vol. 3777: O.B. Lupanov, O.M. Kasim-Zade, A.V. Chaskin, K. Steinhöfel (Eds.), Stochastic Algorithms: Foundations and Applications. VIII, 239 pages. 2005.

Vol. 3776: S.K. Pal, S. Bandyopadhyay, S. Biswas (Eds.), Pattern Recognition and Machine Intelligence. XXIV, 808 pages. 2005.

Vol. 3775: J. Schönwälder, J. Serrat (Eds.), Ambient Networks. XIII, 281 pages. 2005.

Vol. 3774: G. Bierman, C. Koch (Eds.), Database Programming Languages. X, 295 pages. 2005.

Vol. 3773: A. Sanfeliu, M.L. Cortés (Eds.), Progress in Pattern Recognition, Image Analysis and Applications. XX, 1094 pages. 2005.

Vol. 3772: M.P. Consens, G. Navarro (Eds.), String Processing and Information Retrieval. XIV, 406 pages. 2005.

Vol. 3771: J.M.T. Romijn, G.P. Smith, J. van de Pol (Eds.), Integrated Formal Methods. XI, 407 pages. 2005.

Vol. 3770: J. Akoka, S.W. Liddle, I.-Y. Song, M. Bertolotto, I. Comyn-Wattiau, W.-J. van den Heuvel, M. Kolp, J. Trujillo, C. Kop, H.C. Mayr (Eds.), Perspectives in Conceptual Modeling. XXII, 476 pages. 2005.

Vol. 3769: D.A. Bader, M. Parashar, V. Sridhar, V.K. Prasanna (Eds.), High Performance Computing – HiPC 2005. XXVIII, 550 pages. 2005.

Vol. 3768: Y.-S. Ho, H.J. Kim (Eds.), Advances in Multimedia Information Processing - PCM 2005, Part II. XXVIII, 1088 pages. 2005.

Vol. 3767: Y.-S. Ho, H.J. Kim (Eds.), Advances in Multimedia Information Processing - PCM 2005, Part I. XXVIII, 1022 pages. 2005.

Vol. 3766: N. Sebe, M.S. Lew, T.S. Huang (Eds.), Computer Vision in Human-Computer Interaction. X, 231 pages. 2005.

Vol. 3765: Y. Liu, T. Jiang, C. Zhang (Eds.), Computer Vision for Biomedical Image Applications. X, 563 pages. 2005.

Vol. 3764: S. Tixeuil, T. Herman (Eds.), Self-Stabilizing Systems. VIII, 229 pages. 2005.

Vol. 3762: R. Meersman, Z. Tari, P. Herrero (Eds.), On the Move to Meaningful Internet Systems 2005: OTM 2005 Workshops. XXXI, 1228 pages. 2005.

Vol. 3761: R. Meersman, Z. Tari (Eds.), On the Move to Meaningful Internet Systems 2005: CoopIS, DOA, and ODBASE, Part II. XXVII, 653 pages. 2005.

Vol. 3760: R. Meersman, Z. Tari (Eds.), On the Move to Meaningful Internet Systems 2005: CoopIS, DOA, and ODBASE, Part I. XXVII, 921 pages. 2005.

Vol. 3759: G. Chen, Y. Pan, M. Guo, J. Lu (Eds.), Parallel and Distributed Processing and Applications - ISPA 2005 Workshops. XIII, 669 pages. 2005.

Vol. 3758: Y. Pan, D.-x. Chen, M. Guo, J. Cao, J.J. Dongarra (Eds.), Parallel and Distributed Processing and Applications. XXIII, 1162 pages. 2005.

Vol. 3757: A. Rangarajan, B. Vemuri, A.L. Yuille (Eds.), Energy Minimization Methods in Computer Vision and Pattern Recognition. XII, 666 pages. 2005.

Vol. 3756: J. Cao, W. Nejdl, M. Xu (Eds.), Advanced Parallel Processing Technologies. XIV, 526 pages. 2005.

Kolibri 360 GmbH
Ferdinand-Jühlke-Straße 7
99095 Erfurt, Deutschland
produktsicherheit@kolibri360.de